Eng.d by D.C.Hinman, from the original painting by Col. Trumbull in the Gallery at Yale College.

SURRENDER OF LORD CORNWALLIS, AT YORKTOWN, VA. OCT. 19th 1781.

Entered according to act of Congress in the year 1844 by D.C.Hinman, in the Clerks office of the Dist.t of Conn.

VIRGINIA

SIC SEMPER TYRANNIS

HISTORICAL COLLECTIONS

OF

VIRGINIA;

CONTAINING

A COLLECTION OF THE MOST INTERESTING FACTS, TRADITIONS,
BIOGRAPHICAL SKETCHES, ANECDOTES, &c.

RELATING TO

ITS HISTORY AND ANTIQUITIES,

TOGETHER WITH

GEOGRAPHICAL AND STATISTICAL DESCRIPTIONS.

TO WHICH IS APPENDED,

AN HISTORICAL AND DESCRIPTIVE SKETCH

OF THE

DISTRICT OF COLUMBIA.

ILLUSTRATED BY

OVER 100 ENGRAVINGS,

GIVING

VIEWS OF THE PRINCIPAL TOWNS,—SEATS OF EMINENT MEN,—
PUBLIC BUILDINGS,—RELICS OF ANTIQUITY,—HISTORIC
LOCALITIES, NATURAL SCENERY, ETC., ETC.

BY HENRY HOWE.

[Arms of Virginia.]

SIC SEMPER TYRANNIS

[Thus always with tyrants.]

HERITAGE BOOKS
2011

HERITAGE BOOKS

AN IMPRINT OF HERITAGE BOOKS, INC.

Books, CDs, and more—Worldwide

For our listing of thousands of titles see our website
at
www.HeritageBooks.com

A Facsimile Reprint
Published 2011 by
HERITAGE BOOKS, INC.
Publishing Division
100 Railroad Ave. #104
Westminster, Maryland 21157

— Publisher's Notice —
In reprints such as this, it is often not possible to remove blemishes from
the original. We feel the contents of this book warrant its reissue despite
these blemishes and hope you will agree and read it with pleasure.

International Standard Book Numbers
Paperbound: 978-0-7884-0811-3
Clothbound: 978-0-7884-8767-5

PREFACE.

THE primary object of the following pages is to narrate the most prominent events in the history of Virginia, and to give a geographical and statistical view of her present condition. Similar volumes* have appeared on Pennsylvania, Massachusetts, Connecticut, New York, and New Jersey. The favorable reception of these in their respective states, has led to the opinion that one upon Virginia —the mother of states and statesmen, the "Old Dominion," so rich in historic lore—would meet not only the approval of Virginians, but be favorably received by others.

Early in the year 1843 we commenced travelling over the state, collecting materials and taking sketches for illustrations. Every section of the commonwealth was visited. The better to effect our purpose, we occasionally journeyed hundreds of miles on foot, often sharing alike the hospitality of the planter and the mountaineer, and cheered onward by pleasant interviews with some of her most intelligent citizens. Much valuable information has been thus obtained, by observation and inquiry, and interesting but scattered details of her history and antiquities collected in a form to ensure their preservation. Written communications, moreover, have been received, embodying facts enhancing the value of this publication, and placing us under lasting obligation to their authors.

This work has three departments. The first—an outline, or general history— comprises an abstract of leading events from the first settlement of Virginia to the present time; the first five chapters of which are from the admirably written historical sketch in Martin's Gazetteer,[†] and the last by a gentleman personally familiar with most of the events related. The second consists of miscellanies, intended to throw light upon the past and present condition of the commonwealth. The third and principal department, is arranged in counties, in alphabetical order, where each is successively described. In this are the descriptions of towns, literary institutions, historic localities, seats and memoirs of eminent Virginians, antique structures, natural scenery, anecdotes, local history, and events but glanced at in the outline sketch, fully detailed.

---

* The first—on Connecticut—was published in 1836; the one on Massachusetts, 1838; New York, 1841; Pennsylvania, 1843, and New Jersey, 1844. Connecticut and Massachusetts were prepared by John W. Barber—the pioneer in works on this plan; New York and New Jersey by John W. Barber and Henry Howe; and Pennsylvania by Sherman Day.

† This work, published in 1836, was the first issued descriptive of Virginia, since the celebrated notes of Mr. Jefferson. Our publishers having purchased the copyright, we have availed ourselves of it in preparing this volume.

Thus the volume comprehends a history and a gazetteer. Its advantages over formal histories are, that the events and their localities are given together, serving more strongly to impress the memory; the past and present are in juxtaposition, and many events given which regular history, in her stately march, does not step aside to notice—events usually considered of minor importance, but forming the undercurrent of history, and useful in illustrating the advancement and condition of society.

Written history forms but a small part of occurrences. The vicissitudes of war have been considered more worthy of narration, than those things promoting the wellbeing of man. Says an eminent essayist: " The perfect historian considers no anecdote, no peculiarity of manner, no familiar saying, as too insignificant for his notice, which is not too insignificant to illustrate the operation of laws, of religion, and of education, and to mark the progress of the human mind."

The great variety of subjects presented, and the almost impossibility of producing such a publication without errors and imperfections, has created a degree of diffidence in submitting it to the public. It will doubtless come before many possesing better means of information, and more knowledge on some subjects introduced, than could reasonably be expected in us.

Besides drawing largely from a great variety of publications, we are enabled to present much not previously published, as well as that inaccessible to the mass of readers. We do not, however, consider ourselves responsible for every sentiment introduced in these pages. In order to form a correct judgment, it is useful to hear the opinions of those who differ from us in their religious or political sentiments.

The drawings for the numerous engravings were, with a few exceptions only, taken by us on the spot. We trust they have an honest look, and faithfully represent their originals. Some biographical sketches are doubtless omitted, not less important than many inserted, while others have not due prominence. In some few cases we have supposed the reader to be familiar with them, while in others it arises from the extreme difficulty of obtaining the desired information.

The history of Virginia is of deep interest; but one imperfectly chronicled. Much is left to the investigation of the antiquarian, and many a thrilling episode is lost in the lapse of generations. Yet enough remains to stimulate to the loftiest patriotism; while the memory of her illustrious sons is cherished with just pride by our common country.

INDEX.

☞ The counties being arranged in alphabetical order in this work, supersedes the neces sity of placing them in the index.

CITIES AND TOWNS.

GENERAL OR OUTLINE HISTORY.

CHAPTER I.

INTRODUCTION—PROGRESS OF COMMERCE—ROANOKE SETTLEMENTS.

Discovery of America.—England.—Want of commerce in early times.—Voyages of the Cabots.—Progress of English discovery—Frobisher—Gilbert—Raleigh.—Failure of the Roanoke settlements...... *Page* 11

CHAPTER II.

SETTLEMENT AT JAMES TOWN—SUFFERINGS OF THE COLONIES—ADVENTURES OF SMITH.

New company raised—its charter.—James Town.—Machinations against Smith.—Difficulties of the colony.—Smith taken prisoner—his release.—Arrival of Newport.—Discovery of earth believed to be gold.—Departure of Newport.—Survey of the Chesapeake and its waters by Smith.—Smith made president.—Second arrival of Newport.—Judicious conduct of Smith.—New charter.—New arrival of emigrants.—Badness of the selection.—New settlements.—Accident to Smith—his departure—his character.. *Page* 22

CHAPTER III.

PROGRESS OF THE COLONY—MASSACRE OF 1622—DISSOLUTION OF THE LONDON COMPANY.

State of the colony at Smith's departure—its conduct and subsequent sufferings.—Arrival of Gates—of Lord De La Ware—his departure.—Arrival of Dale.—Martial law.—Gates governor.—Grants of land to individuals.—New charter.—Marriage of Pocahontas.—Friendly relations with the Indians.—Cultivation of tobacco.—Tenure of lands.—Tyranny of Argall.—Propriety of reform in the government.— Yeardley governor.—First colonial assembly in 1619.—Introduction of women.—Introduction of negroes by the Dutch in 1620.—Constitution brought over by Sir Francis Wyatt.—Relations with the Indians.— Massacre of the 22d of March, 1622—its consequences.—Struggles between the king and the company. —Commissioners sent to Virginia.—Firmness of the Virginians.—Dissolution of the company.. *Page* 34

CHAPTER IV.

CHAPTER V.

CHAPTER VI.

CHAPTER VII.

CHAPTER VIII.

MISCELLANIES.

2

OUTLINE

HISTORY OF VIRGINIA.

CHAPTER I.

INTRODUCTION, PROGRESS OF COMMERCE, ROANOKE SETTLEMENTS.

Discovery of America.—England.—Want of Commerce in early times.—Voyages of the Cabots.—Progress of English discovery—Frobisher—Gilbert—Raleigh.—Failure of the Roanoke settlements.

THE claims of the Icelanders, the Welsh, and even the Norwegians,* to the discovery of America, seem in modern times to be universally set aside in favor of a native of a milder clime. Indeed, the evidence by which their respective claims were sought to be established was so vague, contradictory, and unsatisfactory,† and their discoveries, if proved, so entirely accidental, and useless to mankind, that it is not at all astonishing that all the merit should be given to that individual whose brilliant genius first demonstrated *a priori* the existence of a continent in the western waters, and whose adventurous daring‡ led him to risk his life in the search of a world, of the existence of which he was only informed by his science, with little aid of any human experience; or that posterity should give to COLUMBUS the undivided glory of an exploit for which he received only the ignominy of his contemporaries, and to Italy the honor due the birthplace of so distinguished a son, from whose brilliant achievements she has received little else.

In 1460, the Portuguese discovered the Cape de Verd islands, and afterwards extended their discoveries farther south. This near prospect of an easier and more direct route to India, had already begun to excite the jealousy of the Venetians, who then nearly monopolized the trade of India, and to elevate the hopes of the Portuguese, who expected to enjoy a portion of the wealth and luxury which the Venetians derived from that trade; when the minds of both, and indeed of all Europe, were turned in another

---

* Winterbotham's America, vol. I. p. 1 and 2, and Hinton's United States.

† Bancroft's Hist. U. States, vol. I. p. 6, and notes.

‡ "L'Italie reparut, avec les divins tresors que les Grecs fugitifs rapportèrent dans son sein; le ciel lui révéla ses lois; *l'audace de ses enfants découvrit un nouvel hémisphère.*"—De Staël—Corinne.

direction by the occurrence of an event in the history of maritime discovery, compared with which all others sunk into insignificance.

This event was the discovery of America, by Christopher Columbus. The education of this daring mariner, his disappointments and dangers, his difficulties and his brilliant success, or the melancholy story of his sad reverses, and the example afforded in him of the ingratitude of kings, it is not the purpose of the writer to narrate. He refrains from recounting so temptingly interesting a narrative, because it would lead him too far from his purpose, which is only to narrate succinctly the progress of navigation and discovery to the time of the first colony settled in Virginia,—and because the same story has been so well told by Robertson, Irving, and others, that it ought to be familiar to all.

Oct. 11, 1492.

Notwithstanding the advances in navigation which have been enumerated, the art of ship-building was still in such a rude and imperfect state, that the vessels in which Columbus embarked on an unknown sea, a modern mariner, with all the advantages of modern science, would scarcely venture in, to cross the Atlantic. The largest was a vessel of no considerable burden,* and the two others scarcely superior in burden to large boats, and the united crews of the three only amounted to *ninety men*, including officers, and a few gentlemen, adventurers from Isabella's court.

But notwithstanding these inadequate means for the prosecution of maritime discovery, the ardor of enterprise was so much excited by the brilliant achievements of Columbus, the greedy thirst for gain, and hope of finding some country abounding in gold, together with the eager desire which still prevailed of discovering some passage through the great continent of America, which might lead to India, that in twenty-six years from the first discovery of land by Columbus, the Spaniards had visited all of the islands of the West Indies—they had sailed on the eastern coast of America from the Rio de la Plata to the western extremity of the Mexican Gulf—they had discovered the great Southern Ocean, and had acquired considerable knowledge of the coast of Florida. It is also said that these voyages in search of a nearer passage to the East Indies, had extended much farther north, but not however until that country had been discovered by the seamen of another nation, of whose exploits in the field of maritime adventure we shall presently speak.

The great interior was still unknown, the whole western and the extreme southeastern coasts were still undiscovered, and the long line of coast from Florida to Labrador had only been seen, and touched upon in a few places.

England did not at an early period make those advances in navigation, to which the eminent advantages of her insular situation

---

invited, and gave no promise of that maritime distinction, and commercial wealth, to which the wise policy of her subsequent rulers have led her to attain. From the times of the conquest to the discovery of America, England had been engaged in perpetual wars, either foreign or domestic; and thus, while the southern portion of Europe and the free cities on the Rhine were advancing so rapidly in opulence and power, England was destitute of even the germ of that naval strength to which she is so much indebted for her present greatness. Every article of foreign growth or fabric which she consumed, was wafted to her shores in the barks of other nations, and the subsequent mistress of the seas scarcely dared to float her flag beyond the limits of her own narrow jurisdiction. Scarcely an English ship traded with Spain or Portugal before the beginning of the fifteenth century, and it required another half century to give the British mariner courage enough to venture to the east of the Pillars of Hercules.*

Feeble as the marine of England then was, her reigning monarch, Henry VII., did not lack the spirit required for undertaking great enterprises, and accident only deprived him of the glory of being the patron of the discoverer of America. Columbus, after the failure of his own native country of Genoa to encourage his great enterprise, and his second rebuff from his adopted country, Portugal, fearing another refusal from the king of Castile, to whose court he then directed his steps, dispatched his brother Bartholomew to England to solicit the aid of Henry VII., who being then at peace, was supposed to have leisure to undertake a great enterprise which promised such renown to himself and emolument to England. Bartholomew was captured by pirates on his voyage, and robbed of all his effects, which, with an illness that followed, prevented him from presenting himself at court, after he arrived in England, until he could provide himself with suitable apparel Feb. 13, 1488.† by his skill in drawing maps and sea-charts. He brought himself to the notice of Henry by presenting him with a map, and upon his representing to him the proposal of Columbus, he accepted it with "a joyful countenance, and bade him fetch his brother." So much delay had been produced by the circumstances mentioned, that Bartholomew, hastening to Castile, learned at Paris, from Charles, king of France, that his brother Christopher's efforts had already been crowned with the most brilliant success.

When we reflect upon the difficulties which were thrown in the way of Columbus at the court of Ferdinand and Isabella, even after they became convinced of the practicability of his scheme,

---

* Robertson's Virginia, p. 18, 19.

† This date is preserved in some curious verses upon the map, of which we give a specimen : "Bartholmew Colon de Terra Rubra." "The yeere of Grace, a thousand and four hundred and fourscore" "And eight, and on the thirteenth day of February more," "In London published this worke. To Christ all laud therefore." Hacklyt, vol. III p. 22.

and the yet more arduous difficulties which he encountered on his voyage, from the mutinous timidity of his crew, we may well doubt whether Henry's courage would have sustained him in the actual accomplishment of the enterprise, or whether England at that time afforded mariners sufficiently hardy to have persevered a sufficient length of time in a seemingly endless voyage upon an unknown sea.

Fortunately, perhaps, for mankind, the courage of England was not put to the test of making the first great adventure; and whether she would have succeeded in that or not, she was not destitute of sufficient courage to undertake an enterprise of very considerable magnitude at that day, soon after the existence of land in our western hemisphere had been discovered.

June 24, 1497.

The merit of this new enterprise is also due to a native of Italy, and his motive was the same which prevailed in most of the adventures of the time,—the desire to discover a new route to India.

Giovanni Gaboto, better known by his anglicised name of John Cabot, a Venetian merchant who had settled at Bristol, obtained from Henry a charter for himself and his three sons, Lewis, Sebastian, and Santius, allowing them full power and authority to sail into all places in the eastern, western, or northern sea, under the banners of England, with five ships, at their own proper costs and charges, to discover countries before unknown to Christians, to plant the banners of England in all such places, and to take possession of them, to hold as vassals of England, to have the exclusive monopoly of the trade of all such places, paying to the king one-fifth of the clear profits of every voyage. All other persons were prohibited from visiting such places, and the Cabots were bound always to land on their return only at Bristol.

Under this patent, containing "the worst features of colonial monopoly and commercial restriction," John Cabot, and his celebrated son Sebastian, embarked for the west. The object of Cabot being to discover the passage to India, he pursued a course more northwardly than any selected by previous navigators, and the first land he reached was the coast of Newfoundland, which on that account he named Prima Vista; next the Island of St. John; and finally the continent, among the "polar bears,.the rude savages and dismal cliffs of Labrador;" and this seems to have been the only fruit of the first British voyage to America.

In the following year a new patent was given to John Cabot, and the enterprise was conducted by his adventurous and distinguished son, Sebastian. In this expedition, which was undertaken for the purposes of trade as well as discovery, several merchants of London took part, and even the king himself. Cabot sailed in a northwest course, in hopes of finding a northwest passage to India, as far probably as the 58th or 60th degree of latitude, until he was stopped by the quantities of ice which he encountered, and the extreme severity of the weather;

Feb. 3, 1498.

he then turned his course southward and followed the coast, according to some writers to the coast of Virginia, and in the opinion of some, as far as the coast of Florida. The only commodities with which he returned to England, as far as our accounts inform us, were three of the natives of the newly discovered countries. He found, upon his return, the king immersed in his preparations for a war with Scotland, which prevented his engaging in any further prosecution of his discoveries, or entertaining any design of settlement.

It is not our purpose to notice the Portuguese discoveries under Cotereal, the French under Verrazzani and Cartier, or their abortive attempt at settlements in Canada and New England. Nor shall we notice the extensive inland expedition of the Spaniards under Soto from Florida, through the states of Georgia, Alabama, Mississippi, across the Mississippi, and into Louisiana,—or the attempts of the French at settlement in Florida and the Carolinas,— these matters belong rather to the history of the United States, than to the sketch of the history of Virginia which we propose to give. We pass at once to the British attempts at colonization in America.

The progress of maritime adventure extended rapidly. The evidence exists of several English voyages having been made not only to the coast of North America, but the Levant, the harbors 1548. of northern Africa and Brazil. The visits to the fisheries of Newfoundland had become frequent; and the commerce from that source had become of such importance, and had been the subject of such long and oppressive exactions, as to require the action of parliament for their prohibition.

India was still the great object with the merchants, and the dis- 1550. covery of a nearer passage than that offered by the Cape of Good Hope, the great desideratum with mariners. The northwestern passage had been attempted thrice by the Cabots in vain; a northeastern expedition was fitted out, and sailed under the command of Willoughby and Chancellor. Willoughby with his ship's company were found in their vessel frozen to death in a Lapland harbor; Chancellor with his vessel entered the port of 1554. Archangel, and "discovered" the vast empire of Russia, till then unknown to Western Europe. This discovery led to the hope of establishing an intercourse by means of caravans 1568. across the continent to Persia, and thence to the distant empire of Cathay.

Elizabeth afforded every encouragement to the maritime enterprises of her subjects, and especially encouraged the newly estab- 1576. lished intercourse with Russia. The hope of discovering a northwest passage was by no means as yet relinquished. Martin Frobisher, after revolving in his mind the subject for fifteen years, believed that it might be accomplished, and "determined and resolved within himself to go and make full proof thereof," "knowing this to be the only thing in the world that was left yet undone, whereby a notable mind might be made famous and fortunate." Frobisher was too poor to supply himself with the means of carrying his designs into execution; but after much solicitation at court he was patronised by Dudley, Earl of Warwick, who supplied him with two small barks, the one of twenty and the other of twenty-five tons burden, and a pinnace of ten tons. With this little fleet he set sail. The expedition was entirely unfortunate. One of his barks deserted and returned home, the pinnace went down in a storm, "whereby he lost only four men :" with such small vessels and crews did the hardy mariners of that day venture to cross the Atlantic. The Admiral's mast was sprung, and the top-mast blown overboard, by the same storm in which he lost the pinnace; but, nothing daunted, he persevered, and entered Hudson's Bay. The only thing accomplished by the voyage was the taking possession of the cold and barren wilderness in the name of Elizabeth, carrying home some of the gravel and stones, one of the latter of which, resembling gold, or probably having some gold artificially mingled with it after it reached London, caused the gold refiners nearly to go mad, and the merchants to undertake one of the wildest expeditions recorded in the annals of discovery; besides this show of gold, which was pronounced very rich for the quantity, the only other acquisition was a poor native, whose simplicity was imposed upon by the most treacherous devices, until he was decoyed to the English vessel, and then seized by force, and carried away from his friends. He bit off his tongue from despair, and died soon after his arrival in England, from cold taken on the voyage.

The mania which the story of the little bit of gold produced in London caused a fleet of several vessels to be fitted out, of 1577. which the queen herself furnished one, to bring home the rich produce of these icy mines. The ships returned with black earth, but no gold.

The spirit of avarice was not to be stopped in her career by a single failure; a new fleet of fifteen vessels was fitted out, 1578. and to Martin Frobisher was given the command. A colony was to be planted for the purpose of working the mines, while twelve vessels were to be sent home with ore. After almost incredible difficulties, encountered amid storms and "mountains of floating ice on every side," the loss of some vessels, and the desertion of others, they reached the northern Potosi, and the ships were well laden with the black earth; but the colonists, being disheartened by their hardships, declined settling on the coast, and all returned to England. We are not informed of the value of the proceeds of the cargo.

While the British queen and her merchants were indulging themselves in fancies as brilliant and as evanescent as the icebergs which encumbered the scene of the delusion, Sir Humphrey Gilbert, a man of insuperable energy and fearless enterprise, formed a design of promoting the fisheries, and engaging in useful colonization.

With this view he obtained a patent of the same character with most of those which were granted to the early pro-moters of colonization in America, conferring unbounded privileges upon the proprietor, and guarantying no rights to the colonists. The first expedition, in which Gilbert had expended much of his private fortune, failed,—from what cause is uncertain.

June 11, 1578.

1579.

The second expedition, undertaken four years afterwards, was still more unfortunate; for it lost to the world the gallant and accomplished projector of the expedition. Five vessels sailed from Plymouth on Tuesday, the 11th of June, 1583. Two days afterward, the vice-admiral complained of sickness aboard, and returned with the finest ship in the fleet to Plymouth. The admiral, nevertheless, continued his course with his little squadron, and took possession, with the feudal ceremony, of Newfoundland, to be held by him as a fief of the crown of England, in accordance with the terms of his charter.

1583.

The looseness of morals displayed by the mariners of that day is truly disgusting, and increases our wonder at the daring of men who could venture so far from home, in such frail barks, with almost a certainty of encountering on the great highway, in their fellow-men, greater perils than were presented by all the terrors of the deep. Robbery by sea was too common, and often committed in violation of the most sacred obligations, even upon persons engaged in the very act of relieving the distress of the depredators.* Gilbert seems to have been cursed with a remarkably riotous and insubordinate company. The sick and disaffected were left at Newfoundland to be sent home with the Swallow, and the admiral proceeded with his three remaining barks.

On Tuesday the 20th of August they sailed from the harbor of St. Johns, and on the 29th, in about latitude 44 degrees, the largest remaining vessel, by the carelessness of the crew, struck, and went to pieces, and the other barks were forced by a high sea and a lee shore to struggle for their own preservation, which they accomplished with difficulty,—alleging, at the same time, that they could see none of the crew of the wreck floating upon timbers, but all seemed to have gone down when the ship broke up. A few, however, escaped to Newfoundland in the ship's pinnace, as was afterwards discovered.

This calamity, followed by continual storms, in an unknown and shoaly sea, enhanced by an extreme scantiness of provisions, and want of clothes and comforts in the two little barks which yet remained, induced the admiral, at the earnest solicitation of his men, to return homeward. Sir Humphrey Gilbert was vehemently persuaded by the crew of the Golden Hind to remain with them during the voyage; but, as some malicious taunts had been thrown out by some evil-disposed person, accusing

Aug. 31.

---

* See a remarkable instance in Hacklyt, vol. III., 191, 196, &c.

3

him of being afraid of the sea, he chose to continue to sail in his little pinnace, the Squirrel, which was burdened beyond her strength.

After the vessels had left the Azores to the south, and reached the latitude of England, they encountered violent and continued storms. On Monday, the 9th of September, the Squirrel was nearly cast away, but recovered, and the admiral was seen sitting abaft with a book in his hand, and heard to cry out to those in the Hind, "We are as near to heaven by sea as by land." That same night, at 12 o'clock, the Squirrel being in advance, her light suddenly disappeared, and her hardy crew, with their gallant commander, Sept. 22. sleep forever in the deep. The Hind reached Falmouth in safety, but after encountering eminent peril to the last moment.*

The daring spirit of the mariners of that day is amazing. Sir Walter Raleigh, the step-brother of Sir Humphrey Gilbert, so far from being intimidated by the melancholy fate of his relative, or disheartened by the unprofitable and disastrous termination of March 25, 1584. most of the voyages to America, undertook in the very next year an expedition to the coast of the present United States. He easily obtained one of the usual un-limited patents from Elizabeth, and, leaving the cold north, with its barren snows, its storms, icebergs, and certain evils, together with its imaginary wealth, he spread his sails for the sweet south, where he was sure to find a fertile soil and a delightful climate, though his ship's company might not all be enriched by the dis-covery of gold.

On the second of July they found shoal water, "and smelt so sweet and strong a smell, as if they had been in the midst of some delicate garden abounding with all kinds of odoriferous flowers."

On the 13th they entered Ocracock inlet, on the coast of the present state of North Carolina, and landed on Wocoken Island. They commenced an intercourse with the natives, who proved to be bold, confiding, intelligent, and honorable to their friends, but treacherous, revengeful, and cruel towards their enemies.

The English explored a little the surrounding islands and bays, and returned home in September, carrying with them two natives, Manteo and Wanchese. The glowing description given by the adventurers, on their return, of the beauty of the country, the fer-tility of the soil, and pleasantness of the climate, delighted the queen, and induced her to name the country of which she had taken possession, Virginia, in commemoration of her unmarried life.

It might be expected that so favorable an account would soon 1585. lead to a new expedition. Accordingly, another was pre-pared for the succeeding year, consisting of seven vessels.

* Hacklyt, III., 184 to 202.

Ralph Lane was appointed by Raleigh governor of the colony, which consisted of one hundred and eight persons. Sir Richard Grenville took command of the fleet, and several learned and accomplished men attended the expedition, one of whom has transmitted to posterity many interesting particulars of the nature of the country, and the habits, manners, and government of its inhabitants.

The English soon began to maltreat the harmless, unpretending, July 11, 1586. and simple natives, and they, on the other hand, to grow jealous of the power of the overbearing strangers. They soon learned the inordinate passion of the newcomers for gold, and, taking advantage of their credulity, inflicted upon them the labor of many fruitless expeditions in search of pretended mines,—hoping at the same time, by these divisions, to weaken the power of the little colony to such a degree that they might be able to destroy it in detachment; but the English were too cautious for this, and went too short a distance, and in force too powerful for the Indians to encounter with the great disparity of arms. The greatest advantage which accrued from these expeditions, and indeed from the whole attempt at a settlement, was the discovery of Chesapeake Bay.

The little colony, finding no gold, and receiving no supplies from England, had begun to despond, when most unexpectedly Sir Francis Drake arrived, on his return from his expedition against the Spaniards in South America, with a fleet of three and twenty ships. The sagacity of Drake perceived in a moment what was necessary for the colony, and his generosity supplied them with provisions, vessels, and other things necessary to maintain their position, extend their researches, and, if necessary, to return to England; but the accomplishment of his purpose was defeated by a violent storm which suddenly arose, and nearly wrecked his whole fleet, driving the vessel of provisions intended for the colony to sea, and destroying the vessels which had been set apart to be left for their use. He would have supplied others; but the colony, June 19. with their governor at their head, earnestly requesting permission to return to England, he complied with their wishes. Thus terminated the first English settlement in America.

This little colony, during its sojourn with the Indians, had acquired something of their fondness for the use of tobacco, and learned to regard it with almost the same superstitious reverence, as a powerful medicinal agent. Upon their return, they introduced the use of this plant into England; and a weed at first disgusting and nauseating to all who use it, has become gradually the favorite luxury (and indeed with many a necessary of life) of all classes of society, and of both the young and the old throughout the world, —and this, after experience has proved that in most cases it is an injury rather than a benefit to the health.

A few days after Lane's departure, an English vessel arrived on the coast with every necessary for the colony, but finding it deserted, returned home. Sir Richard Grenville arrived soon after with three ships, well furnished with stores for the colony; but not finding it, he also returned, leaving fifteen men on Roanoke Island, to keep possession in the name of Great Britain.

The genius of Sir Walter Raleigh was not of a nature to suc-
1587. cumb to slight failures, or ordinary difficulties. The suc-
ceeding year another colony was dispatched to settle in Virginia; and that they might consider their settlement perma-nent, and Virginia their home, many persons with wives and fami-lies were sent.

Jan. 7. A charter of incorporation was granted for a town, to be called the City of Raleigh, a name revived in after times in the present metropolis of North Carolina. John White was appointed governor, and, with eleven assistants, constituted the administration for the control of the colony. Ample provision was made by the noble and liberal proprietor for the comfort of the colonists, and a plentiful stock of instruments of husbandry pro-vided, to enable them to supply their own future wants, and estab-lish themselves on the only footing which could possibly be expected to be permanent.

April 26. The company embarked in April, and arrived in July at the place where they expected to find the fifteen un-fortunate men whom Grenville had left. But their grounds were grown up in weeds, their tenantless dwellings had become the abode of the wild animals of the forest, and their scattered bones, blanching in the sun, were the last sad memorials which told their fate to their anxious countrymen. Whether they fell by civil dis-sensions among themselves, by famine or disease, or were yet more miserably cut off by the overpowering numbers of a savage host, taking advantage of their desolate situation, (deprived of sympa-thy, and destitute of the hope of succor,) is one of the mysteries of history which the ken of man may not unravel.

The sagacity of Raleigh had directed the new settlement to be made on the shores of the magnificent Chesapeake, and there was the new city to be built; but the naval officer, preferring trade
July 23. with the West Indies to exploring the coast, left White on Roanoke Island, and compelled him to establish himself there.

The colony soon became involved in difficulties with the natives,
July 28. partly from accident, and partly from the previously en-gendered hostility of some of the tribes. Indeed, it would seem impossible a priori, (even if we had not, unfortunately, too much experience of the fact,) that two nations of such different degrees of civilization, manners, and habits, with such different designs, could long remain together in peace, harmony, and on the footing of equals. It would seem to be the nature of man that the ignorant tribe should be jealous, treacherous, and vindictive,—that the more civilized should be greedy, rapacious, and overbearing. And when a spirit of suspicion is once excited, the imprudence of

CAPTAIN JOHN SMITH.

From a portrait showing him in the fashionable dress of the period in which he lived.

a single individual too often involves in a quarrel all of the citizens of the little communities : nothing is extenuated, and nothing is attributed to accident ; but suspicion in the injured party supplies the place of malice in the aggressor. These difficulties made the colonists feel more anxiously their dependence upon England, and forced upon them a melancholy foreboding, that without frequent and effectual assistance from the mother country, they could not long sustain themselves in a strange and distant land, the natives of which had become bitterly hostile. Under this impression, when their last ship was about to depart from England, they forced their reluctant governor, by excessive importunity, to desert his charge, in order that he might lend his personal aid and influence in sending them succor from home. He sailed with the Aug. 27. ship, but not until after his daughter, Eleanor Dare, the wife of one of the assistant governors, had presented him with the first white child born on the continent of North America. Aug. 18. This child was christened Virginia Dare, and, with her mother, was esteemed a sufficient pledge of the exertions of the governor in aid of the colony, and of his speedy return.

White found all England engaged in anxious preparation to 1588. meet the threatened Spanish invasion, but this did not prevent the generous Raleigh from dispatching him with two ships of supplies for the relief of the colony. But the spirit of gain overcame the spirit of humanity, and even the tender ties of April 22. parental affection : instead of going at once to the colony, he employed himself in taking Spanish prizes, and was at last himself overcome and rifled, which compelled him to return to England, much to the chagrin of the noble proprietor, and probably the destruction of the neglected colony.

The Invincible Armada of Spain had to be overcome, and the safety of England herself to be secured, before another effort could be made to succor the little colony at Roanoke ; and when this was accomplished, leisure found the noble patron of the enterprise too much impoverished by his previous unprofitable exertions to fit out, at his own expense, another expedition. He was obliged to assign an extensive portion of his powers to a company of merchants and others who might carry his schemes into execution ; but with his profuse liberality, the active spring which had quickened previous expeditions was gone, the spirit of gain rather than of glory presided over the destinies of infant America, and it 1590. was not until another year had elapsed, that White was sent in quest of his subjects and his daughter.

When he arrived the colony was gone ; an inscription on the bark of a tree, indicating Croatan as the place whither they had gone, was the last record of their existence seen by a civilized eye. Conjecture has pointed to an amalgamation with the tribe of Hatteras Indians as the history of their destiny, and old Indian traditions and the physical characteristics of that tribe are said to confirm the idea; but while humanity may indulge a hope, credulity itself must entertain a doubt of the truth of the hypothesis.

White returned to England as soon as he found out that the colony was gone, and Raleigh is said to have sent five several times in vain, to search for his liege-men, but no tidings were ever received of their existence or their fate. Thus terminated the attempts at settlement on the coast of North Carolina, then called Virginia; the scene next opens upon the broad bosom of the "mother of the waters."*

CHAPTER II.

SETTLEMENT AT JAMESTOWN—SUFFERINGS OF THE COLONISTS—ADVENTURES OF SMITH.

New Company raised—its charter.—Jamestown.—Machinations against Smith.—Difficulties of the colony.—Smith taken prisoner—his release.—Arrival of Newport.—Discovery of earth believed to be gold.—Departure of Newport.—Survey of the Chesapeake and its waters by Smith.—Smith made president.—Second arrival of Newport.—Judicious conduct of Smith.—New charter.—New arrival of emigrants.—Badness of the selection.—New settlements.—Accident to Smith—his departure—his character.

WE have now approached the period in which the British were destined to make a permanent settlement in America. England already possessed a population considered redundant, in consequence of the inadequate means of support afforded by her limited commerce and inefficient agriculture. The pacific and timid character of James I.' threw out of employment many of the brave spirits who had served under Elizabeth, and left them the choice of only two means of acquiring wealth or distinction,—and these were either to draw a mercenary sword in the quarrels of strangers, or to serve their king and country by transplanting their energy and enterprise to a new world.

BARTHOLOMEW GOSNOLD chose the latter. He was a person of rank and intelligence, and had already acquired distinction by his courage and skill in arms. He solicited his friends for aid for many years in vain, but at length attracted the attention of the distinguished adventurer Capt. JOHN SMITH, EDWARD MARIA WINGFIELD, a merchant, and ROBERT HUNT, a clergyman, who, after taking a year for reflection, entered zealously into his projects.

Nothing, however, could be effected until persons of wealth and distinction could be found to patronise by their favor and aid by

---

* This is the translation usually given of the Indian name "Chesapeake," but Chilly McIntosh, the celebrated Georgia Creek chief, now removed west of the Mississippi, with his tribe, told the writer another meaning, which he said was the true one, but which the writer has forgotten; but which was, however, not so unlike the one given above but that the same word might well convey the two different impressions, in different idioms of the same language.

their capital the enthusiasm of the adventurers. Sir FERDINAND GORGES, a man of wealth, rank, and influence, had been informing himself, by conversation with several American Indians who had been carried to England by previous voyages, and by every other means in his power, of the nature of the country; and from the information he obtained became exceedingly anxious to possess a domain on the western side of the Atlantic. He persuaded Sir JOHN POPHAM, lord chief-justice of England, to unite in his views. RICHARD HACKLYT, the distinguished compiler of narratives of maritime adventures, and one of the assignees of Raleigh, had not yet relinquished his hopes of a permanent settlement in America, notwithstanding the frequent previous discouraging failures, and cheerfully joined in this new scheme of American colonization. The exertions of these energetic and distinguished individuals speedily raised a company, and procured a charter from King James.

As this was the first charter under which a permanent settlement was made, it may be worth attention to notice some of its prominent features. The charter bears date on the tenth of April, sixteen hundred and six.* It grants all the country from four-and-thirty to five-and-forty degrees of north latitude, and all islands within one hundred miles of the coast. This immense extent of country was divided by the charter between two companies, for the more speedy accomplishment of their purpose,—which have been ever since designated as the London and the Plymouth companies. The London company wished to establish a colony between the 34th and 41st degrees of latitude, and the Plymouth between the 38th and 45th, and the grants were made in conformity to their wishes. But as there was room for collision between the 38th and 41st degrees of latitude, the colony which first settled was to possess the land for fifty miles north and south of its location, and the other colony was forbidden to settle within one hundred miles of the colony first planted. Each of the colonies was to be governed by a council of thirteen† persons, under the management and direction of a council of thirteen in England, which was to regulate both colonies. The council in the colonies were to govern according to laws, ordinances, and instructions prescribed by the king himself. The colonies had full power given to search for and work mines, paying to the king a fifth part of the gold and silver obtained, and a fifteenth of the copper; and they were further allowed to coin money to pass current in the colonies. They were also empowered to levy a duty of two and a half per cent. upon the property of the king's subjects trading within their limits, and five per cent. upon all others so trading, for the use of the colony for twenty-one years, and afterwards for the use of the king.

Certain articles of necessity were allowed to be carried to the colonies from any part of the king's dominions free of duty for the first seven years; and the colonists and their descendants were to have forever the privileges, franchises, and immunities of native-born Englishmen.

The English council was to have power to name the persons who were to compose the colonial council, and the latter elected their own president, and supplied vacancies in their own body. The religion of the church of England was established; lands were to descend as at common law; manslaughter, adultery, and dangerous tumults and seditions, were to be punished with death. The president and council constituted the supreme tribunal in all cases. The property of the colonists was to <u>continue in joint</u> stock for five years.

One hundred and nine years from the discovery of the North American continent by Cabot, three small vessels, whose joint tonnage amounted to only one hundred

Dec. 19, 1606.

* See this charter preserved in Stith,—Henning's Stat. at Large, p. 60, and in T. Rynier.

† It appears afterwards that only seven were appointed; no reason is assigned for the change.

and sixty tons burden, sailed for the coast of Virginia with a colony of one hundred and five men. They were detained for six weeks in sight of England by adverse winds. The voyage was prosecuted under the command of Captain Newport, who sailed by the old route of the Canaries and the West India islands; thus consuming the valuable time and provisions of the colonists, in a voyage unnecessarily long and circuitous. He did not arrive in the Chesapeake until the 26th of April.

Dissensions had sprung up in the course of the voyage, which there was no competent authority to quell, as the absurd affectation of diplomatic mystery on the part of King James had sealed up his instructions, and the names of those who were to constitute the council, in a box which was not to be opened until after they arrived in Virginia.

The southern cape of the Chesapeake received the name of Henry, and the northern that of Charles, after the names of the sons of James. After landing on Cape Henry, the box of instructions was opened, and Smith* was found to be named as one of the council, but he was excluded by the jealous malignity of the rest. Wingfield was chosen president.

Soon after passing the capes, they reached the mouth of a large and beautiful river, which they named after their sovereign James, but which the natives called Powhatan. About fifty miles from the mouth of this river, they selected a spot for their settlement, May 13. to which they gave the name of *James Town.* There could not, perhaps, be a company more unfitted for the duty which it had to perform, than that which now commenced the foundation of the British empire in America. The colonists were in a wilderness, surrounded by savages, without a fortification to repel their incursions, possessed of a scanty supply of provisions, without means of planting,—and without a habitation to protect them from the weather, save such as they might themselves erect; yet in the whole company there were but *four* carpenters, and *twelve* laborers, to *fifty-four gentlemen.* At first, however, this rare collection of pioneers fell to work with spirit, each to his appropriate duty. The president, who seems to have been a very weak man, and ill-suited for his station, was too jealous of his own men to allow exercises at arms, or a fortification to be erected; and the only protection provided, was a sort of half-moon formed of the boughs of trees, by the exertions of Kendall. Newport, Smith, and twenty others were sent to discover the head of the river. In six days they arrived at a town called Powhatan, belonging to King Powhatan, situated at the falls of the river, near the site of the present city of Richmond. They were kindly treated by the Indians. When the expedition returned, they found that Jamestown had been attacked by the savages, and seventeen

---

* The council named, was Bart. Gosnold, John Smith, Edward Wingfield, Christopher Newport, John Ratcliffe, John Martin, and George Kendall.

men wounded, and a boy killed. They were attacked while at work, and their arms out of order; so that the whole were only saved from destruction by the timely aid of the vessels. After this experience of his folly, the president permitted the place to be fortified; and the labor necessary to effect this, with so small a force, while it was necessary, at the same time, to guard their workmen by day, to watch by night, to prepare ground for corn, and lumber to relade the ships, may be better conceived than described. After a stay of six weeks, Newport prepared to depart, and the council affecting a tender regard for the character of Smith, whom they had falsely accused of a treacherous design to usurp royal authority in the colony, and kept out of his seat in the council under these charges, now proposed, that he might not be utterly ruined by a trial, to send him home to the council, to be disposed of as they might think proper. But Smith, conscious of innocence of the absurd charge, boldly defied them, and demanded a trial. His accusers suborned witnesses, who, instead of answering the expectations of their employers, only exposed the subornation. The company were so incensed at the infamous conduct of his accusers, that they condemned the president to pay him £200, which, when received, he generously threw into the common stock. Newport sailed on the 15th of June, leaving one hundred men in Virginia.

The condition of the men thus left, was the most melancholy that can well be imagined. They consisted, for the most part, of men entirely unused to labor or hardship; who were doomed to encounter every kind of difficulty, in the midst of summer, in a hot and sickly climate. In ten days from the departure of Newport, scarce ten men could stand, from sickness and weakness. The food was scanty in quantity, and of the most unwholesome quality. The allowance of each man was half a pint of wheat, and as much barley, boiled in water, which was served out from a common kettle, and which having been closely stowed in the ship's hold for twenty-six weeks, in a warm and moist atmosphere, was reduced to a condition any thing but tempting. Smith, the narrator of these sufferings, humorously remarks: "If we had been as free from all sins, as from gluttony and drunkenness, we might have been canonized for saints." As might be supposed in such an unfortunate state of affairs, great mortality prevailed, and fifty men were buried between May and September; and those that survived relied principally for their subsistence upon sturgeon and sea-crabs. The suffering, in this state of affairs, must have been greatly aggravated by the knowledge that the president was indulging himself in every luxury which the stores afforded—and his detection in an attempt to escape in the pinnace, from the suffering colony. This last act of treachery was more than the little colony could endure; and weak as it was, it deposed him, and Kendall, his accomplice. Ratcliffe was made president. The council do not seem to have exercised the power granted them in their charter, of filling up vacancies, and it was now reduced to three—*Ratcliffe, Smith,* and *Martin; Gosnold* had perished, *Newport* sailed for England, and *Wingfield* and *Kendall* had been deposed.

The president and Martin being unpopular men, and very deficient in judgment and energy, committed the control of affairs nearly entirely to Smith, who, by his example and his skill in managing men, speedily reduced affairs to order, induced the men to work, and provided comfortable habitations. His next object was to obtain a supply of corn for the immediate necessity of the people, which he did effectually, by frightening the people of

4

Kecoughtan, an Indian village, situated near the site of the present town of Hampton—after first trying every means to purchase their provision. Smith now constituted the only hope, not only for the existence of the colony, as such, but for the lives of the individuals of whom it consisted. Their recent wretchedness was not a sufficient warning to them to preserve order, and to husband their resources with prudence, now that plenty was provided; but they lived as wastefully as if they had boundless magazines at command. Smith, seeing this, caused the pinnace to be fitted up for a cruise; and, in the mean time, availed himself of the opportunity to become acquainted with the country lying on the Chickahominy.

During one of these temporary absences of Smith, Wingfield and Kendall, who had lived in disgrace since they were deposed, laid a plot to carry off the pinnace to England, which the fortunate return of Smith, before they had time to effect their purpose, prevented. But not even then were they defeated without firing on the pinnace, by which means Kendall lost his life.

Smith having gained possession of the pinnace, ascended the Chickahominy, and procured an abundance of corn. Winter coming on soon after, afforded an amply supply of game and wild fowl, so that plenty was once more restored, and thought no longer entertained of going to England.

Little souls cannot look upon the greatest exploits of nobler creatures, without suffering a captious and jealous malignity to detract from their merit. The very beings whom Smith had preserved by his good conduct, now murmured against him their absurd complaints—because he had not discovered the head of the Chickahominy, although he had returned only to supply them with food. His spirit could not brook reproach, however undeserved, for any thing which was yet possible to be accomplished. He again ascended the Chickahominy as far as was practicable in the pinnace, and leaving it in a position which he supposed to be safe, he advanced yet higher, with two whites and two Indians, in a canoe. He left his men with his little boat, and taking only his Indian guide, advanced into the forest with his gun to procure them provision. Unfortunately, in disobedience to his orders, the men in the pinnace went ashore, and one of them was taken by the Indians, who learned from their prisoner whither the captain had gone. The savages pursued him, and slew the men left with the canoe while they slept. They next sought Smith, but found him no easy prey; for, tying his guide to his arm as a buckler to keep off their arrows, he defended himself so gallantly that they dared not approach him until, falling accidentally into a marsh, he was at length forced by cold and fatigue to surrender. The savages conducted him to their chief, Opechankanough, king of Pamunkee. Smith endeavored to impress the king with a high idea of his powers, by presenting him with a mariner's compass, explaining its uses, and instructing him in the rudiments of astronomy, by explaining the motion of the earth, its shape, and the motion of the sun, moon, and planets; truths which it is difficult to believe he could make the savage comprehend, especially as he had but little knowledge of their language. It is more probable that the king was pleased with the ivory case of the compass, and the mysterious play of the needle, which he could see but not touch, and which moved without an apparent cause. Accordingly, we find when his men had tied Smith to a tree and were about to slay him, the king did not attempt to prevent it by explaining the motion of the earth around the sun, but merely held up the compass, the sight of which seems to have been sufficient to disarm their wrath.

For six or seven weeks Smith was led about in triumph by these simple people, and exhibited to the tribes between the James and Potomac rivers, during the whole of which time he was in hourly apprehension of being put to death; but was generally well treated, and provided with most of the luxuries which their simple state afforded. At length he was brought before their emperor, Powhatan, who received him with all the formal pomp and 'state known to his savage court. A long consultation was held by the council there assembled, upon the disposition to be made of him, which terminated unfavorably. He was seized by a number of the savages, and his head laid upon two great stones which had been brought there for the purpose. His executioners had already raised their clubs to dash out his brains, and thus at once end his toil and difficulties, and cut off the only hope of the colony, when an advocate appeared, as unexpected as would have been the appearance of an angel sent immediately from heaven to ask his release. This was Pocahontas, the emperor's favorite daughter, who generously stepped forth and entreated, with tears, that Smith might be spared. And when she found this unavailing with the inexorable judges, she seized his head, and placed it under her own, to protect it from the blows. This sight so moved Powhatan, that he permitted Smith to live, intending to retain him to make trinkets and utensils for his family and himself. But a few days afterwards Powhatan told him they would be friends again, and sent him back to Jamestown, with an offer of a large district of country in exchange for two great guns and a grindstone; but the party who were to carry these things found them so heavy, and were so much terrified by the effect of the guns, when discharged at a tree, that they were well satisfied to return without them, having received a few paltry baubles and trinkets. Smith's return again prevented a party from running off with the pinnace; which so incensed them that they laid a plot to slay him, by a mock trial for the death of the two men he had left in the canoe, and who were slain by the savages; but he was too prompt for the conspirators, whom he seized and kept close prisoners until he had an opportunity of sending them to England for trial. The colony was now only preserved from perishing by the kindness of Pocahontas, who brought ample supplies every four or five days.

During this time the little colony had not been forgotten by the company in England, but Newport, soon after his return, was again dispatched, in company with another vessel, commanded by Francis Nelson, furnished with all things which could be imagined necessary either for the crews or the colonists. Nelson, when in sight of Cape Henry, was driven by a storm so far to sea, that he was obliged to land in the West Indies to refit and renew his supply of water. Newport arrived without an accident. Before the arrival of this supply, Smith had established a regular intercourse with the savages, and bought their provisions at moderate prices, which the high estimation in which he was held by them, and the awe which his name inspired, enabled him to fix for himself. But now the poor colonists were so grateful to the mariners who had come to their relief, that they were permitted to trade at such prices as they thought proper, by which means, it followed, in a short time, that a pound of copper would not purchase what had before sold for an ounce. Newport thought proper to pay a visit of ceremony to Powhatan, who received the party with great dignity and state. During this visit, a contest of wits took place between the two parties, in which Powhatan evinced infinitely greater diplomatic skill than Captain Newport; and by working upon his pride, was very near consummating a highly advantageous bargain; but he in his turn was outwitted by the ingenuity of Smith, who, having passed many baubles before his eyes, and finding that his attention was attracted by some blue beads, affected to value them exceedingly, and intimated that they were not to be worn except by the greatest personages. This inflamed the desire of the emperor to such an extent, that he cheerfully gave several hundred bushels of corn for a pound or two of these rare jewels, whose beautiful color resembled the pure ether of heaven. The same stratagem was afterwards played off by Smith, with equal success, upon Opechankanough, king of Pamunkee.

Unfortunately, when Smith and Newport returned to Jamestown with this new supply, and added it to their former store, it took fire and the greater part was consumed, together with many of their dry-thatched dwellings, a portion of their palisade fortifications, and some of their arms, bedding, and apparel.

Instead of returning home with all possible expedition, Newport remained fourteen weeks in the colony, consuming the precious provisions which should have been applied to the support of the unfortunate individuals he was to leave behind him. Unfortunately, too, he had brought out some gold refiners in his ship, who having discovered a glittering earth near Jamestown, thought it gold; and all hands were diverted from their useful toil, for the purpose of lading his ship with this worthless article. To such an extent did this mania prevail, that Smith says, "there was no talk, no hope, no work, but dig gold, wash gold, refine gold, load gold." Newport, having completed his cargo, at length returned home. Soon after his departure, the Phœnix, the vessel of Nelson, which had been given up for lost, arrived, with all his men in safety, and a good stock of provisions; which he freely and fairly gave to the colonists to the extent of his ability. The next subject for consideration was the return cargo; to obtain which, the president wished Smith to examine the commodities to be found in the country above the falls; others wished the lading to be of the same gold with which Newport was freighted; but Smith, more prudent than either, succeeded in loading the Phœnix with cedar, which was the first available cargo sent from Virginia to England.

Smith accompanied the Phœnix, as far as Cape Henry, in a small open barge with fourteen men, with which equipment he proposed to accomplish his long cherished object of exploring the Chesapeake and its tributary waters. It is not our purpose to follow him through his two wonderful voyages, undertaken for this purpose, but we will merely present an outline of his course from the pen of an able modern author,* from whom we have before quoted. "Two voyages, made in an open boat, with a few companions, over whom his superior courage, rather than his station as a magistrate, gave him authority,

June 2, 1608.

occupied him about three months of the summer, and embraced a navigation of nearly three thousand miles. The slenderness of his means has been contrasted with the dignity and utility of his discoveries, and his name has been placed in the highest rank with the distinguished men who have enlarged the bounds of geographical knowledge, and opened the way by their investigations for colonies and commerce. He surveyed the bay of the Chesapeake to the Susquehannah, and left only the borders of that remote river to remain for some years longer the fabled dwelling-place of a giant progeny. The Patapsco was discovered and explored, and Smith probably entered the harbor of Baltimore. The majestic Potomac, which at its mouth is seven miles broad, especially invited curiosity; and passing beyond the heights of Mount Vernon and the City of Washington, he ascended to the falls above Georgetown. Nor did he merely explore the river and inlets. He penetrated the territories, established friendly relations with the native tribes, and laid the foundation for future beneficial intercourse. The map which he prepared and sent to the company in London is still extant, and delineates correctly the great outlines of nature. The expedition was worthy the romantic age of American history." The map is indeed astonishingly accurate. We cannot forbear adding the corroborating testimony of the distinguished Robertson* upon this subject, which is also quoted and approved by Marshall.† "He brought with him an account of that large portion of the American continent now comprehended in the two provinces of Virginia and Maryland, so full and exact, that after the progress of information and research for a century and a half, his map exhibits no inaccurate view of both countries, and is the original upon which all subsequent descriptions have been formed."

When Smith returned to Jamestown he found that little had been done, and a whole summer, which was a season of plenty, was wasted in idleness by the folly and imbecility of the president, whose conduct was so outrageous that the company had been at last forced to depose and imprison him.

Sept. 7, 1608.

Smith was now elected president, and his energetic conduct speedily brought affairs into good order, and repaired as far as possible the injuries occasioned by the misconduct of his predecessor.

Sept. 10.

Soon after Smith's election Newport again arrived, with the preposterous order, supposed to have been procured by his own representations, not to return without a lump of gold, discovery of a passage to the south sea, or one of the lost company sent out by Sir Walter Raleigh. He also absurdly brought some costly articles for the royal household of Powhatan, which served only to inflate the pride, without conciliating the affection of that prince. Some Poles and Dutchmen were also brought for the purpose of

* See Robertson's Hist. of Va. p. 71.
† Marshall's Introduction to Life of Washington, p. 41.

manufacturing pitch, tar, glass, ashes, &c., which would have been well enough if the colony had been in a condition always to defy famine, but which it was impossible to accomplish now, when every man's exertions were necessary to procure a sufficiency of food. Notwithstanding Smith's remonstrances, Newport insisted upon his trip of discovery above the falls of James River, for the purpose of discovering a route to the south sea, although Powhatan had assured them that the story they had heard of there being a sea in that direction was utterly false. The party returned, as Smith had predicted, disappointed and disheartened. Since this project had failed, Smith having first procured a supply of provisions, which Newport and the rest with all their vain boasting and their costly presents had failed to do, and knowing that it was as impossible to find a lump of gold, or one of Raleigh's company, as it was to find the south sea on James River, set himself to work to supply a cargo of tar, pitch, boards, ashes, and such articles as they had it in their power to procure, although with great difficulty and labor. So effectually did he exert himself, and so much authority had he acquired over the delicate gentlemen under his control, whose tender hands blistered with the use of the axe, that in a short time he had provided a sufficient cargo for Captain Newport, who at length departed, leaving two hundred souls in the colony. By the return of the vessel Smith wrote to the council a letter detailing the cause of their mishaps, assuring them that they need not expect a sudden acquisition of wealth, and that nothing was to be obtained but by labor. He complained of the want of judgment and economy in the expenditure for the benefit of the colony, which prevented them from reaping an advantage of greater value than a hundred pounds judiciously expended would purchase, from an actual outlay by the company of two or three thousand. He also especially complained of the habits and character of the men sent out, and entreated them when they sent again, rather to send "but thirty carpenters, husbandmen, gardeners, fishermen, blacksmiths, masons, and diggers up of tree-roots, well provided, than a thousand such as they had; for unless they could both lodge and feed them, they would perish with want before they could be made good for any thing."

From the departure of the ship until the next arrival, the men 1609. were only preserved from perishing by the most active and unremitting exertions of their president, the detail of whose conduct in his intercourse with the savages, and his management of the ill-assorted, disorderly, turbulent spirits under his control, is one of the most interesting stories in history, and proves him to have been a man of extraordinary abilities.

Although the fond anticipations of the Virginia company had been entirely disappointed, a spirit seems to have prevailed, which was rather disposed to surmount all difficulties by increased exertion, than to succumb to the accumulated misfortunes which had already been encountered.

The company seemed to have perceived their error in expecting a sudden acquisition of wealth from their American possessions ; and the defects in the government established by the first charter. To remedy these evils a new charter was obtained, in which many individuals and corporate bodies were included, of great wealth, power, and reputation.

May 23, 1609.

By the new charter the power which had before been reserved by the king was now transferred to the company itself ; which was to have the power of choosing the supreme council in England, and of legislating in all cases for the colony. The powers of the governor were enlarged from those of a mere president of the council, to supreme and absolute civil and military control ; the instructions and regulations of the supreme council being his only guide or check. There can be no doubt but that this was the only practicable government which could be offered to a colony in the situation and composed of the materials which then existed in Virginia. The members of the council had only been so many petty tyrants,—the indolent and weak thwarting the exertions of the industrious and intelligent, and the cowardly and factious disputing the authority and impugning the motives of such as were brave and honorable. In truth, whenever any thing good had thus far been done, it was by the exercise of absolute authority by a mind superior to the rest ; and whatever had gone wrong, might with truth be attributed almost as much to the opposing views of the various members of the council, as to the disposition of some to do wrong.

Lord De La Ware received the appointment of governor for life under the new charter, and an avarice which would listen to no possibility of defeat, and which already dreamed of a flourishing empire in America, surrounded him with stately officers, suited by their titles and nominal charges to the dignity of an opulent kingdom. The condition of the public mind favored colonization ; swarms of people desired to be transported ; and the adventurers with cheerful alacrity contributed free-will offerings. The widely diffused enthusiasm soon enabled the company to dispatch a fleet of nine vessels, containing more than five hundred emigrants. Newport was made admiral, and was joint commissioner with Sir Thomas Gates and Sir George Somers to administer the affairs of the colony until the arrival of the governor. But these three individuals, with a ceremonious punctilio characteristic of little minds, seeking that distinction from artificial positions in society which they cannot obtain by their own merit, could not agree in a contest for precedence, and hence were compelled, as a compromise, all to go in the same ship : thus exposing the colony to all the danger of anarchy rather than that one should appear by the ship he occupied to be a greater man than the other.

They accordingly embarked with their commission, their directions, and much of the provision, in the *Sea Venture.* When near the coast of Virginia they encountered a violent storm which destroyed one small vessel, and drove the Sea Venture so far to sea that she stranded on the rocks of the Bermudas. Seven ships arrived in safety.

When Smith heard of the arrival of this immense fleet, he at first supposed it belonged to Spain, and was sent to take possession of the colony ; he accordingly made all things ready, with his usual promptness and energy of character, to give them a warm reception, and little fear was entertained of the result. Smith had by this time by his good conduct brought the savages so completely into subjection, by their admiration for his qualities and fear of his power, that they had become subjects and servants, planting and working for him as he required ; and now, when it was thought he was about to be attacked by the Spaniards, they lent him all the aid in their power.

The company in England had not attended to the wise advice of Smith in the selection of their colonists, for it must be remarked that he had no friend at home, while his enemies were suffered there to make their own representations. In the new batch of officers Ratcliffe and Archer were sent back, who had been sent home in disgrace for their idle, dissolute, and mutinous conduct. They prejudiced the minds of the other officers so much against Smith, on the voyage, that they hated him mortally before they had seen him. The historian of the times regrets that the fleet was not composed of Spaniards instead of Englishmen, and thinks it would have been better for the colony.

The newly-imported "unruly gallants, packed hither by their friends to escape ill destinies," taking sides with Ratcliffe, Archer, and their confederates against the president, whose commission they affected to consider as having been superseded by the new commission, conducted themselves very riotously, and refused to remain in subordination to any authority. Smith bore this for some time patiently, expecting every moment the arrival of the new commission, and wishing, when that event happened, to depart for England, and leave the scene of his great sufferings and glorious exertions; being willing to quit the service of a company, who could so unceremoniously dispense with his authority, for the purpose of putting individuals over him who had no claims upon them, and who knew nothing of the management of the colony. Fortunately the commissioners had been stranded, and did not arrive, and Smith could no longer suffer affairs to remain in confusion. After his resolution was taken, he quickly laid by the heels the most factious, who had been perpetually plotting his destruction, and engaging in all kinds of mischief, until he could have leisure to do them justice.

The number still remaining at large in Jamestown being too great for that position, and more than could be well supported or easily managed, he dispatched West with a hundred and twenty of the best men he could select, to form a settlement at the falls; and Martin, with nearly as many more, to Nansemond; providing them with a fair proportion of food and other necessary articles. Martin managed badly; his jealous fears induced him to attack the savages in his neighborhood, who had treated him well, and take possession of a large quantity of their corn and other property—while his cowardly caution or criminal tenderness permitted them to rally, and in their turn attack his men with impunity, to kill and wound several, and retake all they had lost. He sent to Jamestown for a reinforcement, which he did not employ when he received, but hastened thither himself, covering under the protection of Smith's prowess, and leaving his men to their fate.

The president set out for the falls, a few days after West had departed, and found that he had located himself in an exceedingly inconvenient station, subject to inundation, and surrounded by other intolerable inconveniences. He offered a fair proposition to Powhatan, for the purchase of his place called Powhatan, which he was willing to accept; but the disorderly spirits he had sent thither, who were dreaming that the country immediately above them was full of gold, to which they wished no one to have access but themselves, refused the place or to ratify the contract, despising alike his kindness and his authority. The president, with his five men, went boldly among them, and seized the ringleaders of the mutiny; but the whole number of a hundred and twenty gathering in upon him, forced him to retire, but not without seizing one of their boats, with which he took possession of the ship, in which their provision was lodged. Fortunately for Smith, he was sustained by the mariners, who had learned his character from his old soldiers and their own observations of his conduct, as well as by several of the officers, who had learned the error of their first prejudices, deserted his adversaries, and become his firm friends. The Indians came to Smith, whom they considered as their friend and protector, complaining bitterly of the maltreatment of the party at the falls, stating that they were worse than their old enemies the Monocans, from whom it was the duty of the party to protect them; and seeing their turbulent disobedience, they offered their aid to chastise them. Smith remained nine days longer trying to heal these differences, and to convince them of the absurdity of their "gilded hopes of the South sea mines." But finding all in vain, he set out for Jamestown. Such visionary and disorderly persons were the first *civilized* inhabitants of the present polished, intelligent, and hospitable city of Richmond. No sooner was Smith's voyage commenced down the river, than the savages attacked those he left behind him, and slew many, and so frightened the rest, that they suffered the prisoners they held in custody to escape. The terrified wretches fled for safety to Smith, whose ship had grounded, and submitted, without stipulation, to his mercy. He seized six or seven of the ringleaders, and imprisoned them; the rest he placed in the savage fort Powhatan, which from the beauty of its position, the excellence of its houses and fortifications, and other advantages, was called Nonsuch. He also satisfied the savages. This fair prospect was again marred by the imbecility of West, who listened to the deceitful tales and whining entreaties of the prisoners, and released them, which again threw all things into disorder; the evil disposed being the more encouraged in their mutinous conduct now, by the possession of their provisions and stores, which had been returned to them at the time of their previous submission. They abandoned Non-such, and returned to their former inconvenient station at West's fort. Smith, finding it impossible to restore tranquillity, again set sail down the river.

In his progress an unfortunate accident occurred, which deprived the colony of his services, and was near depriving him of life. His powder-bag accidentally exploded while he was sleeping, and tore the flesh from his body and thighs in a horrible manner. The pain was so acute that he threw himself into the river to cool the burning sensation, and was near drowning before he could be recovered. He had yet to go nearly one hundred miles in this situation, before he could reach a surgeon, or have any soothing application applied to his wound.

When he returned to Jamestown, the time for the trial of Ratcliffe and Archer was approaching, and these worthies, fearing the result, hired an assassin to murder him in his bed, but the heart of the wretch failed him ere he could fire the fatal shot. Failing in this, their next hope was to save their lives, by possessing themselves of the government; but in this they were disappointed by Smith, who, having in vain urged all those he thought most worthy to accept the presidency, resigned it to Mr. Percy, who was about to sail for England, but was induced to stay under the present embarrassing circumstances, to prevent the supreme control of the colony from falling into the hands of the miscreants who aspired to it.

Smith, finding himself disabled by his wound, the pain of which almost deprived him of his reason, and seeing that there was not

5

sufficient surgical skill in the colony to restore him, determined to depart for England. He well knew that, in his disabled state, the colony was no place for him; for it had required his utmost exertion in health to suppress faction at home, keep the Indians in awe, and, by the most unceasing activity, supply the colony with provision. He departed under the most mortifying circumstances; "his commission was suppressed, he knew not why—himself and soldiers to be rewarded, he knew not how—and a new commission granted, they knew not to whom." After his determination was known, the ships, which were to have departed the next day, were retained three weeks, while the mutinous captains were perfecting some colorable charges to send home against him. Never had the colony sustained such a loss. His conduct and his character will be best given in the language of those who knew him best. A writer, who was with him in his troubles, speaking of the attempt to usurp the government immediately before his departure, says:

"But had that unhappy blast not happened, he would quickly have qualified the heat of those humors and factions, had the ships but once left them and us to our fortunes; and have made the provision from among the savages, as we neither feared Spaniard, savage, nor famine; nor would have left Virginia nor our lawful authority, but at as dear a price as we had bought it and paid for it. What shall I say but thus: we left him, that in all his proceedings, made justice his first guide, and experience his second, even hating baseness, sloth, pride, and indignity, more than any danger, —that never allowed more for himself, than his soldiers with him that upon no danger would send them where he would not lead them himself;—that would never see us want what he either had, or could by any means get us;—that would rather want than borrow, or starve than not pay;—that loved action more than words, and hated falsehood and covetousness worse than death; whose adventures were our lives, and whose loss our deaths."

CHAPTER III.

PROGRESS OF THE COLONY—MASSACRE OF 1622—DISSOLUTION OF THE
LONDON COMPANY.

State of the colony at Smith's departure—its conduct and consequent sufferings.—Arrival of Gates—of Lord De La Ware—his departure.—Arrival of Dale.—Martial Law. —Gates Governor.—Grants of land to individuals.—New charter.—Marriage of Pocahontas.—Friendly relations with the Indians.—Cultivation of Tobacco.—Tenure of lands.—Tyranny of Argall.—Propriety of Reform in the government.—Yeardley Governor.—First colonial assembly in 1619.—Introduction of women.—Introduction of negroes by the Dutch in 1620.—Constitution brought over by Sir Francis Wyatt. —Relations with the Indians.—Massacre of the 22d of March, 1622—its consequences.—Struggles between the king and the company.—Commissioners sent to Virginia.—Firmness of the Virginians.—Dissolution of the company.

WHEN Smith left the colony, it contained four hundred and ninety odd persons. The harvest was newly gathered, and there was provision for ten weeks in the stores. The savages were in a good state of subjection, and readily yielded at a reasonable price whatever they could spare. All things were in such a condition that prudent management might have ensured the most brilliant success, but the wildest confusion and anarchy prevailed. The new president was so ill that he could not attend to business, and twenty others endeavored to hold the reins of government. When the savages found that Smith was gone, they speedily attacked and broke up the establishments at Powhatan and Nansemond, driving in the remnant of the men their butcheries left, to subsist upon the rapidly wasting provisions of Jamestown. Ratcliffe with a vessel and thirty men attempting to trade with Powhatan, was by his carelessness cut off, and he himself with all his company perished except two, who were saved by the humanity of Pocahontas. West with a crew of thirty escaped in a ship to become pirates.[*] The miserable company, now left without control or authority, and composed with a few exceptions of "gentlemen, tradesmen, serving-men, libertines, and such-like, ten times more fit to spoil a commonwealth, than either begin one, or but help to maintain one," now gave free rein to all their evil dispositions. Each one sought only to gratify his passions or preserve his own life, without regard to the wants or sufferings of the rest. There was no union, no concert, no harmony. Vice stalked abroad in her naked deformity, and her handmaids, misery and famine, followed in her train. The savages attacked and slew the whites upon every occasion, and forming a systematic plan to starve the remainder, they would supply no further provisions; after they had bought every disposable article at the fort, even to most of their arms, at such a price as they chose to exact. The corn was speedily consumed; next followed the domestic animals, poultry, hogs, goats, sheep, and finally the horses; all were consumed, even to their skins. The only resource was in roots, acorns, berries, and such other unwholesome stuff as could be found; nay, so pinching was the hunger, that savages who had been slain and buried were disinterred to be consumed, and even some of the whites who had perished were used to preserve life by the rest. Of nearly five hundred that Smith left, in six months only sixty emaciated beings remained alive; and these were without the possibility of support for longer than ten days.

When Gates and Sumner were shipwrecked on the Bermuda rocks, their good management saved the life of every individual, and a large proportion of their provision and stores. On this island, although uninhabited, nature was so bountiful, and presented spontaneously such a rich variety of productions suitable to the sustenance of man, that three hundred and fifty men lived in ease and abundance for nearly ten months. The disagreeable idea of remaining thus upon an island, cut off from all intercourse with the rest of the world, stimulated them to the exertion necessary to build two barks, with such rude instruments as they possessed, from the wreck of their old ship and the cedars of the island. In these they embarked for Virginia, expecting to find, in the comforts

[*] Smith in book 4, p. 2, says, "sailed for England."—Bancroft, 156, says, on the authority of Stith, "became pirates."

and plenty of a flourishing colony, ample solace for all their toils and difficulties. What,

May 23. then, was their astonishment, when they reached Jamestown, (after a more prosperous voyage than they could have expected in their crazy vessels,) to meet, instead of the warm and joyful welcome of their countrymen, in the full fruition of health and plenty, only the greedy cravings of a few miserable wretches, begging for a sufficiency of food to preserve their existence. Not anticipating this melancholy situation, they had only provided themselves with enough provision for their voyage, and were unable to relieve the necessities of their fellow-creatures, whose sufferings it was so painful to witness. It was impossible, in this situation, to remain longer in the colony. All were embarked on board the vessels, Jamestown was abandoned, and it was with difficulty that its departing citizens could be prevented from setting fire to the habitations in which they had suffered so much misery. All the provisions which could be raised did not amount to more than would support them for 16 days, at the most limited allowance; yet with this they set out with the hope to reach Newfoundland, where they expected to be relieved by the British fishing-vessels.

But although it had been the will of Heaven to permit the colonists to receive an awful chastisement for their misconduct, yet it was not decreed by the Ruler of all human affairs that the colony should be entirely abandoned, and so much labor and suffering be useless to mankind, or so fine a country left in its original wild and unimproved condition. Before Gates and his associates had reached the mouth of James River, they were met by Lord De La Ware, with three ships, having on board a number of new settlers, an ample stock of provisions, and every thing requisite for defence or cultivation. By persuasion and authority he prevailed upon

June 10, 1610. them to return to Jamestown, where they found their fort and houses and magazines in the same situation in which they had been left. A society with so bad a constitution, and such a weak and disordered frame, required skilful and tender nursing to restore it to vigor. Lord De La Ware was fully competent to his station. He held a long consultation to ascertain the cause of the previous difficulties, and concluded, after listening to their mutual accusations, by a speech full of wholesome advice, recommending the course they should pursue, and assuring them that he should not hesitate to exercise his lawful authority in punishing the insubordinate, dissolute, and idle. By unwearied assiduity, by the respect due to an amiable and beneficent character, by knowing how to mingle severity with indulgence, and when to assume the dignity of his office, as well as when to display the gentleness natural to his own temper, he gradually reconciled men corrupted by anarchy to subordination and discipline, he turned the attention of the idle and profligate to industry, and taught the Indians again to reverence and dread the English name. Under such an administration, the colony began

March 28, 1611. once more to assume a promising appearance, when, unhappily for it, a complication of diseases brought on by the climate obliged Lord De La Ware to quit the country, the government of which he committed to Mr. Percy. The colony at this time consisted of about two hundred men; but the departure of the governor was a disastrous event, which produced not only a despondency at Jamestown, but chilled the zealous warmth of the London company, and caused a decided reaction in the popular mind in England, which was exhibited in the manner in which popular feeling delights to display itself—by exhibiting the Virginia colony as a subject of derision upon the stage.

Before the departure of Lord De La Ware, the company in England had dispatched Sir Thomas Dale with supplies ; and it May 10. was well he arrived so soon, for the company were already fast relapsing to their former state of idleness and improvidence, and had neglected to plant corn, which he caused to be done immediately. The company having found all their previous systems of government inefficient, granted to Sir Thomas Dale more absolute authority than had been granted to any of his predecessors,—impowering him to rule by martial law, a short code of which, founded on the practice of the armies in the Low Countries, (the most rigid school at that time in Europe,) they sent out with him. This system of violent and arbitrary government was recommended by Sir Francis Bacon, the most enlightened philosopher, and one of the most eminent lawyers of his age. It proves the depth of his sagacity ; for it would have been absurd to apply the refined speculative theories of civil government to a set of mutinous, undisciplined, idle, ignorant creatures, shut up in a fort, surrounded by hostile nations, and dependent upon their own exertions for support. Surely, in such a case a strong government was as necessary as in a ship at sea, and more so than in ordinary military stations, where habitual discipline preserves order and ensures respect to the officers.

The governor who was now intrusted with this great but necessary power, exercised it with prudence and moderation. By the vigor which the summary mode of military punishment gave to his administration, he introduced into the colony more perfect order than had ever been established there ; and at the same time he tempered its vigor with so much discretion, that no alarm seems to have been given by this innovation.

In May, Sir Thomas Dale wrote to England full information of the weakness of the colony, but recommending in strong terms the importance of the place. His favorable representations were fully confirmed by Lord De La Ware and Sir Thomas Gates. The hopes of the company were resuscitated, and in August, Gates arrived at Jamestown with six ships and three hundred emigrants. The colony, which now consisted of seven hundred men, was surrendered into the hands of Gates ; and Dale, by his permission, made a settlement with three hundred and fifty chosen men upon a neck nearly surrounded by the river, which, in honor of Prince Henry, he called Henrico.

One of the greatest checks to industry which had hitherto existed in the colony was the community of property in the provisions and stores. The idle and dissipated, seeing that they were to have a full share, had no stimulus to exertion, and the industrious were disheartened by seeing the larger portion of the fruits of their industry consumed by the idle members of the little society. So discouraging was this state of things to exertion, that frequently, in the best times, the labor of thirty did not accomplish more than was done under a different system by three. Gates perceived the evil and applied the remedy. He distributed a certain portion of land to each individual to be worked for his own benefit, still paying, however, a small portion of his produce to the general store to provide against contingencies. This policy was found so advantageous that every encouragement was afforded to individual enterprise in the acquisition of wealth. But little respect was paid to the rights of the Indians; for some depredation or injury from the tribe of Apamatuck, they were dispossessed of their corn and their cabins, which, "considering the position commodious," were unceremoniously appropriated by the English to their own benefit.

The colony now having extended considerably, assumed a more regular form, by pur-
March 12, 1612. suing a more consistent system of policy; and beginning to promise permanency, a new charter was granted by James. This confirmed and enlarged all the privileges and immunities which had been previously granted, extended the time of exemption from duties, and enlarged their territory and jurisdiction to all islands and seats within three hundred miles of the coast. This included the newly discovered, fertile Bermudas, which were soon after sold by the company to one hundred and twenty of its members.

This new charter made some changes in the constitution of the company, by giving more power to the company itself and less to the council; it also conferred the power of raising money by lottery for the benefit of the colony, which was the first introduc-
March, 1621. tion of this pernicious system of taxation into England, and which was soon after prohibited by act of Parliament, but not until the company had raised nearly thirty thousand pounds by the privilege.

As the new system of policy had increased the independence and preserved the numbers of the colony, so had it increased its strength and the respect of the savages. One powerful tribe now voluntarily sought British protection, and became British subjects; another was brought to a close and friendly alliance by a tenderer tie than fear could afford.

Captain Argall, in a voyage to the Potomac for the purpose of purchasing corn, fell in with an old chief named Iapazaws, to whom Powhatan had intrusted Pocahontas, which he disclosed to Argall, and offered to sell her to him for a copper kettle. The bargain was made, and Pocahontas being enticed on board by the cunning of her guardian, was carried off without once suspecting the treachery of the old hypocrite. The authorities at Jamestown availed themselves of the possession of this lucky prize to endeavor to extort from Powhatan a high ransom; but the old emperor, though he really loved his daughter, seemed to be so highly affronted at the indignity offered him, that he preferred fighting those who had robbed him of his daughter to purchasing her freedom. But while this matter was in agitation, a treaty of a different character was going forward between the young princess herself and Mr. Rolfe, a highly respectable young gentleman of Jamestown, who, struck by her beauty, and fascinated by her manners, so far superior to the rest of her race, wooed and won her affections, and obtained a promise of her hand. The news of this amicable adjustment of all difficulties soon reached the ears of Powhatan, and met with his cordial approbation. He sent the uncle and two brothers of Pocahontas to witness the nuptial ceremonies at Jamestown, which were solemnized with great pomp, according to the rites of the English church. From this marriage several of the most highly respected families in Virginia trace their descent. Happy would it have been for both races, if this amalgamation had been promoted by other instances, but this is the only case upon record. This marriage secured the permanent friendship of Powhatan, and all under his influence; and the Chickahominies, his next neighbors, when they heard of it, sent deputies, and submitted by solemn treaty to become subjects to King James, and to submit to his governor in the colony,—to pay tribute,—and furnish men to fight against whatever enemies should attack the colony; only stipulating that at home they should continue to be governed by their own laws.

We have already mentioned a partial distribution of lands by Sir Thomas Dale, for the purpose of encouraging individual industry; it may be well to explain more in detail the tenure by which lands were held by individuals. At the favored Bermudas plantation, near the mouth of the Appomattox, either on account of the greater merit, longer service, or some favorable circumstances attending the expense of the emigration of the tenants, the lands were held by a rent of two and a half barrels of corn annually to the general stock, and one month's service, which was not to be in time of sowing or of harvest. Those who had been brought over at the expense of the company, had three acres of land allotted them, and two bushels of corn from the public store, and with this scanty allowance were required to support themselves by one month's labor; the other eleven being required by the company. This species of laborers had decreased in 1617 to fifty-four, including all classes; and these were finally released entirely from their vassalage by Sir George Yeardley, in 1617. The original bounty to emigrants coming at their own expense, or that of others than the company, had been one hundred acres of land; but after the colony became better settled, it was reduced to fifty, the actual occupancy of which gave a right to as many more. The payment of twelve pounds and ten shillings to the treasurer of the company, entitled the adventurer to a grant of one hundred acres, the occupancy of which also secured a right to as many more.*

The labor of the colony, which had been for a long time misdirected in the manufacture of ashes, soap, glass, and tar, in which they could by no means compete with Sweden and Russia, and also in planting vines which require infinite labor and attention, and for which subsequent experiments have indicated the climate to be unfit, was at length directed, by the extended use of *tobacco* in England,† almost exclusively to the cultivation of that article. This commodity always finding a ready price, and affairs being now so regulated that each one could enjoy the fruits of his labor, was cultivated so assiduously, as to take off the attention of the planters too much from raising corn, so that it became scarce, and supplies had again to be looked for from England, or purchased of the Indians. The fields, gardens, public squares, and

1615.

---

* Smith, Book IV. p. 18. Bancroft, I. p. 167. Burke.

† Note by Robertson.—"It is a matter of some curiosity, to trace the progress of the consumption of this unnecessary commodity. The use of tobacco seems to have been first introduced into England about the year 1586. Possibly a few seafaring persons may have acquired a relish for it, by their intercourse with the Spaniards, previous to that period; but it could by no means be denominated a national habit anterior to that date. Upon an average of the seven years immediately preceding the year 1622, the whole import of tobacco into England amounted to a hundred and forty-two thousand and eighty-five pounds weight. Stith, p. 246. From this it appears that the taste had spread with a rapidity which is remarkable. But how inconsiderable is that quantity to what is consumed now in Great Britain!" or now!!

even the streets of Jamestown, were planted with tobacco, and thus becoming an article of universal desire, it became, to a great extent, the circulating medium of the colony. Not only private debts, but salaries and officers' fees were paid in tobacco; and the statute-book to this day rarely mentions the payment of money, that it does not add, as an equivalent, "or tobacco"

Early in the year 1614, Sir Thomas Gates had returned to England, leaving the colony, which then consisted of about four hundred men, under the command of Sir Thomas Dale, who in his turn desiring to visit England and his family, left the colony in 1616, under the protection and control of Sir Thomas Yeardley. With Dale, Mr. Rolfe and his interesting bride, Pocahontas, sailed. By a communication from Smith, her amiable and valuable conduct was made known at court, and every attention was shown her, both by the queen and many of the nobility. This excellent princess, whose deportment was so far superior to that which the condition of her race would authorize one to expect, that it won for her universal admiration and esteem, was destined never more to behold her father or her native land. She died at Gravesend, where she was preparing to embark with her husband and child for Virginia. Peace to her gentle spirit! Her memory will not perish while the commonwealth of Virginia endures, or noble and generous actions are valued by her sons.

Yeardley's administration was similar to that of his predecessors, enforcing obedience from his own men, and the respect of the savages. He was succeeded, in 1617, by Captain Argall, who was a rough seaman, accustomed to the despotic sway of his own ship, naturally tyrannical in his disposition, cruel and covetous, in short, a person utterly unfit to be trusted with the administration of the arbitrary government which then existed in Virginia. For although we have considered such a government the only practicable one which could have been then established, yet it required the utmost firmness in the governor, tempered by mildness, prudence, and discretion, to make it tolerable. Such had been the case under the administration of Gates, Dale, and Yeardley, and under them the colony had prospered more than it had ever done before; but such was not the disposition of this new governor. Instead of holding the severity of the laws in terrorem over them, and not actually resorting to the extent of his power, except in cases of extreme necessity, he sought to bring innocent actions within the letter of the law, which indeed was not very difficult with the bloody military code which then existed. These arbitrary exertions of power were principally used in the gratification of his inordinate rapacity, which, in its indiscriminate grasp, sought not only to clutch the property of the colonists, but also trespassed upon the profits of the company. Not satisfied with perverting the labor of the free colonists to his own use or pleasures, he consumed the time of the servants of the company upon his own plantations. At length his conduct was so flagitious, in the case of one Brewster, who was left by Lord Delaware to manage his

POCAHONTAS.

The above is copied from an engraving said to be an exact copy of an original drawing of the "LADY REBECCA," or Pocahontas, as she is usually called. It shows her in the fashionable English dress of the time in which she lived. The following is inscribed around and underneath the original portrait.

"MATOKA ALS REBECCA FILIA POTENTISS PRINC: POWHATANI IMP: VIRGINIÆ."

"Matoaks als Rebecka, daughter to the mighty Prince Powhatan, Emperour of Attanough-komouck als Virginia, converted and baptised in the Christian faith, and wife to the wor^ll Mr. Joh Rolff." "Ætatis suæ 21 A. D. 1616."

estate, and who only sought to prevent Argall from utterly despoiling it, that neither the colony nor company could bear his tyranny longer, but he was deposed and Sir George Yeardley sent in his place. Yet he contrived to escape punishment, by the mismanagement of some and the connivance of others, and preserved all of his ill-gotten booty.

One of the first acts of Yeardley was to emancipate the remaining servants of the colony. The labor now being free, each man enjoying the fruits of his own industry, and anxious to increase his store, there was no fear of scarcity, and no time or 1619. opportunity for mutiny among the scattered and industrious planters. With the increasing strength and independence* of the colony, all fear of the savages had vanished. It is manifest that in these altered circumstances, a modification of the despotic government ought to have been made, because its severity was no longer necessary, and while the power existed it might be abused, as the colony seriously experienced in the case of Argall. The only use of government is to ensure the safety of the state from external foes, to secure justice and the free disposition of person and property to each individual, and sometimes to aid in the prosecution of such objects of general utility as individual enterprise cannot accomplish. The moment the colonists began to take an interest in the country, by the enjoyment of their own labor, and the possession of property, it was right that they should have some share in that government, in the prudent conduct of which they were most interested. Yeardley was aware of this, for without any authority from home which we can trace, he called together a General Assembly consisting of two members from every town, borough, or hundred, besides the governor and council, which met at Jamestown, near the end of June, 1619. In this assembly seven corporations were represented, and four more were laid off in the course of the same summer.

In this first North American legislature, wherein were " debated all matters thought expedient for the good of the colony," several acts were passed which were pronounced by the treasurer of the company to be " well and judiciously carried," but which are unfortunately lost to posterity. This was an eventful year to the colony, for in addition to their assembly, a college was established in Henrico, with a liberal endowment. King James had exacted £15,000 from the several bishops of his kingdom for the purpose of educating Indian children, and 10,000 acres of land were now added by the company ; and the original design was extended to make it a seminary of learning also for the English. One hundred idle and dissolute persons, in custody for various misdemeanors, were transported by the authority of the king and against the wishes of the company to Virginia. They were distributed through the colony as servants to the planters ; and the degradation of the colonial character produced by such a process, was endured for the assistance derived from them in executing the various plans of industry, that were daily extending themselves. This beginning excited in the colonists a desire for using more extensively other labor than their own, an opportunity for the gratification of which, unfortunately, too soon occurred. In this eventful year, too, a new article was introduced into the trade of the company with the colony, by the good policy of the treasurer, Sir Edward Sandys, which produced a material change in the views and feelings of the colonists with regard to the country. At the accession of Sir Edwin to office, after twelve years labor, and an expenditure of eighty thousand pounds by the company, there were in the colony no more than six hundred persons, men, women, and children. In one year he provided a passage for twelve hundred and sixty-one new emigrants. Among these were ninety agreeable young women, poor but respectable and incorrupt, to furnish wives to the colonists. The wisdom of this policy is evident,—the men had hitherto regarded Virginia only as a place of temporary sojourn for the acquisition of wealth, and never dreamed of making a permanent residence in a place where it was impossible to enjoy any of the comforts of domestic life. They had consequently none of those endearing ties of home and kindred to bind them to the country, or attach them to its interests, which are so necessary to make a good citizen. This new commodity was transported at the expense of the colony, and sold to the young planters, and the following year another consignment was made of sixty young maids of virtuous

---

* The savages now sometimes purchased corn of the English, instead of supplying them as formerly.

education, young, handsome, and well recommended. A wife in the first lot sold gen
erally for one hundred pounds of tobacco, but as the value of the new article became
known in the market, the price rose, and a wife would bring a hundred and fifty pounds
of tobacco. A debt for a wife was of higher dignity than other debts, and to be paid
first. As an additional inducement to marriage, married men were generally preferred
in the selection of officers for the colony. Domestic ties were formed, habits of thrift
ensued, comforts were increased, and happiness diffused ; the tide of emigration swelled :
within three years fifty patents for land were granted, and three thousand five hundred
persons found their way to Virginia.

In the month of August of this year an event occurred which stamped its impress
1620. upon the constitution of Virginia, and indeed of the whole southern portion of
America so deeply, that it will be difficult to erase it save by the destruction of
society. This was the introduction of twenty African slaves by a Dutch vessel, which
availed itself of the freedom of commerce, which had been released from the shackles
of the company's monopoly in the early part of this year, to rivet forever the bonds of
slavery upon a portion of their fellow-creatures and their descendants. The indented
and covenanted servants which had been long known in Virginia, and whose condition
was little better than that of slavery, was a small evil and easily removed, because they
were of the same color and country with their masters ; when they were emancipated
they leaped at once from their shackles to the full dignity of freedom. No one scorned
to associate with them, and no one spurned their alliance ; if honorable and worthy in
other respects, they were equal to their masters, and might even rise to distinction. But
not so the poor African. Nature has fixed upon him a stamp which cannot be erased
or forgotten, the badge of his bondage is borne with him, when his fetters have crumbled
to the dust.

The overbearing disposition of King James created a powerful
popular party in England, which being unable to establish a liberal
government at home, was determined to secure for free principles a
safe asylum in the colonies. The accomplishment of this determination was accelerated by the disposition of the king to intermeddle
with this very subject. He was exceedingly jealous of the company,
in which the patriot party prevailed, and suspicious of the liberal
principles discussed in its meetings with uncontrolled freedom : he
feared it as the school of debate, and nursery of parliamentary
leaders. Upon the resignation of Sir Edwin Sandys of his office
May 17, 1620. as treasurer, the king determined to try the extent
of his influence in the election of a successor to
this first office in the company. He accordingly sent in a nomination of four individuals, to one of whom he desired the office to be
given ; but he proved unsuccessful in his attempt at dictation, and
none of his nominees were elected, but the choice fell upon the Earl
of Southampton.

The company having thus vindicated its own privileges, proceeded next to guaranty freedom to the colonists, by a constitution
remarkably liberal for the time and circumstances. This charter
of freedom, the principles of which the Virginians never could be
brought subsequently to relinquish, has been preserved to posterity
in "Summary of the ordinance and constitution of the treasurer,
council and company in England, for a council of state, and
another council to be called the General Assembly in Virginia,
contained in a commission to Sir Francis Wyatt (the first governor
under that ordinance and constitution) and his council," dated July
24, 1621.

The council of state was to be chosen by the treasurer, council and company in England, with the power of removal at pleasure; their duty was to advise and assist the governor, and to constitute a portion of the General Assembly. This General Assembly was to be called by the governor once a year, and not oftener, unless on very extraordinary and important occasions; it was to consist, in addition to the council of state, of two burgesses, out of every town, hundred, or other particular plantation, to be respectively chosen by the inhabitants; in which council all matters were to be decided, determined, and ordered, by the greater part of the voices then present, reserving to the governor always a negative voice. " And this General Assembly was to have full power, to treat, consult, and conclude, as well of all emergent occasions concerning the public weal of the said colony, and every part thereof, as also to make, ordain, and enact such general laws and orders, for the behoof of said colony, and the good government thereof, as from time to time might seem necessary."

The General Assembly and council of state were required to imitate and follow the policy of the form of government, laws, customs, and manner of trial, and of the administration of justice, used in the realm of England, as near as might be, as the company itself was required to do, by its charter. No law or ordinance was to continue in force or validity unless it was solemnly ratified in a general quarterly court of the company, and returned under seal; and it was promised that as soon as the government of the colony should once have been well framed and settled, that no orders of court should afterwards bind the colony, unless they were ratified in the same manner by the General Assembly.

When Sir Francis arrived, he found that negligence and security among the colonists, which is the inevitable consequence of a long peace. Old Powhatan had died in 1618, honored by the esteem and respect of all who knew him—his own people holding in grateful remembrance his prowess and policy in youth, and his mildness in age—and his English friends and brethren admiring his firm support of his dignity, his paternal affection, his mild simplicity, and his native intelligence. He was succeeded in his power by Opechancanough, his younger brother, who was cunning, treacherous, revengeful, and cruel. He renewed the former treaties, with every assurance of good faith, and wore the mask of peace and friendship so successfully as completely to lull the whites to security. But this crafty prince had always viewed with peculiar jealousy and hate the progress of the colony. He had given much trouble, and engaged in frequent hostilities, while he was king of Pamunkee, and it was not to be supposed that he would patiently submit to the continued and rapid encroachments of the whites upon his lands, to the entire extermination or banishment of his people, now that he possessed the empire of his brother. But to meet them in the field was impossible, the disparity in arms was too great, and the numbers in fighting men now equal; the attempt would be madness and desperation, and lead to that extermination of his race which he wished to avoid. His only resource was to strike some great and sudden blow which should annihilate the power of the colony at once. He had applied to a king who resided on tho Eastern Shore, to purchase a subtle poison which grew only in his dominions, but this king being on good terms with the whites, and wishing to enjoy their trade, refused to gratify him. His next resource was in a general massacre, to take effect upon all of the scattered plantations on the same day. The situation of the whites favored this design; they not only placed confidence in the words of the savages, which had now been so long faithfully kept, but in their weakness and cowardice. They had extended their plantations over a space of one hundred and forty miles, on both sides of James River, and made some settlements in the neighborhood of the Potomac; in short, wherever a rich spot invited to the cultivation of tobacco, there were they established, and an absence of neighbors was preferred. The planters were careless with their arms, never using their swords, and their fire-arms only for game. The old law making it criminal to teach a savage the use of arms was forgotten, and they were fowlers and hunters for many of the planters, by which means they became well acquainted with the use of arms and the places in which they were kept. One great object with the settlers, and with the company, in whose instructions we find it perpetually enjoined, had been the conversion of the Indians to the Christian religion. To promote this pious object, they had always been received in the most friendly manner; they became market people to the planters, and they were fed at their tables, and lodged in their bed-chambers as friends and brothers.

Opechancanough had renewed the treaty with Governor Wyatt, and took every other means in his power to avoid suspicion. He told a messenger, about the middle of March, that the sky should fall ere he would violate the treaty of peace; only two days before the fatal 22d, the English were guided in safety and kindness through the forest by the unsuspected Indians; and a Mr. Browne, who had been sent to live among them to learn their language, was sent safely to his friends;—nay, so well was the dread secret kept, that the English boats were borrowed to transport the Indians over the river to consult on the "devilish murder that ensued;" and even on the day itself, as well as on the evening before, they came as usual unarmed into the settlements with deer, turkeys, fish, fruits, and other provisions to sell, and in some places sat down to breakfast with the English. The concert and secrecy of this great plot is the more astonishing, when we reflect that the savages were not living together as one nation, and did not have for most purposes unity of action, but were dispersed in little hamlets containing from thirty to two hundred in a company; "yet they all had warning given them one from another in all their habitations, March 22, 1622. though far asunder, to meet at the day and hour appointed for the destruction of the English at their several plantations; some directed to one place, some to another, all to be done at the time appointed, which they did accordingly: some entering their houses under color of trading, so took their advantage; others drawing them abroad under fair pretences, and the rest suddenly falling upon those that were at their labors." They spared no age, sex, or condition, and were so sudden in their indiscriminate slaughter that few could discern the blow or weapon which brought them to destruction. Their familiarity with the whites led them with fatal precision to the points at which they were certain to be found, and that "fatal morning fell under the bloody and barbarous hands of that perfidious and inhuman people, three hundred and forty-seven men, women, and children, principally by their own weapons." Not content with this destruction, they brutally defaced and mangled the dead bodies, as if they would perpetrate a new murder, and bore off the several portions in fiendish triumph. Those who had treated them with especial kindness, and conferred many benefits upon them, who confided so much in them that to the last moment they could not believe mischief was intended, fared no better than the rest. The ties of love and gratitude, the sacred rights of hospitality and reciprocal friendship, oaths, pledges, and promises, and even the recent and solemn profession of fidelity to an all-merciful and omnipotent God, were broken asunder or forgotten in obedience to the command of their chief, for the execution of a great but diabolical stroke of state policy. With one, and only one, of all who had been cherished by the whites, did gratitude for their kindness and fidelity to his new religion prevail over his allegiance to his king and affection for his people. A converted Indian who resided with a Mr. Pace, and who was treated by him as a son, revealed the plot to him in the night of the 21st. Pace immediately secured his house and rowed himself up to Jamestown, where he disclosed it to the governor, by which means that place and all the neighboring plantations, to which intelligence could be conveyed, was saved from destruction; for the cowardly Indians when they saw the whites upon their guard immediately retreated. Some other places were also preserved by the undaunted courage of the occupants, who never failed to beat off their assailants, if they were not slain before their suspicions were excited. By these means was Virginia preserved from total annihilation in a single hour, by this well-conceived, well-concealed, and well-executed plot of her weak and simple adversaries. The larger portion of the colony was saved: for a year after the massacre it contained two thousand five hundred persons; but the consternation produced by it, caused the adoption of a ruinous policy. Instead of marching at once boldly to meet the adversary, and driving him from the country, or reducing him to subjection by a bloody retaliation, the colonists were huddled together from their eighty plantations into eight, the college, manufactories, and other works of public utility were abandoned, and cultivation confined to a space almost too limited, merely for subsistence. These crowded quarters produced sickness, and some were so disheartened that they sailed for England.

In England this disastrous intelligence, so far from dispiriting the company, excited their sympathies to such a degree, that it aroused them to renewed exertion, and a more obstinate determination to secure, at all hazards, a country which had cost so much blood and treasure. Supplies were promptly dispatched; and even the king was moved to the generosity of giving some old rusty arms from the tower, which he never meant to use, and promising further assistance, which he never meant to render.

Serious discussions now took place in the courts of the company as to the course proper to be pursued with the Indians, and some advocated their entire subjection, in imitation of the example of the Spaniards,—which policy would surely have been more merciful than that war of extermination which was carried into effect, whether by deliberate design or a system of temporary expedients does not appear. Smith offered the company to protect all their planters from the James to the Potomac, with a permanent force of one hundred soldiers and thirty sailors, with one small bark, and means to build several shallops; and there is no doubt but that he would have accomplished it, by which means the planters could have employed themselves much more successfully in attending to their crops, than when they had to keep perpetual watch, and occasionally to take up arms to defend themselves or make an attack upon the enemy. Smith received for answer that the company was impoverished, but that he had leave to carry his proposal into effect, if he could find means in the colony and would give the company half the booty he should acquire: upon which answer he observes, that except some little corn, he would not give twenty pounds for all the booty to be made from the savages for 20 years. The colonists, although they could not be soon again lulled to their former security, speedily recovered from their recent panic, and on July of the same year sallied forth with three hundred men to seize the corn and inflict other punishment on the Indians. But they suffered themselves to be deceived by false pretences until the corn was removed from their reach, so that they got but little ; they succeeded, however, in burning many of their villages and destroying much of their property, by which they said they were likely to suffer much during the ensuing winter. We find that a law was passed on the following session, by the General Assembly, requiring that on the beginning of July next, the inhabitants of every corporation should fall upon the adjoining savages, as had been done the last year ; and enacting that those who were hurt should be cured at the public charge, and such as were maimed should be maintained by the country, according to their quality. We find it also further enacted in 1630, "that the war begun upon the Indians be effectually followed, and that no peace be concluded with them ; and that all expeditions undertaken against them should be prosecuted with diligence." This state of fierce warfare continued to rage with uninterrupted fury until a peace was concluded in 1632, under the administration of Gov. Harvey. In the course of this warfare the Indians were not treated with the same tenderness with which they had generally been before the massacre, but their habitations, cleared lands, and pleasant sites, when once taken possession of, were generally retained by the victors, and the vanquished forced to take refuge in the woods and marshes.

While these events were transpiring in the colony, an important 1623. change in the character of their government was about to take place in England. The company had been unsuccessful : the fact could no longer be denied. They had transported more than nine thousand persons, at an expense exceeding a hundred thousand pounds ; and yet, in nearly 18 years, there were only about two thousand persons in the colony, and its annual exports did not exceed twenty thousand pounds in value. The king took advantage of the present unfortunate state of affairs, to push his plans for the dissolution of the company. He carefully fomented the dissensions which arose, and encouraged the weaker party, which readily sought the aid of his powerful arm. He had long disliked the democratic freedom of their discussions, and had of late become envious of their little profits on the trade of the colonists, which he felt every disposition to divert into his own coffers ; and he determined to make good use of the present state of despondency in most of the company, and unpopularity with the public, to effect his designs. Wishing, however, to gain his end by stealth, and 1623. secret influence with their officers, rather than by open violence, he again tried his strength in the nomination of four individuals from whom the company were to choose their treasurer. But he was again signally defeated, and the Earl of Southampton re-elected by a large majority, the king's candidates receiving only eight votes in seventy.

Failing in this, it was manifest that the company was not to be browbeaten into submission to his dictation, and he only considered how the charter of the company might be revoked, with the least violation to the laws of England. To effect this with plausible decency some allegation of improper conduct was to be made, and some proof ferreted out. The first of these objects was effected by two long petitions by members of the royal faction in the company, setting forth at full length every evil which had accrued to the colony, from its earliest establishment to that hour, and charging all upon the mismanagement of the company. For many of these charges there was too much truth, and the faults of the company could be easily seen after the accidents had happened; but whether they were not necessarily incidental to the situation of things in Virginia, or they might have been avoided by the king or a corporation differently constituted, are questions difficult to answer; but these petitions contained, mingled with these truths, a great proportion of glaring falsehood as to the physical and moral condition of the colony. They had been prepared and presented with great secrecy; but the company contrived to obtain copies of them, and refuted their slanders by the most irrefragable testimony, many facts being in the cognizance of the members themselves, and others established by the evidence of respectable persons who had long resided in Virginia. This mass of evidence was laid before the king, in the vain hope that he might be induced to disregard the petitions; but part of his object was now gained, the charges were made, the next step was to procure a semblance of proof: for this purpose, in a few days, in answer to the prayer in one of the petitions, he issued a commission, under the great seal, to seven persons, to inquire into all matters respecting Virginia, from the beginning of its settlement.

The better to enable these commissioners to conduct their investigations, by an order of the privy council, all the records of the company, of whatsoever nature, were seized, the deputy treasurer was imprisoned, and on the arrival of a ship from Virginia, all the papers on board were inspected.

The report of these commissioners has never transpired, but it October, 1623. was, without doubt, such as the king wished and expected; for by an order in council he made known, that having taken into his princely consideration the distressed state of Virginia, occasioned by the ill-government of the company, he had resolved, by a new charter, to appoint a governor and twelve assistants to reside in England; and a governor and twelve assistants to reside in Virginia; the former to be nominated by his majesty in council, the latter to be nominated by the governor and assistants in England, and be appointed by the king in council; and that all proceedings should be subject to the royal direction. This was a return at one step to the charter of 1606. The company was called together to consider upon this arbitrary edict, under an alternative similar to the one given to witches upon their trial: if they could swim with a heavy weight about their necks, they were burned as guilty; if they sunk and drowned, they were acquitted: the king gave the company the privilege of accepting his proposition and resigning its charter, or of refusing and having the charter annulled.

The company, which had refused to gratify the king in the choice of its officers, was less disposed to comply with this suicidal requisition. The astounding order was read over three several times before they could convince themselves that their ears informed them correctly of its purport. At length the vote was taken, and one hundred and twelve votes were against the relinquishment, and twenty-six, the precise number of the king's faction, in favor of it. The company asked further time for a more deliberate decision, as there had not been sufficient notice, few members were present, and it was one of those matters of importance which could not be decided, by the terms of their charter, except at a regular quarterly meeting; but the council would not listen to the proposition, ordering the company to meet again in three days, and give a clear, direct, and final answer. In obedience to this order, an extraordinary court was summoned, and the question of surrender submitted to their consideration, upon which only nine of the seventy present voted in its favor; an answer was returned that they would defend their charter. The knowledge of these proceedings transpiring produced a shock to the credit of the company, which palsied for the time the spirit of commercial enterprise; to remedy this evil the privy council declared that the private property of every one should be protected, and secured by additional guarantees if necessary; that they should proceed with their regular business; and all ships bound for Virginia should sail. To endeavor to discover something more authentic against the company than his secret conclave of commissioners had yet been able to obtain, the king now thought proper to Oct. 24, 1623. send John Harvey, John Pory, Abraham Piersey, Samuel Matthews, and John Jefferson, as commissioners to Virginia, " To make more particular and diligent inquiry touching divers matters, which concerned the state of Virginia; and in order to facilitate this inquiry, the governor and council of Virginia were ordered to assist the commissioners, in this scrutiny, by all their knowledge and influence."

The commissioners early in the ensuing year arrived in the 1624. colony. In all of this controversy between the king and the company, the colony not supposing its chartered rights were likely to be violated by either party, and feeling little interest in the discussion of rights which belonged entirely to others, and which they never supposed they were to possess; had acted with entire neutrality, and cared little whether they were to be under the general superintendence of the courts of the company, or a council chosen by the king, so long as they could regulate their own affairs by their own General Assembly.*

In such a mood would the commissioners have found the colony and General Assembly, had they not procured copies of the two slanderous petitions, in spite of all the precautions of the king, and the secrecy of his council and commissioners. Although they felt little interest in the controversy, they felt great interest in defending themselves from defamation, and their country from false and malicious representations, well calculated to disparage and depreciate it in the estimation of those with whom they wished it to Feb. 20, 1624. stand fairest. In six days from their meeting they had prepared spirited and able answers to these petitions; declaring in their preamble, " that they, holding it a sin against God and their own sufferings, to permit the world to be abused with false reports, and to give to vice the reward of virtue,—They, in the name of the whole colony of Virginia, in their General Assembly met, many of them having been eye-wit-

---

* The king and company quarrelled, and, by a mixture of law and force, the latter were ousted of all their rights, without retribution, after having expended £100,000 in establishing the colony, without the smallest aid from the government. King James suspended their powers by proclamation of July 15, 1624, and Charles I. took the government into his own hands. Both sides had their partisans in the colony; but in truth the people of the colony in general thought themselves little concerned in the dispute. There being three parties interested in these several charters, what passed between the first and second it was thought could not affect the third. If the king seized on the powers of the company, they only passed into other hands, without increase or diminution, while the rights of the people remained as they were. Jefferson's Notes on Va., p. 152-3.

nesses and sufferers in those times, had framed, out of their duty to their country and love of truth, the following answer given to the praises of Sir T. Smith's government, in the said declaration."

They next drafted a petition to the king, which, with a letter to the privy council and the other papers, were committed to the care of Mr. John Pountis, a member of the council, who was selected to go to England to represent the general interests of the colony before his majesty and the privy council; and whose expenses were provided for by a tax of four pounds of the best merchantable tobacco for every male person sixteen years of age, who had been in the country for one year. This gentleman unfortunately died on his passage. The letter to the privy council marks very strongly the value which they set even at that early day upon the right of legislating for themselves; the principal prayer in it being, " that the governors may not have absolute power, and that they might still retain the liberty of popular assemblies, than which, nothing could more conduce to the public satisfaction and public utility."

A contest of wits was commenced between the commissioners and the Assembly. The former, under various pretexts, withheld from the latter a sight of their commission, and the other papers with which they had been charged; and the governor and the Assembly thought proper to preserve an equal mystery as to their own proceedings. In this dilemma Mr. Pory, who was one of the commissioners, and who had been secretary to the company, and discharged from his post for betraying its councils to the earl of Warwick, now suborned Edward Sharpless, a clerk of the council, to give him copies of the proceedings of that body and of the Assembly. This treachery was discovered, and the clerk was punished with the loss of his ears; while an account was sent home to the company, expressive of the greatest abhorrence at the baseness and treachery of Pory. The commissioners finding their secret manœuvring defeated, next endeavored, by the most artful wheedling, to induce the Assembly to petition the crown for a revocation of the charter. In reply to this the Assembly asked for their authority to make such a proposition, which of course they could not give without betraying their secret instructions, and were compelled to answer the requisition in general terms and professions. The Assembly took no farther notice of the commissioners, but proceeded with their ordinary legislation.

Thirty-five acts of this Assembly have been preserved to the present time, and exhibit, with great strength, the propriety and good sense with which men can pass laws for the regulation of their own interests and concerns. One of these acts establishes at once, in the most simple and intelligible language, the great right of exemption from taxation without representation ; it runs in these words :—" The governor shall not lay any taxes or impositions upon the colony, their lands or commodities, other way than by the authority of the General Assembly, to be levied and employed as the said Assembly shall appoint." By a subsequent act it was declared that the governor should not withdraw the inhabitants from their private labors to any service of his own, upon any color whatsoever and in case the public service required the employment of many hands, before the holding of a General Assembly, he was to order it, and the levy of men was to be made by the governor and whole body of the council, in such manner as would be least burdensome to the people and most free from partiality. To encourage good conduct, the old planters who had been in the colony since the last arrival of Gates, were exempted from taxation or military duty. Many acts of general utility were passed; the members of the Assembly were privileged from arrest ; lands were to be surveyed and their boundaries recorded, which is no doubt the origin of our highly beneficial recording statutes ; vessels arriving were prohibited from breaking their cargoes until they had reported themselves ; inspectors of tobacco were established in every settlement ; the use of sealed weights and measures was enforced ; provision was made for paying the public debt, " brought on by the late troubles ;" no person was, upon the rumor of supposed change and alteration, to presume to be disobedient to the present government, or servants to their private officers, masters, or overseers, at their uttermost perils.

Wise regulations were likewise made to prevent surprises by the Indians; every house was to be fortified with palisadoes; no man should go or send abroad without a party sufficiently armed, or to work without their arms, with a sentinel over them; the inhabitants were forbidden to go aboard ships or elsewhere in such numbers as to endanger the safety of their plantations; every planter was to take care to have sufficient arms and ammunition in good order; watch was to be kept by night; and no planter was to suffer powder to be expended in amusement or entertainments. To promote corn-planting, and ensure plenty of provision, no limit was fixed to its price; viewers were appointed to see that every man planted a sufficiency for his family, and all trade with the savages for corn was strictly prohibited.

Having thus given a specimen of colonial spirit, and colonial legislation, we return to the little intrigues of James, who was striving by every means in his power to become possessed of the control of the colony; partly to gratify his love of arbitrary authority and of money, and partly to gratify his royal self-complacency, by framing a code of laws for a people with whose character and condition he was utterly unacquainted, and who, from the specimens recently given, appeared to be fully competent to the management of their own affairs, without the dictation or advice of this royal guardian; who, while he displayed the craft without the talent of a Philip, aspired to the character of a Solon. The recent acts of the king led to a solemn council of the company on the state of their affairs, in which they confirmed by an overwhelming majority the previous determination to defend their charter, and asked for a restitution of their papers for the purpose of preparing their defence. This request was pronounced reasonable by the attorney-general, and complied with. While these papers were in the hands of the company, they were transcribed, and the copy has been fortunately preserved, and presents a faithful record of many portions of Virginia history, which it would be otherwise impossible to elucidate.*

The king had caused a quo warranto to be issued against the company soon after the appointment of his com-

Nov. 10, 1624. missioners to go to Virginia, and the cause was tried in the King's Bench, in Trinity Term of 1624. A cause which their royal master had so much at heart could not long be doubtful with judges entirely dependent upon his will for their places; it is even credibly reported that this important case, whereby the rights of a powerful corporation were divested, and the possibility of a remuneration for all of their trouble and expense forever cut off, was decided upon a mere technical question of special pleading !†

---

* Burke, p. 274-5. Stith compiled his history principally from these documents.
† Note to Bancroft, p. 207. Stith, p. 329, 330, doubts if judgment was passed. The doubt may be removed. " Before the end of the same term, a judgment was declared by the Lord Chief Justice Ley, against the company and their charter, only upon *failer or mistake in pleading.*" See a Short Collection of the most Remarkable Passages from the Original to the Dissolution of the Virginia Company: London, 1651, p. 15. See also Hazard, vol. I. p. 19; Chalmers, p. 62; Proud's Pennsylvania, vol. I., p. 107.

In the mean time the commissioners had returned, and reported very favorably of the soil and climate of Virginia, but censuring deeply the conduct of the company,—recommending the government of the original charter of 1606, and declaring that a body so large and so democratic in its forms as the company, could never persevere in a consistent course of policy, but must veer about as the different factions should prevail. In this it must be admitted that there was much truth, and all hopes of profit having for some time expired, and the company only being kept up by the distinguished men of its members, from patriotic motives and as an instrument of power for thwarting the king, in which capacity its present unpopularity rendered it of little use—it was now suffered to expire under the judicial edict, without a groan. The expiration of the charter brought little immediate change to the actual government of the colony:—a large committee was formed by the king, consisting principally of his privy council, to discharge the functions of the extinct company; Sir Francis Wyatt was reappointed governor, and he and his council only empowered to govern " as fully and amply as any governor and council resident there, at any time within the space of five years last' past"— which was the exact period of their representative government. The king, in appointing the council in Virginia, refused to appoint embittered partisans of the court faction, but formed the government of men of moderation.

So leaving Virginia free, while his royal highness is graciously pleased to gratify his own vanity in preparing a new code of laws to regulate her affairs, we pass on to a new chapter.

CHAPTER IV.

PROGRESS OF THE COLONY FROM THE DISSOLUTION OF THE LONDON COMPANY, TO THE BREAKING OUT OF BACON'S REBELLION IN 1675.

Accession of Charles I.—Tobacco trade.—Yeardley governor—his commission favorable—his death and character.—Lord Baltimore's reception.—State of religion—legislation upon the subject.—Invitation to the Puritans to settle on Delaware Bay.— Harvey governor.—Grant of Carolina and Maryland.—Harvey deposed—restored.— Wyatt governor.—Acts of the Legislature improperly censured.—Berkeley governor. —Indian relations.—Opechancanough prisoner—his death.—Change of government in England.—Fleet and army sent to reduce Virginia.—Preparation for defence by Berkeley.—Agreement entered into between the colony and the commissioners of the commonwealth.—Indian hostilities.—Matthews elected governor.—Difficulties between the governor and the legislature—adjusted.—State of the colony and its trade.—Commissioners sent to England.—The Restoration.—General legislation.

THE dissolution of the London Company was soon followed by
March 27, 1625. the death of James, and the accession of his son,
Charles I. The king troubled himself little about
the political rights and privileges of the colony, and suffered them

to grow to the strength of established usage by his wholesome neglect; while he was employed in obtaining a monopoly of their tobacco. This valuable article, the use of which extended with such unaccountable rapidity, had early attracted the avidity of King James. The 19th article of the charter of 1609 had exempted the company, their agents, factors, and assignees, from the payment of all subsidies and customs in Virginia for the space of one and twenty years, and from all taxes and impositions forever, upon any goods imported thither, or exported thence into any of the realms or dominions of England; except the five per cent. usual by the ancient trade of merchants. But notwithstanding the express words of this charter, a tax was laid by the farmers of the customs, in the year 1620, upon the tobacco of the colony; which was not only high of itself, but the more oppressive because it laid the same tax upon Virginia and Spanish tobacco, when the latter sold in the market for three times the price of the former. In the same year the same prince was guilty of another violation of the charter, in forcing the company to bring all of their tobacco into England; when he found that a portion of their trade had been diverted into Holland, and establishments made at Middleburg and Flushing. The charters all guarantied to the colony all of the rights, privileges, franchises, and immunities of native born Englishmen, and this act of usurpation was the first attempt on the part of the mother country to monopolize the trade of the colony. The next year the king, either his avidity being unsatisfied, or not liking the usurped and precarious tenure by which his gains were held, inveigled the Virginia and Somer Isles company into an arrangement, by which they were to become the sole importers of tobacco; being bound, however, to import not less than forty nor more than sixty thousand pounds of Spanish varinas, and paying to the king, in addition to the sixpence duty before paid, one-third part of all the tobacco landed in the realms. The king, on his part, was to prohibit all other importation and all planting in England and Ireland; and that which was already planted was to be confiscated.

When the company petitioned parliament to prolong its existence, in opposition to the efforts of the king, they failed—but that portion of their petition, which asked for the exclusive monopoly of Sep. 29, 1624. tobacco to Virginia and the Somer Isles, was granted, and a royal proclamation issued accordingly. Whether this exclusiveness was understood with the limitation in the previous contract between the king and the two companies, it is impossible to say, as the original documents are not accessible to the writer.* But the probabilities are greatly against the limitation.

Charles had not been long on the throne before he issued a

---

* Burke, I. 291, and Bancroft, I. 206—quoting Stith, Cobbett's Parliament. Hist. and Hazard.

April 9, 1625. proclamation, confirming the exclusive privileges of the Virginia and Somer Isles tobacco ; and prohibiting a violation of their monopoly, under penalty of censure by the dread star-chamber. This was soon followed by another, in which he carefully set forth the forfeiture of their charter by the company, and the immediate dependence of the colony upon the crown ; concluding by a plain intimation of his intention to become their sole factor.

Soon after this, a rumor reached the colonies that an individual was in treaty with the king for an exclusive contract for tobacco ; one of the conditions of which would have led to the importation of so large an amount of Spanish tobacco, as would have driven that of the colonists from the market. The earnest representations of the colony on this subject caused an abandonment of the scheme ; but in return, the colony was obliged to excuse itself from a charge of trade with the Low Countries, and promise to trade only with England. But the king's eagerness for the possession of this monopoly was not to be baffled thus. He made a formal proposition to the colony for their exclusive trade, in much the same language as one tradesman would use to another ; and desired that the General Assembly might be convened for the purpose of considering his proposition. The answer by the Mar. 26, 1628. General Assembly to this proposition is preserved. It sets forth in strong, but respectful language the injury which had been done the planters, by the mere report of an intention to subject their trade to a monopoly : they state the reasons for not engaging in the production of the other staples mentioned by the king ; and dissent from his proposition as to the purchase of their tobacco ; demanding a higher price and better terms of admission, in exchange for the exclusive monopoly which he wished.

In the mean time, the death of his father rendered it necessary 1626. for Sir Francis Wyatt to return to Europe, to attend to his private affairs ; and the king appointed Sir George Yeardley his successor. This was itself a sufficient guarantee of the political privileges of the colony ; as he had had the honor of calling the first colonial assembly. But in addition to this, his powers were, like those of his predecessor, limited to the executive authority exercised by the governor within five years last past. These circumstances taken in connection with the express sanction given by Charles to the power of a legislative assembly, with regard to his proffered contract for tobacco, sufficiently prove that he had no design of interfering with the highly prized privilege of self-government enjoyed by the colonists : and fully justifies the General Assembly in putting the most favorable construction upon the king's ambiguous words, announcing his determination to preserve inviolate all the "former interests" of Virginia, which occur in his letter of 1627.

Thus were those free principles established in Virginia, for which the mother country had to struggle for some time longer.

The colony rose in the estimation of the public, and a thousand new emigrants arrived in one year; which of course much enhanced the price of provision.

Death now closed the career of Yeardley. The character of his administration is exhibited in the history of the colony;

Nov. 14, 1627.

and the estimate placed upon his character by those who were best acquainted with his conduct, and who were little disposed to flatter undeservedly either the living or the dead, is to be found in a eulogy written by the government of Virginia to the privy council, announcing his death. In obedience to the king's commission to the council, they elected Francis West governor, the day after the burial of Yeardley. He held the commission until the 5th of March, 1628, when, designing to sail for England, John Pott was chosen to succeed him. Pott did not continue long in office, for the king, when the death of Yeardley was known, issued his commission to Sir John Harvey, who arrived some time between October, 1628, and March, 1629.

In the interval between the death of Yeardley and the arrival of Harvey, occurred the first act of religious intolerance which defiles the annals of Virginia.

Lord Baltimore, a Catholic nobleman, allured by the rising reputation of the colony, abandoned his settlement in Newfoundland and came to Virginia; where, instead of being received with the cheerful welcome of a friend and a brother, he was greeted with the oath of allegiance and supremacy; the latter of which, it was well known, his conscience would not allow him to take.

Much allowance is to be made for this trespass upon religious freedom before we attribute it to a wilful violation of natural liberty. The times and circumstances ought to be considered. The colony had grown into life while the violent struggles between the Romish and Protestant churches were yet rife. The ancient tyranny and oppression of the Holy See were yet fresh in the memory of all; its cruelties and harsh intolerance in England were recent; and yet continuing in the countries in which its votaries had the control of the civil government. The light of Protestantism itself was the first dawn of religious freedom; and the thraldom in which mankind had been held by Catholic fetters for so many ages, was too terrible to risk the possibility of their acquiring any authority in government. Eye-witnesses of the severities of Mary were yet alive in England, and doubtless many of the colonists had heard fearful relations of the religious sufferings during her reign, probably some had suffered in their own families: most of them had emigrated while the excitement against the Papists was still raging in England with its greatest fury, and continually kept in action by the discovery, or pretended discovery, of Popish plots to obtain possession of the government. Was it wonderful, then, that a colony which, with a remarkable uniformity of sentiment, professed a different religion, should be jealous of a faith which sought by every means in its power to obtain supreme control, and used that control for the extermination, by the harshest means, of all other creeds?

The colony in Virginia was planted when the incestuous and monstrous connection of church and state had not been severed in any civilized country on the globe; at a period when it would have been heresy to attempt such a divorce, because it required all the aid of the civil power to give men sufficient freedom to "profess, and by argument to maintain," any other creed than one—and that one the creed of Rome. The anxiety of the British government upon this subject, so far from being unnatural, was highly laudable, since all its efforts were necessary to sustain its new-born power of professing its own creed. The awful effect of Catholic supremacy, displayed in a neighboring kingdom, afforded a warning too terrible* to be easily forgotten; and it would have been as unwise to allow the Catholics equal civil privileges at that day, as it would be impolitic and unjust now to exclude them. We find this regard for religious

---

* The massacre of the Protestants by the Catholics on St. Bartholomew's day, in France, in 1572.

freedom, (for emancipation from the Pope's authority was a great step in religious freedom,) carefully fostered in the colonies. Every charter requires the establishment of the church of England, and authorizes the infliction of punishment for drawing off the people from their religion, as a matter of equal importance with their allegiance. For at that period, before any important differences between the Protestants had arisen, when but two religions were struggling for existence, not to be of the church of England was to be a Papist, and not to acknowledge the secular supremacy of the king, was to bow to the authority of the pope. The Catholics, as the only subject of terror, were the only subjects of intolerance; no sufficient number of dissenters had availed themselves of the great example of Protestantism, in rejecting any creed which did not precisely satisfy their consciences, to become formidable to mother church; nor had she grown so strong and haughty in her new-fledged power, as to level her blows at any but her first great antagonist.*

The colony in Virginia consisted of church of England men; and many of the first acts of their legislature relate to provision for the church. Glebe lands were early laid off, and livings provided. The ministers were considered not as pious and charitable individuals, but as officers of the state, bound to promote the true faith and sound morality, by authority of the community by which they were paid, and to which they were held responsible for the performance of their duty. The very first act of Assembly which was passed, required that in every settlement in which the people met to worship God, a house should be appropriated exclusively to that purpose, and a place paled in to be used solely as a burying-ground; the second act imposed a penalty of a pound of tobacco for absence from divine service on Sunday, without sufficient excuse, and fifty pounds for a month's absence; the third, required uniformity, as nearly as might be, with the canons in England; the fourth, enjoined the observance of the holy days, (adding the 22d of March, the day of the Massacre, to the number,) dispensing with some, "by reason of our necessities;" the fifth, punished any minister absenting himself from his church above two months in the year, with forfeiture of half his estate—and four months, his whole estate and curacy; the sixth, punished disparagement of a minister; the seventh, prohibited any man from disposing of his tobacco or corn, until the minister's portion was first paid. This sacred duty discharged, the Assembly next enact salutary regulations for the state. We find at the session of 1629, the act requiring attendance at church on the Sabbath, specially enforced, and a clause added, forbidding profanation of that day by travelling or work; also an act, declaring that all those who work in the ground shall pay tithes to the minister. We find requisition of uniformity with the canons of the English church not only repeated, in every new commission from England, but re-enacted by the legislature of 1629–30, and in 1631–32, as well as in the several revisals of the

---

* The persecution of the Puritans was an exception to this. They were persecuted with considerable rigor, but their numbers were small, consisting only of two churches, and most of those who then existed went to Holland with their leaders, John Robinson and William Brewster, in 1607 and 8, and settled in Amsterdam, whence they removed to Leyden in 1609, whence they sailed to America in 1620, and landed in Cape Cod Harbor on the 7th of November, and settled Plymouth on the 31st of December following.—Holmes' Am. An. 156–203.

laws. In the acts of 1631–32, we find many acts conveying the idea advanced of ministers being considered public officers ; and churchwardens required to take an oath, to present offences against decency or morality, which made them in effect censors of the public morals. In these acts, it is made the duty of ministers to teach children the Lord's prayer, commandments, and the articles of faith ; also to attend all persons dangerously sick, to instruct and comfort them in their distress ; to keep registers of christening, marriages, and deaths ; and to preserve in themselves strict moral conduct, as an advancement to religion and an example to others. We find, also, frequent acts passed providing for the payment of ministers, until the session of 1657–58, when church and state seem to have been effectually divorced ; for, though no act of religious freedom was passed, but all were still expected, rather than compelled, to conform to the church of England, yet the compulsory payment of ministers was abandoned, and all matters relating to the church were left entirely to the control of the people.

From the review which we have given of the religious condition of England and the colony, it must be manifest that the tender of the oath of supremacy to Lord Baltimore, was not only a religious but a civil duty in the council, which they could by no means have omitted, without a violation of their own oaths, laws, and charters. But if any further proof were necessary, to show that it flowed from this source, and not from a disposition to religious intolerance—it is afforded by the liberal invitation given in the instructions to Captain Bass to the Puritans, who had settled at New Plymouth, to desert their cold and barren soil, and come and settle upon Delaware Bay, which was in the limits of Virginia.

Harvey met his first General Assembly in March, and its acts, 1629. as those of several succeeding sessions, only consist of the usual business acts of the colony. We have now approached a period in our history, upon which the few scattered and glimmering lights which exist, have rather served to mislead than to guide historians. It is a period replete with charges made by historians, of the most heinous character, against the governor, with no evidence upon record to support them. The truth is, that Sir John Harvey was deposed and sent home by the colony for some improper conduct ; but what that was, does not fully appear, and historians seem to have thought it their duty to supply the defect in the record, by abusing his administration as arbitrary and tyrannical from the first : the charge is without evidence, and every probability is against its truth. During the whole of his administration, the General Assembly met and transacted their business as usual. The fundamental laws which they had passed, to which we have before referred, restraining the powers of the governor, and asserting the powers of the Assembly, were passed again as of course. There could manifestly be no oppression from this source. The General Assembly ordered the building of forts, made the contracts, provided the payments, provided garrisons and soldiers for the field when necessary, and disbanded them when the occasion for their services had ceased. The Assembly and the soldiers were planters, and they could be little disposed to oppress themselves, their families and friends. The only evidence which exists against Harvey, is the fact of his being deposed, and sent home with commissioners to complain of his conduct to the king; but this did not occur until 1635, after the extensive grants had been made to Lord Baltimore and others, which dismembered the colony, and were so displeasing to the planters; and we shall see that aid or connivance in these grants were the probable causes of Harvey's unpopularity.

The first act of tyranny towards the colony which we find recorded against Charles, was his grant in 1630 to Sir Robert Heath of a large portion of the lands of the colony—commencing at the 36th degree of latitude, and including the whole southern portion of the United States, under the name of Carolina. But as this country was not settled until long afterwards, and the charter became void by non-compliance with its terms, it could not be regarded as injurious by the colony, except as an evidence of the facility with which their chartered rights could be divested. Another instance of a more objectionable character soon occurred. Cecilius Calvert, Lord Baltimore, obtained a grant of that portion of Virginia which is now included in the state of Maryland, and immediately commenced a settlement upon it, notwithstanding the value which the Virginians set upon it, and their having actually made settlements within its limits. William Claiborne, who had been a member of the council, and secretary of state for Virginia, had obtained a license from the king to "traffic in those parts of America where there was no license," which had been confirmed by Harvey. In pursuance of this authority he had settled himself at Kent Island, near the city of Annapolis, and seemed by no means inclined tamely to relinquish his possessions. He resisted the encroachments of Maryland by force. This was the first controversy between the whites which ever took place on the waters of the Chesapeake. Claiborne was indicted, and found of guilty of murder, piracy, and sedition; and to escape punishment he fled to Virginia. When the Maryland commissioners demanded him, Harvey refused to give him up, but sent him to England to be tried. It is highly probable that the conduct of Harvey in giving up instead of protecting Claiborne, incensed the colony against him; for they clearly thought the Maryland charter an infringement of their rights, and they were little inclined to submit to imposition from any quarter.

The account which we have of the trial of Harvey is extremely meager, detailing neither the accusations nor the evidence, but only the fact. The manner of proceeding, however, as it appears on the record, is as little like that of an enslaved people, as it is like a "transport of popular rage and indignation." The whole

1632.

matter seems to have been conducted with calm deliberation, as a
free people acting upon the conduct of an unworthy servant. The
first entry upon the subject runs thus : " An assembly to be called
to receive complaints against Sir John Harvey, on the petition of
many inhabitants, to meet 7th of May." Could as much coolness,
deliberation, and publicity be given to action against a tyrant who
had already trodden liberty under foot ? or is a transport of popular rage so slow in action ? The next entry upon this subject is
the following : " On the 28th of April, 1635, Sir John Harvey
thrust out of his government, and Capt. John West acts as governor, till the king's pleasure known." It appears that before the
Assembly met which was to have heard complaints against Harvey, he agreed in council to go to England to answer them ; and
upon that, West was elected governor.

How long West governed is uncertain ; but it appears by a
paper among the records, that Harvey was governor again in January, 1636. It appears that Charles regarded the conduct of the
colony as an unwarrantable piece of insolence, little short of treason, and would not even hear them, lest the spectacle of so noble
an example might inflame the growing discontents in his own
kingdom, which finally rose to such a pitch, as not only to take the
same unwarrantable liberty of deposing him, but even laid violent
hands upon his sacred person. He accordingly sent the commissioners home with their grievances untold, and Harvey was rein-
stated in his power without undergoing even a trial. The conduct
of the colony appears to have been a salutary lesson to him, and
he probably feared that for the next offence they would take
justice into their own hands ; for we hear no complaints of him
during his administration, which expired in November, 1639. Sir
Francis Wyatt succeeded him.

In 1634 the colony was divided into eight shires,* which were
to be governed as the shires in England: lieutenants were to be
appointed in the same manner as in England, and it was their
especial duty to pay attention to the war against the Indians.
Sheriffs, sergeants, and bailiffs, were also to be elected as in England. In 1628–9 commissions were issued to hold monthly courts
in the different settlements, which was the origin of our county
court system.

At the first assembly which was held after the return of Wyatt,
several acts were passed, which, from the inattention of historians
to the circumstances of the times, have received universal reprobation, but which, when properly considered, will be found to be
marked with great shrewdness, and dictated by the soundest
policy.

The act declares that, " tobacco by reason of excessive quantities being made, being
so low, that the planters could not subsist by it, or be enabled to raise more staple com-

---

* Viz., James City, Henrico, Charles City, Elizabeth City, Warwick River, Warros
quoyoke, Charles River, and Accomack.

modities, or pay their debts : therefore it was *enacted*, that the tobacco of that year be viewed by sworn viewers, and the rotten and unmerchantable, and *half the good*, to be burned. So the whole quantity made would come to 1,500,000 lbs., without stripping and smoothing ; and the next two years 170 lbs. tobacco per poll, stripped and smoothed, was to be made, which would make, in the whole, about 1,300,000 lbs., and all *creditors* were to take 40 *lbs. for a hundred.*" By a second act, it was declared that " no man should be obliged to perform above half his covenants about freighting tobacco in 1639." Nothing could be more absurd than such acts at the present day, and hence they have been pronounced absurd at that time. But let us look to the circumstances. Except the little tobacco made in the Somer Isles, Virginia at that time had the monopoly of the English market. The taste for tobacco was new, existed with few, and could not be suddenly extended ; consequently the consumption could not be increased in proportion to the increase of supply, but those who used it would obtain it at a price proportionably less. Thus a superabundant supply so glutted the market as to reduce the article to a price ruinous to the planters. On the other hand, with those who had acquired a taste for tobacco, it was nearly indispensable, and if less than a usual crop was made, the demand enhanced the value of the remainder beyond that of the full crop ; hence the propriety of burning half of the good tobacco. This seems to have been perceived, and we have seen no fault found with the first portion of the act ; but the latter part, forcing creditors to take less than their full dues, has been pronounced flagrantly unjust. But if this had not been done, what would have been the condition of the planter ? If he had made a hundred pounds, and owed fifty, the burning and his creditor would deprive him of his whole crop, while the creditor receiving the fifty pounds at its enhanced value, would receive more than double what was due him. This would have been highly oppressive to the debtor, and made the whole act redound entirely to the benefit of the creditor. Whereas, making him take forty pounds in the hundred, when that forty was enhanced to more than the value of the hundred, was no hardship.

In the early stages of the colony, the planters wanted the comforts of life from England, and not money, for money could purchase nothing in America. It would have been wasteful extravagance to have brought it. The Virginians had but one article of export, —all trading vessels came for tobacco,—hence that would purchase every thing, and became, on that account, useful to every man, and an article of universal desire, as money is in other countries, and hence the standard of value and circulating medium of the colony. We find, when money first began to be introduced, as the keeping accounts in tobacco was inconvenient to the foreign merchants who came to trade, an act was passed with the following preamble :—" Whereas it hath been the usual custom of merchants and others dealing intermutually in this colony, to make all bargains, contracts, and to keep all accounts in tobacco, and not in money," &c. It then goes on to enact that in future they should be kept in money, and that in all pleas and actions the value should be represented in money. This was in 1633. But it was found so inconvenient to represent value by an arbitrary standard, the representative of which did not exist in the colony, that another act was passed in January, 1641, declaring that,—" Whereas many and great inconveniences do daily arise by dealing for money, Be it enacted and confirmed by the authority of this present Grand Assembly, that all money-debts made since the 26th day of March, 1642, or which hereafter shall be made, shall not be *pleadable or recoverable* in any court of justice under this government." An exception was afterwards made in 1642-3, in favor of debts contracted for horses or sheep, but money-debts generally were not even made recoverable again until 1656. We thus see that tobacco was the currency, and an excess as injurious as an over-issue of bank-paper, depreciating itself in the market, or, in common parlance, causing every thing to rise We see, moreover, the cause of the excessive care taken in burning bad tobacco, since that was as important to the uniformity of their currency as the exclusion of counterfeits in a money currency. All the viewings, censorships, inspections, regulations of the amount to be cultivated by each planter, each hand,—the quantity to be gathered from each plant,—the regulations prescribed as to curing it,—are to be regarded more as *mint regulations* than as regulations of agricultural industry. Indeed, we find the attempt to sell or pay bad tobacco, is made a crime precisely as it is now to sell or pay counterfeit money. This act of Assembly then allowed debtors to discharge themselves by paying half their debts *in amount*, did, in effect, make them pay all *in value*, and can by no means be compared to the acts of states or princes in debasing the coin, and allowing it to retain its old nominal value, or by introducing valueless paper money ; in these cases, the debt is paid nominally, or in words, but not in *value*, whereas in Virginia it was not paid nominally, as it had been contracted for so many *pounds* of tobacco, but it was paid in *fewer* pounds, rendered of *greater actual value* than the debt would have amounted to if paid in *pounds* before the burning of half the quantity made.

Wyatt remained governor only for one year and a few months, when he was succeeded by Sir William Berkeley. Historians who have not been aware of the intermediate administration of Wyatt and have heard no complaint of Berkeley, have delighted to deck his character in the gayest colors, in contrast to the black character which they have drawn of Harvey. There can be no doubt that he was esteemed an accomplished and chivalric gentleman; but his accession brought no increase of political freedom to Virginia, and his commission did not differ from those of his predecessors. On the contrary, the instructions which he brought, so far from granting new franchises, imposed new, severe, and unwarrantable restrictions on the liberty of trade; England claiming that monopoly of colonial commerce, which was ultimately enforced by the navigation act, and which was a perpetual source of contention, until all differences were finally healed by the revolution.

Berkeley arrived in February, 1642; an assembly met in March, and soon after passed a solemn protest against a petition which Sir George Sandys had presented to Parliament for the restoration of the company. This paper is drawn with great ability, and sets forth the objections to the petition in very strong and striking terms. They enlarge especially upon the wish and power of the company to monopolize their trade; the advantages and happiness secured to them by their present form of government, with its annual assemblies and trial by jury; the fact, that a restitution of the power of the company would be an admission of the illegality of the king's authority, and a consequent nullification of the grants and commissions issued by him; and the impossibility of men, however wise, at such a distance, and unacquainted with the climate or condition of the country, to govern the colony as well as it could be governed by their own Grand Assembly. The king, in reply to this, declared his purpose not to change a form of government in which they received so much content and satisfaction.

Other important matters were settled at this legislature. A tax for the benefit of the governor was abolished. The punishment by condemnation to temporary service was abolished, which had existed ever since the foundation of the colony; and this protection to liberty was considered as so important to the Assembly, that they declared it was to be considered as a record by the inhabitants of their birthright as Englishmen, and that the oppression of the late company was quite extinguished. The governor probably received some benefit from these considerations, for he is praised for giving his assent to an act in which he preferred the public freedom to his particular profit. A nearer approach was made to the laws and customs of England in proceedings of courts and trials of causes. Better regulations were prescribed for discussing and deciding land titles. The bounds of parishes were more accurately marked. A treaty with Maryland, opening the trade of the Chesapeake, was matured; and peace with the Indians confirmed. Taxes were proportioned more to men's estates and abilities than to the numbers, by which the poor were much relieved, "but which through the strangeness thereof could not but require much time and debating." They published a list of their acts in order to show to the colony that they had not swerved from " the true intent of their happy constitution," which required them to " enact good and wholesome laws, and rectify and relieve such disorders and grievances as are incident to all states and republics ; but that their late consultations would redound greatly to the benefit of the colony and their posterity." In the conclusion of that list, they state, that the gracious inclination of his majesty, ever ready to protect them, and now more particularly assured to them, together with the concurrence of a happy Parliament in England, were the motives which induced them to take this opportunity to " establish their liberties and privileges, and settle their estates, often before assaulted and threatened, and lately invaded by the corporation ; and to prevent the future designs of monopolizers, contractors, and pre-emptors, ever usurping the benefit of their labors ; and they apprehended that no time could be misspent, or labor misplaced, in gaining a firm peace to themselves and posterity, and a future immunity and ease to themselves from taxes and impositions, which they expected to be the fruits of their endeavors."

The Indians had been driven back, and weakened by a perpetual succession of hostilities, from the time of the great massacre, until the year 1644. During the latter years of this period, we have little account of their proceedings, but the rapid increase of the settlements had driven them from the rich borders of the rivers in the lower country, higher into the interior, and the new grants were every day driving them still farther from the homes of their fathers. This incessant warfare, while it weakened them 1644. as a nation, had increased their cunning and skill in partisan warfare. Opechancanough, though now so old that he had to be carried in a litter, and so feeble that he could not raise his eyelids without assistance, still retained sufficient strength of mind to embody a combination of the various tribes under his control, and make a sudden and violent attack upon many of the frontier settlements at once. Little is known of the circumstances attending this second great massacre. An act of Assembly of 1645, making the eighteenth day of April a holiday and day of thanksgiving, for escape from the Indians, marks the period of the massacre. Other evidence makes the number of their victims three hundred.[*] The precautions which the whites had been taught to take by the previous massacre, in trading with them only at particular places, in always going armed, in never admitting them to the same familiarity, effectually prevented them, with all their caution in approach, and violence of attack, from committing as great slaughter as they had upon the former occasion. The whites do not seem to have been stricken with a panic now as formerly, but quickly sallied upon their assailants, and drove them back so rapidly that their venerable chieftain himself had to be deserted by his attendants, and was taken by Sir William Berkeley, at the head of a squadron of light cavalry. He was carried to Jamestown, and manifested, in his imprisonment, the same haughty dignity which had always distinguished him. He preserved a proud and disdainful silence, and such indifference to the passing scenes, that he rarely requested his eyelids to be raised. In this melancholy condition, he was basely shot in the back by his sentinel, with whom recollection of former injuries overcame

---

[*] Bancroft, p. 224.—Burke, v. II. p. 55, says—on authority of Beverley—" five hundred."

all respect for helpless age, or former greatness. The only subject which called forth any show of regret from him was a flash of angry indignation, at being exposed in his dying hours to the idle and curious gaze of his enemies.

So little regard was now paid to the Indian hostilities, that, on the following June, Sir William Berkeley sailed for England, and the council elected Richard Kemp to occupy his post until his return. In the mean time, the warfare with the Indians continued without remission. It appears by an act of the latter part of the year 1644, that many of the inhabitants, probably on the frontiers, had been collected in large bodies; but leave was then given them to dispose of themselves " for their best advantage and convenience, provided that in places of danger there should not be less than ten men allowed to settle."

Sir William Berkeley again took possession of his government Oct. 5, 1646. in June, 1645; and in the following year a treaty of peace was concluded with the Indians, by which Necotowance, the successor of Opechancanough, acknowledged that he held his kingdom of the crown of England, and agreed that his successors should be appointed or confirmed by the king's governor; on the other hand, the Assembly, on behalf of the colony, undertook to protect him against rebels and all enemies whatsoever. In this treaty, the Indians were permitted to dwell on the north side of York River, but ceded to the whites all the country from the falls of the James and York to the bay, forever; and any Indian coming upon that territory was to suffer death, unless he bore the badge of a messenger. The Indians were also to surrender all prisoners, negroes, and arms taken. Other articles were added, prescribing the form of intercourse. Thus were the aborigines at length finally excluded from their father-land, leaving no monument of their having existed, save the names of the waters and mountains, and the barrows containing the ashes of their ancestors.*

Thus the colony of Virginia acquired the management of all its concerns; war was levied, and peace concluded, and territory acquired, in conformity to the acts of the representatives of the people; while the people of the mother country had just acquired these privileges, after a long and bloody conflict with their former sovereign. Possessed of security and quiet, abundance of land, a free market for their staple, and, practically, all the rights of an independent state—having England for its guardian against foreign oppression, rather than its ruler—the colonists enjoyed all the prosperity which a virgin soil, equal laws, and general uniformity

---

* I know of no such thing existing as an Indian monument—of labor on the large scale. I think there is no remain as respectable as would be a common ditch for the draining of lands; unless, indeed, it would be the barrows, of which many are to be found all over the country. That they were repositories of the dead, has been obvious to all; but on what particular occasion constructed, was a matter of doubt.—Jefferson's Notes on Va., p. 132.

of condition and industry, could bestow. Their numbers increased ; the cottages were filled with children, as the ports were with ships and emigrants. At Christmas, 1648, there were trading in Virginia, ten ships from London, two from Bristol, twelve Hollanders, and seven from New England. The number of the colonists was already twenty thousand, and they, who had sustained no griefs, were not tempted to engage in the feuds by which the mother country was divided. They were attached to the cause of Charles, not because they loved monarchy, but because they cherished the 1649. liberties of which he had left them in the undisturbed possession ; and after his execution, though there were not wanting some who favored republicanism, the government recognised his son without dispute.

The loyalty of the Virginians did not escape the attention of June, 1650. the royal exile : from his retreat in Breda he transmitted to Berkeley a new commission, and Charles the Second, a fugitive from England, was still the sovereign of Virginia.

But the Parliament did not long permit its authority to be denied. Having, by the vigorous energy and fearless enthusiasm of republicanism, triumphed over all its enemies in Europe, it turned its attention to the colonies ; and a memorable ordinance at once empowered the council of state to reduce the rebellious colonies to obedience, and at the same time established it as a law that foreign ships should not trade at any of the ports "in Barbadoes, Antigua, Bermudas, and Virginia." Thus giving the first example of that wholesale blockade, afterwards rendered so notorious by the celebrated orders in council during the wars of the French revolution. Maryland, which was not expressly included in the ordinance, had taken care to acknowledge the new order of things ; and Massachusetts, alike unwilling to encounter the hostility of Parliament, and jealous of the rights of independent legislation, by its own enactment, prohibited all intercourse with Virginia till the supremacy of the commonwealth should be established,—although the order, when it was found to be injurious to commerce, was promptly repealed, even while royalty still flourished at Jamestown.

A powerful fleet, with a considerable body of land forces on board, sent out to bring the colonies to submission, having subdued Barbadoes and Antigua, cast anchor before Jamestown. Sir William Berkeley and his hardy colonists had not been inactive : the growing strength of the colony had recently been increased by the acquisition of many veteran cavaliers from the king's army, and it now presented no contemptible force. Several Dutch ships which were lying in the river, and which, as trading contrary to the prohibition of Parliament, were armed, to provide against surprise by the commonwealth's fleets, were also pressed into service. This show of resistance induced the commissioners of Parliament to hesitate, before they attempted to reduce the colony to obedience by force, and to offer them fair and honorable terms of submission. The terms offered being such as completely satisfied the Virginians that their freedom was to be preserved inviolate, and their present happy constitution guarantied, while they were to suffer nothing for past conduct, they readily acquiesced, since they gained all by such a surrender which they could effect by the most successful warfare. It appears that they never anticipated any thing more than the preservation of their own liberties from wanton violation from the new and untried power which now held the reins of government in England, and could scarcely have been mad enough to hope to effect any thing favorable to the king by their resistance.

The articles of surrender are concluded between the commissioners of the commonwealth, and the council of state and Grand Assembly of Virginia, as equal treating with equal. It secures—

1st. That this should be considered a voluntary act, not forced or constrained by a conquest upon the country ; and that the colonists should have and enjoy such freedoms and privileges as belong to the freeborn people of England.

2dly. That the Grand Assembly, as formerly, should convene and transact the affairs of Virginia, doing nothing contrary to the government of the commonwealth or laws of England.

3dly. That there should be a full and total remission of all acts, words, or writings against the Parliament.

4thly. That Virginia should have her ancient bounds and limits, granted by the charters of the former kings, and that a new charter was to be sought from Parliament to that effect, against such as had trespassed upon their ancient rights. [This clause would seem to be aimed at some of the neighboring colonies.]

5thly. That all patents of land under the seal of the colony, granted by the governor, should remain in full force.

6thly. That the privilege of fifty acres of land for every person emigrating to the colony, should remain in full force.

7thly. That the people of Virginia have free trade, as the people of England enjoy, with all places and nations, according to the laws of the commonwealth ; and that Virginia should enjoy equal privileges, in every respect, with any other colony in America.

8thly. That Virginia should be free from all taxes, customs, and impositions whatsoever ; and that none should be imposed upon them without the consent of their Grand Assembly ; and no forts or castles be erected, or garrison maintained, without their consent.

9thly. That no charge should be required from the country on account of the expense incurred in the present fleet.

10thly. That this agreement should be tendered to all persons, and that such as should refuse to subscribe to it, should have a year's time to remove themselves and effects from Virginia, and in the mean time enjoy equal justice.

The remaining articles were of less importance. This was followed by a supplemental treaty, for the benefit of the governor and council, and such soldiers as had served against the commonwealth in England,—allowing them the most favorable terms.

If this was a conquest, happy would it be for most colonies to be conquered. Every privilege was secured which could possibly be asked, and the liberties of the colony were established more thoroughly than they had ever been ; and the conquest was only less favorable to Virginia than her declaration of independence, by having her rights depending upon the pledged faith of another nation, instead of having them entirely under her own control. The correspondence between the rights now secured, and the rights mentioned in the Declaration of Independence as violated by the British king, is remarkable.

All matters were thus happily and amicably arranged ; and, as Sir William Berkeley was too loyal a subject to be willing to take office under Parliament, Richard Bennett, one of the commissioners, was elected governor. A council was also elected, with powers to act in conformity to the instructions they should receive from the Parliament, the known law of England, and the Acts of Assembly, and such other powers as the Assembly should think proper from time to time to give them. It was declared, at the same session, that it was best that officers should be elected by the Burgesses, " the representatives of the people ;" and after discussion upon the propriety of allowing the governor and council to be members of the Assembly, it was determined that they might, by taking the same oath which was taken by the Burgesses. The Assembly thus having no written constitution as their guide, took upon themselves the office of a convention of the people, and granted or resumed powers as it might seem best for the good of the country.

The whites and the remnants of the neighboring Indian tribes continued to be upon good terms, and the latter were kindly and humanely treated by the guardian care of the Assembly. A slight irruption of the Rappahannocks seems to have been soon terminated. But a new scene in the history of the colony now presented itself. The Rechahecrians, a fierce and warlike tribe, came down from the mountains, and took up a strong position on the falls of James River, with six or seven hundred warriors. This excited no little uneasiness, as it had been very difficult to extirpate the Indians who had formerly possessed the spot. The first expedition against them failed ; a new one was prepared, and the subject Indians being called upon for aid, furnished a hundred warriors, most of whom, with their chief, Totopotomoi, fell fighting gallantly.

When Bennett retired from office, and the Assembly elected Edward Digges his successor, the commissioners of March 31, 1655. the commonwealth had little to do with controlling the destinies of Virginia, but were engaged in settling the affairs and adjusting the boundaries of Maryland.

The Assembly reciting the articles of agreement with the commissioners of Parliament, which admitted that March 13, 1658. the election of all officers of the colony appertained to the Burgesses, the representatives of the people proceeded to the election of a governor and council until the next Assembly ; and the choice fell upon "worthy Samuel Matthews, an old planter, of nearly forty years standing,—a most deserving commonwealth's man, who kept a good house, lived bravely, and was a true lover of Virginia." But this worthy old gentleman seems to have conceived higher ideas of his powers than the Assembly was willing to allow. The Assembly had determined not to dissolve itself, but only to adjourn until the first of November

9

They then proceeded with their ordinary business, making, however, one important change in the constitution,—which was, to
require that all propositions and laws presented by a committee
should be first discussed by the House of Burgesses in private,
before the admission of the governor and council. The governor
and council, on the first of April, sent a message declaring that
they thought fit then to dissolve the Assembly, and requiring the
speaker to dismiss the Burgesses. To this the Assembly returned
for answer, that the act was illegal, and without precedent, and
requested a revocation of it, as they expected speedily to finish
their business. The house then declared, that any member who
should depart should be censured, as betraying the trust reposed
in him by his country ; and that the remainder should act in all
things, and to all intents and purposes, as an entire house ; that
the speaker should sign nothing without the consent of a majority
of the house, and that the members should take an oath not to
disclose the acts or debates of that body. The governor replied
to the communication from the house, that he was willing that the
house should conclude its business speedily, and refer the dispute
as to the legality of his power to dissolve, to the decision of the
Lord Protector. The house unanimously decided this answer to
be unsatisfactory, expressed an earnest desire that public business
might be soon dispatched, and requested the governor and council
to declare the house undissolved, in order that a speedy period
might be put to public affairs.. In reply to this, the governor and
council revoked the order of dissolution, upon their promise of a
speedy conclusion, and again referred the matter of disputed right
to the Lord Protector. The house, still unsatisfied with this answer, appointed a committee to draw up a report in vindication
of the conduct of the Assembly, and in support of its power. In
the report, the Burgesses declare that they have in themselves full
power of election and appointment of all officers in the country,
until they should have an order to the contrary from the supreme
power in England ; that the house of Burgesses, the representatives of the people, were not dissolvable by any power yet extant
in Virginia, except their own ; that the former election of governor and council was null, and that, in future, no one should be admitted a counsellor unless he was nominated, appointed, and confirmed by the house of Burgesses.

They then directed an order to the sheriff of James City county, who was their sergeant-at-arms, that he should execute no warrant, precept, or command, directed to him by any other power or
person than the Speaker of the House. They then ordered, that
" as the supreme power of the country of Virginia had been declared resident in the Burgesses," the secretary of state should be
required to deliver up the public records to the speaker. An oath
was prescribed for the governor and council to take, and the same
governor was elected and most of the same council. Thus were
all difficulties adjusted, and popular sovereignty fully established.

Upon the death of Cromwell, the House of Burgesses unani-
March, 1659. mously recognised his son Richard, and adopted an
address praying a confirmation of their former privileges, in which address the governor was required to join, after
solemnly acknowledging, in the presence of the whole Assembly,
that the supreme power of electing officers was, by the present
laws, resident in the Grand Assembly ; which was alleged to be
required for this reason, that what was their privilege now might
belong to their posterity hereafter.

Matthews died, leaving the colony of Virginia without a gover-.
March, 1660. nor, about the same time that the resignation of
Richard Cromwell left England without a head. In
this emergency the Assembly, reciting that the late frequent distractions in England preventing any power from being generally
confessed ; that the supreme power of the colony should be vested
in the Assembly, and that all writs should issue in its name, until
such a command and commission should come from England as
should by the Assembly be adjudged lawful. Sir William Berkeley was then elected governor, with the express stipulation that
he should call an Assembly once in two years at least, and should
not dissolve the Assembly without its own consent. This old roy-
alist, probably thinking now that there was a prospect of the restoration, accepted the office under the prescribed conditions, and
acknowledged himself to be but the servant of the Assembly.

During the suspension of the royal government in England, Virginia attained unlimited liberty of commerce, which they regulated by independent laws. The ordinance
of 1650 was rendered void by the act of capitulation ; the navigation act of Cromwell
was not designed for her oppression, and was not enforced within her borders. Only
one confiscation appears to have taken place, and that was entirely by the authority of
the Grand Assembly. The war between England and Holland necessarily interrupted
the intercourse of the Dutch with the English colonies ; but, if after the treaty of peace
the trade was considered contraband, the English restrictions were entirely disregarded.
1655. Commissioners were sent to England to undecive Cromwell with regard to the
course Virginia had taken with reference to the boundary of Maryland, with
regard to which he had been misinformed ; and to present a remonstrance demanding
unlimited freedom of trade ; which, it appears, was not refused, for some months before
the Protector's death, the Virginians invited the " Dutch and all foreigners" to trade with
them on payment of no higher duty than that which was levied on such English vessels
as were bound for a foreign port. Proposals of peace and commerce between New-
Netherland and Virginia were discussed without scruple by the respective colonial governments ; and at last a special statute of Virginia extended to every Christian nation,
in amity with England, a promise of liberty of trade and equal justice.

1660. At the restoration, Virginia enjoyed freedom of commerce with the whole world.

Virginia was the first state in the world composed of separate
townships, diffused over an extensive surface, where the govern-
1655. ment was organized on the principle of universal suffrage.
All freemen, without exception, were entitled to vote. The
1656. right of suffrage was once restricted, but it was soon after
determined to be " hard and unagreeable to reason, that
any person shall pay equal taxes and yet have no vote in the election ;" and the electoral franchise was restored to all freemen.

Servants, when the time of their bondage was completed, at once became electors; and might be chosen burgesses. Thus Virginia established upon her soil the supremacy of the popular branch, the freedom of trade, the independence of religious societies, the security from foreign taxation, and the universal elective franchise. If in the following years she departed from either of these principles, and yielded a reluctant consent to change, it was from the influence of foreign authority. Virginia had herself established a nearly independent democracy. Prosperity advanced with freedom; dreams of new staples and infinite wealth were indulged; while the population of Virginia at the epoch of the restoration may have been about thirty thousand. Many of the recent emigrants had been royalists in England, good officers in the war, men of education, of property, and of condition. But the waters of the Atlantic divided them from the political strifes of Europe; their industry was employed in making the best advantage of their plantations; the interests and liberties of Virginia, the land which they adopted as their country, were dearer to them than the monarchical principles which they had espoused in England; and therefore no bitterness could exist between the partisans of the Stuarts and the friends of republican liberty. Virginia had long been the home of its inhabitants—" Among many other blessings," said their statute-book, " God Almighty hath vouchsafed increase of children to this colony; who are now multiplied to a considerable number;" and the huts in the wilderness were as full as the birds' nests of the woods.

The genial climate and transparent atmosphere delighted those who had come from the denser air of England. Every object in nature was new and wonderful.

The hospitality of the Virginians became proverbial. Labor was valuable; land was cheap; competence promptly followed industry. There was no need of a scramble; abundance gushed from the earth for all. The morasses were alive with water-fowl; the forests were nimble with game; the woods rustled with covies of quails and wild turkeys, while they sung with the merry notes of the singing birds; and hogs, swarming like vermin, ran at large in troops. It was " the best poor man's country in the world." " If a happy peace be settled in poor England," it had been said, " then they in Virginia shall be as happy a people as any under heaven." But plenty encouraged indolence. No domestic manufactures were established; every thing was imported from England. The chief branch of industry, for the purpose of exchanges, was tobacco planting; and the spirit of invention was enfeebled by the uniformity of pursuit.

CHAPTER V.

BACON'S REBELLION—HOSTILE DESIGNS OF THE FRENCH.

Indifference to change in England.—Navigation Act.—Convicts.—Conspiracy detected. —Discontents.—Cessation from tobacco planting for one year.—Royal grants.— Virginia's remonstrance.—Success of deputies.—Indian hostilities.—Army raised and disbanded by governor.—People petition for an army—elect Bacon commander -he marches without commission and defeats Indians—pursued by governor, who retreats on hearing of rising at Jamestown.—Governor makes concessions.—Bacon prisoner—is pardoned.—People force commission from governor.—Bacon marches to meet Indians—hears he is declared a rebel by Berkeley—marches to meet him—he flees to Accomac.—Convention called and free government established.—Bacon defeats the Indians.—Berkeley obtains possession of the shipping, and occupies Jamestown—is besieged by Bacon, and driven out.—Jamestown burnt.—Death of Bacon— character of his enterprise.—Predatory warfare—treaty between governor and his opponents.—Cruelty of Berkeley.—King's commissioners.—Departure of Berkeley, and his death.—Acts of Assembly passed during Bacon's influence.—Conduct of king's commissioners.—Culpeper governor.—Discontents.—Conduct of Beverly.— Howard governor.—General conduct of Virginia and progress of affairs.—Plan of Callier for dividing the British colonies.

As Virginia had provided for herself a government substantially free, the political changes in England could have little effect upon her repose, provided no attempt was made to interfere with the freedom of her trade, or her local government. She seemed content to be under the protection, rather than control, of whatever power the people of England thought proper to place at the head of affairs, provided that power did not seek to extend the conceded authority. In this mood she had adhered to Charles I. until the Parliament, by its commissioners, promised a preservation of all her privileges; she acknowledged Cromwell upon a similar promise, and his son Richard under the same idea; upon his resignation she held herself aloof, thus proving how perfect and how independent was her own local government, until the voice of England should declare who should rule; and upon the accession of Charles II. she gave in her allegiance to him. As in all these British changes she remained unconcerned and unmoved, so the last caused neither extraordinary joy nor regret. The colonists, thus free from external sources of uneasiness, proceeded to legislate upon internal matters; providing rewards for the encouragement of silk and other staples; negotiating with Carolina and Maryland for the adoption of uniform measures for the improvement of tobacco, and diminishing its quantity; and providing for the erection of public buildings, the improvement of Jamestown, and other subjects of general utility.

While the colonists were proceeding in this useful occupation, they were alarmed by the intelligence of the re-enaction of the navigation act, odious with new prohibitions, and armed with new penalties. The Virginians had long enjoyed a very beneficial trade with other countries besides England, and had early perceived its advantages, often urging the propriety of

1663.

its continuance, and contending that "freedom of trade was the life of a commonwealth." But the object of the navigation act was to confine its trade exclusively to England, for the encouragement of English shipping, and the emolument of English merchants, as well as the promotion of the king's revenue ; without regard to the gross injury done to the colony by depriving her of the benefit of competition in her harbors. The colony remonstrated in vain, and continued boldly her trade with all such foreigners as would venture to encounter the risk of being taken by the English cruisers, and encountering the penalties of the act.

It appears to have been for some time the practice to send felons and other obnoxious persons to the colony, to expiate their offences by serving the planters for a term of years. At the restoration many of the veteran soldiers of Cromwell, to whom it was anticipated the return of the *ancien régime* would not be particularly palatable, were shipped to Virginia to work off their spleen in the cultivation of tobacco. It appears that this new business was not as agreeable to them as they had found the psalm-singing and plundering of the royalists, under the command of their devout leader ; and they accordingly quickly organized an insurrection, by the operation of which they were to change places with such of their masters as were left alive by the process. But this outbreaking, which seems to have been well planned and extensively organized, was prevented by the compunction of one of their associates, who disclosed the whole affair to the governor the evening before it was to have gone into effect ; and adequate means were Feb. 13. taken to prevent the design. Four of the conspirators were executed. But this evil of importing *jail-birds*, as they were called, increased to such an extent that it was prohibited by the General Court, in 1670, under severe penalties.

The increase in the amount of tobacco raised by the increase of June 5, 1666. the colony and the settlement of Maryland and Carolina, far outstripped the increase of taste for it, rapid as that was, and caused such a glut of the commodity that its price fell to an amount utterly ruinous to the planter. In this the exclusive privilege of purchase which England enjoyed, notwithstanding the extensive contraband trade, no doubt largely contributed ; but this the planters could not prevent, and their only remaining resource was in diminishing the amount of tobacco raised. To effect this various schemes had been devised, but they were all liable to be evaded, and were, if successful, too partial in their operation to effect the object desired. Nothing could be efficient, short of a total *cessation* from planting for one year, and this was at last accomplished after long negotiations with Maryland and Carolina.

Many other staples had been recommended from time to time to the planters, and even encouraged by bounties and rewards, and this year, it was thought, would give them more leisure to attend to the subject. But it is not probable that many engaged in the occupations proposed, which required the investment of capital, the acquisition of skill, and the aid of time to render them profitable; and the year's leisure only served to increase the growing discontent, especially as towards its end Maryland began to be suspected of bad faith.

There were other causes of discontent which probably prevailed between different classes of society. Loud complaint was made of the manner in which taxes were levied, entirely on persons without regard to property, which, as there must have been a very large class of poor free persons now existing, from the frequent emancipation, and expiration of the terms of those who came over as servants, besides those who were free but poor when they came to the country, must have created considerable excitement. An effort was made to remedy this evil by laying a tax on property, but ineffectually; the only result being a small export duty on tobacco, in aid of the general revenue.

While the taxes bore thus hard upon the poorer portion of the community, they also had just reason to complain of exclusion from the right of suffrage by an act of 1670, and from the Legislature, to which none but freeholders could be chosen; as well as of the enormous pay which the Burgesses appropriated to themselves, of one hundred and fifty pounds of tobacco per diem, and one hundred for their horses and servants. The forts were also complained of as a source of heavy expenditure, without any benefit; their chief use, indeed, being rather injurious, as they kept off traders who violated the navigation acts.

But these evils in domestic legislation were trivial, compared with those produced by the criminal prodigality of Charles, who wantonly made exorbitant grants to his favorites of large tracts of lands, without a knowledge of localities, and consequently without regard to the claims or even the settlements of others. To cap the climax of royal munificence, the gay monarch, in, perhaps, a merry mood, granted to Lords Culpeper and Arlington the whole colony of Virginia, for thirty-one years, with privileges effectually royal as far as the colony was concerned, only reserving some mark of homage to himself. This might be considered at court, perhaps, as a small bounty to a favorite, but was taken in a very serious light by the forty thousand people thus unceremoniously transferred. The Assembly, in its extravagance, only took from them a great proportion of their profits; but the king was filching their capital, their lands, and their homes, which they had inherited from their fathers, or laboriously acquired by their own strenuous exertion.

The Legislature sent three deputies to England, to remonstrate with the king against these intolerable grants, to endeavor to procure his assent to some charter which might secure them against such impositions for the future; and if they should fail in the first of these objects, to endeavor to buy out the rights of the patentees. To bear the expense of these three deputies, Mr. Ludwell, Mr.

Morryson, and Mr. Smith, the enormous annual tax of fifty pounds of tobacco was laid upon every titheable person for two years, which, though it was for a popular object, was considered as of itself an intolerable grievance, at which we cannot wonder when we reflect that many who had to pay this tax did not own a foot of land. The amount can only be accounted for, by supposing much of it was to be used as *secret service money*, with such of his majesty's minions as could only see justice through a golden medium.

These deputies exerted themselves with remarkable success, and procured from the king an order for a charter, precisely in conformity to the petition which they presented, and providing against the grievances of which they complained; especially grants from the crown without information from the governor and council in Virginia that such grants would be of no injury; dependence immediately upon the crown of England, and not on any subfeudatory; and exemption from taxation without consent of the Grand Assembly. His majesty ordered the solicitor-general and attorney-general to prepare a bill embodying these and the other matters embraced in their petition, in due legal form, for his signature; but the matter, notwithstanding the most assiduous attention of the deputies, was so long delayed in going through the official forms that it was finally stopped, before its completion, in the Hanaper office, by the news of Bacon's Rebellion.

Soon after the deputies left Virginia, the difficulties of the colony had been increased by the addition of an Indian war, which, although not now, as formerly, a matter causing danger of destruction to the whole colony, and requiring all its strength to repel it, was yet a subject of great terror and annoyance to the frontier.

A standing army of five hundred men, one-fourth of which was to consist of cavalry, was raised by the Legislature, Mar. 7, 1675. and every provision made for their support and regulation; but after it was raised, and in a complete state of preparation to march against the Indians, it was suddenly disbanded by the governor without any apparent cause. This was followed by earnest petitions to the governor from various quarters of the country, to grant a commission to some person to chastise the Indians, the petitioners offering to serve in the expedition at their own expense. This reasonable request was refused, and the people, seeing their country left defenceless to the inroads of a savage foe, assembled of themselves in their primary capacity, in virtue of their right of self-defence, to march against the enemy. They chose for their leader Nathaniel Bacon, junior, a young gentleman of highly respectable family and education, who, although he had returned to Virginia but three years before, from the completion of his studies in England, had already received the honor of a colonel's rank in the militia, and a seat in the Legislature for Henrico, in which county his estate lay,—exposed by its situation to the fury of the Indians. He stood high in the colony, and was possessed of courage, talent, and address, which fitted him well for such an enterprise. After Bacon had been selected by this volunteer army as their leader, his first step was to apply to the governor for a commission, in order, if possible, to have the sanction of the legitimate authorities for his conduct. The governor evaded this rational and respectful request, by saying that he could not decide upon so important a matter without his council, which he summoned to consult, at the same time artfully hinting to Bacon the injury which he might probably do himself by persevering in his course. Bacon dispatched messengers to Jamestown to receive the commission, which he did not doubt would be ultimately granted; and as public impatience would not abide the dilatory proceedings of the governor, and he was probably nettled at the insinuations addressed to his selfishness, in the governor's communication,—he proceeded on his expedition, authorized only by the will of the people, the danger of the country, and the anxious wish of those who trusted their lives to his control.

Sir William Berkeley, (whose conduct, notwithstanding the high encomiums bestowed upon him, seems to have been marked in ordinary times only by a haughty condescension, which in his excellency was called suavity of manners, and in those times of difficulty, by vacillating imbecility,) after temporizing in the most conciliating manner with Bacon until his departure, now denounced him and his followers as mutineers and traitors, for daring to defend their country after his excellency had refused them a commission; and gathering together such forces as he could collect, consisting principally of the wealthy aristocrats in the settled country, who probably liked the mode of taxation which was least injurious to them, and who suffered little from Indian incursions upon the frontier, he marched to put down the rebellious troops. He had not proceeded further than the falls of James River, when he received intelligence of a rising in the neighborhood of Jamestown of a more formidable nature than Bacon's, which compelled him to retreat and take care of affairs at home. This new ebullition of feeling was headed by Ingram and Walklate, and was probably produced by the indignation of the common people at the absurd conduct of the governor in first refusing a commission to Bacon, and then marching to destroy him, while engaged in so useful an occupation. Be this as it may, we find them insisting upon dismantling the forts, which were intolerably oppressive, without producing any good effect against an enemy whose progress was by stealth, whose onset was sudden and furious, and whose retreat was immediate. Against such an enemy active operations in the field were required, and the vigorous prosecution of the war in his own country. The forts, probably, were regarded by the poor as instruments of power in the hands of the rich; which they kept up by oppressive acts, while they took measures to put down Bacon's operations, which constituted the only hope which the people had for protection. The governor was obliged to yield to the storm. The forts were ordered to be dismantled, and the obnoxious assembly was dissolved, and writs issued for a new election, in which, for the first time, freemen, as distinguished from freeholders, were elected.

In the mean time, Bacon had been very successful in defeating the Indians, destroying their towns, and taking them captive ; and was returning leisurely to Jamestown when he heard of the revolution there. This induced him to leave his little army, and, with a few followers, embark for Jamestown ; but he was taken on his voyage by Gardiner, who was cruising to intercept him, and sent a prisoner to the governor. Bacon had been elected a member for Henrico in the new legislature, and was pardoned and permitted to take his seat upon his confessing the impropriety and disobedience of his conduct, praying pardon of the governor, and promising future obedience. Credible report says, that he was induced to make this full and humiliating acknowledgment upon a promise by the governor, not only of pardon, but of a commission : and, indeed, without supposing it the result of a compromise, it is difficult to account either for this act or his subsequent conduct. The causes which induced his next step are not sufficiently explained by the historians of the times, but it was probably produced by the solicitations of his friends in the legislature, who found that they could gain no redress of grievances. He collected troops in the country, and marched to Jamestown ; he surrounded the state house with his enraged soldiers, demanding a commission for him ; which, by the earnest solicitation of the council and assembly, was at length obtained from the governor, together with a full act of indemnity for his present conduct, and a letter, highly applauding his designs and his proceedings, addressed to the king, and signed by the burgesses, the council, and the *governor*.

Thus relieved from all former sources of fear, and provided against future contingencies, Bacon again sallied forth towards the frontier. But the governor had not long been relieved from his presence before he dissolved the assembly, and retiring into Gloucester, again declared Bacon a rebel, and his army traitors, and raised the standard of opposition. Upon being informed of this, Bacon immediately fell back by forced marches upon Gloucester, and compelled his puissant excellency to retreat with precipitation to Accomac. This county was at that time considered as a distinct territory, although under the control of Virginia, and Bacon, taking advantage of this against an unpopular governor, called a convention for the purpose of settling the government, declaring that the governor had abdicated. This convention met at Middle Plantation on the 3d of August, 1676, and declared that the government was vacant by the abdication of Sir William Berkeley, and that, by invariable usage, the council or the people might fill the vacancy until the king's pleasure should be known. Writs were then issued by five* members of the council for a new election of burgesses. The convention next declared Sir William Berkeley guilty of aiding and abetting certain evil disposed persons in fomenting and stirring up the people to civil war; and that they would aid in discovering all such evil disposed persons, and opposing their forces, until the king be fully informed of the state of the case; and that they would aid Bacon and his army against the common enemy, and in suppressing the horrid outrages and murders daily committed by them.

Bacon having now provided a regular government for the country, proceeded once more against the Indians, who had formed a confederacy and gained several advantages since his retreat. He destroyed the Pamunky, Chickahominy, and Mattaponi towns and their corn, in retaliation of the late excesses. The Indians retreated before him, with occasional skirmishes, until they reached their place of general rendezvous near the falls of James River. He there found their whole force posted on an eminence overhanging a stream, which, from the sanguinary nature of the conflict, has been since called Bloody Run. They were protected by a stockade fort, which was stormed by the impetuous ardor of Bacon and his followers, who made great slaughter among them, encumbered as they were with their old men, women, and children.

In the mean time, Berkeley had not met with that warm reception which he had anticipated among the loyalists of Accomac; but, on the other hand, he had been presented with a strong and spirited remonstrance against the objectionable acts of Parliament, and a requisition that they should be suspended, at least so far as regarded that portion of the country. How the matter terminated we are not informed.

The governor was not allowed to remain undisturbed in Accomac, until he could again succeed in raising a force which might give trouble. Bacon's party was in possession of all the vessels in the colony, and two of his friends, Giles Bland and William Carver, went with their force to cut off supplies from the governor, or, as his friends surmised, to surprise him. But if such was their object they were defeated, for Captain Larimore, from whom one of the vessels had been taken, gave intimation to the governor's friends that he would betray his vessel into the hands of a party sufficiently strong to keep possession. The proposal was acceded to, and at midnight six and twenty men, obeying Larimore's signal, were along side of his ship, and had possession almost before the crew were aroused from their slumbers; the other vessels were then easily taken. Thus, Sir William finding himself in possession of the whole naval force of the colony, while Bacon was absent on his expedition against the Indians, he collected together

---

* Burke, vol. II, p. 179, says, " by Bacon and four other members of the council," but the member of the council was Nathaniel Bacon, sen., and the general was Nathaniel Bacon, jun., delegate for Henrico.—Hening, vol. II. p. 544-5.

a force of some six hundred men, consisting mostly of aristocratic gentlemen and their servile dependents, and took possession once more of Jamestown. As usual, his first act in returning to power, was to disavow his acts in favor of Bacon as made under duress, and again to declare him a rebel, and his soldiers traitors.

Bacon was on his return from his successful campaign when this news reached him ; most of his followers had dispersed, but he hastened on with the remainder, without regard to their fatigues in the recent campaign. He arrived before Jamestown late in the evening, fired his artillery and sounded a defiance, and then coolly dismounted and laid off his trenches. His men that very night, by the aid of trees, earth, and brushwood, formed a tolerable breastwork, and the next morning advanced to the palisadoes of the town, and fired upon the guard, without loss. Sir William Berkeley, well knowing that time would increase the force of his adversary, while it diminished his own, next resolved to try the effects of a sally ; and some of his men at first behaved with some show of courage, but the whole body soon retreated in disorder before the well-directed fire of Bacon's men, leaving their drum and their dead as trophies to the victors. Bacon would not allow the victory to be followed up, as it would have placed his men under the range of the guns of the shipping. To prevent the use which might be made by this auxiliary, he planted several great guns so as to bear on the ships,· which served also to alarm, though they could not annoy the town.

Now the marked difference which existed between the character of Bacon's troops and those of the governor was exhibited, and that, too, in a manner well calculated to exhibit the character of Bacon's proceedings. Berkeley's troops, consisting principally of mercenary wretches, whom he had scraped together by the hopes of plunder, deserted every day when they found that the governor was determined to defend the place, and that they were likely to get more blows than booty in the contest, until at last the governor was left with little more than twenty gentlemen, whose sense of honor would not allow them to desert his person. Bacon's troops, on the other hand, were daily reinforced by accessions from the country people, who clearly considered him as an intrepid soldier, who had delivered them from the butcheries of the savages ; and a patriot, who was now endeavoring to put down an odious and oppressive government.

The governor, finding his followers reduced to so small a number that it would be madness to attempt to defend the place, at length yielded to the earnest solicitations of those about him, and deceiving his adversaries as to his real design, by exhibiting evidences of a contemplated attack, he went on board a ship at midnight, and was seen next morning riding at anchor, beyond the reach of the guns in the fort at Jamestown. Bacon, with his followers, after their week's siege, marched into the empty town the next morning, the governor and his party having carried off or destroyed every article of value. The possession of Jamestown, in this situation, was of no advantage to Bacon or his followers. The men who had left their homes to defend their country from the incursions of the Indians, could not remain together for the purpose of defending the capital from their hostile governor, who was quietly waiting in the river for them to depart, in order that he might again resume possession. What could be done with a town which could not be defended, and, if defended, was of no value to the possessors; but which was all-important to the enemy? The answer to this question was manifest, and Bacon's proposal for its destruction was received with acclamation; several of his followers, who owned the most valuable houses, applying the firebrand with their own hands to their own property. The sight of the flames started Sir William Berkeley on a cruise to Accomac; and Bacon having overcome all opposition to the government established by the convention, dismissed the troops to their homes.

We have little account of Bacon's proceedings after this successful termination of his labors; we presume he did not do much, as he was ill of a disease caught by sleeping exposed in the trenches before Jamestown, which in a short time terminated his existence. He died at the house of a Mr. Pate, in Gloucester county. Thus died the distinguished individual, who overcame both the foreign and domestic enemies of his country, and left it enjoying the blessings of a free government. Had he lived precisely a century later, he would have been one of the distinguished heroes of the revolution, and historians would have delighted as much in eulogizing his conduct, as they have, under existing circumstances, in blackening his character. He accomplished all which it was possible for him to do. He never opposed the British government, but only foreign enemies, and domestic mal-administration, which he succeeded in defeating. He seems always to have acted by the consent and with the wish of the people, and never to have sought self-aggrandizement. It was manifestly impossible for him to elevate himself to absolute power in Virginia, without the consent of the government of England, and the people of Virginia; and the idea of resisting both of these powers was absurd. For all the evils which accrued to the country after his death, and the restoration of Sir William Berkeley, he has been unjustly made responsible, while he has received no credit for his good conduct, or the beneficial acts passed by the legislature during his ascendency. In short, we can see no difference between his course, and that pursued in the previous expulsion of Sir John Harvey from the government, or the subsequent treatment of Lord Dunmore, and many other royal governors, at the commencement of the revolution. The only difference between the patriots of 1676 and 1776, was in the establishment of a free government, subject to the general control of Great Britain, which was all that could be done in 1676, and the establishment of a free government independent of Great Britain, which was accomplished in 1776. The unfortunate death of Bacon, and the power of the mother country, destroyed in a great measure the benefit of the exertion of the little band of patriots of the first period, while the benefits of the latter have continued to exist. The loyal writers, after the re-establishment of Berkeley, sought to hide his pusillanimity by extolling his virtues, and blackening his adversary, in which they have been blindly followed by other writers, who have attributed the subsequent misery to the previous rebellion, instead of to the avarice, malignity, and revenge of the governor and his party, seeking to overawe and suppress popular indignation, and break the strength of the popular party, by the forcible exertion of arbitrary authority, as well as to avenge themselves for the indignities to which their own folly subjected them. On the other hand, the patriots of the revolution have only received the just reward of their merit, in the lavish praises of a grateful posterity; and the loyal party of their day has been justly handed down to universal execration.

The death of Bacon, by leaving the republicans without a head, revived the courage of the governor so far, that he ventured in his ships to move about upon the bay and rivers, and attack the inhabitants wherever he could find them defenceless, and snatch a little plunder to gratify his needy followers ; always retiring when the opposite party appeared to oppose him. This predatory species of warfare preventing the quiet pursuit of agricultural labors, and destroying all the comfort and happiness of society, without producing any beneficial result, soon grew wearisome to both parties. Sir William Berkeley, whose cruelties, especially to his prisoners, had gone far to keep up the enthusiasm of popular excitement, finding that his name had ceased to strike that awe which habitual respect for one high in authority had formerly given it, and that his punishments excited indignation rather than terror, felt disposed to take advantage, by milder means, of the returning pacific disposition on the part of a people whose stubborn tempers could not be brought into obedience by force. With this view, he treated his prisoners with more liberality, published an act of general indemnity, and proposed a treaty of peace to Ingram and Walklate, the principal leaders of the opposing party since the death of Bacon. So anxious were the people to be relieved from the present confusion and anarchy, and the governor once more to rule with uncurbed sway, that a treaty was speedily concluded, only stipulating, on the part of the governor, a general oblivion, and indemnity of past offences ; and, on the part of his opponents, a surrender of their arms, and a restoration of such property as they had taken. Thus easily did these unfortunate men deliver themselves again into the lion's power, after having defeated him at all points, and inflicted deep and irremediable wounds upon his inflated vanity, and pompous mock-dignity. The governor, when he had his enemies in his power, instead of trying to heal the wounds of the bleeding state by mildness and conciliation, only added to its sufferings by a bloody retribution for all the trouble which he had been made to endure. Fines and confiscations, for the benefit of his excellency, became the order of the day, and an occasional execution, as an extra treat to his vengeance. He at first attempted to wrest the honest juries of the county to his purpose, but in vain, —ten prisoners were acquitted in a single day. Finding that his enemies were thus likely to escape his grasp, by the unflinching integrity and sense of justice prevailing among the people, he determined to avoid the use of a court constituted upon principles of the English constitution, which he found so little subservient to his will, and tried his next victims under martial law. He here found a court of more congenial spirits. The commissioners of the king give an account of some of these trials, such as they were carried on even after their arrival, which mark well the spirit of the times. " We also observed some of the royal party, that sat on the bench with us at the trial, to be so forward in impeaching, accusing, reviling, the prisoners at bar, with that inveteracy, as if they had been the worst of witnesses, rather than justices of the commission ; both accusing and condemning at the same time. This severe way of proceeding represented to the assembly, they voted an address to the governor, that he would desist from any further sanguinary punishments, for none could tell when or where it would terminate. So the governor was prevailed on to hold his hands, after *hanging* twenty-three."

A notable way which the governor adopted to replenish his purse, after the disasters of the war, was to relieve the *rebels* from a trial in one of his courts-martial, in which they were to be condemned, upon their paying him a great portion of their estates, by way of compromise. This method of disposing of men's estates, without trial or conviction, was protested against by his majesty's commissioners, as a gross violation of the laws of England, but which Sir William's friends seem to think only a just retribution for the losses sustained by himself and the royal party during the *rebellion.* Enormous fines, payable in provision, were also found a convenient method of providing for the king's troops which had been sent over to subdue the colony.

His majesty's commissioners fortunately arrived in time to stay the wrath of the vindictive old man, who would, as an eye-witness says, "he verily believes, have hanged half the county if they had let him alone." They urged him in vain to publish the king's proclamation of a general pardon and indemnity; and then proceeded to hold their commission for hearing and redressing grievances. As the proceedings of the governor diffused a gloom, the generality of which was co-extensive with the immense numbers that were engaged in the rebellion, so did the proceedings of the commissioners spread a universal joy. Crowds of persons now came forward to present their grievances—widows and orphans to ask for the confiscated estates of their husbands and fathers, who had been butchered by the military tribunals of the governor; others came in to complain of the seizing of their estates without the form of a trial; and many, who had submitted themselves upon the governor's proclamation of indemnity and pardon, complained of subsequent imprisonment and confiscations of their property.

The commissioners state in their report to the king and council, that "in the whole course of their proceedings they had avoided receiving any complaints of public grievances, but by and under the hand of the most credible, loyal, and sober persons of each county with caution; that they did not do it in any mutinous manner, and without mixture of their old leaven, but in such sort as might become dutiful subjects, and sober, rational men to present." When they found that all their representations to Sir William Berkeley, to endeavor to induce him to restore the confiscated estates, which were in the possession of himself or his most faithful friends, were in vain, they ascertained as many of the possessors as possible, and made them give security to take care of them until his majesty should determine as to the restitution which they should recommend him to make. The commissioners also devised several matters of utility for the peace, good government, and safety of the colony; which they recommended his majesty to adopt. Sir William Berkeley returned in the fleet to England, leaving Sir Herbert Jeffries, who had been sent over with the commissioners, as governor. Upon his arrival, he found that his cruel conduct in Virginia was looked upon with horror by most of his former friends and the council, and was not sustained by the king, subservient loyalty to whom had been the source and spring of his high-handed measures. The old knight, thus finding himself execrated in Virginia, and despised in England, soon languished and died under the load of infamy with which he had crushed the fair fame of his earlier years. Thus ended the life of Sir William Berkeley—a governor, whose early character historians have delighted to honor, and whose subsequent conduct they have sought to excuse: but of whom we can find nothing better upon record, than the negative merit of not opposing the legislature in its schemes of government in the early part of his reign ; but whose latter years are disgraced by cowardly imbecility, and stained with crime.

Before we take leave of the transaction which has been termed, in complaisance to the royal governor, Bacon's rebellion, it may not be amiss to cast a hurried glance at the laws passed by the legislature which met under his influence ; which must go far with posterity in determining, whether the name of rebels or patriots would be most consistent with the character of their acts. They strike first at the most important and pressing subject, and the one which had been most neglected—the Indian war. They provide efficient means for conducting it, and for regulating the army. The next act prescribed regulations for Indian trading, the abuse of which was thought to have been very mischievous. They next pray his majesty's governor and council, that the lands which had been set apart at the last peace exclusively for the Indians, and which had been or might be subsequently deserted by them, might not be granted away to individuals, but might be used for the purpose of defraying the expenses of the war. The fourth act looks very little like an encouragement of rebellion—reciting that tumults, riots, and unlawful assemblies, had recently been frequent ; they make it the duty of every officer, civil and military, in the country to aid in suppressing them, and the duty of all citizens to assist such officers under penalty of punishment for refusal ; and the *governor* is specially requested to assemble a force at the public charge with all possible expedition, to suppress such tumults, and inflict condign punishment upon the offenders, which, says the act, "will conduce to the great safety and peace of this country, and enable us the better to defend ourselves against the barbarous and common enemy." This single act sheds more light upon the history of the times, and exhibits more plainly the history of the views of the principal actors, than any, or perhaps all, other documents ; we see in it the reason why no private persons took advantage of the unsettled state of affairs to disturb the public peace, and that there was no tumult or armed force, except the regular army, raised by the assembly and put under Bacon's command ; and no rebellious assembly, except the miscreant crew raised by Berkeley in opposition to the government established by the people.

Having thus provided for safety from foes without and for peace within, the assembly next proceeded to the investigation of abuses by civil officers. Under this head they made several provisions for the prevention of abuses, which have been found so well devised, that they have continued in use to the present day. They next provide against the long continuance of vestries in office ; for the election of burgesses by freemen as well as freeholders ; and against false returns of burgesses. Their eighth act provides against abuses committed by the justices in laying county levies ; and requires, that a number of discreet men, chosen by the people, equal in number to the justices appointed by the governor, should act with the justices in laying the county levy. They next empowered the county courts to select their own collectors of county levies and dues ; and prohibit any member of the council from sitting on the county court bench. Passing some acts of less general importance, but which were wise and useful, we come to an act of general pardon and indemnity for all crimes committed between the 1st of March and 25th of June, passed " out of a hearty and pious desire to put an end to all suits and controversies, that by occasion of the late fatal distractions have arisen," "and to bury all seeds of future discord and remembrance of any thing whereby the citizens might be obnoxious to any pains or penalties whatsoever."

Their last act deprives Edward Hill and John Stith for ever of the right to hold any office of trust, judicature, or profit, because it was notoriously manifest that they had been the greatest instruments in raising, promoting, and stirring up the late differences and misunderstanding that had arisen between the honorable governor and his majesty's good and loyal subjects. The acts of this Assembly were signed by Berkeley in all due form, but were subsequently all declared void, though many of them were re-enacted by the Legislature, which, under the influence and control of Berkeley, declared them void.

Although the people of Virginia had laid down their arms, they were not subdued, but continued to manifest, through their Legislature, the same undaunted tenacity of their rights which had ever characterized them. This was exhibited towards the king's commissioners in one of the boldest defences of privilege which the records of any nation can exhibit, and shows how strongly imbued with the spirit of freedom the people must have been, when they could snuff the approach of tyranny at such a distance, and put themselves on their defence against their friends, lest their enemies might take advantage of their concessions. The king's commissioners were empowered to call for persons and papers, for the purpose of prosecuting more effectually their inquiries into the grievances of the colony. In conformity with their powers they called upon the secretary of the Legislature for its journals, but were surprised to find, that although their proceedings were popular, and their object was to investigate and redress grievances of which these very men complained, that they refused to allow them to inspect their journals, returning for answer, that it was a dangerous precedent, which might be used in violation of their privileges. At this time, the governor and commissioners had complete physical power over the colony, by the entire absence of any thing like organized opposition, and from the presence of the king's troops ; and availing themselves of this power, they did not hesitate to wrest the journals of the Assembly from the hands of its officer by force. Upon which the Virginia Assembly published a bold and manly declaration, setting forth, "that his majesty's commissioners having called for and forced from the clerk of the Assembly, all the original journals of the Assembly, which power they supposed his majesty would not grant them, for that they find not the same to have been practised by any of the kings of England, and did therefore take the same to be a violation of their privileges, desiring withal satisfaction to be given them, that they might be assured no such violation of their privileges should be offered for the future." The king was so much displeased with this declaration, that although he pardoned the members of the Legislature, he directed the record of it to be erased, and required the governor to propose a bill to the next General Assembly condemning the proceeding, and declaring the right of his majesty and his officers to call for all the public records and journals, whenever they shall think it necessary for his royal service.

Sir Herbert Jeffries deserves the merit due to an advantageous treaty with the Indians, and a successful opposition to the petty intrigues of the loyalists. He died in 1678, leaving the colony in the hands of the lieutenant-governor, Sir Henry Chickerly, during whose administration magazines and forts were established at the heads of the four great rivers, to overawe the savages, and a silly act passed prohibiting the importation of tobacco from Carolina and Maryland, for the purpose of transhipment, which practice, if they had suffered it to continue, might have proved very profitable to the colony, besides putting the tobacco trade more exclusively into its own hands. In the succeeding spring, Sir Henry delivered the government to Lord Culpeper. The first act of his lordship was to declare full and unqualified indemnity to all for their conduct in Bacon's rebellion, and allowing reparation to those who should be reproached for their conduct upon that occasion. This popular act, added to the pleasing and conciliatory manners of his lordship, so won upon the good-natured simplicity of the Assembly, that they passed an act which probably no force could have extorted from them. They raised the duties and made them perpetual, instead of annual, as before, and, what was at once surrendering up the great bulwark of that freedom, for the safety of which they had been so long contending, they made the duties henceforth subject to his majesty's sole direction and disposal.

The king rewarded Culpeper's address in obtaining this acquisition to his power, by the addition of a thousand pounds to his salary, and one hundred and sixty pounds per annum for his rent. The Assembly, too, as if they could not do enough for a royal governor who could condescend to smile upon them, granted his excellency a regular duty proportionate to the tonnage of every vessel trading to Virginia. Culpeper having thus obtained a considerable increase to his revenue by his trip to Virginia, proceeded to England, to enjoy it, leaving the colony once more with Sir Henry Chickerly.

The discontents of the people again began to extend to a degree which could scarcely be kept within bounds. The troops which had been sent over to suppress Bacon's rebellion were still kept up. There were no barracks, and the people positively refused to receive these idle and troublesome drones into their houses, although they were regularly billeted by the government. The low price of tobacco, too, was a never-failing source of complaint, as well as the commercial regulations which aided in producing it. The colony had urged Culpeper to exert his influence at court to procure a *cessation* from planting, to which they had for some time in vain endeavored to obtain the assent of Carolina and Maryland.

To these evils another was now added, which struck another blow at commerce. The idea had been conceived that the colony could not prosper without towns, and to promote their growth the planters, living principally on the shores of the magnificent Chesapeake, and the broad navigable rivers of Virginia, were required to bring their produce to particular spots for the purpose of being shipped. Thus taxing the planter with unnecessary freight and commission for the benefit of such idlers as might congregate in the towns. These acts were enforced by heavy penalties, and as they contributed very much to the benefit of the town's people, the penalty for the violation was rigorously enforced. These prose-cutions drove many traders from the country, and the poor plant-ers, to whom it was physically impossible to convey their crops to these paper-towns, were doomed to see their crops rotting on their hands by this injudicious legislation, or, if they attempted to evade the law, have them wrested from them in the shape of penalties. These several subjects of complaint induced the people of several counties to petition the deputy governor to call an assembly, to endeavor to provide a remedy for the evils. At the meeting of the Assembly, there was much debate and declamation upon the con-dition of the country, but no measure of relief was adopted. By order of the king, however, the two companies of infantry were paid off and disbanded, which put an end to one of the subjects of difficulty. The dissolution of the Assembly without effecting any thing, caused the impatience of the poor and ignorant people of several of the counties to break through all restraint, and expend their wrath in the destruction of tobacco-plants, at a season of the year when it was too late to sow more seed. Sir Henry Chickerly, with commendable moderation, only took measures to stop these misguided people, without resorting to harsh punishments ; but lest it should be drawn into a precedent, the Legislature not long after-wards made it treason. In the mean time, Lord Culpeper ar-rived, and his haughty bearing to the Council and the Burgesses soon gave intimation to them that his lordship's feelings towards the colony had undergone a change. He enlarged, in his speech to the Assembly, much upon the favor of his majesty in disband-ing the troops, and spoke of permission which he had obtained to raise the value of the current coin ; he then went on to declare that the colonists did not deserve these gracious favors, but rather punishment for their recent turbulence ; he also expressed his majesty's great dissatisfaction at the refusal of the journals, and desired that that portion of their proceedings should be expunged.

The Assembly expressed their gratitude for the concessions which had been made by the king, but at the same time, with admirable good sense, and a knowledge of the prin-ciples of commerce, which shows that they were not acting blindfold with regard to the alterations in the price of tobacco heretofore alluded to, protested, by a large majority, against raising the value of the coin ; stating, as a reason, that the exercise of this dan-gerous power would be made a precedent, and specie, which of course as the standard of other value should be as fixed as possible itself, would be blown about by the breath of the governor, and the people would have no certainty of the value of the coin in their pockets. They stated, moreover, that it was the duty of the legislature to enact all laws for the regulation of commerce, and, of course, to prescribe the current price of specie, and they accordingly introduced a bill for that purpose ; but this bill, which was necessary, as the coins of many different countries were in circulation, was stopped short in its progress by the governor, who declared that it was trespassing upon executive prerog-ative, and that he would veto any bill which the legislature might pass upon the subject. He then proceeded to fix the value himself by proclamation, raising the current price considerably, but making exception of his own salary and the revenue of the king.

This exception was, in effect, nothing more or less than a new tax of the most odious and oppressive character, and the colony plainly recognised it as such, and refused to regard the exceptions, but paid the revenue as other debts, according to the new stand-ard. And the governor, afraid to bring such a case before any court of law, which he well knew would expose his contemptible meanness, and yet afraid to allow his procla-mation to be openly disregarded, which would have put an end at once to the authority of his edicts, was compelled, by the dilemma, to lower the value of the coin as suddenly as he had raised it. This was at once realizing all the worst anticipations of the legis-lature as to the arbitrary fluctuations in the standard of value, besides being highly un-just and oppressive to such persons as had made payment of debts according to the new standard, and such as had given credit during the time of the alteration. The gov-ernors had, by some means, been suffered to exercise the power of dissolving the Assem-blies, and this having now grown into a usage, was a favorite method of silencing their clamors ; and they having rashly made the provision for the revenue perpetual, and put the control of that subject into the king's hands, were bound hand and foot, and could not control executive usurpation by stopping the wheels of government. The governor now made use of this dangerous power and dissolved the Assembly. The governor, thus left without a watch or control over his actions, proceeded to a vigorous exercise of ex-ecutive powers. The unfortunate plant-cutters, who had merely been imprisoned, and such of them dismissed from time to time as would give assurance of penitence, and promise a peaceable demeanor, were now proceeded against with the utmost rigor, for what the king was pleased to call their treasonable conduct. But the noblest victim for tyrannical persecution was Robert Beverly, the former clerk of the Assembly, who had refused to give up its papers without authority from "his masters, the house of Burgess-es." For some reason, it seems that an inspection of journals was demanded by the council again in 1682, and Beverly again refusing to deliver them, was thrown into pri-son, in a king's ship, the Duke of York, then lying in the river, his persecutors being afraid to trust him to the keeping of the jails among his countrymen. While he was in prison, a committee of the council was appointed to seize the papers, which he, foresee-ing this event, had secreted. The pretences for this imprisonment were the most frivo-lous that can well be imagined ; he is accused of fomenting discord, and stirring up the late partial insurrections, but the only specific act of which he was accused, was setting on foot petitions for an Assembly. Under these arbitrary proceedings, he was detained a prisoner, denied the writ of habeas corpus, and hurried about from prison to prison, until the governor at last thought proper, after two years searching for charges, to com-mence a regular prosecution.

The accusation consisted of three heads :—

1st. That he had broken open public letters directed to the Secretary's office, with the writs enclosed for calling an Assembly, in April, 1682, and took upon him the exer-cise of that part of the government which belongs to the Secretary's office, and was con-trary to his ;—

2d. That he had made up the journal, and inserted his majesty's letter therein (which was first communicated to the house of Burgesses at their prorogation) after their pro-rogation ;—

3d. That he had refused to deliver copies of the journal of the house of Burgesses in 1682, to the lieutenant-governor and council, saying, "that he might not do it without leave of his masters."

This was all which could be charged against this faithful officer, after so long an im-prisonment, and so long a preparation for the prosecution. But of course they will not bear scrutiny, being only a flimsy veil thrown over their designs, rather indicating a wish to hide the naked deformity of the prosecution, than actually concealing it.

Before this notable prosecution was ended, Lord Culpeper for-feited his commission, and was superseded by Lord Howard, who took the oaths of office on the 28th of February, 1684. His first measure was to call an assembly, which, as a popular act, induced the colony to hope some degree of mildness in his administration ; but these hopes were soon dissipated. He pursued the unfortunate plant-cutters with renovated vigor, and such of them as had been excepted in a proclamation of general pardon were now executed, and their estates, after paying officer's fees, appropriated to the governor's own use.

The assembly met and refused to proceed with business for the want of a clerk, as their former clerk was in prison, and they refused to elect another. In this situation of affairs the matter seems to have been compromised, the governor no doubt despairing of his conviction upon the absurd charges made, and Beverly and his friends willing to end his long imprisonment and sufferings, by asking pardon, at the same time not giving up the papers or the principles for which he suffered. Be this as it may, Beverly threw himself upon the mercy of the court, declining to employ counsel or make any defence, and was pardoned. Probably these long-continued sufferings, with other persecutions afterwards endured, injured the constitution of Beverly, for we find that he died prior to April, 1687. His noble conduct induced king James, the then reigning monarch, to deprive the Burgesses of the election of their own clerk, ordering the governor to elect him, and requiring the assembly to make the clerk, so elected, the usual allowance for his services.

The accession of James II. was proclaimed with the usual demonstrations of respect in the colony, and complimentary assurances of loyalty on the one side, and gracious regard on the other, were exchanged between his subjects and the assembly. But nothing was done to secure the freedom of the colony, and Lord Howard took advantage of the succeeding recess of the assembly, to enlarge the fees and perquisites of his office, and to impose new ones without the advice or authority of the assembly. This body, which met in November, immediately took into consideration these arbitrary exactions, and passed spirited resolutions in reprobation of them, and made provision for the defence of the citizens from similar encroachments in future. To these acts the governor applied his negative, without assigning any reason. Lord Howard, not satisfied with thus stopping the legislation of the colony, proceeded in effect to acts of executive legislation, by issuing a proclamation, in obedience, he said, to the king's instructions, repealing several acts of the legislature, which were themselves repeals of former acts, and declaring the acts repealed by that body to be revived, and in full force, as before the passage of the repealing acts. This proclamation the assembly protested against as illegal and unwarrantable, as utterly subversive of the government, annihilating the right of the popular branch, and bringing all to bow in humble submission to the mercy of the prerogative. The spirited conduct of the Burgesses could not be endured by the governor, and he prorogued them. The governor had sent to James an account of the conduct of this assembly. This representation produced in reply from James, a furious, quarrelsome order, calling their conduct mutinous, and attributing it to their "unquiet dispositions and sinister intentions to protract the time of their sitting to the great oppression of his subjects, from whom they received wages;" concluding by an order for the prosecution of their clerk Beverly, to whom he ascribes all of these evils.

Feb. 15, 1685.

Oct. 20, 1686.

In the same year, several persons were imprisoned and punished for treasonable expressions. The council was now as servile as the governor could wish, and he proceeded without interruption in his system of arbitrary innovation upon the established usages of the colony, and the liberties of its citizens.

The province of New York belonged to the king as proprietor as well as sovereign; and, in order to strengthen this his own estate, he sent orders for all the other colonies to assist in building forts, and supplying garrisons for its western frontier, alleging that these measures were equally necessary for the protection of all. In conformity to these orders a message was received from governor Dungan, requiring the quota of Virginia; but the legislature refused to appropriate a man or a farthing for purposes from which they were to derive no benefit, but rather an injury, as the protection of the north-western frontier would drive the Indians further south, where they might commit their depredations upon the unprotected citizens with more impunity. *(Nov. 10, 1687.)*

While the colony was contending against their governor, a revolution in England had dethroned the sovereign, and placed William and Mary upon the throne. This change, while it placed the council, which had made many loyal professions to James, in an awkward position, was an event producing unalloyed joy to the people of Virginia, as they could now hope for justice to be done to their oppressive governor. *(1689.)*

Soon after this occurrence, the war broke out between the allied powers and Louis XIV. of France, and the colony was ordered to place itself in the best posture of defence.

The complaints of the Virginia legislature against their governor at length were taken up by the privy council, and although the charges against Howard were not tried, yet redress against his usurpation was granted, at the same time that the principles upon which they contended that their rights had been violated, were denied to be correct. Howard pleading ill-health, was not deprived of his commission for not returning to the colony; but as it was necessary that there should be a governor upon the eve of a war, Sir Francis Nicholson was sent over. His conduct was mild and conciliatory, and consequently popular; among other highly beneficial acts passed under his government, was one for the establishment of a college, which was very liberally endowed.

He was succeeded by Sir Edmund Andros as governor-in-chief, who is represented to have been actuated in his administration by a sound judgment and a liberal policy; to have been exact, diligent, and methodical in the management of business; of a conciliatory deportment, and great generosity. Sir Francis Nicholson was again made governor-in-chief, in November, 1698. He was an ambitious man, who had served in the capacity of a governor and deputy governor in several of the colonies, and taken great pains to become popular, and to make *(Sept. 20, 1692.)*

himself well acquainted with the situation of all the colonies, their wants, their trade, and their capabilities, with a view to unite them, if possible, under one government, over which he hoped to obtain the appointment of governor-general. The pressure of war, with the combined force of the French and Indians, which seemed now about to fall upon the colonies, and rendered some union necessary for the purpose of defence, seemed highly favorable to his design.

The French, at an early day, conceived a correct idea of the importance of the British colonies in America. The Count De Callier, governor of Montreal, during his residence in Canada, after a long experience, derived from observations on the spot, had formed the bold project of separating in two the English colonies by the capture of New York. The success of this scheme would manifestly have destroyed that concert so necessary to harmony and efficiency of co-operation, and left the other colonies liable to be cut off in detail, and would effectually establish the safety of Canada, by enabling the French to keep in check the powerful savage confederation, composed of the Five Nations, which had lately, by a furious irruption, laid waste the country, even to the gates of Montreal and Quebec. This plan of Callier's was adopted by the French government. A fleet was sent to the bay of New York, with orders to retain possession of it until December, when, if no further orders were received, it was to sail for Port Royal, land its munition and stores, and return to France. The land force were to have marched from Quebec by the route of the Sorel River and Lake Champlain. This expedition was defeated by a destructive inroad of the Five Nations, which carried death and desolation over the whole country, even to the very gates of the capital. This unforeseen occurrence rendered it necessary to retain the whole force at home, in measures of self-defence, and saved New York, without her having to strike a blow in her own behalf.

Sept. 1692.

The British government, daily becoming more sensible of the importance of the North American colonies, and seeing the danger to which they were exposed by the plan of De Callier, set on foot a plan of general defence in the year 1695, adjusting the quotas of each colony to the ratio of its population, and forwarding the scale to the different governors, to recommend for the adoption of the respective colonial assemblies. Several of the colonies rejected this scheme, because several of those which were thought most exposed wished to employ it as their own interest dictated. Among the refractory was Virginia, which could not be prevailed upon, by all the art and ingenuity of the governor, aided by his great enthusiasm in this his favorite plan, to vote a cent to the enterprise, to his inconceivable chagrin and mortification. Nicholson, finding his own efforts utterly unavailing, laid the matter before the king, and urged the propriety of forcing Virginia to see her true interests upon this occasion. William, in reply, recommended a new consideration of the matter by the General Assembly, alleging, upon the authority of Nicholson's report, "that New York was the barrier of Virginia against the Indians and French of Canada; and as such, it was but justice she should defend it." The assembly deemed it but due respect to his majesty to take the subject again into consideration, but found no reason to change their former opinion, declaring "that neither the forts then in being, nor any others that might be built in the province of New York, could in the least avail in the defence or security of Virginia; for that either the French, or the northern Indians, might invade the colony, and not come within a hundred miles of such fort."

The failure of this great subject irritated the governor beyond expression; and excited in his mind the most inordinate antipathy to the assembly. He charged the conduct of the assembly to a spirit of rebellion, and inveighed against what he called its parsimony, in the most unmeasured terms, offering to pay the quota of Virginia out of his own pocket, and boasting afterwards that he had done it; but, at the same time, taking the obligation of the gentleman to whom he gave the bills, that no use should be made of them until the queen should remit money to pay them. This affectation of generosity was designed to gain popularity with the other colonies.

CHAPTER VI.

EVENTS FROM THE YEAR 1705 TO THE TERMINATION OF THE FRENCH AND INDIAN WAR.

Gov. Nicholson superseded by Nott, and he by Jennings.—Administration of Gov. Spotswood—he effects a passage over the Blue Ridge.—Drysdale governor—succeeded by Gooch.—Death of Rev. James Blair.—Notice of Col. Wm. Byrd.—Gooch's charge to the Grand Jury, against Presbyterians, Methodists, &c.—Burning of the Capitol at Williamsburg.—Revision of the Colonial Laws.—Departure of Gooch.— Dinwiddie governor.—Encroachments of the French.—Mission of George Washington beyond the Alleganies, to the French Commandant of a Fort—its inauspicious results.—Gov. Dinwiddie prepares to repel the encroachments of the French—Expedition against them under Col. Fry, and the erection of Fort Duquesne.—Washington's skirmish with Jumonville—he erects Fort Necessity—he surrenders to the French, and marches back to Virginia.—The Burgesses pass a vote of thanks to him. Gov. Dinwiddie resolves to prosecute the war—the futility of his projects.—Arrival of Gen. Braddock.—Braddock's defeat.—Bravery of Washington and the Virginia troops.—Frontiers open to incursions from the savages.—Fauquier governor.— Troops destined for the conquest of Duquesne rendezvous at Raystown.—Defeat of Major Grant, and heroism of Capt. Bullet.—Fort Duquesne evacuated.—End of the War.

THE first half of the eighteenth century, to the breaking out of the French and Indian war, is extremely barren of incident in the history of Virginia. Very little more can be given than a list of the various colonial governors, with the dates of their appointments and removals, and a synopsis of their characters. This brevity arises from the fact that it was mainly a time of peace, which usually leaves but little of striking incident to record, of marked interest to the general reader,—although a narration of laws, and causes which advance or retard the welfare of society, or those things which exhibit a true portraiture of it, would arrest the attention of the political economist, and, to some degree, of all. Again, the annals of Virginia, during this period, are brief and unsatisfactory; and, doubtless, much highly valuable material is, in consequence, forever lost. Probably a thorough inspection of documents in possession of the British government would throw much light upon this period, and the colonial history of Virginia generally, and settle some points which, for lack of information, are now in controversy.

Gov. Nicholson continued in office until 1705, when he was superseded by Edward Nott, who survived his appointment but a few months. The death of Nott devolved the government on Edmund Jennings, the president, and the council. A commission, meanwhile, had issued, appointing Brigadier Gen. Hunter lieutenant-governor, under the Earl of Orkney; but he having been taken on his passage by the French, Col. Alexander Spotswood was appointed his successor. His administration commenced in 1710. He was an accomplished and enterprising man; and had his suggestions to the British ministry been fully and promptly executed, they would have proved highly useful to the interests of Britain in America, at a time when France was endeavoring to wrest from her the trade and riches of the new world. Early in his administration, Spotswood, at the head of a troop of horse, effected a passage over the Blue Ridge, which had previously been considered an impenetrable barrier to the ambition of the whites, and discovered the beautiful valley which lies beyond. In commemoration of this event, he received from the king the honor of knighthood, and was presented with a miniature golden horseshoe, on which was inscribed the motto, "*Sic jurat transcendere montes*"—"Thus he swears to cross the mountains."

In 1723, Spotswood was succeeded by Sir Hugh Drysdale. In 1739, when hostilities were commenced again against Spain, and soon after against France, Spotswood was again called into service, and honored with the command of the colonial troops; but he did not live to enjoy the returning smiles of royal favor. Drysdale was succeeded in office by Gooch, a brigadier-general on the British establishment, who passed acts of the Assembly for the first time in 1727. During his administration, he commanded the colonial troops in the unsuccessful expedition against Carthagena. In 1743, died the Rev. James Blair, the first president of William and Mary. He was an eminent and learned divine, to whose exertions the institution owed much of its prosperity. His death occasioned a vacancy in the council, which was filled by William

12

Fairfax, son of the proprietor of the Northern Neck. Col. Wm. Byrd, also a member of the council, died about this period. He was a wealthy gentleman, of extensive acquirements, and one of the commissioners who had been appointed to run the dividing line between Virginia and North Carolina. His journal of the survey, which has descended to our times, is "marked by a spirit of unaffected humor, that does equal honor to his heart and understanding."

In April, 1745, Gov. Gooch made an address to the grand jury of the General Court, in opposition to the Presbyterians, Methodists, and other denominations of Christians, who had at this time become numerous in Virginia. It illustrates the state of religious intolerance at that time, and, singular as it may seem to us of the present day, it met with the approval of the most gifted minds in the colony, "among whom were some that afterwards became distinguished champions of an unqualified freedom in every thing that related to the human mind."*

In the year 1746, the public buildings in Williamsburg were burnt ; and the subject was shortly after agitated of removing the seat of government to some more central part of the colony. In the session of 1748, the assembly appointed the following named gentlemen a committee to revise the colonial laws :—Peyton Randolph, Philip Ludwell, Beverly Whiting, Carter Burwell, and Benjamin Waller. Gooch, who had been governor of Virginia for upwards of 20 years, sailed for England in 1749, "amidst the blessings and tears of the people, among whom he had lived as a wise and beneficent father." The government now devolved on Robinson, the president of the council. At his death a few days after, Thomas Lee, who had succeeded him in the presidency, was advanced to the chair of government.

In the year 1752, Governor Dinwiddie arrived in Virginia. Since the failure of De Callier's design upon New York, in 1692, the French in Canada and Louisiana, acting in concert, continued to extend their forts and strengthen their power by alliances with the Indians ; thus at once endeavoring to unite their possessions, to monopolize the Indian trade, and to limit the British settlements. Gov. Dinwiddie, viewing with just alarm the encroachments of the French, in Oct., 1753, dispatched George Washington, then but 21 years of age, on a mission to the French commandant of a fort on a branch of French Creek, about 15 miles south of Lake Erie.

This commission was delicate and hazardous, and required experience in the modes of travelling through the woods, and a knowledge of the Indian character. The distance was nearly 600 miles, over rugged mountains and mostly through a howling wilderness. The party consisted of eight persons : Jacob Vanbraam, interpreter, Mr. Gist, guide, and four others, two of whom were Indian traders. After much toil in an inclement season, in marching over snow-covered mountains and crossing rivers on frail rafts, they at length reached the junction of the Monongahela with the Allegany. Washington examined the place, and by his recommendation the fortification was erected there that afterwards became so much celebrated.

---

* For this address see Burke's History of Va., vol. III., p. 119.

Twenty miles below the Forks of the Ohio, at Logstown, he called together some of the Indian chiefs and delivered to them the governor's message, soliciting a guard to the French encampments. The principal sachem was Tanacharison, alias the Half-King. The sachems having met in council, Washington addressed them, explaining the objects of his mission. The Half-King made a pacific reply, and, in company with him and three other Indians, Washington finally set off and reached the French fort. M. de St. Pierre, the commandant, received him courteously. Washington presented his commission and letter from Gov. Dinwiddie. This letter asserted that the lands on the Ohio belonged to the British crown, and urged a speedy and peaceful departure of the French. St. Pierre's reply was respectful, but uncomplying and determined. He said that the message should have been sent to the French governor in Canada, and that he would not retire unless ordered by him. While there, Washington was very politely entertained ; but the French commandant used artifice to detain the Indians. Finally, after much perplexity, the whole party embarked in a canoe on their return, and proceeded down as far as Venango, which they reached in six days. The passage was full of peril from rocks, shallows, and drifting trees. At Venango they found their horses, in an emaciated condition. To lighten their burden, Washington proceeded on foot, in an Indian walking dress, in company with Messrs. Gist and Vanbraam, the horses being under the direction of the drivers. After three days travel, Washington, with Mr. Gist, left the party and went on ahead, each with a loaded knapsack and a gun. The next day they met an Indian, whom they engaged to pilot them to the forks of the Allegany. The Indian acted very suspiciously, and it was soon conjectured from his conduct that he intended to murder them. They managed, however, to get rid of him, and travelled all night. The next evening, at dusk, they arrived at the Allegany river. Weary and exhausted, they passed the night on the bank, making their bed on the snow, and exposed to the inclemencies of the weather. When morning arrived they prepared to cross the river.

"There was no way of getting over," says Washington, "but on a raft ; which we set about making with but one poor hatchet, and finished just after sunsetting. This was a whole day's work. We next got it launched, and went on board of it ; then set off. But, before we were half way over, we were jammed in the ice in such a manner, that we expected every moment our raft would sink, and ourselves perish. I put out my setting-pole to try to stop the raft, that the ice might pass by ; when the rapidity of the stream threw it with so much violence against the pole, that it jerked me out into ten feet water. But I fortunately saved myself by catching hold of one of the raft-logs. Notwithstanding all our efforts, we could not get the raft to either shore, but were obliged, as we were near an island, to quit our raft and make to it."

This was a desert island. They passed the night in extreme suffering, from the intense cold, and Mr. Gist's hands and feet were frozen. When morning dawned, a gleam of hope appeared. The ice had congealed to the eastern shore sufficiently hard to allow them to cross to it. At length, after an absence of sixteen weeks, they arrived at Williamsburg.

The intentions of the French being now understood, the Governor of Virginia acted with energy to resist their encroachments. The journal of Washington was also published. It was reprinted in London, and considered by the government as unfolding the hostile views of the French, and the first proof of their intentions. A regiment was raised in Virginia, under the command of Colonel Joshua Fry, for the purpose of erecting a fort at the forks of the Ohio. Washington was appointed second in command, with the rank of lieutenant-colonel. A small party of Captain Trent's company was hastily sent forward to commence the fort, but were interrupted by the arrival of Captain Contrecœur, with a thousand French and Indians, who drove away the English, and erected Fort Duquesne. This was the first act of open hostility. The news reached Colonel Washington while he was posted at Will's creek (at which place Fort Cumberland was afterwards erected) with three companies, waiting the arrival of Colonel Fry with the remainder of the regiment and the artillery. He wrote immediately for reinforcements, and pushed forward with his companies towards the Monongahela, as fast as the process of cutting a new road through the wilderness would permit. His intention was to reach the mouth of Redstone, there to wait for the arrival of the artillery and reinforcements under Colonel Fry, and then drop down the Monongahela by water, to the Forks. He had designed to descend the Yough'ogheny, but after an examination of the falls, abandoned the design.

"Learning that the French were coming out to meet him, Washington hurried forward to the Great Meadows, and threw up a hasty intrenchment. This place is ten miles east from Uniontown, a few rods south of the present national road, between the fifty-second and fifty-third miles from Cumberland. Commanded, as it is, by elevated ground on both sides, within one hundred yards of the fort, it would seem to be injudiciously chosen for defence; but Washington knew the French and Indians could bring no artillery, and the meadows being entirely free from timber, the enemy would be compelled to emerge upon the open plain, beyond the protection of the woods, before he could efficiently attack the fort. Washington learned from Tanacharison, the half-king, a chief of the Six Nations, and from Mr. Gist, that La Force was out, from Fort Duquesne, with a party of French and Indians, and their tracks had been seen within five miles of the Great Meadows. He immediately dispatched a party of seventy-five on horseback, to reconnoitre their position, but they were not to be found. Washington writes on 29th May, 1754:

"About nine o'clock the same night, I received an express from the half-king, who was encamped with several of his people about six miles off, that he had seen the tracks of two Frenchmen crossing the road; and that, behind, the whole body were lying not far off, as he had an account of that number passing Mr. Gist's. I set out with forty men before ten, and it was from that time till near sunrise before we reached the Indians' camp, having marched in small paths through a heavy rain, and a night as dark as it is possible to conceive. We were frequently tumbling one over another, and often so lost that fifteen or twenty minutes' search would not find the path again."

"When we came to the half-king, I counselled with him, and got his assent to go hand in hand and strike the French. Accordingly he, Monocawacha, and a few other Indians, set out with us, and when we came to the place where the tracks were, the half-king sent two Indians to follow their tracks, and discover their lodgment, which they did at half a mile from the road, in a very obscure place surrounded with rocks. I thereupon, in conjunction with the half-king and Monocawacha, formed a disposition to attack them on all sides—which we accordingly did; and, after an engagement of about fifteen minutes, we killed ten, wounded one, and took twenty-one prisoners. The principal officers taken, are M. Drouillon and M. La Force, of whom your honor has often heard me speak, as a bold, enterprising man, and a person of great subtlety and cunning. With these are two cadets."

"In this engagement we had only one man killed, and two or three wounded, (among whom was Lieutenant Waggener, slightly)—a most miraculous escape, as our right wing was much exposed to their fire, and received it all."

In his journal he had also noted:

"As I marched on with the prisoners, (after the action,) they informed me that they had been sent with a summons for me to depart—a specious pretext, that they might discover our camp, and reconnoitre our force and situation. This was so evident, that I was astonished at their assurance in telling me that they came as an embassy. By their instructions, they were to obtain a knowledge of the roads, rivers, and country, as far as the Potomac. Instead of coming as ambassadors—public, and in an open manner—they came secretly, and sought out the most hidden retreats, much better suited for deserters than ambassadors. Here they encamped; here they remained concealed for whole days together, within five miles of us. They sent out spies to reconnoitre our camp. The whole body then moved back two miles. Thence they sent messengers, as directed in the instructions, to acquaint M. Contrecœur with the place we were in, and with our disposition, that he might forward his detachments to enforce the summons as soon as it should be given. An ambassador has no need of spies; his character is always sacred. Since they had so good an intention, why should they remain two days within five miles of us, without giving me notice of the summons, or of any thing which related to their embassy? This alone would be sufficient to raise the strongest suspicions; and the justice is certainly due them, that, as they wished to conceal themselves, they could not have chosen better places than they did."

"They pretend that they called to us, as soon as we were discovered; which is absolutely false—for I was at the head of the party in approaching them, and I can affirm, that as soon as they saw us they ran to their arms, without calling, which I should have heard if they had done so."

And in a subsequent letter to Governor Dinwiddie, Washington says, speaking of some deserters from the French: "These deserters corroborate what the others said, and we suspected. La Force's party were sent out as spies, and were to show that summons if discovered or overpowered by a superior party of ours. They say the commander was blamed for sending so small a party."[*]

"Washington having sent his prisoners to the governor, prepared his intrenchments, by erecting a stockade, for receiving a more formidable attack from the French, which he had good reason to expect, after they should have heard of the loss of Jumonville's party. To this stockade he gave the name of *Fort Necessity.* Colonel Fry had died in Virginia, and the chief command devolved on Colonel Washington. Captain Mackay, of the royal army, with an independent company of one hundred men, arrived at the Great Meadows. Washington, leaving him in command of the fort, pushed on over Laurel-hill, cutting the road with extreme labor through the wilderness, as far as Gist's plantation. This tedious march occupied them two weeks. During the march, they were joined by the Half-king, and a numerous body of Indians, with their families, who had espoused the English cause.

"A strong detachment was at length announced, as being on their march from Fort Duquesne, under the command of Monsieur de Villiers. It was at first determined to receive them at Gist's; but on further information of the enemy's force, supposed to

---

[*] "No transaction in the life of Washington has been so much misrepresented, or so little understood, as this skirmish with Jumonville. It being the first conflict of arms in the war, a notoriety was given to it, particularly in Europe, altogether disproportioned to its importance. War had not yet been declared between Great Britain and France, and, indeed, the diplomatists on both sides, were making great professions of friendship. It was the policy of each nation to exaggerate the proceedings of the other on their colonial frontiers, and to make them a handle for recrimination and complaints, by throwing upon the adverse party the blame of committing the first acts of aggression. Hence, when the intelligence of the skirmish with Jumonville got to Paris, it was officially published by the government, in connection with a memoir and various papers; and his death was called a murder. It was said, that while bearing a summons, as a civil messenger, without any hostile intentions, he was waylaid and assassinated. The report was industriously circulated, and gained credence with the multitude. Mr. Thomas, a poet, and scholar of repute, seized the occasion to write an epic, entitled, '*Jumonville,*' in which he tasked his invention to draw a tragical picture of the fate of his hero. The fabric of the story, and the incidents, were alike fictitious. But the tale passed from fiction to history, and to this day it is repeated by the French historians, who in other respects render justice to the character of Washington; and who can find no other apology for this act than his youth and inexperience, and the ferocity of his men.

"The mistakes of the French writers were not unknown to Washington; but, conscious of having acted in strict conformity with his orders and military usage, he took no pains to correct them, except in a single letter to a friend, written several years afterwards, which related mostly to the errors in the French account of the subsequent action of the Great Meadows. Unfortunately, all his correspondence, and the other papers which he wrote during this campaign, were lost the next year at the battle of the Monongahela, and he was thus deprived of the only authentic materials that could be used for explanation and defence. The most important of these papers have recently been found, [by Mr. Sparks, in his researches in England,] and they afford not only a complete vindication of Colonel Washington in this affair, but show that it met with the unqualified approbation of the governor and legislature of Virginia, and of the British ministry."—*Sparks' Life and Writings of Washington*—where the incidents of this campaign are ably and fully delineated, and the conduct of Washington, both in this affair and the capitulation at the Great Meadows, are clearly explained and triumphantly vindicated against the charges of the French.

be nine hundred men, it was determined to retreat to Fort Necessity, and, if possible, to Wills' creek. Their provisions were short, their horses worn down, and it was with excessive labor and fatigue that they reached the fort, after a forced march of two days. Here only a small quantity of flour was found; but supplies were hourly expected, and it was therefore determined to fortify the place as well as circumstances would permit, and abide the event.

"On the 3d July the enemy appeared, and commenced firing from the woods, but without effect. Washington had drawn up his men outside of the fort, with the view of inviting an encounter in the open field. This the French and Indians declined, hoping to draw him into the woods. It rained constantly during the day, and the muskets became wet, and were used with difficulty. Washington's troops withdrew within the trenches, and fired as opportunities occurred. In the evening the French proposed a parley, which Washington at first declined, suspecting a design to gain an entrance to the fort, and discover his weakness; but he afterwards consented to send an officer to them. Captain Vanbraam, a Dutchman, who pretended to understand French, was sent to them, and returned with proposals, in the French language, for capitulation. These proposals, after being modified in some particulars by the besieged party, were agreed to. The garrison was to be permitted to leave the fort with the honors of war, taking their baggage, except their artillery, with them. They were not to be molested by the French, nor, as far as it could be prevented, by the Indians. Since their cattle and horses had been killed in the action, they were to be permitted to conceal such of their effects as could not be carried away, and to leave a guard with them until they could return with horses to take them away; but on condition that they should not, within one year, attempt any establishment there, or on that side of the mountains. The prisoners taken *at the time of Jumonville's death,*[*] were to be returned, and Captains Vanbraam and Stobo were to be retained by the French as hostages, until the return of the prisoners.[†] On the following morning, Washington, with

[*] "In the French proposals this expression was insidiously written, '*à l'assassinat de M. Jumonville;*' and as Vanbraam, the stupid interpreter, did not explain the force of the expression to Washington, the capitulation was signed in that shape."

[†] It seems (according to Burke) that La Force, one of the prisoners taken by Washington in the skirmish in May, had made strenuous exertions to instigate the Indians to hostilities, and that he had been travelling on the frontiers of Virginia to obtain information of its resources. When taken, there were found upon him papers, in part disclosing the designs and policy of France.

Viewing him in the character of a spy, Governor Dinwiddie threw him into prison at Williamsburg. To redeem this man, was the principal design of De Villier in demanding these hostages. La Force escaped from prison, and the people of the country were alarmed. "The opinion," says Burke, "that before prevailed of his extraordinary address and activity, his desperate courage, and fertility in resources, was by this new feat wrought into a mingled agony of terror and astonishment. Already had he reached King and Queen courthouse, without any knowledge of the country through which he passed, without a compass, and not daring to ask a question, when he attracted the notice of a back-woodsman. Their route lay the same way; and it occurred to La Force, that by the friendship and fidelity of this man, he might escape in spite of the difficulties and dangers of his situation. Some questions proposed by La Force, relative to the distance and direction of Fort Duquesne, confirmed the woodsman in his suspicions, and he arrested him as he was about to cross the ferry at West Point. In vain did La Force tempt the woodsman with an immediate offer of money, and with promises of wealth and preferment, on condition that he accompanied him to Fort Duquesne. He was proof against every allurement, inconsistent with his duty, and he led him back to Williamsburg. The condition of La Force, after this attempt, became in the highest degree distressing. He was loaded with a double weight of irons, and chained to the floor of his dungeon.

"Such was the situation of affairs when Colonel Washington, after his resignation, arrived in Williamsburg. Here, for the first time, he heard of the imprisonment and persecution of La Force, and he felt himself compelled to remonstrate with Mr. Dinwiddie against them, as an infraction of the articles of capitulation, and of the laws of honor acknowledged by soldiers. His application was strongly backed by the sympathy of the people, which now began to run strongly in favor of the prisoner; but the governor was inexorable. Meanwhile, the hostages, Stobo and Vanbraam, had been ordered, for greater security, to Quebec, and in retaliation of the sufferings of La Force, they too were confined in prison, but without any additional severity. Almost at the same moment that La Force had broken his prison, Stobo and Vanbraam, by efforts equally extraor-

the garrison, left the fort, taking such baggage as they could carry, and transporting the wounded upon their backs. The Indians, contrary to the stipulation, annoyed them exceedingly, and pilfered their baggage. After a toilsome march, they at length arrived at Wills' creek, where they found rest and refreshment."

From thence Washington proceeded to Williamsburg, and communicated the events of the campaign to Governor Dinwiddie.

As soon as the House of Burgesses assembled, they passed a vote of thanks to Col. Washington and his officers, for their bravery and gallant conduct. Thus ended the first campaign of Washington. "Although as yet a mere youth, with small experience, unskilled in war, and relying on his own resources, he had behaved with the prudence, address, courage, and firmness of a veteran commander. Rigid in discipline, but sharing the hardships, and solicitous for the welfare of his soldiers, he had secured their obedience and won their esteem, amidst privations, sufferings, and perils, that have seldom been surpassed."

Gov. Dinwiddie resolved to prosecute the war, but being wholly ignorant of military affairs, his preliminary measures, in undertaking to organize an army, were injudicious. In August, he wrote to Washington, who was at Winchester, to fill up the companies of his regiment by enlistment, and lead them without delay to Wills' creek, where Col. Innes, with some troops from the Carolinas and New York, were building Fort Cumberland. From thence, it was the governor's project that the united forces should immediately cross the Alleganies and drive the French from Fort Duquesne, or build another fort beyond the mountains. Washington, astonished at the absurdity of the scheme, contemplated at a season when the mountains would be covered with snow, and the army enfeebled and destitute of supplies, made such a strong remonstrance that the project was abandoned.

The governor was opposed by the assembly, who would not yield to all his demands, and he never ceased to complain of their " republican way of thinking." He had lately prorogued them, to punish their obstinacy, and wrote to the ministry that he was satisfied the French would never be effectually opposed unless the colonies were compelled, independently of assemblies, to contribute to the common cause. When the Burgesses again met, they contributed £20,000 for the public service, which was soon increased to £30,000 by specie sent from England.

In possession of funds, the governor now enlarged the army to ten companies of 100 men each, and placed them upon the establishment of independent companies, by which the highest officers in the Virginia regiment, among whom was Washington, would be

dinary, had escaped from Quebec, and were passing the causeway leading from the city, at the moment that the governor of Canada was airing in his carriage. Stobo succeeded in effecting his escape ; but Vanbraam, fainting with fatigue and hunger, and despairing of being able to effect his escape, called out to the governor from beneath the arch of the causeway, where he concealed himself, and desired to surrender. The governor received him in his carriage, and remanded him to prison, but without any extraordinary severity. Even these facts were not unknown to Mr. Dinwiddie ; yet, without being touched by so generous an example, he persisted in his unjustifiable rigor towards La Force."

captains. He thereupon resigned his commission and retired from the service.

Early in the ensuing spring, (1755,) Major-Gen. Edward Braddock arrived in the country with the 44th and 48th regiments of royal troops, under Sir Peter Halkett and Col. Dunbar. The people seemed elated with joy, and in their imagination the intruding French seemed about to be driven back like a torrent upon the frontiers of Canada. Col. Washington, who now was to take an active part in the fearful scenes to be enacted, accepted the appointment of aid-de-camp to Gen. Braddock. At Wills' Creek, (Fort Cumberland,) the royal forces were joined by about 1000 Virginians, but the army was detained for want of horses, wagons, and forage. By the energy of Dr. Franklin, then postmaster-general of the provinces, the deficiency was supplied. The army moved at length on the 8th and 9th of June, but soon found themselves so encumbered with baggage and wagons, that it was determined, at the suggestion of Washington, to divide the force, pushing forward a small, but chosen band, with such artillery and light stores as were necessary, leaving the heavy artillery, baggage, &c., to follow by slow and easy marches.

The general, with 1,200 chosen men, and Sir Peter Halkett, as brigadier, Lieut. Col. Gage, (afterwards Gen. Gage,) Lieut. Col. Burton, and Major Sparks, went forward, leaving Col. Dunbar to follow with the remainder of the troops and baggage. Col. Washington, who had been very ill with a fever, was left in charge of Col. Dunbar, but with a promise from Gen. Braddock that he should be brought up with the advanced corps before they reached Fort Duquesne. He joined it at the mouth of the Yough'-ogheny, on the 8th July. On the 9th, the day of Braddock's defeat, he says, "I attended the general on horseback, though very low and weak. The army crossed to the left bank of the Monongahela, a little below the mouth of Yough'ogheny, being prevented by rugged hills from continuing along the right bank to the fort."

"Washington was often heard to say during his lifetime, that the most beautiful spectacle he ever beheld was the display of the British troops on this eventful morning.—Every man was neatly dressed in full uniform; the soldiers were arranged in columns and marched in exact order; the sun gleamed from their burnished arms; the river flowed tranquilly on their right, and the deep forest overshadowed them with solemn grandeur on their left. Officers and men were equally inspirited with cheering hopes and confident anticipations."

"In this manner they marched forward until about noon, when they arrived at the second crossing place, ten miles from Fort Duquesne. They halted but a little time, and then began to ford the river and regain its northern bank. As soon as they had crossed they came upon a level plain, elevated only a few feet above the surface of the river, and extending northward nearly half a mile from its margin. Then commenced a gradual ascent at an angle of about three degrees, which terminated in hills of a considerable height at no great distance beyond. The road from the fording place to Fort Duquesne led across the plain and up this ascent, and thence proceeded through an uneven country at that time covered with wood.

"By the order of march, a body of 300 men under Col. Gage made the advanced party, which was immediately followed by another of 200. Next came the general with the columns of artillery, the main body of the army, and the baggage. At one o'clock, the whole column had crossed the river, and almost at this moment a sharp firing was heard upon the advanced parties, who were now ascending the hill, and had proceeded about a hundred yards from the termination of the plain. A heavy discharge of musketry was poured in upon their front, which was the first intelligence they had of the proximity of an enemy, and this was suddenly followed by another on the right flank. They were filled with the greater consternation, as no enemy was in sight, and the firing seemed to proceed from an invisible foe. They fired in turn, however, but quite at random, and obviously without effect.

"The general hastened forward to the relief of the advanced parties; but before he could reach the spot which they occupied, they gave way and fell back upon the artillery and the other columns of the army, causing extreme confusion, and striking the whole mass with such a panic that no order could afterwards be restored. The general and the officers behaved with the utmost courage, and used every effort to rally the men, and bring them to order, but all in vain. In this state they continued nearly three hours, huddled together in confused bodies, firing irregularly, shooting down their own officers and men, and doing no perceptible harm to the enemy. The Virginia* provincials were the only troops who seemed to retain their senses, and they behaved with a bravery and resolution worthy of a better fate. They adopted the Indian mode, and fought each man for himself, behind a tree. This was prohibited by the general, who endeavored to form his men into platoons and columns, as if they had been manœuvring on the plains of Flanders. Meantime the French and Indians, concealed in the ravines and behind trees, kept up a deadly and unceasing discharge of musketry, singling out their objects, taking deliberate aim, and producing a carnage almost unparalleled in the annals of modern warfare. The general himself received a mortal wound,† and many of his best officers fell by his side.

"During the whole of the action, as reported by an officer who witnessed his conduct, Col. Washington behaved with 'the greatest courage and resolution.' Captains Orme and Morris, the two other aids-de-camp, were wounded and disabled, and the duty of distributing the general's orders devolved on him alone. He rode in every direction, and was a conspicuous mark for the enemy's sharpshooters. 'By the all-powerful dispensa-

---

* Washington said—"The Virginia troops showed a good deal of bravery, and were nearly all killed; for, I believe, out of three companies that were there, scarcely 30 men are left alive. Capt. Peyrouny, and all his officers down to a corporal, were killed. Capt. Polson had nearly as hard a fate, for only one of his was left. In short, the dastardly behavior of those they call regulars, exposed all others that were inclined to do their duty, to almost certain death; and, at last, in despite of all the efforts of the officers to the contrary, they ran as sheep pursued by dogs, and it was impossible to rally them. . . . . It is conjectured, (I believe with much truth,) that two-thirds of our killed and wounded received their shot from our own cowardly regulars, who gathered themselves into a body, contrary to orders, ten or twelve deep—would then level, fire, and shoot down the men before them."

† "There had long existed a tradition that Braddock was killed by one of his own men, and more recent developments leave little or no doubt of the fact. A recent writer says:

"'When my father was removing with his family to the west, one of the Fausetts kept a public house to the eastward from, and near where Uniontown now stands, as the county seat of Fayette, Penn. This man's house we lodged in about the tenth of October, 1781, twenty-six years and a few months after Braddock's defeat, and there it was made any thing but a secret that one of the family dealt the death-blow to the British general.

"'Thirteen years afterwards I met Thomas Fausett in Fayette co., then, as he told me, in his 70th year. To him I put the plain question, and received a plain reply, "I did shoot him!" He then went on to insist, that, by doing so, he contributed to save what was left of the army. In brief, in my youth, I never heard the fact either doubted or blamed, that Fausett shot Braddock.'

"Hon. Andrew Stewart, of Uniontown, says he knew, and often conversed with Tom Fausett, who did not hesitate to avow, in the presence of his friends, that he shot Gen. Braddock. Fausett was a man of gigantic frame, of uncivilized half-savage propensities, and spent most of his life among the mountains, as a hermit, living on the game which he killed. He would occasionally como into town, and get drunk. Sometimes he would repel inquiries into the affair of Braddock's death, by putting his fingers to his lips and uttering a sort of buzzing sound; at others, he would burst into tears, and appear greatly agitated by conflicting passions.

"In spite of Braddock's silly order, that the troops should not protect themselves behind trees, Joseph Fausett had taken such a position, when Braddock rode up, in a passion, and struck him down with his sword. Tom Fausett, who was but a short distance from his brother, saw the whole transaction, and immediately drew up his rifle and shot Braddock through the lungs, partly in revenge for the outrage upon his brother, and partly, as he always alleged, to get the general out of the way, and thus save the remainder of the gallant band, who had been sacrificed to his obstinacy, and want of experience in frontier warfare."—*Day's Penn.*

tions of Providence,' said he, in a letter to his brother, ' I have been protected beyond all human probability or expectation, for I had four bullets through my coat, and two horses shot under me, yet I escaped unhurt, although death was levelling my companions on every side of me.'* So bloody a contest has rarely been witnessed. The number of officers in the engagement was 86, of whom 26 were killed, and 37 were wounded. The killed and wounded of the privates amounted to 714. On the other hand, the enemy's loss was small. Their force amounted, at least, to 850 men, of whom 600 were Indians. According to the returns, not more than 40 were killed. They fought in deep ravines, concealed by the bushes, and the balls of the English passed over their heads.

" The remnant of Braddock's army being put to flight, and having re-crossed the river, Col. Washington hastened to meet Col. Dunbar, and order up horses and wagons for the wounded. Three days were occupied in retreating to Gist's plantation. The enemy did not pursue them. Satiated with carnage and plunder, the Indians could not be tempted from the battle-field, and the French were too few to act without their aid. The unfortunate general, dying of his wounds, was transported first in a tumbril, then on a horse, and at last was carried by the soldiers. He expired the fourth day, and was buried in the road near Fort Necessity. A new panic seized the troops ; disorder and confusion reigned ; the artillery was destroyed ; the public stores and heavy baggage were burnt, no one could tell by whose orders ; nor were discipline and tranquillity restored, till the straggling and bewildered companies arrived at Fort Cumberland.

" Such was the termination of an enterprise, one of the most memorable in American history, and almost unparalleled for its disasters and the universal disappointment and consternation it occasioned. Notwithstanding its total and even disgraceful failure, the bitter invectives everywhere poured out against its principal conductors, and the reproaches heaped upon the memory of its ill-fated commander, yet the fame and character of Washington were greatly enhanced by it. It was known that he gave prudent counsel to General Braddock, which was little heeded. During the march, a body of. Indians offered their services, which, at the earnest request and recommendation of Washington, were accepted, but in so cold a manner, and the Indians were treated with so much neglect, that they withdrew, one after another, in disgust. On the evening preceding the action, they came again to camp and renewed their offer. Again Col. Washington interposed, and urged the importance of these men as scouts and outguards, their knowledge of the grounds and skill in fighting among woods. Relying on the prowess of his regular troops, and disdaining such allies, the general peremptorily refused to receive them, in a tone not more decided than ungracious. Had a scouting party of a dozen Indians preceded the army after it crossed the Monongahela, they would have detected the enemy in the ravines, and reversed the fortunes of the day."†

After the defeat of Braddock, Col. Dunbar, who succeeded to the command, marched his troops to Philadelphia. The whole frontier, even to the Blue Ridge, was now harassed and horror-stricken by the bloody incursions of the French Indians. Col. Washington, in his capacity as adjutant-general of militia, circulated orders for them to assemble in their respective districts for exercise and review. Volunteer companies were organized, and the martial spirit of the people revived. Addresses were made to them from the pulpit, in one of which, the eloquent Samuel Davies of Hanover, after complimenting the bravery shown by the Virginia troops, added the following encomium, which seems almost

---

* When Washington went to the Ohio, in 1770, to explore wild lands near the mouth of the Kenhawa River, he met an aged Indian chief, who told him, through an interpreter, that during the battle of Braddock's field, he had singled him out as a conspicuous object, fired his rifle at him many times, and directed his young warriors to do the same ; but none of his balls took effect. He was then persuaded that the young hero was under the special guardianship of the Great Spirit, and ceased firing at him. He had now come a long way to pay homage to the man who was the particular favorite of heaven, and who could never die in battle.

† Sparks' Life of Washington, from which much important information relating to this war is inserted in this chapter.

prophetic. " As a remarkable instance of this, I may point out to the public that heroic youth, Col. Washington, whom I cannot but hope Providence has hitherto preserved in so signal a manner for some important service to his country."

In consequence of the desperate state of affairs, Gov. Dinwiddie convened the Assembly on the 4th of August. They voted £40,-000 for the public service, and enlarged their regiment to sixteen companies. Money was also granted to Col. Washington and the other officers and privates, " for their gallant behavior and losses," in the late disastrous battle. To Col. Washington was given the command of all the forces raised and to be raised in Virginia, with the unusual privilege of selecting his own field-officers. He now applied himself with his wonted energy to the discharge of the high responsibility conferred upon him. Lieut. Col. Adam Stephens, and Major Andrew Lewis, were the field officers next in rank. Washington's head quarters were at Winchester. After putting affairs in train, he performed a tour of inspection among the mountains, visiting all the outposts in the frontier, from Fort Cumberland to Fort Dinwiddie, on Jackson's river. He then started for Williamsburg, to confer with the governor on the plan of operations, when he was overtaken below Fredericksburg by an express, announcing a new irruption of the savages upon the back settlements. He hastened back, mustered a force, and gave a timely and effectual check to the invaders, but not such as to quiet the fears of the settlers, many of whom, with their families, fled into the lower country, and increased the general terror.

The defects of the militia system were such as to put the patience of Col. Washington to a severe trial. He represented in strong language, to the government of the colony, these defects, and their fatal consequences, and at last prevailed. A new law was passed providing a remedy, but too late in the year for him to undertake offensive operations.

In April of the ensuing year, (1756,) when the Assembly again met at Williamsburg, Col. Washington hastened thither to mature a plan for defence during the summer. Had the several colonies united, the intruding French might have been driven from the Ohio ; but local jealousies prevented a union, and Virginia saw that the most strenuous exertions were necessary to defend their long line of frontier. The Assembly determined to augment the army to 1500 men. A bill was passed for drafting militia to supply the deficiency of recruits. Col. Washington returned to Winchester. But a few men were stationed there, most of the regiment being scattered at different posts for the better protection of the frontiers. The enemy, encouraged by the successes of the preceding year, were continually on the alert, and accounts were daily received of fresh massacres by them. Scouting parties, and even forts were attacked, and some of the bravest troops killed. Serious apprehensions were felt for the safety of Winchester. The number of troops was wholly insufficient for the protection of the

settlers. Col. Washington, deeply affected by the scenes he witnessed, addressed a letter to the governor, in which he said:

"I see their situation, I know their danger, and participate their sufferings, without
having it in my power to give them further relief than uncertain promises. In short, I
see inevitable destruction in so clear a light, that, unless vigorous measures are taken
by the Assembly, and speedy assistance sent from below, the poor inhabitants now in
forts must unavoidably fall, while the remainder are flying before the barbarous foe.
In fine, the melancholy situation of the people, the little prospect of assistance, the gross
and scandalous abuses cast upon the officers in general, which is reflecting on me in particular, for suffering misconduct of such extraordinary kind, and the distant prospect,
if any, of gaining reputation in the service, cause me to lament the hour that gave me
a commission, and would induce me, at any other time than this of imminent danger,
to resign, without one hesitating moment, a command from which I never expect to
reap either honor or benefit; but, on the contrary, have almost an absolute certainty of
incurring displeasure below, while the murder of helpless families may be laid to my account here.

"The supplicating tears of the women, and moving petitions of the men, melt me
with such deadly sorrow, that I solemnly declare, if I know my own mind, I could offer
myself a willing sacrifice to the butchering enemy, provided that would contribute to
the people's ease."

These agonizing sensations were heightened by base calumnies
against the army, and indirectly against the commander-in-chief,
which seemed for a while to gain public credence.

"By degrees," says Sparks, "the plot was unravelled. The governor, being a Scotchman, was surrounded by a knot of his Caledonian friends, who wished to profit by this
alliance, and obtain for themselves a larger share of consideration than they could command in the present order of things. The discontented, and such as thought their
merits undervalued, naturally fell into this faction. To create dissatisfaction in the
army, and cause the officers to resign from disgust, would not only distract the councils
of the ruling party, but make room for new promotions. Col. Innes, the governor's
favorite, would ascend to the chief command, and the subordinate places would be reserved for his adherents. Hence false rumors were set afloat, and the pen of detraction
was busy to disseminate them. The artifice was easily seen through, and its aims were
defeated by the leaders on the patriotic side, who looked to Col. Washington as a pillar
to support their cause."

The campaign being solely a defensive one, no opportunities
were allowed for obtaining laurels. The scenes of the past year
were re-enacted, the savages continued their murderous incursions,
there was the same tardiness in enlistments, the same troubles with
the militia, and to increase the difficulties, the governor, tenacious
of his authority, intrusted insufficient power to Col. Washington.
"Totally unskilled in military affairs, and residing 200 miles from
the scene of action, he yet undertook to regulate the principal
operations; sending expresses back and forth, and issuing vague,
contradictory orders, seldom adapted to circumstances—frequently
impracticable. The summer and autumn were passed in skirmishes
with the Indians, repairing the old forts, and building new ones.
By the advice of Col. Washington, a large fort was begun at
Winchester, as a depository for the military stores, and a rallying
point for the settlers and troops, should they be driven from the
frontiers. It was called Fort Loudoun, in honor of the Earl of
Loudoun, who had now succeeded Gen. Shirley in the American
command." Traces of this fortification remain to the present day.

As the year drew to a close, Col. Washington drew up a paper of the military affairs of the province, which he transmitted to Lord Loudoun. It contained a history of the war and valuable suggestions for future operations. It was courteously received. In March, (1757,) Washington attended a meeting, at Philadelphia, of several governors and principal officers, summoned by Lord Loudoun, to consult upon a comprehensive plan for the next campaign. It was decided that the principal efforts should be made on the lakes and Canada border, while the southern and middle colonies were left on the defensive. Col. Washington strenuously recommended an expedition against Fort Duquesne. Had his views been adopted it would have saved the expense of another campaign, and secured the borders from the savage incursions. From this conference Washington returned to Winchester, where he had spent the two preceding years. His routine of duties was the same. The Indians still continued their hostilities.

The assembly, prorogued to the 27th of October, (1757,) was dissolved on the 9th of November, and writs were issued for a new assembly to meet on the 22d of the same month. A day of fasting and prayer was appointed.

While the Assembly were deliberating upon measures of defence, the French general, Montcalm, took the posts of Oswego and Ontario, and his savage allies continued their murderous inroads upon the frontiers. Col. Armstrong, at the head of about 300 provincials, attacked one of their towns situated about 25 miles above Fort Duquesne, killed 40 Indians, and rescued eleven prisoners.

Dinwiddie sailed for England in January, 1758, much to the satisfaction of the people of Virginia. Originally a petty clerk of customs in the West Indies, he had brought himself under the notice of government by the detection of an enormous system of fraud on the part of his principal, and was thereupon immediately rewarded by the appointment of governor of Virginia. In this situation, charges were brought against him of extorting illegal fees, and appropriating the public funds to his private purposes. His public course was vacillating, his deportment arrogant, and he was wholly devoid of those qualities becoming his station, and particularly requisite at the perilous time he was intrusted with such high powers. Lord Loudoun had been commissioned as his successor, but his military duties at the north prevented him from entering upon the duties of his office. His place was filled, temporarily, by John Blair, president of the council, until the arrival, on the 7th of June, of Gov. Francis Fauquier.

Mr. Pitt having acceded to the British ministry in the spring of this year, (1758,) he resolved to prosecute the war with energy in America. Gen. Forbes was appointed to the command of an expedition against Fort Duquesne. To further his plans, he wrote a circular letter to several of the colonies to incite them to action, and offering certain supplies at the expense of the king. The Virginia Assembly augmented their force to 2000 men. They were divided into two regiments: the first under Col. Washington, who still continued commander-in-chief of all the Virginia troops; the second under Col. Byrd. Early in July, Washington marched from Winchester with the principal part of the Virginia troops, to Fort Cumberland. Six companies of the 1st regiment proceeded by another route, and joined Col. Boquet at Raystown, the general place of rendezvous for the 6000 troops destined for the conquest of Duquesne. While at Fort Cumberland, Col. Washington learned that Gen. Forbes thought of constructing a new road to Duquesne, instead of following the one made by Braddock. He made the most strenuous objection against the plan, "when," as he said, there was "scarce time left to tread the beaten track, universally confessed to be the best passage through the mountains." His efforts were in vain. Col. Boquet was ordered by Gen. Forbes, who was absent, to send forward parties to work upon the new road. "Six weeks had been thus spent, when Gen. Forbes arrived at Raystown, about the middle of September. Forty-five miles only had been gained by the advanced party, then constructing a fort at Loyal Hanna, the main army being still at Raystown, and the larger part of the Virginia troops at Fort Cumberland. At that moment the whole army might have been before the walls of Fort Duquesne, if they had marched as advised by Washington. An easy victory would have ensued; for it was ascertained that the French at that time, including Indians, numbered not more than 800 men."

From Loyal Hanna, Colonel Boquet rashly detached Major Grant, a British officer, with a force of 800 men, to reconnoitre in the vicinity of Fort Duquesne.

"This officer reached a hill near the fort during the night, and having posted his men in different columns, he sent forward a party to examine the works and discover the situation of the enemy. He also detached Major Andrew Lewis with a baggage guard about two miles in his rear; and having made such other arrangements as he deemed necessary, he believed himself secure, and, with more parade than prudence, ordered the *réveille*, or alarm, to be beaten. During all this time silence reigned in the fort, which Grant imputed to the terrors imposed by his appearance. But the calm was a dreadful precursor of a storm, which burst with resistless fury and unexpected ruin. The moment the Indians and French were ready for the attack, they issued from the fort, spreading death and dismay among the provincial troops. As soon as the attack was announced by the firing of guns, Major Lewis, with his rear-guard, advanced to the assistance of Grant, leaving only fifty men, under the command of Captain Bullet, to guard the baggage. Their united forces, however, were unable to withstand the impetuous assault of the savages, whose warwhoop is always a forerunner of havoc and destruction. The fire of the rifle requires coolness and deliberation, whereas the tomahawk and scalping-knife are fitted for sanguinary dispatch. No quarter was given by the Indians. Major Grant saved his life only by surrendering to a French officer. In the same way the brave Major Lewis escaped, after defending himself against several Indians successively. The two principal officers being now in the hands of the enemy, the rout became general among their troops. In their pursuit, the Indians exercised every cruelty which savage ferocity could inflict upon the hapless victims whom the sad fortune of the day delivered into their hands. The situation of the retreating troops, at this time, must appear truly desperate. They were in an enemy's country, far from any English settlement, as well as from any immediate prospect of succor; routed and dispersed by a bloody and vindictive foe, whose intimate knowledge of the woods and superior agility seemed to threaten a total destruction of the party. Their escape, however, was effected by the prudence and heroism of Captain Bullet, of the baggage guard, by a manœuvre no less fortunate for his men than honorable to himself. This officer, immediately on discovering the rout of the troops, dispatched on the strongest horses the most necessary part of the baggage, and disposing the remainder on an advantageous part of the road, as a kind of breastwork, he posted his men behind it, and endeavored not only to rally the fugitives as they came up, but by a well-directed fire to check the violence of the pursuers. Finding the enemy growing too strong to be withstood by his feeble force, he ordered his men, according to previous agreement, to reverse their arms and march up in front of their assailants, holding out a signal for capitulation, as if going to surrender. The impatience of the Indians to bathe their tomahawks in English blood, would scarcely allow them to suspend their attacks, while the latter appeared in the act of suing for mercy. The moment they had arrived within about eighty yards of the enemy, Bullet gave the word to fire :—a dreadful volley was instantly poured upon the Indians, and was followed by a furious charge with fixed bayonets. The enemy were unable to resist this bold and unexpected attack, and believing that the army of the English was at hand, they fled with precipitation ; nor did they stop until they reached the French regulars. Bullet, instead of pursuing them, wisely retreated towards the main body of the army, collecting in his march the wounded and wandering soldiers, who had escaped from the field of battle without knowing whither to direct their course In this fatal action, about twenty officers, and two hundred and seventy-three private soldiers, were either killed or taken prisoners.

" The Virginia troops on this occasion behaved with courage, and suffered severely in the action ; but the gallant conduct of Captain Bullet is almost without a parallel in American history. His situation, after the defeat of Grant, to an officer of less discernment must have appeared desperate. To resist the triumphant savages with a handful of men, would seem madness ; and to have fled without any hopes of escape, would have been folly. In this dilemma, with scarcely time to deliberate, Bullet adopted the only plan which could preserve himself and his men from the most cruel death, or the most distressing captivity."

The dilatory and unwise method of carrying on the expedition alarmed the Virginia Assembly for the fate of the expedition, and they resolved to recall their troops and place them upon the protection of their own frontier. But subsequent information occasioned them to revoke these resolves.

On General Forbes' arrival at Raystown he called a council of war, and, at his desire, Col. Washington drew up a line of march. Washington, at his own request, was placed in the advance, with a division of 1000 men. "The month of November had set in before General Forbes, with the artillery and main body of the army, arrived at Loyal Hanna. More than 50 miles, through pathless and rugged wilds, still intervened between the army and Fort Duquesne. A council of war was held, and it was decided to be unadvisable, if not impracticable, to prosecute the campaign any further till the next season, and that a winter encampment among the mountains, or a retreat to the frontier settlements, was the only alternative that remained. Thus far all the anticipations of Washington had been realized." A mere accident reversed this decision. Three prisoners were taken, who gave such representations of the weak state of the garrison that it was determined to push on.

On the 25th of November, 1758, the army took peaceable possession of Fort Duquesne, or rather the place where it stood, for the enemy had burnt and abandoned it the day before, and gone down the Ohio in boats. This fortress, after being repaired and garrisoned, was named Fort Pitt, now the site of the flourishing city of Pittsburg, which place was then considered within the jurisdiction of Virginia. The remains of Major Grant's men were buried by Gen. Forbes in one common tomb, the whole army assisting at the solemn ceremony.

Gen. Forbes returned to Philadelphia, where he died in a few weeks, and Washington soon directed his course to Williamsburg, as a member of the General Assembly from Frederick county. The capture of Duquesne restored quiet and general joy throughout the colony. The war was soon prosecuted at the North with vigor. In the succeeding summer of 1759, Niagara and Crown Point fell into the possession of the British crown, and on the 18th of September, Quebec surrendered to the brave and gallant Wolfe. The treaty of Fontainbleau, in November, 1762, put an end to the war.

CHAPTER VII.

FROM THE TERMINATION OF THE FRENCH AND INDIAN WAR TO THE SURRENDER OF CORNWALLIS.

Encroachments of Britain upon the American colonies.—Spirited conduct of Virginia thereon.—Patrick Henry's resolution on the right to tax America.—Death of Governor Fauquier.—Arrival of Lord Bottetourt.—Continued aggressions of the mother country.—Death of Bottetourt.—Lord Dunmore governor.—Dunmore's war.—Battle of Point Pleasant.—Speech of Logan.—End of the Indian war.—Meeting of the Continental Congress.—Dunmore removes the gunpowder of the colony from the magazine at Williamsburg.—Patrick Henry marches down at the head of a body of volunteers and forces the Receiver-general to make compensation.—Battle of Lexington.—Dunmore flees on board the Fowey man-of-war.—Termination of the Royal government in Virginia.—Meeting of the Virginia Convention.—Dunmore, with the British fleet, attacks Hampton.—Affair in Princess Anne.—Defeat of the enemy at Great Bridge.—Norfolk burnt.—Delegates in Congress instructed by the General Convention of Virginia to propose the Declaration of Independence.—A Constitution for the State Government adopted.—Patrick Henry governor.—Joyous reception in Virginia of the news of the Declaration of Independence.—Dunmore driven from Gwynn's Island.—First meeting of the Legislature under the State Constitution.—Indian war.—Col. Christian makes peace with the Creek and Cherokee nations.—Revision of the State laws.—Glance at the war at the north.—Col. Rogers Clark takes Kaskaskias and Fort St. Vincent.—Illinois erected into a county.—Virginia cedes her Western Territory to the United States.—Sir Henry Clinton appointed Commander-in-chief of the British army.—He transfers the seat of the war to the south.—Sir George Collier, with a British fleet, enters Hampton Roads.—Fort Nelson abandoned.—The enemy take possession of Portsmouth, and burn Suffolk.—They embark for New York.—The reduction of Virginia determined on by the enemy.—Gen. Leslie invades Virginia, and lands at Portsmouth.—The government prepares to resist the enemy.—Leslie leaves Virginia.—Battle of the Cowpens.—Arnold invades Virginia, lands at Westover, and marches to Richmond.—He returns to Westover, and arrives at Portsmouth.—Washington forms a plan to cut off his retreat.—Clinton detaches Gen. Philips to the assistance of Arnold.—Defenceless situation of Virginia.—Philips takes possession of Petersburg, and commits depredations in the vicinity.—Death of Gen. Philips.—Cornwallis enters Petersburg.—Tarleton's expedition to Charlotteville.—Various movements of the two armies.—Cornwallis concentrates his army at York and Gloucester.—Surrender of Cornwallis.

" QUESTIONS touching the power of the British Parliament to interfere with the concerns of the colonies had arisen more than once before the war, and during its continuance the delicate question arose, of the proportions which the several colonies should pay for the common defence. The British ministry proposed that deputies should meet and determine the amount necessary, and draw on the British treasury, which in turn should be reimbursed by an equal tax on all the colonies, to be laid by Parliament; but the colonies were afraid to let the lion put his paw in their pockets, even to take back his own; and this being no time to raise difficulties, the colonial legislatures were left to their own discretion in voting supplies, which they did with a liberality so disproportioned to their ability, as to excite the praise, and in some instances to induce a reimbursement on the part of the mother country. Virginia had always resisted any interference on the part of Parliament, especially in the navigation acts, and asserted as early as 1624, that she only had the undoubted right 'to lay taxes and impositions, and none other,' and afterwards refused to let any member of the council of Governor Berkeley, in the height of his popularity, *assist* them in determining the amount of the public levy. Again in 1676, even stronger language was used and acquiesced in by the king, to whom it was immediately addressed.

"The slight taxes imposed for the regulation of commerce, and the support of a post-office, were borne by the colonies without a murmur, being considered only a fair compensation for a benefit received. In March, 1764, the ministers declared it 'expedient to raise a revenue on stamps in America, to be paid into the king's exchequer.' The discussion of this was postponed until the next year in Parliament, but commenced immediately in America, and the proposition was met by every form of respectful petition and indignant remonstrance; which were, however, equally unavailing, and the stamp act passed in 1765. The passage of this act excited universal and indignant hostility throughout the colonies, which was displayed in the forms of mourning and the cessation of business; the courts refused to sanction the act by sitting, and the bar by using the stamps. In the succeeding Virginia legislature, Patrick Henry introduced and carried, among others, the following resolution:—

"*Resolved*, That the General Assembly of this colony, together with his majesty, or substitute, have, in their representative capacity, the only exclusive right and power to lay taxes and impositions upon the inhabitants of this colony: and that every attempt to vest such power in any person or persons whatsoever, other than the General Assembly aforesaid, is illegal, unconstitutional, and unjust, and has a manifest tendency to destroy British as well as American freedom."

"After the passage of Henry's resolutions, the governor dissolved the Assembly; but the people re-elected the friends, and excluded the opposers of the resolutions. The spirited conduct of Virginia fired the ardor of the other colonies; they passed similar resolutions, and a general Congress was proposed. The deputies of nine states met in New York on the 1st of October; they drafted a declaration of rights, a petition to the king, commons, and lords.

14

The stamp act was repealed, and Virginia sent an address of thanks to the king and parliament."

Francis Fauquier, Lieut. Governor of Virginia, died in 1767, and the government devolved on John Blair, until the arrival of Lord Bottetourt, the following year.

" The joy of the colonies at the repeal of the stamp act was short-lived. British ministers imagined that they could cheat the colonies out of their opposition to taxation without representation, by laying an import duty instead of a direct tax; and accordingly, a duty was laid upon glass, tea, paper, and painter's colors; but this was equally against the spirit of the British constitution, and met with a warmer and more indignant resistance on the part of the colonies, who now began to believe they had little hope from the justice of parliament. The legislature of Virginia passed very spirited resolutions, which it ordered to be sent only to the king; upon the passage of which the governor dissolved it; and the members immediately met and entered unanimously into a non-importation agreement.

" The British ministers perceived their error, and determined to pause in their violence; to effect this object the governors were directed to inform the colonies, that his majesty's ministers did not intend to raise a revenue in America, and the duties objected to should be speedily repealed. These assurances, made to Virginia by Lord Bottetourt, a governor whom they highly respected, served, with his own good conduct, for a time to allay her suspicions of the ministry; but the course they pursued towards Massachusetts was more than sufficient to rekindle her jealousy. She passed a protest, declaring that partial remedies could not heal the present disorders, and renewed their non-importation agreement. In 1771 Bottetourt died, and Virginia erected a statue to his memory, which still stands in the town of Williamsburg. Wm. Nelson, then president of the council, occupied the chair of government until the arrival of Lord Dunmore, in 1772. The delay of Lord Dunmore in New York for some months after his appointment to the gubernatorial chair of Virginia, excited the prejudices of the colony, which his sending a man of some military distinction as a clerk, and raising a salary and fees for him out of the colony, were by no means calculated to dissipate. The first legislature that met compelled the governor to dispense with the emoluments of his secretary, Capt. Foy; and the next, after thanking him for his activity in apprehending some counterfeiters of the colony paper, strongly reproved him for dispensing with the usual forms and ceremonies with which the law has guarded the liberty of the citizen. The same legislature, having provided for the soundness and security of the currency, the punishment of the guilty, and required the governor to respect the law, turned their eyes to their sister colonies, and appointed a committee of correspondence* to

---

* This committee were Peyton Randolph, Robert Carter Nicholas, Richard Bland,

inquire into the various violations of their constitutional rights by the British ministry. While Virginia was employed in animating her sister states to resistance, her governor was employed in the ignoble occupation of fomenting jealousies and feuds between the province, which it should have been his duty to protect from such a calamity, and Pennsylvania, by raising difficult questions of boundary, and exciting the inhabitants of the disputed territory to forswear allegiance to the latter province ; hoping thus, by affording a more immediately exciting question, to draw off the attention of these two important provinces from the encroachments of Great Britain. This scheme, as contemptible as it was iniquitous, wholly failed, through the good sense and magnanimity of the Virginia council. Lord North, full of his feeble and futile schemes of *cheating* the colonies out of their rights, took off the obnoxious duties with the exception of three pence per pound on tea ; and, with the ridiculous idea that he might fix the principle upon the colonies by a precedent, which should strip it of all that was odious, offered a draw-back equal to the import duty. This induced the importation of tea into Boston harbor, which, being thrown overboard by some of the citizens, called down upon their city all the rigor of the celebrated Boston port bill. A draft of this bill reached the Virginia legislature while in session; an animated protest, and a dissolution of the assembly by the governor, of course followed. On the following day the members convened in the Raleigh tavern, and, in an able and manly paper, expressed to their constituents and their government those sentiments and opinions which they had not been allowed to express in a legislative form. This meeting recommended a cessation of trade with the East India Company, a Congress of deputies from all the colonies, ' declaring their opinion, that an attack upon one of the colonies was an attack upon all British America,' and a convention of the people of Virginia. The sentiments of the people accorded with those of their late delegates ; they elected members who met in convention at Williamsburg, on the 1st of August, 1774. This convention went into a detailed view of their rights and grievances, discussed measures of redress for the latter, and declared their determination never to relinquish the former ; they appointed deputies to attend a general Congress, and they instructed them how to proceed. The Congress met in Philadelphia, on the 4th of September, 1774. While Virginia was engaged in her efforts for the general good, she was not without her peculiar troubles at home. The Indians had been for some time waging a horrid war upon the frontiers, when the indignation of the people at length compelled the reluctant governor to take up arms, and march to suppress the very savages he was thought to have encouraged and excited to hostility by his intrigues.

Richard Henry Lee, Benjamin Harrison, Edmund Pendleton, Patrick Henry, Dudley Digges, Dabney Carr, Archibald Carey, and Thomas Jefferson.

" Lord Dunmore marched the army in two divisions : the one under Col. Andrew Lewis he sent to the junction of the Great Kanawha with the Ohio, while he himself marched to a higher point
on the latter river, with pretended purpose of destroying the Indian towns and joining Lewis at Point Pleasant; but it was believed with the real* object of sending the whole Indian force to
annihilate Lewis' detachment, and thereby weaken the power and
break down the spirit of Virginia. If such was his object he was
signally defeated through the gallantry of the detachment, which
met and defeated the superior numbers of the enemy at Point
Pleasant, after an exceeding hard-fought day, and the loss of nearly
all its officers. The day after the victory, an express arrived from
Dunmore with orders for the detachment to join him at a distance
of 80 miles, through an enemy's country, without any conceivable
object but the destruction of the corps. As these orders were
given without a knowledge of the victory, Col. Lewis was proceeding to the destruction of the Shawanese villages, when he
was informed the governor had made peace.

" When the treaty was commenced, Cornstalk, the celebrated Shawanese chieftain,
made a speech, in which he charged upon the whites the cause of the war, in consequence, principally, of the murder of Logan's family. Logan was a Mingo chief.
' For magnanimity in war, and greatness of soul in peace, few, if any, in any nation,
ever surpassed Logan.' ' His form was striking and manly, his countenance calm and
noble, and he spoke the English language with fluency and correctness.' Logan did
not make his appearance among the Indian deputies. ' He disdained to be seen among
the suppliants. But, lest the sincerity of a treaty should be disturbed, from which so
distinguished a chief absented himself, he sent, by Gen. John Gibson,† the following
speech, to be delivered to Lord Dunmore.'

" ' I appeal to any white man to say, if ever he entered Logan's cabin hungry, and he
gave him not meat: if ever he came cold and naked, and he clothed him not. During
the course of the last long and bloody war, Logan remained idle in his cabin, an advocate
for peace. Such was my love for the whites, that my countrymen pointed, as they passed,
and said, ' Logan is the friend of white men.' I had even thought to have lived with
you, but for the injuries of one man. Colonel Cresap,‡ the last spring, in cold blood, and
unprovoked, murdered all the relations of Logan, not even sparing my women and children. There runs not a drop of my blood in the veins of any living creature. This
called on me for revenge. I have sought it : I have killed many : I have fully glutted
my vengeance : for my country I rejoice at the beams of peace. But do not harbor a
thought that mine is the joy of fear. Logan never felt fear. He will not turn on his
heel to save his life. Who is there to mourn for Logan ?—Not one.' "

The affairs between Britain and her American colonies were
now verging to a crisis. The hostile attitude of the latter, soon
occasioned orders to be issued to their governors to remove the
military stores out of their reach. Accordingly, on the 20th of
April, 1775, Dunmore secretly removed the gunpowder from the

---

* See Memoir of Indian wars, &c., by the late Col. Stuart of Greenbrier, presented
to the Virginia Historical and Philosophical Society by Charles A. Stuart, of Augusta county, and the Chronicles of Border Warfare, by Alexander C. Withers, for a
strong corroboration of these suspicions.

† The authenticity of this speech has been much questioned. The reader will find
the deposition of Gen. Gibson in the American Pioneer, which gives full and satisfactory
confirmation of its genuineness.

‡ Various evidence is given, in the Pioneer, that it was Capt. Michael Cresap, not
Col. Cresap, who murdered the Indians on the Ohio.

magazine at Williamsburg, to the Magdalen man-of-war, anchored off Yorktown. Thereupon, the volunteers of Williamsburg immediately flew to arms, and could with difficulty be restrained from seizing the person of the governor. The people of the town sent a deputation to Dunmore, who remonstrated with him for this act, especially at a time when they feared an insurrection of the slaves. His reply " was everywhere considered as a mean and scandalous evasion." Fearful of the consequences of his conduct, he established a guard of negroes at his palace. Exasperated to the highest degree, he openly swore, " by the living God," that if any injury was offered to himself, or the officers who had acted under his direction in the affair of the gunpowder, he would proclaim freedom to the slaves, and reduce Williamsburg to ashes. These savage threats wrought the indignation of the people to the highest pitch, which spread like electricity throughout the colony. Over six hundred people of the upper country armed themselves, assembled at Fredericksburg, and offered their services to defend, if necessary, Williamsburg from the threatened attack of Dunmore. Thousands also, in all parts of Virginia, stood ready, at a moment's warning, to lend their aid. In the mean time, those ardent patriots, Peyton Randolph and Edmund Pendleton, transmitted their advice to the Fredericksburg meeting to abstain, for the present, from hostilities, until Congress should decide on a general plan of resistance.

" On the receipt of this advice, they held a council, consisting of over one hundred members, who, by a majority of one only, concluded to disperse for the present. They, however, drafted an address, which was almost tantamount to a declaration of independence, in which they ' firmly resolved to resist all attempts against their rights and privileges, from whatever quarter they might be assailed. They pledged themselves to each other to be in readiness, at a moment's warning, to *reassemble, and*, BY FORCE OF ARMS, *to defend the laws, the liberties, and the rights of this or any* SISTER COLONY, *from unjust and wicked invasion.* They then sent dispatches to troops assembled in Caroline, Berkeley, Frederick, and Dunmore counties, thanking them for their offer of service, and acquainting them with their determinations. The address was read at the head of each company, and unanimously approved. It concluded with these impressive words GOD SAVE THE LIBERTIES OF AMERICA!' "

The volunteers of Hanover, however, determined to recover the powder, or perish in the attempt. With Patrick Henry at their head, they marched from Hanover town to Doncastle's ordinary, within 16 miles of the capitol, their numbers swelled by accessions of volunteers from King William and New Kent. They here disbanded, (May 4th,) and returned to their homes, Patrick Henry having received ample compensation for the powder from Richard Corbin, the king's receiver-general. Two days after the above, Dunmore issued a proclamation against " a certain Patrick Henry, of the county of Hanover, and a number of deluded followers," and forbade all persons to countenance him, or others concerned in like combinations. On the 11th, Henry left Virginia to attend the Continental Congress, of which he was a member.

By this time, every county in Virginia was fairly aroused to the dangers that beset them. County committees were formed, who anticipated measures of defence, by arming and raising minute-men, and taking all practicable means to make an effectual resist-ance. The people sympathized with the sufferings of the Bos-tonians, and the citizens of Williamsburg assembled, and unani-mously resolved to subscribe money for their aid. The news of the battle of Lexington reached Virginia about this time.

The proclamation of Dunmore had scarce made its appearance, when some persons privately entered the magazine and carried away a great number of arms and military equipments. New causes of irritation between the governor and the people were con-tinually arising.

When Patrick Henry marched down to make reprisals for the gunpowder, Dunmore dispatched a messenger to the Fowey man-of-war, anchored off Yorktown, for aid. A detachment of 40 ma-rines and sailors was sent to Williamsburg, where they remained about 10 days. Previous to their landing at Yorktown, Capt. Mon-tague sent a letter from on board the Fowey to Col. Thomas Nel-son, threatening to fire upon the town if the troops were molested or attacked,—a message which still further increased the indigna-tion of the people.

On the 1st of June the governor convened the Assembly, and addressed them in a speech. With this commenced a political correspondence between him and the House of Burgesses, which was, on the part of the latter, a clear and forcible defence of the rights of the colonies. On the 8th of June, the governor, with his family, fled on board the Fowey, off Yorktown, from ill-grounded apprehensions of his safety at Williamsburg. Several communi-cations passed between him and the Assembly, relative to public business generally, the late disturbances respecting the removal of the gunpowder, and the governor's proclamation and course of conduct.

Dunmore " refused, upon invitation of the Assembly, to return to his palace or to sign bills of the utmost importance to the colony, and refused to perform this branch of duty, unless the Assembly would come and hold their meetings under the guns of his ship at Yorktown. In this emergency, the governor was declared to have abdicated, and the president of the council appointed to act in his place. His lordship, on the termination of the intercourse between himself and the Assembly, which was towards the close of June, sailed down the river." Thus ended the royal government in Vir-ginia.

The Assembly now dissolved, and, pursuant to agreement, the delegates, on the 17th of July, met in convention at Richmond, to organize a provincial form of government and a plan of defence. The following illustrious characters composed the committee of safety :—Edmund Pendleton, George Mason, John Page, Richard Bland, Thomas Ludwell Lee, Paul Carrington, Dudley Digges, James Mercer, Carter Braxton, William Cabell, and John Tabb. The convention made arrangements to raise troops for defence, and the general committee met at Hanover Town, in Hanover county, on business connected with the military establishment, and then adjourned to Williamsburg about the last of September. Previously, the committee of safety recommended to the district committees to direct the contractors in each district to provide, among other things, a stand of colors, bearing on one side the name of the district, on the other, " *Virginia for Constitutional Liberty.*"

In October, by Dunmore's orders, a party of men, under cover of their men-of-war, landed at Norfolk, and forcibly carried on board their vessels the press and types of a newspaper imbued with the patriotic principles of the day. Shortly after, Dunmore marched to Kempsville, in Princess Anne, destroyed some fire-arms deposited there, and took prisoner Capt. Matthews, of the minute-men. About this time an attack was made on Hampton, by some vessels commanded by Capt. Squires, who had threatened to burn the town. The enemy were beaten off with loss, while not a single Virginian was killed.

In the mean time, numbers of armed people from the upper country were arriving at Williamsburg. Dunmore, hearing that the 2d Virginia Regiment and the Culpeper Battalion had been ordered to Norfolk, directed the Kingfisher and three large tenders to move up to Burwell's Ferry, to prevent their crossing the James. These vessels, on their arrival, finding an American skipper at the landing, commenced firing upon her, and in a peremptory tone ordered her to come alongside the Kingfisher. Some Virginian riflemen, on the bank, directed her master not to obey the order. Upon this the man-of-war commenced a brisk fire upon the vessel, but without effect. Twice the Kingfisher sent a large boat full of men to take possession, and twice they were beaten off by the unerring aim of the riflemen. Foiled in this attempt, the enemy the next day attempted to land a boat filled with armed men at Jamestown. They were again repulsed by some rifle sentinels on the shore. In this month (November) Dunmore, with a superior force, surprised about 200 militia of Princess Anne, on their march to join the troops. Their colonel, with several others, was made prisoner.

Under date of November 7th, Dunmore issued his proclamation, in which he proclaimed martial law, declared all capable of bearing arms who did not resort to his majesty's standard traitors, and offered freedom to all slaves " appertaining to rebels" who would join his majesty's troops. On this Dunmore had staked his best hopes. Had he had a formidable force at hand to execute his threats, some apprehensions might have been excited. But as it was, it only harmonized public opinion, increased public irritation, and engendered a burning detestation of the means to which their late governor unblushingly stooped to awe them into submission. His lordship set up his standard in Norfolk and Princess Anne, issued orders to the militia captains to raise a body of troops to oppose the colonial army, prescribed, and, in some cases, extorted an oath of allegiance. A multitude of motley partisans flocking to his standard, he designed to destroy the provisions collected at Suffolk for the Virginia troops. To prevent this, Col. Woodford, on the 20th of November, detached 215 light troops, under Col. Scott and Major Marshall, to that place, and on the 25th arrived there with the main body of the Virginia troops.

About this time evidence was brought to light of a diabolical scheme, matured by Dunmore, against that colony of which he pretended to be a friend. This was a co-operation of the various Indian tribes with the tories on the frontiers. John Connelly, a Pennsylvanian, an artful, enterprising man, was the projector of the intrigue. In July he nearly matured the plan with the governor. Ample rewards were offered to the militia captains inclined to the royal cause, and willing to act under Connelly. To connect its extensive ramifications, he was dispatched to General Gage, at Boston, and returned about the 15th of October, with instructions from the latter. These invested him with the rank of Lieut.-Colonel of a regiment of loyalists, to be raised on the frontier. Fort Pitt was to be the rendezvous of all the forces to act under him, among which were several companies of the Royal Irish, then at Fort Gage, in the Illinois country. From thence they would march through Virginia, and join Dunmore on the 20th of April at Alexandria, where an army was to land under the cannon of ships-of-war and possess themselves of the town. For a time, fortune favored this formidable plot, in the prosecution of which Connelly often travelled long distances in various directions. Suspicions were at length aroused : an emissary of the governor's was arrested, upon whom were found papers partly disclosing the plot. These led to the arrestation of Connelly He, with two confederates, Allen Cameron and Dr. John Smyth, both Scotchmen, were taken near Hagerstown, Maryland, on their way to Detroit. Upon searching their baggage, a general plan of the whole scheme was found, with large sums of money, and a letter from Dunmore to one of the Indian chiefs. " Thus was a plot, originally contrived with profound and amazing secrecy, and in its subsequent stages managed with consummate skill, brought by patriotic vigilance to an untimely issue."

The only avenue from Suffolk to Norfolk—to which place he was destined—by which Col. Woodford could march, was by the Great Bridge, about 12 miles from the latter. The enemy were posted there in a stockade fort, on his arrival with the Virginian troops. Woodford constructed a breastwork within cannon-shot of the fort.

On the 9th of December, Capt. Fordyce, at the head of a party of British grenadiers, in attempting to storm the breastwork, was repulsed by a most destructive and bloody fire. After this, Dunmore, with most of his followers, took refuge on board his vessels. The Virginians marched into Norfolk, and annoyed the enemy by firing into their vessels. In retaliation, Dunmore cannonaded the town, and on the night of the 1st of January, 1776, landed a party, who, under cover of their cannon, set fire to the houses on the river which had sheltered the provincials. The committee of safety ordered Col. Robert Howe to destroy the remainder of the town, to prevent the British from making it a permanent post. Norfolk, then the most populous town in Virginia, contained near 6,000 inhabitants.

Colonels Woodford and Stevens assisted Col. Howe in the command at Norfolk. Besides the two regiments already raised, the Convention resolved to raise seven more. Six of these were placed on the continental establishment, to whose officers Congress granted commissions, in order, beginning with Col. Henry, of the 1st, and ending with Col. Buckner, of the 6th Regiment.*

Col. Patrick Henry resigned his commission, much to the regret of the regiment, and was thereupon chosen a member of the Convention from Hanover.

The General Convention of Virginia met at the capital, May 6th, 1776, and appointed Edmund Pendleton, President, and John Tazewell, Clerk. Since the flight of Dunmore, the House of Burgesses had met twice, pursuant to adjournment, but on neither occasion was there a quorum. They now met on the same day with the Convention, but "did neither proceed to business, nor adjourn as a House of Burgesses." Considering their meeting as illegal, not in conformity with a summons from a governor, they unanimously dissolved themselves. "Thus was the tottering fabric of the royal government utterly demolished in Virginia; to substitute in its stead a structure of more elegant and more solid form, was now the task of the Convention."

On the 15th of this month, the convention, after appealing to "the Searcher of hearts" for the sincerity of their former declarations in favor of peace and union with the mother country, adopted unanimously the following resolution:

"That the delegates appointed to represent this colony in General Congress, be instructed to propose to that respectable body, *to declare the united colonies free and independent States*, absolved from all allegiance to, or dependence on the crown or parliament of Great Britain; and that they give the assent of this colony to such declaration, and whatever measures may be thought necessary by Congress for forming foreign alliances, and a confederation of the colonies, at such time, and in the manner that to them shall seem best: provided, that the power of forming governments for, and the regulations of the internal concerns of each colony, be left to the colonial legislatures."

The convention appointed a committee to prepare a *Declaration of Rights*, and a *Plan of Government*, for the colony. The former was adopted on the 12th of June. On the 29th a constitution was unanimously adopted; "the first which was framed with a view to a permanent separation from Great Britain since those of South Carolina and New Hampshire, which alone preceded it, were to continue only until a reconciliation could be effected between the mother country and the colonies. This plan of government was proposed by the celebrated George Mason,† and had been adopted in committee before the arrival of one which Mr. Jefferson, then in Congress, had prepared. They however accepted Mr. Jefferson's preamble, which is nearly the same as the recital of wrongs in the Declaration of Independence."‡

---

* The following were appointed field-officers :—

Regiment.	Colonels.	Lieut.-Colonels.	Majors.
Third,	Hugh Mercer,	George Weedon,	Thomas Marshall.
Fourth,	Adam Steven,	Isaac Read,	R. Lawson.
Fifth,	William Peachy,	Wm. Crawford,	J. Parker.
Sixth,	Mordecai Buckner,	Thomas Elliott,	J. Hendricks.
Seventh,	Wm. Dangerfield,	Alex. M'Clanahan,	Wm. Nelson.
Eighth,	Peter Muhlenburg,	A. Bowman,	P. Helvistone.
Ninth,	Thomas Fleming,	George Matthews,	M. Donavon.

† The Declaration of Rights was also drawn up by him.   ‡ Tucker's Life of Jefferson.

The following appointments were made under the constitution: Patrick Henry, Esq., governor. John Page, Dudley Digges, John Tayloe, John Blair, Benjamin Harrison of Berkeley, Bartholomew Dandridge, Charles Carter of Shirley, and Benjamin Harrison of Brandon, counsellors of state. Thomas Whiting, John Hutchings, Champion Travis, Thomas Newton, jun., and George Webb, Esquires, commissioners of admiralty. Thomas Everard and James Cocke, Esquires, commissioners for settling accounts. Edmund Randolph, Esq., attorney-general.

On the 5th of July the convention adjourned. Though the session was brief, it was an important one. Among other acts besides the formation of a government, they passed an ordinance for erecting salt works in the colony: for establishing a board of commissioners to superintend and direct the naval affairs of the colony: for raising six troops of horse: for arranging the counties into districts for electing senators, &c. They also resolved to expunge from the litany such parts as related to the king and royal family, and substituted, in the morning and evening service, such forms of expression as were better suited to the new state of affairs.

The Declaration of Independence, so strongly recommended by the Virginia convention, was passed in Congress on the 4th of July, 1776; and, agreeably to an order of the privy council, it was proclaimed on the 25th of the same month at the capitol, the court-house, and the palace at Williamsburg, amidst the acclamations of the people, and the firing of cannon and musketry.

The energetic measures that had been adopted by the Virginia troops in precluding the flotilla of Dunmore from obtaining supplies, had at last obliged them to burn the intrenchments they had erected near the ruins of Norfolk, and seek a refuge on board their ships, where disease and hunger pursued them. The presence of his lordship in the lower country had given countenance to the disaffected, who were there numerous. A vigorous course was ordered to be pursued towards them. Col. Woodford, stationed at Kemps' Landing, (now Kempsville, Princess Anne,) humanely executed these orders, which were intrusted to him by the committee of safety, through Maj. Gen. Chas. Lee.

Dunmore, with his fleet, left Hampton Roads about the 1st of June, landed and erected fortifications on Gwynn's island, within the limits of what is now Matthew's county. On the 9th of July he was attacked by the Virginians, under Brig. Gen. Andrew Lewis, and forced to abandon the island. Shortly after, Dunmore dispatched the miserable remnant of his followers to Florida and the West Indies, and sailing himself to the north, forever left the shores of Virginia.

The nefarious plot of Connelly was only part of an extensive scheme of operations, which the British had meditated in seeking an alliance with the savages. By their instigation the Indians were harassing the frontiers of the southern states to such a degree that a combination was formed to destroy their settlements on the borders. Col. Christian, on the part of this state, marched with a body of Virginia troops into the Cherokee country, burnt four of their towns, and compelled them to sue for peace.

On the 7th of October, 1776, the Assembly of Virginia met for the first time; Edmund Pendleton was chosen Speaker of the House of Delegates, and Archibald Carey of the Senate. One of the earliest of their labors was the repeal of all acts of Parliament against dissenters, which was the first direct blow struck at the established church in the state.

In the session of this fall, the Assembly appointed Thomas Jefferson, Edmund Pendleton, George Wythe, George Mason, and Thomas Ludwell Lee, Esquires, a committee to revise the State laws, and prepare a code more suitable to the new state of affairs: the execution of the work devolved on the three first.

At the north, the war was progressing with various success. The Americans had been defeated at Long Island, New York came into the possession of the British, and General Montgomery fell before the walls of Quebec, and his army retreated from Canada. Washington's army, reduced to 3,500 effective men, retreated through New Jersey, before the overwhelming force of the enemy, and crossed the Delaware. On the 25th of December, 1776, Washington recrossed the Delaware, and the victories of Trenton and Princeton, the first on the 26th of December, and the last on the 3d of January, at this the darkest period of the revolution, reanimated the hopes of the friends of liberty.

The principal object of the British in the campaign of 1777, was to open a communication between New York city and Canada, and to separate New England from the other states. Early in the year, Burgoyne was sent for this purpose, with 7,000 men, from Canada. He was arrested by Gen. Gates, and on the 17th of October, was compelled to surrender his whole army to him. The capture of Burgoyne spread joy throughout the country. Washington, in the mean while, was in anxious suspense, watching the operations of Sir Wm. Howe, who had sailed from New York with 18,000 men, and a large fleet commanded by Lord Howe. Apprehensive it was a ruse, designed to draw him to the south, and leave the north open to their attacks, Washington proceeded to Bucks co., Penn., and there waited the destination of the enemy.

The British fleet sailed up the Chesapeake, and landed the army in Maryland which soon after defeated the Americans at Brandywine and Germantown. In the former action, the Virginia brigades, under Wayne and Weedon, distinguished themselves. The British did not follow up these victories with vigor. While the Americans lost only a few hundred men, these conflicts improved them in discipline, and better fitted them for the contest.

Although the seat of the war was for so long a period transferred from Virginia, her soil was doomed soon to be again trod by the foot of the invader. Previous, however, to giving an abstract of the military operations which occurred here in the last few years of the revolutionary struggle, we shall glance at a few matters too important to be omitted in even this brief sketch of her history.

While the events above alluded to were transpiring at the north, Virginia was exerting every nerve, in furnishing additional men and means, for the common cause, and adopting energetic measures against the disaffected within her own bosom. Among them were many British merchants, settled in the towns, in whose hands was much of the trade. These were compelled to leave the state, or be taken in custody. An oath of allegiance to the commonwealth, was also required of all free-born male inhabitants over 16 years of age. At this time, a taste for elegant literature and profound research prevailed throughout Virginia. The learned Dr. Small, of William and Mary College, had chiefly contributed to the diffusion of that taste before the war, through the encouragement of Gov. Fauquier, "the ablest character who had then ever filled the chair of government in Virginia." A literary and scientific society was instituted, amid the excitement of revolutionary scenes, of which Mr. John Page* was president, and Prof. James Madison† one of the secretaries. They held a meeting in the capitol, and several valuable philosophical papers were read. The calls of war, unfortunately, prevented a ripe development of the association.

A loan-office was opened at Williamsburg, to effect two resolutions of Congress for the obtaining a loan of continental money for the use of the United States. Another loan-office was established by the state, for borrowing, on the part of the commonwealth, one million of dollars, to supersede the necessity of emitting more paper money.

It was fortunate for Virginia that she had at this time, on her western borders, an individual of rare military genius, in the person of Col. George Rogers Clarke, "*the Hannibal of the West*," who not only saved her back settlements from Indian fury, but planted her standard far beyond the Ohio. The governor of the Canadian settlements in the Illinois country, by every possible method, instigated the Indians to annoy the frontier. Virginia placed a small force of about 250 men under Clarke, who descending the Ohio, hid their boats, and marched northwardly, with their provisions on their backs. These being consumed, they subsisted for two days on roots, and, in a state of famine, appeared before Kuskaskias, unseen and unheard. At midnight, they surprised and took the town and fort, which had resisted a much larger force; then seizing the golden moment, sent a detachment who with equal success surprised three other towns. Rocheblave, the obnoxious governor, was sent to Virginia. On his person were found written instructions from Quebec, to excite the Indians to hostilities, and reward them for the scalps of the Americans. The settlers transferred their allegiance to Virginia, and she, as the territory belonged to her by conquest and charter, in the autumnal session of 1778 erected it into a county to be called Illinois. Insulated in the heart of the Indian country, in the midst of the most ferocious tribes, few men but Clarke could have preserved this acquisition. Hamilton, the governor of Detroit, a bold and tyrannical personage, determined, with an overwhelming force of British and Indians, to penetrate up the Ohio to Fort Pitt, to sweep all the principal settlements in his way, and besiege Kaskaskias. Clarke despaired of keeping possession of the country, but he resolved to preserve this post, or die in its defence. While he was strengthening the fortifications, he received information that Hamilton, who was at Fort St. Vincent, had weakened his force by sending some Indians against the frontiers. This information, to the genius of Clarke, disclosed, with the rapidity of an electric flash, not only safety but new glory. To resolve to attack Hamilton before he could collect the Indians, was the work of a moment,—the only hope of saving the country. With a band of 150 gallant and hardy comrades, he marched across the country. It was in February, 1779. When within nine miles of the enemy, it took these intrepid men five days to cross the drowned lands of the Wabash, having often to wade up to their breasts in water. Had not the weather been remarkably mild, they must have perished. On the evening of the 23d, they landed in sight of the fort, before the enemy knew any thing of their approach. After a siege of eighteen hours it surrendered, without the loss of a man to the besiegers. The governor was sent prisoner to Williamsburg, and considerable stores fell into the possession of the conqueror. Other auspicious circumstances crowned this result. Clarke, intercepting a convoy from Canada, on their way to this post, took the mail, 40 prisoners, and goods to the value of $45,000; and to crown all, his express from Virginia arrived

---

* Afterwards governor of Virginia.   † Subsequently bishop of the Episcopal Church.

with the thanks of the assembly to him and his gallant band, for their reduction of the country about Kaskaskias. This year Virginia extended her western establishments, through the agency of Col. Clarke, and had several fortifications erected, among which was Fort Jefferson, on the Mississippi.

On the 2d of January, 1781, the assembly, in conformity to the wishes of Congress, ceded to the United States her large territory northwest of the Ohio. To this liberal measure, Virginia was induced by a desire of accelerating the general ratification of the articles for the confederation of the Union.

On the accession of Sir Henry Clinton, in the place of Sir William Howe, to the chief command, the war was carried on with greater energy. The reduction of the south seemed an object less difficult, and of as much value as the north ; hence the plan of conquest was somewhat altered. Georgia was threatened with subjection by an expedition under Lieut. Col. Campbell, while Sir Henry Clinton prepared, in person, to invade South Carolina.

The central position of Virginia had hitherto, in a measure, saved her from the incursions of the enemy. Sir Henry Clinton saw that the resistance of the southern states would depend much upon Virginia, and he was determined to humble her pride and destroy her resources. For this purpose an expedition was planned, and early in May, 1779, their squadron, under Sir George Collier, anchored in Hampton Roads. Fort Nelson, just below Portsmouth, was abandoned to them, and on the 11th, the British general, Matthews, took possession of Portsmouth. The enemy destroyed large quantities of naval and military stores at Gosport and Norfolk ; burnt Suffolk, and many private houses, and destroyed upwards of 100 vessels. The army shortly embarked for New York with their plunder.

" This destruction of private property, which ought to be held sacred by civilized nations at war, called for the interference of the Assembly. A resolve was passed in that body, requiring the governor to remonstrate against this cruel mode of carrying on the war. The fall of Charleston, and the success of the British arms in the south, under Lord Cornwallis, portended much evil to Virginia. Her reduction was determined on by the commander-in-chief, and a plan, apparently big with success, was laid for that purpose. As soon as Clinton was informed of the defeat of the southern army by Lord Cornwallis, he dispatched Brigadier-General Leslie, with a force of about three thousand men, against Virginia. The co-operation of this detachment with the army under Cornwallis, who was expected to enter Virginia on the south, appeared fully adequate to the object in view.

" Leslie arrived in the Chesapeake bay in October, 1780, and landing at Portsmouth, took possession of such vessels and other property as could be found on the coast. The defeat of Major Ferguson, who had been ordered to manœuvre through the northern parts of South Carolina, and was expected to join Cornwallis at Charlotte, caused the latter to alter his plans, and prevented his junction with Leslie. Some time elapsed before Leslie could obtain information of the situation of Cornwallis, and the circum stances that occurred to prevent the important junction with that officer. Meanwhile the governor of Virginia was earnestly employed in preparing to oppose the invaders. Thomas Jefferson, successor of Patrick Henry, was then governor of the state, and the assembly, composed of men selected for their wisdom and patriotism, was in session. At this crisis, General Greene, who had been appointed to succeed Gates in the command of the southern army, arrived in Richmond, on his way to the south. As much reliance had been placed on the supplies to be received from Virginia, Greene was not a little embarrassed to find her in such a weak and exposed situation. After making such arrangements as he deemed necessary, he continued his journey to the south, leaving Baron Steuben to direct the defence of the state. General Gates had removed his head-quarters to Charlotte, and there he surrendered into the hands of Greene the command of the southern army. In the mean time, General Leslie, leaving the shores of Virginia, sailed for Charleston, where he found orders requiring him to repair with his army to Camden. On the 19th of December he began his march, with about fifteen hundred men, to effect a junction with the army under Cornwallis. This he accomplished without difficulty. On the 11th of January, Cornwallis advanced towards North Carolina. Wishing to disperse the force under General Morgan, who had been manœuvring in the western parts of the state, he dispatched Colonel Tarleton in pursuit of him. The splendid victory of the Cowpens checked the ardor of the pursuers, and revived the drooping spirits of the Americans. The southern army was, however, unable to face their enemy in the field; and the movements of Cornwallis indicating a design to bring Greene to action, compelled the latter to retreat towards Virginia. This he safely accomplished, notwithstanding the vigorous pursuit of the British general, who had destroyed his baggage in order to effect his movements with more celerity. The van of the British army arrived just after the rear of the American had passed the Dan, which forms the dividing line between the two states. The next day General Greene wrote to Mr. Jefferson, governor of Virginia, and to Baron Steuben, giving information of his situation, and requesting reinforcements.

"Early in December, 1780, Governor Jefferson received a letter from General Washington, informing him that preparations were making by the enemy at New York, for an expedition to the south, which was probably designed against Virginia. On the 30th, Brigadier-General Arnold, with near fifty sail of vessels, arrived in the Chesapeake, and embarking in lighter vessels, proceeded up James River. On receiving news of this approaching squadron, Mr. Jefferson dispatched General Nelson to collect and arrange a force with as much haste as possible, while Baron Steuben, with about two hundred men, marched to Petersburg. On the 4th of January, Arnold landed his force, consisting of about nine hundred men, at Westover, the seat of Mr. Byrd, and marched to Richmond without opposition. Thus was the metropolis of Virginia exposed to the insult and depredation of a traitor ; her stores and archives plundered, and her governor compelled to seek security by immediate flight. From Richmond, Lieutenant-Colonel Simcoe was dispatched to Westham, where he destroyed the only cannon foundry in the state. At this place they also destroyed the military stores, which had, on the alarm caused by Arnold's approach, been removed from Richmond. After two days spent in pillaging public and private property, General Arnold returned to Westover, where on the 10th he re-embarked his men, and descended the river. On his way he landed detachments at Mackay's mill, and at Smithfield, where they destroyed some public stores ; and on the 20th, arrived at Portsmouth.

"Major-General Steuben, assisted by General Nelson, having collected a considerable force, marched in pursuit of Arnold. But the movements of the latter were too rapid to be interrupted by the tardy advances of undisciplined militia. They were, however, able to prevent similar incursions, and by remaining in the vicinity of Portsmouth, they confined the enemy to their entrenchments. On hearing of the invasion of Virginia by the traitor Arnold, and his encampment at Portsmouth, General Washington formed a plan to cut off his retreat. He intimated to Count Rochambeau and Admiral D'Estouches, the importance of an immediate movement of the French fleet to the Chesapeake ; and at the same time detached the Marquis De la Fayette, with twelve hundred men, to Virginia. The French admiral, not entering fully into the views of Washington, detached only a small part of his squadron, who, from their inability to effect the desired purpose, returned to the fleet at Rhode Island. The situation of Arnold had induced Sir H. Clinton to detach to his aid Major-General Phillips, to whom the command of the British forces in Virginia was committed. The united detachments under Arnold and Phillips formed a body of about three thousand five hundred men. Being able to act on the offensive, General Phillips left one thousand men in Portsmouth, and proceeded with the remainder up James River, for the purpose of completing the destruction of the internal strength and resources of the state. Opposite to Williamsburg he landed, and from thence sent to Yorktown a detachment, who destroyed the naval stores in that place. Re-embarking, they ascended the river to City Point, where James River receives the waters of the Appamattox. At this place Phillips landed, and directed his march to Petersburg, which stands on the bank of the last-mentioned stream, about twelve miles from its junction with the former.

"Virginia was at this time in a defenceless situation ; all the regular force of the state was under Greene, in South Carolina, and her whole reliance was upon militia, of whom about two thousand were now in the field. This force, half of which was stationed on each side of James River, was under the command of Baron Steuben and General Nelson. Steuben directed the southern division, on whom the defence of Petersburg devolved, and from which place he was compelled to retreat by the superior force of Phillips. During his stay in Petersburg, General Phillips destroyed the warehouses, and spread terror and devastation, the constant attendants of British invasion, through the town. Leaving Petersburg, he crossed the Appamattox into Chesterfield, and detaching Arnold to Osborne's to destroy the tobacco at that place, he proceeded himself to Chesterfield court-house, where he destroyed the barracks and stores which had been formed there for the accommodation of recruits designed for the southern army. The two divisions of the army uniting again, marched into Manchester, where was renewed the scene of pillage and devastation transacted in Petersburg and Chesterfield. The fortunate arrival of the Marquis De la Fayette at Richmond, with a body of regular troops, saved the metropolis from a similar fate. From Manchester, General Phillips proceeded down the river to Bermuda hundred, opposite City Point, where his fleet remained during his incursion. Here he re-embarked his troops, and fell down the river, while the marquis followed on the north side to watch his movements. He soon learned that Phillips, instead of returning to Portsmouth, had suddenly relanded his army on the south side of the river, one division at Brandon, and the other at City Point, and was on his march to Petersburg. It immediately occurred to the marquis, that a junction with Cornwallis, who was then approaching Virginia, was the object which Phillips had in view, and to prevent which he determined to throw himself, by forced marches, into Petersburg before the arrival of that general. Phillips, however, reached that place first, and Lafayette halting, recrossed the river, and posted himself a few miles below Richmond. The death of General Phillips, soon after his arrival in Petersburg, devolved the command of the army again on General Arnold.

"Cornwallis was now on his way to Petersburg, and having crossed the Roanoke, he detached Colonel Tarleton to secure the fords of the Meherrin, while Colonel Simcoe, with the rangers, was sent for the same purpose to the Nottoway. The enemy effected his passage over these rivers without interruption, and on the 20th of May entered Petersburg. In addition to this united force, which seemed fully sufficient to crush every germ of opposition in Virginia, General Leslie had again made his appearance on the coast, with a reinforcement of two regiments and two battalions, part of which was stationed in Portsmouth, under the command of that officer. The Marquis De la Fayette continued near Richmond, with a force of about four thousand men, nearly three-fourths of whom were militia. Steuben, who was on the south side of James River, proceeding with about six hundred levies to reinforce General Greene, was suddenly recalled, and ordered to take a position at the Point of Fork, where were deposited some military stores. General Weedon was requested to collect a force near Fredericksburg, for the purpose of protecting an important manufactory of arms at Falmouth. In addition to these different forces, General Wayne was on his way to Virginia, with a detachment from the northern army of about nine hundred men. The strength of the enemy was, however, too great for any force Virginia could bring into the field, and her fate, as far as superior numbers and discipline could influence it, seemed now to be decided.

"Cornwallis, after resting four days in Petersburg, proceeded down the south side of Appamattox and James rivers, until he came opposite Westover, where he determined to cross. Lafayette, informed of the enemy's movement, left his encampment below Richmond, and retreated behind the Chickahomony River, keeping the direction towards Fredericksburg. The enemy pursued him across that stream, anxious to bring him to battle before his junction with Wayne. Lafayette, however, escaped the impending blow, and hastening across the Pamunky and Mattapony, the confluence of whose streams form York River, he endeavored to gain the road on which Wayne was approaching. The British commander, failing in his project of bringing the marquis to battle, thought proper to change his course, and determined to penetrate with his detachments the interior of the state. Lieutenant-Colonel Simcoe was directed to attack Baron Steuben at Point of Fork, (a point of land formed by the junction of the Rivanna and Fluvanna rivers,) and destroy the stores at that place ; while Colonel Tarleton advanced to Charlottesville, where the General Assembly was then convened.

"Simcoe succeeded in driving Steuben from his post, and destroying the magazines under his protection ; while Tarleton pushed on to Charlottesville, eager to add to his numerous exploits the capture of a corps of republican legislators. His approach, however, was discovered by the Assembly in time for the members to make their escape. Mr. Jefferson, the governor, on hearing of their approach, sought an asylum in the wilds of the mountain adjacent to his house. After destroying some military stores, which had been deposited in Charlottesville as a place of safety, Tarleton proceeded down the Rivanna, towards the Point of Fork, near to which Cornwallis had arrived with the main body of the army. Uniting with his army the different detachments, the British commander marched to Richmond, which he entered on the 16th of June. Meanwhile Lafayette had formed a junction with Wayne, and was watching with a cautious eye the movements of the foe.

"After halting a few days in Richmond, Cornwallis resumed his march towards the coast, and on the 25th of the month arrived in Williamsburg, while the marquis, with a force of between four and five thousand men, followed close on his rear. From that place the British commander detached Colonel Simcoe to the Chickahomony, for the purpose of destroying some boats and stores on that river. Colonel Butler, with a detachment from the American camp, was immediately sent against this party, and a severe conflict ensued, in which each side claimed the victory. After remain-

16

ing about a week in Williamsburg, the British commander prepared to cross the river, and selected James City island as the most
eligible place to effect a passage. In the mean time, Lafayette
and the intrepid General Wayne pressed close on his rear, with a
view to strike as soon as the enemy should be weakened by the
van having crossed the river. Under a mistaken belief that the
separation of the enemy's force had actually taken place, an attack
was made on the whole strength of the British army drawn up in
order of battle. The approach of night saved the American army,
who effected a retreat after losing, in killed, wounded and prisoners, upwards of a hundred men. From a belief that a grand attack was intended on New York by the combined army, Sir H.
Clinton had ordered Cornwallis to take a position near Portsmouth
or Williamsburg, on tide-water, with a view to facilitate the transportation of his forces to New York, or such aid as might be
deemed necessary. In obedience to this command, Cornwallis
selected York and Gloucester as the most eligible situations, where
he immediately concentrated his army. The bold and discerning
mind of Washington soon formed a plan to strike his lordship while
encamped at York—a plan no less wisely devised than successfully
executed. The arrival of the French fleet in the Chesapeake, at
this juncture, contributed essentially to the completion of his designs. Count De Grasse, on obtaining intelligence from Lafayette of the situation of the enemy, immediately detached four ships
of the line to block up York River. Washington, fearful that
Cornwallis might attempt to retreat to the south, sent orders to Lafayette to take effective measures to prevent his escape ; and also
wrote to Mr. Jefferson, who was still governor of Virginia, urging
him to yield every aid which his situation could afford, and which
the importance of the object required. On the 14th of September,
General Washington arrived in Williamsburg, which was now the
head-quarters of Lafayette, and proceeding to Hampton, the plan
of siege was concerted with the Count De Grasse. About the 25th
of the month the troops of the north arrived, and formed a junction
with those under De la Fayette. The whole regular force thus
combined, consisted of about twelve thousand men. In addition to
these, there was a body of Virginia militia under the command of
the brave and patriotic General Nelson. The trenches were
opened by the combined forces on the 6th of October, at the distance of six hundred yards from the enemy's works. On the 19th
the posts of York and Gloucester were surrendered to the combined
forces of America and France."

The news of the surrender of Cornwallis spread universal joy
throughout the country. The termination of the war was evidently
near,—a war for constitutional liberty. In its trying scenes, Virginia was among the foremost. When the colonies had gone too
far to allow a hope for an honorable submission, she was the first
to adopt a perfectly independent constitution—the first to recommend the Declaration of Independence : her great son was the first

among the leaders of the armies of the nation, and her officers and soldiers, whether in the shock of battle, or marching half-clad, ill-fed, and barefooted, amid the snows of the north, through pestilential marshes, and under a burning sun at the far south, evinced a bravery and fortitude unsurpassed.

CHAPTER VIII.

FROM THE CLOSE OF THE AMERICAN REVOLUTION TO THE PRESENT TIME.

End of the war.—Action of the Virginia Convention upon the Federal Constitution.— Origin of the Federal and Democratic parties.—Opposition to the Alien and Sedition Laws in Virginia.—Report of Mr. Madison thereon.—War of 1812.—Revision of the State Constitution in 1829-30.—Action of Virginia upon the subject of Slavery in 1831-2.—Policy of the state in reference to Internal Improvement and Education.

ALTHOUGH active military operations were prolonged in various parts of the country, especially at the south, after the capture o Cornwallis's army, it may be said that the war was effectually extinguished in Virginia by that memorable event. Most of the troops which had been raised for the defence of the state were in a short time disbanded, and although the negotiations for peace between the two countries were rather slow in their progress, yet the conviction soon became general, that the signal defeat of the enemy at Yorktown would lead to that happy result. The statesmen of Virginia took an active part in the discussions which followed the treaty of peace, growing out of the acknowledged incompetency of the articles of confederation to bind the states together by ties sufficiently strong. The firmest patriots were alarmed at the symptoms of approaching dissolution, and none were more conspicuous in their efforts to avert that catastrophe than the great man who led the armies of the Republic, and achieved its independence. The Convention which assembled in Richmond, in June, 1788, to ratify the federal constitution, was composed of some of the most illustrious men in the state. The names of Marshall,* Madison,* Monroe,* Mason,† Nicholas,‡ Henry,§ Ran-

---

* Chief-Justice Marshall, and Presidents Madison and Monroe.
† There were two Masons in the convention : George Mason, a man of transcendent talents, and an active participator in the formation of the first Constitution of Virginia, in 1776 ; and Stevens Thompson Mason, who was also a man of fine abilities, and a Senator in Congress during Washington's administration.
‡ There were two gentlemen of the name of Nicholas ; Wilson Carey Nicholas, afterwards governor of Virginia, and George Nicholas, his brother, who removed to Kentucky, and was a prominent man in that state. They have an only surviving brother, Judge Philip N. Nicholas, of Richmond.
§ The celebrated Patrick Henry.

dolph,* Pendleton,† Lee,‡ Washington,§ Wythe,‖ Innes,¶ Harrison,** Bland,†† Grayson,‡‡ and a host of others, shed a lustre upon the deliberations of that august body, which has never been surpassed in the annals of the commonwealth. "The debates as given to the public, though no doubt imperfect, exhibit a display of eloquence and talents, certainly at that time unequalled in the country."§§

Yet it may appear strange to the present generation, that such was the diversity of opinion which prevailed, and so serious were the apprehensions entertained by many, that too much power was conceded to the general government by the instrument proposed for adoption, that it was only ratified by a lean majority of ten, out of 168 members, who voted on the final question. The opposite political opinions which were developed on that occasion, were strongly impressed upon the public mind, and traces of their influence may be easily distinguished in the subsequent history of parties in Virginia. The name of federalist, which was originally applied to those who were in favor of adopting the Constitution, was afterwards used to designate the party which favored that construction of the instrument supposed to give greater efficiency to the powers it conferred ; while those, for the most part, who were hostile to the new form of government, preferred to be distinguished by the title of democrats, or republicans.‖‖ These distinctions, were aggravated and widened by the subsequent action of Congress, and especially by the passage of the Alien and Sedition laws, in Mr. Adams's administration. These measures encountered the most decided opposition in Virginia. Mr. Madison, who was one of the ablest and most distinguished advocates of the federal constitution, conceived that its true meaning had been grossly perverted by the measures referred to—and having been

---

* Edmund Randolph, a distinguished lawyer ; governor of Virginia, and a member of Washington's first Cabinet.

† Edmund Pendleton, an eminent jurist, and president of the Court of Appeals.

‡ Henry Lee, an active partisan officer of the revolution, and afterwards governor of the state. He was the historian of the Southern war.

§ Bushrod Washington, nephew of George Washington, and a judge of the Supreme Court of the United States.

‖ The venerable Judge Wythe, Chancellor of the state.

¶ James Innes, an eloquent and eminent lawyer, and attorney-general of the state.

** Benjamin Harrison, the father of President Harrison ; a signer of the Declaration of Independence, and governor of the state in 1781.

†† Theodorick Bland, an active officer of the revolution, in the family of Washington.

‡‡ Mr. Grayson, an eminent lawyer and statesman, of surpassing merit.

§§ Political and Civil History of the United States ; by the Hon. Timothy Pitkin, of Connecticut.

‖‖ The great orator, Patrick Henry, was one of the most prominent opponents to the adoption of the federal constitution ; but after its adoption, he determined to support the government in the exercise of those powers which he believed to have been legitimately conferred, but against the giving of which he had so earnestly contended. Accordingly he was elected to the Legislature, in the spring of 1799, resolved to sustain in that body the constitutionality of the Alien and Sedition laws. His death, which occurred before the meeting of the Legislature, spared him the great and perhaps unequal conflict.—*See Wirt's Life of Henry.*

elected to the state legislature for the session of 1799, prepared
his celebrated report, which received the sanction of that body,
by a considerable majority. This report, ever since its adoption,
has been regarded by the state-rights, or democratic party, as a
political text-book, or authoritative exposition of the federal constitution; yet it is affirmed by their opponents, that its reasons and
deductions have been frequently applied to cases which were not
within the contemplation of its original framer, or of many others, who sanctioned its application to the Alien and Sedition
laws.

Passing over the minor events in the annals of the state, it may
be sufficient to observe, that she gave a constant and cordial support to the measures of her presidents, Jefferson and Madison,
which were preliminary to the war of 1812, declared against Great
Britain. During the existence of that war, she contributed liberally her treasure, and the services of her people, to the defence of
the country. To say nothing of the distinguished men and numerous recruits with which she supplied the land and naval forces
of the Union, instances were not wanting of the display of heroic
valor within her own borders, in repelling the predatory and sanguinary depredations of the enemy. Hampton, Craney Island, the
White House, and various other points on the Potomac, will long
be remembered as scenes of gallant enterprise or patient endurance
of the hardships of war. Her sons from the mountains and valleys of her extensive western domain, marched with alacrity to
the seaboard, and submitted, without murmuring, to the toils and
perils of the camp; and hundreds paid the forfeit of their lives in
a climate which, to them, habit and nature had rendered uncon-
genial and fatal.

Although the state was a cordial and zealous supporter of the
war, and perhaps suffered less than some of the more exposed of
her sister commonwealths, yet she was by no means disinclined to
peace; although, in the opinion of many, the terms upon which
that blessing was acquired were not precisely consistent with the
objects for which the war was declared. This, however, is one of
the usual contingencies upon which the mortal conflicts of nations
are waged. They fight for principle, but are obliged to make
peace from necessity; and there is no truth which is taught us by
experience more salutary, than that peace, even with its attendant disadvantages, is more tolerable, than war, which places
every thing at hazard, and is always followed by multiplied horrors.

Nothing, perhaps, occurred of sufficient consequence to be noticed by the general annalist or historian, after the peace of 1815,
until the period which brought about the General Convention of
1829, assembled for the purpose of revising the state constitution;
a frame of government which had been established prior to the
Declaration of Independence, and which was, therefore, consecrated
in the affections of a large portion of the people by being asso-

ciated with revolutionary scenes and recollections. It is not to be
denied, however, that some of the complaints of those who were
clamorous for reform, were in themselves reasonable, even if no
serious inconvenience and mischief had been experienced in practice. The grievance which had been most earnestly dwelt upon
in the popular discussions, was the great inequality of representation in the state legislature. Counties of unequal size, wealth,
and population, were represented in the state councils by an equal
number of delegates ; and although perhaps the interests of large
sections or divisions were fully protected in the practical operation
of government, yet the sense of local wrong was too powerful to
be resisted. The call of a convention was sanctioned by a majority of the people, and that body assembled in Richmond in October, 1829. No set of men of more varied talents, or of riper
experience and wisdom, had been organized as a public body in
Virginia, since the meeting of the state convention which ratified
the federal constitution ; and there are many conspicuous names
found in the proceedings of both those distinguished assemblies.[*]
How strikingly different were the results of the deliberations of
the two conventions ! The first in the order of time contributed
essentially to cement the union of the states, by the substitution of
a solid fabric of government for a feeble confederation, which, in
the language of the day, had been aptly compared to a " rope of
sand." The labors of the latter, in the opinion of able minds, have
not only resulted in no essential good, but in much practical mischief. Whether the opinion be or be not well-founded, it is not
necessary to decide ; but it is certain that the amended constitution has dissatisfied many, and that propositions have already been
made to the legislature to adopt preliminary measures for a third
convention.

Virginia having the most extensive territory of any of the states
of the Union, and being the largest slaveholder, has always been
peculiarly sensitive in regard to that species of property. As far
back as the first administration of Gov. Monroe, at the commencement of the present century, a well-organized insurrection of the
slaves in the immediate vicinity of the seat of government, was
only prevented from resulting in the most frightful consequences
to the persons and property of the whites, by the timely interposition of Providence. From the best authenticated accounts, founded upon evidence taken at the time by the constituted authorities,
a large body of slaves, supposed to be a thousand in number, headed by skilful leaders, and provided with the means of offensive

---

* Ex-presidents Madison and Monroe, and Chief-Justice Marshall, were members of both conventions. Among the conspicuous leaders in the last, may be mentioned the names of B. W. Leigh, and his brother, Judge Leigh, John Randolph of
Roanoke, Gov. Giles, Chapman Johnson, Judge Philip P. Barbour, Judge Stanard,
Charles F. Mercer, Jno. R. Cooke, Richard Morris, Judge Summers, Judge Scott, Philip
Dodridge, Judge Green, Littleton W. Tazewell, Gen. Robert B. Taylor, Gov. Pleasants, Judge Abel P. Upshur, and many others.

warfare, assembled by preconcert, in the night, about six miles from Richmond, and resolved to attack the town before daybreak. No suspicion having been excited, the police was feeble and inert ; the inhabitants were lulled into perfect security, and nothing, it is believed, saved them from massacre and pillage, but a sudden and violent storm, accompanied by heavy rains, which rendered impassable a stream lying between the insurgents and the city. A young negro, attached to his master and family, was seized with compunction for his criminal designs, and swam the stream, at the hazard of life, to give information of the plot. The whole city was roused—troops were ordered out—the insurrection was suppressed, and the ringleaders expiated their offence on the gallows. The severity of the punishment inflicted upon these unhappy sufferers, it was supposed, for a long period of time, would prevent any similar disturbance in the state ; but unhappily, in the year 1831, during the administration of Gov. Floyd, a still more alarming insurrection occurred in the county of Southampton, which was attended by the most tragical results. A fanatical slave by the name of Nat Turner, with his brother, who was still more fanatical, and who styled himself the prophet, rallied a band of desperate followers, and, in open day, carried death and desolation into all the surrounding neighborhoods. Whole families of men, women, and children, were slaughtered without mercy, under circumstances of peculiar barbarity ; and the insurrection was only suppressed by the prompt interference of the military authority. After the fullest investigation, the conduct of these sanguinary wretches could not be accounted for upon any of the usual motives which govern men in a servile condition. As slaves, they were not treated with particular unkindness or severity ; and the only plausible solution of the problem is to be found in the suggestions of a wild superstition, excited by the unnatural and extraordinary appearance of the sun at that particular period—a phenomenon which was recorded at the time, and is still well recollected.

This painful and startling event made a deep impression upon the public mind. Men began to think and reason about the evils and insecurity of slavery ; the subject of emancipation was discussed both publicly and privately, and was prominently introduced into the popular branch of the legislature at the ensuing session of 1831-32. The House of Delegates contained, at that time, many young members of shining abilities, besides others of maturer years and more established reputation ; and the debate which sprang up, upon the abstract proposition declaring it expedient to abolish slavery, was characterized by all the powers of argument and all the graces of eloquence. It was a topic eminently fitted to arouse the strongest passions of our nature, and to enlist the long-cherished prejudices of a portion of the Virginia people. After an animated contest, the question was settled by a kind of compromise, in which the evils of slavery were distinctly recognised, but that views of expediency required that further action on the subject should be postponed. That a question so vitally important would have been renewed with more success at an early subsequent period, seems more than probable, if the current opinions of the day can be relied on; but there were obvious causes in operation which paralyzed the friends of abolition, and have had the effect of silencing all agitation on the subject. The abolitionists in the northern and eastern states, gradually increasing their strength as a party, became louder in their denunciations of slavery, and more and more reckless in the means adopted for assailing the constitutional rights of the south. The open and avowed security given to fugitive slaves, not only by the efforts of private societies, but by public official acts in some of the free states, together with the constant circulation of incendiary tracts, calculated to endanger the safety of slave-holding communities, have awakened a spirit of proud and determined resistance; and it is now almost impossible to tell when the passions shall have sufficiently cooled for a calm consideration of the subject.

If Virginia has not successfully rivalled some of the more wealthy and populous states in the cause of general education, and in works of internal improvement, she has at least devoted to those important objects all the resources she could command without impairing her credit by too great a pecuniary responsibility. It is an honorable trait, that she has been careful to fulfil her engagements in the most embarrassing times.

MISCELLANIES,

HISTORICAL, STATISTICAL, AND DESCRIPTIVE.

THE annexed concise geographical and statistical description of Virginia, is abridged from Sherman & Smith's Gazetteer of the United States, and contains the results of the statistics and census of 1840, published by the general government.

Virginia is 370 miles long, and 200 broad at its greatest width, containing 64,000 square miles, or 40,960,000 acres. The population in 1790, was 747,610 in 1800, 886,149; in 1810, 974,622; in 1820, 1,065,366; in 1830, 1,211,272; in 1840, 1,239,797, of which 448,987 were slaves. Of the free white population, 371,223 were white males; 369,745 ditto, females; 23,814 were colored males; 26,020 ditto, females. Employed in agriculture, 318,771; in commerce, 6,361; in manufactures and trades, 54,147; navigating the ocean, 582; ditto, canals, rivers, and lakes, 2,952; learned professions, &c., 3,866.

The state is divided into 123 counties and 2 districts—Eastern and Western. The Eastern district comprises that part of the state east of the Blue Ridge, and has 67 counties. Population in 1840: whites, 369,398; free colored, 42,294; slaves, 395,250; total, 806,942. The Western district comprises that part of the state west of the Blue Ridge, and has 56 counties. Population: whites, 371,570; free colored, 7,548; slaves, 53,737; total, 432,855.

Richmond is the capital of the state, situated on the north side of James River, at the head of tidewater, and just below its lower falls. This state has a great variety of surface and soil. From the Atlantic to the lower falls on the river, which includes a tract of from 110 to 130 miles in width, the country is low and flat, in some places marshy, but extensively sandy, covered with the pitch-pine. On the margin of the rivers, the soil is often rich. This is denominated the low country, and is unhealthy from August to October. Between the head of tidewater and the Blue Ridge, the country becomes uneven and hilly, and more so as it approaches the mountains. The soil in this region is some of it sandy and poor; some of it is fertile, particularly on the margins of the rivers. Towards the mountains the country is stony and broken, though the soil is often rich. The first ridge of mountains in this state is generally about 150 miles from the ocean. Beyond this the country is mountainous, traversed by successive ridges of the Alleghany, which occupies a greater breadth of country in Virginia than in any other state. Between the various ridges, however, there are long valleys or table-lands, parallel with them, often of considerable breadth, and containing some of the best and most pleasant land in Virginia. The farms are here smaller than in other parts of the state, better cultivated, and there are fewer slaves. The climate in this region is very healthy.

The soil in the tidewater country is generally poor, producing Indian corn, oats, and peas. Wheat is raised in some parts of it, and a little rice in the swamps in its southern part. Between tidewater and the mountains is the tobacco-country; but in the northern upland counties wheat has extensively superseded tobacco; and south of James River, sufficient cotton is raised for home consumption. The southeastern counties produce apples and peaches in great abundance. Among the mountains, the farmers raise large numbers of cattle and hogs. Indian corn is cultivated throughout the state. The country west of the mountains, towards the Ohio, is rough and wild—sometimes, but not generally, fertile; but very rich as a mineral region.

There were in this state in 1840, 326,438 horses and mules; 1,024,148 neat cattle; 1,293,772 sheep; 1,992,155 swine; poultry to the value of $754,698. There were produced 10,109,716 bushels of wheat; 87,430 of barley; 13,451,062 of oats; 1,482,799 of rye; 243,822 of buckwheat; 34,577,591 of Indian corn; 2,538,374 pounds of wool; 10,597 of hops; 65,020 of wax; 2,944,660 bushels of potatoes; 364,708 tons of hay; 25,594 of hemp and flax; 75,347,106 pounds of tobacco; 2,956 of rice; 3,494,483 of cotton; 3,191 of silk cocoons; 1,541,833 of sugar. The products of the dairy were valued at $1,480,488; of the orchard $705,765; value of lumber produced $538,092; 13,911 gallons of wine were made.

The mineral wealth of Virginia is very great. Gold, copper, lead, iron, coal, salt, limestone, and marble are found, together with a number of valuable mineral springs. An attention to the business of mining has recently been excited, and in 1840, 2,000 persons were employed in it. The belt of country in which gold is found, extends through Spotsylvania county and the adjacent country, and in a southwest direction passes into North and South Carolina, Georgia, and Alabama. The gold in this state is not sufficiently concentrated to render it profitable, excepting in a few places, to engage in mining it. The coal fields in Virginia are very extensive, and afford both the bituminous and anthracite. Large quantities have been obtained and exported from the vicinity of Richmond. Salt springs have been found in various places, and salt has been extensively manufactured on the Great Kanawha River, near Charleston. The state abounds in mineral springs, which are much resorted to; the principal are, the White and Blue Sulphur, in Greenbriar; the Salt and Red Sulphur, and Sweet, in Monroe; Hot and Warm, in Bath; Berkeley, in Morgan; Fauquier White Sulphur, in Fauquier; Shannondale, in Frederick; Alum, in Rockbridge; Jordan's White Sulphur, in Frederick; Red, in Alleghany; Grayson, in Carroll; Bottetourt, in Roanoke; Holston, in Scott; Augusta Springs; and Daggers Springs, in Bottetourt.

The staple productions of the state are wheat and tobacco. The Potomac River separates this state from Maryland. James River is the largest which belongs to this state. It is 500 miles in length, and flows from the mountains in the interior, behind the Blue Ridge, through which it passes. It is navigable for sloops 120 miles, and for boats much further, and enters into Chesapeake Bay. The Appomattox is 130 miles long, and enters James River 100 miles above Hampton Roads, and is navigable 12 miles, to Petersburg. The Rappahannock rises in the Blue Ridge, is 130 miles long, is navigable 110 miles for sloops, and enters into the Chesapeake. York River enters the Chesapeake 30 miles below the Rappahannock, and is navigable 40 miles for ships. The Shenandoah enters the Potomac just before its passage through the Blue Ridge. Of the rivers west of the mountains, the Great Kanawha rises in North Carolina, passes through this state, and enters the Ohio. The Little Kanawha also enters the Ohio. The Monongahela rises in this state, though it runs chiefly in Pennsylvania.

The lower part of Chesapeake Bay lies wholly in this state, is 15 miles wide at its mouth, and enters the Atlantic between Cape Charles and Cape Henry. Norfolk, 8 miles from Hampton Roads, has a fine harbor, much the best in the state, spacious, safe, and well defended ; and it is the most commercial place in Virginia ; but Richmond and Petersburg are more populous, and have an extensive trade. Besides these, Wheeling, Lynchburg, Fredericksburg, and Winchester, are the principal places.

The exports of this state, in 1840, amounted to $4,778,220 ; and the imports to $545,685. There were 31 commercial and 64 commission houses engaged in foreign trade, with a capital of $4,299,500 ; 2,736 retail drygoods and other stores, with a capital of $16,684,413 ; 1,454 persons employed in the lumber trade, with a capital of $113,210 ; 931 persons engaged in internal transportation, who, with 103 butchers, packers, &c., employed a capital of $100,680 ; 556 persons employed in the fisheries, with a capital of $28,383.

The manufactures of Virginia are not so extensive as those of some states inferior to it in territory and population. There were, in 1840, domestic or family manufactures to the amount of $2,441,672 ; 41 woollen manufactories and 47 fulling-mills, employing 222 persons, producing articles to the amount of $147,792, with a capital of $112,350 ; 22 cotton manufactories, with 42,262 spindles, employing 1,816 persons, producing articles to the amount of $446,063, with a capital of $1,299,020 ; 42 furnaces producing 18,810 tons of cast-iron, and 52 forges &c., producing 5,886 tons of bar-iron, the whole employing 1,742 persons, and a capital of $1,246,650 ; 11 smelting houses employed 131 persons, and produced gold to the amount of $51,758, employing a capital of $103,650 ; 5 smelting houses employed 73 persons, and produced 878,648 pounds of lead, employing a capital of $21,500 ; 12 paper manufactories, producing articles to the amount of $216,245, and other paper manufactories producing $1,260, the whole employing 181 persons, and a capital of $287,750 ; 3,342 persons manufactured tobacco to the amount of $2,406,671, employing a capital of $1,526,080 ; hats and caps were manufactured to the amount of $155,778, and straw bonnets to the amount of $14,700, the whole employing 340 persons, and a capital of $85,640 ; 660 tanneries employed 1,422 persons, and a capital of $838,141 ; 982 other leather manufactories, as saddleries, &c., produced articles to the amount of $626,597, and employed a capital of $341,957 ; 4 glass-houses and 2 glass-cutting establishments employed 164 persons, producing articles to the value of $146,500, with a capital of $132,000 ; 33 potteries employed 64 persons, producing articles to the amount of $31,380, with a capital of $10,225 ; 36 persons produced drugs, paints, &c., to the amount of $66,633, with a capital of $61,727 ; 445 persons produced machinery to the amount of $429,858 ; 150 persons produced hardware and cutlery to the amount of $50,504 ; 262 persons manufactured 9,330 small-arms ; 40 persons manufactured granite and marble to the amount of $16,652 ; 1,004 persons produced bricks and lime to the amount of $393,253 ; carriages and wagons were manufactured to the amount of $647,815, employing 1,592 persons, and a capital of $311,625 ; 1,454 distilleries produced 865,725 gallons, and 5 breweries produced 32,960 gallons, employing 1,631 persons, and a capital of $187,212 ; 764 flouring-mills produced 1,041,526 barrels of flour, and with other mills employed 3,964 persons, producing articles to the amount of $7,855,499, with a capital of $5,184,669 ; ships were built to the amount of $136,807 ; 675 persons manufactured furniture to the amount of $289,391 ; 402 brick or stone, and 2,604 wooden houses were built, employing 4,694 persons, and cost $1,367,393 ; 50 printing offices, and 13 binderies, 4 daily, 12 semi-weekly, and 35 weekly newspapers, and 5 periodicals, employed 310 persons, and a capital of $168,850. The whole amount of capital employed in manufactures in the state was $11,360,861.

William and Mary College, at Williamsburg, is the oldest in the state, and one of the oldest in the country, and was founded in 1691. Hampden Sidney College, in Prince Edward county, was founded in 1783, and is flourishing. Washington College, at Lexington, was founded in 1812. Randolph Macon College, was founded at Boydton in 1832. Emory and Henry College, Washington county, was founded in 1839. Rector College, Prunty Town, Taylor county, was founded in 1839. Bethany College, Brooke county, was founded in 1841. There are theological schools at Richmond, in Prince Edward county, and in Fairfax county. But the most important literary institution in the state, is the University of Virginia, at Charlottesville, founded in 1819. Its plan is extensive, its endowment has been munificent, and it is a prosperous institution. In all these, with a few smaller institutions, there were in 1840, 1,097 students ; there were in the state, also, 382 academies, with 11,083 students ; 1,561 common and primary schools, with 35,331 scholars ; and 58,787 white persons over 20 years of age who could neither read nor write.

The Baptists, the most numerous religious denomination, have about 437 churches; the Presbyterians 120; the Episcopalians, 65 ministers; the Methodists 170. There are also a few Lutherans, Catholics, Unitarians, Friends, and Jews.

In January, 1840, there were in this state 8 banks and branches, with a capital of $3,637,400, and a circulation of $2,513,412. At the close of the same year the public debt amounted to $6,857,161. There is a state penitentiary located at Richmond.

The first constitution of Virginia was formed in 1776. This was altered and amended by a convention assembled for that purpose, in 1830. The executive power is vested in a governor, elected by the joint vote of the two houses of the General Assembly. He is chosen for three years, but is ineligible for the next three. There is a council of state, elected in like manner for three years, the seat of one being vacated every year. The senior councillor is lieutenant-governor. The senators can never be more than 36, and the delegates than 150; and both are apportioned anew among the counties every 10 years, commencing with 1841. The senators were elected for 4 years, and the seats of one fourth of them are vacated every year. The delegates are chosen annually. All appointments to any office of trust, honor, or profit, by the legislature, are given openly, or *viva voce*, and not by ballot. The judges of the supreme court of appeals, and of the superior courts, are elected by the joint vote of both houses of the general assembly, and hold their offices during good behavior, or until removed by a joint vote of two-thirds of the legislature.

The right of suffrage is extended to every resident white male citizen of 21 years of age, entitled to vote by the former constitution; or who owns a freehold valued at $25; or a joint interest in a freehold to that amount; or who has a life-estate, or a reversionary title to land valued at $50, having been so possessed for 6 months; or who shall own, or be in occupation of, a leasehold estate, having been recorded 2 months, for a term not less than 5 years, to the annual value or rent of $200; or who for 12 months shall have been a housekeeper and head of a family, and paid the taxes assessed by the commonwealth.

Virginia has undertaken several important works of internal improvement, by chartering private companies, several of which have been liberally aided by the state. The Dismal Swamp Canal connects Chesapeake Bay with Albemarle Sound, extending from Deep Creek to Joyce's Creek, 23 miles, at a cost of $879,864. It has branches of 11 miles. The Alexandria Canal extends 7¼ miles, from Georgetown to Alexandria. The James River and Kanawha Canal extends 146 miles, from Richmond to Lynchburg. The Richmond, Fredericksburg, and Potomac Railroad extends 75 miles, to Aquia Creek. Louisa branch, 25 miles from Richmond, proceeds 49 miles, to Gordonsville. Richmond and Petersburg Railroad, from Richmond, extends 23 miles, to Petersburg. Petersburg and Roanoke Railroad extends from Petersburg, 59 miles, to Weldon. Greensville Railroad extends from near Hicksford, for 18 miles, to Gaston, N. C. City Point Railroad extends from Petersburg, 12 miles, to City Point. Chesterfield Railroad extends from Coal Mines, 13½ miles, to Richmond. Portsmouth and Roanoke Railroad extends from Portsmouth, 8 miles, to Weldon, N. C. Winchester and Potomac Railroad extends from Harper's Ferry, 32 miles, to Winchester.

ORIGIN OF THE APPELLATION "OLD DOMINION."*

There is in the possession of the Massachusetts Historical Society, a coin of the following description: on one side is a head, and the words " Georgius III. Rex.;" on the other side is a shield, on which are quartered the arms of England, Scotland, Ireland, and *Virginia*. The whole surmounted by a crown, and encircled with the word, " Virginia, 1773."

A similar coin was dug up a few years since, and the following statement was published with the description of it: During the usurpation of Cromwell, the colony of Virginia refused to acknowledge his authority, and declared itself independent. Shortly after, finding that Cromwell threatened to send a fleet and an army to reduce Virginia to subjection, and fearing the ability of this feeble state to withstand this force, she sent, in a small ship, a messenger to Charles II., then an exile in Breda, Flanders. Charles accepted the invitation to come over, and be king of Virginia, and was on the eve of embarking when he was recalled to the throne of England. As soon as he was restored to the crown of England, in gratitude for the loyalty of Virginia, he caused her coat of arms to be quartered with those of England, Scotland, and Ireland, as an independent member of the empire.

---

* From the Savannah Georgian.

The above coin is clearly confirmatory of these facts. Hence the origin of the phrase "Old Dominion," frequently applied to Virginia.

History does not confirm all these statements, though it establishes some, and sufficiently discloses, in the conduct of Virginia during the Protectorate of Cromwell, a cause for the origin of the name *Old Dominion*, frequently applied to Virginia. The facts, as gathered from a variety of creditable historians, appear to be these :

After the death of king Charles I., and the installation of Oliver Cromwell as Protector, the colony of Virginia refused to acknowledge his authority ; and Parliament having subdued opposition elsewhere, were not disposed to submit to such a resistance of its authority by the 20,000 inhabitants of Virginia. It issued an ordinance declaring them notorious robbers and traitors ; prohibited all intercourse with the refractory colonists, either by the people of England, the inhabitants of the other American settlements, or with foreign nations ; and finally, sent over a fleet, under Sir George Ayscue, to overpower the provincial royalists, and extinguish the last traces of monarchial authority that still lingered in extremities of the empire. The commissioners appointed to accompany this expedition were empowered to try, in the first instance, the efficacy of pardons and other conciliatory propositions, in reducing the colonists to obedience ; but if their pacific overtures should prove ineffectual, they were then to employ every species of hostile operations.

From Barbadoes, Captain Ayscue dispatched Capt. Dennis with a small squadron to the Chesapeake, to land his forces, and drive Sir William Berkeley out of Virginia ; for during the whole preceding struggle of Charles I. and the Parliament, the Virginians were firm on the side of their king, and enacted a declaration, "that they were born under a monarchy, and would never degenerate from the condition of their birth, by being subject to any other government." After the king was beheaded, they acknowledged the authority of the fugitive prince, and actually continued the provincial government under a commission which he sent to Sir William Berkeley from his retreat at Breda. The young prince was not, however, actually invited over to establish a kingdom in Virginia ; though, according to Clarendon, Sir William Berkeley was so assured of the loyalty of the inhabitants, and so impressed with confidence of ultimate success, that he wrote to him, "*almost inviting him to America !*" In these acts consisted the enmity of the Parliament to the governor ; and for this open defiance of its power, Virginia was to be ravaged by a fleet in her waters, and insidious assassins on her soil. Historians differ greatly as to the proceedings of Sir William, after the arrival of the fleet within the Capes of Virginia. Several, as Beverly, (p. 45 ;) Oldmixon, (i. 375 ;) Burke, (European Settlements, ii. 223 ;) Graham, (i. 99,) have asserted that he made a great show of resistance, assisted by the Dutch ships in the harbor, and the royalists, who were a majority of the population.

Bancroft, (i. 223,) citing contemporary authorities of the highest value, says, no sooner had the Guinea frigate entered within the waters of the Chesapeake, than (quoting from Clarendon) all thoughts of resistance were laid aside. It marks, continues Bancroft, the character of the Virginians ; that they refused to surrender to force, but yielded by a voluntary deed and mutual compact." " By the articles of surrender a complete indemnity was stipulated for all past offences ; and the colonists recognising the authority, were admitted into the bosom of the English commonwealth, and expressly assured of an equal participation in all the privileges of the free people of England. In particular, it provided that the Provincial Assembly should retain its wonted functions, and that the people of Virginia should have as free trade as the people of England to all places and all nations," and " shall be free from all taxes, customs, and impositions whatsoever, without the consent of their own Assembly." Berkeley disdained to make any stipulation for himself, with those whom his principles of loyalty taught him to regard as usurpers. Without leaving Virginia, he withdrew to a retired situation, where he continued to reside as a private individual, universally beloved and respected till a new revolution was to summon him once more to defy the republican forces of England and restore the ascendancy of royalty in the colony.

This was in March, 1652: and affairs continued much in this state until 1660. In the mean time, Richard Bennet, Edward Digges, and Samuel Matthews, had been severally elected by the Burgesses, Governor of Virginia, under allegiance to Oliver Cromwell, and on his death, 1658, to Richard Cromwell. But in 1660, Gov. Matthews died ; and the people, discontented with some commercial restrictions imposed by the Protectorate, did not wait for a new commission from England, but elected Sir William Berkeley, and " by an obliging violence compelled him to accept the government." He, however, refused to act under the usurpation of the Cromwells, and would not consent, unless they joined with him in joining their lives and fortunes for the king who was then an exile.

"This," says Beverly, "was their dearest wish, and therefore, with a unanimous voice, they told him that they were ready to hazard all for the king." Now, this was actually before the king's return to England, and proceeded from a broad principle of loyalty for which they had no example. Sir William Berkeley embraced their choice, *and forthwith proclaimed Charles II. king of England, Scotland, Ireland, and Virginia,* and caused all processes to be issued in his name. *Thus his majesty was actually king in Virginia before he was in England.* On the restoration of the king he sent Sir William a new commission, and granted him permission to visit England.

He was received by the monarch with much kindness ; and there is recorded a tradition, that the king, in compliment to that colony, wore at his coronation a robe made of the silk which was sent from thence. Such is a condensed narration of the causes and incidents which gave to Virginia the honored title of the "OLD DOMINION."

SLAVERY AND TOBACCO.

The following relates to the introduction of slaves, and the cultivation of tobacco, with their influence on the character and condition of the inhabitants of Virginia. It is drawn from the Life of Jefferson, by Prof. George Tucker, of the University of Virginia; a work written with perspicuity and candor, and incidentally elucidating important points in the civil and political history of the state.

In 1744, at the period of the birth of Mr. Jefferson, the settlements had extended about 200 miles from the sea-coast, and in the northern part of the colony, had passed the Blue Ridge. The population was then about 200,000, of whom from a quarter to a third were slaves.

The cultivation of tobacco, and the introduction of slaves, soon after Virginia was settled, have had a marked influence upon the habits, character, and fortunes of the country. The introduction of tobacco, in England, about 20 years before the settlement of Jamestown, led to a rapid extension of its use.. A demand being thus created, and a heavy price paid, encouraged the first settlers of Virginia to cultivate it for market, to the neglect of other crops. It long continued the sole article of export, and from the inadequate supply of the precious metals, it became the general measure of value, the principal currency of the colony. In 1758, the quantity exported had increased to about 70 millions of pounds, since which time the product has somewhat diminished.

"As this plant requires land of the greatest fertility, and its finer sorts are produced only in virgin soil, which it soon exhausts, its culture has been steadily advancing westwardly, where fresh land is more abundant, leaving the eastern region it has impoverished to the production of Indian corn, wheat, and other grain. Its cultivation has thus generally ceased in the country below the falls of the great rivers, and in its progress to the west, the centre of the tobacco region is now two hundred miles from the coast.

"The business of cultivating tobacco, and preparing it for market, requires such continual attention, and so much, and so many sorts of handling, as to allow to the planter little time for any of the other useful processes of husbandry ; and thus the management of his dairy and orchard, and the useful operations of manuring, irrigation, and cultivating artificial grasses, are either conducted in a slovenly way, or neglected altogether. The tobacco district nowhere exhibits the same external face of verdure, or marks of rural comfort and taste, as are to be seen in those countries in which its culture has been abandoned.

"But the most serious consequence of the tobacco cultivation is to be found in the increase of slaves ; for though it did not occasion their first introduction, it greatly encouraged their importation afterwards. It is to the spirit of commerce, which in its undistinguished pursuit of gain, ministers to our vices no less than to our necessary wants, that Virginia owes this portentous accession to her population. A Dutch ship from the coast of Guinea entered James River, in 1620, thirteen years after the first settlement of Jamestown, and sold twenty of her slaves to the colonists.

"The large profits which could be made from the labor of slaves, while tobacco sold at three shillings sterling a pound, equal to about ten times its ordinary price now, greatly encouraged their further importation, by giving to the planters the means of purchasing as well as the inclination ; and the effect would have been much greater, if they had not been continually supplied with labor from the paupers, and sometimes the convicts, who were brought from England and sold to the planters for a term of years, to defray the expenses of their transportation.

" This supply of English servants, together with the gradual fall in the price of tobacco, had so checked the importation of slaves, that in the year 1671, according to an official communication from the governor, Sir William Berkeley, while the whole population was but 40,000, the number of indented servants was 6,000, and that of the slaves was but 2,000. The importations of the latter, he says, did not exceed two or three cargoes in seven years, but that of servants, of whom he says, ' most were English, few Scotch, and fewer Irish,' he estimates at 1,500 annually.

" But in process of time, slave labor was found preferable to that of indented white servants, partly because the negro slaves were more cheaply fed and clothed than the laborers who were of the same race as the masters, but principally because they were less able to escape from bondage, and were more easily retaken. The colonial statute book affords abundant evidence of the frequency and facility with which the indented servants ran away from their masters ; and the extent of the mischief may be inferred from the severity of its punishment. In 1642, runaway servants were liable, for a second offence, to be branded on the cheek ; though fifteen years afterwards the law was so far mitigated as to transfer this mark of ignominy to the shoulder. In 1662, their term of service, which did not often exceed four or five years, might, for the offence of running away, be prolonged, at the discretion of a magistrate, and the master might superadd ' moderate corporeal punishment.' In the following year, this class of persons, prompted by the convicts who had been sent over after the restoration of Charles the Second, formed a conspiracy of insurrection and murder, which was discovered just in time to be defeated. Seven years afterwards, in 1670, the governor and council took upon themselves to prohibit the further importation of convicts, whom they call ' jail birds ;' and they assign this conspiracy as one of their motives for the order. The privilege, too, enjoyed by the servant of complaining to the magistrate for the harsh treatment of his master, either as to food, clothing, or punishment, formed, no doubt, a further ground of preference for slaves, who had no such inconvenient rights.

" Under the united influence of these circumstances the number of negro slaves so increased, that in 1732, the legislature thought proper to discourage their further importation by a tax on each slave imported ; and not to alarm the commercial jealousy of England, the law, conforming to the notions of the age, formally provided for what no mode of levying the tax could have prevented, that the duty should be paid by the purchaser. This duty was at first five per cent. on the value of the slave, but in a few years afterwards, (1740,) it was increased to ten per cent., from which it was never reduced. It did not, however, prevent large importations, for we find the number to have increased in 119 years, in the ratio of 1 to 146 ; that is, from 2,000 in the year 1671, to 293,427 in 1790 ; while in the same period the whites had increased only as 1 to 12, or from 38,000 to 454,881. In the forty years which have elapsed, from the first to the last census, it is gratifying to perceive that the increase of the free population in Virginia has been somewhat greater than that of the slaves, in the proportion of 63 per cent. to 60, and that this comparative gain seems to be gradually increasing.

" As Eastern Virginia is everywhere intersected by navigable rivers, which are skirted on either side by rich alluvial lands, the early settlers, whose plantations were principally along the margins of the rivers, were able to carry on a direct intercourse with foreign countries, from their separate dwellings. Thus commerce, by the very diffusion of its most important natural facilities, did not here concentrate in a few favorable spots, and foster the growth of towns, as in most of the other colonies ; and at the beginning of the revolution, Williamsburg, the seat of government, and the largest town in Virginia, itself the most populous of the colonies, did not contain 2,000 inhabitants. But as the bees which form no hive, collect no honey, the commerce, which was thus dispersed, accumulated no wealth. The disadvantages of this dispersion were eventually perceived by the colonists, and many efforts were made by the legislature to remedy the mischief by authorizing the establishment of towns on selected sites, and giving special privileges and immunities to those who built, or those who resided on them. Their purpose was also favored, and even stimulated by the government, from fiscal considerations. But most of these legislative efforts failed, and none were very successful. Thus in 1680, as many as twenty towns were authorized by act of assembly, being one for each county ; yet at not more than three or four of the designated spots is there even a village remaining to attest the propriety of the selection.

" There were indeed wanting in the colony all the ordinary constituents of a large town. Here were no manufactories to bring together and employ the ingenious and industrious. The colonists, devoting themselves exclusively to agriculture, owned no shipping, which might have induced them to congregate for the sake of carrying on their foreign commerce to more advantage : here was no court, which by its splendor and amusements might attract the gay, the voluptuous, and the rich : there was not even a class of opulent landlords, to whom it is as easy to live on their rents in town as in the country, and far more agreeable. But the very richest planters all cultivated their own land with their own slaves ; and while those lands furnished most of the materials of a generous, and even profuse hospitality, they could be consumed only where they were produced, and could neither be transported to a distance, nor converted into money. The tobacco, which constituted the only article of export, served to pay for the foreign luxuries which the planter required ; yet, with his social habits, it was barely sufficient for that purpose, and not a few of the largest estates were deeply in debt to the Scotch or English merchants, who carried on the whole commerce of the country. Nor was this system of credit more eagerly sought by the improvident planter, than it was given by the thrifty and sagacious trader ; for it afforded to him a sure pledge for the consignment of the debtor's crop, on the sales of which his fair perquisites amounted to a liberal profit, and if he was disposed to abuse his trust, his gains were enormous. The merchants were therefore ready to ship goods, and accept bills of exchange on the credit of future crops, while their factors in the colony took care in season to make the debt safe by a mortgage on the lands and slaves of the planter. Some idea of the pecuniary thraldom to which the Virginia planter was formerly subjected may be formed from the fact, that twice a year, at a general meeting of the merchants and factors in Williamsburg, they settled the price of tobacco, the advance on the sterling cost of goods, and the rate of exchange with England. It can scarcely be doubted that the regulations were framed as much to the advantage of the merchants as they believed it practicable to execute. Yet it affords evidence of the sagacious moderation with which this delicate duty was exercised, that it was not so abused as to destroy itself.

" This state of things exerted a decided influence on the manners and character of the colonists, untrained to habits of business and possessed of the means of hospitality. They were open-handed and open-hearted ; fond of society, indulging in all its pleasures, and practising all its courtesies. But these social virtues also occasionally ran into the kindred vices of love of show, haughtiness, sensuality—and many of the wealthier class were to be seen seeking relief from the vacuity of idleness, not merely in the allowable pleasures of the chase and the turf, but in the debasing ones of cock-fighting, gaming, and drinking. Literature was neglected, or cultivated by the small number who had been educated in England, rather as an accomplishment and a mark of distinction, than for the substantial benefits it confers.

"Let us not, however, overrate the extent of these consequences of slavery. If the habitual exercise of authority, united to a want of steady occupation, deteriorated the character of some, it seemed to give a greater elevation of virtue to others. Domestic slavery, in fact, places the master in a state of moral discipline, and according to the use he makes of it, is he made better or worse. If he exercises his unrestricted power over the slave, in giving ready indulgence to his humors or caprice—if he habitually yields to impulses of anger, and punishes whenever he is disobeyed, or obeyed imperfectly, he is certainly the worse for the institution which has thus afforded aliment to his evil propensities. But if, on the other hand, he has been taught to curb these sallies of passion, or freaks of caprice, or has subjected himself to a course of salutary restraint, he is continually strengthening himself in the virtues of self-denial, forbearance, and moderation, and he is all the better for the institution which has afforded so much occasion for the practice of those virtues.* If, therefore, in a slave-holding country, we see some of the masters made irascible, cruel, and tyrannical, we see many others as remarkable for their mildness, moderation, and self-command ; because, in truth, both the virtues of the one and the vices of the other are carried to the greater extreme by the self-same process of habitual exercise."

INDIANS OF EASTERN VIRGINIA.†

According to the account of Captain John Smith, that part of Virginia that lies between the sea and the mountains, was inhabited by forty-three different tribes of Indians. Thirty of these were united in a grand confederacy under the emperor Powhatan. The dominions of this mighty chief, who was long the most powerful rival, and most impla-

---

* The character of the Presidents which Virginia has furnished, may be appealed to for a confirmation of this view ; and many living illustrations will readily present themselves to all who have a personal knowledge of the southern states.

† This article is from the various histories of Virginia.

cable foe, with whom the English had to contend, extended over that part of the country that lies south of the Potomac, between the coast and the falls of the rivers.

In comparison with civilized countries, this extensive territory contained but a scanty population. The Powhatan confederacy consisted of but about eight thousand inhabitants.

Indian in a summer dress.   *Indian Priest.*

Besides this confederacy, there were two others which were combined against that of Powhatan. These were the Mannahoacks and Manakins; the former of whom, consisting of eight tribes, occupied the country lying between Rappahannock and York rivers; and the latter, consisting of five tribes, was settled between York and James rivers, above the falls. Besides these, were the Nottoways, the Meherricks, the Tuteloes, and several other scattering and independent tribes.

The hereditary dominions of Powhatan lay on James River, which originally bore his name.* He had a seat on this river, about a mile below the falls, where Richmond now stands, and another at Werowocomoco on the north side of York River, within the present county of Gloucester.

This monarch was remarkable for the strength and vigor of his body, as well as for the energies of his mind. He possessed great skill in intrigue and great courage in battle. His equanimity in the career of victory, was only equalled by his fortitude in the hour of adversity. If he had many vices incident to the savage life, he had some virtues seldom found among the civilized. He commanded a respect rarely paid by savages to their werowance, and maintained a dignity and splendor worthy the monarch of thirty nations. He was constantly attended by a guard of forty warriors, and during the night a sentry regularly watched his palace. Though unlimited by custom in the number of his wives, his seraglio exhibited the apathy of the Indian character. When he

---

* Powhatan, Arrowhattock, Appamattock, Pamunkey, Youghtanund, and Mattapoment, descended to him from his ancestors.

slept, one of his women sat at his head and another at his feet. When he dined they attended him with water, or brought him a bunch of feathers to wipe his hands. His regalia, free from the glitter of art, showed only the simple royalty of the savage. He wore a robe composed of skins, and sat on a throne spread with mats, and decked with pearls and with beads. The furniture of his palace, like the qualities of his mind, was adapted to war, and the implements of death, rather than of pleasure, garnished his halls.

The figures in the annexed engraving, representing an Indian in his summer dress, and an Indian priest, were copied from those given in Beverly's History of Virginia, published in London, in 1722. The figure on the left, (the Indian in his summer dress,) is thus described:

The upper part of his hair is cut short to make a ridge, which stands up like the comb of a cock, the rest is either shorn off or knotted behind his ear. On his head are stuck three feathers of the wild turkey, pheasant, hawk, or such like. At his ear is hung a fine shell, with pearl drops. At his breast is a tablet or fine shell, smooth as polished marble, which also hath sometimes etched on it a star, half-moon, or other figure, according to the maker's fancy; upon his neck and wrists hang strings of beads, peak, and roenoke. His apron is made of a deer skin, gashed around the edges, which hang like tassels' or fringe; at the upper end of the fringe is an edging of peak, to make it finer. His quiver is of a thin bark; but sometimes they make it of the skin of a fox, or young wolf, with the head hanging to it, which has a wild sort of terror in it; and to make it yet more warlike they tie it on with the tail of a panther, buffalo, or such like, letting the end hang down between their legs. The pricked lines on his shoulders, breast, and legs, represent the figures painted thereon. In his left hand he holds a bow, and in his right an arrow. The mark upon his shoulder-blade, is a distinction used by the Indians in travelling, to show the nation they are of—and perhaps is the same with that which Baron Lahontan calls the arms and heraldry of the Indians. Thus, the several lettered marks are used by several other nations about Virginia, when they make a journey to their friends and allies.

The habit of the *Indian priest*, is a cloak made in the form of a woman's petticoat; but instead of tying it about their middle, they fasten the gatherings about their neck, and tie it upon the right shoulder, always keeping one arm out to use upon occasion. This cloak hangs even at the bottom, but reaches no lower than the middle of the thigh; but what is most particular in it is, that it is constantly made out of a skin dressed soft, with the pelt or fur on the outside, and reversed; insomuch that when the cloak has been a little worn, the hair falls down in flakes, and looks very shagged and frightful.

The cut of their hair is likewise peculiar to their function; for 'tis all shaved close, except a thin crest, like a cock's comb, which stands bristling up, and runs in a semicircle from the forehead up along the crown to the nape of the neck. They likewise have a border of hair over the forehead, which, by its own natural strength, and by the stiffening it receives from grease and paint, will stand out like the peak of a bonnet.

The face of the Indian, when arrived at maturity, is a dark brown and chesnut. By a free use of bear's grease, and a continual exposure to the sun and weather, it becomes harder and darker. This, however, is not the natural complexion. In infancy they are much fairer.* Their hair is almost invariably of a coal black, straight, and long; their cheek bones are high, and their eyes black and full of a character of wildness and ferocity that mark their unappeasable thirst of vengeance, and their free and uncontrolled indulgence of every fierce and violent passion. But the education of an Indian, which commences almost with his birth, teaches him that dissimulation, which masks the thought and smooths the countenance, is the most useful of virtues; and there is a continual effort to check the fierce sallies of the eye, and keep down the consuming rage of his bosom. His eye, therefore, is generally averted or bent downwards. The terrible complacency of the tiger is no inapt illustration of an Indian visage.

The figure of an Indian is admirably proportioned beyond any thing that has hitherto been seen of the human form. Tall, straight; their muscles hardened by the continual action of the weather; their limbs supple by exercise, and perhaps by the use of oil, they

---

* " They are very swarthy," says Charlevoix, speaking of the Canadians, " and of a dirty dark red. But this is not their natural complexion. The frequent frictions they use give them this red, and it is surprising that they are not blacker; being continually exposed to the smoke in winter, to the great heat in summer, and in all seasons to the inclemencies of the air." .

outstrip the bear, and run down the buck and the elk. No such thing is to be found as a dwarfish, crooked, bandylegged, or otherwise misshapen Indian.

The power and qualities of their minds are such as we should expect from their state of society. In a state of nature the mind of man differs but little from the animals around him. Occupied in supplying his wants or gratifying his resentments, he has but little time or inclination for the labors of calculation or the refinements of abstraction. The sensible objects with which he is most conversant, impress themselves on his memory in the order and degrees of their importance; but their classification, and the faculty of generalizing them by an idea and term that shall take in all the particulars and classes, are the result of deep thought and intense reflection. For this, leisure and application are necessary. But the time of the Indian, after returning successful from the chase, or victorious from the battle, is too valuable to be employed in such trifles. His duty it is to spread the feast; to hear the praises of the old men, and the congratulations of the women; to attend the great council of the nation, and to sing the history of his own exploits. If any time remain after discharging those duties, he exercises himself in shooting the arrow or throwing the tomahawk; or stretched at length along the grass, enjoys that luxury of indolence which constitutes the supreme blessing of his existence.

The idea of numbers is, therefore, very limited among the tribes. Some of them can reckon a thousand, while others cannot exceed ten; to express any greater number they are compelled to resort to something indefinite. As numerous as the pigeons in the woods, or the stars in the heavens, is a mode of expression for any greater number. For the same reason, their language has no term for the abstract ideas of time, space, universal, &c. There is, however, a conjecture, which, if true, will prove that the Indians of Virginia had a more copious arithmetic. It is suggested that Tomocomoco or Uttomac-comac was sent to England by Powhatan, for the purpose of procuring an exact account of the number of the people of England. Tomocomoco made the attempt till his arithmetic failed; but before he would be sent on such an errand, he must have been able to reckon the Powhatans, and these, according even to the lowest estimates, amounted to eight thousand.

It has been said that the Indian is the most improvident of animals; that, satisfied with his present enjoyments, he wastes no thought on the morrow, and that repeated calamities have added nothing to his care or foresight. This may have been true of some of the tribes in South America, or in the islands. The North American, and more especially the Virginian, always had their public stock hoarded. Powhatan and the other sachems carried on a continual trade with the first colonists for corn, and we find that Raleigh, Baltimore, and Penn, derived their principal support from similar sources. But the quantity of labor and industry required for raising this superfluity was comparatively nothing. A few did not, as in established societies, work for the support of the whole, and for the purpose of enabling the rich to vend their surplus commodities in foreign markets. Here every man labored for himself, or for the common stock, and a few days in every year were sufficient for the maintenance of each man, and by consequence, of all the members of the tribe.

The Indians of Virginia have no written laws, but their customs, handed down from age to age in the traditions of their old men, have all the force of the best-defined and positive institutions. Nor is this respect acquired by the fear of punishment. The aborigines of Virginia, whatever may be pretended, enjoyed complete freedom. Their sachems made their own tools and instruments of husbandry. They worked in the ground in common with the other Indians. They could enter into no measure of a public nature without the concurrence of the matchacomoco or grand council; and even after this body had decided on the merits of the question, the consent of the people at large was necessary to sanction their proceedings. If the voice of this council be in favor of war, the young men express their approbation by painting themselves of various colors, so as to render their appearance horrible to their enemies. In this state they rush furiously into the council: they begin the war dance, accompanying their steps with fierce gestures, expressive of their thirst of vengeance; and describing the mode in which they will surprise, wound, kill, and scalp their enemies. After this they sing their own glories; they recount the exploits of their ancestors, and the ancient glories of their nation.

The Indian festival dance, says Beverly, is performed by the "dancers themselves forming a ring, and moving round a circle of carved posts, that are set up for that purpose; or else round a fire, made in a convenient part of the town; and then each has his rattle in his hand, or what other thing he fancies most, as his bow and arrows, or his tomahawk. They also dress themselves up with branches of trees, or some other strange accoutrements. Thus they procced, dancing and singing, with all the antic postures they can invent ; and he is the bravest fellow that has the most prodigious gestures."

Indian Festival Dance

When any matter is proposed in the national council, it is common for the chiefs of the several tribes to consult thereon apart with their counsellors, and when they have agreed, to deliver the opinion of the tribe at the national council, and as their government seems to rest wholly on persuasion, they endeavor, by mutual concessions, to obtain unanimity. Their only controls are their manners and their moral sense of right and wrong, which, like tasting and smelling, in every man makes part of his nature.

An offence against these is punished by contempt, by exclusion from society, or when the case is serious, as in murder, by the individuals whom it concerns.

The Indians of Virginia had no idea of distinct and exclusive property ; the lands were in common, and every man had a right to choose or abandon his situation at pleasure. Their mode of computation, as with us, was by units, tens, and hundreds. There is no light on the records by which we may discover its limits or extent. Analogy affords no helps on this occasion. The Iroquois could reckon a thousand, while other tribes, almost in their neighborhood, could count no further than ten.

They reckon their years by winters, or cohonks, as they call them, which was a name taken from the note of the wild geese, intimating so many times of the wild geese coming to them, which is every winter.

They distinguish the several parts of the year by five seasons, viz. : the budding or blossoming of the spring ; the earing of the corn, or roasting ear time ; the summer, or highest sun ; the corn-gathering, or fall of the leaf ; and the winter, or *cohonks*.

They count the months by the moons, though not with any relation to so many in a year as we do ; but they make them return again by the same name, as the moon of stags, the corn moon, the first and second moon of cohonks."

They have no distinction of the hours of the day, but divide it only into three parts, the rise, the power, and lowering of the sun ; and they keep their accounts by knots on a string, or notches on a stick, not unlike the Peruvian Quippoes.

If we believe the accounts of Smith and Beverly, the Indians of Virginia were grossly superstitious, and even idolatrous. The annexed engraving is a representation of their idol *Okee, Quioccos*, or *Kiwasa*, copied from one in Beverly's History. "They do not look upon it as one single being, but reckon there are many of the same nature ; they likewise believe that there are tutelar deities in every town."

Although they have no set days for performing the rites of religion, they have a number of festivals, which are celebrated with the utmost festivity. They solemnize a day for the plentiful coming of their wild fowl, such as geese, ducks, teal, &c. ; for the returns of their hunting seasons ; and for the ripening of certain fruits. But the greatest annual festival they have is at the time of their corn-gathering, at which they revel several days together. To these they universally contribute, as they do to the gathering of the corn : on this occasion they have their greatest variety of pastimes, and more especially their war dances and heroic songs ; in which they boast that their corn being now gathered, they have store enough for their women and children, and have nothing to do but go to war, travel, and to seek for new adventures.

There is a second annual festival, conducted with still greater solemnity. It commences with a fast, which exceeds any thing of abstinence known among the most mortified hermits. This fast is succeeded by a feast. The old fire is put out, and a new fire, called the drill fire, elicited by the friction of two pieces of wood. They sprinkle sand on the hearths, and, to make the lustration complete, an emetic is taken by the whole nation. At this meeting all crimes, except murder, are pardoned, and the bare mention of them afterwards is considered as disreputable. At the close of this festival, which continues four days, a funeral procession commences, the signification of which is that they bury all the past in oblivion, and the criminals having tasted of the decoction of casina, are permitted to sit down by the men they have injured.

The ceremony of huskanawing returns after an interval of fourteen or sixteen years, or more frequently, as the young men happen to arrive at maturity. This is intended as a state of probation, preparatory to their being initiated into the class of warriors and counsellors. The candidates are first taken into the thickest part of the forest, and kept in close and solitary confinement for several months, with scarcely any sustenance besides an infusion or decoction of some intoxicating roots. This diet, added to the severity of the discipline, invariably induces madness, and the fit is protracted for eighteen days. During the paroxysms they are shut up in a strong enclosure, called an huskanaw pen, "one of which," says Beverly, "I saw belonging to the Pamaunkie Indians, in the year 1694. It was in shape like a sugar-loaf, and every way open like a lattice for the air to pass through." When their doctors suppose they have drunk a

Indian Idol.

sufficient portion of the intoxicating juice, they gradually restore them to their senses by lessening the quantity of the potion, and before they recover their senses they are brought back to the town. This process is intended to operate like Lethe on their memory: "To release the youth from all their childish impressions, and from that strong partiality to persons and things which is contracted before reason takes place. So that when the young men come to themselves again, their reason may act freely without being biased by the cheats of custom and education. Thus they also become discharged from any ties by blood; and are established in a state of equality and perfect freedom, to order their actions and dispose of their persons as they think proper, without any other control than the law of nature."

Marriage, or the union of husband and wife, stood precisely on the same footing as among the other American tribes. A man might keep as many wives as he could support: but in general they had but one, whom, without being obliged to assign any reason, they might at any time abandon, and immediately form a new engagement. The rights of the woman are the same, with this difference, that she cannot marry again until the next annual festival.

Courtship was short, and, like their marriage, unembarrassed by ceremony. If the presents of a young warrior are accepted by his mistress, she is considered as having agreed to become his wife, and without any further explanations to her family, she goes home to his hut. The principles that are to regulate their future conduct are well understood. He agrees to perform the more laborious duties of hunting and fishing ; of felling the tree, erecting the hut, constructing the canoe, and of fighting the enemies of the tribe. To her, custom had assigned almost all the domestic duties ; to prepare the food ; to watch over the infancy of the children. The nature of their lives and circumstances added another, which, with more propriety, taking in a general view, should have been exercised by the male. It belonged to the women to plant the corn, and attend all the other productions of an Indian garden or plantation. But the labor required for raising these articles was trifling, and the warriors, being engaged in hunting and war, had neither leisure nor inclination to attend to objects of such inferior consideration.

To compensate for this seeming hardship or neglect, the women had several valuable privileges, that prove their importance, and the respect entertained for them by the men. All the honors of an Indian community are *maternal*, and the children, in the event of a separation, belong to the wife. The husband is considered only as a visitor ; and, should any difference arise, he takes up his gun and departs. Nor does this separation entail any disgrace upon the parties.

If any credit be due to the accounts of our early historians, the women in the Powhatan confederacy had considerable weight. Some of the tribes had even female sachems, a regulation which could not have been tolerated by freemen and warriors, if, as has been imagined by some historians, they had been regarded only as objects of contempt and ill-usage. What agitation and sorrow were not excited by the death of Pocahontas, and how anxious the inquiries of her family respecting her health and her feelings, her content and her return !

It was no uncommon spectacle to see groups of young women, almost naked, frisking with wanton modesty in the wild gambols of the dance. Even the decent Pocahontas did not disdain to mingle in those pastimes. Crowned with a wreath of leaves and flowers, she sometimes led the chorus and presided in the dance. Nor should this be regarded as a deviation from the rules of modesty and innocence. They acted agreeably to the usage of their country and the dictates of nature. Every object inspired happiness and content, and their only care was to crowd as many pleasures as possible into the short span of a fleeting existence.

The following summary account of the Indians in Virginia, as they were about the year 1700, is from Beverly's History of Virginia.

The Indians of Virginia, east of the Blue Ridge, are almost wasted, but such towns or people as retain their names and live in bodies, are hereunder set down ; all which together cannot raise five hundred fighting men. They live poorly, and much in fear of the neighboring Indians. Each town, by the articles of peace, 1677, pays three Indian arrows for their land, and twenty beaver-skins for protection, every year.

In Accomack are eight towns, viz : Matomkin is much decreased of late by the small-pox, that was carried thither. Gingoteque ; the few remains of this town are joined with a nation of the Maryland Indians. Kiequotank is reduced to a very few men. Matchopungo has a small number yet living. Occahanock has a small number yet living. Pungoteque ; governed by a queen, but a small nation. Oanancock has but four or five families. Chiconessex has very few, who just keep the name. Nanduye : a seat of the empress ; not above twenty families, but she hath all the nations of the shore under tribute. In Northampton, Gangascoe, which is almost as numerous as all the foregoing nations put together. In Prince George, Wyanoke is extinct. In Charles City, Appamattox, extinct. In Surry, Nottaways, which are about a hundred bowmen, of late a thriving and increasing people. By Nansamond : Menheering, has about thirty bowmen, who keep at a stand. Nansamond : about thirty bowmen : they have increased much of late. In King William's county, Pamunkie has about forty bowmen, who decrease. Chickahomonie, which had about sixteen bowmen, but lately increased. In Essex : Rappahannock, extinct. In Richmond : Port Tabago, extinct. In Northumberland : Wiccomocco has but few men living, which yet keep up their kingdom, and retain their fashion ; yet live by themselves, separate from all other Indians, and from the English.

The following able article, from Tucker's Life of Jefferson, relates to the " Abolition of Entails.—Primogeniture.—Their effects considered.—Church establishment in Virginia—its gradual abolition.—Entire freedom of religion."

On the 11th of October, 1776, three days after Mr. Jefferson had taken his seat in the legislature, he brought in a bill for the establishment of Courts of Justice, which was subsequently approved by the House and passed. Three days afterwards, he introduced a bill to convert estates in tail into fee-simple. This, he avows, was a blow at the aristocracy of Virginia.

In that colony, in the earlier periods of its history, large grants of land had been obtained from the crown by a few favored individuals, which had been preserved in their families by means of entails, so as to have formed, by degrees, a patrician class among the colonists. These modes of continuing the same estates in the same family, found a protection here which they could not obtain in the mother country ; for, by an act passed in the year 1705, the practice of docking entails, which had previously prevailed in Virginia as in England, was expressly prohibited ; and whenever the peculiar exigencies of a family made it necessary that this restraint or alienation should be done away, it could be effected only by a special act of Assembly.

The class which thus provided for the perpetuation of its wealth, also monopolized the civil honors of the colony. The counsellors of the state were selected from it, by reason of which the whole body commonly had a strong bias in favor of the crown, in all questions between popular right and regal prerogative. It is but an act of justice to this class to state, that although some of them might have been timid and hesitating in the dispute with the mother country—disposed to drain the cup of conciliation to the dregs—yet, others were among the foremost in patriotic self-devotion and generous sacrifices ; and there was but a small proportion of them who were actually *tories*, as those who sided with Great Britain were then denominated.

Mr. Jefferson was probably influenced less by a regard to the conduct of the wealthy families in the contest, than by the general reason which he thus gives: " To annul this privilege, and instead of an aristocracy of wealth, of more harm and danger than benefit to society, to make an opening for the aristocracy of virtue and talent, which nature has wisely provided for the direction of the interests of society, and scattered with an equal hand through all its conditions, was deemed essential to a well-ordered republic."

The repeal of this law was effected, not without a struggle. It was opposed by Mr. Pendleton, who, both from age and temper, was cautious of innovation ; and who, finding some change inevitable, proposed to modify the law so far as to give to the tenant in tail the power of conveying in fee-simple. This would have left the entail in force, where the power of abolishing it was not exercised ; and he was within a few votes of saving so much of the old law.

This law, and another subsequently introduced by Mr. Jefferson, to abolish the preference given to the male sex, and to the first-born, under the English common law, have effectually answered their intended purpose of destroying the gross inequality of fortunes which formerly prevailed in Virginia. They have not merely altered the distribution of that part of the landed property, which is transmitted to surviving relatives by the silent operation of the law, but they have also operated on public opinion, so as to influence the testamentary disposition of it by the proprietors, without which last effect the purpose of the Legislature might have been readily defeated. The cases are now very rare, in which a parent makes, by his will, a much more unequal distribution of his property among his children than the law itself would make. It is thus that laws, themselves the creatures of public opinion, often powerfully react on it.

The effects of this change in the distribution of property are very visible. There is no longer a class of persons possessed of large inherited estates, who, in a luxurious and ostentatious style of living, greatly exceed the rest of the community ; a much larger number of those who are wealthy, have acquired their estates by their own talents or enterprise ; and most of these last are commonly content with reaching the average of that more moderate standard of expense which public opinion requires, rather than the higher scale which it tolerates.*

Thus, there were formerly many in Virginia who drove a coach and six, and now

---

* A large portion of the matter on this page was appropriated by Lord Brougham, in his Miscellanies, without any acknowledgment whatsoever.

such an equipage is never seen. There were, probably, twice or three times as many four-horse carriages before the revolution, as there are at present; but the number of two-horse carriages may now be ten, or even twenty times as great, as at the former period. A few families, too, could boast of more plate than can now be met with; but the whole quantity in the country has now increased twenty, if not fifty fold.

Some nice but querulous observers, have thought that they perceived a correspondent change in the manners and intellectual cultivation of the two periods; and, while they admit that the mass of the people may be less gross, and more intelligent than the back-woodsman, the tobacco-roller,* or the rustic population generally under the regal government, yet they insist that we have now no such class as that which formerly constituted the Virginia gentleman of chivalrous honor and polished manners—at once high-minded, liberal, delicate, and munificent; and that as to mental cultivation, our best educated men of the present day cannot compare with the Lees, the Randolphs, the Jeffersons, Pendletons, and Wythes, of that period.

This comparison, however, cannot easily be made with fairness; for there are few who have lived long enough to compare the two periods, and those few are liable to be biased on one side or the other, according to their early predilections and peculiar tastes. But apart from these individual influences, there is a general one to which we are all exposed. Time throws a mellow light over our recollections of the past, by which their beauties acquire a more touching softness, and their harsher parts are thrown into shade. Who that consults his reason can believe, if those scenes of his early days, to which he most fondly looks back, were again placed before him, that he would again see them such as memory depicts them? His more discriminating eye, and his less excitable sensibility, would now see faults which then escaped his inexperience, and he would look tranquilly, if not with indifference, on what had once produced an intoxication of delight. Yet such is the comparison which every one must make between the men and things of his early and his later life; and the traditionary accounts of a yet earlier period are liable to the same objection, for they all originate with those who describe what they remember, rather than what they actually observed. We must, therefore, make a liberal allowance for this common illusion, when we are told of the superior virtues and accomplishments of our ancestors.

The intellectual comparison may be more satisfactorily made. While it is admitted that Virginia could, at the breaking out of the Revolution, boast of men that could hold a respectable rank in any society; yet, after making allowance for the spirit-stirring occasion, which then called forth all their talents and faculties, there seems to be no reason to suppose that there is any inferiority in the present generation. It must be recollected, that by the more general diffusion of the benefits of education, and the continued advancement of mental culture, we have a higher standard of excellence in the present day than formerly, and in the progressive improvement which our country has experienced in this particular, the intellectual efforts which in one generation confer distinction, would in that which succeeds it scarcely attract notice. It may be safely said, that a well-written newspaper essay would then have conferred celebrity on its author, and a pamphlet would then have been regarded as great an achievement in letters as an octavo volume at present. Nor does there pass any session of the legislature, without calling forth reports and speeches, which exhibit a degree of ability and political information, that would, forty years ago, have made the author's name reverberate from one end of British America to the other. The supposed effect of this change in the distribution of property, in deteriorating manners, and lowering the standard of intellectual merit, may then well be called in question.

Another law, materially affecting the polity of the state, and the condition of society, owes its origin in part to Mr. Jefferson. This was the act to abolish the church establishment, and to put all religious sects on a footing. The means of effecting this change were very simple. They were merely to declare that no man should be compelled to support any preacher, but should be free to choose his sect, and to regulate his contribution for the support of that sect at pleasure.

From the first settlement of Virginia, the Church of England had been established

---

* The tobacco was formerly not transported in wagons, as at present, but by a much simpler process. The hogshead, in which it was packed, had a wooden pin driven into each head, to which were adjusted a pair of rude shafts, and thus, in the way of a garden roller it was drawn to market by horses. Those who followed this business of tobacco-rolling, formed a class by themselves—hardy, reckless, proverbially rude, and often indulging in coarse humor at the expense of the traveller who chanced to be well-dressed, or riding in a carriage.

in the colony. The inhabited parts were laid off into parishes, in each of which was a minister, who had a fixed salary in tobacco, together with a glebe and a parsonage house. There was a general assessment on all the inhabitants, to meet the expenses. Mr. Jefferson thus explains the success of rival sects:—

" In process of time, however, other sectarisms were introduced, chiefly of the Presbyterian family ; and the established clergy, secure for life in their glebes and salaries, adding to these generally the emoluments of a classical school, found employment enough in their farms and school rooms for the rest of the week, and devoted Sunday only for the edification of their flock, by service and a sermon, at their parish church. Their other pastoral functions were little attended to. Against this inactivity, the zeal and industry of sectarian preachers had an open and undisputed field ; and by the time of the Revolution, a majority* of the inhabitants had become dissenters from the established church, but were still obliged to pay contributions to support the pastors of the minority. This unrighteous compulsion, to maintain teachers of what they deemed religious errors, was grievously felt during the regal government and without a hope of relief."

The successive steps by which an institution, which was deeply rooted in the affections of many of the principal citizens, was deprived of its power and property, without disturbing the public tranquillity, may be not unworthy of notice.

In the bill of rights which was drawn by George Mason, June 12, 1776, the principle of religious freedom is distinctly asserted in the last article, which declares, " that religion, or the duty which we owe to our Creator, and the manner of discharging it, can only be directed by reason and conviction, not by force or violence ; and, therefore, all men are equally entitled to the free exercise of religion, according to the dictates of conscience." But the constitution itself, passed June 29th, is silent on the subject of religion, except that it renders " all ministers of the Gospel" incapable of being members of either House of Assembly, or of the Executive Council.

At the first session of the legislature, in the same year, under the new constitution, numerous petitions were received for abolishing the general assessment for the established church ; and at this session, Mr. Jefferson drafted and supported a law for the relief of the dissenters, which, he says, brought on the severest contests in which he was ever engaged. Here, too, he encountered the formidable opposition of Mr. Pendleton and Mr. R. C. Nicholas, both zealous churchmen. The bill finally passed, but modified by its opponents. It declared all *acts of Parliament*, which proscribe or punish the maintenance of any opinions in matters of religion, the forbearing to repair to church, or the exercising any mode of worship whatsoever, to be of no validity within the commonwealth ; it exempts dissenters from all contributions for the support of the established church ; and, as this exemption might in some places make the support of the clergy too burdensome on the members of the church, it suspends, until the end of the succeeding session, all acts which provide salaries for the clergy, (except as to arrears then due,) and leaves them to voluntary contributions. But, at the same time, it reserves to the established church its glebe lands and other property, and it defers "to the discussion and final determination of a future Assembly," the question, whether every one should not be subjected by law to a general assessment for the support of the pastor of his choice ; or, " every religious society should be left to voluntary contributions." The church party had previously succeeded so far as to obtain a declaration in committee, " that religious assemblies ought to be regulated, and that provision ought to be made for continuing the succession of the clergy, and superintending their conduct."

In the following years, the question of providing for the ministers of religion by law, or leaving it to individual contributions, was renewed ; but the advocates of the latter plan were only able to obtain, at each session, a suspension of those laws which provided salaries for the clergy—the natural progress in favor of liberal sentiments being counterbalanced by the fact, that some of the dissenting sects, with the exception of the Bap*ists, satisfied with having been relieved from a tax which they felt to be both unjust and degrading, had no objection to a general assessment; and, on this question, voted with the friends of the church. But the advocates of religious freedom finally prevailed, and after five suspending acts, the laws for the support of the clergy were, at the second session of 1779, unconditionally repealed. And although Mr. Jefferson was not then a member of the legislature, it is probable that his influence, as governor of the commonwealth, was sufficiently exerted towards its repeal. But to protect the rights of conscience, it was not deemed enough to remove past injustice, it was thought also prudent to prevent its recurrence. Among the bills, therefore, reported by the re-

---

* This probably greatly overrates their number.

visers, was the celebrated act of religious freedom, drawn by Mr. Jefferson; which not merely reasserts the principles of religious liberty contained in the bill of rights, but aims to give them permanence, by an argument equally clear, simple, and conclusive.

This bill, with many others, was not acted upon by the legislature for several years; but in the mean time, the friends of the Episcopal church prepared to make one more effort to recover a portion of its ancient privileges, by a general assessment. Their first object was to get an act of incorporation for the church, to enable it the better to retain and defend the large property it held, as well as to facilitate further acquisitions. A resolution having passed by a large majority, in favor of incorporating "all societies of the Christian religion" which desired it, leave was immediately given to bring in a bill "to incorporate the Protestant Episcopal Church," by which the minister and vestry in each parish were made a body corporate, for holding and acquiring property, and regulating the concerns of the church, and which finally passed into a law. The plan of a general assessment met with more difficulty. The petitions which had been got up among the people gave it the show of popularity, and it received the powerful aid of Patrick Henry's eloquence. Thus supported, it seemed likely to obtain a majority, when those who were opposed to the measure on principle, for the purpose of gaining time, proposed to refer the matter to the people before the legislature acted upon it, and they succeeded in postponing it. George Mason, George Nicholas, and others of this party, then proposed to Mr. Madison to prepare a remonstrance to the next legislature against the assessment, to be circulated through the state for signatures. This was done, and the paper which he prepared exhibited the same candid, dispassionate, and forcible reasoning, which had ever characterized the productions of his pen, convincing those who before doubted, so that there was a general disapprobation of the measure among all sects and parties; and, at the next session, the table could scarcely hold the petitions and remonstrances against the proposed assessment. Such a manifestation of the public will was not to be resisted. The measure was abandoned, and Mr. Jefferson's bill, with some slight alterations, was then passed without difficulty.

To conclude this history of religious establishments in Virginia: the law could not fairly claim the praise of impartiality, so long as a single church had the benefits of incorporation; and the injustice was the greater, if, as the other sects maintained, most of the large property it held it owed to the public bounty. In two years afterwards the act allowing religious incorporations was repealed, but with a saving to all religious societies of the property they possessed, with the right of appointing trustees for its management. In 1799, all these laws, as well as those made for the benefit of the dissenters and the church, were repealed, as inconsistent with the bill of rights and the principles of religious freedom; and lastly, in 1801, the overseers of the poor in each county were authorized to sell all its glebe lands, as soon as they shall become vacant by the death or the removal of the incumbent for the time; but reserving the rights of all private donations before 1777. By the execution of this act, the last vestige of legal privilege which this church had over other sects, was completely eradicated.

LISTS OF VIRGINIANS WHO HAVE HELD HIGH PUBLIC STATIONS.

List of Governors of the State of Virginia.

June 29, 1776....Patrick Henry.	Dec., 1816....James P. Preston.
" 1, 1779....Thomas Jefferson.	" 1819....Thomas M. Randolph.
" 12, 1781....Thomas Nelson.	" 1822....James Pleasants.
Nov. 30, 1781....Benj. Harrison.	" 1825....John Tyler. (late Pres. of U S.)
Dec., 1784....Patrick Henry.	March, 1827....Wm. B. Giles.
" 1786....Edmund Randolph.	" 1830....John Floyd.
" 1788....Beverley Randolph.	" 1834....Littleton W. Tazewell, resigned
" 1791....Henry Lee.	30th April, 1836.
" 1794....Robert Brooke.	April, 1836....Wyndham Robertson, Lieut.-Governor—acting Governor.
" 1796....James Wood.	
" 1799....James Monroe.	March, 1837....David Campbell.
" 1802....John Page.	" 1840....Thomas W. Gilmer; resigned,
" 1805....Wm. H. Cabell.	March, 1841.
" 1808....John Tyler.	" 1841....John Rutherford, Lieut.-Governor
Jan. 4, 1811....James Monroe.	and acting Governor.
Dec. 5, 1811....Geo. W. Smith, burnt in the theatre, Dec. 26.	" 1842....John M. Gregory, Lieut.-Governor and acting Governor.
Jan. 3, 1812....James Barbour.	Jan., 1843....James McDowell.
Dec., 1814....Wilson Carey Nicholas	

The following are lists of Virginians who have held high public stations under the general government. They are complete only to the year 1842.

Presidents of the United States.—George Washington, elected 1789; died Dec. 14, 1799, aged 67. Thomas Jefferson, elected 1801; died July 4, 1826, aged 83. James Madison, elected 1809; died June 28th, 1836, aged 84. James Monroe, elected 1817; died July 4, 1831, aged 72. William Henry Harrison, elected in 1841; died April 4, 1841, aged 68. John Tyler, 1841.

Vice-Presidents of the United States.—Thomas Jefferson, elected 1797. John Tyler, elected 1841.

Secretaries of State.—Thomas Jefferson, 1789. Edmund Randolph, 1794; died Sept. 12, 1813. John Marshall, 1800; died July 6, 1835, aged 79. James Madison, 1801. James Monroe, 1811. Henry Clay, (born in Va.,) 1825. Abel P. Upshur, 1843; died Feb. 28, 1844. John Forsyth, (born in Va.,) 1834; died Oct. 22, 1841, aged 61.

Secretaries of War.—James Monroe, 1814. James Barbour, 1825; died June 8, 1842, aged 66.

Secretaries of the Navy.—Abel P. Upshur, 1841. Thomas W. Gilmer, 1843; died Feb. 28, 1844. John Y. Mason, 1844.

Attorney-Generals.—Edmund Randolph, 1789. Charles Lee, 1795; died June 24, 1815, aged 58. William Wirt, (D. C.,) 1817; died Feb. 18, 1834, aged 61. Peter V. Daniel, appointed in 1833, but declined.

Chief-Justices of the Supreme Court.—John Marshall, 1801 to 1835.

Associate do.—John Blair, 1789 to 1796; died Aug. 31, 1800, aged 68. Bushrod Washington, 1798 to 1829; died June 14, 1832, aged 73. Thomas Todd, 1807 to 1826; died Feb. 1826. Philip P. Barbour, 1836 to 1841; died Feb. 25, 1841, aged 60. Peter V. Daniel, 1841.

Foreign Ministers.—James Monroe, Minister Plenipotentiary to Great Britain in 1803, 1806, and 1808. James Barbour, do. to do. in 1828. Andrew Stevenson, do. to do. in 1836. William Short, Chargé de Affaires to France in 1790. James Monroe, Minister Plenipotentiary to do. in 1794. Patrick Henry, Min. Plen. to do. in 1799; did not accept. Wm. C. Rives, Min. Plen. and Envoy Extraordinary to do. in 1829. Wm. Short, Minister Resident in Spain, 1794. James Monroe, Min. Plen. to Spain, 1804. John Forsyth, (born in Va.,) Min. Plen. 1819. Hugh Nelson, Min. Plen. and En. Ex. to Spain, 1823. Wm. Short, Min. Res. to Netherlands, 1792. John Graham, Min. Plen. to Brazil, 1819. Thomas L. L. Brent, Chargé de Affaires to do., 1825. Henry Clay, (born in Va.,) to Prussia, 1823. John Randolph, about 1831, Min. Plen. to Russia. Richard C. Anderson, Min. Plen. to Colombia, 1823. Wm. Boulware, Chargé de Affaires Two Sicilies, 1841. Wm. Brent, Chargé d'Affaires to Buenos Ayres, 1844. Henry A. Wise, Minister to Brazil in 1844. Wm. M. Blackford, Chargé d'Affaires to New Grenada, 1842. Wm. Crump, Chargé d'Affaires to Chili, 1844.

U. S. Senators, from the adoption of the Constitution.—Wm. S. Archer, 1842 to 1847. James Barbour, 1815 to 1825. Richard Brent, 1809 to 1815. John W. Eppes, 1817 to 1819; died Sept. 1830, aged 50. Wm. B. Giles, 1804 to 1816; died Dec. 8, 1830. William Grayson, 1789 to 1790; died March 12, 1790. Richard H. Lee, 1789 to 1792; died 19th June, 1794, aged 62. Benjamin Watkins Leigh, 1834 to 1838. A. T. Mason, 1815 to 1817; died 6th Feb. 1819, aged 33. James Monroe, 1790 to 1794. Andrew Moore, 1804 to 1809. Wilson C. Nicholas, 1799 to 1804; died 10th Oct. 1820. James Pleasants, 1819 to 1822. John Randolph, 1825 to 1827; died 24th May, 1833, aged 60. William C. Rives, 1832 to 1834, 1836 to 1839, 1842 to 1845. John Taylor, about 1803. Henry Tazewell, 1794 to 1799. Littleton W. Tazewell, 1824 to 1833. John Tyler, 1827 to 1836. Abraham B. Venable, 1803 to 1804; perished in the Richmond Theatre, 26th Dec. 1811. John Walker, 1790.

Members of the Old Congress from 1774 to 1788, inclusive.—Thomas Adams, 1778 to 1780. John Banister, 1778 to 1779. Richard Bland, 1774 to 1776; died in 1778. Theodorick Bland, 1780 to 1783; died in 1790, aged 48. Carter Braxton, 1776; died 1797, aged 61. Edward Carrington, 1785 to 1786; died 1810, aged 61. John Fitzhugh, 1779 to 1780; died in 1809, aged 83. Wm. Grayson, 1784 to 1787. Cyrus Griffin, 1778 to 1781, 1787 to 1788; died in 1810, aged 62. Samuel Hardy, 1783 to 1785. John Harvie, 1778 to 1779. Benjamin Harrison, 1774 to 1778; died in 1791. James Henry, 1780 to 1781; died in 1805. Patrick Henry, 1774 to 1776. Thomas Jefferson, 1775 to 1777, 1783 to 1785. Joseph Jones, 1777 to 1778, 1780 to 1783. Arthur Lee, 1781 to 1784; died 14th Dec. 1782, aged 42. Francis L. Lee, 1775 to 1780; died 1797, aged 63. Henry Lee, 1785 to 1788; died in 1818, aged 62. Richard H. Lee, 1774 to 1780, 1784 to 1787; died in 1794, aged 62. James Madison, jr., 1780 to 1783, 1786 to 1788; died in 1836. James Mercer, 1779 to 1780. James Monroe, 1783 to 1786; died July 4, 1831. Thomas Nelson, 1775 to 1777, 1779 to 1780; died Jan. 4. 1789. aged 50. Mann Page, 1777. Edmund Pendleton, 1774 to 1775; died in 1803, aged 82. Edmund Randolph, 1779 to 1782; died in 1813. Peyton Randolph, 1774 to 1775; died 22d Oct. 1775, aged 52. Meriwether Smith, 1778 to 1782. George Washington, 1774 to 1775. George Wythe, 1775 to 1777; died 6th June, 1806, aged 80.

Members of the Convention from Va. which formed the Constitution of the United States.—John Blair, James Madison, Jr., George Mason, James M'Clurg, Edmund Randolph, George Washington, and George Wythe. Messrs. Mason, M'Clurg, Randolph, and Wythe, did not sign the constitution.

List of members from Virginia, of the U. S. House of Representatives, from the adoption of the Federal Constitution to the 4th of March, 1845.

Alexander, Mark	1819–33	Bayley, T. H.	1843
Allen, John J.	1833–35	Bayley, Thomas M.	1813–15
Allen, Robert	1827–33	Beale, J. M. H.	1833–37
Archer, Wm. S.	{ 1820–33 { 1833–35	Beirne, Andrew Bland, Theodore	1837–41 1789–90
Armstrong, Wm.	1825–33	Botts, John M.	1839–43
Atkinson, A.	1843–45	Bouldin, Thomas T.	1829–33
Austin, Archibald	1817–19	Bouldin, J. W.	1833–39
Baker, John	1811–13	Breckenridge, James	1809–17
Ball, Wm. L.	1817–24	Brent, Richard	{ 1795–99 { 1801–03
Banks, Linn	1837–43		
Barbour, John S.	1823–33	Browne, John	1789–92
Barbour, Philip P.	{ 1814–25 { 1827–30	Burwell, Wm. A. Cabell, Samuel J.	1806–21 1795–03
Barton, Richard W	1841–43	Caperton, Hugh	1813–15
Bassett, Burwell	{ 1805–13 { 1815–19 { 1821–31	Cary, George B. Chapman, A. A. Chinn, Joseph W.	1841–43 1843 1831–35

Chilton, Samuel	1843
Claiborne, John	1805–08
Claiborne, Nathaniel H.	1825–37
Claiborne, Thomas	{ 1793–99 { 1801–05
Clark, Christopher	1804–06
Clay, Matthew	1797–13
Clopton, John	{ 1795–99 { 1801–16
Coke, Richard	1829–33
Coles, Isaac	{ 1789–91 { 1793–97
Coles, Walter	1835–45
Colston, Edward	1817–19
Craig, Robert B.	1829–33
Craig, Robert	1835–41
Crump, John	1826–27
Davenport, Thomas	1825–35

Dawson, John	1797-14
Doddridge, Philip	1829-32
Draper, Joseph	1830-31 / 1833-33
Dromgoole, Geo. C.	1835-41 / 1843-45
Eggleston, John	1798-01
Eppes, John W.	1803-11 / 1813-15
Estill, Benjamin	1825-27
Evans, Thomas	1797-01
Floyd, John	1817-29
Fulton, John H.	1833-35
Garland, David S.	1809-11
Garland, James	1835-41
Garnett, James M.	1805-09
Garnet, Robert S.	1817-27
Gholson, Thomas	1808-16
Gholson, James H.	1833-35
Giles, Wm. B.	1790-98 / 1801-02
Gilmer, Thomas W	1841-43
Goggin, Wm. L.	1839
Goode, Samuel	1799-01
Goode, W. O.	1841-43
Goodwin, Peterson	1803-18
Gordon, Wm. F.	1829-35
Gray, Edwin	1799-13
Gray, John C.	1820-21
Griffin, Samuel	1789-95
Griffin, Thomas	1803-05
Hancock, George	1793-97
Harrison, Carter B.	1793-99
Harris, Wm. A.	1841-43
Hawes, Aylett	1811-17
Hays, Samuel L.	1841-43
Heath, John	1793-97
Hill, John T.	1839-41
Holleman, Joel	1839-41
Holmes, David	1797-09
Hopkins, G. W.	1835
Hubard, Edm. W.	1841
Hungerford, John P.	1813-17
Hunter, R. M. T.	1837-43
Jackson, Edward B.	1820-23
Jackson, John George	1795-97 / 1799-10 / 1813-17
Johnson, James	1813-20
Johnson, Joseph	1823-27 / 1835-41
Johnson, Chas. C.	1831-32
Jones, James	1819-23
Jones, John W	1835-45
Jones, Walter	1797-99 / 1803-11
Kerr, John	1813-17

Lee, Henry	1799-01
Lee, Richard Bland	1789-95
Leffler, Isaac	1827-29
Leftwich, Jabez	1821-25
Lewis, Joseph	1803-17
Lewis, Wm. J.	1817-19
Love, John	1807-11
Lucas, Edward	1833-37
Lucas, Wm. F.	1839-41 / 1843-45
Loyall, George	1831-37
Machir, James	1797-99
Madison, James	1789-97
Mallory, Francis	1837-39 / 1841-43
Marshall, John	1799-00
Mason, John Y.	1831-37
Mason, James M.	1837-39
Maxwell, Lewis	1827-33
McCarty, Wm. M	1839-41
McComas, Wm.	1833-37
M'Coy, Wm.	1811-33
M'Kinley, Wm.	1810-11
Mercer, Chas. Fenton	1817-39
Moore, Andrew	1789-97 / 1803-04
Moore, Thomas L.	1820-23
Moore, S. McD.	1833-35
Morgan, Daniel	1797-99
Morgan, Wm. S.	1835-39
Morrow, John	1805-09
Nelson, Hugh	1811-23
Nelson, Thomas M.	1816-19
Nevel, Joseph	1793-95
New, Anthony	1793-05
Newton, Thomas	1801-29 / 1831-33
Newton, W.	1843-45
Nicholas, Wilson Carey	1807-09
Nicholas, John	1793-01
Page, John	1789-97
Page, Robert	1799-01
Parker, Josiah	1789-01
Parker, Severn E.	1819-21
Patton, John M.	1830-37
Pennybacker, I. S.	1837-39
Pindall, James	1818-19
Pleasants, James	1817-20
Powell, Alfred H.	1811-19
Powell, Cuthbert	1825-27
Powell, Levin	1841-43
Preston, Francis	1799-01
Randolph, John	1793-97 / 1799-13 / 1815-17 / 1819-25 / 1827-29

Randolph, Thomas M.	1803-07
Rives, Francis E.	1837-41
Rives, William C.	1823-29
Roane, John	1827-31 / 1835-37
Roane, John J.	1831-33
Roane, John T.	1809-15
Roane, Wm. H.	1815-17
Robertson, John	1833-39
Rutherford, Robert	1793-97
Samuel, Green B.	1839-41
Sheffey, Daniel	1809-17
Smith, Arthur	1821-25
Smith, Ballard	1815-21
Smith, John	1801-15
Smith, Wm.	1821-27
Smyth, Alexander	1817-25 / 1827-30
Steenrod, Lewis J.	1839-45
Stephenson, James	1803-05 / 1809-11 / 1822-25
Steuart, Archibald	1837-39
Stuart, Alex. H. H.	1841-43
Stevenson, Andrew	1821-33
Stratton, John	1801-03
Strother, George F.	1817-20
Summers, George W.	1841-45
Swearingin, Thomas V.	1819-22
Swoope, Jacob	1809-11
Taliaferro, John	1801-03 / 1811-13 / 1824-31 / 1835-43
Tate, Magnus	1815-17
Taylor, Robert	1825-27
Taylor, Wm. P.	1833-35
Taylor, Wm.	1843
Tazewell, Littleton W.	1800-01
Thompson, Philip R.	1801-07
Trezvant, James	1825-31
Trigg, Abram	1797-09
Trigg, John	1797-04
Tucker, Henry St. George	1815-19
Tyler, John (late President of U. S.)	1816-21
Venable, A. B.	1791-99
Walker, Francis	1793-95
White, Alexander	1789-93
White, Francis,	1813-15
Williams, Jared	1819-25
Wilson, Alexander	1804-09
Wilson, Edgar C.	1833-35
Wilson, Thomas	1811-13
Wise, Henry A.	1833-43

List of persons who have lived 110 years and over.

	Place	When died.	Age.
William M'Kim,	Richmond,	1818	130
John de la Somet,		1700	130
Wonder Booker, (a negro,)	Prince Edward co.	1819	126
Eleanor Spicer,	Accomac co.	1773	121
Charles Lauge,	Campbell co.	1821	121
Charles Roberts,	Bullskin,	1796	116
Philip Crull,	Fairfax co.	1813	115
Wm. Taylor,	Pittsylvania co.	1794	114
Frank, (a negro,)	Woodstock,	1820	114
Alex. Berkley,	Charlotte co.	1825	114
Priscilla Carmichael,	Surry co.	1818	113
Sarah Carter,	Petersburg,	1825	112
Mrs. A. Berkley,	Charlotte,	1826	111
Wm. Wootten,		1773	111
A negro,	Richmond,	1818	136
Mrs. Harrison,	Brunswick co.	1805	110
John Cuffee, (a slave,)	Norfolk,	1836	120
John, (a negro,)	Washington, D. C.	1838	115
Gilbert, (a negro,)	Augusta co.	1844	112

OBITUARY.

Below are obituary notices, drawn from the Obituary in the American Almanac, of public individuals, natives and residents of Virginia and the District of Columbia, who have died within the last ten or twelve years. The perusal will create retrospections, too often lost amid the engrossing scenes of the present, and the demands of the future.

1832

Oct. 13.—At Norfolk, *John E. Holt*, nearly twenty years mayor of that borough.

Nov. 19.—At Washington city, aged 60, *Philip Doddridge*, a member of Congress, a distinguished lawyer, and one of the ablest men in the body of which he was a member.

1833.

Jan. 29.—At Warrenton, N. C., in his 64th year, *John Hall*, recently judge of the Supreme Court of N. Carolina. He was born in Staunton, Va., and when a young man removed to N. C. His life was pure, and his integrity unspotted.

May 24.—At Philadelphia, aged 60, *John Randolph of Roanoke.*

Nov. 17.—At Columbus, S. C., aged about 90, *Colonel Thomas Taylor.* He was born in Amelia co., Va., in 1743. He has been styled "the patriarch of the states-right party of South Carolina."

Dec. 21.—At Twiford, in Westmoreland co., Va., in his 74th year, *John P. Hungerford.* He was an officer in the revolutionary war, and afterwards a member of Congress.

1834.

Feb. 11.—In the Capitol at Washington, *Thomas Tyler Bouldin*, M. C. Before he was elected a member of Congress, he had been a lawyer of high rank, an able and upright judge ; and he was highly respected for his integrity.

Feb. 18.—At Washington city, in his 62d year, the *Hon. William Wirt*, the author of the Life of Patrick Henry, and of the British Spy.

April 13.—At Norfolk, *Gen. Robert B. Taylor*, an eminent lawyer, and a judge of the General or District Court of Va. ; a man greatly respected, and much lamented.

Oct.—At Petersburg, of cholera, aged about 48, *Gen. William H. Brodnax*, of Dinwiddie Co., Va., distinguished as a lawyer and a philanthropist, and for several years a very prominent member of the House of Delegates. He signalized himself in the debates on the abolition of slavery in 1831, advocating a gradual and cautious abolition ; and also, in opposition to the doctrines of President Jackson's Proclamation of Dec., 1832.

Near Monongahela, Va., aged 97, *Col. John Evans ;* a commander of a regiment of militia in the revolution, and a member of the convention that formed the first constitution.

1835.

March 2.—In Bath co.,Va., aged about 77, *Gen. Samuel Blackburn*, a soldier of the revolution, an eminent lawyer, and for many years a conspicuous member of the legislature. At his death he liberated his slaves, forty-six in number, charging his estate with the expense of transporting them to Liberia.

April 7.—At Philadelphia, in his 73d year, *James Brown*, who was born in Virginia in Oct. 1766. In 1812, he was elected a member of the U. S. Senate from Louisiana, and in 1823 appointed minister to France. He was distinguished as a lawyer and a statesman.

April 25.—Aged about 40, *Jonathan P. Cushing*, President of Hampden-Sidney College, which office he had held for fourteen years. He was born in New Hampshire. The institution over which he presided was greatly indebted to his well-directed zeal, talents, and influence, and he was highly esteemed for his virtues. By his will he emancipated his slaves, sixty in number, providing amply for their removal to Liberia ; and also gave about $40,000 to establish schools in Albemarle, and the adjoining county

May 13.—In Brunswick county, in his 84th year, *Rev. Edward Dromgoole*, father of the Hon. George C. Dromgoole ; a minister of the gospel sixty-three years, and a magistrate and member of the county court forty-five years.

July 1.—At Richmond, in his 77th year, *Maj. James Gibbon*, collector of customs of the port of Richmond, and a gallant officer of the revolutionary army, known as "the hero of Stony-Point." Col. Gibbon, on the 16th of July, 1779, then a lieutenant, led one of the two "forlorn hopes," of twenty men, when Gen. Wayne carried the fortress of Stony-Point by storm. Of his twenty men, seventeen were killed or wounded. He was greatly respected and esteemed, and his remains were interred with the highest honors.

July 6.—At Philadelphia, in his 80th year, *John Marshall*, Chief-Justice of the United States.

June 28.—At Baltimore, Md., aged about 50, of a fractured skull, from the fall of a chimney, *Thomas Marshall*, of Fauquier Co., the eldest son of Chief-Justice Marshall, being on a journey to attend the death-bed of his father. He graduated in Princeton in 1803 ; was distinguished as a scholar, a lawyer, and a member of the legislature ; and was highly esteemed for his talents, his many virtues, and his exemplary and useful life.

May 26.—At Columbia, S. C., aged 70, *Gen. Francis Preston*, of Washington Co., Va., a member of Congress from 1793 to 1797, and father of the Hon. William C. Preston.

Nov.—At Lexington, Va., *George Baxter*, a distinguished lawyer.

Nov.—In Caroline co., aged about 48, *John Dickenson*, an eminent lawyer.

Oct. 7.—In Alabama, *Charles Tait*, in his 68th year. He was born in Louisa county, but removed at an early age to Georgia, where he was, for several years, a judge of the Superior Court, and a senator in Congress, from 1809 to 1819.

Dec. 3.—At Washington city, aged 47, *Richard Wallack*, a distinguished lawyer.

1836.

March 22.—At Washington, D. C., in his 82d year, *Gen. Mountjoy Baily*, an officer of the revolution.

Jan. 28.—At Abingdon, *John H. Fulton*, a respected member of the 23d Congress.

April 29.—In Logan co., Ohio, *Gen. Simon Kenton*, aged 82, a native of Virginia. He was a companion of Col. Boone, in exploring the west, and in commencing its settlement, and he endured many hardships.

March 25.—At Belmont, Loudon co., Va., aged 76, *Ludwell Lee*, second son of Richard Henry Lee, a gentleman highly respected.

Nov. 9.—At his residence, in Goochland co., Va., aged 67, *James Pleasants*, M. C. from 1811 to 1819; U. S. Senator from 1819 to 1822 : governor of Virginia from 1822 to 1825, and a member of the convention for 1829-30, for amending the state constitution. He was twice appointed to the bench, but declined, from a distrust of his own qualifications. He was a man of rare modesty, greatly respected and esteemed for public and private virtues

Oct. 10.—In Albemarle co., Va., aged upwards of 70, *Mrs. Martha Randolph*, widow of Gov. Thomas M. Randolph, and the last surviving daughter of Thomas Jefferson ; a lady distinguished for her talents and virtues.

1837.

Jan. 8.—At his seat in Culpeper co., aged 63, *Dabney Carr*, a judge of the Virginia Court of Appeals ; a man much respected and esteemed for his amiable character, his talents, learning, industry, solidity of mind, and uncommonly fine colloquial powers.

Aug. 16.—At the Sweet Springs, *John Floyd*, M. C. from 1817 to 1819, and governor of Virginia from 1829 to 1834.

April 12.—In Beaver co., Penn., *Gen. Abner Lacock*, in his 67th year. He was born in Virginia, removed early in life to Pennsylvania, and was, from 1813 to 1819, a member of the U. S. Senate.

June 28, 1836.-At Montpelier, Orange co. Va. in his 86th year, *James Madison*, the 4th President of the United States.

March 18, 1836.—In Albemarle, Va, *Hugh Nelson*, formerly speaker of the House of Delegates, a judge of the General Court, a member of Congress from 1811 to 1823, and afterwards U. S. Minister to Spain.

June 3.—In Virginia, in his 53d year, *Allen Taylor*, judge of the General Court, 17th Circuit.

Jan. 7.—At Needham, in his 70th year, *Creed Taylor*, late chancellor of the Richmond and Lynchburg District.

Nov. 5.—Aged 57, *David Briggs*, an eminent attorney, formerly mayor of Fredericksburg, and counsellor of state.

Nov. 20.—At his father's residence, in Bedford co., *John Thompson Brown*, of Petersburg, Va., aged 36. He was for several years a very distinguished member of the legislature, was rising rapidly at the bar, and was regarded as one of the most eminent men of his age in the state.

Oct. 7.—At Yorktown, aged 64, *Major Thomas Griffin*, second in command at the battle of Hampton, and M. C. in 1803-5.

Nov. 30, 1836.—At Bellegrove, *Major Isaac Hite*, an officer in the revolutionary war.

Dec. 15.—At Gosport, in his 85th year, *Capt. John Cox*, who, early in the revolution, was commissioned as a captain in the naval service of Virginia, and was one of the most distinguished and efficient patriots in the contest.

Dec. 2.—In Goochland co., aged 62, *Dr. Andrew Kean*, one of the most eminent physicians of. Virginia.

Sept. 8.—In Albemarle co., aged 85, *Mrs. Lucy Marks*, the mother of Meriwether Lewis, who, with William Clarke, explored the Rocky Mountains ; a woman of uncommon energy and strength of mind.

Sept. 19.—At Clinton, Fauquier co., aged 83, *Capt. William Payne*, who commanded the Falmouth Blues for several years in the early part of the revolution ; and a company of volunteers at the siege of Yorktown.

July 22.—In Kanawha co., aged 71, *Philip R. Thompson*, M. C. from Virginia in 1801-7.

1838.

March 26.—In Missouri, *Gen. William H. Ashley*, first lieutenant-governor of that state, and a native of Powhatan co., Va.

May 7.—At Washington, D. C., *Abraham Bradley*, for many years assistant postmaster-general.

Feb. 2.—In Stafford co., *John Coulter*, formerly a judge of the Circuit Court and Court of Appeals.

Jan. 9.—At Staunton, aged 36, *John J. Craig*, a man much respected ; distinguished for his talents as a lawyer, and a member of the legislature.

Feb. 6.—At Charlotte, C. H., aged 40, *Nash Le Grand*, for several years a member of the state council.

Jan. 6.—At Richmond, Va., suddenly, aged about 35, *Edward V. Sparhawk*, editor of the Petersburg Intelligencer ; a gentleman of fine talents, extensive acquirements, and a highly respectable and useful member of society.

Dec.—At Richmond, aged 60, *John Brockenbrough*, judge of the Court of Appeals.

Sept. 1.—At St. Louis, in his 69th year, *William Clarke*, a native of Virginia, companion of Meriwether Lewis in the expedition across the Rocky Mountains, and governor of Missouri Territory, from 1813 to 1820.

Sept. 15.—At Huntsville, Ala., *Col. William Lindsay*, a native of Va., and a highly respectable man and officer of the U. S. army.

Dec. 21.—At Alexandria, D. C., *Thompson F. Mason*, judge of the Criminal Court of the District of Columbia.

1839.

April 8.—At Wheeling, *Alexander Caldwell*, judge of the U. S. Court in the Western District of Va.

Nov. 3.—In Hanover co., in his 72d year, suddenly, while feeling the pulse of a dying patient, *Dr. Carter Berkeley*, a lineal descendant of Sir William Berkeley, a graduate of the Edinburgh Medical School, a distinguished physician, and much respected for his upright, benevolent, and religious character.

Nov. 20.—At Lynchburg, in his 69th year, *William Daniel*, a conspicuous member of the legislature in 1798-99 ; and, for the last twenty-three years, a judge of the General and Circuit Courts ; a man much respected for his talents and legal knowledge.

Nov.—At New Orleans, *Capt. Gilbert T. Francis*, a native of Va. His life was romantic and eventful, and he passed through surprising adventures in foreign countries. Though of defective education, his great energy of character and extensive travels made him the most entertaining of companions.

Oct. 2.—In Culpeper co., in his 88th year, *Col. David Jameson*, an active militia officer of the revolution ; afterwards a member of the House of Delegates, a respected magistrate, and a member of the county court.

1840.

May 20.—At Richmond, aged about 75, *Daniel Call*, brother-in-law to Chief-Justice Marshall, an able and eminent lawyer, author of 6 vols. of law reports, known as " Call's Reports."

Jan.—At Richmond, aged about 88, *Chas. Shirley Carter*, an eminent lawyer and advocate, attorney of the state in the Circuit Court of Henrico co. ; formerly a distinguished member of the legislature.

Oct.—At the University of Virginia, aged about 48, *Chas. Bonnycastle*, Prof. of Mathematics. He was a native of England, and a son of John Bonnycastle, the author of a celebrated algebra. He was a man of profound and vigorous mind, and author of a valuable work upon Inductive Geometry.

Nov. 14.—At the University of Va., (of a pistol-shot discharged by a disguised student,) aged 39, *John A. G. Davis*, Prof. of Law in the University. He was a man of a high order of intellect, of untiring industry, of amiable and philanthropic character, and he was an exemplary member of the Episcopal church. He published, in 1838, a valuable law-book—" A Treatise on Criminal Law, and a Guide to Justices of the Peace." As a successful instructor, he could hardly be surpassed ; and it is thought, since graduates of his law-school have taken their places at the bar, the profession in Virginia has breathed a more enlarged spirit, and displayed a wider and a higher tone.

Dec.—At Nashville, Tenn., *Felix Grundy*, a native of Berkeley co., Va., and a distinguished member of the U. S. Senate from Tennessee.

Nov.—In Va., aged about 63, *Richard E. Parker*, a judge of the Supreme Court of Appeals.

Jan. 19.—At Morven, Loudon co., in his 75th year, *Thomas Swan*, an eminent lawyer, and formerly attorney of the U. S. for the Dist. of Columbia. " He attained the highest rank in his profession, uniting to the most extensive learning the most effective eloquence as a pleader. His influence over juries, arising from this cause, and partly from the universal confidence in the purity of his character, is believed to have been seldom, if ever, surpassed, in the instance of any other American advocate."

1841.

Feb. 25.—At Washington, D. C., aged about 60, *Philip P. Barbour*, of Orange co., an associate judge of the Supreme Court of the U. S.

April 24.—In Va., aged 77, *George Baxter*, D.D., Prof. in the Union Theo. Sem. in Prince Edward co. ; formerly president of Wash. College, at Lexington, and one of the most eminent and respected Presbyterian clergymen in Virginia.

Oct. 22.—At Washington, D. C., (of bilious fever,) aged 61, *John Forsyth*, of Georgia, a man of talents and eloquence, and secretary of state in Mr. Van Buren's administration. He was born in Fredericksburg, Va., in 1781.

April 4.—At Washington city, in his 69th year, *William Henry Harrison*, President of the U. States. He was born in Charles City co., Va., on the 9th of Feb. 1773.

June 10.—At Washington city, in his 92d year, *Richard Harrison*, late auditor of the treasury, and a man highly respected.

April 27.—At Washington city, aged about 80, *Rev. Andrew T. McCornish*, a respected clergyman, for 23 years minister of the first Episcopal church formed in Washington.

June.—At Washington city, *George Washington Montgomery*, who was born in Valencia, in Spain, of a distinguished Irish family, and a man of superior talents and education. He came in early life to this country, and was long employed in the department of State. He was the author of Bernardo del Carpio, " an exquisite historical novel of the 8th century, and the translation of Irving's Conquest of Granada."

Sept. 1.—Near Georgetown, D. C., in his 88th year, *Joseph Nourse*, register of the U. S. Treasury from 1789 to 1829, and one of the vice-presidents of the American Bible Society, and a man much respected. He was born in London in 1754 ; emigrated with his family to Virginia, and entered the revolutionary army in 1776, and served in different departments connected with it till the close of the war.

1842.

Feb. 24.—In Madison co., *Hon. Linn Banks*, from 1818 to 1838 speaker of the House of Delegates.

June 8.—In Orange co., *Hon. James Barbour*, ex-governor of Virginia, aged 66.

Aug. 13.—*John P. Emmett*, Esq., Prof. of Chem. in the University of Va. He was the son of the late Thomas Addis Emmett, and a man of talents and learning.

Jan. 5.—At Savannah, Ga., *Col. Thomas Haynes*, aged 55, who was born in Va. He was treasurer of Georgia, and commanded respect and great public influence.

1843.

Nov. 23.—In Fauquier co., *Thomas Fitzhugh*, aged 81. He was a highly respected citizen, and had been for many years presiding judge of the County Court.

Dec. 14.—In Washington city, *Chas. W. Goldsborough*, chief of the bureau of provisions and clothing of the navy department, and author of a naval history of the U. S. He was one of the oldest and most respected inhabitants of the city.

Nov. 30.—In Rappahannock co., *Maj. John Roberts*, aged 85. He served in the revolutionary army, and negotiated the exchange for the prisoners obtained by the convention at Saratoga in 1777. Afterwards he was a member of the legislature for 13 successive years, and had great influence in its deliberations.

Aug. 27.—At the White Sulphur Springs, *Hon. Lewis Summers*, of Kanawha, aged 65, for 24 years one of the judges of the General Court of Va.

1844.

Feb. 10.—At Fredericksburg, *Carter Beverley*, Esq., aged 72.

Feb. 28.—By the accident on board the U. S. steamer Princeton, *Thomas W. Gilmer*, of Charlottesville, secretary of the navy. His various public trusts he discharged with great ability. He was respected in public, and beloved in private life.

March 29.—At Norfolk, *Com. E. Pendleton Kennedy*, of the U. S. N., aged 65. At the time of his death, he was commander of the line-of-battle ship Pennsylvania.

Feb. 28.—By the accident on board the steamer Princeton, *Com. Beverley Kennon*, chief of the bureau of construction, repairs, and equipment, in the navy department. He had long been attached to the naval service, in which he had attained a distinguished reputation.

Feb. 28.—By the accident on board the Princeton, *Hon. A. P. Upshur*, secretary of state, aged 54. He was born in Northampton co. in 1790.

EXTRACTS FROM THE ANCIENT LAWS OF VIRGINIA.

1662.—Every person who refuses to have his child baptized by a lawful minister, shall be amerced 2000 lbs. of tobacco ; half to the parish, half to the informer.

The whole liturgy of the Church of England shall be thoroughly read at church or chapel, every Sunday ; and the canons for divine service and sacraments duly observed.

Church-wardens shall present at the county court, twice every year, in December and April, such misdemeanors of swearing, drunkenness, fornication, &c., as by their own knowledge, or common fame, have been committed during their being church-wardens.

To steal, or unlawfully to kill any hog that is not his own, upon sufficient proof, the offender shall pay to the owner 1000 lbs. of tobacco, and as much to the informer; and in case of inability, shall serve two years, one to the owner, and one to the informer.

The man and woman committing fornication, shall pay each 500 lbs. of tobacco, and to be bound to their good behavior. If either of them be a servant, the master shall pay the 500 lbs. of tobacco, and the servant shall serve half a year longer than his time. If the master shall refuse to pay, then the servant to be whipped. If a bastard be got and born, then the woman to serve her master two years longer than her time, or pay him 2000 lbs. of tobacco; and the reputed father to give security to keep the child.

No marriage shall be reputed valid in law but such as is made by the minister, according to the laws of England. And no minister shall marry any person without a license from the governor or his deputy, or thrice publication of bans, according to the rubrick in the common-prayer book. The minister that doth marry contrary to this act, shall be fined 10,000 lbs. of tobacco.

All persons keeping tipling-houses without license, shall be fined 2000 lbs. of tobacco; half to the county, and half to the informer.

No master of any ship, vessel, &c., shall transport any person out of this colony without a pass, under the secretary's hand, upon the penalty of paying all such debts as any such person shall owe at his departure, and 1000 lbs. of tobacco to the secretary.

The court in every county shall cause to be set up near the court-house, a pillory, a pair of stocks, a whipping-post, and a ducking-stool, in such place as they shall think convenient: which not being set up within six months after the date of this act, the said court shall be fined 5000 lbs. of tobacco.

In actions of slander occasioned by a man's wife, after judgment passed for damages, the woman shall be punished by ducking, and if the slander be such as the damages shall be adjudged at above 500 lbs. of tobacco, then the woman shall have ducking for every 500 lbs. of tobacco adjudged against her husband, if he refuse to pay the tobacco.

Enacted that the Lord's Day be kept holy, and no journeys be made on that day, unless upon necessity. And all persons inhabiting in this country having no lawful excuse, shall every Sunday resort to the parish church or chapel, and there abide orderly during the common prayer, preaching, and divine service, upon the penalty of being fined 50 lbs. of tobacco by the county court.

This act shall not extend to Quakers, or other recusants, who totally absent themselves, but they shall be liable to the penalty imposed by the stat. 23 Eliz., viz. £20 sterling for every month's absence, &c.; and all Quakers assembling in unlawful conventicles, shall be fined, every man so taken, 200 lbs. of tobacco, for every time of such meeting.

All ministers officiating in any public cure, and six of their family, shall be exempted from public taxes.

1663.—If any Quakers, or other separatists whatsoever, in this colony, assemble themselves together to the number of five or more, of the age of sixteen years, or upwards, under the pretence of joining in a religious worship not authorized in England or this country, the parties so offending, being thereof lawfully convicted by verdict, confessions, or notorious evidence of the fact, shall, for the first offence, forfeit and pay 200 lbs. of tobacco; for the second offence, 500 lbs. of tobacco, to be levied by warrant from any justice of the peace, upon the goods of the party convicted; but if he be unable, then upon the goods of any other of the separatists or Quakers then present. And for the third offence, the offender being convicted as aforesaid, shall be banished the colony of Virginia.

Every master of a ship or vessel, that shall bring in any Quakers to reside here, after the 1st of July next, shall be fined 5000 lbs. of tobacco, to be levied by distress and sale of his goods, and enjoined to carry him, her, or them, out of the country again.

Any person inhabiting this country, and entertaining any Quaker in or near his house, to preach or teach, shall, for every time of such entertainment, be fined 5000 lbs. of tobacco.

1668.—The 27th of August, appointed for a day of humiliation, fasting, and prayer, to implore God's mercy; if any person be found upon that day gaming, drinking, or working, (works of necessity excepted,) upon presentment by the church-wardens, and proof, he shall be fined 100 lbs. of tobacco, half to the informer, and half to the poor of the parish.

1670.—None but freeholders and housekeepers shall have any voice in the election of Burgesses—every county not sending two Burgesses to every session of the Assembly, shall be fined 10,000 lbs. of tobacco, to the use of the public.

1676.—The allowance of every Burgess for the future, shall be 120 lbs. of tobacco and cask, per day ; to commence two days before every Assembly, and continue two days after. And for their travelling charges, there shall be allowed to those that come by land, 10 lbs. of tobacco per day for every horse so used. And for water passage, they shall be allowed proportionably.

1679.—The first offence of hog stealing, shall be punished according to the former law ; upon a second conviction, the offender shall stand two hours in the pillory, and lose his ears ; and for the third offence, he shall be tried by the laws of England, as in case of felony.

1680.—No licensed attorney shall demand or receive, for bringing any cause to judgment in the general court, more than 500 lbs. of tobacco and cask ; and in the county court, 150 lbs. of tobacco and cask ; which fees are allowed him without any pre-agreement.

If any attorney shall refuse to plead any cause in the respective courts aforesaid, for the aforesaid fees, he shall forfeit as much as his fees should have been.

LIFE IN WESTERN VIRGINIA.

Much of Western Virginia is yet a new country, and thinly settled ; and in some of the more remote and inaccessible counties, the manner of living and the habits of the people are quite primitive. Many of these mountain counties are so far from markets, that it is a common saying among the inhabitants that they can only sell those things which will "*walk away*"—meaning cattle, horses, swine, &c. Of the latter, immense droves are sent to the east annually from this country, and Tennessee, Kentucky, and Ohio. The feeding of the swine, as they pass through the country in the autumn of each year, supplies a market for much of the corn which is produced. Aside from this, there is but little inducement for each one to raise more grain than his own family will consume ; and consequently, there is but little room for enterprise on the part of the agriculturist. His products, when they sell at all, bring but a trivial sum. For instance, corn, the chief product, brings but from 17 to 25 cents per bushel ; oats, 12 1-2 cts. do. ; pork, beef, and venison, $2 to $2 50 neat per 100 lbs. ; and other things in proportion. This pay, too, is frequently in store-goods, on which the merchant, owing to his small amount of custom, charges heavy profits. For foreign luxuries, the agriculturist pays the highest prices,—the expense of transportation from the north—where they are usually purchased by the merchant—to the wild parts of Western Virginia, being 3 or 4 cents per pound : so for bulky articles, as sugar, coffee, &c., the consumer is obliged to pay several cents a pound more than an inhabitant of the older portions of the state. He, however, graduates his wants to his means ; and although he may not have the fine house, equipage, dress, &c., of the wealthy planter, yet he leads a manly life, and breathes the pure air of the hills with the contented spirit of a freeman. Living

> " Far from the maddening crowd's ignoble strife,
> *His* sober wishes never *learn* to stray ;
> Along the cool, sequestered vale of life,
> *He keeps* the noiseless tenor of his way."

The inhabitants of the mountain counties are almost perfectly independent. Many a young man with but a few worldly goods, marries, and, with an axe on one shoulder and a rifle on the other, goes into the recesses of the mountains, where land can be had for almost nothing. In a few days he has a log-house and a small clearing. Visit him some fine day thirty years afterwards, and you will find he has eight or ten children— the usual number here—a hardy, healthy set ; forty or fifty acres cleared, mostly cultivated in corn ; a rude square log bin, built in cob-house fashion, and filled with corn in *the cob*, stands beside his cabin ; near it is a similar structure, in which is a horse ; and scattered about are half a dozen hay-ricks ; an immense drove of hogs, and some cattle, are roaming at large in the adjoining forest. And if it is what is called "*mast year*" —that is, if the forests abound in nuts, acorns, &c.—these animals will be found to be very fat, and display evidence of good living

LIFE IN EASTERN VIRGINIA.
The Home of the Planter.

LIFE IN WESTERN VIRGINIA.
The Home of the Mountaineer.

Enter the dwelling. The lady of the house, and all her children, are attired in home-spun. Her dress is large, of convenient form, and entirely free from the fashionable lacing universal elsewhere. It is confined together with buttons, instead of hooks and eyes. She looks strong and healthy—so do her daughters—and as rosy and blooming as "flowers by the way-side." Her sons, too, are a sturdy-looking set, who soon (if not now) will be enabled to fell a tree or shoot a deer with facility. The house and furniture are exceedingly plain and simple, and, with the exception of what belongs to the cupboard, principally manufactured in the neighborhood. The husband is absent, hunting. At certain seasons of the year, what time he can spare from his little farm he passes in the excitement of the chase, and sells the skins of his game.

Soon he enters with a buck or bear he has shot, (for he is a skilful marksman,) or perhaps some other game. He is fifty years of age, yet in his prime—a stout, athletic man; his countenance is bronzed by exposure, and his frame seems almost of iron; he is robed in a hunting-shirt of picturesque form, made, too, of homespun, and ornamented with variegated fringe; and a pair of moccasins are on his feet. He receives you with a blunt, honest welcome, and as he gives you his hand, his heart goes with it; for he looks upon you as a friend; he has passed his life among the mountains, in the midst of a simple-hearted people, who have but little practical knowledge of the deceit which those living in densely-populated communities, among the competitive avocations of society, are tempted to practice. His wife prepares dinner. A neat white cloth is spread, and soon the table is covered with good things. On it is a plate of hot corn-bread, preserves of various kinds, bacon, venison, and more than probable three varieties of meat. Your host may ask a blessing—thanks to the itinerating system of the Methodists, which has even reached this remote spot—his wife pours you out a "dish of coffee," the great luxury of the country, and frequently used at every meal: it is thickened with cream—not milk—and sweetened with sugar from the maple grove just front of the house. The host bids you help yourself, and, if not squeamish, you "go into it," and enjoy that plain, substantial meal better than you ever did a dinner at Astor's.

Now mount your nag and be off! As you descend the mountain-path faintly discerned before you, and breathe the pure, fresh air of the hills, cast your eyes upon the most impressive of scenes, for Nature is there in all her glory. Far down in the valley, to the right, winds a lovely stream; there hid by the foliage overarching its bright waters—anon it appears in a clearing—again, concealed by a sweep of the mountain you are descending—still beyond, it seems diminished to a silvery thread. To the right and front is a huge mountain, in luxuriant verdure, at places curving far into the plain,—and at those points, and at the summits, bathed in a sea of golden light,—at others, receding, thrown into dark, sombre, forbidding shades. Beyond are mountains piled on mountains, like an uptossed sea of ridges, until they melt away in distance, and imagination fancies others still farther on. High in blue ether float yon clouds of snowy white, and far above them, in majestic flight, sails the bird of the mountain, with an air as wild as free, as the spirit of liberty. How every thing is rejoicing all around! Innumerable songsters are warbling sweetest music; those wild flowers, with scarce the morning dew from off their lips, are opening their bright cheeks to the sun; and even the tiny insects flitting through the air, join in the universal hallelujah! Now fast losing the scene, you are entering the dark, solemn forest, densely matted above with vines, almost excluding the light of day. You are soon at the base of the mountains, and from the copse before you out starts a deer! the graceful animal pricks up its ears, distends its nostrils in fear, and, gathering its slender limbs ready for a spring, then bounds away, over hillocks and through ravines, and is seen no more. The stream, broad and shallow, is wending its way across your road with gentle murmurings,—splash! splash! goes your horse's feet into the water; forty times in ten miles does it cross your road, and in various places for many hundred yards your course is directly through it. There are no bridges upon it: there are comparatively few in Western Virginia.

* * * * * * * * * *

The above picture of a mountaineer, with a sketch of the wild and romantic scenery among which he lives, is a common, though not a universal one; but between him and the wealthy inhabitant of a large village, who lives in the enjoyment of every blessing, are all grades. Many cannot read or write, and many that can, know nothing of geography and other branches. The country is too thinly settled to carry out a system of common schools, although the state makes liberal appropriations for that purpose. The mountaineer who lives not within half a day's travel of a school-house, cannot afford, like the wealthy lowland planter, to hire a private instructor, and pay him a heavy salary.

Among these mountain fastnesses is much latent talent, which requires only an opportunity for its development. Many of the people are of Scotch-Irish descent, and possess the bravery and other noble traits of their ancestry. Almost entirely isolated from the world, fashion, with her iron sway, has not stereotyped manners, modes of thought, and expression; and, therefore, an amusing originality and ingenuity in metaphor is frequently displayed. The educated of this mountain region are often men of high intelligence, fine address, and are possessed of all that which gives zest to social intercourse.

To further illustrate the subject we are upon, the manners and customs of the mountaineers, we will introduce an article—already elsewhere published by us—giving our adventures in one of the wildest counties in the state:

A Religious Encampment in a Forest.

Towards the close of an autumnal day, while travelling through this thinly-settled region, I came up with a substantial looking farmer, leaning on a fence by the road-side. I accompanied him to his house to spend the night. It stood in a field, a quarter of a mile from the road, and was one of the better sort of log-dwellings, inasmuch as it had two stories and two or three small windows. In its rear was a small log structure, about fifteen feet square, the weaving-shop of the family. On entering the house, I found a numerous family, all clothed in substantial garments of their own manufacture. The floor was unadorned by a carpet, and the room devoid of superfluous furniture; yet all that necessity required to make them comfortable. One needs but little experience like this to discover how few are our real wants, how easily most luxuries of dress, equipage, and furniture can be dispensed with. After my arrival, two or three chickens were knocked down in the yard, and ere long supper was ready. It consisted of chickens, bacon, hoe-cake, and buckwheat cakes. Our beverage was milk, which is used at all meals in Virginia, and coffee thickened with cream and sweetened by maple sugar.

Soon as it grew dark, my hostess took down a small candle-mould for three candles, hanging from the wall on a frame-work just in front of the fire-place, in company with a rifle, long strings of dried pumpkins, and other articles of household property. With this, she "run" her lights for the evening. On retiring, I was conducted to the room overhead, to which I ascended by stairs out of doors. My bed-fellow was the county sheriff, a young man of about my age; and as we lay together, a fine field was had for astronomical observations through the chinks of the logs. On my informing him that this was one of the first log dwellings in which I had ever spent a night, he regarded me with astonishment, and proceeded to enlighten me upon life in the backwoods, giving me details I could scarcely credit, but which subsequent experience fully verified. The next morning, after rising, I was looking for the washing apparatus, when he tapped me on the shoulder as a signal to accompany him to a brook just back of the house, in whose pure, crystal waters we performed our morning ablutions, and wiped ourselves dry with a coarse towel.

After breakfast, through the persuasion of the sheriff, who appeared to have taken a sort of fancy to me, I agreed to go across the country by his house. He was on horseback—I on foot. For six miles, our route lay through a pathless forest, on leaving which we passed through " the Court-House," the only village in the county, composed of about a dozen houses, mostly log, and a brick court-house. A mile beyond, my companion pointed to a small log structure as the place where he was initiated into the mysteries of reading and writing. It was what is called, in Virginia, " an old field schoolhouse," an expression, originating in the circumstance that these buildings, in the older portions of the state, are erected upon worn-out lands. Soon after, we came to a Methodist encampment. The roads are here too rude to transport tents, hence the Methodists and Baptists, in this country, build log structures which stand from year to year, and afford much better shelter than tents. This encampment was formed of three continuous lines, each occupying a side of a square, and about one hundred and fifty feet in length. Each row was divided into six or eight cabins, with partitions between. The height of the rows on the inner side of the enclosed area, was about ten feet ; on the outer about six, to which the roof sloped shed-like. The door of each cabin opened on the inner side of the area, and at the back was a log chimney, which came up even with the roof. At the upper extremity of the enclosure formed by these three lines of cabins, was a shed, say thirty by fifty feet, in which was a coarse pulpit and log seats ; a few tall trees were standing in the area, and many stumps scattered here and there. The whole establishment was in the depth of a forest, and wild and rude as can well be imagined. Religious pride would demand a more elegant temple ; but where could the humble more appropriately worship ? We read that

> " The groves were God's first temples. Ere man learned
> To hew the shaft, and lay the architrave,
> And spread the roof above them,—ere he framed
> The lofty vault, to gather and roll back
> The sound of anthems ; in the darkling wood,
> Amid the cool and silence, he knelt down
> And offered to the Mightiest solemn thanks
> And supplication."

In many of these sparsely-inhabited counties, there are no settled clergymen, and rarely do the people hear any other than the Methodist and Baptist preachers. Here is the itinerating system of Wesley exhibited in its full usefulness. The circuits usually are of three weeks duration, in which the clergymen preach about every day : so it rarely happens, in some neighborhoods, when they have public worship, that it is on the Sabbath. Most of these preachers are men of indefatigable energy, and often endure great privations.

After sketching the encampment, I came in a few minutes to the dwelling of the sheriff. Close by it, were about a dozen mountaineers, and several highland lassies, seated around a log corn-bin, twelve feet square, ten high, and open at the top, into which these neighbors of my companion were casting ears of corn, fast as they could husk them. Right merrily did they perform the task. The men were large and hardy, —the damsels plump and rosy, dressed in good, warm, homespun garments, which, instead of being hooked and eyed, were buttoned up behind. The sheriff informed me that he owned about two thousand acres of land around his dwelling, and that its whole value was about one thousand dollars, or fifty cents per acre ! I entered his house, which was of logs, one story in height, about twenty feet square, and divided into two small rooms, without any windows or openings for them, and no place to let in light, except by a door in its front, and one in the rear. I soon partook of a meal, in which we had quite a variety of luxuries, among which was *bear's meat.* A blessing was asked at table by one of the neighbors. After supper, the bottle, as usual at corn-huskings, was circulated. The sheriff learning I was a Washingtonian, with the politeness of one of nature's gentlemen, refrained from urging me to participate. The men drank very moderately. Indeed, in my travels over nearly the whole of Virginia, I have seen far less intemperance than in my similar wanderings at the north. We all drew around the fire, the light of which was the only one we had. Hunting stories, and kindred topics, served to talk down the hours until bed-time. There were in the room two beds. One was occupied by a married couple the other by myself ; but there were no curtains between.

On awaking in the morning, I saw two ladies cooking breakfast in my bed-room, and three gentlemen seated over the fire, watching that interesting operation.

Having completed my toilet, my host, from a spring hard by, dipped a pitcher and poured the water into my hands, for me to wash myself. After breakfast, I bade the sheriff farewell, buckled on my knapsack, and left. He was a generous, warm-hearted man, and on my offering a remuneration, he replied, "you are welcome ; call again when this way."

In the course of two hours, I came to a cabin by the way-side. There being no gate, I sprang over the fence, entered the open door, and was received with a hearty welcome. It was a humble dwelling, the abode of poverty. There was a neatness in the arrangement of the few articles of furniture extremely pleasing. In a corner stood two beds, one hung with curtains, and both spread with coverlets of snowy white, forming a contrast to the dingy log walls, rude furniture, and rough boarded floor of this, the only room of the dwelling. Around a cheerful fire was seated an interesting family group. In one corner, on the hearth, sat the mother, who had given up her chair to me, smoking a pipe. Next to her was a little girl, in a little chair, holding a little kitten. In the opposite corner sat the father, a venerable old man of Herculean stature, robed in a hunting-shirt, and with a countenance as majestic and impressive as a Roman senator. In the centre of the group was a young maiden, about eighteen, modest and retiring, not beautiful, except in that moral beauty virtue gives. She was reading to them from a little book. She was the only one in the family who could read, and she could do so but imperfectly. In that book, which cost perhaps two shillings, was the whole secret of the neatness and happiness found in this lowly cot. That little book was the New Testament !

I conversed with the father. He was, he said, " a poor mountaineer, ignorant of the world." He was, it is true ; but he had the independence of a man—the humility of a Christian. As I left the cottage, the snow-flakes were slowly falling, and I pursued my lonely way through the forest, with buoyant feelings, reflecting upon this beautiful exhibition of the religion of the meek and lowly One. How exquisite are these lines, as applied to a similar scene :

> "Compared with this, how poor Religion's pride,
>   In all the pomp of method and of art,
> When men display to congregations wide
>   Devotion's every grace, except the heart.
> But happy we, in some *cot* far apart,
>   May hear, well pleased, the language of the soul."

LIFE IN EASTERN VIRGINIA.

In the foreground of the engraving illustrating the Home of the Planter, is a colored woman strutting across the yard with a tub of water on her head. Near her is a group of white and black miniature specimens of humanity, playing in great glee. In the middle ground is the mansion of the planter, pleasantly embowered in a grove of locusts. The mansion itself has the chimneys on the outside, a peculiar feature in the domestic architecture of the southern states. Under the shade of the porch sits the planter, with a pail of water by his side, from which, in warm weather, he is accustomed to take frequent draughts. At the door are a gentleman and lady, about making a social visit. On the right are the quarters of the blacks, where is seen the overseer, with some servants. In the distance is shown a river ; the finest plantations being generally on the fertile banks of some calm, flowing stream. This completes the picture, which we trust will prove a familiar one to most of our readers.

It is, perhaps, unnecessary to describe in detail the life of a planter, as it is incidentally illustrated in several places in this volume. The term planter, originally applied in this state to those who cultivated the tobacco-plant, is now an expression commonly used in reference to all agriculturists of the lowlands. This class forms the great bulk of the inhabitants, and from it have arisen most of the distinguished statesmen who have shed such lustre upon the name of Virginia. Settled, as this portion of the state was, by old English cavaliers, their descendants have many of the same traits of character. The introduction of slaves has given them the leisure to cultivate the elegancies of life, to mix much in social intercourse, and to become familiar with all current political topics. From this, too, has arisen much of the hospitality for which the planter is proverbial. Nowhere are the wishes and wants of the stranger guest more regarded, and nowhere is the character of a true gentleman held more sacred. The planter is also noted for his frankness and sincerity. And why should he not be ? He does not engage in the strife and turmoil of trade. He has no business secrets. His better nature has not been shocked, and his feelings blunted, by familiarity with the devices of the business world. Hence, his address is frank and free, and there is often a child-like simplicity and ingenuousness of manner that charms the stranger, and wins his strongest affections. The current of the planter's life runs smooth ; and if possessed of a sufficiency, none can live more independently, more free from the distracting cares which often cut short the days of the man of business, and render his pilgrimage here one constant scene of struggle and perplexity.

- We herewith present a description of the condition of the slaves. It is from the pen of a judge of one of the Virginia courts, and was published in a work a few years since. It is in the form of answers to certain queries made by the author of that work :

"I am not certain that I understand the scope of the first inquiry : 'The laws for the government of the master and the slave in Virginia.' Properly speaking, there are no laws affecting this relation. Both are under the protection of the law to a certain extent. The master would be punished for any mayhem or felony committed on the slave ; but it has been decided that no prosecution will lie against him, even for excessive beating, not amounting to mayhem or felony. It has never been found necessary to enact laws for the government of the master in his treatment of the slave, for reasons that will appear hereafter.

"We have many laws respecting slaves, controlling them in certain particulars. Thus, they are not allowed to keep or carry military weapons—nor to leave home without a written permission—nor to assemble at any meeting-house or other place in *the night*, under pretence of religious worship—nor at any school, for the purpose of being taught to read or write—nor to trade and go at large as freemen—nor to hire themselves out—nor to preach or exhort. Some of the penalties for a violation of these laws are imposed upon the master, for permitting his slave to do certain acts ; in other cases, the slave is liable to be taken before a justice of the peace, and punished by stripes, never exceeding thirty-nine.

"Slaves emancipated by their masters, are directed to leave the state within twelve months from the date of their emancipation.

"These laws, and every other having the appearance of rigor towards the slave, are nearly dead letters upon our statute book, unless during times of excitement, or since the efforts of the abolitionists have reanimated them. I have, until lately, scarcely known an instance in which they have been enforced.

"It is equally rare to witness the trial of a slave for any except very serious crimes. There are many offences committed by them, for which a freeman would be sent to the penitentiary, that are not noticed at all, or punished by a few stripes under the directions of the master.

"When tried for a crime, it is before a court of at least five magistrates, who must be unanimous to convict. They are not entitled to a trial by jury, but it is acknowledged on all hands that this is a benefit, and not a disadvantage. The magistrates are more respectable than common jurors ; and, being generally slave-holders themselves, they feel a certain sympathy with the prisoner, or, at all events, an absence of that prejudice to which common jurors are very subject.

"Slaves may be taught, and many of them are taught, in their owner's family. They are allowed to attend religious worship conducted by white ministers, and to receive from them religious instruction. In point of fact, they go where they please on Sundays, and at all other times when they are not engaged in labor.

"2. 'The rights and duties of slaves,' as a distinct class, are not defined by law. They depend upon usage or custom, which controls the will of the master. Thus, the law does not recognise their right to hold property, but no instance is known of the master's interfering with their little acquisitions ; and it often happens, that they are considerable enough to purchase themselves and family. In such cases I have never known the master to exact from the slave the full price that he might have obtained from others. In the same manner, the quantity and quality of food and clothing, the hours of labor and rest, the holidays, the privileges, &c., of the slave, are regulated by custom, to depart materially from which, would disgrace the master in public opinion.

"3. 'The domestic relations of the master and slave.' On this subject the grossest misrepresentations have been made. It seems to be imagined at the North that our society is divided *horizontally*. All above the line, tyrants—all below it, trembling, crouching slaves. Nothing can be more unlike the real picture. The intercourse between the master and slave is kind, respectful, and approaching to intimacy. It must be recollected, that they have been brought up together, and often form attachments that are never broken. The servants about the house are treated rather as humble friends than otherwise. Those employed differently have less intercourse with the white family; but, when they meet, there is a civil, and often cordial greeting on both sides. The slaves generally look upon their masters and mistresses as their protectors and friends. Born slaves, and familiarized with their condition, they have no wish to change it when left to themselves. When they compare it with that of the poor laboring whites in their own neighborhood, no envy is excited, but an opposite sentiment. The slave of a gentleman, universally considers himself a superior being to ' *poor white folks.*' They take pride in their master's prosperity; identify his interest with their own; frequently assume his name, and even his title, and speak of his farm, his crops, and other possessions, as their own; and well, indeed, may they employ this language, for they know that the greater part of the profits is liberally devoted to their use.

"In their nature the slaves are generally affectionate; and particularly so to the children of the family, which lays the foundation of the attachments I have spoken of, continuing through life. The children are always favorites, and the feeling is reciprocated. It is a great mistake to suppose that the children are permitted to tyrannize over the slaves, young or old; and that they learn in this way domineering habits. Some may, but more frequently there is rather too much familiarity between the white females and children of a family, and the slaves of the same description. The children play together on terms of great equality; and if the white child gives a blow, he is apt to have it returned with interest. At many tables you will find the white children rising from them, with their little hands full of the best of every thing, to carry to their nurses or playmates; and I have often known them to deny themselves for the sake of their favorites. These propensities are encouraged, and every thing like violence or tyranny strictly prohibited. The consequence is, that when the young master (or mistress) is installed into his full rights of property, he finds around him no alien hirelings, ready to quit his service upon the slightest provocation, but attached and faithful friends, known to him from his infancy, and willing to share his fortunes, wherever they may carry him. The connection is more that of the Scottish clansman, than of the English serf in times past; and it influences all their future intercourse. The old gray-headed servants are addressed by almost every member of the white family as uncles and aunts. The others are treated with at least as much respectful familiarity as if they were white laborers, and I should say with more. Fully aware of their standing and consequence, they never hesitate to apply to their masters and mistresses in every difficulty. If they have any want, they expect to be relieved—if they are maltreated, they ask redress at their hands. Seldom or never are appeals of this kind made in vain. Injury to the slave from any quarter, is regarded as an injury to the master. On no subject is a Virginian more sensitive; for he considers himself bound, by every moral obligation, to protect and defend his slave. If he is carried before a justice for any offence, the master accompanies him; if he is arraigned before the courts, the master employs counsel, and does every thing in his power to see that he has justice. In fact, the disposition is to screen the slave by every possible means, even when his guilt is apparent, and I have known this carried to very unjustifiable lengths. In short, as far as my observation has extended, and I have been in free as well as slave states, I do not hesitate to affirm, that the domestic relations of the master and slave are of a more familiar, confidential, and even respectful character, than those of the employer and hireling elsewhere.

"4. ' The usual duration of the labor of the slave,' is from sunrise to sunset, with the exception of about one hour and a half allowed for breakfast, and from 12 to 2 o'clock for dinner. In harvest-time they get out somewhat earlier. But any extraordinary diligence during this period is more than made up by their being allowed, at its termination, a few days to labor for themselves, or for others who have not finished, and from whom they receive wages. The women in this part of the state do very little field-work. They are engaged in spinning, cooking for the out-hands, and taking care of the children. Few women are worth their victuals and clothes. Their labors are very light and profitless. A white laboring woman will do double as much.

"5. ' The liberty usually allowed him, his holidays and amusements, the manner in which they usually pass their evenings and holidays.' Under these heads may be classed various privileges enjoyed by the slave. When he is not at work he is under no restriction or surveillance. He goes where he pleases, seldom taking the trouble to ask for a pass; and if he is on the farm at the appointed hours, no inquiry is made how he has employed the interval. The regular holidays are two at Easter, two at Whitsuntide, and a week at Christmas. These he enjoys by prescription; and others, such as Saturday evenings, by the indulgence of his master. He passes them in any way he pleases. Generally, they are spent in visiting from house to house, and in various amusements. His favorite one, if he can raise a violin, is dancing. But this, unfortunately, is going out of fashion, both with whites and blacks, and no good substitute has been found for it. They, however, assemble at their cabins to laugh, chat, sing, and tell stories, with all imaginable glee. No present care seems to annoy, no anticipated sorrow to deject them, but they surrender themselves fully and entirely to the enjoyment of the passing moments. They know that, under all circumstances, their masters must provide for them. Of course they have no anxiety about their families, or the failure of crops, or the course of the seasons, or the horrors of debt, or any other of the many circumstances which embitter the life of the freeman, and render sad or thoughtful the gayest disposition.

"Other of the slaves, who are more provident, employ a portion of their holidays and evenings in working for themselves. Each head of a family, or married man or woman, has a cabin allotted for his or her accommodation. These cabins are usually made of logs, chinked and plastered, with plank or dirt floors. Some proprietors build them of brick or stone, or framed wood, but I do not believe the slaves generally prefer them. They like the large, open fireplace of the cabin, where a dozen or more can sit round the blazing hearth, filled with as much wood as would supply a patent stove for ten days. Stoves they abominate, and small Rumfordized fireplaces. Near their cabins they have ground allotted for their garden and *patch* of corn. In their gardens they have every vegetable they choose to cultivate, besides raising pumpkins, broom-corn, &c. In their masters' corn-fields. Most of them are permitted to raise a hog, to dispose of as they please; and these hogs are invariably the largest and fattest on the farm. They also raise fowls of every description, and sell them for the most part to their owners, at a fair price. Their allowance of food is never diminished on these accounts. Their hog, their fowls, their vegetables, their brooms, and baskets, and flag-chairs, and many other articles, they are allowed to sell, for the purpose of purchasing Sunday clothes and finery, to show off at meetings and other public occasions. In this way, those who are at all industrious, are enabled to appear as well dressed as any peasantry in the world.

"6. 'The provision made for their food and clothing, for those who are too young or too old to labor.' The slaves always prefer Indian corn-meal to flour. Of this, the old and young, in this part of Virginia, are allowed just as much as they can eat or *destroy*. They have, besides, a certain quantity of bacon given out every week, amounting to about half a pound a day for each laborer or grown person. When they have beef or fish, the allowance of bacon is less; but, as it is the food they love best, they have always a portion of it. Besides this, they have milk and vegetables on most farms in abundance, without touching their own stores. The old and infirm fare like the rest, unless their situation requires coffee, sugar, &c., which are always provided. The young slaves have also their meats, but less in quantity, and they depend more upon bread, milk, and vegetables. To look at them, you would see at once they are well fed. On small farms the slaves fare better than on large ones, there being little difference in the food of the whites and blacks, except in articles of mere luxury. But, on the largest, their usual allowance is that which I have mentioned. They have three meals a day, and it is rare to see them eating what they call dry bread at any one.

"Their allowance of clothing is quite uniform; and consists of a hat, a blanket, two suits of clothes, three shirts or shifts, and two pair of shoes, a year. The winter suit is of strong linsey cloth; the summer, of linen for the men, and striped cotton for the women. The men's cloth is dressed and fulled. The children have linsey and cotton garments, but no shoes or hat, until they are ten or eleven years old, and begin to do something. Their beds are sometimes of feather, generally of straw, and are well furnished; some prefer to lie like the Indians, on their blankets.

"Comparing their situation with respect to food and clothing with our own white laborers, I would say that it is generally preferable. In each case, much depends on the industry and management of the party; but there is this difference, that the slave, however lazy or improvident, is furnished with food and clothing at regular periods, which the white man of the same temperament is unable to procure. When the white man, too, is so old and infirm that he can no longer labor, his situation is truly deplorable, if he has laid up nothing for support. Bt the old and infirm slave is still supported by his master, with the same care and attention as before. He cannot even set him free without providing for his maintenance, for our law makes his estate liable.

"7. 'Their treatment when sick.' Being considered as valuable property, it might naturally be concluded that they would be properly attended to when sick. But better feelings than any connected with their value as property, prompt the white family to pay every attention to the sick slave. If it is deemed at all necessary, a physician is immediately called in. On large farms he is frequently employed by the year; but, if not, he is sent for whenever there is occasion for his services. If the slave is a hireling, our law compels the owner, not the hirer, to pay the physician's fees, so that the latter has every motive of interest to send for a physician, without being liable for the expense. Where there are many slaves together, the proprietor sometimes erects an hospital, provided with nurses and the usual accommodations. In all cases coming under my observation, whatever is necessary for the comfort of the sick is furnished, as far as the master has means. They are frequently visited by the white family, and whatever they wish to have is supplied. Such indulgence, and even tenderness, is extended to them on these occasions, that it sometimes induces the lazy to feign sickness; but I have never known them, in these suspected cases, to be hurried to their work until their deception became manifest, or the report of the physician justified it. It is my decided conviction, that the poor laborers of no country under heaven are better taken care of than the sick slaves in Virginia. There may be, and no doubt are, exceptions to many of these observations; but I speak of their general treatment as I have known it, or heard it reported.

"8. 'Their rewards and punishments.' Of rewards, properly speaking, the slaves have few—of indulgences they have many; but they are not employed as rewards, for all usually partake in them without discrimination. The system of rewards has not, to my knowledge, been fairly tried. Sometimes slaves who have conducted themselves well, or labored diligently, are allowed more time than others to attend to their own affairs, or permitted to trade on their own account, paying some small sum; and they are treated, of course, with greater respect and confidence than the idle and worthless. But I know of no instance in which specific rewards have been offered for specific acts of good conduct. In this respect they are treated much like soldiers and sailors.

"As to their punishments, they are rare, and seldom disproportioned to the offence. Our laws are mild, and make little discrimination between slaves and free whites, except in a few political offences. The punishments inflicted by the master partake of the same character. The moral sense of the community would not tolerate cruelty in a master. I know of nothing that would bring him more surely into disgrace. On a farm where there may be one hundred slaves, there will not, perhaps, be one punished on account of his work during the year, although it is often done in a careless, slovenly manner, and not half as much as a white laborer would do. For insolent and unruly conduct to their overseers, for quarrelling and fighting with each other, for theft and other offences, which would send the white man to the whipping-post or penitentiary, they are punished more frequently, but always with moderation. Very often they escape altogether, when the white man would certainly be punished. I have lived in different parts of Virginia for more than 30 years, since my attention has been directed to such subjects; and I do not recollect half a dozen instances in which I ever saw a grown slave stripped and whipped. Such a spectacle is almost as rare as to see a similar punishment inflicted on a white man. When it is considered that, except for the highest grade of crimes, the punishment of the slave is left pretty much (practically) to his master's discretion, I am persuaded it will be found that they are in this respect in no worse condition than laborers elsewhere. No other punishment is inflicted except stripes or blows. They are not imprisoned, or placed upon short allowance, or condemned to any cruel or unusual punishments from which white persons are exempted.

"The worst feature in our society, and the most revolting, is the purchase and sale of slaves; and it is this which renders their situations precarious and uncomfortable, and occasions them more uneasiness than all other causes combined. On this subject I will submit a few observations before I close this letter. So far as the traffic is confined to the neighborhood, it is of little consequence, and is often done for the accommodation of the slave. It breaks no ties of kindred, and occasions only a momentary pang, by transferring the slave from the master who, perhaps, is no longer able to keep him, to one as good, who is able, or who purchases because he owns his wife or child, &c. It is the sale to negro-buyers by profession, which is in general so odious to the slave, although there are instances in which these artful men prevail with them to apply to their owners to be sold. Such sales, except in the rare instance just alluded to, are never voluntarily made of slaves whose conduct and character are good. Masters will not part with their slaves but from sheer necessity, or for flagrant delinquencies, which in other countries would be punished by deportation at least. Thousands retain them when they know full well that their pecuniary condition would be greatly improved by selling, or even giving them away. It is the last property the master can be induced to part with. Nothing but the dread of a jail will prevail with him. Negro-traders, although there are many among us, are universally despised by the master, and detested by the body of the slaves. Their trade is supported by the misfortunes of the master, and the crimes or misconduct of the slave, and not by the will of either party, except in a few instances. Sometimes the slave, after committing a theft or other crime, will abscond, for fear of detection; or will be enticed away from his master's service by holding out to him false hopes; and perhaps the negro-buyer himself is the decoy. If caught, he is generally sold, for the sake of the example to other slaves. From these sources the negro-buyers are supplied; but it does not happen, in one case out of a thousand, that the master willingly sells an honest, faithful slave. The man doing so would be looked upon as a sordid, inhuman wretch; and be shunned by his neighbors and countrymen of respectable standing.

"I believe, if any plan could be fallen upon to remove our slaves to a place where they would be willing to go, and where their condition would be probably improved, that many, very many masters would be ready to manumit them. An opinion is entertained by increasing numbers, that slave labor is too expensive to be continued in a grain-growing state, if its place can be supplied by freemen. In other words, that the free laborer would cost less, and work harder, than the slave. But the slaves themselves are unwilling to go to Liberia, and very few would accept their freedom on that condition. Some, already emancipated, remain in the state, incurring the constant risk of being sold as slaves. To send them to any part of our own country without worldly knowledge or capital, is deemed by most masters false humanity; and to retain them here in the condition of free negroes is impossible.

"Until some plan can be suggested to remove these difficulties, under the guidance and direction of the constituted authorities, we are averse to all agitation of the subject. We know it will be attended with danger to one class, and will increase the burdens and privations of the other. Hence our indignation at the movements of the Northern abolitionists, who are meddling with a subject they know nothing about. Let them come among us, and see the actual condition of the slaves, as well as of the whites, and I am persuaded that all whose intentions are really good, would, on their return, advise their deluded co-operators to desist from agitation."

STATISTICS AND CENSUS OF THE COUNTIES OF VIRGINIA.

THE subjoined statistical table of the various counties of Virginia, is from the U. S. statistics and census of 1840. It presents a view of the relative agricultural, manufacturing, and mercantile wealth of the various counties.

Explanation of the Table.—The columns of neat cattle, sheep, and swine, show the number of *thousands* of those animals. The columns of wheat, rye, Indian corn, oats, and potatoes, give the number of *thousand bushels* annually produced. The columns of tobacco and cotton, give the number of *thousand pounds* produced. The columns of capital in stores, and in manufactures, give the number of *thousand dollars* thus invested. The column of scholars in *schools and academies*, as well as those of the slaves and population, are carried out in full.

It will be observed there are some blanks. These are left so, either from the fact that there are no statistics of sufficient amount for record, or that the marshals employed to take them, made no returns to the general government.

Counties.	Neat cattle.	Sheep.	Swine.	Wheat.	Rye.	Indian corn.	Oats.	Potatoes.	Tobacco.	Cotton.	Capital in stores.	Cap. in manufactories.	Scholars in schools.	Slaves.	Population.
Accomac . .	14	10	27	14		643	453	113			125	73	751	4,630	17,096
Albemarle .	15	21	35	327	117	712	216	29	2409		302	261	786	13,809	22,924
Alleghany .	3	4	5	25	9	71	59	9	42		2	29	88	547	2,749
Amelia . .	6	8	13	51		245	106	58	1871	6	42	21	206	7,023	10,320
Amherst . .	8	6	17	113	11	381	145		2106	2	78	112	674	5,577	12,576
Augusta . .	21	20	34	324	92	384	245	48			117	138	693	4,145	19,628
Bath . . .	9	11	8	31	27	118	79	32			32	40	196	347	4,300
Bedford . .	16	15	31	206	7	537		22	3442		70	11	197	8,864	20,203
Berkley . .	9	13	25	287	38	391	136				123	356	727	1,919	10,972
Botetourt . .	9	13	21	197	22	299	185		708		152	23		2,925	11,679
Braxton . .	3	3	6	9		67	21		4		11	21		064	2,575
Brooke . .	5	34	11	140	5	135	144	63			83	450	746	091	7,948
Brunswick .	11	6	19	27		329	116		2141	13	56	25	282	8,805	14,346
Buckingham .	12	15	22	169	1	439	227	21	2453	11	191	226	656	10,014	18,786
Cabell . . .	9	10	20	39	½	379	96	17	6		67	32	339	567	8,163
Campbell . .	11	14	21	178		482	228	23	3257	4	1690	398	585	1,045	21,030
Caroline . .	10	9	19	81	13	576	120	19	774	20	132	5	589	9,314	17,813
Charles City	2	2	6	36		118	45	4		2	16	11	140	2,433	4,774
Charlotte . .	10	15	22	65		509	247	15	4181	19	134	44	585	9,260	14,595
Chesterfield .	7	7	17	34		285	156	10	680	6	20	935	420	6,781	17,148
Clarke . .	6	8	15	258	17	267	91	20				60	281	3,325	6,353
Culpeper .	11	15	20	122	14	390	128	21	29		126	78	769	6,069	11,393
Cumberland .	6	10	10	61		247	122		2896	23	163	107	263	6,781	10,399
Dinwiddie .	10	8	20	37		284	137	18	2219	71	1921	781	894	9,947	22,558
Elizabeth City	2	1	5	19		80	14	11		¼	46	23	274	1,708	3,706
Essex . . .	7	7	13	74	¼	419	40	15	4	15	140	53	378	6,756	11,309
Fairfax . .	13	6	10	27	6	158	67	8	13				265	3,453	9,370
Floyd . . .	6	8	13	24	13	73	77	20	18		11	4	160	321	4,453
Fauquier .	26	35	37	362	35	670	307	57	55		381	126	1521	10,708	21,897
Fluvanna . .	5	6	9	62		182	71	8	1279		126	97	418	4,146	8,812
Franklin . .	12	12	32	97	7	430	184	18	2508	3	119	74	367		15,832
Frederick . .	7	13	13	173	31	300	135	37			237	226	274	2,302	14,242
Fayette . .	4	5	7	11	4	105	64	15			20	30		133	3,924
Giles . . .	7	10	13	45	35	163	69	17	13		34	33	223	574	5,307
Gloucester .	8	5	14	56		307	62	13	8		87	28	314	5,791	10,715
Goochland .	6	5	11	80		259	170	10	4501	5	80	2	139	5,500	9,760
Grayson .	14	18	22	28	17	219	143	34			40	5	252	492	9,087
Greene . .	3	3	7	40	13	124	33	8	490	1	21	24	372	1,740	4,232
Greenbrier .	14	19	12	69	43	207	198	32			112	69	231	1,214	8,695
Greensville .	5	4	16	9		230	93	11	346	573	39	27	200	4,102	6,366
Halifax . .	14	17	31	78		598	281	16	6209	22	171	209	809	14,216	25,936
Hampshire .	15	27	18	179	52	471	174	71			158	63	577	1,403	12,295
Hanover . .	10	9	14	48	18	350	177	26	615	23	20	36	417	8,394	14,968
Hardy . . .	24	15	13	87	18	411	41	32			69	75	218	1,131	7,622
Harrison . .	5	3	33	136	7	421	226	62	23		99	131	436	693	17,699
Henrico . .	5	2	12	39	3	248	138	12	33	1	5340	1884	1862	13,237	33,076
Henry . . .	6	5	16	40		206	74	12	1623	3	33	14	466	2,852	7,335
Isle of Wight	6	½	23	4		291	29	77		31	67	36	397	3,786	9,972
Jackson . .	5	3	11	28		117	40	5	5		16	2	153	87	4,890
James City .	3	1	5	17		86	35	3	8	6	21	6	129	1,947	3,779
Jefferson . .	12	67	72	517	43	99	72	151			320	344	737	4,157	14,082
Kanawha . .	7	4	8	14		203	23	8			117	50	408	2,560	13,567
King and Queen	8	3			3	343	36	14	8	42	21	60	548	5,937	10,862
King George .	5	5	7	38	4	254	37	6	23	4	21		189	3,382	5,927
King William	6	5	13	59	6	350	45	17	11	56	54	51	349	5,780	9,258
Lancaster .	3	2	8	26			44	7		10	30	2	140	2,478	4,628
Lee	10	10	34	37	7	446	103	23	23		17	31	138	580	8,441
Lewis . . .	12	15	20	47	5	253	80	24	12		59	31	219	124	8,151
Logan . . .	5	2	10	7		871	28	11	9		28		370	150	4,309

21

Counties.	Neat cattle.	Sheep.	Swine.	Wheat.	Rye.	Indian corn.	Oats.	Potatoes.	Tobacco.	Cotton.	Capital in stores.	Cap. in manufactories.	Scholars in schools.	Slaves.	Population.
Loudon	27	32	39	573	82	892	225	53	1		275	196	1274	5,273	20,431
Louisa	11	13	20	221	1		158	15	2431		111	70	591	9,010	15,433
Lunenburg	7	9	16	27		275	138	10	2640	19	111		230	6,707	11,055
Madison	7	9	13	101	24	272	33	13	149	9	48	133	397	4,308	8,107
Mason	8	9	17	70	2	299		20	9		33	8	241	808	6,777
Marshall	5	7	9	83	2	146	103	30			19	13	70	46	6,937
Matthews	4	2	9	9		171	54	17		25	34	35	349	3,309	7,442
Mecklenburg	14	14	32	77		472	224	25	4124	19	303	50	520	11,915	20,724
Mercer	3	4	5	13	5	56	28	8	3		4	65	24	98	2,233
Middlesex	4	3	7	17	1	122	21	8	1	3	26	29	202	2,209	4,392
Monongalia	16	29	20	166	6	381	320	62	15		66	43	653	260	17,368
Monroe	12	20	14	68	39	209	124	23			229	65	179	868	8,422
Montgomery	10	13	17	106	21	209	114	18	241		126	59	442	1,473	7,405
Morgan	3	4	6	38	14	63	42	17	1		44	9	347	134	4,253
Nansemond	7	4	23	5		316	34	80		154	157	70	424	4,530	10,795
New Kent	4	3	9	22		140	51	8		4	21		287	3,385	6,230
Nicholas	4	5	5	4	3	56	38	11	4		40	7	77	72	2,515
Norfolk	8	3	19	3		260	35	35		1	1985	250	1085	7,845	21,092
Northampton	4	5	12	½		297	197	52		6	39	41	186	3,620	7,715
Northumberl'nd	6	4	12	28		179	55	20		12	56	10	180	3,243	7,924
Nottoway	6	7	10	42		249	70	8	2213	21	55	49	195	7,071	9,719
Nelson	8	8	20	128	36	327	91	19	2229	1	258	50	345	5,967	12,287
Ohio	4	27	10	125	2	254	146	43			465	520	1089	212	13,357
Orange	7	11	15	98	8	395	92	21	416	2	95	115	348	5,364	9,125
Page	5	5	13	105	30	156	29	15	7		99	87	257	781	6,194
Patrick	7	6	24	28	3	223	69	13	618		21	14	120	1,842	8,032
Pendleton	14	21	13	66	36	130	51	36			63	51	235	462	6,940
Pittsylvania	19	19	42	142	6	679	334	24	6439	18	200	222	1012	11,588	26,398
Pocahontas	7	10	5	18	21	41	50	21			12	28	133	219	2,922
Powhatan	5	7	9	54		189	138	7	1850		28	43	219	5,129	7,924
Preston	7	12	9	3	18	43	130	35	4		109	45		91	6,866
Prince Edward	8	12	15	57		304	129	13	3107	11	124	204	517	8,576	14,069
Princess Anne	11	7	21	7		299	85	37		1	2	10	238	3,087	7,285
Prince William	7	8	9	47	4	180	105	6	5		66	22	118	2,767	8,144
Prince George	3	3	6	31		177	35	6	115	23	5	12	117	4,004	7,175
Pulaski	7	10	12	46	17	144	80	15			54	32	136	954	3,739
Randolph	10	14	9	27	7	151	87	30	7		65	27	108	216	6,208
Rappahannock	9	13	18	180		310	94	24	5		93	35	502	3,663	9,257
Roanoke	5	6	11	141	14	182	98	6	599		47	40	196	1,553	5,449
Rockbridge	13	20	26	264	70	505	249	36	294		169	131	883	3,510	14,284
Rockingham	20	24	39	375	91	470	248	41	37		304	174	844	1,899	17,344
Russell	14	15	27	59	8	294	142	21			29	29	41	700	7,878
Scott	10	14	24	40	2	294	112	17	7		31	22	206	344	7,303
Shenandoah	11	12	16	164	32	298	105	35			186	178	355	1,033	11,618
Smythe	9	11	16	52	7	221	178	34			29	8	298	838	6,522
Southampton	10	8	44	10	3	554	71	88	25	851	56	6	449	6,555	14,525
Spottsylvania	8	8	12	58		303	102	10	353	4	395	153	640	7,590	15,161
Stafford	5	5	9	31	4	212	68	12	34	760	18	2	195	3,596	8,454
Surrey	4	4	13	9		185	36	34	5	64	47	7	186	2,853	6,480
Sussex	9	8	24	19		405	104		176	477	36	6	363	6,384	11,229
Tazewell	10	11	15	34	13	150	126	16		45	41	11		786	6,290
Tyler	6	12	13	53	2	223	58	35	1		29	42	416	85	6,954
Warwick	2	1	4	11		46	9	2		1	63	218	52	831	1,456
Warren	5	7	13	148	17	219	58	16			83	115	234	1,434	5,627
Washington	14	19	32	107	8	397	296	60			304	43	551	2,058	13,001
Westmoreland	5	4	6	60	1	244	28	7	1	5	67	10	153	3,590	8,019
Wood	8	14	12	71		204	85	22	87		99	17	626	624	7,923
Wythe	14	18	23	86	47	234	152	38			173	72	309	1,618	9,375
York													170		4,720

ACCOMAC COUNTY.

This is the northernmost of the two counties forming the "eastern shore of Virginia," which is cut off from the rest of the state by Chesapeake Bay. Accomac was formed from Northampton co., in 1672. The term *Accawmacke*—as it was anciently spelt—is derived from a tribe of Indians who once inhabited this region. It is about 48 miles long, and 10 wide; its surface is level, and the soil, though generally light, is in many parts fertile. It produces well, wheat, corn, cotton, oats, &c., and an abundance of table vegetables. Pop. 1830, 19,656; 1840, whites 9,518, slaves 4,630, free colored 2,848; total 17,096.

Accomac C. H., or Drummondstown, in the heart of the county, 212 miles E. of Richmond, contains about 40 dwellings. Horntown, Modest-town, and Pungoteague, are small villages.

Upon the Atlantic coast are numerous islands, stretching along the whole length of the "eastern shore." The two northernmost are Chincoteague and Assateague. The first is about 8 miles long, and contains nearly a hundred families. About one-third of their bread-corn is raised upon the island; the sea and wrecks furnish the remainder of their subsistence. Assateague, though many times larger, has but few inhabitants, and is unfit for the cultivation of corn. Its rich bent-growing lands are subject to inundation from the spring tides. The scenery around Chincoteague is in many places inexpressibly sublime, and the view of the ocean and the surrounding cluster of islands, from the elevated sand-hills of Assateague, is enchanting. The Farmer's Register, from which this article is abridged, says that the Hebrides of Scotland, so profitable to their proprietors, do not possess a hundredth part of the advantages of these Atlantic islands for all the purposes of comfortable living and extensive stock-raising; yet, for want of enterprise, they are neglected. These islands are flat, sandy, and soft, producing abundance of excellent grass.

Some thirty years since, an immense number of wild horses were raised upon these islands, with no other care than to brand and castrate the colts. Their winter subsistence was supplied abundantly by nature. The tall, heavy rich grass of the flatlands affording them green food nearly the whole of the winter, the tops of which alone were killed by the frosts, mild as usual so near the ocean. It was customary to have annual gatherings in June, to drive these wild horses into pens, where they were seized by islanders accustomed to such adventures, who pushed fearlessly in among them. On being broken, more docile and tractable animals could not be found. The horses have been gradually diminishing, until on one island they are nearly extinct, and the rustic splendor, the crowds, and the wild festivity of the Assateague *horse-pennings*, are among the things that were.

The multitudes of both sexes that formerly attended these occasions of festal mirth were astonishing. The adjoining islands were literally emptied of their simple and frolic-loving inhabitants, and the peninsula itself contributed to swell the crowd. For fifty miles above and below the point of meeting, all the beauty and fashion of a certain order of the female population, who had funds or favorites to command a passage, were sure to be there. All who loved wild adventure, whose hearts danced at the prospect of a distant water excursion, and a scene of no ordinary revel, where the ocean rolled his billows almost to their feet; all who had a new gown to show, or a pretty face to exhibit, who could dance well or sing; belles that sighed for beaux, or beaux that wanted sweethearts ; all who loved to kiss or be kissed, to caress or be caressed ; all, in short, whose hearts delighted in romance without knowing its name, hurried away to this anxiously-expected scene of extravagant jollity, on the narrow thread of beach that the ocean seemed every moment to usurp. The imagination can scarcely conceive the extravagant enthusiasm with which this exciting sport was anticipated and enjoyed. It was a frantic carnival, without its debauchery. The young of both sexes had their imaginations inflamed by the poetical narratives of their mothers and maiden aunts, who in their more juvenile days were wont to grace those sylvan fetes of the mad flight of wild horses careering away along a narrow, naked, level sand-beach, at the top of their speed, with manes and tails waving in the wind, before a company of mounted men upon the fleetest steeds, shouting and hallooing in the wildest notes of triumph, and forcing the animals into the angular pen of pine logs prepared to enclose them. And then the deafening peals of loud huzzas from the thousand half-frenzied spectators, crowding into a solid mass around the enclosure, to behold the beautiful wild horse in all his native vigor, subdued by man, panting in the toils, and furious with heat, rage, and fright; or hear the clamorous triumphs of the adventurous riders, each of whom had performed more than one miracle of equestrian skill on that day of glorious daring ; and the less discordant neighing of colts that had lost their mothers, and mothers that had lost their colts, in the *mêlée* of the sweeping drive, with the maddened snorts and whinnying of the whole gang—all, all together formed a scene of unrivalled noise, uproar, and excitement, which few can imagine who had not witnessed it, and none can adequately describe.

But the play of spirits ended not here. The booths were soon filled, and loads of substantial provision were opened, and fish and water-fowl, secured for the occasion, were fried and barbecued by hundreds, for appetites whetted to marvellous keenness by early rising, a scanty breakfast, exercise, and sea air. The runlets of water, and the jugs of more exhilarating liquor, were lightened of their burdens. Then softer joys succeeded ; and music and dance, and love and courtship, held their undisputed empire until deep in the night, when all sought shelter and repose on board of their boats, moored by the shore, or among their island friends, who gladly entertained them with characteristic hospitality. Many a winter's evening tale did the incidents of those merry-making occasions supply, and many a peaceful young bosom, of retired rural beauty, was assailed with other emotions than the rough sports of an Assateague horse-penning inspired ; and from one anniversary of this half-savage festivity to another, all was talk of the joy and transports of the past, and anticipations of the future.

ALBEMARLE.

ALBEMARLE was formed, in 1744, from Goochland. Its length, from sw. to NE., is 35 miles, and its mean width 20 miles. The northern part is drained by the Rivanna and its branches ; the southern by the Hardware and its branches. The surface is generally hilly or mountainous, the scenery picturesque, and much of the soil highly productive in corn and tobacco. Pop. 1830, 22,618 ; 1840, whites 10,512, slaves 13,809 ; total 22,924.

Scottsville is on the N. bank of the James River canal, 20 miles from Charlottesville, and 79 from Richmond. It is the largest and most flourishing village on the canal, between Richmond and Lynchburg, and does a heavy business; it contains 1 Presbyterian, 1 Methodist, and 1 Reformed Baptist church, and about 160 houses.

Charlottesville, the county seat, is 121 miles from Washington City, and 85 northwesterly from Richmond. It is beautifully situated in a fertile and well-watered valley, on the right bank of the Rivanna River. It contains many mercantile and mechanical estab-

UNIVERSITY OF VIRGINIA, AT CHARLOTTESVILLE.

lishments, and has greatly improved within the last few years. The religious societies are Episcopal, Presbyterian, Baptist, and Methodist. The population is not far from 2000 : much of the society of the town and county is highly refined. Albemarle has given birth to several eminent men: among whom may be mentioned Jefferson, the late Gov. Gilmer, Dr. Gilmer, author of "Sketches and Essays of Public Characters," Meriwether Lewis, and others.

The UNIVERSITY OF VIRGINIA is one mile west of Charlottesville, and although of a deservedly high reputation, it is an institution of recent origin. The legislature of the state, at the session of. 1817–18, adopted measures for establishing the university, which, however, did not go into operation until 1825. The institution was erected and endowed by the state ; and it owes its origin and peculiar organization to Mr. Jefferson. It has a fine collection of buildings, consisting of four parallel ranges about 600 feet in length, and 200 feet apart, suited to the accommodation of 9 professorships, and upwards of 200 students ; which, together with the real estate, cost over $300,000. It possesses valuable libraries, amounting to 16,000 vols., and is amply provided with philosophical and chemical apparatus, together with a fine cabinet of minerals and fossils, and an anatomical and miscellaneous museum. The observatory, a short distance from the university, is furnished with the requisite astronomical instruments. "The plan of the university differs materially from that of other institutions in the Union. The students are not divided into four classes, with a course of studies embracing four years ; but the different branches are styled *schools*, and the student is at liberty to attend which he pleases, and *graduate* in each when prepared. In order to attain the title of "Master of Arts of the University of Virginia," the student must graduate in the several schools of mathematics, ancient languages, moral philosophy, natural philosophy, chemistry, and in some two of the modern languages. The chairman of the faculty is annually chosen from the faculty, by the board of visitors. This board is appointed by the governor and council every four years, and chooses its own rector. This institution is, in every respect, organized and justly regarded as an university of the first class. The number of students, including the law and medical departments, is not far from 200."

The British and German prisoners taken at Saratoga, in the revolution, and known as the "*Convention troops*," were sent to Charlottesville in the beginning of the year 1779. On their first arrival a momentary embarrassment was felt for the want of necessary accommodations. A British officer by the name of Anbury, whose travels have been published, was among the prisoners. On this point he says :

But on our arrival at Charlottesville, no pen can describe the scene of misery and confusion that ensued ; the officers of the first and second brigades were in the town, and our arrival added to their distress ; this famous place we had heard so much of, consisted only of a court-house, one tavern, and about a dozen houses; all of which were crowded with officers,—those of our brigade, therefore, were obliged to ride about the country, and entreat the inhabitants to take us in. As to the men, the situation was truly horrible, after the hard shifts they had experienced in their march from the Potomack; they were, instead of comfortable barracks, conducted into a wood, where a few log huts were just begun to be built, the most part not covered over, and all of them full of snow; these the men were obliged to clear out, and cover over to secure themselves from the inclemency of the weather, as quick as they could, and in the course of two or three days, rendered them a habitable, but by no means a comfortable retirement. What added greatly to the distresses of the men, was the want of provisions, as none had as yet arrived for the troops, and for six days they subsisted on the meal of indian corn made into cakes. The person who had the management of every thing, informed us that we were not expected till spring. Never was a country so destitute of every comfort; provisions were not to be purchased for ten days: the officers subsisted upon salt pork and indian corn made into cakes; not a drop of any kind of spirit, what little there had been, was already consumed by the first and second brigades; many officers, to comfort themselves, put red pepper into water, to drink by way of cordial.

Upon a representation of our situation, by Brigadier-General Hamilton, to Colonel Bland, who commanded the American troops, he promised to render the situation of the men as comfortable as possible, and with all expedition. As to the officers, upon signing a parole, they might go to Richmond, and other adjacent towns, to procure themselves quarters; accordingly, a parole was signed, which allowed a circuit of near one hundred miles. And after the officers had drawn lots, as three were to remain in the barracks with the men, or at Charlottesville, the principal part of them set off for Richmond, many of them are at plantations, twenty or thirty miles from the barracks. I am quartered with Major Master and four other officers of our regiment, about twenty miles from the barracks; the owner has given up his house, and gone to reside at his overseer's, and for the use of his house, we pay him two guineas a week. On the arrival of the troops at Charlottesville, the officers, what with vexation, and to keep out the cold, drank rather freely of an abominable liquor, called peach brandy, which, if drunk to excess, the fumes raise an absolute delirium, and in their cups, several were guilty of deeds that would admit of no apology; the inhabitants must have actually thought us mad, for in the course of three or four days, there were no less than six or seven duels fought.

The Baroness de Riedesel was also with the convention troops. This gifted and heroic lady, also says, in her memoirs :

At first they suffered many privations; they were billeted in block-houses without windows or doors, and but poorly defended from the cold. But they went diligently to work to construct better dwellings, and in a short time the place assumed the appearance of a neat little town. In the rear of each house they had trim gardens, and enclosed places for poultry. Afterwards, when the old provisions were consumed, they received fresh meat, and flour to make bread; and as this latter was of better quality, they could even make cakes and pies. They wanted nothing but money, of which the English sent but little; and as it was difficult to purchase any thing on credit, the soldiers were in many perplexities on that account.

Mr. Jefferson, who then resided in the vicinity, did his utmost to render the situation of the troops and officers as pleasant as possible. To the latter, he offered the hospitalities of his mansion, threw open his library for their inspection, and contributed, by neighborly intercourse and attention, to render them happy. His efforts in their behalf called forth the strongest expressions of gratitude and esteem. These troops remained here until October, 1780, when the state being invaded by Leslie, the public safety demanded the removal of the British portion of them to Fort Frederick, in Maryland. The Germans, however, continued longer.

In May, 1781, when Cornwallis invaded Virginia, the legislature adjourned from Richmond to Charlottesville, as a place of greater safety. In June, the celebrated partisan officer, Tarleton, was detached to Charlottesville, with 180 cavalry of his legion, and 70 mounted infantry, with directions to surprise the General Assembly, seize the person of Jefferson, then the governor, and to do other mischief. He was then to join Simcoe, who had been detached to the Point of Fork, in Fluvanna county. The subjoined details of this event, are from Tucker's Life of Jefferson :

A gentleman who was in the neighborhood of the British army, and who suspected Tarleton's object, was able, by means of a fleet horse, and a nearer road, to give two hours notice of his approach.* As it was, all the members of the Assembly, except

---

* Another incident contributed to defeat Colonel Tarleton's purpose. The following

seven, effected their escape, and reassembled on the 7th of June, at Staunton, about forty miles west of Charlottesville. Tarleton, hearing that there were many gentlemen of the lower country then at the houses of Dr. Walker, and Mr. John Walker, which lay near his route, for a moment lost sight of his principal object, and resolved to make them prisoners. He accordingly divided his force, and sent a part to Mr. John Walker's, while he himself stopped at the house of Dr. Walker. Several gentlemen were here made captives.

When Tarleton approached within ten miles of Charlottesville, he detached a party of horse, under captain M'Leod, to Monticello, to seize Mr. Jefferson. But he had, about sunrise, received the intelligence of Tarleton's approach. Several members of the legislature, including the speakers of both houses, were then his guests, and they hastened to Charlottesville, to adjourn the legislature. Mrs. Jefferson and her three children hurried off in a carriage to Colonel Edward Carter's, about six miles to the south. Mr. Jefferson followed afterwards on horseback, and had not left his house ten minutes before the British entered it. His property, books, and papers, were all respected, with the exception of the waste which was committed in his cellars, by a few of the men, without the knowledge of the commanding officer. Tarleton entered Charlottesville on the 4th of June, four days after Mr. Jefferson's term of office expired. He, on the next day, rejoined Lord Cornwallis, who had established his head-quarters at Elk Hill, a plantation near the Point of Fork, belonging to Mr. Jefferson. Here every sort of wanton mischief was perpetrated. Besides making a free use of the cattle, and carrying off all the horses fit for service, as was to be expected, the throats of the young horses were cut, the growing crops of corn and tobacco were destroyed; those of the preceding year, together with the barns which contained them, and all the fences on the plantation were burnt. Other plantations shared a similar fate, though not to the same extent. Thirty thousand slaves were taken from Virginia by the British in these invasions, of whom twenty-seven thousand were computed to have died of the small-pox, or camp fever. The whole amount of property carried off, and destroyed, during the six months preceding Cornwallis's surrender, has been estimated at £3,000,000 sterling.

Monticello,* the seat of Thomas Jefferson, is three miles southeast of Charlottesville. The annexed glowing description, is from Wirt's Eulogy upon Adams and Jefferson:

The Mansion House, at Monticello, was built and furnished in the days of his prosperity. In its dimensions, its architecture, its arrangements and ornaments, it is such a one as became the character and fortune of the man. It stands upon an elliptic plain, formed by cutting down the apex of a mountain, and, to the west, stretching away to the north and the south, it commands a view of the Blue Ridge for a hundred and fifty miles, and brings under the eye one of the boldest and most beautiful horizons in the world; while on the east, it presents an extent of prospect bounded only by the spherical form of the earth, in which nature seems to sleep in eternal repose, as if to form one of her finest contrasts with the rude and rolling grandeur of the west. In the wide prospect, and scattered to the north and south, are several detached mountains, which contribute to animate and diversify this enchanting landscape; and among them, to the south Willis's mountain, which is so interestingly depicted in his Notes. From this summit, the philosopher was wont to enjoy that spectacle, among the sublimest of Nature's operations, the looming of the distant mountains; and to watch the motions of the planets, and the greater revolution of the celestial sphere. From this summit, too, the patriot could look down with uninterrupted vision, upon the wide expanse of the world around, for which he considered himself born; and upward to the open and vaulted heavens, which he seemed to approach, as if to keep him continually in mind of his high responsibility. It is indeed a prospect in which you see and feel, at once, that nothing mean or little could live. It is a scene fit to nourish those great and high-souled principles which formed the elements of his character, and was a most noble and appropriate post for such a sentinel, over the rights and liberties of men.

Approaching the house on the east, the visiter instinctively paused to cast around one thrilling glance at this magnificent panorama: and then passed to the vestibule, where, if he had not been previously

---

facts are stated on the authority of a gentleman who received them from Dr. Walker himself: On Tarleton's arrival at his house, he had ordered breakfast to be prepared for the colonel and the officers; but the operations of the cook appearing to be unusually tardy, and his guest manifesting great impatience, he went to the kitchen himself to inquire the cause of the delay; and was there told by the cook that he was then engaged in preparing *the third breakfast*, the two first having been taken from him by some of Colonel Tarleton's men; on which the doctor told his guest, that if he wished for breakfast, he must place a guard of soldiers to protect the cook, which was accordingly done. The time that was thus lost, it appeared, on comparing notes afterwards, saved the delegates from capture.

* Monticello, in Italian, signifies "*Little Mountain.*"

informed, he would immediately perceive that he was entering the house of no common man. In the spacious and lofty hall which opens before him, he marks no tawdry and unmeaning ornaments: but before, on the right, on the left, all around, the eye is struck and gratified by objects of science and taste, so classed and arranged, as to produce their finest effect. On one side, specimens of sculpture set out in such order as to exhibit, at a coup d'œil, the historical progress of that art, from the first rude attempts of the aborigines of our country, up to that exquisite and finished bust of the great patriot himself, from the master hand of Carracci. On the other side the visiter sees displayed a vast collection of specimens of the Indian art, their paintings, weapons, ornaments, and manufactures; on another an array of the fossil productions of our country, mineral and animal; the polished remains of those colossal monsters that once trod our forests, and are no more; and a variegated display of the branching honors of those "monarchs of the waste," that still people the wilds of the American continent.

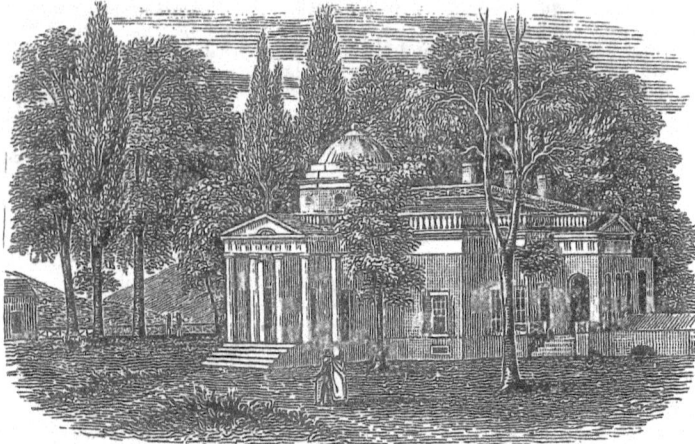

Monticello, the seat of Thomas Jefferson.

From this hall he was ushered into a noble saloon, from which the glorious landscape of the west again bursts upon his view; and which, within, is hung thick around with the finest productions of the pencil—historical paintings of the most striking subjects, from all countries, and all ages; the portraits of distinguished men and patriots, both of Europe and America, and medallions, and engravings in endless profusion.

While the visiter was yet lost in the contemplation of these treasures of the arts and sciences, he was startled by the approach of a strong and sprightly step, and turning with instinctive reverence to the door of entrance, he was met by the tall, and animated, and stately figure of the patriot himself—his countenance beaming with intelligence and benignity, and his outstretched hand, with its strong and cordial pressure, confirming the courteous welcome of his lips. And then came the charm of manner and conversation that passes all description—so cheerful—so unassuming—so free, and easy, and frank, and kind, and gay,—that even the young and overawed, and embarrassed visiter forgets his fears, and felt himself by the side of an old and familiar friend.

The subjoined memoir of the author of the Declaration of American Independence is abridged principally from the American Portrait-Gallery.

THOMAS JEFFERSON was born at Shadwell, in this county, April 2d, 1743. His ancestors were among the early settlers of Virginia, and his father, Peter Jefferson, was an influential public man, who, at his death, left his son an ample fortune. Jefferson passed through his collegiate course at William and Mary, with distinction, and became a student of law under the celebrated George Wythe. When of age, he was admitted to the bar, and was soon elected a representative from Albemarle to the legislature. From youth his mind was imbued with the most liberal political sentiments. On one of his seals, about this time, was engraved the motto, "*Resistance to tyrants is obedience to God.*" These feelings strengthened with the position of public affairs.

In 1772 he married Miss Wayles, an amiable and accomplished lady. She died in about ten years, leaving two infant daughters. In 1773, Jefferson devised and arranged

Fac-simile of Thomas Jefferson's Signature.

JEFFERSON

the first organized system of colonial resistance, which was the formation of committees of correspondence in the different provinces. Its adoption was strikingly beneficial. As the crisis of public affairs approached, not content with his constant labors as a member of the legislature, he wrote and published " A Summary View of the Rights of British America." For this publication Lord Dunmore threatened to prosecute him on a charge of high treason, and dissolved the legislature who had sustained the same doctrines. When the conciliatory propositions of the British ministry were sent out in the following year, the committee of the legislature presented a reply from the pen of Jefferson, which has ever been considered a state paper of the highest order. In June, 1775, he took his seat as a delegate to the General Congress. In the succeeding summer, Jefferson was chairman of the committee, and drew up the Declaration of Independence, which, after a few alterations, was adopted by Congress, July 4th, 1776. In the autumn of this year, he was appointed one of the commissioners to the court of France ; but ill-health, and considerations of a public nature, prevented his acceptance. He shortly after resigned his seat in Congress, and being elected to the first legislature under the new constitution of Virginia, he introduced, and, with the aid of able coadjutors, carried through important laws, founded on just and great principles of the social compact. The first of these was a bill preventing the importation of slaves ; this he followed up by destroying entails and abolishing the rights of primogeniture, the overthrow of the church establishment, which had been introduced in imitation of that of England. Besides these, he reduced to a system the various irregular enactments of the colonial government and mother country. It was a most severe labor. It consisted of 126 bills, comprising and remodelling the whole statutory law ; and though not all enacted as he contemplated, they have formed the admirable basis of the jurisprudence of Virginia.

In June, 1779, he was elected governor of Virginia, and re-elected the next year. It was a season of imminent peril ; the state was invaded by Tarleton and Arnold, and he himself made the object of particular pursuit. At the expiration of his term, the legislature passed a unanimous resolution expressive of their high opinion of his ability and integrity. In June, 1783, he was again elected to Congress, and there prepared the beautiful address, made by Congress to Washington, on taking leave of public life. He was, also, the chairman of a committee appointed to form a plan for temporary government in the vast and then unsettled western territory. He introduced a clause forbidding the existence of slavery in it after the year 1800. In the summer of 1784, he was sent as a minister plenipotentiary to France. He remained in Europe until Nov., 1789, during which time he visited England, and, in concert with Mr. Adams, ineffectually endeavored to effect a commercial treaty with Britain. While in France, he was engaged in many diplomatic negotiations of considerable importance to his country. Among men of letters, and high political distinction, he was received with marked kindness, and he graced the most brilliant social circles of Paris. When he returned to the United States, he occupied the office of secretary of state under Washington, instead of resuming, as he had intended, the post of minister to France. Of the great mass of the constitution, which had been formed during his absence, he approved, though there were points in it, in which he thought there was no adequate security for political rights. In its practical interpretations, he adopted the more popular view ; and he became the head of the party which sustained it. While in the department of state, he laid down the great, and ever since approved, maxims relative to our foreign intercourse. Among other negotiations, he became especially engaged in one with the ministers from the French republic, which seriously involved the political rights of the United States as a neutral nation, and led to the adoption of that policy of preserving peace, commerce, and friendship with all nations, but entering into entangling alliances with none. His report on an uniform system of currency, weights, and measures, was one of those measures of domestic policy appropriate to his office, and is said to have abounded with the most enlightened views. He also presented to Congress a valuable memoir on the subject of the cod and whale fisheries. His last act as secretary of state, was a report on the nature and extent of the privileges and restrictions of the commercial intercourse of the United States with other countries, and on the best means of counteracting them. It attracted much attention, and was a document of great ability. It was the foundation of a series of resolutions proposed by Mr. Madison, sanctioning the views it embraced, and it became, in fact, the ostensible subject on which the federal and republican parties distinctly arrayed themselves against each other.

In Dec., 1793, Jefferson resigned his office and retired to Monticello. The Duke de Liancourt, a French traveller, has given in his work a pleasing narrative of the manner in which the life of the retired statesman was passed. " His conversation," he says,

" is of the most agreeable kind, and he possesses a stock of information not inferior to any other man. In Europe he would hold a distinguished rank among men of letters, and as such he has already appeared there. At present, he is employed with activity and perseverance in the management of his farms and buildings ; and he orders, directs, and pursues, in the minutest detail, every branch of business relating to them. I found him in the midst of harvest, from which the scorching heat of the sun does not prevent his attendance. His negroes are nourished, clothed, and treated as well as white servants could be. Every article is made on his farm ; his negroes being cabinet-makers, carpenters, and masons. The children he employs in a nail factory ; and the young and old negresses spin for the clothing of the rest. He animates them all by rewards and distinctions. In fine, his superior mind directs the management of his domestic concerns with the same abilities, activity, and regularity, which he evinced in the conduct of public affairs, and which he is calculated to display in every situation of life." It was at this period of retirement that he was unanimously elected president of the American Philosophical Society.

Jefferson was not, however, long permitted to enjoy the tranquillity of private life. On the retirement of Washington from the presidency, Mr. Jefferson was selected by the democratic party as their candidate for that office, and Mr. Adams by the federal party. The highest number of votes appearing for the latter, he was declared president and Jefferson vice-president. For the succeeding four years most of his time was passed tranquilly at Monticello. When the period for another election arrived he was again a candidate for the presidential chair. On canvassing the votes of the electors, it was found that Mr. Jefferson and Mr. Burr had each seventy-three votes, Mr. Adams sixty-five, and C. C. Pinckney sixty-four. As the constitution provided that the person having the greatest number of votes should be president, and Mr. Jefferson and Mr. Burr, having an equal number, it became the duty of the House of Representatives, voting by states, to decide between these two gentlemen. The ballot was taken several days in succession. The federal party, generally, supported Mr. Burr ; the democratic party Mr. Jefferson. On the thirty-sixth ballot Mr. Jefferson was elected president, and Mr. Burr vice-president.

On the 4th of March, 1801, Mr. Jefferson entered on his first presidential term. In his inaugural address, he stated, with great eloquence of language and admirable clearness and precision, the political principles by which he intended to be governed in the administration of public affairs.

His administration embraces a long and interesting period in the history of our country, and measures of lasting importance were carried through. The aggressions of the Tripolitans were promptly chastised ; the encroachments of the agents of the Spanish government to deprive us of the right of navigating the Mississippi, were repelled ; Louisiana was purchased ; the internal policy of the Union underwent important changes ; measures were adopted for the speedy discharge of the public debt ; the judiciary was restored to the original plan ; strict economy was observed in carrying on the government, and useless offices suppressed.

So much was his administration approved, that when his term of service expired, he was again elected by a very large majority. He had scarcely entered on his office when the conspiracy of Burr was discovered. The foreign relations of the Union, however, assumed an importance exceeding all domestic affairs. The aggressions of Great Britain and France upon our commerce left no honorable course but that of retaliation. On the 22d of December, 1807, the Embargo Act was passed, on the recommendation of Mr. Jefferson. In January, 1809, overtures were made by the British government indicative of a disposition to recede from the ground they had assumed ; and these were preceded by a repeal of their most objectionable measures. In this situation were the foreign relations of the United States when Mr. Jefferson's second term of office expired, on the 3d of March, 1809, and his political career closed.

He had been engaged, almost without interruption, for forty years, in the most arduous public duties. From this time, until his death, he resided at Monticello. His home was the abode of hospitality, and the seat of dignified retirement ; he forgot the busy times of his political existence, in the calm and congenial pleasures of science, and his mind, clear and penetrating, wandered with fresh activity and delight through all the regions of thought. Among the plans for the public welfare in which he was engaged, the establishment of the University of Virginia was with him a favorite scheme. The legislature approved of his plan, and appointed him rector. Until the time of his death, his most cherished hopes and endeavors were for its success.

Mr. Jefferson died July 4th, 1826, at the age of 83 years. His family and servants were called around his dying bed. After declaring himself gratified by their affectionate solicitude, and having distinctly articulated these words, "I resign myself to my God, and my child to my country," he expired without a groan.

The neighborhood of Monticello affords innumerable monuments of the benevolence and liberality of Mr. Jefferson; and on his own estate, such was the condition of his slaves, that in their comfort, his own interest was too often entirely forgotten. His attachment to his friends was unvarying, and few public men have had warmer. His domestic habits were simple, his application was excessive, and he conducted all his business with great exactness and method. His correspondence was wonderfully extensive.

In person, Mr. Jefferson was six feet two inches in height, erect and well formed, though thin; his eyes were light, and full of intelligence; his hair, originally of a yellowish red, was in his latter years silvered with age; his complexion was fair, his forehead broad, and the whole face square and expressive of deep thinking; his countenance was remarkably intelligent, and open as day, its general expression full of good will and kindness, and when the occasion excited it, beaming with enthusiasm; his address was cordial, confirming the good will of his lips; his motions were flexible and easy, his step firm and sprightly; and such were his strength and agility, that he was accustomed in the society of children, of which he was fond, to practise feats that few could imitate. His manner was simple, mingled with native dignity, but cheerful, unassuming, frank, and kind; his language was remarkable for vivacity and correctness; and in his conversation, which was without apparent effort, he poured forth knowledge, the most various, from an exhaustless fountain, yet so modestly and engagingly that he seemed rather to seek than to impart information.

He lies buried in a small burying, near the road, which winds around it to Monticello. It has a slight enclosure, and is surrounded by the native wood. In it lie the remains of members of the family, some two or three of whom have tablets of marble. On his own grave, his executor has erected a granite obelisk, eight feet high, and on a piece of marble, inserted on its southern face, are inscribed the three acts for which he thought he best deserved to be remembered by posterity. This inscription was found among his papers after his death, in his own handwriting, and it is in these words:

> HERE LIES BURIED
> ## THOMAS JEFFERSON,
> AUTHOR OF THE DECLARATION OF AMERICAN INDEPENDENCE,
> OF THE STATUTE OF VIRGINIA FOR RELIGIOUS FREEDOM,
> AND FATHER OF THE UNIVERSITY OF VIRGINIA.

"Mr. Jefferson's religious creed," says Tucker, "as described in his correspondence, cannot perhaps be classed with that of any particular sect, but was nearer the Socinian than any other. In the last years of his life, when questioned by any friends on this subject, he used to say he was a Unitarian."

Meriwether Lewis, the son of a wealthy farmer, was born near Charlottesville, in 1774. At 18 years of age, he relinquished his academic studies and engaged in agriculture. Two years after, he acted as a volunteer, to suppress the whiskey insurrection, from which situation he was removed to the regular service. From about 1801 to 1803, he was the private secretary of Mr. Jefferson, when he, with Wm. Clarke, went in their celebrated exploring expedition to the Rocky Mountains. Mr. Jefferson, in recommending him to this duty, gave him a high character, as possessing courage, inflexible perseverance, intimate knowledge of the Indian character, fidelity, intelligence, and all those peculiar combinations of qualities that eminently fitted him for so arduous an undertaking. They were absent three years, and were highly successful in the accomplishment of their duties. When, shortly after his return, in 1806, he was appointed governor of the territory of Louisiana, and finding it the seat of internal dissensions, he by his moderation, firmness, and impartiality, brought matters into a systematic train. He was subject to constitutional hypochondria, and while under the influence of a severe attack shot himself on the borders of Tennessee, in 1809, at the age of 35. This event was ascribed to the protest of some bills, which he drew on the public account. The account of his expedition, which he wrote, was published in 1814. The mother of Mr. Lewis died in this county, only a few years since. She possessed very strong powers of mind.

WILLIAM WIRT, the distinguished author of the British Spy, who was born at Bladensburg, for a time resided in this county. In 1792, when 20 years of age, he commenced the practice of law at Fairfax, in the neighboring county of Culpeper.

" In 1795, he married the eldest daughter of Dr. George Gilmer, a distinguished physician, and took up his residence at Pen Park, the seat of his father-in-law, near Charlottesville ; and here he was introduced to the acquaintance of Jefferson, Madison, Monroe, and other persons of celebrity.

" In 1799 his wife died, and he was soon after elected clerk of the House of Delegates. Having performed the duties of his office two years, he was in 1802 appointed chancellor of the Eastern District of Virginia, and then took up his residence at Williamsburg ; and the same year he married the daughter of Col. Gamble, of Richmond. He soon after resigned his chancellorship, and at the close of the year 1803 removed to Norfolk, and entered upon the assiduous practice of his profession. Just before he removed to Norfolk, he wrote the letters published in the Richmond Argus, under the title of ' the British Spy,' which were afterwards collected in a small volume, and have passed through many editions. In 1806 he took up his residence in Richmond, and in the following year he greatly distinguished himself in the trial of Col. Burr. In 1812 he wrote the greater part of a series of essays, which were originally published in the Richmond Enquirer, under the title of ' The Old Bachelor,' and have since, in a collected form, passed through several editions. The ' Life of Patrick Henry,' his largest literary production, was first published in 1817. In 1816 he was appointed, by Mr. Madison, the U. S. Attorney for Virginia ; and in 1817, by Mr. Monroe, attorney-general of the United States, a post which he occupied with distinguished reputation until 1829, through the entire administrations of Monroe and Adams. In 1830, he took up his residence in Baltimore for the remainder of his life. He died Feb. 18th, 1834, at Washington City, in his 62d year. As a public and professional man, Mr. Wirt ranked among the first of his time ; and in all the relations of private life, as a man and a Christian, he was most exemplary, and was regarded with singular affection and veneration."

ALLEGHANY.

ALLEGHANY was formed in 1822, from Bath, Bottetourt, and Monroe. Its mean length is twenty-six, mean breadth twenty miles. Most of this county is a high mountain valley, drained by the head waters of the James. The main Alleghany chain forms its boundary on the west ; Peter's mountain and Warm Spring mountain divide the county into two nearly equal parts, having only a narrow gap at Covington, and Middle Mountain and Rich Patch form its southeastern boundary. The passage of Jackson's River through Waite's mountain, is a sublime feature of the natural scenery of the county. Population in 1830, 2,816 ; 1840, whites 2,142, slaves 547, free colored 60 ; total, 2,749.

Covington, the county-seat, lies one hundred and ninety-six miles west of Richmond, at the head of the James River navigation, on Jackson's River, fifteen above its confluence with the Cow-Pasture, both of which by their union constitute the James. It contains, at present, about fifty dwellings. At some future period, it is contemplated that the James River Canal will be continued to here ; in which case, it will be the depôt between the land and water communication in the chain of the James River and Kanawha improvements, and will then command the trade of a large and fertile region of country. Near Covington, a fort, called Fort Young, was built in the early settlement of the country, as a protection against the Indians.

Peter's Mountain derived its name from Peter Wright, a famous hunter at the time of the first settlement, who was accustomed to hunt upon it. He resided near the present site of Covington. Near the house of Mr. John Lewis, there is, on the roadside, a large shelving rock, called Peter's Rock, where, says tradition, he sought shelter in a snow storm. There he lay for several days, until the snow was four feet deep, when he was obliged to eat his moccasins to prevent starving. He at length discovered and shot a deer, which furnished him with food. He left, at his death, two sons, both of whom emigrated to the west many years since.

There was an eccentric female, who lived in this section of the country towards the latter part of the last century. Her name was *Ann Bailey.* She was born in Liverpool, and had been the wife of an English soldier. She generally went by the cognomen of Mad Ann. During the wars with the Indians, she very often acted as a messenger, and conveyed letters from the fort, at Covington, to Point Pleasant. On these occasions she was mounted on a favorite horse of great sagacity, and rode like a man, with a rifle over her shoulder, and a tomahawk and a butcher's-knife in her belt. At night she slept in the woods. Her custom was to let her horse go free, and then walk some distance back on his trail, to escape being discovered by the Indians. After the Indian wars she spent some time in hunting. She pursued and shot deer and bears with the skill of a backwoodsman. She was a short, stout woman, very masculine and coarse in her appearance, and seldom or never wore a gown, but usually had on a petticoat, with a man's coat over it, and buckskin breeches. The services she rendered in the wars with the Indians, endeared her to the people. Mad Ann, and her black pony Liverpool, were always welcome at every house. Often, she gathered the honest, simple-hearted mountaineers around, and related her adventures and trials, while the sympathetic tear would course down their cheeks. She was profane, often became intoxicated, and could box with the skill of one of the fancy. Mad Ann possessed considerable intelligence, and could read and write. She died in Ohio many years since.

In 1764, a party of about fifty Indians came into this region, and then dividing into two, one went towards the Roanoke and Catawba settlements, and the other in the direction of Jackson's River, where each committed murders and depredations. Captain Paul, who commanded at Fort Dinwiddie, went in pursuit of the latter party, and accidentally came upon the other, about midnight, encamped on New River, at the mouth of Indian Creek. In an instant after firing upon them, Captain Paul and his men rushed forward to secure the wounded and prevent further escapes, as most of them had ran. One of the party raised his tomahawk to strike, as he supposed, a squaw, who sat composedly awaiting the result. As the tomahawk was descending, Captain Paul threw himself between the assailant and his victim, and received the blow on his arm, exclaiming : " It is a shame to hurt a woman, even a squaw !" She proved to be Mrs. Catharine Gunn, an English woman, an acquaintance of Captain Paul, taken prisoner on the Catawba a few days before, when her husband and two children were killed. On being asked why she had not made known she was a prisoner, by crying out, she replied : " I had as soon be killed as not—my husband is murdered—my children are slain—my parents are dead. I have not a relation in America—every thing dear to me here is gone—I have no wishes, no hopes, no fears—I would not have risen to my feet to have saved my life."

AMELIA.

AMELIA was formed in 1734, from part of Prince George. Its length is about 30, mean breadth 10 miles. It is drained by the Appomattox. The surface is agreeably diversified ; the soil on the hills poor and usually much worn, on the bottoms fertile, and it has generally much deteriorated from its original fertility, owing to the injudicious modes of cultivation pursued by its early settlers. Pop. 1830, 11,031 ; in 1840, whites 3,074, slaves 7,023, free colored, 223 ; total, 10,320.

There are no villages in the county of any note. Amelia C. H., which is centrally situated, 45 miles sw. of Richmond, contains but a few dwellings.

WILLIAM ARCHER, Col.-commandant of the county, made himself so conspicuous by his zeal in the revolutionary cause, that he was made prisoner by Tarleton, on his return from his excursion to New London. He was conveyed to one of the prison-ships at Norfolk, so well known for the sufferings of which they were the scenes. There he was retained until he became a victim of the small-pox. He was finally permitted to land, but in so advanced a stage of the disease that he died in a few days, without restoration to his family. One of his sons, Lieut. Joseph Archer, was killed at the battle of Brandywine. Another of his sons, Major John Archer—the father of the present member of the U. S. Senate, the Hon. Wm. S. Archer—was an aid to one of the American generals. He was sent to remove public stores, when a detachment from the army of Lord Cornwallis made the celebrated dash on Charlottesville. Delaying too long in the discharge of his duty, he was overtaken in the rapid advance of the enemy. The English officer to whom he surrendered his sword, received and passed it entirely through his body. The speedy retreat of the enemy permitting immediate assistance, he had the good fortune to recover, and lived many years.

Major JOSEPH EGGLESTON was a native of Amelia. He was a highly meritorious officer of Lee's legion, and served through the whole of the southern campaigns. At the conclusion of the war he turned his attention to literature. He was a member of Congress in 1798-9, where he served with credit. He was cut off in the flower of his age, by the effects of an amputation of a disordered limb.

The residence of the late distinguished WILLIAM BRANCH GILES, was near the margin of the Appomattox, in this county. He sprang from humble, but respectable parentage, and was educated at Princeton. He was for many years a member of Congress from Virginia, both in the Senate and House of Representatives, where he arrived, as a debater, to very high rank.

" He resigned his seat in the Senate, in 1815. He was governor of Virginia from 1826 to 1829, and died in 1830, at an advanced age. He published a speech on the embargo laws in 1808; political letters to the people of Virginia, in 1813; a series of letters, signed a Constituent, in the Richmond Enquirer of Jan. 1818, against the plan for a general education; in April, 1824, a letter of invective against President Monroe and Henry Clay, for their 'hobbies,' the South American cause, the Greek cause, Internal Improvements, and the Tariff in Nov. 1825; he addressed a letter to Judge Marshall, disclaiming the expressions, not the general sentiments in regard to Washington, ascribed to him in the Life of Washington. He has also appeared before the public as the correspondent of John Quincy Adams." Mr. Giles was also one of the most distinguished members of the convention that revised the constitution of Virginia, in 1830.

In 1843, there died in this county, at an advanced age, a negro preacher of considerable local celebrity, who went by the name of UNCLE JACK. He was kidnapped, and brought from Africa at seven years of age, and landed at Osborne's, on James River, from what it is supposed was the last slave-ship which deposited its cargo in Virginia. Such was his worth of character, that, on the death of his master, several benevolent individuals by their contributions purchased his freedom. One, who kne·   · well, said, " I regard this old African as a burning light, raised up by Christia   .uciples alone, to a degree of moral purity seldom equalled and never exceeded in any country." The late Rev. Dr. Rice also remarked, " The old man's acquaintance with the scriptures is wonderful. Many of his interpretations of obscure passages of scripture are singularly just and striking. In many respects, indeed, he is the most remarkable man I ever knew."

His views of the leading doctrines of Christianity were thorough and evangelical. His preaching abounded with quotations surprisingly minute, and his illustrations were vivid and correct. His knowledge of human nature was profound; and hence his extensive usefulness among the African population, as well as an extensive circle of whites. His language was pure English, without the vulgarities of the blacks. In his intercourse with all classes he was governed by Christian humility, and he abhorred cant and grimace. " He uniformly opposed, both in public and private, every thing like noise and disorder in the house of God. His colored audience were very prone to indulge themselves in this way. But, whenever they did, he uniformly suspended the exercises until they became silent. On one of these occasions, he rebuked his hearers substantially, as follows: ' You noisy Christians remind me of the little branches after a heavy rain. They are soon full—then noisy—and as soon empty. I had a great deal rather see you like the broad, deep river, which is quiet because it is broad and deep.' "

Of this worthy and strong-minded old man, we take the liberty of annexing a few anecdotes, drawn from his memoir in the Watchman of the South. In speaking of the excitement and noise at a protracted meeting, he remarked, "I was reminded of what I have noticed in the woods: when the wind blows hard, the *dry leaves* make a great deal more noise than the green ones." When persons scoffed at his religion, his usual diffidence and reserve would give way to a firm and bold defence, and most happily would he "answer a fool according to his folly." A person addicted to horse-racing and card-playing stopped him one day on the road, and said—"Old man, you Christians say a great deal about the way to heaven being very narrow. Now, if this be so, a great many who profess to be travelling it will not find it half wide enough." "That's very true," was the reply, "of all who have merely a name to live, and all like you." "Why refer to me?" asked the man; "if the road is wide enough for any, it is for me." "By no means," replied Uncle Jack; "when you set out you will want to take along a card-table, and a race-horse or two. Now, there's no room along this way for such things, and what would you do, even in heaven, without them?" An individual accustomed to treat religion rather sportively, and who prided himself upon his morality, said to him, "Old man, I am as good as I need be; I can't help thinking so, because God blesses me as much as he does you Christians, and I don't know what more I want than he gives me." To this the old preacher replied, with great seriousness, "Just so with the hogs. I have often looked at them, rooting among the leaves in the woods, and finding just as many acorns as they needed; and yet I never saw one of them look up to the tree from whence the acorns fell." In speaking of the low state of religion, he said, "there seems to be great coldness and deadness on the subject of religion everywhere; the fire has almost gone out, and nothing is left but a few smoking chumps, lying about in places."

The laws of Virginia prohibit religious as well as other assemblies of slaves, unless at least two white persons are present. Such, however, was the universally acknowledged happy influence of Uncle Jack's meetings, that in his case it was not deemed necessary to enforce the law. On one occasion, some mischievous persons undertook to arrest and whip him and several of his hearers. After the arrest, one of the number thus accosted Uncle Jack: "Well, old fellow, you are the ringleader of all these meetings, and we have been anxious to catch you; now, what have you got to say for yourself?" "Nothing at all, master," was the reply. "What! nothing to say against being whipped! how is that?" "I have been wondering for a long time," said he, "how it was that so good a man as the Apostle Paul should have been whipped three times for preaching the gospel, while such an unworthy man as I am should have been permitted to preach for 20 years, without ever getting a lick." It is hardly necessary to add, that these young men immediately released him.

His influence over the members of his church was almost unbounded. As evidence of the fact, take the following :—

A gentleman who resided in the neighborhood, on walking out over his farm, detected one of his servants, who belonged to Uncle Jack's flock, in some very improper conduct. The only notice he took of it, was to threaten that he would inform that spiritual man. When he arose on the following morning and came to the door, he found this servant waiting and anxious to see him. "Why, Tom," said he, "what is the matter; why don't you go to your work?" "Why, master," replied the servant, "if you would please whip me yourself, and don't tell Uncle Jack."

We would like to extend this notice, but want of space forbids. Uncle Jack died at the age of nearly 100 years. He was one of those characters, that, under propitious circumstances, might have left an undying name. But in the limited sphere of his influence, his humble and consistent life won for him the affections of the best people in the community

---

AMHERST.

Amherst was formed in 1761, from Albemarle. It is about 22 miles long, and 19 wide. The James River forms its sw. and se. boundary, and the Blue Ridge its northwest. The James River Canal passes through the se. part of the county. The soil is naturally fertile, and of a dark, rich, red hue, and the scenery

beautifully diversified.   Pop. in 1830, 12,072; in 1840, whites
6,426, slaves 5,577, free colored 373; total, 12,576.

Amherst C. H., on the road from Lynchburg to Charlottesville,
about 15 miles N. of the former, and New Glasgow, are small
villages.

Pass of the James River through the Blue Ridge.

The pass of the James River through the Blue Ridge, is on the
line of this and the county of Rockbridge.   There a canal, seven
miles in length, has been constructed around Balcony Falls, which
will form the bed of the James River Canal, whenever that work
is continued westward.   The stage road from Lynchburg to the
Natural Bridge winds along the side of the mountain, through
wild and romantic scenery, which, to the lowlander accustomed
only to the flatlands and pine-barrens of eastern Virginia, is
striking.   As he enters the gap from the east, the road gradually

follows its tortuous course up the mountain's side, until it gains an elevation of hundreds of feet above the river, which it appears to nearly overhang. Gigantic mountains hem him in on every side ; while far, from the dark ravine below, comes up the roar of the rapids. A little mountain rivulet, from amid the primeval forest, dashes across his path, and, leaping from rock to rock, hurries on to swell the stream below. Emerging from the pass, a beautiful and fertile country opens before him, and still westward the blue outlines of distant mountains in Rockbridge meet his view.

AUGUSTA.

Augusta was formed from Orange, in 1738. " Previously, all that part of Virginia lying west of the Blue Ridge was included in Orange ; but in the fall session of this year it was divided into the counties of Frederick and Augusta. Frederick county was bounded by the Potomac on the north, the Blue Ridge on the east, and a line to be run from the head spring of Hedgman to head spring of the Potomac, on the south and west ; the remainder of Virginia, west of the Blue Ridge, to constitute Augusta. This immense territory, at the present time, comprises four entire states, and nearly 40 counties in western Virginia. As the population increased, the limits of Augusta were reduced until it reached its present boundaries in 1790." It is about 35 miles long, and 30 broad. The surface is generally uneven, and in the E. and W. mountainous. There are, however, some extensive bottoms of very fertile land. It is drained by tributaries of the James and Shenandoah rivers. Pop. 1830, 19,925 ; 1840, whites 15,072, slaves 4,145, free colored 421 ; total 19,628.

There are several fine villages in the county, besides the large and flourishing town of Staunton. Greenville and Middlebrook, the first 12 miles ssw. and the last 11 miles sw. of Staunton, contain each about sixty dwellings. Waynesboro', at the western base of the Blue Ridge, on the main stage road from Charlottesville to Staunton, 12 miles easterly from the latter, is a wealthy and flourishing village, containing about 100 dwellings. Mount Sydney, 10 miles NE. of Staunton, contains about 40 dwellings. Mount Solon, Spring Hill, Mount Meridian, and New Hope, are small places, at the first of which there is considerable manufacturing carried on. There the Moss Creek Spring rises from a hill, and furnishes the power for a forge, a furnace, and 1 paper and 1 merchant mill.

The Augusta Springs are 12 miles NW. of Staunton. The water is strongly impregnated with sulphuretted hydrogen, and is said to equal the celebrated springs of Harrowgate, England. The improvements at this place are ample, and the situation extremely picturesque. About 12 miles sw. of Staunton, is one of those ebbing and flowing springs, so common in western Virginia.

Virginia Lunatic Asylum at Staunton.

Staunton, the county-seat, lies 116 ms. northwesterly from Richmond, 163 from Washington City, on one of the extreme head branches of the E. fork of Shenandoah River, in a fine valley between the Blue Ridge and north mountain chains.

Institution for the Deaf and Dumb and the Blind, at Staunton, Va.

It contains 1 newspaper printing office, 2 female seminaries, 2 male academies, 1 Presbyterian, 1 Episcopal, 1 Lutheran, and 1 Methodist church, and a population of about 2,200. It has many mercantile and mechanical establishments, and does a large business with the surrounding country. An excellent macadamised road leads from here to Winchester. The Western Lunatic Asylum is located at this place, and is a noble pile of brick buildings. By the U. S. census of 1840, the whole number of insane and idiotic persons in Virginia was 892, or 1 to every 866 persons. The Virginia Institution for the Deaf and Dumb and the Blind, has been established within a few years. A beautiful brick building is now erecting for it, near the town, on an elevated and picturesque site. By the U. S. census for 1840, the number of deaf and dumb in the state was 603, or 1 to every 2,056 of the population; the number of blind 802, or one to every 1390 of the population.

"When Tarleton, in the war of the revolution, pursued the legisture to Charlottesville, to which place they had adjourned from Richmond, they again fled and met at Staunton, where they finished their session. At some future day it will probably become the seat of government. It was at this place that two large conventions were held, to deliberate on forming the constitution of Virginia. The last met in July, 1825, and made an appeal to the legislature, who thereupon submitted the question to the people, and it finally resulted in the adoption of the new constitution."

This county has been the birth-place or the residence of several prominent characters. Among them may be mentioned the Hon. Daniel Sheffey; Gen. Robert Porterfield, a gallant officer of the revolution; and Judge Archibald Stuart, father of the Hon. Alex. H. H. Stuart.

DANIEL SHEFFEY was born at Frederick, Md., in 1770, and was bred a shoemaker, in his father's shop. His education was inconsiderable; but possessing an ardent desire for knowledge, he passed his leisure in reading, and became particularly fond of astronomical and mathematical studies. Arrived at manhood, he travelled on foot, with his "kit" on his back, to Winchester. From thence he walked through the valley of Virginia, stopping at various villages on his route, and earning sufficient money by his trade, to pay his expenses, until he at last arrived at Abbeville, Wythe county. He was a stranger, friendless and destitute. "Here he commenced his trade once more. The novelty and originality of his character, and the flashes of genius which enlivened his conversation, often compelled his new-tried friends to look on the eccentric youth with wonder." Becoming popular, he was received into the office of Alexander Smyth, Esq., and after being admitted to the bar of Wythe county, was employed in the most important suits. After some years he settled in Staunton, and obtained a lucrative practice. He often represented Augusta in the House of Delegates, and, in 1811, was chosen as a member of Congress. "His speech, in favor of a renewal of the charter of the first bank of the United States, was a masterly combination of sound judgment and conclusive facts: for three hours profound silence reigned; and the most experienced statesmen were astonished at this exhibition of his talents." He was opposed to the declaration of war in 1812. On one occasion, he gave John Randolph, whose bitter sarcasm few could withstand, a most severe retort. In commenting upon a speech of Mr. Sheffey's, he said that "the shoemaker ought not to go beyond his last." In an instant Sheffey retorted, "if that gentleman had ever been on the bench, he never would have left it."

Mr. Sheffey was a plain man; his accent German, his pronunciation not agreeable; yet the most refined audience always paid him profound attention. He seized upon the strong points of a case, and maintained them with unconquerable zeal. "Like Patrick Henry, he was the artificer of his own fortune, and like him, in after-life, lamented that in his early days the lamp of life had shed but a feeble ray along the path which it was his destiny to travel."* He died in 1830.

Cyclopean Towers, Augusta Co.

The Cyclopean towers, which are near the Augusta Springs, are among the greatest curiosities of nature in the Union. Yet for many years they were known only in the vicinity, and bore the rude appellation of "the chimneys." They are about 60 or 70 feet in height. We annex the following from a published description by a gentleman who visited the towers in 1834, and gave them

* Southern Literary Messenger.

their present name. It commences with a description of the country as he approached towards them:

After passing over a hilly and picturesque country, the road opened upon a fertile valley; which though in places narrow, was of considerable length—and when seen from an elevated position, appeared like the bed of an ancient lake, or as it really is, the alluvial border of a flowing stream. The strata of limestone hills followed their usual order of parallel lines to the great mountains of our continent, as though a strong current had once swept through this magnificent valley, forming in'its course islands and promontories, which are now discoverable in numerous short hills and rocky bluffs, that are either naked and barren, or covered with a growth of stately trees. It was at such a projection, that we first descried the gray summits of what seemed a ruinous castle—resembling those which were raised in feudal times to guard the passes of the Rhine, or like such as are still seen in mouldering majesty on many an Alpine rock. These summits or towers, of which there were seven, lifted their heads above the lofty elms, like so many antique chimneys in the midst of a grove ; but, on approaching them nearer, our pleasure was greatly increased to find them rise almost perpendicularly from the bed of a stream, which, winding around their base, serves as a natural moat to a building not made with mortal hands.

These rocks in their formation resemble the palisades on the Hudson River—but are more regular in their strata, which appears to have been arranged in huge masses of perfect workmanship, with projections like cornices of Gothic architecture, in a state of dilapidation. Those who are acquainted with the structure of the Cyclopean walls of the ancients, would be struck with the resemblance.

A narrative of the circumstances connected with the settlement of Augusta county, by the Lewis family, collected from authentic records, and traditions of the family, and communicated for this work by a gentleman of the county:

John Lewis was a native and citizen of Ireland, descended from a family of Huguenots, who took refuge in that kingdom from the persecutions that followed the assassination of Henry IV., of France. His rank was that of an Esquire, and he inherited a handsome estate, which he increased by industry and frugality, until he became the lessee of a contiguous property, of considerable value. He married Margaret Lynn, daughter of the laird of Loch Lynn, who was a descendant of the chieftains of a once powerful clan in the Scottish Highlands. By this marriage he had four sons, three of them, Thomas, Andrew, and William, born in Ireland, and Charles, the child of his old age, born a few months after their settlement in their mountain home.

The emigration of John Lewis to Virginia, was the result of one of those bloody affrays, which at that time so often occurred to disturb the repose, and destroy the happiness of Irish families. The owner of the fee out of which the leasehold of Lewis was carved, a nobleman of profligate habits and ungovernable passions, seeing the prosperity of his lessee, and repenting the bargain he had concluded, under pretence of entering for an alleged breach of condition attempted by the aid of a band of ruffians, hired for his purpose, to take forcible possession of the premises. For this end, he surrounded the house with his ruffians, and called upon Lewis to evacuate the premises without delay, a demand which was instantly and indignantly refused by Lewis ; though surprised with a sick brother, his wife, and infant children in the house, and with no aid but such as could be afforded by a few faithful domestics. With this small force, scarce equal to one-fourth the number of his assailants, he resolved to maintain his legal rights at every hazard. The enraged nobleman commenced the affray by discharging his fowling-piece into the house, by which the invalid brother of Lewis was killed, and Margaret herself severely wounded. Upon this, the enraged husband and brother, rushed from the house, attended by his devoted little band, and soon succeeded in dispersing the assailants, though not until the noble author of the mischief, as well as his steward, had perished by the hand of Lewis. By this time the family were surrounded by their sympathizing friends and neighbors, who, after bestowing every aid in their power, advised Lewis to fly the country, a measure rendered necessary by the high standing of his late antagonist, the desperate character of his surviving assailants, and the want of evidence by which he could have established the facts of the case. He therefore, after drawing up a detailed statement of the affair, which he directed to the proper authorities, embarked on board a vessel bound for America, attended by his family and a band of about thirty of his faithful tenantry. In due time, the emigrants landed on the shores of Virginia, and fixed their residence amid the till then unbroken forests of west Augusta. John Lewis's settlement was a few miles below the site of the town of Staunton, on the banks of the stream which still bears his name. It may be proper to remark here, that when the circumstances of the affray became known, after due investigation, a pardon was granted to John Lewis, and patents are still extant, by which his majesty granted to him a large portion of the fair domain of western Virginia.

For many years after the settlement at Fort Lewis, great amity and good will existed between the neighboring Indians and the white settlers, whose numbers increased apace, until they became quite a formidable colony. It was then that the jealousy of their red neighbors became aroused, and a war broke out, which, for cool though desperate courage and activity on the part of the whites, and ferocity, cunning, and barbarity on the part of the Indians, was never equalled in any age or country. John Lewis was, by this time, well stricken in years, but his four sons, who were now grown up, were well qualified to fill his place, and to act the part of leaders to the gallant little band, who so nobly battled for the protection of their homes and families. It is not my purpose to go into the details of a warfare, during which scarcely a settlement was exempt from monthly attacks of the savages, and during which Charles Lewis, the youngest son of John, is said never to have spent one month at a time out of active and arduous service. Charles was the hero of many a gallant exploit, which is still treasured in the memories of the descendants of the border riflemen, and there are few families among the Alleghanies where the name and deeds of Charles Lewis are not familiar as household words. On one occasion, Charles was captured by the Indians while on a hunting excursion, and after having travelled some two hundred miles, barefoot, his arms pinioned behind him, goaded on by the knives of his remorseless captors, he effected his escape. While travelling along the bank of a precipice some twenty feet in height, he suddenly, by a strong muscular exertion, burst the cords which bound him, and plunged down the steep into the bed of a mountain torrent. His persecutors hesitated not to follow. In a race of several hundred yards, Lewis had gained some few yards upon his pursuers, when, upon leaping a prostrate tree which lay across his course, his strength suddenly failed, and he fell prostrate among the weeds which had grown up in great luxuriance around the body of the tree. Three of the Indians sprang over the tree within a few feet of where their prey lay concealed; but with a feeling of the most devout thankfulness to a kind and superintending Providence, he saw them one by one disappear in the dark recesses of the forest. He now bethought himself of rising from his uneasy bed, when lo! a new enemy appeared, in the shape of an enormous rattlesnake, who had thrown himself into the deadly coil so near his face that his fangs were within a few inches of his nose; and his enormous rattle, as it waved to and fro, once rested upon his ear. A single contraction of the eyelid—a convulsive shudder—the relaxation of a single muscle, and the deadly beast would have sprung upon him. In this situation he lay for several minutes, when the reptile, probably supposing him to be dead, crawled over his body and moved slowly away. " I had eaten nothing," said Lewis to his companions, after his return, " for many days; I had no fire-arms, and I ran the risk of dying with hunger, ere I could reach the settlement; but rather would I have died, than made a meal of the generous beast." During this war, an attack was made upon the settlement of Fort Lewis, at a time when the whole force of the settlement was out on active duty. So great was the surprise, that many of the women and children were captured in sight of the fort, though far the greater part escaped, and concealed themselves in their hiding places, in the woods. The fort was occupied by John Lewis, then very old and infirm, his wife, and two young women, who were so much alarmed that they scarce moved from their seats upon the ground floor of the fort. John Lewis, however, opened a port-hole, where he stationed himself, firing at the savages, while Margaret reloaded the guns. In this manner he sustained a siege of six hours, during which he killed upwards of a score of savages, when he was relieved by the appearance of his party.

Thomas Lewis, the eldest son of John Lewis and Margaret Lynn, labored under a defect of vision, which disabled him as a marksman, and he was, therefore, less efficient during the Indian wars than his brethren. He was, however, a man of learning and sound judgment, and represented the county of Augusta for many years in the House of Burgesses; was a member of the convention which ratified the constitution of the United States, and formed the constitution of Virginia, and afterwards sat for the county of Rockingham in the House of Delegates of Virginia. In 1765, he was in the House of Burgesses, and voted for Patrick Henry's celebrated resolutions. Thomas Lewis had four sons actively participating in the war of the revolution; the youngest of whom, Thomas, who is now living, bore an ensign's commission when but fourteen years of age

Andrew, the second son of John Lewis and Margaret Lynn, is the Gen. Lewis who commanded at the battle of Point Pleasant. (See his memoir in Bottetourt co.)

Charles Lewis, the youngest of the sons of John Lewis, fell at the head of his regiment, when leading on the attack at Point Pleasant. Charles was esteemed the most skilful of all the leaders of the border warfare, and was as much beloved for his noble and amiable qualities as he was admired for his military talents.

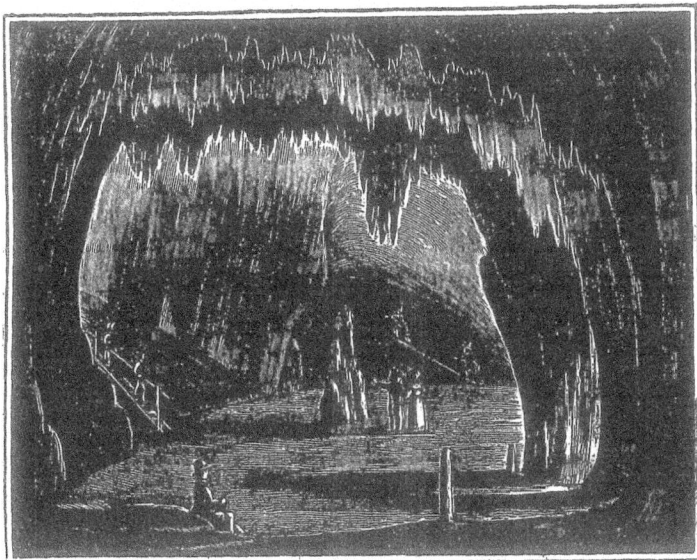

View in Weyer's Cave.

William, the third son, was an active participator in the border wars, and was an officer of the revolutionary army, in which one of his sons was killed, and another maimed for life. When the British force under Tarleton drove the legislature from Charlottesville to Staunton, the stillness of the Sabbath eve was broken in the latter town by the beat of the drum, and volunteers were called for to prevent the passage of the British through the mountains at Rockfish Gap. The elder sons of Wm. Lewis, who then resided at the old fort, were absent with the northern army. Three sons, however, were at home, whose ages were 17, 15, and 13 years. Wm. Lewis was confined to his room by sickness, but his wife, with the firmness of a Roman matron, called them to her, and bade them fly to the defence of their native land. "Go my children," said she, "I spare not my youngest, my fair-haired boy, the comfort of my declining years. I devote you all to my country. Keep back the foot of the invader from the soil of Augusta, or see my face no more." When this incident was related to Washington, shortly after its occurrence, he enthusiastically exclaimed, "Leave me but a banner to plant upon the mountains of Augusta, and I will rally around me the men who will lift our bleeding country from the dust, and set her free."

I have frequently heard, when a boy, an anecdote related by an old settler, somewhat to this effect: The white, or wild clover, is of indigenous growth, and abounded on the banks of the rivers, &c. The red was introduced by John Lewis, and it was currently reported by their prophets, and believed by the Indians generally, that the blood of the red man slain by the Lewises and their followers, had dyed the trefoil to its sanguine hue. The Indians, however, always did the whites the justice to say, that the red man was the aggressor in their first quarrel, and that the white men of western Virginia had always evinced a disposition to treat their red brethren with moderation and justice.

Weyer's Cave, is 17 miles N. of Staunton, in a hill a short distance west of the Blue Ridge. It derives its name from Bernard Weyer, who discovered it in 1804, while hunting.

Within a few hundred yards of it, is Madison's cave, described by Jefferson. This, however, has superior attractions. No language can convey an adequate idea of the vastness and sublimity of some, or the exquisite beauty and grandeur of other of its innumerable apartments, with their snowy-white concretions of a thousand various forms. Many of these, with their striking and picturesque objects, have names exceedingly inappropriate, which to mention would degrade any description, however well written, by the association of the beautiful and sublime, with the vulgar and hackneyed. Washington Hall, the largest apartment, is 250 feet in length. A foreign traveller who visited the cave at an annual illumination, has, in a finely written description, the following notice of this hall:

"There is a fine sheet of rock-work running up the centre of this room, and giving it the aspect of two separate and noble galleries, till you look above, where you observe the partition rises only 20 feet towards the roof, and leaves the fine arch expanding over your head untouched. There is a beautiful concretion here, standing out in the room, which certainly has the form and drapery of a gigantic statue; it bears the name of the Nation's Hero, and the whole place is filled with those projections, appearances which excite the imagination by suggesting resemblances, and leaving them unfinished. The general effect, too, was perhaps indescribable. The fine perspective of this room, four times the length of an ordinary church; the numerous tapers, when near you, so encumbered by deep shadows as to give only a dim religious light; and when at a distance, appearing in their various attitudes like twinkling stars on a deep dark heaven; the amazing vaulted roof spread over you, with its carved and knotted surface, to which the streaming lights below in vain endeavored to convey their radiance; together with the impression that you had made so deep an entrance, and were so entirely cut off from the living world and ordinary things; produces an effect which, perhaps, the mind can receive but once, and will retain forever."

"Weyer's Cave," says the writer above quoted, "is in my judgment one of the great natural wonders of this new world; and for its eminence in its own class, deserves to be ranked with the Natural Bridge and Niagara, while it is far less known than either. Its dimensions, by the most direct course, are more than 1,600 feet; and by the more winding paths, twice that length; and its objects are remarkable for their variety, formation, and beauty. In both respects, it will, I think, compare, without injury to itself, with the celebrated Grotto of Antiparos. For myself, I acknowledge the spectacle to have been most interesting; but, to be so, it must be illuminated, as on this occasion. I had thought that this circumstance might give to the whole a toyish effect; but the influence of 2,000 or 3,000 lights on these immense caverns is only such as to reveal the objects, without disturbing the solemn and sublime obscurity which sleeps on every thing. Scarcely any scenes can awaken so many passions at once, and so deeply. Curiosity, apprehension, terror, surprise, admiration, and delight, by turns and together, arrest and possess you. I have had before, from other objects, one simple impression made with greater power; but I never had so many impressions made, and with so much power, before. If the interesting and the awful are the elements of the sublime, here sublimity reigns, as in her own domain, in darkness, silence, and deeps profound."

There died in this county, in February, 1844, a slave, named Gilbert, aged 112 years. He was a servant to Washington at the time of Braddock's defeat, and was afterwards present, in the same capacity, at the surrender of Cornwallis.

BATH.

BATH was formed in 1791, from Augusta, Bottetourt, and Greenbriar. It is about 35 miles long and 25 broad. It is watered by the head-branches of the James, Cow Pasture and Jackson Rivers. Some of the valley lands are very fertile, but the greatest proportion of the county is uncultivated, and covered with mountains. Pop. 1830, 4,008; 1840, whites 3,170, slaves 347, free colored 83; total 4,300.

Warm Springs, the county-seat, is 164 miles W. of Richmond, and 40 miles N. E. of the White Sulphur Springs of Greenbriar.

Besides the county buildings, and the elegant hotels for the accommodation of visiters at the springs, there are but a few dwellings. The situation of the place is delightful, in a narrow and fertile valley, between two high mountains, and offers numerous attractions to its many visiters.

The tradition respecting the discovery of the springs is, that a party of Indians hunting, spent a night in the valley. One of their number discovering the spring, bathed in it, and being much fatigued, he was induced, by the delicious sensation and warmth imparted by it, to remain all night. The next morning he was enabled to scale the mountain before his companions. As the country became settled, the fame of the waters gradually extended : and at first, visiters from the low country dwelt here in rude huts. For a long time, both this and the Hot Spring were only surrounded by brush, and open at top. The subjoined analysis of these waters was made by Prof. Rogers :

"The bath is an octagon, 38 feet in diameter, and 16 feet 9 inches inside—its area is 1163.77 feet. The ordinary depth of water being 5 feet, the cubic capacity is 5818.86 feet, or 43533.32 gallons. Notwithstanding *the leaks,* this quantity of water will flow into the reservoir in one hour. The average *temperature* of the bath is 98 deg. Fahrenheit. The gas which rises in the bath consists of *nitrogen,* with minute quantities of *sulphuretted hydrogen* and *carbonic acid.*

"Besides this gas, each gallon of water contains 4.5 cubic inches of gas, consisting of nitrogen, 3.25 cubic inches ; sulphuretted hydrogen, 0.25 do. ; carbonic acid, 1.00 do.

"The saline contents of one gallon of the water, are as follows : muriate of lime, 3.968 ; sulphate of magnesia, 9.984 ; carbonate of lime, 4.288 ; sulphate of lime, 5.466 ; a trace of soda, no doubt, in the state of muriate.

"While the Warm Springs afford the most luxurious bath in the world, they contain neutral salts and various gases, which act as a gentle aperient, diuretic and sudorific, and give tone and vigor to the human system. It is well ascertained in other countries, that waters of a high temperature tend more to strengthen the digestive organs than those of a low temperature ; but it is found, by actual experiment, that the water at the Warm Springs retains a considerable portion of its useful qualities when bottled in the spring, and then cooled by immersing the bottles in cold water, or even ice ; and this plan is adopted by many of those who have a repugnance to the use of warm water."

The approach to the Warm Springs from the east, is over the mountain of the same name. The road which leads across it is five miles, four-fifths of which is on the east side of the ridge, where to the traveller a succession of deep precipices and glens present themselves, environed with gloomy woods and obscure bottoms. From the summit of the mountain at the Warm Spring Rock, which is much visited, there is a sublime view of parallel ridges of mountains, extending for 40 or 50 miles, one behind the other, as far as the eye can reach, " like a dark blue sea of giant billows, instantly stricken solid by nature's magic wand." Some 70 years since, the principal route of emigration was across this mountain, at which time there was no wagon-road over it. The emigrants came in wagons to " the camping-ground," a level spot near what is now Brinckley's tavern, at the eastern base of the mountain. From thence they transported their baggage to the west on pack-horses, while their wagons returned east loaded with venison, hams, &c.

One mile west of the little village of Milboro' Spring, and 12 miles east of the Warm Springs, on the road between the two places, in a high ledge on the bank of the Cow-Pasture River, is the celebrated "*blowing-cave,*" described in Jefferson's Notes. The mouth of the cave is 20 or 30 feet above the road, in shape semi-circular, and in height about 4 feet. It has been explored for a

24

considerable distance. It is said that a small dog who entered found his way out through some unknown passage. When the internal and external atmosphere are the same, there is no perceptible current issuing from it. In intense hot weather, the air comes out with so much force as to prostrate the weeds at the entrance. In a warm day in June, in 1843, as Dr. John Brockenbrough, the principal proprietor of the Warm Springs, was passing in his carriage, he sent a little child to the mouth of the cave, who let go before it a handkerchief, which was blown by the current over the horses' heads in the road, a distance of 30 or 40 feet. In intense cold weather, the air draws in. There is a *flowing and ebbing spring* on the same stream with the blowing-cave, which supplies water-power for a grist-mill, a distillery, and a tan-yard. It flows irregularly. When it commences, the water bursts out in a body as if let loose from a dam.

Gen. Samuel Blackburn, who resided in this county, was born about the year 1758. He was one of the most successful orators and criminal lawyers of his time in Virginia. He was the father of the anti-duelling law of the state, which we believe was the first passed in the country after the war of the revolution. Among other penalties, it prohibited any one who had been engaged in a duel from holding offices of trust in the gift of the state. Some years after, a gentleman who had challenged another was elected to the legislature. When he came forward to take the customary oath, his violation of this law was urged against him. Some, however, contended that the circumstances of the case were so aggravating that its provisions ought to be disregarded, and fears were entertained that this sentiment might prevail. Then it was that Gen. Blackburn, who was a member, came forward with a speech of great power in opposition. The result was the triumph of the law in the rejection of the member. Gen. B. died in 1835, aged about 77. He was a man of much benevolence. At his death, he by will manumitted all his slaves, and provided for their transportation to Liberia.

The *Hot Springs* are 5 miles from the Warm, in the same beautiful valley with the latter. These springs stand high in public favor. There are several baths here, called the Hot Spouts. Their highest temperature is 106 degrees.

"The beneficial effects of hot spouts, topically applied, are so miraculous, in many painful and obstinate complaints, that words cannot adequately describe them ; therefore the prisoners of pain are strongly recommended to expose their rheumatic joints, gouty toes, and enlarged livers, to the comfortable outpourings of these healing steams. The water of the Hot Springs contains nitrogen and carbonic acid, carbonate of lime, sulphate of lime, sulphate of soda, sulphate of magnesia, muriate of soda, silica, and a trace of oxide of iron. It may be taken internally with much advantage, particularly as a sure and gentle diuretic.

"The effect of this bath on rheumatic and gouty affections, and on old deep-seated and chronic complaints, that medicine does not seem to reach, is very beneficial. It restores the surface to a good condition, and promotes the healthy action of the skin ; and every person who drinks the water of the various sulphur springs, should afterwards stop here two or three weeks, and try the virtue of the boiler. There is, near the hotel, a hot and cold spring issuing so near each other, that you can dip the thumb and forefinger of the same hand into hot and cold water at the same time."

BARBOUR.

Barbour was formed in 1843, from Harrison, Lewis, and Randolph, and named from the distinguished Barbour family : it is 30 miles long and 15 wide. The eastern part is mountainous, the western hilly, and much of the soil is fertile and adapted to grazing. It is thickly settled at the heads of Simpson's and Elk creeks, and on Buchannon and Tygart's Valley Rivers. Estimated population 5,000. Philippi, the county-seat,—formerly Boothe's Ferry of Randolph,—is situated 240 miles NW. of Richmond, and 30 SE. of Clarksburg, on the east bank of Tygart's Valley River, in a fertile country. It contains about a dozen dwellings, and has in its vicinity an abundance of coal and iron ore of an excellent quality.

The tract of country comprehended in the limits of this county, was the first permanently settled in northwestern Virginia. The following, relating to the settling of this portion of Virginia, is drawn from Withers' Border Warfare, published in 1831,—a work from which we have obtained considerable information respecting this portion of the state.

The comparative security which succeeded the treaty of 1765, contributed to advance the prosperity of the Virginia frontiers, and soon induced the settling of several places on the Monongahela and its branches, and on the Ohio river. The first settlement was that made on the Buchannon, a fork of the Tygart's Valley River, and was induced by the flattering account given by two brothers, who had dwelt there under rather unpleasant circumstances.

In 1761, four soldiers deserted from Fort Pitt, and after some wanderings, encamped in the glades over to the head of the Yougho'gany, where they remained about twelve months. Two of them, in an excursion among the settlers at Looney creek, were recognised and apprehended as deserters; but John and Samuel Pringle escaped to their camp in the glades, where they remained till some time in the year 1764.

During this year, and while in the employ of John Simpson, (a trapper who had come there in quest of furs,) they determined on removing further west. Simpson was induced to this by the prospect of enjoying the woods free from the intrusion of other hunters, (the glades having begun to be a common hunting-ground for the inhabitants of the South Branch;) while a regard for their personal safety, caused the Pringles to avoid a situation in which they might be exposed to the observation of other men.

In journeying through the wilderness, and after having crossed Cheat River, at the Horse-Shoe, a quarrel arose between Simpson and one of the Pringles; and notwithstanding that peace and harmony were so necessary to their mutual safety and comfort, yet each so far indulged the angry passions which had been excited, as at length to produce a separation.

Simpson crossed over the Valley River, near the mouth of Pleasant creek, and passing on to the head of another water-course, gave to it the name of Simpson's creek. Thence he went westwardly, and fell over on a stream which he called Elk: at the mouth of this he erected a camp, and continued to reside for more than twelve months. During this time he neither saw the Pringles, nor any other human being; and at the expiration of it, went to the South Branch, where he disposed of his furs and skins, and then returned to and continued at his encampment at the mouth of Elk, until permanent settlements were made in its vicinity.

The Pringles kept up the Valley River till they observed a large right-hand fork, (now Buchannon,) which they ascended some miles; and at the mouth of a small branch, (afterwards called Turkey run,) they took up their abode in the cavity of a large sycamore tree. The stump of this is still to be seen, and is an object of no little veneration with the immediate descendants of the first settlers.

The situation of these men, during a residence here of several years, although rendered somewhat necessary by their previous conduct, could not have been very enviable. Deserters from the army, a constant fear of discovery filled their minds with inquietude. In the vicinity of a savage foe, the tomahawk and scalping-knife were ever present to their imaginations. Remote from civilized man, their solitude was hourly interrupted by the frightful shrieks of the panther, or the hideous howlings of the wolf. And though the herds of buffalo, elk, and deer, which gambolled sportively around, enabled them easily to supply their larder; yet, the want of salt, of bread, and of every species of kitchen vegetable, must have abated their relish for the otherwise delicious loin of the one, and haunch of the others. The low state of their little magazine, too, while it limited their hunting to the bare procuration of articles of subsistence, caused them, from a fear of discovery, to shrink at the idea of being driven to the settlements for a supply of ammunition. And not until they were actually reduced to two loads of powder, could they be induced to venture again into the vicinity of their fellow-men. In the latter part of the year 1767, John left his brother, and intending to make for a trading post on the Shenandoah, appointed the period of his return.

Samuel Pringle, in the absence of John, suffered a good deal. The stock of provisions left him became entirely exhausted—one of his loads of powder was expended in a fruitless attempt to shoot a buck—his brother had already delayed his return several days longer than was intended, and he was apprehensive that he had been recognised, taken to Fort Pitt, and would probably never get back. With his remaining load of powder, however, he was fortunate enough to kill a fine buffalo; and John soon after returned with the news of peace, both with the Indians and French. The two brothers agreed to leave their retirement.

Their wilderness habitation was not left without some regret. Every object around had become more or less endeared to them. The tree, in whose hollow they had been so frequently sheltered from storm and tempest, was regarded by them with so great reverence, that they resolved, so soon as they could prevail on a few others to accompany them, again to return to this asylum of their exile.

In a population such as then composed the chief part of the South Branch settlement this was no difficult matter. All of them were used to the frontier manner of living; the most of them had gone thith-er to acquire land; many had failed entirely in this object, while others were obliged to occupy poor and broken situations off the river, the fertile bottoms having been previously located. Add to this the pas-sion for hunting, (which was a ruling one with many,) and the comparative scarcity of game in their neighborhood, and it need not excite surprise that the proposition of the Pringles to form a settlement in such a country as they represented that on Buchannon to be, was eagerly embraced by many.

In the fall of the ensuing year, (1768,) Samuel Pringle, and several others who wished first to examine for themselves, visited the country which had been so long occupied by the Pringles alone. Being pleas-ed with it, they in the following spring, with a few others, repaired thither with the view of cultivating as much corn as would serve their families the first year after their emigration. And having examined the country, for the purpose of selecting the most desirable situations, some of them proceeded to im-prove the spots of their choice. John Jackson (who was accompanied by his sons, George and Edward) settled at the mouth of Turkey run, where his daughter, Mrs. Davis, now lives—John Hacker higher up on the Buchannon River, where Bush's fort was afterwards established, and Nicholas Heavenor now lives —Alexander and Thomas Sleeth, near to Jackson's, on what is now known as the Forenash plantation. The others of the party (William Hacker, Thomas and Jesse Hughes, John and William Radcliff, and John Brown) appear to have employed their time exclusively in hunting; neither of them making any improvement of land for his own benefit. Yet were they of very considerable service to the new settle-ment. Those who had commenced clearing land, were supplied by them with abundance of meat, while in their hunting excursions through the country, a better knowledge of it was obtained, than could have been acquired had they been engaged in making improvements.

In one of these expeditions they discovered, and gave name to Stone-coal creek; which flowing west-wardly, induced the supposition that it discharged itself directly into the Ohio. Descending this creek, to ascertain the fact, they came to its confluence with a river, which they then called, and has since been known as the West Fork. After having gone some distance down the river they returned by a different route to the settlement, better pleased with the land on it and some of its tributaries, than with that on Buchannon.

Soon after this, other emigrants arrived under the guidance of Samuel Pringle. Among them were John and Benjamin Cutright, who settled on Buchannon, where John Cutright the younger, now lives; and Henry Rule, who improved just above the mouth of Fink's run. Before the arrival of Samuel Prin-gle, John Hacker had begun to improve the spot which Pringle had chosen for himself. To prevent any unpleasant result, Hacker agreed that if Pringle would clear as much land on a creek which had been recently discovered by the hunters, as he had on Buchannon, they could then exchange places. Comply-ing with this condition, Pringle took possession of the farm on Buchannon, and Hacker of the land im-proved by Pringle on the creek, which was hence called Hacker's creek. John and William Radcliff then likewise settled on this stream—the former on the farm where the Rev. John Mitchel now lives; the latter at the place now owned by William Powers, Esq. These comprise all the improvements which were made on the upper branches of the Monongahela, in the years 1769 and 1770.

At the close of the working season of 1769, some of these adventurers went to their families on the South Branch; and when they returned to gather their crops in the fall, found them entirely destroyed. In their absence the buffaloes, no longer awed by the presence of man, had trespassed on their enclo-sures and eaten their corn to the ground; this delayed the removal of their families till the winter of 1770.

Soon after the happening of this event, other settlements were made on the upper branches of the Monongahela River. Capt. James Booth and John Thomas established themselves on what has been since called Booth's creek—the former at the place now owned by Jesse Martin, and the latter where William Martin at present resides, and which is, perhaps, the most valuable landed estate in northwest-ern Virginia, off the Ohio River.

Previous, however, to the actual settlement of the country above the forks of the Monongahela, some few families (in 1767) had established themselves in the vicinity of Fort Redstone, now Brownsville, in Pennsylvania.

BEDFORD.

Bedford was formed from Lunenburg county, in 1753. It is 35 miles long, with an average breadth of 25. The surface is un-even, and the soil is naturally very fertile, but has been injured by the injudicious cultivation of tobacco. It is bounded on the north by the James River, and on the south by the Staunton. Goose and Otter creeks flow through it, the latter of which gives name to the noted Peaks of Otter. Population in 1830, 20,253; in 1840, whites 11,016, slaves 8,864, free colored 323—total 20,203.

Liberty, the county-seat, is on the Lynchburgh and Salem turn-pike, 26 miles sw. of the former, and contains five mercantile stores, one Baptist, one Presbyterian, one Episcopal, and one Meth-odist church, a large and handsome court-house, built in 1834, and a population of about 600. This neat and flourishing village is the admiration of travellers,—being surrounded by a beautiful, rolling, fertile country, bounded by a back-ground of great sublimity. The Blue Ridge, running to the right and left across the horizon for many miles, here towers to its greatest height in the celebrated peaks of Otter, which, although seven miles distant, appear in the immediate vicinity. These apparently isolated peaks, with one or two exceptions, are the loftiest mountains in the southern states. The estimated height of the most elevated,

The Peaks of Otter from near Liberty.

the northern peak, is 4200 feet above the plain, and 5307 feet above the level of the ocean, which is more than a mile in height. The most southerly, or the conical peak, is much visited. A writer in the Southern Literary Messenger gives the following glowing description of a trip to the peaks:

After riding about a mile and a quarter, we came to the point beyond which horses cannot be taken, and dismounting our steeds, commenced ascending on foot. The way was very steep, and the day so warm, that we had to halt often to take breath. As we approached the summit, the trees were all of a dwarfish growth, and twisted and gnarled by the storms of that high region. There were, also, a few blackberry bushes, bearing their fruit long after the season had passed below. A few minutes longer brought us to where the trees ceased to grow; but a huge mass of rocks, piled wildly on the top of each other, finished the termination of the peak. Our path lay for some distance around the base of it, and under the overhanging battlements; and rather descending for awhile until it led to a part of the pile, which could with some effort be scaled. There was no ladder, nor any artificial steps—and the only means of ascent was by climbing over the successive rocks. We soon stood upon the wild platform of one of nature's most magnificent observatories—isolated, and apparently above all things else terrestrial, and looking down upon, and over, a beautiful, variegated, and at the same time grand, wild, wonderful, and almost boundless panorama. Indeed, it was literally boundless; for there was a considerable haze resting upon some parts of "the world below;" so that, in the distant horizon, the earth and sky seemed insensibly to mingle with each other.

I had been there before. I remember when a boy of little more than ten years old, to have been taken to that spot, and how my unpractised nerves forsook me at the awful sublimity of the scene. On this day it was as new as ever; as wild, wonderful, and sublime, as if I had never before looked from those isolated rocks, or stood on that lofty summit. On one side, towards eastern Virginia, lay a comparatively level country, in the distance, bearing a strong resemblance to the ocean; on the other hand, were ranges of high mountains, interspersed with cultivated spots, and then terminating in piles of mountains, following in successive ranges, until they were lost also in the haze. Above and below, the Blue Ridge and Alleghanies ran off in long lines; sometimes relieved by knolls and peaks, and in one place above us making a graceful curve, and then again running off in a different line of direction. Very near us stood the rounded top of the other peak, looking like a sullen sentinel for its neighbor. We paused in silence for a time. We were there almost cut off from the world below, standing where it was fearful even to look down. It was more hazy than at the time of my last visit, but not too much so to destroy the interest of the scene.

There was almost a sense of pain, at the stillness which seemed to reign. We could hear the flapping of the wings of the hawks and buzzards, as they seemed to be gathering a new impetus after sailing through one of their circles in the air below us. North of us, and on the other side of the Valley of Virginia, were the mountains near Lexington, just as seen from that beautiful village—the Jump, North, and House Mountains succeeding each other; they were familiar with a thousand associations of our childhood, seeming mysteriously, when away from the spot, to bring my early home before me—not in imagination, such as had often haunted me when I first left it to find another in the world, but in substantial reality. Further on down the valley, and at a great distance, was the top of a large mountain, which was thought to be the great North Mountain, away down in Shenandoah county—I am afraid to say how far off. Intermediate between these mountains, and extending opposite and far above us, was the Valley of Virginia, with its numerous and highly cultivated farms. Across this valley, and in the distance, lay the remotest ranges of the Alleghany and the mountains about; and I suppose beyond the White Sulphur Springs. Nearer us, and separating eastern and western Virginia, was the Blue Ridge, more than ever showing the propriety of its cognomen of the "backbone;" and on which we could distinctly see two zigzag turnpikes, the one leading to Fincastle, and the other to Buchanan; and over which latter we had travelled a few days before. With the spyglass we could distinguish the houses in the village of Fincastle, some twenty-five or thirty miles off, and the road leading to the town.

Turning towards the direction of our morning's ride, we had beneath us Bedford county, with its smaller mountains, farms and farm-houses—the beautiful village of Liberty, the county roads, and occasionally a mill-pond, reflecting the sun like a sheet of polished silver. The houses on the hill at Lynchburg, twenty-five or thirty miles distant, are distinctly visible on a clear day, and also Willis' Mountain away down in Buckingham county.

I had often visited Bedford, and had been more or less familiar with it from childhood; but at our elevation, distances were so annihilated, and appearances so changed, that we could scarcely recognise the most familiar objects. After some difficulty, we at length made out the residence of Dr. M., we had that morning left, and at that moment rendered more than usually interesting, by containing, in addition to the other very dear relatives, two certain ladies, who sustained a very interesting connexion with the doctor and myself, and one of whom had scarcely laid aside the blushes of her bridal hour.

A little beyond this, I recognised the former residence of a beloved sister, now living in a distant southern state. It was the same steep hill ascending to the gate, the same grove around the house, as when she lived there, and the same as when I played there in my boyhood. And it was the first time I had seen it since the change of owners. I then saw it from the Peaks of Otter: but it touched a thousand tender cords; and I almost wept when I thought, that those I once there loved were far away, and that the scenes of my youthful days could not return.

Myself and companions had, some time before, gotten on different rocks, that we might not interrupt each other in our contemplations. I could not refrain, however, from saying to one of them, " What little things we are! how factitious our ideas of what is extensive in territory and distance!" A splendid estate was about the size I could step over; and I could stand and look at the very house whence I used often to start in days gone by, and follow with my eye my day's journey to the spot where, wearied and worn down, I dismounted with the setting sun. Yet I could look over what seemed so great a space, with a single glance. I could also look away down the Valley of Virginia, and trace the country, and, in imagination, the stage-coach, as it slowly wound its way, day and night for successive days, to reach the termination of what I could throw my eye over in a moment. I was impressively reminded of the extreme littleness with which these things of earth would all appear, when the tie of life which binds us here is broken, and we shall be able to look back and down upon them from another world. The scene and place are well calculated to excite such thoughts.

It is said that John Randolph once spent the night on these elevated rocks, attended by no one but his servant; and that, when in the morning he had witnessed the sun rising over the majestic scene, he turned to his servant, having no other to whom he could express his thoughts, and charged him, " never from that time to believe any one who told him there was no God."

I confess, also, that my mind was most forcibly carried to the judgment-day; and I could but call the attention of my companions to what would, probably, then be the sublime terror of the scene we now beheld, when the mountains we saw and stood upon, should all be melted down like wax; when the flames should be driving over the immense expanse before us; when the heavens over us should be " passing away with a great noise;" and when the air beneath and around us should be filled with the very inhabitants now dwelling and busied in that world beneath us.

BERKELEY.

Berkeley was formed in 1772, from Frederick. Its mean length is 22½ miles; mean breadth, 13 miles. The surface is much broken and mountainous. Back and Opequan creeks run through the county and empty into the Potomac. Some of the land bordering these streams and the Potomac River, is very fertile. Anthracite coal is found in the western section of this county. Population: 1830, 10,528; 1840, whites 8,760, slaves 1,919, free colored 293; total

10,972. Darksville and Gerardstown contain each from 30 to 40 dwellings. Martinsburg, the county-seat, lies on the line of the Baltimore and Ohio Railroad, 169 miles NNW. of Richmond, 77 from Washington, and 20 from Harper's Ferry.

Central View in Martinsburg.

It is compactly built, and contains 2 newspaper printing offices; 7 stores; a market; 1 Presbyterian, 1 Lutheran, 1 Episcopal, 1 German Reformed, 1 Methodist, and 1 Catholic church; and a population of about 1700. This town was laid out by Adam Stephen, Esq., and established by law in 1778, when the following gentlemen were appointed trustees: James M'Alister, Joseph Mitchell, Anthony Noble, James Strode, Robert Carter Willis, William Patterson, and Philip Pendleton. It derived its name from the late Col. T. B. Martin. The Baltimore and Ohio Railroad passes through the village.

The public building, in the centre of the view, is the court-house, which was built a year after the formation of the county, in the reign of George III. The jail at this place is rarely tenanted, and but one individual has been sent to the penitentiary within the last 12 years. Traces of the road cut by Braddock's army on their unfortunate expedition to the west, are discernible near the town. In St. Clair's defeat, about 80 citizens of the county were killed. In the vicinity of Leetown, (in the adjoining county of Jefferson,) there lived within a few miles of each other, after the war of the revolution, three general officers of the American army—Alexander Stephens, Horatio Gates, and Charles Lee. The will of the latter is now in the clerk's office, in this county. The accompanying extract from it, is in keeping with its eccentric author:

"I desire most earnestly that I may not be buried in any church or church-yard, or within a mile of any Presbyterian or Anabaptist meeting-house, for since I have resided in this country, I have kept so much bad company while living, that I do not choose to continue it when dead."

General Lee's unbounded ambition led him to envy the great fame of Washington, and it was supposed his aim was to supersede him in the supreme command. He wrote a pamphlet, filled with scurrilous imputations upon the military talents of the commander-in-chief. In consequence, he was challenged by Col. Laurens, one of Washington's aids, and was wounded in the duel which ensued. Degraded in the opinions of the wise and virtuous, he retired to this section of country, where, secluded from society, he lived in a rude hovel, without windows or plastering, or even a decent article of furniture, and with but few or no companions but his books and dogs. In 1780, Congress resolved that they had no further occasion for his services in the army. In the autumn of 1782, wearied with his forlorn situation and broken in spirits, he went to Philadelphia, where, in his lodgings in an obscure public-house he soon died, a martyr to chagrin and disappointment. In his dying moments, he was, in imagination, on the field of battle: the last words he was heard to utter were, "*Stand by me, my brave grenadiers !*"

Gen. Gates, of whom the prediction of Gen. Lee was verified, "that his *northern laurels* would be covered with *southern willow,*" was, after the disastrous battle of Camden, suspended from military command until 1782, when the great scenes of the war were over. Gates was one of the infamous cabal who designed to supplant Washington : but he lived to do justice to the character of that great man.

After the war, Gates lived about seven years on his plantation in Virginia, the remainder of his life he passed near New York city. In 1800, he was elected to the legislature of that state by the anti-federal party. He died in 1806, aged 78 years. " A few years before his death, he generously gave freedom to his slaves, making provision for the old and infirm, while several testified their attachment to him by remaining in his family. In the characteristic virtue of a planter's hospitality, Gates had no competitor, and his reputation may well be supposed to put this virtue to a hard test. He had a handsome person, and was gentlemanly in his manners, remarkably courteous to all, and carrying good humor sometimes beyond the nice limit of dignity." Both Lee and Gates were natives of England, and all three, Lee, Gates, and Stephens, had command of Virginia troops.

Many of the early settlers of the county were Scotch-Irish, who were Presbyterians. " It is said that the spot where Tuscarora meeting-house now stands, is the first place where the gospel was publicly preached and divine service performed, west of the Blue Ridge. This was, and still remains, a Presbyterian edifice. Mr. Semple, in his history of the Virginia Baptists, states that in the year 1754, Mr. Stearns, a preacher of this denomination, with several others, removed from New England. 'They halted first at Opequon, in Berkeley county, Va., where he formed a Baptist church, under the care of the Rev. John Gerard.' This was probably the first Baptist church founded west of the Blue Ridge."

There is an interesting anecdote, related by Kercheval, in his account of Indian incursions and massacres in this region, of a young and beautiful girl, named Isabella Stockton, who was taken prisoner in the attack on Neally's fort, and carried and sold to a Canadian in Canada. A young Frenchman, named Pluta, becoming enamored with her, made proposals of matrimony. This she declined, unless her parents' consent could be obtained—a strong proof of her filial affection and good sense. The Frenchman conducted her home, readily believing that his generous devotion and attachment to the daughter would win their consent. But the prejudices then existing against the French, made her parents and friends peremptorily reject his overtures. Isabella then agreed to elope with him, and mounting two of her father's horses, they fled, but were overtaken by her two brothers in pursuit, by whom she was forcibly torn from her lover and protector and carried back to her parents, while the poor Frenchman was warned that his life should be the forfeit of any farther attempts.

The Hon. FELIX GRUNDY was born on the 11th of Sept., 1777, in a log house on Sleepy Creek, in this county. His father was a native of England. When Felix was but two years of age, his family removed to what is now Brownsville, Penn., and in 1780 to Kentucky, where he lived from childhood to maturity, and in 1807 or 1808, removed to Tennessee.

Mr. Grundy was one of the most distinguished lawyers and statesmen of the western states. When in the councils of the nation, he had but few superiors. He was always a zealous and most efficient supporter of the democratic party. "His manners were amiable, his conversation instructive, abounding in humor and occasionally sarcastic. His cheerful disposition gained him friends among his political opponents, and rendered him the delight of the domestic circle. His morals were drawn from the pure fountain of Christianity, and, while severe with himself, he was charitable to others. Integrity and justice controlled his transactions with his fellow-men."

"COL. CRAWFORD emigrated from Berkeley county in 1768, with his family, to Pennsylvania. He was a captain in Forbes' expedition, in 1758. He was the intimate friend of Washington, who was frequently an inmate of his humble dwelling, during his visits to the then west, for the purpose of locating lands and attending to public business. Col. Crawford was one of the bravest men on the frontier, and often took the lead in parties against the Indians across the Ohio. His records and papers were never preserved, and very little else than a few brief anecdotes remain to perpetuate his fame. At the commencement of the Revolution, he raised a regiment by his own exertions, and held the commission of colonel in the continental army. In 1782, he accepted, with great reluctance, the command of an expedition to ravage the Wyandott and Moravian Indian towns on the Muskingum. On this expedition, at the age of 50, he was taken prisoner, and put to death by the most excruciating tortures."

BRAXTON.

BRAXTON was formed in 1836, from Lewis, Kanawha, and Nicholas, and named from Carter Braxton, one of the signers of the Declaration of American Independence : it is about 45 miles long, with a mean width of 20 miles. It is watered by Elk and Little Kanawha Rivers, and their branches. The country is rough, but well watered, and fertile. Pop. 1840, whites 2,509 : slaves 64 free col'd. 2 ; total, 2,575.

Sutton, the county-seat, on Elk River, 289 miles w. of Richmond, is a small village ; the only public buildings being those belonging to the county. The locality called Bulltown, where there is a post-office, was so named from the fact that about sixty years since, it was the residence of a small tribe of Indians, the name of whose chief was Captain Bull.

BROOKE.

BROOKE was formed from Ohio co., in 1797. It is the most northerly county in the state, and is a portion of the narrow neck of land lying between Pennsylvania and the Ohio River called the "panhandle." Its mean length is 31 miles, mean breadth 6 1-2. The surface is hilly, but much of the soil is fertile. The county abounds in coal. Large quantities are quarried on the side hills on the Ohio. There is not at the present time, (Sept. 1843,) a licensed tavern in the county, for retailing ardent spirits, and not one distillery; nor has there been a criminal prosecution for more than two years. Pop. 1830, 7,040; 1840, whites 7,080, slaves 91, free col'd. 77; total, 7,948.

Fairview, or New Manchester, lies on the Ohio, 22 miles N. of Wellsburg, on an elevated and healthy situation. It contains about 25 dwellings. The churches are Presbyterian and Methodist. Holliday's Cove is a long and scattering village, about 7 miles above Wellsburg, in a beautiful and fertile valley, of a semi-circular form. It contains 1 Union church, 1 Christian Disciples' church, an academy, and about 60 dwellings. Flour of a superior quality is manufactured at the mills on Harmon's Creek, in this valley. Bethany is beautifully situated, 8 miles E. of Wellsburg. It contains a few dwellings only. It is the residence of Dr. Alexander Campbell, the founder of the denomination generally known as "the Campbellite Baptists:" a name, however, which they themselves do not recognise, taking that of "Disciples, or Christian Baptists."

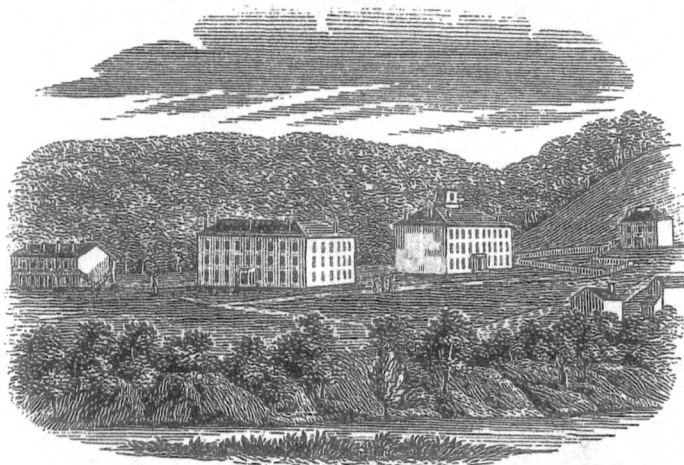

Bethany College, Brooke County.

Bethany College was founded by Dr. Alexander Campbell, in 1841. Its instructors are the president, (Dr. Campbell,) and 4 professors. The institution is flourishing, numbering something like a hundred pupils, including the preparatory department. The buildings prepared for their reception are spacious and convenient.

The following historical sketch of "the Disciples of Christ," with a view of their religious opinions, is from Hayward's Book of Religions:

The rise of this society, if we only look back to the drawing of the lines of demarcation between it and other professors, is of recent origin. About the commencement of the present century, the Bible alone, without any human addition in the form of creeds or confessions of faith, began to be preached by many distinguished ministers of different denominations, both in Europe and America.

With various success, and with many of the opinions of the various sects imperceptibly carried with them from the denominations to which they once belonged, did the advocates of the Bible cause plead for the union of Christians of every name, on the broad basis of the apostles' teaching. But it was not until the year 1823 that a restoration of the *original gospel* and *order of things*, began to be advocated in a periodical edited by Alexander Campbell, of Bethany, Virginia, entitled " The Christian Baptist."

He and his father, Thomas Campbell, renounced the Presbyterian system, and were immersed, in the year 1812. They, and the congregations which they had formed, united with the Redstone Baptist Association, protesting against all human creeds as bonds of union, and professing subjection to the Bible alone. This union took place in the year 1813. But, in pressing upon the attention of that society and the public the all-sufficiency of the *sacred* Scriptures for every thing necessary to the perfection of Christian character,—whether in the private or social relations of life, in the church, or in the world,—they began to be opposed by a strong creed-party in that association. After some ten years' debating and contending for the Bible alone, and the apostles' doctrine, Alexander Campbell, and the church to which he belonged, united with the Mahoning association, in the Western Reserve of Ohio; that association being more favorable to his views of reform.

In his debates on the subject and action of baptism with Mr. Walker, a seceding minister, in the year 1820, and with Mr. M'Calla, a Presbyterian minister of Kentucky, in the year 1823, his views of reformation began to be developed, and were very generally received by the Baptist society, as far as these works were read.

But in his " Christian Baptist," which began July 4, 1823, his views of the need of reformation were more fully exposed; and, as these gained ground by the pleading of various ministers of the Baptist denomination, a party in opposition began to exert itself, and to oppose the spread of what they were pleased to call heterodoxy. But not till after great numbers began to act upon these principles, was there any attempt towards separation. After the Mahoning association appointed Mr. Walter Scott, an evangelist, in the year 1827, and when great numbers began to be immersed into Christ, under his labors, and new churches began to be erected by him and other laborers in the field, did the Baptist associations begin to declare non-fellowship with the brethren of the reformation. Thus, by constraint, not of choice, they were obliged to form societies out of those communities that split, upon the ground of adherence to the apostles' doctrine. The distinguishing characteristics of their views and practices are the following:—

They regard all the sects and parties of the Christian world as having, in greater or less degree, departed from the simplicity of faith and manners of the first Christians, and as forming what the apostle Paul calls " the apostacy." This defection they attribute to the great varieties of speculation and metaphysical dogmatism of the countless creeds, formularies, liturgies, and books of discipline, adopted and inculcated as bonds of union, and platforms of communion in all the parties which have sprung from the Lutheran reformation. The effect of these synodical covenants, conventional articles of belief, and rules of ecclesiastical polity, has been the introduction of a new nomenclature,—a human vocabulary of religious words, phrases, and technicalities, which has displaced the style of the living oracles, and affixed to the sacred diction ideas wholly unknown to the apostles of Christ.

To remedy and obviate these aberrations, they propose to ascertain from the Holy Scriptures, according to the commonly received and well-established rules of interpretation, the ideas attached to the leading terms and sentences found in the Holy Scriptures, and then to use the words of the Holy Spirit in the apostolic acceptation of them.

By thus expressing the ideas communicated by the Holy Spirit, in the terms and phrases learned from the apostles, and by avoiding the artificial and technical language of scholastic theology, they propose to restore a pure speech to the household of faith; and, by accustoming the family of God to use the language and dialect of the Heavenly Father, they expect to promote the sanctification of one another through the truth, and to terminate those discords and debates which have always originated from the words which man's wisdom teaches, and from a reverential regard and esteem for the style of the great masters of polemic divinity; believing that speaking the same things in the same style, is the only certain way to thinking the same things.

They make a very marked difference between faith and opinion; between the testimony of God and the reasonings of men; the words of the Spirit and human inferences. Faith in the testimony of God, and obedience to the commandments of Jesus, are their bond of union, and not an agreement in any abstract views or opinions upon what is written or spoken by divine authority. Hence all the speculations, questions, debates of words, and abstract reasonings, found in human creeds, have no place in their religious fellowship. Regarding Calvinism and Arminianism, Trinitarianism and Unitarianism, and all the opposing theories of religious sectaries, as *extremes* begotten by each other, they cautiously avoid them, as equidistant from the simplicity and practical tendency of the promises and precepts, of the doctrine and facts, of the exhortations and precedents, of the Christian institution.

They look for unity of spirit and the bonds of peace in the practical acknowledgment of one faith, one Lord, one immersion, one hope, one body, one Spirit, one God and Father of all; not in unity of opinions, nor in unity of forms, ceremonies, or modes of worship.

The Holy Scriptures of both Testaments they regard as containing revelations from God, and as all necessary to make the man of God perfect, and accomplished for every good word and work; the New Testament, or the living oracles of Jesus Christ, they understand as containing the Christian religion; the testimonies of Matthew, Mark, Luke, and John, they view as illustrating and proving the great proposition on which our religion rests, viz., that Jesus of Nazareth is the Messiah, the only begotten and well-beloved Son of God, and the only Saviour of the world; the Acts of the Apostles as a divinely authorized narrative of the beginning and progress of the reign or kingdom of Jesus Christ, recording the full development of the gospel by the Holy Spirit sent down from heaven, and the procedure of the apostles in setting up the Church of Christ on earth; the Epistles as carrying out and applying the doctrine of the apostles to the practice of individuals and congregations, and as developing the tendencies of the gospel in the behavior of its professors; and all as forming a complete standard of Christian faith and morals, adapted to the interval between the ascension of Christ and his return with the kingdom which he has received from God; the Apocalypse, or Revelation of Jesus Christ to John, in Patmos, as a figurative and prospective view of all the fortunes of Christianity, from its date to the return of the Saviour.

Every one who sincerely believes the testimony which God gave of Jesus of Nazareth, saying, " This is my Son, the beloved, in whom I delight," or, in other words, believes what the evangelists and apostles have testified concerning him, from his conception to his coronation in heaven as Lord of all, and who is willing to obey him in every thing, they regard as a proper subject of immersion, and no one else. They consider immersion into the name of the Father, Son, and Holy Spirit, after a public, sincere, and intelligent confession of the faith in Jesus, as necessary to admission to the privileges of the kingdom of the Messiah, and as a solemn pledge, on the part of Heaven, of the actual remission of all past sins, and of adoption into the family of God.

The Holy Spirit is promised only to those who believe and obey the Saviour. No one is taught to expect the reception of that heavenly Monitor and Comforter, as a resident in his heart, till he obeys the gospel.

Thus, while they proclaim faith and repentance, or faith and a change of heart, as preparatory to immersion, remission, and the Holy Spirit, they say to all penitents, or all those who believe and repent of their sins, as Peter said to the first audience addressed after the Holy Spirit was bestowed, after the glorification of Jesus, "Be immersed, every one of you, in the name of the Lord Jesus, for the remission of sins, and you shall receive the gift of the Holy Spirit." They teach sinners that God commands all men, everywhere, to reform, or turn to God; that the Holy Spirit strives with them, so to do, by the apostles and prophets; that God beseeches them to be reconciled, through Jesus Christ; and that it is the duty of all men to believe the gospel, and turn to God.

The immersed believers are congregated into societies, according to their propinquity to each other, and taught to meet every first day of the week, to break the loaf, which commemorates the death of the Son of God, to read and hear the living oracles, to teach and admonish one another, to unite in all prayer and praise, to contribute to the necessities of saints, and to perfect holiness in the fear of the Lord.

Every congregation chooses its own overseers and deacons, who preside over and administer the affairs of the congregations; and every church, either from itself, or in coöperation with others, sends out, as opportunity offers, one or more evangelists, or proclaimers of the word, to preach the word, and to immerse those who believe, to gather congregations, and to extend the knowledge of salvation where it is necessary, as far as their means allow. But every church regards these evangelists as its servants; and, therefore, they have no control over any congregation, each congregation being subject to its own choice of presidents or elders, whom they have appointed. Perseverance in all the work of faith, labor of love, and patience of hope, is inculcated, by all the disciples, as essential to admission into the heavenly kingdom.

Such are the prominent outlines of the faith and practices of those who wish to be known as the Disciples of Christ; but no society among them would agree to make the preceding items either a confession of faith or a standard of practice, but, for the information of those who wish an acquaintance with them, are willing to give, at any time, a reason for their faith, hope, and practice.

View of Wellsburg, Brooke County.

Wellsburg, the seat of justice for the county, is beautifully situated on the Ohio River, 337 miles from Richmond and 16 above Wheeling. It is a thriving, business place, and contains 9 mercantile stores, 2 academies, 1 Presbyterian, 1 Methodist, 1 Christian Baptist, and 1 Episcopal church, 1 white flint-glass works, 1 glass-cutting establishment, 1 paper-mill, 1 large cotton factory, 2 extensive potteries, 1 steam saw-mill, 5 large warehouses, 1 newspaper printing office, 6 extensive flouring-mills in it and the vicinity, 1 woollen factory, a branch of the N. W. Va. Bank, and a population of over 2,000. Inexhaustible beds of stone-coal abound on all sides of the place, which is furnished at a few cents per bushel to the numerous manufactories located here. About 50,000 barrels of flour are annually exported from here to New Orleans, in steam and flat boats.

Wellsburg was laid out in 1789, by Charles Prather, the original proprietor, from whom it was named Charleston. There being two other towns in the state of a similar name, it was afterwards changed to its present name from Alexander Wells, who built a flour warehouse at the point, the first ever erected on the Ohio. The first settlers came before the revolution: they were three brothers, Isaac, George, and Friend Cox, who built a fort, as a protection against the Indians, about a mile above the village. Most of the early settlers were from New England. The inhabitants in the town and vicinity, at an early date, whose names are recollected, were Wm. M'Farland, Capt. Oliver Brown, Capt. Samuel Brown, Dr. Joseph and Philip Dodridge, James and Thomas Marshall, Major M'Mahon, who was killed in Wayne's campaign, Samuel Brady, the famous Indian hunter, James and Hezekiah Griffeth, Isaac Reeves, and James Perry. About a mile below town, on the river, at a place now called Indian Side, a Mrs. Buskirk was killed and scalped by the Indians. The Mingo tribe of Indians had a settlement three miles above Wellsburg, on the opposite side of the river.

PHILIP DODRIDGE, who died at Washington, in 1832, while a member of Congress, was from Wellsburg. He was scarcely less celebrated in western Virginia, for his eloquence and splendid talents, than was Patrick Henry, in his day, in the oldest portions of the state. Dr. S. P. Hildreth, in the American Pioneer, has given the subjoined sketch:

Mr. Dodridge, as is well known to the early inhabitants of western Pennsylvania and Virginia, was for many years one of the most noted men in that region, for his splendid talents at the bar; and has probably never been excelled, if he has been equalled, for his discrimination in fathoming the depths of an intricate case, or his powerful and logical reasoning in unfolding it. His father was among the earliest settlers of northwestern Virginia, in the vicinity of what was then called Charleston, but now Wellsburg. His constitution being not very robust, at the age of sixteen or eighteen years he was taken from the plough, put to school, and commenced the study of Latin. His vigorous mind drank in knowledge with the rapidity of thought, or as a dry sponge absorbs water. It soon became a habit with him to exercise his memory, in changing the common conversation around him into the idiom of his studies; and following his father in his evening and morning devotions, he soon learned to render his prayers into very good Latin, and to converse with his teacher fluently. This close application to his books, although it invigorated his mental powers, yet enfeebled his body, and it became necessary for a while to suspend his studies. At this period, the region in which he lived had become so much improved as to afford considerable surplus produce beyond the wants of the inhabitants, the only market for which was to be found on the Mississippi River or at New Orleans. Some of his cousins, young men of his own age, having loaded a boat with flour, invited him to go with them, and recruit his enfeebled frame by a voyage to the south. Nothing very interesting occurred until they reached Natchez, at that time in the possession of the Spaniards. They were very strict in their police, forbidding any strangers or boatmen to go up into the town, seated on a high bluff, without a written permission from the commandant or governor of the place. Young Dodridge feeling the ill effects of confinement to the narrow limits of the boat, and that he needed exercise, determined to take a walk and visit the town on the hill. He had ascended about half way, when he was met by a well-dressed man, who accosted him in the Spanish language. Dodridge did not fully understand him, but thought it similar to the Latin, and answered him in that tongue. It so happened that the individual who addressed him was no less a personage than the governor of Natchez, and was weiï versed in the Latin, having been liberally educated in Spain. They soon fell into a very familiar and animated discourse, without Philip's once suspecting the station of his new acquaintance. Learning that he had visited the Mississippi country on account of his delicate health, and that he was now walking for exercise, after long confinement to the boat, and withal astonished and delighted to have discovered so learned a man in an up-country boatman, he invited him to his house. The sprightly wit and uncommon intellect of the young stranger soon won his whole heart, and interested the Spanish commandant deeply in his welfare. His admiration was not the less excited, from having pointed out to him on a large map of the western country, which hung against the wall, the spot near the head of the Ohio River, where he was born, and from whence he departed on the present voyage. While thus agreeably engaged, a black servant drove up to the door with a neat Spanish carriage and pair of horses, accompanied with an invitation from the governor to step in and ride as far as he pleased. With many thanks, not the less acceptable to his benefactor from their being clothed in the Latin tongue, Philip accepted the offered kindness, and extended his ride to some distance around the suburbs of Natchez. When about to depart, he was invited to call every day as long as he remained, and the carriage and servant should be ready for his service. This pleasing intercourse was continued for about a week; and when he finally took his leave, the governor gave him letters of introduction to several of the first men in New Orleans, accompanied with many flattering expressions of his admiration for his uncommon acquirements, and the pleasure his acquaintance had afforded him; thus demonstrating the homage that is ever paid by the wise and good to learning and worth, even when accompanied with poverty and among strangers. His companions looked with wonder and astonishment at the gracious reception and attention paid to their cousin by the governor, while they were barely allowed to step on shore, and not suffered to leave the vicinity of the landing. Philip laughingly told them it was all owing to his good looks, which they could hardly believe, as in this particular they were decidedly superior to their cousin. On reaching New Orleans, his letters procured him ready admission to the tables and the society of the most prominent men in the city; and the few weeks he staid there were passed in a round of amusements, freely bestowed by the hospitable Spaniards. At his departure they loaded him with their good wishes and assurances, that they should never forget his name, or the pleasure they had received from the brilliant sallies of his humor and wit.

The Rev. DR. JOSEPH DODRIDGE, a brother of the above, was an Episcopal clergyman, in Wellsburg. He was the author of the work, entitled, "Notes on the settlement and Indian Wars of the western parts of Virginia and Pennsylvania, from the year 1763 until the year 1783, inclusive, together with a view of the state of society and manners of the first settlers of that country." From this interesting and graphic volume, we have, in our work, made several extracts. We here present the reader with his description of the weddings among the early pioneers:

For a long time after the first settlement of this country, the inhabitants in general married young. There was no distinction of rank, and very little of fortune. On these accounts the first impression of love resulted in marriage; and a family establishment cost but a little labor, and nothing else. A description of a wedding, from the beginning to the end, will serve to show the manners of our forefathers, and mark the grade of civilization which has succeeded to their rude state of society in the course of a few years. At an early period, the practice of celebrating the marriage at the house of the bride began, and, it should seem, with great propriety. She also had the choice of the priest to perform the ceremony.

A wedding engaged the attention of a whole neighborhood; and the frolic was anticipated by old and young with eager expectation. This is not to be wondered at, when it is told that a wedding was almost the only gathering which was not accompanied with the labor of reaping, log-rolling, building a cabin, or planning some scout or campaign.

In the morning of the wedding-day, the groom and his attendants assembled at the house of his father, for the purpose of reaching the mansion of his bride by noon, which was the usual time for celebrating the nuptials, which for certain must take place before dinner

Let the reader imagine an assemblage of people, without a store, tailor, or mantua-maker, within a hundred miles; and an assemblage of horses, without a blacksmith or saddler within an equal distance. The gentlemen dressed in shoe-packs, moccasins, leather breeches, leggins, linsey hunting-shirts, and all home-made. The ladies dressed in linsey petticoats, and linsey or linen bed-gowns, coarse shoes, stockings, handkerchiefs, and buckskin gloves, if any. If there were any buckles, rings, buttons, or ruffles, they were the relics of old times; family pieces, from parents or grand-parents. The horses were caparisoned with old saddles, old bridles or halters, and pack-saddles, with a bag or blanket thrown over them; a rope or string as often constituted the girth, as a piece of leather.

The march, in double file, was often interrupted by the narrowness and obstructions of our horse-paths, as they were called, for we had no roads; and these difficulties were often increased, sometimes by the good, and sometimes by the ill-will of neighbors, by falling trees, and tying grape-vines across the way. Sometimes an ambuscade was formed by the wayside, and an unexpected discharge of several guns took place, so as to cover the wedding-party with smoke. Let the reader imagine the scene which followed this discharge; the sudden spring of the horses, the shrieks of the girls, and the chivalric bustle of their partners to save them from falling. Sometimes, in spite of all that could be done to prevent it, some were thrown to the ground. If a wrist, elbow, or ankle happened to be sprained, it was tied with a handkerchief, and little more was thought or said about it.

Another ceremony commonly took place before the party reached the house of the bride, after the practice of making whiskey began, which was at an early period; when the party were about a mile from the place of their destination, two young men would single out to run for the bottle; the worse the path, the more logs, brush, and deep hollows, the better, as these obstacles afforded an opportunity for the greater display of intrepidity and horsemanship. The English fox-chase, in point of danger to the riders and their horses, is nothing to this race for the bottle. The start was announced by an Indian yell; logs, brush, muddy hollows, hill and glen, were speedily passed by the rival ponies. The bottle was always filled for the occasion, so that there was no use for judges; for the first who reached the door was presented with the prize, with which he returned in triumph to the company. On approaching them, he announced his victory over his rival by a shrill whoop. At the head of the troop, he gave the bottle first to the groom and his attendants, and then to each pair in succession to the rear of the line, giving each a dram; and then putting the bottle in the bosom of his hunting-shirt, took his station in the company.

The ceremony of the marriage preceded the dinner, which was a substantial backwoods feast, of beef, pork, fowls, and sometimes venison and bear-meat, roasted and boiled, with plenty of potatoes, cabbage, and other vegetables. During the dinner the greatest hilarity always prevailed, although the table might be a large slab of timber, hewed out with a broadaxe, supported by four sticks set in auger-holes; and the furniture, some old pewter dishes and plates; the rest, wooden bowls and trenchers; a few pewter spoons, much battered about the edges, were to be seen at some tables. The rest were made of horns. If knives were scarce, the deficiency was made up by the scalping-knives, which were carried in sheaths suspended to the belt of the hunting-shirt.

After dinner the dancing commenced, and generally lasted till the next morning. The figures of the dances were three and four-handed reels, or square setts and jigs. The commencement was always a square four, which was followed by what was called jigging it off; that is, two of the four would single out for a jig, and were followed by the remaining couple. The jigs were often accompanied with what was called cutting out; that is, when either of the parties became tired of the dance, on intimation the place was supplied by some one of the company without any interruption of the dance. In this way a dance was often continued till the musician was heartily tired of his situation. Towards the latter part of the night, if any of the company, through weariness, attempted to conceal themselves, for the purpose of sleeping, they were hunted up, paraded on the floor, and the fiddler ordered to play, "Hang out till to-morrow morning."

About nine or ten o'clock, a deputation of the young ladies stole off the bride, and put her to bed. In doing this, it frequently happened that they had to ascend a ladder instead of a pair of stairs, leading from the dining and ball-room to the loft, the floor of which was made of clapboards, lying loose, and without nails. As the foot of the ladder was commonly behind the door, which was purposely opened for the occasion, and its rounds at the inner ends were well hung with hunting-shirts, petticoats, and other articles of clothing, the candles being on the opposite side of the house, the exit of the bride was noticed but by few. This done, a deputation of young men in like manner stole off the groom, and placed him snugly by the side of his bride. The dance still continued ; and if seats happened to be scarce, which was often the case, every young man, when not engaged in the dance, was obliged to offer his lap as a seat for one of the girls ; and the offer was sure to be accepted. In the midst of this hilarity the bride and groom were not forgotten. Pretty late in the night, some one would remind the company that the new couple must stand in need of some refreshment ; black Betty, which was the name of the bottle, was called for, and sent up the ladder ; but sometimes black Betty did not go alone. I have many times seen as much bread, beef, pork, and cabbage, sent along with her, as would afford a good meal for half a dozen hungry men. The young couple were compelled to eat and drink, more or less, of whatever was offered them.

It often happened that some neighbors or relations, not being asked to the wedding, took offence ; and the mode of revenge adopted by them on such occasions, was that of cutting off the manes, foretops, and tails of the horses of the wedding company.

On returning to the infare, the order of procession, and the race for black Betty, was the same as before. The feasting and dancing often lasted for several days, at the end of which the whole company were so exhausted with loss of sleep, that several days rest were requisite to fit them to return to their ordinary labors.

Should I be asked why I have presented this unpleasant portrait of the rude manners of our forefathers—I in my turn would ask my reader, why are you pleased with the histories of the blood and carnage of battles ? Why are you delighted with the fictions of poetry, the novel, and romance ? I have related truth, and only truth, strange as it may seem. I have depicted a state of society and manners which are fast vanishing from the memory of man, with a view to give the youth of our country a knowledge of the advantages of civilization, and to give contentment to the aged, by preventing them from saying, " that former times were better than the present."

Capt. Samuel Brady resided at one time at Wellsburg. He was tall, rather slender, and very active, and of a dark complexion. When in the forest, engaged in war or hunting, he usually wore, instead of a hat, a black handkerchief bound around his head.

He bore towards the Indians an implacable hatred, in consequence of the murder of his father and brother by them, and took a solemn oath of vengeance. Gen. Hugh Brady, of the U. S. army, is either a brother or nephew of him. He was at the siege of Boston ; a lieutenant at the massacre of Paoli ; and in 1779–80–81, while Gen. Broadhead held command at Fort Pitt, was captain of a company of rangers. To fully detail his adventures would require a volume, and we have space but for a few anecdotes, drawn from various sources, illustrative of his courage and sagacity,

A party of Indians having made an inroad into the Sewickly settlement, and committed barbarous murders and carried off some prisoners, Brady set off in pursuit with only five men and his *pet* Indian. He came up with them, and discovered they were encamped on the banks of the Mahoning. Having reconnoitred their position, Brady returned to and posted his men, and in the deepest silence all awaited the break of day. When it appeared, the Indians arose and stood around their fires ; exulting, doubtless, in the scalps they had taken, the plunder they had acquired, and the injury they had inflicted on their enemies. Precarious joy—short-lived triumph ! The *avenger of blood* was beside them ! At a signal given, seven rifles cracked, and five Indians were dead ere they fell. Brady's well-known war-cry was heard, his party was among them, and their guns (mostly empty) were all secured. The remaining Indians instantly fled and disappeared.

Brady being out with his party, on one occasion had reached Slippery Rock Creek, a branch of the Beaver, without seeing signs of Indians. Here, however, he came on an Indian trail in the evening, which he followed till dark without overtaking the Indians. The next morning he renewed the pursuit, and overtook them while they were engaged at their morning meal. Unfortunately for him, another party of Indians were in his rear. They had fallen upon his trail, and pursued him, doubtless, with as much ardor as his pursuit had been characterized by ; and at the moment he fired upon the Indians in his front, he was, in turn, fired upon by those in his rear. He was now between two fires, and vastly outnumbered. Two of his men fell ; his tomahawk was shot from his side, and the battle-yell was given by the party in his rear, and loudly returned and repeated by those in his front. There was no time for hesitation ; no safety in delay; no chance of successful defence in their present position. The brave captain and his rangers had to flee before their enemies, who pressed on their flying footsteps with no lagging speed. Brady ran towards the creek. He was known by many, if not all of them; and many and deep were the scores to be settled between him and them. They knew the country well: he did not; and from his running towards the creek they were certain of taking him prisoner. The creek was, for a long distance above and below the point he was approaching, washed in its channel to a great depth. In the certain expectation of catching him there, the private soldiers of his party were disregarded; and throwing down their guns, and drawing their tomahawks, all pressed forward to seize their victim. Quick of eye, fearless of heart, and determined never to be a captive to the Indians, Brady comprehended their object, and his only chance of escape, the moment he saw the creek; and by one mighty effort of courage and activity, defeated the one and effected the other. He sprang across the abyss of waters, and stood, rifle in hand, on the opposite bank, in safety. As quick as lightning his rifle was primed; for it was his invariable practice in loading to prime first. The next minute the powder-horn was at the gun's muzzle; when, as he was in this act, a large Indian, who had been foremost in the pursuit, came to the opposite bank, and with the manliness of a generous foe, who scorns to undervalue the qualities of an enemy, said in a loud voice, and tolerable English, " Blady make good jump !" It may indeed be doubted whether the compliment was uttered in derision; for the moment he had said so he took to his heels, and, as if fearful of the return it might merit, ran as crooked as a worm-fence—sometimes leaping high, at others suddenly squatting down, he appeared no way certain that Brady would not answer from the lips of his rifle. But the rifle was not yet loaded. The captain was at the place afterwards, and ascertained that his leap was about 23 feet, and that the water was 20 feet deep. Brady's next effort was to gather up his men. They had a place designated at which to meet, in case they should happen to be separated; and thither he went, and found the other three there. They immediately commenced their homeward march, and returned to Pittsburg about half defeated. Three Indians had been seen to fall from the fire they gave them at breakfast.

In Sept., 1782, immediately after the Indians had been defeated in their attempt to take the fort at Wheeling, they sent 100 picked warriors to take Rice's Fort, which was situated on Buffalo Creek, about 12 or 15 miles from its mouth. This fort* consisted of some cabins and a small blockhouse, and, in dangerous times, was the refuge of a few families in the neighborhood.

---

* " The reader will understand by this term, not only a place of defence, but the residence of a small number of families belonging to the same neighborhood. As the Indian mode of warfare was an indiscriminate slaughter of all ages, and both sexes, it was as requisite to provide for the safety of the women and children as for that of the men.

" The fort consisted of cabins, blockhouses, and stockades. A range of cabins commonly formed one side at least of the fort. Divisions, or partitions of logs, separated the cabins from each other. The walls on the outside were ten or twelve feet high, the slope of the roof being turned wholly inward. A very few of these cabins had puncheon floors, the greater part were earthen. The blockhouses were built at the angles of the fort. They projected about two feet beyond the outer walls of the cabins and stockades. Their upper stories were about eighteen inches every way larger in dimension than the under one, leaving an opening at the commencement of the second story to prevent the enemy from making a lodgment under their walls. In some forts, instead of blockhouses, the angles of the fort were furnished with bastions. A large folding gate, made of thick slabs, nearest the spring, closed the fort. The stockades, bastions, cabins, and blockhouse walls, were furnished with port-holes at proper heights and distances. The whole of the outside was made completely bullet-proof.

" It may be truly said that necessity is the mother of invention; for the whole of this work was made without the aid of a single nail or spike of iron; and for this reason, such things were not to be had. In some places, less exposed, a single blockhouse, with a cabin or two, constituted the whole fort. Such places of refuge may appear very trifling to those who have been in the habit of seeing the formidable military garrisons of Europe and America; but they answered the purpose, as the Indians had no artillery. They seldom attacked, and scarcely ever took one of them."—*Dodridge's Notes.*

The Indians surrounded the fort at night ere they were discovered, and soon made an attack, which continued at intervals until 2 o'clock in the morning. In the intervals of the firing the Indians frequently called out to the people of the fort, " Give up, give up, too many Indian. Indian too big. No kill." They were answered with defiance. " Come on, you cowards ; we are ready for you. Show us your yellow hides and we will make holes in them for you." They were only six men in the fort, yet such was their skill and bravery, that the Indians were finally obliged to retreat with the loss of a number of their men.

" Thus was this little place defended by a Spartan band of six men, against 100 chosen warriors, exasperated to madness by their failure at Wheeling Fort. Their names shall be inscribed in the list of the heroes of our early times. They were Jacob Miller, George Lefler, Peter Fullenweider, Daniel Rice, George Felebaum, and Jacob Lefler, jun. George Felebaum was shot in the forehead, through a port-hole at the second fire of the Indians, and instantly expired, so that in reality the defence of the place was made by only five men."

BOTETOURT.

BOTETOURT was formed in 1769 from Augusta, and named from Gov. Botetourt. Its length is 44 miles, with mean breadth of 18 miles. The Blue Ridge forms its E. boundary, and much of the county is mountainous. The James River runs through the N. part. Much of the soil is fertile.

Fincastle from Grove Hill.

FINCASTLE, the county-seat, lies 175 miles west of Richmond. This town was established by law in 1772, on forty acres given for the purpose by Israel Christian, and named after the seat of Lord Botetourt in England. It is compactly built in a beautiful rolling country. It contains 5 mercantile stores, 1 newspaper printing office, 2 academies ; 1 Presbyterian, 1 Baptist, 1 Episcopal, and 1 Methodist church ; and a population of about 700. The above view shows the principal part of the village as it appears from Anderson's or Grove Hill. The public building on the left is the Episcopal, and that on the right the Presbyterian church. The

North mountain, 5 miles distant, appears in the background. Pattonsburg and Buchanon lie immediately opposite each other, on the James River, 12 miles N. of Fincastle. They are connected together by a fine bridge, and in a general description would be considered as one village. They are beautifully situated in a valley, between the Blue Ridge and Purgatory mountain, at the head of navigation on James River, though in high water, batteaux go up as far as Covington in Alleghany co. These villages were incorporated in 1832–3, and contain at present 1 newspaper printing office, a branch of the Va. bank, 5 stores, a tobacco inspection, 2 tobacco factories ; 1 Free, 1 Presbyterian, and 1 Episcopal church ; and a population of about 450. Eventually the James River Canal will pass through here to Covington, and probably a macadamized road from Staunton to Knoxville, Tennessee.

Dagger's Springs are situated in the northern part of the county, near the James River, 18 miles from Fincastle, 16 from Buchanon, 22 from Lexington. The scenery in the vicinity is very fine. Some years since extensive improvements were made there for the accommodation of the guests.

"The most active mineral ingredients in the water are carbonated alkalies. In this it differs materially from the White and Salt Sulphur, and is more nearly assimilated in its qualities to the Red and Gray Sulphur. It is, however, more decidedly alkaline than either of those springs. This peculiarity will ever recommend it to persons subject to acidities of the stomach, and to the other concomitants of dyspepsia, while the large quantity of hydrogen that it contains will render it useful in all of those complaints for which sulphur-water is usually prescribed."

At the small village of Amsterdam, 5 miles S. of Fincastle, there is a large brick church, lately built by the Dunkards. The Dunkers at Amsterdam are descendants of Germans who emigrated to Pennsylvania. The following, regarding the tenets and practices of this sect, is from a published account :

The Tunkers are a denomination of Seventh-Day Baptists, which took its rise in the year 1724. It was founded by a German, who, weary of the world, retired to an agreeable solitude, within sixty miles of Philadelphia, for the more free exercise of religious contemplation. Curiosity attracted followers, and his simple and engaging manners made them proselytes. They soon settled a little colony, called Ephrata, in allusion to the Hebrews, who used to sing psalms on the border of the river Euphrates. This denomination seem to have obtained their name from their baptizing their new converts by plunging. They are also called *Tumblers*, from the manner in which they perform baptism, which is by putting the person, while kneeling, head first under water, so as to resemble the motion of the body in the action of tumbling. They use the trine immersion, with laying on the hands and prayer, even when the person baptized is in the water. Their habit seems to be peculiar to themselves, consisting of a long tunic or coat, reaching down to their heels, with a sash or girdle round the waist, and a cap or hood hanging from the shoulders. They do not shave the head or beard.

The men and women have separate habitations and distinct governments. For these purposes, they erected two large wooden buildings, one of which is occupied by the brethren, the other by the sisters of the society ; and in each of them there is a banqueting-room, and an apartment for public worship ; for the brethren and sisters do not meet together even at their devotions.

They used to live chiefly upon roots and other vegetables, the rules of their society not allowing them flesh, except upon particular occasions, when they hold what they call a love-feast ; at which time the brethren and sisters dine together in a large apartment, and eat mutton, but no other meat. In each of their little cells they have a bench fixed, to serve the purpose of a bed, and a small block of wood for a pillow. They allow of marriages, but consider celibacy as a virtue.

The principal tenet of the Tunkers appears to be this—that future happiness is only to be obtained by penance and outward mortifications in this life, and that, as Jesus Christ, by his meritorious sufferings, became the Redeemer of mankind in general, so each individual of the human race, by a life of abstinence and restraint, may work out his own salvation. Nay, they go so far as to admit of works of supererogation, and declare that a man may do much more than he is in justice or equity obliged to do, and that his superabundant works may, therefore, be applied to the salvation of others.

This denomination deny the eternity of future punishments, and believe that the dead have the gospel preached to them by our Saviour, and that the souls of the just are employed to preach the gospel to those who have had no revelation in this life. They suppose the Jewish Sabbath, sabbatical year, and year of jubilee, are typical of certain periods after the general judgment, in which the souls of those who are not then admitted into happiness are purified from their corruption. If any, within those smaller periods, are so far humbled as to acknowledge the perfections of God, and to own Christ as their only Saviour, they are received to felicity ; while those who continue obstinate are reserved in torments, until the grand period, typified by the jubilee, arrives, in which all shall be made happy in the endless fruition of the Deity.

They also deny the imputation of Adam's sin to his posterity. They disclaim violence, even in cases of self-defence, and suffer themselves to be defrauded, or wronged, rather than go to law. Their church government and discipline are the same with other Baptists, except that every brother is allowed to speak in the congregation; and their best speaker is usually ordained to be the minister. They have deacons and deaconesses from among their ancient widows and exhorters, who are all licensed to use their gifts statedly. The Tunkers are not so rigid in their dress and manner of life as formerly; still they retain the faith of their fathers, and lead lives of great industry, frugality, and purity.

In 1761, about sixty Shawanee warriors penetrated the settlements on James River, committed several murders, and carried off several prisoners, among whom were Mrs. Renix and her five children. The Indians were overtaken in their retreat by a party of whites, and nine of their number killed, after which they proceeded towards their villages without further molestation. The remainder of the story is given by Withers:

In Boquet's treaty with the Ohio Indians, it was stipulated that the whites detained by them in captivity were to be brought in and redeemed. In compliance with this stipulation, Mrs. Renix was brought to Staunton in 1767 and ransomed, together with two of her sons, William, the late Col. Renix, of Greenbrier, and Robert, also of Greenbrier—Betsy, her daughter, had died on the Miami. Thomas returned in 1783, but soon after removed, and settled on the Scioto, near Chilicothe. Joshua never came back; he took an Indian wife, and became a chief among the Miamies—he amassed a considerable fortune, and died near Detroit in 1810.

Hannah Dennis was separated from the other captives, and allotted to live at the Chilicothe towns. She learned their language, painted herself as they do, and in many respects conformed to their manners and customs. She was attentive to sick persons, and was highly esteemed by the Indians, as one well skilled in the art of curing diseases. Finding them very superstitious, and believers in necromancy, she professed witchcraft, and affected to be a prophetess. In this manner she conducted herself, till she became so great a favorite with them that they gave her full liberty, and honored her as a queen. Notwithstanding this, Mrs. Dennis was always determined to effect her escape, when a favorable opportunity should occur; and having remained so long with them, apparently well satisfied, they ceased to entertain any suspicions of such a design.

In June, 1763, she left the Chilicothe towns, *ostensibly* to procure herbs for medicinal purposes, (as she had before frequently done,) but *really* to attempt an escape. As she did not return that night her intention became suspected, and in the morning some warriors were sent in pursuit of her. In order to leave as little trail as possible, she had crossed the Scioto River three times, and was just getting over the fourth time, 40 miles below the town, when she was discovered by her pursuers. They fired at her across the river without effect; but, in endeavoring to make a rapid flight, she had one of her feet severely cut by a sharp stone.

The Indians then rushed across the river to overtake and catch her, but she eluded them by crawling into the hollow limb of a large fallen sycamore. They searched around for her some time, frequently stepping on the log which concealed her, and encamped near it that night. On the next day they went on to the Ohio River, but finding no trace of her, they returned home.

Mrs. Dennis remained at that place three days, doctoring her wound, and then set off for home. She crossed the Ohio River, at the mouth of Great Kenawha, on a log of drift-wood, travelling only during the night for fear of discovery. She subsisted on roots, herbs, green grapes, wild cherries, and river mussels—and, entirely exhausted by fatigue and hunger, sat down by the side of Greenbrier River, with no expectation of ever proceeding further. In this situation she was found by Thomas Athol and three others from Clendennin's settlement, which she had passed without knowing it. She had been then upwards of twenty days on her disconsolate journey, alone, on foot; but, till then, cheered with the hope of again being with her friends.

She was taken back to Clendennin's, where they kindly ministered to her, till she became so far invigorated as to travel on horseback, with an escort, to Fort Young on Jackson's River, from whence she was carried home to her relations.

Gen. ANDREW LEWIS resided on the Roanoke, in this county. He was one of the six sons of that Lewis who, with Mackey and Salling, had been foremost in settling Augusta co., and the most distinguished of a family who behaved so bravely in defending the infant settlements against the Indians.

In Braddock's war, he was in a company in which were all his brothers, the eldest, Samuel Lewis, being the captain. This corps distinguished themselves at Braddock's defeat. They, with some other of the Virginia troops, were in the advance, and the first attacked by the enemy. Severed from the rest of the army, they cut their way through the enemy to their companions, with the loss of many men. His conduct at Major Grant's defeat, in his attack upon Fort Duquesne, acquired for him the highest reputation for prudence and courage. He was at this time a major. In this action, the Scotch Highlanders, under Grant, were surrounded by the Indians; when the work of death went on quite rapidly, and in a manner quite novel to the Highlanders, who, in all their European wars, had never before seen men's heads *skinned*. When Major Lewis was advancing to the relief of Grant with his 200 provincials, he met one of the Highlanders under speedy flight, and inquiring of him how the battle was going, he said they were " a' beaten, and he had seen Donald M'Donald up to his hunkers in mud, and a' *the skeen af his heed.*" Both Lewis and Grant were made prisoners. Before Lewis was taken into the fort, he was stripped of all his clothes but his shirt. An elderly Indian insisted upon having that ; but he resisted, with the tomahawk drawn over his head, until a French officer, by signs, requested him to deliver it, and then took him to his room, and gave him a complete dress to put on. While they were prisoners, Grant addressed a letter to Gen. Forbes, attributing their defeat to Lewis. This letter being inspected by the French, who knew the falsehood of the charge, they handed it to Lewis. He waited upon Grant,* and challenged him. Upon his refusal to fight, he spat in his face in the presence of the French officers, and then left him to reflect upon his baseness. Major Lewis was with Washington July 4, 1754, at the capitulation of Fort Necessity, when, by the articles agreed upon, the garrison was to retire and return without molestation to the inhabited parts of the country ; and the French commander promised that no embarrassment should be interposed either by his own men or the savages. While some of the soldiers of each army were intermixed, an Irishman, exasperated with an Indian near him, "cursed the copper-colored scoundrel," and raised his musket to shoot him. Lewis, who had been twice wounded in the engagement, and was then hobbling on a staff, raised the Irishman's gun as he was in the act of firing, and thus not only saved the life of the Indian, but probably prevented a general massacre of the Virginia troops. He was the commander and general of the Virginia troops at the battle of Point Pleasant, (see Mason co.,) fought the 10th of May, 1774. In this campaign the Indians were driven west of the Ohio. Washington, in whose regiment Lewis had once been a major, had formed so high an opinion of his bravery and military skill, that, at the commencement of the revolutionary war, he was induced to recommend him to Congress as one of the major-generals of the American army—a recommendation which was slighted, in order to make room for Gen. Stephens. It is also said, that when Washington was commissioned as commander-in-chief, he expressed a wish that the appointment had been given to Gen. Lewis. Upon this slight in the appointment of Stephens, Washington wrote to Gen. Lewis a letter, which is published in his correspondence, expressive of his regret at the course pursued by Congress, and promising that he should be promoted to the first vacancy. At his solicitation, Lewis accepted the commission of brigadier-general, and was soon after ordered to the command of a detachment of the army stationed near Williamsburg. He commanded the Virginia troops when Lord Dunmore was driven from Gwynn's Island, in 1776, and announced his orders for attacking the enemy by putting a match to the first gun, an eighteen pounder, himself.

Gen. Lewis resigned his command in 1780 to return home, being seized ill with a fever. He died on his way, in Bedford co., about 40 miles from his own house on the Roanoke, lamented by all acquainted with his meritorious services and superior qualities.

" Gen. Lewis," says Stuart, in his Historical Memoir, " was upwards of six feet high, of uncommon strength and agility, and his form of the most exact symmetry. He had a stern and invincible countenance, and was of a reserved and distant deportment, which rendered his presence more awful than engaging. He was a commissioner, with Dr. Thomas Walker, to hold a treaty, on behalf of the colony of Virginia, with the six nations of Indians, together with the commissioners from Pennsylvania, New York, and other eastern provinces, held at Fort Stanevix, in the province of New York, in the year 1768. It was then remarked by the governor of New York, that ' the earth seemed to tremble under him as he walked along.' His independent spirit despised sycophantic means of gaining popularity, which never rendered more than his merits extorted."

BRUNSWICK.

Brunswick was formed, in 1720, from Surry and Isle of Wight. It is nearly a square of 26 miles on a side. The southwest angle

---

* This was the same Col. Grant who, in 1775, on the floor of the British Parliament, said that he had often acted in the same service with the Americans—that he knew them well, and, from that knowledge, ventured to predict " that they would never dare face an English army, as being destitute of every requisite to constitute good soldiers."

touches the Roanoke, and a small section is drained by that stream ; but the body of the county is comprised in the valleys of Meherrin and Nottoway Rivers and declines to the east. Large quantities of tobacco and corn are raised, together with some cotton. Pop. 1830, 15,770 ; 1840, whites 4,978, slaves 8,805, free colored 563 ; total, 14,346.

Lawrenceville, the county-seat, is 73 miles w. of s. from Richmond. It is a neat village, pleasantly situated on a branch of Meherrin River, and contains 2 churches and about 25 dwellings. Lewisville contains about 15 dwellings.

In the upper end of the county, in the vicinity of Avant's and Taylor's creeks, have been found many Indian relics, and this portion of the county yet shows traces of having been inhabited by Indians. It is supposed that when the country was first settled, there was a frontier fort, or trading establishment, a few miles below Pennington's Bridge, on the Meherrin : an iron cannon now lies on a hill near the spot, and in the neighborhood runs a road, called to this day " the fort road." There are also excavations in the earth constructed for wolf-pits, by the early settlers. Tradition says they were formed in the following manner : A hole was dug ten or twelve feet deep, small at the top, and growing wider on all sides as it descended, sloping inwards so much that no beast could climb up. Two sticks were fastened together in the middle at right angles ; the longer one confined to the ground, and the shorter—to the inner end of which was attached the bait—swinging across the middle of the pit, so that when the wolf attempted to seize it, he was precipitated to the bottom.

BUCKINGHAM.

BUCKINGHAM was formed in 1761, from Albemarle. It is 34 miles long, with a mean breadth of 24. The James River runs on its N. and W. and the Appomattox on its S. boundary. Willis' and Slate Rivers rise in the south part. On the margin of the streams the land is fertile, but the intervening ridges are frequently sterile and desolate, and in many sections uninhabited. The surface is generally level, and the only mountain of note is Willis', from which is an almost uninterrupted prospect over a vast extent of level country. The Buckingham White Sulphur Spring is 12 miles SE. of the court-house, and there are also one or two other mineral springs in the county, none of which have as yet attained any celebrity. Buckingham is rich in minerals ; some dozen gold mines have been in operation, only three or four of which have proved profitable. Limestone found in the county is beginning to be used in agriculture, and iron ore abounds. Upon Hunt's Creek, within 2 miles of James River Canal, is an inexhaustible slate quarry of superior quality. The principal literary institutions of the county are a Collegiate Institute for females, under the patronage of the Methodist church, and the Slate River Academy, which has two professors, and is liberally supported. Tobacco, corn, wheat, and oats, are the principal products. Pop. 1830, 18,351; 1840, whites 7,323, slaves 10,014, free colored 449; total, 18,786.

Maysville, the county-seat, 79 miles west of Richmond, near the centre of the county, on Slate River, 26 miles from its junction with the James, is a neat village, containing 1 church, 4 stores, and about 200 inhabitants. New Canton contains about 40 dwellings. Curdsville, a flourishing village, has 1 Episcopal church, 6 stores, and about 250 inhabitants.

PETER FRANCISCO, a soldier of the Revolution, and celebrated for his personal strength, lived and raised his family in Buckingham, where he died a few years since. His origin was obscure. He supposed that he was a Portuguese by birth, and that he was kidnapped when an infant, and carried to Ireland. He had no recollection of his parents, and the first knowledge he preserved of himself was in that country when a small boy. Hearing much of America, and being of an adventurous turn, he indented himself to a sea-captain for seven years, in payment for his passage. On his arrival he was sold to Anthony Winston, Esq., of this county, on whose estate he labored faithfully until the breaking out of the revolution. He was then at the age of 16, and partaking of the patriotic enthusiasm of the times, he asked and obtained permission of his owner to enlist in the continental army. At the storming of Stony-Point, he was the first soldier, after Major Gibbon, who entered the fortress, on which occasion he received a bayonet wound in the thigh. He was at Brandywine, Monmouth, and other battles at the north, and was transferred to the south under Greene, where he was engaged in the actions of the Cowpens, Camden, Guilford Court-House, &c. He was a very brave man, and possessed such confidence in his prowess as to be almost fearless. He used a sword having a blade five feet in length, which he could wield as a feather, and every swordsman who came in contact with him, paid the forfeit of his life. His services were so distinguished, that he would have been promoted to an office had he been enabled to write. His stature was 6 feet and an inch, and his weight 260 pounds. His complexion was dark and swarthy, features bold and manly, and his hands and feet uncommonly large. Such was his personal strength, that he could easily shoulder a cannon weighing 1100 pounds; and our informant, a highly respectable gentleman now residing in this county, in a communication before us, says: "he could take me in his right hand and pass over the room with me, and play my head against the ceiling, as though I had been a doll-baby. My weight was 195 pounds!" The following anecdote, illustrative of Francisco's valor, has often been published:—

"While the British army were spreading havoc and desolation all around them, by their plunderings and burnings in Virginia, in 1781, Francisco had been reconnoitring, and while stopping at the house of a Mr. V......, then in Amelia, now Nottoway county, nine of Tarleton's cavalry came up, with three negroes, and told him he was their prisoner. Seeing he was overpowered by numbers, he made no resistance. Believing him to be very peaceable, they all went into the house, leaving him and the paymaster together. 'Give up instantly all that you possess of value,' said the latter, 'or prepare to die.' 'I have nothing to give up,' said Francisco, 'so use your pleasure.' 'Deliver instantly,' rejoined the soldier, 'those massy silver buckles which you wear in your shoes.' 'They were a present from a valued friend,' replied Francisco, 'and it would grieve me to part with them. Give them into your hands I never will. You have the power; take them, if you think fit.' The soldier put his sabre under his arm, and bent down to take them. Francisco, finding so favorable an opportunity to recover his liberty, stepped one pace in his rear, drew the sword with force from under his arm, and instantly gave him a blow across the scull. 'My enemy,' observed Francisco, 'was brave, and though severely wounded, drew a pistol, and, in the same moment that he pulled the trigger, I cut his hand nearly off. The bullet grazed my side. Ben V.....' (the man of the house) very ungenerously brought out a musket, and gave it to one of the British soldiers, and told him to make use of it. He mounted the only horse they could get, and presented it at my breast. It missed fire. I rushed on the muzzle of the gun. A short struggle ensued. I disarmed and wounded him. Tarleton's troop

of *four hundred* men were in sight. All was hurry and confusion, which I increased
by repeatedly hallooing, as loud as I could, *Come on, my brave boys; now's your time ;
we will soon dispatch these few, and then attack the main body !*   The wounded man

Francisco's Encounter with Nine British Dragoons.

[This representation of Peter Francisco's gallant action with nine of Tarleton's cavalry, in sight of a
troop of 400 men, which took place in Amelia county, Virginia, 1781, is respectfully inscribed to him, by
James Webster and James Warrell.—Published Dec. 1st, 1814, by James Webster of Pennsylvania.]

flew to the troop; the others were panic struck, and fled. I seized V-·····, and would
have dispatched him, but the poor wretch begged for his life; he was not only an object of my contempt, but pity. The eight horses that were left behind, I gave him to
conceal for me.   Discovering Tarleton had dispatched ten more in pursuit of me, I
made off. I evaded their vigilance. They stopped to refresh themselves. I, like an
old fox, doubled, and fell on their rear. I went the next day to V-····· for my horses ;
he demanded two, for his trouble and generous intentions. Finding my situation dangerous, and surrounded by enemies where I ought to have found friends, I went off with
my six horses. I intended to have avenged myself of V ···· at a future day, but Providence ordained I should not be his executioner, for he broke his neck by a fall from
one of the very horses.' "
    Several other anecdotes are related of the strength and bravery of Francisco. At
Gates' defeat at Camden, after running some distance along a road, he took to the woods
and sat down to rest; a British trooper came up and ordered him to surrender. With
feigned humility, he replied he would, and added, as his musket was empty, he had no
further use for it. He then carelessly presented it sideways, and thus throwing the soldier off his guard, he suddenly levelled the piece, and driving the bayonet through his ab-
domen, hurled him off his horse, mounted it, and continued his retreat. Soon he overtook
his colonel, William Mayo, of Powhatan, who was on foot. Francisco generously dismounted and gave up the animal to his retreating officer, for which act of kindness the
colonel subsequently presented him with a thousand acres of land in Kentucky.
    Francisco possessed strong natural sense, and an amiable disposition. He was, withal,
a companionable man, and ever a welcome visitor in the first families in this region of the
state. He was industrious and temperate, and always advocated the part of the weak

and unprotected. On occasions of outbreaks at public gatherings, he was better in rushing in and preserving public peace, than all the conservative authorities on the ground. Late in life, partly through the influence of his friend, Chas. Yancey, Esq., he was appointed sergeant-at-arms to the House of Delegates, in which service he died, in 1836, and was interred with military honors in the public burying-ground at Richmond.

CABELL.

CABELL was created in 1809, from Kanawha, and named from Wm. H. Cabell, Gov. of Va., from 1805 to 1808. It is 35 miles long, with a mean breadth of 20 miles. A considerable portion of the county is wild and uncultivated, and somewhat broken. The river bottoms are fertile, and settled upon. Pop. 1830, 5,884 ; 1840, whites 7,574, slaves 567, free colored 22 ; total, 8,163. Barboursville, the county-seat, lies on the Guyandotte river, 7 1-2 miles from its mouth, and 352 miles wnw. of Richmond. The turnpike, leading from the eastern part of the state, by the great watering-place, to the Kentucky line, passes through this village, which contains about 30 dwellings. Guyandotte lies on the Ohio, at the mouth of the Guyandotte River. It is much the most important point of steamboat embarkation, as well as debarkation, in western Virginia, with the exception of Wheeling. It is a flourishing village, containing 1 church, 6 or 8 stores, a steam saw-mill, and a population of about 800.

Cabell county was settled at a comparatively late period. Thomas Hannon was one of the earliest settlers, having removed, in 1796, from Botetourt county to Green Bottom, about 18 miles above Guyandotte, when the first permanent settlement was made. Soon after Guyandotte was settled, at which place Thomas Buffington was one of the earliest settlers.

A portion of the beautiful flatland of what is called Green Bottom, lying partly in this and Mason county, a few years since, before the plough of civilization had disturbed the soil, presented one of those vestiges of a city which are met with in central America, and occasionally in the southern and western forests of the United States. The traces of a regular, compact, and populous city with streets running parallel with the Ohio River, and crossing and intersecting each other at right angles, covering a space of nearly half a mile, as well as the superficial dimensions of many of the houses, are apparent, and well defined. Axes and saws of an unique form—the former of iron, the latter of copper—as well as other implements of the mechanic arts, have been found. These remains betoken a state of comparative civilization, attained by no race of the aborigines of this country now known to have existed. Who they were, or whence they sprung, tradition has lost in the long lapse of ages. It is a singular fact, that these remains are rarely, if ever, found elsewhere than upon the river bottoms, or flat level lands.

27

CAMPBELL.

CAMPBELL was formed from Bedford in 1784, and named in honor of Gen. William Campbell, a distinguished officer of the American revolution. In form, it approximates to a square of about 25 miles on a side; its surface is broken, and its soil productive. Staunton River runs on its s., and the James on its NW. boundary; both of these streams are navigable for boats far above the county limits, thus opening a communication with Chesapeake Bay and Albemarle Sound. Pop. 1830, 20,330; 1840, whites 10,213, slaves 10,045, free colored 772; total, 21,030.

Besides the large and flourishing town of Lynchburg, there are in the county several small villages, viz.: Campbell C. H., 12 miles s. of Lynchburg, Brookneal, Leesville, and New London.

Lynchburg, the fifth town in population in Virginia, is situated on a steep declivity on the south bank of James River, in the midst of bold and beautiful scenery, within view of the Blue Ridge and the Peaks of Otter, and 116 miles westerly from Richmond. This town was established in October, 1786, when it was enacted " that 45 acres of land, the property of John Lynch, and lying contiguous to Lynch's Ferry, are hereby vested in John Clarke, Adam Clement, Charles Lynch, John Callaway, Achilles Douglass, William Martin, Jesse Burton, Joseph Stratton, Micajah Moorman, and Charles Brooks, gentlemen, trustees, to be by them, or any six of them, laid off into lots of half an acre each, with convenient streets, and established a town by the name of Lynchburg." The father of the above-mentioned John Lynch was an Irish emigrant, and took up land here previous to the revolution. His place, then called Chesnut Hill, afterwards the seat of Judge Edmund Winston, was two miles below here. At his death the present site of Lynchburg fell to his son John, by whose exertions the town was established. The original founder of Lynchburg was a member of the denomination of Friends, and a plain man, of strict integrity and great benevolence of character. He died about 20 years since, at a very advanced age. At the time of the formation of the town, there was but a single house, the ferry-house, which stood where the toll-house to the bridge now is. A tobacco warehouse and 2 or 3 stores were thereupon built under the hill, and it was some time before any buildings were erected upon the main street. The growth of the place has been gradual. In 1804, a Methodist Episcopal church was erected upon the site of the present one, and shortly after a market was established. The first Sabbath-school in the state was formed in the church above mentioned, in the spring of 1817, by George Walker, James McGehee, and John Thurman. The next churches built were the First Presbyterian, the Baptist, the Protestant Episcopal, the Protestant Methodist, the Second Presbyterian, and a Friends' meeting-house in the outskirts of the town. The Catholic and Universalist churches were erected in 1843.

"The Lynchburg Water Works, for furnishing the town with an unfailing supply of pure and whole-some water, were constructed in 1828-29, under the direction of Albert Stein, Esq., engineer, at an ex-pense of $50,000. The height—unprecedented in this country—to which it was necessary to raise the water, renders this one of the most interesting undertakings of the kind in the United States.

"An arm of the James, formed by an island about 2 miles in length, is crossed, a short distance above the limits of the corporation, by a dam 10 feet high. A canal of half a mile in length conveys the water to the pump-house on the river bank, at the foot of 3d alley. A double forcing-pump, on the plan of De la Hire, worked by a large breast wheel, impels the water through the ascending pipe, which is 2000 feet long, to a reservoir containing 400,000 gallons, situated between 4th and 5th streets, and *at the elevation of 253 feet above the level of the river.* Fire-plugs are connected with the distributing pipes, at every in-tersection of the alleys with 2d and 3d streets, and afford an admirable security against the danger of fire. The height of the reservoir, above these streets, gives a jet of water by means of hose pipes, of from 60 to 80 feet elevation, and throws it, in bold and continuous streams, over the roofs of the highest houses.

"The water-power created by the dam for the water works, is amply sufficient for working a large additional amount of machinery, and waits only for a clearer perception by capitalists, of the manufac-turing advantages of this town, to be brought into extensive use. The cheapness of labor, the abund-ance of provisions, and the extent and wealth of the country looking this way for supplies of domestic, as well as of foreign goods, unite with the vast water-power actually prepared and ready for any appli-cation, in inviting the attention of men of capital and enterprise to this important subject." These works are gradually enlarged, from year to year, to meet the wants of an increasing population.

The annexed account of the celebration of laying the corner stone of the water works, is from a news-paper of that date :—

Interesting Event.—On Saturday last, [August 23d, 1828,] an event deeply interesting to Lynchburg took place ; one in which the convenience, health, and safety of us all, are involved. The corner stone of the Lynchburg Water Works was laid—works, the magnitude of which exceed any ever attempted in Virginia····The stone was laid with civic, masonic, and military ceremonies. About 9, A. M., the pro-cession was formed at the Presbyterian church, at the lower end of Main street, in the following order :—
The military ; the reverend clergy ; the engineer ; the members of the common council, preceded by the watering committee ; the judge of the General Court for the circuit, and mayor of the Corporation ; the recorder and aldermen ; the Masonic fraternity ; citizens.

When the procession, under the directions of the marshals of the day—Major James B. Risque, Col. Maurice H. Langhorne, and Captains R. R. Phelps, Samuel I. Wiat, and A. M. Gilliam—reached the ground, the artillery and rifle companies formed a hollow square, within which were the masons, the adjacent banks being thronged with spectators.

The impressive ceremonies commenced with a prayer appropriate to the occasion, by the Rev. W. S. Reid, followed by solemn music. The Rev. F. G. Smith then implored of the Supreme Architect of the Universe, a blessing on the undertaking. The Masonic fraternity proceeded to lay the corner stone ; the plate bears the following inscription :—

This Stone, the foundation of a work executed by order of the common council of Lynchburg, for supplying the town with water, was laid under the direction of John Victor, John Thurman, John Early, David G. Murrell, and Samuel Claytor, by the Rt. W. Howson S. White, D.D., G. Master, and the Wor-shipful Maurice H. Garland, M. of Marshall Lodge, No. 39, of Free and Accepted Masons, on the 23d August, A.M. 5828, A.D. 1828, in presence of the Mayor, Recorder, Aldermen, and Common Councilmen, of said Town ; the members of said Lodge ; the Artillery and Rifle Companies, commanded by Captains J. E. Norvell and James W. Pegram, and numerous citizens, Albon McDaniel, Esq., Mayor, John Thur-man, Esq., President of the Council, Albert Stein, Esq., Engineer.

Mr. John Victor, the chairman of the watering committee, delivered an address ; after which the military fired a salute, and the gratified beholders returned to their homes, all, we hope, determined to use their efforts to carry on the work to a successful termination. We cordially unite with Mr. V. in saying, "Let us join hands, nothing doubting that we too can accomplish what others have so often done."

We conclude this sketch of Lynchburg, by giving its statistics, as published in a communication to the Lynchburg Republican, in 1843 :

The census of 1840, showed a population of upwards of five thousand. Since that time, there has been a considerable accession to the number of buildings ; from which we may safely assume that our present population reaches, if it does not exceed 6,000. The extent of the tobacco trade of Lynchburg may be judged of from the fact that upwards of fifteen thousand hogsheads have already been inspected here the present year—a number which far exceeds all previous calculation. We have about 30 tobacco factories and stemmeries, giving employment to about 1000 hands ; three flouring-mills, manufacturing, I am told, about 20,000 barrels of flour annually ; 1 cotton factory, operating 1,400 spindles ; iron found-ries, which consume, probably, 100 tons pig-iron annually. More than 100,000 bushels of wheat are sold here yearly. 300 tons bar-iron ; 200 tons pig metal, sold to the country ; 1000 tons plaster of Paris. About 50 dry-goods and grocery stores—selling, in the aggregate, more than one million of dollars worth of goods. Some of our stores are so extensive and elegant, as not to suffer by a comparison with those of Philadelphia and New York.—4 apothecaries and druggists ; several cabinet manufactories ; 4 saddle and harness manufactories ; 10 blacksmith-shops ; several excellent hotels ; 5 jewellers' establishments ; 2 printing offices.

There are here branches of the Bank of Virginia, and the Farmer's Bank of Virginia, and also 3 Sa-vings' Banks. Seven flourishing Sabbath-schools, with from 700 to 1000 scholars. One debating society, with a library of several thousand volumes, &c. &c. &c. From the hasty view I have presented, and which, by no means does justice to the industry and enterprise of our citizens, it will be seen that we have already the elements of a flourishing city. But I have said nothing of the magnificent line of canal now in the "full tide of successful experiment," between this place and Richmond, from which we are distant 147 miles by water. This splendid work, the pride and boast of Virginia, opens to Lynchburg the brightest era which has ever yet dawned upon her fortunes ; securing to us a safe, speedy, and cheap navigation for the immense produce shipped annually to Richmond and the north—and destined, as the writer believes, to furnish a great thoroughfare for the countless thousands of produce and merchandise for the western and southwestern part of our state, as well as Tennessee, Alabama, &c.

Lynch Law.—Col. Charles Lynch, a brother of the founder of Lynchburg, was an officer of the American revolution. His residence was on the Staunton, in the sw. part of this county, now the seat of his grandson, Chas. Henry Lynch, Esq. At that time, this country was very thinly settled, and infested by a lawless band of tories and desperadoes. The necessity of the case involved desperate measures, and Col. Lynch, then a leading whig, apprehended and had them punished, without any superfluous legal ceremony. Hence the origin of the term "*Lynch Law.*" This practice of Lynching continued years after the war, and was applied to many cases of mere suspicion of guilt, which could not be regularly proven. "In 1792," says Wirt's Life of Henry, "there were many suits on the south side of James River, for inflicting Lynch's law." At the battle of Guilford Court-House, a regiment of riflemen, raised in this part of the state, under the command of Col. Lynch, behaved with much gallantry. The colonel died soon after the close of the war. Charles Lynch, a governor of Louisiana, was his son.

The Old Court-House, at New London.

New London is on the Salem turnpike, 11 miles sw. of Lynchburg. It contains 2 churches, a classical academy, and a few dwellings. It was founded several years prior to the American revolution. About the period of the war, it was a place of considerable importance, and contained, says the Marquis de Chastellux, in his travels, "at least 70 or 80 houses." There was here then, an arsenal, a long wooden structure, which stood opposite Echol's tavern. The establishment has long since been removed to Harper's Ferry. There was also a long building, used as a magazine in the war, which was under the guard of some soldiers. In July, 1781, Cornwallis detached Tarleton to this place, for the purpose of destroying the stores and intercepting some light troops reported to be on their march to join Lafayette. But neither stores nor troops were found, and on the 15th, he rejoined his lordship in Suffolk county. Early in the war, there were several Scotch merchants largely engaged in business here. Refusing to take the

LYNCHBURG.

The above shows Lynchburg as it appears from the northern banks of James river. On the left, is shown the bridge across the river and in front, the town, which is finely situated on rising ground, in the midst of bold and romantic scenery.

oath of allegiance, they were compelled to break up and leave the country. This, with the superior location of Lynchburg, gave a permanent shock to its prosperity, and it is now a broken down village, fast going to decay.

New London was at first the county-seat of Lunenburg. In 1753, on the formation of Bedford, it was made the county-seat of the latter. Still later, under the old district system, the superior court was held here. There is now standing in the town, an interesting relic of a more prosperous era—the old court-house—which, in its pristine days, was the scene of important events; but it is now dilapidated, tumbling to ruins, and is used as a barn. Humble as this building is at present, once admiring audiences, moved by the magic eloquence of Patrick Henry, were assembled within its walls. Here it was, that he delivered his celebrated speech in the Johnny Hook case, the account of which is thus given by his biographer :

Hook was a Scotchman, a man of wealth, and suspected of being unfriendly to the American cause. During the distresses of the American army, consequent on the joint invasion of Cornwallis and Phillips in 1781, a Mr. Venable, an army commissary, had taken two of Hook's steers for the use of the troops. The act had not been strictly legal ; and on the establishment of peace, Hook, on the advice of Mr. Cowan, a gentleman of some distinction in the law, thought proper to bring an action of trespass against Mr. Venable, in the district court of New London. Mr. Henry appeared for the defendant, and is said to have deported himself in this cause to the infinite enjoyment of his hearers, the unfortunate Hook always excepted. After Mr. Henry became animated in the cause, says a correspondent, he appeared to have complete control over the passions of his audience : at one time he excited their indignation against Hook ; vengeance was visible in every countenance ; again, when he chose to relax and ridicule him, the whole audience was in a roar of laughter. He painted the distresses of the American army, exposed almost naked to the rigor of a winter's sky, and marking the frozen ground over which they marched with the blood of their unshod feet ; where was the man, he said, who had an American heart in his bosom, who would not have thrown open his fields, his barns, his cellars, the doors of his house, the portals of his breast, to have received with open arms, the meanest soldier in that little band of famished patriots ? Where is the man ?—There he stands—but whether the heart of an American beats in his bosom, you, gentlemen, are to judge. He then carried the jury, by the powers of his imagination, to the plains around York, the surrender of which had followed shortly after the act complained of : he depicted the surrender in the most glowing and noble colors of his eloquence—the audience saw before their eyes the humiliation and dejection of the British, as they marched out of their trenches—they saw the triumph which lighted up every patriotic face, and heard the shouts of victory, and the cry of Washington and liberty, as it rung and echoed through the American ranks, and was reverberated from the hills and shores of the neighboring river—"but, hark ! what notes of discord are these which disturb the general joy, and silence the acclamations of victory —they are the notes of John Hook, hoarsely bawling through the American camp, beef ! beef ! beef !"

The whole audience were convulsed : a particular incident will give a better idea of the effect, than any general description. The clerk of the court, unable to command himself, and unwilling to commit any breach of decorum in his place, rushed out of the court-house, and threw himself on the grass, in the most violent paroxysm of laughter, where he was rolling, when Hook, with very different feelings, came out for relief into the yard also. "Jemmy Steptoe," he said to the clerk, "what the devil ails ye, mon ?" Mr. Steptoe was only able to say, that he could not help it. "Never mind ye," said Hook, "wait till Billy Cowan gets up : he'll show him the la'." Mr. Cowan, however, was so completely overwhelmed by the torrent which bore upon his client, that when he rose to reply to Mr. Henry, he was scarcely able to make an intelligible or audible remark. The cause was decided almost by acclamation. The jury retired for form sake, and instantly returned with a verdict for the defendant. Nor did the effect of Mr. Henry's speech stop here. The people were so highly excited by the tory audacity of such a suit, that Hook began to hear around him a cry more terrible than that of *beef;* it was the cry of *tar and feathers;* from the application of which, it is said, that nothing saved him but a precipitate flight and the speed of his horse.

About half a mile N. of the village is the seat of the above mentioned "Jemmy Steptoe." He was clerk of Bedford 40 years : an intimate friend of Jefferson, who was a frequent visitor at his residence. He died in 1826, esteemed for his amiable and generous disposition.

"Poplar Forest," 3 miles NE. of New London, is the name of the seat of William Cobbs, Esq., which was originally the property of Jefferson, and occasionally his residence in the summer months. It is an octagonal brick edifice, built by him, on the same plan with Monticello, although much smaller. Its situation is commanding, within sight of the Blue Ridge, and the grounds around are beautifully laid out, and adorned with shrubbery.

Immediately after Tarleton's incursion to Charlottesville, when Jefferson narrowly escaped being made prisoner, he retired with his family to *Poplar Forest,* where, riding upon his farm some time after, he was thrown from his horse and seriously injured. " While Mr. Jefferson was confined at Poplar Forest," says Tucker, " in consequence of the fall from his horse, and was in consequence incapable of any active employment, public or private, he occupied himself with answering the queries which Mons. De Marbois, then secretary of the French legation to the United States, had submitted to him respecting the physical and political condition of Virginia ; which answers were afterwards published by him, under the title of ' *Notes on Virginia.*' When we consider how difficult it is, even in the present day, to get an accurate knowledge of such details in our country, and how much greater the difficulty must then have been, we are surprised at the extent of the information which a single individual had thus been enabled to acquire, as to the physical features of the state—the course, length, and depth of its rivers ; its zoological and botanical productions ; its Indian tribes ; its statistics and laws. After the lapse of more than half a century, by much the larger part of it still gives us the fullest and most accurate information we possess of the subjects on which it treats. Some of its physical theories are, indeed, in the rear of modern science ; but they form a small portion of the book, and its general speculations are marked with that boldness, that utter disregard for received opinions, which always characterized him ; and the whole is written in a neat, flowing style, always perspicuous, and often peculiarly apt and felicitous."

Jefferson's notes were printed in Paris, in 1784, soon after his arrival there as minister to the court of France. Says the same author: " One of the first objects which engaged his attention, was the printing his notes on Virginia. He had, for the sake of gratifying a few friends with copies, wished to publish them in America, but was prevented by the expense. He now found they could be printed for about a fourth of what he had been asked at home. He therefore corrected and enlarged them, and had 200 copies printed. Of these he presented a few in Europe, and sent the rest to America. One of them having fallen into the hands of a bookseller in Paris, he had it translated into French, and submitted the translations to the author for revision. It was a tissue of blunders, of which only the most material he found it convenient to correct ; and it was thus printed. A London bookseller having requested permission to print the original, he consented, " to let the world see that it was not really so bad as the French translation had made it appear."

CAROLINE.

CAROLINE was formed in 1727, from Essex, King and Queen, and King William. It is 30 miles long by 20 broad. The Rappahannock flows on its north, the Pamunkey on its south boundary, and the Mattapony runs near its centre. The surface is broken, and the soil various, but the low grounds of these streams are extremely fertile, and admirably adapted to the culture of corn, wheat, and tobacco. Caroline was formerly divided into three parishes; Drysdale and St. Mary's, created in 1727, and St. Margaretts in 1744; in each of which a church was placed—the latter only remains. The Baptists are now the prevailing denomination. Pop. 1830, 17,774; 1840, whites 6,725, slaves 9,314, free colored 774: total, 17,813.

The principal villages are Bowling Green and Port Royal. The first is situated on the main road from Fredericksburg to Richmond, 22 miles from the former, and a short distance only E. of the railroad between these two places. It is the seat of justice for the county, and was originally called New Hope. Its fine location, on a beautiful level green, has given rise to its present name. It contains 2 churches and about 40 dwellings. Port Royal, on the Rappahannock, 22 miles below Fredericksburg, is a somewhat larger village. It was founded in 1744, and possesses a fine harbor, capable of admitting vessels drawing 11 feet of water. The Concord Academy is an institution in this county in excellent repute.

EDMUND PENDLETON was born in this county in 1741, and died in Richmond in 1803. He was president of the Court of Appeals, and of the Virginia convention of 1775. He was twice appointed a member of Congress. In 1788 he was chosen president of the convention of Virginia which met to consider the adoption of the Federal constitution. When the Federal government was organized, he was selected by Congress to be district judge for Virginia, but declined the appointment. Wirt says "He had in a great measure overcome the disadvantages of an extremely defective education, and by the force of good company, and the study of correct authors, had attained to great accuracy and perspicuity of style. . . . His manners were elevated, graceful, and insinuating. His person was spare, but well proportioned, and his countenance one of the finest in the world; serene, contemplative, benignant; with that expression of unclouded intelligence, and extensive reach, which seemed to denote him capable of any thing that could be effected by the power of the human mind. His mind itself was of a very fine order. It was clear, comprehensive, sagacious, and correct; with a most acute and subtle faculty of discrimination; a fertility of expedient which never could be exhausted; a dexterity of address which never lost an advantage and never gave one; and a capacity for continued and unremitting application which was perfectly invincible. As a lawyer, and a statesman, he had few equals and no superiors. For parliamentary management, he was without a rival. With all these advantages of person, manners, address, and intellect, he was also a speaker of distinguished eminence. He had that silver voice of which Cicero makes such frequent and honorable mention; an articulation uncommonly distinct; a perennial stream of transparent, cool, and sweet elocution; and the power of presenting his arguments with great simplicity and striking effect. He was always graceful, argumentative, persuasive; never vehement, rapid, or abrupt. He could instruct and delight; but he had no pretensions to those high powers which are calculated to "shake the human soul."

General WILLIAM WOODFORD, a revolutionary officer of high merit, was born in Caroline. He early distinguished himself in the French and Indian war. Upon the assembling of the Virginia troops at Williamsburg in 1775, consequent upon the hostile attitude of Lord Dunmore, he was appointed colonel of the second regiment. In the military operations immediately subsequent, in that section of the state, his name is honorably mentioned in history, particularly at the battle of Great Bridge, fought Dec. 9th, upon which occasion he had the chief command, and gained a signal victory over the enemy. He was finally promoted to the command of the 1st Va. brigade, in which station he served through the war. He was in various actions, in one of which, the battle of Brandywine, he was wounded. He was made prisoner by the British in 1780, during the siege of Charleston, and taken to New York, where he died on the 13th of November of that year, in the 46th year of his age.

Caroline was also the birth-place of Col. JOHN TAYLOR, "one of the most zealous of the republican party," and an intimate associate of Jefferson. "He represented Virginia in the United States Senate, and was distinguished among the great and good men which this ancient commonwealth has produced. He did much towards advancing the science of agriculture in his native state, and was ever forward in promoting objects conducive to the public good. As a statesman, he is perhaps better known by his Construction Construed; and an Inquiry into the Principles of the Government of the United States, which he published in 1814. He also published several other treatises on various subjects. He died in this county, Aug. 20th, 1824, ripe in years and honor." A county formed in western Virginia, in the session of 1843-4, was named in honor of him.

CARROL.

CARROL was formed in 1842, from the southwestern part of Grayson, and named from Charles Carrol of Carrolton. It is a wild and mountainous tract, and is watered by the New River and some of the head-branches of the Holston.

The Grayson Sulphur Springs, formerly in Grayson, are now within the limits of this county. The improvements at this place are quite recent; but since they have been made, it has grown into popular favor, and attracts more visitors than could have been expected from its remote situation. "The efficacy of the waters in dyspepsia and rheumatism is such as to promise a certain cure."

Grayson Sulphur Springs.

The springs are located immediately on the west side of the Blue Ridge, on the bank of New River, about 20 miles s. of Wytheville, in the midst of scenery of a remarkably wild and romantic character, similar to that of Harper's Ferry, in a region perhaps as healthy as any in our country, abounding with fish and a variety of game. An analysis is subjoined, made by Professors Rogers, of the University of Virginia, and Aiken, of Baltimore.

ANALYSIS.—Carbonate of soda, 4^1; carbonate of magnesia, 3; carbonate of lime, 8; sulphate of lime, 2; sulphate of magnesia, 3; chloride of sodium, 2; chloride of calcium, 3; chloride of magnesium, $1\frac{3}{4}$; sulphate of soda, $4\frac{1}{2}$; sulphureted hydrogen carbonic acid gases.

CHARLES CITY.

CHARLES CITY was one of the eight original shires into which Virginia was divided in 1634. It then extended on both sides of James River, since which its limits have been much reduced. The James River bounds it on the s., and the Chickahominy on the E. and N. The surface is rolling. There are no villages in it; its advantageous situation with respect to trade with the neighboring cities preventing their formation. Pop. 1830, 5,500; 1840, whites 1,171, slaves 2,433, free colored 670: total, 4,774.

Westover, long the seat of the distinguished family of Byrds, is on the James River. It was originally the residence of Col. Wm. Byrd, where he long lived. In his time, it was "a beautifully decorated and princely mansion, which even at this late day exhibits admirable remains of his taste, and his magnificent scale of expenditure for its gratification." Col. Byrd was the author of "The History of the Dividing Line," and one of the most accomplished men in Virginia at his day. He was a worthy inheritor of the opinions and feelings of its old cavaliers. He was for 37 years a member, and at last became president of the council of the colony. He died in 1744, at the age of 70 years. His grave is covered by a white marble monument, which yet stands at Westover. The Marquis de Chastellux, who was here in 1782, gives, in his travels, a glowing description of Westover, which he says surpassed all the seats in the country round about "in the magnificence of the buildings, the beauty of its situation, and the pleasures of society." He eulogizes Mrs. Byrd as a lady of great sense, and an agreeable countenance, who fulfilled the duties incumbent upon her, as the head of a large household, with uncommon skill. To her negroes she did all in her power to render them happy, and served "them herself as a doctor in time of sickness."

Three times, in the course of the revolutionary war, the enemy landed at Westover, under Cornwallis and Arnold.

On the evening of Jan. 8th, 1781, the enemy, who were at Barclay and Westover, sent Lieut.-Col. Simcoe, with a detachment of the Queen's Rangers, to Charles City court-house, where they surprised a party of 150 militia, of whom they killed one, wounded three, and took several prisoners. We here subjoin the account of this event, as given in the journal of Simcoe:

Gen. Arnold directed a patrol to be made on the night of the 8th of January towards Long Bridge, in order to procure intelligence. Lieut.-Col. Simcoe marched with forty cavalry, for the most part badly mounted, on such horses as had been picked up in the country; but the patrol had not proceeded above two miles before Sergeant Kelly, who was in advance, was challenged: he parleyed with the videttes till he got nearer to them, when, rushing at them, one he got hold of, the other flung himself off his horse and escaped into the bushes. A negro was also taken, whom these videttes had intercepted on his way to the British army. From these people information was obtained that the enemy was assembled at Charles City court-house, and that the corps which had appeared in the day-time opposite Westover, nearly to the amount of 400 men, lay about 2 miles in advance of their main body, and on the road to Westover. The party were immediately ordered to the right-about, and to march towards them. Lieut. Holland, who was similar in size to the vidette who had been taken, was placed in advance; the negro had promised to guide the party so as to avoid the high road, and to conduct them by an unfrequented pathway which led close to the creek, between the body which was supposed to be in advance, and that which was at Charles City court-house. Lieut. Col. Simcoe's intention was to beat up the main body of the enemy, who, trusting to those in front, might reasonably be supposed to be off their guard; in case of repulse he meant to retreat by the private way on which he escaped, and should he be successful, it was optional to attack the advance party or not on his return. The patrol passed through a wood, where it halted to collect, and had scarcely got into the road when the advance was challenged: Lieut. Holland answered, "A friend,"—gave the countersign procured from the prisoner—"It is I, me, Charles," the name of the person he personated; he passed one vidette, whom Sergt. Kelly seized, and himself caught hold of the other, who in a struggle proved too strong for him, got free, presented and snapped his carbine at his breast; luckily it did not go off, but the man galloped away, and at some distance fired the signal of alarm. The advance division immediately rushed on, and soon arrived at the court-house; a confused and scattered firing began on all sides;

Lieut.-Col. Simcoe sent the bugle-horns, French and Barney, through an enclosure to the right, with orders to answer his challenging, and sound when he ordered; he then called loudly for the light infantry, and hallooed "Sound the advance;" the bugles were sounded as had been directed, and the enemy fled on all sides, scarcely firing another shot. The night was very dark, and the party totally unacquainted with the ground; part of the dragoons were dismounted, and mixed with the hussars; some of the enemy were taken, others wounded, and a few were drowned in a mill-dam. In saving three armed militia-men from the fury of the soldiers, Lieut.-Col. Simcoe ran a great risk, as their pieces were loaded, pointed to his breast, and in their timidity they might have discharged them. From the prisoners he learned that the whole of their force was here assembled, and that there was no party in advance: the soldiers were mounted as soon as possible, nor could they be permitted to search the houses where many were concealed, lest the enemy should gain intelligence of their numbers, and attack them; and this might easily be done, as the darkness of the night prevented the Rangers from seeing around them, while they were plainly to be distinguished by the fires which the enemy had left. It appeared that the militia were commanded by Gen. Nelson, and consisted of seven or eight hundred men: they were completely frightened and dispersed, many of them not stopping till they reached Williamsburg. Sergt. Adams, of the hussars, was mortally wounded. This gallant soldier, sensible of his situation, said, "My beloved colonel, I do not mind dying, but for God's sake do not leave me in the hands of the rebels." Trumpeter French and two hussars were wounded. About a dozen horses were seasonably captured.

Berkeley, the birth-place of President Harrison.

[This building stands upon the James River, a few hundred yards from its brink. It is an old-fashioned edifice, constructed of brick, and surrounded by a grove of poplars, intermingled with other trees. It is now the residence of the widow of the late Benjamin Harrison, Esq.]

WILLIAM HENRY HARRISON, the ninth President of the United States, was born at Berkeley, Feb. 9th, 1773. His ancestors settled in Virginia in 1640, and the family name was always among the most prominent in her history.

His father, Benjamin Harrison, was a conspicuous patriot of the revolution. When a very young man, he honorably represented his native district in the House of Burgesses for many years, and on the 14th of Nov., 1764, was one of those of its distinguished members chosen to prepare an address to the king, a memorial to the lords, and a remonstrance to the House of Commons, in opposition to the stamp act. He was a delegate from Virginia to the first Continental Congress, which assembled at Philadelphia, Sept. 1st, 1774, when he had the gratification of seeing his brother-in-law, Peyton Randolph, placed in the presidential chair. "At the congress of the following year, 1775, after the death of Mr. Randolph, it was the wish of nearly all the southern members that Mr. Harrison should succeed him in the presidency; but as the patriotic John Hancook, of Massachusetts, had likewise been nominated, Mr. Harrison, to avoid any sectional jealousy or unkindness of feeling between the northern and southern delegates at so momentous a crisis, with a noble self-denial and generosity relinquished his own claims, and insisted on the election of Mr. Hancock, who accordingly had the honor of being unanimously chosen to that high office. Mr. Harrison still, however, continued one of the most active and influential members of the Continental Congress. On the 10th of June, 1776, as chairman of the committee of the whole house, he introduced the resolution which declared the independence of the colonies ; and on the ever-memorable *fourth of July*, he reported the more formal Declaration of Independence, to which celebrated document his signature is annexed. The legislature of Virginia returned Mr. Harrison four times as a delegate to Congress. On the expiration of his last term of congressional service, he was immediately elected to the House of Burgesses from his own county, and was at once chosen speaker of that body—an office he held uninterruptedly until the year 1782, when he was elected governor of Virginia, and became one of the most popular officers that ever filled the executive chair. This eminent patriot died in the year 1791."

William Henry Harrison was left under the guardianship of Robert Morris, the distinguished financier, and was educated at Hampden Sydney College, and turned his attention to the study of medicine. " The hostilities of the Indians on the northwestern frontier having begun to excite general attention, the young student resolved to relinquish his professional pursuits, and join the army destined to the defence of the Ohio frontier. In 1791, soon after the death of his father, who died in April of the same year, he received from President Washington, when only in his 19th year, the commission of ensign ; in 1792 he was promoted to the rank of lieutenant, and he fought under Gen. Wayne, who spoke of his gallant conduct in a very flattering manner. After the desperate battle of the Miami Rapids, he was promoted to the rank of captain, and was placed in the command of Fort Washington. In 1797 he resigned his commission in the army, and was immediately appointed secretary of the NW. territory. In 1799, at the age of 26, he was elected a delegate from this territory to Congress, and in this office he performed very important services for his constituents. On the erection of Indiana into a territorial government, he was appointed its first governor, and he held this office by reappointment until 1813. In addition to the duties in the civil and military government of the territory, he was commissioner and superintendent of Indian Affairs ; and in the course of his administration he concluded thirteen important treaties with the different tribes. On the 7th of Nov., 1811, he gained over the Indians the celebrated battle of Tippecanoe, the news of which was received throughout the country with a burst of enthusiasm. During the last war with Great Britain, he was made commander of the northwestern army of the United States, and he bore a conspicuous part in the leading events of the campaign of 1812–13—the defence of Fort Meigs, and the victory of the Thames. In 1814 he was appointed, in conjunction with his companion in arms, Gov. Shelby, and Gen. Cass, to treat with the Indians in the northwest ; and in the following year, he was placed at the head of a commission to treat with various other important tribes.

" In 1816, Gen. Harrison was elected a member of Congress from Ohio ; and in 1828 he was sent minister plenipotentiary to the Republic of Columbia. On his return, he took up his residence at North Bend, on the Ohio, 16 m. below Cincinnati, where he lived upon his farm in comparative retirement until he was called by the people of the United States to preside over the country as its chief magistrate." Of 294 votes for president, he received 234. He died April 4th, 1841, just a month after his inauguration. His death caused a deep sensation throughout the country.

JOHN TYLER, the father of the late President of the United States, resided in this county. " He was one of the leading revolutionary characters of Virginia, was many years a member of the House of Delegates, and in 1781 succeeded Mr. Benjamin Harrison as speaker. After being governor of Virginia, to which office he was elected in 1808, he was judge of the District Court of the United States for Virginia, and died at his seat in Charles City co., Jan. 6th, 1813. He was simple in his manners, distinguished for the uprightness and fidelity with which he discharged his official duties, and enjoyed in an uncommon degree the esteem and confidence of his fellow-citizens."

JOHN TYLER, the 10th President of the United States, and the *sixth* from Virginia, was born on the James River in this co., in 1790, about 5 m. below Berkeley. Four miles lower down on the river is his present residence.

CHARLOTTE.

CHARLOTTE was formed in 1794, from Lunenburg. It is 22 miles long, with a mean breadth of 18 miles. The surface is diversified; the soil on the river bottoms fertile, but on the ridges mostly barren; it is watered by numerous creeks and rivulets, all tributary to Staunton river, except the head branches of the Meherrin, on the E. and SE. Pop. 1830, 15,252; 1840, whites 5,130; slaves 9,260; free colored 307; total, 14,595.

Charlotte C. H., or Marysville, 98 miles sw. of Richmond, and 30 SE. of Lynchburg, near the centre of the county, contains 1 Baptist, 1 Presbyterian, and 1 Methodist church, and about 50 dwellings. Keysville, and Rough Creek Church, are small places in the county.

Charlotte has been the residence of three distinguished Virginians, viz.: Patrick Henry, John Randolph, and the late Judge Paul Carrington, senr.

The residence of the latter was near the junction of the L. Roanoke, with the Staunton, on an elevated and beautiful site. He was a member of the bar of Charlotte, in 1765. After Lord Dunmore had abdicated the government of Virginia, a convention met in Richmond, in the year 1775, to organize a provincial form of government, and a plan of defence for the colony. Mr. Carrington was one of the committee of public safety to whom this plan was submitted. He subsequently became a judge of the court of appeals, in which office he remained until a few years before his death.

Red Hill, the Seat of Patrick Henry.

Red Hill is on the southwest angle of the county. There lived and died PATRICK HENRY; the man who, Jefferson said, " was the greatest orator that ever lived;" and to whom Randolph applied the words of sacred writ, as being one " who spake as never man spake."

Red Hill is now the seat of his son, John Henry, Esq. The larger part of the main building, shown on the left, has been added since the decease of its illustrious occupant.*

---

* Patrick Henry, when governor, resided at Williamsburg, Richmond; at Salisbury,

It is beautifully situated on an elevated ridge, the dividing line of Campbell and Charlotte, within a quarter of a mile of the junction of Falling River with the Staunton. From it the valley of the Staunton stretches southward about three miles, varying from a quarter to nearly a mile in width, and of an oval-like form. Through most fertile meadows, waving in their golden luxuriance, slowly winds the river, overhung by mossy foliage, while on all sides gently sloping hills, rich in verdure, enclose the whole, and impart to it an air of seclusion and repose. From the brow of the hill, west of the house, is a scene of an entirely different character; the Blue Ridge, with the lofty Peaks of Otter, appear in the horizon at a distance of nearly sixty miles. At the foot of the garden, under a dense cluster of locust and other trees, enclosed by a wooden paling, are the graves of Patrick Henry and his wife, overrun with myrtle, and without any monuments over them.

Under the trees seen on the left of the picture, in full view of the beautiful valley beneath, the orator was accustomed in pleasant weather to sit mornings and evenings, with his chair leaning against one of their trunks, and a can of cool spring-water by his side, from which he took frequent draughts. Occasionally, he walked to and fro in the yard from one clump of trees to the other, buried in revery, at which times he was never interrupted. Among the relics in the house is the *arm-chair* in which he died, and a knife given to him when a boy by his uncle, Patrick Henry, which he carried through life, and had in his pocket at the moment of his death. In the parlor hangs his portrait, a masterly production, by Sully, representing him pleading in the British *debt cause*. The dress is black, cravat white, and a red velvet mantle is thrown over the shoulders.* He appears three-quarters face, leaning partly back, with his spectacles thrown over his forehead; and the expression is one of deep solemnity and impressiveness.

Under the description of Hanover county, the reader will find a succinct memoir of Henry; and in that of New London, Campbell county, and of the city of Richmond, are views of buildings memorable as the scenes of some of his celebrated oratorical efforts. We now give some reminiscences, collected by us from a reliable source while in this section of the state. They are mainly detached facts, without connection, and must necessarily be given in that manner.

When fourteen years of age, Mr. Henry went with his mother in a carriage to the Fork church in Hanover, to hear preach the celebrated Samuel Davies, afterwards president of Princeton college. His eloquence made a deep impression on his youthful mind, and he always remarked, he was the greatest orator he ever heard. When a member of the Continental Congress, he said the first men in that body were Washington, Richard Henry Lee, and Roger Sherman; and later in life, Roger Sherman and George Mason, the greatest statesmen he ever knew. When governor, he had printed and circulated in Richmond, at his own expense, Soame Jenyns' View of Christianity, and Butler's Analogy of Natural and Revealed Religion. Sherlock's sermons, he affirmed, was the work which removed all his doubts of the truth of Christianity; a copy of which, until a short time since, was in the possession of his children, filled with marginal notes. He read it every Sunday evening to his family, after which they all joined in sacred music, while he accompanied them on the violin. He never quoted poetry. His quotations were from the Bible, and his illustrations from the Bible, ancient and modern history. He was opposed to the adoption of the Federal constitution, because he thought it gave too much power to the general government; and in conversation with the father of a late venerable senator from Prince Edward, he remarked with emphasis: "The President of the United States will always come in at the head of a party. He will be supported in all his acts by a party. You do not now think much of the patronage of the President; but the day is coming when it will be tremendous, and from this power the country may sooner or later fall."

In the British *debt* cause, of which Wirt gives a full account, Mr. Henry made great preparation. He shut himself up in his office for three days, during which he did not see his family; his food was handed by a servant through the office-door. The Countess of Huntington, then in this country, was among the auditors, and remarked, after hearing the arguments of the several speakers,† "that if every one of them had spoken in

---

Chesterfield county, and at Leatherwood, Henry co. Afterwards, he dwelt on the Appomattox, in Prince Edward; at Long Island, Campbell co., and removed to Red Hill in 1795, four years previous to his death.

* His usual dress while in the legislature.

† They were, on the part of plaintiff, Messrs. Ronald, Baker, Wickham, and Starke: and on that of the defendant, Messrs. Henry, Marshall, Innis, and Alex. Campbell, a

Westminster Hall, they would have been honored with a peerage." Mr. Henry had a diamond ring on his finger, and, while he was speaking, the Countess exclaimed to the Judge, Iredell—who had never before heard him—"The diamond is *blazing !*" "Gracious God!" replied he, "he is an orator indeed." In this cause he injured his voice so that it never recovered its original power.

The following anecdote was related by President Madison, at the conclusion of the late war, to a party of gentlemen assembled at his residence in Washington. In the revolutionary war, certificates were given by the legislature to the Virginia line on continental establishment, stating the amount due to them, which was to be paid at a future time. The necessities of the soldiers, in many instances, compelled them to part with the certificates to speculators for a trivial sum. Madison brought a bill before the legislature to put a stop to it. He had previously asked Mr. Henry if he was willing to support it. The reply was "yes;" but having no further communication with him on the subject, Mr. Madison feared he had forgotten the circumstance. After the bill was read, he turned to where Mr. Henry sat, with an anxious eye, upon which the latter immediately arose and addressed the house. Mr. Madison said that upon that occasion he was particularly eloquent. His voice reminded him of a trumpeter on the field of battle, calling the troops to a charge. He looked alternately to the house and the audience, and saw they were with the orator ; and, at the conclusion, one of the chief speculators in tickets, then in the galleries, exclaimed in an audible voice—"That bill ought to pass !"—it did pass, and unanimously.

We conclude this article by the subjoined extract from "the Mountaineer," a series of Essays, originally published in 1813 in the Republican Farmer, at Staunton, and written by Conrad Speece, D.D., pastor of the Augusta church :

Many years ago, I was at the trial, in one of our district courts, of a man charged with murder. The case was briefly this: the prisoner had gone, in execution of his office as a constable, to arrest a slave who had been guilty of some misconduct, and bring him to justice. Expecting opposition in the business, the constable took several men with him, some of them armed. They found the slave on the plantation of his master, within view of the house, and proceeded to seize and bind him. His mistress, seeing the arrest, came down and remonstrated vehemently against it. Finding her efforts unavailing, she went off to a barn where her husband was, who was presently perceived running briskly to the house. It was known his always kept a loaded rifle over his door. The constable now desired his company to remain where they were, taking care to keep the slave in custody, while he himself would go to the house to prevent mischief. He accordingly ran towards the house. When he arrived within a short distance of it, the master appeared coming out of the door with his rifle in his hand. Some witnesses said that as he came to the door he drew the cock of the piece, and was seen in the act of raising it to the position of firing. But upon these points, there was not an entire agreement in the evidence. The constable, standing near a small building in the yard, at this instant fired, and the fire had a fatal effect. No previous malice was proved against him ; and his plea upon the trial was, that he had taken the life of his assailant in necessary self-defence.

A great mass of testimony was delivered. This was commented upon with considerable ability by the lawyer for the commonwealth, and by another lawyer engaged by the friends of the deceased for the prosecution. The prisoner was also defended, in elaborate speeches, by two respectable advocates. These proceedings brought the day to a close. The general whisper through a crowded house was, that the man was guilty and could not be saved.

About dusk, candles were brought, and Henry arose. His manner was exactly that which the *British Spy* describes with so much felicity ; plain, simple, and entirely unassuming. "Gentlemen of the jury," said he, "I dare say we are all very much fatigued with this tedious trial. The prisoner at the bar has been well defended already ; but it is my duty to offer you some further observations in behalf of this unfortunate man. I shall aim at brevity. But should I take up more of your time than you expect, I hope you will hear me with patience, when you consider *that* blood *is concerned.*"

I cannot admit the possibility that any one who never heard Henry speak should be made fully to conceive the force of impression which he gave to these few words, "*blood is concerned.*" I had been on my feet through the day, pushed about in the crowd, and was excessively weary. I was strongly of opinion, too, notwithstanding all the previous defensive pleadings, that the prisoner was guilty of murder ; and I felt anxious to know how the matter would terminate. Yet when Henry had uttered these words, my feelings underwent an instantaneous change ; I found every thing within me answering at once, yes, since blood is concerned, in the name of all that is righteous, go on ; we will hear you with patience until the rising of to-morrow's sun. This bowing of the soul must have been universal ; for the profoundest silence reigned, as if our very breath had been suspended. The spell of the magician was upon us, and we stood like statues around him. Under the touch of his genius, every particular of the story assumed a new aspect, and his cause became continually more bright and promising. At length he arrived at the fatal act itself. "You have been told, gentlemen, that the prisoner was bound by every obligation to avoid the supposed necessity of firing, by leaping behind a house near which he stood at that moment. Had he been attacked with a club, or with stones, the argument would have been unanswerable, and I should feel myself compelled to give up the defence in despair. But surely I need not tell you, gentlemen, how wide is the difference between sticks or stones, and double-triggered *loaded rifles cocked at your breast.*" The effect of this terrific image, exhibited in this great orator's peerless manner, cannot be described. I dare not attempt to delineate the paroxysm of emotion which it excited in every heart. The result of the whole was, that the prisoner was acquitted ; with the perfect approba-

cousin of the poet. This case "was discussed with so much learning, argument, and eloquence, as to have placed the bar of Virginia, in the estimation of the federal judges (if the reports of the day may be accredited,) above all others in the United States."

tion, I believe, of the numerous assembly who attended the trial. What was it that gave such transcendent force to the eloquence of Henry? His reasoning powers were good: but they have been equalled, and more than equalled, by those of many other men. His imagination was exceedingly quick, and commanded all the stores of nature as materials for illustrating his subject. His voice and delivery were inexpressibly happy. But his most irresistible charm was the vivid feeling of his cause with which he spoke. Such feeling infallibly communicates itself to the breast of the hearer.

Roanoke, the seat of John Randolph.

The residence of the late John Randolph is near the Staunton, in the southern part of the county, several miles above its junction with the Dan, and about thirteen below Charlotte court-house.

The name, *Roanoke*, is derived from a small creek running through the plantation. The buildings are in a dense forest, which has scarce ever echoed to the woodman's axe. On leaving the main road, the traveller threads his way through the woods by a narrow path, for about half a mile, when, a few rods distant, the dwellings and out-houses suddenly appear through the foliage, without any cultivated land or clearing in view, seeming, from the wild seclusion and primitive aspect of the spot, to have been the abode of a recluse, rather than of a statesman, whose fame extended beyond the limits of his native land.

The two buildings in front were occupied by Mr. Randolph, and those in the rear by his domestics. That on the right is clapboarded, and is much the most commodious; it was the one in which he dwelt in summer. On the ground-floor are two rooms, one containing his books, the other is the drawing-room, adorned with convenient and neat furniture. The library is large, well selected, and contains many rare works. Most of the books bear evidence of careful perusal, and the striking passages are marked with the pencil. Among the many pictures and portraits in these rooms is one of Pocahontas. The arms are bare to the elbow, displaying an arm and a hand of exquisite beauty. The hair and eye are a raven black,—the latter remarkably expressive, and the whole countenance surpassing lovely, and beaming with intelligence and benignity.

The dwelling on the left was his winter residence, and the one in which he usually partook of his meals. It is a log structure, which is entered through a shed, paved with water-worn pebbles and supported by unhewn posts. Notwithstanding its extreme simplicity, it is richly furnished. These rooms are also hung with portraits. One of them is a fine drawing of his servant Jupiter—or, as he is commonly called, Juba—dressed as a sportsman, with a double-barrelled gun on his shoulder. Over the fireplace in the bedroom is a portrait of Mr. Randolph, when twelve years of age. It is a fine oil painting, from the easel of the celebrated Gilbert Stuart. In the fresh rosy complexion, and round chubby face of this beautiful little boy, it would be difficult to trace any resemblance to the thin, cadaverous lineaments of the original in his latter years. John and Juba, the favorite servants of Randolph, yet reside in the small huts shown in the background.

The first is a man of strong mind, and the general expression, and the high, well-developed forehead, denote an intellect of greater than an ordinary cast; but the latter —the affectionate and faithful Juba—was more appreciated for the qualities of his heart. As we mounted our horses, on leaving Roanoke, at the close of a fine summer's day in 1843, we said to him : " Juba, you lost a fine master when Mr. Randolph died." " Ah !" replied he, " he was more than a father to me."

About 100 yards to the right of where the foregoing view was taken, is the grave of Randolph. It is in the midst of the forest, with no marble memorial ; but two tall pines hang their rude limbs over the spot, and the wind mournfully sighs through their branches.

Fac-simile of the signature of John Randolph of Roanok

JOHN RANDOLPH OF ROANOKE[*] was born June 2d, 1773, at Cawson's, Prince George county, the family seat of his mother. He was descended in the seventh generation from Pocahontas, the Indian princess. This lady died at Gravesend, England, in 1617, at the age of twenty-three. Thomas Rolf, her son, became a citizen of Virginia, and left at his death a daughter, who married Col. Robert Bolling, by whom she had one son and five daughters. They married respectively, Col. John Fleming, Dr. Wm. Gay, Mr. Thomas Eldridge, Mr. James Murray, and Col. Richard Randolph. John Randolph of Roanoke, was the son of John Randolph, a wealthy country gentleman, who died at Matoax, his residence on the Appomattox, near Petersburg, where he lies burried. John Randolph of Roanoke's mother was Frances Bland, daughter of Col. Theodorick Bland, jun., who was a brother of Richard Bland, a member of the continental congress. Surviving her first husband, she married secondly, St. George Tucker, the eminent jurist. John Randolph's half-brothers, now surviving, are Beverley T. Tucker, professor of law at William and Mary, and Henry St. George Tucker, professor of law at the University of Va.

The mother of John Randolph was an exemplary and pious member of the Episcopal denomination, and a lady of sprightliness and talent. She brought up her son strictly, " teaching him," as he often remarked, " the Lord's prayer and the ten commandments." John Randolph passed a short time at three colleges : Princeton, Columbia, and William and Mary ; but he used to say, that he acquired all his knowledge from his library at Roanoke, and by intercourse with the world.

In the spring of 1799, Mr. Randolph presented himself to the electors of Charlotte as a candidate for Congress, in competition with Mr. Clement Carrington, a federalist, and Mr. Powhatan Bolling, a democrat. On the same occasion he encountered Patrick Henry, then a candidate for the state senate, and opposed to those measures Mr. Randolph advocated. They met at the court-house, and supported a long and animated discussion. Mr. Henry was then in his 67th year ; the measure of his fame was full ; the late proceedings of the Virginia assembly, in relation to the alien and sedition laws, had filled him with alarm—" had planted his pillow with thorns, and he had quitted his retirement to make one more, his *last*, effort for his country." Enfeebled by age and ill-health, with a linen cap upon his head, he mounted the hustings, and commenced with difficulty ; but as he proceeded, his eye lighted up with its wonted fire, his voice assumed its wonted majesty ; gradually accumulating strength and animation, his eloquence seemed like an *avalanche* threatening to overwhelm his adversary. Many present considered it his best effort. Mr. Moulton remarked, that many of its passages were indelibly impressed upon his memory. In the course of the speech, Mr. Henry said, " The alien and sedition laws were only the fruits of that constitution, the adoption of which he opposed. . . . . If we are wrong, let us all go wrong together," at the same time clasping his hands and waving his body to the right and left. His auditory unconsciously *waved* with him. As he finished he literally descended into the arms of the obstreperous throng, and was borne about in triumph, when Dr. John H. Rice exclaimed, " *the sun has set in all his glory.*"

---

[*] Hugh A. Garland, Esq., of Petersburg, is preparing a biography of John Randolph, from whom will doubtless be given an authentic and full memoir.

As Mr. Henry left the stand, Mr. Randolph, with undaunted courage, arose in his place. He was then about 26 years of age—a mere boy from college, who had, probably, never yet addressed a political assembly—of a youthful and unprepossessing appearance. The audience, considering it presumptuous for him to speak after Mr. Henry, partially dispersed, and an Irishman present exclaimed, " Tut! tut! it won't do, it's nothing but the bating of an old tin pan after hearing a fine church organ."   But if " the sun of the other had *set* in all his glory," his was about to *rise* with, perhaps, an equal brilliancy. He commenced : " his singular person and peculiar aspect,; his novel, shrill, vibratory intonations ; his solemn, slow-marching, and swelling periods ; his caustic crimination of the prevailing political party; his cutting satire ; the *tout ensemble* of his public *début*, soon calmed the tumultuous crowd, and inclined all to listen to the strange orator, while he replied at length to the sentiments of their old favorite.   When he had concluded, loud huzzas rang through the welkin.

" This was a new event to Mr. Henry.   He had not been accustomed to a rival, and little expected one in a beardless boy : for such was the aspect of the champion who now appeared to contend for the palm which he was wont to appropriate to himself. He returned to the stage and commenced a second address, in which he soared above his usual vehemence and majesty.   Such is usually the fruit of emulation and rivalship. He frequently adverted to his youthful competitor with parental tenderness ; compliment-ed his rare talents with the liberality of profusion ; and, while regretting what he depre-cated as the political errors of youthful zeal, actually wrought himself and audience into an enthusiasm of sympathy and benevolence that issued in an ocean of tears.   The gesture, intonations, and pathos of Mr. Henry, operated like an epidemic on the trans-ported assembly.   The contagion was universal.   An hysterical phrensy pervaded the audience to such a degree, that they were at the same moment literally weeping and laughing.   At this juncture the speaker descended from the stage.   Shouts of applause rent the air, and were echoed from the skies.   The whole spectacle as it really was, would not only mock every attempt at description, but would almost challenge the im-agination of any one who had not witnessed it.   With a recollection of the event, Mr Randolph, eighteen years afterwards, in his place in the House of Representatives of the U. S., speaking of the general-ticket law, which was carried by the democratic party by a majority of five votes only in the popular branch of the Virginia Assembly, said : ' Had Patrick Henry lived, and taken his seat in the Assembly, that law would never have passed.   In that case the electoral vote of Virginia would have been divided, and Mr. Jefferson lost his election !   Five votes !   Mr. Chairman !   Patrick Henry was good for five times five votes.' "*

In this contest Mr. Henry was elected to the Senate of Virginia, but did not live to take his seat ; and Mr. Randolph was returned to Congress, in which body he was at different intervals for more than twenty-four years, including the time he served in the United States Senate.   Well did the people of Charlotte obey the last injunction of Patrick Henry in the speech above described, when he said, " He is a young man of promise ; *cherish* him, he will make an invaluable man."

Such was Mr. Randolph's youthful appearance, that when he made his first appearance at the clerk's table of the House of Representatives to qualify, that gentleman could not refrain from inquiring his age : "*Ask my constituents*, sir," was the reply.   Mr. Ran-dolph soon became one of the leaders of the republican party in Congress, and a de-cided politician of the Jeffersonian school.   He later was distinguished by his opposition to the embargo and non-intercourse acts, and the gun-boat system of Mr. Jefferson.

In Madison's administration, Mr. Randolph opposed the declaration of war with Great Britain ; but when fears were entertained of the invasion of Virginia, at the time of the burning of Washington, he offered himself to the governor for any post he chose to as-sign him.   He was given an office in the corps of topographical engineers, which he filled as long as the corps remained in service.   In the administration of Mr. Monroe, he op-posed with ability the Greek resolutions, and the internal improvement system of the general government.   During the administration of J. Q. Adams, he was elected to the U. S. Senate, where he again arrayed himself in opposition to the friends of the presi-dent.   It was then that he used those violent remarks which occasioned the duel be-tween himself and Mr. Clay.

The account of this duel, which we extract, has been given to the public in a letter of Gen. James Hamilton, who accompanied Mr. Randolph to the field on this occasion, in conjunction with Col. Tattnal, then a member of Congress from Georgia :

---

* From the Memoir of Patrick Henry, by E. H. Cummins, A. M.—in the 2d Amer-ican edition of the New Edinburgh Encyclopedia, published in 1817

The night before the duel, Mr. Randolph sent for me in the evening. I found him calm, but in a singularly kind and confiding mood. He told me that he had something on his mind to tell me. He then remarked, " Hamilton, I have determined to receive, without returning, Clay's fire ; nothing shall induce me to harm a hair of his head ; I will not make his wife a widow, or his children orphans. Their tears would be shed over his grave ; but when the sod of Virginia rests on my bosom, there is not, in this wide world, one individual to pay this tribute upon mine." His eyes filled, and resting his head upon his hand, he remained some moments silent. I replied, " My dear friend," (for ours was a sort of posthumous friendship, bequeathed by our mothers,) " I deeply regret that you have mentioned this subject to me, for you call upon me to go to the field and to see you shot down, or to assume the responsibility, in regard to your own life, in sustaining your determination to throw it away. But on this subject a man's own conscience and his own bosom are his best monitors. I will not advise ; but under the enormous and unprovoked personal insult you have offered Mr. Clay, I cannot dissuade. I feel bound, however, to communicate to Col. Tattnal your decision." He begged me not to do so, and said, " he was very much afraid that Tattnal would take the studs and refuse to go out with him." I however sought Col. Tattnal, and we repaired, about midnight, to Mr. Randolph's lodgings, whom we found reading Milton's great Poem. For some moments he did not permit us to say one word in relation to the approaching duel ; and he at once commenced one of those delightful criticisms on a passage from this poet, in which he was wont so enthusiastically to indulge. After a pause, Col. Tattnal remarked, " Mr. Randolph, I am told you have determined not to return Mr. Clay's fire ; I must say to you, my dear sir, if I am only to go out to see you shot down, you must find some other friend." Mr. Randolph remarked that it was his determination. After much conversation on the subject, I induced Col. Tattnal to allow Mr. Randolph to take his own course, as his withdrawal, as one of his friends, might lead to very injurious misconstructions. At last Mr. Randolph, smiling, said, " Well, Tattnal, I promise you one thing ; if I see the devil in Clay's eye, and that with malice prepense he means to take my life, I may change my mind."—A remark I knew he merely made to propitiate the anxiety of his friend.

Mr. Clay and himself met at 4 o'clock the succeeding evening, on the banks of the Potomac. But he saw " no devil in Clay's eye," but a man fearless, and expressing the mingled sensibility and firmness which belonged to the occasion.

I shall never forget this scene as long as I live. It has been my misfortune to witness several duels, but I never saw one, at least in its sequel, so deeply affecting.

The sun was just setting behind the blue hills of Randolph's own Virginia. Here were two of the most extraordinary men our country in its prodigality had produced, about to meet in mortal combat. * * * While Tattnal was loading Randolph's pistol, I approached my friend, I believed for the last time ; I took his hand ; there was not in its touch the quickening of one pulsation. He turned to me and said, " Clay is calm, but not vindictive. I hold my purpose, Hamilton, in any event—remember this." On handing him his pistol, Col. Tattnal sprung the hair-trigger. Mr. Randolph said, " Tattnal, although I am one of the best shots in Virginia, with either a pistol or gun, yet I never fire with the hair-trigger ; besides, I have a thick buckskin glove on, which will destroy the delicacy of my touch, and the trigger may fly before I know where I am." But from his great solicitude for his friend, Tattnal insisted upon hairing the trigger. On taking their position, the fact turned out as Mr. Randolph anticipated : his pistol went off before the word, with the muzzle down.

The moment this event took place, Gen. Jesup, Mr. Clay's friend, called out that he would instantly leave the ground with his friend, if this occurred again. Mr. Clay at once exclaimed it was entirely an accident, and begged that the gentleman might be allowed to go on. On the word being given, Mr. Clay fired without effect, Mr. Randolph discharging his pistol in the air. The moment Mr. Clay saw that Mr. Randolph had thrown away his fire, with a gush of sensibility he instantly approached Mr. R. and said, with an emotion I never can forget, " I trust in God, my dear sir, you are untouched ; after what has occurred, I would not have harmed you for a thousand worlds." Deeply affected by this scene, I could not refrain from grasping Mr. Clay by the hand, and said, " My good sir, we have been long separated, but after the events of to-day, I feel that we must be friends for ever."

The magnanimous conduct of Mr. Randolph on the occasion of this duel excited general admiration. Shortly afterwards he retired from Congress, and in 1829 he was elected a member of the convention for revising the state constitution. Every morning he went to the capitol in Richmond, where the convention met, clad in mourning, with a black suit, and hat and arms bound with crape. " Have you lost a friend ?" was the frequent query. " Oh no !" replied he, in his peculiarly melancholy tones ; " I go in mourning for *the old constitution : I* fear I have come to witness *its death and funeral.*" When he returned from the convention, he intended to retire from public life, and made, as he supposed, his farewell address to his constituents at Charlotte court-house. From the memory of a gentleman present, we give a slight sketch of his remarks :

He commenced by saying, " he had lately been very unpleasantly situated ; that he was in a convention where Virginian was contending with Virginian for power, and that he had taken part in the strife. Fellow-citizens, you know *brothers never could divide an estate !* The convention agreed to a constitution he had there voted for, and should presently go into the court-house and vote for again. But he disliked it. They had extended the right of suffrage ; he never could agree to it—never thought it right. There many plans for a constitution were submitted ; every man thought himself a constitution-maker—every man thought himself a George Mason. But my main business is to take leave of you, and what shall I say ? Twenty-eight years ago you took me by the hand when a beardless boy, and led me into Congress Hall. The clerk asked me if I was of lawful age ; I told him to ask you. You said you had a faithful representative ; I said *no man ever had such constituents.* You have supported me through evil report and through good report. I have served you to the best of my ability, but fear I have been an unprofitable servant ; and if justice were meted out to me, should be beaten with *many stripes.* People of Charlotte ! which of you is without SIN ?"—at the same time shaking his long bony finger, "that javelin of rhetoric," (as it has been termed,) at them in his peculiarly impressive manner. "But I know," continued he, "I shall get a verdict of acquittal from my earthly tribunal: I see it! I read it in your countenances. But it is time for me to retire, and prepare to stand before another, a higher tribunal, where a verdict of acquittal will be of infinite more importance than one from an earthly tribunal. Here is the trust you placed in my hands twenty-eight years ago"—at the same time, suiting the action to the idea, bending forward as though rolling a great weight towards them, and exclaiming—"*Take it back! take it back!*" He then mounted his horse and rode off.

Early in the administration of President Jackson, he was appointed a minister-plenipotentiary to Russia. He suddenly returned from his mission, came into Charlotte, and raised his standard in opposition to the executive. Death, however, soon terminated his labors. He died at Philadelphia, May 24th, 1833, whither he had gone to embark on board of a vessel for Europe, for the benefit of his health. His physician published a long and thrilling narrative of his last days. We have, however, but sufficient space to quote the concluding scene:

"After the lapse of about an hour or more, and about 50 minutes before his decease, I returned to his sick room; but now the scene was changed. His keen, penetrating eye had lost its expression; his powerful mind had given way, and he appeared totally incapable of giving any correct directions relative to his worldly concerns. To record what now took place may not be required, further than to say, that almost to the last moment some of his eccentricities could be seen lingering about him. He had entered within 'the dark valley of the shadow of death,' and what was now passing within his chamber was like the distant voice of words which fell with confusion on the ear. The further this master-spirit receded from view, the sounds became less distinct, until they were lost in the deep recesses of the valley, and all that was mortal of Randolph of Roanoke was hushed in death."

Mr. Randolph never married. He was once engaged to a distinguished heiress; but when the day appointed for the wedding arrived, he declined, and she subsequently married a gentleman of distinction. Yet, from the following anecdote, it would seem that he had no great predilections for a life of celibacy. Respecting an epistle to a friend, congratulating him upon his marriage, written by Mr. Randolph early in life, one who saw it has said: "a letter of more beautiful simplicity and feeling, I never read. I recollect that while the writer dwelt upon the happiness and advantages to be expected from a wedded life, he spoke feelingly of never expecting to enjoy them himself."

The portrait of Mr. Randolph when a boy, shows him to have been a beautiful child. When a young man, he was tall, ungainly, flaxen-haired, and his complexion of a parchment hue. The expression was unprepossessing; but when animated, his countenance changed in a moment, and that which was before dull and heavy, flashed up with the brightest beams of intellect. His personal appearance late in life is here given from a published account, omitting the extravagances of the original:

I had frequently heard and read descriptions of Randolph: and one day, as I was standing in one of the public streets of Baltimore, I remarked a tall, thin, unique-looking being, hurrying towards me with a quick impatient step, evidently much annoyed by a crowd of boys following close upon him, absorbed in silent and curious wonder. He stopped to converse with a gentleman, which gave me an opportunity, unnoticed, to observe the Roanoke orator for a considerable length of time, and really he was the most remarkable looking person I ever beheld.

His limbs, long and thin, were encased in a pair of small-clothes, so tight that they seemed part and parcel of the limbs of the wearer. Handsome white stockings were fastened with great tidiness at the knees by a small gold buckle, and over them, coming about half-way up to the calf, were a pair of what I believe are called hose, coarse and country-knit. He wore shoes: they were old-fashioned, and fastened only with buckles —huge ones. In walking, he placed his feet in the straight-forward Indian manner. It was then the fashion to wear a fan-tailed coat, with a small collar, and buttons far apart behind, and a few on the breast. Mr. Randolph's were the reverse of this; the coat was swallow-tailed, the collar immensely large, and the buttons crowded together. His waist was remarkably slender, and around it his coat was buttoned very tight, and held together by one button. His neck was enveloped in a large high white cravat, without any collar being perceptible, although it was then the fashion to wear them very large. His complexion was dark and cadaverous, and his face exceedingly wrinkled. His lips were thin, compressed, and colorless; the chin, beardless as a boy's, was broad for the size of his face, which was small; his nose was straight, with nothing remarkable in it, except it was too short. He wore a fur cap, which he took off, standing a few minutes uncovered. I observed that his head was quite small; a characteristic which is said to have marked many men of talent—Byron and Chief Justice Marshall, for instance.

To accurately delineate the character of Mr. Randolph, would require the pen of a master, and a long acquaintance with him. While in Congress, he had but few personal friends, but those few, it has been said, " he riveted to his heart with hooks of steel." His attachments and hatred were alike strong. His affection for his servants was great; and his treatment, kind and generous, excited that gratitude which is a marked feature in the African race. The return of " Massa Randolph" from Congress was greeted with the utmost demonstration of joy.

The conversational powers of Mr. Randolph were extraordinary, and when he chose, there was irresistible fascination in his voice and manner. His knowledge of books and men too was extensive. A friend on board the steamboat with him, on his passage from Baltimore to Philadelphia, a few days before his death, stated to the writer, that among the crowd that at one time surrounded him, as he reclined upon a settee in the cabin, was a gentleman, now a foreign minister; an individual who, as a writer, has done more to enhance the reputation of American literature abroad than any other. Him, the statesman, enfeebled in body and mind by disease, was addressing. He hung upon his lips as if drawn by a charm, and appeared like a child before its teacher.

It has been said, that when in the halls of legislation, " he never spoke without commanding the most intense interest. At his first gesture, or word, the house and galleries were hushed into silence and attention. His voice was shrill and pipe-like, but under perfect command; and in its lower tones, it was music. His tall person, firm eye, and peculiarly ' expressive fingers,' assisted very much in giving effect to his delivery. His eloquence, taking its character from his unamiable disposition, was generally exerted in satire and invective; but he never attempted pathos without entire success. In quickness of perception, accuracy of memory, liveliness of imagination, and sharpness of wit, he surpassed most men of his day; but his judgment was feeble, or rarely consulted."

The aphorism, "a prophet is not without honor save in his own country," did not apply to him. He was always an object of wonder and curiosity to all. He often stopped at the hotel of Wyatt Cardwell, Esq., at Charlotte C. H. On those occasions, the multitude, though frequently seeing him, would crowd the windows and doors to get a glimpse of that man, about whose genius, eccentricities, and physical aspect, there was so much of the incomprehensible.

Mr. Randolph was opposed to that feature in the Federal constitution which gave so much power to the president. To that, by his friends, has been ascribed his opposition to every executive.

He went for the independence of the representative. A quotation from one of his speeches, supplied by the memory of one present, is here in point. " I was at Federal Hall. I saw Washington, but could not hear him take the oath to support the Federal constitution. The constitution was in its *chrysalis state*. I saw what Washington did not see; but two other men in Virginia saw it—George Mason and Patrick Henry—*the poison under its wings*."

Mr. Randolph had a great veneration for religion, and a most intimate knowledge of the Bible. His strongest illustrations were often from Sacred writ, and he could converse upon it in the most interesting manner. He was peculiarly a being of impulse, often reminding one, by his eccentricities, of the saying of Cicero, " that there was but a hair's-breadth between a great genius and a madman." When excited, he sometimes inadvertently used the name of the Almighty irreverently, upon which, instantly checking the torrent of his impetuosity, he would with deep humility ask forgiveness, exclaiming, " God forgive!" Towards the latter part of life, he was accustomed to call his servants together on Sundays, when he would preach to them with almost surpassing eloquence. He was charitable to the poor in his neighborhood, and beloved by them. He was wealthy, and left 318 slaves and 180 horses. At different times he made several wills, both written and nuncupative, by some of which he liberated slaves. They have become the subject of litigation the most complicated, expensive, and interminable.

Mr. Randolph has been described as one who " possessed a mind fertilized by every stream of literature; but the use he made of his great acquirements, was calculated to make enemies rather than friends; and, as he once said, ' no man ever had such constituents'—a fact which, of itself, speaks volumes in his praise. If he originated no great national benefits, nor did any great positive national good, he prevented many evils; and in doing so, he became the benefactor of his country, although not to the extent he might otherwise have been."

CHESTERFIELD.

CHESTERFIELD was formed from Henrico, in 1748. It is 28 miles long, with an average width of about 18; the surface is broken, and, excepting on the margin of the streams, the soil is generally sterile. It is particularly celebrated for its immense beds of coal, which have been worked from a very early day. The James River forms its N. and the Appomattox its s. boundary; and the great line of railroads, from the north to the south, passes through its eastern portion. Pop. 1830, 11,689; 1840, whites 7,859, slaves 8,702, free colored 587; total, 17,148.

Manchester lies on the James, immediately opposite Richmond, with which it is connected by the railroad and Mayo's bridges. In the American revolution it was visited by the enemy, and then had but a few houses. Ten years ago it contained a population of 1500, since which it has not increased. The town is very much scattered; there are several tobacco and one or more large cotton manufactories. Its beautiful situation has induced wealthy men, doing business in Richmond, to make it their residence, who have erected some splendid private mansions within its limits. Bellona Arsenal, on the river, 12 miles above Richmond, was established in 1816. Formerly it was a depôt for military stores, and was garrisoned by a company of U. S. troops. Adjacent is the Bellona foundry, one of the oldest cannon foundries in the Union. Hallsboro' is a small village in the w. part of the county. Salisbury, now the seat of Mrs. Johnson, in this county, was once the residence of Patrick Henry.

Warwick, which is on the river, was, previous to the revolution, larger than Richmond, and one of the principal shipping ports on the river. Formerly large vessels came up there, and it was the point where all the coal of this county was shipped. The Marquis de Chastellux thus describes it, as it was in 1782: "We skirted James River to a charming place called *Warwick*, where a group of handsome houses form a sort of village, and there are several superb ones in the neighborhood; among others, that of Col. Carey, on the right bank of the river, and Mr. Randolph's [at Tuckahoe] on the opposite shore." In the revolution, the barracks of the American troops at the court-house of this county, were burnt by the enemy.

On the N. bank of the Appomattox, above the falls, and about a mile from Petersburg, is Matoax, where resided John Randolph, senr., the father of John R. of Roanoke. The name Matoax, (or Matoaca,) was the private name of Pocahontas. Of the house nothing now remains. Here John Randolph of Roanoke passed the years of his boyhood. The Bland papers, from which this article is abridged, remark that, "he is said in after-life, when involved in the turmoil of politics, to have recurred with fond regret to his early days at Matoax, and in particular to his angling amusements there. Numerous arrowheads, stone tomahawks, and other Indian relics found there, would seem to indicate it as formerly a favorite haunt of the natives." Subjoined are translations from Latin inscriptions engraved on three tombstones, under a clump of oaks, near the site of the Matoax house:

John Randolph, Esq., died 28th October, 1775, aged 34. Let not a tomb be wanting to his ashes, nor memory to his virtues.

Jesus, the Saviour of mankind. When shall we cease to mourn for Frances Bland Tucker, wife of St. George Tucker? She died 18th January, 1788, aged 36.

Martha Hall, died 4th of March, 1784. Whom Hymen slighted, Pollux and Apollo courted.

The coal-region of eastern Virginia is supposed to be about 50 miles long and 12 broad, and occupies part of this and several of the adjacent counties. Here, however, the mining has been the most successfully prosecuted, and at present the mines in Chesterfield daily raise, in the aggregate, about 250 tons. We had the pleasure, in the summer of 1843, of visiting one of the mines, and at the time published a letter in a public print, giving an account of our visit. A portion of it is copied below :

Learning that the Midlothian mines were the most extensively and as skilfully wrought as any, I paid them a visit; but my remarks as to the management and quality of the coal, will in general apply as well to the remainder. Four shafts have been sunk by this company since 1833 ; in two, coal has been reached, one at a depth of 625, and the other at 775 feet. The sinking of the deepest occupied three years of labor, at a cost of about $30,000. The materials were raised by mules, and it is supposed a like depth was never before attained by horse-power in any country. These shafts, eleven feet square each, are divided by timbers into four equal chambers. At the deep shaft, two steam-engines on the surface operate in raising coal ; at the other, one. The extra engine at the deep shaft draws coal up an inclined plane down in the mine, to the bottom of the shaft. This plane reaches the lowest point of the mine, about 1,000 feet or a fifth of a mile from the surface. The coal having thus been brought to the pit, the other engine raises it perpendicularly to the surface, when the baskets containing it are placed on little cars on a small hand-railway, and are pushed by the negroes a few rods to where it is emptied, screened, and shovelled into the large cars on the railroad, connecting with tide-water near Richmond, 12 miles distant. While the engine attached to the plane is drawing up coal, it is so arranged that pumps, by the same motion, are throwing out the "surface water," which, by means of grooves around the shaft, is collected in a reservoir made in the rock, 360 feet below the surface This water is conducted about twenty feet above ground, to a cistern, from which it is used by the different engines.

Through the kindness of the president of the company, I was allowed to descend into the mines. I was first conducted to a building where I put on a coarse suit, which is perhaps worthy of description. Firstly, imagine a figure about five feet and a half in height, incased in a pair of pants of the coarsest "hard-times" cloth, coming up nearly to his shoulders, with legs as large as the wearer's body. Throw over these a coat of the same material, with a very short skirt, and over its collar place a shirt-collar of sail-cloth, turned over "à la Byron," being the upper termination of a garment operating most unmercifully as a flesh-brush upon the tender skin of its wearer. Mount this interesting figure in a pair of negro shoes, crown him with a low black wool hat, stuck just on the top of his head ; beneath it place a countenance sunburnt and weatherbeaten to the hue of unscraped sole-leather, relieved on each side by huge masses of long light hair, and you have a tolerable portrait of the writer as he was about making his *début*, at 4 P. M., July 13th, A. D. 1843, into the deep pit of the Midlothian coal-mine, in Chesterfield county, "Ole Virginny."

My friend, guide, and self, each with a lighted lamp, sprang into a basket suspended by ropes over pulleys and frame-work, above a yawning abyss seven hundred and seventy-five feet deep. The signal was given—puff! puff! went the steam-engine, and down, down, went we. I endeavored to joke to conceal my trepidation. It was stale business. Rapidly glided past the wooden sides of the shaft,—I became dizzy,—shut my eyes,—opened them and saw, far, far above, the small faint light of day at top. In one minute—it seemed five—we came to the bottom with a *bump !* The under-ground superintendent made his appearance, covered with coal-dust and perspiration ; his jolly English face and hearty welcome augured well for our subterranean researches. Him we followed, each with a lighted lamp, through many a labyrinth, down many a ladder, and occasionally penetrating to the end of a drift, where the men were at work shovelling coal into baskets on the cars running on railroads to the mouth of the pit, or boring for blasts. We witnessed one or two. The match was put, we retreated a short distance,—then came the explosion, echoing and re-echoing among the caverns,—a momentary noise of falling coal, like a sudden shower of hail, succeeded, and then all was silence.

The drifts, or passages, are generally about sixteen feet wide, and ten feet high, with large pillars of coal intervening about sixty feet square. I can give the idea by comparing the drifts to the streets, and the pillars to the squares of a city in miniature. When the company's limits are reached, the pillars will be taken away. The general inclination of the passages is about 30°. Frequently obstacles are met with, and one has to descend by ladders, or by steps, cut in solid rock. Doors used in ventilation were often met with, through which we crawled. Mules are employed under ground in transporting the coal on the small railways, coursing nearly all the drifts. They are in excellent condition, with fine glossy coats of hair, nearly equal well-kept race-horses, which is supposed to result from the sulphur in the coal, and the even temperature of the mines. Well-arranged stables are there built, and all requisite attention paid them. Some of the animals remain below for years, and when carried to the strong light of day, gambol like wild horses.

Partitions of thin plank, attached to timbers put up in the centre of the main drifts, are one of the principal means by which the mines are ventilated, aided by a strong furnace near the upcast shaft. Near this is a blacksmith-shop. The atmospheric air is admitted into the mines down the deepest shaft, and after coursing the entire drifts, and ascending to the rise-workings of the mines, is thence conducted to the furnace, where it is rarefied, and ascends to the surface, having in its progress become mixed with the carbureted hydrogen gas emitted from the coal. When this gas is evolved in unusual quantities, greater speed is given to the air by increasing the fire. If the partitions in the drifts (known as brattice-work) should be broken, the circulation would be impeded, and the gas so strongly impregnate the air, as in its passage over the furnace to ignite, and result in destructive consequences. Or, should too much gas be thrown out of the coal when the circulation is impeded from any cause, it would explode on the application of a common lamp. In such cases, the Davy lamp is used. I heard the gas escaping from the coal make a hissing noise, and I saw it set on fire in crevices of the walls by the lamp of our conductor; and although a novice in these matters, enough was seen to convince me of the skill of Mr. Marshall, the company's under-ground superintendent, in managing the ventilation.

Some years since, when ventilation was less understood than at present, an explosion took place in a neighboring mine of the most fearful character. Of the fifty-four men in the mine, only two, who happened to be in some crevices near the mouth of the shaft, escaped with life. Nearly all the internal works of the mine were blown to atoms. Such was the force of the explosion, that a basket then descending, containing three men, was blown nearly one hundred feet into the air. Two fell out, and were crushed to death, and the third remained in, and with the basket was thrown some seventy or eighty feet from the shaft, breaking both his legs and arms. He recovered, and is now living. It is believed, from the number of bodies found grouped together in the higher parts of the mine, that many survived the explosion of the inflammable gas, and were destroyed by inhaling the carbonic acid gas which succeeds it. This death is said to be very pleasant; fairy visions float around the sufferer, and he drops into the sleep of eternity like one passing into delightful dreams.

To a person unacquainted with mining, no true conception can be formed of the interior of a large and well-arranged coal-mine, unless by examination; and none but a thorough adept can give a description of its complicated arrangements. The art of coal-mining has progressed rapidly in this vicinity within a few years; but, unfortunately, the trade is now depressed. The Midlothian coal has a beautiful lustre, similar to the anthracite. It is believed that no bituminous coal unites qualities so generally adapted to all purposes. It has been extensively used in the production of gas and coke, in the manufacture of iron, glass, copper, chemicals, for locomotives, steamboats—and for smiths and forges it has no superior. As domestic fuel it is equal to the best English coals, and far superior to them in strength and durability. It is strange, that with all these qualities, a preference should be given at the north to English coal. This is accounted for from the fact that formerly large quantities of inferior coal were shipped to the northern ports from the north side of James River, and created strong prejudices against Virginia coal generally.

The Midlothian mines employ, in all their operations, some 150 negroes.* They are

* Shortly after we were at the Midlothian mine, the Rev. Mr. Jeter, of Richmond, made it a visit, and having held divine worship there, published an interesting and graphic narration of the scene. A part of his description here follows:

The intelligence of the meeting had spread throughout the cavern, and all had gathered for the service. The news had gone beyond the pit, and brought down several from above. By means of logs, puncheons and boxes, the congregation were mostly seated in a wide and well-ventilated drift. The small brilliant lamps, of which every collier has one, were suspended along the walls of our chapel, creating a dazzling light. The congregation consisted of about 80 colored, and 10 white persons. The blacks at my request sung a song. Their singing was greatly inferior to that of their colored brethren in the tobacco factories at Richmond. I lined a hymn, which was sung, offered a prayer, and preached from John iii. 16. The

well-fed, clothed, and treated, and in case of sickness are sent to a comfortable hospital, under the care of a steward, and daily attended by physicians. I could not but almost envy their well-developed muscular figures. The negroes prefer this labor to any other, enjoy many perquisites, and generally the labor of the week is performed in five days. Singular as it may seem, persons engaged in mining become exceedingly attached to it. I never knew a person more enamored with his profession than our conductor. He eloquently descanted, in a rich brogue, upon the pleasure he experienced in the mine. Was he sick, the pure air of the pit—the thermometer being about 60° throughout the year—would restore him. Was he hot, there he could become cool. Was he cold, there become warm. Was he low-spirited, his employment would bring relief. In fine, " the pure air of the pit" was a universal panacea, the elixir of life, the infallible remedy for all human ills. If his opinion were general, farewell Saratoga, White Sulphur, and Rockaway—your glories would be eclipsed by the glories of this!

Our conductor, as he took us about, all zeal to show us every thing, and a determination that we should not depart until all was seen, would have kept us there I know not how long, had not the cry of " All's well !" resounding from cavern to cavern, echoing in the recesses and dying in the distance, proclaimed that it was 7 o'clock, the day's work finished, and time for us to ascend. Glad was I, for although I had gone through but a small portion of the drifts, yet the *four miles* I did travel, of such " *going*," was enough even for as old a pedestrian as myself. I returned as I came, entered the dressing-house, and on looking in the glass, saw a face blackened with coal-dust, which, on a due application of soap and water, I recognised as an old acquaintance. Being duly washed, combed, and dressed, I leisurely wended my way to a fine old mansion on the hill, embowered in a grove of waving locusts, the abode of elegant hospitality. There, seated under the porch, with the delicious feeling a comfortable seat always inspires when one is greatly fatigued, I passed " twilight's witching hour,"—my senses lulled by delightful music from the adjoining parlor : anon, recovering from my revery, I listened to the amusing adventures of Col. A., from Texas, or treasured up the particulars of mining operations, and anecdotes given by Major W. The music I must not give : heavenly sounds produced by fairy fingers, are too ethereal to be materialized by the printer's imp ! but I will give, in conclusion, an anecdote of the Major's, of a most *tragical occurrence*. Usually comedy, but now tragedy will be the finale, ere the curtain drops.

Some years since, a gentleman was one autumnal evening hunting in this county in the vicinity of some old coal-pits. Straying from his companions, he accidentally slipped down the side of an abandoned pit, and caught by one arm a projecting branch on its slope. The pit was supposed to be about two hundred feet in perpendicular depth, and its bottom a pile of rocks. He heard in the distance the cries of his companions, and the yell of the hounds in the chase. He shouted for help, but no answering shout was returned, save the echo of his own voice among the recesses of the surrounding forest. Soon his companions were far away. Death awaited him—an awful death. His mind was intensely excited, and keenly alive to the terrors of his situation. He thought of his friends—of all he loved on earth ! and thus to separate; oh ! 'twas agony. Hoarsely moaned the wind through the dying leaves of autumn ; coldly shone the moon and stars on high, inanimate witnesses of human frailty fast losing its hold upon this life. Nature could sustain herself no longer, he bade " farewell to earth," grew weaker and weaker, released his grasp and fell—fell about *six inches !* This brought him to the bottom of the pit, as you, patient reader, are at the bottom of a long letter—all about *coal* too.

---

circumstances were impressive and awful. I desired to do good—I spoke without premeditation, and I was listened to with devout attention. When I had closed my sermon, I requested my friend N. to follow in exhortation and prayer. He arose, attired in the uncouth dress of the mine; and solemn as was the scene, and as much as my heart was in unison with it, I could not avoid smiling at the oddity of his appearance. The diversion, however, was momentary only. The exhortation was pertinent, and the prayer fervent. Many of us felt that God was present. The colored friends sang another song. I was desirous of knowing how many professors of religion there were among them; and first having all seated, I requested those who were professing Christians to arise. Thirty arose ; they are all, or nearly all, members of the Baptist church. I was gratified to learn from the managers, that many of them are orderly and consistent in their deportment; and, generally, that there is a marked difference between those who do, and those who do not profess religion. A few words of advice and encouragement closed the service. The like had never been known in these parts. Mr. Marshall, who had spent many years in the English mines, said that he had frequently heard social prayer in the pits, but had never before known a sermon delivered in one. To address the living, on the solemn subjects of death, judgment, and eternity, 800 feet beneath the sleeping-place of the dead, in a pit which bears so striking a resemblance to that region of outer darkness into which the impenitent shall be cast, cannot but interest and affect the heart.

CLARKE.

CLARKE was formed in 1836, from Frederick, and named from Gen. Geo. Rogers Clarke; it is 17 miles long, and 15 wide. Its surface is undulating, and the soil not surpassed in fertility by any other county in the state. The Shenandoah runs through the eastern part, at the foot of the Blue Ridge, and the Opequon near its western line. Pop., whites 2,867, slaves 3,325, free colored 161; total, 6,353.

Washington's Office and Lodgings at " Soldier's Rest."

Berryville, the county-seat, is 160 miles NW. of Richmond, and 12 east of Winchester. It was established Jan. 15, 1798, on 20 acres of land belonging to Benjamin Berry and Sarah Strebling, and the following gentlemen appointed trustees: DANIEL MORGAN, William M'Guire, Archibald Magill, Rawleigh Colston, John Milton, Thomas Strebling, George Blackmore, Charles Smith, and Bushrod Taylor. It now contains an Episcopal church, and about 35 dwellings. About the year 1744, (says Kercheval,) Joseph Hampton and two sons came from the eastern shore of Maryland, settled on Buck marsh, near Berryville, and lived the greater part of the year in a hollow sycamore tree. They enclosed a piece of land and made a crop, preparatory to the removal of the family.

The village of Berryville is often called *Battletown,* from having been the scene of many of those pugilistic combats for which Gen. Daniel Morgan, of revolutionary memory, was remarkable.

This officer resided, for a time, about half a mile N. of Battletown, at a seat called "*Soldier's Rest.*" It is a plain two-story dwelling, originally built by a Mr. Morton, and afterwards added to by Morgan. It is now the residence of Mr. John B. Taylor.

Morgan subsequently built another, a beautiful seat, now standing in this county, two miles NE. of White Post, which he very appropriately named Saratoga. It was erected by Hessians taken prisoners at Saratoga. About 200 yards from "Soldier's Rest," stands an old log hut, which well-authenticated tradition states was occupied by Washington while surveying land in this region for Lord Fairfax. It is about 12 feet square, and is divided into two rooms ; one in the upper, and the other in the lower story. The lower apartment was then, and is now, used as a milk-room. A beautiful spring gushes up from the rocks by the house, and flows in a clear, crystal stream, under the building, answering admirably the purpose to which it is applied, in cooling this apartment. Many years since, both the spring and the building were protected from the heat of the summer's sun, by a dense copse of trees. The upper, or attic room, which is about 12 feet square, was occupied by Washington as a place of deposite for his surveying instruments, and as a lodging—how long, though, is not known. The room was lathed and plastered. A window was at one end, and a door—up to which led a rough flight of steps —at the other. This rude hut is, perhaps, the most interesting relic of that great and good man, who became "first in the hearts of his countrymen." It is a memento of him in humble life, ere fame had encircled his brows with her choicest laurels, before that nation, now among the highest through his exertions, had a being ; but the vicissitudes and toils of his youth—as beautifully described in the annexed extract from Bancroft— combined to give energy to his character, and that practical, every-day knowledge, which better prepared him for the high and important destiny that awaited him :

At the very time of the Congress of Aix-la-Chapelle, the woods of Virginia sheltered the youthful George Washington, the son of a widow. Born by the side of the Potomac, beneath the roof of a West-moreland farmer, almost from infancy his lot had been the lot of an orphan. No academy had welcomed him to its shades, no college crowned him with its honors : to read, to write, to cipher—these had been his degrees in knowledge. And now at sixteen years of age, in quest of an honest maintenance, encountering intolerable toil ; cheered onward by being able to write to a schoolboy friend, "Dear Richard, a doubloon is my constant gain every day, and sometimes six pistoles ;" "himself his own cook, having no spit but a forked stick, no plate but a large chip ;" roaming over spurs of the Alleghanies, and along the banks of the Shenandoah ; alive to nature, and sometimes "spending the best of the day in admiring the trees and richness of the land ;" among skin-clad savages, with their scalps and rattles, or uncouth emi-grants "that would never speak English ;" rarely sleeping in a bed ; holding a bear-skin a splendid couch ; glad of a resting-place for the night upon a little hay, straw, or fodder, and often camping in the forests, where the place nearest the fire was a happy luxury ;—this stripling surveyor in the woods, with no companion but his unlettered associates, and no implements of science but his compass and chain, con-trasted strangely with the imperial magnificence of the Congress of Aix-la-Chapelle. And yet God had selected not Kaunitz, nor Newcastle, not a monarch of the house of Hapsburg, nor of Hanover, but the Virginia stripling, to give an impulse to human affairs, and, as far as events can depend upon an indi-vidual, had placed the rights and the destinies of countless millions in the keeping of the *widow's son.*

Col. Charles M. Thruston, a patriotic clergyman of the Episcopal denomination, who became an officer of the revolutionary army, resided for many years on a beautiful farm in this county, called Mount Sion, one mile above the Shenandoah. For a biographical sketch, see Gloucester county.

Four miles NE. of Millwood is the "Old Chapel," built in 1796, in which the Rt. Rev. Wm. Meade, Bishop of the Episcopal church in Va., officiated for many years. It is a venerable-looking stone edifice, partly in a grove, and has adjoining it a grave-yard, in which lie buried many respectable people of the neighboring country.

Gen. Rogers Clarke, from whom this county derived its name, was an officer of the revolution, of undaunted coolness and courage. In addition to the facts given on p. 116, we have a single anecdote to relate, published in the "Notes of an Old Officer." At the treaty of Fort Washington, where Clarke had but 70 men, 300 Shawnees appeared in the council chamber. Their chief made a boisterous speech, and then placed on the table a belt of white and black wampum, to intimate they were ready for either peace or war, while his 300 savages applauded him by a terrific yell. At the table sat Clarke, with only two or three other persons. Clarke, who was leaning on his elbow with apparent unconcern, with his rattan coolly pushed the wampum on to the floor. Then rising as the savages muttered their indignation, he trampled on the belt, and with a look of stern defiance and a voice of thunder, that made the stoutest heart quail, bade them instantly quit the hall. They involuntarily left, and the next day sued for peace. Gen. Clarke died in Kentucky, in 1817.

The subject of the above notice had a brother, Gen. Wm. Clarke, who was scarcely less distinguished. He was born in this state in 1770. When 14 years old, he removed with his father's family to Kentucky, where the city of Louisville now stands. It then consisted only of a few cabins surrounding a fort, then recently established by his brother, Gen. Rogers Clarke. He entered the army, and was lieutenant in 1790. He was the companion of Lewis on the expedition to the Pacific. In 1806, he was appointed governor of the territory of Upper Louisiana, and governor of Missouri from 1813 to 1820, when it was admitted into the Union. He held various offices, among which was that of superintendent of Indian affairs. He made many important treaties with the Indians. He well understood their character and won their most unbounded confidence. " His name was known to the most remote tribes, and his word was every where reverenced by them. They regarded him as a father, and his signature, which was known to the most remote tribes, whenever shown was respected." He died in 1838, aged 68, at St. Louis, where he had resided for over 30 years.

Millwood, 11 miles southeasterly from Winchester, contains an Episcopal church, and about 30 dwellings. It is the centre of a beautiful and fertile country, and enjoys a considerable trade with it. White Post,* 12 miles SE. of Winchester, contains a church, 2 mercantile stores, and 16 dwellings.

Greenway Court, the seat of Lord Fairfax.

Thirteen miles southeast from Winchester, near the village of White Post in this county, is Greenway Court, the seat of the late Lord Fairfax, the proprietor of the Northern Neck of Virginia; and at present the residence of the Rev. Mr. Kennerly.

Part of the immense tract among the rich valleys of the Alleghany mountains, were surveyed by Washington, and divided into lots, to enable the proprietor to claim his quit-rents and give legal titles. Washington set off on his first surveying expedition in March, 1748, just a month from the day he was sixteen years old, in company with George Fairfax, the eldest son of William Fairfax, whose daughter, Washington's eldest brother, Lawrence, had married. Sparks, in his Life of Washington, gives the annexed account of the proprietor of the Northern Neck:

Lord Fairfax, a distant relative of William Fairfax, was a man of an eccentric turn of mind, of great private worth, generous, and hospitable. He had been accustomed to the best society, to which his rank entitled him, in England. While he was at the

---

* So named from a *white post* which Lord Fairfax planted as a guide to his dwelling —one mile distant.

University of Oxford he had a fondness for literature, and his taste and skill in that line may be inferred from his having written some of the papers in the *Spectator*. Possessing by inheritance a vast tract of country,* situate between the Potomac and Rappahannock Rivers, and stretching across the Alleghany mountains, he made a voyage to Virginia to examine this domain. So well pleased was he with the climate and mode of life, that he resolved, after going back to England and arranging his affairs, to return and spend his days amidst this wild territory. At the time (1748) of which we are now speaking, he had just arrived to execute his purpose, and was residing with his relatives at Belvoir. This was his home for several years; but he at length removed over the Blue Ridge, built a house in the Shenandoah Valley, called *Greenway Court*, and cultivated a large farm. Here he lived in comparative seclusion, often amusing himself with hunting, but chiefly devoted to the care of his estate, to acts of benevolence among his tenants, and to such public duties as devolved upon him in the narrow sphere he had chosen; a friend of liberty, honored for his uprightness, esteemed for the amenity of his manners, and his practical virtues.

The prominent building shown in the view at Greenway Court, was appropriated to the use of the steward of Fairfax. It was the commencement of a series of buildings which Lord Fairfax had intended to erect, but did not live to complete.

His lordship lived and died in a single clap-board story and a half house, which stood just in front of the modern brick dwelling of Mr. Kennerly, and was destroyed in 1834. There are now several of the original buildings standing at the place: among them is a small limestone structure, where quit-rents were given and titles drawn, of his lordship's domains. Fairfax had, probably, 150 negro servants, who lived in log huts scattered about in the woods.

A few years since, in excavating the ground near the house, the servants of Mr. Kennerly discovered a large quantity of joes and half-joes, amounting to about $250; they were what is termed *cob-coin*, of a square form, and dated about 1730. They were supposed to have been secreted there by Lord Fairfax. Under a shelving rock, 9 feet from the surface, there was also found a human skeleton of gigantic stature; supposed to be that of an Indian.

When Lord Dunmore went on his expedition against the Indians in 1774, he came on as far as this place with a portion of his troops, and waited here about a fortnight for reinforcements. His soldiers encamped in what was then a grove—now a meadow—about 300 yards N. of Mr. Kennerly's present residence. The spot is indicated by a deep well, supposed to have been dug by them; an old magazine, destroyed in 1843, stood near the well. Washington, when recruiting at Winchester, often visited this place.

Lord Fairfax had but little cultivated ground around his premises, and that was in small patches without taste or design. The land was left for a park, and he lived almost wholly from his rents. The following, as well as much of the foregoing, respecting him, is traditionary: His lordship was a dark, swarthy man, several inches over 6 feet in height, and of a gigantic frame and personal strength. He lived the life of a bachelor, and fared coarse, adopting in that respect the rough customs of the people among whom he was. When in the humor, he was generous—giving away whole farms to his tenants, and simply demanding for rent some trifle, for instance, a present of a turkey for his Christmas dinner. He was passionately fond of hunting, and often passed weeks together in the pleasures of the chase. When on these [expeditions, he made it a rule, that he who got the fox, cut off his tail, and held it up, should share in the jollification which was to follow, free of expense. Soon as a fox was started, the young men of the company usually dashed after him with great impetuosity, while Fairfax leisurely

---

* The domain of Lord Fairfax, called the Northern Neck of Virginia, included the immense territory now comprising the counties of Lancaster, Northumberland, Richmond, Westmoreland, Stafford, King George, Prince William, Fairfax, Loudoun, Fauquier, Culpeper, Clarke, Madison, Page, Shenandoah, Hardy, Hampshire, Morgan, Berkeley, Jefferson, and Frederick. Charles II. granted to the ancestors of Lord Fairfax, all lands lying between the head-waters of the Rappahannock and Potomac to the Chesapeake Bay; a territory comprising about one quarter of the present limits of Virginia. For a full history of the Northern Neck, the reader is referred to Kercheval's History of the Valley of Virginia.

waited behind, with a favorite servant who was familiar with the water-courses, and of a quick ear, to discover the course of the fox. Following his directions, his lordship would start after the game, and, in most instances, secure the prize, and stick the tail of the fox in his hat in triumph.

Lord Fairfax died at the advanced age of ninety-two, in the autumn of 1782, soon after the surrender of Cornwallis, an event he is said to have much lamented. He was buried at Winchester, under the communion-table of the old Episcopal church. [See Winchester.]

CULPEPER.

CULPEPER was formed in 1748, from Orange, and named from Lord Culpeper, governor of Virginia from 1680 to 1683. It has an average length of about 20, with a breadth of 18 miles, and has been much reduced from its original limits. The Rappahannock runs upon its NE. and the Rapid Ann upon its SE. and SW. boundaries. The surface is beautifully diversified, and the soil of a deep red hue and very fertile. Pop. 1830, 24,026 ; 1840, whites 4,933, slaves 6,069, free colored 491 ; total 11,393.

Besides the Court-House there are the villages of Jeffersonton and Stevensburg ; the first contains a Baptist church and about 50 dwellings, the last about 30 dwellings. Fairfax, the county-seat, was named after Lord Fairfax, the original proprietor of the county. It was founded in 1759 ; it is 98 m. from Richmond, and 82 from Washington city, and contains 1 Episcopal, 1 Presbyterian, and 1 Baptist church, 5 stores, and about 700 inhabitants. In one of the books in the clerk's office, in the ancient and venerable-looking court-house in this village, is the annexed entry :

20th July, 1749, (O. S.)—GEORGE WASHINGTON, GENT., produced a commission from the President and Master of William and Mary College, appointing him to be surveyor of this county, which was read, and thereupon he took the usual oaths to his majesty's person and government, and took and subscribed the abjuration oath and test, and then took the oath of surveyor, according to law.

Culpeper was distinguished early in the war of the revolution for the services of her gallant MINUTE-MEN, who, as Mr. Randolph said in the U. S. Senate, " were raised in a minute, armed in a minute, marched in a minute, fought in a minute, and vanquished in a minute."

Immediately on the breaking out of the war in 1775, Patrick Henry, then commander of the Virginia troops, sent to this section of the colony for assistance. Upon his summons, 150 men from Culpeper, 100 from Orange, and 100 from Fauquier, rendezvoused here and encamped in a field now the property of John S. Barber, Esq., half a mile west of the court-house. An old oak now standing, marks the spot. These were the first minute-men raised in Virginia. They formed themselves into a regiment, choosing Lawrence Taliaferro of Orange, colonel ; Edward Stevens of Culpeper, lieutenant-colonel ; and Thomas Marshall of Fauquier—the father of Chief-Justice Marshall—major. The flag used by the Culpeper men is depicted in the accompanying engraving, with a rattlesnake in the centre. The head of the snake was intended for Virginia, and the 12 rattles for the other 12 states. This corps were dressed in green hunting-shirts, with the words " LIBERTY OR DEATH !"[*] in large white letters on their bosoms.

---

[*] A wag, on seeing this, remarked it was too severe for him ; but that he was willing to enlist if the words were altered to " Liberty or be *crippled !*"

They wore in their hats buck-tails, and in their belts tomahawks and scalping-knives Their savage, warlike appearance, excited the terror of the inhabitants as they marched through the country to Williamsburg. Shortly after their arrival at that place, about

THE CULPEPER MINUTE MEN

LIBERTY,   OR DEATH!

DONT TREAD ON ME

150 of them—those armed with rifles—marched into Norfolk co., and were engaged in the battle of the Great Bridge. Among them was Chief-Justice Marshall, then a lieutenant, and Gen. Edward Stephens.

In the course of the war, 8 companies of 84 men each, were formed in Culpeper for the continental service. They were raised by the following captains: John Green,* John Thornton, George Slaughter, Gabriel Long, Gabriel Jones, John Gillison,† ———— M'Clanahan,‡ and Abraham Buford.§

Virginia raised, in the beginning of the war, 15 continental regiments of about 800 men, besides 3 state regiments of regular troops, not subject to be ordered out of the state. Besides these were Lee's legion, composed of two companies of cavalry and two of infantry, a regiment of artillery under Col. Harrison, Col. Baylor's and Col. Bland's regiments of cavalry, and the corps of horse raised by Col. Nelson. These, we believe, comprised most if not all the regular troops raised by the state. They became reduced to one quarter of their original number before the war was over, particularly by disease and the casualties of battle in the southern campaigns. From this statement—supplied from the memory of a surviving officer of the Virginia line—it will be seen that Culpeper bore her full share of the burden of war. On the same authority we state, that in skirmishes, when the numbers were equal, the American troops were superior to the British. The former took aim; the latter fired with their pieces brought on a level with the hip. Hence the superiority of the Americans on these occasions. They despised the English as being no marksmen.

Capt. PHILIP SLAUGHTER, now (1844) residing in this co., is probably the only officer living in Virginia who served in the continental establishment throughout the revolution. At the age of 17 years he entered the Culpeper minute-men as a private, and marched with them to Williamsburg shortly after the hegira of Dunmore. Having received the commission of lieutenant, he marched to the north in the fall of 1776 with the 11th Virginia continental regiment. Daniel Morgan was then colonel of this corps, and of a volunteer rifle regiment. There Slaughter remained until the commencement of the year 1780, and was in the battles of Brandywine, Germantown, Monmouth, and at the storming of Stony Point. He spent the winter of 1777–78 at Valley Forge. His mess-

---

* John Green was afterwards a colonel. While storming a breastwork he was wounded in the shoulder and made a cripple for life. He died about 30 years ago.

† John Gillison, while gallantly leading on his men to attack the enemy at Brandywine, to prevent them making prisoners the company of Capt. Long, was struck in the forehead by a musket ball. The surgeon examined the wound, and then lifting up his hands, exclaimed, "Oh, captain! it is a noble wound. Right in the middle of the forehead, and no harm done." The wound soon healed, and left a scar of which any soldier might have been proud.

‡ Capt. M'Clanahan was a Baptist clergyman, and at first regularly preached to his men. His recruits were drawn principally from his own denomination, in conformity with the wishes of the legislature, who invited the members of particular religious societies, especially Baptists and Methodists, to organize themselves into separate companies under officers of their own principles. The Baptists were among the most strenuous supporters of liberty.

§ Abraham Buford was the Col. Buford defeated by Tarleton, May 29th, 1780, at the Waxhaws, near the borders of North Carolina.

mates were Lieut. Robert (afterwards Gen.) Porterfield, Capt. Chas. Porterfield, Capt. Johnson, and Lieut. John (afterwards Chief-Justice) Marshall. There they were all reduced to great deprivations in the want of food and clothing. They bore their sufferings without murmur, being fortified by an undaunted patriotism. Most of the officers gave to their almost naked soldiers nearly the whole of their clothing, reserving only that they themselves had on. Slaughter was reduced to a single shirt. While this was being washed, he wrapped himself in a blanket. From the breast of his only shirt he had wristbands and a collar made, to complete his uniform for parade. Many of his brother officers were still worse off, having no under garment at all ; and not one soldier in five had a blanket. They all lived in rude huts, and the snow was knee-deep the whole winter. Washington daily invited the officers in rotation, to dine with him at his private table ; but for want of decent clothing, few were enabled to attend. Slaughter being so much better provided, frequently went in the place of others, that, as he said. "his regiment might be represented." While in this starving condition, the country people brought food to the camp. Often the Dutch women were seen riding in, sitting on bags on their horses' backs, holding two or three bushels each of apple pies, baked sufficiently hard to be thrown across the room without breaking. These were purchased eagerly, eaten with avidity, and considered a great *luxury.*

Slaughter performed the duties of captain, paymaster, and clothier. He was promoted to a captaincy in 1778, he then being not 20 years of age. He has in his possession a brief journal of the movements of the troops during the time he was in service, and certificates of his soldier-like conduct from Chief-Justice Marshall, Gen. Robert Porterfield, and Col. Jamieson.

As tending to show the chivalrous feelings among the Virginia officers, we will state, that one of them, on his promotion to a captaincy, wrote the name of the lady to whom he was engaged upon his commission, declaring, at the same time, that it should never be disgraced with *her* name upon it. It *never* was disgraced. The same officer, while in camp in New Jersey, heard that a wealthy gentleman was laying siege to the affections of his betrothed, and was advised to return home. Failing in his application for a furlough, he dispatched a sergeant on horseback with a letter—there being no mails—to the friend in Virginia from whom he received the information, making further inquiries. The distance there and back was 500 miles. The messenger returned with an answer that quieted the apprehensions of the officer, and he married the lady after the war.

Capt. Slaughter has held various civil offices, among which was that of high sheriff of Culpeper. He has married twice, had 19 children, and numbers among his descendants nearly 100 souls. From the lips of this venerable and patriotic old man, we have received most of the information embodied in the two preceding pages.

It is well known that dissenters generally, and the Baptist clergymen in particular, were persecuted for opinion's sake in Virginia previous to the war of the revolution. (On this point more particularly, see Middlesex county.) One among the many sufferers by this mistaken mode of what was deemed the suppression of error, was the Rev. James Ireland, a worthy clergyman of the Baptist persuasion, who was forcibly seized and imprisoned in the jail of this county. While there confined, several attempts were made to murder him, of which he has given the following narrative :

A number of my persecutors resorted to the tavern of Mr. Steward, at the court-house, where they plotted to blow me up with powder that night, as I was informed, but all they could collect was half a pound. They fixed it for explosion, expecting I was sitting directly over it, but in this they were mistaken. Fire was put to it, and it went off with considerable noise, forcing up a small plank, from which I received no damage. The next scheme they devised was to smoke me with brimstone and Indian pepper. They had to wait certain opportunities to accomplish the same. The lower part of the jail door was a few inches above its sill. When the wind was favorable, they would get pods of Indian pepper, empty them of their contents, and fill them with brimstone and set them burning, so that the whole jail would be filled with the killing smoke, and oblige me to go to cracks and put my mouth to them, in order to prevent suffocation. At length a certain doctor, and the jailer, formed a scheme to poison me, which they actually effected.

This last-mentioned act of diabolical malevolence, came near costing Mr. Ireland his life. He was made extremely ill, and his constitution never recovered from the injury. He however bore up against these persecutions with Christian fortitude. He said, in giving an account of his persecutions:

My prison then, was a place in which I enjoyed much of the Divine presence; a day seldom passed without some signal token of the Divine goodness towards me, which generally led me to subscribe my letters in these words, " *From my Palace in Cul-peper.*"

In a family burying-ground, half a mile N. of Culpeper C. H., is a monument bearing the following inscription:

IN MEMORY OF

GENERAL EDWARD STEVENS,

WHO DIED

AUGUST THE 17TH, 1820,

At his seat in Culpeper, in the 76th year of his age.

This gallant officer and upright man, had served his country with reputation in the Field and Senate of his native state. He took an active part, and had a principal share in the war of the revolution, and acquired great distinction at the battles of Great Bridge, Brandywine, Germantown, Camden, Guilford Court-House, and Siege of York; and although zealous in the cause of American Freedom, his conduct was not marked with the least degree of malevolence, or party spirit. Those who honestly differed with him in opinion, he always treated with singular tenderness. In strict integrity, honest patriotism, and immoveable courage, he was surpassed by none, and had few equals.

Gen. Stevens resided in the village of Culpeper C. H., in the house on the corner of Coleman and Fairfax streets, now occupied by Mrs. Lightfoot. Aside from the above, we have but little to add respecting this highly meritorious officer. The histories of the revolution make such honorable mention of him, that it is evident his epitaph is no fulsome eulogy. At the battle of Guilford Court-House, " the brave and gallant Stevens," animated his men by words, and still more by his example. Resolved to make even the timid perform their duty, he placed several riflemen in the rear, with peremptory orders to shoot down any of his militia that should attempt to escape before a retreat was ordered. In this action he received a ball in the thigh, but he enjoyed the reflection that his men had made a noble stand, and displayed an honorable firmness in opposing the enemy, by whom they were at last, after an obstinate conflict, driven back by an overwhelming force at the bayonet's point.

CUMBERLAND.

CUMBERLAND was formed in 1748, from Goochland. It is 32 miles long and about 10 broad, with the Appomattox running on its s., the James River on its N. boundary, and Willis River through its NW. portion. The surface is undulating, and the soil productive. Pop. 1830, 11,689; 1840, whites 3,263, slaves 6,791, free colored 355; total, 10,399.

Cartersville, on the James River, contains a church and about 50 dwellings. Ca Ira, 5 miles w. of the C. H., has an Episcopal church and 10 dwellings. Cumberland court-house is in the southern part of the county, about 52 miles from Richmond. The village has not increased since the Marquis de Chastellux was here, about the year 1782. In his travels, he says:

Besides the court-house and a large tavern, its necessary appendage, there are seven or eight houses, inhabited by gentlemen of fortune. I found the tavern full of people, and understood that the judges were assembled to hold a *court of claims*, that is to say, to hear and register the claims of sundry persons who had furnished provisions for the army. We know that in general, but particularly in unexpected invasions, the American troops had no established magazines, and as it was necessary to have subsistence for them, provisions and forage were indiscriminately laid hold of, on giving the holders a receipt, which they called a *certificate*. During the campaign, while the enemy were at hand, little attention was given to this sort of loans, which accumulated incessantly, without the sum total being known, or any means taken to ascertain the proofs. Virginia being at length loaded with these certificates, it became necessary, sooner or later, to liquidate these claims. The last assembly of the state of Virginia had accordingly thought proper to pass a bill, authorizing the justices of each county to take cognizance of these certificates, to authenticate their validity, and to register them, specifying the value of the provisions in money, according to the established tariff. I had the curiosity to go to the court-house to see how this affair was transacted, and saw it was performed with great order and simplicity. The judges wore their common clothes, but were seated on an elevated tribunal, as at London in the Court of King's Bench, or Common Pleas.

Gen. Charles Scott, a distinguished officer of the revolution, and subsequently governor of Kentucky, was born near the line of this and Powhatan county. The present residence of Mr. Thomas Palmer, in the upper part of that county, was built by him.

Scott raised the first company of volunteers in Virginia, south of the James River, that entered into actual service; and so distinguished himself prior to 1777, that when Powhatan county was formed in that year, the county-seat was named in honor of him. When governor of Kentucky, he had some severe battles with the Indians, in which he lost two sons. Immediately after St. Clair's defeat, Gen. Scott, at the head of a body of Kentucky cavalry, reconnoitred the battle-ground. Finding the Indians still there, rejoicing over their victory in a drunken revelry, he surprised and fell upon them. Being totally unprepared, they were routed with great slaughter. About two hundred of them were killed, and he recovered six hundred muskets, and all the artillery and baggage remaining in the field. This, the most brilliant affair of the war, in a measure "dispelled the gloom occasioned by the misfortune of St. Clair, and threw, by the power of contrast, a darker shade of disgrace over that unfortunate general's miscarriage."

Scott was a man of strong natural powers, but somewhat illiterate and rough in his manners. He was eccentric, and many amusing anecdotes are related of him. When a candidate for governor, he was opposed by Col. Allen, a native of Kentucky, who, in an address to the people when Scott was present, made an eloquent appeal. The friends of the latter, knowing he was no orator, felt distressed for him, but Scott, nothing daunted, mounted the stump, and addressed the company, nearly as follows:

"Well, boys, I am sure you must all be well pleased with the speech you have just heard. It does my heart good to think we have so smart a man raised up among us here. He is a native Kentuckian. I see a good many of you here that I brought out to this country when a wilderness. At that time we hardly expected we should live to see such a smart man raised up among ourselves. You, who were with me in those early times, know we had no time for education, no means of improving from books. We dared not then go about our most common affairs without arms in our hands, to defend ourselves against the Indians. But we guarded and protected the country, and now every one can go where he pleases; and you now see what smart fellows are growing up to do their country honor. But I think it would be a pity to make this man governor; I think it would be better to send him to Congress. I don't think it requires a very smart man to make a governor; if he has sense enough to gather smart men about who can help him on with the business of state. It would suit a worn-out old wife of a man like myself. But, as to this young man, I am very proud of him; as much so as any of his kin, if any of them have been here to-day, listening to his speech." Scott then descended from the stump, and the huzzas for the old soldier made the welkin ring.

Scott had the greatest veneration for Washington; and while governor of Kentucky, he visited Philadelphia during the session of Congress. Attired in the rough garb of the backwoods, with a hunting-shirt, buckskin leggings, and a long beard, he gave out that he was going to visit the president. He was told that Washington had become puffed up with the importance of his station, and was too much of an aristocrat to welcome him in that garb. Scott, nothing daunted, passed up to the house of the president, who, with his lady, happened to be at the window, and recognising the old soldier, rushed out, and each taking him by the arm, led him in. "Never," said Scott, "was

I better treated. I had not believed a word against him ; and I found that he was
' old hoss'* still.''

Major JOSEPH SCOTT, a brother of the above, was an officer of the revolutionary
army, and was appointed marshal of Virginia by Jefferson, under the following circumstances : Major Joseph Eggleston, from Amelia, who had been a meritorious officer of
Lee's legion through the whole of the southern campaigns, and a member of Congress in
1798–99, was tendered the office by the president. This he declined, but recommended
his old friend and companion in arms, Major Scott, then a steward upon the estate of
John Randolph. The first intimation Scott had of the matter was the reception of the
appointment, which was extremely gratifying ; he being at the time in necessitous circumstances.

DINWIDDIE.

DINWIDDIE was formed in 1752, from Prince George, and named
from Robert Dinwiddie, governor of Va. from 1752 to 1758. The
surface is rolling, and its form hexagonal, with a diameter of about
28 miles. The Appomattox runs on its N., the Nottaway on its S.
boundary, and the great southern railroad through its eastern portion. Pop. 1830, 21,901; 1840, whites 9,847, slaves 9,947, free
colored 2,764 ; total, 22,558. The court-house is centrally situated upon a branch of the Nottaway.

The large, wealthy, and flourishing town of Petersburg, is situated at the northeastern angle of the county, on the south bank of
the Appomattox, 22 miles S. of Richmond, and 9 S. w. of City
Point, on the line of the great southern railroad, with which last-
named place there is also a railroad communication. The harbor
admits vessels of considerable draught, and even ships come up as
far as Walthall's Landing, 6 miles below the town, where there is
a branch railroad about 3 miles in length, connecting with the
Richmond and Petersburg railroad. It contains 2 Epis., 2 Pres.,
2 Meth., 1 Bap., and 1 Catholic church, besides those for colored
people. It exports largely tobacco and flour, and there were, in
1843, belonging to this place, the following cotton manufactories,
viz : Merchants co., Matoaca co., Ettricks co., Mechanics co., Bat-
tersea co., Canal Mills, Washington Mill, and the Eagle Mill. The
goods here manufactured have a high reputation. There is also a
very large number of tobacco factories. There were inspected
here in 1843, 11,942 hogsheads of tobacco. Petersburg contains
branches of the Bank of Va., Farmers Bank of Va., and the Exchange Bank of Va. The tonnage in 1840, was 3,098. There
were 6 commercial and 8 commission houses engaged in foreign
trade, capital $875,000 ; 121 retail stores, capital $1,026,250 ; 2
lumber yards, cap. $6,000 ; 1 furnace, 6 forges, 1 woollen facto-
ry, 1 pottery, 2 rope-walks, 2 flouring-mills, 1 grist-mill, 2 saw-
mills, 2 printing offices, 1 semi-weekly newspaper. Cap. in manufacturing $726,555. Pop. in 1830, 8,322 ; 1840, 11,136.

As early as 1645–6, a fort called Fort Henry, was established at the falls of the Ap-

---

* " *Old hoss*," was a term frequently applied by the soldiers of the revolution to their commander
in-chief.

pomattox, where Petersburg now is, for the defence of the inhabitants on the south side of James river.

In 1675, war being declared against the Indians, 500 men were ordered to proceed to the frontier, and eight forts garrisoned. Among these was the one near the falls of the Appomattox, at Major General Wood's, "or over against him at one ffort or defensible place at *ffleets*, of which Major Peter Jones be captain or chief commander."

In 1728, fifty-three years after, Col. Byrd, on his return from the expedition in which he was engaged as one of the Virginia commissioners, in running the line between this state and North Carolina, mentions the site of Petersburg, as follows: "At the end of thirty good miles, we arrived in the evening at Col. Bolling's, where from a primitive course of life we began to relax into luxury. This gentleman lives within hearing of the falls of Appomattox river, which are very noisy whenever a flood happens to roll a greater stream than ordinary over the rocks. The river is navigable for small craft as high as the falls, and, at some distance from them, fetches a compass and runs nearly parallel with James River, almost as high as the mountains."

By an act passed in 1646, it appears that 600 acres of land adjacent to Fort Henry, together with all the "houses and edifices" appurtenant thereto, were at that time granted to Captain Abraham Wood in fee-simple; yet he was not the earliest settler; for, by the same act, it appears that the land on which the fort stood, together with part of the adjacent 600 acres, had been granted to Thomas Pitt. He may, therefore, be considered the earliest proprietor of the site of Petersburg, it having been granted to him previous to 1646. The town derived its name from Peter Jones, who opened a trading establishment with the Indians at an early day, a few rods west of what is now the junction of Sycamore and Old streets. The locality was called *Peter's Point*, subsequently changed to *Petersburg*.

This Peter Jones was an old friend and fellow-traveller of Col. William Byrd, of Westover; and in 1733, accompanied the latter on a journey to Roanoke, on which occasion the plan of establishing Richmond and Petersburg was conceived. Byrd says, in his journal, "When we got home, we laid the foundation of two large cities—one at Shacco's, to be called Richmond, and the other at the point of Appomattox River, to be called Petersburg. These Major Mayo offered to lay off into lots, without fee or reward. The truth of it is, these two places being the uppermost landing of James and Appomattox rivers, are naturally intended for marts, where the traffic of the outer inhabitants must centre. Thus we did not build castles only, but cities, in the air."

In the October session, in 1748, in the 22d year of the reign of King George II., the towns of Petersburg and Blandford were established. Four years later an act was passed, allowing a bridge to be built by subscription over the Appomattox, at Bolling's Point, "to the land of John Bolling, gentleman;" which was probably the first bridge ever built over the river. In 1762, in the preamble to an act enlarging the town, it is stated that it "had very greatly increased, and become a place of considerable trade." At that time Robert Bolling, Roger Atkinson, William Eaton, John Bannister, Robert Ruffin, Thomas Jones, Henry Walker, George Turnbull, and James Field, gentlemen, were appointed trustees for laying out the town. In 1784, Petersburg was incorporated, and Blandford, Pocahontas, and Ravenscrofts, united with it.

In the war of the revolution, Petersburg was twice visited by the enemy. On the 22d of April, 1781, the British, under Gen. Phillips, left Williamsburg, sailed up the James, and on the 24th landed at City Point. "The next day," says Girardin's Hist. of 'Va., "they marched up to Petersburg, where Baron Steuben received them with a body of militia, somewhat under 1000 men. Although the enemy were 2,300 strong, Steuben opposed their progress. For two hours, he skilfully and bravely disputed the ground with them; the assailants were twice broken, and precipitately ran back until supported by fresh troops. During the interval of time just stated, they gained but a mile, and that by inches. The inferiority of the Virginians in numbers obliged them to withdraw about 12 miles up the Appomattox, till more militia should be assembled. They retired in good order over a bridge, which was taken up as soon as the militia passed, so as to secure their retreat. The whole loss of the Virginians, in killed, wounded, and taken, amounted to about 60. That sustained by the enemy, was conjectured to be more considerable."[*]

From an article entitled "*Reminiscences of the British at Bol-*

---

[*] Lieut.-Col. Simcoe, in his "Journal of the operations of the Queen's Rangers," states the loss of the British at one man killed and 10 wounded, of the light infantry.

lingbrook,"* published in the Southern Literary Messenger of January, 1840, we extract some interesting facts :

There is, perhaps, no house in Virginia connected with a greater number of military revolutionary recollections, than Bollingbrook, in the town of Petersburg.

On the approach of the enemy, a large portion of the people of the town made their escape. General Phillips took up his residence at Bollingbrook. He and the officers of his family are said to have treated Mrs. Bolling with a good deal of courtesy, and (some add) addressed her always as Lady Bolling. Arnold is recollected as a handsome man, that limped in his gait.† He was fond of caressing the children of the family, and dandled them on his knee.

Both the houses on Bollingbrook hill were occupied by British officers.‡ Mrs. Bolling was allowed the use of a room in the rear of the east building. Two sentinels were placed at each door of the house with crossed bayonets. The British soldiery repeatedly set on fire the fences about Bollingbrook, and frequently " all around was in a light blaze."§ Upon these occasions, Mrs. Bolling was obliged to send her servants to arrest the flames, and she was thus kept in a state of continual apprehension and alarm.

On the next day after his arrival, (to wit, the 26th of April,) General Phillips (according to Arnold's letter to Sir Harry Clinton) burnt 4000 hhds. of tobacco. The warehouses which belonged to Mrs. Bolling, at her solicitation, were spared on condition that the inhabitants should remove the tobacco from them, which was accordingly done, by extraordinary exertions, during the night of the 25th. This conflagration must have presented a striking and picturesque spectacle. The scarlet-dressed soldiers moving about amidst the flames, scattering the fire-brands, and officiating in the work of destruction—the burning of the shipping on the river, reflecting its lurid glare on Pocahontas and Blandford—heightened the effect of the scene.

Arnold, *on dit*, cautioned Mrs. Bolling to be careful in her intercourse with General Phillips, not to irritate him, as he was a man of an ungovernable temper. This lady, during that period of terror, suffered an intense solicitude and anxiety, which discovered itself in her unconsciously darning the needles, with which she was knitting, into the bed by which she sat. Her conduct during this trying crisis, displayed a heroism which doubtless won the respect of the British officers ; who are in general " men of honor and cavaliers."

After committing devastations at Osborne's, Manchester, Warwick, &c., the enemy set sail, and proceeded down James River, until, receiving (near Hog Island) countermanding orders, they returned up the river. On the 7th of May, they landed in a gale of wind at Brandon ; and on the 9th, marched 30 miles, and entered Petersburg late in the night. They came so unexpectedly as to surprise ten American officers, who were there for the purpose of collecting boats to convey the army of the Marquis de Lafayette across the James River.

General Phillips entered Petersburg this second time, sick of a bilious fever ;—he arrived on the 9th of May, and breathed his last on the 13th, at Bollingbrook. He lay sick in the west room front of the east building. During the illness of General Phillips, the town was cannonaded by Lafayette from Archer's hill,‖ and it is commonly reported that he died while the cannonade was going on. It seems, however, more probable, that this cannonade occurred on the 10th, when Lafayette (according to Arnold's letter) " appeared with a strong escort on the opposite side of the river,¶ and having stayed some time to reconnoitre, returned to Osborne's." Cannon-balls fired upon that occasion, were preserved in the town some years ago, and may be yet extant. The Americans being aware that Bollingbrook was head-quarters, directed their shot par-

---

* These reminiscences were written by Chas. Campbell, Esq., of Petersburg, a gentleman better informed upon the history of eastern Virginia than any one we have met in the course of our investigations, and to whom we are indebted for much valuable information.

† From a wound received at Saratoga, where Phillips was made captive with Burgoyne's army.

‡ There was then a tavern somewhere near the corner of Old and Market streets, called the " Golden Ball," at which a number of the British quartered.

§ Chastellux says, speaking of the enclosure, " It was formerly surrounded by rails, and she raised a number of fine horses there, but the English burnt the fences, and carried away a great number of the horses."

‖ On the north side of the river opposite the town.

¶ The Appomattox.

PETERSBURG.

The above view was taken on an eminence about half a mile north of the central part of the town. In the centre of the view is seen the depot of the Richmond and Petersburg railroad; on the right, a glimpse of the Appomattox river, and beyond, the principal part of Petersburg.

ticularly at that house,* a measure which, considering the sickness of General Phillips, would hardly have been justifiable, but for the horrid series of devastations in which he had just been engaged, in company with that odious traitor Arnold. This officer, in the early part of the cannonade, was walking across the yard, until a ball having passed very near him, he hastened into the house, and directed all the inmates to go down into the cellar for shelter.† General Phillips was removed down there. Mrs. Bolling also took refuge there, with one or two ladies who were with her. Anburey‡ (if memory serves) mentions that during the firing of the American artillery, Phillips, being then at the point of death, exclaimed—" Wont they let me die in peace ?"

Gen. Phillips died on the 13th of May, and was buried in the grave-yard adjoining Blandford church. There reposes one, of whom Mr. Jefferson said—" he is the proudest man, of the proudest nation on earth."

On the 20th of May, 1781, just one week after the death of Phillips, Lord Cornwallis entered Petersburg on his route from Wilmington, North Carolina. He remained in Petersburg only three or four days, and, as is understood, made his head-quarters at Bollingbrook. General O'Hara, it appears, was quartered at what is commonly styled the " Long Ornary,"—about a mile to the west of Petersburg, on the main road. Mrs. Bolling found it necessary to visit this officer at that place, for the purpose of recovering certain negroes and horses, which had been taken from her, and were then there. The general consented to restore the slaves, but with respect to the horses proved quite inexorable. He is described as a harsh, uncouth person. He was wounded at the battle of Guilford, and surrendered Lord Cornwallis' sword at Yorktown.

At the siege of Toulon, in a sortie made by the youthful Napoleon, a grenadier in the darkness of the night drew a wounded prisoner down into a ditch ; that prisoner was Major-General O'Hara, of " Long Ornary" memory, commander-in-chief of the British forces.

On the 21st of October, 1812, 103 young men from this place and vicinity embarked in the service of their country, and consecrated their valor at the battle of Fort Meigs, on the 5th of May, 1813. They were extensively known as the " *Petersburg Volunteers.*" They remained in service one year, and on their discharge received the following highly commendatory testimonial of their gallant and soldier-like conduct.

GENERAL ORDERS.

Head-Quarters, Detroit, 17th October, 1813.

The term of service for which the *Petersburg Volunteers* were engaged having expired, they are permitted to commence their march to *Virginia,* as soon as they can be transported to the south side of the lake.

IN granting a discharge to this *patriotic and gallant corps,* the General feels at a loss for words adequate to convey his sense of their exalted merits ; almost exclusively composed of individuals who had been nursed in the lap of ease, they have, for twelve months, borne the hardships and privations of military life in the midst of an inhospitable wilderness, with a cheerfulness and alacrity which has never been surpassed. Their conduct in the field has been excelled by no other corps ; and while in camp, they have set an example of subordination and respect for military authority to the whole army. The General requests Capt. M'RAE, his subalterns, non-commissioned officers, and privates, to accept his warmest thanks, and bids them an affectionate farewell.

By command, ROBERT BUTLER,

Acting Assistant Adjutant-General

Herewith is a list of this corps : the italicised letters attached to their names signify

---

* Two balls struck the house, one of which being spent, lodged in the front wall of the house ; the other passed through the house, and killed a negro woman (old Molly) who was standing by the kitchen door, in the act of reviling the American troops.

† On the approach of the enemy, Old Tom, a house servant, was provident enough to bury certain silver plate, money, &c., in the cellar ; there is also a vague rumor of an earthenware tea-pot, full of gold. While Arnold was down in the cellar, he was not aware that he was in such desirable company. There is still in preservation in the town, a set of China-ware, which was interred at this time.

‡ In his travels in the interior of North America.

as follows : *k.* killed at Fort Meigs ; *w.* wounded at Fort Meigs ; *d.* died ; *p.* promoted ; and *p. a.* promoted in the army.

Captain :
Richard M'Rae.

Lieutenants :
William Tisdale, 1st.
Henry Gary, 2d. *d.*

Ensign :
Shirley Tisdale, *p.*

Sergeants :
James Stevens, *d.*
Robert B. Cook. *p.*
Samuel Stevens, *w.*
John Henderson, *p. a.*

Corporals :
N'bn. B. Spotswood, *p*
John Perry, *d.*
Joseph Scott, *w.*
Thomas G. Scott, *w.*
Joseph C. Noble,
G. T. Clough, *k.*

Musicians :—Daniel Eshon, *w.* ; James Jackson, *w.*

Privates :

Andrew Andrews, *d.*	Samuel Cooper, *w.*	James Jeffers,	Wm. P. Rawlings, *d.*
Richard Adams,	James Cureton, *d.*	William Lacey, *d.*	Evans Rawlings,
John Bignall,	William R. Chives, *w.*	Herbert C. Lofton, *w.*	George Richards,
Edward Branch, *p.*	George Craddock,	Benjamin Lawson,	Geo. P. Raybourne, *d.*
Richard H. Branch,	Laven Dunton,	Alfred Lorain,	John Shore, *k.*
Thos. B. Bigger, *p. a.*	Wm. B. Degraffenreidt,	William Lanier, *d.*	John Shelton,
Robert Blick, *w.*	George P, Digges,	William R. Leigh, *w,*	Richard Sharp,
George Burge,	Grieve Drummond, *w.*	David Mann,	John H. Smith,
William Burton,	A. O. Eggleston, *p. a.*	Nich. Massenburg, *k.*	John Spratt,
Daniel Booker,	James Farrar, *p.*	Anthony Mullen,	Robert Stevens,
Richard Booker, *p. a.*	John Frank,	Benjamin Middleton,	Edward Stith, *w.*
George Booker, *k.*	Edmund Gee, *d.*	Roger Mallory,	Thomas Scott, *w.*
Joseph R. Bentley,	James Gary,	Joseph Mason, *w.*	John H. Saunders,
John W. Bentley,	Frederick Gary,	Edwd. Mumford, *p. a.*	Daniel Worsham,
Edmund Brown, *w.*	George Grundy,	Samuel Miles, *d.*	Charles Wynne,
Thomas Clarke,	George W. Grymes,	James Pace,	Nath. H. Wills, *w.*
Reuben Clements,	Leroy Graves,	James Peterson,	Thomas Worsham,
Moses Clements,	Edmund M. Giles, *p. a.*	Richard Pool,	Samuel Williams, *k*
Jas. G. Chalmers, *w.*	William Harrison,	Benjamin Pegram,	James Williams,
Edward Cheniworth, *d.*	Nathaniel Harrison,	Thomas W. Perry, *w.*	John F. Wiley,
James Cabiness,	Jacob Humbert,	John Potter, *p. a.*	David Williams.
Edward H. Cogbill,	John C. Hill,	John Rawlings,	

A pleasant anecdote is related of the volunteers in a late number of the Pioneer,[*] as having occurred at Point Pleasant, while they were passing through that place to the frontier. The author of the story was then on his way from western New York, with his family, bound for Cincinnati. After he had been there about a week, the volunteers arrived. The anecdote we give in his own words :

Being unable to pass the Ohio on account of the running of the ice, they encamped near the village, and remained about two weeks, during which time the writer had an opportunity of learning their character, which soon became of great service to him. Soon as the ice permitted, they struck their tents and began to cross the river, rejoicing in the prospect of soon reaching the post of danger. Some five or six of these soldiers, impatient of delay, were about to take a skiff which belonged to the writer, who was then young, inexperienced, and of such very fiery temperament as not to be very passive when his rights were invaded, and therefore began rather abruptly, perhaps, to remonstrate with them ; and on their persisting in taking the skiff, high words ensued, in which he called them a set of *scoundrels.* The words were scarcely uttered, when he was surrounded by half the company, all of whom seemed to feel that the indignity was offered to the whole company. As more and more still gathered around him, they said : ' We have a right to use any means in our power to get on where our country calls us. We bear the character of gentlemen at home : you have called us scoundrels ; this you must retract, and make us an apology, or we will tear you in pieces.' Thinking I knew their character, I instantly resolved on the course to be pursued, as the only means of saving myself from the threatened vengeance of men exasperated to the highest pitch of excitement. Assuming an apparent courage, which I confess I did not feel as strongly as I strove to evince, I turned slowly round upon my heels, looking them

[*] The American Pioneer is a monthly periodical, now published at Cincinnati, by John S. Williams. It is devoted to collecting and publishing incidents relative to the early settlement and successive improvement of the country. Its *materiel* is furnished by numerous correspondents, interested in historical researches. We take pleasure in directing public attention to this excellent work.

full in the face, with all the composure I could command, without uttering a word. By this time several of the citizens were standing on the outside of the crowd that surrounded me. The volunteers, not knowing I was a stranger there, thought I had turned round in search of succor from the citizens, and with a view of making my escape—said to me, 'You need not look for a place of escape ; if all the people of the county were your friends, they could not liberate you—nothing but an apology can save you.' The citizens were silent witnesses of the dilemma in which the Yankee, as they called me, was involved. I replied, 'I am not looking for a place of escape—I am looking on men who say they have volunteered to fight their country's battles—who say they are gen-

The Blandford Church.

tlemen at home—who doubtless left Petersburg, resolved, if they ever returned, to do so with laurels of victory round their brows. And now, I suppose, their first great victory is to be achieved before they leave the shores of their native state, by sixty or seventy of them tearing *one man* to pieces. Think, gentlemen, if indeed you are *gentlemen*, how your fame will be blazoned in the public prints—think of the immortality of such a victory! You can tear me in pieces ; and, like cannibals, eat me, when you have done. I am entirely in your power ; but there is one thing I *cannot* do. You are soldiers, so am I a soldier ; you ask terms of me no soldier can accept ; you *cannot*, with a threat over my head, extort an apology from me ; therefore, I have only to say, the greatest scoundrel among you, strike the first blow! I make no concession.' The result was more favorable than I had anticipated. I had expected to have a contest with some *one* of them, for I believed the course I had taken would procure me friends enough from among themselves, to see me have, what is called 'fair play' in a fisticuff battle. But I had effected more. I had made an appeal to the pride, the bravery, and the noble generosity of Virginians—too brave to triumph over an enemy in their power—too generous to permit it to be done by any of their number. A simultaneous exclamation was heard all around me, '*He is a soldier ; let him alone*'—and in a moment they dispersed."

Blandford is said to be older than Petersburg. It was formerly superior in architecture and fashion, and might properly have been called "the court end" of the town ; but her glory has departed, and her sister settlement, Petersburg, has absorbed her vitality. Its old church,

> "Lone relic of the past! old mouldering pile,
> Where twines the ivy round its ruins gray,"

is one of the most interesting and picturesque ruins in the country. Its form is similar to that of the letter T with a short column. Its site is elevated, overlooking the adjacent town, the river, and a landscape of beauty.

Within the limits of Petersburg, " on the north bank of the Appomattox, within a few feet of the margin of the river, is a large, dark-gray stone, of a conical form, about five feet in height, and somewhat more in diameter. On the side which looks to the east, three feet above the ground, there is an oval excavation about twelve inches across, and half as many in depth. The stone is solitary, and lifts itself conspicuously above the level of the earth. It is called the BASIN OF POCAHONTAS, and except in very dry weather, is seldom without water."

JOHN BURK, a lawyer, was a native of Ireland, and settled in Petersburg, where he wrote and published, in 1804, three volumes on the history of Virginia, bringing it down to the commencement of the American revolution. While here, he wrote plays for an histrionic society in the town, and on the boards of its amateur theatre, acted parts in them. His work on the state he did not live to complete. At a public table Burk used some expressions derogatory to the French nation. A French gentleman accidentally present, named Coburg, a stranger in the country, offended by the remarks, challenged him. They fought at Fleet's Hill, on the opposite bank of the Appomattox, and Burk was killed. The 4th and remaining volume, published in 1816, was written by Skelton Jones and Louis Hue Girardin, the latter of whom was a Frenchman, and, it is stated, wrote under the supervision of Jefferson at Monticello, who, familiar with the era to which it related, imparted valuable information.

GEN. WINFIELD SCOTT, the present commander-in-chief of the U. S. Army, was born near Petersburg, June 13th, 1785. As an officer and a soldier his name stands conspicuous in the annals of our country.

ELIZABETH CITY.

ELIZABETH CITY was one of the eight original shires into which Virginia was divided in 1634. Its form is nearly a square of 18 miles on a side. The land is generally fertile; and that portion known as "the back river district," comprising about one-third of its area, is remarkably rich. There were in 1840, whites 1,954, slaves 1,708, free colored 44 ; total 3,706.

Hampton, the county-seat, is 96 miles SE. of Richmond. It is on Hampton Roads, 18 miles from Norfolk, 24 from Yorktown, 36 from Williamsburg. Hampton is the residence of many of the pilots of James River. It contains 2 Methodist, 1 Baptist church, and one Episcopalian church. The Methodist society was established in 1789, and the Baptist in 1791. It has 18 stores and shops, and a population of about 1200.

Hampton is an old town, and one of historic interest. Its site was visited by Capt. John Smith in 1607, on his first exploratory voyage up the Potomac, previous to the settlement of Jamestown. Burk says, "While engaged in seeking a fit place for the first settlement, they met five of the natives, who invited them to their town, *Kecoughtan* or *Kichotan*, where Hampton now stands. Here they were feasted with cakes made of Indian corn, and 'regaled with tobacco and a dance.' In return, they presented the natives beads and other trinkets." Hampton was established a town by law in 1705, the same year with Norfolk. The locality was settled in 1610, from Jamestown.* The Episcopal church is the old-

---

* Jones' " Present State of Virginia."

est public building in the town, and is said to be the third oldest church in the state. The oldest inscription in the grave-yard attached to this venerable edifice, is that of Capt. Willis Wilson, who died Nov. 19th, 1701. Among the public men who lie buried there is Dr. George Balfour, who died at Norfolk, in 1830. He was a member of the medical staff in the U. S. Army; and " braved the perils of the west under the gallant Wayne, who, at a subsequent period, on Presque Isle, breathed his last in his arms. In 1798, on the organization of the Navy, he was appointed its senior surgeon, and performed the responsible duties of that office until 1804, when he retired to private practice in Norfolk." Major James M. Glassell, who died Nov. 3, 1838, and Lieut. James D. Burnham, who died March 6, 1828, both of whom were of the U. S. Army, are interred there. Tradition says, that anciently, the king's coat-of-arms was placed upon the steeple ; but that in 1776, shortly after the Declaration of Independence, the steeple was rent lengthwise by lightning, and the insignia of royalty hurled to the earth.

On the Pembroke farm, near Hampton, are four ancient monuments of black marble. Each is 6 feet long and 3 wide, and surmounted with a coat-of-arms. Annexed are the inscriptions :

Here lies ye body of John Nevill, Esq., Vice Admiral of His Majesty's fleet and commander-in-chiefe of ye squadron cruising in ye West Indies, who dyed on board ye Cambridge, ye 17 day of August, 1697, in the ninth yeare of the reign of King William ye third, aged 57 years.

In hopes of a blessed resurrection, here lies ye body of Thomas Curle, gent., who was born Nov. 24, 1641, in ye parish of Saint Michael, in Lewis, in ye county of Surry, in England, and dyed May 30, 1700.
When a few years are come then shall I go ye way whence I shall not return.—Job, 16 ch. 22 v.

Here lyeth ye body of ye Reverend Mr. Andrew Thompson, who was born at Stonehive in Scotland, and was minister of this parish 7 yeares, and departed this life ye 11 Sep. 1719, in ye 46 yeare of his age, leaving ye character of a sober and religious man.

This stone was given by His Excellency Francis Nicholson, Esq , Lieutenant and Governor-General of Virginia, in memory of Peter Heyman, Esq., grandson to Sir Peter Heyman of Summerfield in ye county of Kent—he was collector of ye customs in ye lower district of James River, and went voluntarily on board ye king's ship Shoreham, in pursuit of a pyrate who greatly infested this coast—after he had behaved himself 7 hours with undaunted courage, was killed with a small shot, ye 29 day of April, 1700. In the engagement he stood next the governor upon the quarter deck, and was here honorably interred by his order.

Hampton was attacked by the British in the war of the revolution, and also invaded by them in the late war.

The first was in Oct. 1775, and was, says Burk, dictated by revenge on the part of Lord Dunmore, for two schooners which had been burnt by two enterprising young men of the name of Barron. These men, afterwards distinguished for their courage and success in maritime adventure against the British, commanded, at this time, two pilot boats—a species of vessel constructed chiefly with an attention to sailing—and kept the fleet of Dunmore constantly on the alert by the rapidity of their movements. If pursued, by keeping close in with the shore, they took refuge in Hampton. The people of the town, fearing an attack, had applied to the committee of safety for assistance, who sent down " Col. Woodford, with 100 mounted riflemen of the Culpeper battalion, without any other incumbrance than their provisions and blankets. But before the arrival of Woodford, captain Squires, with six tenders full of men, appeared in Hampton creek, and commenced an attack on the town. He imagined that the mere display of his squadron would have paralyzed the courage of the new-raised troops, and that no resistance would have been attempted. Under this impression, the boats, under cover of a fierce cannonade, rowed towards the shore for the purpose of setting fire to the houses, and carrying off whatever property should be spared from the conflagration. A few moments disclosed the vanity of these expectations. A shower of bullets soon compelled the boats to return to the ships, while the riflemen, disposed in the houses and the bushes along the beach, proved that even the tenders were not secure against their fatal precision. Checked by a resistance so fierce and unexpected, the tenders hauled further into the stream, and further operations were suspended until a reinforcement, which was hourly expected, would render an assault more certain and decisive.

"Meanwhile Woodford, who had used the most extraordinary expedition, arrived at daybreak with his riflemen, and as it was certainly known that the enemy would renew the attack, a new disposition was made of the American troops. The enemy's fleet had spread themselves with the view of dividing the force of the Americans; and though it was intended perhaps only as a diversion, it was not improbable that an attempt would be made to land troops at a considerable distance in the rear of the Americans. To guard against this, Woodford disposed the minute-men, with a part of the militia, in his rear; the remainder of the militia was distributed at different points on the creek, to act as parties of observation, according to circumstances, while he himself took post with the riflemen in the houses, and every other low and covered position that presented itself on the beach.

"At sunrise the enemy's fleet was seen standing in for the shore, and having at length reached a convenient position, they lay with springs on their cables, and commenced a furious cannonade. Double-headed and chain shot, and grape, flew in showers through all parts of the town; and as the position of the ships enabled them to enfilade, it was thought impossible to defend it, even for a few minutes. Nothing could exceed the cool and steady valor of the Virginians; and although, with very few exceptions, wholly unacquainted with military service, they displayed the countenance and collection of veterans. Woodford's commands to his riflemen, previous to the cannonade, were simply to fire with coolness and decision, and observe the profoundest silence. The effects of this advice were soon visible; the riflemen answered the cannonade by a well-directed fire against every part of the line, and it soon appeared that no part of the ship was secure against their astonishing precision. In a short time the enemy appeared to be in some confusion; their cannonade gradually slackened, and a signal was given by the commander to slip their cables and retire. But even this was attended with the most imminent danger. No man could stand at the helm in safety; if the men went aloft to hand the sails, they were immediately singled out. In this condition two of the schooners drifted to the shore. The commander of one of these in vain called on his men to assist in keeping her off; they had all retired to the hold, and declared their utter refusal to expose themselves to inevitable destruction. In this exigency, deserted by his men, he jumped into the water and escaped to the opposite shore. The rest of the fleet had been fortunate enough to escape, although with some difficulty, and returned to Norfolk."[*]

After the British fleet were defeated in their attempt upon Norfolk, in June, 1813, by the gallant defence of Craney Island, they proceeded to attack Hampton, which was defended by a garrison of 450 militia, protected by some slight fortifications. The annexed account of this event is from Perkins' History of the Late War:

Admiral Cockburn, on the 25th of June, with his forces, advanced towards the town in barges and small vessels, throwing shells and rockets, while Sir Sidney Beckwith effected a landing below with two thousand men. Cockburn's party were repulsed by the garrison, and driven back behind a point, until General Beckwith's troops advanced and compelled the garrison to retire. The town being now completely in the possession of the British, was given up to pillage. Many of the inhabitants had fled with their valuable effects; those who remained suffered the most shameful barbarities. That renegado corps, composed of French prisoners accustomed to plunder and murder in Spain, and who had been induced to enter the British service by promises of similar indulgence in America, were now to be gratified, and were let loose upon the wretched inhabitants of Hampton without restraint. For two days the town was given up to

---

[*] The inhabitants had sunk five sloops before the town.

unrestrained pillage ; private property was plundered and wantonly destroyed ; unarmed and unoffending individuals grossly abused ; females violated ; and, in one instance, an aged sick man murdered in the arms of his wife, who, at the same time, was dangerously wounded. A collection of well-attested facts, made by a committee of Congress respecting the outrages at Hampton, stand on their journals as lasting monuments of disgrace to the British nation.

Hampton has been the birth-place of several distinguished naval officers. Among them were the two Barrons,* of the Virginia navy, who performed several gallant exploits in the revolution. The grandfather of Com. Lewis Warrington, who, in 1814, while in command of the Peacock, captured the Epervier, was pastor of the old Episcopal church in this town. Major Finn, of the army, was from this place. Capt. Meredith and Capt. William Cunningham, of the Virginia navy in the revolution, were also born at Hampton. The first was a remarkably bold and enterprising officer, and on one moonlight night ventured to sail out to sea in a small vessel, passing through a British fleet anchored in Hampton Roads. The following notice of the latter is abridged from the U. S. Military and Naval Magazine :

At the beginning of the war of the revolution, Capt. Cunningham enlisted in one of the minute companies, and continued in that service until Virginia armed a few fast-sailing pilot-boat schooners. Thus was the navy of that state commenced. It, however, varied materially ; sometimes amounting to as many as 50 vessels, and occasionally to only one. Among them was the schooner Liberty, which was never captured, although several times sunk in the rivers to conceal her from the enemy. Capt. Cunningham embarked and remained in the Liberty, as her first lieutenant, until the war assumed a more regular form. Capt. Cunningham purchased a small schooner, and engaged in traffic to the West Indies. Sea-officers were encouraged to engage in commerce as the only means of procuring the munitions of war.

On these occasions, he encountered great risk from the enemy's fleets. Once, in the month of June, he suddenly came upon an English frigate, off Cape Henry, in a dense fog. The English commander ordered him to strike his colors, and haul down his light sails, or he would sink him. By a judicious and skilful stratagem, he made the enemy believe that he intended to surrender. He, therefore, suspended his threatened firing. At the moment they discovered that Cunningham intended to escape, the jib-boom of the frigate caught in the topping-lift of the schooner's main-boom. Capt. C. sprang up to the stern, with a knife, to free his vessel. While in the act of cutting the rope, a British marine shot him through the arm. Nothing daunted, he deliberately effected his object, and amid a shower of grape, his vessel shot away from the frigate, and was in a few moments out of sight.

Some time after, Capt. Cunningham joined the army on the south side of James River, and had the misfortune, while on a foraging expedition, to be taken by the enemy and carried into Portsmouth. He had then been recently married.

One day he said to an uncle of his, (also a prisoner,) that he would see his wife the next evening, or perish in the attempt. " My dear Will, are you mad ?" was the reply.

The prison in which he was confined was a large sugar-house, at the extreme south end of the town, enclosed by a strong stockade fence. At sunset every evening, the guard, composed of 40 or 50 men, were relieved by fresh troops, and on their arrival, the two guards, with their officers, were paraded in front of the prison, on each side of the pathway to the gate. At this hour, the ceremony observed on the occasion was in progress ; the relieved guard had stacked their arms, and were looking up their baggage ; the fresh guard were relieving sentinels, and, in a degree, at their ease. This was the time selected by Capt. C. The sentinel had just begun to pace his sacred ground, and awful, indeed, was the moment. Capt. C. was justly a great favorite with the prisoners, who all, in silent terror, expected to see their beloved companion pinned to the earth by many bayonets, for expostulation had been exhausted. "*My wife, or death !*" was his watchword. The sentinel's motions had been sagaciously calculated upon, and as he turned from

* One of these was the father of the present Com. James Barron, of the U. S. Navy.

the prison, Capt. C. darted out, and butted him over at his full length, and ran past him through the gate. It was now nearly dark. All was uproar and confusion. Cunningham soon reached a marsh near the house, and was nowhere to be found. Volley after volley was fired after him, and some of the balls whistled over his head. Ere long he arrived at the southern branch of Elizabeth River, which he swam over a little below the navy-yard at Gosport, and finally reached the place whither his wife had fled.

Lieut. Church, who had served as Capt. C.'s first, was determined that his commander should not alone encounter the danger of an escape. He, therefore, followed him; and strange as it may appear, he was never heard of, or accounted for.

Old Point Comfort, on which stands fortress Monroe, is 2½ miles from Hampton, and about 12 in a direct line from Norfolk. It is a promontory, exactly on lat. 37°, and with the opposing point, Willoughby, forms the mouth of James River.

The name was given to it in 1607 by the first colonists of Virginia, who, on their exploratory voyage up the James, previous to landing at Jamestown, called it *Point Comfort* " on account of the good channel and safe anchorage it afforded." The prefix of " *Old*," was afterwards given to distinguish it from " New Point Comfort."

A fort was built on the Point a few years after the first settlement of the country. The following act for its erection was passed in March, 1629–30. " Matter of ffortifications was againe taken into consideration, and Capt. Samuel Mathewes was content to undertake the raysing of a ffort at Poynt Comfort; whereupon, Capt. Robert Ffelgate, Capt. Thomas Purfury, Capt. Thomas Graies, Capt. John Uty, Capt. Tho. Willoby, Mr. Tho. Heyrick, and Leu't. Wm. Perry, by full consent of the whole Assembly, were chosen to view the place, conclude what manner of fforte shall bee erected, and to compounde and agree with the said Capt. Mathewes for the building, raysing, and finishing the same," &c.

Count de Grasse, the admiral of the French fleet, threw up some fortifications on old Point Comfort a short time previous to the surrender at York.

The salutary experience, dearly bought in the lessons of the late war, when these waters were the resort of British fleets, has doubtless had much influence in prompting the erection of the fortresses of Monroe and Calhoun. The first is one of the largest single fortifications in the world, and is generally garrisoned by a regiment of U. S. troops. The channel leading in from the Capes of Virginia to Hampton Roads, is at Old Point Comfort reduced to a very narrow line. The shoal water, which under the action of the sea, and reacted upon by the bar, is kept up in an unremitting ripple, has given the name of *Rip Raps* to this place. When the bar is passed, Hampton Roads affords one of the finest anchorages, in which navies could ride in safety. Fort Calhoun, or the castle of the Rip Raps, is directly opposite fort Monroe, at the distance of 1900 yards. The two forts are so constructed as to present immense batteries of cannon at an approaching hostile ship; and the probabilities are, that long before she had completed the bendings of the channel, she would be a wreck, or a conflagration from the hot shot thrown into her. The Rip Raps structure is a monument of the genius of the engineers by whom it was planned. It is formed upon an island, made from the sea by casting in rocks in a depth of 20 feet of water, until, by gradual accumulation, it emerged above the tides. The present aspect of the place is rough and savage; the music of the surrounding elements of air and sea, is in keeping with the dreariness and desolation of the spot.

The beach at Old Point, affords excellent bathing-ground; this, with a fine hotel, and other attractions, make the place much resorted to in the summer months. The officers' quarters occupy several neat buildings within the area of the fort, where there is a fine level parade-ground, ornamented by clumps of live-oak, which is the most northern point in the Union in which that tree is found.

GEORGE WYTHE, a signer of the Declaration of Independence, was born in this county in 1726. "His education was principally directed by his mother. The death of both his parents before he became of age, and the uncontrolled possession of a large fortune, led him for some time into a course of amusement and dissipation. At the age of thirty, however, his conduct underwent an

View of the Harbor of NORFOLK and PORTSMOUTH, from Fort Norfolk.

Fort Monroe is seen in front, on OLD POINT COMFORT, and in the distance, Fort Calhoun, at the Rip Raps.

entire change. He applied himself vigorously to the study of the law; and soon after his admission to the bar, his learning, industry, and eloquence, made him eminent. For several years previous to the revolution, he was conspicuous in the House of Burgesses; and in the commencement of the opposition to England, evinced an ardent attachment to liberty. In 1764, he drew up a remonstrance to the House of Commons, in a tone of independence too decided for that period, and which was greatly modified by the Assembly before assenting to it. In 1775, he was appointed a delegate to the Continental Congress in Philadelphia. In the following year he was appointed, in connection with Mr. Jefferson and others, to revise the laws of Virginia—a duty which was performed with great ability. In 1777, he was appointed Speaker of the House of Delegates, and during the same year judge of the high court of chancery. On a new organization of the court of equity, in the subsequent year, he was appointed sole chancellor— a station which he filled for more than twenty years. In 1787, he was a member of the convention which formed the federal constitution, and during the debates acted, for the most part, as chairman. He was a strenuous advocate of the instrument adopted. He subsequently presided twice, successively, in the college of electors in Virginia. His death occurred on the 8th of June, 1806, in the 81st year of his age. It was supposed that he was poisoned; but the person suspected was acquitted by a jury. In learning, industry, and judgment, Chancellor Wythe had few superiors. His integrity was never stained, even by a suspicion; and from the moment of his abandonment of the follies of his youth, his reputation was unspotted. The kindness and benevolence of his heart were commensurate with the strength and attainments of his mind."

ESSEX.

Essex was formed in 1692, from a part of (old) Rappahannock county. It lies on the s. side of the Rappahannock, about 30 miles NE. of Richmond. Its length is 28 miles; mean breadth 10 miles. In the western part it is slightly hilly, and its soil, except on the margin of the streams, generally sandy. The county, however, produces large crops of corn, considerable wheat and oats, and some cotton and tobacco. Pop. in 1840, whites 3,955, slaves 6,756, free colored 598; total, 11,309.

Tappahannoc, port of entry and seat of justice for the county, lies on the Rappahannock, 50 miles from its mouth in Chesapeake Bay, and contains about 30 dwellings. It has a good harbor, and all the shipping belonging to the towns on the river is entered at the custom-house in this place; tonnage in 1840, 4,591. Loretto is a small village one mile from the Rappahannock, in the NE. part of the county.

FAIRFAX.

FAIRFAX was formed in 1742, from Prince William, and named after Lord Fairfax, the proprietor of "the Northern Neck." The part of Virginia included in the District of Columbia was formed from Fairfax. The county is watered by the Potomac and the Occoquan, and their branches. Pop., whites 5,469, slaves 3,453, free colored 448; total, 9,370,

Fairfax Court House is near the centre of the county, 21 miles from Washington City; it contains the county buildings, and about 200 inhabitants. Centerville is a village of about the same population, on a high and healthy situation near the southwestern angle of the county.

Much of the land of this county, and, indeed, of the whole of the tide-water country of Virginia, is flat and sandy. Some parts, it is true, are very fertile and produce large crops; but these are so intermixed with extensive tracts of waste land, worn out by the excessive culture of tobacco, and which are almost destitute of verdure, that the country has frequently the aspect of barrenness. A ruinous system has prevailed to a great extent, of working the same piece of land year after year until it was exhausted, when new land was cleared, in its turn to be cultivated a few seasons and then abandoned. In some parts of the country the lands thus left waste throw up a spontaneous growth of low pines and cedars, whose sombre aspect, with the sterility of the soil, oppresses the traveller with feelings of gloom. However, land thus shaded from the rays of the sun, recovers in time its former fertility.

Several years since, some of the enterprising farmers of German origin from Dutchess county, New York, commenced emigrating to this county and purchased considerable tracts of worn-out land, which they have, in many instances, succeeded in restoring to their original fertility. Good land can be bought for $8 or $10 per acre; tolerable fair for about $3; which, in a few years, can be brought up with clover and plaster. Some of the finest farms in New York are upon lands, which, a few years ago, were sand, blowing about in the wind. The worn-out Virginian lands are not so bad as this, and, with a fine climate, are as easily restored. The success thus far attending the experiment is encouraging, and emigration still continues. These farmers make this movement better than going west, for they are sure of a good market, without the whole value of their produce being exhausted by the expense of transportation. Slave-labor is not employed in resuscitating land; the farmers work themselves, with their sons and hired men.

The following extracts are from Davis's Four and a Half Years in America, published in 1803. Davis was a school-teacher in the section of country which he describes. His work is dedicated, by permission, to Jefferson :—

I prosecuted my walk to *Newgate*, where, on the piazza of Mr. Thornton's tavern, I found a party of gentlemen from the neighboring plantations carousing over a bowl of toddy, and smoking cigars. No people could exceed these men in politeness. On my ascending the steps to the piazza, every countenance seemed to say, This man has a double claim to our attention, for he is a stranger in the place. In a moment there was room made for me to sit down; a new bowl was called for, and every one who addressed me did it with a smile of conciliation. But no man asked me where I had come from, or whither I was going. A gentleman in every country is the same; and, if good breeding consists in sentiment, it was found in the circle I had got into.

The higher Virginians seem to venerate themselves as men; and I am persuaded there was not one in company who would have felt embarrassed at being admitted to the presence and conversation of the greatest monarch on earth. There is a compound of virtue and vice in every human character; no man was ever yet faultless; but whatever may be advanced against Virginians, their good qualities will ever outweigh their defects; and when the effervescence of youth has abated, when reason asserts her empire, there is no man on earth who discovers more exalted sentiments, more contempt of baseness, more love of justice, more sensibility of feeling, than a Virginian.

No walk could be more delightful than that from Occoquan to Colchester, when the moon was above the mountains. You traverse the bank of a placid stream, over which impend rocks, in some places bare, but more frequently covered with an odoriferous plant that regales the traveller with its fragrance. So serpentine is the course of the river, that the mountains which rise from its bank may be said to form an amphitheatre; and nature seems to have designed the spot for the haunt only of fairies, for here grow flowers of purple dye, and here the snake throws her enamelled skin. But into what regions, however apparently inaccessible, has not adventurous man penetrated? The awful repose of the night is disturbed by the clack of two huge mills, which drown the echoes of the mocking-bird, who nightly tells his sorrows to the listening moon.

Art is pouring fast into the lap of nature the luxuries of exotic refinement. After clambering over mountains, almost inaccessible to human toil, you come to the junction of the Occoquan with the noble river of the Potomac, and behold a bridge, whose semi-elliptical arches are scarcely inferior to those of princely London. And on the side of this bridge stands a tavern, where every luxury that money can purchase is to be obtained at first summons; where the richest viands cover the table, and where ice cools the Madeira that has been thrice across the ocean. * * * Having slept one night at this tavern, I rose with the sun and journeyed leisurely to the mills, catching refreshment from a light air that stirred the leaves of the trees. About eight miles from the Occoquan mills is a house of worship, called *Powheek church;* a name it claims from a run that flows near its walls. Hither I rode on Sundays and joined the congregation of parson Weems, a minister of the Episcopal persuasion, who was cheerful in his mien, that he might win men to religion. A *Virginian* church-yard, on a Sunday, resembles rather a race-course than a sepulchral ground; the ladies come to it in carriages, and the men after dismounting from their horses make them fast to the trees. But the steeples to the Virginian churches were designed not for utility but ornament; for the bell is always suspended to a tree a few yards from the church. It is also observable, that the gate to the church-yard is ever carefully locked by the sexton, who retires last. * * * Wonder and ignorance are ever reciprocal. I was confounded, on first entering the church-yard at Powheek, to hear

Steed threaten steed with high and boastful neigh.

Nor was I less stunned with the rattling of carriage-wheels, the cracking of whips, and the vociferations of the gentlemen to the negroes who accompanied them. But the discourse of parson Weems calmed every perturbation; for he preached the great doctrines of salvation, as one who had experienced their power. * * * In his youth Mr. Weems accompanied some young Americans to London, where he prepared himself by diligent study for the profession of the church. * * * Of the congregation at Powheek church, about one half was composed of white people, and the other of negroes. Among many of the negroes were to be discovered the most satisfying evidences of sincere piety, an artless simplicity, passionate aspirations after Christ, and an earnest endeavor to know and do the will of God.

The church described in the foregoing sketch is still standing and an object of interest from having been the one Washington regularly attended for a long series of years while resident at

Mount Vernon, distant some 6 or 7 miles. The particular location
of the church is ascribed to him. At a very early age he was an
active member of the vestry ; and when its location was under
consideration and dispute, surveyed and made a map of the whole
parish, and showed where it ought to be erected. The Rt. Rev.
Wm. Meade, Bishop of Va., in an official tour taken three or four
years since, thus describes its appearance as it was at that time ;
since which it has been repaired :

My next visit was to Pohick church, in the vicinity of Mount Vernon, the seat of
Gen. Washington. I designed to perform service there on Saturday as well as Sunday,
but through some mistake no notice was given for the former day. The weather, indeed, was such as to prevent the assembling of any but those who prize such occasions
so much as to be deterred only by very strong considerations. It was still raining when
I approached the house, and found no one there. The wide opened doors invited me to
enter, as they do invite, day and night through the year, not only the passing traveller,
but every beast of the field and fowl of the air. These latter, however, seemed to have
reverenced the house of God, since few marks of their pollution are to be seen throughout it. The interior of the house, having been well built, is still good. The chancel,
communion-table, tables of the law, etc., are still there and in good order. The roof
only is decayed ; and at the time I was there, the rain was dropping on these sacred
places, and on other parts of the house. On the doors of the pews, in gilt letters, are
still to be seen the names of the principal families which once occupied them. How
could I, while for an hour traversing those long aisles, entering the sacred chancel, ascending the lofty pulpit, forbear to ask : And is this the house of God which was built
by the Washingtons, the Masons, the McCarties, the Grahams, the Lewises, the Fair-
faxes—the house in which they used to worship the God of our fathers according to the
venerable forms of the Episcopal Church, and some of whose names are yet to be found
on those deserted pews ? Is this, also, destined to moulder piecemeal away—or, when
some signal is given, to become the prey of spoilers, and to be carried hither and thither,
and applied to every purpose under heaven ?

The Rev. M. L. Weems, to whom allusion has been made, was
the rector of Mount Vernon parish at the time Washington attended this church. He was the author of a life of Washington,
and also one of Marion. His memoir of Washington has been a
very popular work, and has passed through 30 or 40 editions. It
is a volume extremely fascinating to the youthful mind. " He
turns all the actions of Washington to the encouragement of virtue, by a careful application of numerous exemplifications drawn
from the conduct of the founder of our republic, from his earliest
life."

From a clerical friend of the late Mr. Weems, we have gathered these facts respecting him : The wants of a large family occasioned Mr. Weems to abandon preaching for
a livelihood, and he became a book-agent for the celebrated Matthew Carey of Philadelphia. He travelled extensively over the southern states, and met with almost unpre-
cedented success—selling, in one year, 3000 copies of a high-priced Bible. He also sold
other works, among which were those of his own writing. He was accustomed to be
present at courts and other large assemblages, where he mingled with the people ; and
by his faculty of adapting himself to all circumstances, he generally drew crowds of listen-
ers, whom he would address upon the merits of his works, interspersing his remarks with
anecdotes and humorous sallies. He wrote and sold a pamphlet entitled " The Drunk-
ard's Looking-Glass," illustrated by cuts, showing the progressive stages of the drunk-
ard, from his first taking the social glass until the final scene of his death. With this
in hand he entered taverns, and addressing the inmates, would mimic the extravagances
of an inebriate, and sell the pamphlet. His eccentricities and singular conduct lowered
his dignity, and occasioned the circulation of many false and ridiculous tales unbecoming
his clerical profession. He was a man of much benevolence, and a great wit. When
travelling, he sometimes received and accepted invitations to preach. His sermons were

generally moral essays, abounding with humor. On one occasion, when at Fredericks-burg, he preached from the text, " We are fearfully and wonderfully made,"—which ser-mon he abruptly concluded by saying, " I must stop ; for should I go on, some of the young ladies present would not sleep *a wink* to-night." Mr. Weems was of the medium stature, his hair white and long, and his countenance expressive and sprightly. He was energetic in his movements, and polite. He proved useful in his vocation, being careful not to circulate any works but those of a good moral tendency. He died at an advanced age, many years since, leaving a highly respectable and well-educated family.

Residence and Tomb of Washington, Mount Vernon.

An English traveller in this country, about the close of the revo-lution, gives the following list of the seats on the Potomac existing at that time :

" On the Virginia side of the Potomac, are the seats of Mr. Alex-ander, Gen. Washington, Col. Martin, Col. Fairfax, Mr. Lawson, near the mouth of Oquaquon, Col. Mason, Mr. Lee, near the mouth of Quantico, Mr. Brent,* Mr. Mercer, Mr. Fitzhugh, Mr. Alexan-der, of Boyd Hole and all Chotank, Col. Frank Thornton, on

---

* Burnt by the enemy early in the revolutionary war.

33

Marchodock, Mr. Thacker Washington, Mrs. Blair, Mr. M'Carty, Col. Phil. Lee, of Nominey," &c.

Mount Vernon is on the Potomac, 8 miles from Alexandria, and 15 from Washington City. The mansion is built of wood, cut in imitation of free stone. The central part was built by Lawrence Washington, brother to the general; the wings were added by Gen. Washington. It is named after Admiral Vernon, in whose expedition Lawrence Washington served.

The following graphic description of a visit to Mount Vernon, from the pen of a New Englander, we extract from a recent number of the Boston Daily Advertiser and Patriot:

I had this morning, for the first time, crossed the Potomac, and was under the full influence of the sense that I was in a new land, and amid all the historical associations of the "Ancient Dominion." The day was soft and balmy, and, though early in March, was as warm as our budding days of May. We were in a portion of the great primeval forest of America. The crows cawed from the tops of the ancient, half-decayed trees ; and the naked trunks and branches of the sycamore, and the strange spreading forms of the other giants of the wood, were beautifully relieved by the evergreen of the pines and cedars. A solemn stillness filled the air. An ancient, sad, half-degenerate, but most venerable and soul-stirring character was impressed upon all around us.

After a few miles of riding through the forest, with occasional openings and cultivated spots, in one of which a negro was following his plough through the furrows, my friend pointed out a stone sunk in the ground by the road-side, which, he said, marked the beginning of the Mount Vernon estate. Still, we rode on for a couple of miles of beautiful country, left much in its natural condition, without even a fence to line the road-side, with a delightful variety of surface, before the gate and porter's lodge came in sight.

Instead of an iron gate upon stone posts, there was a simple wooden gate, swinging from posts of wood, without paint, turned to a gray color, and shutting with a wooden latch. An aged negro came out from the porter's house, courtesied as we passed, and answered civilly the questions as to her health, and whether her mistress was at home. All was characteristic of the domestic institutions of Virginia, even to the woman's standing still, and letting the gate swing to and latch itself. We had still half a mile before us, and the simple carriage-path led us over hills and down dales, with a surface as diversified as that of Mount Auburn, while the trees were more grand and forest-like, though thinly scattered, and with less variety and richness. We crossed a brook, passed through a ravine, and felt ourselves so completely in the midst of aboriginal, untouched nature, that the sight of the house and its cluster of surrounding buildings, came like a surprise upon me. The approach to the house is towards the west front. The high piazza, reaching from the roof to the ground, and the outline of the building, are familiar to us from the engravings ; but its gray and time-worn aspect must be mentioned to those whose eyes are accustomed to the freshness of white walls, green blinds, and painted bricks. We rode up to the piazza, but an unbroken silence reigned, and there was no sign of life, or of any one stirring. Turning away, we passed among the adjoining houses, occupied by the blacks, from one of which a servant, attracted by the sound of our horses' hoofs, came out, and being recognised by my friend, took our horses from us, and we walked towards the house. The door from the piazza opened directly into a large room, which we entered. It was no mere habit that lifted the hat from my head, and I stepped lightly, as though upon hallowed ground. Finding that no one had seen us, my friend went in search of the family, and left me to walk through the halls. From the first room I passed into another, from which a door led me out upon the eastern piazza. A warm afternoon breeze shook the branches of the forest which closes in upon the house on two sides, and breathed across the lawn and rising knolls with a delicious softness. Under this piazza, upon its pavement of flat stones, Washington used to walk to and fro, with military regularity, every morning, the noble Potomac in full view, spreading out into the width of a bay at the foot of the mount, and the shore of Maryland lining the eastern horizon. By the side of the door hung the spy-glass, through which he watched the passing objects upon the water. Little effort was necessary to call up the commanding figure of the hero, as he paced to and fro, while those pure and noble thoughts, which made his actions great, moved with almost an equal order through his simple and majestic understanding.

My friend approached and told me he had learned that the family were at dinner, and we left the house privately and walked towards the tomb. At a short distance from the house, in a retired spot, stands the new family tomb, a plain structure of brick, with a barred iron gate, through which are seen two sarcophagi of white marble, side by side, containing the remains of Washington and his consort. This had been recently finished, as appeared from the freshness of the bricks and mortar, and the bare spots of earth about it, upon which the grass had not yet grown. It is painful to see change and novelty in such connections; but all has been done by the direction of Washington's will, in which he designated the spot where he wished the tomb to be. The old family tomb, in which he was first placed, is in a more picturesque situation, upon a knoll, in full view of the river; but the present one is more retired, which was reason enough to determine the wishes of a modest man. While we were talking together here, a person approached us, dressed in the plain manner of a Virginia gentleman upon his estate. This was the young proprietor. After his greeting with my friend, and my introduction, he conducted us to the old tomb, which is the one represented in the prints scattered through the country. It is now going to decay, being unoccupied, is filling up, and partly overgrown with vines and shrubs. The change was made with regret, but a sacred duty seemed to require it. It is with this tomb that our associations are connected, and to this the British fleet is said to have lowered its flags while passing up the Potomac to make the attack upon the capitol.

To one accustomed to the plantation system and habits of Virginia, this estate may have much that is common with others; but to persons unused to this economy, the whole is new and striking. Of things peculiar to the place, are a low rampart of brick, now partly overgrown, which Washington had built around the front of the house, and an underground passage leading from the bottom of a dry well, and coming out by the river side at the foot of the mount. On the west side of the house are two gardens, a green-house, and—the usual accompaniments of a plantation—seed-houses, tool-houses, and cottages for the negroes—things possessing no particular interest, except because they were standing during Washington's life, and were objects of his frequent attention. I would not be one to countenance the making public of any thing pertaining to those who have received a visitor in confidence and good faith. And I hope not to transgress when I say, that if he can judge from what may be seen among those who bear the name and inherit the estate of the hero, no Massachusetts man need fear that the bond which united the two ancient historical commonwealths, is at all weakened; or that those memory-charge, cabalistic words, Massachusetts and Virginia, have lost any of their force with the true sons of either. Among the things of note shown us in the house, was the key of the Bastile, sent to Washington from France at the time of the destruction of the prison. Along the walls of the room hung engravings, which were mostly battle or hunting-pieces. Among them I noticed a print of Bunker Hill, but none of any battle in which Washington himself was engaged. The north room was built by Washington for a dining-room, and for the meetings of his friends and political visitors. The furniture of the room is just as when he used it, and leads us back to the days when there were met within these walls the great men of that generation who carried the states through the revolution, laid the foundations of the government, and administered it in its purer days. The rooms of the house are spacious, and there is something of elegance in their arrangement; yet the whole is marked by great simplicity. All the regard one could wish seems to have been shown to the sacredness of these public relics, and all things have been kept very nearly as Washington left them. Money made in the stocks can purchase the bedizenry of our city drawing-rooms; but these elevating associations, which no gold can buy, no popular favor win, which can only be inherited, these are the heir-looms, the traditionary titles and pensions, inalienable, not conferred, which a republic allows to the descendants of her great servants.

Let every American, and especially every young American, visit this place, and catch, if he can, something of its spirit. It will make an impression upon him which he may keep through life. It will teach him the story and lessons of the past so as no printed page can teach them. From amid the small machinery of day and week politics, he may learn what was once the tone of public life. It will enlarge his patriotism, elevate his notions of the public service, and call out some sense of veneration and loyalty towards the institutions of his country and the memory of her mighty dead; so that YOUNG AMERICA may, as there is some hope she may, bring back the elements which dignified the first eight years of our constitutional history.

As the afternoon rew to a close, and we were obliged to take our leave, regret from parting from our courteous entertainers, was lost in the grand and solemn impression made by all around us. Nothing was real. Every thing acted through the imagination. Each object was dim with associations, and seemed but the exponent of some thought or emotion, the shadow of something great and past. The whole was enchanted ground ; and the occupants seemed privileged persons, whom the guardian spirits of the place allowed to remain its tenants and keepers. When the young proprietor took leave of us at the piazza, he stood where Washington had stood to welcome and to part from the immortal men of France and America. He stood there his representative to a third generation. It may well be supposed that as we rode slowly home, our thoughts were in no ordinary course. We repassed the gate, the rivulet, and the open field, but still we were on enchanted ground. So impressed was I with this feeling, that had I met a procession of the great men of the past, riding slowly towards the mansion of their companion in arms and in the cabinet, it would have seemed only a natural consummation. It was not until we had reached the town, and our horses' hoofs struck upon the pavement, that the illusion was fairly broken.

The following was found inscribed on the back of a small portrait of Washington at Mount Vernon. It was written by some unknown visitor, supposed to have been an English traveller :

> WASHINGTON,
> The Defender of his Country.—The Founder of Liberty :
> The Friend of Man.
> History and Tradition are explored in vain,
> For a Parallel to his Character.
> In the Annals of Modern Greatness
> He stands alone ;
> And the noblest names of antiquity,
> Lose their Lustre in his Presence.
> Born the Benefactor of Mankind,
> He united all the qualities necessary
> To an illustrious career.
> Nature made him great,
> He made himself virtuous.
> Called by his country to the defence of her Liberties,
> He triumphantly vindicated the rights of humanity :
> And on the Pillars of National Independence
> Laid the foundations of a great republic.
> Twice invested with supreme magistracy,
> By the unanimous voice of a free people
> He surpassed in the Cabinet
> The Glories of the Field.
> And voluntarily resigning the Sceptre and the Sword,
> Retired to the shades of Private Life.
> A spectacle so new and so sublime
> Was contemplated with the profoundest admiration.
> And the name of WASHINGTON,
> Adding new lustre to humanity,
> Resounded to the remotest regions of the earth.
> Magnanimous in youth,
> Glorious through life,
> Great in Death.
> His highest ambition, the Happiness of Mankind ;
> His noblest Victory, the conquest of himself.
> Bequeathing to posterity the inheritance of his fame,
> And building his monument in the hearts of his countrymen.
> HE LIVED—The Ornament of the 18th Century.
> HE DIED—Regretted by a Mourning World.

Gunston Hall, which was the seat of the celebrated GEORGE MASON, stands on an elevated and commanding site overlooking the Potomac.

Mr. Jefferson said that he was " of the first order of wisdom, among those who acted on the theatre of the revolution, of expansive mind, profound judgment, cogent in argument, learned in the lore of our former constitution, and earnest for the republican change on democratic principles. His eloquence was neither flowing nor smooth ; but his language was strong, his manner most impressive, and strengthened by a dash of biting criticism when provocation made it seasonable." Mr. Mason was the framer of the constitution of Virginia, and a member of the convention which formed the federal constitution, but he did not sign that instrument. In conjunction with Patrick Henry,

WASHINGTON

he opposed its adoption in the Virginia convention, believing that it would tend to the conversion of the government into a monarchy. He also opposed the slave trade with great zeal. He died at his seat in the autumn of 1792, aged 67 years.

The annexed epitaph was copied from a tombstone on the banks of Neabsco Creek, in October, 1837. It is, without doubt, the *oldest* monumental inscription in the United States. From the earliness of the date, 1608, it is supposed that the deceased was a companion of Capt. John Smith on one of his exploratory voyages.

Here lies ye body of Lieut. William Herris, who died May ye 16th, 1608 : aged 065 years ; by birth a Britain, a good soldier ; a good husband and neighbor.

FAUQUIER.

FAUQUIER was created in 1759, from Prince William, and named from Francis Fauquier, Gov. of Va. from 1758 to 1767. Its greatest length is 45 miles, mean breadth 16. The surface is agreeably diversified, and the soil, when judiciously cultivated, susceptible of high improvement, and very productive. In the county exist valuable beds of magnesia and soapstone, and there are several gold mines worked by the farmers with tolerable profit, at intervals of leisure from their agricultural labors. Pop., whites 10,501, slaves 10,708, free colored 688 ; total, 21,891.

Warrenton, the county-seat, is 102 miles NNW. from Richmond. It is a beautiful village in the heart of the county, adorned with shade-trees, standing upon an eminence commanding a fine view of some of the spurs of the Blue Ridge. It contains about a dozen mercantile stores, 1 Episcopal, 1 Presbyterian, and 1 Methodist church, a fine male academy where ancient and modern languages are taught, a female academy in excellent repute, a newspaper printing office, the county buildings, among which is a handsome court-house, (shown in the annexed view,) and a population of about 1,400. An excellent macadamized road leads from here to Alexandria. Among the anecdotes we have gathered " by the way," the one herewith presented is, perhaps, worthy of insertion. Some thirty or more years since, at the close of a long summer's day, a stranger entered this village. He was alone and on foot, and his appearance was any thing but prepossessing. His garments, coarse and dust-covered, indicated an individual in the humbler walks. From a cane resting across his shoulders was suspended a handkerchief containing his clothing. Stopping in front of Turner's tavern, he took from his hat a paper and handed it to a gentleman standing on the steps : it read as follows—

The celebrated historian and naturalist, VOLNEY, needs no recommendation from
G. WASHINGTON

There are several other villages in Fauquier. Upperville, at the foot of the Blue Ridge, in the NW. angle of the county, is a new and flourishing village in a very rich agricultural country, on

the main road from Winchester to Alexandria. It contains 1 Met.,
1 Epis., and 1 Baptist church, and a population of about 500. Paris

Central View in Warrenton.

and Somerville contain each about 40, and New Baltimore 20
dwellings.

The Fauquier White Sulphur Springs are 6 miles sw. of Warrenton. The improvements are very extensive, and the grounds
beautifully adorned with shrubbery. These springs are very popular, and of easy access from the eastern cities.

JOHN MARSHALL, late
Chief Justice of the
United States, was born
at a locality called Ger-
mantown, in this coun-
ty, 9 miles below War-
renton. The house in
which he was born is not in existence. When he was quite young, the family moved to
Goose's Creek, under Manassa's Gap, near the Blue Ridge, and still later to Oak Hill,
where the family lived at the commencement of the revolution. His father, Thomas
Marshall, was a planter of limited means and education, but of strong natural powers,
which, cultivated by observation and reflection, gave him the reputation of extraordinary
ability. He served with distinction in the revolution, as a colonel in the continental
army. John was the eldest of fifteen children. The narrow fortune of Col. Marshall,
and the sparsely inhabited condition of Fauquier, compelled him to be almost exclusively the teacher of his children, and to his instructions the Chief-Justice said, "he
owed the solid foundation of all his success in life." He early implanted in his eldest
son a taste for English literature, especially for poetry and history. At the age of twelve,
John had *transcribed* the whole of Pope's Essay on Man, and some of his Moral Essays ; and had committed to memory many of the most interesting passages of that distinguished poet.

At the age of 14 he was placed with the Rev. Mr. Campbell, in Westmoreland, where,
for a year, he was instructed in Latin, and had for a fellow-student James Monroe. The
succeeding year was passed at his father's, where he continued the study under the Rev.
Mr. Thompson, a Scotch gentleman, which "was the whole of the classical tuition he
ever obtained. By the assistance of his father, however, and the persevering efforts of
his own mind, he continued to enlarge his knowledge, while he strengthened his body by
' hardy, athletic exercises in the open air. He engaged in field sports ; he indulged his

solitary meditations amidst the wildest scenery of nature; he delighted to brush away the earliest dews of the morning.' " To these early habits in a mountain region he owed a vigorous constitution. The simple manner of living among the people of those regions of that early day, doubtless contributed its share. He ever recurred with fondness to that primitive mode of life, when he partook with a keen relish balm tea and mush; and when the females used thorns for pins.

In the summer of 1775 he was appointed Lieut. in the " Minute Battalion," and had an honorable share in the battle of Great Bridge. In July, 1776, he was appointed 1st Lieut. in the 11th Virginia regiment, on the continental establishment, which marched to the north in the ensuing winter; and in May, 1777, he was promoted to a captaincy. He was in the skirmish at Iron Hill, and at the battles of Brandywine, Germantown, and Monmouth. He was one of that body of men, never surpassed in the history of the world, who, unpaid, unclothed, unfed, tracked the snows of Valley Forge with the blood of their footsteps in the rigorous winter of 1778, and yet turned not their faces from their country in resentment, or from their enemies in fear.

That part of the Virginia line which was not ordered to Charleston, (S. C.,) being in effect dissolved by the expiration of the term of enlistment of the soldiers, the officers (among whom was Captain Marshall) were, in the winter of 1779-80, directed to return home, in order to take charge of such men as the state legislature should raise for them. It was during this season of inaction that he availed himself of the opportunity of attending a course of law lectures given by Mr. Wythe, afterwards chancellor of the state; and a course of lectures on natural philosophy, given by Mr. Madison, president of William and Mary College in Virginia. He left this college in the summer vacation of 1780, and obtained a license to practise law. In October he returned to the army, and continued in service until the termination of Arnold's invasion. After this period, and before the invasion of Phillips, in February, 1781, there being a redundancy of officers in the Virginia line, he resigned his commission.

During the invasion of Virginia, the courts of law were not reopened until after the capitulation of Lord Cornwallis. Immediately after that event, Mr. Marshall commenced the practice of law, and soon rose into distinction at the bar.

In the spring of 1782, he was elected a member of the state legislature, and in the autumn of the same year, a member of the executive council. In January, 1783, he married Miss Ambler, the daughter of a gentleman who was then treasurer of the state, and to whom he had become attached before he left the army. This lady lived for nearly fifty years after her marriage, to partake and enjoy the distinguished honors of her husband. In 1784, he resigned his seat at the council-board in order to return to the bar; and he was immediately afterwards again elected a member of the legislature for the county of Fauquier, of which he was then only nominally an inhabitant, his actual residence being at Richmond. In 1787 he was elected a member from the county of Henrico; and though at that time earnestly engaged in the duties of his profession, he embarked largely in the political questions which then agitated the state, and indeed the whole confederacy.

Every person at all read in our domestic history must recollect the dangers and difficulties of those days. The termination of the revolutionary war left the country impoverished and exhausted by its expenditures, and the national finances at a low state of depression. The powers of Congress under the confederation, which even during the war were often prostrated by the neglect of a single state to enforce them, became in the ensuing peace utterly relaxed and inefficient.

Credit, private as well as public, was destroyed. Agriculture and commerce were crippled. The delicate relation of debtor and creditor became daily more and more embarrassed and embarrassing; and, as is usual upon such occasions, every sort of expedient was resorted to by popular leaders, as well as by men of desperate fortunes, to inflame the public mind, and to bring into odium those who labored to preserve the public faith, and to establish a more energetic government. The whole country was soon divided into two great parties, the one of which endeavored to put an end to the public evils by the establishment of a government over the Union, which should be adequate to all its exigencies, and act directly on the people; the other was devoted to state authority, jealous of all federal influence, and determined at every hazard to resist its increase.

It is almost unnecessary to say, that Mr. Marshall could not remain an idle or indifferent spectator to such scenes. As little doubt could there be of the part he would take in such a contest. He was at once arrayed on the side of Washington and Madison. In Virginia, as everywhere else, the principal topics of the day were paper money, the

collection of taxes, the preservation of public faith, and the administration of civil justice. The parties were nearly equally divided upon all these topics; and the contest
concerning them was continually renewed. In such a state of things, every victory
was but a temporary and questionable triumph, and every defeat still left enough of hope
to excite to new and strenuous exertions. The affairs, too, of the confederacy were
then at a crisis. The question of the continuance of the Union, or a separation of the
states, was freely discussed; and, what is almost startling now to repeat, either side of
it was maintained without reproach. Mr. Madison was at this time, and had been for
two or three years, a member of the House of Delegates, and was, in fact, the author of
the resolution for the general convention at Philadelphia to revise the confederation.
He was at all times the enlightened advocate of union, and of an efficient federal government, and he received on all occasions the steady support of Mr. Marshall. Many have
witnessed with no ordinary emotions, the pleasure with which both of these gentlemen
looked back upon their co-operation at that period, and the sentiments of profound respect with which they habitually regarded each other.

Both of them were members of the convention subsequently called in Virginia for the
ratification of the federal constitution. This instrument having come forth under the
auspices of General Washington and other distinguished patriots of the revolution, was
at first favorably received in Virginia, but it soon encountered decided hostility. Its
defence was uniformly and most powerfully maintained there by Mr. Marshall. He was
then not thirty years old. It was in these debates that Mr. Marshall's mind acquired
the skill in political discussion which afterwards distinguished him, and which would of
itself have made him conspicuous as a parliamentarian, had not that talent been overshadowed by his renown in a more soberly illustrious though less dazzling career. Here,
too, it was that he conceived that deep dread of disunion, and that profound conviction
of the necessity for closer bonds between the states, which gave the coloring to the whole
texture of his opinions upon federal politics in after-life.

The constitution being adopted, Mr. Marshall was prevailed upon to serve in the
legislature until 1792. From that time until 1795, he devoted himself exclusively to his
profession. In 1795, when Jay's Treaty was "the absorbing theme of bitter controversy," he was elected to the House of Delegates, and his speech in its defence, says
Judge Story, "has always been represented as one of the noblest efforts of his genius.
His vast powers of reasoning were displayed with the most gratifying success......
The fame of this admirable argument spread through the Union. Even with his political enemies it enhanced the estimate of his character; and it brought him at once to
the notice of some of the most eminent statesmen who then graced the councils of the
nation."

Soon after he, with Messrs. Pinkney and Gerry, were sent by President Adams as
envoys extraordinary to France. The Directory refused to negotiate, and though the
direct object of the embassy failed, much was effected by the official papers the envoys
addressed to Talleyrand, her minister of foreign relations, in showing France to be in
the wrong. These papers—models of skilful reasoning, clear illustration, accurate detail, and urbane and dignified moderation—have always been attributed to Marshall, and
bear internal marks of it. Such was the impression made by the dispatches, that on the
arrival of Mr. Marshall in New York, in June, 1798, his entry had the éclat of a triumph. A public dinner was given to him by both houses of congress, "as an evidence
of affection for his person, and of their grateful approbation of the patriotic firmness with
which he sustained the dignity of his country during his important mission;" and the
country at large responded with one voice to the sentiment pronounced at this celebration: "*Millions for defence, but not a cent for tribute.*"

Mr. Marshall was elected to Congress in 1799. He had been there not three weeks,
when it became his lot to announce the death of Washington. Never could such an
event have been told in language more impressive or more appropriate. "MR. SPEAKER,
—The melancholy event, which was yesterday announced with doubt, has been rendered
too certain. Our Washington is no more! The hero, the patriot, and the sage of America;
the man on whom in times of danger every eye was turned, and all hopes were placed,
lives now only in his own great actions, and in the hearts of an affectionate and afflicted
people," &c., &c.

That House of Representatives abounded in talent of the first order for debate; and
none were more conspicuous than John Marshall. Indeed, when the law or constitution were to be discussed, he was, confessedly, the first man in the house. When he
discussed them, he exhausted them; nothing more remained to be said; and the impression of his argument effaced that of every one else.

In 1800 he was appointed secretary of state, an office which he held but a few months. He was appointed chief-justice of the Supreme Court of the United States, January 31, 1801 ; " not only without his own solicitation, (for he had in fact recommended another to the office,) but by the prompt and spontaneous choice of President Adams, upon his own unassisted judgment. The nomination was unanimously confirmed by the Senate. How well he filled that office is known to his countrymen. We shall not attempt to protract our account of the last thirty-five years of Judge Marshall's life. It was spent in the diligent and upright, as well as able discharge of his official duties ; sometimes presiding in the Supreme Court at Washington, sometimes assisting to hold the circuit federal courts in Virginia and North Carolina. His residence was in Richmond, whence it was his frequent custom to walk out, a distance of three or four miles, to his farm. He had also a farm in his native county, Fauquier, which he annually visited, and where he always enjoyed a delightful intercourse with numerous relations and friends. Twice in these thirty-five years, he may be said to have mingled in political life ; but not in party politics. In 1828 he was a member of a convention, held in Charlottesville, to devise a system of internal improvement for the state, to be commended to the legislature. In 1829 he was a member of the convention to revise and amend the state constitution, where he delivered a speech regarded as an unrivalled specimen of lucid and conclusive reasoning.

"No man more highly relished social, and even convivial enjoyments. He was a member of a club which for forty-eight summers has met once a fortnight near Richmond, to pitch quoits and mingle in relaxing conversation ; and there was not one more delightedly punctual in his attendance at these meetings, or who contributed more to their pleasantness ; scarcely one who excelled him in the manly game, from which the ' Quoit Club' drew its designation. He would hurl his iron ring of two pounds weight, with rarely erring aim, fifty-five or sixty feet ; and at some *chef-d'œuvre* of skill in himself or his *partner*, would spring up and clap his hands with all the light-hearted enthusiasm of boyhood. Such is the old age which follows a temperate, an innocent, and a useful life."

Chief-Justice Marshall died at Philadelphia, July 6th, 1835, in his 80th year. " The love of simplicity and dislike of ostentation, which had marked his life, displayed itself also in his last days. Apprehensive that his remains might be encumbered with the vain pomp of a costly monument, and a laudatory epitaph, he, only two days before his death, directed the common grave of himself and his consort, to be indicated by a plain stone, with this simple and modest inscription :"

JOHN MARSHALL, son of THOMAS and MARY MARSHALL, was born on the 24th of September, 1755 ; intermarried with MARY WILLIS AMBLER the 3d of January, 1783 ; departed this life the —— day of ————, 18—.

This unostentatious inscription, with the blanks only filled, is carved on the plain white marble monument erected over his remains, in the grave-yard at Shoccoe Hill, Richmond.

The late Francis W. Gilmer, a young man of the finest promise, of whom it is said, " had he not prematurely been cut off by the hand of death, would have ranked with the foremost men of his age and country," thus described the intellectual character of Judge Marshall :—

His mind is not very richly stored with knowledge ; but it is so creative, so well organized by nature, or disciplined by early education, and constant habits of systematic thinking, that he embraces every subject with the clearness and facility of one prepared by previous study to comprehend and explain it. So perfect is his analysis, that he extracts the whole matter, the kernel of inquiry, unbroken, clean, and entire. In this process, such are the instinctive neatness and precision of his mind, that no superfluous thought, or even word, ever presents itself, and still he says every thing that seems appropriate to the subject. This perfect exemption from needless incumbrance of matter or ornament, is in some degree the effect of an aversion to the labor of thinking. So great a mind, perhaps, like large bodies in the physical world, is with difficulty set in motion. That this is the case with Mr. Marshall's, is manifest from his mode of entering on an argument, both in conversation and in public debate. It is difficult to rouse his faculties ; he begins with reluctance, hesitation, and vacancy of eye ; presently, his articulation becomes less broken, his eye more fixed, until, finally, his voice is full, clear, and rapid ; his manner bold, and his whole face lighted up, with the mingled fires of genius and passion ; and he pours forth the unbroken stream of eloquence, in a current deep, majestic, smooth, and strong. He reminds one of some great bird, which flounders and flounces on the earth for a while, before it acquires *impetus* to sustain its soaring flight.

The foregoing memoir of Marshall is abridged from an exceedingly interesting one in the Southern Literary Messenger for February, 1836, which is partly original and partly compiled from the eulogies on his life and character, by Horace Binney, Judge Story, and Edgar Snowden. We have, in addition, collected a few reminiscences and anecdotes from different gentlemen, of high respectability, which we presume to be authentic:

Marshall was noted for extreme plainness of person and address, and a child-like simplicity of character. His carelessness of his personal attire, in early life particularly, is well known, and on one occasion, (as stated in the Literary Messenger,) while travelling, occasioned his being refused admittance into a public house. On the occasion which we are now to relate, it caused him the loss of a generous fee. Marshall, when just rising on the professional ladder, was one morning strolling through the streets of Richmond, attired in a plain linen roundabout and shorts, with his hat under his arm, from which he was eating cherries, when he stopped in the porch of the Eagle hotel, indulged in some little pleasantry with the landlord, and then passed on. Mr. P., an elderly gentleman from the country, then present, who had a case coming on before the court of appeals, was referred by the landlord to Marshall, as the best advocate for him to employ ; but the careless, languid air of the young lawyer, had so prejudiced Mr. P. that he refused to engage him. On entering court, Mr. P. was a second time referred by the clerk of the court, and a second time he declined. At this moment entered Mr. V., a venerable-looking legal gentlemen, in a powdered wig and black coat, whose dignified appearance produced such an impression on Mr. P. that he at once engaged him. In the first case which came on, Marshall and Mr. V. each addressed the court. The vast inferiority of his advocate was so apparent, that at the close of the case, Mr. P. introduced himself to young Marshall, frankly stated the prejudice which had caused him, in opposition to advice, to employ Mr. V. ; that he extremely regretted his error, but knew not how to remedy it. He had come into the city with one hundred dollars, as his lawyer's fee, which he had paid, and had but five left, which, if Marshall chose, he would cheerfully give him, for assisting in the case. Marshall, pleased with the incident, accepted the offer, not, however, without passing a sly joke at the *omnipotence* of a powdered wig and black coat.

Marshall was accustomed to go to market, and frequently unattended. "Nothing was more usual than to see him returning at sunrise, with poultry in one hand and vegetables in the other." On one of these occasions, a would-be fashionable young man from the North, who had recently removed to Richmond, was swearing violently because he could hire no one to take home his turkey. Marshall stepped up, and ascertaining of him where he lived, replied, "That is my way, and I will take it for you." When arrived at his dwelling, the young man inquired, "What shall I pay you?" "Oh, nothing," was the rejoinder, "you are welcome ; it was on my way, and no trouble." "Who is that polite old gentleman who brought home my turkey for me ?" inquired the other of a by-stander, as Marshall stepped away. "That," replied he, "is John Marshall, Chief-Justice of the United States." The young man, astounded, exclaimed, "Why did he bring home my turkey?" "To give you a severe reprimand, and learn you to attend to your own business," was the answer.

The venerable Capt. Philip Slaughter, now (May, 1844) living in Culpeper, was a messmate of Marshall's in the revolution. He says Marshall was the best tempered man he ever knew. During their sufferings at Valley Forge, nothing discouraged, nothing disturbed him ; if he had only bread to eat it was just as well ; if only meat it made no difference. If any of the officers murmured at their deprivations, he would shame them by good-natured raillery, or encourage them by his own exuberance of spirits. He was an excellent companion, and idolized by the soldiers and his brother officers, whose gloomy hours were enlivened by his inexhaustible fund of anecdote.

For sterling honesty no man ever exceeded Marshall. He never would, knowingly, argue in defence of injustice, or take a legal advantage at the expense of moral honesty. A case of the latter is in point. He became an endorser on a bond amounting to several thousand dollars. The drawer failed, and Marshall paid it, although he knew it could be avoided, inasmuch as the holder had advanced the amount at more than legal interest.

He possessed a noble generosity. In passing through Culpeper, on his way to Fauquier, he fell in company with Mr. S., an old fellow-officer in the army of the revolution. In the course of conversation, Marshall learned that there was a lien upon the estate of his friend to the amount of $3000, about due, and he was greatly distressed at the prospect of impending ruin. On bidding farewell, Marshall privately left a check for the amount, which being presented to Mr. S. after his departure, he, impelled by a chivalrous independence, mounted, and spurred on his horse until he overtook his friend. He thanked him for his generosity, but refused to accept it. Marshall strenuously persisted in its acceptance, and the other as strongly persisted in not accepting. Finally it resulted in a compromise, by which Marshall took security on the lien, but never called for pay.

GEN. SIMON KENTON was born in this county, May 15th, 1755. His parentage was humble, and his education was entirely neglected. At the early age of 16, he became entangled in the snares of a young coquette, and soon had a severe battle with a rival by the name of Leitchman. Supposing he had killed him, he fled to Kentucky, and became one of the boldest pioneers of that then wilderness country, and one of the bravest that ever encountered the wiles of the Indians. His life was one of eventful incident. On being taken prisoner by them, on one occasion, he was eight times exposed to the gauntlet—three times tied to the stake to be burnt, and often thought himself on the eve of a terrible death. But Providence at last interposed in his favor, and he escaped. He was a spy in Dunmore's war. He acted in the same capacity under the gallant Col. George Rogers Clarke, in the revolution. He shared in Wayne's victory, and distinguished himself through the whole of the Indian wars of that day. He died in Ohio, in 1837, aged 82. His once gigantic form was broken by age; and his last days, it is said, were spent in poverty and neglect.

FAYETTE.

FAYETTE was formed in 1831, from Logan, Greenbrier, Nicholas, and Kanawha. Its greatest length is 47 miles; greatest width 30. New River, a main branch of the Great Kanawha, runs through the county its whole length. Much of the surface of the county is mountainous. The principal mountains are the Gauley, (a continuation of Cumberland mountain,) Big and Little Sewel. The great turnpike through the Kanawha valley passes over some of the most lofty of these mountains. "There are extensive bodies of good arable land, in some places partaking of the character of what along the Alleghany mountains is denominated *glades*, and in the west, prairies. The average price of unimproved, or wild lands of good quality, is one dollar per acre. We are satisfied that these lands, in point of natural fertility, and adaptation to the culture of grain, grasses, fruits, &c., is superior to the best counties east of the Blue Ridge." Pop., whites 3,773, slaves 133, free colored 18; total 3,924.

Fayetteville, the county-seat, is 289 miles westerly from Richmond, and contains a few dwellings. The turnpike leading from Charleston, on the south side of the Kanawha River, passes through the place, and terminates at the Red Sulphur Springs in Monroe county. Gauley Bridge is situated at the falls of the Great Kanawha, just below the junction of the Gauley and New Rivers, 36 miles above Charleston. There are here a store or two and several mills. The Kanawha at this spot is 500 yards wide, and has a fall of 22 feet over a ledge of rocks extending entirely across the stream. This is one of the wildest and most picturesque regions of the state. It is the last navigable point on the Kanawha, and presents one of the best sites for machinery in Virginia. A traveller who visited these falls, thus describes his impressions:

We reached the hotel at which we were to pause, about midnight. It is near to the Kanawha Falls; and from the beauty of the neighborhood has many visitors. I took a hasty cup of coffee, and weary as I was, went with another gentleman to see the Falls. We could hear them in the distance; but we had to go round in order to reach them. The chief of our way was over shattered rock, offering a good access by day, but requiring care at night, from the sharp pitches of some parts, and from the numerous circular holes bored in them by the eddies of the water. They are not to be spoken of with Niagara, or even with Shauffausen, but the whole scene was striking and interesting, the more so, undoubtedly, in the still hour of night. I seated myself on a shelf of rock whence the waters made their principal leap. Darkness had spread its curtain on the sleeping objects in the distance. The pale moon had run her race, and was just falling behind the hills; her last lights fell faintly on my face and the head of waters, but left the precipices and pools before me in heavy shadows. At my feet the river was dashing, and lifting up its voice from the depths beneath to Him who holds the waters in the hollow of his hand. It had done so for ages past; it would do so for ages to come. Here the poor Indian had stood, but will never stand again, thinking he heard in those waters the voice of Deity, and gazing on the face of that orb with wonder, till the spirit of worship was stirred within him. Here also I stood, and shall never stand again, wistfully looking through the visible and audible to the unseen but present object of adoration and praise.

On New River, along which passes the Kanawha turnpike, and within 10 m. of its junction with the Gauley, the traveller passes by the summit of a high cliff of rocks, long known as the *Hawk's Nest*, but more recently called *Marshall's Pillar*, in honor of the late venerable chief-justice, who, as one of the state commissioners in 1812, stood upon its fearful brink, and sounded its exact depth to the river margin, which is about 1000 ft. Standing upon the verge of this precipice, the river, diminished by distance in the deep valley below to a silvery thread between two borders of green, appears to wash the base of the cliff; yet it requires a powerful arm to cast a stone into its waters. The sublime and elevating emotions which this scene is calculated to inspire, are given in the following chaste and beautiful language of a foreign traveller:

We returned to the inn. I had an hour and a half of rest; and was found with my companions on the way, soon after 3 o'clock. Most of the company showed that they had only been awakened, like a child, to be put in a new position, and their heads were nodding about in all directions. About 7 o'clock, however, we approached a spot which is of great reputed beauty, and we pledged the coachman to stop, that we might have a fair sight of it. You leave the road by a little by-path, and after pursuing it for a short distance, the whole scene suddenly breaks upon you. But how shall I describe it? The great charm of the whole is greatly connected with the point of sight, which is the finest imaginable. You come suddenly to a spot which is called the Hawk's Nest. It projects on the scene, and is so small as to give standing *to only some half dozen persons.* It has on its head an old picturesque pine; and it breaks away at your feet abruptly and in perpendicular lines, to a depth of more than 1000 feet. On this standing, which, by its elevated and detached character, affects you like the Monument, the forest rises above and around you. Beneath and before you is spread a lovely valley. A peaceful river glides down it, reflecting, like a mirror, all the lights of heaven—washes the foot of the rocks on which you are standing—and then winds away into another valley at your right. The trees of the wood, in all their variety, stand out on the verdant bottoms, with their heads in the sun, and casting their shadows at their feet; but so diminished, as to look more like the pictures of the things than the things themselves. The green hills rise on either hand and all around, and give completeness and beauty to the scene; and beyond these appears the gray outline of the more distant mountains, bestowing grandeur to what was supremely beautiful. It is exquisite. It conveys to you the idea of perfect solitude. The hand of man, the foot of man, seem never to have touched that valley. To you, though placed in the midst of it, it seems altogether inaccessible. You long to stroll along the margin of those sweet waters, and repose under the shadows of those beautiful trees; but it looks impossible. It is solitude, but of a most soothing, not of an appalling character—where sorrow might learn to forget her griefs, and folly begin to be wise and happy.

MARSHALL'S PILLAR.

On Big Beaver Creek, in this county, are the remains of an ancient
fortification, which occupies an area of about 20 square rods. The
walls were built of stone, and, it is supposed, were 6 ft. high, and
at the base 7 ft. thick. The reader will find a plan, drawn by A.
Beckley, and a description by Isaac Craig, in the American Pioneer
for Sept. 1842.

FLOYD.

FLOYD was formed in 1831 from Montgomery, and was named
from John Floyd, governor of Virginia from 1829 to 1834. It is
35 m. long, with a mean width of 15 m. It is watered by Little
River, a branch of New River. The surface is mountainous, and
the soil generally more adapted to grazing than grain. Horses,
oxen, hogs, and sheep, are the principal staples. There were in 1840,
whites 4.123, slaves 321, free colored 9 ; total, 4,453. Jackson-
ville, or Floyd C. H., is a small village 215 m. sw. of Richmond.

The Buffalo Knob, in this county, is a very lofty eminence, from the top of which the
view is sublime. On the north, east, and west, the beholder is amazed at the boundless
succession of mountains rising beyond mountains—while far away to the south, the plain
seems to stretch to an interminable length. On the east, the knob is accessible on
horseback, being two miles in height from the beginning of the ascent to the highest
point ; on the west it breaks off precipitately, and presents the shape of the animal
whose name it bears. This mountain is seen 60 or 80 miles, towering above all others.
On the highest point is a space of about 30 acres, which is so elevated that not any trees
grow there ; and in the warmest days of summer, the visitor requires thick clothing to
protect him from the cold. The spot is covered with fine grass, strawberry-vines, and
gooseberry and currant-bushes. The fruit upon them is of superior flavor, but it does
not ripen until two or three months later than that upon the lowlands.

FLUVANNA.

FLUVANNA was formed in 1777, from Albemarle. It is 26 m.
long, and 16 wide. The Rivanna enters it from Albemarle, and
flowing SE. through the co., divides it nearly equally. The surface
is generally broken, excepting between the James and the Rivanna, where there is a large tract of barren level land. The soil on
the rivers is good, and that on the James extremely fertile. Gold
has been found and worked near Palmyra. Much tobacco is
raised in the county, and of a superior quality. Pop., whites 4,445,
slaves 4,146, free colored 221 ; total, 8,812.

Palmyra, the county-seat, lies on the Rivanna, 62 miles westerly
from Richmond. It contains about 20 dwellings. Columbia, on
the Rivanna, at its junction with the James, is a village somewhat
larger. At the Union Mills, on the Rivanna, in the NW. part of
the county, is an extensive cotton factory, situated in the midst of
beautiful mountain and river scenery.

At the confluence of the two branches of the James, in this county, is a point of land called the Point of Fork, where, in the latter part of the revolution, a state arsenal was established, and a large quantity of military stores collected. When the state was invaded by Cornwallis, Baron Steuben had charge of this post. When Tarleton was detached to Charlottesville, Lieut.-Col. Simcoe was sent to destroy the magazines at the Point of Fork, and he was ultimately to be joined by Tarleton, to assist his intended operations. The following details of this excursion are from Girardin:

With their accustomed eagerness and activity, the two indefatigable and dreaded partisans entered upon the execution of their respective tasks. This double movement rendered Steuben's situation unusually perilous. The extreme difficulty of obtaining prompt and correct information respecting the British and their schemes—the severe precautions which Simcoe took for securing every person met or seen on his route, effectually concealed his march from the baron. The latter, however, became apprized of Tarleton's rapid advance. Imagining himself the immediate object of it, he lost no time in transporting his stores to the south side of the Fluvanna, intending himself speedily to follow, with the whole division under his command. When Simcoe reached the Point of Fork the American stores had been removed, and Steuben's detachment had crossed the river, except about 30 men, then awaiting the return of the boats to embark and join their friends. These men unavoidably fell into the hands of the British cavalry. The river was deep and unfordable, and all the boats had been secured on the south side of it: Simcoe's main object was, therefore, frustrated. Under the mortification arising from this disappointment, a singular stratagem occurred to his wily mind. It was to impress the baron with the belief that the troops now at the Point of Fork were the advance of the British army, ready to overwhelm him ; and thus to work upon his fears so far as to induce him to sacrifice most of the stores which had been transported over the Fluvanna. For this purpose he encamped on the heights opposite to Steuben's new station, advantageously displaying his force, and by the number of his fires suggesting a probability of the main body, headed by Cornwallis, having actually reached the neighborhood. The baron, who had been informed that the corps under Tarleton threatened his left, now fancied himself in imminent danger. Retreating precipitately during the night, he marched near 30 miles from the Point of Fork, abandoning to the enemy such stores as could not be removed. In the morning, Simcoe observing the success of his stratagem, and wishing to give it still further effect, procured some small canoes, and sent across the river Capt. Stephenson, with a detachment of light infantry, and Cornet Wolsey with four hussars. The former was directed to destroy the stores and arms which the baron had left behind in the hurry and confusion of his premature retreat ; and the latter, to mount his hussars, who had carried their saddles over with them, on such straggling horses as he was likely to find, to patrol some miles on the route taken by Steuben—in short, to exhibit every appearance of eager and formidable pursuit. Both these orders were successfully executed. Stephenson performed, without delay or annoyance, the task of destruction assigned to him ; and Wolsey so confirmed the belief of Steuben that the whole British army was close in his rear, that he accelerated his march, retiring still further from the river. His object was to resume his original destination, and join Gen. Greene ; but he received fresh orders not to leave the state, so long as Cornwallis should continue there. On the militia under Lawson, a similar injunction was laid. British historians have greatly exaggerated the loss sustained by the Americans at the Point of Fork. Of their thrasonic accounts, undoubted evidence is in the hands of the author of this narrative.

FRANKLIN.

FRANKLIN was formed in 1784, from Bedford and Henry: its length is 30, with a mean breadth of 20 miles. The Roanoke runs on its south boundary, and the county is intersected by numerous small creeks. The surface is rolling, and the Blue Ridge forms its western boundary. The soil is on a clay foundation, and is well adapted to farming. The county produces very large crops of tobacco, Indian corn, oats, wheat, and some cotton. The tanning business is extensively carried on. Population in 1830, 14,911; 1840, 15,832. Rocky Mount, the county-seat, lies 179 miles sw. of Richmond: it derives its name from an abrupt precipice in the vicinity. The town contains about 30 dwellings, and near it is an extensive iron furnace. Union Hall is a smaller post-village, at the intersection of the road from Pittsylvania C. H. to Rocky Mount. Iron ore, some of which is of a superior quality, is found in various parts of the county.

FREDERICK.

FREDERICK was formed in 1738, from Orange: it is 25 miles long, with a mean width of 18 miles. The soil is highly productive, and its surface diversified. Opequan, Sleepy, and Back Creeks rise in this county, and flow into the Potomac. A rail-road extends from Winchester to the Baltimore and Ohio Rail-Road at Harper's Ferry. Population, whites 11,119, slaves 2,302, free colored 821; total, 14,242.

Newtown, or Stephensburg, is a neat and thriving village, 8 miles south of Winchester, on the macadamized road to Staunton. There are about 100 dwellings, 2 churches, a market-house, about a dozen shops for the manufacture of wagons, (for which the place is noted,) together with other mechanical and mercantile establishments, and a population of about 800. Stephensburg was established by law in 1758, and named after Peter Stephens, its founder, who came to Virginia with Joist Hite in 1732. It was settled almost exclusively by Germans, whose descendants long preserved the customs and language of their ancestors. Middletown lies 5 miles s. of Stephensburg, on the same road. It contains 1 Methodist and 1 Episcopal church, and about 60 dwellings. Gainsboro', Brucetown, and Whitehall, are small places, the first of which contains 2 churches, and about 30 dwellings. *Jordan's White Sulphur Springs*, 6 miles n. of Winchester, have lately come into notice, and are growing in popular favor. The waters are said to resemble the celebrated White Sulphur Springs of Greenbrier.

Winchester, the county-seat, is 74 miles from Washington city, 146 from Richmond, and 30 from Harper's Ferry. Next to Wheeling. it is the largest town west of the Blue Ridge. It is in the beautiful and fertile valley of Virginia, and is surrounded by a rich and abundant country. The town is well and substantially built, the streets cross each other at right angles, and are generally paved, and the houses are mostly of brick or stone. As a whole, it is very compact, and has a business, city-like aspect. The public buildings are a court-house, jail, market-house, masonic hall,

and a lyceum. There are 2 newspaper printing offices, an academy, 2 banks—the Farmers' Branch Bank and the Bank of the

Loudon-street, Winchester

Valley—a Savings Institution, about 50 stores of different kinds,
and a variety of mechanical and manufacturing establishments,
12 churches—2 Presbyterian, 1 Episcopal,* 2 Baptist, 2 Methodist,
2 Lutheran, 1 German Reformed, 1 Friends, and 1 Catholic—and
a population in 1840 of 3,454. A rail-road connects Winchester
with Harper's Ferry.

"Tradition informs us that the ground on the edge of the present site of Winchester,
was occupied by a large and powerful tribe of Indians, called the Shawnees, or Shawanees, and some springs at that point are called the *Shawnee Springs* at this day. The
earliest accounts of the settlement of Winchester state that there were two houses on its
present location as early as 1738, situated near the town run; but its establishment as a
town commenced in Feb., 1752, in the 25th year of the reign of George II., when the
General Assembly passed an 'act for the establishment of the town of Winchester.'
In 1758 it was enlarged in consideration of an additional quantity of land being laid off
in lots by Col. James Wood, now called in the plot of the town, Wood's addition. Trustees were then appointed, consisting of Lord Fairfax, Col. Martin, and others ; vide
Henning's Statutes at Large, vol. 7, p. 135. Additions to the town were also made by
Lord Fairfax. Col. Wood is therefore entitled to the honor of being the founder. Win-
chester is mentioned by General Washington as being one of the points in his route, in
his celebrated mission, by order of Governor Dinwiddie, to the French authorities on the
Ohio. He came from Alexandria to Winchester, where he procured baggage horses, &c.
This was in November, 1753.

* The first Episcopal Church, in the Valley of Virginia, was erected in Winchester.
The following relating to it is from Hawks' History of the Protestant Episcopal Church
in Virginia, published in 1836. "Morgan Morgan was a native of Wales, whence he
emigrated in early life to the province of Pennsylvania. In the year 1726, he removed
to what is now the county of Berkeley, in Virginia, and built the first cabin which was
reared on the south side of the Potomac, between the Blue Ridge and the North Mountain. He was a man of exemplary piety, devoted to the Church ; and in the year 1740,
associated with Dr. John Briscoe and Mr. Hite, he erected the first Episcopal Church
in the valley of Virginia. This memorial of his zeal, it is believed, is still standing,
and now forms that part of the parish of Winchester which is known as 'Mill Creek
Church.'"

"In the French and Indian warfare that succeeded, Washington fixed his head-quarters at Winchester, which was then a frontier settlement, the North mountain, a few miles west of Winchester, being the boundary. From the fear occasioned by the attacks of the French and Indians, this place was almost the only settlement west of the Blue Ridge, which range of mountains was, as late as 1756, the northwestern fron-tier. At that period, public stores, to a large amount, were deposited at Winchester for the frontier settlement. After the distinguished action at Great Meadows, July 4, 1754, Washington returned with his regiment to Winchester to recruit; soon after which, he was joined by a few companies from Maryland and North Carolina; after which rein-forcement they were ordered, by the lieutenant-governor, to march immediately over the Alleghany to drive the French from Fort Duquesne, or build one in its vicinity. After the disastrous defeat of Braddock, Washington, with the remains of the brave Virginia troops, retreated to Westchester. Upon the invasion of the frontiers by the French and Indians, Washington, then on his way to Williamsburg, the seat of government, was overtaken by an express, below Fredericksburg, with the intelligence that the French and Indians had broken in upon the frontier settlements, and were murdering and cap-turing women and children, burning houses, destroying crops, &c., and that the troops stationed among them were insufficient for their protection. He immediately hastened back to Winchester, where the utmost confusion and alarm prevailed. His attempts to raise the militia were unsuccessful. He sent urgent orders to the county lieutenants, east of the Blue Ridge, to hasten their militia to Winchester; but before these orders could be executed, the enemy, which had done so much injury, and caused so much alarm, had recrossed the Alleghany mountain. Col. Washington, after repeated inef-fectual efforts to arouse the government to act on the offensive, and adopt a more efficient system of warfare, by sending a force sufficient to destroy Fort Duquesne, at length prevailed, and Gen. Forbes was ordered to undertake the campaign for its reduction. On the 24th of May, 1758, orders were issued to Washington's regiment to rendezvous at Winchester, and be in readiness to march in 15 days. June 24, the Virginia troops, in pursuance to the orders they had received, moved in detachments from Winchester to Fort Cumberland, where they assembled early in July. Upon the reduction of Fort Du-quesne—when its name was changed to Pitt, in honor of the then British Minister—Col. Washington, after furnishing 200 men from his regiment to garrison the fort, marched the rest back to Winchester, whence he soon proceeded to Williamsburg to take his seat in the House of Delegates, of which he had been elected a member by the *county of Frederick*, while at Fort Cumberland. During these contests a fort was built at Win-chester, the remains of which are still visible at the north end of the principal street. In Henning's Statutes, vol. 7, page 33, we find the 16th clause of a law passed March, 1756, which refers to this fort, and the appropriation for its erection, in these words: 'And whereas, it is now judged necessary that a fort should be immediately erected in the town of Winchester, county of Frederick, for the protection of the adjacent inhab-itants against the barbarities daily committed by the French and their Indian allies; be it therefore enacted, that the governor, or commander-in-chief of the colony for the time being, is hereby empowered and desired to order a fort to be built with all possible dis-patch, in the aforesaid town of Winchester; and that his honor give such orders and instructions for the immediate effecting and garrisoning the same, as he shall think necessary for the purpose aforesaid.' The act also appropriates the sum of £1000 for carrying the above provision into effect. This fort was called Fort Loudon, in honor of the British general, Lord Loudon, who had been appointed to the command of the British troops in America."

The annexed sketch is a representation of the remains of Fort Loudon, engraved from a drawing in the possession of the "Virginia Historical and Philosophical Society." "It appears to have been a field-work, or redoubt, having four bastions, whose flanks and faces were each 25 feet, with curtains 96 feet." The dotted lines represent the present course of Loudon street. It is stated in the History of the Valley, upon authority entitled to the highest respect, the gentleman furnishing the information referred to having been informed by Washington's officers, that Washington marked out the site of this fort and superintended its erection; that he bought a lot in Winchester, had a blacksmith shop erected on it, and brought from Mount Vernon his own blacksmith to make the necessary iron-work for the fort. The very spot is pointed out where Washington's own residence was situated. It is stated that his chamber was above the gateway of the fort, in a situation commanding a view of the principal street of the town. This fort covered an area of half an acre, and there is still much of its embankments and mounds remaining. There is also a well, from which water now rises to the surface, sunk through the solid rock 103 feet. The labor of throwing up this fort, and sinking this well, was said to have been performed by Washington's regiment. The fort contained a strong garrison ; and it is stated, by one of the oldest inhabitants of Winchester, to have mounted six 18 pounders, six 12 pounders, six 6 pounders, 4 swivels, and 2 howitzers ; and to this day grape-shot and cannon-balls are found there. These cannon were removed from Winchester early in the war of the revolution. This fort was said to have been once reconnoitred by a French officer, but never was attacked by the enemy.

There were a large number of Hessian and German prisoners confined at Winchester in the war of the revolution. In 1780, barracks were erected for them 4 miles west of the town. In 1781, their numbers had increased to 1600.

Major Peter Helphistine, of Winchester, was a native of Germany, and a patriot of the American revolution. He was a major in the 8th Virginia regiment, commanded by Col. Muhlenberg. This corps was composed of young men of German extraction, and frequently called the German regiment. In a campaign at the south, he contracted a disease from exposure, returned, and died in Winchester, and now lies buried in the Lutheran grave-yard.

Gen. Daniel Roberdeau, an officer of the revolution, also lies buried in one of the grave-yards in Winchester. His monument states his death as having taken place Jan. 5, 1795, at the age of 68 years. He was from the Isle of France, and a Huguenot. His descendants are scattered over Virginia. He first settled in Pennsylvania, where he built a fort at Wyoming, at his own expense, which was destroyed by the Indians. He was a follower of Whitefield, and a modest and estimable man.

Lord Fairfax was buried under the old Episcopal church, which was on the public square. The land on which it stood was given by him to the society, for the construction of the church. This structure, which was of stone, was taken down about 12 or 14 years since. The bones of Fairfax were removed, and placed under the new Episcopal church. In this house there is a monumental slab to his memory. At the time of his disinterment, a large mass of silver was found, which was the mounting to his coffin. There is now in Winchester an old building used as a stable, which was once a tavern, in which it is said Fairfax occasionally held levees. His permanent residence was at Greenway Court, 13 miles se. of Winchester. (See p. 235.)

The following incident, in the life of Chief-Justice Marshall, is stated to have taken place at McGuire's hotel in Winchester, which stood on the site of the one shown on the right of the foregoing view in Loudon-street. It was a plain, unpainted building, and was destroyed many years since. The account given below was originally published in the Winchester Republican :

It is not long since a gentleman was travelling in one of the counties of Virginia, and about the close of the day stopped at a public house to obtain refreshment, and spend the night. He had been there but a short time, before an old man alighted from his gig, with the apparent intention of becoming his fellow-guest at the same house. As the old man drove up, he observed that both the shafts of his gig were broken, and that they were held together by withes formed from the bark of a hickory sapling. Our traveller observed further, that he was plainly clad, that his knee-buckles were loosened, and that something like negligence pervaded his dress. Conceiving him to be one of the honest yeomanry of our land, the courtesies of strangers passed between them, and they entered the tavern. It was about the same time that an addition of three or four young gentlemen was made to their number—most, if not all of them, of the legal profession. As soon as they became conveniently accommodated, the conversation was turned by the latter upon an eloquent harangue which had that day been displayed at the bar. It was replied by the other, that he had witnessed, the same day, a degree of eloquence no doubt equal, but that it was from the pulpit. Something like a sarcastic rejoinder was made to the eloquence of the pulpit ; and a warm and able altercation ensued, in which the merits of the Christian religion became the subject of discussion. From six o'clock until eleven, the young champions wielded the sword of argument, adducing with ingenuity and ability, every thing that could be said pro and con. During this protracted period, the old gentleman listened with all the meekness and modesty of a child; as if he was adding new information to the stores of his own mind; or perhaps he was observing, with philosophic eye, the faculties of the youthful mind, and how new energies are evolved by repeated action; or, perhaps, with patriotic emotion, he was reflecting upon the future destinies of his country, and on the rising generation upon whom these future destinies must devolve; or, most probably, with a sentiment of moral and religious feeling, he was collecting an argument which—characteristic of himself—no art would be "able to elude, and no force resist." Our traveller remained a spectator, and took no part in what was said.

At last one of the young men, remarking that it was impossible to combat with long and established prejudices, wheeled around, and with some familiarity exclaimed, "Well, my old gentleman, what think you of these things?" If, said the traveller, a streak of vivid lightning had at that moment crossed the room, their amazement could not have been greater than it was with what followed. The most eloquent and unanswerable appeal was made for nearly an hour, by the old gentleman, that he ever heard or read. So perfect was his recollection, that every argument urged against the Christian religion was met in the order in which it was advanced. Hume's sophistry on the subject of miracles was, if possible, more perfectly answered than it had already been done by Campbell. And in the whole lecture there was so much simplicity and energy, pathos and sublimity, that not another word was uttered. An attempt to describe it, said the traveller, would be an attempt to paint the sunbeams. It was now a matter of curiosity and inquiry who the old gentleman was. The traveller concluded it was the preacher from whom the pulpit eloquence was heard—but no—it was the CHIEF JUSTICE OF THE UNITED STATES.

———

In the Presbyterian grave-yard, at Winchester, is the grave of Gen. Daniel Morgan. His monument is a horizontal slab, raised a few feet above the ground. It bears the following inscription:

> Major-General DANIEL MORGAN
> departed this life
> On July the 6th, 1802,
> In the 67th year of his Age.
> Patriotism and valor were the
> prominent Features of his character,
> And
> the honorable services he rendered
> to his country
> during the Revolutionary war,
> crowned him with Glory, and will
> remain in the Hearts of his
> Countrymen
> a Perpetual Monument
> to his
> Memory.

The military history of the brave commander of the celebrated rifle corps of the revolution,—whom to confront was almost instant death —is generally well known. At the end of the war, Gen. Morgan retired to his estate, named Saratoga, a few miles from Winchester.

Dan'l Morgan [signature] After the expedition against the insurgents in the Whiskey insurrection, he was selected from this district to Congress, where he served two sessions. In 1800 he removed to Winchester, where, after a confinement of two years from extreme debility, he expired. The house where he resided and died, was the frame building now (1844) occupied by the Rev. Mr. Boyd, in the NW. part of the town. His widow moved to Pittsburg. His two daughters married officers of the revolution.

A writer in a recent number of the Winchester Republican has, in an article descriptive of the Winchester grave-yards, some interesting facts respecting Gen. Morgan, which we here annex:

This "thunderbolt of war," this "brave Morgan, who never knew fear," was, in camp, often wicked and very profane, but never a disbeliever in religion. He testified that himself. In his latter years General Morgan professed religion, and united himself with the Presbyterian church in this place, under the pastoral care of the Rev. Mr. (now Dr.) Hill, who preached in this house some forty years, and may now be occasionally heard on Loudon street. His last days were passed in this town; and while sinking to the grave, he related to his minister the experience of his soul. "People thought," said he, "that Daniel Morgan never prayed;"—"People said old Morgan never was afraid;" —"People did not know." He then proceeded to relate in his blunt manner, among many other things, that the night they stormed Quebec, while waiting in the darkness and storm with his men paraded, for the word *to advance*, he felt unhappy; the enterprise appeared more than perilous; it seemed to him that nothing less than a miracle could bring them off safe from an encounter at such an amazing disadvantage. He stepped aside and kneeled by the side of a munition of war—and then most fervently prayed that the Lord God Almighty would be his shield and defence, for nothing less than an almighty arm could protect him. He continued on his knees till the word passed along the line. He fully believed that his safety during that night of peril was from the interposition of God. Again, he said, about the battle of the Cowpens, which covered him with so much glory as a leader and a soldier—he had felt afraid to fight Tarleton with his numerous army flushed with success—and that he retreated as long as he could—till his men complained—and he could go no further. Drawing up his army in three lines, on the hill side; contemplating the scene—in the distance the glitter of the advancing enemy—he trembled for the fate of the day. Going to the woods in the rear, he kneeled in an old tree-top, and poured out a prayer to God for his army, and for himself, and for his country. With relieved spirits he returned to the lines, and in his rough manner cheered them for the fight; as he passed along, they answered him bravely. The terrible carnage that followed the deadly aim of his lines decided the victory. In a few moments Tarleton fled. "Ah," said he, "people said old Morgan never feared;"—"they thought old Morgan never prayed, they did not know;"—"old Morgan was often miserably afraid." And if he had not been, in the circumstances of amazing responsibility in which he was placed, how could he have been brave?

The last of his riflemen are gone: the brave and hardy gallants of this valley, that waded to Canada and stormed Quebec, are all gone—gone, too, are Morgan's sharpshooters of Saratoga. For a long time two, that shared his captivity in Canada, were seen in this village, wasting away to shadows of their youth, celebrating with enthusiasm the night of their battle, as the year rolled round—Peter Lauck and John Schultz. But they have answered the roll-call of death, and have joined their leader; the hardy Lauck wondering that Schultz, the feeblest of the band, whom he had so often carried through the snows of Canada, should outlive him. There is interest round the last of such a corps.

GILES.

GILES was formed in 1806, from Monroe and Tazewell, and named from Wm. B. Giles, Gov. of Va. from 1826 to 1829; it is 50 miles

long, with a mean width of 14 miles. The surface is very mountainous ; several lofty ridges of the Alleghany chain pass through
the county, and much of the scenery is wild. In the mountain
valleys, and the low grounds of the streams, the land is very fertile. The New River, one of the main branches of the Kanawha,
passes through and fertilizes a large tract in the county. Pop.,
whites 4,684, slaves 574, free colored 49 ; total, 5,307.

Parisburg, or Giles C. H., lies 238 miles southwesterly from
Richmond, three-fourths of a mile from the bank of New River,
just above where it passes through Peter's mountain. The situation of the town is picturesque, being at the extremity of a mountain called " Angel's Rest." It was laid off in 1806, and contains
at present about 30 dwellings, mostly built of stone. Nine miles
from Parisburg, on New River, are situated the *Hygeian Springs*,
the waters of which are highly spoken of.

On the opposite bank of New River, both above and below
the springs, the rocks present the most majestic appearance : there
being several *natural pillars* that rise perpendicularly to the height
of from thirty to two hundred feet, and natural arches ; one pillar
is denominated " Pompey's Pillar," near which is " Cæsar's Arch ;"
the pillar and arch nearly join.

The celebrated *Salt Pond* is five miles from these springs—sometimes known as the
White Sulphur Springs of Giles—and ten miles E. of Parisburg. It is a natural and
beautiful lake of pure *fresh* water, on the summit of the Salt Pond mountain, one of
the highest spurs of the Alleghany. This pond is about a mile long and one-third of a
mile wide. At its termination it is dammed by a huge pile of rocks, over which it runs :
but which once passed through the fissures only. In the spring and summer of 1804,
immense quantities of leaves and other rubbish washed in and filled up the fissures, since
which it has risen full 25 feet. Previous to that time it was fed by a fine large spring
at its head ; that then disappeared, and several small springs now flow into it at its upper end. When first known, it was the resort of vast numbers of elk, buffalo, deer, and
other wild animals, for drink ; hence its name of " salt pond." It has no taste of salt,
and is inhabited by fine trout.

The above description of the Salt Pond is from the mss. for the
2d edition of Kercheval's History of the Valley of Virginia. From
the same source we derive the annexed particulars of an Indian
incursion into this region, and of the captivity of Mrs. Hall :

In the year 1774 the Indians commenced their outrages in the vicinity of Sinking
Creek, on the New River, in Giles county. In July of this year John Lybrook, (now
living, 1836,) with several other children, while at play near the stream were discovered
by four Indians. One ahead of his party pursued young Lybrook, who escaped by jumping a gully twelve feet wide. The rest of the children sprang into a canoe and were
followed by the Indians, who killed and scalped five of them. A sister of Lybrook, a
girl of thirteen, jumped out of the canoe and ran, pursued by one of the Indians. Her
life was saved by a remarkably fierce dog, who, attracted by her screams, jumped upon
the savage and threw him down, hung and jerked violently upon him while the girl got
out of danger. The Indian struck at him with his war club, and finally knocked him
down ; the dog then ran to the canoe and guarded the dead children until the people took
them away for burial. The animal refused to follow them—immediately ran off, and
soon raised a most piteous howl. This attracted some of the party to the spot, who
found a little brother of Mr. Lybrook, aged about 6 years, with his scull severely fractured and his brains oozing out, and scalped. He lived about 24 hours and then expired.

Mrs. Margaret Hall, now living, when about 10 years old was taken prisoner by the
Indians on New River and conveyed to their towns, with whom she remained 18 years,

until after Wayne's victory. The Shawnese, by whom she was taken, transferred her to the Delaware tribe, where she was adopted into the family of an Indian chief. The Indians were somewhat civilized. In this respect the Shawnese were superior to the Delawares. The Indians had a few cattle, and made butter, fritters, and pancakes. Shortly before Mrs. Hall returned home an Indian chief fell violently in love with her, and urged his suit, and upon her refusal to marry him threatened to kill her. Her foster-mother used her persuasions in his favor, and the young squaws presented their congratulations upon the offer. Annoyed by his solicitations she fled early one morning, on horseback, to a village about 70 miles distant, where her foster-sister and brother had removed. She arrived about sunset, and found her foster-brother absent. There she was pursued by the young warrior, who told her she must immediately consent to marry him or he would take her life. She refused, and he made a lunge at her with a long knife; at which her foster-sister threw herself between them and received a slight wound in the side, the point of the knife striking a rib. The Indian girl instantly seized the knife by the blade, wrenched it from him, broke it, and threw it away. A fight ensued, while the subject of it sat petrified with fear. Her sister bade her run and hide, as he would probably kill them both. The girl proved the conqueror, gave him a severe drubbing, and drove him from the field. Her foster-brother, on returning home from a hunting excursion, told her not to be uneasy, called him a dog, and threatened to kill him if he made any further attempts. The fellow never annoyed her again, and was subsequently killed at Wayne's victory. Mrs. Hall is now living in Giles county, about 4 miles from the Troy Sulphur Springs.

The following account of "*the Lucas family*," was written by a gentleman of Christiansburg, and published in the Richmond Compiler in the summer of 1842. It shows in this family a depth of depravity rarely equalled:

The scene of the lives and depredations of this notorious family is in Giles county, on Doe Creek, a small branch of New River which heads in the celebrated salt pond mountain, and from its obscurity and loneliness, and the character of its inhabitants, has always been avoided by civilized man.

The father of Lucas is now about 93 years of age, and is, no doubt, a hoary-headed old villain, although he has, during a long life, been adroit enough to commit no crime of which the law could take cognizance. I will give one trait in the character of this old sinner, which will suffice to show what kind of man he is. On the recent trial of his son "*Dave*," when his life was in jeopardy, this old man, on being asked what was the character of his son David, responded that he believed "Dave would kill any man for twenty-five cents."

The first in this family of blood—perhaps unparalleled in civil society—was the first son of "*Old Ran*," as he is universally called. (His name, perhaps, is Randolph; but I presume he has never seen or heard of the baptismal fount.) Well, this first-born of "Old Ran," named "Jerry," as long ago as the late war, became criminally connected with a man's wife, who was in the service of his country as a military man at Norfolk. In a week after the man returned home. "Jerry Lucas," at the earnest solicitation of the fiendish woman, under pretence of friendship, invited him home from muster with him. He was afterwards found murdered, behind a log, with about two hundred weight of stone upon his body. Lucas confessed that the evening they left the muster-ground he beat his victim over the head with a club until he supposed he was dead, and went to his house and stayed all night with his wife. To make assurance doubly sure, he returned in the morning to see if the man was dead. He found him sitting, leaning against a tree, and covered with gore. The poor fellow begged for his life, told Lucas to take his wife, and he would leave the country as soon as he was able, and would never say any thing about what he had done to him. The savage Lucas was inexorable, murdered, and concealed him. For this murder he was hung at Giles Court House, in the fall of 1814. Old Ran, his father, sat under the gallows when he was hanging, and amused himself by eating gingerbread. Jerry's paramour escaped punishment for want of testimony.

"Dave," the second son of "Old Ran," the most notorious of these villains, commenced his career of crime about 1820, at the age of 19, by stealing a horse, for which he was sentenced to the penitentiary for five years, during which time he escaped, in company with another convict, to his home, was retaken, and served out his time.

Not long after his return home, he robbed a small pedler of all his wares, for which he was again sentenced to the penitentiary for three years. At the time of his last conviction, a cousin of Dave's, a lad of sixteen or seventeen years of age, was convicted of some crime and also sent to the penitentiary for three years. They were discharged at the same time, and left the penitentiary together. The boy has never been heard of since; and Lucas, in some of his drunken frolics, boasted that as they came on home, he killed the boy and threw his body into the river. He told the boy's father, that when he ran his knife into him, he bawled like a calf. So it seems he murdered the boy for the wretched pittance given him on leaving the penitentiary to defray his expenses home.

On the night Dave returned last from the penitentiary, a large stack-yard, and a barn full of grain, were burnt in his neighborhood, belonging to witnesses on behalf of the commonwealth in his several convictions, which he subsequently admitted were set on fire by him. Dave's next exploit was at a militia-muster, in September, 1841. In a quarrel and fight with his sister's son, he killed him with a blow. He was acquitted, on trial, owing to some extenuating circumstances. Since his recent confinement, he has admitted he ought to have been punished for this murder, as he had, at the time he struck the blow, a pound of lead concealed in his hand.

The next crime of which Dave is accused, is founded on the following strong circumstances: Some years ago, a man who had been on north with a drove of cattle, merely as a driver, was returning home through Dave's neighborhood, on foot. Shortly after he passed, Lucas was seen to follow him with a rifle, and in a few minutes a report of a gun was heard in that direction. Dave returned with blood on his clothes, and there was seen, on the same day, a large quantity of blood in the road. But, as the drover was an entire stranger, no investigation was had. Very recently a man's dog, in the vicinity, came to his master with a human skull in his mouth.

Dave's last crime, and for which the world has been freed from the monster, was the murder of John Poff, a poor laborer, who had been working at the Kanawha salt-works a few months, and who, with the proceeds of his labor in his wallet, was travelling alone, and on foot, to his family and home in Floyd county. Dave fell in with him late in the day, and invited him to go home with him, saying he could entertain him as well as any one. Poor Poff consented, and soon met his fate.

Dave killed him within 200 yards of his residence, and so obscure is the place, that he lay nearly a week above ground without discovery; and what was certainly a strange infatuation, apparently no pains or care was taken to conceal the foul deed. He was tried, and found guilty by the jury in 15 minutes from their retirement from the court-room. There were 17 witnesses on the part of the commonwealth. The criminal had no witness, and refused to employ counsel. The court assigned him counsel, but his case was so plain and flagrant that the counsel submitted it to the jury without argument. He was sentenced, and hung, at Giles Court-House, Friday, June 24th, 1842. The wretched man died as he had lived, without any outward signs of compunction. He made no particular confession when under the gallows; on the contrary, swore when in this awful situation, in answer to something said by one of the attending clergy; and finally, while the sheriff was adjusting the rope around his neck, attempted to bite his ear. He met death with such a demoniac grin, that among the many thousands present not one tear of sorrow or sympathetic feeling was manifested.

The next on the list of this family of criminals is John Lucas, " Old Ran's" third son. He also has killed his man, and his full cousin too; for it seems they are like old Cain, their hands appear to be raised against their own kin. John and his cousin engaged in a fight, caused by the cousin tauntingly saying, " Your brother Dave is in the penitentiary," which so enraged John that he struck him a blow with his heavy rifle, with so much force as to cleave his skull to the very teeth, breaking stock and barrel off in the middle, and causing instant death. Dave being, in part, cause of this quarrel and its disastrous consequences to John, perhaps accounts for the recklessness of his behavior on hearing of Dave's final fate, and may have been strong in his mind when he made the observation, " that it would have been to the credit of the family if Dave had been hung many years ago."

John was tried for his life; but as the murder occurred, on the part of the murdered man, under aggravating circumstances, John was sent to the penitentiary. He is a very good *fac simile* of the Lucas family. They are truly a savage-looking race. There are yet two brothers, younger than those already mentioned, who have not yet rendered themselves so conspicuous in the annals of crime. What their fate will be time only can tell. They promise fair to be genuine chips of the old block, and although young, are already the terror of the neighborhood. " Old Ran" has also daughters, for these

Ill weeds are very prolific ; but they are worse than the sons—save the mark—and there-by hangs a tale. But it is a tale not meet to be told among Christians, and we pass it over.

GLOUCESTER.

GLOUCESTER was formed in 1642, from York. It lies on Chesa-peake Bay, and on the N. side of York River. Much barley was formerly raised in the county ; but, from some unknown cause, the lands have ceased to be adapted for its cultivation. Indian corn is the principal product. Pop., whites 4,412, slaves 5,791, free colored 612 ; total 10,715.

Gloucester, the county-seat, lies immediately opposite Yorktown, on the N. side of York River. It is a small, decayed village, con-taining only a few dwellings. During the siege of York, it was one of the outposts of Cornwallis, and the scene of some minor military operations. There exist remains of redoubts thrown up at that time. The earliest settlers in the co. were from Gloucester-shire in England—who not only transferred the names of places, but the streams also ; hence they have here their Severn, and other rivers, and local denominations.

Rosewell, the seat of John Page, Esq., governor of Va. in 1802, is on the York, nearly opposite the mouth of Queen's creek. It is perhaps the noblest old mansion in the state, and is a most venera-ble relic of antiquity. It is a cube of 90 feet, is four stories high, and its appearance strikingly massive. The roof is flat, and lead-ed. "It has been said that Mr. Jefferson and Gov. Page, in the summer evenings, sometimes enjoyed conversation and the moon-light scene there. From the top of Rosewell house, the view stretches nearly ten miles up and down the river York, which is there about three miles wide—a superb and lovely sheet of water, as bright, as pure, and as sparkling blue as the waters of the ocean. Before the house spreads a fair lawn—around the house are a few trees : this enhances its simple grandeur, standing, as it were, in the dignified solitude of some antique castle." Gov. Page was distinguished for his talents and patriotism, and fulfilled his numerous trusts, as governor of the state, representative in Con-gress, &c., with honor. He died at Richmond, Oct. 11th, 1808, in the 65th year of his age.

Gloucester has connected with its early history some most inter-esting facts. Nathaniel Bacon, the leader of what has been de-nominated " *Bacon's Rebellion*," died and was buried in this county. The spot is not known, inasmuch as, in the language of a writer (T. M.) of that day, his body "was so made away as his bones were never found, to be exposed on a gibbet as was purposed—stones being laid on his coffin—supposed to be done by Laurence."

In a late number of the Southern Literary Messenger, Charles

Campbell, Esq., of Petersburg, has an article conclusively proving that it was in this county that Pocahontas rescued Capt. Smith. Beneath is an extract from his communication touching this point:

Next to Jamestown, Werowocomoco is perhaps the spot most celebrated in the early chronicles of Virginia. As Jamestown was the seat of the English settlers, so Werowocomoco was the residence of the great Indian chief, Powhatan. It was the scene of many interviews and rencontres between the settlers and the savages. It was at Werowocomoco that supplies for the colony were frequently obtained; here that Smith once saw suspended on a line between two trees, the scalps of 24 Payanketanks, recently slain; here that Powhatan was crowned by Newport; and here that occurred the most touching scene in the whole colonial drama—the rescue of Smith by Pocahontas. Werowocomoco is on the York River, in the county of Gloucester. It may surprise some readers to hear, that the rescue of Smith took place on the York, since, in the general neglect of our early history, it seems to have been taken for granted by many that it took place on James River. Smith and Stith, in their histories, put the matter beyond dispute. Smith, Book II., p. 117, describes the Pamaunkee [now York] River, as follows:

"Fourteen myles northward from the river Powhatan is the river Pamaunkee, which is navigable 60 or 70 myles, but with catches and small barkes 30 or 40 myles farther. At the ordinary flowing of the salt water, it divideth itselfe into two gallant branches. On the south side inhabit the people of Youghtanund, who have about 60 men for warres. On the north branch Mattapanient, who have 30 men. Where this river is divided, the country is called Pamaunkee, [now West Point,] and nourisheth neare 300 able men. *About 25 myles lower, on the north side of this river, is Werowocomoco, where their great king inhabited when I was delivered him prisoner.*"

Again, Book II., p. 142, Smith says:

"At Werowocomoco, on the north side of the river Pamaunkee, [York,] was his [Powhatan's] residence when I was delivered him prisoner, some 14 myles from James Towne where, for the most part, he was resident."

Stith, as quoted by Burk's History of Virginia, Vol. I., p. 111, describes its position as follows:

"Werowocomoco lay on the north side of York river, in Gloncester county, nearly opposite to the mouth of Queen's creek, and about 25 miles below the fork of the river."

Upon a short visit made to that part of Gloucester county a year or two ago, I was satisfied that Shelly, the seat of Mrs. Mann Page, is the famous Werowocomoco. Shelly is on the north bank of the York River, in the county of Gloucester, said to be about 25 miles from West Point at the head of the river, and is nearly opposite the mouth of Queen's creek, lying somewhat above. It is true the word "nearly" is indefinite, and it might be supposed that Werowocomoco, perhaps, lay a little below the point opposite the mouth of Queen's creek instead of a little above. But the marshy, oozy character of the bank of the York below Shelly, rendering it apparently uninhabitable, seems to forbid the supposition. Werowocomoco, then, it may be taken for granted, was either at Shelly, or at some point above Shelly. But as Shelly *is* nearly opposite the mouth of Queen's creek, it is obvious that the further you proceed up the river, the less appropriate will become the expression "nearly opposite."

Carter's creek, emptying into the York at Shelly, forms a safe harbor for canoes. Smith, in a passage already quoted, mentions that Werowocomoco is 14 miles from Jamestown. In Book III., p. 194, he says, that "he went over land to Werowocomoco some 12 miles; there he passed the river of Pamaunkee in a salvage canow." Now, as it was 14 miles from Jamestown to Werowocomoco, and 12 to the point on the south bank of the York where Smith embarked in a canoe, it follows that Werowocomoco was only two miles from that point; and Shelly, I take it, is just about two miles from where it is probable Smith went into the canoe on that occasion.

Shelly adjoins Rosewell, (formerly the seat of John Page, Esq., sometime governor of Virginia,) and was originally part of the Rosewell plantation; and I learned from Mrs. Page, of Shelly, that Gov. Page always held Shelly to be the ancient Werowocomoco, and accordingly he, at first, gave it that name, but afterwards, on account of the inconvenient length of the word, dropped it, and adopted the title of Shelly, on account of the extraordinary accumulation of shells found there. The enormous beds of oyster-shells deposited there, particularly just in front of the Shelly-house, indicate it to have been a place of great resort among the natives. The situation is highly picturesque and beautiful; and looking, as it does, on the lovely and majestic York, it would seem, of all others, to have been the befitting residence of the lordly Powhatan.

Charles Mynn Thruston, who was born in this county in 1738, was a descendant of the old English cavaliers; and his ancestors were among the first settlers of Gloucester. Mr. Thruston was educated at William and Mary. When 20 years of age, he acted as a lieutenant of provincials, in the campaign which resulted in the evacuation of Fort Duquesne. He afterwards studied for the ministry, and was chosen rector of a parish in his native county. In 1769 he removed to Frederick county, where he continued in the practice of his profession until the commencement of hostilities with the mother country. He had been among the most prominent in repelling the attempt to introduce the Stamp Act in Virginia, and he now embarked in the common cause with an unconquerable zeal. He exerted himself to procure arms and ammunition, and addressed the people at public gatherings by the most spirit-stirring and eloquent harangues. Not content with this, parson Thruston threw aside the gown, and seizing the sword, raised a volunteer company, composed of the *élite* of the young men of the county; and he being chosen captain, they marched to join Washington in New Jersey. He made a bold and vigorous attack on a strong Hessian picket near Amboy. In this action his arm was shattered by a musket-ball, and he was carried, fainting with the loss of blood, from the field. He was afterwards promoted to the rank of colonel; but as the regiment to which he was appointed could not be raised, he became a supernumerary, and was obliged to retire from the service. He never resumed his pastoral functions. He held various public offices, among which was that of presiding judge of the court of Frederick county, and member of the legislature. In 1809, the wants of a numerous family occasioned him to remove to the west, where he died in 1812, aged 73. The battle of New Orleans was fought upon the place of his burial. The ruthless invader perished upon the tomb of the soldier-parson, who had employed tongue, pen, and sword in the cause of American freedom, and perilled fortune and life under the star-spangled banner. The venerable Judge Thruston, of Washington, over whose head the snows of 80 winters have passed, and left an intellect unscathed and vigorous, is a son of the warrior-parson of Gloucester.

GOOCHLAND.

Goochland was formed in 1727, from Henrico, and named from a colonial governor of Virginia. It lies on the north side of James River, and is 30 miles long, with an average width of 10 miles. The surface is undulating, and in some places broken; the soil is various, and much of it exhausted, though naturally good; that on the James is of great fertility. It is drained by several small streams, several of which afford water-power.

The county produces large crops of tobacco, corn, and oats. Bituminous coal of an excellent quality is extensively mined, and also small quantities of gold. Pop., whites 3,570, slaves 5,500, free colored 690; total 9,760.

There are no villages in the county of any note. The Court-House, which is 30 miles west of Richmond, and 1 mile N. of James River, contains a few dwellings only.

Gen. Nathaniel Massie, one of the early pioneers of Kentucky, and a man of indefatigable energy, was a native of this county. He was at the head of a band of adventurous spirits who formed, in 1791, the earliest settlement in the Virginia military district, and the fourth in Ohio, at what is now the town of Manchester.

The late Gov. James Pleasants, who died in this county in 1836, was a man highly valued both in public and private life.

GRAYSON.

Grayson was formed in 1793, from Wythe, and named after a distinguished member of the Virginia convention that ratified the federal constitution. This is a wild and thinly-settled mountainous tract, lying on the North Carolina line, at the southeastern corner of western Virginia. It is drained by the New River and its branches. Its limits were reduced in 1842 by the formation of Carrol county. Pop. in 1840, whites 8,542, slaves 492, free colored 53; total, 9,087.

Grayson C. H. lies 261 miles sw. of Richmond, and contains a few dwellings only.

GREENBRIER.

Greenbrier was formed in 1777, from Botetourt and Montgomery, and named from its principal stream. Its mean length is 46 miles, mean breadth 32½, and area 1409 square miles. The surface is broken, and part of it mountainous. The mountains are infested with reptiles, such as the rattlesnake, copperhead, blacksnake, &c.; there are some deer, wild turkeys, pheasants, wolves, wild-cats, panthers, bears, and a variety of small game. The horses raised in this region are distinguished for durability. The land on Greenbrier River, which runs centrally through the county, is very fertile; the mean elevation of the farms above the ocean is at least 1,500 feet. There was manufactured in this county in 1840, 114,932 pounds of maple sugar. Pop., whites 7,287, slaves 1,214, free colored 194; total, 8,695.

Frankfort, 10 miles ne. of Lewisburg, contains a Methodist church and about 50 dwellings. In March, 1669, Col. John Stuart, Robert McClenachan, Thomas Renick, and Wm. Hamilton, settled here. They, as well as all those that immediately followed, were from Augusta county. This was the first permanent settlement in the county.

Lewisburg, the seat of justice for the county, lies on the James River and Kanawha turnpike; 214 miles west of Richmond, 263 from Washington; about 150 from Guyandotte, on the Ohio River, 9 miles w. of the White Sulphur, and 13 from the Blue Sulphur Springs. This town was established by law in October, 1782, and the act appointed the following gentlemen trustees, viz.: Samuel Lewis, James Reid, Samuel Brown, Andrew Donnelly, John Stuart, Archer Mathews, Wm. Ward, and Thomas Edgar. It contains 6 mercantile stores, 1 newspaper printing office, 1 Baptist, 1 Presbyterian, and 1 Methodist church, 1 academy, and a population of about 800. It is a flourishing village, the most important in this whole region, and the place where the western branch of the court of appeals hold their sittings.

Lewisburg stands on the site of the old Savannah Fort, and is the place where the army of Gen. Lewis rendezvoused in 1774, previous to the battle of Point Pleasant. They constructed the first road ever made from here to Point Pleasant on the Ohio, distant about 160 miles. The old fort at this place stood about 100 yards SE. of the site of the present court-house, on land now (1843) belonging to Mr. Thomas B. Reynold, and the widow of Mr. Wm. Mathews. It was erected about the year 1770.

The first church—a Presbyterian—erected at Lewisburg, was about the year 1795. It is a stone edifice, and is now occupied by that denomination. Previously, the same society had a log church, about a mile and a half NW. of the village, near the present residence of Mr. Chas. Rogers. Their first clergyman was the Rev John M'Cue. There were then some Baptists in the county; their clergyman was the Rev. John Alderson. Lewisburg derived its name from the Lewis family. In olden time it was called "the Savannah," being a kind of a prairie.

The following details respecting the early settlement of the county, the difficulties with the Indians, &c., are from Stuart's "Memoir of the Indian Wars and other Occurrences:"

About the year 1749, a person, who was a citizen of the county of Frederick, and subject to paroxysms of lunacy, when influenced by such fits, usually made excursions into the wilderness, and in his rambles westwardly, fell in on the waters of Greenbrier River. At that time, the country on the western waters was but little known to the English inhabitants of the then colonies of America, being claimed by the French, who had commenced settlements on the Ohio and its waters, west of the Alleghany mountains. The lunatic being surprised to find waters running a different course from any he had before known, returned with the intelligence of his discovery, which did abound with game. This soon excited the enterprise of others. Two men from New England, of the name of Jacob Marlin and Stephen Sewell, took up a residence upon Greenbrier River; but soon disagreeing in sentiment, a quarrel occasioned their separation, and Sewell, for the sake of peace, quit their cabin, and made his abode in a large hollow tree. In this situation they were found by the late General Andrew Lewis, in the year 1751. Mr. Lewis was appointed agent for a company of grantees, who obtained from the governor and council of Virginia, an order for one hundred thousand acres of land lying on the waters of Greenbrier River; and did, this year, proceed to make surveys to complete the quantity of said granted lands; and finding Marlin and Sewell living in the neighborhood of each other, inquired what could induce them to live separate in a wilderness so distant from the habitations of any other human beings. They informed him that difference of opinion had occasioned their separation, and that they had since enjoyed more tranquillity and a better understanding; for Sewell said, that each morning when they arose and Marlin came out of the great house and he from his hollow tree, they saluted each other, saying, Good-morning, Mr. Marlin, and Good-morning, Mr. Sewell, so that a good understanding then existed between them; but it did not last long, for Sewell removed about forty miles further west, to a creek that still bears his name. There the Indians found him and killed him.

Previous to the year 1755, Mr. Lewis had completed for the grantees, under the order of council, upwards of fifty thousand acres;—and the war then commencing between England and France, nothing further was done in the business until the year 1761, when his majesty issued his proclamation commanding all his subjects within the bounds of the colony of Virginia, who were living, or who had made settlements on the western waters, to remove from them, as the lands were claimed by the Indians, and good policy required that a peaceable understanding should be preserved with them, to prevent hostilities on their part. The order of council was never afterwards carried into effect, or his majesty's consent obtained to confirm it.

At the commencement of the revolution, when the state of Virginia began to assume independence, and held a convention in 1776, some efforts were made to have the order of council established under the new order of things then beginning to take place. But it was not confirmed; and commissioners were appointed, in 1777, to grant certificates to each individual who had made settlements on the western waters, in the state of

Virginia, previous to the year 1768 and since, with preference according to the time of improvements; which certificates gave the holder a right to four hundred acres for his settlement claim, and the pre-emption of one thousand more, if so much were found clear of prior claims, and the holder chose to accept it. The following year, 1778, Greenbrier was separated from Botetourt county, and the county took its name from the river, which was so named by old Colonel John Lewis, father to the late General, and one of the grantees under the order of council, who, in company with his son Andrew, exploring the country in 1751, entangled himself in a bunch of green briers on the river, and declared he would ever after call the river Greenbrier River.

After peace was confirmed between England and France, in the year 1761, the Indians commenced hostilities, in 1763, when all the inhabitants in Greenbrier were totally cut off by a party of Indians, headed by the Cornstalk warrior. The chief settlements were on Muddy creek. These Indians, in number about sixty, introduced themselves into the people's houses under the mask of friendship, and every civility was offered them by the people, providing them victuals and accommodations for their entertainment, when, on a sudden, they killed the men, and made prisoners of the women and children. From thence they passed over into the Levels, where some families were collected at the house of Archibald Clendenin, (where the Hon. Balard Smith now lives.) There were between fifty and one hundred persons, men, women, and children. There the Indians were entertained, as at Muddy creek, in the most hospitable manner. Clendenin having just arrived from a hunt, with three fat elks, they were plentifully feasted. In the mean time, an old woman, with a sore leg, was showing her distress to an Indian, and inquiring if he could administer to her relief; he said he thought he could; and drawing his tomahawk, instantly killed her and all the men almost, that were in the house. Conrad Yolkom only escaped, by being some distance from the house, when the outcries of the women and children alarmed him. He fled to Jackson's River and alarmed the people, who were unwilling to believe him, until the approach of the Indians convinced them. All fled before them; and they pursued on to Carr's creek, in Rockbridge county, where many families were killed and taken by them. At Clendenin's a scene of much cruelty was performed; and a negro woman, who was endeavoring to escape, killed her own child, who was pursuing her crying, lest she might be discovered by its cries. Mrs. Clendenin did not fail to abuse the Indians with terms of reproach, calling them cowards, &c., although the tomahawk was drawn over her head, with threats of instant death, and the scalp of her husband lashed about her jaws. The prisoners were all taken over to Muddy creek, and a party of Indians retained them there till the return of the others from Carr's creek, when the whole were taken off together. On the day they started from the foot of Keeney's Knob, going over the mountain, Mrs. Clendenin gave her infant child to a prisoner woman to carry, as the prisoners were in the centre of the line, with the Indians in front and rear, and she escaped into a thicket, and concealed herself until they all passed by. The cries of the child soon made the Indians inquire for the mother, who was missing; and one of them said he would soon bring the cow to her calf. Taking the child by the heels he beat its brains out against a tree, and throwing it down in the path, all marched over it, till its guts were all trampled out with the horses. She told me she returned that night, in the dark, to her own house, a distance of more than ten miles, and covered her husband's corpse with rails, which lay in the yard, where he was killed in endeavoring to escape over the fence, with one of his children in his arms; and then she went into a corn-field, where great fear came upon her, and she imagined she saw a man standing by her, within a few steps. The Indians continued the war till 1764, and with much depredation on the frontier inhabitants, making incursions as far as within a few miles of Staunton.

An end was put to the war in the fall of that year by the treaty which Col. Boquet held with the Indians, near Muskingum. In the spring of 1774, another Indian war—known as Dunmore's war —broke out. In the fall of that year, a portion of the army under Gen. Lewis, destined to act against the Indians, assembled at Camp Union, (now Lewisburg,) and from thence marched on through the wilderness to the mouth of the Great Kanawha, where they met and defeated the Indians under their famous leader, the brave and generous Cornstalk. For an account of this action, the battle of Point Pleasant, see Mason county.

In 1778, an attack was made by about 200 Indians, upon Donnally's Fort. This fort stood about 100 yards E. of the present residence of Mr. Anthony Rader, on Rader's run, 10 miles N. of Lewisburg. It was a double log-house, with a chimney in the centre, and was surrounded by a stockade of split logs. The house was destroyed about the year 1825, at which time many bullets were found in the timbers. Dick Pointer, the old negro who acted so gallantly in its defence, died only a few years since. The state had purchased his freedom in reward for his services. He was buried with the honors of war. The account of the attack on Donnally's Fort is here given from the memoir of Mr. Stuart:

Intelligence having been conveyed to Col. Donnally of the approach of the Indians, he lost no time to collect in all his nearest neighbors that night, and sent a servant to my house to inform me. Before day about twenty men, including Hammond and Prior, were collected at Donnally's, and they had the advantage of a stockade fort around and adjoining the house. There was a number of women and children, making in all about sixty persons in the house. On the next day they kept a good look-out, in momentary expectation of the enemy.

Colonel Samuel Lewis was at my house when Donnally's servant came with the intelligence; and we lost no time in alarming the people, and to collect as many men for defence as we could get at Camp Union all the next day. But all were busy; some flying with their families to the inward settlements, and others securing their property, so that in the course of the day, we had not collected near one hundred men. On the following day we sent out two scouts to Donnally's, very early in the morning, who soon returned with intelligence that the fort was attacked. The scouts had got within one mile, and heard the guns firing briskly. We determined to give all the aid we could to the besieged, and every man who was willing to go was paraded. They amounted to sixty-eight in all, including Colonel Lewis, Captain Arbuckle, and myself. We drew near Donnally's house about two o'clock, P. M., but heard no firing. For the sake of expedition we had left the road for a nearer way, which led to the back side of the house, and thus escaped falling into an ambuscade, placed on the road some distance from the house, which might have been fatal to us, being greatly inferior to the enemy in numbers. We soon discovered Indians, behind trees in a rye-field, looking earnestly at the house. Charles Gatliff and I fired upon them, when we saw others running in the rye, near where they stood. We all ran directly to the fort. The people, on hearing the guns on the back side of the house, supposed that it was another party of Indians, and all were at the port-holes ready to fire upon us; but some discovering that we were their friends, opened the gate, and we all got in safe. One man only was shot through his clothes.

When we got into the fort, we found that there were only four men killed. Two of them who were coming to the fort, fell into the midst of the Indians, and were killed. A servant of Donnally's was killed early in the morning on the first attack; and one man was killed in a bastion in the fort. The Indians had commenced their attack about daylight in the morning, when the people were all in bed, except Philip Hammond and an old negro. The house formed one part of the fort, and was double, the kitchen making one end of the house, and there Hammond and the negro were. A hogshead of water was placed against the door. The enemy had laid down their guns at a ota ble, about fifty yards from the house, and made their attacks with tomahawks and war-clubs. Hammond and the negro held the door till they were splitting it with their tomahawks : they suddenly let the door open, and Hammond killed the Indian on the threshold, who was splitting the door. The negro had a musket charged with swan-shot, and was jumping about in the floor asking Hammond where he should shoot ? Hammond bade him fire away among them; for the yard was crowded as thick as they could stand. Dick fired away, and I believe, with good effect; for a war-club lay in the yard with a swan-shot in it. Dick is now upwards of eighty years old, has long been abandoned by his master, as also his wife, as aged as himself, and they have made out to support their miserable existence, many years past, by their own endeavors. This is the negro, to whom our Assembly, at its last session, refused to grant a small pension to support the short remainder of his wretched days, which must soon end, although his humble petition was supported by certificates of the most respectable men in the county, of his meritorious service on this occasion, which saved the lives of many citizens then in the house.

The firing of Hammond and Dick awakened the people in the other end of the house, and up stairs, where the chief of the men were lying. They soon fired out of the windows on the Indians so briskly, that when we got to the fort, seventeen of them lay dead in the yard, one of whom was a boy about fifteen or sixteen years old. His body was so torn by the bullets that a man might have run his arm through him, yet he lived almost all day, and made a most lamentable cry. The Indians called to him to go into the house.

After dark, a fellow drew near to the fort and called out in English that he wanted to make peace. We invited him in to consult on the terms, but he declined our civility. They departed that night, after dragging eight of their slain out of the yard; but we never afterwards found where they buried them. They visited Greenbrier but twice afterwards, and then in very small parties, one of which killed a man and his wife, of the name of Munday, and wounded Capt. Samuel McClung. The last person killed was Thomas Griffith; his son was taken, but going down the Kenawha, they were pursued, one of the Indians was killed, and the boy was relieved, which ended our wars in Greenbrier with the Indians, in the year 1780.

The WHITE SULPHUR SPRING of Greenbrier, the most celebrated of all the watering-places of Virginia, is 9 miles easterly from Lewisburg, about 170 from the Ohio River at Point Pleasant, 242 sw. of Washington City, and 205 w. of Richmond. It is thus described by a late visitor:

The White Sulphur Spring is situated some 6 or 8 miles from the height of the Alleghany, on the western declivity, in an extensive valley beautifully embosomed with hills and mountains. It was known to the Indians as one of the most important licks of the deer and the elk. As early as 1772, a woman was brought here on a litter 40 miles, whose disease had baffled all medical skill. A tree was felled, and a trough dug and filled with the mineral water, which was heated by putting hot stones into it. In this the patient was bathed, while, at the same time, she drank freely of the fountain. In a few weeks she went from her bark cabin perfectly restored. The fame of this cure attracted many sick persons to the spring, and they soon commenced throwing up rude log cabins. But the dreariness of the mountains, the badness of the roads, and the poverty of the accommodations, repelled all but the desperate from these health-giving waters till 1818, when they fell into the hands of Mr. Calwell, the present enterprising owner. From that time the place has continued rapidly to improve. Mr. Calwell's estate includes from ten to twelve thousand acres, much of which is fine interval soil. All the buildings, for one or two miles around the spring, belong to him. Nature has done every thing to make this an enchanting spot. The valley opens about half a mile in breadth, winding in length from east to west, with graceful undulations, beyond the eye's reach. The fountain issues from the foot of a gentle slope, terminating in the low interval upon a small and beautiful river. The ground ascends from the spring eastward, rising to a considerable eminence on the left, and spreading east and south into a wide and beautiful lawn. The lawn and walks cover perhaps fifty acres. A few rods from the spring, at the right, are the hotel, the dining-hall, the ball-room: all the rest of the ground is occupied mainly with cabins. These are rows of contiguous buildings, one story high, mostly of wood, some of brick, and a few of hewed logs white-washed. The framed cabins are all painted white. Directly to the right of the spring, and very near it, is Spring row; further eastward, with a continuous piazza shaded with vines, is Virginia row; at right-angles with this, crossing the lawn in the middle, is South Carolina row; heading the eastern extremity of the lawn is Bachelor's row; on the north side of the lawn, beginning nearest the spring, are Alabama, Louisiana, Paradise, and Baltimore rows—the last of which is the most elegant in the place. Without the enclosure, southward from the fountain, is Broadway; and a little west from this, on the Guyandot road, is Wolf row. The appearance of these cabins, painted, decorated, looking forth from the green foliage, and tastefully arranged, is beautiful and imposing.

I have an analysis of the spring by Professor Rogers, the distinguished state geologist, but am not permitted to communicate the proportions, as he wishes to reserve that fraction of interest for his forthcoming work. The solid matter procured by evaporation from 100 cubic inches, weighs 63.54 grains, composed of sulphate of lime, sulphate of

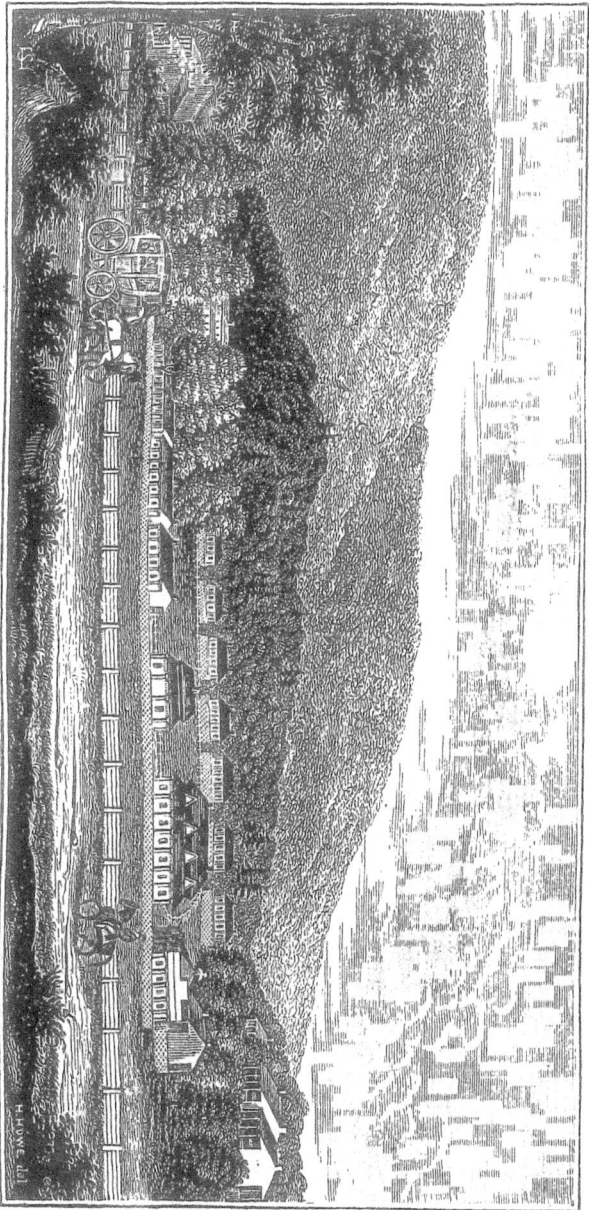

VIEW AT THE WHITE SULPHUR SPRINGS OF GREENBRIER.

The above view, taken near Mastin's hotel, shows only a portion of the erections at this, one of the most popular watering places in the Southern States. Virginia Row is shown in front, Baltimore Row beyond, and Greenbrier Mountain in the distance.

magnesia, sulphate of soda, carbonate of lime, carbonate of magnesia, chloride of magnesium, chloride of sodium, chloride of calcium, peroxide of iron, phosphate of lime, sulphate and hydrate of sodium, organic matter, precipitated sulphur, iodine. The gaseous matter consists of sulphurated hydrogen, carbonic acid, nitrogen, and oxygen. It is obvious, from this analysis, that the water must exert a very positive agency upon the system. Its remedial virtues extend chiefly to diseases of the liver, kidneys, alimentary canal, and to scrofula, rheumatism, and neuralgia.

The fountain is covered with a stately Doric dome, sustained by twelve large pillars, and surmounted with a colossal statue of Hygeia, looking towards the rising sun.

The *Blue Sulphur Spring*, in this county, is also quite popular. The improvements are extensive, and the location one of much natural beauty. The water tastes like that of the White Sulphur. Subjoined is the analysis:

ANALYSIS.—*Solid ingredients in the Blue Sulphur Water.*—Sulphate of lime; sulphate of magnesia; sulphate of soda; carbonate of lime; carbonate of magnesia; chloride of magnesium; chloride of sodium; chloride of calcium; hydro-sulphate of sodium and magnesium; oxide of iron, existing as proto-sulphate; iodine, sulphur, organic matters. *Gaseous ingredients.*—Sulphurated hydrogen; carbonic acid; oxygen; nitrogen.

The spring is a very bold one, furnishing fifteen gallons of water to a minute; there is a great deal of red, white, and black, and other deposites from the water.

GREENE.

GREENE was formed in 1838, from the western part of Orange, and named after Gen. Nathaniel Greene, of the revolution. It is 15 miles long, and 10 wide. The Blue Ridge runs on its western line. It is watered by branches of the Rivanna and the Rapid Ann. Its surface is mountainous and broken, and the soil in the valleys fertile. The principal products are tobacco, Indian corn, and wheat. A small quantity of cotton is produced. Population in 1840, whites 2,447, slaves 1,740, free colored 45; total, 4,232.

Stanardsville, the county-seat, is in the western part, 95 miles northwesterly from Richmond, and 18 miles w. of Orange C. H. The village is pleasantly situated, and contains about 35 dwellings.

GREENSVILLE.

GREENSVILLE was formed in 1784, from Brunswick. It is 28 miles long, with a variable breadth of from 8 to 24 miles. The Nottoway River runs on its N. boundary, and the Meherrin through it centrally. On the first-named stream anciently dwelt the Nottoway Indians; on the last, the Meherrins and Tuteloes, "who were connected with the Indians of Carolina, probably with the Chowanocs." Large quantities of cotton are raised in this county. Population in 1840, whites 1,928, slaves 4,102, free colored 136; total 6,366.

Hicksford, the county-seat, lies 62 miles south of Richmond, on

the line of the great southern rail-road, which here crosses the Meherrin by a bridge 300 feet long, supported by stone piers. Besides
the public buildings, it contains from 12 to 20 dwellings, and several stores and hotels.

In the march of Cornwallis into Virginia, after the battle of Guilford Court-House, a
company of militia under a Captain Robinson were made prisoners on the Meherrin,
below Hicksford, without firing a shot, by a body of cavalry under Lieut.-Col: Simcoe,
who had been detached from Petersburg by Arnold, to gain information of Cornwallis.
The whole party, the captors and captured, repaired to an adjacent tavern, where, in a
conference among the British officers, it was announced to the prisoners that they were to
be paroled. " Pray, gentlemen," demanded one of them, in great consternation, " what
kind of *a death is* that ?"

HALIFAX.

Halifax was formed in 1752, from Lunenburg. Its length is 33
miles, and mean breadth 23 miles. The Roanoke runs on its n.
and ne. boundary; and the Dan and its branches flow through it
centrally. The soil is fertile, and large quantities of excellent tobacco, corn, and oats, are raised. Population in 1840, whites
11,145, slaves 14,216, free colored 575; total, 25,936.

Banister, or Halifax C. H., lies 127 miles southwesterly from
Richmond. It is a long, scattering village, well elevated by a
gradual ascent of three quarters of a mile from Banister River; it
contains a population of about 300. Brooklyn, Meadsville, Scotts-
burg, and Barksdale, contain each a few dwellings.

HAMPSHIRE.

Hampshire was established in 1754, from Frederick and Augusta.
Its mean length is about 33 miles, and mean breadth 30 miles.
A large proportion of the county is mountainous, and much of the
high mountain-land is untillable. The principal streams are the
South and the North Branch of Potomac, the Potomac, and the
Great Cacapon. On all of these there are extensive and fertile low
grounds. Near the Maryland line are immense fields of bitumi-
nous coal, and deposites of iron ore in various parts of the county.
Population, whites 10,703, slaves 1,403, free colored 189; total
12,295.

Romney, the county-seat, is situated in the heart of the county,
on the South Branch of Potomac, 188 miles nw. of Richmond, and
39 miles from Winchester. It is a small village, yet one of considerable business, and has a branch of the Bank of the Valley,
several stores, and about 350 inhabitants. It was established by
law in 1762, and laid off by Lord Fairfax, its founder, into streets
and half-acre lots. The Parkersburg turnpike passes through it.

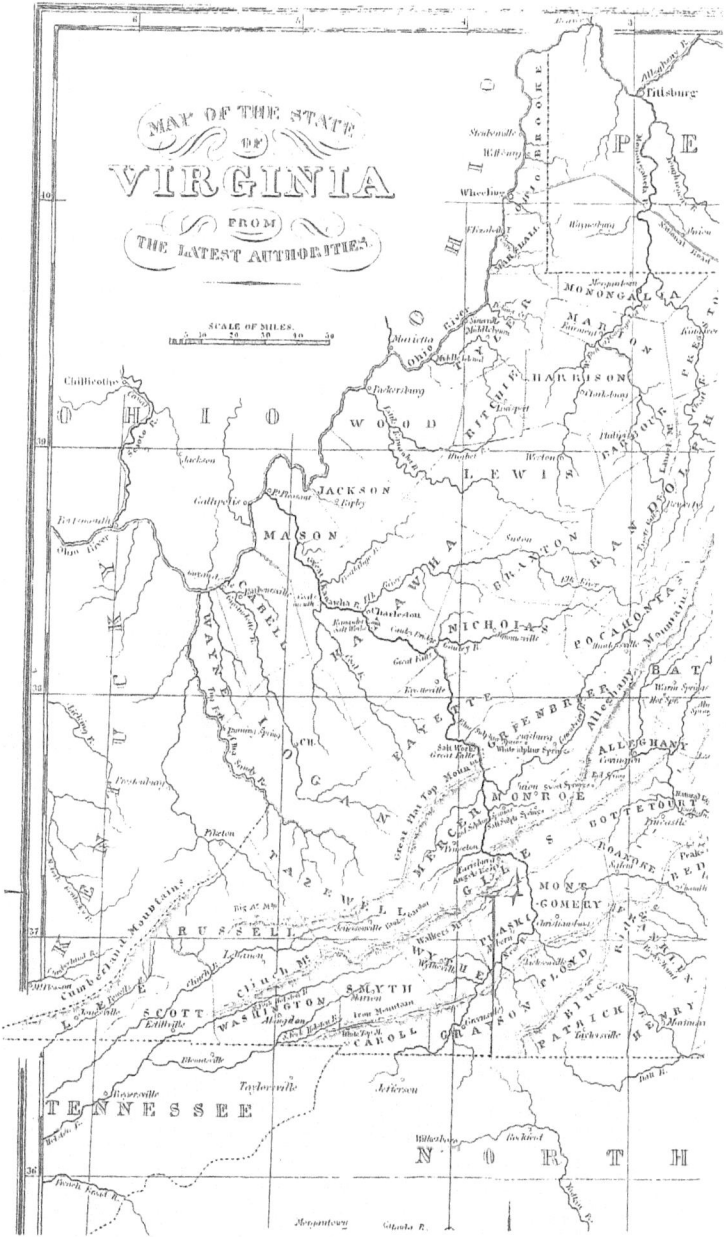

MAP OF THE STATE OF VIRGINIA FROM THE LATEST AUTHORITIES

SCALE OF MILES.

PENNSYLVANIA

Johnstown Portage Rail Road Hollidaysburg Juniata R. HARRISBURG Reading

Bedford Chambersburg Gettysburg York Lancaster Philadelphia Chester

Union Cumberland M A R Hancock Bath Frederick Mercer de Grace Elk Town New Castle Salem

HAMPSHIRE MORGAN BERKELEY Romney Winchester LOUDON Harper's Ferry Rail Road BALTIMORE ANNAPOLIS

HARDY SHENANDOAH Washington Alexandria Cambridge

PAGE New Market Luray RAPPAHANNOCK George T. WASHINGTON Pt. Frederick

ROCKINGHAM Harrisonburg MADISON ORANGE CAROLINE Eastville

AUGUSTA Staunton GREENE LOUISA HANOVER WESTMORELAND RICHMOND

NELSON Lexington FLUVANNA GOOCHLAND Egyptanneck LANCASTER MIDDLESEX

BEDFORD New Canton BUCKINGHAM CUMBERLAND POWHATAN HENRICO RICHMOND NEW KENT

Lynchburg PRINCE EDWARD NOTTOWAY CHESTERFIELD CHARLES SURRY

CAMPBELL CHARLOTTE Petersburg PRINCE GEORGE

LUNENBURG DINWIDDIE SUSSEX ISLE OF WIGHT NORFOLK Cape Henry

MECKLENBURG BRUNSWICK GREENSVILLE SOUTHAMPTON

Danville Roanoke R. Meherrin R. Nottoway R.

Roxboro Oxford Elizabeth City Hertford

H C A R O L I N A Edenton

Windsor ALBEMARLE SOUND

RALEIGH Plymouth

Longitude East 1 from Washington.

Frankfort, Springfield, Cold Stream Mill, and Paddytown, are small villages.

The Ice Mountain.

The Ice Mountain of Hampshire is one of the greatest natural curiosities in Virginia. It rises from the eastern bank of the North River, a branch of the Capon, and is distant 26 miles NW. from Winchester, and 16 miles E. of Romney. It is in height 400 or 500 feet.

The west side of the mountain, for about a quarter of a mile, is covered with a mass of loose stone of a light color, which reaches down to the bank of the river. This part of the mountain is represented in the accompanying engraving. By removing the loose stone, pure crystal ice can always be found in the warmest days of summer. It has been discovered even as late as the 15th of September; but never in October, although it may exist throughout the entire year, and be found, if the rocks were excavated to a sufficient depth. The body of rocks where the ice is found is subject to the full rays of the sun from nine o'clock in the morning until sunset. The sun does not have the effect of melting the ice as much as continued rains. At the base of the mountain is a spring of water colder by many degrees than spring water generally is. "Very near this spring," says Kercheval, "the owner of the property has removed the stone, and erected a small log dairy, for the preservation of his milk, butter, and fresh meats. When the author saw this little building, which was late in the month of April, the openings between the logs, (on the side next the cavity from which the stone had been taken out,) for eighteen inches or two feet from the floor, were completely filled with ice, and about one-half the floor was covered with ice several inches thick. Mr. Deevers, who is the owner of the property, informed the author that milk, butter, or fresh meats of every kind, are perfectly safe from injury for almost any length of time, in the hottest weather. If a fly venture in, he is immediately stiffened with the cold and becomes torpid. If a snake in his rambles happens to pass over the rocks covering the ice, he soon loses all motion, and dies. Christopher Heiskell, Esq., informed the author that several instances had occurred of the snakes being found dead among the rocks covering the ice. An intelligent young lady at the same time stated that she had seen instances of this character. In truth, it was upon her first suggesting the fact, that the author was led to make inquiry of Mr. Heiskell. And Mr. Deevers stated that he had several times removed torpid flies from his dairy into a more temperate atmosphere, when they soon recovered life and motion, and flew off."

Mr. C. B. Hayden, in a recent number of Silliman's Journal,

thus accounts for the phenomenon of the preservation of ice in this mountain :

The solution, I conceive, is to be found in the large and unusual collection of rocks, which from their porous homogeneous texture are extremely poor conductors of heat. One side of the mountain consists of a massive wall many hundred feet in thickness, and heaped up against this as an abutment, is a mass of rocks containing several thousand cubic feet. As the mountain has a general direction from NE. to SW., the talus heap containing the ice has a NW. exposure. The cavernous nature of this heap would admit the free entrance of atmospheric waters, which during the winter would form ice in the interior of the mass. The ice thus situated would be protected from external heat by the surrounding rocks, as ice in a refrigerator is isolated and protected from the external temperature, by the non-conducting sides of the refrigerator. The Ice Mountain only requires for the explanation of its phenomenon, the application of the familiar principle upon which is constructed the common refrigerator, which temporarily effects what the Ice Mountain permanently does—a temperature independent of external causes. The Ice Mountain is, in fact, a huge sandstone refrigerator, whose increased and unusual effects beyond those of the ordinary refrigerator, are due to the increased and unusual collection of poor conducting materials which form its sides.

There are several other curiosities of nature in this county. They are Caudy's Castle, the Tea-Table, and the Hanging Rocks.

Caudy's Castle was so named from having been the retreat of an early settler when pursued by the Indians. It is a fragment of a mountain in the shape of a half cone, with a very narrow base, which rises from the banks of the Capon to the height of about 500 feet, and presents a sublime and majestic appearance. The Tea-Table is about 10 miles below Caudy's Castle, in a deep ragged glen, three or four miles east of the Capon. This table is of solid rock, and presents the form of a man's hat standing on its crown. It is about 4 feet in height and the same in diameter. From the top issues a clear stream of water, which flows over the brim on all sides, and forms a fountain of exquisite beauty. The Hanging Rocks are about 4 miles north of Romney. There the Wappatomka River has cut its way through a mountain of about 500 feet in height. The boldness of the rocks, and the wildness of the scene, excite awe in the beholder.

A bloody battle, says tradition, was once fought at the Hanging Rocks, between contending parties of the Catawba and Delaware Indians, and it is believed that several hundred of the latter were slaughtered. Indeed, the signs now to be seen at this place exhibit striking evidences of the fact. There is a row of Indian graves between the rock and public road, along the margin of the river, of from 60 to 70 yards in length. It is believed that but very few of the Delawares escaped.

HANOVER.

HANOVER was formed in 1720, from New Kent. Its length is 45 miles; main width, 14 miles. It is watered by the Pamunkey, the Chickahominy, and their branches. The surface is generally level, and the soil of every extreme, from the best river alluvion to barren sand. Inexhaustible beds of marl exist in the county, and are extensively used in agriculture, now in an improving condition. The Fredericksburg and Richmond rail-road runs N. and S. through the central part. The Louisa rail-road commences at the "Junction" on the line of the above-mentioned rail-road, 24 miles N. of Richmond, and runs through the western part of Hanover. Pop., whites 6,262, slaves 8,394, free colored 312; total, 14,968.

Hanover C. H. is 20 miles N. of Richmond. Hanover town, on the Pamunkey, in the E. part of the county, was settled before Richmond, and anciently called Page's Warehouse. It once had a large population, and was a place of considerable business, even within the memory of those living. At one time there were 1600 hogsheads of tobacco annually exported from it. Then the Pamunkey was navigable for sloops and schooners, since which the channel has much filled up. When the Assembly of the state were agitating the subject of removing the capitol from Williams-

Birthplace of Henry Clay.

burg, they came within a few votes of deciding upon Hanover Town instead of Richmond. The site is now a cultivated field, and shows but a few traces of its having been a town. Newcastle, which is 4 or 5 miles lower down on the Pamunkey, was also, at the same time, a considerable village. It now consists of a single house. It is the spot where Patrick Henry assembled his volunteers at the time Dunmore took the gunpowder from the magazine at Williamsburg. This section of the county is a beautiful agricultural tract, on which there was once much tobacco raised.

Patrick Henry, Henry Clay, and Col. Baylor, were all natives of Hanover county. The latter was at one time aid to Washington. His regiment of light dragoons, which were from Virginia, while sleeping in a barn near the line of New Jersey and New York, were surprised, Sept. 28th, 1778, and nearly all of them cruelly massacred. Col. Baylor was dangerously wounded, and made prisoner. He was noted for his bravery. The *birthplace* of Henry Clay is in a poor piny region, called the Slashes of Hanover, about 3 miles from the court-house, on the turnpike to Richmond.

The Rev. SAMUEL DAVIES, "the father* of the Presbyterian church in Virginia," was

* We take this expression, "father of the Presbyterian church in Virginia," from a periodical. Mr. Davies was not so, strictly speaking; but he did more than any other person in disseminating the doctrines of, and making converts to this church, at an early day. The father of the Presbyterian church in America was the Rev. Francis Makemie. He was a Scotch-Irish Presbyterian, "from the neighborhood of Ramelton, in Donegal, in the north of Ireland, and was first introduced to the presbytery in January, 1680." Reid's History of the Presbyterian Church in Ireland, from which the above is derived, also says: "He settled in Accomac county, on the eastern shore of Virginia, where he died in 1701. He was the first Presbyterian minister who settled in America, and with a

born in Delaware, in 1724, in humble circumstances. In 1748, he accepted a call from the Presbyterians of this neighborhood to settle among them. He gained great credit for his knowledge, address, and eloquence, in an argument which he had with Peyton Randolph, the king's attorney-general, on the subject of the rights of Protestant dissenters from the established church in Virginia. When he went to England in 1753, he obtained from the king and council a declaration, under authority, that the provisions of the act of toleration did extend to Virginia. The Old Fork Church in which he preached is, or was lately, standing on the South Anna Branch, near Ground Squirrel Bridge, in this county.

The home of Mr. Davies was in this county, about 12 miles from Richmond ; but his occasional labors were greatly extended over a considerable part of the colony ; and he acquired an influence greater, probably, than any other preacher of the gospel in Virginia ever possessed. It was the influence of fervent piety and zeal, directed by a mind of uncommon compass and force. He took no little pains to instruct the negroes, and to this day the descendants of his negro converts manifest the happy effects of the pious instructions of their parents.

In 1753, Mr. Davies accompanied the Rev. Gilbert Tennent on a mission to England, to solicit donations for the College of New Jersey, at Princeton, where he met with a success that astonished himself. He preached frequently, and with great applause. The following anecdote is related of him : The king, (George II.,) being curious to hear a preacher from the wilds of America, attended on one occasion, when he was so much struck with his commanding eloquence that he expressed his astonishment loud enough to be heard half-way over the house. Davies observing that the king was attracting more attention than himself, paused, and looking his majesty full in the face, gave him, in an emphatic tone, the following rebuke : " *When the lion roareth, let the beasts of the forest tremble ; and when the Lord speaketh, let the kings of the earth keep silence.*" The king shrunk back in his seat and remained quiet during the remainder of his discourse ; and the next day sent for Mr. Davies, and gave him fifty guineas for the college, observing at the same time to his courtiers : " *he is an honest man ! an honest man !*"

Shortly after the return of Mr. Davies, in 1755, the presbytery of Hanover was erected, and he was appointed to open the presbytery, which was directed to meet in Hanover, on the 3d of December of that year. The limits of the presbytery originally comprehended the whole of Virginia, and a considerable part, if not the whole, of North Carolina. Through this extensive region there were scattered numerous settlements of Protestant dissenters, besides many who had originally belonged to the established church, but had chosen to leave it and to join the dissenters. Of this whole dissenting interest, Mr. Davies was the animating soul. He made his influence to be felt everywhere ; he transfused his own spirit into the bosoms of his associates, and roused them by the force of his example. His popularity in Virginia was almost unbounded ; so that he was invited and urged to preach in almost all the settled portions of the colony.

But he did not content himself merely with the discharge of pastoral duties. The country was alarmed and agitated to the highest degree, by the French and Indian war. At this time he delivered several patriotic sermons, one of which, under the title of " Religion and Patriotism the constituents of a good soldier," was addressed in Hanover to Capt. Overton's company of independent soldiers. In it he uttered the prophetic remark respecting Washington. (See p. 99.) On another occasion he preached a sermon " to the militia of Hanover county, in Virginia, at a general muster, May 8th, 1759, with a view to raise a company for Capt. Samuel Meredith." At its close, a company was made up in a few minutes, and many more offered their names than the law allowed. As Mr. Davies left the muster-ground for the tavern, to get his horse, the whole corps followed him, pressing around to catch every word that fell from his lips. Observing their desire, he again addressed them from the tavern porch until he was exhausted with speaking.

The celebrated Patrick Henry has spoken in terms of enthusiasm of Mr. Davies. It has been supposed that he first kindled the fire, and afforded the model of Henry's elocution, as he lived from his 11th to his 22d year in the neighborhood where the patriotic sermons of Mr. Davies were delivered, which produced as powerful effec`s as those ascribed to the orations of Demosthenes.

In 1759, Mr. Davies accepted the appointment of president of New Jersey College,

---

few other brethren from Ulster, constituted the *first regular presbytery that was organized in the new world.*" Hodge's History of the Presbyterian Church in America, states that he settled in Accomac anterior to 1790, when his name first appears upon the county records, and that he died in 1708.—H. H.

at Princeton. The services he rendered as president of that institution were very important. President Davies died on the 4th of February, 1762, having remained in office about eighteen months. He was about fourteen years in public life, and died in the thirty-seventh year of his age. He possessed the advantages of superior genius ; and was much distinguished as a laborious scholar. He dreaded to preach without proper preparation. When pressed to speak extemporaneously he sometimes replied : " It is a dreadful thing to talk nonsense in the name of the Lord." He declared that " every discourse of his which he thought worthy of the name of a sermon, cost him four days hard study in the preparation." It was by this combination of talent and diligence that he became the most eloquent and accomplished pulpit-orator that our country ever produced, and he was more successful as a preacher than almost any other individual of his day. Since his death, his sermons have passed through numerous editions, both in this country and Britain, and probably there are no sermons in the language more extensively read or more deservedly popular.*

The Marquis de Chastellux, an officer attached to the French army in America in the revolutionary war, has in his travels left us some interesting notices respecting this county. He says :

As you approach Newcastle, the country becomes more gay. This little capital of a small district contains 25 or 30 houses, some of which are pretty enough. We continued our journey to Hanover court-house. We arrived before sunset, and alighted at a tolerably handsome inn ; a very large saloon, and a covered portico, are destined to receive the company who assemble every three months at the *court-house*, either on private or public affairs.... The county of Hanover, as well as that of New Kent, had still reason to remember the passage of the English. Mr. Tilghman, our landlord, though he lamented his misfortune in having lodged and boarded Lord Cornwallis and his retinue, without his lordship's having made the least recompense, could not yet help laughing at the fright which the unexpected arrival of Tarleton spread amongst a considerable number of gentlemen, who had come to hear the news, and were assembled in the court-house. A negro on horseback came full gallop to let them know that Tarleton was not above three miles off. The resolution of retreating was soon taken ; but the alarm was so sudden, and the confusion so great, that every one mounted the first horse he could find, so that few of those curious gentlemen returned upon their own horses. The English who came from Westover had passed the Chickahominy at Button's Bridge, and directed their march towards the South Anna, which Lafayette had put between them and himself.

The next morning the Marquis left the court-house, and arrived about noon at *Offley*, near the North Anna River, the seat of the then ex-governor Nelson, where he passed two or three days in the enjoyment of the hospitalities of the family. He eulogizes the patriotism and zeal of the governor, whose acquaintance he had made at the siege of York, and compliments the beauty, artlessness, and music of the young ladies, describing them as " pretty nymphs, more timid and wild than those of Diana."

The Marquis then goes on to describe the venerable ex-secretary Nelson, the father of Gov. Nelson, whose elegant house, being occupied by Lord Cornwallis during the siege of York, was at last almost entirely destroyed by the cannon-shot of the Americans. The two sons of the secretary were in the American army, and sent a flag to the British general requesting permission for their father to leave the town, which request Cornwallis humanely granted. The tranquillity which had succeeded these unhappy times, by giving him leisure to reflect upon his losses, had not embittered the recollection. He lived happily on his plantation, where in six hours he could assemble seventy of his posterity, all inhabitants of Virginia.

PATRICK HENRY, the second son of John and Sarah Henry, and one of nine children, was born on the 29th of May, 1736, at the family seat, called Studley, in Hanover county. At the age of ten years he was taken from the school where he had learned to read and write, and taught Latin by his father, who had opened a grammar-school in his own house. At the same time he acquired some proficiency in mathematics. Passionately addicted to the sports of the field, he could not brook the toil and confinement of study. And the time which should thus have been employed, was often passed in

* The memoir of President Davies is principally abridged from a biographical sketch in President Green's work on the College of New Jersey.

the forest with his gun, or over the brook with his angling-rod. " His companions frequently observed him lying along, under the shade of some tree that overhung the sequestered stream, watching for hours, at the same spot, the motionless cork of his fishing-
line, without one encouraging symptom of success, and without any apparent source of
enjoyment, unless he could find it in the ease of his position, or in the illusions of hope ;
or, which is most probable, in the stillness of the scene, or the silent workings of his own
imagination." This love of solitude in his youth was a marked trait in his character.

Fac-simile of the signature of Patrick Henry.

The wants of a large family compelled his father to find employment for his sons.
At the age of fifteen Patrick was put behind the counter of a country merchant, and the
year following entered into business with his elder brother, William, with whom was to
devolve its chief management ; but such were his idle habits, that he left the burden of
the concern to Patrick, who managed wretchedly. The drudgery of business became
intolerable to him, and then, too, " he could not find it in his heart" to disappoint any
one who came for *credit ;* and he was very easily satisfied with apologies for non-pay-
ment. He sought relief from his cares by having recourse to the violin, flute, and
reading. An opportunity was presented of pursuing his favorite study of the human
character, and the character of every customer underwent this scrutiny.

One year put an end to the mercantile concern, and the two or three following Patrick
was engaged in settling up its affairs. At eighteen years of age he married Miss Shelton, the daughter of a neighboring farmer of respectability, and commenced cultivating
a small farm ; but his aversion to systematic labor, and want of skill, compelled him to
abandon it at the end of two years. Selling off all his little possessions at a sacrifice, he
again embarked in the hazardous business of merchandise. His old business habits still
continued, and not unfrequently he shut up his store to indulge in the favorite sports of
his youth. His reading was of a more serious character ; history, ancient and modern,
he became a proficient in. Livy, however, was his favorite ; and having procured a copy,
he read it through at least once a year in the early part of his life. In a few years his
second mercantile experiment left him a bankrupt, and without any friends enabled to assist him further. All other means failing, he determined to try the law. His unfortunate
habits, unsuitable to so laborious a profession, and his pecuniary situation unfitting him
for an extensive course of reading, led every one to suppose that he would not succeed.
With only six weeks' study, he obtained a license to practise, he being then twenty-four
years of age. He was then not only unable to draw a declaration or a plea, but incapable, it is said, of the most common and simple business of his profession. It was not
until his twenty-seventh year, that an opportunity occurred for a trial of his strength at
the bar. In the mean time the wants and distresses of his family were extreme. They
lived mostly with his father-in-law, Mr. Shelton, who then kept a tavern at Hanover
court-house. Whenever Mr. Shelton was from home, Henry took his place in the tavern,
which is the identical public-house now standing at Hanover court-house. The occasion on which his genius first broke forth, was the controversy between the clergy and
the legislature and people of the state, relating to the stipend claimed by the former.
The cause was popularly known as the *parsons' cause.* A decision of the court on a demurrer in favor of the claims of the clergy, had left nothing undetermined but the amount
of damages in the cause which was pending. Soon after the opening of the court, the
cause was called. The scene which ensued is thus vividly described by Wirt :

The array before Mr. Henry's eyes was now most fearful. On the bench sat more than twenty clergymen, the most learned men in the colony, and the most capable, as well as the severest critics before
whom it was possible for him to have made his *début.* The court-house was crowded with an overwhelming multitude, and surrounded with an immense and anxious throng, who, not finding room to
enter, were endeavoring to listen without, in the deepest attention. But there was something still more
awfully disconcerting than all this ; for in the chair of the presiding magistrate, sat no other person than
his own father. Mr. Lyons opened the cause very briefly : in the way of argument he did nothing more
than explain to the jury, that the decision upon the demurrer had put the act of 1750 entirely out of the
way and left the law of 1748 as the only standard of their damages ; he then concluded with a highly-

wrought eulogium on the benevolence of the clergy. And now came on the first trial of Patrick Henry's strength. No one had ever heard him speak, and curiosity was on tiptoe. He rose very awkwardly, and faltered much in his exordium. The people hung their heads at so unpromising a commencement; the clergy were observed to exchange sly looks with each other; and his father is described as having almost sunk with confusion from his seat. But these feelings were of short duration, and soon gave place to others of a very different character. For now were those wonderful faculties which he possessed for the first time developed; and now was first witnessed that mysterious and almost supernatural transformation of appearance, which the fire of his own eloquence never failed to work in him. For as his mind rolled along, and began to glow from its own action, all the *exuviæ* of the clown seemed to shed themselves spontaneously. His attitude by degrees became erect and lofty. The spirit of his genius awakened all his features. His countenance shone with a nobleness and grandeur which it had never before exhibited. There was a lightning in his eyes which seemed to rivet the spectator. His action became graceful, bold, and commanding; and in the tones of his voice, but more especially in his emphasis, there was a peculiar charm, a magic, of which any one who ever heard him will speak as soon as he is named, but of which no one can give any adequate description. They can only say that it struck upon the ear and upon the heart, *in a manner which language cannot tell*. Add to all these, his wonder-working fancy, and the peculiar phraseology in which he clothed its images; for he painted to the heart with a force that almost petrified it. In the language of those who heard him on this occasion, " he made their blood run cold, and their hair to rise on end."

It will not be difficult for any one who ever heard this most extraordinary man, to believe the whole account of this transaction which is given by his surviving hearers; and from their account, the courthouse of Hanover county must have exhibited, on this occasion, a scene as picturesque as has been ever witnessed in real life. They say that the people, whose countenances had fallen as he arose, had heard but a very few sentences before they began to look up; then to look at each other with surprise, as if doubting the evidence of their own senses; then, attracted by some strong gesture, struck by some majestic attitude, fascinated by the spell of his eye, the charm of his emphasis, and the varied and commanding expression of his countenance, they could look away no more. In less than twenty minutes they might be seen, in every part of the house, on every bench, in every window, stooping forward from their stands, in death-like silence; their features fixed in amazement and awe, all their senses listening and riveted upon the speaker, as if to catch the last strain of some heavenly visitant. The mockery of the clergy was soon turned into alarm, their triumph into confusion and despair, and at one burst of his rapid and overwhelming invective, they fled from the bench in precipitation and terror. As for the father, such was his surprise, such his amazement, such his rapture, that, forgetting where he was, and the character which he was filling, tears of ecstasy streamed down his cheeks, without the power or inclination to repress them.

The jury seem to have been so completely bewildered, that they lost sight not only of the act of 1748, but that of 1758 also; for, thoughtless even of the admitted right of the plaintiff, they had scarcely left the bar when they returned with a verdict of *one penny damages*. A motion was made for a new trial; but the court, too, had now lost the equipoise of their judgment, and overruled the motion by a unanimous vote. The verdict, and judgment overruling the motion, were followed by redoubled acclamation, from within and without the house. The people, who had with difficulty kept their hands off their champion from the moment of closing his harangue, no sooner saw the fate of the cause finally sealed than they seized him at the bar, and, in spite of his own exertions and the continued cry of " order," from the sheriffs and the court, they bore him out of the court-house, and raising him on their shoulders, carried him about the yard in a kind of electioneering triumph.

From this time Mr. Henry's star was in the ascendant, and he at once rose to the head of his profession in that section. In the autumn of 1764, having removed to Roundabout, in Louisa county, he was employed to argue a case before a committee on elections of the House of Burgesses. He distinguished himself by a brilliant display on the right of suffrage. Such a burst of eloquence from a man of so humble an appearance, struck the committee with amazement, and not a sound but from his lips broke the deep silence of the room.

In 1765, he was elected a member of the House of Burgesses, when he introduced his celebrated resolutions on the Stamp Act. Among his papers there was found, after his decease, one sealed and thus endorsed :

" Enclosed are the resolutions of the Virginia Assembly, in 1765, concerning the Stamp Act. Let my executors open this paper." On the back of the paper containing the resolutions was the following endorsement: " The within passed the House of Burgesses in May, 1765. They formed the first opposition to the Stamp Act, and the scheme of taxing America by the British parliament. All the colonies, either through fear, or the want of opportunity to form an opposition, or from influence of some kind or other, had remained silent. I had been for the first time elected a burgess a few days before, was young, inexperienced, unacquainted with the forms of the house and the members who composed it. Finding the men of weight averse to opposition, and the commencement of the tax at hand, and that no person was likely to step forth, I determined to venture; and alone, unaided and unassisted, on the blank leaf of an old law-book, wrote the within. Upon offering them to the house, violent debates ensued. Many threats were uttered, and much abuse cast on me by the parties for submission. After a long and warm contest, the resolutions passed by a very small majority, perhaps one or two only. The alarm spread throughout America with astonishing quickness, and the ministerial party were overwhelmed. The great point of resistance to British taxation was universally established in the colonies. This brought on the war, which finally separated the two countries, and gave independence to ours. Whether this will prove a blessing or a curse, will depend upon the use our people make of the blessings which a gracious God hath bestowed on us. If they are wise, they will be great and happy. If they are of a contrary character, they will be miserable. Righteousness alone can exalt them as a nation. Reader, whoever thou art, remember this; and in thy sphere, practise virtue thyself, and encourage it in others.
" P. HENRY."

It was in the midst of the above-mentioned debate that he exclaimed, in tones of thunder, " Cæsar had his Brutus—Charles the First his Cromwell—and George the

Third—(' Treason !' cried the speaker—' Treason ! treason !' echoed from every part of the house. Henry faltered not for a moment ; taking a loftier attitude, and fixing on the speaker an eye of fire, he finished his sentence with the firmest emphasis)—"*may profit by their example. If this* be treason, make the most of it." Henceforth Mr.

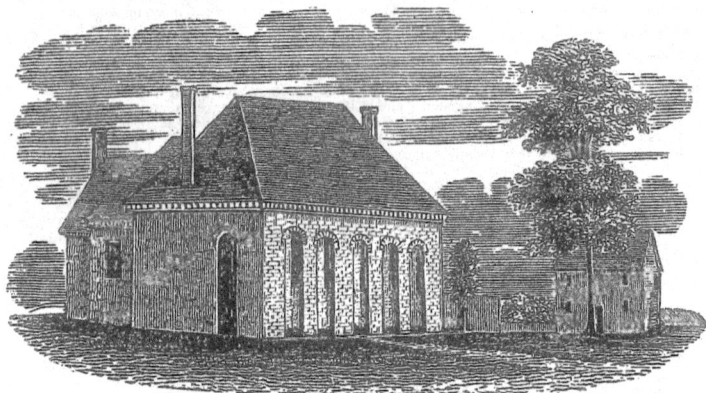

The old Court-House, Hanover.

[The Hanover Court-House is over a century old, and is built of imported brick. It is the building in which Patrick Henry made his celebrated speech in " *The Parsons' Cause.*"]

Henry was the idol of the people of Virginia, and his influence as one of the great champions of liberty, extended throughout America. In 1769 he was admitted to the bar of the general court. Without that legal learning which study alone can supply, he was deficient as a mere lawyer. But before a jury, in criminal cases particularly, his genius displayed itself most brilliantly. His deep knowledge of the springs of human action, his power of reading in the flitting expressions of the countenance what was passing in the hearts of his hearers, has rarely been possessed by any one in so great a degree. In 1767 or '68, Mr. Henry removed back to Hanover, and continued a member of the House of Burgesses until the close of the revolution, acting upon its most important committees, and infusing a spirit of bold opposition in its members to the pretensions of Britain. He was a delegate to the first Colonial Congress, which assembled Sept. 4, 1774, at Philadelphia.

Upon Lord Dunmore's seizing the gunpowder at Williamsburg, in the night after the battle of Lexington, Henry summoned volunteers to meet him ; and marching down towards the capitol, compelled the agent of Dunmore to give a pecuniary compensation for it. This was the first military movement in Virginia. The colonial convention of 1775 elected him the colonel of the first regiment, and the commander of " all the forces raised and to be raised for the defence of the colony." Soon resigning his command, he was elected a delegate to the convention, and not long after, in 1776, the *first* governor of the commonwealth, an office he held by successive re-elections until 1779, when, without an intermission, he was no longer constitutionally eligible. While holding that office he was signally serviceable in sustaining public spirit during the gloomiest period of the revolution, providing recruits, and crushing the intrigues of the tories.

On leaving the office of governor, he served, until the end of the war, in the legislature, when he was again elected governor, until the state of his affairs caused him to resign in the autumn of 1786. Until 1794 he regularly attended the courts, where his great reputation obtained for him a lucrative business. In 1788 he was a member of the convention of Virginia which so ably and eloquently discussed the constitution of the United States. He employed his masterly eloquence, day after day, in opposition to the proposed constitution. His hostility to it proceeded entirely from an apprehension that the federal government would swallow the sovereignty of the states ; and that ultimately the liberty of the people would be destroyed, or crushed, by an overgrown and ponderous consolidation of political power. The constitution having been adopted, the government organized, and Washington elected President, his repugnance measurably abated. The chapter of amendments considerably neutralized his objections : but, nevertheless, it is believed that his acquiescence resulted more from the consideration of a citizen's duty, confidence in the chief magistrate, and a hopeful reliance on the wisdom and virtue of the people, rather than from any material change in his opinions."

In 1794 Mr. Henry retired from the bar. In 1796 the post of governor was once more tendered to him, and refused. In 1798 the strong and animated resolutions of the Virginia Assembly, in opposition to the alien and sedition laws, which laws he was in favor of, " conjured up the most frightful visions of civil war, disunion, blood, and anarchy ; and under the impulse of these phantoms, to make what *he* considered a virtuous effort for his country, he presented himself in Charlotte county as a candidate for the House of Delegates, at the spring election of 1799," although he had retired to private life three years previously.

His speech on this occasion, before the polls were opened, was the last effort of his eloquence. " The power of the noon-day sun was gone ; but its setting splendors were not less beautiful and touching." Mr. Henry was elected by his usual commanding majority, and the most formidable preparations were made to oppose him in the Assembly. But " the disease which had been preying upon him for two years now hastened to its crisis ; and on the 6th of June, 1799, this friend of liberty and man was no more."

By his first wife he had six children, and by his last, six sons and three daughters. He left them a large landed property. He was temperate and frugal in his habits of living, and seldom drank any thing but water. He was nearly six feet in height, spare, and raw-boned, and with a slight stoop in his shoulders ; his complexion dark and sallow ; his countenance grave, thoughtful, and penetrating, and strongly marked with the lines of profound reflection, which with his earnest manner, and the habitual knitting and contracting of his brows, gave at times an expression of severity. " He was gifted with a strong and musical voice, and a most expressive countenance, and he acquired particular skill in the use of them. . . . He could be vehement, insinuating, humorous, and sarcastic, by turns, and always with the utmost effect. He was a natural orator of the highest order, combining imagination, acuteness, dexterity, and ingenuity, with the most forcible action, and extraordinary powers of face and utterance. As a statesman, his principal merits were sagacity and boldness. His name is brilliantly and lastingly connected with the history of his country's emancipation."

" In private life, Mr. Henry was as amiable as he was brilliant in his public career. He was an exemplary Christian, and his illustrious life was greatly ornamented by the religion which he professed. In his will he left the following testimony respecting the Christian religion : ' I have now disposed of all my property to my family. There is one thing more I wish I could give them, and that is the Christian religion. If they have that, and I had not given one shilling, they would be *rich ;* and if they have not that, and I had given them the whole world, they would be *poor*.' "

HARDY.

Hardy was formed in 1786, from Hampshire, and named from Samuel Hardy, a member of Congress from 1783 to 1785. He was a young man of promising talents, who died suddenly. Its mean length is 42, breadth 17 miles. The surface of the county is traversed, in a NE. direction, by the South Branch and other tributaries of the Potomac ; with lateral chains of mountains intervening, and extending in the same direction with the rivers. The surface is much broken, and, for the most part, very rocky and sterile ; but tracts of excellent land lie on the streams, and in the mountain-valleys. There are some valuable banks of iron ore in the county. Pop., whites 6,100, slaves 1,131, free colored 391 ; total, 7,622.

Trout Run, or Wardensville, is a small village on Trout Run, in the eastern section of the county, 26 miles from the county-seat. It was laid off in 1827. In the place and vicinity are several flour mills and iron works. Moorefield, the county-seat, is 178 miles NW. of Richmond, and 50 miles southwesterly from Winchester. This village is situated on the South Branch of the Potomac, at the junction of the south fork, in a valley of surpassing fertility, and contains a population of about 400. It was established by law, in 1777, on land belonging to Conrad Moore, from whom it derived its name. The act appointed, as trustees to lay out the town, Garret Vanmeter, Abel Randall, Moses Hutton, Jacob Read, Jonathan Heath, Daniel M'Neil, and Geo. Rennock. Petersburg is a small village on the South Branch of the Potomac.

On the Wappatomaka have been found numerous Indian relics, among which was a highly finished pipe, representing a snake coiled around the bowl. There was also discovered the under jaw-bone of a human being (says Kercheval) of great size, which contained eight jaw-teeth in each side, of enormous size ; and, what is more remarkable, the teeth stood transversely in the jaw-bone. It would pass over any man's face with entire ease.

The FAIRFAX STONE, the southern point of the western boundary between Maryland and Virginia, is on the westerly angle of this county. It was planted Oct. 17, 1746

There are several natural curiosities in this county worthy of note. They are the Regurgitary Spring, the Lost River, and the Devil's Garden.

The *Regurgitary Spring* is on the summit of a high mountain, a few miles from Petersburg. It flows and ebbs every two hours. When rising, it emits a noise similar to the gurgling of liquor from the bung-hole of a barrel, which continues two hours, and sends out sand and pebbles. It then ebbs two hours, at the end of which time the water entirely disappears.

The Devil's Garden. A strip of ground between two lofty ranges of mountains, rises gradually for about three miles, when it abruptly terminates at its southern extremity by an isolated and perpendicular pile of granitic rocks, of about 500 feet in height. At this place there is a figure in solid rock, resembling, in its upper part, the bust of a man. It is on a piece of ground thickly strewn with rocks, which, from the dark frowning appearance of the image, standing as the presiding deity of this savage spot, has given rise to the name it bears. Near his " satanic majesty," a door opens into a cavern, containing about a dozen rooms. *The Lost River* is so called from having, in the aggregate, a subterranean passage of three miles under several mountains.

This section of the country suffered severely in the Indian wars, previous to the revolution. Some incidents of bravery deserve a record :

Near Petersburg, a party of Indians attacked, just before daybreak, the dwelling of Samuel Bingham. Himself, wife, and parents, slept below, and a hired man in the loft above. A shot was first fired into the cabin, wounding his wife. Bingham sprang to his feet, bade the others to get under the bed, and requested the hired man to come down to his assistance, who, however, did not move. As the Indians rushed in at the door, he laid about him, with his rifle, with so much desperation that he finally cleared the room. Daylight appearing, he discovered that he had killed five, and the remaining two were seen retreating. He having broken his rifle ·in the mêlée, seized one which had been left by the Indians, and wounded one of the fugitives. Tradition relates that the other fled to the Indian camp, and reported that they had a fight with a devil, who had killed six of his companions, and that if they went, he would kill them all.

There was a memorable battle fought with the Indians, called the battle of Trough Hill. The whites were surrounded, and greatly outnumbered, but they fought with Spartan-like bravery ; and cutting their way through the savages, retreated to Fort Pleasant with the loss of many killed and wounded. In retreating, they were obliged to swim a river. Some, too badly wounded for this, loaded their rifles and deliberately awaited the approach of the savages from behind some cover, and dealt certain death to the first who approached, and then calmly yielded to the tomahawk.

When Cornwallis entered Virginia, a party of tories, at the head of whom was a Scotchman named Claypole, and his two sons, raised the British standard, and gained a large party on Lost River, and on the south fork of the Wappatomaka. It was their intention to join Cornwallis. It was, however, crushed in the bud by a force from Winchester, under General Daniel Morgan; and several of the young men, ashamed of their conduct, volunteered and marched to aid in the capture of the British at Yorktown.

HARRISON.

HARRISON was created in 1784, from Monongalia, and named in honor of Benjamin Harrison, governor of Virginia from 1781 to 1784, and father of the late President of the U. States. The surface is much broken, and much of the soil on the streams fertile. The bounds have been reduced within a few years by the formation of Marion, Ritchie, Barbour, and Taylor counties. Pop. in 1840, whites 16,850, slaves 693, free colored 126; total, 17,699.

Bridgeport, 6 miles east of Clarksburg, contains 1 Methodist and 1 Baptist church, and 25 dwellings. Lewisport, Milford, and Shinnston, are small villages in the county.

Clarksburg, the county-seat, lies 253 miles northwesterly from Richmond, and 70 east of the Ohio River, at the junction of Elk creek with the west fork of the Monongahela. The village stands on a rolling table-land, surrounded by an amphitheatre of hills, while Elk creek, meandering through and around the town, imparts additional beauty to the scene. Clarksburg was established by law, Oct., 1785, and William Carpenter, John Myers, William Haymond, John M'Ally, and John Davisson, gentlemen, were appointed the trustees. It is now a flourishing town, and contains 7 mercantile stores, 2 newspaper printing offices, 2 fine classical academies, 1 Methodist, and 1 Presbyterian church, and a population of about 1100. There are inexhaustible supplies of coal in the immediate neighborhood; and being in the midst of a fertile country, possessing great mineral wealth in its iron, salt, &c., it possesses the elements of prosperity. This immediate vicinity was settled a few years before the commencement of the revolutionary war. The early settlers in this region of country suffered greatly in the wars with the Indians, until Wayne's treaty in 1795. Withers' Chronicles of Border Warfare and History of Northwestern Virginia, published at Clarksburg in 1831, details many soul-harrowing cases of savage barbarity.

JESSE HUGHS was one of the bold pioneers who acted a conspicuous part against the Indians. He was bred from infancy in the hotbed of Indian warfare, and resided in Clarksburg. He was a light-built, spare man, and remarkably active on foot, and from his constant practice of hunting, became one of the best woodsmen and Indian hunters of his day. The annexed anecdotes we derive from the American Pioneer:

About the year 1790, the Indians one night came secretly upon the settlement of Clarksburg, and stole some horses. Next morning at daylight a party of about 25 men started in pursuit, and came upon the Indian trail, and judged from appearances there were only 8 or 10 of them. The captain and a majority, in a hasty council, were for pursuing the trail. Hughs opposed it, and advised them to let him pilot them by a near way to the Ohio, and intercept the Indians in their retreat. But this they would not listen to. He then showed them the danger of following their trail; and that in that case they would be waylaid,—that the Indians would choose a secure position, shoot two or three of them, and escape. The commander, jealous of Hughs' influence, broke up the council, by exclaiming: " All the *men* may follow me—let the *cowards* go home !" and dashed off at full speed. Hughs felt the insult, but followed with the rest. The result proved as he had predicted. Two Indians in ambush on the top of a cliff, fired and mortally wounded two of the party in the ravine, and escaped. Now convinced of their error, they put themselves under Hughs; but on arriving at the Ohio, they saw that the savages had crossed it. Hughs then got some satisfaction of the captain for his insult to him. He told them *he* wanted to find who the cowards were; that if any would go with him, or even one, he would cross the river in the pursuit. They all refused. He then said he would go alone, and get a scalp, or leave his own with them. Alone he crossed the river, and the next morning came upon their camp. They were all absent hunting except one Indian, who was left to guard the camp. He, unsuspecting danger, was fiddling on some dry bones, and singing, to pass the time, when Hughs crept up and shot him ; and, with the poor fellow's scalp, returned to his home some 70 miles distant, through the wilderness.

At a time of great danger from the incursions of the Indians in Virginia, when the citizens of the neighborhood were in a fort at Clarksburg, Hughs one morning observed a lad very intently fixing his gun. "Jim," said he, "what are you doing that for ?" " I am going to shoot a turkey that I hear gobbling on the hillside," said Jim. " I hear no turkey," said Hughs. " Listen," says Jim; " there, didn't you hear it ? listen again." " Well," says Hughs, after hearing it repeated, " I'll go and kill it." " No you won't," says Jim, " it is my turkey; I heard it first." " Well," says Hughs, "but you know I am the best marksman ; and besides, I don't want the turkey, you may have it." The lad then agreed to let Hughs go and kill it for him. Hughs went out of the fort on the side that was farthest from the supposed turkey, and taking along the river, went up a ravine and came in on the rear ; and, as he expected, he espied an Indian sitting on a chestnut stump, surrounded by sprouts, gobbling, and watching to see if any one would come from the fort to kill the turkey. Hughs crept up behind him, and shot him, before the Indian knew of his approach. He took off the scalp and went into the fort, where Jim was waiting for his prize. " There, now," says Jim, " you have let the turkey go. I would have killed it if I had gone." " No," says Hughs, " I didn't let it go ;" and taking out the scalp, threw it down. " There, take your turkey, Jim, I don't want it." The lad was overcome, and nearly fainted, to think of the certain death he had escaped, purely by the keen perception and good management of Mr. Hughs.

HENRICO.

HENRICO was one of the eight original shires into which Virginia was divided in 1634. Its mean length is 27 miles; mean breadth 10¾ miles. Excepting the lands on the James and Chickahominy, the soil is generally light and unproductive. The surface is moderately undulating, terminating in abrupt precipices, both on the Chickahominy and James River bottoms. Over one million of bushels bituminous coal are annually mined in the western section of the county. A rail-road connects the mines with James River. Population, including Richmond, whites 16,900, slaves 13,237, free colored 2,939 ; total, 33,076.

As early as 1611, Sir Thomas Dale established a town on the James River, which, in honor of Prince Henry, he called *Henrico*. From this originated the name of the county. It contained three streets of framed houses, with a good church, besides storehouses, watchhouses, &c., and was defended by a palisade and several forts. "Upon the verge of the river bank," says Stith, in his History of Virginia, published about a century since, " stood five houses inhabited by the *better sort of people*, who kept continual sentinel for the town's security.

" About two miles from the town, into the main, he ran another palisade, from river to river, near two miles in length, guarded with several forts, with a large quantity of corn ground impaled, and sufficiently secured. Besides these precautions, there may still be seen, upon the river bank, within the island, the ruins of a great ditch, now overgrown with large and stately trees; which, it may be supposed, was defended with a palisade, to prevent a surprise on that side, by crossing the river; and for a still further security to the town, he intended, but never quite finished, a palisade on the south side of the river, as a range for the hogs; and he called it Hope in Faith and Coxendale. It was about two miles and a half long, and was secured by five of their sort of forts, called Charity fort, Elizabeth fort, fort Patience, and Mount Malady, with a guest-house for sick people, upon a high and dry situation, and in a wholesome air, in the place where Jefferson church now stands. On the same side of the river also, Mr. Whitaker, their preacher, chose to be seated; and he impaled a fine parsonage, with a hundred acres of land, calling it Rock Hall."

Richmond, the metropolis of Virginia, is situated on the north side of James River, at the *Great Falls*, distant 117 miles from Washington City, 342 from New York, 557 from Boston, 520 from Cincinnati, 1055 from New Orleans, 423 from Charleston, 351 from Wheeling, 116 from Lynchburg, 62 from Fredericksburg, 106 from Norfolk, 146 from Winchester, and 23 from Petersburg.

Although Richmond is comparatively a modern town, yet its site is frequently alluded to in the early history of Virginia. The first mention of it is in 1609, when Master West, in a scarcity of provisions, went up from Jamestown to the Falls of James River, as the place was then called, to procure food, but found nothing edible except acorns. In the same year West was sent with a colony of 120 men, to settle at the falls. Capt. John Smith, then president of the colony, visiting West's settlement found his people planted " in a place not only subject to the river's inundation, but round environed with many intolerable inconveniences." This was, perhaps, where Rockett's now is, just below Richmond.

"To remedy these inconveniences, Smith, by means of a messenger, proposed to Powhatan to purchase from him the place of that name.* The settlers, however, disdainfully rejected Smith's plan, and became so mutinous upon the occasion that Smith landed among them and committed the ringleaders to confinement. At length, however, overpowered by their numbers, he being only supported by five, was forced to retire to a vessel in the river. At this time the savages daily supplied Smith with provisions, in requital for which the disorderly English stole their corn, plundered their gardens, beat them, broke into their wigwams and made them prisoners, so that the poor Indians complained to Smith that those whom he had planted there as their protectors were worse than their enemies the Monocans. Smith embarked for Jamestown. No sooner had he sailed, than a handful of Indians assaulted West's people, and slew many of them. However, before Smith had proceeded a mile and a half down the river, his vessel ran aground, whereupon he summoned the malecontents to a parley, and with such a panic were they struck at the assault of a few savages, that they submitted themselves to the president's mercy. He arrested the ringleaders, and established the rest at Powhatan in the Indian palisade fort there, which was so well fortified with poles and bark of trees as to defy all the savages of Virginia. They found, also, there, dry wigwams, and near 200 acres of land ready to be planted. And from the strength and beauty of the place, they called it 'Nonsuch' Smith being now on the eve of his departure, West arrived, which renewed all the troubles, and the upshot was that they abandoned Nonsuch and returned to the Falls. Smith, finding all his efforts frustrated, embarked for Jamestown in his boat, for the vessel had sailed two days before."

In 1644–5, the Assembly of Virginia ordered a fort to be erected at the Falls of James River, to be called " fforte Charles." In 1646 an act was passed, of which the following is an extract:—

" And, whereas, there is no plantable land adjoyning to ffort Charles, and therefore no encouragement for any vndertaker to maintaine the same, It is, therefore, thought fitt and inacted, That if any person or persons purchasing the right of Capt. Thomas Harris shall or will seate or inhabitt on the south side of James River right opposite to the said fforte, see it be done this or the ensueing yeare, That hee or they so vndertakeing as aforesaid shall have and enjoy the houseing belonging to the said ffort for the vse of timber, or by burning them for the nailes or otherwise, as also shall be exempted from the publique taxes for the term of three yeares, provided that the number exceed not tenn, as also shall have and enjoy the boats and ammunition belonging to the said ffort."

---

* The town where this monarch resided was called after him, Powhatan. It consisted of about a dozen houses, and stood about two miles below the site of Richmond.

In March, 1675-6, war was declared against the Indians. Five hundred men were ordered to proceed to the frontier, and eight forts garrisoned. " Fifty-five men out of James City county to be garrisoned neare the ffalls of James River, at Captain Byrd's, or at one ffort or place of defence over against him at Newletts, [or Howletts,] of which fforte Coll. Edward Ramsay be captaine or cheife commander."

In 1676, a party of Indians, evacuating a fort on the Potomac where they had been besieged by the colonists, " took their route over the head of that river, and thence over the heads of Rappahannock and York Rivers, killing whom they found of the upmost plantations, until they came to the head of James River, where (with Bacon and others) they slew Mr. Bacon's overseer, whom he much loved, and one of his servants, whose blood he vowed to avenge, if possible "*

" Bacon's Quarter Branch and Bloody Run, near Richmond, still call to mind Bacon and his rebellion. The term *Bacon's Quarter*, indicates that his plantation lay there. Bloody Run, according to tradition, is so called from a bloody battle Bacon fought there with the Indians. We have not been able to find any thing in the history of those times to confirm this tradition, and it would seem more probable that Bloody Run derived its name from the battle in which Hill was defeated, and Totopotomoi slain. The stream is a small one, and is said during the battle to have run blood."†

In 1679, certain privileges were granted Capt. Wm. Byrd, upon the condition that he should settle fifty able-bodied and well-armed men in the vicinity of the falls, to act as a protection to the frontier against the Indians.

In the Westover mss. Col. Byrd mentions his plantations at the falls, as follows : " September 18th, (1732,) for the pleasure of the good company of Mrs. Byrd and her little governor, my son, I went about half-way to the falls in my chariot. There we halted not far from a purling stream, and upon the stump of a propagate oak picked the bones of a piece of roast beef. By the spirit which it gave me, I was the better able to part with the dear companions of my travels, and to perform the rest of my journey on horseback by myself. I reached Shacco's before two o'clock, and crossed the river to the mills. I had the grief to find them both stand as still for the want of water, as a dead woman's tongue for want of breath. It had rained so little for many weeks above the falls, that the Naiads had hardly water enough left to wash their faces. However, as we ought all to turn our misfortunes to the best advantage, I directed Mr. Booker, my first minister there, to make use of the lowness of the water for blowing up the rocks at the mouth of the canal. * * * The water now flowed out of the river so slowly, that the miller was obliged to pond it up in the canal, by setting open the flood-gates at the mouth, and shutting those close at the mill. By this contrivance, he was able at any time to grind two or three bushels, either for his choice customers or for the use of my plantations. Then I walked to the place where they broke the flax, which is wrought with much greater ease than the hemp, and is much better for spinning. From thence I paid a visit to the weaver, who needed a little of Minerva's inspiration to make the most of a piece of cloth. Then I looked in upon my Caledonian spinster, who was mended more in her looks, than in her humor. * * On the next day, after I had swallowed a few poached eggs, we rode down to the mouth of the canal, and from thence crossed over to the broad-rock island in a canoe. Our errand was to view some iron ore, which we dug up in two places. That on the surface seemed very spongy and poor, which gave us no great encouragement to search deeper, nor did the quantity appear to be very great. However, for my greater satisfaction, I ordered a hand to dig there for some time this winter. We walked from one end of the island to the other, being about half a mile in length, and found the soil very good, and too high for any flood less than Deucalion's to do the least damage. There is a very wild prospect both upwards and downwards, the river being full of rocks, over which the stream tumbled with a murmur loud enough to drown the notes of a scolding wife. This island would make an agreeable hermitage for any good Christian, who had a mind to retire from the world."

Richmond was established a town by law in the reign of George II., May, 1742, on land belonging to Col. William Byrd, who died in 1744. The locality was anciently called Byrd's Warehouse. That gentleman, at the time, had a warehouse near where the Exchange Hotel now is. The seat of a Col. Byrd is thus described in Burnaby's Travels in North America in 1759-60. He " has a small place called Belvidere, upon a hill at the lower end of these falls, (James River,) as romantic and elegant as any thing I have ever seen. It is situated very high, and commands a fine prospect of the

---

* T. M.'s account of Bacon's Rebellion.　　　† From mss. of Charles Campbell, Esq.

RICHMOND.

The Capital, City Hall & the Governor's House are seen in the central part - the State Penitentiary is seen on the extreme left.

river, which is half a mile broad, forming cataracts in the manner above described. There are several little islands scattered carelessly about, very rocky and covered with trees, and two or three villages in view at a small distance. Over all these you discover a prodigious extent of wilderness, and the river winding majestically along through the midst of it."

In 1777, the assailable situation of Williamsburg to the aggressions of the enemy, occasioned the Assembly of the state to remove the troops, arms, and ammunition, together with the public records, to Richmond ; and, partially from the same cause, and the extension of the population westward, an act was passed, May, 1779, to remove the seat of government here. At this time, Richmond was an insignificant place, scarcely affording sufficient accommodations for the officers of government. The legislature bestowed upon it the name of a city; but it was then only a city in embryo, with scarcely any thing of interest except the grandeur of its natural scenery. The analogy of the situation of the place to that of Richmond-on-the-Thames, in England, suggested the name the town bears. The public buildings were temporary. The *old capitol*, which was private property, stood on the site now occupied by the custom-house, and some of the adjacent buildings. It was a wooden structure, long since destroyed.

Richmond was invaded by the traitor Arnold in 1781. The subjoined account is from Tucker's Life of Jefferson :

On the 3d of January the fleet came to anchor at Jamestown, and on the 4th it reached Westover, where about 900 men, but then supposed to be a much larger force, landed under the command of the notorious Arnold, and proceeded on their march towards Richmond. Until then, it was not known whether that town or Petersburg was the object of attack. The governor, [Jefferson,] on the same day, called out the *whole* of the militia from the adjacent counties ; but having no means of present resistance, he endeavored to secure that part of the public property which could be removed, by having it transported to the south bank of James River. Such of it as had been previously sent to Westham, six miles above Richmond, was also ordered to cross the river. That night the enemy encamped at Four-mile creek, 12 miles below Richmond. At half after seven o'clock at night, the governor set out for Westham, and, having stopped to hasten the transportation of the arms and stores, he proceeded to join his family at Tuckahoe, eight miles further, which place he reached after midnight.

The next morning, having taken his family across the river, and sent them to a place of safety, he rode down to Britton's, opposite to Westham, and gave further orders concerning the public property, the transportation of which had been continued through the whole night, and part of the next day, until the approach of the enemy. He then proceeded to Manchester, from whence he had a full view of the invading force. They had reached Richmond at 1 o'clock in the afternoon of that day, at which time there were only 200 militia, including those of the town, embodied.

The governor wishing to advise with Baron Steuben, then commanding the new levies in the state intended for the south, and which then amounted to 200 recruits, went to Chetwood's, his head-quarters, a few miles from Manchester, but learning he was at Col. Fleming's, the governor proceeded to that place, where he continued that night. While there, some of the citizens of Richmond waited on him, to tender an offer from Arnold not to burn the town, provided British vessels were permitted to come to it unmolested, and take off the tobacco there deposited. The offer was unhesitatingly rejected. As soon as Arnold reached Richmond, he sent a detachment under Col. Simcoe to destroy the cannon foundry above the town—which having done, they advanced to Westham ; but finding that all the public property sent thither had been transported over the river, they returned to Richmond the same day. On the 6th, the governor returned to Britton's, and having given orders respecting the public archives, rejoined his family in the evening at Fine creek. The British, after burning some public and some private buildings, as well as a large quantity of tobacco, left Richmond about 24 hours after they entered it, encamped at Four-mile creek, and on the 7th, at Berkley and Westover ; having thus penetrated 33 miles into the country from the place of debarkation, and completed their incursion, without loss, in 48 hours from the time of their landing. On the 7th, the governor went to Manchester, where he remained that night, and the next day returned to Richmond.

The bare communication of the fact, that a force of 1,000, or at most 1,500 men, was able to invade a country containing at that time a population of more than half a million, and 50,000 enrolled militia—march to its metropolis—destroy all the public and much of the private property found there, and in its neighborhood—and to leave the country with impunity, is, at first, calculated to excite our surprise, and to involve both the people, and those who administered its affairs, in one indiscriminate reproach. But there seems to be little ground for either wonder or censure, when it is recollected that these 50,000 militia were scattered over a surface of more than as many square miles; that the metropolis, which was thus insulted, was but a village, containing scarcely 1,800 inhabitants, half of whom were slaves; and that the country itself, intersected by several navigable rivers, could not be defended against the sudden incursions of an enemy whose naval power gave it the entire command of the water, and enabled it to approach within a day's march of the point of attack.

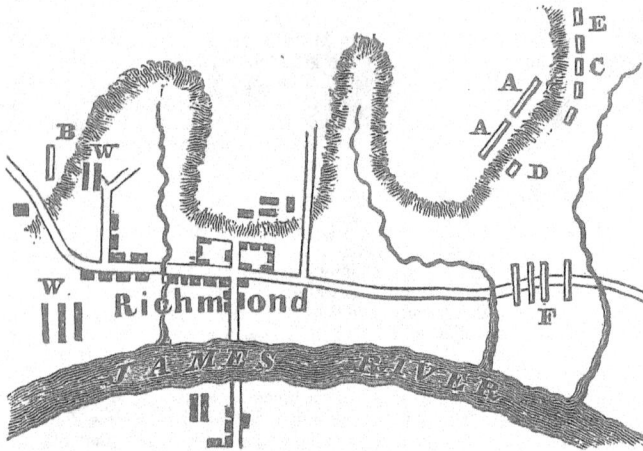

Skirmish at Richmond, Jan. 5th, 1781.

A. Rebel Infantry.—B. Rebel Cavalry.—C. Queen's Rangers.—D. Queen's Rangers' Cavalry.—E. Yagers.—F. British Army.—W. Warehouses.

We here give a narration of the invasion of Richmond, from Simcoe's Journal. Lieut.-Col. Simcoe was the celebrated commander of a partisan corps called the Queen's Rangers. Late in life he was lieutenant-governor of Upper Canada. Although a gentlemanly man, he was noted for his prejudices against the United States. The engraving given is mainly important as delineating Richmond as it then was:

On the arrival at Westover, the troops were immediately disembarked: at first, from the reports of the country of the force that was assembling to defend Richmond, Gen. Arnold hesitated whether he should proceed thither or not, his positive injunctions being not to undertake any enterprise that had much risk in it; but Lieut.-Cols. Dundas and Simcoe, concurring that one day's march might be made with perfect security, and that by this means more perfect information might be obtained, the troops were immediately put in motion, and proceeded towards Richmond, where the enemy was understood to have very considerable magazines. It was above 30 miles from Westover; several transports had not arrived, and Gen. Arnold's force did not amount to 800 men. On the second day's march, while a bridge was replacing over a creek, the advanced guard only having passed over, some of the enemy's militia, who had destroyed it the evening before, and were to assemble with others to defend it, were deceived by the dress of the Rangers, and came to Lieut.-Col. Simcoe, who immediately reprimanded them for not coming sooner, held conversation with them, and then sent them prisoners to Gen. Arnold. Within seven miles of Richmond, a patrol of the enemy appeared, who, on being discovered, fled at full speed: the Queen's Rangers, whose horses were in a miserable condition from the voyage, could not pursue them. Soon after, Lieut.-Col. Simcoe halted, having received the clearest information that a road, made passable by wood

carts, led through the thickets to the rear of the heights on which the town of Richmond was placed, where they terminated in a plain, although they were almost inaccessible by the common road. On giving this information to Gen. Arnold, he said it was not
worth while to quit the road, as the enemy would not fight. On approaching the town,
Gen. Arnold ordered the troops to march as open, and to make as great an appearance,
as possible ; and the ground was so favorable, that a more skilful enemy than those who
were now reconnoitring, would have imagined the numbers to have been double. The
enemy at Richmond appeared drawn up on the heights to the number of two or three
hundred men : the road passed through a wood at the bottom of these heights, and then
ran between them and the river into the lower town. Lieut.-Col. Simcoe was ordered
to dislodge them : he mounted the hill in small bodies, stretching away to the right, so
as to threaten the enemy with a design to outflank them ; and as they filed off, in appearance to secure their flank, he directly ascended with his cavalry, where it was so
steep that they were obliged to dismount and lead their horses. Luckily, the enemy
made no resistance, nor did they fire ; but on the cavalry's arrival on the summit, retreated to the woods in great confusion. There was a party of horsemen in the lower
town, watching the motion of Lieut.-Col. Dundas, who, the heights being gained, was
now entering it. Lieut.-Col. Simcoe pushed on with the cavalry, unnoticed by the
enemy in the lower town, till such time as he began to descend almost in their rear,
when an impassable creek stopped him, and gave the enemy time to escape to the top
of another hill beyond the town. Having crossed over lower down, he ascended the hill,
using such conversation and words towards them as might prevent their inclination to
retreat. However, when the Rangers were arrived within twenty yards of the summit,
the enemy, greatly superior in numbers, but made up of militia, spectators, some with
and some without arms, galloped off ; they were immediately pursued, but without the
least regularity : Capt. Shank and Lieut. Spencer, who had met with good horses in the
country, far distanced the rest of the cavalry. Lieut.-Col. Simcoe left an officer to
mark the position he meant his infantry to take on their arrival, and collecting all the
men he could overtake, followed Capt. Shank, anxious lest his ardor should prove fatal :
he had pursued the enemy four or five miles, six or seven of whom he had taken, with
several horses—a very well-timed capture. On Lieut.-Col. Simcoe's return, he met with
orders from Gen. Arnold to march to the foundry at Westham, six miles from Richmond,
and to destroy it ; the flank companies of the 80th, under Major Gordon, were sent as
a reinforcement. With these, and his corps, he proceeded to the foundry : the trun-
nions of many pieces of iron cannon were struck off ; a quantity of small arms, and a
great variety of military stores, were destroyed. Upon consultation with the artillery-
officer, it was thought better to destroy the magazine than to blow it up. This fatiguing
business was effected, by carrying the powder down the cliffs, and pouring it in the
water ; the warehouses and mills were then set on fire, and many explosions happened
in different parts of the buildings, which might have been hazardous, had it been relied
on that all the powder was regularly deposited in one magazine ; and the foundry, which
was a very complete one, was totally destroyed. It was night before the troops returned
to Richmond ; the provisions which had been made for them were now to be cooked :
fatigued with the march, the men in general went to sleep ; some of them got into private houses, and there obtained rum.

Morse, the geographer, thus describes Richmond in 1789, ten
years after it was made the capital :

It "contains about 300 houses. The new houses are well built. A large and elegant
state-house, or capitol, has lately been erected on the hill. The lower part of the town
is divided by a creek, over which there is a bridge which, for Virginia, is elegant. A
handsome and expensive bridge, between 300 and 400 yards in length, has lately been
thrown across James River at the foot of the falls, by Col. John Mayo, a respectable
and wealthy planter, whose seat is about a mile from Richmond. This bridge connects
Richmond with Manchester ; and as the passengers pay toll, it produces a handsome
revenue to Col. Mayo, who is the sole proprietor. The falls above the bridge are seven
miles in length. A canal is cutting on the north side of the river, which is to terminate
in a basin of about two acres, in the town of Richmond. The opening of this canal
promises the addition of much wealth to Richmond." In the year 1794, the canal was
so far completed that the difficulty of passing the rapids was removed. At this period,
the principal merchants of Richmond, and, indeed, of all the large towns in Eastern
Virginia, were Scotch and Scotch Irish. The inhabitants of this town have been
described by Paulding as being then generally " a race of most ancient and respectable

planters, having estates in the country, who chose it for their residence for the sake of social enjoyment. They formed a society now seldom to be met with in any of our cities. A society of people not exclusively monopolized by money-making pursuits, but of liberal education, liberal habits of thinking and acting; and possessing both leisure and inclination to cultivate those feelings, and pursue those objects which exalt our nature, rather than increase our fortune."

Richmond has increased steadily in population and wealth since it became the metropolis of the state. The population, in 1800, was 5,737; in 1810, 9,785; in 1820, 12,067; in 1830, 16,060; in 1840, 20,153. " Its situation is beautiful, and even romantic. Shockoe and Richmond Hills stand opposite to each other, with Shockoe creek, a bold and lively stream, between them. The city is spread over those hills; and along the margin of the river the hills have been thrown into various undulations, and present a great many points from which different views may be taken, highly beautiful.

" The picturesque falls and rapids of the river, which extend more than six miles; the islands; the town of Manchester, connected by two bridges with Richmond; the rich plantations adjoining the town; the river, winding and stretching below to a great extent; the waving hills on its north side, and the valley through which Shockoe creek passes, are the principal objects on which the eye fixes; and from every eminence they are seen in some new form, and under some new coloring of light and shade; the whole presenting the three great requisites of landscape, viz., grandeur, beauty, and variety. Besides, Richmond is one of the healthiest cities in the United States. The annual amount of deaths, on an average, is *one* in *eighty-five*."

With some trifling exceptions, the streets of Richmond intersect each other at right angles. The city plot has been greatly extended within a few years, and it now has an outline of 7½ miles in length, and an area of 3½ square miles, the larger portion of which is unoccupied by buildings. James River, immediately in front of the principal improvements, is interrupted by a ledge of rocks, which occasions a considerable fall in the stream. Some of these rocks rise into beautiful little islands. The navigable communication around the falls, by means of a canal and locks, opened many years since, now forms the outlet of James River Canal, with which it is connected by a capacious basin, situated near the centre of business in the city.

In the western division of the city, on Shockoe Hill, stands the capitol, on a commanding situation, in the centre of a beautiful square of about eight acres. It is a spacious and showy building. The statue of Washington, in the area of the capitol, was the work of Houdon, a French sculptor. It was made by the order of the Virginia Assembly, at Paris, under the direction of Jefferson, a few years after the close of the American revolution. The costume of this statue is the military dress of the revolution. One hand holds a cane, the other rests upon the fasces, with which are united the sword and ploughshare, and over it a martial cloak. The inscription, by James Madison, on the pedestal, is as follows:

> GEORGE WASHINGTON. The General Assembly of the Commonwealth of Virginia have caused this statue to be erected, as a monument of affection and gratitude to GEORGE WASHINGTON; who, uniting to the endowments of the *hero* the virtues of the *patriot*, and exerting both in establishing the liberties of his country, has rendered his name dear to his fellow-citizens, and given the world an immortal example of true glory. Done in the year of Christ, one thousand seven hundred and eighty-eight, and in the year of the commonwealth the twelfth.

Near the statue of Washington is a marble bust of Lafayette. In one angle of capitol square stands the city-hall, decorated at each end by a fine Doric portico of four columns. Near the eastern part of capitol square is a house erected for the residence of the governor of the state. In another part of Richmond is seen the county court-house. In the western suburbs of the city is the state penitentiary, a large building in the form of a hollow square, 300 feet long and 110 feet broad, with several acres of ground connected with it. In the suburbs of the city, on the N., is the almshouse, a spacious building, surrounded by extensive grounds. Among the other public buildings are a county and city jail, an orphan asylum, a theatre, a museum, two markets, an armory 320 by 280 feet, an academy, and a masonic hall. The city is supplied by water, which is elevated, by water-power and two forcing-pumps, into three large reservoirs, containing 1,000,000 gallons each, from which it is distributed over the city, and forms a great resource in case of fire, as well as a supply for the inhabitants. The cost of these works was about $120,000. There are three banks in the city.

Richmond is well situated for commerce. Vessels drawing 10 feet of water come to Rocket's, about a mile below the centre of the city; and those drawing 15 feet, to War-wick, 3 miles below the city. The falls in James River are obviated by the canal, and above them it is navigable to Lynchburg. Regular lines of packets connect this city with New York and other places, and it is connected by steamboats to Norfolk. The principal articles of exportation are wheat, flour, and tobacco. The exports amount to about $3,000,000 annually. The tonnage of this port in 1840, was 6,911.

The manufactures of Richmond are also extensive. The falls of the James River afford a water-power of unlimited extent. There were in 1840, 17 foreign commercial and 29 commission-houses, cap. $3,062,000; 256 retail stores, cap. $1,646,450; 3 lumber-yards, cap. $24,000; 4 furnaces, and 8 forges, &c., cap. $317,900; machinery produced amounted to $128,000; 1 cotton factory, 5,810 sp., cap. $175,000; tobacco manufactories, cap. $492,250; 1 paper factory, cap. $75,000; 3 flouring-mills, 2 grist-mills, 3 saw-mills, total cap. $61,000; 8 printing-offices, 1 bindery, 2 daily, 6 weekly, and 2 semi-weekly newspapers, and 1 periodical, cap. $48,700. Total cap. in manu-factories, $1,372,950.

Richmond contains 23 churches—4 Protestant Episcopal, 4 Baptist, 4 Methodist, 3 Presbyterian, (one of them a Bethel,) 1 Catholic, 1 German Lutheran, 1 Disciples, or Campbellite, 1 Universalist, 1 Friends, or Quakers, 1 African, 2 Jewish Synagogues.

The Monumental (Episcopal) Church is a handsome octagonal edifice, erected upon the spot once occupied by the Richmond Theatre, which was burnt in 1811. The remains of the unfortunate victims in that sad catastrophe, are deposited in a marble urn which stands in the front portico of the church, and from which it derives its name. The Right Rev. Bishop Moore preached here during his whole residence in Richmond.

The Monumental congregation are now building a new structure, to which they in-tend removing, to be called St. Paul's Church. Its model is St. Luke's, in Philadelphia, of the Corinthian order, much elaborated. The spire is to be 208 feet high.

The subjoined account of the burning of the Richmond Theatre, was published in the Richmond Standard the following day.

Last night the play-house in this city was crowded with an unusual audience. There could not have been less than 600 persons in the house. Just before the conclusion of the play, the scenery caught fire, and in a few minutes the whole building was wrapped in flames. It is already ascertained that sixty-one persons were devoured by that most terrific element. The editor of this paper was in the house when the ever-to-be-remem-bered deplorable accident occurred. He is informed that the scenery took fire in the back part of the house, by the raising of a chandelier; that the boy who was ordered by some of the players to raise it, stated that if he did so, the scenery would take fire, when he was commanded in a peremptory manner to hoist it. The boy obeyed, and the fire instantly communicated to the scenery. He gave the alarm in the rear of the stage, and requested some of the attendants to cut the cords by which the combustible materials were suspended. The person whose duty it was to perform this became panic-struck, and sought his own safety. This unfortunately happened at a time when one of the performers was playing near the orchestra, and the greatest part of the stage, with its horrid danger, was obscured from the audience by a curtain.

The flames spread with almost the rapidity of lightning; and the fire falling from the ceiling upon the performer, was the first notice the audience had of their danger. Even then, many supposed it a part of the play, and were a little time restrained from flight by a cry from the stage that there was no danger. The performers and their attendants in vain endeavored to tear down the scenery; the fire flashed in every part of the house with a rapidity horrible and astonishing; and, alas! gushing tears and unspeakable anguish deprived me of utterance. No person who was not present can form any idea of this unexampled scene of distress. The editor, having none of his family with him and not being far from the door, was among the first who escaped.

Burning of the Richmond Theatre.

[The above engraving of the burning of the theatre at Richmond, on the night of December 26th, 1811, is a reduced copy from one published at Philadelphia, by B. S. Tanner, in the February following.]

No words can express his horror when, on turning round, he discovered the whole building to be in flames. There was but one door for the greatest part of the audience to pass. Men, women, and children were pressing upon each other, while the flames were seizing upon those behind. The editor went to the different windows, which were very high, and implored his fellow-creatures to save their lives by jumping out of them. Those nearest the windows, ignorant of their danger, were afraid to leap down, while those behind them were seen catching on fire, and writhing in the greatest agonies of pain and distress. At length those behind, urged by the pressing flames, pushed those who were nearest to the window, and people of every description began to fall one upon another, some with their clothes on fire, some half roasted. Oh, wretched me! Oh, afflicted people! Would to God I could have died a thousand deaths in any shape, could individual suffering have purchased the safety of my friends, my benefactors, of those whom I loved! . . . The editor, with the assistance of others, caught several of those whom he had begged to leap from the windows. One lady jumped out when all her clothes were on fire. He tore them burning from her, stripped her of her last rags, and, protecting her nakedness with his coat, carried her from the fire. Fathers and mothers were deploring the loss of their children, children the loss of their parents; husbands were heard to lament their lost companions, wives were bemoaning their burnt husbands. The people were seen wringing their hands, beating their heads and breasts; and those that had secured themselves, seemed to suffer greater torments than those enveloped in the flames.

Oh! distracting memory! Who that saw this can think of it again, and yet retain his senses! Do I dream? No, no! Oh, that it were but a dream. My God! who that saw his friends and nearest connections devoured by fire, and laying in heaps at the door, will not regret that he ever lived to see such a sight? Could savages have seen this memorable event it would even soften their hearts.

A sad gloom pervades this place, and every countenance is cast down to the earth.

The loss of a hundred thousand friends on the field of battle could not touch the heart like this. Enough. Imagine what cannot be described. The most distant and implacable enemy, and the most savage barbarians, will mourn our unhappy lot. All of those in the pit escaped, and had cleared themselves from the house, before those in the boxes could get down; and the door was for some time empty. Those from above were pushing each other down the steps, when the hindermost might have got out by leaping into the pit. A gentleman and lady, who otherwise would have perished, had their lives saved by being providentially thrown from the second boxes. There would not have been the least difficulty in descending from the first boxes into the pit.

St. John's Church.

In addition to the list now given, it is believed that at least sixty others perished, whose names are not yet ascertained:

George W. Smith, governor, A. B. Venable, president of the bank, Benjamin Botts, wife, and niece, Mrs. Tayloe Braxton, Mrs. Patterson, Mrs. Gallego, Miss Conyers, Lieut. J. Gibbon, in attempting to save Miss Conyers; Mrs. E. Page, Miss Louisa Mayo, Mrs. William Cook, Miss Elvina Coutts, Mrs. John Lesley, Miss M. Nelson, Miss Nelson, Miss Page, Wm. Brown, Miss Julia Hervey, Miss Whitlock, George Dixon, A. Marshall (of Wythe) broke his neck in attempting to jump from a window, Miss Ann Craig, Miss Stevenson, (of Spottsylvania,) Mrs. Gibson, Miss Maria Hunter, Mrs. Mary Davis, Miss Gerard, Thomas Lecroix, Jane Wade, Mrs. Picket, Mrs. Heron, Mrs. Laforest and niece, Jo. Jacobs, Miss Jacobs, Miss. A. Bausman, Miss M. Marks, Edward Wanton, jr., two Misses Trouins, Mrs. Gerer, Mrs. Elicott, Miss Patsey Griffin, Mrs. Moss and daughter, Miss Littlepage, Miss Rebecca Cook, Mrs. Girardin and two children, Miss Margaret Copeland, Miss Gwathmey, Miss Clay, daughter of M. Clay, member of Congress, Miss Gatewood, Mrs. Thomas Wilson, Wm. Southgate, Mrs. Robert Greenhow, Mrs. Convert and child, Miss Green, Miss C. Raphael.

At a meeting of the commissioners appointed by the Common Hall to superintend the interment of the remains of their friends and fellow-citizens, who unfortunately lost their lives in the conflagration of the theatre, the following resolutions were adopted:

1st. That the citizens of Richmond and Manchester, and the citizens at present residing in either of those places, be requested to assemble to-morrow, the 28th inst., at 10 o'clock, P. M., at the Baptist meeting-house, for the purpose of attending the funeral.

2d. That the following be the order of procession:—corpses, clergy, mourners and ladies, executive council, directors of the bank, judiciary, members of the legislature, Court of Hastings, Common Hall, citizens on foot, citizens on horseback.

| WM. HAY, Jr., | JOHN ADAMS, |
| J. G. GAMBLE, | GAB. RALSTON, |

ST. JOHN'S CHURCH, on Richmond Hill, is the oldest colonial place of worship in the town. It is preserved with religious care, and has been somewhat modernized by the addition of a tower. This church stands in the centre of a grave-yard, embosomed by trees, where all around in crowded hillocks are the mansions of the dead.

It was here, in the Virginia convention of '75, that Patrick Henry thundered against the common oppressor of America, and uttered that immortal sentence, " *Give me liberty, or give me death !*"

The celebrated Virginia convention of '88, that met to ratify the federal constitution, assembled within its walls. The transcendent talents engaged in its discussion, " tempted industry to give up its pursuits, and even dissipation its objects," for the high intellectual feast here presented. Among the crowd from far and near, who filled the hall, " no bustle, no sound was heard, save only a slight movement when some new speaker arose, whom they were all eager to see as well as to hear; or when some master-stroke of eloquence shot thrilling along their nerves, and extorted an involuntary and inarticulate murmur. Day after day was this banquet of the mind and the heart spread before them, with a delicacy and variety which could never cloy." Among its illustrious members were Madison, Marshall, and Monroe; and " there were those sages of other days, Pendleton and Wythe ; there was seen the Spartan vigor and compactness of George Nicholas ; and there shone the radiant genius and sensibility of Grayson ; the Roman energy and the Attic wit of George Mason was there ; and there also the classic taste and harmony of Edmund Randolph ; ' the splendid conflagration' of the high-minded Innis ; and the matchless eloquence of the immortal Henry !"

The medical department of Hampden Sidney College was established in the year 1838, and has succeeded beyond the expectations of its most sanguine friends. The necessity of an institution where the young men of Virginia might prosecute the study of medicine without incurring the expense of a winter's residence in a northern city, had long been keenly felt, and the *projet* was carried into effect by a few enterprising members of the faculty resident in Richmond. Unassisted by legislative appropriation, this college struggled nobly through an infancy of six years, and " now presents to the student of the healing-art advantages not to be surpassed by any other establishment in the Union." The hospitals of the penitentiary and almshouse are under the supervision of the professors ; and the most abundant opportunities for clinical study are thus afforded. Attached to the college building is an extensive infirmary. The college building recently erected, is a fine specimen of the Egyptian style of architecture, admirably arranged for the purposes of lecture and dissection. The following is the faculty :—Augustus L. Warner, M. D., Dean of the faculty, John Cullen, M. D., Jeffries Wyman, M. D., S. Maupin, M. D., L. W. Chamberlayne, M. D., R. L. Bohannan, M. D.

St. Vincent's College, under the control of the Catholic clergy, is pleasantly situated about a mile east of the city. The Rev. Bishop Whelan is president. There is a very respectable number of students, who attend mass every morning at the chapel in Richmond.

Richmond College, a Baptist institution, was incorporated by act of legislature in the year 1832. The Rev. Robert Ryland is president of the institution. It contains five or six professors, and about one hundred students. The buildings are delightfully situated, about a mile west of the city, on the Fredericksburg rail-road.

The Richmond Academy, Wm. Burk principal, is a school for the preparation of youth for college in the higher branches of classical and mathematical education. There are five teachers, and some ninety or one hundred pupils. The pupils are allowed the privilege of being enrolled in a corps of cadets, at their option, in which the exercises of drill and military tactics are taught by a competent professor.

The Orphan Asylum is an institution under the direction of the " Ladies' Humane Association," for the education and support of female orphans. A large number of this unfortunate class are maintained there annually. A commodious and elegant building has been recently erected, out of a munificent bequest of the late Edmund Walls, Esq.

There is also, in Richmond, a Lancasterian free school for the use of the poor.

The following are slips cut from newspapers. The first was published a few years since, under the signature of C. C., and is a graphic sketch of the Virginia convention of 1829–30. The second is an inscription on a monument at Turkey island, in this county. The last is from the Virginia Gazette of August —, 1776 :

CONVENTION OF VIRGINIA.—I attended the debates of this body a fortnight. The capitol, in which the convention sat, is a fine building, nobly situated—more so than any other I have seen in this country. Richmond is a picturesque place ; the James looks beautiful there in a spring morning ; the rocks and islands, and foaming rapids, and murmuring falls, and floating mists, all light and glorious, under a clear blue sky. The convention boasted several men of distinction—Madison, Monroe, Giles, Marshall, Randolph, Leigh, Tazewell, &c. Mr. Madison sat on the left of the speaker, Mr. Monroe on the right. Mr. Madison spoke once for half an hour ; but although a pin might have been heard to drop, so low was his tone, that from the gallery I could distinguish only one word, and that was, "Constitution." He stood not more than six feet from the speaker. When he rose, a great part of the members left their seats and clustered around the aged statesman, thick as a swarm of bees. Mr. Madison was a small man, of ample forehead, and some obliquity of vision, (I thought the effect probably of age,) his eyes appearing to be slightly introverted. His dress was plain ; his overcoat a faded brown surtout. Mr. Monroe was very wrinkled and weather-beaten—ungraceful in attitude and gesture, and his speeches only common-place. Mr. Giles wore a crutch—was then governor of the state. His style of delivery was perfectly conversational—no gesture, no effort ; but in ease, fluency, and tact, surely he had not there his equal ; his words were like honey pouring from an eastern rock. Judge Marshall, whenever he spoke, which was seldom, and only for a short time, attracted great attention. His appearance was revolutionary and patriarchal. Tall, in a long surtout of blue, with a face of genius, and an eye of fire, his mind possessed the rare faculty of condensation ; he distilled an argument down to its essence. There were two parties in the house ; the western or radical, and the eastern or conservative. Judge Marshall proposed something in the nature of a compromise. John Randolph was remarkably deliberate, distinct, and emphatic. He articulated excellently, and gave the happiest effect to all he said. His person was frail and uncommon—his face pale and withered—but his eye radiant as a diamond. He owed, perhaps, more to his manner than to his matter ; and his mind was rather poetical than logical. Yet in his own peculiar vein, he was superior to any of his cotemporaries. Benjamin Watkins Leigh cut a distinguished figure in the convention, as the leader of the lowland party. His diction is clear, correct, elegant, and might be safely committed to print just as spoken. Yet high as he stands, he is not perhaps in the highest rank of speakers. He never lightens, never thunders ; he can charm, he can convince, but he can hardly overwhelm. Mr. Tazewell I never saw up but once, for a moment, on a point of order ; a tall, fine-looking man. P. P. Barbour presided over the body with great dignity and ease. Of these seven extraordinary men, four have since died, to wit : Monroe, Giles, Randolph, and Marshall. Mr. Leigh is now a United States senator, and Mr. Tazewell governor of Virginia.

———

The foundation of this pillar was laid in the calamitous year 1771, when all the great rivers of this country were swept by inundations never before experienced ; which changed the face of nature, and left traces of their violence that will remain for ages.

———

On Monday last, being court-day, the DECLARATION OF INDEPENDENCE was publicly proclaimed in the town of Richmond, before a large concourse of respectable freeholders of Henrico county, and upwards of 200 militia, who assembled on that grand occasion. It was received with universal shouts of joy, and re-echoed by three volleys of small-arms. The same evening the town was *illuminated*, and the members of the committee held a club, where many patriotic toasts were drunk. Although there were near one thousand people present, the whole was conducted with the utmost decorum, and the satisfaction visible in every countenance, sufficiently evinces their determination to support it with their lives and fortunes.

> Now will America's sons her fame increase,
> In arms and science, with glory, honor, and peace.

———

"EDMUND RANDOLPH was an eminent lawyer, and a warm friend of the revolution. After having filled several honorable stations in the state, he was, in 1779, elected to a seat in Congress, and held it until 1782. In 1787, he was a member of the convention which formed the federal constitution, but voted against its adoption. The next year he was chosen governor of Virginia, and in 1789, was appointed attorney-general of the United States ; and in 1794, secretary of state, which office he resigned the succeeding year. He died Sept. 12th, 1813." His personal and intellectual characteristics are described in the British Spy.

" The old Stone House," Main-street.

"The old Stone House," is situated on the northern side of Main-street, a few rods below the market. It is the oldest dwelling standing in Richmond, and among the first ever built in the town.

It is the residence and property of Mrs. Elizabeth Welsh, and has been in the same family for six generations. Mr. Jacob Ege, her great-grandfather, was a native of Germany, who settled upon this spot when there were few or no inhabitants on the site of the town, and previous to the erection of Byrd's warehouse. Mr. Ege had originally intended to have settled further up the country, but was so well pleased with the place, that he took up some land for a garden, and built this house. When President Monroe was a young man, attending school in Richmond, he boarded here. Mr. Samuel Ege, the father of Mrs. Welsh, resided in this house during the revolution. At that time it was one of the best houses in Richmond. It has been honored by the visits of Washington, Jefferson, Lafayette, Madison, Henry, and other distinguished personages. This part of the town was first settled, and it gradually extended to the capitol, which building was commenced in 1780, and was several years in constructing. It was a question whether it should be on Richmond Hill, or where it now is. It was decided by a gentleman's giving all the land included in the capitol square.

When the British, under Arnold, invaded Richmond in 1781, Mr. Ege was absent on duty, as a commissary in the American army. The first his wife (Mrs. Welsh's mother) knew of their approach, was the seeing a body of their cavalry galloping down Richmond Hill, then much steeper than at present. She described it as the most beautiful sight she ever witnessed. One of their officers quartered with her. The enemy broke open the stores, and emptied the liquors and provisions into the gutters. The spirits ran into the creek and gutters. The cows and hogs, having partaken of the liquid, were seen staggering about the streets.

HENRY.

HENRY was formed in 1776, from Pittsylvania, and named in honor of Patrick Henry. It is in form approaching a square of about 18 miles on a side. Its extreme sw. angle is crossed by the two branches of Mary's River; but the greater part of the area of the county is included in the valley of Smith's River, which enters the county near its NW. angle, and forms a junction with the

Dan near its se. angle. Tobacco, Indian corn, oats, and wheat, are the principal staples. Pop. in 1840, whites 4,243, slaves 2,852, free colored 240 ; total, 7,335.

Martinsville, the county-seat, lies near the n. bank of Smith's River, about 70 miles sw. of Lynchburg, and 194 miles from Richmond. It is but a small village, situated on a beautiful eminence, commanding an extensive view of the surrounding country, and well supplied with excellent springs.

ISLE OF WIGHT.

Isle of Wight was one of the eight original shires into which Virginia was divided in 1634. Its name originally was *Warrosquyoake shire*, which it retained three years only, when its present one was given to it. The county is 37 miles long, with a mean width of 11 : it has many creeks and swamps upon its surface, and a great variety of soil, though it is generally thin and sandy. Pop. in 1840, whites 4,918, slaves 3,786, free colored 1,268 ; total, 9,972.

Smithfield is in the northern part of the county, 65 miles southeasterly from Richmond, 15 above Hampton Roads, and 3 miles from James River. It lies on an elevated bank on the margin of Pagan creek, a bold and navigable stream, commanding a beautiful view of both land and water scenery—the country for 10 miles on the opposite bank of the James is in full view. This town was established in February, 1752, ten years after the founding of Richmond. Arthur Smith, Esq., the original owner of the land, had then laid it out into streets and lots, and being "an healthy place, and open to trade and navigation," it had begun to be built and settled upon. By the provisions of the act, Robert Burwell, Arthur Smith, William Hodsden, James Baker, James Dunlop, James Arthur, and Joseph Bridger, gentlemen, were appointed trustees. Smithfield at present contains 10 or 12 stores, 1 Episcopalian, 1 Baptist, and 1 Methodist church, and a population of about 1000. The village is ornamented with shade-trees ; and the numerous porches to the dwellings impress the stranger favorably as to the social and neighborly habits of its people. Several vessels sail from Smithfield with the exports of the county. Among these is bacon, cured here, which has long been celebrated, and commands the preference in all markets. Mayfield is a small village in the western part of the county.

Within an hour's ride from Smithfield, near the road to Suffolk, in the depths of the forest, stands an ancient church in ruins. It is alike an object of interest from its secluded situation, and its great antiquity. We have before us a communication from a highly respectable gentleman of this vicinity, which gives strong evidence that it was built in the reign of Charles I., between the years 1630

and 1635. Tradition, too, states that it was the second church
erected in Virginia. The brick, lime, and timber, were imported
from England. The timber is English oak, and was framed be-

Ancient Church, near Smithfield.

fore shipment. The whole structure was built in the most substantial manner ; and even now, the wood-work, where not exposed
to rain, is perfectly sound, and the mortar sufficiently hard to strike
fire when in collision with steel. The structure is of brick, has a
lofty tower, and is in good preservation. Its walls are overrun with
a delicate net-work of vines.

In its day, it was a splendid edifice. One window, of about 25
feet in height, was composed of painted glass, representing scrip-
tural subjects. It was probably abandoned about the period of the
American revolution, when the Episcopal church, for a time, became nearly extinct in Virginia. Within the last twenty-five years
it has been temporarily occupied by a sect called O'Kellyites.
There is a project, which may be carried into effect, to repair it. If
successful, generations yet unborn will meet within its time-hal-
lowed walls, where, even now, more than two centuries have
elapsed since their forefathers first raised the hymn of praise to
the living God.

JACKSON.

JACKSON was formed in 1831, from Mason, Kanawha, and Wood:
its length is 33, and its mean breadth 24 miles. The surface is

hilly, and the soil well adapted to grazing. The bottom lands on Mill creek and its branches are of the first quality. From the interior of the county, the principal exports are cattle and pork; along the Ohio, which bounds it on the west, the people export large quantities of staves, hoop-poles, and lumber of all kinds. Pop. in 1840, whites 4,803, slaves 87; total, 4,890.

Ripley, the county-seat, lies 336 miles northwesterly from Richmond, and 12 from the Ohio River, on the Great Mill creek, at its confluence with Sycamore creek. Although but recently established, it is a thriving village, containing 2 mercantile stores, and about 30 dwellings. Ravenswood, 10 miles NE. of Ripley, on the Ohio, contains 1 church, 1 store, 1 steam saw-mill, and about 15 dwellings.

JAMES CITY.

JAMES CITY was one of the eight original shires into which Virginia was divided in 1634. It has York River on its northern, and the James on its southern boundary. Its length is 23 miles, mean breadth 8 miles. Pop., whites 1,325, slaves 1,947, free colored 507; total, 3,779.

Ruins at Jamestown.

Jamestown, the first settlement in British America, was settled by Capt. John Smith and his companions, May 13th, 1607. The site is a point of land projecting into the James. The water is gaining on the shore, and the time may arrive when the waves will roll over it. Of this deeply interesting spot, little remains but a church-yard, and the tower of an ancient church—a venerable memento of antiquity, carrying back the mind of the traveller, as he hurries by in a passing steamer, to scenes long since vanished "down time's lengthening way." How appropriate and beautiful are the reflections of the British Spy at this spot:

It is difficult [says he] to look at this venerable steeple, surrounded as it is with these awful proofs of the mortality of man, without exclaiming, in the pathetic solemnity of our Shakspeare,

> "The cloud-capt towers, the gorgeous palaces,
> The solemn temples, the great globe itself,
> Yea, all which it inherits, shall dissolve ;
> And, like this insubstantial pageant faded,
> Leave not a wreck behind."

Whence, my dear S . . . . . , arises the irrepressible reverence and tender affection with which I look at this broken steeple ? Is it that my soul, by a secret, subtle process, invests the mouldering ruin with her own powers ; imagines it a fellow-being ; a venerable old man, a Nestor, or an Ossian, who has witnessed and survived the ravages of successive generations, the companions of his youth, and of his maturity, and now mourns his own solitary and desolate condition, and hails their spirits in every passing cloud ? Whatever may be the cause, as I look at it, I feel my soul drawn forward as by the cords of gentlest sympathy, and involuntarily open my lips to offer consolation to the drooping pile.

Where, my S . . . . . . , is the busy, bustling crowd which landed here two hundred years ago ? Where is Smith, that pink of gallantry, that flower of chivalry ? I fancy that I can see their first slow and cautious approach to the shore ; their keen and vigilant eyes piercing the forest in every direction, to detect the lurking Indian, with his tomahawk, bow and arrow. Good heavens ! what an enterprise ! how full of the most fearful perils ! and yet how entirely profitless to the daring men who personally undertook and achieved it ! Through what a series of the most spirit-chilling hardships had they to toil !—How often did they cast their eyes to England in vain ! and with what delusive hopes, day after day, did the little famished crew strain their sight to catch the white sail of comfort and relief ! But day after day the sun set, and darkness covered the earth ; but no sail of comfort or relief came. How often in the pangs of hunger, sickness, solitude, and disconsolation, did they think of London ; her shops, her markets groaning under the weight of plenty ; her streets swarming with gilded coaches, bustling hacks, with crowds of lords, dukes, and commons, with healthy, busy, contented faces of every description ; and, among them, none more healthy, or more contented, than those of their ungrateful and improvident directors ! But now—where are they all ? the little famished colony which landed here, and the many-colored crowd of London— where are they, my dear S . . . . . ? Gone, where there is no distinction ; consigned to the common earth. Another generation succeeded them ; which, just as busy and as bustling as that which fell before it, has sunk down into the same nothingness. Another, and yet another billow, has rolled on, each emulating its predecessor in height ; towering for its moment, and curling its foaming honors to the clouds ; then roaring, breaking, and perishing on the same shore.

It is not known, precisely, when the church, the tower of which remains, was built. A church was erected very soon after its first settlement, which the Westover ms. says "cost no more than £50." The following extracts from Smith's History, will throw some light upon the subject :

And so we returned all well to *Iames* towne, where this new supply being lodged with the rest, accidentally fired their quarters, and so the towne, which being but thatched with reeds, the fire was so fierce as it burnt their pallisado's, (though eight or ten yards distant,) with their armes, bedding, apparell, and much priuate prouision. Good Master Hunt, *our preacher*, lost all his liberary, and all he had but the cloathes on his backe : yet none neuer heard him repine at his losse. This happned in the winter, in that extreame frost, 1607.—Smith, *book* 3, (*Richmond edition*,) p. 168.

The spring approaching, and the ship departing, Mr. *Scrivener* and Captaine Smith divided betwixt them the rebuilding *Iames* towne ; the repairing our pallisadoes ; the cutting downe trees ; preparing our fields ; planting our corne, and to rebuild our church, and to recover our store-house. All men thus busie at their seuerall labors, Master Nelson arrived with his lost *Phœnix.—Book* 3, *p.* 170.

The Phœnix arrived, says Sparks, in his Life of Smith, in the spring of 1608. Smith says, under the chapter headed " The gouernment deuolued to Captaine Samuel Argall 1617 :"

In March they set saile, 1617, [from England,] and in May he [Argall] arrived at Iames towne, where hee was kindly entertained, by Captaine *Yearley* and his companie, in a martiall order, whose right-hand file was led by an Indian. In *Iames* towne he found but fiue or six houses, the *church* downe, the pallizado's broken, the bridge in pieces, the well of fresh water spoiled, the storehouse vsed for the church ; the market-place and streets, and all other spare places planted with tobacco ; the saluages as fre-quent in their houses as themselues, whereby they become expert in our armes, and had a great many in their custodie and possession ; the colony dispersing all about, planting tobacco.

From the above, it is evident that previous to 1617, or 10 years after the first settlement of Jamestown, there were two churches destroyed. This tower now standing may have belonged to the second church, and survived its destruction. It could not have been part of the first, for that " cost no more than £50 ;" or it may have been the tower of a third. We can only surmise that the tower has been standing about 230 years. It is unnecessary to detail further the early history of Jamestown, as it is delineated in the general history of Virginia in this volume.

Two actions were fought in this vicinity in the revolution. The first was June 25th, 1781, and took place at Spencer's ordinary, in the forks of the roads leading to Jamestown and Williamsburg. The subjoined account is from Girardin :

Lafayette, attentive to the movements of his adversary, no sooner observed his retreat from Richmond, than he himself moved onward ; displaying, however, the same salutary circumspection as before, and uniformly keeping his main body at the distance of about twenty miles from the foe. Cornwallis reached Williamsburg on the 25th of June. During his halt in that place, hearing that the Americans had some boats and stores on Chickahominy River, he charged Lieut.-Col. Simcoe with the destruction of these. The latter, attended by his corps and a party of yagers, easily performed the task. Lafayette, after passing through Richmond and New Kent Court House in pur-suit of Cornwallis, had taken post on Tyre's plantation, about twenty miles from Wil-liamsburg. There he was informed, by his exploring parties, of Simcoe's expedition to the Chickahominy, and immediately detached Lieut.-Col. Butler, of the Pennsylvania line, with orders to strike the British partisan on his return. Butler was well known for his skill and courage. His achievements at Saratoga had placed him by the side of Morgan, and he had uniformly and gloriously maintained this high ground. The con-fidence of Lafayette could not be better placed. On the present occasion, where only a partial engagement was sought, the detachment confided to him consisted, besides his continentals, of the rifle-corps under the Majors Call and Willis, and about one hun-dred and twenty horsemen. This last force was commanded by Major M'Pherson, of Pennsylvania. He mounted some infantry behind his dragoons, and, seeking Simcoe with unusual ardor and speed, overtook him near Spencer's plantation, six or seven miles above Williamsburg. A sharp conflict immediately ensued, in which the British yagers and the American cavalry were alternately repulsed. The arrival of the riflemen, headed by.Call and Willis, gave to the action additional fierceness ; but the superiority of the hostile cavalry, compelled Butler's van to fall back upon the body of continentals stationed in the rear. Here the contest ended ; Simcoe resuming his retreat, and Butler not choosing to pursue him because he was informed that Cornwallis, upon hearing the first fire, had ordered his main body to the support of the returning detachment. The official accounts of the two generals widely differ as to the loss sustained by each party in this action. Lafayette states the enemy's loss at sixty killed and one hundred wounded. Cornwallis says that three officers and thirty privates only were killed and wounded. Among the killed, a Lieutenant Jones seems to have excited peculiar regret. The loss of the Americans in killed and wounded has not been recorded ; but if we credit the statement of the British commander, three of their officers, with twenty-eight privates, were taken prisoners.

When Cornwallis first arrived in this vicinity, he prepared to cross over the James, at Jamestown, and march to Portsmouth. After halting nine days at Williamsburg, his lordship advanced, on the 4th of July, 1781, to Jamestown Island. The 5th and 6th were employed in transporting his baggage, &c., while the main army still continued in their encampment. Lafayette having received false information that only a covering party remained on this side of the river with Cornwallis, determined to make an attack, the success of which was deemed infallible. The events are thus detailed by Girardin :

The British commander received information of Lafayette's approach about noon on the 6th, and took every measure in his power to confirm the belief that his rear-guard only now remained. He drew up the major part of his army in compact order on the main land, deployed a few troops on the island so as to magnify their apparent numbers, drew in his light parties, and directed his piquets to suffer themselves to be insulted and driven in. By this coincidence of circumstances calculated to delude, an error was perpetuated which exposed the American army in Virginia to the most imminent peril of utter annihilation.

About three in the afternoon, Lafayette's army began to move from Greenspring. This late hour was judiciously and happily fixed upon. If only a strong hostile party should be found at Jamestown, the remaining part of the day would suffice for its destruction ; if, on the contrary, the main body of Cornwallis's troops should be encountered, the intervening shades of the approaching night would shield the Americans from ruin. In their advance to the enemy, not more than one mile and a half distant, Lafayette's troops had to pass over a causeway, extending from the house at Greenspring to the Williamsburg road, through a tract of low and sunken ground impracticable to either infantry or cavalry. The time consumed in the passage of this defile retarded the approach of the Americans to the British till near sunset. The rifle corps under Call and Willis, and a patrol of dragoons, formed the front of the assailants. These were followed by the cavalry of Armand and Mercer's troop, headed by Major M'Pherson. The continental infantry, under Wayne, supported the whole. Steuben was left at Greenspring with the militia, forming a reserve obviously too remote from the acting corps for any efficient purpose. When the advancing column reached the road, parties of riflemen were thrown on its flanks, while the cavalry continued to move in front. The action was soon commenced by a desultory fire of the enemy's yagers. M'Pherson and Mercer being then ordered to take the command of the rifle corps, rapidly led them on to the attack, and drove in the hostile piquets, with much confusion and some loss on the side of the British. This advantage was keenly pursued by the American riflemen, who, taking post in a ditch covered by a rail fence, recommenced their fire with considerable effect. Two battalions of continental infantry, led on by Majors Galvan and Willis, supported by two pieces of artillery under the direction of Captain Savage, now joined the riflemen, and assisted them in successfully maintaining for some time a most arduous conflict against the enemy, who now advanced in a body headed by Lieut.-Col. Yorke on the right, and Lieut.-Col. Dundas on the left. The superiority of the foe, however, was too great to be long resisted : the riflemen first gave way, then the cavalry, and finally the light infantry. They all fell back upon Wayne, as did also Capt. Savage with his two field-pieces. The brave leader of the Pennsylvania line had drawn up his men in compact order, under cover of an adjacent wood. He repeatedly directed them to charge the enemy with fixed bayonets, but local circumstances prevented the execution of this order, and allowed only a close and murderous fire. Lafayette, who by this time had discovered his mistake, and became convinced that he had to contend with the main body of the British army, observing that Wayne was nearly outflanked on both sides, ordered him to retreat to the second line of continentals, drawn up about half a mile in his rear. The darkness of the night favored this retreat. It was, however, found necessary to abandon the two field-pieces ; after which the morass in front of Greenspring was recrossed, and the acting corps, together with the reserve, proceeded to a more remote and safer encampment. Whether from his apprehension of some ambuscade, or from what was with him a more powerful consideration than fear, a desire, of quickly transmitting to Sir Henry Clinton the required assistance, Cornwallis attempted no pursuit, but in the course of the night crossed over into Jamestown Island, and soon afterwards proceeded to Portsmouth.

In this affair, one hundred and eighteen of the continental troops, among whom were ten officers, were killed, wounded, or taken. The British state their loss, both in killed and wounded, at five officers and seventy privates.

Williamsburg, the seat of justice for the county, is 58 miles from Richmond, 12 from Yorktown, 68 from Norfolk, and 7 from Jamestown. It is finely situated, on a level plain, between the York and James, immediately on the division line between James City and York counties. It is laid out in parallel streets, with a square in the centre of several acres, containing the county buildings. Through it runs the principal street, which is very wide, and about a mile in length; at one end of which is the college, and at the other the ruins of the old capitol.

Williamsburg, in its most palmy days, contained only a population of about 2,000. It has at present 1 Episcopal, 1 Baptist, and 1 Methodist church, and about 1,600 inhabitants. The Eastern Lunatic Asylum is located here. It consists of a lofty and extensive pile of brick buildings, enclosed by a wall, in a pleasant area of several acres. The number of patients is generally over one hundred; and the institution is ably conducted, under the superintendence of Dr. John M. Galt.

There is an air of repose about this village city, so interesting from its historic associations. It is the oldest incorporated town in Virginia. This immediate vicinity was first known as the Middle Plantations, and the town was first settled in 1632, from the adjoining settlements, principally from Jamestown. In 1698, the seat of government was removed here from that place. From a work* published a short time after, we make the following extract, principally relative to this place:

The first metropolis, Jamestown, was built in the most convenient place for trade, and security against the Indians; but often received much damage, being twice burnt down, after which it never recovered its perfection—consisting at present of nothing but abundance of brick rubbish and three or four good inhabited houses, though the parish is of pretty large extent, but less than others. When the state-house and prison were burnt down, Governor Nicholson removed the residence of the governor, with the meetings of the general courts and general assemblies, to Middle Plantation, seven miles from Jamestown, in a healthier and more convenient place, and freer from the annoyance of moschetoes. Here he laid out the city of Williamsburg—in the form of a cipher, made of W and M—on a ridge at the head springs of two great creeks, one running into James, and the other into York River, which are each navigable for sloops within a mile of the town; at the head of which creek are good landings, and lots laid out, and dwelling-houses and warehouses built; so that this town is most conveniently situated, in the middle of the lower part of Virginia, commanding two noble rivers, not above four miles from either, and is much more commodious and healthful than if built upon a river.

Public buildings here of note are, the college, the capitol, the governor's house, and the church.

The college front, which looks due east, is double, and is 136 feet long. It is a lofty pile of brick buildings, adorned with a cupola. At the north end runs back a large wing, which is a handsome hall, answerable to which the chapel is to be built; and

* "The Present State of Virginia, by Hugh Jones, A. M., chaplain to the honorable Assembly, and lately minister of Jamestown, &c., in Virginia." This work is a small 12mo. of about 150 pages. It is very scarce. The only copies we have seen are in the libraries of Gov. Tazewell, and Peter Force, Esq., of Washington city.

there is a spacious piazza on the west side, from one wing to the other. It is approached by a good walk, and a grand entrance by steps, with good courts and gardens about it, with a good house and apartments for the *Indian* master and his scholars, and out-houses; and a large pasture enclosed like a park, with about 150 acres adjoining, for occasional uses.

The building is beautiful and commodious, being first modelled by Sir Christopher Wren, adapted to the nature of the country by the gentlemen there; and since it was burnt down it has been rebuilt, nicely contrived, altered, and adorned, by the ingenious direction of Governor Spotswood; and is not altogether unlike Chelsea Hospital.

This royal foundation was granted and established by charter, by King William and Queen Mary, and endowed by them with some thousand acres of land, with duties upon furs and skins, and a penny a pound for all tobacco transported from Virginia and Maryland to the other plantations; to which have been made several additional bene-factions: as that handsome establishment of Mr. Boyle, for the education of Indians, with the many contributions of the country, especially a late one of £1000 to buy negroes for the college use and service.

The society is a corporation, established for a president, six masters, or professors, with a hundred scholars, more or less.

The salary of the president, Mr. James Blair, has been lately ordered to be reduced from £150 to £100 per annum.

The salary of the fellows—one of which I have been for several years—is £80 per annum each; with 20s. entrance, and 20s. a year for pupilage, for each scholar. The payments are sometimes made in current Spanish money, and sometimes in sterling bills.

When the college shall be completely finished, and scholarships founded, then is the trust to be transferred from the trustees to the president and masters; but at present it is managed by a certain number of governors or visitors—one of which is yearly chosen rector—appointed first by the trustees, elected out of the principal and worthiest inhabitants. These appoint a person to whom they grant several privileges and allow-ances, to board and lodge the masters and scholars at an extraordinary cheap rate. This office is at present performed in the neatest and most regular and plentiful manner by Mrs. Mary Stith, a gentlewoman of great worth and discretion, in good favor with the gentry, and great esteem and respect with the common people.

The Indians who are upon Mr. Boyle's foundation have now a handsome apartment for themselves and their master, built near the college. The young Indians, procured from the tributary or foreign nations with much difficulty, were formerly boarded or lodged in the town, where abundance of them used to die, either through sickness, change of provision, and way of life; or, as some will have it, often for want of proper necessaries, and due care taken with them. Those of them that have escaped well, and been taught to read and write, have, for the most part, returned to their home, some with, and some without baptism, where they follow their own savage customs and hea-thenish rites. A few of them have lived as servants among the English, or loitered and idled away their time in laziness and mischief. But it is a great pity that more care is not taken of them after they are dismissed from school. They have admirable capaci-ties when their humors and tempers are perfectly understood.

Fronting the college, at near its whole breadth, is extended a whole street, mathemat-ically straight—for the first design of the town's form is changed to a much better—just three quarters of a mile in length, at the other end of which stands the *Capitol*, a noble, beautiful, and commodious pile, as any of its kind, built at the cost of the late queen, and by direction of the governor. In this is the secretary's office, with all the courts of law and justice, held in the same form, and near the same manner, as in Eng-land, except the ecclesiastical courts. Here the governor and twelve counsellors sit as judges in the general courts, in April and October, whither trials and causes are re-moved from courts held at the court-houses, monthly, in every county, by a bench of justices and a county clerk. Here are also held the Oyer and Terminer courts, one in summer and the other in winter, added by the charity of the late queen, for the preven-tion of prisoners lying in jail above a quarter of a year before their trial. Here are also held court martials, by judges appointed on purpose for the trial of pirates; likewise courts of admiralty, for the trial of ships for illegal trade. The building is in the form of an H nearly; the secretary's office and the general court taking up one side below stairs; the middle being a handsome portico, leading to the clerk of the assembly's office, and the House of Burgesses on the other side; which last is not unlike the House of Commons. In each wing is a good staircase, one leading to the council-chamber, -where the governor and council sit in very great state, in imitation of the king and council, or the lord chancellor and House of Lords. Over the portico is a large room where conferences are held, and prayers are read by the chaplain to the general assembly; which office I have had the honor, for some years, to perform. At one end of this is a lobby, and near it is the clerk of the council's office; and at the other end are several chambers for the committees of claims, privileges, and elections; and over all these are several good offices for the receiver-general, for the auditor, and treasurer, &c.; and upon the middle is raised a lofty cupola with a large clock.

The whole is surrounded with a neat area, encompassed with a good wall, and near it is a strong sweet prison for criminals; and on the other side of the open court another for debtors, when any are removed from the other prisons in each county; but such prisoners are very rare, the creditors being there generally very merciful, and the laws so favorable for debtors that some esteem them too indulgent.

The cause of my being so particular in describing the *capitol*, is because it is the best and most commodious pile of its kind that I have seen or heard of.

Because the state-house, James Town, and the college have been burnt down, therefore is prohibited in the *capitol*, the use of fire, candles, and *tobacco*.

Parallel to the main street mentioned is a street on each side of it, but neither quite so long nor so broad; and at proper distances are small cross-streets, for the convenience of communication. Near the middle stands the *church*, which is a large strong piece of brick-work in the form of a cross, nicely regular and convenient, and adorned as the best churches in London. This from the parish is called Bruton church, where I had the favor of being lecturer. Near this is the large *octagon tower*, which is the magazine, or repository of arms and ammunition, standing far from any house except James Town court-house; for the town is half in James Town county, and half in York county. Not far from hence is a large area for a market-place; near which is a playhouse and good bowling-green.

From the church runs a street northward, called Palace-street; at the other end of which stands the palace, or governor's house, a magnificent structure, built at the public expense, finished and beautified with gates, fine gardens, offices, walks, a fine canal, orchards, &c., with a great number of the best arms, nicely posited, by the ingenious contrivance of the most accomplished Colonel Spotswood. This likewise has the ornamental addition of a good cupola or lantern, illuminating most of the town upon birth-nights, and other nights of occasional rejoicings. At the *capitol*, at public times, may be seen a great number of handsom, well-dressed, compleat gentlemen; and at the governor's house, upon birth-nights, and at balls and assemblies, I have seen as fine an appearance, as good diversion, and as splendid entertainments in Governor Spotswood's time, as I have seen anywhere else.

These buildings here described are justly reputed the best in all English America, and are exceeded by few of their kind in England. . . . .

Williamsburg is now incorporated and made a market-town, and governed by a mayor and alderman; and is well stocked with rich stores of all sorts of goods, and well furnished with the best provisions and liquors. Here dwell several very good families, and more reside here at their own houses in public times. They live in the same neat manner, dress after the same modes, and behave themselves exactly as the gentry in London; most families of any note having a coach, chariot, berlin, or chaise. The number of artificers here is daily augmented, as are the convenient ordinaries or inns, for the accommodation of strangers. The servants here, as in other parts of the county, are English, Scotch, Irish, or negroes. The town is regularly laid out in lots or square portions, sufficient each for a house and garden, so that they don't build contiguous, whereby may be prevented the spreading danger of fire; and this also affords a free passage for the air, which is very grateful in violent hot weather.

Here, as in other parts, they build with brick, but most commonly with timber lined with ceiling, and cased with feather edged plank, painted with white-lead and oil, covered with shingles of cedar, &c., tarred over at first; with a passage generally through the middle of the house, for an air-draught in summer. Thus their houses are lasting; dry and warm in winter, and cool in summer; especially if there be windows enough to draw the air. Thus they dwell comfortably, genteelly, pleasantly, and plentiful, in this delightful, healthful, and, I hope, thriving *city of Williamsburg*.

The foregoing description of Williamsburg, published 120 years since, in many points resembles it at the present time. From then until 1779, when the seat of government was removed to Richmond, the town was the centre of the fashion, wealth, and learning of the "Old Dominion;" the influence of which has left its impress upon the place, and the manners and characteristics of its present inhabitants. Being then " the residence of the governor—the immediate representative of the sovereign—the royal state in which he lived, the polite and brilliant circle which he always had about him, diffused their influence through the city and the circumjacent country, and filled Williamsburg with a degree of emulation,

William and Mary College, Williamsburg.

taste, and elegance, of which we can form no conception by the appearances of the present day. During the session of the House of Burgesses, too, these stately modes of life assumed their richest forms; the town was filled with a concourse of visitors, as well as citizens, attired in their gayest colors; the streets exhibited a continual scene of animated and glittering tumult; the houses, of costly profusion."

Several of the buildings above described are yet standing: among which is the church and the octagon tower known as the " old magazine." In the church, a few years since, was to be seen the gubernatorial pew of Sir Alexander Spotswood, governor of Virginia from 1710 to 1723. It was raised from the floor, covered with a canopy, around the interior of which his name was written in gilt letters.

William and Mary College, now the principal support of the town, is, with the exception of Harvard University, the oldest literary institution in the Union. It is distinguished for the very large proportion of its graduates who have arisen to eminence; some of whom have held the highest stations in the nation.

" The college library contains somewhat less than four thousand volumes, of which many are theological. Some of the books were presented by Robert Dinwiddie, and have his coat of arms affixed, the crest, an eagle, and the motto, ' *Ubi libertas, ibi patria*.' In others was inscribed the name of Major-General Alexander Spots-wood.   Some were the gift of the former presidents of the college, and others of the Assembly of Virginia.   Catesby's Natural History of Carolina, Florida, and the Bahama Islands, was given (as appears from a note on the first page, in the hand-writing of Thomas Jefferson) on condition that it should never go out of the college.   This work was printed London, 1754, with colored plates, in two volumes folio, in English and French."

The college was founded in 1692, in the reign of William and Mary, who granted it a donation of 20,000 acres of land.

In 1793, the Assembly ordered that it should be built at Williamsburg.   "The college received a penny a lb. duty on certain tobaccos exported from Virginia and Maryland, which had been levied by the statute of the 25th of Charles II.   The Assembly also gave it, by temporary laws, a duty on liquors imported, and skins and furs exported.   From these resources it received upwards of 3000 pounds, communibus annis.   The buildings are of brick, and sufficiently large for the accommodation of 100 students.   By its charter, dated the 8th of February, 1692, it was placed under the direction of not less than twenty visitors, and to have a president and six professors, who were incorporated.   It was formerly allowed a representative in the General Assembly.   Under this charter, a professorship of the Greek and Latin languages, a professorship of mathematics, one of moral philosophy, and two of divinity were established.   To these were annexed, for a sixth professorship, a considerable donation, by Mr. Boyle of England, for the instruction of the Indians and their conversion to Christianity.   This was called the professorship of Brafferton, from an estate of that name in England purchased with the moneys given.   The admission of the learners of Latin and Greek filled the college with children.   This rendering it disagreeable, and degrading to young men already prepared for entering on the sciences, they were discouraged from resorting to it, and thus the school for mathematics and moral philosophy, which might have been of some service, became of very little   The revenues, too, were exhausted in accommodating those who came only to acquire the rudiments of science.   After the revolution, the visitors, having no power to change those circumstances in the constitution of the college, which were fixed by the charter, and being, therefore, confined in the number of professorships, undertook to change the object of the professorships.   They excluded the two schools for divinity, and that for the Greek and Latin languages, and substituted others.   At present it has nineteen acting visitors, and is under the superintendency of a president and five professors, embracing the professor of humanity, who has charge of the classical department.   There is also a law department in this institution;" and in the town a flourishing male and female boarding-school.

The Rev. James Blair, D. D., was named president of William and Mary College in the charter, but is said not to have entered upon the duties of his office until 1729 ; he died in 1742, and was succeeded by the Rev. William Stith, (author of a history of Virginia,) who died in 1750. The Rev. James Madison, D. D., (Bishop of Va.,) was president from 1777 to 1812. His successors have been the Rev. W. H. Wilmer, Dr. J. Augustine Smith, Rev. Dr. Adam Empie, and Thomas R. Dew, A. M., the present incumbent. There were, in 1840, in the college 98 students ; in the law school 32 students.

———

In the beautiful square, fronting the college, stands the statue of Lord Botetourt, one of the colonial governors. It is much mutilated, though still presenting a specimen of elegant sculpture. He appears in the court-dress of that day, with a short sword at his side. It was erected in 1774, at the expense of the colony, and removed in 1797 from the old capitol to its present situation. Its pedestal bears the following inscription :—

The Right Honorable Norborne Berkley, Baron de Botetourt, his Majesty's late Lieutenant : and Governor-General of the Colony and Dominion of Virginia. *Right side.*—Deeply impressed with the warmest sense of gratitude for his Excellency's, the Right Honorable Lord Botetourt's, prudent and wise administration, and that the remembrance of those many public and social virtues which so eminently adorned his illustrious character might be transmitted to posterity, the General Assembly of Virginia, on the xx. day of July, Ann. Dom., MDCCLXXI. resolved with one united voice to erect this statue to his Lordship's memory. Let wisdom and justice preside in any country, the people must and will be happy. *Left side.*—America, behold your friend, who leaving his native country declined those additional honors which were there in store for him, that he might heal your wounds and restore tranquillity and happiness to this extensive continent. With what zeal and anxiety he pursued these glorious objects, Virginia thus bears her grateful testimony.

Lord Botetourt was distinguished for love of piety and literature. His arrival as governor of the colony, in Oct., 1768—as is shown in the subjoined extract from the Virginia Gazette of that date—was greeted with public rejoicings becoming the loyal subjects of his majesty :—

Last Tuesday evening arrived in Hampton Roads, in eight weeks from Portsmouth, the Rippon man-of-war, of 60 guns, Samuel Thompson, Esq., commander, having on board his Excellency, the Right Hon. NORBORNE Baron de BOTETOURT, his majesty's Lieut. and Gov.-General of this Colony and Dominion. Next morning his Excellency landed at *Little England*, and was saluted with a discharge of the cannon there. After tarrying a few hours and taking a repast, his Excellency set out about noon for this city, where he arrived about sunset. His Excellency stopped at the Capitol, and was received at the gate by his Majesty's Council, the Hon. the Speaker, the Attorney-General, the Treasurer, and many other gentlemen of distinction, after which, being conducted to the Council Chamber and having his commissions read, was qualified to exercise his high office by taking the usual oaths. His Excellency then swore in the members of his Majesty's Council, after which he proceeded to the *Raleigh Tavern*, and supped there with his Majesty's Council. His Excellency retired about ten, and took up his lodgings at the palace, which had been put in order for his reception. Immediately upon his arrival the city was illuminated, and all ranks vied with each other in testifying their gratitude and joy, that a Nobleman of such distinguished merit and abilities is appointed to preside over and live among them.

———

In the succeeding paper the following Ode was published :—

RECITATIVE.

VIRGINIA, see, thy GOVERNOR appears!
 The *peaceful olive* in *his* brow *he* wears!
  Sound the shrill trumpets, beat the rattling drums;
From *Great Britannia's* isle *his* LORDSHIP comes.
Bid Echo from the waving *woods* arise,
And joyful acclamations reach the skies;
Let the loud *organs* join their tuneful roar,
And bellowing *cannons* rend the pebbled shore:
Bid smooth *James River* catch the cheerful sound,
And roll it to *Virginia's* utmost bound;
While *Rappahannock* and *York's* gliding stream,
Swift shall convey the sweetly pleasing theme
To distant *plains*, where pond'rous *mountains* rise,
Whose cloud-capp'd verges meet the bending skies.
 The LORDLY PRIZE the *Atlantic* waves resign,
And now, *Virginia*, now the BLESSING'S *thine:*
His listening ears will to your *trust* attend,
And be your GUARDIAN, GOVERNOR, and FRIEND.

AIR.

He comes: his EXCELLENCY comes,
 To cheer *Virginian* plains!
Fill your brisk bowls, ye loyal sons,
 And sing your loftiest strains.
Be this your glory, this your boast,
LORD BOTETOURT'S the favorite toast;
 Triumphant wreaths entwine;
Fill full your bumpers swiftly round,
And make your spacious rooms rebound
 With music, joy, and wine.

RECITATIVE.

Search every garden, strip the shrubby bowers,
And strew *his* path with sweet autumnal flowers!
Ye *virgins*, haste, prepare the fragrant rose,
And with triumphant laurels crown *his* brows.

DUET.
 Enter Virgins with flowers, laurels, &c.

See, we've stript each flowery bed;
Here's laurels for his LORDLY HEAD;
And while *Virginia* is *his* care,
May *he* protect the virtuous *fair.*

AIR.

Long may he live in *health* and *peace,*
And ev'ry hour *his joys* increase.
To this let ev'ry swain and lass
Take the sparkling, flowing glass;
Then join the sprightly dance, and sing,
Health to our GOVERNOR, and GOD *save the* KING.

VIRGINS.
Health to our GOVERNOR.

BASS SOLO.
Health to our GOVERNOR.

CHORUS.
Health to our GOVERNOR, and GOD SAVE THE KING!

Facing the public square is the house—shown on the right of
the annexed view—in which, a few years since, resided President Tyler. On the square stands the *Old Magazine*, built about
120 years ago, and memorable as being the building from which
Lord Dunmore, in 1775, removed the powder belonging to the

colony on board the Magdalen man-of-war, which arbitrary act
threw the whole of Virginia into a state of ferment, and occa-

The Old Magazine.

sioned the first assembling of an armed force in the colony in opposition to royal authority.

At the head of a small, but beautiful grassy court, called the
Palace Green, are two small brick structures, the remains of the
Palace of Lord Dunmore, the last of the colonial governors. That
on the right was the office, and the one on the left the guard-house.
The main building occupied the space between them; it was of
brick, 74 feet long, and 68 feet wide. Here Lord Dunmore resided

Remains of Lord Dunmore's Palace.

in great state, surrounded by the pomp and pageantry of vice-
royalty. At that time the adjacent grounds, comprising 360 acres,
were beautifully laid out, with carriage-roads winding through

them. Numerous lindens were imported from Scotland and planted; one or two of which now remain, and are almost unrivalled in magnificence and beauty. The palace was accidentally destroyed by fire during its occupancy by some French troops, immediately after the surrender of Cornwallis at Yorktown.

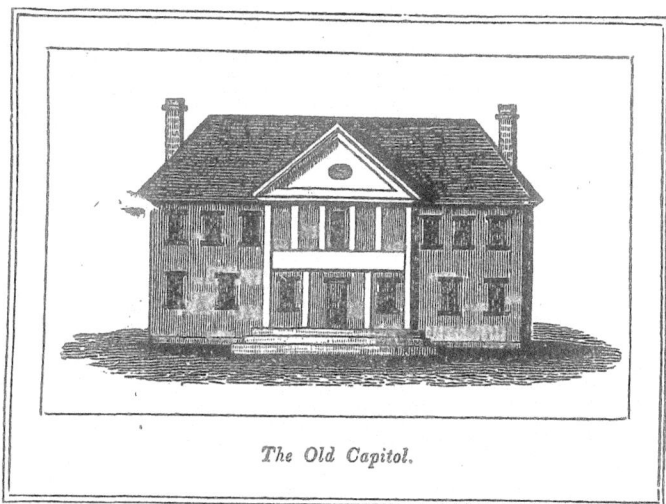

The Old Capitol.

The first building erected in Williamsburg for a capitol was burnt in the year 1746, and shortly after another was built, which in its turn was consumed by fire, in April, 1832. Of this structure, now known as the "OLD CAPITOL," nothing remains but a few scattered bricks. Fortunately, we are enabled to present an engraving, from a drawing preserved by a lady of the place. Within its walls did the great and patriotic of Virginia's sons deliberate in the darkest period of the nation's history. There were those resolves made, and that course of action pursued, which made Virginia foremost in opposition to the arbitrary measures of Britain. It was there that Patrick Henry made his *début* in the House of Burgesses, when, attired in a coarse apparel, with the air of "an obscure and an unpolished rustic," he arose and astonished all by "the rugged might and majesty of his eloquence," teaching "the proud aristocracy" of that body the superiority of native talent over the learning of schools and the glitter and assumptions of high life. It was there, also, that occurred that touching incident in the life of Washington, who, (says Wirt,) after closing his glorious career in the French and Indian war, was complimented by the speaker, Mr. Robinson, for his gallantry; but in such glowing terms, that when he arose to express his acknowledgments for the honor, he blushed, and stammered, and trembled, unable to give distinct utterance to a single syllable; when the speaker, observing his

42

trepidation, relieved him by a masterly stroke of address, saying with a conciliating smile, "*Sit down, Mr. Washington; your modesty is equal to your valor, and that surpasses the power of any language that I possess.*"

The "OLD RALEIGH TAVERN" is yet occupied as a public-house; over the portico of which is the bust of Sir Walter Raleigh. It is memorable from being the place "where many important committees of the legislature met, where some of our most distinguished patriots concerted measures for aiding in the arduous struggle for liberty, and where it is said Richard Henry Lee and others originated the plan to establish corresponding committees throughout many or all of the colonies."

———

The subjoined description of the characteristics of Virginians about 120 years since, is from the work of Hugh Jones, previously quoted. He appears pleased with every body and every thing around him, while the colonies more remote, instead of looming up brightly by "the enchantment of distance," are presented to his imagination in the most sombre and forbidding hues. The description is a curiosity in its way, and is written in a quaint, hyperbolical style, quite amusing:

The habits, life, customs, computations, &c., of the Virginians, are much the same as about London, which they esteem their home; and for the most part, have contemptible notions of England, and wrong sentiments of Bristol and the other outports, which they entertain from seeing and hearing the common dealers, sailors, and servants, that come from these towns, and the country-places in England and Scotland, whose language and manners are strange to them. For the planters, and even the native negroes, generally talk good English, without idiom or tone, and can discourse handsomely on most common subjects. Conversing with persons belonging to trade and navigation from London, for the most part, they are much civilized, and wear the best of cloaths, according to their stations; nay, sometimes too good for their circumstances, being for the generality comely, handsome persons, of good features and fine complexions—if they take care—of good manners and address. The climate makes them bright, and of excellent sense, and sharp in trade; an idiot or deformed native being almost a miracle. Thus they have good natural notions, and will soon learn arts and sciences; but are generally diverted, by business or inclination, from profound study and prying into the depth of things; being ripe for management of their affairs before they have laid so good a foundation for learning, and had such instructions and acquired such accomplishments, as might be instilled into such naturally good capacities. Nevertheless, through their quick apprehension, they have a sufficiency of knowledge and fluency of tongue, though their learning for the most part be but superficial. They are more inclinable to read men by business and conversation, than to dive into books, and are, for the most part, only desirous of learning what is absolutely necessary, in the shortest and best method. . . . . As for education, several are sent to England for it, though the *Virginians*, being naturally of good parts, as I have already hinted, neither require nor admire as much learning as we do in Britain; yet more would be sent over, were they not afraid of the small-pox, which most commonly proves fatal to them. But indeed, when they come to England, they are generally put to learn to persons that know little of their temper, who keep them drudging on what is of least use to them, in pedantick methods too. tedious for their volatile genius. . . . . If New England be called a receptacle of Dissenters and an Amsterdam of religion, Pennsylvania a nursery of Quakers, Maryland the retirement of Roman Catholics, North Carolina the refuge of runaways, and South Carolina the delight of Buccaneers and Pyrates, Virginia may be justly esteemed the happy retreat of true Britons, and true Churchmen for the most part; neither soaring too high, nor dropping too low, consequently should merit the greater esteem and encouragement.

The common planters leading easy lives, don't much admire labor, or any manly exercise, except horse-racing, nor diversion, except cockfighting, in which some greatly delight. This easy way of living, and the heat of the summer, makes some very lazy, who are then said to be climate-struck. The saddle-horses, though not very large, are hardy, strong, and fleet; and will pace naturally and pleasantly at a prodigious rate. They are such lovers of riding, that almost every ordinary person keeps a horse: and I have known some spend the morning in ranging several miles in the woods to find and catch their horses, only to ride two or three miles to church, to the court-house, or to a horse-race, where they generally appoint to meet upon business, and are more certain of finding those that they want to speak or deal with, than at their home.

No people can entertain their friends with better cheer and welcome; and strangers and travellers are here treated in the most free, plentiful, and hospitable manner, so that a few inns or ordinaries on the road are sufficient.

The first newspaper printed in British America was in Boston, in 1704, and in 1719 the second was issued, in the same city. In 1725 a newspaper was first printed in New York; from this time they were gradually extended through the continent.

"In 1671, Sir William Berkeley 'thanks God there are no free schools nor printing, [in Virginia,]—and hopes we shall not have these hundreds of years to come.' The first printing-press erected in Virginia, in 1682, was shortly after put down."

The first newspaper published in Virginia was the Virginia Gazette, the first number of which was issued at Williamsburg, August 6th, 1736. It was then a sheet about 12 inches by six, and was printed and published by W. Parks, at 15s. per annum. In his introduction, after mentioning that papers had been established elsewhere in the colonies, as well as in Europe, he says: "From these examples, the encouragement of several gentlemen, and the prospect I have of success in this *ancient* and *best-settled* colony, VIRGINIA, I am induced to set forth weekly newspapers here; not doubting to meet with as good encouragement as others, or at least such as may enable me to carry them on." This same Wm. Parks printed, in 1729, Stith's History of Virginia and the Laws of Virginia, at this place. His paper was under the influence of the government. Parks died in 1750, and the paper was discontinued for a time. In Feb., 1751, this paper was renewed by Wm. Hunter. He died in 1761. It was then enlarged, and published by Joseph Royle; after whose death it was carried on by Purdie and Dixon, who continued it until the commencement of the revolution; and Purdie, alone, published it several years during the revolutionary contest.

Mr. Jefferson in answer to an inquiry observes, ." till the beginning of our revolutionary disputes we had but one press; and that having the whole business of the government, and no competitor for public favor, nothing disagreeable to the governor could find its way into it. We procured Rind to come from Maryland to publish a free paper." Accordingly, in May, 1766, a second paper, entitled also "The VIRGINIA GAZETTE," "published by authority, open to all parties, but influenced by none," was issued at this place by Wm. Rind. The clause, "published by authority," was omitted at the end of the first year. Rind dying in August, 1773, the paper was continued by his widow, Clementina Rind, and at her death by John Pinckney. Another "Virginia Gazette" was first published at Williamsburg in 1775, and continued weekly, for several years, by John Clarkson and Augustine Davis.*

From these papers we make the subjoined extracts:

Williamsburg, Nov. 12, 1736.—On this day sen'night, being the 5th of November, the president, masters, and scholars, of *William* and *Mary* college went, according to their annual custom, in a body, to the governor's, to present his honor with two copies of Latin verses, in obedience to their charter, as a grateful acknowledgment for two valuable tracts of land given the said college by their late *K. William* and *Q. Mary.* Mr. President delivered the verses to his honor; and two of the young gentlemen spoke them. It is further observed there were upwards of 60 scholars present; a much greater number than has been any year before since the foundation of the college.

---

* For most of the facts above stated we are indebted to Thomas's History of Printing.

Sept. 10, 1736.—This evening will be performed at the *Theatre*, by the young gentlemen of the college, The *Tragedy* of CATO ; and on Monday, Wednesday, and Friday next, will be acted the following comedies, by the gentlemen and ladies of this country, viz : The BUSY BODY, The RECRUITING OFFICER, and The BEAUX STRATAGEM.

Williamsburg, Sept. 21, 1739.—An epitaph on Miss M. Thacker, (daughter of Col. Edwin Thacker, of Middlesex,) who died at Williamsburg, on Wednesday last :

> Pensively pay the tribute of a tear,
> For one that claims our common grief lies here.
> Good-natured, prudent, affable, and mild,
> In sense a woman, in deceit a child.
> Angels, like us, her virtues shall admire,
> And chant her welcome thro' the Heavenly choir.

Sept. 21, 1739.—EDWARD MORRIS, *Breeches-Maker* and *Glover*, from London, is set up in his business, near the college, in Williamsburg, where he makes and sells the best *buckskin breeches*, either of the common tanned color, black, or other cloth colors, after the English manner. Also buckskin gloves with high tops. Any persons that have occasion to make use of him, in any of the above particulars, may depend upon kind usage, and at very reasonable rates.

Williamsburg, March 3, 1768.—Early this morning, died at the palace, after a tedious illness, which he bore with the greatest patience and fortitude, the Hon. FRANCIS FAUQUIER, Esq., Lieut. Gov. and commander-in-chief of the colony, over which he has presided near ten years, much to his own honor, and the ease and satisfaction of the inhabitants. He was a gentleman of the most amiable disposition, generous, just, and mild, and possessed, in an eminent degree, of all the social virtues. He was a Fellow of the Royal Society, and died in his 65th year.*

May 26, 1768.—For the benefit of Mrs. Parker, by permission of the *worshipful the Mayor of Williamsburg*, at the OLD THEATRE, near the Capitol, by the VIRGINIA COMPANY OF COMEDIANS, on Friday, the 3d of June, will be presented the BEGGAR'S OPERA, and the ANATOMIST, or SHAM DOCTOR.

Williamsburg, April 13, 1768.—A hog was brought to town this week, from Sussex, as a show, raised by Mr. Henry Tyler there, who, though only four years old, is near three feet and a half high, about nine and a half long, and, it is supposed, weighs near twelve hundred pounds. He much exceeds any animal of the kind ever raised on this continent, and, indeed, we do not remember to have heard of any so large in England.

Oct. 5, 1768.—Yesterday, PEYTON RANDOLPH, Esq., our worthy representative, gave a genteel dinner at the RALEIGH Tavern, to the electors of this city, after which many loyal and patriotic toasts were drank, and the afternoon spent with cheerfulness and decorum.

From the Virginia Gazette of 1776 are extracted the following marriage notices, which, according to the custom of the time, are accompanied with a few poetic lines :

EDMUND RANDOLPH, Esq., Attorney-General of Virginia, to Miss BETSEY NICHOLAS, a young lady whose amiable sweetness of disposition, joined with the finest intellectual accomplishments, cannot fail of rendering the worthy man of her choice completely happy.

> Fain would the aspiring muse attempt to sing
> The virtues of this amiable pair ;
> But how shall I attune the trembling string,
> Or sound a note which can such worth declare ?
> Exalted theme ! too high for common lays !
> Could my weak verse with beauty be inspired,
> In numbers smooth I'd chant my BETSEY's praise,
> And tell how much her RANDOLPH is admired.
> To light the hymeneal torch since they've resolved,
> Kind Heaven I trust will make them truly blest ;
> And when the *Gordian knot* shall be dissolved,
> Translate them to eternal peace and rest.

---

* A paper of a late, late says he was buried in the north aisle of the church.

Mr. WILLIAM DERRICOAT, of Hanover, to Miss SUCKEY TOMKIES, of Gloucester, daughter of Col. Francis Tomkies.

> Her's the mild lustre of the blooming morn,
> And his the radiance of the rising day.
> Long may they live, and mutually possess,
> A steady love and genuine happiness.

On Sunday last, Mr. BEVERLY DIXON to Miss POLLY SAUNDERS, a very agreeable young lady.

> Hymen, thy brightest torch prepare,
> Gild with light the nuptial bower,
> With garlands crown this lovely pair,
> On them thy choicest blessings shower
> Cupids lightly sport and play,
> Hymen crowns the happy day;
> Sprightly graces too descend,
> And the beauteous bride attend.
> Here no sordid interest binds,
> But purest innocence and love
> Combined unite their spotless minds,
> And seal their vows above.

Captain SAMUEL DENNY, of the artillery, to Miss FALLEN, of Northumberland

> May peace and love the sacred band unite,
> And equal joy, yield equal sweet content.

JAMES MADISON, D. D., Bishop of the Episcopal Church in Virginia, and President of William and Mary College, was born near Port Republic, in Rockingham county, in 1749. His father was the district clerk of West Augusta. He graduated with the highest honors at William and Mary, then studied law with the celebrated George Wythe, and after being licensed to practise, turned his attention to theology, and was admitted to holy orders. He was chosen professor of mathematics, in William and Mary, in 1773. In 1777, at the early age of 28, he was elected president, and soon after visited England. "In 1788, as Bishop elect of Virginia, he went again to England for Episcopal ordination, and was consecrated at Lambeth, Sept. 19, 1790. On his return, he united the performance of his duties of bishop with those of president and professor. Until the close of his life, such were his literary and scientific pursuits, that he was occupied in lectures from four to six hours every day. After a severe illness, he died, March 6, 1812, in the 63d year of his age. His published works are, a Thanksgiving Sermon, 1781; a letter to J. Morse, 1795; an address to the Episcopal Church, 1799; and an able and very eloquent discourse on the death of Washington. The reputation of Bishop Madison is that of a refined gentleman, an accomplished scholar, and an enlightened and liberal Christian philanthropist."

"PEYTON RANDOLPH, first president of the American Congress, was a native of Virginia, and one of the most distinguished lawyers and patriots of the state. He was, as early as 1756, appointed king's attorney of the colony, and held the office for many years. In 1766, he was elected speaker of the House of Burgesses, and in 1773, a member of the committee of correspondence. The following year, he was appointed a delegate to the Congress which assembled at Philadelphia, and was elected its president; and also presided in the Congress of 1775, till obliged to return to Virginia, when Hancock was chosen his successor. He soon resumed his seat in Congress, but died suddenly of an apoplectic fit on the 22d of October, 1775, aged 52 years."

In speaking of his death, Girardin observes: "That illustrious citizen, distinguished at first by the eminence of his forensic station, and afterwards by the ability, zeal, integrity, and dignity, which he displayed in the higher offices of public life, had several times been elected speaker of the House of Burgesses. On the 20th of March, he was unanimously appointed president of the first convention; and on the 11th of August following, first nominated one of the delegates for Virginia to the general Congress. A new and well-merited honor awaited him there; without one dissentient voice, he was called to preside over that great and venerable body. ... The remains of this worthy patriot were afterwards brought from Philadelphia to Williamsburg by Edmund Randolph, his nephew, and in November, 1776, deposited in the family vault in the college chapel, with suitable funeral ceremonies. A short time before his departure for the general Continental Congress, the convention, observing with great concern that he was very much indisposed, recommended him to retire for the present from the fatigues of public duty, tendering to him at the same time their unfeigned thanks for his unre-

mitted attention to the important interests of his country, and his unwearied application
to, and able, faithful, and impartial discharge of the duties of his office; and assuring
him that he had the warmest wishes of the convention for a speedy return to health,
and an uninterrupted enjoyment of every felicity."

JEFFERSON.

JEFFERSON was formed in 1801, from Berkeley; its mean length
is 22 miles, breadth 12 miles. The Potomac forms its northeastern
boundary; the Shenandoah enters the county near its southeastern border, and flowing in a northeast direction, parallel with the

Harper's Ferry, from the Blue Ridge.

Blue Ridge, enters the Potomac at Harper's Ferry. The face of
the country is rolling, and the soil almost unequalled in fertility
by any other county in Virginia. "It was settled principally by
old Virginia families from the eastern part of the state; and the
inhabitants still retain that high, chivalrous spirit, and generous
hospitality, for which that race was so remarkable in the palmy
days of their prosperity." Pop. in 1840, whites 9,323, slaves
4,157, free colored 602; total, 14,082.

Middleway, 7 miles southwest of Charlestown, contains 1 Presbyterian, and 1 Methodist church, 3 mercantile stores, and about
500 inhabitants. Leetown is at the western end of the county, and
contains a few dwellings. It derives its name from the celebrated
Gen. Charles Lee, who once resided there.

Harper's Ferry is distant 173 miles from Richmond, 57 from Washington city, and 30 from Winchester, with which it is connected by a rail-road. This thriving manufacturing village is situated at the junction of the Potomac and Shenandoah Rivers. Its name is derived from a ferry, long since established across the Potomac, where the river breaks through the Blue Ridge ; at this place it is about 1200 feet in height. The name of the place was originally Shenandoah Falls.

"The scenery at Harper's Ferry is, perhaps, the most singularly picturesque in America. To attain the view here given, it was necessary to climb the Blue Ridge by a narrow winding path immediately above the bank of the Potomac. The view from this lofty summit amply repays the fatigue incurred by its ascent. The junction of the two rivers is immediately beneath the spectator's feet ; and his delighted eye, resting first upon the beautiful and thriving village of Harper's Ferry, wanders over the wide and woody plains, extending to the Alleghany mountains. President Jefferson, who has given the name to a beautiful rock immediately above the village, has left a powerful description of the scenery of Harper's Ferry. He says :

" ' The passage of the Potomac through the Blue Ridge, is, perhaps, one of the most stupendous scenes in nature. You stand on a very high point of land ; on your right comes up the Shenandoah, having ranged along the foot of a mountain a hundred miles to seek a vent. On your left approaches the Potomac, in quest of a passage also ; in the moment of their junction, they rush together against the mountain, rend it asunder, and pass off to the sea. The first glance of this scene hurries our senses into the opinion that this earth has been created in time ; that the mountains were formed first ; that the rivers began to flow afterwards ; that in this place particularly, they have been dammed up by the Blue Ridge of mountains, and have formed an ocean which filled the whole valley ; that, continuing to rise, they have at length broken over at this spot, and have torn the mountain down from its summit to its base. The piles of rock on each hand, particularly on the Shenandoah—the evident marks of their disrupture and avulsion from their beds by the most powerful agents of nature, corroborate the impression. But the distant finishing which nature has given to the picture, is of a very different character ; it is a true contrast to the foreground ; it is as placid and delightful as that is wild and tremendous ; for the mountain being cloven asunder, she presents to your eye, through the clefts, a small catch of smooth blue horizon, at an infinite distance in the plain country, inviting you, as it were, from the riot and tumult warring around, to pass through the breach and participate of the calm below. Here the eye ultimately composes itself ; and that way, too, the road happens actually to lead. You cross the Potomac above the junction, pass along its side through the base of the mountain for three miles, its terrible precipices hanging in fragments over you, and within about twenty miles reach Fredericktown, and the fine country round that. This scene is worth a voyage across the Atlantic ; yet here, as in the neighborhood of the Natural Bridge, are people who have passed their lives within half a dozen miles, and have never been to survey these monuments of a war between rivers and mountains, which must have shaken the earth itself to its centre.' "

There are many points of view from which the scenery appears romantic and beautiful. Among these, that seen from Jefferson's Rock, which is on a hill overhanging the town, is very fine. The top of this rock is flat, and nearly twelve feet square ; its base, which does not exceed five feet in width, rests upon the top of a larger rock ; and its height is about five feet. The whole mass is so nicely balanced, that the application of a small force will cause it to vibrate considerably. On this rock once reposed another rock, on which Mr. Jefferson, during a visit to this place, inscribed his name. In the extraordinary political excitement of 1798-9, between the federal and the democratic parties, a Capt. Henry, who was stationed here with some U. S. troops, at the head of a band of his men hurled off the apex of this rock.

At Harper's Ferry, on the Maryland side, "there is said to be a wonderful likeness of Washington in the stupendous rocks which overhang the Potomac. The nose, lips, and chin are admirably formed, and bear the semblance of studied art. The forehead is obscure ; yet there is sufficient to give the mind a just idea of the noble form and dignified carriage, with the mildness of feature, which the original possessed so pre-eminently as to inspire all men with a profound reverence towards this august personage."

Harper's Ferry is compactly, though irregularly built, around the foot of a hill; but the engraving annexed shows but a small portion of it. It contains about a dozen mercantile stores, several mechanical and manufacturing establishments, 1 Presbyterian, 1 Catholic, 1 Methodist, and 1 Free Church; and, including the suburbs, has a population of over 3,000. The Chesapeake and Ohio Canal passes along the left bank of the Potomac, and the Baltimore and Ohio rail-road passes through the town. The town is connected with the Maryland side by a fine bridge across the Potomac, of about 800 feet in length. The United States Armory and the National Arsenal, at Harper's Ferry, are worthy of attention. In the latter, 80,000 or 90,000 muskets are usually kept, which, as they are sent away, are replaced by others from the factories.

Dwelling of Rumsey, the first Steamboat Inventor.

Shepherdstown is situated on the Potomac, in the northwestern part of the county, 5 miles north of the Baltimore and Ohio rail-road, and about 12 miles above Harper's Ferry. It was established by law in November, 1762, laid off by Capt. Thomas Shepherd, and named Mecklenburg: its first settlers were German mechanics. It contains 6 or 8 mercantile stores, 3 merchant mills, 1 Episcopal, 1 Presbyterian, 1 German-Reformed, and 1 Lutheran church, and a population of about 1,600. There is a small stream, of considerable fall, which runs through the town, immediately opposite to which is an inlet-lock to the Chesapeake and Ohio Canal.

This town is remarkable as being the place where the *first steamboat was constructed and navigated*. Previous to detailing the experiments at this place, we shall introduce a brief historical sketch of navigation by steam:

" Who invented the steamboat?" is a question which has occasioned much controversy—an achievement of which nations, as well as individuals, have been covetous.

Several of the early experimenters in steam appear to have conceived of the idea. The first account we have on the subject, is given in a work recently published in Spain, containing original papers relating to the voyage of Columbus, said to have been preserved in the royal archives at Samancas, and among the public papers of Catalonia, and those of the secretary at war for the year 1543. This narrative states that " Blasco de Garay, a sea-captain, exhibited to the emperor and king Charles V., in the year 1543, an engine by which ships and vessels of the largest size could be propelled, even in a calm, without the aid of oars or sails. Notwithstanding the opposition which this project encountered, the emperor resolved that an experiment should be made, as in fact it was, with success, in the harbor of Barcelona, on the 17th of June, 1543. Garay never publicly exposed the construction of his engine ; but it was observed, at the time of his experiment, that it consisted of a large caldron, or vessel of boiling water, and a moveable wheel attached to each side of the ship. The experiment was made on a ship of 209 tons, arrived from Calibre to discharge a cargo of wheat at Barcelona ; it was called the Trinity, and the captain's name was Peter de Scarza. By order of Charles V., and the prince Philip the Second, his son, there were present at the time, Henry de Toledo, the governor, Peter Cardona, the treasurer, Ravago, the vice-chancellor, Francis Gralla, and many other persons of rank, both Castilians and Catalonians ; and among others, several sea-captains witnessed the operation—some in the vessel, and others on the shore. The emperor and prince, and others with them, applauded the engine, and especially the expertness with which the ship could be tacked. The treasurer, Ravago, an enemy to the project, said it would move two leagues in three hours. It was very complicated and expensive, and exposed to the constant danger of bursting the boiler. The other commissioners affirmed, that the vessel could be tacked twice as quick as a galley served by the common method, and that, at its slowest rate, it would move a league in an hour. The exhibition being finished, Garay took from the ship his engine, and having deposited the wood-work in the arsenal of Barcelona, kept the rest to himself. Notwithstanding the difficulties and opposition thrown in the way by Ravago, the invention was approved ; and if the expedition in which Charles V. was then engaged had not failed, it would undoubtedly have been favored by him. As it was, he raised Garay to a higher station, gave him a sum of money (200,000 maravedies) as a present, ordered all the expenses of the experiment to be paid out of the general treasury, and conferred upon him other rewards."

The editor of the Franklin Journal, from which this extract has been made, observes, " when the ' Public Records' shall appear in an *authentic form*, their evidence must be admitted ; *until then*, he should not be inclined to commence the history of the invention of the steamboat so far back as 1543. For, circumstantial as the account is, it seems to have been written since the days of Fulton."

He is not alone in this opinion, as it is generally regarded as a mere fiction, the offspring of an individual jealous of his country's reputation. This, too, it must be remembered, is stated to have occurred 54 years previous to the birth of the Marquis of Worcester, to whom history assigns the credit of being the original inventor of the steam-engine. When we consider how slow is the progress of invention—how it took several generations of ingenious men, each of whom successively contributed his share in improving upon the first crude conception of Worcester, ere it could be successfully applied—how rude the state of mechanic arts three centuries since, and the difficulties of perfecting so complicated a work of mechanism as the steam-engine—it seems incredible that one mind alone should have overcome them all, and, at a single leap, done that which has taken the successive light and talent of generations of men, and all the mechanical skill and knowledge of the 19th century, to consummate.

The most prominent and authentic account of the early projects of applying steam as a motive power to the propelling of vessels, is given in a treatise printed in London in 1737, entitled " Description and draught of a new-invented machine, for carrying vessels out of, or into any harbor, port, or river, against wind and tide, or in a calm : for which his majesty George II. has granted letters patent for the sole benefit of the author, for the space of 14 years ; by Jonathan Hulls." The draught or drawing prefixed, is a plate of a stout boat, with chimney smoking, a pair of wheels rigged out over each side of the stern, moved by means of ropes passing around their outer rims ; and to the axis of these wheels are fixed six paddles to propel the boat. From the stern of the boat a tow-line passes to the foremast of a two-decker, which the boat thus tows through the water. There is no evidence that Hulls ever applied his conceptions to practice.

Previous to the great and successful experiment of Fulton, in 1807, several attempts were made in this country and in Europe, to navigate vessels by steam. The first in order of time, was made by the subject of this sketch ; the second was John Fitch, who, in 1789, succeeded in propelling his steamboat by paddles, at the rate of eight miles an hour, on the Delaware. In his autobiography he says, " I know of nothing so perplexing and vexatious to a man of feelings, as a turbulent wife and steamboat building. I experienced the former, and quit in season ; and had I been in my right senses, I should undoubtedly have treated the latter in the same manner. But for one man to be teased with both, he must be looked upon as the most unfortunate man of this world." Fitch died at Bardstown, Kentucky, about the year 1796. It was his wish to be buried on the banks of the Ohio, that he might repose " where the song of the boatman would enliven the stillness of his resting-place, and the music of the steam-engine sooth his spirit." How melancholy is the sentiment found in his journal : " The day will come when some more powerful man will get fame and riches from my invention ; but nobody will believe that poor John Fitch can do any thing worthy of attention." As early as 1783, both Rumsey and Fitch had exhibited models to Gen. Washington.

Shortly after the experiment of Fitch, a Mr. Symington succeeded in propelling a steamboat on the Clyde, in Scotland.

John Stevens, of Hoboken, commenced his experiments in 1797. With various forms of vessels and machinery, he impelled boats at the rate of five or six miles an hour. In the year 1797, Chancellor Livingston built a steamboat on the Hudson, and he applied to the legislature of New York for an exclusive privilege. Being unable to comply with the conditions of their grant—viz., that he should propel a vessel by steam at the rate of three miles an hour, within a year—the project was, for a time, dropped. He afterwards associated with Stevens, and being aided by Nicholas Rosevelt, they carried on their experiments until Livingston was sent minister to France. Mr. Stevens continued his experiments until several years later, when Mr. Livingston obtained a renewal of the exclusive grant from the legislature of New York. Mr. Stevens, with the assistance of his son, now applied himself with increased assiduity to the project, and succeeded in 1807, only a few days later than Mr. Fulton's convincing experiment, in propelling a steamboat at the required velocity. Mr. Fulton had, in 1803, made a successful experiment upon the Seine, with a boat which moved at the rate of four miles per hour.

Another of these indefatigable experimenters in navigation by steam, was Oliver Evans, of Philadelphia, the inventor of the high-pressure steam-engine, the only one which can be successfully applied to locomotives. " In the year 1804, Mr. Evans, by order of the board of health of Philadelphia, constructed at his works, situated a mile and a half from the water, a machine for cleaning docks. It consisted of a large flat, or scow, with a steam-engine of the power of five horses on board, to work machinery in raising the mud into scows. This was considered a fine opportunity to show the public that his engine could propel both land and water conveyances. When the machine was finished, he fixed, in a rough and temporary manner, wheels with wooden axletrees, and, of course, under the influence of great friction. Although the whole weight was equal to 200 barrels of flour, yet his small engine propelled it up Market-st., and round the circle to the water-works, where it was launched into the Schuylkill. A paddle-wheel was then applied to its stern, and it thus sailed down that river to the Delaware, a distance of 16 miles, leaving all vessels that were under sail at least half way, (the wind being ahead,) in the presence of thousands of spectators—which he supposed would have convinced them of the practicability of steamboats and steam-carriages. But no allowance was made by the public for the disproportion of the engine to its load, nor for the rough manner in which the machinery was fixed, or the great friction and ill form of the boat ; but it was supposed that this was the utmost it could perform. In 1802, Evans built a steamboat to ply on the Mississippi between New Orleans and Natchez. The boat being ready, a drought left it high and dry, and the steam-engine was placed temporarily in a saw-mill. The mill was like to deprive some who sawed lumber of profitable jobs ; and, on the third attempt, it was burnt by incendiaries. Thus were the projectors ruined, and a laudable attempt to establish steamboats on the Mississippi, three or four years before Fulton's experiment, defeated."

JAMES RUMSEY, who is believed to be the first person that ever succeeded in propelling a boat by steam, was a native of Maryland. When a young man, he removed to Shepherdstown, where he devoted much of his time to mechanics.

He was, at one period of his life, engaged as a merchant in company with a Mr.

Orrick, at Bath, in Morgan county. In September, 1781, it appears from a letter of his, now before us, that he was employed by the Potomac company, of which Washington was a member, to improve the navigation of the Potomac River. In the summer of the year 1783, he directed his attention to the subject of steamboats; and in the autumn of 1784 succeeded in a private, but very imperfect experiment, in order to test some of the principles of his invention. In the October session of that year, he obtained the passage of an act from the Virginia Assembly, guarantying to him the exclusive use of his invention in navigating the waters of that state, for the space of 10 years from date.* In January, 1785, he obtained a patent from the General Assembly of Maryland, for navigating their waters. Through the whole of this year he was engaged in working at his boat, but was not ready for a public trial until 1786, the year following. In this experiment he was eminently successful. He succeeded in propelling his boat, by steam alone, at Shepherdstown, *against the current of the Potomac, at the rate of four or five miles an hour.*

There are now several persons living who were on board at this time: among these is Mrs. Ann Baker, the mother-in-law of the late Gov. Gilmer. Washington, it is said, was also among the passengers. In his correspondence, compiled by Sparks, is a letter to Rumsey, dated anterior to the public experiment in 1786, advising him to hasten the construction of his boat, so as to prevent being forestalled by another individual, and to convince the public of its practicability. Also, in a letter to Hugh Williamson, M. C., dated Mount Vernon, March 15th, 1785, Washington says, in alluding to Rumsey's boat: "If a model of a thing, in miniature, is a just representation of a greater object in practice, there is no doubt of the utility of the invention. A view of his model, with the explanation, removed the principal doubt I ever had of the practicability of propelling against a stream, by the aid of mechanical power; but as he wanted to avail himself of my introduction of it to the public attention, I chose, previously, to see the actual performance of the model in a descending stream, before I passed my certificate, and having done so, all my doubts are satisfied."

While at Shepherdstown, Mr. Rumsey dwelt in a small log-house, now standing near the town jail in the outskirts of the village. It is the same building represented in the engraving. He was supplied with funds for the undertaking by his brother-in-law, Charles Morrow, which proved the ruin of the latter. The boat was built upon the banks of the Potomac, about half a mile above the town. She was called by the townspeople, not the steamboat, but "*the flying-boat;*" and Mr. Rumsey himself received, from the same source, the appellation of "*Crazy Rumsey.*" There is a place upon the banks of the Potomac, formerly called "Rumsey's Walk," where Rumsey was often seen for hours walking to and fro, in deep meditation upon his favorite project. A portion of the boiler of his boat is now in the possession of Alexander R. Boteler, Esq., of Shepherdstown, to whose kindness we are indebted for some of the facts in this article.

"Stuart's Anecdotes of the Steam-Engine," an English publication, thus describes his boat:

"Rumsey's boat was about 50 feet in length, and was propelled by a pump worked by a steam-engine, which forced a quantity of water up through the keel; the valve was then shut by the return of the stroke, which at the same time forced the water through a channel or pipe, a few inches square, (lying above or parallel to the kelson,) out at the stern under the rudder, which had a less depth than usual, to permit the exit of the water. The impetus of this water forced through the square channel against the exterior water, acted as an impelling power upon the vessel. The reaction of the effluent water propelled her at the rate above mentioned, when loaded with three tons in addition to the weight of her engine, of about a third of a ton. The boiler was quite a curiosity, holding no more than five gallons of water, and needing only a pint at a time. The whole machinery did not occupy a space greater than that required for four barrels of flour. The fuel consumed was not more than from four to six bushels of coal in twelve hours. Rumsey's other project was to apply the power of a steam-engine to long poles, which were to reach the bottom of the river, and by that means to push a boat against a rapid current."

"After the experiment above alluded to, Rumsey being under the strong conviction that skilful workmen and perfect machinery were alone wanting to the most perfect suc cess, and sensible that such could not be procured in America, resolved to go to England. With slender means of his own, and aided, or rather *mocked*, by some timid and unsteady patronage, he there resumed with untiring energy his great undertaking. He proceeded to procure patents of the British government for steam navigation : these patents bear date in the beginning of the year 1788. Several of his inventions, in one modified form or another, are now in general use ; as, for instance, the cylindrical boiler, so superior to the old tub or still-boilers, in the presentation of fire surface, and capacity for holding highly rarefied steam, is described, both single and combined, in his specifications, and is identical in principle with the tub-boiler which he used in his Potomac experiment.

" Difficulties and embarrassments of a pecuniary nature, and such as invariably obstruct the progress of a new invention, attended him in England. He was often compelled to abandon temporarily his main object, and turn his attention to something else, in order to raise means to resume it. He undertook, with the same power, but by its more judicious application, to produce higher results in several water-works, in all which he succeeded, realizing thereby some reputation as well as funds to apply to his favorite project.

" At another time, in order to avoid a London prison, and the delay, if not the defeat of all his high hopes, he was compelled to transfer, at what he considered a ruinous sacrifice, a large interest in his inventions,—a contract which entangled and embarrassed him through life. Still, however, he struggled on, undismayed, and had constructed a boat of about one hundred tons burden, and pushed forward his machinery so near to the point of completion, as to be able to indicate a day not very distant for a public exhibition."[*]

Death, however, put an end to his career, in Liverpool, at a most flattering point in his life, and under circumstances of the most touching character.

Rumsey had consented, at the suggestion of some gentlemen, to give a public exposition of his *projet*, for the purpose of enlisting the patronage of the public in his behalf. The evening came, and, to his astonishment, the hall was filled to overflowing with the learning, and fashion, and beauty of Liverpool. He was overwhelmed at this unlooked-for token of interest ; and he seems to have been so conquered by his feelings, as to be unequal to the occasion. He saw that his most ardent hopes were upon the eve of accomplishment, and that the helping hand of power was to be extended to' him in his penury, and carry through in triumph the cherished object of his life. He arose to begin his lecture—his agitation was observed by a gentleman, who handed him a glass of water—he returned his thanks in a few incoherent sentences, sank in his chair, and never spake more. He was seized with an apoplectic fit, and died within two days after. Thus died poor Rumsey, another of those *martyrs of civilization*, of which those benefactors of the human race who have labored in the department of mechanical invention —whose works constitute the peculiar glory of our time—form so long a roll.

Rumsey had obtained the patronage of some enterprising individuals, and the boat ne constructed was set in motion after his death, on the Thames, in 1793.

A sharp controversy, at one time, existed between Rumsey and Fitch, as to the originality of their respective inventions. Neither, however, can claim originality as to the idea, as has been shown. The Hon. Robert Wickliffe, Sen., of Kentucky, in a communication on this subject to the American Pioneer, (Vol. I., p. 34,) says that about the year 1780, Fitch accidentally met Rumsey in Winchester, and imparted to him his idea of propelling boats by steam. Admitting the fact, it proves nothing more than that from Fitch, Rumsey derived the bare idea : the principles of their machinery were different. Without deciding upon the respective merits of either, both certainly claim admiration for their perseverance, as well as sympathy for their misfortunes.

Gen. WILLIAM DARKE was born in Pennsylvania, in 1736. When he was five years of age, he removed with his parents to Virginia, within five miles of Shepherdstown.

---

* The last quotation is from the speech of Mr. Rumsey, of Kentucky, before the Congressional House of Representatives, on the occasion of offering the following resolution, afterwards unanimously passed, Feb. 9, 1839. " Resolved, by the Senate and House of Representatives, &c. &c., That the President be, and he is hereby requested, to present to James Rumsey, jun., the son and only surviving child of James Rumsey, deceased, a suitable gold medal, commemorative of his father's services and high agency in giving to the world the benefit of the steamboat." For the speech above referred to, see the National Intelligencer of that date.

THE SHANNONDALE SPRINGS.

This popular watering place is beautifully situated on the Shenandoah river in Jefferson County. The establishment is shown on the right, and at the distance of a few miles, the Blue Ridge appears.

H. HOWE, del.

He was gifted by nature with an herculean frame; his manners were rough; his mind was strong, but uncultivated; and his disposition frank and fearless. In his 19th year, he was with the Virginia provincials at Braddock's defeat. He then returned and continued engaged in agricultural pursuits. When the revolutionary war broke out, he joined the American army. He was taken prisoner at Germantown, and remained so until Nov. 1, 1780. In the succeeding spring he repaired to Winchester to recruit his regiment. He was colonel-commandant of the Hampshire and Berkeley regiments at the siege of York, and nobly sustained the character he had previously won for bravery and heroic daring. After the war he returned to agriculture. He was chosen, with Gen. Stevens, to represent Berkeley county in the Virginia convention of 1788, and voted for the federal constitution. Subsequently, he was repeatedly elected to the legislature. At St. Clair's defeat, Col. Darke commanded the left wing of the army. When the Indians were making their most desperate onsets, and the whites were falling in heaps before his eyes, St. Clair at this crisis ordered Darke to charge with the bayonet, who drove the enemy from his position with his usual gallantry, but, for want of riflemen, could not continue the pursuit. The Indians again penetrated to the camp; Darke, assisted by Butler and Clarke, made a second charge, with success—recovered the artillery, and drove the enemy before them. But these exertions were not sustained, so that a concentrated effort could not be made, and the loss of officers increased every moment. Among these was Capt. Joseph Darke, his youngest son, who was mortally wounded. His father saw him fall, paused for a moment, and then rushed to the contest. The retreat soon commenced, and Darke arrived that evening at Fort Jefferson, distant 30 miles, with his son on a horse-litter, although he himself was wounded in the thigh, and liable to be overtaken and slain. A council of war was held at Fort Jefferson, and Darke urged the expediency of an immediate attack, and contended that the Indians might be beaten, because they were flushed with victory and unprepared for the contest. But he was overruled. Darke died Nov. 20th, 1801.

————

Charlestown, the seat of justice for the county, is on the line of the rail-road from Winchester to Harper's Ferry, 8 miles from the latter, and 22 from the former. This town was established in October, 1786, and named from the Christian name of its first proprietor, Col. Charles Washington, a brother of George Washington. Eighty lots were divided into lots and streets, and the following named gentlemen were appointed trustees: John Augustine Washington, William Drake, Robert Rutherford, James Crane, Cato Moore, Magnus Tate, Benjamin Rankin, Thornton Washington, William Little, Alex. White, and Richard Ranson. Col. Charles Washington resided in a log-house, which stood a short distance from the town. A fine spring marks the spot. The whole of the land in the vicinity of Charlestown originally belonged to the Washington family, and a considerable portion still remains in the possession of their descendants. Col. Chas. Washington was the only brother of Washington that settled west of the Blue Ridge. He was an amiable, modest, and dignified gentleman, and in his appearance, as well as character, resembled his illustrious brother.

Braddock's army, in their route to the west, passed through this region; one mile west of the village, on the land of Bushrod Washington, Esq., there is a well dug by them.

The annexed view was taken in the central part of the village, looking down the principal street; the public building on the right, is the court-house, recently erected. The town is flourishing, and contains 11 mercantile stores, a branch of the Bank of the Valley, an academy, newspaper printing-office, 1 Presbyterian, 1 Episcopal, and 1 Methodist church, and a population of about 1,400.

Central view in Charlestown, Jefferson co.

Washington's Masonic Cave is two and a half miles southeast of Charlestown. It is divided into several apartments, one of which is called the lodge-room. Tradition informs us that Washington, with others of the masonic fraternity, held meetings in this cavern. In the spring of 1844 the masons in this vicinity had a celebration there.

Ruins of Trinity Church, Norborne Parish.

About two miles southwest of Charlestown, near the line of the rail-road to Winchester, in an open, cultivated field, stand the remains of an ancient church. It is a venerable and picturesque ruin, overrun with vines, which, clinging in their beauty and verdure to the crumbling walls, gently wave in the passing winds. The cedar-wood of the windows is yet sound and fragrant, and on the walls are carved the names of visitors. Its age is unknown. The dead of other generations, who repose at its base, are despoiled of the monuments that once marked their resting-place, and gave token to the stranger of the names, and ages, and virtues of the departed.

The Shannondale Springs are situated upon the Shenandoah River, near the Blue Ridge. They are easier of access from the

Atlantic cities, than any others in Virginia. The cars from Baltimore will convey the traveller, in seven hours, through Harper's Ferry to Charlestown, at which place coaches run to the springs, a distance of five miles. The scenery of this place is most beautiful and magnificent, to which the engraving annexed by no means does justice.

The late Dr. DE BUTTS analyzed the Shannondale water in 1821. An examination was made from a quantity of the solid contents of both springs, obtained by evaporation. One hundred grains from the principal fountain afforded the following results :— sulphate of lime, 63 ; carbonate of lime, 10.5 ; sulphate of magnesia, (epsom salt,) 23.5 ; muriate of magnesia, 1 ; muriate of soda, 1 ; sulphate of iron, 0.3 ; carbonate of iron, 0.7. GASEOUS CONTENTS :—sulphureted hydrogen, quantity not ascertained ; carbonic acid, quantity not ascertained. SOLID CONTENTS : 30 grains to the pint. TEMPERATURE : 55° of Fahrenheit.

Conformably to the preceding analysis, the Shannondale water may be properly classed with the *Saline Chalybeates*, a combination of the most valuable description in the whole range of mineral waters, and closely resembling the celebrated Bedford waters in composition, operation, and efficacy.

KANAWHA.

KANAWHA was formed in 1789, from Greenbrier and Montgomery : it is about 60 miles long, with a mean breadth of 40 miles. Gauley River unites with New River, and forms the Great Kanawha upon the eastern border of the county. The Kanawha then flows through the county in a NW. direction, receiving in its passage through the county, Elk, Pocatalico, and Coal Rivers. The surface of the county is much broken. It is famous for its mineral treasures, salt, coal, &c. Pop., in 1840, whites 10,910, slaves 2,560, free colored 97 ; total, 13,567.

The first settlement in what is now Kanawha county, was made about twenty miles above Charleston, at Kelly's creek, by a man after whom that creek was named. One of the first settlers was Lewis Tachet, concerning whom, and the marauding parties of Indians that harassed the early settlers, there are many traditions in the Kanawha valley. He erected a fort at the mouth of Cole River, which was destroyed by a party of Indians from the towns on the Scioto, in 1788, when his family were made prisoners. In 1798 there was a fort built immediately above the mouth of Elk, on the site of Charleston. Among the earliest settlers were also the Morrisses from Culpeper, whose descendants, mostly of the first respectability, now form perhaps nearly a tenth of the population of the county. Joseph Carroll, the Clendenins, John Young, William Droddy, Andrew Donnally, Michael See, and John Jones, were also very early settlers. For many years they subsisted chiefly on buffalo, bear, elk, deer, and raccoon meat, and Indian corn broken in stone mortars. In the Indian dialect, Kanawha signifies "*river of the woods.*" Pocatalico, a considerable tributary of that stream, signifies "*plenty of fat doe.*"

Charleston, the seat of justice for the county, is 308 miles w. of Richmond, and 46 miles E. of the Ohio River. It is a neat and flourishing village on the north bank of the Kanawha. Charleston was named after Charles Clendenin, an early settler, and an owner of the soil forming its site. The first house of worship was built by the Methodists, the second by the Presbyterians, in 1830, and the third by the Episcopalians, in 1835. There are in the place, 11 dry-goods and 6 grocery stores, 2 saw and grist mills, a newspaper printing-office, a branch of the Bank of Virginia, and a population of about 1,500. The district court of the United States is held at this place twice a year. Within the present century Charleston has arisen from the wilderness. Where, within the memory of man, a few scattered log-huts once arrested the traveller's eye, he now sees commodious and, in some instances, elegant buildings, the abodes of comfort and refinement. The

HORSE BOAT FERRY.

View in Charleston, Kanawha county.

Kanawha is here a beautiful sheet of water, more than 300 yards wide, and is navigated by steamboats. The state turnpike, the principal thoroughfare from Richmond to Guyandotte on the Ohio, passes through the town. Fine sandstone and bituminous coal abound in the vicinity.

Terra Salis, or Kanawha Salines, is a flourishing town about 6 miles above Charleston, containing 4 dry-goods and 2 grocery stores, an extensive iron-foundry, 1 Episcopal, 1 Presbyterian, and 1 Methodist church, and a population of about 800.

The Kanawha salt-works commence on the river, near Charleston, and extend on both sides for about 15 miles, giving employment, directly and indirectly, to about 3,000 persons. The view annexed was taken opposite the residence of Col. Reynolds, 6 or 8 miles above Charleston, and gives an idea of the character of the scenery in which the salt-works are situated. The description below (written several years since) is from the pen of a gentleman, now occupying a prominent office in the government of the state.

It is nearly 20 miles below the falls before the Kanawha valley widens into something like a plain, and opens its beautiful vista to the eye. The mountains which enclose it on either side become gradually depressed into hills; and, for the first time, the dense, dark volumes of smoke which ascend from the salt-furnaces, announce the busy and bustling scene which enlivens the highway to the village of Charleston. What a scene of animation, indeed, contrasted with the deep solitudes from which the traveller has but just emerged. Here he is feasted with a continued succession of green meadows and cultivated fields, teeming with flocks and herds, and adorned by commodious and even elegant mansions. The chimneys of the salt manufactories pour

View of the Salt-Works on the Kanawha.

forth, at short intervals of space, their curling masses of black vapor, while swarms of laborers, and others connected with these establishments, are continually passing to and fro, presenting a pleasing *coup d'œil* of incessant activity and industry. Nature, indeed, seems to have been prodigal in her bounties to this interesting region. The contiguous forests having been almost stripped to supply fuel to the salt-furnaces ; the precious mineral so necessary to human comfort, must have remained for ever useless but for the discovery of inexhaustible beds of coal, so convenient of access as to make the cost of procuring it scarcely worth considering. Sometimes, by suitable platforms and inclined culverts, it is thrown from the mountain-side immediately to the door of the manufactory, and when more remote from the place of consumption, it is transported with equal ease, in wagons or cars, over rail-roads constructed for the purpose.

The whole product of the salt district is estimated at 1,200,000 bushels annually ; and this product must continue to swell with the increasing demand, and with the employment of additional capital. It is a curious fact, and worthy of philosophical inquiry, that while the salt water is obtained by boring at a depth of from 3 to 500 feet below the bed of the Kanawha, it invariably rises to a level with the river. When the latter is swollen by rains, or the redundant waters of its tributaries, the saline fluid, enclosed in suitable gums on the shore, ascends like the mercury in its tube, and only falls when the river is restored to its wonted channel. How this mysterious correspondence is produced, is a problem which remains to be solved. Theories and speculation I have heard on the subject, but none seem to me to be precisely consonant with the principles of science.

The discovery of salt water in this region was led to by a large buffalo-lick on the NE. side of the river, 5 miles above Charleston. In this lick the first salt-well was sunk, in 1809.

Several vestiges remain on the Kanawha, which show that the Indians were acquainted with and made use of the salt water. Remains of rude pottery are found in abundance in the neighborhood, respecting which there is but little doubt that they are the remains of vessels used by them for the evaporation of the salt water. That the neighborhood of the Big Lick was their favorite resort, is evinced by the traces of their idle hours to be found upon the neighboring rocks. A short distance below the Big

Lick was, some years since, a rock called *the pictured or calico rock*, on which the natives had sculptured many rude figures of animals, birds, &c. This rock was finally destroyed to make furnace chimneys. Another similar sculptured rock is, or was lately, on the sw. side of the river, upon the summit of the nearest hill. The article annexed, originally published in the Lexington Gazette in 1843, above the signature of H. R., describes a curiosity peculiarly interesting to the scientific, and promising to have a wonderful influence upon the prosperity of this region.

THE GAS WELLS OF KANAWHA.—These wonderful wells have been so lately discovered, that as yet only a brief and imperfect notice of them has appeared in the newspapers. But they are a phenomenon so very curious and interesting, that a more complete description will doubtless be acceptable to the public.

They are, in fact, a new thing under the sun; for in all the history of the world, it does not appear that a fountain of strong brine was ever before known to be mingled with a fountain of inflammable gas, sufficient to pump it out in a constant stream, and then, by its combustion, to evaporate the whole into salt of the best quality.

We shall introduce our account of these wells by some remarks on the geological structure of the country at the Kanawha salt-works, and on the manner in which the salt water is obtained.

The country is mountainous, and the low grounds along the river are altogether alluvial, the whole space, of about a mile in width, having been at some time the bed of the river. The rocks are chiefly sandstone of various qualities, lying in beds, or strata, from two inches to several feet in thickness. These strata are nearly horizontal, but dipping a little, as in other parts of the country, towards the NW. At the salt-works they have somehow been heaved up into a swell above the line of general direction, so as to raise the deep strata nigher to the surface, and thus to bring those in which the salt water is found within striking-distance.

Among the sand-rocks are found layers of slate and coal; this latter being also, by the same upheaving, made more conveniently accessible than in most other parts of the country.

The salt water is obtained by sinking a tight curb, or gum, at the edge of the river, down about twenty feet, to the rock which underlies the river, and then boring into the rock. At first the borings did not exceed two hundred feet in depth, but the upper strata of water being exhausted, the wells were gradually deepened, the water of the lower strata being generally stronger than the upper had ever been. Until last year, (1842,) none of the wells exceeded six or seven hundred feet in depth. Mr. Tompkins, an enterprising salt-maker, was the first to extend his borings to a thousand feet, or more. His experiment was attended with a most unexpected result. He had somewhat exceeded a thousand feet, when he struck a crevice in the rock, and forth gushed a powerful stream of mingled gas and salt water. Generally, the salt water in the wells was obtained in rock merely porous, and rose by hydrostatic pressure to the level of the river. To obtain the strong water of the lower strata, unmixed with the weak water above, it is the practice to insert a copper tube into the hole, making it fit tightly below by means of wrapping on the outside, and attaching the upper end to the pump, by which the water is drawn up to the furnaces on the river bank.

When Mr. Tompkins inserted his tube, the water gushed out so forcibly, that instead of applying the pump, he only lengthened his tube above the well. The stream followed it with undiminished velocity to his water-cistern, sixty feet above the level of the river.

In the next place, he inserted the end of the spout from which the water and gas flowed, into a large hogshead, making a hole in the bottom to let out the water into the cistern. Thus the light gas was caught in the upper part of the hogshead, and thence conducted by pipes to the furnace, where it mingled with the blaze of the coal fire. It so increased the heat as to make very little coal necessary; and if the furnace were adapted to the economical use of this gaseous fuel, it would evaporate all the water of the well, though the quantity is sufficient to make five hundred bushels of salt per day. The same gentleman has since obtained a second gas-well, near the former, and in all respects similar to it. Other proprietors of wells have also struck gas-fountains by deep boring. In one of these wells the gas forces the water up violently, but by fits, the gush continuing for some two or three hours, and then ceasing for about the same length of time. In another of these wells there has been very recently struck, a gas-fountain that acts with such prodigious violence as to make the tubing of the well in the usual way impossible; when the copper tube was forced down through the rushing stream of brine and gas, it was immediately flattened by the pressure; and the auger-hole must be enlarged to admit a tube sufficiently strong and capacious to give vent to the stream without being crushed. In another well, a mile and a half from any gas-well, a powerful stream of gas has been recently struck. It forces up the water with great power; but, unfortunately for the proprietor, the water is too weak to be profitably worked. It appears from this fact, that the gas is not inseparably connected with strong brine. When struck before good salt water is reached, it will operate injuriously, for no water obtained below it can rise at all, unless the pressure of the gas be taken off by means of a strong tube extending below it.

Several wells have been bored to a depth equal to that of the gas-wells, without striking the gas; the source of which seems to lie below, perhaps far below, the depth of the wells. This light, elastic substance, wheresoever and howsoever generated, naturally presses upwards for a vent, urging its way through every pore and crevice of the superincumbent rocks; and the well-borer's auger must find it in one of the narrow routes of its upward passage, or penetrate to its native coal-bed, before it will burst forth by the artificial vent.

The opinion just intimated, that the gas originates in deep coal-beds, is founded on the fact that it is the same sort of gas that constitutes the dangerous *fire-damp* of coalpits, and the same that is manufactured out of bituminous coal for illuminating our cities. It is a mixture of carbureted and sulphureted hydrogen. Philosophers tell us that bituminous coal becomes anthracite by the conversion of its bitumen and sulphur into this gas, and that water acts a necessary part in the process. Whether the presence of salt water causes a more rapid evolution of the gas, the present writer will not undertake to say; but, somehow, the quantity generated in the salt region of Kanawha is most extraordinary.

It finds in this region innumerable small natural vents. It is seen in many places bubbling up through the sand at the bottom of the river, and probably brings up salt water with it, as in the gas-wells, but in small quantity. The celebrated *burning spring* is the only one of its natural vents apparent on dry land. This stream of gas, unaccompanied by water, has forced its way from the rocks below, through seventy or eighty feet of alluvial ground, and within eighty yards of the river bank. It is near this burning spring where the principal gas-wells have been found. But, twenty-five years ago, or more, a gas-fountain was struck in a well two hundred feet deep, near Charleston, seven miles below the Burning Spring. This blew up, by fits, a jet of weak salt water twenty or thirty feet high. On a torch being applied to it, one night, brilliant flames played and flashed about the watery column in the most wonderful manner.

The Hon. LEWIS SUMMERS, (says a Kanawha paper,) was born of highly respectable parentage in Fairfax co., Nov. 7th, 1778. He entered upon the duties of active life during the presidency of the elder Adams. With the ardor which distinguished the Virginia youth at that period, he used his influence to achieve the civic victory which bore Mr. Jefferson into the presidential chair; and, through a long life, adhered to the political principles of his younger days with an undeviating constancy. In 1808, he removed to Gallipolis, Ohio, and served for several years in the senate and legislature of that state. In 1814, he took up his permanent residence in this county. In 1817–18, he served in the legislature of Virginia, and in Feb., 1819, he was chosen one of the judges of the general court, and a judge of the Kanawha judicial circuit. For some time he was a member of the board of public works of Va.; and in 1829 he was elected a member of the convention to revise the constitution of the state.

In all these relations his own strong, original, and vigorous mind, has been indelibly impressed upon the times and events with which he was connected. As a judge, he was most able and faithful. As a statesman, his efforts were perseveringly directed to the best interests of his country. Most of all that Virginia has accomplished in the great work of internal improvement, has been ascribed to his exertions.

In that most remarkable assemblage, the state convention for the amendment of the constitution of Va., which sat in 1829–30, the sterling, vigorous, and practical character of Judge Summers' mind made him, before the close of its deliberations, one of the most useful, if not one of the most conspicuous members of that illustrious body. As the able champion of the true principles of elective government, he, in that assembly, performed services and acquired a reputation which will ever cause his memory to be cherished with warm and respectful affection by the people of western Virginia.

Mr. Summers died at the White Sulphur Springs, August 27th, 1843, after having been for more than 24 years one of the judges of the general court of Va. He was interred in Charleston.

KING AND QUEEN.

KING AND QUEEN was formed from New Kent in 1691, the third year of the reign of William and Mary. The Mattapony runs on its sw. and the Piankatank on a portion of its NE. boundary. Its length is 40 miles, mean width 11 miles. Immense beds of marl run through the county, and furnish an inexhaustible source of improvement to the soil. No county in the state contains memorials of greater magnificence. On the Mattapony, a beautiful stream, are the vestiges of many ancient and once highly-improved seats, among which are Laneville, Pleasant Hill, Newington, Mantapike, Mantua, Rickahoe, White Hall, &c., known as the former residences of the Braxtons, Corbins, Robinsons, &c. Cotton and Indian corn are extensively produced. Pop. in 1840, whites 4,426, slaves 5,937, free colored 499 ; total, 10,862.

The Court-House is near the Mattapony, 53 miles NE. from Richmond. Newtown in the N., and Little Plymouth in the s. part of the county, are small places ; the former, which is the largest, has about 20 dwellings. Dunkirk, now a post-office only, was, 30 or 40 years since, a village of considerable trade ; but its unhealthiness and other causes have nearly obliterated it.

This county is the birthplace of CARTER BRAXTON, one of the signers of the Declaration of Independence. He was born at Newington, September 10th, 1736. His father was a wealthy planter, and his mother a daughter of Robert Carter, at one time president of the council of the colony. Mr. Braxton, having graduated at William and Mary at the age of nineteen, married Miss Judith Robinson, an accomplished lady, and daughter of a wealthy planter of Middlesex. His style of living was according to the general mode of southern hospitality of that day, and subjected him to great expense.

As early as 1765, he was a member of the House of Burgesses when Patrick Henry's celebrated resolutions were passed. In 1769, when Gov. Botetourt, in consequence of the bold and spirited measures introduced, suddenly dissolved the Assembly, Mr. Braxton was one of the members who retired to a private room and signed a written non-importation agreement. In the next house, he was on three of the standing committees. He was elected a member from King William to the first Virginia convention, in 1774. At the period of the disturbance caused by the removal of the gunpowder from the magazine at Williamsburg by Lord Dunmore, Mr. Braxton was essentially instrumental in effecting a settlement on the part of his lordship which pacified the excited populace. He was a very active and useful member of the last House of Burgesses ever convened in Virginia by royal authority, and was employed upon the committees of the house to whom were referred the subjects of dispute between his lordship and the legislature. Mr. Braxton was a member of the convention chosen by the people which met in Richmond in July, 1775, and was placed upon the committee of public safety. In December of the same year, he was appointed the successor of Peyton Randolph in Congress, that gentleman having died a short time previous. He was omitted in the election of members to Congress subsequent upon the Declaration of Independence. But on a meeting of the General Assembly, the first under the new constitution, of which he was a member, he, with Mr. Jefferson, received a vote of thanks from the Assembly, " for the eloquence, ability, and integrity with which they executed the important trust reposed in them, as two of the delegates of the count͏ꞏ ͏ꞏͺͭ ͏ꞏͭͳͺ Wirͭ͏ꞏͺͺꞏ in the general Congress." He was a member of Congress from 1777 to 1783, and in 1785. From 1786 to 1791 he was a member of the council of the state, and from 1794 until the day of his death, Oct. 6th, 1797. Mr. Braxton's services, it will be seen, were highly important. The confidence and attachment of his constituents were unequivocally manifested in every vicissitude of circumstance, some of which were of the most afflictive kind, even to the close of his life.

KING GEORGE.

KING GEORGE was formed in 1720, from Richmond county. It lies between the Potomac and the Rappahannock, and is 18 miles long, with a mean breadth of 10; its surface is hilly, and its soil diversified. Its principal products are Indian corn, oats, wheat, tobacco, and some cotton. Pop. in 1840, whites 2,269, slaves 3,382, free colored 276; total, 5,927.

King George C. H., situated near the centre of the county, 82 miles NNE. from Richmond, and 76 sw. of Washington, contains about a dozen houses. Port Conway, on the Rappahannock, opposite Port Royal, and Millville on the line of this and Westmoreland counties, are small villages

---

KING WILLIAM.

KING WILLIAM was formed in 1701 from King and Queen. The mean length of the county is 32 miles; mean breadth 8¼ miles. The county lies between the Pamunkey and Mattapony, which unite at the SE. angle of the county, and form the York. The land on the borders of these streams is very fertile, and their waters afford convenient navigation, as well as fine shad and herring fisheries. Pop. in 1840, whites 3,150, slaves 5,780, free colored 338; total, 9,258. King William C. H. lies 27 miles NE. of Richmond, 2 miles from the Mattapony. It contains but a few dwellings beside the public buildings, which are of brick, and stand in a handsome square. Ayletts is a small village at the head of navigation, on the Mattapony, 30 miles above its junction with the Pamunkey.

The Pamunkey and the Mattapony meet at the southerly angle of the county. and form York River. The place of their junction is named West Point. It was the place of habitation of Opechancanough, the brother of Powhatan, and king of Pamunkee. "He was the author of the great massacre in 1622, the 'Sicilian Vespers' of the colony. When very old and infirm, and nearly blind, he headed his people in battle, borne on a litter; he was at length captured by Governor Berkeley, with a party of horse, and finally assassinated by a private hand while a prisoner at Jamestown, displaying to the last moment the fortitude of a 'stoic of the woods,' unimpaired by age, and unshaken by calamity." In "Bacon's Rebellion," the followers of Bacon occupied West Point, and strongly fortified it.

West Point was, anciently, a large village: it has now but one good house, and the ruins of several others. There is the remnant of the Mattapony tribe of Indians, now dwindled down to only 15 or 20 souls. Further up on the Pamunkey, at what is called Indian Town, are about 100 descendants[1] of the Pamunkeys. Their Indian character is nearly extinct, by intermixing with the whites and negroes. Their land is in the hands of trustees appointed to hold it for the tribe. They manufacture pottery and baskets very neatly. A traveller, as long ago as 1759, thus speaks of this Indian settlement:

> On the north side of Pamunkey River stands the Pamunkey Indian town, where at present are the few remains of that large tribe ; the rest having dwindled away through intemperance and disease. They live in little wigwams, or cabins, upon the river ; and have a very fine tract of land of about 2000 acres, which they are restrained from alien- ating by act of Assembly. Their employment is chiefly hunting or fishing for the neigh- boring gentry. They commonly dress like the Virginians, and I have sometimes mista- ken them for the lower sort of that people.

On the banks of Moncuen creek, just above Warranuncock island, now known as Goodwin's island, are two Indian mounds or tumuli, somewhat reduced in size by cultivation, yet eight or ten feet high, and about sixty feet in diameter. Evident traces exist of an Indian settlement in the vicinity, on the Pampitike estate.

LANCASTER.

LANCASTER was formed in 1652. It lies on the N. side of the Rappahannock, at its mouth, and is 24 miles long, with a mean breadth of 8 miles. Pop. in 1840, whites 1,903, slaves 2,478, free colored 247 ; total, 4,628.

Lancaster C. H., situated near the centre of the county, 83 miles NE. of Richmond, contains a population of about 100. Kilmarnock is a small village on a creek putting up from Chesapeake Bay. Pain's Cross Roads, in the SE. part of the county, was, 20 years since, a place of considerable trade ; but at present it has a few dwellings only.

In the year 1762, James Waddel, the BLIND PREACHER described in Wirt's British Spy, was settled over the churches of Lancaster and Northumberland. His residence in the latter part of his time here, was on Curratoman River. For a more full notice of this extraordinary divine, see Orange county.

LEE.

LEE was formed in 1792, from Russell, and named after Henry Lee, Gov. of Va. from 1791 to 1794 ; it lies in the southwestern angle of the state, bordering on Tennessee and Kentucky. Its greatest length is 75 miles ; breadth 10 miles. The Cumberland mountains run on the Kentucky line, the Powell mountain is on a part of the SE. boundary, and there are several other ridges in the county, known as Stone, Chesnut, Wallens, &c. Powell's River runs lengthwise through the county into Tennessee. Much of the land is of a very black, rich soil. The staples are beef, pork, and horses. The people of this county make their own sugar and molasses from the maple sugar tree, which grows in great abundance. Pop. in 1840, whites 7,829, slaves 580, free colored 32 ; total, 8,441.

Jonesville, the county-seat, lies 284 miles from Richmond, 65 from Knoxville, Tenn., and 60 from Barboursville, Kentucky, on one of the branches of Powell's River. It stands on a beautiful eminence, in the midst of wild mountain scenery. It was founded in 1793, and contains a church, 5 stores, and about 40 dwellings. The following account of a duel which took place in this county in the year 1823, is from a newspaper of the time :

A remarkable duel took place in Lee county, on Sunday, Dec. 7th, which has been the subject of much conversation here...... Two negro men, belonging to two gentlemen, had been smitten by the charms of a sable beauty, and neither being willing to yield to the other, they determined, like gentlemen, to decide their pretensions by a duel. The arrangement was accordingly made, and they met in a distant and retired wood, unattended by seconds, and without the knowledge of any other person—each armed with a trusty rifle. Their proceedings appear to have been conducted with a strict honor, the more remarkable in such case, as it was exhibited by slaves. The ground was measured off about fifteen paces ; the antagonists took their posts ; the word was given, by one of them, and both instantly fell—one shot through the heart, and the other through the right breast. The former expired immediately ; the latter, with great difficulty and pain, crawled to a small path not far from the scene of combat ; but unable to go further, he remained by it in the hope that some one would pass and find him. He lay there, under all the suffering which his wound and exposure inflicted, until the following Tuesday, before he was found. Depressed and debased as that unfortunate race is, there are occasional instances in which they exhibit traits of character which elevate them above the sphere to which our policy compels us to confine them. The strict observance of honorable conduct, and the cool, determined courage of these negroes, afford an example which ought to make some gentlemen of high condition blush

LEWIS.

LEWIS was formed in 1816, from Harrison, and named in honor of Col. Charles Lewis, who fell at the battle of Point Pleasant. It is 60 miles long, with a mean width of about 20 miles. It is watered by the Little Kanawha and west fork of Monongahela ; the surface is rocky, hilly, and in some parts mountainous: on the streams there is considerable fertile land. Stone-coal of an excellent quality abounds in some parts of the county. In 1843, portions of its territory were set off to the new counties of Barbour and Ritchie. Large quantities of sugar, and some tobacco, are raised in this county ; the greatest staple is Indian corn. Pop. in 1840, whites 7,989, slaves 124, free colored 38 ; total, 8,151.

Weston, the county-seat, is situated at the west fork of Monongahela, 281 miles northwesterly from Richmond, and 50 from the Ohio River, and contains about 60 dwellings.

LOGAN.

Logan was formed in 1824, from Giles, Kanawha, Cabell, and Tazewell, and named from the Mingo chief. It is about 70 miles long, with a mean width of 35 miles. It is watered by Guyandotte, Tug Fork of Big Sandy, and branches of the Great Kanawha. The surface is generally mountainous, and the soil adapted to grazing. It is one of the largest, wildest, and most sparsely inhabited counties in the state, with a population of less than 2 persons to a square mile. Pop. in 1840, whites 4,159, slaves 150 ; total, 4,309.

Lawnsville, or Logan C. H., is 351 miles west of Richmond, in a fertile bottom in a bend of the river Guyandotte, surrounded by mountains abounding in stone-coal and iron ore. It was laid off in 1827, and contains a few dwellings only.

The destruction of the Roanoke settlement in the spring of 1757, by a party of Shawnees, gave rise to a campaign into this region of country, called by the old settlers "the Sandy creek voyage." This expedition was for the purpose of punishing the Indians, and to establish a military post at the mouth of the Great Sandy, to counteract the influence of the French at Gallipolis with the Indians. It was composed of four companies, under the command of Andrew Lewis. The captains were Audley Paul, Wm. Preston, (ancestor of the late Gov. P.,) Wm. Hogg, and John Alexander, father of Archibald Alexander, D. D., president of Princeton Theological Seminary. The party were ordered, by a messenger from Gov. Fauquier, to return. They had then penetrated nearly to the Ohio, without accomplishing any of the objects of their expedition. When the army on their return arrived at the Burning spring, in the present limits of this county, they had suffered much from extreme cold, as well as hunger: their fear of alarming the Indians having prevented them from either hunting or kindling fires Some buffalo hides, which they had left at the spring on their way down, were cut into tuggs or long thongs, and eaten by the troops, after having been exposed to the heat from the flame of the spring. Hence they called the stream near by, now dividing Kentucky from Virginia, *Tugg River*, which name it yet bears. Several who detached themselves from the main body, to hunt their way home, perished. The main body, under Col. Lewis, reached home after much suffering; the strings of their moccasins, the belts of their hunting-shirts, and the flaps of their shot-pouches, having been all the food they had eaten for several days.

LOUDON.

Loudon was formed in 1757, from Fairfax, and named in honor of the Earl of Loudon, commander of the military affairs in America during the latter part of the French and Indian war. It is about 28 miles long, and 22 broad. The Blue Ridge, forming its western boundary, rises to an altitude of 1000 to 1400 feet above tide-water, and from 300 to 700 above the adjacent country. Another range, of equal height, called the Short Hills, in the NW. part of the county, runs parallel with the Blue Ridge about 12 miles. The Kittoctan mountain runs centrally through the county, parallel with the above. This county contains all varieties of soil, from rich alluvion to an unproductive clay. The eastern portion is most unproductive, in consequence of a wretched system of farming hitherto practised, of cropping with corn and tobacco, without endeavoring to improve the soil ; some of it, formerly fertile, is now thrown out to common as useless. The middle and western portion of the county has generally a good soil. Plaster of Paris and clover act finely in improving the soil. Pop. in 1840, whites 13,840, slaves 5,273, free colored 1,318; total, 20,431.

Central View in Leesburg.

Leesburg, the county-seat, lies in the northern part of the county, 34 miles NW. of Washington, and 153 miles N. of Richmond. It was named from the Lee family, who were among the early settlers of the county: it was established in September, 1758, in the 32d year of the reign of George II. Mr. Nicholas Minor, who owned 60 acres around the court-house, had then laid it off into streets and lots, some of which, at the passage of the act, had been built upon. The act constituted the Hon. Philip Ludwell Lee, Esq., Thomas Mason, Esq., Francis Lightfoot Lee, James Hamilton, Nicholas Minor, Josias Clapham, Æneas Campbell, John Hugh, Francis Hague, and William West, gentlemen, trustees for the town. Leesburg is well and compactly built, its streets are well paved, and it is supplied with fine water, conducted into the town in pipes from a neighboring spring at the base of a mountain. It contains the county buildings, (of which the court-house is shown in the above view,) 1 Presbyterian, 1 Episcopalian, and 1 Methodist church, a bank, a very handsome academy recently erected, 1 newspaper printing-office, and a population of about 1500. During the French and Indian war, Braddock's army passed through here. Traces of the road cut by them are still discernible, about a mile s. of the village. Braddock remained in Leesburg several days; the house he occupied (now down) stood in Loudon street. Washington, who was here, also put up in that portion of the town. Middleburg, near the line of Fauquier county, 16 miles ssw. of Leesburg, is a flourishing village, surrounded by a fertile country. It contains 6 or 8 mercantile stores, 1 Epis., 1

Met., and 1 free church used by Baptists, and a population of about
500. Waterford, 6 miles NW. of Leesburg, contains 4 mercantile
stores, 1 Friends' meeting-house, 1 free church, and about 70 dwellings. There are, beside these, several small villages in the county,
containing from 6 to 25 dwellings ; among them are Aldie, Bloom-
field, Hillsborough, Lovettsville, Mount Gilead, Montville, Phil-
mont, Snickersville, and Union.

"A very considerable contrast is observable in the manners of
the inhabitants in the different sections of the county. That part
lying NW. of Waterford was originally settled by Germans, and is
called the German settlement ; and the middle of the county, sw.
of Waterford and w. of Leesburg, was mostly settled by emigrants
from the middle states, many of whom were Friends. In these
two sections the farms are small, and cultivated by free labor."
The Quakers in this state, as well as elsewhere, suffered much
persecution at an early day. By referring to page 151 of this
volume, the reader will perceive the severity of the laws passed
against them in the early history of Virginia. In the revolution,
their non-conformity to the military laws of the state, from con-
scientious motives, brought them into difficulty, as will be seen in
the annexed extract from Kercheval :—

At the beginning of the war, attempts were made to compel them to bear arms and
serve in the militia ; but it was soon found unavailing. They would not perform any
military duty required of them : not even the scourge would compel them to submit to
discipline. The practice of coercion was therefore abandoned, and the legislature enacted a law to levy a tax upon their property, to hire substitutes to perform militia duty
in their stead. This, with other taxes, bore peculiarly heavy upon them. Their personal property was sold under the hammer to raise these public demands ; and before
the war was over, many of them were reduced to great distress in their pecuniary circumstances.

This selling of Quakers' property afforded great opportunity for designing individuals
to make profitable speculations. They continued to refuse to pay taxes for several
years after the war, holding it unlawful to contribute their money towards discharging
the war debt. This being at length adjusted, no part of our citizens pay their public
demands with more punctuality, (except their muster-fines, which they still refuse to
pay.) Owing to their industrious and sober habits, they soon recovered from their pecuniary distress produced by the war, and are, generally speaking, the most independent
part of our community. Vast numbers of them have migrated to the western country,
and several of their meetings are entirely broken up. They continued their ancient
practice of depending upon their household manufactures for their clothing ; and it was
a long time before they gave in to the practice of purchasing European goods. A few
of them entered into the mercantile business ; several others erected fine merchant mills ;
others engaged in mechanical pursuits ; but the great body of them are farmers, and
are generally most excellent cultivators of the soil.

All who have read Lee's "Memoirs of the War," will doubtless
recollect the thrilling narration of the pretended desertion of JOHN
CHAMPE, sergeant-major of Lee's celebrated partisan legion. He
perilled his life, and, what was far more sacred to this high-minded
soldier, his *reputation*, to bring the traitor Arnold into the power
of the Americans, and thus save the life of the unfortunate Andre ;
but his well-laid plans were frustrated. Champe was a native of
this county. Near the close of the revolution he returned to Lou-

don, but removed thence after some years to Kentucky, where he died. When Champe arrived in New York, he was placed in the company of a Captain Cameron, in Arnold's legion. A portion of Cameron's private journal, published in the British United Service Journal, gives some interesting anecdotes of Champe. Among others, it seems that his old captain after the war married in Virginia, and while travelling through Loudon with his servant, was benighted in a severe thunder-storm in the woods. Their situation was one of peril. They at last descried a light glimmering through the trees, and found it to proceed from a log-house, in which they sought shelter. They were most cordially received by its owner, as will be seen in the annexed extract from the journal of Capt. Cameron :

He would not permit either master or man to think of their horses, but insisting that we should enter the house, where fire and changes of apparel awaited us, he himself led the jaded animals to a shed, rubbed them down, and provided them with forage. It would have been affectation of the worst kind to dispute his pleasure in this instance, so I readily sought the shelter of his roof, to which a comely dame bade me welcome, and busied herself in preventing my wishes. My drenched uniform was exchanged for a suit of my host's apparel ; my servant was accommodated in the same manner, and we soon afterwards found ourselves seated beside a blazing fire of wood, by the light of which our hostess assiduously laid out a well-stocked supper table. I need not say that all this was in the highest degree comfortable. Yet I was not destined to sit down to supper without discovering still greater cause for wonder. In due time our host returned, and the first glance which I cast towards him satisfied me that he was no stranger. The second set every thing like doubt at rest. Sergeant Champe stood before me ; the same in complexion, in feature, though somewhat less thoughtful in the expression of his eye, as when he first joined my company in New York.

I cannot say that my sensations on recognising my ci-devant sergeant were altogether agreeable. The mysterious manner in which he both came and went, the success with which he had thrown a veil over his own movements, and the recollection that I was the guest of a man who probably entertained no sense of honor, either public or private, excited in me a vague and undefined alarm, which I found it impossible on the instant to conceal. I started, and the movement was not lost upon Champe. He examined my face closely ; and a light appearing to burst in all at once upon his memory, he ran forward towards the spot where I sat.

" Welcome, welcome, Captain Cameron," said he, " a thousand times welcome to my roof ; you behaved well to me while I was under your command, and deserve more of hospitality than I possess the power to offer ; but what I do possess is very much at your service, and heartily glad am I that accident should have thus brought us together again. You have doubtless looked upon me as a twofold traitor, and I cannot blame you if you have. Yet I should wish to stand well in your estimation, too ; and therefore I will, if you please, give a faithful narrative of the causes which led both to my arrival in New York, and to my abandonment of the British army on the shores of the Chesapeake. But I will not enter upon the subject now. You are tired with your day's travel ; you stand in need of food and rest. Eat and drink, I pray you, and sleep soundly ; and to-morrow, if you are so disposed, I will try to put my own character straight in the estimation of the only British officer of whose good opinion I am covetous."

There was so much frankness and apparent sincerity in this, that I could not resist it, so I sat down to supper with a mind perfectly at ease ; and having eaten heartily, I soon afterwards retired to rest, on a clean pallet which was spread for me on the floor. Sleep was not slow in visiting my eyelids : nor did I awake until long after the sun had risen on the morrow, and the hardy and active settlers, to whose kindness I was indebted, had gone through a considerable portion of their day's labor.

I found my host next morning the same open, candid, and hospitable man that he had shown himself on first recognising me. He made no allusion, indeed, during breakfast, to what had fallen from him over night ; but when he heard me talk of getting my horses ready, he begged to have a few minutes' conversation with me. His wife, for such my hostess was, immediately withdrew, under the pretext of attending to her household affairs, upon which he took a seat beside me and began his story.

Oak Hill, the Seat of President Monroe.

Oak Hill, the seat of the late James Monroe, President of the United States, is situated 9 miles s. of Leesburg, on a commanding eminence enveloped in a beautiful grove of oaks, locusts, and poplars. The place is now in the possession of Samuel L. Governeur, Esq., a son-in-law of Mr. Monroe. The main building, with a Grecian front, is of brick, and was built by Mr. Monroe while in the presidential chair. The one on the left is a wooden dwelling of humble pretensions, and was occupied by him previous to his inauguration. The memoir annexed is from the Encyclopædia Americana.

Fac-simile of the signature of James Monroe.

JAMES MONROE, the fifth President of the United States, was born in Westmoreland county, April 28th, 1758. He graduated at William and Mary, and having entered as a cadet in the American army in 1776, he was soon after appointed lieutenant. He was in the battle of Harlaem Heights, White Plains, and Trenton. At the latter, perceiving that the enemy were endeavoring to form a six-gun battery at the head of King-street, Lieut. Monroe, with Capt. Wm. Washington, rushed forward with the advance-guard, drove the artillerists from their guns, and took two pieces which they were in the act of firing. These officers were both wounded in this successful enterprise, and for his gallant conduct, Lieut. Monroe was promoted to a captaincy. He was aid to Lord Stirling in the campaigns of 1777 and 1778, and was at Brandywine, Germantown, and Monmouth, in which actions he distinguished himself. By the recommendation of Washington, he was appointed to raise a regiment, of which he was to be given the command; but in the exhausted state of Virginia, he failed to raise his regiment, and therefore resumed the study of the law under Jefferson, then governor of the state. He was active as a volunteer in the militia, and in the subsequent invasions of Virginia, and in 1780 visited the southern army, under De Kalb, as a military commissioner, at the request of Mr. Jefferson.

In 1782, he was a member of the Virginia legislature, and of the executive council, and in 1783, at the age of 24, a member of Congress, in which he served three years. He was always at his post, and engaged in the most arduous duties. He introduced a resolution to vest in Congress the power to regulate the trade with all the states, and other important resolutions. He was appointed a commissioner to settle the boundary between New York and Massachusetts. In 1787 he was again a member of the Virginia legislature, and in 1788, of the Virginia convention. From 1790 to 1794 he was a member of the United States senate. From 1794 to 1796 he was minister plenipotentiary to France, and he was recalled by Washington, under an implied censure. In 1799, under the nomination of Mr. Madison, he was appointed governor of Virginia. In 1803 he was minister extraordinary to France, to act in conjunction with Mr. Livingston, the resident minister.

This mission was of the utmost consequence, as it terminated in the acquisition of Louisiana. In the same year, he was appointed minister to London, and in 1804, to Spain. In 1806, in conjunction with the late William Pinckney, he was appointed minister to London, where he pursued the negotiations with the Fox ministry. Mr. Monroe having been prominently brought forward as a candidate for the presidency, as the successor of Mr. Jefferson, returned from London ; but soon after withdrew from the canvass. In 1810 he was again elected to the legislature, and again appointed governor. He was appointed secretary of state, Nov. 26, 1811. The war department being in a very embarrassed state, on the departure of its head, Gen. Armstrong, Mr. Monroe undertook it, and made extraordinary and very useful exertions to help the war on the lakes, and the defence of New Orleans. After he had reduced to order the war department, he resumed the duties of the department of state ; which he continued to exercise until, in 1817, he was chosen successor to James Madison in the presidency. In 1821, he was re-elected by a vote unanimous, with a single exception, one vote in New Hampshire having been given to J. Q. Adams.

Mr. Monroe was wise and fortunate in the selection of his ministers. He went further than either of his two immediate predecessors, in maintaining the necessity of an efficient general government, and in strengthening every arm of the national defence. He encouraged the army, increased the navy, and caused those foreign naval expeditions to be sent out to the West Indies, the Mediterranean, the coast of Africa, and the shores of South America, which have given instruction to our officers, augmented our seamen, protected the national commerce, and caused the country to be universally respected by distant nations. He ordered the principal headlands, and exposed points along our borders and sea-coasts, to be accurately surveyed, plans of fortifications drawn, and the reports made up, with a view to the ultimate complete defence of the frontiers of the United States, both on the land and sea-side. He directed inquiries, surveys, and plans, as to the most suitable sites for the northern and southern naval depôts for the repair and accommodation of our fleets, in time of war and peace. The cession of Florida, by Spain, to the United States, was effected during his administration. It was during his administration, that the emancipated Spanish and Portuguese colonies were formally recognised by the United States. He assumed high constitutional ground in favor of internal improvement and the United States Bank. He was mainly instrumental in promoting the pension law for the relief of indigent revolutionary soldiers. During his administration the illustrious Lafayette visited these shores as the guest of the nation. He took the most energetic measures in favor of the abolition of the slave-trade, and continued to encourage the establishment of the principles of commerce with all nations, upon the basis of free and equal reciprocity.

It is a high compliment to the firmness, judgment, and sagacity of Mr. Monroe, that he proclaimed to the world the determination of the United States not to suffer any European government to interfere with the internal concerns of the independent South American governments. The well-timed expression of this sentiment put an end to all rumors of any armed intervention in the affairs of Spanish America. Col. Monroe retired from the office of president at the end of his second term.

In the late stages of his life, he was associated with the ex-presidents Jefferson and Madison, in founding the University of Virginia. Subsequently, he was chosen a member of the convention of 1829–30, for revising the state constitution, and presided over its deliberations. He did not disdain to act as justice of the peace in Loudon.

Mr. Monroe died at New York, July 4th, 1831, the anniversary of American Independence, like the ex-presidents Jefferson and Adams. Col. Monroe's biography is intimately and honorably connected with the civil and military history of the United States. He was one of the leaders of the democratic or Jefferson party, and involved in most of the party questions and occurrences by which the country was divided and agitated. He possessed a very energetic, persevering spirit; a vigorous mind, and extraordinary powers of application. In his unlimited devotion to public business, he neglected his private affairs. He retired from office extremely deep in debt; a situation from which he was relieved, though when almost too late, by liberal appropriations of Congress to satisfy the large claims which he preferred on the government for moneys disbursed, and debts incurred on its account.

LOUISA.

Louisa was formed from Hanover in 1742: its mean length is 30, mean breadth 18 miles. The county is watered by the North and South Anna Rivers and their numerous branches. The surface is hilly; the soil, originally of middling fertility, has been injured by injudicious agriculture. Several gold mines have been opened in the county, but not worked with much profit: in 1840 the gold mined was worth $3,000. Pop. in 1840, whites 6,047, slaves 9,010, free colored 376; total, 15,433.

Louisa C. H., 60 miles NW. of Richmond, on the line of the Louisa rail-road, is a small village containing a few dwellings only. There are no places of note in the county.

Louisa has been the scene of no important historical incident. Its citizens bore their full share in the Indian and French war of 1755, and in the war of the revolution. Tarleton with his cavalry passed up by the court-house in 1781, on his expedition into Albemarle: and when Lafayette had united with Wayne at the Raccoon Ford, on the Rapid Ann, and turned to pursue the British general from whom he had been retreating, he made a forced and rapid march across this county, from Brock's bridge on the North Anna, to the Fluvanna line, in order to intercept the enemy. The road which he opened for this purpose is still known as " *the Marquis's road;*" passing southwesterly three or four miles above the Green Spring. In the same year, two tories who had attached themselves, as marauders, to the British army, were summarily hung by one Holland and another man, near the Goochland boundary, twenty-one miles south from Louisa C. H., with the countenance and before the eyes of the neighboring people. Louisa first sent Patrick Henry as a delegate to the House of Burgesses in 1765, soon after his removal from Hanover; and she again elected him in 1776–7, till he returned to his native county.

As the Virginia House of Burgesses had the merit of originating that powerful engine of resistance—corresponding committees between the legislatures of the different colonies—so Louisa had the honor of furnishing the member, in the person of DABNEY CARR, Esq., who introduced the measure March 12th, 1773. The resolutions adopted were entered upon the public journals, one of which placed Mr. Carr on the standing committee of correspondence and inquiry. Wirt says of him :

In supporting these resolutions, Mr. Carr made his *début*, and a noble one it is said to have been. This gentleman, by profession a lawyer, had recently commenced his practice at the same bar with Patrick Henry; and although he had not yet reached the meridian of life, he was considered by far the most formidable rival in forensic eloquence that Mr. Henry had ever yet had to encounter. He had the advantage of a person at once dignified and engaging, and the manner and action of an accomplished gentleman. His education was a finished one ; his mind trained to correct thinking ; his conceptions quick, and clear, and strong ; he reasoned with great cogency, and had an imagination which enlightened beautifully, without interrupting or diverting the course of his argument. His voice was finely toned, his feelings acute ; his style free, and rich, and various ; his devotion to the cause of liberty verging on enthusiasm ; and his spirit firm and undaunted, beyond the possibility of being shaken. With what delight the House of Burgesses hailed this new champion, and felicitated themselves on such an access to their cause, it is easy to imagine. But what are the hopes and expectations of mortals !

" Ostendent terris hunc tantum fata, neque ultra
" Esse sinent—''

In two months from the time at which this gentleman stood before the House of Burgesses, in all the pride of health, and genius, and eloquence—he was no more : lost to his friends and to his country, and disappointed of sharing in that noble triumph which awaited the illustrious band of his compatriots.

LUNENBURG.

LUNENBURG was formed in 1746 from Brunswick : its length is 25, mean breadth 16 miles. The Meherrin runs on its southern boundary, and the Nottoway on its northern. Pop. in 1840, whites 4,132, slaves 6,707, free colored 216 ; total, 11,055.

Lewiston, the county-seat, situated in an elevated and healthy part of the county, 78 miles sw. of Richmond, was laid off in 1817 by act of Assembly, when there was but one family residing here. It now contains about 20 dwellings.

When the British invaded Virginia in 1781, Tarleton, with his legion, passed through this county and committed depredations upon the people. His men entered private dwellings, and wantonly ripped open beds and scattered their contents, notwithstanding the tears and remonstrances of the females, whose husbands and brothers were mostly with the army. The Rev. Mr. Craig, a strenuous whig, owned a fine mill a few miles from the C. H., where flour was manufactured for the American troops. To this mill Tarleton was guided by a young tory. The old parson, hearing of the proximity of the enemy, was busily engaged in rolling the last barrel of flour with the U. S. mark into the mill-pond, when Tarleton appeared at the head of his men. They burnt the mill, a trace of the dam of which is now to be seen, and compelled the good old parson to off with his coat and assist in slaughtering his pigs for their use. They carried off his slaves, but they, with a single exception, returned, reporting that they were harshly used by the enemy.*

* From mss. of R. F. Astrop, Esq., containing historical and descriptive matter relating to this section of the state.

MADISON.

MADISON was formed in 1792, from Culpeper. It is about 23 miles long, and 13 miles wide. It lies at the eastern foot of the Blue Ridge, from which extend several mountains into the western part of the county, some of the smaller of which are very fertile. The tobacco raised on the highlands is of a superior quality: between the mountains are fine valleys of rich bottom land. The county is watered by the Rapid Ann and its branches. Pop. in 1840, whites 3,729, slaves 4,308, free colored 70 ; total, 8,107.

Madison, the county-seat, is 97 miles NNW. of Richmond. It is situated in the heart of the county, on a high and elevated ridge, and commands a beautiful and picturesque view of the Blue Ridge and the neighboring mountains. It contains 4 mercantile stores, 1 Baptist and 1 Episcopal church, and about 50 dwellings. At the post-offices of Rapid Ann Meeting-House and Leon are a few dwellings ; the first contains a Baptist and a Free church.

The late HON. LINN BANKS, of this county, " for 20 successive years was speaker of the House of Delegates, an office for which he was so peculiarly qualified, that he was selected to fill it in all the mutations of party. He retired from the legislature in 1838, and was elected to Congress in that year, to complete the unexpired term of Mr. Patton, who was chosen counsellor. He was re-elected in 1839, and again in 1841. He served in the extra session of 1841, and then agreed with his competitor, to submit their cause to the people of his district. He consequently resigned his seat, which was obtained by his opponent, the majority against him being small. He was found drowned (Feb. 24th, 1842) in a stream which he had to cross in going from Madison Court-House to his residence, a few months after he was thus consigned to private life."

MASON.

MASON was formed in 1804 from Kanawha, and named from the celebrated statesman George Mason. It is about 30 miles long and 22 broad. The Ohio forms its western boundary, and the Great Kanawha passes centrally through it. The surface is broken, and much of the soil of a good quality. Pop., whites 5,923, slaves 808, free colored 46 ; total, 6,777.

Buffalo, in the SE. part of the county, on the E. bank of the Kanawha, 21 miles from its mouth, contains a Presbyterian church and about 20 dwellings.

Point Pleasant, the county-seat, is situated at the junction of the Great Kanawha with the Ohio, 370 miles west of Richmond. It contains 1 Episcopalian and 1 Presbyterian church, 3 mercantile stores, 1 steam flour, and 1 steam saw-mill, 2 tanneries, and about 50 dwellings.

There was once an Indian town of the Shawnee tribe at the mouth of Old Town creek, near Point Pleasant, on the land of Thomas Lewis, Esq., the clerk of the county It was deserted by them, it is supposed, about the year 1760. In ploughing there in 1798, about 80 gun-barrels were found. An anvil, a vice, hammers, and other blacksmith's tools have been disinterred. Mr. Lewis, the county clerk, has opened several of the small mounds which abound in this section, and found a gun-barrel, a camp kettle, a butcher knife, tomahawk, a pewter basin, a variety of beads, and human skeletons.

——

Point Pleasant is on the site of the bloodiest battle ever fought with the Indians in Virginia,—*the battle of Point Pleasant*—which took place in Dunmore's war, Oct. 10th, 1774.

To illustrate more clearly this desperate action, we present our readers with a plan of the battle-ground, with explanatory references, obtained by us while at Point Pleasant, in the autumn of 1843 : *a.* A small pond and ravine where the action commenced, and where Col. Charles Lewis was mortally wounded. From this place, at right angles to the Ohio, to Crooked creek, both armies, early in the action, were extended through the woods. After a while the Indian line extended further down on the creek. *d.* Position of the fort built after the battle. All the officers who fell in the battle were buried at or near this spot, in what is now known as the Point Lot. *b.* The court-house. *c.* Cornstalk's grave. He was originally buried near the Kanawha ; but a few years since his remains were disinterred, and removed to their present resting-place.

Plan of the battle of Point Pleasant.

The subjoined account of this action, is from the work of Withers :

The army destined for this expedition was composed of volunteers and militia, chiefly from the counties west of the Blue Ridge, and consisted of two divisions. The northern division, comprehending the troops collected in Frederick, Dunmore, (now Shenandoah,) and the adjacent counties, was to be commanded by Lord Dunmore in person ; and the southern, comprising the different companies raised in Botetourt, Augusta, and the adjoining counties east of the Blue Ridge, was to be led on by Gen. Andrew Lewis. These two divisions, proceeding by different routes, were to form a junction at the mouth of the Big Kanawha, and from thence penetrate the country northwest of the Ohio River, as far as the season would admit of their going, and destroy all the Indian towns and villages which they could reach.

About the first of September, the troops placed under the command of Gen. Lewis rendezvoused at Camp Union, (now Lewisburg,) and consisted of two regiments, commanded by Col. William Fleming of Botetourt, and Col. Charles Lewis of Augusta, and containing about four hundred men each. At Camp Union they were joined by an independent volunteer company under Col. John Field of Culpeper, a company from Bedford under Capt. Buford, and two from the *Holstein settlement*, (now Washington county,) under Capts. Evan Shelby and Harbert. These three latter companies were part of the forces to be led on by Col. Christian, who was likewise to join the two main divisions of the army at Point Pleasant, so soon as the other companies of his regiment could be assembled. The force under Gen. Lewis, having been thus augmented to eleven hundred men, commenced its march for the mouth of Kanawha on the 11th of September, 1774.

From Camp Union to the point proposed for the junction of the northern and southern divisions of the army, a distance of one hundred and sixty miles, the intermediate country was a trackless forest, so rugged and mountainous as to render the progress of the army at once tedious and laborious. Under the guidance of Capt. Matthew Arbuckle, they, however, succeeded in reaching the Ohio River, after a march of nineteen days ; and fixed their encampment on the point of land immediately between that river and the Big Kanawha. The provisions and ammunition, transported on pack-horses, and the beeves in droves, arrived soon after.

When the southern division arrived at Point Pleasant, Governor Dunmore, with the forces under his command, had not reached there; and unable to account for his failure to form the preconcerted junction at that place, it was deemed advisable to await that event ; as by so doing a better opportunity would be afforded to Col. Christian of coming up with that portion of the army which was then with him. Meanwhile Gen. Lewis, to learn the cause of the delay of the northern division, dispatched runners by land in the direction of Fort Pitt, to obtain tidings of Lord Dunmore, and to communicate them to him immediately. In their absence, however, advices were received from his lordship, that he had determined on proceeding across the country, directly to the Shawnee towns; and ordering Gen. Lewis to cross the river, march forward, and form a junction with him near to them. These advices were received on the 9th of October, and preparations were immediately begun to be made for the transportation of the troops over the Ohio River.

Early on the morning of Monday, the tenth of that month, two soldiers left the camp, and proceeded up the Ohio River, in quest of deer. When they had progressed about two miles, they unexpectedly came in sight of a large number of Indians rising from their encampment, and who, discovering the two hunters, fired upon them and killed one; the other escaped unhurt, and running briskly to the camp, communicated the intelligence, " that he had seen a body of the enemy, covering four acres of ground, as closely as they could stand by the side of each other." The main part of the army was immediately ordered out under Cols. Charles Lewis,* and William Fleming ; and having formed into two lines, they proceeded about four hundred yards, when they met the Indians, and the action commenced.

At the first onset, Col. Charles Lewis having fallen, and Col. Fleming being wounded, both lines gave way and were retreating briskly towards the camp, when they were met by a reinforcement under Col. Field,† and rallied. The engagement then became general, and was sustained with the most obstinate fury on both sides. The Indians perceiving the " tug of war" had come, and determined on affording the colonial army no chance of escape, if victory should declare for them, formed a line extending across the point, from the Ohio to the Kanawha, and protected in front by logs and fallen timber. In this situation they maintained the contest with unabated vigor, from sunrise till towards the close of evening ; bravely and successfully resisting every charge which was made on them ; and withstanding the impetuosity of every onset, with the most invincible firmness, until a fortunate movement on the part of the Virginia troops decided the day.

Some short distance above the entrance of the Kanawha River into the Ohio, there is a stream called Crooked creek, emptying into the former of these, from the northeast, whose banks are tolerably high, and were then covered with a thick and luxuriant growth of weeds. Seeing the impracticability of dislodging the Indians by the most vigorous attack, and sensible of the great danger which must arise to his army, if the contest were not decided before night, Gen. Lewis detached the three companies which were commanded by Capts. Isaac Shelby, George Matthews, and John Stuart, with orders to proceed up the Kanawha River and Crooked creek, under cover of the banks and weeds, till they should pass some distance beyond the enemy ; when they were to emerge from their covert, march downward towards the point, and attack the Indians in their rear. The manœuvre thus planned was promptly executed, and gave a decided victory to the colonial army. The Indians finding themselves suddenly and unexpectedly encompassed between two armies, and not doubting but that in their rear was the looked-for reinforcement under Col. Christian, soon gave way, and about sundown commenced a precipitate retreat across the Ohio, to their towns on the Scioto. The victory, indeed, was decisive, and many advantages were obtained by it ; but they were not cheaply bought. The Virginia army sustained in this engagement a loss of seventy-five

---

* Few officers were ever more, or more deservedly, endeared to those under their command than Col. Charles Lewis. In the many skirmishes which it was his fortune to have with the Indians, he was uncommonly successful ; and in the various scenes of life through which he passed, his conduct was invariably marked by the distinguishing characteristics of a mind of no ordinary stamp. His early fall on this bloody field was severely felt during the whole engagement; and to it has been attributed the partial advantages gained by the Indian army near the commencement of the action. When the fatal ball struck him, he fell at the root of a tree; from whence he was carried to his tent, against his wish, by Capt. William Morrow and a Mr. Bailey, of Capt. Paul's company, and died in a few hours afterwards.

† An active, enterprising, and meritorious officer, who had been in service in Braddock's war, and profited by his experience of the Indian mode of fighting. His death checked for a time the ardor of his troops, and spread a gloom over the countenances of those who accompanied him on this campaign.

killed, and one hundred and forty wounded—about one-fifth of the entire number of the troops.

Among the slain were Cols. Lewis and Field; Capts. Buford, Morrow, Wood, Cundiff, Wilson, and Robert McClannahan; and Lieuts. Allen, Goldsby, and Dillon, with some other subalterns. The loss of the enemy could not be ascertained. On the morning after the action, Col. Christian, who had arrived after the battle was ended, marched his men over the battle-ground, and found twenty-one of the Indians lying dead; and twelve others were afterwards discovered, where they had been attempted to be concealed under some old logs and brush.

From the great facility with which the Indians either carry off or conceal their dead, it is always difficult to ascertain the number of their slain; and hence arises, in some measure, the disparity between their known loss and that sustained by their opponents in battle. Other reasons for this disparity are to be found in their peculiar mode of warfare, and in the fact that they rarely continue a contest, when it has to be maintained with the loss of their warriors. It would not be easy otherwise to account for the circumstance, that even when signally vanquished, the list of their slain does not, frequently, appear more than half as great as that of the victors. In this particular instance, many of the dead were certainly thrown into the river.

Nor could the number of the enemy engaged be ever ascertained. Their army is known to have been composed of warriors from the different nations north of the Ohio, and to have comprised the flower of the Shawanee, Delaware, Mingo, Wyandotte, and Cayuga tribes; led on by men, whose names were not unknown to fame,[*] and at the head of whom was Cornstalk, sachem of the Shawanees, and king of the northern confederacy.

This distinguished chief and consummate warrior, proved himself on that day to be justly entitled to the prominent station which he occupied. His plan of alternate retreat and attack was well conceived, and occasioned the principal loss sustained by the whites. If at any time his warriors were believed to waver, his voice could be heard above the din of arms, exclaiming, in his native tongue: "Be strong! be strong!" and when one near him, by trepidation and reluctance to proceed to the charge, evinced a dastardly disposition, fearing the example might have a pernicious influence, with one blow of his tomahawk he severed his skull. It was, perhaps, a solitary instance in which terror predominated. Never did men exhibit a more conclusive evidence of bravery in making a charge, and fortitude in withstanding an onset, than did these undisciplined soldiers of the forest in the field at Point Pleasant. Such, too, was the good conduct of those who composed the army of Virginia on that occasion, and such the noble bravery of many, that high expectations were entertained of their future distinction. Nor were those expectations disappointed. In the various scenes through which they subsequently passed, the pledge of after eminence then given was fully redeemed · and the names of Shelby, Campbell, Matthews, Fleming, Moore, and others, their compatriots in arms on the memorable tenth of October, 1774, have been inscribed in brilliant characters on the roll of fame.[†]

Having buried the dead, and made every arrangement which their situation admitted, for the comfort of the wounded, intrenchments were thrown up, and the army commenced its march to form a junction with the northern division, under Lord Dunmore. Proceeding by the way of the Salt Licks, Gen. Lewis pressed forward with astonishing rapidity, (considering that the march was through a trackless desert;) but before he had gone far, an express arrived from Dunmore with orders to return immediately to the mouth of the Big Kanawha. Suspecting the integrity of his lordship's motives, and urged by the advice of his officers generally, Gen. Lewis refused to obey

---

[*] Such were Redhawk, a Delaware chief,—Scoppathus, a Mingo,—Elinipsico, a Shawanee, and son to Cornstalk,—Chiyawee, a Wyandotte, and Logan, a Cayuga.

[†] The following gentlemen, with others of high reputation in private life, were officers in the battle at Point Pleasant. Gen. Isaac Shelby, the first governor of Kentucky, and afterwards secretary of war; Gen. William Campbell, and Col. John Campbell, heroes of King's Mountain and Long Island; Gen. Evan Shelby, one of the most favored citizens of Tennessee, often honored with the confidence of that state; Col. William Fleming, an active governor of Virginia during the revolutionary war; Gen. Andrew Moore, of Rockbridge, the only man ever elected by Virginia from the country west of the Blue Ridge, to the senate of the United States; Col. John Stuart, of Greenbrier; Gen. Tate, of Washington county, Virginia; Col. William McKee, of Lincoln county, Kentucky; Col. John Steele, since a governor of the Mississippi Territory; Col. Charles Cameron, of Bath; Col. Bazaleel Wells, of Ohio; and Gen. George Matthews, a distinguished officer in the war of the revolution, the hero of Brandywine, Germantown, and of Guilford, a governor of Georgia, and a senator from that state in the Congress of the United States. The salvation of the American army at Germantown is ascribed, in Johnstone's life of Gen. Greene, to the bravery and good conduct of two regiments, one of which was commanded by Gen., then Col. Matthews.

these orders, and continued to advance till he was met (at Kilkenny Creek, and in sight of an Indian village, which its inhabitants had just fired and deserted) by the governor, (accompanied by White Eyes,) who informed him that he was negotiating a treaty of peace, which would supersede the necessity of the further movement of the southern division, and repeating the order for its retreat.

The army under Gen. Lewis had endured many privations and suffered many hardships. They had encountered a savage enemy in great force, and purchased a victory with the blood of their friends. When arrived near to the goal of their anxious wishes, and with nothing to prevent the accomplishment of the object of the campaign, they received those orders with evident chagrin, and did not obey them without murmuring. Having, at his own request, been introduced severally to the officers of that division, complimenting them for their gallantry and good conduct in the late engagement, and assuring them of his high esteem, Lord Dunmore returned to his camp; and Gen. Lewis commenced his retreat.

This battle (says Col. Stuart, in his historical memoir) was, in fact, the beginning of the revolutionary war, that obtained for our country the liberty and independence enjoyed by the United States—and a good presage of future success; for it is well known that the Indians were influenced by the British to commence the war to terrify and confound the people, before they commenced hostilities themselves the following year at Lexington. It was thought by British politicians, that to excite an "Indian war would prevent a combination of the colonies for opposing parliamentary measures to tax the Americans." The blood, therefore, spilt upon this memorable battle, will long be remembered by the good people of Virginia and the United States with gratitude.

The brave and noble Shawanee chief, Cornstalk, was atrociously murdered at Point Pleasant, in the summer of 1777. The governor of Virginia offered a reward for the apprehension of the murderers, but without effect. Point Pleasant, which was first settled in 1774, did not flourish for many years. It had no church, the state of society was bad, and it was the popular superstition that the place was cursed for this fiend-like act. The particulars here detailed of this event, are from the modest, unostentatious memoir of Col. John Stuart:—

In the year 1777, the Indians, being urged by British agents, became very troublesome to frontier settlements, manifesting much appearance of hostilities, when the Cornstalk warrior, with the Redhawk, paid a visit to the garrison at Point Pleasant. He made no secret of the disposition of the Indians; declaring that, on his own part, he was opposed to joining in the war on the side of the British, but that all the nation, except himself and his own tribe, were determined to engage in it; and that, of course, he and his tribe would have to run with the stream, (as he expressed it.) On this Captain Arbuckle thought proper to detain him, the Redhawk, and another fellow, as hostages, to prevent the nation from joining the British.

In the course of that summer our government had ordered an army to be raised, of volunteers, to serve under the command of General Hand; who was to have collected a number of troops at Fort Pitt, with them to descend the river to Point Pleasant, there to meet a reinforcement of volunteers expected to be raised in Augusta and Botetourt counties, and then proceed to the Shawanee towns and chastise them so as to compel them to a neutrality. Hand did not succeed in the collection of troops at Fort Pitt; and but three or four companies were raised in Augusta and Botetourt, which were under the command of Colonel George Skillern, who ordered me to use my endeavors to raise all the volunteers I could get in Greenbrier, for that service. The people had begun to see the difficulties attendant on a state of war and long campaigns carried through wildernesses, and but a few were willing to engage in such service. But as the settlements which we covered, though less exposed to the depredations of the Indians, had showed their willingness to aid in the proposed plan to chastise the Indians, and had raised three companies, I was very desirous of doing all I could to promote the business and aid the service. I used the utmost endeavors, and proposed to the militia officers to volunteer ourselves, which would be an encouragement to others, and by such means to raise all the men who could be got. The chief of the officers in Greenbrier agreed to the proposal, and we cast lots who should command the company. The lot fell on Andrew Hamilton for captain, and William Renick lieutenant. We collected in all, about forty, and joined Colonel Skillern's party, on their way to Point Pleasant.

When we arrived, there was no account of General Hand or his army, and little or no provision made to support our troops, other than what we had taken with us down the Kanawha. We found, too, that the garrison was unable to spare us any supplies, having nearly exhausted, when we got there, what had been provided for themselves. But we concluded to wait there as long as we could for the arrival of General Hand, or some account from him. During the time of our stay two young men, of the names of Hamilton and Gilmore, went over the Kanawha one day to hunt for deer; on their return to camp, some Indians had concealed themselves on the bank among the weeds, to view our encampment; and as Gilmore came along past them, they fired on him and killed him on the bank.

Captain Arbuckle and myself were standing on the opposite bank when the gun fired; and while we were wondering who it could be shooting, contrary to orders, or what they were doing over the river, we saw Hamilton run down the bank, who called out that Gilmore was killed. Gilmore was one of the company of Captain John Hall, of that part of the country now Rockbridge county. The captain was a relation of Gilmore's, whose family and friends were chiefly cut off by the Indians in the year 1763, when Greenbrier was cut off. Hall's men instantly jumped into a canoe and went to the relief of Hamilton, who was standing in momentary expectation of being put to death. They brought the corpse of Gilmore down the bank, covered with blood and scalped, and put him into the canoe. As they were passing the river, I observed to Captain Arbuckle that the people would be for killing the hostages, as soon as the canoe would land. He supposed that they would not offer to commit so great a violence upon the innocent, who were in nowise accessary to the murder of Gilmore. But the canoe had scarcely touched the shore until the cry was raised, Let us kill the Indians in the fort; and every man, with his gun in his hand, came up the bank pale with rage. Captain Hall was at their head, and leader. Captain Arbuckle and I met them, and endeavored to dissuade them from so unjustifiable an action; but they cocked their guns, threatened us with instant death if we did not desist, rushed by us into the fort, and put the Indians to death.

On the preceding day, the Cornstalk's son, Elinipsico, had come from the nation to see his father, and to know if he was well, or alive. When he came to the river opposite the fort, he hallooed. His father was at that instant in the act of delineating a map of the country and the waters between the Shawanee towns and the Mississippi, at our request, with chalk upon the floor. He immediately recognised the voice of his son, got up, went out, and answered him. The young fellow crossed over, and they embraced each other in the most tender and affectionate manner. The interpreter's wife, who had been a prisoner among the Indians, and had recently left them, on hearing the uproar the next day, and hearing the men threatening that they would kill the Indians, for whom she retained much affection, ran to their cabin and informed them that the people were just coming to kill them; and that, because the Indians who killed Gilmore had come with Elinipsico the day before. He utterly denied it; declared that he knew nothing of them, and trembled exceedingly. His father encouraged him not to be afraid, for that the *Great Man above* had sent him there to be killed and die with him. As the men advanced to the door, the Cornstalk rose up and met them; they fired upon him, and seven or eight bullets went through him. So fell the great Cornstalk warrior,—whose name was bestowed upon him by the consent of the nation, as their great strength and support. His son was shot dead as he sat upon a stool. The Redhawk made an attempt to go up the chimney, but was shot down. The other Indian was shamefully mangled, and I grieved to see him so long in the agonies of death.

The Cornstalk, from personal appearance and many brave acts, was undoubtedly a hero. Had he been spared to live, I believe he would have been friendly to the American cause; for nothing could induce him to make the visit to the garrison at the critical time he did, but to communicate to them the temper and disposition of the Indians, and their design of taking part with the British. On the day he was killed we held a council, at which he was present. His countenance was dejected; and he made a speech, all of which seemed to indicate an honest and manly disposition. He acknowledged that he expected that he and his party would have to run with the stream, for that all the Indians on the lakes and northwardly, were joining the British. He said that when he returned to the Shawanee towns after the battle at the Point, he called a council of the nation to consult what was to be done, and upbraided them for their folly in not suffering him to make peace on the evening before the battle. "What," said he, "will you do now? The Big Knife is coming on us, and we shall all be killed. Now you must fight, or we are undone." But no one made an answer. He said, "then let us kill all our women and children, and go and fight till we die." But none would answer. At length he rose and struck his tomahawk in the post in the centre of the town-house: " I'll go," said he, " and make peace ;" and then the warriors all grunted out, "ough, ough, ough," and runners were instantly dispatched to the governor's army to solicit a peace, and the interposition of the governor on their behalf.

When he made his speech in council with us, he seemed to be impressed with an awful premonition of his approaching fate ; for he repeatedly said, " When I was a young man and went to war, I thought that might be the last time, and I would return no more. Now I am here among you ; you may kill me if you please ; I can die but once ; and it is all one to me, now or another time." This declaration concluded every sentence of his speech. He was killed about one hour after our council.

There is living upon Thirteen Mile creek, Mr. Jesse Van Bebber, an aged pioneer in this county. His life, like his own mountain-stream, was rough and turbulent at its commencement ; but as it nears its close, calm and peaceful, beautifully reflecting the Christian virtues. From conversation with him, we gathered many interesting anecdotes and incidents, illustrating the history of this region, some of which here follow :

Battle of Point Pleasant.—During the action, those troops from the more eastern part of the state, unaccustomed to fighting with the Indians, were all the day engaged in making a breastwork at the junction of the Kanawha with the Ohio, so that the army, if defeated, should have a secure retreat. Ignorant of how the action would terminate, they worked as if for their lives, and before the day was finished had a strong fortification erected. When the alarm was given that the Indians were near, Gen. Lewis deliberately lighted his pipe, and then coolly gave the orders to his brother, Col. Chas. Lewis, to advance upon them. The soldiers in Col. Fleming's regiment used a stratagem that proved very effectual. They concealed themselves behind trees, and then held out their hats, which the Indians mistakingly shot at. The hat being at once dropped, the Indian would run out from his covert to scalp his victim, and thus met a sure death from the tomahawk of his adversary. The whites in this action being all backwoodsmen, were more successful marksmen than the savages ; a fact in part owing to the want of the mechanical skill in the Indians, requisite to keeping their rifles in order. At the close of the action, the Indians went off hallooing, as if coming on to renew the attack. This stratagem deceived the whites, and enabled them to retreat in more safety. They recrossed the Ohio on rafts, three miles above, near the old Shawanee town.

Fort at Point Pleasant.—A fort was erected at Point Pleasant just after the battle, at the mouth of the Kanawha. It was a rectangular stockade, about eighty yards long, with blockhouses at two of its corners. It was finally destroyed, and a smaller one erected about fifty rods further up the Ohio, on the site of the store of James Capehart. It was composed of a circle of cabins, in which the settlers lived.

Eulen's Leap.—In the spring of '88 or '89, Ben Eulen, who was then insane, was out hunting in the woods below Point Pleasant, when he was discovered and pursued by an Indian. He threw away his rifle, an elegant silver-mounted piece, to arrest the attention of the Indian, and gain time. The Indian stopped to pick it up. Eulen unexpectedly came to a precipice, and fell head foremost through a buckeye, struck a branch, which turned him over, and he came upon his feet. The fall was fifty-three feet perpendicular. He then leaped another precipice of twelve feet in height, and escaped.

Anecdotes of the Van Bebbers.—A few years after the close of the revolution, a daughter of Capt. John Van Bebber, named Rhoda, aged 17, and Joseph Van Bebber, a young lad of 13, a brother of our informant, had crossed over in a canoe one morning, to the west side of the Ohio, opposite Point Pleasant, on an errand to Rhoda's father, then living temporarily in a house that side of the stream, when a party of Indians suddenly made their appearance. Dave, a black man belonging to Capt. Van Bebber, gave the alarm, and rushed into the house. The Indians attacked the house, but were driven off by Dave and Capt. Van Bebber, with the loss of two or three of their number. Joseph and Rhoda, in their terror, hastened to the canoe, whither the Indians pursued them, killed and scalped the young lady, and took Joseph a prisoner to Detroit. Rhoda's scalp the Indians divided into two, and sold them to the Indian traders at Detroit for $30 each ; their object in purchasing them was to encourage the savages in their incursions, so as to prevent a settlement of the country by the whites, and thus monopolize the Indian trade. Joseph afterwards stated that the barrel in which the scalps were put was nearly full of the horrid trophies. He remained with the Indians two years, during which he learned their language, and acted as interpreter between them and the traders. He at length made his escape, and lived with a trader until after Wayne's victory, when he returned home. While at Detroit, he became acquainted with the notorious Simon Girty, then a British pensioner for services in the revolution. He said Girty was an affable man, but extremely intemperate. Girty denied to him that he was the instigator of the death of Col. Crawford ; but that he went so far to save him that his own life was in danger.

In the fall of '88 or '89, Matthias Van Bebber, aged 18, and Jacob, aged 12 years, were out a short distance from Point Pleasant, with a horse, when they were waylaid by four Indians. Jacob was leading the horse, and Matthias was a short distance ahead, with a rifle across his shoulder, when the Indians fired two guns at Matthias. One of the balls struck him over the eyes, and rendered him momentarily blind ; he sprang one side, and fell into a gully. The boy Jacob, on hearing the report of the guns, fled, and three of the Indians went in pursuit. Matthias, in the mean time, sprang up and took to a tree. The remaining Indian did the same. Matthias brought up his gun to an aim, the Indian dodged, and the former took the opportunity and escaped into the fort. The Indians, after a tight chase of half a mile, caught the lad, who, being very active, would have escaped had his moccasins not been too large. The Indians retreated across the Ohio with their prisoner. He was a sprightly little fellow, small of his age, and the Indians, pleased with him, treated him kindly. On the first night of their encampment, they took him on their knees, and sang to him. He turned away his head to conceal his tears. On arriving at their town, while running the gauntlet between the children of the place, one Indian boy, much larger than himself, threw a bone, which struck him on the head. Enraged by the pain, Jacob drew back, and running with all his force, butted him over, much to the amusement of the Indian warriors. He was adopted into an Indian family, where he was used with kindness. On one occasion his adopted father whipped him, though slightly, which affected his Indian mother and sister to tears. After remaining with the Indians about a year, he escaped, and for five days travelled through the wilderness to his home. When he had arrived at maturity, he was remarkable for his fleetness. None of the Indians who visited the Point could ever equal him in that respect.

Indian incursion.—In May, 1791, a party of eighteen whites were attacked by about thirty Indians, about one mile north of the fort at Point Pleasant, near the field now belonging to David Long. The whites were defeated. Michael See and Robert Sinclair were killed. Hampton and Thomas Northrop, and a black boy, belonging to See, were taken prisoners. This boy was a son of Dick Pointer, who acted so bravely a few years before at the attack on Donnally's fort, in Greenbrier. He became an Indian chief, and in the late war with Great Britain took part with the friendly Indians against the enemy.

MARSHALL.

MARSHALL was formed in 1835, from Ohio county, and named from Chief-Justice Marshall : it is about 20 miles long and 18 wide. The surface is uneven and mountainous ; the mountains rise, in many places, 300 and 400 feet above the level of the Ohio, and are cultivated frequently on their summits and part way down their slopes—the soil there being often nearly as rich as the river bottoms. The wild lands of the county are valued from $3 to $8 per acre ; the cultivated mountain, from $15 to $20 ; and the river bottom, on the Ohio and the streams generally, from $30 to $40. Pop., whites 6,854, slaves 46, free colored 37 ; total, 6,937.

Grave Creek is situated upon a plain on the Ohio, 12 miles below Wheeling, at the mouth of Grave Creek. It is divided into
two distinct villages. Elizabethtown, the upper village, is the
county-seat; the lower village is called Moundsville. Unitedly
they contain 1 newspaper printing office, 2 mercantile stores, a
classical academy, an extensive steam flouring-mill, and a population of about 1,200. West Union, 16 miles NE. of the C. H., near
the Pennsylvania line, contains a few dwellings.

The Grave of Capt. Foreman.

Grave Creek was first settled in 1770, by Joseph Tomlinson, an
emigrant from Maryland. In 1772, he discovered the mammoth
mound at this place; and about this time several other families
from Maryland emigrated here. During the succeeding years,
the inhabitants suffered considerably from the Indians, and erected
forts for their security.

About four miles above the village of Grave Creek, on the
bank of the Ohio, is a monument bearing the following inscription:

This humble stone is erected to the memory of Capt. Foreman and twenty-one of his
men, who were slain by a band of ruthless savages—the *allies* of a *civilized* nation of
Europe—on the 25th of Sept., 1777.

So sleep the brave who sink to rest,
By all their country's wishes blest.

The account of the massacre which the monument is designed to commemorate, is thus given in a communication to the American Pioneer:

About the time of the attack at Wheeling, which occurred in September, (1777,) Capt. Foreman and his men were surprised at the head of Grave creek narrows; the account of which event, as given in the Border Warfare, differs somewhat from the way Robin Harkness, my uncle, related it, who was with Capt. Foreman at the time. I will, therefore, give it as related by him. A smoke was discovered down the river in the direction of the fort at Grave creek, which induced those at Wheeling to believe that the Indians had not yet left the country, and that the fort at Grave creek had been set on fire. In order to make discoveries, on the 25th of September Capt. Foreman, with 45 men, set out for Grave creek. Having arrived there, and seeing the fort standing, and discovering no signs of the Indians, they returned. On arriving at the foot of the Narrows, a contention arose between Capt. Foreman and a man by the name of Lynn, who had been sent with him as a spy, about which road they should take, the river or ridge. Lynn urged the probability of the Indians having been on the opposite shore, and had more than likely seen them pass down; and the most likely place for waylaying them was in the narrows, and therefore urged the necessity of going the ridge road. Foreman, being indisposed to take the counsel of Lynn, proceeded along the base of the hill. During the contention, Robin Harkness sat upon a log, having very sore eyes at the time, and took no part in the dispute; but when Capt. Foreman started, he followed him. Lynn, however, with seven or eight other frontiers-men, went the ridge road. While passing along a narrow bottom at the head of the narrows, the foremost of Capt. Foreman's men picked up some Indian trinkets, which immediately excited a suspicion that Indians were near, which caused a halt. Before them some five or six Indians stepped into the path, and behind them about the same number; and at the same moment a fire was poured in upon them from a line of Indians under cover of the river bank, and not over fifteen steps from the white men. Those that escaped the first fire fled up the hill; but it being steep and difficult to climb, they were exposed for some time to the fire of the Indians. Lynn and his comrades, hearing the fire when they were below them on the ridge, ran along until opposite. They then proceeded to the brink of the hill, where they saw a man ascending near them, who had got nearly to the top when he received a shot in his thigh, which broke it. Lynn and his comrades ran down and lifted him up, carried him over the hill, and hid him under a cleft of rocks, and then proceeded to Wheeling. As Robin Harkness was climbing the hill near the top, and pulling himself up by a bush, a ball struck it and knocked the bark off against him, which alarmed him, as he supposed it to be the ball; he however proceeded on and escaped unhurt. In this fatal ambuscade, twenty-one of Capt. Foreman's party were killed, and several much wounded: among the slain were Capt. Foreman and his two sons. The Indian force was never ascertained; but it was supposed to have been the same party that attacked Fort Henry, at Wheeling, which was supposed to have been upwards of 300 strong. On the ensuing day, the inhabitants of the neighborhood of Wheeling, under the direction of Col. Zane, proceeded to the fatal spot to bury those who had fallen, and at the same time to get the man who was wounded and hid under the rocks, who was still alive and finally recovered.

Within a quarter of a mile from the Ohio, on the river flats at Grave Creek, in full view of the passing steamers, is the mammoth mound. On the summit is an observatory, erected by Mr. A. B. Tomlinson in 1837. From his communication in the American Pioneer, we derive the following facts:

The Mammoth Mound is 69 feet high, and about 900 feet in circumference at its base. It is a frustum of a cone, and has a flat top of about 50 feet in diameter. This flat, until lately, was slightly depressed—occasioned, it is supposed, by the falling in of two vaults below. A few years since a white oak, of about 70 feet in height, stood on the summit of the mound, which appeared to die of age. On carefully cutting the trunk transversely, the number of concentric circles showed that it was about 500 years old.

'In 1838, Mr. Tomlinson commenced at the level of the surrounding ground, and ran in an excavation horizontally 111 feet, when he came to a vault that had been excavated in the earth before the mound was commenced. This vault was 12 feet long, 8 wide, and 7 in height. It was dry as any tight room. Along each side and the two ends, stood upright timbers, which had supported transverse timbers forming the ceiling. Over the timbers had been placed unhewn stone ; but the decay of the timbers* occasioned the fall of the stones and the superincumbent earth, so as to nearly fill the vault. In this vault were found two skeletons, one of which was devoid of ornament—the other was surrounded by 650 ivory beads, resembling button-moles, and an ivory ornament of about six inches in length, which is one inch and five eighths wide in the centre, half an inch wide at the ends, and on one side flat and on the other oval-shaped. A singular white exudation of animal matter overhangs the roof of this vault.

The Mammoth Mound at Grave Creek.

Another excavation was commenced at the top of the mound downwards. Midway between the top and bottom, and over the vault above described, a second and similar vault was discovered, and, like that, caved in by the falling of the ceiling, timbers, stones, &c. In the upper vault was found the singular hieroglyphical stone hereafter described, 1700 ivory beads, 500 sea-shells of the involute species, that were worn as beads, and five copper bracelets about the wrists of the skeleton. The shells and beads were about the neck and breast of the skeleton, and there were also about 150 pieces of isinglass strewed over the body.

The mound is composed of the same kind of earth as that around it, being a fine loamy sand, but differs very much in color from that of the natural ground. After penetrating about eight feet with the first or horizontal excavation, blue spots began to appear in the earth of which the mound is composed. On close examination, these spots were found to contain ashes and bits of burnt bones. These spots increased as they approached the centre : at the distance of 120 feet within, the spots were so numerous and condensed as to give the earth a clouded appearance, and excited the admiration of all who saw it. Every part of the mound presents the same appearance, except near the surface. The blue spots were probably occasioned by depositing the remains of bodies consumed by fire.

In addition to the relics in the mammoth mound, there has been a great number and variety of relics found in the neighborhood : many of them were discovered with skeletons which were nearly decayed. Mr. Tomlinson has some beads, found about two

---

* At the top and bottom, where the timbers had been placed, were particles of charcoal—an evidence that fire, instead of iron, had been used in severing the wood. This goes to show that the constructors of the mound were not acquainted with the use of iron ; and the fact that none of that metal was found in the vault, strongly corroborates the opinion. Some of the stones were water-worn, probably from the river ; others were identical with a whet-stone quarry on the Ohio side of the river, two miles north.—H. H.

miles from this great mound, that are evidently a kind of porcelain, and very similar, if not identical in substance with artificial teeth set by dentists. He has also an image of stone, found with other relics about eight miles distant. It is in human shape, sitting in a cramped position, the face and eyes projecting upwards. The nose is what is called Roman. On the crown of the head is a knot, in which the hair is concentrated and tied. The head and features particularly is a display of great workmanship and ingenuity. It is eleven inches in height, but if it were straight would be double that height. It is generally believed to have been an idol.

Mr. Henry R. Colcraft, [Schoolcraft,] whose researches upon the Indian antiquities of the west have placed him at the head of the list of scientific inquirers upon this subject, visited Grave Creek in August, 1843, and devoted several days to the examination of the antique works of art at that place. The result of his investigations is partially given in a communication to the New York Commercial Advertiser, copied below. We were subsequently at Grave Creek, and obtained an impression in wax of the hieroglyphical stone to which he alludes. An accurate engraving from this impression we insert in its proper place in his article :

I have devoted several days to the examination of the antiquities of this place and its vicinity, and find them to be of even more interest than was anticipated. The most prominent object of curiosity is the great tumulus, of which notices have appeared in western papers ; but this heavy structure of earth is not isolated. It is but one of a series of mounds and other evidences of ancient occupation at this point, of more than ordinary interest. I have visited and examined seven mounds situated within a short distance of each other. They occupy the summit level of a rich alluvial plain, stretching on the left or Virginia bank of the Ohio, between the junctions of Big and Little Grave creeks with that stream. They appear to have connected by low earthen intrenchments, of which plain traces are still visible on some parts of the commons. They included a well, stoned up in the usual manner, which is now filled with rubbish.

The summit of this plain is probably 75 feet above the present summit-level of the Ohio. It constitutes the second bench or rise of land above the water. It is on this summit, and one of the most elevated parts of it, that the great tumulus stands. It is in the shape of a broad cone, cut off at the apex, where it is some fifty feet across. This area is quite level, and commands a view of the entire plain, and of the river above and below, and the west shores of the Ohio in front. Any public transaction on this area would be visible to multitudes around it, and it has, in this respect, all the advantages of the Mexican and Yucatanese teocalli. The circumference of the base has been stated at a little under 900 feet ; the height is 69 feet.

The most interesting object of antiquarian inquiry is a small flat stone, inscribed with antique alphabetic characters, which was disclosed on the opening of the mound. These

characters are in the ancient rock alphabet of 16 right and acute-angled single strokes, used by the Pelasgi and other early Mediterranean nations, and which is the parent of the modern Runic as well as the Bardic. It is now some four or five years since the completion of the excavations, so far as they have been made, and the discovery of this relic. Several copies of it soon got abroad which differed from each other, and, it was supposed, from the original. This conjecture is true. Neither the print published in the Cincinnati Gazette in 1839, nor that in the American Pioneer in 1843, is correct. I have terminated this uncertainty by taking copies by a scientific process, which does not leave the lines and figures to the uncertainty of man's pencil.

The existence of this ancient art here could hardly be admitted, otherwise than as an insulated fact, without some corroborative evidence in habits and customs, which it would be reasonable to look for in the existing ruins of ancient occupancy. It is thought some such testimony has been found. I rode out yesterday three miles, back to the range of high hills which encompass this sub-valley, to see a rude tower of stone standing on an elevated point, called Parr's Point, which commands a view of the whole plain, and which appears to have been constructed as a watch-tower, or lookout, from which to descry an approaching enemy. It is much dilapidated. About six or seven feet of the work is still entire. It is circular, and composed of rough stones, laid without mortar, or the mark of a hammer. A heavy mass of fallen walls lies around, covering an area of some forty feet in diameter. Two similar points of observation, occupied by dilapidated towers, are represented to exist, one at the prominent summit of the Ohio and Grave creek hills, and another on the promontory on the opposite side of the Ohio, in Belmont county, Ohio.

It is well known to all acquainted with the warlike habits of our Indians, that they never evinced the foresight to post a regular sentry, and these rude towers may be regarded as of contemporaneous age with the interment of the inscription.

Several polished tubes of stone have been found in one of the lesser mounds, the use of which is not very apparent. One of these now on my table is twelve inches long, one and a fourth wide at one end, and one and a half at the other. It is made of a fine, compact, lead-blue steatite, mottled, and has been constructed by boring, in the manner of a gun-barrel. This boring is continued to within about three-eighths of an inch of the larger end, through which but a small aperture is left. If this small aperture be looked through, objects at a distance are more clearly seen. Whether it had this telescope or others, the degree of art evinced in its construction is far from rude. By inserting a wooden rod and valve, this tube would be converted into a powerful syphon or syringe.

I have not space to notice one or two additional traits which serve to awaken new interest at this ancient point of aboriginal and apparently mixed settlement.

MARION.

MARION was formed in 1842, from Harrison and Monongalia, and named from General Francis Marion. It is about 40 miles long, with a mean width of 13 miles. It is watered by the west fork of the Monongahela and its branches. The county is well timbered, and adapted to grazing; its surface is hilly, and much of the soil fertile. Fairmont, formerly called Middletown, is the county-seat; it is 278 miles NW. of Richmond, 40 miles E. of the Ohio, 22 N. of Clarksburg, and 18 S. of Morgantown. It was established by law in 1820, and is now a flourishing village, pleasantly situated on the west bank of the Monongahela, near the southern line of the county. It contains 5 mercantile stores, 1 Methodist and 1 Presbyterian church, several flouring and other mills in it and vicinity, and about 70 dwellings. The face of the surrounding country is somewhat hilly; the soil is generally of a rich loamy clay, producing all the staples common to the middle states. The forests abound with the finest timber, and the earth is stored with iron ore, and the best stone-coal, the latter of which is largely exported. Palatine lies opposite Fairmont, on the Monongahela. It is a new and flourishing village, containing 2 stores, some mills, and about 25 dwellings. Holtsville, Newport, and Milford, are small but flourishing places on the Monongahela, below Fairmont. As this county comes within the limits of the tract described in Doddridge's Notes, we make an extract depicting the customs of those primitive times:

The settlements on this side of the mountains commenced along the Monongahela, and between that river and the Laurel ridge, in the year 1772. In the succeeding year they reached the Ohio River. The greater number of the first settlers came from the upper parts of the then colonies of Maryland and Virginia. Braddock's trail, as it was called, was the route by which the greater number of them crossed the mountains. A less number of them came by the way of Bedford and Fort Ligonier, the military road from Pennsylvania to Pittsburg. They effected their removals on horses furnished with pack-saddles. This was the more easily done, as but few of these early adventurers into the wilderness were encumbered with much baggage.

Land was the object which invited the greater number of these people to cross the mountain, for, as the saying then was, "It was to be had here for taking up;" that is, building a cabin and raising a crop of grain, however small, of any kind, entitled the occupant to four hundred acres of land, and a pre-emption right to one thousand acres more adjoining, to be secured by a land-office warrant. This right was to take effect if there happened to be so much vacant land, or any part thereof, adjoining the tract secured by the settlement right.

At an early period the government of Virginia appointed three commissioners to give certificates of settlement rights. These certificates, together with the surveyor's plat, were sent to the land-office of the state, where they lay six months, to await any caveat which might be offered. If none was offered, the patent then issued.

There was, at an early period of our settlements, an inferior kind of land title denominated a "tomahawk right," which was made by deadening a few trees near the head of a spring, and marking the bark of some one or more of them with the initials of the name of the person who made the improvement. I remember having seen a number of those "tomahawk rights" when a boy. For a long time many of them bore the names of those who made them. I have no knowledge of the efficacy of the tomahawk improvement, or whether it conferred any right whatever, unless followed by an actual settlement. These rights, however, were often bought and sold. Those who wished to make settlements on their favorite tracts of land, bought up the tomahawk improvements, rather than enter into quarrels with those who had made them. Other improvers of the land, with a view to actual settlement, and who happened to be stout veteran fellows, took a very different course from that of purchasing the "tomahawk rights." When annoyed by the claimants under those rights, they deliberately cut a few good hickories, and gave them what was called in those days a "laced jacket," that is, a sound whipping.

Some of the early settlers took the precaution to come over the mountains in the spring, leaving their families behind to raise a crop of corn, and then return and bring them out in the fall. This I should think was the better way. Others, especially those whose families were small, brought them with them in the spring. My father took the latter course. His family was but small, and he brought them all with him. The Indian meal which he brought over the mountain was expended six weeks too soon, so that for that length of time we had to live without bread. The lean venison and the breast of wild turkeys we were taught to call bread. The flesh of the bear was denominated meat. This artifice did not succeed very well. After living in this way for some time we became sickly, the stomach seemed to be always empty and tormented with a sense of hunger. I remember how narrowly the children watched the growth of the potato tops, pumpkin and squash vines, hoping from day to day to get something to answer in the place of bread. How delicious was the taste of the young potatoes when we got them! What a jubilee, when we were permitted to pull the young corn for roasting ears. Still more so, when it had acquired sufficient hardness to be made into jonny-cakes by the aid of a tin grater. We then became healthy, vigorous, and contented with our situation, poor as it was.

My father, with a small number of his neighbors, made their settlements in the spring of 1773. Though they were in a poor and destitute situation, they nevertheless lived in peace; but their tranquillity was not of long continuance. Those most atrocious murders of the peaceable, inoffensive Indians at Captina and Yellow Creek, brought on the war of Lord Dunmore in the spring of the year 1774. Our little settlement then broke up. The women and children were removed to Morris's Fort, in Sandy Creek glade, some distance to the east of Uniontown. The fort consisted of an assemblage of small hovels, situated on the margin of a large and noxious marsh, the effluvia of which gave the most of the women and children the fever and ague. The men were compelled by necessity to return home, and risk the tomahawk and scalping-knife of the Indians, in raising corn to keep their families from starvation the succeeding winter.

Those sufferings, dangers, and losses, were the tribute we had to pay to that thirst for blood which actuated those veteran murderers who brought the war upon us! The memory of the sufferers in this war, as well as that of their descendants, still looks back upon them with regret and abhorrence, and the page of history will consign their names to posterity with the full weight of infamy they deserve.

My father, like many others, believed that, having secured his legal allotment, the rest of the country belonged of right to those who chose to settle in it. There was a piece of vacant land adjoining his tract, amounting to about 200 acres. To this tract of land he had the pre-emption right, and accordingly secured it by warrant; but his conscience would not permit him to retain it in his family; he therefore gave it to an apprentice lad whom he had raised in his house. This lad sold it to an uncle of mine for a cow and a calf, and a wool hat.

Owing to the equal distribution of real property directed by our land laws, and the sterling integrity of our forefathers in their observance of them, we have no districts of "sold land," as it is called, that is, large tracts of land in the hands of individuals, or companies, who neither sell nor improve them, as is the case in Lower Canada, and the northwestern part of Pennsylvania. These unsettled tracts make huge blanks in the population of the country where they exist.

The division-lines between those whose lands adjoined, were generally made in an amicable manner, before any survey of them was made, by the parties concerned. In doing this they were guided mainly by the tops of ridges and water-courses, but particularly the former. Hence the greater number of farms in the western parts of Pennsylvania and Virginia bear a striking resemblance to an amphitheatre. The buildings occupy a low situation, and the tops of the surrounding hills are the boundaries of the tract to which the family mansion belongs.

Our forefathers were fond of farms of this description, because, as they said, they are attended with this convenience, "that every thing comes to the house down hill."

Most of the early settlers considered their land as of little value, from an apprehension that after a few years' cultivation it would lose its fertility, at least for a long time. I have often heard them say that such a field would bear so many crops, and another so many, more or less than that. The ground of this belief concerning the short-lived fertility of the land in this country, was the poverty of a great proportion of the land in the lower parts of Maryland and Virginia, which, after producing a few crops, became unfit for use, and was thrown out into commons.

My reader will naturally ask where were their mills for grinding grain? Where their tanneries for making leather? Where their smith-shops for making and repairing their farming utensils? Who were their carpenters, tailors, cabinet workmen, shoemakers, and weavers? The answer is, those manufacturers did not exist, nor had they any tradesmen who were professedly such. Every family were under the necessity of doing every thing for themselves as well as they could. The hommony-block and hand-mills were in use in most of our houses. The first was made of a large block of wood about three feet long, with an excavation burned in one end, wide at the top and narrow at the bottom, so that the action of the pestle on the bottom threw the corn up to the sides towards the top of it, from whence it continually fell down into the centre. In consequence of this movement, the whole mass of the grain was pretty equally subjected to the strokes of the pestle. In the fall of the year, while the Indian corn was soft, the block and pestle did very well for making meal for jonny-cake and mush, but were rather slow when the corn became hard.

The sweep was sometimes used to lessen the toil of pounding grain into meal. This was a pole of some springy elastic wood, thirty feet long or more; the butt end was placed under the side of a house, or a large stump. This pole was supported by two forks, placed about one-third of its length from the butt end, so as to elevate the small end about fifteen feet from the ground; to this was attached, by a large mortise, a piece of a sapling, about five or six inches in diameter, and eight or ten feet long. The lower end of this was shaped so as to answer for a pestle. A pin of wood was put through it at a proper height, so that two persons could work at the sweep at once. This simple machine very much lessened the labor, and expedited the work. I remember that, when a boy, I put up an excellent sweep at my father's. It was made of a sugar-tree sapling. It was kept going almost constantly, from morning till night, by our neighbors for several weeks. In the Greenbrier country, where they had a number of saltpetre caves, the first settlers made plenty of excellent gunpowder by the means of those sweeps and mortars.

A machine still more simple than the mortar and pestle, was used for making meal, while the corn was too soft to be beaten. It was called a grater. This was a half-circular piece of tin, perforated with a punch from the concave side, and nailed by its edges to a block of wood. The ears of corn were rubbed on the rough edges of the holes, while the meal fell through them on the board or block to which the grater was nailed, which, being in a slanting direction, discharged the meal into a cloth or bowl placed for its reception. This, to be sure, was a slow way of making meal, but necessity has no law.

The hand-mill was better than the mortar and grater. It was made of two circular stones, the lowest of which was called the bed-stone, the upper one the runner. These were placed in a hoop, with a spout for discharging the meal. A staff was let into a hole in the upper surface of the runner, near the outer edge, and its upper end through a hole in a board fastened to a joist above, so that two persons could be employed in turning the mill at the same time. The grain was put into the opening in the runner by hand. These mills are still in use in Palestine, the ancient country of the Jews. To a mill of this sort our Saviour alluded, when, with reference to the destruction of Jerusalem, he said: "Two women shall be grinding at a mill, the one shall be taken and the other left." This mill is much preferable to that used at present in Upper Egypt for making the dhoura bread. It is a smooth stone, placed on an inclined plane, upon which the grain is spread, which is made into meal by rubbing another stone up and down upon it.

Our first water-mills were of that description denominated tub-mills. It consists of a perpendicular shaft, to the lower end of which a horizontal wheel of about four or five feet in diameter is attached; the upper end passes through the bed-stone, and carries the runner after the manner of a trundlehead. These mills were built with very little expense, and many of them answered the purpose very well. Instead of bolting cloths, sifters were in general use. They were made of deerskins, in the state of parchment, stretched over a hoop, and perforated with a hot wire.

Our clothing was all of domestic manufacture. We had no other resource for clothing, and this indeed was a poor one. The crops of flax often failed, and the sheep were destroyed by the wolves. Linsey, which is made of flax and wool—the former the chain, and the latter the filling—was the warmest and most substantial cloth we could make. Almost every house contained a loom, and almost every woman was a weaver.

Every family tanned their own leather. The tan-vat was a large trough sunk to the upper edge in the ground. A quantity of bark was easily obtained every spring in clearing and fencing land. This, after drying, was brought in, and in wet days was shaved and pounded on a block of wood, with an axe or mallet. Ashes were used in place of lime, for taking off the hair. Bears' oil, hogs' lard, and tallow, answered the place of fish oil. The leather, to be sure, was coarse; but it was substantially good. The operation of currying was performed by a drawing-knife with its edge turned, after the manner of a currying-knife. The blacking for the leather was made of soot and hogs' lard.

Almost every family contained its own tailors and shoemakers. Those who could not make shoes, could make shoepacks. These, like moccasins, were made of a single piece of leather, with the exception of a tongue-piece on the top of the foot. This was about two inches broad, and circular at the lower end. To this the main piece of leather was sewed with a gathering stitch. The seam behind was like that of a moccasin. To the shoepack, a sole was sometimes added. The women did the tailor-work. They could all cut out and make hunting-shirts, leggins, and drawers.

The state of society which existed in our country at an early period of its settlement, is well calculated to call into action every native mechanical genius. This happened in this country. There was in almost every neighborhood some one, whose natural ingenuity enabled him to do many things for himself and his neighbors, far above what could have been reasonably expected. With the few tools which they brought with them into the country, they certainly performed wonders. Their ploughs, harrows with wooden teeth, and sleds, were in many instances well made. Their cooper-ware, which comprehended every thing for holding milk and water, was generally pretty well executed. The cedar-ware, by having alternately a white and red stave, was then thought beautiful; many of their puncheon floors were very neat, their joints close, and the top even and smooth. Their looms, although heavy, did very well. Those who could not exercise these mechanic arts, were under the necessity of giving labor or barter to their neighbors in exchange for the use of them, so far as their necessities required.

MATHEWS.

MATHEWS was created in 1790, from Gloucester, and named in honor of a meritorious officer of the Virginia troops in the revolution, and subsequently governor of Georgia. This county is a peninsula, extending into Chesapeake Bay, united to the main by a narrow neck of land scarcely a mile wide, and its boundaries are almost entirely of water. It is 20 miles long, and in its widest section not nine miles. The principal streams are the Piankatank, East, and North Rivers. About 60,000 acres of the land are of a medium fertility. Marl exists in some parts. Formerly ship-building was carried on to such an extent, that agriculture was almost entirely neglected. The county is supplied with meal by wind and tide mills. Owing to the land being almost a dead level, there are no streams of fresh water running through the county; hence in long dry seasons every cattle hole, at which the stock water, dry up, and they suffer much from thirst. Pop., in 1840, whites 3,969, slaves 3,309, free colored 174; total, 7,442.

Mathews C. H., or Westville, is near the centre of the county, on a small stream putting up from East River, 100 miles E. of Richmond. It is a port of entry, and contains about 30 dwellings.

Gwyn's Island is on the east side of the county, in Chesapeake Bay, at the mouth of Piankatank River; it contains about 2000 acres, and a population of about 200. There is a tradition that Pocahontas, in attempting to swim across the Piankatank, was near drowning, but was rescued by an individual, to whom, as a token of her gratitude, she gave this island.

Several months after the burning of Norfolk, Lord Dunmore left Hampton Roads with his whole fleet, landed about the 1st of June at Gwyn's Island, where he fortified himself. His force, consisting of about 500 men, including negroes, whom he had induced by false promises to leave their masters, was attacked by the Virginians under Gen. Lewis, and compelled to abandon the place. Shortly after, Dunmore left the coast of Virginia forever.

The annexed account of the attack upon Dunmore, and his expulsion from Gwyn's Island, is from the Virginia Gazette of July 29th, 1776:—

We got to the island on Monday, the 8th, and next morning, at 8 o'clock, began a furious attack upon the enemy's shipping, camp, and fortifications, from two batteries, one of five, six, and nine-pounders; the other mounting two eighteen-pounders. What forces the enemy had, were encamped on a point of the island nearly opposite to our five-gun battery, covered by a battery of four embrasures, and a breastwork of considerable extent. Besides this, they had two other batteries, and a stockade fort higher up the haven, where troops were stationed to prevent our landing. In the haven were three tenders; one a sloop, (the Lady Charlotte,) mounting six carriage-guns; a schooner of two carriages, six swivels and cohorn; and a pilot-boat, badly armed, who had orders from Captain Hammond, of the Roebuck, to prevent our boats passing over to the island, and to annoy the rebels by every means in their power. Gen. Lewis announced his orders for attacking the enemy, by putting a match to the first gun, an eighteen-pounder, himself; and the Dunmore being then nearest to us, at the distance of about 500 yards, it passed through her hull, and did considerable damage. Our five-gun battery likewise began playing on the fleet, the enemy's camp, and works; and the fire soon became so hot that the Dunmore was obliged to cut her cables and haul off, after receiving ten shot, some of which raked her fore and aft. The Otter lay next to her, and it was expected would have taken her birth, but the first shot we gave her, took place supposed between wind and water, and she immediately slipped her cable likewise, and hauled out on a careen, without firing a gun. By this time all the fleet any way near the shore, began to slip their cables in the utmost confusion; and had the wind set in with a flood-tide, we must have taken great numbers of them. Our eighteen-pounders did great execution from the upper battery, which raked the whole fleet; and Captain Denny, who commanded the other battery, soon silenced the enemy at the point, knocking down several tents, which put their camp into a great confusion. At half after 9 the firing ceased, which was renewed again at 12, with double vigor, from both batteries; and nothing prevented our pushing to the island, during the cannonade, but the want of vessels.

The general being determined to cross the next day, gave orders for all the small crafts to be collected together from the neighboring creeks that night, and two brass field-pieces, six-pounders, to be carried to a place called Lower Wind Mill Point, to attack the tender that lay there, and facilitate our crossing. Accordingly, in the morning Captain Harrison, who had the direction of those field-pieces, began playing upon the tenders, which he galled so much, that the schooner ran up a small creek which indented the island, where the crew abandoned her, and the sloop got aground in reach of our cannon; upon which the general ordered Captain Smith, of the 7th regiment, with his company, to man the canoes and board her, which was done with alacrity. However, before our men came up with her, the crew got into their boat, and pushed for the island. But Captain Smith, very prudently passing the tender, pursued them so close, that before they could reach the shore, he exchanged a few shot with them, and took part of them prisoners. The enemy's look-outs, perceiving our men close upon the lower part of the island, cried out, "The shirt-men are coming!" and scampered off. The pilot-boat made no resistance.

General Lewis then ordered two hundred men, under Colonel M'Clanahan, to land on the island, which was performed as expeditiously as our small vessels would admit of. On our arrival, we found the enemy had evacuated the place with the greatest precipitation, and were struck with horror at the number of dead bodies, in a state of putrefaction, strewed all the way from their battery to Cherry Point, about two miles in length, with a shovel full of earth upon them; others gasping for life; and some had crawled to the water edge, who could only make known their distress by beckoning to us. By the small-pox, and other malignant disorders which have raged on board the fleet for many months past, it is clear they have lost, since their arrival at Gwyn's Island, near five hundred souls. I myself counted one hundred and thirty graves, or rather holes loosely covered over with earth, close together, many of them large enough to hold a corporal's guard. One in the middle was neatly done up with turf, and is supposed to contain the remains of the late Lord Gosport. Many were burnt alive in brush huts, which, in their confusion, had got on fire. In short, such a scene of misery, distress, and cruelty, my eyes never beheld; for which the authors, one may reasonably conclude, never can make atonement in this world. The enemy left behind them, in their battery, a double fortified nine-pounder, a great part of their baggage, with several tents and marquees, beside the three tenders, with their cannon, small arms, &c. Also the anchors and cables of the Dunmore, Otter, and many others, to the amount, it is supposed, of twelve hundred pounds. On their leaving the island, they burnt some valuable vessels which had got aground. Mr. John Grymes' effects on the island have fallen into our hands, consisting in thirty-five negroes, horses, cattle, and furniture.

Major Byrd, on the approach of our canoes to the island, was huddled into a cart in a very sick and low condition, it is said, and carried down to Cherry Point, where he embarked. The second shot the Dunmore received, cut her boatswain in two, and wounded two or three others; and she had scarcely recovered from the shock, when a nine-pounder from the lower battery entered her quarter, and beat in a large timber, from the splinters of which Lord Dunmore got wounded in the legs, and had all his valuable china smashed about his ears. It is said his lordship was exceedingly alarmed, and roared out, "Good God, that ever I should come to this!"

We had our information from one of his people that came ashore after the engagement, and was taken by our scouts. He likewise said, that many were killed in the fleet, which had sustained some thousand pounds worth of damage. The Fowey and Roebuck were the lowermost ships, besides which there were one hundred and odd sail of large vessels, which took their departure on Thursday afternoon, and are supposed to have gone into Potomac.

In this affair, we lost not a man but poor Captain Arundel, who was killed by the bursting of a mortar of his own invention, although the general and all the officers were against his firing it. His zeal for the service cost him his life.

MECKLENBURG.

MECKLENBURG was created in 1764, from Lunenburg. Its length is 36, mean width 18 miles. The Meherrin runs on its northern line, and the Roanoke through its southern portion. On the Roanoke is much extremely fertile land. The soil of the county is generally fertile, and although the ridges are thin and poor, yet it is a free soil, and annually produces about four millions of pounds of tobacco. Pop., whites 7,754, slaves 11,915, free colored 1,055 ; total, 20,724.

Boydton, the county-seat, is 109 miles sw. of Richmond, and 6 from the Roanoke River, on an elevated and healthy site. It contains 4 mercantile stores, 17 mechanic shops, 1 tannery, 1 jeweller, 1 apothecary, 1 Methodist, 1 Episcopal, and 1 Presbyterian church, and a population of about 400. About a mile from Boydton is RANDOLPH MACON COLLEGE, an institution in high repute, established in 1832, and under the superintendence and patronage of the Methodist Episcopal church. It has 4 professors and about a hundred students. L. C. Garland, A. M., is the president. A preparatory school is attached to the college, under the control and management of the faculty.

Clarksville is 12 miles sw. of Boydton, at the junction of Dan and Staunton Rivers. It has increased more in the last ten years than any other village in Virginia. In 1835 it had but 14 dwellings : it now contains 10 mercantile stores, 20 mechanic shops, 2 tobacco inspections and warehouses, 1 tannery, 1 Baptist, 1 Methodist, and 1 Presbyterian church, and about 1000 inhabitants. Over 2000 hogsheads of tobacco are annually inspected here, and a large number of batteaux are constantly plying on the river, loaded with the products of the country.

MERCER.

MERCER was formed in 1837, from Giles and Tazewell, and named from Gen. Hugh Mercer, who fell at Princeton. It is 40 miles long, with a mean breadth of about 15 miles. It is watered by New River and its branches ; the main stream being its NE. boundary. It is a wild and thinly settled tract, and much of the surface is mountainous and hilly. It is principally a stock-raising county ; the woodlands affording a fine range for cattle. Pop., whites 2,127, slaves 98, free colored 8 ; total, 2,233.

At the formation of the county there was not a village in it : the erection of the county buildings has formed the nucleus of a small village called Princeton, situated 28 miles from Giles C. H., 35 from Tazewell C. H., and 42 from Monroe C. H., and containing 1 Baptist and 1 Methodist church, 1 store, and about a dozen dwellings.

MIDDLESEX.

MIDDLESEX was formed in 1675, from Lancaster. This county is a long narrow strip of land lying between its two boundary rivers; its greatest length is 39 miles, its mean breadth is 5 miles. The lands immediately on the Rappahannock, Piankatank, and Dragon, are fertile. Many branches of the Rappahannock make up into the county, affording convenience to the farmer in sending his produce to Baltimore and Norfolk, the usual markets for the produce of this section. Pop. in 1840, whites 2,041, slaves 2,209, free colored 142 ; total, 4,392.

Urbanna, the county-seat, is a sea-port, located about 18 miles above the mouth of the Rappahannock, near the entrance of Urbanna creek into that stream, and 84 miles northeasterly from Richmond. It was established a town by law the same year with Norfolk, 1705. It is a small village, containing several stores and about a dozen dwellings. This village was the residence of the celebrated botanist and physician, JOHN MITCHELL, who emigrated to this country from England in the early part of the last century, and distinguished himself by his philosophical and medical essays, and historical writings.

The prevailing religious denomination of this county is the Baptist : indeed, for the last sixty years, Virginia has been distinguished for containing a larger number of Baptists than any other state in the Union. It is not known that any of the original settlers of Virginia were of this denomination. The first church gathered in the colony was at Burley, in the county of the Isle of Wight, about the year 1714, more than a century after the landing at Jamestown, which church is supposed to have continued 40 or 50 years, when many of its members removed to North Carolina, and soon increased greatly. They were all *General Baptists ;* but in a few years after their removal they began to embrace the Calvinistic sentiments. The next appearance of the Baptists in this state was in the counties of Berkeley, Rockingham, and Loudon, from the year 1743 to 1756. This period dates the origin of the Regular Baptists in Virginia ; but they did not flourish to any considerable extent until 1760. " Their first preachers came from the north, and some few arose in the south : all met with opposition from those in power. ' The ministers (says Leland) were imprisoned, and the disciples buffeted.' This is but too true. No dissenters in Virginia experienced for a time harsher treatment than did the Baptists. They were beaten and imprisoned ; and cruelty taxed its ingenuity to devise new modes of punishment and annoyance."

Outrageous mobs disturbed their congregations and preachers. A snake and a hornet's nest were thrown into their meetings, and even in one case fire-arms were brought to disperse them. " When the Baptists first appeared in Virginia and North Carolina they were received by men in power as beneath their notice ; and in some places persecution in a legal shape was never resorted to. But in many others, alarmed by their rapid increase, the men in power strained every penal law in the Virginia code to obtain ways and means to put down these disturbers of the public peace, as they were called. It

seems by no means certain, that any law in force in Virginia authorized the imprisonment of any person for preaching. The law for the preservation of the peace was so in-
terpreted as to answer this purpose; and accordingly, whenever the preachers were apprehended it was done by a peace-warrant. About thirty preachers were honored with
a dungeon, and a few others beside."*

Among the first, if not the first Baptist preacher in this county, was John Waller,
born in Spottsylvania in 1741, and a descendant of the honorable family of that name
in England. In his youth he let himself loose to every species of wickedness, and acquired for himself the infamous appellation of *Swearing Jack Waller*, and was sometimes called the *Devil's Adjutant*. He was furious against the Baptists. He was a
member of a grand jury who presented one of their ministers for preaching. The jury
being dismissed, the clergyman thanked them for the honor they had done him, and
added : "While I was wicked and injurious you took no notice of me; but since I have
altered my course of life, and endeavored to reform my neighbors, you concern yourselves
much about me. I shall take the spoiling of my goods joyfully." The meekness of
spirit manifested by this man towards his persecutors, so touched the heart of Waller
that it finally resulted in his conversion. In 1770 he was ordained pastor of a church
established in his neighborhood. Accompanied by a companion he travelled into this
county, preaching wherever he went. "His name sounded far and wide. By the un-
godly he was considered as a bold, inexorable fanatic, that would do much mischief unless restrained. The Baptists and their adherents looked upon him as sent for the defence of their cause, and with much confidence rallied around him as their leader. His
persecutions in several counties were of the most painful character." He was confined
in the jail of Urbanna, in this county, forty-six days.

Mr. Waller continued laboring with great success in the cause. In 1773 he removed
to South Carolina, where he died in 1802, at the age of 62. He had been "a minister
of God's word for about 35 years, and in that time had been in four different jails 113
days, besides receiving reproachings, buffetings, stripes, &c. Nor was his labor in vain
in the Lord. While in Virginia, he baptized more than 2,000 persons, assisted in the
ordination of 27 ministers, and in the constitution of 18 churches."†

"The usual consequences followed ; persecution made friends for its victims ; and the
men who were not permitted to speak in public, found willing auditors in the sympathizing crowds who gathered around the prisons to hear them preach from the grated
windows. It is not improbable that this very opposition imparted strength in another
mode, inasmuch as it at least furnished the Baptists with a common ground on which
to make resistance ; and such common ground was in a great degree wanting in their
creed ; for, not to speak of their great division into Regulars and Separates, some 'held
to predestination, others to universal provision ; some adhered to a confession of faith,
others would have none but the Bible ; some practised laying on of hands, others did
not ;' and in fact the only particular in which there seems to have been unanimity,
was in the favorite exclusive opinion of the sect, that none but adult believers are fit subjects of baptism, and that immersion is the only effectual or authorized mode of admin-
istering that sacrament."‡

At the commencement of the American revolution, the Baptists had gained considerable influence and power among the people. The dissenters, both the Baptists and
Presbyterians, were generally republicans. The Baptists addressed the convention of
the state, "and informed that body," says Hawks, "that their religious tenets presented
no obstacle to their taking up arms and fighting for the country ; and they tendered the
services of their pastors in promoting the enlistment of the youth of their religious persuasion." It was owing partly to the efforts of the Baptists that the established church
was abolished in Virginia. In 1785, just previous to the passage of "the Act for
establishing Religious Freedom," Mr. Madison's able remonstrance was presented to the
General Assembly "against the general assessment," pointing out the dangers to religious liberty and to religion that lurked in the scheme. It was not until this time that
the dissenting clergymen were allowed by law to perform marriage or funeral rites ;
although many, presuming on a future sanction of government, had, by the advice of
Patrick Henry, done so, as being the best means of obtaining a law to that end.
Many petitions had been and were presented to the legislature, in many different forms.
Among the rest, the following lines accompanied the petition sent by the Baptists. It
was addressed "To the Honorable General Assembly," as

---

* Benedict's "History of the Baptists."   † Taylor's "Lives of Virginia Baptist Ministers."
‡ Hawks' "History of the Prot. Ep. Ch. in Va."

"THE HUMBLE PETITION OF A COUNTRY POET."

Now liberty is all the plan,
The chief pursuit of every man,
Whose heart is right, and fills the mouth
Of patriots all, from north to south ;
May a poor bard, from bushes sprung,
Who yet has but to rustics sung,
Address your honorable House,
And not your angry passions rouse ?

Hark ! for awhile your business stop ;
One word into your ears I'll drop :
No longer spend your needless pains,
To mend and polish o'er our chains ·
But break them off before you rise,
Nor disappoint our watchful eyes.

What say great Washington and Lee ?
"Our country is, and must be free."
What say great Henry, Pendleton,
And Liberty's minutest son ?
'Tis all one voice—they all agree,
"God made us, and we must be free."

Freedom we crave with every breath,
An equal freedom, or a death.

The heavenly blessing freely give,
Or make an act we shall not live.
Tax all things ; water, air, and light,
If need there be ; yea, tax the *night*,
But let our brave heroic minds
Move freely as celestial winds.

Make vice and folly feel your rod,
But leave our consciences to God :
Leave each man free to choose his form
Of piety, nor at him storm.

And he who minds the civil law,
And keeps it whole without a flaw,
Let him, just as he pleases, pray,
And seek for heav'n in his own way ;
And if he miss, we all must own,
No man is wrong'd but he alone.

About three miles from Urbanna is one of those decayed churches so common in lower Virginia. It is called "the Middle Church." A finely written description of this old church, including monumental inscriptions from the church-yard, is in the Southern Literary Messenger for May, 1842. We annex a single paragraph :

More than a century, yea, near two centuries have passed since the ringing of the mason's trowel broke the stillness of the surrounding forest, when the walls of this temple of the living God rose like a flower in the wilderness of Middlesex, and invited the way-farer to its sacred precincts. More than half a century has gone by since last the solemn organ pealed forth its sublime symphonies, and the anthems of the choir told upon the feelings of rapt worshippers,—now the church is a desolate ruin ; and the choir, and the worshippers—where are they ? There is scarcely a vestige of the interior left ; the pulpit, the tablets, the altar, the chancel, the ——, all gone ! The house is roofless, windowless. The walls alone are standing. The walls surrounding the spot constituting the church-yard, are in ruins too, portions only remaining to mark their boundaries. The tombs are nearly all in a dilapidated condition ; but of many, there is enough left to mark them as having been monuments of the most exquisite sculpture.

MONONGALIA.

MONONGALIA was formed in 1776, from the district of West Augusta. It is 50 miles long, with a mean width of 11 miles. The county is watered by the Monongahela and its branches. Laurel Hill, the last western regular ridge of the Alleghany, lies in the eastern part; the remainder of the county is generally hilly. Much of the soil is fertile. The principal exports are stock, iron, lumber, and some flour. In 1842, its limits were reduced by the formation of Marion. Population in 1840—whites 16,962, slaves 260, free colored 146, total, 17,368.

Morgantown, the county-seat, is 295 miles NW. of Richmond, 35 NNE. of Clarksburg, and about 60 S. of Pittsburg, Penn. It was established in 1785, on the lands of Zaquell Morgan, when, by the act, Samuel Hanway, John Evans, David Scot, Michael Kearnes, and James Daugherty, gentlemen, were appointed trustees. This

flourishing and wealthy village is handsomely situated on the
Monongahela—navigable to this place in steamers—in a fertile
country, and rich in mineral wealth, iron, coal, &c. It contains
various mills, several mercantile stores, 1 or 2 newspaper printing-
offices, a female academy, 1 Methodist and 1 Presbyterian church,
and about 150 dwellings. Jamestown, Granville, Blacksville, and
Smithfield, are villages in the county, none of which contain over
35 dwellings. Jackson's iron-works, on Cheat River, are among
the most valuable in the state. On the road leading from Clarksburg and Beverly, 5 miles from Morgantown, on the plantation of
Henry Hamilton, there is a large flat rock about 150 feet long and
50 wide, with numerous engravings of animals, well executed—
such as panthers of full size, buffalo-tracks, horse-tracks, deer-
tracks, turkey-tracks, eels, fish, women as large as life, human
tracks, otters, beavers, snakes, crows, eagles, wild-cats, foxes,
wolves, raccoons, opossums, bears, elks, &c.

An attempt was made at a settlement in the present limits of
this county, as early as the French war, an account of which is
here given from Withers:

Dr. Thomas Eckarly and his two brothers came from Pennsylvania, and camped at
the mouth of a creek emptying into the Monongahela eight or ten miles below Morgantown; they were Dunkards, and from that circumstance on which they
fixed themselves for awhile, has been called Dunkard's creek. While their camp continued at this place, these men were engaged in exploring the country; and ultimately
settled on Cheat River, at the Dunkard bottom. Here they erected a cabin for their
dwelling, and made such improvements as enabled them to raise the first year, a crop
of corn sufficient for their use, and some culinary vegetables: their guns supplied them
with an abundance of meat, of a flavor as delicious as the refined palate of a modern
epicure could well wish. Their clothes were made chiefly of the skins of animals,
and were easily procured; and although calculated to give a grotesque appearance to a
fine gentleman in a city drawing-room, yet were they particularly suited to their situation, and afforded them comfort.

Here they spent some years entirely unmolested by the Indians, although a destructive war was then waging, and prosecuted with cruelty, along the whole extent of our
frontier. At length, to obtain an additional supply of ammunition, salt, and shirting,
Dr. Eckarly left Cheat with a pack of furs and skins, to visit a trading-post on the
Shenandoah. On his return he stopped at Fort Pleasant, on the South Branch, and
having communicated to its inhabitants the place of his residence, and the length of time
he had been living there, he was charged with being in confederacy with the Indians,
and probably at that instant a spy, examining the condition of the fort. In vain the
Doctor protested his innocence, and the fact that he had not even seen an Indian in the
country; the suffering condition of the border settlements rendered his account, in their
opinion, improbable, and he was put in confinement.

The society of which Dr. Eckarly was a member, was rather obnoxious to a majority
of the frontier inhabitants. Their intimacy with the Indians, although cultivated with
the most laudable motives, and for noble purposes, yet made them objects at least of
distrust to many. Laboring under these disadvantages, it was with difficulty that Dr.
Eckarly prevailed on the officer of the fort to release him; and when this was done, he
was only permitted to go home under certain conditions—he was to be escorted by a
guard of armed men, who were to carry him back if any discovery were made preju-
dicial to him. Upon their arrival at Cheat, the truth of his statement was awfully confirmed. The first spectacle which presented itself to their view, when the party came
in sight of where the cabin had been, was a heap of ashes. On approaching the ruins,
the half-decayed and mutilated bodies of the poor Dunkards were seen in the yard; the
hoops on which their scalps had been dried were there, and the ruthless hand of desolation had waved over their little fields. Dr. Eckarly aided in burying the remains of his
unfortunate brothers, and returned to the fort on the South Branch.

In the fall of 1758, Thomas Decker and some others commenced a settlement on the Monongahela River, at the mouth of what is now Decker's creek. In the ensuing spring it was entirely broken up by a party of Delawares and Mingoes, and the greater part of its inhabitants murdered.

There was at this time, at Brownsville, a fort then known as Redstone Fort, under the command of Captain Paul. One of Decker's party escaped from the Indians who destroyed the settlement, and making his way to Fort Redstone, gave to its commander the melancholy intelligence. The garrison being too weak to admit of sending a detachment in pursuit, Captain Paul dispatched a runner with the information to Captain John Gibson, then stationed at Fort Pitt. Leaving the fort under the command of Lieut. Williamson, Captain Gibson set out with thirty men to intercept the Indians on their return to their towns.

In consequence of the distance which the pursuers had to go, and the haste with which the Indians had retreated, the expedition failed in its object; they however accidentally came on a party of six or seven Mingoes, on the head of Cross creek, in Ohio, near Steubenville. These had been prowling about the river, below Fort Pitt, seeking an opportunity of committing depredations. As Captain Gibson passed the point of a small knoll, just after daybreak, he came unexpectedly upon them. Some of them were lying down; the others were sitting round a fire, making thongs of green hides. Kiskepila, or Little Eagle, a Mingo chief, headed the party. So soon as he discovered Captain Gibson, he raised the war-whoop and fired his rifle; the ball passed through Gibson's hunting-shirt, and wounded a soldier just behind him. Gibson sprang forward, and swinging his sword with herculean force, severed the head of Little Eagle from his body. Two other Indians were shot down, and the remainder escaped to their towns on the Muskingum.

When the captives who were restored under the treaty of 1763 came in, those who were at the Mingo towns when the remnant of Kiskepila's party returned, stated that the Indians represented Gibson as having cut off Little Eagle's head with a *long knife.* Several of the white persons were then sacrificed to appease the manes of Kiskepila, and a war-dance ensued, accompanied with terrific shouts, and bitter denunciations of revenge on "*the big-knife warrior.*" This name was soon after applied to the Virginia militia generally; and to this day they are known among the northwestern Indians as the "*Long Knives,*" or "*Big Knife nation.*"

MONROE.

MONROE was formed in 1799, from Greenbrier, and named from President Monroe; its mean length is 31 miles, mean breadth 18½ miles. New River forms its southwestern boundary, and receives in its course the Greenbrier River, Indian Creek, and some minor streams. Much of the county is mountainous; but as a whole, it is a thriving agricultural section, having a large proportion of fertile soil, well adapted to grazing. Pop., whites 7,457, slaves 868, free colored 97; total, 8,422.

Union, the county-seat, lies 229 miles west of Richmond. It is a beautiful little village, situated in a picturesque and fertile valley, 14 miles west of the Alleghany mountains, and contains 3 mercantile stores, 1 Methodist, and 1 Presbyterian church, and a population of about 400. Peterstown, named from its first settler, Christian Peters, lies in the south angle of the county, on Rich's Creek, near the point where New River breaks through the Alleghany, and about 20 miles southerly from Union, in a wild, romantic country. Its site is well adapted for machinery, and it contains about 25 dwellings. Gap Mills, 8 miles N. of the C. H., contains 1 fulling,

1 flour, 1 saw, and 1 oil mill, 1 woollen factory, 1 distillery, 1 tannery, and a few dwellings.

This county is favored with several noted and popular mineral springs. They are the Salt Sulphur, the Sweet, and the Red Sulphur Springs; the improvements at all of which are extensive. The descriptions below are from published sources:

The RED SULPHUR SPRINGS are situated on Indian creek, about 40 miles sw. of the White Sulphur, and 16 from the Salt Sulphur. The spring is near one side of a little triangular plain, almost buried in mountains. The water is clear and cool—its temperature being 54° Fahrenheit—is very strongly charged with sulphureted hydrogen gas, and contains portions of several neutral salts. The water is believed to be directly sedative, indirectly tonic, alterative, diuretic, and diaphoretic.

The water has been found efficacious in all forms of consumption, scrofula, jaundice, and other bilious affections, chronic dysentery and diarrhœa, dyspepsia, diseases of the uterus, chronic rheumatism and gout, dropsy, gravel, neuralgia, tremor, syphilis, scurvy, erysipelas, tetter, ringworm, and itch; and it has long been celebrated as a vermifuge.

The SALT SULPHUR SPRINGS are 25 miles from the White Sulphur, and 3 miles from the village of Union, on Indian Valley creek. There are at this place three springs—the Sweet, the Salt Sulphur, and the New Spring. The last contains a large portion of iodine, and is highly beneficial for scrofula, and those affections for which iodine is generally given. The two first are somewhat alike in their properties. The analysis of the Salt Sulphur is thus given by Prof. Rogers:

SOLID INGREDIENTS.—Sulphate of lime, sulphate of magnesia, sulphate of soda, carbonate of lime, carbonate of magnesia, chloride of sodium, chloride of magnesium, chloride of calcium, iodine, probably combined with sodium—sulpho-hydrate of sodium and magnesium, sulphur, mingled with a peculiar organic matter—peroxide of iron derived from proto-sulphate.

GASEOUS INGREDIENTS.—Sulphureted hydrogen, nitrogen, oxygen, carbonic acid. The bubbles of gas that are seen adhering to the sides of the spring, are composed almost entirely of nitrogen. The temperature of this is 50° Fahrenheit.

The Salt Sulphur, like almost all the sulphurous waters, being a stimulant, should consequently not be employed in acute or highly inflammatory affections. Nor in those in which there exists much active determination of blood to the head, or at least not until this determination has been guarded against by previous diet, purgation, and, if necessary, blood-letting. But in all chronic affections of the brain, nervous system, some diseases of the lungs, stomach, bowels, liver, spleen, kidneys, and bladder, it is one of the most valuable of our remedial agents. In diseases of the joints (gout and rheumatism) and skin'; in mercurial sequelæ; in hæmorrhoidal affections; and in chronic diseases of the womb, it is also a remedy of immense importance.

The SWEET SPRINGS are situated in a wide and beautiful valley, 18 miles from the White Sulphur, and 29 from Fincastle. The following description of the medicinal properties of the Sweet Spring waters, is taken from Dr. Bell, on baths and mineral waters:

The water of the spring rises into a large cylindrical reservoir, from opposite sides of which it flows out by small pipes: one conveying water to the bath for the men, the other to that for the ladies. The men's bath is of a quadrangular form, surrounded by a wall, and open at the top; it is of tolerable extent, and clear, the bottom being of gravel, and the water constantly flowing in, and as constantly passing out, after it reaches a certain height. The temperature of the spring is 73° Fahr., the same as that which in England, by a strange blunder, is called Bristol hot wells. There is a considerable resemblance between the two in other respects, as well in the abundant evolution of the carbonic acid gas, as in the earthy and saline matters held in solution. In the Virginia spring, however, iron has been detected, whereas the Bristol hot wells has none in its composition. If we can rely on the rather crude analysis of Bouelle, one quart of the water of the Sweet Spring contains—

Saline substances in general, 12 to 15 grains; earthy substances, 18 to 24 do.; iron, ½ to 1 do.

The saline substances are sulphate of magnesia, muriate of soda, and muriate of lime, with a little sulphate of lime. The earthy substances consist of sulphate of lime, a small portion of carbonate of magnesia and lime, with a small portion of silicious earth. The name is calculated to convey erroneous impressions of their taste, which is like a solution of a small quantity of a calcareous or magnesian carbonate. The excess of carbonic acid gives, however, the waters a briskness, productive of a very different effect on the palate from what an imperfect mixture of the earths would produce. The first effects of this water, due to its temperature and gaseous contents, when drunk, are a feeling of warmth at the stomach, with a sensation of fulness at the head and some giddiness. Taken at stated intervals in moderate quantity, it will produce a moisture on the skin and increase the flow of urine. If the stomach be in a good state, it gives additional appetite and imparts fresh vigor to the system. The Sweet Spring water is serviceable in the varieties of dyspepsia accompanied by gastrodynia or spasm, with pains occurring at irregular intervals, and heart-burn—when the extremities are cold, and the skin torpid. In secondary debility of the digestive canal, from the exhausting heat of summer, or in chronic diarrhœa, and dysentery without fever, or not sustained by hepatic inflammation, much good will be produced by the internal use of these waters.

The harassing cough to which young persons are occasionally subject, and which often has its origin in an enfeebled state of the stomach, or in scrofulous habits from enlargement of the bronchial glands, as also the *tussis humoralis* of old people, will all be materially benefited by the use of these waters. The relief afforded in such cases as these has usually given Bristol hot wells its reputation in the cure of pulmonary consumption. Females of what are termed a nervous habit of body, will find their strength and health restored by drinking these waters, as well as bathing in the manner to be soon mentioned. Irregularity in the uterine functions will often soon disappear after the restoration of the digestive system to its former energy. As we should have inferred from the excess of carbonic acid, and the presence of the earthy carbonates in the water, it is useful in calculus and nephritic complaints.

About a mile north of the Sweet Spring, is the RED SPRING of Alleghany. This spring is a popular one, and the waters are said to be peculiarly efficacious in rheumatic complaints.

MONTGOMERY.

MONTGOMERY was formed in 1776, from Fincastle county,* and named from Gen. Montgomery: it is about 23 miles long, and 22 broad. New River runs on its southwestern border, which, with the head-waters of Roanoke River, drain the county. The face of the county is broken and mountainous, though the streams are bordered with excellent soil, which yield heavy crops of corn and wheat. Pop. in 1840, whites 5,825, slaves 1,473, free colored 87; total, 7,405.

Christiansburg, the county-seat, lies 203 miles southwesterly from Richmond, 46 miles from Fincastle, and 47 from Wytheville, on the main stage-road from Richmond to Nashville, Tenn. It was established by law Oct. 10, 1792, and the following gentlemen appointed trustees: Christian Snido, Byrd Smith, James Barnett, Hugh Crockett, Samuel Eason, Joseph Cloyd, John Preston, James Charlton, and James Craig. It contains 4 stores, 1 Presbyterian and 1 Methodist church, and a population of about 400. Blacksburg, 9 miles north of the C. H., contains 1 Presbyterian and 1 Methodist church, and a population of about 250. Lafayette, in the north part of the county, at the junction of the two forks of the Roanoke, contains a Methodist church, and about 45 dwellings.

---

* Fincastle county was formed in 1772 from Botetourt, and extinguished in 1776 by the formation of Washington, Montgomery, and Kentucky counties from its territory.

MORGAN.

MORGAN, named from Gen. Daniel Morgan, was formed in 1820 from Hampshire and Berkeley: its mean length is 22 miles, mean width 16 miles. Great Cacapon and Sleepy creek flow northwardly through the county, and empty into the Potomac. The Baltimore and Ohio rail-road passes through the northern part. Much of the surface is broken and rocky; but there is considerable good soil upon the streams. Pop. in 1840, whites 4,113, slaves 134, free colored 6; total, 4,253.

Bath, or Berkeley Springs, the county-seat, is a small village near the Potomac, and on the line of the Baltimore and Ohio rail-road, 180 miles from Richmond, 93 from Washington, 45 w. of Harper's Ferry, and 40 N. of Winchester. The springs at this place are much frequented by invalids, and others in search of health or pleasure. Though the waters are but slightly impregnated with the mineral ingredients, they are in high repute, and are said to be very beneficial in many diseases.

NANSEMOND.

THIS county was in existence as early as 1639-40; at which time an act was passed defining its boundaries. It bore at first the name of Upper Norfolk. In 1645-6 its name was changed to *Nansimum*, which word is spelt by Capt. John Smith, *Nandsamund*. It is 35 miles long, with an average breadth of 15 miles. The rail-road from Portsmouth to Weldon, N. C., passes through the county. The Dismal swamp extends along the eastern edge of the county, and a small part of Lake Drummond is within its limits. A good portion of the land belonging to the Dismal Swamp Company, is situated within the county. The growth of the swamp consists of juniper, cypress, gum, ash, maple, and pine. The company manufacture and export large quantities of shingles. Agriculture is not so thriving in this county as in many others. Marl is found in many places. The leading articles of trade are tar, turpentine, and staves. Pop. in 1840, whites 4,858, slaves 4,530, free colored 1,407; total, 10,795.

Chuckatuck, on the stage-road from Suffolk to Smithfield, and Somerton, near the northern line, contain each a few dwellings.

Suffolk, the county-seat, is on the Nansemond River, on the line of the Portsmouth and Roanoke rail-road, 18 miles sw. of Norfolk, and 85 from Richmond. This town was established by law in 1742, and has generally been thriving, and a place of considerable business. Vessels of 100 tons come up the river to this town. It contains 1 Episcopal, 1 Baptist, and 2 Methodist churches, and a population of about 1,200. Smith, an English traveller, who was through here in 1784, forty-two years after the town was established, thus describes it :

Suffolk contains about a hundred houses, and carries on a pretty brisk trade, having a considerable share of the commerce of the northern counties of North Carolina. Suffolk stands on a soil so very sandy, that in every step in the street the sand comes above your ankles, which renders it extremely disagreeable. To remedy this inconvenience in some small degree, near their doors they have emptied barrels of tar or pitch, which spreads wide—the sand incorporating with it, and forming a hard, solid consistence, some kind of apology for pavement, and thereby renders walking much more tolerable. The houses in Suffolk are low, being generally not more than one story high, which is indeed the ground story only. The trade of this place consists chiefly of turpentine, tar, pitch, tobacco, and pork, which is killed, salted, and barrelled up here ; also lumber, Indian corn, and some wheat.

In the year 1779, Sir Henry Clinton projected a plan to humble the pride and destroy the resources of Virginia. He sent a powerful fleet, which anchored in Hampton Roads, landed a heavy force under Gen. Matthews, which took possession of Portsmouth and Norfolk, and committed extensive devastations. It was on this expedition, May 13th, that Suffolk was burnt, the account of which here given, is from Girardin :

No sooner was intelligence received of the arrival of the British in Hampton Roads, than the militia of Nansemond county were called to arms. Suffolk was the place of general rendezvous. About two hundred men assembled there, with such weapons as they could procure from their own homes. Few of them had muskets, and still fewer ammunition. This, however, they obtained from Capt. Bright, who commanded the letter of marque, the brig Mars. Bright also furnished two pieces of ordnance, which were immediately mounted upon the carriages of carts. The whole of this little army, headed by Col. Willis Riddick, proceeded about eight miles on the Norfolk road, and, on the evening of the 11th of May, encamped in a large uncultivated field, in front of Capt. James Murdaugh's house. Before this movement, three well-mounted young Virginians, Josiah Riddick, Thomas Granbury, and Thomas Brittle, had been dispatched to reconnoitre the enemy. They were surprised and made prisoners, just below Hall's mills, in Norfolk county—conveyed to New York, where they remained for eighteen months in a state of captivity. Thus did the party under Col. Riddick continue in entire ignorance of the numbers and motions of the enemy.

To a tavern, about a mile below the encampment of the militia, Captains King and Davis had repaired for the night. In front of this tavern was a lane with draw-bars at its extremity. These were soon heard to rattle ; alarmed at this noise, King and Davis seized their muskets, and flew to the door. King leaped out, and fired to give the alarm. The British platoon discharged, and shot Davis through the heart. King, well acquainted with the country, soon reached the Virginian camp, and informed his comrades of approaching hostility. The violence of the wind, blowing in an unfavorable direction, had prevented them from hearing the report even of the British musketry, discharged so near them. Col. Willis Riddick, not suspecting the approach of the foe, had retired to his own house. The command, therefore, devolved upon Col. Edward Riddick. The militia retraced their steps to Suffolk, which they reached before the dawn. Two officers, mounted on fleet horses, were then dispatched to ascertain the situation and force of the enemy. Four miles below Suffolk they halted, and immediately after sunrise, in the entrance of a lane, about one quarter of a mile long, had a full view of the advancing foe, and distinctly counted 600 infantry. They rode back in full speed, and, upon calling the militia to arms, about one hundred only obeyed the call. The others had dispersed. A retreat became unavoidable—every man was admonished to take care of himself. Most of the inhabitants had already left their homes. Few could save their effects. Such as delayed their flight, in attempting to secure their property, were taken prisoners. Ruthless devastation attended the British. They set fire to the town, and nearly the whole was consumed. Several hundred barrels of tar, pitch, turpentine, and rum, had been deposited on lots contiguous to the wharves. The heads of the barrels being knocked out, and their contents, which flowed in a commingled mass, catching the blaze, descended to the river, like torrents of burning lava. As the wind blew from the wharves with great violence, these substances, with difficulty soluble in water, rapidly floated to the opposite shore in a splendid state of conflagration, which they communicated to the thick and decaying herbage of an extensive marsh, the growth of the preceding year. This immense sheet of fire, added to the vast columns of undulating flames which ascended from the burning houses in the town—the explosion, at intervals, of the gunpowder in the magazines—the consequent projection through the air of large pieces of ignited timber, which flew, like meteors, to an astonishing distance—all contributed to form a collective scene of horror, and sublimity, and desolation, such as could not be viewed without emotions not to be described.

NELSON.

Nelson was formed in 1807, from Amherst, and named from Thomas Nelson, governor of Virginia in 1781. It is about 26 miles long, and 20 broad. The face of the country is broken and mountainous, particularly as it approaches the Blue Ridge. The mountains contain generally a fine rich soil; and their intervening valleys, and the low grounds upon the streams, are fertile. Tobacco was formerly more cultivated than at present, but the less land-exhausting crops of wheat and rye have succeeded. An increased attention is being paid to husbandry, and the old injudicious modes of culture are being done away with. As a whole, the county is a fertile and wealthy one. Population in 1840, whites 6,168, slaves 5,967, free colored 152 ; total, 12,287.

Lovingston, the county-seat, is on a branch of the Tye River, near the centre of the county, on the stage-road from Lynchburg to Charlottesville, 105 miles northwesterly from Richmond. It is beautifully situated in a cove surrounded by romantic mountainous scenery. The religious denominations are Methodist, Baptist, and Presbyterian. It has several mercantile stores, and a population of about 300. At New Market, at the influx of the Tye River into the James, in the southern part of the county, there is a tobacco inspection, where several hundred hogsheads of tobacco are annually inspected. The annual amount of tobacco produced in the county, is over two millions of pounds. Faber's Mills, in the west part, contains a Baptist church and a few dwellings.

NEW KENT.

New Kent was formed in 1654, from York. The boundaries were then defined as follows: "It is ordered that the upper part of York county shall be a distinct county called New Kent, from the west side of Scimino creek to the heads of Pamunkey and Mattaponie River, and down to the head of the west side of Poropotanke creek." The Pamunkey runs on its northern and the Chickahominy on its southern boundary : to each of these the respective portions of the county incline. New Kent is about 26 miles long and 9 broad. Population in 1840, whites 2,472, slaves 3,385, free colored 373 ; total, 6,230.

New Kent C. H., or Bassettville, is 30 miles E. of Richmond, and 3 miles s. of the Pamunkey. It contains several stores and taverns, and about a dozen dwellings.

Beautifully situated on the banks of the Pamunkey, is the mansion known as "*the White House.*" It stands on the site of the one in which Washington was married. From Custis's Life of Mrs. Martha Washington, we extract the account of his courtship and marriage :

It was in 1758 that Washington, attired in a military undress, and attended by a body servant, tall and *militaire* as his chief, crossed the ferry called Williams's, over the Pamunkey, a branch of the York River. On the boat touching the southern or New Kent side, the soldier's progress was arrested by one of those personages who give the beau idéal of the Virginia gentleman of the old régime, the very soul of kindness and hospitality. It was in vain the soldier urged his business at Williamsburg, important communications to the governor, &c. Mr. Chamberlayne, on whose domain the militaire had just landed, would hear of no excuse. Col. Washington was a name and character so dear to all Virginians, that his passing by one of the castles of Virginia, without calling and partaking of the hospitalities of the host, was entirely out of the question. The colonel, however, did not surrender at discretion, but stoutly maintained his ground till Chamberlayne, bringing up his reserve, in the intimation that he would introduce his friend to a young and charming widow, then beneath his roof, the soldier capitulated, on condition that he should dine—only dine—and then, by pressing his charger and borrowing of the night, he would reach Williamsburg before his excellency could shake off his morning slumbers. Orders were accordingly issued to Bishop, the colonel's body servant and faithful follower, who, together with the fine English charger, had been bequeathed by the dying Braddock to Major Washington, on the famed and fated field of Monongahela. Bishop, bred in the school of European discipline, raised his hand to his cap, as much as to say, " Your orders shall be obeyed."

The colonel now proceeded to the mansion, and was introduced to various guests, (for when was a Virginia domicil of the olden time without guests?) and, above all, to the charming widow. Tradition relates that they were mutually pleased, on this, their first interview—nor is it remarkable ; they were of an age when impressions are strongest. The lady was fair to behold, of fascinating manners, and splendidly endowed with worldly benefits. The hero was fresh from his early fields, redolent of fame, and with a form on which " every god did seem to set his seal, to give the world assurance of a man."

The morning passed pleasantly away, evening came, with Bishop, true to his orders and firm at his post, holding the favorite charger with one hand, while the other was waiting to offer the ready stirrup. The sun sunk in the horizon, and yet the colonel appeared not. " 'Twas strange, 'twas passing strange ;" surely he was not wont to be a single moment behind his appointments—for he was the most punctual of all men.

Meantime, the host enjoyed the scene of the veteran at the gate, while the colonel was so agreeably employed in the parlor ; and proclaiming that no visitor ever left his home at sunset, his military guest was, without much difficulty, persuaded to order Bishop to put up the horses for the night. The sun rode high in the heavens the ensuing day, when the enamored soldier pressed with his spur his charger's side, and speeded on his way to the seat of government, where, having dispatched his public business, he retraced his steps, and, at the White House, the engagement took place, with preparations for marriage.

And much hath the biographer heard of that marriage, from the gray-haired domestics who waited at the board where love made the feast and Washington the guest. And rare and high was the revelry at that palmy period of Virginia's festal age ; for many were gathered to that marriage, of the good, the great, the gifted, and they, with joyous acclamations, hailed in Virginia's youthful hero a happy and prosperous bridegroom.

" And so you remember when Colonel Washington came a courting of your young mistress?" said the biographer to old Cully, in his hundredth year. " Ay, master, that

I do," replied the ancient family servant, who had lived to see five generations; " great times, sir, great times—shall never see the like again!" " And Washington looked something like a man, a proper man—hey, Cully ?" " Never seed the like, sir—never the like of him, though I have seen many in my day—so tall, so straight ! and then he sat on a horse and rode with such an air ! Ah, sir, he was like no one else. Many of the grandest gentlemen, in the gold lace, were at the wedding ; but none looked like the man himself." Strong, indeed, must have been the impression which the person and manner of Washington made upon the " rude, untutored mind" of this poor negro, since the lapse of three-quarters of a century had not sufficed to efface it.

The precise date of the marriage the biographer has been unable to discover, having in vain searched among the records of the vestry of St. Peter's church, New Kent, of which the Rev. Mr. Munson, a Cambridge scholar, was the rector, and performed the ceremony, it is believed, about 1759. A short time after their marriage, Colonel and Mrs. Washington removed to Mount Vernon, on the Potomac, and permanently settled there.

"This union," says Sparks, " was in every respect felicitous.° It continued forty years. To her intimate acquaintance and to the nation, the character of Mrs. Washington was ever a theme of praise. Affable and courteous, exemplary in her deportment, remarkable for her deeds of charity and piety, unostentatious, and without vanity, she adorned by her domestic virtues the sphere of private life, and filled with dignity every station in which she was placed."

Previous to his acquaintance with Mrs. Custis, Washington had been pleased with other ladies. The author above quoted on this point says, that in 1756, " While in New York, he was lodged and kindly entertained at the house of Mr. Beverley Robinson, between whom and himself an intimacy of friendship subsisted, which, indeed, continued without change, till severed by their opposite fortunes twenty years afterwards in the revolution. It happened that Miss Mary Philips, a sister of Mrs. Robinson, and a young lady of rare accomplishments, was an inmate in the family. The charms of this lady made a deep impression upon the heart of the Virginia colonel. He went to Boston, returned, and was again welcomed to the hospitality of Mr. Robinson. He lingered there till duty called him away ; but he was careful to intrust his secret to a confidential friend, whose letters kept him informed of every important event. In a few months intelligence came, that a rival was in the field, and that the consequences could not be answered for, if he delayed to renew his visits to New York. Whether time, the bustle of a camp, or the scenes of war had moderated his admiration, or whether he despaired of success, is not known. He never saw the lady again till she was married to that same rival, Captain Morris, his former associate in arms, and one of Braddock's aids-de-camp.

" He had before felt the influence of the tender passion. At the age of seventeen, he was smitten by the graces of a fair one, whom he called a ' lowland beauty,' and whose praises he recorded in glowing strains, while wandering with his surveyor's compass among the Alleghany mountains. On that occasion he wrote desponding letters to a friend, and indited plaintive verses, but never ventured to reveal his emotions to the lady who was unconsciously the cause of his pains."

On the eastern bank of Ware creek, a tributary of York River, and the dividing line of New Kent and James City counties, is the " STONE HOUSE," as it is called, which is perhaps the most curious relic of antiquity in Virginia. A writer—C. C. of Petersburg—in a late number of the Southern Literary Messenger, gives the following sketch :

The Stone House is distant from the mouth of Ware creek five miles, from Williamsburg fifteen, and from Jamestown twenty-two. The walls and chimney, which remain, are composed of sandstone. The house is eighteen and a half feet by fifteen in extent. It consists of a basement room under ground and a story above. On the west side is a doorway six feet wide, giving entrance to both apartments. There are loop-holes in the walls, measuring on the inside twenty by ten inches, on the outside twenty by four. The walls are in the basement two feet thick, in the upper story eighteen inches thick. The masonry bears marks of having been executed with great care and nicety. The house stands in an extensive waste of woods, on a high knoll or promontory, around the foot of which winds Ware creek. The structure fronts on the creek, being elevated one hundred feet above its level, and standing back three hundred feet from its margin. The spot is approached only by a long circuitous defile, the comb of a ridge, in some places so narrow that two carts could not pass abreast. This defile is, besides, involved in such a labyrinth of dark ridges of forest and deep gloomy ravines, mantled with laurel, that it is said to be next to impossible to find the way without the aid of a guide. Nor is the place more accessible by water. The surrounding country is described as the most broken and desert tract to be found east of the Blue Ridge.

Ancient Stone Structure on Ware Creek.

The singular structure of the old "Stone House," and its wild, secluded, desolate site, have naturally given rise to several traditions and conjectures as to its origin and purpose. It is said that there is a neighborhood tradition, that the house was erected as early as thirteen years after the landing at Jamestown—and that it was built by the famous pirate Blackbeard, as a depository of his plunder. This hypothesis, however, involves a serious anachronism ; since it is well established that Blackbeard did not figure in the waters of Virginia until about the year 1717—more than a century after the landing at Jamestown.

Another fanciful conjecture is, that the "Stone House," like the cave where Dido entertained Æneas, was a sort of rendezvous meeting-place of Captain Smith and Pocahontas ! This is rather too romantic.

Another conjecture, much more plausible than either of those above mentioned, is that the house was built by the adherents of Bacon in his rebellion, who, after their leader's death, still held out so pertinaciously against Governor Berkeley. This surmise, however, would seem to be unfounded. Firstly, it is well known that those followers of Bacon occupied West Point at the head of York River, strongly fortified it, and made it their place of arms. That post in their hands actually proved impregnable against repeated assaults of the governor's forces under Ludwell. And Sir William Berkeley, at length fatigued by their resolute defence, in order to induce their surrender, was obliged to offer the rebels there a general pardon, which nothing less than the last necessity could have extorted from him. The position occupied by Bacon's adherents at West Point being so strong and every way convenient, there could have been no motive to prompt them to build another fortification on Ware creek.

In the next place, it is altogether improbable that the vindictive vigilance of Berkeley would have suffered Bacon's followers unmolested to erect such a work as the "Stone House," whose elaborate construction would seem rather to indicate that it was built in the leisure of peace, than in the anxious precipitancy of a hard-pressed and hopeless rebellion.

Lastly, of Bacon's rebellion there are several minute circumstantial accounts, and it is improbable that Beverly, T. M., and others, would have omitted a fact so interesting as the erection of a fortified work on Ware creek, when they were detailing so many other particulars of less consequence.

So much for these conjectures. I now beg leave to suggest another, founded on the following passage :

" *We built also a fort for a retreat neere a convenient river, upon a high commanding hill, very hard to be assalted and easie to be defended, but ere it was finished this defect caused a stay.* In searching our casked corne, we found it halfe rotten and the rest so consumed with so many thousands of rats that increased so fast, but their originall was from the ships, as we knew not how to keepe that little we had. This did drive us all to our wits end, for there was nothing in the country but what nature afforded." * * " *But this want of corne occasioned the end of all our works,* it being worke sufficient to provide victuall."—*Smith's Hist. of Va.,* B. III., p. 227.

Upon lately meeting with this passage in Smith, I was forcibly struck with the coincidence between the fort thus spoken of by him and the " Stone House." If the conjecture be well founded, it will entitle that structure to the claim of being the oldest house in Virginia, if not in the United States, as the fort mentioned by Smith was erected about the year 1608–9, only two or three years after the landing at Jamestown, which would make it about two hundred and thirty-four years old. Smith says, " We built also a fort for a retreat ;" that is, a retreat from the Indians in case Jamestown should have been overpowered. " Neere a convenient river." The " Stone House" is about a hundred yards from Ware creek. " A convenient river,"—by the description given above, it is seen that no situation could have been more eligible. It may be worth while to observe that the name of the river is not given ; now, in all probability, Ware creek at that early day had not been named by the English, being an unimportant stream. " Upon a high commanding hill ;" this answers exactly to the site of the " Stone House." " Very hard to be assalted and easie to be defended ;" all the descrip- tions of the " Stone House" fully confirm these particulars. " But ere it was finished this defect caused a stay," &c. * * " But this want of corne occasioned the end of all our works," &c. Now the " Stone House" is apparently incomplete, and there is neither roof nor floor ; this unfinished appearance seems to have puzzled some of its visitors. Smith's statement, however, that it was left unfinished, may at once solve the enigma.

From all these corroborating circumstances, there seems to be good reason to con- clude that the " Stone House" is the fort mentioned by Smith. Its antiquity, the asso- ciations connected with it, the superstitious fancies to which it has given rise, and its wild and sequestered situation, all conspire to render the old " Stone House" an attrac- tive object to the tourist and the antiquary, and, perhaps, not uninteresting even to the novelist and poet.

NICHOLAS.

Nicholas was formed in 1818, from Kanawha, Greenbrier, and Randolph. It is 44 miles long, with a mean width of 20 miles. It is watered by Gauley and Elk Rivers,—the latter of which is a beautiful flowing stream, susceptible, at a small expense, of being made navigable to its source. The soil and climate present great variety ; being in some parts very warm and fertile, in others cold, barren, and mountainous. Pop. in 1840, whites 2,440, slaves 72, free colored 3 ; total, 2,515.

Summerville, the county-seat, 310 miles from Richmond, and about 70 from the Ohio, contains about 25 dwellings.

NORFOLK.

Norfolk was formed in 1691, from Lower Norfolk, afterwards changed to the name of Nansemond. Its length from N. to S. is 32 miles, mean width 17 miles. The Portsmouth and Roanoke rail-

MARKET SQUARE, NORFOLK.

In the centre of the view is shown the market, and in the distance, on the opposite bank of Elizabeth river—the common harbor of Norfolk and Portsmouth—a part of the town of Portsmouth.

road, which is 77 miles long, commences at Portsmouth, in this county, and terminates on the Roanoke River, at Weldon, N. C. The Dismal Swamp Canal, 22 miles long, connects Chesapeake Bay with Albemarle Sound, North Carolina. The north end empties into Deep creek, a branch of Elizabeth River; and the south into Joice's creek, a branch of the Pasquotank River. This canal passes for 20 miles through the Great Dismal Swamp, and has been a work of great labor and difficulty. It was commenced in 1787, under a joint charter of the two states; but was not finished until a few years since. It is one of the best canals in the Union, is navigated by sloops and schooners, and does much business. Lake Drummond, near the centre of the Dismal Swamp, in times of great drought is its only feeder. In addition, a new cut of $2\frac{1}{3}$ miles long, from the town of Deep Creek direct to the Elizabeth River, has lately been made, which saves a circuit of several miles. Hampton Roads lies on the N. border of the county. Pop. in 1840, whites 11,280, slaves 7,845, free colored 1,967; total, 21,092.

Norfolk borough is situated 106 miles from Richmond, 230 from Washington city, and 8 miles above Hampton Roads, on the N. bank of Elizabeth River, near the junction of its southern and eastern branches. It was first established by law as a town in October, 1705, in the 4th year of the reign of Queen Anne; at which time its favorable situation for trade had gathered a considerable population.

In the Westover mss., Col. Byrd, in the History of the Dividing Line between Virginia and North Carolina, thus describes Norfolk in 1728:

Norfolk has most the air of a town of any in Virginia. There were then near 20 brigantines and sloops riding at the wharves, and oftentimes they have more. It has all the advantages of situation requisite for trade and navigation... The town is so near the sea that its vessels may sail in and out in a few hours. Their trade is chiefly to the West Indies, whither they export abundance of beef, pork, flour, and lumber. The worst of it is, they contribute much towards debauching the country by importing abundance of rum, which, like gin in Great Britain, breaks the constitutions, vitiates the morals, and ruins the industry of most of the poor people of this country. This place is the mart for most of the commodities produced in the adjacent parts of North Carolina. They have a pretty deal of lumber from the borderers on the Dismal, who make bold with the king's land thereabouts, without the least ceremony. They not only maintain their stocks upon it, but get boards, shingles, and other lumber out of it in great abundance.

The town is built on a level spot of ground upon Elizabeth River, the banks whereof are neither so high as to make the landing of goods troublesome, nor so low as to be in danger of overflowing. The streets are straight, and adorned with several good houses, which increase every day. It is not a town of ordinaries and public houses, like most others in this country, but the inhabitants consist of merchants, ship-carpenters, and other useful artisans, with sailors enough to manage their navigation. With all these conveniences, it lies under the two great disadvantages that most of the towns in Holland do, by having neither good air nor good water. The two cardinal virtues that make a place thrive, industry and frugality, are seen here in perfection; and so long as they can banish luxury and idleness, the town will remain in a happy and flourishing condition.

The method of building wharves here is after the following manner. They lay down long pine logs, that reach from the shore to the edge of the channel. These are bound fast together by cross pieces notched into them, according to the architecture of the log-houses in North Carolina. A wharf built thus will stand several years, in spite of the worm, which bites here very much, but may be soon repaired in a place where so many pines grow in the neighborhood.

Norfolk was formed into a borough* Sept. 15th, 1736, by royal charter from George II. Samuel Boush, one of the principal land-holders, was made mayor† until a vacancy occurred either by his death or resignation. Sir John Randolph was appointed recorder, and the following gentlemen aldermen—George Newton, Samuel Boush, Jr., John Hutchins, Robert Tucker, John Taylor, Samuel Smith, Jr., James Ivey, and Alexander Campbell.

Ten years after, the inhabitants of the borough evinced their loyalty in their rejoicings at the defeat of the Pretender at the battle of Culloden, fought April 6th, 1746 ; an account of which is preserved in the Virginia Gazette, published at Williamsburg, and copied below :

Williamsburg, July 31.—We have very credible information from the borough of Norfolk, that on the 23d inst. they made extraordinary rejoicings there upon the good news of the defeat of the rebels by His Royal Highness, the Duke of Cumberland. The account we have of it is as follows :

The effigy of the Pretender, in the full proportion of a man, in a Highland dress resembling that which he appeared in, by the account given by a person in town who saw him a few months ago, was placed in a two-armed chair, and the following cavalcade marshalled, viz :

1st. Three drummers.

2d. A piper.

3d. Three violins.

4th. Six men with long white rods, with slips of paper like sashes over their shoulders, and different mottoes wrote on them in capital letters, as Liberty, Property, and No Pretender, No Wooden Shoes, &c.

5th. A man in woman's clothes, dressed like a nurse, carrying a warming-pan with a child peeping out of it.

6th. The Pretender in a two-armed chair, drawn in a cart.

7th. Six men, two and two, with drawn cutlasses.

Lastly. A vast crowd of people of the town and country, who thus marched in procession through all the streets till they came (about one o'clock) to the centre of the three main streets, where a gibbet being erected for that purpose, the cart was drawn under it, and his Protectorship was immediately exalted to the general view and satisfaction of the spectators. Liquor was provided for the better sort, and the populace had great plenty in casks standing with one head out.

On drinking the health of His Majesty, KING GEORGE II., a royal salute was made of 21 guns, planted in two different places, which was answered by a number of others from vessels in the harbor. Then followed other loyal healths, as the Royal Family, His Royal Highness the Duke, the Governor, *Virginia,* success to His Majesty's arms, &c., each health being proclaimed by the guns at the two different parts of the town, and vessels in the harbor. Thus the gentlemen continued at the court-house till the evening, when the windows all over town were beautifully illuminated. Then a large bonfire was kindled around the gibbet, and in a few minutes the effigy dropped into the flames. Then there was another royal salute, accompanied with loud huzzas and acclamations of joy. To conclude, that the ladies might also partake of the rejoicings on this extraordinary occasion, the gentlemen entertained them with a ball, and the evening concluded with innocent mirth and unaffected joy, becoming a people loyal to their king, and zealous for their country's good.

The harbor of Norfolk admits vessels of the largest size, and is equal to any in the country. It may be considered the great naval depôt of the Union ; and the borough, together with Portsmouth, is the residence of a greater number of naval officers than any other port in the country. There are, generally, several vessels of war lying at anchor in her harbor, beside those at the Navy Yard.

Previous to the late war, Norfolk monopolized almost all the trade with the British West Indies, which was a source of much profit. From that period, excepting the years 1816, '17, and '18, during which the restriction was removed, her commerce was in a

---

* Norfolk became a city by act of the legislature, April 24th, 1845.

† There is in the possession of a gentleman at Norfolk a silver mace, weighing several pounds, presented to the corporation by Sir John Randolph. It was carried before the Mayor on going to court, and in public processions.

languishing condition until the completion of the Dismal Swamp Canal. Its facilities for trade have been greatly increased by the completion of this work and the Portsmouth and Roanoke Railroad. It enjoys considerable foreign commerce, chiefly in corn, lumber, cotton, and naval stores. The plan of the town is some-

St. Paul's Church, Norfolk.

what irregular. Most of the streets are wide and well built, with handsome brick and stone buildings. The surface of the town is an almost dead level, and the private residences of many of its inhabitants, away from the business streets, are very neat, and have annexed spacious gardens adorned with shrubbery.

An erroneous impression has prevailed abroad that Norfolk is unhealthy: yet the stranger having this idea cannot but be surprised at the unusual number of fine, rosy-cheeked, healthy-looking children whom he meets in the streets. "The deaths in Norfolk for the year ending May 31st, 1844, as reported by the health-officer, amounted to 209, in a population of 11,000, or $1\frac{7}{8}$ per cent. —a pretty favorable indication of the salubrity of the position. The deaths in London are 3 per cent. of the population; in Philadelphia $2\frac{1}{2}$ per cent. In both of these cities are masses of poor, destitute, vicious, and worked-to-death people, which necessarily accounts for their greater mortality. In Norfolk, however, there is a large slave population, yet the same rule does not apply."

The principal public buildings are a custom-house, court-house, jail, a marine hospital, almshouse, academy, masons' lodge, 2 Episcopal, 1 Methodist, 1 Catholic, 1 Baptist, and 1 Presbyterian church, beside 2 churches for colored people. There is a theatre, 1 Lancasterian, and about 40 other schools, an orphan asylum, 4 banks—the Exchange Bank of Virginia, Virginia Bank, Farmers' Bank of Va., and a Savings' Bank—and a population of about 12,000. It has more foreign commerce than any other place in the state. The tonnage in 1840 was 19,079. There were then, by the U. S. statistics, 8 foreign commercial and 8 commission houses, cap. $202,000; 35 retail stores, cap. $1,590,500; cap. in

manufactures, $178,300.   Population in 1775, about 6,000 ; 1810,
9,193 ; 1820, 9,478 ; 1830, 9,816; 1840, 10,920, of whom about
one-half were blacks.

The most beautiful building in the town is the Norfolk academy,
which is an elegant structure after the temple of Theseus, standing on a spacious green.

It is an academy of the highest class, under the charge of a principal and three assistant professors. The principal, W. F. Hopkins, A. M., was formerly professor of
chemistry at the U. S. Military Academy at West Point.   Under his charge it is very
flourishing.   The pupils, for the purpose of exercise, are formed into a military corps.
Annexed to this institution is a preparatory department.   St. Paul's church is the oldest
building in Norfolk.   It was erected in 1739.   When the town was burnt by the British
in the revolution, it was almost the only building that escaped destruction.   The enemy
robbed the church, and carried the baptismal font, which was of marble, to Scotland.
Upon the end of the church there is still to be seen on the stone-work, the marks of a
cannon-ball fired from the enemy's shipping.   The grave-yard, which was used as early
as 1700, contains many monuments.

In the environs of the town, a beautiful cemetery, containing several acres, has been
laid out by the corporation.   It is surrounded by a high, white wall, and is tastefully
planted with evergreens.   Annexed are inscriptions from some of the monuments :—

Here rest the remains of Capt. Angus Martin, who died Sept. 18th, 1838, aged 75 years. He was a
native of Argyleshire, Scotland. Bred to the sea, he was, at the early age of 18, intrusted with the command of a ship belonging to the port of Greenock ; and crossed the Atlantic one hundred times in his
lifetime, as a mariner, &c. &c.

Sacred to the memory of Robert Monroe Harrison, late a midshipman in the navy of the U. S., and son
of Robert M. Harrison, for many years consul for the U. S. at various places, and now filling that station
at St. Bartholomews.   He was born on the 27th of Dec., 1811, and by the upsetting of one of the U. S.
cutters in this harbor, was drowned, together with his friends and messmates, Mids. J. S. Slidell and
Frederick Rodgers, on the 5th April, 1828.   He was distinguished for his amiable disposition, for the remarkable sprightliness of his genius, and for various and extensive acquirements, which would have done
honor to a riper age.   As an officer he was conspicuous for his zeal and devotion to his duties ; as a gentleman for his accomplished, frank, and manly deportment.   His end was marked by the same firmness
and magnanimity which had characterized his life, resigning himself to a fate which was inevitable.   He
declined the proffered aid of his generous comrades, and exhorted them to use their exertions, which,
alas ! were unavailing, to save themselves.   Thus, in the morning of life, was this brilliant youth cut off
in a career full of promise to his country, and of hope and consolation to his parents.   His remains and
those of his friend, Mid. Slidell, were followed to the grave by one of the largest and most respectable processions of our fellow-citizens ever known, and under circumstances most solemn and affecting, interred
with military honors, on the 13th April, 1828.

Norfolk and its vicinity was the scene of some important military
events in the war of the revolution.   The British fleet, to which
Lord Dunmore had fled at the outbreak of hostilities, made Norfolk harbor its principal rendezvous.

In October, 1775, "a British officer (says Girardin) with 12 or 13 soldiers, and a few
sailors, landed at the county wharf in Norfolk, and, under cover of the men-of-war,
who made every show of firing upon the town in case the party were molested, marched
up the main street to Holt's printing-office, from whence, without opposition or resistance, they carried off the types, with other printing materials, and two of the workmen.
The corporation of Norfolk remonstrated with Dunmore on this outrage ; stated their
ability to have cut off this small party, had they been so disposed ; and requested the
immediate return of the persons and property illegally seized.   Dunmore's answer was
taunting and insulting in the highest degree.   He said that he could not have rendered
the people of Norfolk a greater service, than by depriving them of the means of having
their minds *poisoned*, and of exciting in them ' *the spirit of rebellion and sedition ;*'
that their not having cut off the small party who took Holt's types, he imputed to other
reasons than their peaceable intentions, as their drums were beating to arms without
success the greater part of the time that the party were on shore.   He gave them no
satisfaction on the subject of restoring the persons and property seized and carried off.
Holt, the printer, was not silent on the occasion.   He published in the Williamsburg
papers an eloquent philippic against Dunmore, and a patriotic advertisement, stating his
intention to establish a new press, to be conducted on the same principles as that which
had been destroyed."

The administration of Virginia directed all their attention upon this part of the state, where they perceived the danger most formidable. Dunmore, alarmed at their prepara- tions, constructed batteries and intrenchments at Norfolk, armed the blacks and tories, and forced the country people to drive their cattle and convey provisions to the town. The government of Va. dispatched, with all speed, a detachment of minute-men, under the command of Col. Woodford, into the county.

"Dunmore, apprized (says Botta) of this movement, very prudently occupied a strong position upon the north bank of Elizabeth River, called Great Bridge, a few miles from Norfolk. This point was situated upon the direct route of the provincial troops. Here he threw up works upon the Norfolk side, and furnished them with a numerous artillery. The intrenchments were surrounded on every part with water and marshes, and were only accessible by a long dike. As to the forces of the governor, they were little for- midable : he had only 200 regulars, and a corps of Norfolk volunteers ; the residue con- sisted in a shapeless mass of varlets of every color. The Virginians took post over against the English, in a small village at a cannon-shot distance. Before them they had a long narrow dike, the extremity of which they also fortified. In this state the two parties remained for several days without making any movement."

An ingenious stratagem precipitated the operations. A servant of Major Marshall's, (father of the chief-justice,) being properly instructed, deserted to Dunmore, and re- ported that there were not at the bridge more than 300 *shirt-men*, as the Virginians, who mostly wore hunting-shirts, were contemptuously called. Believing the story, Dun- more dispatched about 200 regulars, and 300 blacks and tories, to the Great Bridge ; who arrived there on the morning of the 9th of December, 1775, and just as the reveille had done beating, made an attack upon the Virginians. They were signally defeated, and lost 102 in killed and wounded. The annexed particulars of this action, called the "*Battle of the Great Bridge*," were published five days after, in the Virginia Gazette :

The Great Bridge is built over what is called the southern branch of Elizabeth River, 12 miles above Norfolk. The land on each side is marshy to a considerable distance from the river, except at the two extremities of the bridge, where are two pieces of firm land, which may not improperly be called islands, being entirely surrounded by water and marsh, and joined to the main land by causeways. On the little piece of firm ground on the further or Norfolk side, Lord Dunmore had erected his fort, in such a manner that his cannon commanded the causeway on his own side, and the bridges between him and us, with the marshes around him. The island on this side of the river contained six or seven houses, some of which were burnt down (those nearest the bridge) by the enemy after the arrival of our troops ; in the others, adjoining the causeway on each side, were stationed a guard every night by Col. Woodford, but withdrawn before day, that they might not be exposed to the fire of the enemy's fort in recrossing the causeway to our camp, this causeway also being commanded by their cannon.

The causeway on our side, in length was about 160 yards, and on the hither extremity our breastwork was thrown up. From the breastwork ran a street gradually ascending, about the length of 400 yards, to a church where our main body was encamped. The great trade to Norfolk in shingles, tar, pitch, and turpentine, from the country back of this, had occasioned so many houses to be built here, whence the articles were conveyed to Norfolk by water. But this by the by. Such is the nature of the place as described to me, and such was our situation, and that of the enemy.

On Saturday the 9th inst., after reveille beating, two or three great guns and some musketry were dis- charged by the enemy, which, as it was not an unusual thing, was but little regarded by Col. Woodford. However, soon after he heard a call to the soldiers to stand by their arms, upon which, with all expedi- tion, he made the proper dispositions to receive them. In the mean time, the enemy had crossed the bridge, fired the remaining houses upon the island, and some large piles of shingles, and attacked our guard in the breastwork. Our men returned the fire, and threw them into some confusion ; but they were instantly rallied by Capt. Fordyce, and advanced along the causeway with great resolution, keeping up a constant and heavy fire as they approached. Two field-pieces, which had been brought across the bridge and placed on the edge of the island, facing the left of our breastwork, played briskly at the same time upon us. Lieut. Travis, who commanded in the breastwork, ordered his men to reserve their fire until the enemy came within fifty yards, and then they gave it to them with terrible execution. The brave Fordyce exerted himself to keep up their spirits, reminded them of their ancient glory, and, waving his hat over his head encouragingly, told them *the day was their own*. Thus pressing forward, he fell within fifteen steps of the breastwork. His wounds were many, and his death would have been that of a hero had he met it in a better cause. The progress of the enemy was now at an end, and they retreated over the causeway with precipitation, and were dreadfully galled in their rear.

Hitherto, on our side only the guard, consisting of twenty-five, and some others, in the whole not amounting to more than ninety, had been engaged. Only the regulars of the 14th regiment, in number 120, had advanced upon the causeway ; and about 230 negroes and tories had, after crossing the bridge, continued upon the island. The regulars, after retreating along the causeway, were again rallied by Capt. Leslie, and the two field-pieces continued playing upon our men. It was at this time that Col. Woodford was advancing down the street to the breastwork with the main body, and against him was now directed the whole fire of the enemy. Never were cannon better served ; yet in the face of them and the musketry, which kept up a continual blaze, our men marched on with the utmost intrepidity. Col. Stevens, of the Culpeper battalion, was sent round to the left to flank the enemy, which was done with so much spirit and activity that a rout immediately ensued. The enemy fled into their fort, leaving behind them the two field-pieces, which, however, they took care to spike up with nails.

Many were killed and wounded in the flight ; but Col. Woodford very prudently restrained his troops from pursuing the enemy too far. From the beginning of the attack, till the repulse at the breastwork, might be 14 or 15 minutes ; till the total defeat, upwards of half an hour. It is said that some of the enemy preferred death to captivity, from fear of being scalped, which Lord Dunmore cruelly told them would be their fate should they be taken alive. Thirty-one killed and wounded fell into our hands, and the number borne off was much greater. Through the whole engagement every officer and soldier behaved with the greatest calmness and courage. The conduct of our sentinels I cannot pass over in silence. Before they quitted their stations, they fired at least three rounds as the enemy were crossing the bridge, and one of them, posted behind some shingles, kept his ground until he had fired eight times, and, after he had received the fire of a whole platoon, made his escape across the causeway to our breastwork. The scene was closed with as much humanity as it was conducted with bravery. The work of death being over, every one's attention was directed to the succor of the unhappy sufferers; and it is an undoubted fact, that Capt. Leslie was so affected with the tenderness of our troops to those capable of assistance, that he gave signs from the fort, of his thankfulness. What is not paralleled in history, and will scarcely be credible, except to such as acknowledge a Providence over human affairs, this victory was gained at the expense of no more than a slight wound in a soldier's hand; and one circumstance which rendered it still more amazing is, that the field-pieces raked the whole length of the street, and absolutely threw double-headed shot as far as the church, and afterwards, as our troops approached, cannonaded them heavily with grape-shot.

An article in a succeeding paper says: "A correspondent on whose information we may depend, informs us that our soldiers showed the greatest humanity and tenderness to the wounded prisoners. Several of them ran through a hot fire to lift up and bring in some that were bleeding, and who they feared would die if not speedily assisted by the surgeon. The prisoners expected to be scalped, and cried out, 'For God's sake, do not murder us.' One of them, unable to walk, cried out in this manner to one of our men, and was answered by him, 'Put your arm around my neck, and I will show you what I intend to do.' Then taking him with his arm over his neck, he walked slowly along, bearing him along with great tenderness, to the breastwork. Capt. Leslie, seeing two of our soldiers tenderly removing a wounded regular from the bridge, stepped upon the platform of the fort, and bowing with great respect, thanked them for their kindness. These are instances of a noble disposition of soul. Men who can act thus, must be invincible."

The repulse of the British at Great Bridge, determined the Virginians to march to Norfolk, "the strong-hold of ministerial power, and the focus of hostile enterprise; and a numerous party under Col. Stevens was immediately detached to Kemp's Landing, with orders to secure, in the neighborhood of that place, every person known to have left Norfolk since the battle of the Great Bridge.

"Among the individuals arrested in consequence of these orders, one William Calvert reported that he was present when Dunmore received the news of the defeat. His lordship, frantic with rage, swore, in his impotent ravings, that he would hang the boy who brought the information. The intrenchments at Norfolk were hastily abandoned, more than 20 pieces of cannon spiked and dismantled, and the fleet resorted to by the late governor and many of the disaffected, with their families and the most portable and valuable of their effects, as the only asylum against the impending vengeance of the patriots. Nothing but trepidation, shame, and despair, was now to be seen among those rash and infatuated boasters who lately hurled defiance and insult in the face of the Virginians—who, with ferocious joy and presumptuous confidence, spoke of easy triumphs over them—considered their noble enthusiasm as a momentary effervescence of popular phrensy—denied their courage, as well as their ability to resist ministerial omnipotence—and in their dreams of ideal conquest, dealt around confiscation, proscription, and death."

In consequence of a pacific declaration, issued by Col. Woodford to the inhabitants of Princess Anne and Norfolk counties, many of the inhabitants resorted to his camp. To those who had joined the enemy through fear alone, all reasonable indulgence was extended; while upon others a vigilant eye was kept. Those taken in arms were each coupled with handcuffs to one of his black fellow-soldiers, as a stigma, and placed in confinement. On the night of the 14th, five days after the battle of Great Bridge, the Virginians entered Norfolk, and the succeeding morning Col. Howe assumed the command.

"Although the greater part of the loyalists of Norfolk and its environs had sought refuge in the governor's fleet, there had, nevertheless, remained a considerable number of them; either on account of their reluctance to leave their properties, or their dread of the sea and of famine, or perhaps because they hoped to find more lenity on the part of their fellow-citizens who made profession of liberty, than they had shown towards them when they had been superior in this country.

"But it is certain that the patriots, on acquiring the ascendency, made them feel it cruelly, and overwhelmed them with all those vexations of which there are so many examples in civil wars, between men of different parties. The governor, transported with rage, and touched by the piteous cries of the loyalists, panted to avenge them. This reciprocal hatred was daily exasperated by the rencontres which took place very frequently between the two parties; the provincials watching at all points of the shore to prevent the royal troops from landing, in order to forage in the country, and the latter, on the contrary, eagerly spying every means to plunder provisions upon the American territory. The multitude of mouths to be fed, kept them constantly in a famishing state. A ship of war arrived in the mean time, in the bay of Norfolk. Lord Dunmore sent a flag on shore to apprize the inhabitants that they must furnish provisions, and cease firing, otherwise he should bombard the town. The provincials answered only by a refusal. The governor then resolved to drive them out of the city with artillery, and to burn the houses situated upon the river. He sent in the morning to give notice of his design, in order that the women, children, and all except combatants might retreat to a place of safety."

On the first of January, 1776, "between three and four o'clock in the afternoon, a heavy cannonade from the frigate Liverpool, two sloops of war, and the ship Dunmore, opened against the town. Under cover of the guns, several parties of marines and sailors were landed, and set fire to the houses on the wharves. As the wind blew from the water, and the buildings were chiefly of wood, the flames rapidly spread. The efforts of the American commanders and their men to stop the progress and ravages of the fire, proved ineffectual. The conflagration raged for nearly three days, and consumed about nine-tenths of the town. Scarcely can even the strongest imagination picture to itself the distress of the wretched inhabitants, most of whom, friends or foes, saw their homes, their property, their all, an indiscriminate prey to the irrepressible fury of the flames. The horrors of the conflagration were heightened by the thunder of cannon from the ships, and musketry of the hostile parties that encountered each other in sharp conflict near the shore, and on the smoking ruins of the devoted town. In these encounters, the British were uniformly repulsed, and driven back to their boats with shame and loss. Of the Americans, by a singular good fortune, none were killed, and only 5 or 6 men wounded, one of whom mortally. Some women and children were, however, reported to have lost their lives. In this affair, the intrepid Stevens still added to his fame. At the head of his hardy, indefatigable, and irresistible band, he rushed with the rapidity of lightning to the water-side, struck a large party of British, who had just landed there, and compelled them to retire, with slaughter and in dismay, to the protection of their wooden walls. In general, during the whole of this afflicting scene, both officers and men evinced a spirit worthy of veterans.

"Such was the melancholy event which laid prostrate the most flourishing and richest town in the colony. Its happy site, combining all those natural advantages which invite and promote navigation and commerce, had been actively seconded by the industry and enterprise of the inhabitants. Before the existing troubles, an influx of wealth was rapidly pouring into its lap. In the two years from 1773 to 1775, the rents of the houses increased from 8,000 to 10,000l. a year. Its population exceeded 6,000 citizens, many of whom possessed affluent fortunes. The whole actual loss, on this lamentable occasion, has been computed at more than three hundred thousand pounds sterling; and the mass of distress attendant on the event is beyond all calculation."

After the conflagration of Norfolk, occasional skirmishes took place between the Virginians and the enemy, in which the latter suffered most severely. "On the 6th of February, Col. Robert Howe, who was now commander of the American troops, abandoned Norfolk, or rather, the site on which Norfolk had stood; for scarcely any vestige of that ill-fated town was now to be seen. After removing the inhabitants, the remaining edifices had been destroyed; and the mournful silence of gloomy depopulation now reigned where the gay, animating bustle of an active emulous crowd had so lately prevailed." Howe stationed his troops at Kemp's, at the Great Bridge, and Suffolk. To the latter place numbers of houseless and distressed fugitives from Norfolk had resorted; humanity and hospitality had thrown open her doors, and every building was crowded with these unfortunate wanderers.

The most energetic measures were resorted to by the committee of safety, to preclude the flotilla of Dunmore from obtaining supplies along the banks of those waters which their presence still infested. By these measures they were compelled to abandon their intrenchments, and after burning the barracks they had erected near the ruins of Norfolk, to seek a refuge on board their vessels, where much suffering awaited them. In the latter part of May they were seen manœuvring in Hampton Roads, and they finally landed and intrenched themselves at Gwyn's island. The signal defeat that awaited them there, is detailed under the head of Mathews county.

On the 9th of May, 1779, a British fleet from New York, conducted by Sir George Collier, anchored in Hampton Roads. The government of the state had erected Fort Nelson a short distance below Portsmouth, on the western bank of Elizabeth River, to secure Portsmouth, Norfolk, and the marine yard at Gosport, from insult. This work was garrisoned by about 150 men, under Major Thomas Matthews, who abandoned it and retreated to the Dismal Swamp. On the 11th, the British took possession of Portsmouth, and detached troops to Norfolk, Gosport, and Suffolk. At the two first they destroyed abundance of naval and military stores, and the last they burnt. They also destroyed, besides much public and private property, upwards of a hundred vessels. They remained but a short time, and then re-embarked for New York.

In October, 1780, Brig. Gen. Leslie, with about three thousand troops from New York, landed at Portsmouth, and took possession of vessels and other property on the coast. He soon left the shores of the state and sailed for Charleston, and shortly after joined Cornwallis. When Arnold invaded Virginia in January, 1781, the waters of Elizabeth River were again entered by the enemy. Portsmouth was for a time the head-quarters of the traitor. Cornwallis was also at Portsmouth just previous to taking post at Yorktown.

Portsmouth, the seat of justice for Norfolk county, is on the left bank of Elizabeth River, immediately opposite Norfolk, with which

there is a constant communication by a ferry, distant three quarters of a mile.   The town was established in February, 1752, on
the land of William Crawford.   Like Norfolk, and several of the
large towns of eastern Virginia, many of its early settlers were
Scotch and Irish, principally engaged in mercantile pursuits.   In
common with Norfolk, it possesses one of the best harbors in the

View in the Harbor of Portsmouth.

Union, in which vessels of war are generally lying at anchor, and
vessels of the largest size come to its wharves.   A short distance
below the town is the U. S. Naval Hospital, a large and showy
building—shown on the right of the above view—built of brick,
and stuccoed.   On the opposite side of the river stand the ruins
of Fort Norfolk; it is on or near the site of Fort Nelson, built in
the war of the revolution.

The U. S. Navy Yard is directly on the southern extremity of
Portsmouth, half a mile from the central part of the town, in that
portion of it called Gosport, where the general government has
built a large and costly dry dock, of the best materials and workmanship, capable of admitting the largest ships.   The construction of vessels at the navy-yard, at times employs as many as
1,400 men; and it is this source that proves one of the principal,
means of the support of the town.   The Portsmouth and Roanoke rail-road commences at this place, and with the connecting
rail-roads forms a communication with Charleston, S. C.   The
Virginia Literary, Scientific, and Military Academy, established
here in 1840, by Capt. Alden S. Partridge, numbers about forty
pupils.   Portsmouth contains a court-house, jail, 6 churches—1
Presbyterian, 1 Episcopal, 1 Catholic, 1 Baptist, 1 Methodist, and

1 do. for blacks—a branch of the Bank of Virginia, and a population of about 7,000. The town is beautifully laid off into squares, and its site is level. With Norfolk, it possesses an excellent fish-market. Shellfish, oysters, crabs, &c., abound. The Lynn Harbor oysters are highly esteemed by epicures.

Navy Yard, Gosport.

The village of Deep Creek is situated at the northern extremity of the Dismal Swamp canal, about 10 miles from Norfolk. It is a depôt of the canal, and contains about 30 dwellings. Its commercial business is principally confined to a trade in large juniper or white cedar shingles, and other lumber from the Dismal Swamp, which gives constant employment to several schooners, plying to the northern cities.

The celebrated swamp called the "*Dismal*," lies partly in Virginia and partly in North Carolina; it extends from north to south nearly 30 miles, and averages, from east to west, about 10 miles. Five navigable rivers and some creeks rise in it. The sources of all these streams are hidden in the swamp, and no traces of them appear above ground. From this it appears that there must be plentiful subterraneous fountains to supply these streams—or the soil must be filled perpetually with the water drained from the higher lands which surround it. The latter hypothesis is most probable, because the soil of the swamp is a complete quagmire, trembling under the feet, and filling immediately the impression of every step with water. It may be penetrated to a great distance by thrusting down a stick, and whenever a fire is kindled upon it, after the layer of leaves and rubbish is burned through, the coals sink down, and are extinguished.

The eastern skirts of the Dismal Swamp are overgrown with reeds, ten or twelve feet high, interlaced everywhere with thorny bamboo briers, which render it almost impossible to pass. Among these are found, here and there, a cypress, and white cedar, which last is commonly mistaken for the juniper. Towards the south there is a very large tract covered with reeds, without any trees, which being constantly green, and waving in the wind, is called the *green sea*. An evergreen shrub, called the gall-bush, grows plentifully throughout, but especially on the borders; it bears a berry which dyes a black color, like the gall of an oak—and hence its name.

51

Near the middle of the swamp, the trees grow much closer, both the cypress and cedar; and being always green, and loaded with large tops, are much exposed to the wind, and easily blown down in this boggy place, where the soil is too soft to afford sufficient hold to the roots. From these causes the passage is nearly always obstructed by trees, which lay piled in heaps, and riding upon each other; and the snags left in them pointing in every direction, render it very difficult to clamber over them.

On the western border of the Dismal Swamp is a pine swamp, above a mile in breadth, the greater part of which is covered to the depth of the knee with water: the bottom, however, is firm, and though the pines growing upon it are very large and tall, yet they are not easily blown down by the wind; so that this swamp may be passed without any hinderance, save that occasioned by the depth of the water. With all these disadvantages, the Dismal Swamp, though disagreeable to the other senses, is, in many places, pleasant to the eye, on account of the perpetual verdure, which makes every season like the spring, and every month like May.

"Immense quantities of shingles and other juniper lumber are obtained from the swamp, and furnish employment for many negroes, who reside in little huts in its recesses.

"Much of the lumber is brought out of the swamp, either through ditches cut for the purpose, in long narrow lighters, or are carted out by mules, on roads made of poles laid across the road so as to touch each other, forming a bridge or causeway. There are very many miles of such road. The laborers carry the shingles, &c., to these roads from the trees, on their heads and shoulders. The Dismal Swamp Canal runs through it from north to south, and the Portsmouth and Roanoke Rail-road passes for five miles across its northern part.

"It looks like a grand avenue, surrounded on either hand by magnificent forests. The trees here, the cypress, juniper, oak, pine, &c., are of enormous size, and richest foliage; and below is a thick entangled undergrowth of reeds, woodbine, grape-vines, mosses, and creepers, shooting and twisted spirally around, interlaced and complicated, so as almost to shut out the sun.

"The engineer who had constructed the road through this extraordinary swamp, found it so formidable a labor as almost to despair of success. In running the line, his feet were pierced by the sharp stumps of cut reeds; he was continually liable to sink ankle or knee deep into a soft muddy ooze; the yellow flies and moschetoes swarmed in myriads; and the swamp was inhabited by venomous serpents and beasts of prey.

"The Dismal Swamp was once a favorite hunting-ground of the Indians; arrow-heads, some knives, and hatchets, are yet found there; and it still abounds in deer, bears, wild turkeys, wild-cats, &c. The water of this swamp is generally impregnated with juniper, and is considered medicinal by the people of the surrounding country, who convey it some distance in barrels. This swamp is much more elevated than the surrounding country, and by means of the Dismal Swamp Canal, might be drained, and thus a vast body of most fertile soil reclaimed; and the canal might be transformed into a rail-road—and the juniper soil, which is vegetable, might, perhaps, be used as peat.

"LAKE DRUMMOND.—There is in the interior of the Dismal Swamp a body of water bearing this name, after the discoverer, who, says tradition, wandering in pursuit of game with two companions, was lost, and in his rambling came upon this lake. His comrades failed to thread their way out. Drummond returned, and gave an account of the sheet of water, which was accordingly called after him."

This lake is much visited by parties from Norfolk and the adjacent portions of North Carolina. There is here, exactly on the line of Virginia and North Carolina, a favorite public house, called "The Lake Drummond Hotel," which has become "the Gretna Green" of this region. The poet Moore, who was in this country in 1804, has made a superstition connected with this lake the subject of a well-known poetical effusion, which we here extract:

A BALLAD.

THE LAKE OF THE DISMAL SWAMP.

Written at Norfolk, in Virginia.

They tell of a young man who lost his mind upon the death of a girl he loved ; and who suddenly disappearing from his friends, was never afterwards heard of. As he frequently said in his ravings that the girl was not dead, but gone to the Dismal Swamp, it is supposed that he had wandered into that dreary wilderness, and had died of hunger, or been lost in some of its dreadful morasses.—*Anon.*

"La Poésie a ses monstres comme la nature."—*D'Alembert.*

"They made her a grave, too cold and damp
For a soul so warm and true ;
And she's gone to the lake of the Dismal Swamp,
Where, all night long, by a firefly lamp,
She paddles her white canoe.

"And her firefly lamp I soon shall see,
And her paddle I soon shall hear ;
Long and loving our life shall be,
And I'll hide the maid in a cypress tree,
When the footstep of death is near !"

Away to the Dismal Swamp he speeds—
His path was rugged and sore,
Through tangled juniper, beds of reeds,
Through many a fen, where the serpent feeds,
And man never trod before !

And when on the earth he sunk to sleep,
If slumber his eyelids knew,
He lay where the deadly vine doth weep
Its venomous tear, and nightly steep
The flesh with blistering dew !

And near him the she-wolf stirr'd the brake,
And the copper-snake breath'd in his ear,
Till he starting cried, from his dream awake,
"Oh ! when shall I see the dusky lake,
And the white canoe of my dear ?"

He saw the lake, and a meteor bright,
Quick over its surface play'd—
"Welcome !" he said ; "my dear one's light !"
And the dim shore echoed for many a night,
The name of the death-cold maid !

Till he hollowed a boat of the birchen bark,
Which carried him off from shore ;
Far he follow'd the meteor spark,
The wind was high and the clouds were dark,
And the boat return'd no more.

But oft from the Indian hunter's camp,
This lover and maid so true,
Are seen at the hour of midnight damp,
To cross the lake by a firefly lamp,
And paddle their white canoe !

On the 22d of June, 1813, a powerful British fleet made an attack on Craney Island, at the entrance to Elizabeth River. They were signally defeated. The event, as given below, is from Perkins' Late War :

Before the British could enter the harbor of Norfolk and approach the town, it was necessary to take possession of Craney Island. On the morning of the 22d, they were discovered passing round the point of Nansemond River, and landing on the main land in a position where the passage was fordable, with a view to pass over and attack the works on the west side of the island, while at the same time a number of barges from the fleet attempted to land in front. These were attacked before they reached the shore, from a battery on the beach, manned by the sailors and marines from the Constellation and the gun-boats. Three of the barges were sunk, most of the men drowned, and the rest compelled to retreat to their shipping. The party which landed at Nansemond, were met and repulsed by the Virginia militia, and driven back to their ships, with the loss, including those in the barges, of upwards of two hundred in killed and wounded. The city of Norfolk, and the neighboring villages of Gosport and Portsmouth, owed their safety to this gallant defence of Craney Island.

RICHARD DALE, a distinguished naval officer of the revolution, was born in this county in 1756. He early showed a predilection for the sea, and at the age of 12 made a voyage to Liverpool, and continued in the merchant service until the breaking out of the revolution. In 1776 he was appointed lieutenant of an armed ship, which belonged to the infant navy of Virginia. While cruising in one of the boats of this vessel in the James, he was captured by a British tender and confined on board of a British prison-ship at Norfolk. He was at this time scarce 20 years of age, and having passed his youth on the ocean, can scarcely be supposed to have been familiar with the great principles of the revolution. An old schoolmate, named Gutteridge, who commanded a British tender, prevailed upon him to make a cruise with him up the Rappahannock. In an engagement with a fleet of pilot-boats, he was wounded in the head by a musket-ball.

After his recovery he sailed for Bermuda, but the vessel he was in was captured by Commodore Barry; an explanation followed, and Dale, convinced of his error, re-entered the American service as a midshipman. Not long after he was again taken prisoner by the British, but was soon exchanged, and was appointed to the U. S. ship Lexington. This vessel being captured, Dale was the third time in the power of the enemy, who threw him and his companions into the Mill Prison at Plymouth. Dale escaped with a companion and travelled to London, when their progress was stopped by a press-gang. They were carried back to Mill Prison, and thrown into a noisome dungeon for forty days. Dale was then released and placed with the rest of the prisoners. He was again thrown into the Black Hole, for singing "rebellious songs." In 1779 this bold mariner escaped to France, and there making the acquaintance of the famous Capt. John Paul Jones, was appointed by him 1st lieutenant in the Bon Homme Richard. The fleet of Jones cruised in the North Sea, and spread terror along the western coast of Scotland. In the almost unparalleled and desperate action between the Bon Homme Richard and the Serapis, Lieut. Dale distinguished himself and received a wound. Dale next served under Captain Nicholson, on board the Trumbull, which was soon captured, and he found himself for the fifth time a prisoner. Being exchanged, he was appointed captain of an armed merchantman, and sailed in her to the close of the war. In 1794, he was one of the six captains appointed from the merchant service to the U. S. navy. In 1801 he commanded the Mediterranean squadron, which protected our commerce from the Barbary corsairs. Having returned to the United States in 1802, he was again appointed to the Mediterranean station, but under circumstances which he conceived injurious to his honor to accept. Commodore Dale, therefore, retired from the navy. The decline of his life was as peaceful as his youth had been stirring and adventurous, and he died in 1826, aged 70 years.

NORTHAMPTON.

Northampton was originally called Accawmacke, and was one of the original 8 shires into which Virginia was divided in 1634. In March, 1642–3, its name was changed to Northampton ; and in 1672 its limits were reduced by the formation of a new county, the present county of Accomac. Northampton is the southern extremity of the long low peninsula forming the eastern side of the Chesapeake, and comprehending eight counties in Maryland and two in Virginia. The shore has numerous small creeks, and numerous islands stretch along the Atlantic. Pop. in 1840, whites 3,341, slaves 3,620, free colored 754 ; total, 7,715.

Eastville, the county-seat, is 151 miles easterly from Richmond, in the centre of the county. It contains about 30 dwellings, and is a place of considerable business. Capeville, 6 miles N. of Cape Charles—the southern point of "the eastern shore"—contains a few houses.

The subjoined description of "the eastern shore" in general, and of this county in particular, was published several years since :

Separated as these counties are from the rest of the state by the spacious bay, which the eye can scarcely see across, and being among the first settled parts of the colony, they are a more unmixed people than is often to be found in our country, and retain more of the usages, and even language of former times, than perhaps any part of the state. The ancient hospitality of Virginia is here found unimpaired ; and the inhabitants have a high relish for good living, which they are also enabled to indulge by a soil and climate extremely favorable to gardening, and by an abundance of excellent fish, oysters, and crabs. They preserve great neatness in their houses and persons, which is a characteristic of persons living in a sandy country. The whole county is as level as a bowling-green, and the roads are good at all seasons of the year. This circumstance has probably increased the social character and habits of the people, as it certainly has their pleasure-carriages. The number of gigs in the county is near three hundred, which is considerably greater than that of the freeholders. It is computed that the county pays about $10,000 a year for its carriages.

The soil of this county is thin, light, and always more or less mixed with sand ; but as it commonly rests on a stiff clay, and the land is too level to be carried off by the rains, or "to wash," to use a term of the upper country, the inhabitants are very much encouraged to pursue an improving course of husbandry; yet in truth they are but indifferent farmers. They cultivate the same land incessantly, one year in Indian corn, and the next in oats, (their two principal crops,) and their lands improve under this severe process, provided they are not also pastured. Whenever a field is not in cultivation, it puts up everywhere a rich luxuriant crop of a sort of wild vetch, called the magotty-bay bean, which shades the land while it is growing, and returns to it a rich coat of vegetable manure. It is by means of this fertilizing plant, and the aliment which is plentifully furnished by the vapors from the sea, that the product of these lands is so much greater than a stranger would be led to expect from the appearance of the soil. The land is so easily cultivated that there are few parts of the state in which more is produced to the man, or the horse, though more may be produced to the acre. On the best farms, a hundred barrels to the hand are often obtained. The fig and the pomegranate flourish without protection during the winter. The former attains the size of a stout tree, sometimes twenty feet high, and its delicious fruit is in greater abundance than the inhabitants can consume. They have not yet learned the art of curing it; or perhaps the species they have is not suited to that operation.

Wind-mills are in use here, but tide-mills, at the mouth of small inlets, are preferred when attainable. These inlets deeply indent the shore, both on the "bay and sea-side," and while they are convenient for fishing, shooting wild-fowls, and as harbors for their boats and small craft, they give a pleasing variety to the landscapes, which are, indeed, as pretty as is compatible with so unvarying a surface. Upon the whole, we know of no part of the state in which the comforts of life are enjoyed in greater number, or higher perfection. They have, too, the sea and land breezes of the West Indies, which temper the sultry heats of summer; and their only annoyances seem to be a few moschetoes, a good many gnats, and now and then a bilious or intermittent fever. There is here an article of culture which is not much met with in other parts of the state—it is the palma christi, called castor bean. It now constitutes a part of almost every farmer's crop, to the extent of eight to ten acres or more. The quantity of the nut or bean produced, is the same as the land would produce in corn. Each bushel yields about two gallons and a half of oil, and sells, at the press, for $1 25 a bushel. This plant is now cultivated in many of the counties on the western shore, and the oil it affords has become a considerable article of export, being preferred to that of the West Indies.

Among the curiosities of this county are the ancient records of the county from 1640, and a marble tomb, or sarcophagus, about five feet high, and as many long, from which we transcribe the following singular inscription:

Under this marble tomb lies the body
of the Hon. John Custis, Esq.,
of the City of Williamsburg,
and Parish of Burton.
Formerly of Hungar's parish, on the
Eastern Shore
of Virginia and county of Northampton,
Aged 71 years, and yet lived but seven years,
which was the space of time he kept
A Bachelor's home at Arlington,
on the Eastern Shore of Virginia.

On the opposite side one reads—

This inscription put on this tomb was by
his own positive orders.

Wm. Cosley Man, in Fenchurch-street,
fecit, London.*

The Hon. ABEL PARKER UPSHUR was the son of Littleton Upshur, and was born in this county, June 17th, 1790. "He received his classical education at Yale and Princeton colleges, and studied law under the instruction of his friend, the late Hon. Wm. Wirt, at Richmond, where he practised his profession from 1810 until 1824, when he removed to Vancluse, his patrimonial residence in this county. In the courts of the eastern shore, he continued the practice of his profession until Dec. 15th, 1826, when he was appointed by the legislature to fill the vacancy on the bench of the general court, caused by the death of his maternal uncle, the late Judge George Parker. He had previously represented his native county in the state legislature. On the 5th of Oct., 1829, he was

---

* Alden, in his "Collection of Epitaphs," published in 1814, says the Hon. John Custis, a gentleman of great opulence, died about 1750, and that this monument was erected and inscribed agreeably to the directions in his will. G. W. P. Custis, Esq., of Arlington, D. C., is one of his descendants.—H. H.

elected a member of the general convention of Virginia. ¡He published a pamphlet containing a review of Judge Story's work on the constitution of the United States, and contributed many articles to the newspapers on the topics of the day. On the reorganization of the judicial system of Virginia, under the new constitution, he was reappointed, April 18, 1831, to a seat on the bench of the general court, and was assigned to the third judicial circuit. This office he continued to fill until the 13th of Sept., 1841, when he was appointed by President Tyler, secretary of the navy. On the 24th of July, 1843, he was transferred, under the same administration, to the office of secretary of state, which he held until the time of his death, Feb. 28th, 1844, which was occasioned by the accident on board the U. S. steamer Princeton."

The Southern Literary Messenger says, that the ancestors of Mr. Upshur settled upon the eastern shore more than two centuries since. His family is one of the oldest in Virginia, and has been remarkable for staid habits and sterling worth. Generation after generation they remained upon the eastern shore, cultivating the soil, and ornamenting society. From the same source we learn that Mr. Upshur was considered one of the most graceful and accomplished orators. His style was unexceptionably good, his arguments forcible, and set forth in sentences remarkable for terse and vigorous language. His speech in the Virginia convention of '29 and '30, is said to have been one of the ablest and best delivered during the sitting. He never took a leading position in politics until called to the presidential cabinet. Mr. Upshur was an able writer, and one of the most polished contributors to the periodical literature of the country.

NORTHUMBERLAND.

NORTHUMBERLAND was formed in 1648. Its length is 30, mean width 12 miles. It is situated in the east part of the state, on Chesapeake Bay, and has the mouth of the Potomac River on its northeast boundary. It is drained by several small streams flowing into the Potomac and Wicomico Rivers, which empty into Chesapeake Bay. Beside the ordinary products of this portion of the state, about 50,000 pounds of sugar are annually produced. Pop., whites 4,034, slaves 3,243, free colored 647 ; total, 7,924.

Northumberland C. H., or Heathsville, is 98 miles NE. of Richmond. It is a handsome village, situated near the head of Coan River, a navigable stream emptying into the Potomac. It contains a Methodist church, several mercantile and mechanical establishments, and about 60 dwellings.

NOTTOWAY.

NOTTOWAY was formed in 1788, from Amelia, and named from the Nottoway tribe of Indians, from whom, also, the river running on its southern boundary received its name. It is drained by tributaries of the Appomattox and the Nottoway. Its length is 22, breadth 12 miles. Over two million pounds of tobacco are annually produced in this county. Pop. in 1840, whites 2,490, slaves 7,071, free colored 158 ; total, 9,719.

Nottoway C. H., on the Little Nottoway, in the central part of the county, 67 miles sw. of Richmond, contains 15 or 20 dwellings. It was at Col. V. ~···.'s, in the northern part of this county, that the celebrated Peter Francisco had a battle with hine of Tarleton's cavalry in 1781; for an account of which see Buckingham.

OHIO.

OHIO was formed in 1776, from the district of West Augusta: it is 14 miles long, with a mean width of 10 miles. It is bounded westerly by the Ohio River, into which empty several creeks of the county. The surface is much broken, but the soil, especially on the water-courses, is very fertile. Over one million bushels of bituminous coal are annually mined in the county. Pop. in 1840, whites 12,842, slaves 212, free colored 303; total, 13,357.

West Liberty is situated 12 miles NE. of Wheeling, and 5 from the Ohio River. It was established in Oct., 1787, and Moses Chaplaine, Zachariah Sprigg, George M'Cullock, Charles Wills, Van Swearingan, James Mitchell, and Benjamin Briggs, gentlemen, were appointed trustees for laying out the town, at which place the county buildings had been erected. It remained the county-seat until Brooke county was formed, in 1797, when the courts were removed to Wheeling.

Wheeling City, the seat of justice for the county, is situated upon an alluvial area on the Ohio River, on both sides of Wheeling creek, 351 miles from Richmond, 264 from Washington city, 56 miles from Pittsburg, and 31 from Washington, Pa. The city is surrounded by bold hills, containing inexhaustible quantities of bituminous coal, from which the numerous manufactories of the town are supplied at a trifling expense. It is furnished with water from the Ohio by water-works. It contains a handsome court-house, a jail, county offices, 2 academies, 2 banks and a savings' institution, a fire and marine insurance company, and 1 Episcopal, 1 Methodist, 1 Baptist, 1 Unionist, 1 German Methodist, 1 Lutheran, and 2 Presbyterian churches, a Friends' meeting-house, and religious societies belonging to the Reformed Baptists or Disciples, Swedenborgians, and Reformed Methodists; 97 stores, 7 commission and forwarding houses, 4 iron foundries, 4 steam-engine factories, 8 glass-houses, in several of which cut-glass is manufactured, 4 woollen and cotton factories, with carding machines, 2 paper-mills, 4 saw-mills, 3 white and sheet-lead and copperas factories, 2 daily, 1 weekly, and 1 semi-monthly newspapers, together with many flouring mills in it and vicinity, and mechanical and manufacturing establishments of a lesser note.

A beautiful and substantial stone bridge crosses Wheeling creek. The city contains about 1000 dwellings; over twenty steamboats are owned here, and all which navigate this portion of the Ohio stop at its wharves. The national road passes through Wheeling, which is one of the greatest thoroughfares in the Union. Zane's island lies on the Ohio, opposite the city, and is crossed by the national road. Wheeling is the largest town in western Virginia.

Bridge over Wheeling Creek

In 1810 its population was 914; in 1820, 1,567; 1830, 5,221; 1840, 7,885. From the advantages of its location, &c., Wheeling must eventually be a place of great business. The vast multitude of emigrants constantly passing through it to the far west, increase its trade, and impart to it an air of bustle and business peculiarly animating.

In 1769, (says Withers,) Col. Ebenezer Zane, his brothers Silas and Jonathan, with some others from the south branch of the Potomac, visited the Ohio for the purpose of making improvements, and severally proceeded to select positions for their future residence. They chose for their residence the site now occupied by the city of Wheeling,* and having made the requisite preparations returned to their former homes, and brought out their families the ensuing year. The Zanes were men of enterprise, tempered with prudence, and directed by sound judgment. To the bravery and good conduct of these three brothers, the Wheeling settlement was mainly indebted for its security and preservation during the war of the revolution. Soon after the settlement of this place, other settlements were made at different points, both above and below Wheeling, and the country on Buffalo, Short, and Grave creeks.

---

* " A very intelligent merchant of this city describes, that in very early time, and doubtless much anterior to that mentioned above, a circumstance took place which presents the strongest probability of the first notice of this spot by a white man, and the best data demonstrative of the circumstance from which the name of Wheeling was conferred upon this city. A European gentleman in the capacity of a Catholic priest, direct from Europe, of the name of *Wheelan*, which was his orthography of the name, who on a missionary excursion through the United States, among the aborigines of this country, on descending the Ohio River, pitched his encampment at the mouth of the present well-known Wheeling creek, in order for the discharge of his missionary duties there, among the red men of the forest. After a few months stay, he proceeded down the river, and left a name behind him, which will distinguish this celebrated spot till time shall be no longer. The founders of the city changed its orthography, since which it is written Wheeling."—*Bowen's Directory of Wheeling for 1839.*

It is stated in a communication to the American Pioneer by Mr. Jno. White, that Wheeling was originally called *Weeling*, which signifies the *place of a head*. The following tradition, explanatory of this, was obtained from Mr. John Brittle, who was taken prisoner by the Delawares, lived with them five years, and acquired their language. "In the earliest period of the settlement of Pennsylvania, some white settlers descended the Ohio River in a boat, and stopping at the mouth of Wheeling creek, were killed by the Delawares. The savages cut off the head of one of their victims, and placing it on a pole, with the face towards the river, called the spot *Weeling*. The Indians informed Mr. Brittle that the head was placed there to guard the river; I presume, to guard the camp from the incursions of the whites. Mr. Brittle said, that if an Indian were asked, after shooting a deer or a bear, where he had hit the animal, he answer—if in the head—would be, ' *weeling*.' "

WHEELING.

The view shows Wheeling as it appears from an eminence on the Ohio side of the river, about a mile and a half below the central part of the town. Wheeling Island is seen on the left, and above it, on the hills in the distance, the National Road.

A traveller in this region in 1802, thus describes Wheeling as it was then :—

Wheeling, situated on one of the high banks of the Ohio, was not in existence 12 years ago. At present it contains about 70 houses, built of planks, which, as in all the rising towns of the United States, are separated by an interval of several toises. This little town is confined by a long hill, from a hundred and eighty to two hundred toises in height, the base of which is not further from the river than two hundred toises. In this interval the houses are built; they form only one street, having one road in the middle. * * * Here are 12 or 15 well-provided stores, from which the inhabitants for 20 miles round are supplied. This small town also participates in the exportation trade carried on between Pittsburg and the western country. Several of the traders of Philadelphia prefer sending their merchandise here, although it is a day's journey further ; but this slight inconvenience is amply compensated by the advantage they derive, in avoiding the long circuit made by the Ohio on quitting Pittsburg, in which the very numerous shallows and the want of rapidity in the current during the summer, retard the navigation.

At Wheeling we lodged with Capt. Reymer, who keeps a tavern at the sign of the Wagon, and takes boarders for two piasters [$2] a week. The living is very good at his house for this money, for provisions are not dear here. Twelve fowls are sold for a piaster, [$1,] and a quintal [100 weight] of flour was not worth more than a piaster and a half.

The most important event in the history of Wheeling, was the siege of *Fort Henry*, at the mouth of Wheeling creek, in September, 1777. The bravery and perseverance of the little band who defended it against more than thirty times their number of savages, led on by the notorious Simon Girty, was such as to rank it among the most memorable events of border warfare. An account of this siege we abridge from the communication of Mr. George S. M. Kiernan, in the American Pioneer :—

Fort Henry stood immediately on the left bank of the Ohio, about a quarter of a mile above Wheeling creek. It is said to have been planned by Gen. George Rogers Clarke, and was constructed under the superintendence of Ebenezer Zane and John Caldwell. It was originally called Fort Fincastle, and was a place of refuge for the settlers in Dunmore's war. The name was afterwards changed to Fort Henry, in honor of Patrick Henry. The fort was built on open ground, and covered a space of about three-quarters of an acre. It was a parallelogram, having a block-house at each corner, with lines of stout pickets, about eight feet high, extending from one block-house to another. Within the enclosure were a storehouse, barrack-rooms, garrison-well, and a number of cabins for the use of families. The principal entrance was through a gateway on the eastern side of the fort, next to the then straggling village of Wheeling, consisting of about 25 log-houses.

The savages, variously estimated at from 380 to 500 warriors, having been abundantly supplied with arms and provisions by the British governor, Hamilton, at Detroit, and led on by Girty, were brought before the walls of Fort Henry before Col. Shepherd, the commandant, knew of their real design. Some symptoms of their propinquity having been discovered, the settlers in the vicinity had, the night previous, sought shelter within the fort.

The garrison numbered only 42 fighting men, all told, counting those advanced in years as well as those who were mere boys. A portion of them were skilled in Indian warfare, and all were excellent marksmen. The storehouse was amply supplied with muskets, but was sadly deficient in ammunition.

The next morning Col. Shepherd dispatched a man, accompanied by a negro, on an errand a short distance from the fort. The white man was brought to the ground by a blow from the firelock of an Indian ; but the negro escaped back into the fort, and gave intelligence that they had been waylaid by a party of Indians in a cornfield.

As soon as the negro related his story, the colonel dispatched Captain Samuel Mason, with fourteen men, to dislodge the Indians from the field. Captain Mason with his party marched through the field, and arrived almost on the bank of the creek without finding the Indians, and had already commenced a retrograde movement when he was suddenly and furiously assailed in front, flank, and rear, by the whole of Girty's army. The captain rallied his men from the confusion produced by this unexpected demonstration of the enemy, and instantly comprehending the situation in which he was placed, gallantly took the lead, and hewed a passage through the savage phalanx that opposed him. In this desperate conflict more than half the little band were slain, and their leader severely wounded. Intent on retreating back to the fort, Mason pressed rapidly on with the remnant of his command, the Indians following closely in pursuit. One by one these devoted soldiers fell at the crack of the enemy's rifle. An Indian who eagerly pursued Captain Mason, at length overtook him; and to make sure his prey, fired at him from the distance of five paces; but the shot, although it took effect, did not disable the captain, who immediately turned about, and hurling his gun at the head of his pursuer, felled him to the earth. The fearlessness with which this act was performed caused an involuntary dispersion of the gang of Indians who led the pursuit; and Mason, whose extreme exhaustion of physical powers prevented him from reaching the fort, was fortunate enough to hide himself in a pile of fallen timber, where he was compelled to remain to the end of the siege. Only two of his men survived the skirmish, and they, like their leader, owed their safety to the heaps of logs and brush that abounded in the cornfield.

As soon as the critical situation of Captain Mason became known at the fort, Captain Ogle, with twelve volunteers from the garrison, sallied forth to cover his retreat. This noble, self-devoted band, in their eagerness to press forward to the relief of their suffering fellow-soldiers, fell into an ambuscade, and two-thirds of their number were slain upon the spot. Sergeant Jacob Ogle, though mortally wounded, managed to escape with two soldiers into the woods, while Captain Ogle escaped in another direction, and found a place of concealment, which, like his brother officer, Captain Mason, he was obliged to keep as long as the siege continued. Immediately after the departure of Captain Ogle's command, three new volunteers left the garrison to overtake and reinforce him. These men, however, did not reach the cornfield until after the bloody scenes had been enacted, and barely found time to return to the fort before the Indian host appeared before it. The enemy advanced in two ranks, in open order, their left flank reaching to the river bank, and their right extending into the woods as far as the eye could reach. As the three volunteers were about to enter the gate, a few random shots were fired at them, and instantly a loud whoop arose on the enemy's left flank, which passed as if by concert, along the line to the extreme right, until the welkin was filled with a chorus of the most wild and startling character. This salute was responded to by a few well-directed rifle-shots from the lower block-houses, which produced a manifest confusion in the ranks of the besiegers. They discontinued their shouting and retired a few paces, probably to await the coming up of their right flank, which, it would seem, had been directed to make a general sweep of the bottom, and then approach the stockade on the eastern side.

At this moment the garrison of Fort Henry numbered no more than twelve men and boys. The fortunes of the day, so far, had been fearfully against them; two of their best officers and more than two-thirds of their original force were missing. The exact fate of their comrades was unknown to them, but they had every reason to apprehend that they had been cut to pieces. Still they were not dismayed; their mothers, sisters, wives, and children, were assembled around them; they had a sacred charge to protect, and they resolved to fight to the last extremity, and confidently trusted in Heaven for the successful issue of the combat.

When the enemy's right flank came up, Girty changed his order of attack. Parties of Indians were placed in such of the village houses as commanded a view of the block-houses; a strong body occupied the yard of Ebenezer Zane, about fifty yards from the fort, using a paling-fence as a cover, while the greater part were posted under cover in the edge of the cornfield, to act offensively or serve as a corps of reserve, as occasion might require. These dispositions having been made, Girty, with a white flag in his hand, appeared at the window of a cabin, and demanded the surrender of the garrison in the name of his Britannic majesty. He read the proclamation of Governor Hamilton, and promised them protection if they would lay down their arms and swear allegiance to the British crown. He warned them to submit peaceably, and admitted his inability to restrain the passions of his warriors when they once became excited with the strife of battle. Colonel Shepherd promptly told him in reply, that the garrison would never surrender to *him*, and that he could only obtain possession of the fort when there remained no longer an American soldier to defend it. Girty renewed his proposition, but before he finished his harangue, a thoughtless youth in one of the block-houses fired a gun at the speaker, and brought the conference to an abrupt termination. Girty disappeared, and in about fifteen minutes the Indians opened the siege by a general dis. charge of rifles.

It was yet quite early in the morning, the sun not having appeared above the summit of Wheeling hill, and the day is represented to have been one of surpassing beauty. The Indians, not entirely concealed from the view of the garrison, kept up a brisk fire for the space of six hours without much intermission. The little garrison, in spite of its heterogeneous character, was, with scarcely an exception, composed of sharp-shooters. Several of them, whose experience in Indian warfare gave them a remarkable degree of coolness and self-possession in the face of danger, infused confidence into the young; and, as they never fired at random, their bullets, in most cases, took effect. The Indians, on the contrary, gloated with their previous success, their tomahawks reeking with the blood of Mason's and Ogle's men, and all of them burning with impatience to rush into the fort and complete their work of butchery, discharged their guns against the pickets, the gate, the logs of the block-houses, and every other object that seemed to shelter a white man. Their fire was thus thrown away. At length some of their most daring warriors rushed up close to the block-houses, and attempted to make more sure work by firing through the logs; but these reckless savages received, from the well-directed rifles of the frontiersmen, the fearful reward of their temerity. About one o'clock the Indians discontinued their fire, and fell back against the base of the hill.

The stock of gunpowder in the fort having been nearly exhausted, it was determined to seize the favorable opportunity offered by the suspension of hostilities, to send for a keg of powder which was known to be in the house of Ebenezer Zane, about 60 yards from the gate of the fort. The person executing this service would necessarily expose himself to the danger of being shot down by the Indians, who were yet sufficiently near to observe every thing that transpired about the works. The colonel explained the matter to his men, and, unwilling to order one of them to undertake such a desperate enterprise, inquired whether any man would volunteer for the service. Three or four young men promptly stepped forward in obedience to the call. The colonel informed them that the weak state of the garrison would not justify the absence of more than one man, and that it was for themselves to decide who that person should be. The eagerness felt by each volunteer to undertake the honorable mission, prevented them from making the arrangement proposed by the commandant; and so much time was consumed in the contention between them, that fears began to arise that the Indians would renew the attack before the powder could be procured. At this crisis, a young lady, the sister of Ebenezer and Silas Zane, came forward and desired that she might be permitted to execute the service. This proposition seemed so extravagant that it met with a peremptory refusal; but she instantly renewed her petition in terms of redoubled earnestness, and all the remonstrances of the colonel and her relatives failed to dissuade her from her heroic purpose. It was finally represented to her that either of the young men, on account of his superior fleetness and familiarity with scenes of danger, would be more likely than herself to do the work successfully. She replied, that the danger which would attend the enterprise was the identical reason that induced her to offer her services, for, as the garrison was very weak, no soldier's life should be placed in needless jeopardy, and that if she were to fall her loss would not be felt. Her petition was ultimately granted, and the gate opened for her to pass out. The opening of the gate arrested the attention of several Indians who were straggling through the village. It was noticed that their eyes were upon her as she crossed the open space to reach her brother's house; but seized, perhaps, with a sudden freak of clemency, or believing that a woman's life was not worth a load of gunpowder, or influenced by some other unexplained motive, they permitted her to pass without molestation. When she reappeared with the powder in her arms, the Indians, suspecting, no doubt, the character of her burden, elevated their firelocks and discharged a volley at her as she swiftly glided towards the gate; but the balls all flew wide of the mark, and the fearless girl reached the fort in safety with her prize. The pages of history may furnish a parallel to the noble exploit of Elizabeth Zane, but an instance of greater self-devotion and moral intrepidity is not to be found anywhere.*

About half past 2 o'clock, the Indians put themselves again in motion, and advanced to renew the siege. As in the first attack, a portion of their warriors took possession of the cabins contiguous to the fort, while others availed themselves of the cover afforded by Zane's paling-fence. A large number posted themselves in and behind a blacksmith-

* This heroine (says Withers) had but recently returned from Philadelphia, where she had received her education, and was totally unused to such scenes as were daily exhibited on the frontier. She married twice, and is, or was a few years since, living in Ohio with her husband, a Mr. Clarke.

shop and stable that stood opposite the northern line of pickets; and another party, probably the strongest of all, stationed themselves under cover of a worm-fence and several large piles of fallen timber on the south side of the fort. The siege was now re-opened from the latter quarter—a strong gang of Indians advancing under cover of some large stumps that stood on the side of the declivity below the fort, and renewing the combat with loud yells and a brisk fire. The impetuosity of the attack on the south side brought the whole garrison to the two lower block-houses, from which they were enabled to pour out a destructive fire upon the enemy in that quarter. While the garrison was thus employed, a party of 18 or 20 Indians, armed with rails and billets of wood, rushed out of Zane's yard and made an attempt to force open the gate of the fort. Their design was discovered in time to defeat it; but they only abandoned it after five or six of their number had been shot down. Upon the failure of this scheme, the Indians opened a fire upon the fort from all sides, except from that next to the river, which afforded no shelter to a besieging host. On the north and the east the battle raged most fiercely; for, notwithstanding the strength of the assailants on the south, the unfavorableness of the ground prevented them from prosecuting with much vigor the attack which they had commenced with such fury.

The rifles used by the garrison, towards evening became so much heated by continued firing, that they were rendered measurably useless; and recourse was then had to muskets, a full supply of which was found in the storehouse. As darkness set in, the fire of the savages grew weaker, though it was not entirely discontinued until next morning. Shortly after nightfall, a considerable party of Indians advanced within 60 yards of the fort, bringing with them a hollow maple log, which they had converted into a field-piece, by plugging up one of its ends with a block of wood. To give it additional strength, a quantity of chains, taken from the blacksmith-shop, encompassed it from one end to the other. It was heavily charged with powder, and then filled to the muzzle with pieces of stone, slugs of iron, and such other hard substances as could be found. The cannon was graduated carefully to discharge its contents against the gate of the fort. When the match was applied it burst into many fragments; and although it made no effect upon the fort, it killed and wounded several of the Indians who stood by to witness its discharge. A loud yell succeeded the failure of this experiment, and the crowd dispersed. By this time the Indians generally had withdrawn from the siege, and fallen back against the hill to take rest and food. Numbers of stragglers, however, lurked about the village all night, keeping up an irregular fire on the fort, and destroying whatever articles of furniture and household comfort they chanced to find in the cabins.

Late in the evening, Francis Duke, a son-in-law of Col. Shepherd, arrived from the Forks of Wheeling, and was shot down by the Indians before he could reach the gate of the fort. About 4 o'clock next morning, (September 28th,) Col. Swearingen, with 14 men, arrived in a periogue from Cross creek, and was fortunate enough to fight his way into the fort without the loss of a man.

About daybreak, Major Samuel McColloch, with 40 mounted men from Short creek, came to the relief of the little garrison. The gate was thrown open, and McColloch's men, though closely beset by the Indians, entered in safety; but McColloch himself was not permitted to pass the gateway: the Indians crowded around him and separated him from his party. After several ineffectual attempts to force his way to the gate, he wheeled about and galloped with the swiftness of a deer in the direction of Wheeling hill.

The Indians might easily have killed him. But they cherished towards him an almost phrensied hatred; for he had participated in so many encounters that almost every warrior personally knew him. To take him alive, and glut their full revenge by the most fiendish tortures, was their object; and they made almost superhuman exertions to capture him. He put spurs to his horse, but soon became completely hemmed in on three sides, and the fourth was an almost perpendicular precipice of 150 feet descent, with Wheeling creek at its base. Supporting his rifle in his left hand, and carefully adjusting his reins with the other, he urged his horse to the brink of the bluff, and then made the leap which decided his fate. In the next moment the noble steed, still bearing his intrepid rider in safety, was at the foot of the precipice. McColloch immediately dashed across the creek, and was soon beyond the reach of the Indians.

After the escape of Major McColloch, the Indians concentrated at the foot of the hill, and soon after set fire to all the houses and fences outside the fort, and killed about 300 head of cattle belonging to the settlers. They then raised the siege, and took up their line of march to some other theatre of action.

During the investiture, not a man within the fort was killed, and only one wounded, and that wound was a slight one. But the loss sustained by the whites during the enemy's inroad was remarkably severe. Of the 42 men who were in the fort on the morning of the 27th, no less than 23 were killed in the cornfield before the siege commenced. The two men who had been sent down the river the previous night in a canoe, were intercepted by the Indians and killed also ; and, if we include Mr. Duke in the list, the loss sustained by the settlement amounted to 26 killed, besides four or five wounded. The enemy's loss was from 60 to 100. Agreeably to their ancient custom, they removed their dead from the field before the siege was raised ; the extent of their loss is therefore merely conjectural.

The defence of Fort Henry, when we consider the extreme weakness of the garrison and the forty-fold superiority of the besieging host, was admirably conducted. Foremost on the list of these brave frontier soldiers was Col. Shepherd, the commandant of the fort, whose good conduct on this occasion gained for him the appointment of county-lieutenant from Gov. Patrick Henry. The brothers Silas and Ebenezer Zane, and John Caldwell, men of influence in the community, and the first settlers at Wheeling, are spoken of as having contributed much to the success of the battle. Besides the names already mentioned, those of Abraham Rogers, John Linn, Joseph Biggs, and Robert Lemmon must not be omitted, as they were among the best Indian-fighters on the frontier, and aided much in achieving the victory of the day. The lady of Ebenezer Zane, together with several other females in the fort, undismayed by the sanguinary strife that was going on, employed themselves in running bullets and preparing patches for the use of the men ; and, by their presence at every point where they could make themselves useful, and by their cheering words of encouragement, infused new life into the soldiers, and spurred them on in the performance of their duty. The noble act of Elizabeth Zane, which has already been related, inspired the men with an enthusiasm which contributed not a little to turn the fortunes of the day. The affair at Fort Henry was emphatically one of the battles of the revolution. The northwestern Indians were as much the mercenary troops of Great Britain as were the Hessians and the Waldeckers, who fought at Bennington, Saratoga, and in New Jersey. If the price received by the Indians for the scalps of American citizens did not always amount to the daily pay of the European minions of England, it was, nevertheless, sufficient to prove that the American savages and the German hirelings were precisely on the same footing as part and parcel of the British army.

A full description of the many feats of bravery displayed by the early settlers of western Virginia in their wars with the Indians, would fill volumes. The preceding account of the siege of Fort Henry, shows how much was effected by a combination of a few individuals against a vastly superior force of savages ; the following extracts from Doddridge, show how much was accomplished by the bravery, skill, and activity of single individuals—some of whom were mere children—in the desperate warfare carried on against the Indians on the western frontier :

Lewis Wetzel.—Lewis Wetzel was the son of John Wetzel, a German, who settled on Big Wheeling, about fourteen miles from the river. He was among the first adventurers into that part of the country. His education, like that of his cotemporaries, was that of the hunter and warrior. When a boy, he adopted the practice of loading and firing his rifle as he ran. This was a means of making him so destructive to the Indians afterwards.

When about thirteen years old, he was taken prisoner by the Indians, together with his brother Jacob, about eleven years old. Before he was taken he received a slight wound in the breast from a bullet, which carried off a small piece of his breast-bone. The second night after they were taken, the Indians encamped at the Big Lick, twenty miles from the river, on the waters of M'Mahan's creek. The boys were not confined. After the Indians had fallen asleep, Lewis whispered to his brother Jacob that he must get up and go back home with him. Jacob at first objected, but afterwards got up and went along with him. When they had got about one hundred yards from the camp, they sat down on a log. "Well," said Lewis, "we can't go home barefooted ; I will go back and get a pair of moccasins for each of us ;" and accordingly did so, and returned. After sitting a little longer, "Now," says he, "I will go back and get father's gun, and then we'll start." This he effected. They had not travelled far on the trail by which they came, before they heard the Indians coming after them. It was a moonlight night. When the Indians came pretty nigh them, they stepped aside into the bushes, let them pass, then fell into their rear, and travelled on. On the return of the Indians they did the same. They were then pursued by two Indians on horseback, whom they dodged in the same way. The next day they reached Wheeling in safety, crossing from the Indian shore to Wheeling island on a raft of their own making. By this time Lewis had become almost spent from his wound.

In the year 1782, after Crawford's defeat, Lewis went with a Thomas Mills, who had been in the campaign, to get his horse, which he had left near the place where St. Clairsville now stands. At the Indian springs, two miles from St. Clairsville, on the Wheeling road, they were met by about forty Indians, who were in pursuit of the stragglers from the campaign. The Indians and white men discovered each other about the same moment. Lewis fired first and killed an Indian, while the Indians wounded Mills in the heel, who was soon overtaken and killed. Four of the Indians then singled out, dropped their guns, and pursued Wetzel. Wetzel loaded his rifle as he ran. After running about half a mile, one of the Indians having got within eight or ten steps of him, Wetzel wheeled round and shot him down, ran, and loaded his gun as before. After going about three quarters of a mile further, a second Indian came so close to him, that when he turned to fire, the Indian caught the muzzle of the gun, and, as he expressed it, " he and the Indian had a severe wring." He however succeeded in bringing the muzzle to the Indian's breast, and killed him on the spot. By this time, he as well as the Indians were pretty well tired; yet the pursuit was continued by the two remaining Indians. Wetzel, as before, loaded his gun, and stopped several times during this latter chase: when he did so, the Indians treed themselves. After going something more than a mile, Wetzel took advantage of a little open piece of ground over which the Indians were passing, a short distance behind him, to make a sudden stop for the purpose of shooting the foremost, who got behind a little sapling which was too small to cover his body. Wetzel shot, and broke his thigh. The wound in the issue proved fatal. The last of the Indians then gave a little yell, and said, " No catch dat man, gun always loaded," and gave up the chase, glad no doubt to get off with his life.

It is said that Lewis Wetzel, in the course of the Indian wars in this part of the country, killed twenty-seven Indians, besides a number more along the frontier settlements of Kentucky.

Adam Poe.—In the summer of 1782, a party of seven Wyandots made an incursion into a settlement some distance below Fort Pitt, and several miles from the Ohio River. Here finding an old man alone in a cabin, they killed him, packed up what plunder they could find, and commenced their retreat. Amongst their party was a celebrated Wyandot chief, who, in addition to his fame as a warrior and counsellor, was, as to his size and strength, a real giant.

The news of the visit of the Indians soon spread through the neighborhood, and a party of eight good riflemen was collected in a few hours for the purpose of pursuing the Indians. In this party were two brothers of the names of Adam and Andrew Poe. They were both famous for courage, size, and activity. This little party commenced the pursuit of the Indians with a determination, if possible, not to suffer them to escape, as they usually did on such occasions, by making a speedy flight to the river, crossing it, and then dividing into small parties, to meet at a distant point in a given time. The pursuit was continued the greater part of the night after the Indians had done the mischief. In the morning the party found themselves on the trail of the Indians, which led to the river. When arrived within a little distance of the river, Adam Poe, fearing an ambuscade, left the party, who followed directly on the trail, to creep along the brink of the river bank, under cover of the weeds and bushes, to fall on the rear of the Indians, should he find them in ambuscade. He had not gone far before he saw the Indian rafts at the water's edge. Not seeing any Indians, he stepped softly down the bank, with his rifle cocked. When about half way down, he discovered the large Wyandot chief and a small Indian, within a few steps of him. They were standing with their guns cocked, and looking in the direction of our party, who by this time had gone some distance lower down the bottom. Poe took aim at the large chief, but his rifle missed fire. The Indians hearing the snap of the gun-lock, instantly turned round and discovered Poe, who being too near them to retreat, dropped his gun, and sprang from the bank upon them, and seizing the large Indian by the clothes on his breast, and at the same time embracing the neck of the small one, threw them both down on the ground, himself being uppermost. The small Indian soon extricated himself, ran to the raft, got his tomahawk, and attempted to dispatch Poe, the large Indian holding him fast in his arms with all his might, the better to enable his fellow to effect his purpose. Poe, however, so well watched the motions of his assailant, that, when in the act of aiming his blow at his head, by a vigorous and well-directed kick with one of his feet, he staggered the savage, and knocked the tomahawk out of his hand. This failure, on the part of the small Indian, was reproved by an exclamation of contempt from the large one.

In a moment the Indian caught up his tomahawk again, approached more cautiously, brandishing his tomahawk, and making a number of feigned blows in defiance and derision. Poe, however, still on his guard, averted the real blow from his head, by throwing up his arm and receiving it on his wrist, in which he was severely wounded ; but not so as to lose entirely the use of his hand. In this perilous moment, Poe, by a violent effort, broke loose from the Indian, snatched up one of the Indians' guns, and shot the small Indian through the breast, as he ran up a third time to tomahawk him. The large Indian was now on his feet, and grasping Poe by a shoulder and leg, threw him down on the bank. Poe instantly disengaged himself, and got on his feet. The Indian then seized him again, and a new struggle ensued, which, owing to the slippery state of the bank, ended in the fall of both combatants into the water. In this situation, it was the object of each to drown the other. Their efforts to effect their purpose were continued for some time with alternate success, sometimes one being under the water and sometimes the other. Poe at length seized the tuft of hair on the scalp of the Indian, with which he held his head under water, until he supposed him drowned. Relaxing his hold too soon, Poe instantly found his gigantic antagonist on his feet again, and ready for another combat. In this they were carried into the water beyond their depth. In this situation they were compelled to loose their hold on each other, and swim for mutual safety. Both sought the shore, to seize a gun and end the contest with bullets. The Indian, being the best swimmer, reached the land first. Poe seeing this, immediately turned back into the water, to escape, if possible, being shot, by diving. Fortunately, the Indian caught up the rifle with which Poe had killed the other warrior. At this juncture, Andrew Poe, missing his brother from the party, and supposing from the report of the gun which he shot, that he was either killed or engaged in conflict with the Indians, hastened to the spot. On seeing him, Adam called out to him to "kill the big Indian on shore." But Andrew's gun, like that of the Indian's, was empty. The contest was now between the white and the Indian, who should load and fire first. Very fortunately for Poe, the Indian in loading drew the ramrod from the thimbles of the stock of the gun with so much violence that it slipped out of his hand, and fell a little distance from him. He quickly caught it up, and rammed down his bullet. This little delay gave Poe the advantage. He shot the Indian as he was raising his gun to take aim at him.

As soon as Andrew had shot the Indian, he jumped into the river to assist his wounded brother to shore ; but Adam, thinking more of the honor of carrying the scalp of the big Indian home as a trophy of victory than of his own safety, urged Andrew to go back, and prevent the struggling savage from rolling himself into the river and escaping. Andrew's solicitude for the life of his brother prevented him from complying with this request. In the mean time, the Indian, jealous of the honor of his scalp even in the agonies of death, succeeded in reaching the river and getting into the current, so that his body was never obtained. An unfortunate occurrence took place during this conflict. Just as Andrew arrived at the top of the bank for the relief of his brother, one of the party who had followed close behind him, seeing Adam in the river, and mistaking him for a wounded Indian, shot at him, and wounded him in the shoulder. He however recovered from his wounds. During the contest between Adam Poe and the Indians, the party had overtaken the remaining six of them. A desperate conflict ensued, in which five of the Indians were killed. Our loss was three men killed, and Adam Poe severely wounded. Thus ended this Spartan conflict, with the loss of three valiant men on our part, and with that of the whole Indian party excepting one warrior. Never on any occasion was there a greater display of desperate bravery, and seldom did a conflict take place, which, in the issue, proved fatal to so great a proportion of those engaged in it.

The fatal result of this little campaign, on the side of the Indians, occasioned a universal mourning among the Wyandot nation. The big Indian and his four brothers, all of whom were killed at the same place, were among the most distinguished chiefs and warriors of their nation.

The big Indian was magnanimous as well as brave. He, more than any other individual, contributed, by his example and influence, to the good character of the Wyandots for lenity towards their prisoners. He would not suffer them to be killed or ill-treated. This mercy to captives was an honorable distinction in the character of the Wyandots, and was well understood by our first settlers, who, in case of captivity, thought it a fortunate circumstance to fall into their hands.

The Johnsons.—In the fall of the year 1793, two boys of the name of John and Henry Johnson, the first thirteen and the latter eleven years old, whose parents lived in Carpenter's station, a little distance above the mouth of Short creek, on the east side of the Ohio River, were sent out in the evening to hunt the cows. At the foot of a hill, at the back of the bottom, they sat down under a hickory tree to crack some nuts. They soon saw two men coming towards them, one of whom had a bridle in his hand. Being dressed like white men, they mistook them for their father and an uncle, in search of horses. When they discovered their mistake, and attempted to run off, the Indians, pointing their guns at them, told them to stop or they would kill them. They halted, and were taken prisoners.

The Indians, being in pursuit of horses, conducted the boys by a circuitous route over the Short creek hills in search of them, until late in the evening, when they halted at a spring in a hollow place, about three miles from the fort. Here they kindled a small fire, cooked and ate some victuals, and prepared to repose for the night. Henry, the youngest of the boys, during the ramble had affected the greatest satisfaction at having been taken prisoner. He said his father was a hard master, who kept him always at hard work, and allowed him no play; but that for his part he wished to live in the woods and be a hunter. This deportment soon brought him into intimacy with one of the Indians, who could speak very good English. The Indians frequently asked the boys if they knew of any good horses running in the woods. Some time before they halted, one of the Indians gave the largest of the boys a little bag, which he supposed contained money, and made him carry it.

When night came on the fire was covered up, the boys pinioned, and made to lie down together. The Indians then placed their hoppis straps over them, and lay down, one on each side of them, on the ends of the straps. Pretty late in the night the Indians fell asleep; and one of them becoming cold, caught hold of John in his arms, and turned him over on the outside. In this situation, the boy, who had kept awake, found means to get his hands loose. He then whispered to his brother, made him get up, and untied his arms. This done, Henry thought of nothing but running off as fast as possible; but when about to start, John caught hold of him, saying, "We must kill these Indians before we go." After some hesitation, Henry agreed to make the attempt. John then took one of the rifles of the Indians, and placed it on a log, with the muzzle close to the head of one of them. He then cocked the gun, and placed his little brother at the breech, with his finger on the trigger, with instructions to pull it as soon as he should strike the other Indian.

He then took one of the Indian's tomahawks, and standing astride of the other Indian, struck him with it. The blow, however, fell on the back of the neck and to one side, so as not to be fatal. The Indian then attempted to spring up; but the little fellow repeated his blows with such force and rapidity on the skull, that, as he expressed it, "the Indian lay still and began to quiver." At the moment of the first stroke given by the elder brother with the tomahawk, the younger one pulled the trigger, and shot away a considerable portion of the Indian's lower jaw. This Indian, a moment after receiving the shot, began to flounce about and yell in the most frightful manner. The boys then made the best of their way to the fort, and reached it a little before daybreak. On getting near the fort they found the people all up and in great agitation on their account. On hearing a woman exclaim, "Poor little fellows, they are killed or taken prisoners!" the oldest one answered, "No, mother, we are here yet."

Having brought nothing away with them from the Indian camp, their relation of what had taken place between them and the Indians was not fully credited. A small party was soon made up to go and ascertain the truth or falsehood of their report. This party the boys conducted to the spot by the shortest route. On arriving at the place, they found the Indian whom the oldest brother had tomahawked, lying dead in the camp: the other had crawled away, and taken his gun and shot-pouch with him. After scalping the Indian, the party returned to the fort; and the same day a larger party went out to look after the wounded Indian, who had crawled some distance from the camp and concealed himself in the top of a fallen tree, where, notwithstanding the severity of his wound, with a Spartan bravery he determined to sell his life as dearly as possible. Having fixed his gun for the purpose, on the approach of the men to a proper distance, he took aim at one of them, and pulled the trigger, but his gun missed fire. On hearing the snap of the lock, one of the men exclaimed, "I should not like to be killed by a dead Indian!" The party concluding that the Indian would, die at any rate, thought best to retreat, and return and look for him after some time. On returning, however, he could not be found, having crawled away and concealed himself in some other place. His skeleton and gun were found some time afterwards.

The Indians who were killed were great warriors, and very wealthy. The bag, which was supposed to contain money, it was conjectured was got by one of the party who went out first in the morning. On hearing the report of the boys, he slipped off by himself, and reached the place before the party arrived. For some time afterwards he appeared to have a greater plenty of money than his neighbors.

The Indians themselves did honor to the bravery of these two boys. After their treaty with Gen. Wayne, a friend of the Indians who were killed, made inquiry of a man from Short creek, what had become of the boys who killed the Indians? He was answered that they lived at the same place with their parents. The Indian replied, "You have not done right; you should make kings of those boys."

ORANGE.

ORANGE was formed in 1734, from Spottsylvania, and derived its name from the color of the soil in its upper or mountainous portion. Its original limits comprised the whole of Virginia west of the Blue Ridge. It is now 22 m. long, with a variable width of from 5 to 20

The Church of the " Blind Preacher."

miles. The Rapid Ann forms its NW. boundary. The surface is hilly, and the soil generally fertile. Gold is found in the county, and in 1840 the value produced amounted to $84,000. Pop. in 1840, whites 3,575, slaves 5,364, free colored 186; total, 9,125.

Orange C. H., is 80 miles NW. of Richmond, and 92 miles from Washington City. It contains 5 mercantile stores, 1 Episcopal and 1 Methodist church, and a population of about 350. Barboursville, 12 miles SW., and Gordonsville, 10 miles S. of the C. H., are small places. The latter is the terminating point of the Louisa rail-road, and about 70 miles from Richmond.

Near the little village of Gordonsville, in the depths of the forest, stands an old church. It is an humble unpainted structure of

53

wood, yet there clings about it a peculiar interest—an interest which all must feel who have read—and who has not?—the pathetic description of the Blind Preacher by the British Spy:

It was one Sunday, (says he,) as I travelled through the county of Orange, that my eye was caught by a cluster of horses tied near a ruinous old wooden house in the forest, not far from the roadside. Having frequently seen such objects before, in travelling through these states, I had no difficulty in understanding that this was a place of religious worship.

Devotion alone should have stopped me, to join in the duties of the congregation; but I must confess that curiosity to hear the preacher of such a wilderness was not the least of my motives. On entering, I was struck with his preternatural appearance. He was a tall and very spare old man. His head, which was covered with a white linen cap, his shrivelled hands, and his voice, were all shaking under the influence of a palsy; and a few moments ascertained to me that he was perfectly blind.

The first emotions which touched my breast were those of mingled pity and veneration. But ah! sacred God! how soon were all my feelings changed! The lips of Plato were never more worthy of a prognostic swarm of bees, than were the lips of this holy man! It was a day of the administration of the sacrament; and his subject, of course, was the passion of our Saviour. I had heard the subject handled a thousand times. I had thought it exhausted long ago. Little did I suppose, that in the wild woods of America I was to meet with a man whose eloquence would give to this topic a new and more sublime pathos than I had ever before witnessed.

As he descended from the pulpit to distribute the mystic symbols, there was a peculiar, a more than human solemnity in his air and manner, which made my blood run cold, and my whole frame shiver.

He then drew a picture of the sufferings of our Saviour; his trial before Pilate; his ascent up Calvary; his crucifixion, and his death. I knew the whole history; but never, until then, had I heard the circumstances so selected, so arranged, so colored! It was all new, and I seemed to have heard it for the first time in my life. His enunciation was so deliberate that his voice trembled on every syllable, and every heart in the assembly trembled in unison. His peculiar phrases had that force of description that the original scene appeared to be, at that moment, acting before our eyes. We saw the very faces of the Jews: the staring, frightful distortions of malice and rage. We saw the buffet; my soul kindled with a flame of indignation, and my hands were involuntarily and convulsively clenched.

But when he came to touch on the patience, the forgiving meekness of our Saviour; when he drew, to the life, his blessed eyes streaming in tears to heaven; his voice breathing to God a soft and gentle prayer of pardon on his enemies, "Father, forgive them, for they know not what they do"—the voice of the preacher, which had all along faltered, grew fainter and fainter, until his utterance being entirely obstructed by the force of his feelings, he raised his handkerchief to his eyes, and burst into a loud and irrepressible flood of grief. The effect is inconceivable. The whole house resounded with the mingled groans, and sobs, and shrieks of the congregation.

It was some time before the tumult had subsided so far as to permit him to proceed. Indeed, judging by the usual, but fallacious standard of my own weakness, I began to be very uneasy for the situation of the preacher. For I could not conceive how he would be able to let his audience down from the height to which he had wound them, without impairing the solemnity and dignity of his subject, or perhaps shocking them by the abruptness of the fall. But—no; the descent was as beautiful and sublime as the elevation had been rapid and enthusiastic.

The first sentence, with which he broke the awful silence, was a quotation from Rousseau, "Socrates died like a philosopher, but Jesus Christ like a God!"

I despair of giving you any idea of the effect produced by this short sentence, unless you could perfectly conceive the whole manner of the man, as well as the peculiar crisis in the discourse. Never before did I completely understand what Demosthenes meant by laying such stress on *delivery*. You are to bring before you the venerable figure of the preacher; his blindness constantly recalling to your recollection old Homer, Ossian, and Milton, and associating with his performance the melancholy grandeur of their geniuses. You are to imagine that you hear his slow, solemn, well-accented enunciation, and his voice of affecting, trembling melody; you are to remember the pitch of passion and enthusiasm to which the congregation were raised; and then the few minutes of portentous, death-like silence, which reigned throughout the house; the preacher removing his white handkerchief from his aged face, (even lyet wet from the recent torrent of his tears,) and slowly stretching forth the palsied hand which holds it, begins the sentence, "Socrates died like a philosopher"—then pausing, raising his other hand, pressing them both clasped together with warmth and energy to his breast, lifting his "sightless balls" to heaven, and pouring his whole soul into his tremulous voice—"but Jesus Christ—like a God!" If he had been indeed and in truth an angel of light, the effect could scarcely have been more divine.

Whatever I had been able to conceive of the sublimity of Massillon, or the force of Bourdaloue, had fallen far short of the power which I felt from the delivery of this simple sentence. The blood, which just before had rushed in a hurricane upon my brain, and, in the violence and agony of my feelings, had held my whole system in suspense, now ran back into my heart with a sensation which I cannot describe—a kind of shuddering delicious horror! The paroxysm of blended pity and indignation to which I had been transported, subsided into the deepest self-abasement, humility, and adoration. I had just been lacerated and dissolved by sympathy for our Saviour as a fellow-creature; but now, with fear and trembling, I adored him as—"a God!"

If this description give you the impression that this incomparable minister had any thing of shallow, theatrical trick in his manner, it does him great injustice. I have never seen, in any other orator, such a union of simplicity and majesty. He has not a gesture, an attitude, or an accent, to which he does not seem forced by the sentiment which he is expressing. His mind is too serious, too earnest, too solicitous, and, at the same time, too dignified, to stoop to artifice. Although as far removed from ostentation as a man can be, yet it is clear from the train, the style, and substance of his thoughts, that he is not only a very polite scholar, but a man of extensive and profound erudition. I was forcibly struck with a short, yet beautiful character which he drew of our learned and amiable countryman, Sir Robert Boyle. He spoke of him as if "his noble mind had, even before death, divested herself of all influence from his frail tabernacle of flesh;" and called him, in his peculiarly emphatic and impressive manner, "a pure intelligence: the link between men and angels."

This man has been before my imagination almost ever since. A thousand times, as I rode along, I dropped the reins of my bridle, stretched forth my hand, and tried to imitate his quotation from Rousseau; a thousand times I abandoned the attempt in despair, and felt persuaded that his peculiar manner and power arose from an energy of soul which nature could give, but which no human being could justly copy. In short, he seems to be altogether a being of a former age, or of a totally different nature from the rest of men. As I recall, at this moment, several of his awfully striking attitudes, the chilling tide, with which my blood begins to pour along my arteries, reminds me of the emotions produced by the first sight of Gray's introductory picture of his bard:

> " On a rock, whose haughty brow,
> Frowns o'er old Conway's foaming flood,
> Robed in the sable garb of wo,
> With haggard eyes the poet stood;
> (Loose his beard and hoary hair
> Streamed, like a meteor, to the troubled air:)
> And with a poet's hand and prophet's fire,
> Struck the deep sorrows of his lyre."

Guess my surprise, when, on my arrival at Richmond, and mentioning the name of this man, I found not one person who had ever before heard of *James Waddel!!*

*   *   *   *   *   *

The above description of the blind preacher has been admired by thousands, and many have supposed it to be fiction. Although years have elapsed since it was written, it is only within a few months that a laudable curiosity has been gratified, to know the history of one whose eloquence drew forth such high encomiums from the accomplished author of the British Spy. This has been done in the memoir of Mr. Waddel, published recently in the Watchman of the South, by James W. Alexander, D. D., late professor in the college at Princeton, and grandson of the blind preacher. From this memoir the following sketch is principally derived:—

James Waddel, D. D., was born in the north of Ireland in 1739, and was brought by his parents, in his infancy, to America. They settled in the southeastern part of Pennsylvania, near the state line, on White Clay creek. To the advice of an excellent and pious mother, Mr. Waddel ascribed his first religious convictions. She was a woman of eminent Christian knowledge and piety, and brought with her to this country the methods of ancient Scottish Presbyterianism. When about 13 years of age, he was sent to and educated at the academy of the celebrated Dr. Finley, at Nottingham, Pennsylvania, where he studied the classics, mathematics, logic, and those branches indispensable for the learned callings. Such was his proficiency, that his distinguished preceptor soon employed him as an assistant. He was afterwards an assistant teacher in another noted Presbyterian school, at Pequea, in Lancaster co., under the elder Smith. After passing a year or more in that seminary, in pursuance of a long-cherished plan—as it is thought, to devote himself to teaching—he set forth on his travels for the south, and finally reached Hanover county, in Virginia. There he made the acquaintance of Col. Henry, the father of Patrick Henry, and the celebrated Samuel Davies. The meeting with Mr. Davies gave a direction to young Waddel's life. We next find him in Louisa, where he assisted the Rev. Mr. Todd in his school, and devoted his leisure to the study of theology. He was licensed as a Probationer, April 2d, 1761, by the (old) Presbytery of Hanover, and in the following year, 1762, accepted a call to the churches of Lancaster and Northumberland. There he found so much hospitality, intelligence, and polish, among those old Virginia gentry, that he would cheerfully have passed his life among them, but for the ill effects of the climate. There was then a brisk trade with Great Britain from the mouths of the rivers, and much genuine piety among the merchants and planters of that region. Mr. Waddel's labors were not slight, as he had three preaching places, viz.: Lancaster C. H., the Forest meeting-house, and the Northumberland meeting-house. About the year 1768, he married Mary Gordon, the daughter of Col. James Gordon, ancestor of Gen. Gordon of Albemarle. The Presbyterian churches of the Northern Neck owed much to the zeal of Col. G., who was an elder in the church, and after his death they visibly declined, and were finally pretty much absorbed in the Baptists. This was in part owing to their estates being open to the ravages of the British vessels, who, carrying off their property, led to the decline of the wealthy Presbyterian families.

About the year 1775, Mr. Waddel removed to the Tinkling Spring church, in Augusta. Although almost broken down by disease, his frame attenuated, and his voice impaired, yet he drew crowds of hearers.

In 1783 he accepted a call, and gave his services to the united congregations of Staunton and Tinkling Spring. He remained in Augusta about seven years, during which his health was entirely renovated. His salary was only £45 per annum, Virginia money.

From thence, Mr. Waddel made a last earthly removal to an estate which he named Hopewell, near the angle of Louisa, Orange, and Albemarle. While here he preached at the " D. S." church, near Charlottesville, at a log-house in Clarkesville, at the Brick church near Orange C. H., and in the small edifice erected by himself, represented in the preceding view. He also again became a teacher. Among his pupils were Meriwether Clark and Governor Barbour.

Although secluded from the literary world, he found means to become thoroughly versed in theology, as well as general literature. Mr. Waddel resided in Louisa about 20 years. There he ended his days, Sept. 17th, 1805, and, according to his request, was buried in his garden. His last hours were such as might have been expected, from a life of eminent piety and singular self-control.

In person Dr. Waddel was tall and erect, and when a young man he is said to have been of striking appearance. His complexion was fair, and his eyes of a light blue ; his mien unusually dignified, and his manners elegant and graceful. His eloquence has become matter of tradition in Virginia. It electrified whole assemblies, transfused to them the speaker's passion at his will ; " a species," says his biographer, " I must be allowed to say, which I have seldom heard but in the south." Under his preaching, audiences were irresistibly and simultaneously moved, like the wind-shaken forest. Especially was his power great in so painting sacred scenes, as to bring the hearer into the very presence of the object. Even his ordinary private intercourse was an uncommon treat to intellectual persons, and occasioned the first men of his time to seek his company. When in scornful argument he was like the sweeping torrent, carrying every thing before it.

It was in 1803, when Mr. Waddel was approaching the end of his life, that Mr. Wirt, under the incognito of a British officer, wrote his celebrated description. It has often been questioned how far the accomplished author gave himself the license of fiction in his sketch. It may, therefore, be observed, that Dr. Waddel was well known in Virginia, his pulpit costume was different from that described, and that the British Spy, instead of being a transient stranger, was well acquainted with Dr. W. and his family. Says Prof. Alexander, " Mr. Wirt stated to me, that so far from adding colors to the picture of Dr. Waddel's eloquence, he had fallen below the truth. He did not hesitate to say that he had reason to believe, that in a different species of oratory he was fully equal to Patrick Henry. He added, that in regard to the place, time, costume, and lesser particulars, he had used an allowable liberty, grouping together events which had occurred apart, and, perhaps, imagining as in a sermon, observations which had been uttered by the fireside." Patrick Henry was accustomed to say, that Waddel and Davies were the greatest orators he ever heard. The elocution of those men was not that taught by masters, or that practised before the mirrors of colleges. A venerable clergyman said, " When other men preach, one looks to see who is affected ; when Dr. Waddel preached, those *not* affected were the exception. Whole congregations were affected." Gov. Barbour declared, that Dr. W. surpassed all orators he ever knew.

Dr. Waddel on some occasions employed his singular faculty in the revolution, in patriotic services, and once addressed Tate's company, at Midway, Rockbridge county, previous to their marching to the south. When the British Spy appeared, the old gentleman was unfeignedly grieved at the laudatory notice of himself, and in reply to a complimentary letter which he received, he dictated the words, *Haud merita laus, opprobrium est*—[*Unmerited praise is a reproach.*]

His independence and zeal brought him into collision with the established church ; and he was one time fined for occupying a parish church. In the latter part of his life he was afflicted with blindness. After several years his sight was partially restored by the operation of couching.

A most touching account of Dr. Waddel's restoration to sight has lately been published in the Literary Messenger. From it we derive the following : For eight years he had been blind, a stranger equally to the cheerful light of day and the cheering faces of kindred and friends. In the lapse of time great changes had taken place. The infant had left the knee to rove among the fields—the youth had started into manhood, and gone forth in the busy scenes of life, without a hope that the eyes of his venerable father would ever rest upon him. Like the evening cloud of summer, a calm and holy resignation settled over the mind of this man of God ; but the dark curtain which hung over the organs of sight seemed destined to rise no more.

After an operation for cataract, which, in the progress of some years, had rendered light sensible, and then objects faintly visible—a well-constructed convex lens, sent by a distant friend, enabled him in a moment to see with considerable distinctness. The scene which followed in his family around was most moving. The father could again see his children, who riveted his attention and absorbed his soul. Among these emotions of intense interest and varied suggestion were visible in the eye, countenance, and hurried movements. The bursts of laughter—the running to and fro—the clapping of hands—the sending for absent friends—and then the silent tear bedewing the cheek in touching interlude—the eager gaze of old servants, and the unmeaning wonder of young ones—in short, the happy confusion and joy was such a scene as a master's pencil might have been proud to sketch. The paroxysm produced by the first application of the glasses having passed away ; behold ! the patriarch in his large arm-chair, with his children around him, scanning with affectionate curiosity the bashful group. There was a visible shyness among the lesser members of the family while undergoing this fatherly scrutiny, not unlike that produced by a long absence. The fondness of a father in contemplating those most dear to him was never more rationally exemplified, or exquisitely enjoyed. And now the venerable old man arose from his seat, and grasped a long staff, which seemed powerfully but momentarily to engage his attention—it had been the companion of his darkest days, the pioneer of his domestic travels, and the supporter of a weak and tottering frame—he then proceeded to the front door to take a view of the mountains, the beautiful southwest range, stretching out in lovely prospect at the distance of about three miles. All followed ; and the mountain-scene, though viewed a thousand times before, was now gazed upon with deeper interest, and presented a greater variety of beauties than ever.

About four miles from Orange C. H., on a slight eminence, is Montpelier, which was the seat of James Madison, President of

the United States from 1809 to 1817.   It is a large brick building.
Its interior is furnished with plain, but rich furniture, and orna-

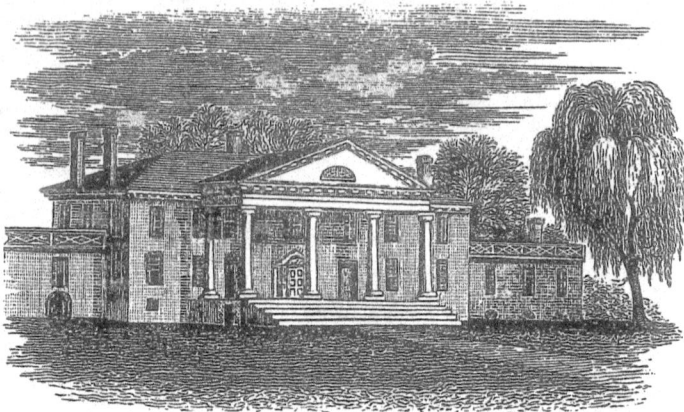

Montpelier, the seat of President Madison.

mented with busts, pictures, &c.   There is an extensive lawn in
the rear of the mansion, beyond which is a large and elegant garden, containing a great variety of both native and exotic plants.
Mr. Madison died at Montpelier, on the 28th of June, 1836, at the
advanced age of eighty-seven, deeply lamented as a national loss.
The following sketch, from the New York Mirror, is by one who
knew him well, and passed many pleasant hours in his society :

Great occasions produce great men.
The records of our own country bear testimony to this truth.   In the early and
in the later ages of her struggles, there
were not wanting men to advise and to
act for a nation's welfare.   Among those who have acted a conspicuous part in building
up our political and civil institutions for more than sixty years, was JAMES MADISON,
who has lately sunk to rest, full of years and honors.
   Mr. Madison was by birth a Virginian, and wholly educated in this country.   He
was intended for a statesman from his youth, and made himself master of constitutional
law, when it was hardly known as a science either in England or in this country.   He
was born on the sixteenth of March, 1751, and, of course, was in all the ardor and
freshness of youth on the breaking out of the revolution.   In 1775, Mr. Madison was
a member of the legislature of Virginia, and at that early age, was distinguished for his
maturity of understanding and sage prudence.   He was soon appointed one of the council of the state.   During the whole eventful struggle, James Madison had the confidence
of the state of Virginia ; and, as a member of her legislature, was listened to with profound attention when he brought forward sundry resolutions for the formation of a general government for the United States, based upon the inefficiency of the old confederation.   From these resolutions grew a convention of delegates from the several states,
who, in conclave, prepared a form of a constitution to be submitted to the several states
for their discussion, approbation, and adoption.   Mr. Madison was a member of this convention, as a delegate from Virginia, and took an active part in the deliberations of that
enlightened body, of which Washington, his colleague, was president.   On the adoption
of this constitution—a wonderful era in the history of the liberties of man—Mr. Madison was elected a member of the first Congress, and took an active part in setting the
machinery in motion.   At this period public opinion was greatly agitated by the crude

and false opinions scattered through the country, through the medium of the opposition presses ; this was grievous to the friends of the constitution, and three mighty minds, Jay, Hamilton, and Madison, formed a holy alliance to enlighten the people upon the great doctrines of the constitution, and breaking through the host of the Philistines, drew the pure waters of truth for the good of the people. The essays from the pens of these worthies, were collected in a volume, called the Federalist, which now stands a monument of the wisdom and patriotism of that age. In the debates of the first Congress, Mr. Madison took a large share. It was an illustrious assemblage of patriots, among whom there often arose a difference of opinion in regard to political policy, but all were lovers of their country, and laboring for her best interests. Here Mr. Madison acted with the Cabots and the Ames' of the east, in perfect harmony. It was reserved for an after age to feel the withering effects of party feuds. These were hardly discovered as long as the father of his country filled the presidential chair. In the administration of his successor, a separation into parties took place, and Mr. Madison ranked himself on the side of Mr. Jefferson and his party. During the presidency of Mr. Jefferson, Mr. Madison was secretary of state, and sustained that office with singular ability. He held a ready pen, had a clear, philosophical perception of the great principles on which the government professed to act, and could readily produce a defence of the course pursued. No secretary ever did, or ever will do more by force of argument, than Mr. Madison, while supporting the measures of Mr. Jefferson.

In March, 1809, Mr. Madison became President of the United States. It was a stormy period. France and England, in their fierce struggles for mastery, forgot the rights of neutral nations, and outraged our independence. Insult followed insult from both countries, for the three first years of his administration ; but he was, from the very elements of his nature, inclined to peace, and had not urged preparations for war. In 1812, war was declared, without preparation, and the executive of the United States had a difficult task to perform. A powerful part of the people were opposed to the war, some for one reason, and some for another, and it required no small degree of moral courage, to steer the ship of state at such a crisis. Mr. Madison was not a military chieftain, and took no pleasure in the glories of a victory, no further than they were beneficial to the interests of his country ; but his moral courage was of the highest order, that which arises from a consciousness of an intention of doing good. There can be no doubt but that so sagacious a statesman as Mr. Madison, saw some of the blessings that were to flow to his country from the evils of war. He knew that nations, at times, hold incorrect opinions, and that the rude shocks of war are the only remedies for these errors. The war had its dark and bright spots on the tablets of fame, but its results were altogether fortunate. The necessity of a navy for national honor and protection, anchored itself into the firm bosom of every patriot, with such a hold as to ride out every billow and whirlwind of faction. By this war we taught that no nation could ever claim to be independent, whose resources were confined to agriculture and commerce alone. By this war we became a manufacturing people to a respectable extent ; but there was as much opposition to this as there was to the war. This goes to show, that it is beyond human reason to foresee what may be best; but all will agree that there should always be wisdom and honesty at the head of our people, to make the most judicious use of every event.

In 1817, when the reign of peace was established, Mr. Madison retired to his farm to enjoy the serenity of rural life ; but here he has not been idle. On the death of Mr. Jefferson, he was made chancellor of the University of Virginia, and, as well as his predecessor, took a deep interest in the prosperity of the institution. When Virginia called a convention to alter her constitution, Mr. Madison, with Chief-Justice Marshall and Mr. Monroe, were found among the sages who had witnessed the birth of that constitution, and were well acquainted with its excellences and defects, and were good judges of the best forms of amendment. Several years ago, a bookseller at Washington got up an edition of the debates in the several conventions called by the states in 1787 and 1788, to deliberate on the adoption of the constitution of the United States. Mr. Madison took a lively interest in this publication, and afforded the editor all the information that he possessed upon the subject.

Mr. Madison was unquestionably the leading member in the Virginia convention, called for the adoption of the constitution of the United States, although there were several distinguished men among them. This body was fortunate enough to have employed a reporter of eminence for the occasion, which was not the case in many other states ; and what the Virginia reporter did not put down in his notes, Mr. Madison's minutes and recollections most readily supplied.

In the convention he had to meet the blaze of Patrick Henry's eloquence, the subtle arguments of Mason, and the chilling doubts of Monroe ; but all were overcome by the clearness of his views, and the force of his reasonings. Mr. Madison was not an orator in the common acceptation of the word ; there were no deep tones in his voice ; no flashes of a fierce and commanding eye ; no elegant gestures to attract the beholder ; all was calm, dignified, and convincing. It was the still, small voice, in which the ora-cles of God were communicated to the prophet. He never talked for the love of display, but simply to communicate his thoughts. He spoke often in debate, when earnest in his cause, but was always heard with profound attention ; not a word of his speeches was lost. He was so perfectly master of his subject, that he had nothing to correct in a retrospective view of it, and was so well understood that he had nothing to explain. His voice was deficient in volume, but it was so well modulated, that its compass was more extensive than that of many speakers of stronger lungs. His conversation was truly a charm. He was familiar with most topics, and he loved both to communicate and receive information. He lived in times when men grew up with strong prejudices and partialities ; but his most familiar guests seldom heard a sentence tinged with them, either at his table or fireside. For nearly twenty years he had been daily preparing for the change of worlds, and at last sunk into the arms of death in as peaceful a sleep as a babe on the bosom of his mother. Nature and religion had cured him of all fears of the grave ; he had no dread of what " dreams might come when he had shuffled off this mortal coil." He had no enmities to settle, for he had quarrelled with no one ; he had no slanders to forgive, for no one ever traduced him. His history contains, indeed, a miracle, for there has not been one of mortal, or of immortal birth, who has acted a con-spicuous part on this earth, but James Madison, whose private reputation has not been assailed.

The late Gov. James Barbour, and the late Judge Philip Pendle-ton Barbour, the sons of Col. Thomas Barbour, were born at the family seat near Montpelier.

JAMES BARBOUR " held the highest trusts in Virginia, as speaker of the House of Delegates, governor of the state, and senator in Congress. Under the general govern-ment he sustained with ability the offices of secretary of war and minister to Great Britain. His political career was a distinguished one, and his character in life secured the esteem of all who knew him. He died June 8th, 1842, aged sixty-six."

PHILIP PENDLETON BARBOUR " was distinguished for his talents, and was indebted to his professional and political eloquence for his success in life. He was a member of Con-gress from 1814 to 1825 ; in 1821 he was elected speaker of the House of Representatives ; in 1825 he was appointed a judge of the Virginia court ; in 1827 he became again a mem-ber of Congress, and served three sessions. In 1836 he was appointed by President Jackson an associate judge of the supreme court of the United States. He died sud-denly, February 25th, 1841, at Washington city, of ossification of the heart, aged about sixty."

PAGE.

PAGE county was formed in 1831, from Rockingham and Shenan-doah, and named from John Page, governor of Virginia from 1802 to 1805. The county is 34 miles long, with a mean width of 11 miles, and consists of one entire valley, with the Shenandoah running its whole length through it, from N. to S., and the Blue Ridge lying on the east, and the Fort or Massanuttin mountain on the west. These mountains ever present a beautiful and pictu-resque appearance, whether viewed robed in the snow, ice, and clouds of winter, the refreshing green of summer, or the gorgeous hues of autumn. The soil of Page is generally of the best quality of limestone valley land; a very considerable portion is bottom, lying on the Shenandoah River, and Hawksbill, and other creeks. The mineral wealth of the county is great; iron abounds, and copper, lead, magnesia, and beautiful marble, are found in many places. Population in 1840, whites 5,195, slaves 781, free colored 216; total, 6,194.

Luray, the county-seat, is 130 miles NW. from Richmond, and 96 from Washington. It is situated on the Hawksbill creek, near the centre of the county. The first house was built here in 1814. It now contains several mercantile stores, 2 or 3 churches, and a population of about 500. About one mile west of the town of Luray, is a cave which is but little inferior in extent, beauty, and magnificence, to Weyer's cave. Its entrance is at the top of a small mountain called Cave Hill, and not being very accessible, is not much visited. The most splendid apartments in it are Congress and Masonic Halls. From a published description of the cave by those who first explored it, we extract the following, relative to these beautiful rooms:

Congress Hall.—After descending, as we supposed, about a quarter of a mile, the passage became very straight and smooth, and gradually enlarged until we perceived that we stood in front of a room whose dimensions, from the light of our candles, we could not discover. The entrance here, as in the room which we first entered, was ten or fifteen feet above the level of the floor. After a few moments, however, by clinging to the projections of spar, which here appeared like large icicles, the whole party stood safely upon the floor of this great room. Here all the wonder and magnificence of the subterranean world burst upon us at once. We found that we stood in a room, the area of whose floor was equal to a quarter of an acre. Immediately before us, and within a few feet of the centre of the room, arose a vast column, or pillar, in some degree combining architectural proportions, and running up about thirty feet, and supporting the dome of this immense hall. This column stands upon a block, or rude pedestal, about three feet in height, and the shaft where it rests upon it is about the thickness of a man's body. It then swells gradually until it becomes, at the distance of twenty feet from its base, about the size of a barrel, whence it continues of the same size, until it gradually enlarges into its capital, where it reaches the dome. Strange to tell, this vast column is almost as regularly fluted or grooved, as if it had been done with the chisel of the sculptor. About fifteen feet from the main pillar stand two smaller ones, about ten feet in height, which consequently do not reach the ceiling; and just at their base, and nearly between them, is a small pool or basin of water. We perceived by the united glare of all our candles, that the whole of the arch of this immense hall was hung with the most beautiful stalactites, and variegated with almost every possible variety of color. In some places it was perfectly white, then red, gray, or yellow, and in others it was as clear and transparent as ice.

In looking around us towards the lights which were dispersed in different parts of the hall, the various small spars or pillars that were pointing up—others that had been detached from the ceiling and lay scattered about the floor—and numerous large blocks of crystallized limestone, produce novel and almost indescribable feelings. It did not require an imagination unusually fervid, to liken this dim picture of the floor to the miniature ruins of some great city, with a few of its spires and steeples pointing up from the ruins; or to some mighty temple, with its shattered and broken columns and fallen walls, with just sufficient of its materials to show the style of its former magnificence.

Masonic Hall.—In this room, about three and a half feet above the level of the floor, is a complete wainscot or chairboard, with apparent mouldings and carved work in complete relief, and extending in one entire and unbroken circle around the room. In the centre of the floor stand three large spars, resembling candlesticks of a mammoth size. These candlesticks arise from the floor of the room, with various enlargements and diminutions resembling carved work, until they reach the exact level of the chairboard, when the spar which resembles the candle, and seems to be set into a socket, runs up about two feet. As if to make the copy more exact, and the resemblance more palpably striking, the candlesticks seem to be of a dusky or bronze color, and the candle or spar arising from it of a clear white. The crystallization on the walls of this room is in beautiful waves and folds, resembling drapery. At one end of the room, a large spar, resembling a bed-post, stood in beautiful relief from the wall, and large folds and waves of drapery, resembling curtains, seemed to hide the rest of the bed.

Here, then, our admiration and astonishment were at their height. Our feelings had been wrought up to a degree of almost painful intensity. Here we stood, hundreds of feet beneath the surface of the earth, and a full half-mile from the first entrance, tread-ing upon a spot and breathing an atmosphere which had not been disturbed since the creation of the world. A place in which the human voice had never before been heard, and on whose beauties the human eye had never rested. There was, in truth, an aw-ful sublimity in the state of our feelings, superinduced not only by what we saw, but in part, perhaps, by a contingent danger to which we were exposed. The falling of the arch, or the rolling of a single rock into some of the narrow passages which we had to retrace, would have shut us up in eternal darkness in this mysterious region of wonders.

Powell's Fort Valley, on the line of this and Shenandoah county, derives its name, says tradition, from an Englishman named Powell, who in early times discovered a silver mine in the West Fort mountain, and commenced coining money, and when at-tempts were made to arrest him, sought shelter in the fastnesses of the mountain. Kercheval says:

The grandeur and sublimity of this extraordinary work of nature, consist in its tre-mendous height and singular formation. On entering the mouth of the fort, we are struck with the awful height of the mountains on each side, probably not less than a thousand feet. Through a very narrow passage, a bold and beautiful stream of water rushes, called Passage creek, which a short distance below works several fine merchant mills. After travelling two or three miles, the valley gradually widens, and for upwards of twenty miles furnishes arable land, and affords settlements for eighty or ninety fami-lies, several of whom own very valuable farms. The two mountains run parallel about 24 or 25 miles, and are called the East and West Fort mountains, and then are merged into one, anciently called Mesinetto, now Masinutton mountain. The Masinutton mountain continues its course about 35 or 36 miles southerly, and abruptly terminates nearly opposite Keisletown, in the county of Rockingham. This range of mountains divides the two great branches of the Shenandoah River, called the South and North forks. This mountain, upon the whole, presents to the eye something of the shape of the letter Y, or perhaps more the shape of the houns and tongue of a wagon.

A few miles above Luray, [says Kercheval,] on the west side of the river, there are three large Indian graves, ranged nearly side by side, thirty or forty feet in length, twelve or fourteen feet wide, and five or six feet high : around them, in a circular form, are a number of single graves. The whole covers an area of little less than a quarter of an acre. They present to the eye a very ancient appearance, and are covered over with pine and other forest growth. The excavation of the ground around them is plainly to be seen. The three first-mentioned graves are in oblong form, probably con-tain many hundreds of human bodies, and were doubtless the work of ages.

PATRICK.

PATRICK was taken from Henry in 1791. It is 25 miles long, with a mean width of 20 ; it is watered by the Dan and its branches. The face of the country is broken, and it has the Alle-ghany on its western boundary, and the Bull and other mountains running across it from E. to W. There is a great diversity of soil; the bottom land on the water-courses is generally of a good quality, and a large portion of the upland, though rocky, is strong. On the south side of Bull mountain the staple is tobacco, and the land there is cultivated by slaves. Some portions of the county are very thinly settled; but latterly there has been some emigration into it, the land being very cheap. Iron ore abounds. Pop. in 1840, whites 6,087, slaves 1,842, free colored 103; total, 8,042.

Taylorsville, or Patrick C. H., on Mayo River, 226 miles southeasterly from Richmond, contains 40 or 50 dwellings.

The natural scenery in the mountainous section of this county is wild and romantic. A late publication thus describes the passage of the Dan down the Alleghany, and "the Bursted Rock:"

The scenery presented by the passage of Dan River down the mountain, and into the flat country, is awful and sublime in the highest degree. The river rises in a plain, traverses it for 8 or 10 miles, till it reaches the declivity of the mountain, dashes down it by a rapid succession of perpendicular falls, and winds its solitary way, unapproached by any footstep save that of the mountain hunter, and hemmed in on every side by immense mountains, descending almost perpendicularly to the water's edge for the distance of several miles, before its banks afford room for settlements. The *Pinnacles of Dan* are found in this interval. To approach them you must ascend the mountain at some convenient gap—upon reaching the top of the mountain, the country becomes comparatively level. The visitor goes along the top under the guidance of some mountaineer, who knows the locality of the pinnacles; he meets with no obstruction except fallen logs, and a most luxuriant growth of weeds, till suddenly he reaches the declivity of the mountain. An immense basin presents itself to his view, surrounded by lofty mountains, almost perpendicular, of which the ridge on which he stands forms a boundary. The depth of the basin is beyond his view, and appears to him to be incalculable. From the midst of the basin two pinnacles, in the shape of a sugar loaf, rise to a level with the surrounding mountains, and of course with the beholder. They appear to be masses of rock rudely piled on each other, with barely soil enough in the crevices to nourish a few bushes. There is no visible outlet to the basin, the narrow chasm through which the river makes its escape being out of view. If the visitor wishes to ascend the main pinnacle, (one being much larger than the other,) he descends from his station the face of the mountain, which is very steep, to a distance which he imagines sufficient to carry him down the highest mountain,—when he reaches a narrow ridge or pass-way not more than thirty feet wide, connecting, at the distance of thirty or forty yards, the pinnacle to the main mountain,—and to his astonishment the river appears at an incalculable distance below him. The ascent of the pinnacle then commences, and an arduous and somewhat perilous one it is. A narrow pathway winds up among the rocks, and in many places the adventurous climber has to pull himself up a perpendicular ascent of five or six feet by the bushes. When he reaches the top, however, he is amply repaid for his labor in ascending. The prospect, though necessarily a limited one, is picturesque and sublime in a high degree. The view of the basin is then complete. The mountains surrounding it nearly of a uniform height; no outlet visible, and the beholder perched upon the summit of an immense natural pyramid in the centre. The river is seen occasionally as it winds around the base of the pinnacle. It attempts to pass on the west side, where the narrow ridge by which the visitor approaches arrests its course; it then winds entirely round the pinnacle close to its base, until it comes to the opposite or southern side of the narrow ridge, passing between the two pinnacles: it then passes round the western and southern side of the smaller pinnacle, and makes its escape as it best can from its apparently hopeless imprisonment. The summit of the pinnacle is about twenty or thirty feet square,—and strange to relate, small bushes of the aspen grow upon it—which is found nowhere else growing wild in this section of country. The echo produced is somewhat remarkable. If a gun be fired off on the top of the pinnacle, you hear nothing for several seconds, when suddenly, in the direction of the narrow pass through which the river flows, a rushing sound is heard, which, although not a correct echo, seems to be the sound of the report escaping through the pass.

The other natural curiosity to which reference has been made, is "the Bursted Rock," which is not very far from the pinnacles, and forms a part of the frowning and sublime scenery which overhangs the Dan, in its passage through the mountain. You approach it as you do the pinnacle along the level top of the mountain, till suddenly your course is arrested by a perpendicular descent of many hundred feet. The face of the precipice is a smooth rock. Far below every thing appears in ruins—rocks piled on rocks, the timber swept from the earth ; and every appearance indicates that a considerable portion of the mountain has been, by some great convulsion of nature, riven and torn from the rest, and precipitated into the valley, or rather chasm below.

PENDLETON.

PENDLETON was formed in 1788, from Augusta, Hardy, and Rockingham, and named from Edmund Pendleton, president of the Virginia convention of 1775. It is 45 miles long, with a mean width of 22 miles. The country is extremely mountainous, and is watered by some of the head branches of the Potomac and the James : the level of arable land from whence flow these streams, it is estimated must exceed 2,000 feet above the ocean. Over one hundred thousand pounds of maple sugar are annually produced. Pop. in 1840, whites 6,445, slaves 462, free colored 33 ; total, 6,940.

Franklin, the county-seat, is 171 miles NW. of Richmond, near the centre of the county, on the south branch of the Potomac ; and contains about 40 dwellings.

Twelve miles northeast of Franklin, on the south fork of the south branch of the Potomac, stood Seybert's fort, in the early settlement of the country.

In this fort, in the year 1758, (says Withers,) the inhabitants of what was then called the "Upper Tract," all sought shelter from the tempest of savage ferocity ; and at the time the Indians appeared before it, there were contained within its walls between thirty and forty persons of both sexes and of different ages. Among them was Mr. Dyer (the father of Col. Dyer, now of Pendleton) and his family. On the morning of the fatal day, Col. Dyer and his sister left the fort for the accomplishment of some object, and although no Indians had been seen there for some time, yet did they not proceed far, before they came in view of a party of forty or fifty Shawnees, going directly towards the fort. Alarmed for their own safety, as well as for the safety of their friends, the brother and sister endeavored by a hasty flight to reach the gate and gain admittance into the garrison ; but before they could effect this, they were overtaken and made captives.

The Indians rushed immediately to the fort and commenced a furious assault on it. Capt. Seybert prevailed (not without much opposition) on the besieged to forbear firing until he should endeavor to negotiate with, and buy off the enemy. With this view, and under the protection of a flag, he went out, and soon succeeded in making the wished-for arrangement. When he returned, the gates were thrown open, and the enemy admitted.

No sooner had the money and other articles stipulated to be given, been handed over to the Indians, than a most bloody tragedy was begun to be acted. Arranging the inmates of the fort in two rows, with a space of about ten feet between them, two Indians were selected, who, taking each his station at the head of a row, with their tomahawks most cruelly murdered almost every white person in the fort ; some few, whom caprice or some other cause induced them to spare, were carried into captivity. Such articles as could be well carried away were taken off by the Indians ; the remainder was consumed, with the fort, by fire.

From Mr. Samuel Kercheval, the author of the "History of the

Valley," we have obtained the following additional facts relating to the attack on this fort :

The Indians were commanded by the blood-thirsty chief Killbuck. Seybert's son, a lad of about fifteen, exhibited great firmness and bravery. He had shot two of the assailants, when their chief called out in English, that if they surrendered, their lives should be spared. At that instant young Seybert was in the act of aiming his rifle at Killbuck, when his father seized it from him, observing, "We cannot defend the fort ; we must surrender to save our lives!" confiding in the faithless promises of Killbuck. The first salutation he received after surrendering, was a stroke in the mouth from the monster Killbuck with the pipe end of his tomahawk, dislocating the old man's teeth ; immediately after which he was massacred with the other victims. Young Seybert was taken off with the other prisoners. *He told Killbuck that he had raised his gun to kill him, but his father had wrested it from him.* The savage laughed and replied, "You little rascal, if you had killed me you would have saved the fort ; for had I fallen, my warriors would have immediately fled, and given up the siege in despair."

PITTSYLVANIA.

PITTSYLVANIA was formed in 1767, from Halifax. It is 35 miles long and 26 broad. It is watered by the Staunton on the N., the Dan on its s., and Banister River in the centre. Much of the soil is excellent, and produces annually over six millions of pounds of tobacco, besides heavy crops of grain. Pop. in 1840, whites 14,283, slaves 11,558, free colored 557 ; total, 26,398.

Competition, the seat of justice for the county, is situated on a branch of Banister River, 162 miles southwesterly from Richmond. The surrounding country is healthy and fertile, and the town itself contains a population of about 300. Danville is a large village on the Dan River, 5 miles from the North Carolina line, and 15 south of Competition. It was established by law in 1793, on the land of "John Barnett, adjoining Winn's Falls." By the provisions of the act, Thomas Tunstale, Matthew Clay, William Harrison, John Wilson, Thomas Fearne, George Adams, Thomas Worsham, Robert Payne, James Dix, John Southerland, John Call, and Thomas Smith, were appointed trustees to lay off the town into lots of half an acre each, with convenient streets. Danville contains 7 mercantile stores, 2 tobacco inspections and warehouses, 4 tobacco factories, 2 banks, 1 male, 1 public, and 1 private female academy, 1 oil, 2 flour, and 2 saw-mills, 2 iron foundries, 1 newspaper printing-office, 18 mechanic shops, 1 Presbyterian, 1 Baptist, 1 Episcopal, and 1 Methodist church, and a population of about 1500. The canal of the Roanoke Company, around the falls of the Dan River, is about one mile long, which affords eligible sites for manufactories to almost any extent, with abundance of water-power at all seasons. The river is navigable for batteaux carrying from 7,000 to 10,000 pounds, as far up as Madison, in North Carolina, 40 miles distant. With some slight improvements, the river is supposed to be susceptible of steamboat navigation to the town.

POCAHONTAS.

POCAHONTAS was formed in 1821, from Bath, Pendleton, and Randolph, and named from the Indian princess : its mean length is 40 and mean width 18 miles. Cheat, Gauley, and Greenbrier Rivers rise in the county, which is one of the most elevated in Virginia. The surface is very broken and mountainous; the southern part is tolerably productive, but towards the northeast the land is more barren. Pop. in 1840, whites 2,684, slaves 219, free colored 19; total, 2,922.

Huntersville, the county-seat, is 190 miles NW. of Richmond, between Greenbrier and Alleghany mountains, on Knapp's creek, 6 miles from its junction with Greenbrier River, and at an elevation of over 1800 feet above the Atlantic. It contains an incorporated academy, 2 or 3 religious societies, and about 30 dwellings. "Eighteen miles from Huntersville, on Elk Ridge, a very high mountain, is a circular hole of about 70 feet diameter, which is considered a curiosity, its waters being perfectly black and of a bituminous taste : it is called ' the black hole.' It is said if wooden poles are thrust in, they will sink to rise no more."

POWHATAN.

POWHATAN was formed in 1777, from Cumberland. Its greatest length is 25, and its greatest width 15 miles. The soil is various; much, however, is fertile. The James and Appomattox—bounding two sides of the county at full length—with their numerous branches afford much fertile low ground. Clover and plaster have been much used in agriculture within a few years. There are some coal-mines in the county, but the distance to market has prevented their being worked advantageously. Pop. in 1840, whites 2,432, slaves 5,129, free colored 363; total, 7,924. Scottville, or Powhatan C. H., lies in the central part of the county, 32 miles w. of Richmond, and contains about 20 dwellings. It was named from Gen. Chas. Scott, a distinguished officer of the revolution, and afterwards governor of Kentucky. A traveller who was here in 1781, says that it then consisted of "only two mean huts, one for the purpose of holding the sessions, the other by way of public house." Smithsville and Jefferson contain each a few dwellings.

In the lower end of this county, about 3 miles from Manakin Town Ferry, on James River, and 17 miles above Richmond, in a healthy and pleasant locality, is Howard's Spring. The waters are something of the character of those of the White Sulphur of Greenbrier, although not so thoroughly impregnated. From its favorable location, it is hoped that this spring will ere long be opened as a watering-place; in which case, it will doubtless secure public favor. It has long been favorably known, and visited with great benefit by invalids of the surrounding country.

This county, near Manakin Town Ferry, was settled by Huguenots, (after the revocation of the edict of Nantz in 1685,) many of whose descendants still remain in that section of Powhatan, and the adjacent parts of Chesterfield; as the Subletts, the Michauxs, the Bernards, the Martins, the Flourneys, &c. Near Keswick, the seat of Major John Clarke, runs Bernard's creek, which takes its name from the Huguenot family of Bernard, who settled near its banks. The Manakin tribe of Indians inhabited this county, and near, or on the land given to the Huguenots, they had a town. Mr. Edward Scott's residence is said to be near the site of that town, and it is his ferry across the James River that goes by the name of the Manakin Town Ferry. Beverly, in his History of Va., published in 1722, thus speaks of these early settlers:

The French refugees, sent in thither by the charitable exhibition of his late majesty King William, are naturalized by a particular law for that purpose. In the year 1699, there went over about 300 of these, and the year following about 200 more, and so on, until there arrived in all between 700 and 800 men, women, and children, who had fled from France on account of their religion. Those who went over the first year were advised to seat on a very rich piece of land about 20 miles above the falls of James River, on the south side of the river; which land was formerly the seat of a great and warlike nation of Indians called *Monacans*, none of which are now left in those parts; but the land still retains their name, and is still called the *Monacan* Town. The refugees that arrived the second year went also to the Monacan Town, but afterwards, upon some disagreement, several dispersed themselves up and down the country; and those that have arrived since have followed their example, except some few that likewise settled at Monacan Town.

The Assembly was very bountiful to those that remained at this town, bestowing on them large donations, money, and provisions for their support. They likewise freed them from every public tax for several years to come, and addressed the governor to grant them a brief, to entitle them to the charity of all well-disposed persons throughout the country; which, together with the king's benevolence, supported them very comfortably till they could sufficiently supply themselves with necessaries, which they now do indifferently well, and have stocks of cattle and hogs.

In the year 1702, they began an essay of wine, which they made of the wild grapes gathered in the woods; the effect of which was strong-bodied claret, of good flavor. I heard a gentleman who tasted it give it great commendation. Now if such may be made of the wild vine in the woods, without pruning, weeding, or removing it out of the shade, what may be produced from a vineyard skilfully cultivated? But I don't hear that they have done any thing since, being still very poor, needy, and negligent.

Gen. WM. H. ASHLEY, of St. Louis, was born in Powhatan county. About the year 1810, being then a poor boy, he emigrated to Missouri, (then Upper Louisiana,) and settled near the lead mines. In 1822, he projected the scheme of the "mountain expedition," by uniting the Indian trade in the Rocky Mountains with the hunting and the trapping business. He enlisted about 300 hardy men in the business, and after various successes and reverses, he and his associates realized handsome fortunes. He also rose to considerable political distinction, and was the first lieutenant-governor of Missouri after its admission into the Union, and a M. C. in 1831-3. He died in 1838, greatly respected for his great enterprise, talents, and worth of character.

Dr. BRANCH T. ARCHER, president of the convention which formed the constitution of Texas, and late secretary of war in that republic, was born in Powhatan.

PRESTON.

PRESTON was formed in 1818, from Monongalia, and named from James P. Preston, a meritorious officer in the late war with Great Britain, and governor of Virginia from 1816 to 1819. Its mean length is 30 miles, and mean breadth 17 miles. Cheat River passes through the county. The general face of the country is mountainous, interspersed, on the eastern and western sides, with large natural meadows called "glades," which afford support for large herds of cattle in summer, and in winter also, when it is mown and cured for food. The glades are destitute of timber, but are covered in summer with grass and weeds, with frequent projecting points of timber, low bushes, &c. The bottom grounds are small but productive, and many of the hill-sides are favorable to grain. Slate and limestone are common; the county is abundantly supplied with bituminous coal, and iron ore is often found. Population in 1840, whites 6,743, slaves 91, free colored 30; total, 6,866.

Kingwood, the county-seat, is 284 miles NW. of Richmond, on a beautiful and healthy eminence, 2 miles west of Cheat River, 20 from Morgantown, 43 from Clarksburg, and 60 from Beverly. It contains several stores, and about 30 dwellings. The German settlement is 18 miles southeasterly from Kingwood.

PRINCE EDWARD.

PRINCE EDWARD was formed in 1753, from Amelia. It is 35 miles long, mean breadth 12 miles. The Appomattox runs on its northern boundary, and with its branches, waters the county. The soil is much like that in this section of the state, naturally good; but injured by continual culture, without any regard to system. Marl, coal, and copper ore, are found in the county. Pop. in 1840, whites 4,923, slaves 8,576, free colored 570; total, 14,069.

Farmsville is situated 70 miles southwesterly from Richmond, on the northern border of the county, on the Appomattox. It was established by law in 1798, on the property of Judith Randolph; and Charles Scott, Peter Johnson, John Randolph, Jr., Philip Holcomb, Jr., Martin Smith, Blake B. W. Woodson, and Creed Taylor, were appointed trustees to lay off the town into half acre lots. Farmsville is now a place of considerable commercial importance; its trade is drawn from Halifax, Lunenburg, Charlotte, Nottoway, and a part of Campbell. It is at the head of batteau navigation on the Appomattox, although boats can go up much higher. It is the fourth tobacco market in Virginia; and the quality of its tobacco is nowhere surpassed. It contains 2 tobacco warehouses, 10 tobacco factories, 7 or 8 mercantile stores, a branch of the Farmers' Bank, 1 newspaper printing-office, 1 Presbyterian, 1 Methodist, and 1 Baptist church, and a population of about 1400. The navigation of the Appomattox is good at all seasons, and its navigation from this place to Petersburg gives employment to about 40 batteaux, carrying from 5 to 7 tons each, of the products of the country. Prince Edward C. H., Jamestown, and Sandy River Church, are small places in the county.

"HAMPDEN SYDNEY COLLEGE originated in an academy in

Prince Edward county, established by the presbytery of Hanover, which was afterwards incorporated as a college. The circumstances leading to the establishment of the academy were these: As Virginia was first settled by members of the Church of England, and the emigration of dissenters not encouraged, it was more than a hundred years ere they were found in any considerable numbers. Some years previous to the revolutionary war, the

Hampden Sydney College.

Rev. Samuel Davies, of Hanover county, in conjunction with others, formed the presbytery of Hanover. The principal mass of Presbyterians then in lower Virginia was in Prince Edward and the neighboring counties, among whom were some French Huguenots. In a few years, as they increased in numbers, they determined to establish a seminary, to be conducted on Presbyterian principles; William and Mary, the only college in the state, being fostered particularly by the Episcopalians. The academy was accordingly established in Prince Edward, at a point convenient for the Presbyterians of Virginia and North Carolina."* This institution was founded in 1774, and was called the Academy of Hampden Sydney. "It was chartered in 1783, and received its present name from those two martyrs of liberty, J. Hampden and A. Sydney. It was established, and has ever been supported, by the private munificence of public-spirited individuals. It has an elevated, healthy, and pleasant situation, one mile from the court-house, and 80 from Richmond. Although the institution has had to encounter many difficulties for want of funds, yet it has generally been in successful operation, and has educated upwards of 2,000 young men; many of whom have been of eminent usefulness, and some of great abilities. More instructors have emanated from this institution than from any other in the southern

---

* Ruffner's ms. History of Washington College.

434   PRINCE EDWARD COUNTY.

country. Connected with the college is a literary and philosophical society, and an institute of education. There are also several societies among the students, which are of great assistance
to them in the prosecution of their studies. The legislative government of the college is vested in 27 trustees, who fill up vacancies in their own body. By the census of 1840, this institution
had 65 students, and 8000 volumes in its library."

The presidents of Hampden Sydney have been—Rev. S. S.
Smith, 1774 ; Rev. J. B. Smith, 1779 to 1789 ; presidents *pro tem.*
to 1797 ; Rev. A. Alexander, D. D., 1797 to 1806 ; Rev. M. Hoge,
D. D., 1807 to 1820 ; J. P. Cushing, A. M., 1821 to 1835 ; Daniel
Carroll, D. D., 1836 ; William Maxwell, LL. D., 1839 to 1844.

The UNION THEOLOGICAL SEMINARY is located in the immediate
vicinity of Hampden Sydney College. " The institution had
its origin in efforts made by the presbytery of Hanover and
the synod of Virginia, as early as 1812, to give their candidates
for the ministry a more complete theological education. It did
not, however, go into operation in a regular form until the year
1824." In 1841–'42 it had 3 professors, 20 students, 175 graduates,
and a carefully-selected library of about 4000 volumes. The
Theological Seminary, and Hampden Sydney College, have spacious and showy brick buildings, sufficient to accommodate a large
number of students.

The Rev. MOSES HOGE, President of Hampden Sydney College, was one of the
most able and venerable clergymen of the Virginia church ; and his memory is now
cherished with peculiar affection by many in the south. During a long life of clerical
service, he maintained a character among the best and greatest men in that country,
for sagacity, theological learning, sound judgment, patriarchal simplicity, and unaffected
meekness and humility. As a preacher, he was not eloquent, in the usual acceptation
of the word ; that is, he was far from the artificial elegancies of rhetoric ; but his fervor
of devotion and of argument often burst forth in a glow and flame which enkindled whole
assemblies. This, together with the sanctity of his manners, made him a great favorite
with John Randolph, who often rode many miles to hear him, and often spent much time
in conversing with him on religious subjects. The widow of Dr. Hoge is now living, at an
advanced age, in Charlotte. Three of his sons became ministers. Of these, the eldest,
the Rev. *James Hoge*, D. D., of Columbus, Ohio, is one of the most distinguished men
in the Presbyterian church. Dr. Moses Hoge was universally respected by his brethren,
as a counsellor and an example ; indeed, it would be difficult to name a man of his profession who had attained to more remarkable mildness, uprightness, or benevolence.
He died in the city of Philadelphia, and his remains were buried in the church-yard of
the Third Presbyterian Church, Pine-street.

Among the Presbyterian clergy of Virginia, an eminent place is due to the late Rev.
JOHN HOLT RICE, D. D. He was born in Bedford county, Nov. 28, 1777, and died in
Prince Edward, Sept. 2, 1831. He was graduated at Washington College, and was
afterwards a tutor in Hampden Sydney, where he was the intimate friend of such men
as Speece, Alexander, and Lyle. He was the founder of the Union Seminary, at the
head of which he passed his last years. For a portion of his life he labored among the
negro slaves ; and the fruits of this remain, in great numbers who not only believe in
Christ, but are well instructed in the reading of the Scriptures, and are in regular connection with the Presbyterian church. Dr. Rice's years of prime were spent as a pastor,
in Richmond. Here he was successful in a high degree, both as a preacher and an
author. The *Evangelical and Literary Magazine* was under his editorial care, and its
most valuable contents are from his pen.

Dr. Rice was characterized by great independence of mind. He abjured all human
authority, and was bold in the expression of his views. Yet he was " swift to hear,
slow to speak." His thirst for knowledge was insatiable, and his learning was in pro-

portion ; but it was the wide range, rather than the minute accuracy of his erudition, which was remarkable. As a writer, he greatly surpassed most of his coevals in ease, fertility, and force. By frequent journeys through the northern and eastern states, he liberalized his views, enjoying valuable intercourse with the first minds in New England, especially with the professors at Andover and New Haven ; yet, from first to last, he was a thorough-paced, enthusiastic Virginia patriot. He was an American of the old stamp, loving and admiring his country with the fervor of a youthful passion ; and he transferred the same regards to the church of which he was an ornament and a champion. His letters to Mr. Madison, and his correspondence with Bishop Ravenscroft, may be adduced in proof. As a pulpit orator, Dr. Rice was not graceful or mellifluous ; but he was more—he was luminous, instructive, convincing, persuasive, and elevating. His greatest discourses, like those of Robert Hall and John M. Mason, were unwritten. In these, as in his life, he evinced the truth, purity, uprightness, and benevolence of the Gospel. Though naturally irascible, he became an example of meekness, and overcame evil with good. His favorite maxim was, Love is Power. There are thousands in Virginia to whom this meager notice will seem far below the truth. Dr. Rice's life was written by Wm. Maxwell, LL.D. (Phil. 1835, one vol. 12mo.)

When Tarleton was in this county, in the revolution, he passed near the residence of Joshua Davison, a gallant dragoon of Lee's legion, who, having received a severe wound in the sword-arm at the Guilford C. H., returned home to recruit. Davison resolved to have a look at the enemy, and, loading an old squirrel-gun, set out in search for them. He followed on their trail a short distance, when he was perceived by a British dragoon, who, rapidly advancing, drew his sword and exclaimed, " Surrender immediately, you rebel rascal, or you die !" " Not so fast, my good friend," replied Davison, " I am not prepared to yield ;" when, raising his squirrel-gun with his left hand, he shot him dead, and seized and carried off his horse and plunder in triumph. Some time after, on being asked if he was satisfied with killing a single man, " By no means," he replied : " I reloaded my piece and went in pursuit ; but my firing had excited such alarm, and Tarleton fled with such expedition, that I never could have overtaken him, or I would have had *another shot.*"*

There died in this county, in 1819, a slave named Wonder Booker, belonging to George Booker, Esq., who had reached his 126th year. " He received his name from the circumstance that his mother was in her 58th year at the time of his birth. He was of great strength of body, and his natural powers, which were far superior to those of people of color in general, he retained in a surprising degree. He was a constant laborer in his master's garden until within eight or ten years of his death."

PRINCESS ANNE.

Princess Anne was formed in 1691, from Norfolk county. It is 30 miles long, with a mean breadth of 12 miles : it has the Atlantic Ocean on the E., and Chesapeake Bay on the N. Cape Henry forms its northeastern angle, and Back Bay, a branch of Currituck sound, sets up in its south part. The county is drained by North River and the east branch of the Elizabeth. Pop., whites 3,996, slaves 3,087, free colored 202 ; total, 7,285.

Princess Anne C. H., situated near the centre of the county, 132 miles SE. of Richmond, contains about 20 dwellings. Kempsville, 10 miles southeasterly from Norfolk, on the eastern branch of Elizabeth River, contains about 30 dwellings. Large quantities of lumber, navy timber, staves, wood, &c., are sent from this place by water to Norfolk.

---

* Garden's Anecdotes of the Revolution.

The record here given of the trial of Grace ¹Sherwood *for witch-craft*, was presented by the late J. P. Cushing, president of Hampden Sydney College, to the Virginia Historical and Philosophical Society, and published in their collections. While it throws some light on the state of society of that time, it evinces that persecution for witchcraft was not alone in our country confined to the Puritans of New England. There, it will be recollected, was shown a noble example of the strength of moral principle on the part of the accused, for they had only to declare themselves guilty and their lives were spared. Rather than do this, many suffered death. Grace Sherwood met a milder fate. The place where she was ducked is a beautiful inlet making up from Lynnhaven Bay, which to this day is called "*Witch's Duck.*"

RECORD OF THE TRIAL OF GRACE SHERWOOD, IN 1705, PRINCESS ANNE COUNTY, FOR WITCHCRAFT.

Princess Anne ss.

At a Court held ye: 3d. of Janry: 170⅝ p. Gent: Mr. Beno: Burro: Collo: Moseley, Mr. John Cornick Capt: Hancock, Capt: Chapman

Justices

Whereas Luke Hill & uxor *somd* Grace Sherwood to this Court in *suspetion* of witchcraft & she fayling to *apear* it is therefore ordr. yt: attachmt. to ye: Sherr do Issue to attach her body to ansr. ye. sd: *som* next Court.

Princess Anne ss.

At a Court held ye. 6th: ffebry: 170⅝ p: Esent. Colo. Moseley, Collo. Adam Thorrowgood Capt: Chapman, Capt. Hancocke Mr. John Cornick, Mr. Richason, Came late

Justices

Suite for *suspition* of Witchcraft brought by Luke Hill agt: Grace Sherwood is ordr: to be referr till to morro:

Princess Ann ss.

At a Court held ye: 7th ffebry: 170⅝ p. Gent. Collo: Moseley Left: Collo: Thorrowgood Mr. John Richason, Mr. John Cornick Capt. Chapman, Capt: Hancock

Justices

Whereas a Complt: was brought agt: Grace Sherwood upon *suspition* of witchcraft by Luke Hill &c. & ye: matter being after a long time debated & ordr. yt: ye: sd. Hill pay all fees of this Complt: & yt: ye: sd. Grace be here next Court to be Searched according to ye: Complt: by a Jury of women to decide ye: sd: Differr: and ye. Sherr: is Likewise ordr. to som an able Jury accordingly.

Princess Ann ss.

At a Court held ye. 7th March 170⅝ Col: Edward Moseley, Lieut: Adam Thorrowgood, Majr. Henry Sprat—Captn: Horatio Woodhouse, Mr. John Cornick Capt: Henry Chapman, Mr. Wm. Smith, Mr. Jno Richason Captn. Geo. Hendcock

Justices

Whereas a Complaint have been to this *Duq* Court by Luke Hill & his wife yt. one Grace Sherwood of ye. County was and have been a long time suspected of witchcraft & have been as such represented wherefore ye. Sherr. at ye. last court was ordr: som a Jury of women to ye. Court to *serch* her on yc. sd. suspicion she assenting to ye. same —and after ye. Jury was impannelled and sworn & sent out to make due inquirery & inspection into all cercumstances after a mature consideration they bring in yr. verditt ; were of ye. Jury have sercath: Grace Sherwood & have found two things like *titts* wth: severall other spotts—Eliza. Barnes, forewoman, Sarah Norris, Margt. Watkins, Hannah *Dimis*, Sarah Goodaerd, Mary Burgess, Sarah Sergeent, Winiford Davis, Ursula Henly, Ann Bridgts, Exable Waplies—Mary Cotle.

At a court held ye. 2nd. May 1706 Present Mr. Jno. Richason, Maj. Henrey Spratt Mr. John Cornick, Capt: Henry Chapman, Mr. Wm Smyth Justices

Whereas a former Complt. was brought agt Grace Sherwood for suspicion of Witchcraft, wth. by ye. attorny Genll: report to his Excly. in Councll was to Generall and not charging her with any perticular act therefore represented to yem: yt. Princess Ann Court might if they thought fitt have her examined de novo & ye. Court being of opinion yt. there is great cause of suspicion doe therefore ordr. yt. ye. Sherr. take ye. said Grace into his safe costody untill she shall give bond & security for her appearance to ye. next Court to be examined De novo & yt: ye. Constable of yt. pr sinkt goe with ye. Sherr: & serch ye. said Graces house & all suspicious places carefully for all Images & such like things as may any way strengthen the suspicion & it is likewise ordered yt. ye Sherr: som an able Jury of women also all evidences as cann give in any thing agt: her in evidence in behalf of our Sovereign Lady ye. Qeen to attend ye. next Court accordingly.

Princess Ann ss.

At a Court held ye. 6th. June 1706. Present Mr. Jno. Richason : Capt Horatio Woodhouse Mr. John Cornick, Capt Henry Chapman, Capt: Wm Smith, Capt: Geo: Hancock

Justices

Whereas Grace Sherwood, of ye. County have been Complained of as a person suspected of witchcraft & now being brought before this Court in Crde: for examinacon ye. have therefore requested Mr. Maxmt: Bonsh to present informacon agt her as Councill in behalf of our sovereign lady ye. Qeen in order to her being brought to a regular triall.

Whereas an Information in behalf of her Mage. was presented by Luke Hill to ye. Court in pursuance to Mr. Genell. Attey's Tomson report on his Excellcy: ordr. in Councill ye. 16th Aprill last about Grace Sherwood being suspected of Witchcraft have thereupon sworn severall evidences agt. her by wth. it doth very likely appear.

Princess Anne ss

At a Court held the 7th: of June 1706. Mr. Jno. Richason, Majr. Henry Spratt Mr. John Cornick, Captn: Chapman Captn. Wm Smyth, Capt: Geo: Hancock

Justices

Whereas at the last Court an ordr. was past yt: ye. Sherr: should sommons an able Jury of women to serch Grace Sherwood on suspicion of witchcraft wch: although ye. same was performed by ye. Sherr: yet they refused, and did not appear it is therefore Ordr. yt. ye. same persons be again somd. by ye. Sherr: for their contempt to be dealt wth: according to ye. utmost severity of ye. law, & yt. a new Jury of women be by him somd. to appear next Court to serch her on ye. aforesd. suspicion & yt. He likewise som all evidences yt. he shall be informed of as materiall in ye. Complaint & yt. She continue in ye. Sherr: Costody unless she give good bond and security for her appearance at ye. next Court and yt. she be of good behaviour towards her Majesty & all her leidge people in ye. meantime.

Princess Anne ss

At a Court held ye. 5th. July Anno Dom: 1706. Present Mr Jno Richason, Captn. Jno Moseley Captn. Henry Chapman, Captn Wm: Smyth

Justices

Whereas for this soverall Courts ye. bussiness between Luke Hill & Grace Sherwood on suspicion of Witchcraft have been for severall things omitted particularly for want of a Jury to serch her & ye. Court being doubtfull that they should not get one ys. Court & being willing to have all means possible tryed either to acquit her or to give more strength to ye. suspicion yt. she might be dealt with as deserved therefore It was Ordr. yt. ys. day by her own consent to be tryed in ye. water by ducking, but ye. weather being very rainy, & bad soe yt. possibly it might endanger her health it is therefore ordr. yt. ye. Sherr. request ye. Justices p e. essvly to appear on Wednessday next by tenn of ye. Clock at ye. Court-house & yt. he secure the body of ye. sd. Grace till ye. time to be forthcoming yn. to be dealt wth. as aforesd.

Princess Ann ss

At a Court held ye. 10th: July 1706. Present: Col: Moseley, Captn Moseley Capt: Woodhouse, Mr John Cornick, Capt Chapman Capt: Wm Smyth— Mr. Richason—came late—

Justices

Whereas Grace Sherrwood being suspected of Witchcraft have a long time waited for a ffit upportunity ffor a ffurther examinacon & by her consent & approbacon of ye. Court it is ordr. yt. ye. Sherr: take all such convenient assistance of boats and men as shall be by him thought ffit to meet at Jno. Harpers plantacon in orde. to take ye. sd. Grace forthwith & *but* her into above mans *debth* & try her how she swims therein, alwayes having care of her life to peserve her from drowning & as soon as she comes out yt. he request as many antient & knowing women as possible he cann to serch her carefully for all teats, Spotts & marks about her body not usuall on others & yt. as they find ye. same to make report on oath to ye. truth thereof to ye. Court & further it is ordr. yt. som women be requested to shift & serch her before she goe into ye. water yt. she carry nothing about her to cause any ffurther serspicion.

(Same Day & only one order between the above order & the following. ☞ I suppose the Court which was then held at the Ferry "Jno. Harper's plantation" & about one mile from witch duck, went to see this ceremony or trial made ♫ Clk:)

Whereas on complaint of Luke Hill in behalf of her Magesty yt. now is agt. Grace Sherrwood for a pe:son suspected of withcraft & having had sundey: evidences sworne agt: her proving many cercumstances & which she could not make any excuse or little or nothing to say in her own behalf only seemed to rely on wt. ye. Court should doe & thereupon consented to be tryed in ye. water & likewise to be serched againe wth. experimts: being tryed & she swiming Wn. therein & bound contrary to custom & ye. Judgts. of all the spectators & afterwards being serched by ffive antient *weamen* who have all declared on oath yt. she is not like ym: nor noe other woman yt. they knew of having two things like titts on her private parts of a Black coller being blacker yn: ye: rest of her body all wth: cercumstance ye. Court weighing in their consideracon doe therefore ordr. yt. ye. Sherr: take ye. sd. Grace into his costody & to comit her body to ye. common Joal of this County their to secure her by irons or otherwise there to remain till such time as he shall be otherwise directed in ordr. for her coming to ye. common goal of ye: Countey to be brought to a ffuture tryall there.

[Copy]*   J. J. BURROUGHS, *C. C.*
Prs. Anne County Clerk's Office, 15 *Sept.* 1832.

In the war of the revolution this county, in common with the country around Norfolk, suffered from the enemy. On the 16th of November, 1775, a skirmish took place between some militia of the county and the enemy, an account of which is subjoined from Girardin :

Hearing that about 200 men of the Princess Anne militia were on their march to join the troops destined for the protection of the lower country, Dunmore had proceeded from Norfolk at the head of a superior force, composed of regulars, fugitive slaves, and disaffected inhabitants, with a view to intercept that patriotic band. The latter, aware of no hostile design, advanced in incautious security to the place of their destination. They were unexpectedly attacked, and compelled to engage under the double disadvantage of an unfavorable ground and inferior numbers. Supported, however, by inherent courage, and warmed by the justice of a noble cause, they for some time fought with great bravery and execution. At last the combined disadvantages just mentioned compelled them to retreat, which they did in perfect order. John Ackiss, one of the minutemen, was killed on the spot. Col. Hutchings and a Mr. Williams, with seven others, were wounded and taken prisoners.†

In the summer of 1777, the counties of Princess Anne and Norfolk became a prey to the depredations of Josiah Philips and his tory-banditti. When pursued, they sought shelter among the disaffected, or fled into their secret haunts in the Dismal Swamp.

---

* The copy of the Record in the above case seems to have been made out with great care by the clerk. The orthography, abbreviations, and other peculiarities of character, have been preserved in type with as much accuracy as possible; still, in some few instances, it has been found difficult to decipher the copy.

† See *Virginia Gazette* of this date.—Some of our documents relate this affair rather differently, and charge part of the militia with misconduct. Candor demands this remark.

He was finally taken, tried, and executed, in 1778. The facts annexed are from Girardin :

A certain Josiah Philips, laborer, of the parish of Lynnhaven, in the county of Princess Anne, a man of daring and ferocious disposition, associating with other individuals of a similar cast, spread terror and desolation through the lower country, committing murders, burning houses, wasting farms, and perpetrating other enormities, at the bare mention of which humanity shudders. Every effort to apprehend him had proved abortive. Strong in the number of his ruffian confederates, or, where force would probably fail, resorting to stratagem and ambush, striking the deadly blow, or applying the fatal torch at the midnight hour, and in those places which their insulated situation left almost unprotected, he retired with impunity to his secret haunts, reeking with blood, and loaded with plunder. The inhabitants of the counties which were the theatre of his crimes, never secure a moment by day or by night, in their fields or their beds, sent representations of their distresses to the governor, claiming the public protection. He consulted with some members of the legislature then sitting, on the best method of proceeding against this atrocious offender. Too powerful to be arrested by the sheriff and his *posse comitatus*, it was not doubted that an armed force might be sent to hunt and destroy him and his accomplices, in their morasses and fastnesses, wherever found ; but the proceeding concluded to be most consonant with the forms and principles of our government was, to pass, during the present session, an act giving him a reasonable, but limited day to surrender himself to justice, and to submit to a trial by his peers according to the laws of the land ; to consider a refusal as a confession of guilt, and divesting him, as an outlaw, of the character of citizen, to pass on him the sentence prescribed by these laws ; and the public officer being defied, to make every one his deputy, especially those whose safety hourly depended on the destruction of the daring ruffian. The case was laid before the legislature. The proofs were ample : his outrages no less notorious than those of the public enemy, and well known to the members of both houses from the lower countries. No one pretended then that the perpetrator of crimes, who could successfully resist the officers of justice, should be protected in the continuance of them by the privileges of his citizenship ; and that, when he baffled ordinary process, nothing extraordinary could be rightfully adopted to protect the citizens against him. No one doubted that society has a right to erase from the roll of its members any one who renders his own existence inconsistent with theirs—to withdraw from him the protection of their laws, and to remove him from among them by exile, or even by death, if necessary. An enemy in lawful war putting to death in cold blood the prisoner he has taken, authorizes retaliation, which would be inflicted with peculiar justice on the individual guilty of the deed were it to happen that he should be taken. And could the murders and robbery of a pirate or outlaw entitle him to more tenderness ? The legislature passed the law, therefore, and without opposition. Philips did not come in before the day prescribed, continued his lawless outrages, was afterwards taken in arms, but delivered over to the ordinary justice of the country. The attorney-general for the commonwealth, the immediate agent of the government, waiving all appeal to the act of attainder, indicted him at the common law as a murderer and robber. He was arraigned on that indictment in the usual forms, before a jury of his vicinage, and no use whatever made of the act of attainder in any part of the proceedings. He pleaded that he was a British subject, authorized to bear arms by a commission from Lord Dunmore ; that he was, therefore, a mere prisoner of war, and under the protection of the law of nations. The court being of opinion that a commission from an enemy could not protect a citizen in deeds of murder and robbery, overruled his plea. He was found guilty by his jury, sentenced by the court, and executed by the ordinary officer of justice ; and all " according to the forms and rules of the common law."

PRINCE GEORGE.

Prince George was formed in 1702, from Charles City. Its average length is about 21, and its breadth about 11 miles. The James forms its NE., and the Appomattox its NW. boundary Pop.

in 1840, whites 2,692, slaves 4,004, free colored 469 ; total, 7,175. The C. H. is situated near the centre of the county, 28 miles southeasterly from Richmond.

City Point is on the James, at the junction of the Appomattox, and although a small village—containing 1 Episcopal and 1 Methodist church, and about 25 dwellings—is a place of considerable importance, being the outport of Richmond and Petersburg. At City Point are several wharves projecting into the James, within a short distance of which ships of the largest class can float. " Not only is a large foreign shipping business done here, but the white sails of domestic commerce daily gladden the eye, as it passes and repasses this port, freighted, in its progress upwards, with the wealth, and productions, and exports of every clime, while its return carries to every port of our happy Union the produce of our soil and our mines." Besides the ordinary shipping, steam, freight, tow, and passage-boats stop here on their way up and down the river. City Point is a much better site for a commercial town than Richmond, and, it is said, would have been the seat of government, had not its owner, a Dutchman, refused to sell on any terms. A rail-road also connects this place with Petersburg. The Appomattox has latterly been discovered to be navigable for vessels of considerable size as far up as Waltham's Landing, half way to Petersburg, at which place there is a short branch rail-road, lately constructed, connecting with the Petersburg and Richmond rail-road.

John Randolph of Roanoke, there is good reason to suppose, was born at Cawson's, in this county, the family seat of his maternal grandfather, Theodorick Bland, Sen. The years of his boyhood were passed at Matoax, near Petersburg.

GEORGE KEITH TAYLOR was, we believe, a native of this county. He was a member of the legislature in '98 and '99, during the famous discussion of the alien and sedition laws, in the advocacy of which he bore a conspicuous part. He was a leader of the federal party, and a confederate of John Marshall, whose sister he married. As an advocate in criminal cases he was distinguished : his oratorical powers have been described as little inferior to those of Patrick Henry ; and, like him, his manner on commencing was unprepossessing. In Gilmer's " Sketches and Essays" there is a note which says that " Mr. Taylor was one of the most eminent lawyers of his state—acute, profound, logical, and persuasive ; of fine wit, of exquisite humor, of brilliant fancy, and of the most amiable disposition."

Col. THEODORICK BLAND, JUN., a worthy patriot and statesman, and a descendant ol Pocahontas, was born in this county about the year 1742. In 1753, when about 11 years of age, he was sent to England to be educated, and in 1761 he repaired to Edinburgh to study medicine. He was among the first persons from Virginia that devoted themselves to the study of medicine—a profession in that day but little cultivated in the colony, and in the improvement of which, from his diligence, he is entitled to the merit of having been one of its earliest pioneers. After an absence of about 12 years from America, he returned to Virginia, and entered upon the practice of his profession. But he was not an indifferent spectator of the political commotions of the day. In December, 1774, in writing to a mercantile friend in England, he says, " I should have vested the small proceeds in goods, but the present political disputes between these colonies and the mother country, which threaten us with a deprivation of our liberties, forbid such a step, and induce us to exert every nerve to imitate the silkworm, and *spin from our own bowels*, although the *web* should be our *winding-sheet*." The battle of Lexington was the subject of a patriotic poetical effusion by him. On the 24th of June, 1775, Dr. Bland was one of a party of 24 gentlemen who, shortly after the flight of Dunmore, removed certain arms from the governor's palace at Williamsburg. In the following December he wrote, apparently for publication, certain philippics against Dunmore, in which the political corruption and private profligacy of his lordship's character are depicted in the blackest hues. In June, 1776, he was captain of the first troop of Virginia cavalry. He was subsequently appointed lieutenant-colonel of horse, and in September, 1777, joined the main army. From a letter, it would appear that towards the close of this year he was a member of the senate of Va. " While in the army, he frequently signalized himself by brilliant actions."* In November, 1778, he superintended the march of the British troops of convention-made prisoners at Saratoga, to Virginia ; and on their arrival, or shortly after, was appointed by Washington to the command of the post at Charlottesville. From 1780 to '83, he was a member of Congress. In 1781, Farmingdale, his residence in Va., was plundered by the enemy. While in Congress he manifested his usual spirit and industry in the public cause, particularly in the financial department. In 1785 he was appointed, by Gov. Henry, lieutenant of this county. He was in that minority in the convention of Va., convened to consult upon the adoption of the federal constitution, that believed it repugnant to the interests of the country, and therefore voted against its ratification. On its adoption, however, he acquiesced in the will of the majority, and was elected to represent his district in the first Congress held under the constitution. While serving in that capacity, he died at New York, June 1st, 1790, aged 48. " In person, Col. Bland was tall—in his latter days corpulent—and of a noble countenance. His manners were marked by ease, dignity, and well-bred repose. In character he was virtuous and enlightened, of exemplary purity of manners and integrity of conduct, estimable for his private worth, and respectable for his public services. His career was distinguished rather by the usefulness of plain, practical qualifications, than by any extraordinary exhibitions of genius. Animated, from his childhood, by a profound love of country, with him patriotism was not an impulse but a principle. In style, he is fluent and correct, and if sometimes too florid or diffuse, he is at others wanting neither in energy of thought nor in elegance of diction. Moderation and good temper pervade his correspondence, and it is nowhere sullied by profanity or indelicacy."†

RICHARD BLAND was another of the many prominent Virginians who acted on the theatre of the revolution. Wirt, in speaking of him before the war, says he " was one of the most enlightened men of the colony. He was a man of finished education, and of the most unbending habits of application. His perfect mastery of every fact connected with the settlement and progress of the colony, had given him the name of the Virginian antiquary. He was also a politician of the first class ; a profound logician, and was also considered as the first writer in the colony ;" but he was a most ungraceful speaker in debate. " He wrote the first pamphlet on the nature of the connection with Great Britain, which had any pretension to accuracy of view on that subject ; but it was a singular one : he would set out on sound principles, pursue them logically, till he found them leading to the precipice which we had to leap ; start back, alarmed ; then resume his ground, go over it in another direction, be led again by the correctness of his reasoning to the same place, and again tack about and try other processes to reconcile right and wrong ; but left his reader and himself bewildered between the steady index of the compass in their hand, and the phantasm to which it seemed to point. Still there was more sound matter in this pamphlet, than in the celebrated Farmer's Letters, which were really but an *ignis fatuus*, misleading us from true principle." Mr. Bland was a member of Congress from 1774 to 1776 ; he died in 1778.

---

* Sketch of Col. Bland, in the History of Va. by J. W. Campbell.
† The foregoing memoir is abridged from that in the introduction of "The Bland Papers, being a selection from the manuscripts of Col. Theodorick Bland, Jr., etc. etc.," edited by Charles Campbell, of Petersburg, and published there, in 1840, by Edmund and Julian C. Ruffin—an octavo volume of about 300 pages, and composed principally of an interesting collection of letters written by the first personages in the country during the revolutionary era.

PRINCE WILLIAM.

PRINCE WILLIAM was formed in 1730, from Stafford and King George. It is about 35 miles long, and 12 wide. The Potomac forms its eastern boundary. Pop. in 1840, whites 4,867, slaves 2,767, free colored 510; total, 8,144.

Brentsville, the county-seat, is situated 101 miles from Richmond, and 33 N. of Fredericksburg, in the heart of the county, at the head of Occoquan River. It is a small village, containing 3 stores and about 20 dwellings. The county buildings are handsomely situated on a public square, containing 3 acres. Thoroughfare and Liberia are small places in the county, containing each a few dwellings. Dumfries is situated on Quantico creek, near the Potomac. It was once the county-seat; but in 1822 the courts were removed to Brentsville, and the old court-house is converted into an Episcopal church. Dumfries is a very old town, and once had considerable commerce; but from a combination of causes it has gone rapidly to decay, and many of the houses have been removed out of town.

Occoquan, situated near the mouth of a river of the same name, was established by law in 1804. It contains a large cotton factory, an extensive flouring mill, several stores, and about 40 dwellings. A handsome bridge is erected over the river at this place. The Occoquan here has a fall of 72 feet in one and a half miles, affording excellent sites for manufactories. This is the market for many of the most important shad and herring fisheries on the Potomac. The scenery around this village is uncommonly picturesque.

———

WILLIAM GRAYSON died at Dumfries, whither he had come on his way to Congress, March 12th, 1790, and his remains were deposited in the family vault, at the Rev. Mr. Spence Grayson's. He was first appointed a member of Congress from Virginia, in 1784, and continued a number of years. "In June, 1788, he was a member of the Virginia convention which was called for the purpose of considering the present constitution of the United States. In this assembly, rendered illustrious by men of the first talents, he was very conspicuous. His genius united with the eloquence of Henry, in opposing the adoption of the constitution. While he acknowledged the evils of the old government, he was afraid that the proposed government would destroy the liberty of the states. His principal objections to it were, that it took from the states the sole right of direct taxation, which was the highest act of sovereignty; that the limits between the national and state authorities were not sufficiently defined; that they might clash, in which case the general government would prevail; that there was no provision against raising such a navy, as was more than sufficient to protect our trade, and thus would excite the jealousy of European powers, and lead to war; and that there were no adequate checks against the abuse of power, especially by the president, who was responsible only to his counsellors and partners in crime, the members of the senate. After the constitution was adopted, Mr. Grayson was appointed one of the senators from Virginia, in the year 1789; his colleague was Richard Henry Lee. His great abilities were united with unimpeached integrity."

———

Immediately after Dunmore was driven from Gwyn's Island, in July, 1776, he sailed up the Potomac to this section of the state. The reception he met with from the inhabitants is thus related by Girardin:

Ascending the Potomac, he left, on many parts of its banks, hideous traces of piratical and depredatory warfare. A little above the mouth of Aquia creek, Mr. William

Brent's elegant brick house was burnt to the ground. The neighboring militia, seized with causeless alarm, retired without opposing the ravages of the lawless freebooters, who, after the destruction of the house, were proceeding to burn a valuable merchant mill, at a small distance, when 30 of the Prince William militia happily arrived, advanced with fearless step, and drove them on board. The spirit and bravery of the people of Stafford county in general, amply redeemed, on subsequent occasions, the momentary disgrace of that unaccountable panic; but the circumstance is yet well remembered in the environs; and we have heard more than once, on the very ruins of the prostrated edifice, the ludicrous account which the senile garrulity of some among the surviving actors in that scene, was ever ready to give. It appears that the Stafford militia mistook the detachment from Prince William for Englishmen, and exerted all the agility and ingenuity of which they were capable to avoid falling into their hands. Dunmore's fleet, consisting of the Roebuck, Mercury, Otter, an armed ship, some gondolas, and several tenders, having taken in fresh water, fell down the river on the ensuing day. They had, in this expedition, met with a severe gale of wind, which drove on shore several small vessels with the friends of the British government on board. These were made prisoners, and sent to Williamsburg under an escort. The third regiment and other troops had been stationed along the banks of the Potomac, to watch the motions of the enemy, while the infant Virginian fleet, consisting of some armed brigs and row-galleys, was cruising for them in the bay. The Roebuck alone could protect Dunmore and his wretched followers. The expected conflict was prevented by the flight of the foe. The excessive heat of the season, the putridity of the water, the scantiness and bad quality of the provisions on board, and the crowded and inconvenient situation of the people there, engendered complicated and malignant diseases, which hourly plunged into a watery tomb multitudes of the motley band. Thus, loaded with the execration of the country; defeated in all his schemes of civil discord, and of servile and savage hostility; hunted from station to station by the resentment of an injured people, naturally prone to loyalty, gratitude, and attachment; pursued, as it were, by Heaven and the elements themselves, Dunmore, with a wounded and humbled spirit, saw himself reduced to flee from these shores, where he had hoped triumphantly to plant the standard of despotism, and to satiate his vindictive and haughty passions with the tears and abjection of the feeble, and the blood of the brave. After burning such vessels as he was able to spare, to prevent their falling into the hands of the Americans, he steered for Lynnhaven Bay with about 40 or 50 sail; and then parting with the miserable companions of his disastrous fate, he sent some of them to St. Augustine, under convoy of the Otter, some to Bermuda, some to the West Indies, and some to Europe. With the rest, he repaired to Sir P. Parker's fleet, and, on the 14th of August, reached Staten Island, where General Howe had lately been joined by his brother, and the fleets under convoy of Commodore Hotham, and the Repulse. Towards the close of this eventful year, he returned to England in the Fowey.

PULASKI.

Pulaski was formed in 1839, from Montgomery and Wythe, and named from Count Pulaski. It is 23 miles long, with a mean width of 18 miles. New River passes through the eastern part, and then, curving to the left, with Little River, divides the county from Montgomery. The face of the country n. and nw. of the C. H., is generally level and adapted to grain and grazing; s. and se. of the C. H., it is more broken; yet on and near New River it is very fertile and productive in wheat. There is considerable mountain land in the county. Beef cattle are at this time the great staple of the county; but horses, swine, sheep, grain, tobacco, and hemp, could be produced in the greatest abundance. Population in 1840, whites 2,768, slaves 954, free colored 17; total, 3,739.

Newbern, the county-seat, is on the great stage-route from Bal-

timore to Nashville, Tenn., 222 miles southwesterly from Richmond, 19 miles from Christiansburg, and 28 from Wytheville. It is
the only village in the county, and one of considerable business
for an inland town : its location is high and airy, giving a fine
view of the neighboring valleys and mountains. It contains 5 mercantile stores, 1 Presbyterian and 1 Methodist church, and a population of about 300. Peak Knob, 4 miles south of Newbern, is a
prominent projection in Draper's mountain, rising about 1,000 feet,
and presenting from its summit a delightful and extensive landscape. Iron ore exists in abundance in this mountain, and also
coal of a good quality. In its vicinity are mineral springs, supposed to possess valuable medicinal qualities. On the north bank
of New River, near Newbern, there is a bluff called *the Glass Windows*, consisting of vertical rocks, nearly 500 feet high. and forming
the immediate bank of the stream for a distance of four miles. They
are considered a great curiosity. The face of these rocks is perforated by a vast number of cavities, which no doubt lead to caves
or cells within the mountain. Some of these cells have been explored and found to contain saltpetre, stalactites, and other concretions.

RANDOLPH.

Randolph was formed in 1787, from Harrison. It is 85 miles
long, with a mean width of 25 miles. This county is made up of
several parallel ranges of mountains, with their intervening valleys : it is drained by the head-waters of Elk River, and the
Monongahela. The mountains are covered with the finest timber,
and abound in coal and iron ore. Much of the soil of the mountains is rich, and they abound in slate, freestone, and limestone.
In some parts are small caves having a kind of copperas, which
is used for a dye ; and along some of the water-courses, alum
projects in icicle-like drops. Salt springs are numerous. Within
the last twelve years, elk and beaver have been seen in small
numbers. Randolph is principally a stock-raising county, and
live stock of every description are annually exported to market.
Population in 1840, whites 5,799, slaves 216, free colored 193;
total, 6,208.

Beverly, the county-seat, is 210 miles NW. of Richmond, 60 s. of
Morgantown, and 45 SE. of Clarksburg. It is situated near Tygart's Valley River, on a handsome plain, and contains a population
of about 200.

An attempt was made as early as 1754, to settle this section of country, by David
Tygart and a Mr. Files. About this time, " these two men, with their families, arrived
on the east fork of the Monongahela, and, after examining the country, selected positions for their future residence. Files chose a spot on the river, at the mouth of a creek
which still bears his name, where Beverly has since been established. Tygart settled a
few miles further up, and also on the river. The valley in which they had thus taken

up their abode, has since been called Tygart's Valley, and the east fork of the Monongahela, Tygart's Valley River.

"The difficulty of procuring bread-stuffs for their families, their contiguity to an Indian village, and the fact that an Indian war-path passed near their dwellings, soon determined them to retrace their steps. Before they carried this determination into effect, the family of Files became the victims of savage cruelty. At a time when all the family were at their cabin, except an elder son, they were discovered by a party of Indians, supposed to be returning from the South Branch, who inhumanly butchered them all. Young Files being not far from the house, and hearing the uproar, approached until he saw too distinctly the deeds of death which were doing; and feeling the utter impossibility of affording relief to his own, resolved, if he could, to effect the safety of Tygart's family. This was done, and the country abandoned by them."*

A writer in the American Pioneer, Mr. Felix Renick, has given some anecdotes of "Big Joe Logston," who lived somewhere in this region in the latter part of the last century. "No Kentuckian," says he, "could ever, with greater propriety than he, have said, 'I can out-run, out-hop, out-jump, throw down, drag out, and whip any man in the country.'" Big Joe removed from the vicinity of the source of the N. branch of the Potomac, to Kentucky, about the year 1790, during the prevalence of the Indian wars. Mr. Renick gives the following account of a desperate fight which he had in that country with two Indians:

Riding along a path which led into a fort, he came to a fine vine of grapes. He laid his gun across the pommel of his saddle, set his hat on it, and filled it with grapes. He turned into the path, and rode carelessly along, eating his grapes; and the first intimation he had of danger, was the crack of two rifles, one from each side of the road. One of the balls passed through the paps of his breast, which, for a male, were remarkably prominent, almost as much so as those of many nurses. The ball just grazed the skin between the paps, but did not injure the breast-bone. The other ball struck his horse behind the saddle, and he sunk in his tracks. Thus was Joe eased off his horse in a manner more rare than welcome. Still he was on his feet in an instant, with his rifle in his hands, and might have taken to his heels; and I will venture the opinion that no Indian could have caught him. That, he said, was not his sort. He had never left a battle-ground without leaving his mark, and he was resolved that *that* should not be the first. The moment the guns fired, one very athletic Indian sprang towards him with tomahawk in hand. His eye was on him, and his gun to his eye, ready, as soon as he approached near enough to make a sure shot, to let him have it. As soon as the Indian discovered this, he jumped behind two pretty large saplings, some small distance apart, neither of which was large enough to cover his body, and, to save himself as well as he could, he kept springing from one to the other.

Joe, knowing he had two enemies on the ground, kept a look-out for the other by a quick glance of the eye. He presently discovered him behind a tree loading his gun. The tree was not quite large enough to hide him. When in the act of pushing down his bullet, he exposed pretty fairly his hips. Joe, in the twinkling of an eye, wheeled, and let him have his load in the part exposed. The big Indian then, with a mighty "Ugh!" rushed towards him with his raised tomahawk. Here were two warriors met, each determined to conquer or die—each the Goliath of his nation. The Indian had rather the advantage in size of frame, but Joe in weight and muscular strength. The Indian made a halt at the distance of fifteen or twenty feet, and threw his tomahawk with all his force, but Joe had his eye on him and dodged it. It flew quite out of the reach of either of them. Joe then clubbed his gun and made at the Indian, thinking to knock him down. The Indian sprang into some brush or saplings, to avoid his blows. The Indian depended entirely on dodging, with the help of the saplings. At length Joe, thinking he had a pretty fair chance, made a side blow with such force, that, missing the dodging Indian, the gun, now reduced to the naked barrel, was drawn quite out of his hands, and flew entirely out of reach. The Indian now gave another exulting

---

* Withers' Border Warfare.

" Ugh !" and sprang at him with all the savage fury he was master of. Neither of them had a weapon in his hands, and the Indian, seeing Logston bleeding freely, thought he could throw him down and dispatch him. In this he was mistaken. They seized each other, and a desperate scuffle ensued. Joe could throw him down, but could not hold him there. The Indian being naked, with his hide oiled, had greatly the advantage in a ground scuffle, and would still slip out of Joe's grasp and rise. After throwing him five or six times, Joe found, that between loss of blood and violent exertions, his wind was leaving him, and that he must change the mode of warfare or lose his scalp, which he was not yet willing to spare. He threw the Indian again, and without attempting to hold him, jumped from him, and as he rose, aimed a fist blow at his head, which caused him to fall back, and as he would rise, Joe gave him several blows in succession, the Indian rising slower each time. He at last succeeded in giving him a pretty fair blow in the burr of the ear, with all his force, and he fell, as Joe thought, pretty near dead. Joe jumped on him, and thinking he could dispatch him by choking, grasped his neck with his left hand, keeping his right one free for contingencies. Joe soon found the Indian was not so dead as he thought, and that he was making some use of his right arm, which lay across his body, and, on casting his eye down, discovered the Indian was making an effort to unsheath a knife that was hanging at his belt. The knife was short, and so sunk in the sheath that it was necessary to force it up by pressing against the point. This the Indian was trying to effect, and with good success. Joe kept his eye on it, and let the Indian work the handle out, when he suddenly grabbed it, jerked it out of the sheath, and sunk it up to the handle into the Indian's breast, who gave a death groan and expired.

Joe now thought of the other Indian, and not knowing how far he had succeeded in killing or crippling him, sprang to his feet. He found the crippled Indian had crawled some distance towards them, and had propped his broken back against a log, and was trying to raise his gun to shoot him, but in attempting to do which he would fall forward, and had to push against his gun to raise himself again. Joe, seeing that he was safe, concluded he had fought long enough for healthy exercise that day, and not liking to be killed by a crippled Indian, he made for the fort. He got in about nightfall, and a hard-looking case he was—blood and dirt from the crown of his head to the sole of his foot, no horse, no hat, no gun—with an account of the battle that some of his comrades could scarce believe to be much else than one of his big stories in which he would sometimes indulge. He told them they must go and judge for themselves. Next morning a company was made up to go to Joe's battle-ground. When they approached it, Joe's accusers became more confirmed, as there was no appearance of dead Indians, and nothing Joe had talked of but the dead horse. They, however, found a trail, as if something had been dragged away. On pursuing it they found the big Indian, at a little distance, beside a log, covered up with leaves. Still pursuing the trail, though not so plain, some hundred yards further, they found the broken-backed Indian, lying on his back, with his own knife sticking up to the hilt in his body, just below the breastbone, evidently to show that he had killed himself, and that he had not come to his end by the hand of an enemy. They had a long search before they found the knife with which Joe killed the big Indian. They at last found it forced down into the ground below the surface, apparently by the weight of a person's heel. This had been done by the crippled Indian. The great efforts he must have made, alone, in that condition, show, among thousands of other instances, what Indians are capable of under the greatest extremities.

Some years after the above took place, peace with the Indians was restored. That frontier, like many others, became infested with a gang of outlaws, who commenced stealing horses and committing various depredations; to counteract which a company of regulators, as they were called, was raised. In a contest between these and the depredators, Big Joe Logston lost his life, which would not be highly esteemed in civil society. But in frontier settlements, which he always occupied, where savages and beasts were to be contested with for the right of the soil, the use of such a man is very conspicuous. Without such, the country could never have been cleared of its natural rudeness, so as to admit of the more brilliant and ornamental exercises of arts, sciences, and civilization.

RAPPAHANNOCK.

RAPPAHANNOCK was formed in 1831, from Culpeper. It is named from the river which runs on its northern boundary. Its soil is fertile, and productive in wheat and corn. Length about 18, breadth 17 miles. Pop. in 1840, whites 5,307, slaves 3,663, free colored 287; total, 9,257.

Washington, the seat of justice, is 123 miles NW. of Richmond, and 75 from Washington city. It is a fine village, near the foot of the Blue Ridge, in a fertile country, and upon one of the head branches of the Rappahannock. It contains a church, an academy, 2 stores, and about 60 dwellings. Sperryville, 6 miles s. of the C. H., Woodville, 10 miles from it, and Flint Hill, contain each about 30 dwellings.

RITCHIE.

RITCHIE was formed in 1843, from Harrison, Lewis, and Wood, and named in honor of Thomas Ritchie, Esq.: it is about 25 miles long, and 20 broad. The surface is generally hilly and broken, and the soil not fertile, except on the streams, where there is considerable champaign country.

Harrisville, the county-seat, lies about 37 miles east of Parkersburg, and 4 miles s. of the NW. turnpike: it contains 2 stores, 1 tannery, 1 Baptist and 1 Methodist church, and about 15 dwellings. Estimated population of the county, 1,800.

ROANOKE.

ROANOKE was formed from Botetourt, in 1838. The name is probably derived from the Indian word *Roenoke*, or *Rawrenoke*, signifying the Indian shell-money. It is a small county, with a mean length of about 20, and mean width of 18 miles. The Blue Ridge forms its eastern boundary; the western parts are mountainous. Much of the soil of the county, particularly on the Roanoke River in the vicinity of Big Lick, is of almost unequalled fertility, and productive in hemp, wheat, and tobacco. Pop. in 1840, whites 3,843, slaves 1,553, free colored 101; total, 5,499.

Salem, the county-seat, is in the valley of Virginia, on the west bank of Roanoke River, 178 miles westerly from Richmond, 25 miles NE. of Christiansburg, and 23 from Fincastle. The navigation of the Roanoke, from Weldon, N. C., to this place, 244 miles, is completed by canals, sluices, &c. Salem is a neat village, and contains 6 stores, 1 Presbyterian, 1 Baptist, and 1 Methodist church,

and a population of about 450.   Big Lick, 7 miles E. of Salem, on
the main stage-road, contains a Baptist church and a few dwellings.   The skeleton of a mammoth was found a few years since
in this vicinity.   Burlington contains a few dwellings.

The Botetourt Springs, in the northern part of the county, 12
miles from Fincastle, are quite popular, and the improvements are
sufficient to accommodate a large number of visitors.   The spring
contains sulphur, magnesia, carbonic acid gas, &c.

ROCKBRIDGE.

ROCKBRIDGE derives its name from the celebrated natural bridge :
it was formed in 1778, from Augusta and Botetourt.   Its mean
length is 31, mean breadth 22 miles.   This county is principally
watered by North River—a branch of James River—and its tributaries.   It flows diagonally through the county, and joins the main
branch of James River at the foot of the Blue Ridge, where their
united waters force a passage through.   Much of the soil is of a
superior quality, and highly cultivated.   It is one of the most
wealthy agricultural counties in the state.   Pop. in 1840, whites
10,448, slaves 3,510, free colored 326 ; total, 14,284.

Brownsburg, 12 miles NE. of Lexington, on the road to Staunton,
contains about 30 dwellings ; near it is the old church, long known
as the New Providence meeting-house.   Fairfield, 13 miles NNE.
of Lexington, contains a Methodist and a free church, and about
25 dwellings.

Lexington, the county-seat, 146 miles from Richmond, 188 from
Washington city, 35 from Lynchburg, 35 from Staunton, and 37
from Fincastle, is beautifully situated on the west bank of North
River, one of the main branches of the James.   It was founded in
1778, and was originally composed almost exclusively of wooden
buildings, most of which were destroyed by fire in 1794.   The
town speedily recovered from the effects of the catastrophe.   It is
now quite compact, many of the buildings are of brick, and some
of the private mansions—among which is that of the ..... governor of Virginia, James M'Dowell, Esq.—are beautifully situated.
A recent English traveller says, " The town, as a settlement, has
many attractions.   It is surrounded by beauty, and stands at the
head of a valley flowing with milk and honey.   House-rent is low,
provisions are cheap, abundant, and of the best quality.   Flowers
and gardens are more prized here than in most places."   Lexing
ton contains 13 mercantile stores, 2 newspaper printing offices,
Washington College, the Virginia Military Institute, a fine classical
school under the charge of Mr. Jacob Fuller, Ann Smith academy,
which is a female institution, 1 Presbyterian, 1 Episcopalian, 1
Baptist, and 1 Methodist church, and about 1,200 inhabitants.

WASHINGTON COLLEGE, AT LEXINGTON.

WASHINGTON COLLEGE, one of the oldest literary institutions south of the Potomac, was established as an academy in the year 1776, under the name of Liberty Hall, by the Hanover Presbytery, (then embracing the whole of the Presbyterian church in Virginia.) Its first rector was the Rev. William Graham, a native of Pennsylvania, and a graduate of Nassau Hall, N. J. Mr. Graham was a man of extensive acquirements, great originality of thought, warm patriotism, and indomitable energy ; and to his exertions, more than to those of any other one man, the institution owes its establishment, and its continuance during the troublous times of our revolutionary struggle. Liberty Hall received its charter from the state in the year 1782, still retaining the name of an academy, although its charter authorized it "to confer literary degrees, to appoint professors, as well as masters and tutors," and, in short, to perform all the acts which properly belong to a college. In the year 1796, it received its first regular endowment, from the hands of the "Father of his country." The legislature of Virginia, "as a testimony of their gratitude for his services," and "as a mark of their respect," presented to Gen. Washington a certain number of shares in the old James' River improvement, a work then in progress ; this Washington, unwilling to accept for his own private emolument, presented to Liberty Hall Academy. To perpetuate the memory of this noble act, the name of the institution was, by the unanimous vote of the trustees, changed to Washington Academy ; and in the year 1812, by an act of the legislature, still further changed to Washington College. Subsequently, John Robinson, Esq., a soldier of Washington, emulating the example of his illustrious leader, bequeathed his whole estate to the college ; and still more recently, the Cincinnati Society of Va., after having accomplished the patriotic purpose for which it was established, bequeathed the residue of its funds to the college, on condition that provision should be made for military instruction in the institution.

George A. Baxter, D. D., succeeded Mr. Graham. About the year 1827, he resigned the presidency, and was succeeded by Louis Marshall, M. D., of Kentucky. Mr. Henry Vethake succeeded him in Feb., 1835. His successor was the present president of the college, the Rev. Henry Ruffner, D. D., who was inaugurated Feb. 22d, 1837.

Like most of the older literary institutions of our country, Washington College has had its seasons of adversity as well as prosperity. At the present time, its prospects appear more flattering than they have done at any previous period since its first establishment. For the last four or five years its number of students has varied from 80 to 100, as large a number as its buildings would accommodate. Additional buildings, now just completed, will enlarge the accommodations so that it can receive about 150 ; probably as large a number as the region from which the college draws its patronage, will furnish for years to come. The faculty of the institution at this time consists of, Henry Ruffner, D. D., president, and professor of ethics and rhetoric ; Philo Calhoun, A. M., prof. of mathematics ; Geo. E. Dabney, A. M., prof. of languages ; Geo. D. Armstrong, A. M., Robinson prof. of natural philosophy and chemistry ; Capt. Thomas H. Williamson, Cincinnati prof. of military tactics. The bill of expenses in the college are : Treasurer's bill for tuition, room-rent, deposite, and matriculation, $42 per annum ; board $7½ to $8 per month ; washing, fuel, candles, bed, &c., about $3 per month. Total, per session of 10 months, about $140.* With such advantages as Washington College enjoys, in its location in the midst of one of the most fertile and healthy portions of the great valley of Virginia, surrounded by a population, moral, frugal, and industrious in their habits, and prizing highly the advantages of a liberal education, we confidently expect that its prosperity will continue ; and that it will continue a lasting monument to the wisdom, as well as the benevolence, of the illustrious man whose name it bears.

THE VIRGINIA MILITARY INSTITUTE.—This is a military academy, established in connection with Washington College by an act of the legislature, passed during the session of 1838-'39. Formerly, a guard of soldiers was maintained at the expense of the state, for the purpose of affording protection to the arms deposited in the Lexington arsenal, for the use of the militia of western Virginia. About the year 1836, some zealous friends of education, among whom we may mention Gov. Jas. McDowell, thinking that the arsenal might be converted into an educational institution, without any increase of expense to the state, and affording at the same time equal security to the public arms, applied to the legislature to make the necessary change. After various delays, this application resulted in the establishment of the Virginia Military Institute, in the year

---

* By an act of the Board of Trustees, indigent students, of good moral character, are admitted without the payment of tuition fees ; and such persons can, with prudence and economy, maintain themselves at college at from $80 to $100 per year.

57

1839. Thus far, its success has been such as to fulfil the wishes of its warmest friends, and to render it a deservedly popular institution in the state.

The course of instruction is a three years' course, requiring for admission a good common school education. It embraces the full course of mathematics and natural science taught in our colleges, with drawing, military tactics, and engineering, and so much of the French and Latin languages as the student's other studies leave him time to acquire during the first two years of his course. The corps of instructors consists of Col. Francis H. Smith, A. M., prof. of mathematics; Maj. John T. L. Preston, A. M., prof. of languages and English literature; Capt. Thomas H. Williamson, instructor in tactics and drawing; Geo. D. Armstrong, A. M., prof. of chemistry, &c., assisted by such cadets as are detailed, from time to time, to assist in the business of instruction. The annual expenses of a student at the institute are about the same as those of one at Washington College. The present number of students is 61, of whom 22 are maintained at the expense of the state.

Alum Springs.

The Alum Springs are 17 miles west of Lexington, on the road to the warm and hot springs of Bath county. The improvements at this place are recent, and the springs, although but comparatively little known, are gaining rapidly in favor with the public.

"The water contains a rare and valuable combination of materials: the principal are iodine, sulphates of iron and alum, magnesia, and sulphuric acid. The water is tonic, increasing the appetite and promoting digestion. It is alterative, exciting the secretions of the glandular system generally, and particularly of the liver and kidneys; it is cathartic, producing copious dark bilious evacuations; and it also effects a determination to the surface, increasing the perspiration.

"From the efficacy of these waters in purifying the blood, they are invaluable in the cure of all diseases of the skin, and all indolent sores, not disposed to a healthy action. In the use of them for such diseases, if the disease of the skin appears to be irritated at first, or if the ulcers become more inflamed, and discharge more freely; let not this circumstance alarm any one, or deter him from persevering in their use. These are the evidences of the good effects of the waters, in expelling the vitiated humors from the blood to the surface; and, until the blood is purified, such diseases cannot be cured In scrofulous ulcers, the use of these waters invariably causes them to discharge more freely, and in a short time of a more healthy appearance. They are a very useful remedy in cholera infantum, or the summer bowel-complaint in children. They immediately give a good appetite, promote digestion, and will effectually correct and cure acidity of the stomach. In amenorrhœa, dysmenorrhœa, and leucorrhœa, the waters are peculiarly efficacious. Most obstinate cases of scrofula, erysipelas, and dyspepsia, have been cured by these waters, which preserve their medicinal qualities when sent away in barrels."

The first settlements in this portion of the valley were made by the Scotch Irish, with a few original Scotch among them. They settled in the neighborhoods around Martinsburg, in Berkeley co., Winchester, and almost the entire counties of Augusta and Rockbridge. The same race went on into North Carolina, and settled in the counties of Orange and Guilford,—especially in the northern and middle parts of the latter county. Rockbridge and Augusta have always been the strongholds of Scotch Irish and Presbyterianism. From the introduction to the history of Washington College, a manuscript volume written by President Ruffner, we have been allowed to introduce the following graphic sketch of the settlement of the valley, and the characteristics of its early inhabitants; some of the facts are elsewhere given in this volume,— a repetition we prefer to breaking the connection:

From the year 1606, when Jamestown was first permanently settled, it required about one hundred years for the infant colony of Virginia to extend itself upwards to the Blue Ridge. The settlements on the upper branches of the Rappahannock, and in the Northern Neck between this river and the Potomac, seem first to have approached the high mountain barrier, whose top, enveloped in a blue mist, had long since attracted the eyes of settlers in the distant plains below. Near the Potomac the ridge is less rugged and forbidding in its aspect than it is further towards the southwest. When it was surmounted by exploring parties of white men, and displayed to their eyes the beauty and fertility of the vale of Shenando, and of the uplands beyond it, the temptation was irresistible, and hardy adventurers resolved to brave every danger for the sake of a possession so alluring. They first planted themselves on the rich low grounds of the Shenando, but soon ventured upon the pleasant uplands beyond the river. Here, in a basin-shaped cavity, they founded the town of Winchester, where fountains of water proved more attractive than fine prospects from the neighboring hills. This, the oldest town in the valley, continued to be a frontier-post until the French were driven out of Canada.

The eastern part of the valley being conveniently situated for emigrants from Pennsylvania, as well as from lower Virginia, the population there came to be a mixture of English Virginians, and German and Scotch Irish Pennsylvanians. Some of the latter were recent emigrants from Europe, who had landed at Philadelphia, and thence made their way by land to the new settlements.

The German Pennsylvanians, being passionate lovers of fat lands, no sooner heard of the rich vales of the Shenando and its branches, than they began to join their countrymen from Europe in pouring themselves forth over the country above Winchester. Finding the main Shenando mostly preoccupied, they followed up the North and South Branches, on both sides of the Massanutten, or Peaked Mountain, until they filled up all the beautiful vales of the country for the space of sixty miles. So completely did they occupy the country, that the few stray English or Irish settlers among them did not sensibly affect the homogeneousness of the population. They long retained, and for the most part do still retain, their German language, and the German simplicity of their manners. Of late years, indeed, a sensible transition has been going on about the borders of their old settlements, and about the villages, where law and trade have caused a mixture of population, and made inroads upon the speech, manners, and dress imported from their fatherland. This change has grieved their old people, who cannot give up the energetic language of their sires, corruptly as they speak it, nor the plain homespun dress of old times, nor see their children give them up without sorrowing for the degeneracy of their race. Not a few of these Germans of the valley have become anglicised by dispersion, where they have been led, by the temptation of good farms, to plunge into the mass of their Scotch Irish neighbors.

How far they might have originally filled up the valley, if the way had been clear, we cannot conjecture; but, ere they had reached the head-branches of the Shenando, their immigrant columns were met by another race, who soon filled up an equal space beyond them in this land of promise.

For the want of towns and roads, the first settlers in the valley were supplied with many needful articles by pedlers who went from house to house. Among these itinerant venders of small wares, was one John Marlin, who traded from Williamsburg to the country about Winchester. His visits to the inhabited parts of this romantic country inspired him with a curiosity to explore the unknown parts towards the southwest. In Williamsburg he got John Salling, a bold weaver, to join him in an exploring expedition. They proceeded through the valley in safety until they reached the waters of the Roanoke, where they were met by a roving party of Cherokees, and of course treated as spies upon the Indian territory. Marlin had the good fortune to escape from the hands of the savages, but Salling was carried as prisoner to their towns upon the upper Tennessee. Here he lived with his captors about three years, until he went with a party of them to the Salt Licks in Kentucky, to hunt the buffalo. Kentucky, like the valley, was a middle ground of contention between the northern and southern tribes. This party of Cherokees was attacked and defeated by some Indians from Illinois. Salling was again captured, and carried to Kaskaskias, where an old squaw adopted him for a son. While thus domiciled in this remote region, he accompanied his new tribesmen on some distant expeditions—once, even to the gulf of Mexico—and saw many countries, and tribes of savages, then wholly unknown in Virginia. But after two years, he was bought of his Indian mother by an exploring party of Spaniards, who wanted him for an interpreter. He was taken by them on their way northwards, until he reached Canada, where he was kindly redeemed by the French governor, and sent to New York; whence he found his way to Williamsburg again, after six years of strange and eventful wanderings.

In Williamsburg, two strangers from Britain, John Lewis and John Mackey, heard Salling's story with admiration. They were particularly struck with his glowing description of the valley of Virginia, a broad space between parallel ridges of mountain; its vales watered by clear streams, its soil fertile, its plains covered only with shrubbery and a rich herbage, grazed by herds of buffalo, and its hills crowned with forests; a region of beauty as yet, for the most part, untouched by the hand of man, and offering unbought homes and easy subsistence to all who had the enterprise to scale the mountain barrier, by which it had been so long concealed from the colonists. Lewis and Mackey joined Salling in making an expedition to this newly-discovered land, in order first to see it, and then, if it fulfilled their expectations, of making a settlement there. They were not disappointed; and having the whole land before them from which to choose, Lewis selected his residence near the Middle River, on a creek which bears his name. Mackey went further up the Middle River, and settled near the Buffalo Gap; but Salling, who in his captivity appears to have acquired a taste for wild solitude, went fifty miles apart from the others, and pitched his habitation in the forks of James River, where a beautiful bottom is overshadowed by mountains.

Lewis, who was evidently a man of energy and forethought, obtained authority to locate 100,000 acres of land in separate parcels in the country around him. While he was exploring the country to select good lands, his neighbor, Mackey, would frequently accompany him for the pleasure of hunting the buffalo. The result was, that Mackey died as he had lived, a poor hunter; but Lewis provided for his family a rich inheritance of lands. The pioneer-tribe of white hunters have generally followed the example of Mackey.

In the spring of the year 1736, Lewis, on a visit to Williamsburg, met with Benjamin Burden, who had lately come over as agent for Lord Fairfax, proprietor of the Northern Neck. Burden accepted Lewis's invitation to accompany him to his new home in the valley. He spent several months with his friend, exploring the country and hunting the buffalo, with Lewis and his sons, Samuel and Andrew. But he was a more provident hunter than Mackey. The party happened once to take a young buffalo-calf, which Samuel and Andrew Lewis turned and gave to Burden, to take with him to Williamsburg. This sort of an animal was unknown in lower Virginia; the calf would, therefore, be an interesting object of curiosity at the seat of government. Burden presented the shaggy young monster to Governor Gooch. The governor was so delighted with this rare pet, and so pleased with the donor, that he promptly favored his views, by entering an order in his official book, authorizing Benjamin Burden to locate 500,000 acres of land, or any less quantity, on the waters of the Shenando and James Rivers, on the conditions that he should not interfere with any previous grants, and that within ten years he should settle at least one hundred families on the located lands. On these conditions, he should be freely entitled to 1,000 acres adjacent to every house, with the privilege of entering as much more of the contiguous lands at one shilling per acre.

Burden returned forthwith to England for emigrants, and the next year, 1737, brought over upwards of one hundred families to settle upon the granted lands. At this time the spirit of emigration was particularly rife among the Presbyterians in the northern parts of Ireland, in Scotland, and in the adjacent parts of England. Most of Burden's colonists were Irish Presbyterians, who, being of Scottish extraction, were often called Scotch Irish. A few of the pure Scotch and northern English were mixed with the early settlers, but all, or nearly all, of the same Presbyterian stamp. Among the primitive emigrants to Burden's grant we meet with the names of some who have left a numerous posterity, now dispersed far and wide from the Blue Ridge to the Mississippi—such as Ephraim M'Dowell, Archibald Alexander, John Patton, Andrew Moore, Hugh Telford, John Matthews, &c.*

The first party were soon joined by others, mostly of their connections and acquaintances in the mother country. These again drew others after them; and they all increased and multiplied, until, ere the first generation had passed away, the land was filled with them. Then they began to send forth colonies to new lands, southward and westward, until now there is scarce a county in the great valley of the Mississippi where some of their descendants may not be found.

Although some lands on the upper branches of the Shenando were not included in Burden's grant, yet from the German settlements upwards to the vale of James River, the population was generally Presbyterian; so that the whole mass, for 60 miles or more along the valley, was scarcely less homogeneous and peculiar than the mass of Germans below them. Few of the old colonists of Virginia migrated to these parts of the valley. They lived by the cultivation of tobacco; tobacco was the sole staple of their trade; tobacco was their money. An Arcadian life among green pastures and herds of cattle, had no charms for them: tobacco was associated with all their ideas of pleasure and of profit. But how was a hogshead of tobacco to be rolled to market through the rugged defiles of the Blue Ridge? Not until roads and navigation offered new facilities for trade, and the Indian weed itself lost some of its importance, did the valley cease to repel settlers from the lowlands of Virginia. Hence the mixture of heterogeneous elements in the population has never, until lately, been sufficient to vary the true-blue hue of their primitive Scotch and Irish Presbyterianism. When, in addition to the names before mentioned, we give others of the more numerous families long settled on Burden's grant—the Prestons, the Paxtons, the Lyles, the Grigsbys, the Stuarts, the Crawfords, the Cumminses, the Browns, the Wallaces, the Willsons, the Carutherses, the Campbells, the M'Campbells, the M'Clungs, the M'Cues, the M'Kees, the M'Cowns, &c. &c.—no one acquainted with the race who imbibed the indomitable spirit of John Knox, can fail to recognise the relationship.

One who is of a different race, may be permitted to speak freely of their characteristics.

They had no sooner found a home in the wilderness, than they betook themselves to clearing fields, building houses, and planting orchards, like men who felt themselves now settled, and were disposed to cultivate the arts of civilized life. Few of them ever ran wild in the forests, or joined the bands of white hunters who formed the connecting link between the savage aborigines and the civilized tillers of the soil. They showed less disposition than the English colonists to engage in traffic and speculative enterprises. Without being dull or phlegmatic, they were sober and thoughtful, keeping their native energy of feeling under restraint, and therefore capable, when exigencies arose, of calling forth exertions as strenuous and as persevering as the occasion might demand.

In their devotion to civil liberty, they differed not from the majority of their fellow colonists. Their circumstances, in a new country planted by themselves, far remote from the metropolitan government, fostered and strengthened their ancestral spirit of freedom. As Presbyterians, neither they nor their forefathers would submit to an ecclesiastical hierarchy; and their detestation of civil tyranny descended to them from the covenanters of Scotland. Hence, in the dispute between the colonists and the mother country, the Presbyterians of the valley—indeed, of the whole country—were almost

---

* Among others (says Withers) who came to Virginia at this time, was an Irish girl named Polly Mulhollin. On her arrival she was hired to James Bell, to pay her passage; and with whom she remained during the period her servitude was to continue. At its expiration, she attired herself in the habit of a man, and, with hunting-shirt and moccasins, went into Burden's grant for the purpose of making improvements and acquiring a title to land. Here she erected thirty cabins, by virtue of which she held one hundred acres adjoining each. When Benjamin Burden the younger came on to make deeds to those who held cabin rights, he was astonished to see so many of the name of Mulhollin. Investigation led to a discovery of the mystery, to the great mirth of the other claimants. She resumed her Christian name and feminine dress, and many of her respectable descendants still reside within the limits of Burden's grant.—H. H.

unanimously Whigs of the firmest and most unconquerable spirit. They were among the bravest and most effective militia, when called into the field. Gen. Washington signified his opinion of them when, in the darkest day of the revolutionary struggle, he expressed his confidence, that if all other resources should fail, he might yet repair with a single standard to West Augusta, and there rally a band of patriots who would meet the enemy at the Blue Ridge, and there establish the boundary of a free empire in the west. This saying of the father of his country has been variously reported ; but we have no reason to doubt that he did, in some form, declare his belief that, in the last resort, he could yet gather a force in western Virginia which the victorious armies of Britain could not subdue. The spirit of these sires still reigns in their descendants, as the day of trial, come when it may, will prove.

Another characteristic of these people was their rigid Calvinistic, or, as some would call it, Puritanical morality. Founded on religious principle, this morality was sober, firm, and consistent, though, in some of its aspects, too stern to be altogether winning, and often unadorned by that refinement of manners which imparts a charm to the exercise of virtue in the common intercourse of life. But much of their austerity should be forgiven, in consideration of the precious substance of virtue within it. Their moral character was a rough diamond, but, nevertheless, a diamond which would brighten most under the hardest rubs.

The root of their morality, as we have intimated, was religious principle, deeply grounded by education, and nurtured by constant attendance on religious exercises. No sooner had they provided necessary food and shelter for their families, than they began to provide for the regular and decent service of God. They built churches and called pastors to the full extent of their ability. While their settlements were sparse and feeble, their churches were necessarily few and far asunder. Consequently, some families had to go an inconvenient distance to church. But they went, notwithstanding, male and female, old and young, on horses, some of them ten or twelve miles, to the house of God regularly on the Lord's day. These were the right sort of people to found a commonwealth that should stand the wear and tear of a hundred ages.

Some of the churches built by the first generation are yet standing, substantial monuments of their pious zeal. They are built of the solid limestone of the valley. Others have been replaced by larger and fairer structures of brick. In building some of the primitive stone churches, before roads, wagons, and saw-mills could facilitate the collection and preparation of materials, they had to adopt some singular modes of conveyance. For example, the Providence congregation packed all the sand used in their church from a place six miles distant, sack by sack, on the backs of horses ! and, what is almost incredible, the fair wives and daughters of the congregation are said to have undertaken this part of the work, while the men labored at the stone and timber. Let not the great-grand-daughters of these women blush for them, however they would deeply blush themselves to be found in such employment. For ourselves, we admire the conduct of these females : it was not only excusable, not only praiseworthy—it was almost heroic. It takes Spartan mothers to rear Spartan men. These were among the women whose sons and grandsons sustained the confidence of Washington in the most disastrous period of the revolution.

Their social intercourse was chiefly religious. When the Lord's Supper was administered in a church, the service usually continued four days. A plurality of ministers was present, and the people would flock to the place from all the country around—those who lived near giving hospitable entertainment to those from a greater distance. It was customary to have two of these sacramental meetings annually in each of the churches—one in the spring and one in the autumn. The meetings of the presbytery, which circulated through the principal churches, drew together a larger concourse, and were celebrated as the chief religious festivals of the country.

But except these solemn festivals, and the weekly meetings at church, the families of the country had little social intercourse, except occasional visits and the occurrence of marriage feasts. Nothing was known of the gay amusements common among the lower Virginians. . . . The careful and religious education of their children was one of the most important features of their domestic policy. Common schools arose among them, therefore, as soon as the state of the population admitted them.

The first academy established in the valley of Virginia was located on Timber Ridge, near the present village of Fairfield, in this county. It is the one alluded to in the preceding . historic sketch of Washington College, and was founded in 1776. Its first rector was the Rev. Wm. Graham.* This institution, the germ whence sprung Washington College, is thus described in the work of Dr. Ruffner :

The schoolhouse was a log cabin. A fine forest of oaks, which had given Timber Ridge its name, cast a shade over it in the summer, and afforded convenient fuel in winter. A spring of pure water gushed from the rocks near the house. From amidst the trees the student had a fine view of the country below, and of the neighboring Blue Ridge. In short, all the features of the place made it a fit habitation of the woodland muse, and the hill deserved its name of Mount Pleasant. Hither about thirty youth of the mountains repaired, " to taste the Pierian spring," thirty-five years after the first settlement of Burden's Grant. Of reading, writing, and *ciphering*, the boys of the country had before acquired such knowledge as primary schools could afford ; but with a few late exceptions, Latin, Greek, algebra, geometry, and such like scholastic mysteries, were things of which they had heard—which they knew perhaps to lie covered up in the learned heads of their pastors—but of the nature and uses of which they had no conception whatever. . . . . It was a log hut of one apartment. The students carried their dinner with them from their boarding-schools in the neighborhood. They conned their lessons either in the school-room, where the recitations were heard, or under the shades of the forest, where breezes whispered and birds sang without disturbing their studies. A horn —perhaps a real cow's horn—summoned the school from play, and the scattered classes to recitation. Instead of broadcloth coats, the students generally wore a far more graceful garment, the hunting-shirt, homespun, homewoven, and homemade, by the industrious wives and daughters of the land. Their amusements were not the less remote from the modern tastes of students—cards, backgammon, flutes, fiddles, and even marbles, were scarcely known among these homebred mountain boys. Firing pistols and ranging the fields with shot-guns to kill little birds for sport, they would have considered a waste of time and ammunition. As to frequenting tippling-shops of any denomination, this was impossible, because no such catchpenny lures for students existed in the country, or would have been tolerated. Had any huckster of liquors, knickknacks, and explosive crackers, hung out his sign in those days, the old puritan morality of the land was yet vigorous enough to abate the nuisance. The sports of the students were mostly gymnastic, both manly and healthful—such as leaping, running, wrestling, pitching quoits, and playing ball. In this rustic seminary a considerable number of young men began their education, who afterwards bore a distinguished part in the civil and ecclesiastical affairs of the country.

SAMUEL HOUSTON, late president of the republic of Texas, was born

* A correspondent has furnished us with the following original anecdote :
In the summer of 1781, Col. Tarleton came near capturing the whole of the Virginia legislature, with Mr. Jefferson, our governor, then assembled at Charlottesville. All of these, however, except seven, made their escape, and reassembled in Staunton, where they resumed their labors, supposing it a place of safety. But soon after they commenced business, a messenger arrived with the information that Col. Tarleton was in full march for that place. Intimidated by their late narrow escape, they precipitately fled, each caring most for his own safety. It so happened that on that day a Presbyterian clergyman from Lexington, 35 miles distant, was on his way to a meeting of his presbytery, at the Augusta church, 8 miles north of Staunton. Meeting with some of his brethren, who informed him of what had occurred, he inquired of them whether any measures had been taken by the legislature before they dispersed, to call out the militia, and being answered in the negative, he expressed great surprise, and said something must be done, and proposed that they should each take different roads, and attend to it at once. This was accordingly done, and the call as promptly obeyed ; and the men assembled at Staunton the same evening, prepared to march with a view of meeting the enemy. The clergyman alluded to reached Lexington, 35 miles distant, the same evening, and having spread the word in different directions, a large company assembled at his house the next morning. To these he delivered an address suited to the occasion. But they were without an officer, and no one being willing to act in that capacity, the clergyman offered his own service, which being accepted, he girt on his sword, and they immediately set out for the scene of action. On reaching Rockfish Gap, (the place where the road leading from Charlottesville to Staunton crosses the Blue Ridge,) they found the mountain covered with riflemen, determined that no hostile foot should enter their borders with impunity. Intelligence, however, soon arrived that Tarleton had changed his course, and was retreating down the country. Some supposed it was a feint, and that he would attempt to cross the mountain at another place, and immediately set out to guard the pass. Others returned home. But the clergyman alluded to, and his company, with others, went in pursuit of the retreating enemy, and joined the Marquis Lafayette below Charlottesville. The campaign, however, being likely to be protracted, they did not continue long with the army, but returned home. The inquiry naturally arises, Who was this clergyman ? Answer—It was the learned and pious *Rev. Wm. Graham*, one of Virginia's most useful and gifted sons—then principal of Liberty Hall Academy, (now Washington College,) whose voice has been heard in almost every part of the valley, announcing the tidings of mercy and who, with hundreds of his spiritual children, is now rejoicing around the throne.

THE NATURAL BRIDGE.

This celebrated curiosity is in the Valley of Virginia, near the centre of the state, one hundred and twenty-two miles west of Richmond. Its mean height, from the stream below to its upper surface, is two hundred and fifteen feet and six inches.

which this vast country boasts. You look opposite to you, and the great and prominent mountains just break away so as to form the foreground to a yet more distant prospect, which is bathed in sunlight and in mist, promising to be equal to any thing you see. Everywhere, above, around, beneath, was the great, the beautiful, the interminable forest. Nothing impressed me so much as this. The forest had often surrounded and overwhelmed me; I had never before such command of it. In a state so long settled, I had expected to see comparatively little of it; but there it was, spreading itself all around like a dark green ocean, and on which the spots that were cleared and cultivated only stood out like sunny islets which adorned its bosom.

On the whole, I had, as you will see, been travelling for three days over most delightful country. For 160 miles you pass through a gallery of pictures, most exquisite, most varied, most beautiful. The ride will not suffer in comparison with a run along the finest portions of the Rhine, or our own drive from Shrewsbury to Bangor. It is often, indeed, compared with Switzerland; but that is foolish; the best scenery in that land is of another and a higher class. I was not at all aware that I should be thus gratified; and therefore, perhaps, had the more gratification. I am thankful that I have seen it, and for the same reasons that I am thankful to have seen something of the west; because they contribute greatly to form just conceptions of America.

The NATURAL BRIDGE is 14 miles southwesterly from Lexington, 172 from Richmond, and 213 from Washington. The mean height of the bridge, from the stream below to its upper surface, is 215 feet 6 inches; its average width is 80 feet, its length 93 feet, and its thickness 55 feet.

"The stupendous arch constituting the bridge is of limestone rock, covered to the depth of from 4 to 6 feet with alluvial and clayey earth, and based upon huge rocks of the same geological character, the summits of which are 90 feet, and their bases 50 feet asunder, and whose rugged sides form the wild and awful chasm spanned by the bridge. The bridge is guarded, as if by the design of nature, by a parapet of rocks, and by trees and shrubbery, firmly embedded in the soil; so that a person travelling the stage road running over it, would, if not informed of the curiosity, pass it unnoticed. It is also worthy of remark, that the creation of a natural bridge at this place has contributed, in a singular manner, to the convenience of man, inasmuch as the deep ravine over which it sweeps, and through which traverses the beautiful 'Cedar creek,' is not otherwise easily passed for several miles, either above or below the bridge; and, consequently, the road running from north to south with an acclivity of 35 degrees, presents the same appearance in soil, growth of trees, and general character, with that of the neighboring scenery."

The Natural Bridge is higher, by 55 feet, than the Falls of Niagara. It is, in the opinion of at least one who has seen both, a greater curiosity, and more an object of wonder. That derives its chief interest from its magnitude, and is but, after all, a vast sheet of falling water;—by comparison with other cataracts only, wonderful. But the Natural Bridge is nature like art, with the proportions of art; on the very spot where art would otherwise have been required for the construction of a bridge. It is unique. No structure exists like it. As "a freak of nature" it is, perhaps, unparalleled, and therefore a greater natural curiosity and more wonderful than Niagara, although not so sublime an object; and, therefore, one does not experience that overwhelming sense of insignificance as in contemplating the latter.

The subjoined eloquent description, originally published in Europe, will strike the intelligent visitor as containing impressions similar to those he received on first viewing the Natural Bridge:

This famous bridge is on the head of a fine limestone hill, which has the appearance of having been rent asunder by some terrible convulsion in nature. The fissure thus made is about ninety feet; and over it the bridge runs, so needful to the spot, and so unlikely to have survived the great fracture, as to seem the work of man ; so simple, so grand, so great, as to assure you that it is only the work of God. The span of the arch runs from 45 to 60 feet wide ; and its height, to the under line, is about 200 feet, and to the head about 240 ! The form of the arch approaches to the elliptical ; and it is carried over on a diagonal line, the very line of all others so difficult to the architect to realize ; and yet so calculated to enhance the picturesque beauty of the object !

There are chiefly three points of sight. You naturally make your way to the head of the bridge first ; and as it is a continuation of the common road, with its sides covered with fine shrubs and trees, you may be on it before you are aware. But the moment you approach through the foliage to the side, you are filled with apprehension. It has, indeed, a natural parapet ; but few persons can stand forward and look over. You instinctively seek to reduce your height, that you may gaze on what you admire with security. Even then it agitates you with dizzy sensations.

You then make your way some fifty feet down into the bosom of the hill, and are supplied with some admirable standings on the projecting rockwork, to see the bridge and all its rich accompaniments. There is, 200 feet below you, the Cedar River, apparently motionless, except where it flashes with light as it cuts its way through the broken rocks. Mark the trees of every variety, but especially the fir, how they diminish as they stand on the margin of its bed ; and how they ascend, step by step, on the noble rockwork, till they overshadow you ; still preserving such delicacy of form and growth, as if they would not do an injury, while they lend a grace. Observe those hills, gathering all around you in their fairest forms and richest verdure, as if to do honor to a scene of surpassing excellence. Now look at the bridge itself, springing from this bed of verdant loveliness, distinct, one, complete ! It is before you in its most picturesque form. You just see through the arch, and the internal face of the further pier is perfectly revealed. Did you ever see such a pier—such an arch ? Is it not most illusive ! Look at that masonry. Is it not most like the perfection of art ; and yet what art could never reach ? Look at that coloring. Does it not appear like the painter's highest skill, and yet unspeakably transcend it ?

This is exquisite. Still you have no just conception of this masterpiece until you get below. You go some little distance for this purpose, as in the vicinity of the bridge the rocks are far too precipitous. A hot and brilliant day is, of all others, the time to enjoy this object. To escape from a sun which scorches you, into these verdant and cool bottoms, is a luxury of itself, which disposes you to relish every thing else. When down, I was very careful of the first impression, and did not venture to look steadily on the objects about me till I had selected my station. At length I placed myself about 100 feet from the bridge, on some masses of rock which were washed by the running waters, and ornamented by the slender trees which were springing from its fissures. At my feet was the soothing melody of the rippling, gushing waters. Behind me, and in the distance, the river and the hills were expanding themselves to the light and splendor of day. Before me, and all around, every thing was reposing in the most delightful shade, set off by the streaming rays of the sun, which shot across the head of the picture far above you, and sweetened the solitude below. On the right and left, the majestic rocks arose, with the decision of a wall, but without its uniformity, massive, broken, beautiful, and supplying a most admirable foreground ; and, everywhere, the most delicate stems were planted in their crevices, and waving their heads in the soft breeze, which occasionally came over them. The eye now ran through the bridge, and was gratified with a lovely vista. The blue mountains stood out in the background ; beneath them, the hills and woods gathered together, so as to enclose the dell below ; while the river, which was coursing away from them, seemed to have its well-head hidden in their recesses. Then there is the arch, distinct from every thing, and above every thing ! Massive as it is, it is light and beautiful by its height, and the fine trees on its summit seem now only like a garland of evergreens ; and, elevated as it is, its apparent elevation is wonderfully increased by the narrowness of its piers, and by its outline being drawn on the blue sky, which appears beneath and above it ! Oh, it is sublime—so strong, and yet so elegant—springing from earth, and bathing its head in heaven ! But it is the sublime not allied to the terrific, as at Niagara ; it is the sublime associated with the pleasing. I sat, and gazed in wonder and astonishment. That afternoon was the shortest I ever remembered. I had quickly, too quickly, to leave the spot for ever ; but the music of those waters, the luxury of those shades, the form and colors of those rocks, and that arch—that arch—rising over all, and seeming to offer a passage to the skies—O, they will never leave me !

James H. Piper, Esq., at present a member of the Virginia senate from Wythe county, when a young man climbed the Natural Bridge. The spot where he ascended is not shown in the engraving. On looking at the place, it seems impossible that a human being could ascend, and had the feat not been accomplished, it would be so considered. This, however, was the only instance, the particulars of which have been variously and erroneously stated. The account below is from the pen of Mr. William A. Caruthers, originally published in the New York Knickerbocker under the caption of—

CLIMBING THE NATURAL BRIDGE ; BY THE ONLY SURVIVING WITNESS OF THAT EXTRAORDINARY FEAT.

I think it was in the summer of 1818, that James H. Piper, William Reveley, William Wallace, and myself, being then students of Washington College, Virginia, determined to make a jaunt to the Natural Bridge, fourteen miles off. Having obtained permission of the president, we proceeded on our way rejoicing. When we arrived at the bridge, nearly all of us commenced climbing up the precipitous sides in order to immortalize our names, as usual.

We had not been long thus employed, before we were joined by Robert Penn of Amherst, then a pupil of the Rev. Samuel Houston's grammar-school, in the immediate neighborhood of the bridge. Mr. Piper, the hero of the occasion, commenced climbing on the opposite side of the creek from the one by which the pathway ascends the ravine. He began down on the banks of the brook so far, that we did not know where he had gone, and were only apprized of his whereabout by his shouting above our heads. When we looked up, he was standing apparently right under the arch, I suppose a hundred feet from the bottom, and that on the smooth side, which is generally considered inaccessible without a ladder. He was standing far above the spot where General Washington is said to have inscribed his name when a youth. The ledge of the rock by which he ascended to this perilous height, does not appear from below to be three inches wide, and runs almost at right angles to the abutment of the bridge ; of course its termination is far down the cliff on that side. Many of the written and traditional accounts state this to be the side of the bridge up which he climbed. I believe Miss Martineau so states ; but it is altogether a mistake, as any one may see by casting an eye up the precipice on that side. The story no doubt originated from this preliminary exploit.

The ledge of rock on which he was standing appeared so narrow to us below, as to make us believe his position a very perilous one, and we earnestly entreated him to come down. He answered us with loud shouts of derision. At this stage of the business Mr. Penn and servant left us. He would not have done so, I suppose, had he known what was to follow ; but up to this time not one of us had the slightest suspicion that Mr. Piper intended the daring exploit which he afterwards accomplished. He soon after descended from that side, crossed the brook, and commenced climbing on the side by which all visitors ascend the ravine. He first mounted the rocks on this side, as he had done on the other, far down the abutment ; but not so far as on the opposite side. The projecting ledge may be distinctly seen by any visitor. It commences four or five feet from the pathway on the lower side, and winds round, gradually ascending, until it meets the cleft of rock over which the celebrated cedar-stump hangs. Following this ledge to its termination, it brought him thirty or forty feet from the ground, and placed him between two deep fissures, one on each side of the gigantic column of rock on which the aforementioned cedar-stump stands. This column stands out from the bridge, as separate and distinct as if placed there by nature on purpose for an observatory to the wonderful arch and ravine which it overlooks. A huge crack or fissure extends from its base to the summit ; indeed, it is cracked on both sides, but much more perceptibly on one side than the other. Both of these fissures are thickly overgrown with bushes, and numerous roots project into them from trees growing on the precipice. It was between these that the aforementioned ledge conducted him. Here he stopped, pulled off his coat and shoes, and threw them down to me. And this, in my opinion, is a sufficient refutation of the story so often told, that he went up to inscribe his name, and ascended so high that he found it more difficult to return than to go forward. He could have returned easily from the point where he disencumbered himself; but the fact that he did thus prepare so early, and so near the ground, and after he had ascended more than double that height on the other side, is clear proof, that to inscribe his name was not, and to climb the bridge is, his object. He had already inscribed his name above Washington himself, more than fifty feet.

Around the face of this huge column, and between the clefts, he now moved, backwards and forwards, still ascending, as he found convenient foothold. When he had ascended about one hundred and seventy feet from the earth, and had reached the point where the pillar overhangs the ravine, his heart seemed to fail him. He stopped, and seemed to us to be balancing midway between heaven and earth. We were in dread suspense, expecting every moment to see him dashed in atoms at our feet. We had already exhausted our powers of entreaty in persuading him to return, but all to no purpose. Now it was perilous even to speak to him, and very difficult to carry on conversation at all, from the immense height to which he had ascended, and the noise made by the bubbling of the little brook as it tumbled in tiny cascades over its rocky bed at our feet. At length he seemed to discover that one of the clefts before mentioned retreated backward from the overhanging position of the pillar. Into this he sprang at once, and was soon out of sight and out of danger.

There is not a word of truth in all that story about our hauling him up with ropes, and his fainting away so soon as he landed on the summit. Those acquainted with the localities will at once perceive its absurdity; for we were beneath the arch, and it is half a mile round to the top, and for the most part up a ragged mountain. Instead of fainting away, Mr. Piper proceeded down the hill to meet us and obtain his hat and shoes. We met about half way, and then he lay down for a few moments to recover himself of his fatigue.

ROCKINGHAM.

ROCKINGHAM was formed in 1778, from Augusta. It is 38 miles long, and 23 broad. The main Shenandoah runs through the eastern portion; North River drains the southern part; north fork of Shenandoah runs through the N. and NW. portion; and Smith's creek, a branch of the latter, the central portion. The western part is very mountainous, and the Peaked mountains lie between Harrisonburg and the Shenandoah. Much of the soil is extremely fertile, and the farming economical and judicious. A large portion of the population is of German origin, and many still speak that language. Pop. in 1840, whites 14,944, slaves 1,899, free colored 501; total, 17,344.

Harrisonburg, the county-seat, is 122 miles northwesterly from Richmond, 25 from Staunton, and 40 from Charlottesville. The town was established in May, 1780, and named from Thomas Harrison, who had laid out 50 acres of his land into streets and lots. It contains 8 mercantile stores, 2 newspaper printing-offices, a market, 1 Methodist, and 2 Presbyterian churches, and about 1100 inhabitants. There is a fine spring of water on the public square, neatly enclosed. The village is handsomely built, flourishing, and is surrounded by a beautiful and fertile country. Mount Crawford, 8 miles s. of the C. H., on the North River, near the head of boat navigation, contains a church and about 30 dwellings. Port Republic, 12 miles s. of the C. H., at the junction of the North and South Rivers, contains a church and about 35 dwellings. Deaton,

4 miles sw., and Edom Mills, 5 miles n. of Harrisonburg, are small places.

This portion of the Shenandoah valley was almost exclusively settled by Germans from Pennsylvania, a few years previous to the French and Indian war. The manner of living among the primitive settlers of the valley of Shenandoah, together with the peculiar customs of the German population, are thus given by Kercheval :

The first houses erected by the primitive settlers were log-cabins, with covers of split clapboards, and weight-poles to keep them in place. They were frequently seen with earthen floors ; or if wooden floors were used, they were made of split puncheons, a little smoothed with the broadaxe. These houses were pretty generally in use since the author's recollection. There were, however, a few framed and stone buildings erected previous to the war of the revolution. As the country improved in population and wealth, there was a corresponding improvement in the erection of buildings.

When this improvement commenced, the most general mode of building was with hewn logs, a shingle roof, and plank floor, the plank cut out with the whipsaw. Before the erection of saw-mills, all the plank used in the construction of houses was worked out in this way. As it is probable some of my young readers have never seen a whipsaw, a short description of it may not be uninteresting. It was about the length of the common mill-saw, with a handle at each end transversely fixed to it. The timber intended to be sawed was first squared with the broadaxe, and then raised on a scaffold six or seven feet high. Two able-bodied men then took hold of the saw, one standing on the top of the log and the other under it, and commenced sawing. The labor was excessively fatiguing, and about one hundred feet of plank or scantling was considered a good day's work for the two hands. The introduction of saw-mills, however, soon superseded the use of the whipsaw, but they were not entirely laid aside until several years after the war of the revolution.

The dress of the early settlers was of the plainest materials—generally of their own manufacture ; and if a modern "belle" or "beau" were now to witness the extreme plainness and simplicity of their fashions, the one would be almost thrown into a fit of the hysterics, and the other frightened at the odd and grotesque appearance of their progenitors.

Previous to the war of the revolution, the married men generally shaved their heads, and either wore wigs or white linen caps. When the war commenced, this fashion was laid aside, partly from patriotic considerations, and partly from necessity. Owing to the entire interruption of the intercourse with England, wigs could not easily be obtained, nor white linen for caps.

The men's coats were generally made with broad backs, and straight short skirts, with pockets on the outside having large flaps. The waistcoats had skirts nearly half way down to the knees, and very broad pocket flaps. The breeches were so short as barely to reach the knee, with a band surrounding the knee, fastened with either brass or silver buckles. The stocking was drawn up under the knee-band, and tied with a garter (generally red or blue) below the knee, so as to be seen. The shoes were of coarse leather, with straps to the quarters, and fastened with either brass or silver buckles. The hat was either of wool or fur, with a round crown not exceeding three or four inches high, with a broad brim.[*] The dress for the neck was usually a narrow collar to the shirt, with a white linen stock drawn together at the ends, on the back of the neck, with a broad metal buckle. The more wealthy and fashionable were sometimes seen with their stock, knee, and shoe buckles, set either in gold or silver with brilliant stones. The author can recollect, when a child, if he happened to see any of those finely-dressed "great folk," as they were then termed, he felt awed in their presence, and viewed them as something more than man.

The female dress was generally the shortgown and petticoat, made of the plainest materials. The German women mostly wore tight calico caps on their heads, and in the summer season they were generally seen with no other clothing than a linen shift and petticoat—the feet, hands, and arms bare. In hay and harvest-time they joined the men in the labor of the meadow and grain-fields. This custom of the females laboring in the time of harvest, was not exclusively a German practice, but was common to all the northern people. Many females were most expert mowers and reapers. Within the

---

[*] The Quakers were remarkable for their broad-brim hats. They were sometimes called "Broadbrims," by way of distinguishing them from other people.

author's recollection, he has seen several female reapers who were equal to the stoutest males in the harvest-field. It was no uncommon thing to see the female part of the family at the hoe or the plough; and some of our now wealthiest citizens frequently boast of their grandmothers, ay, mothers too, performing this kind of heavy labor.

The natural result of this kind of rural life was, to produce a hardy and vigorous race of people. It was this race of people who had to meet and breast the various Indian wars, and the storms of the revolution.

The Dutchman's barn was usually the best building on his farm. He was sure to erect a fine large barn before he built any other dwelling-house than his rude log-cabin. There were none of our primitive immigrants more uniform in the form of their buildings than the Germans. Their dwelling-houses were seldom more than a single story in height, with a large cellar beneath; the chimney in the middle, with a very wide fireplace in one end for the kitchen, in the other end a stove-room. Their furniture was of the simplest and plainest kind; and there was always a long pine table fixed in one corner of the stove-room, with permanent benches on one side. On the upper floor, garners for holding grain were very common. Their beds were generally filled with straw or chaff, with a fine feather-bed for covering in the winter. The author has several times slept in this kind of bed; and to a person unaccustomed to it, it is attended not unfrequently with danger to the health. The thick covering of the feathers is pretty certain to produce a profuse perspiration, which an exposure to cold, on rising in the morning, is apt to check suddenly, causing chilliness and obstinate cough. The author, a few years ago, caught in this way the most severe cold, which was followed by a long and distressing cough; he ever was afflicted with.

Many of the Germans have what they call a drum, through which the stove-pipe passes in their upper rooms. It is made of sheet iron, something in the shape of the military drum. It soon fills with heat from the pipe, by which the rooms become agreeably warm in the coldest weather. A piazza is a very common appendage to a Dutchman's dwelling-house, in which his saddles, bridles, and very frequently his wagon or plough harness, are hung up.

The Germans erect stables for their domestic animals of every species: even their swine are housed in the winter season. Their barns and stables are well stored with provender, particularly fine hay: hence their quadrupeds of all kinds are kept throughout the year in the finest possible order. This practice of housing stock in the winter season is unquestionably great economy in husbandry. Much less food is required to sustain them, and the animals come out in the spring in fine health and condition. It is a rare occurrence to hear of a Dutchman's losing any part of his stock with poverty. The practice of housing stock in the winter is not exclusively a German custom, but is common to most of the northern people, and those descended from immigrants from the north. The author recollects once seeing the cow-stalls adjoining a farmer's dwelling.

The German women, many of them, are remarkably neat housekeepers. There are some of them, however, extremely slovenly, and their dwellings are kept in the worst possible condition. The effluvium arising from this want of cleanliness is in the highest degree disgusting and offensive to persons unaccustomed to such fare. The same remarks are applicable to the Irish; nay, to some native Virginians. The Germans are remarkable for their fine bread, milk, and butter. They consume in their diet less animal flesh, and of course more vegetables, milk, and butter, than most other people. Their "sour krout"* in the winter constitutes a considerable part of their living. They generally consume less, and sell more of the product of their labor, than any other class of citizens. A Dutchman is proverbial for his patient perseverance in his domestic labors. Their farms are generally small, and nicely cultivated. In all his agricultural pursuits his meadows demand his greatest care and attention. His little farm is laid off in fields not exceeding ten or twelve acres each. It is rarely seen that a Dutchman will cultivate more than about ten or twelve acres in Indian corn any one year. They are of opinion that the corn crop is a great exhauster of the soil, and they make but little use of corn for any other purpose than feeding and fattening their swine.

---

* Sour krout is made of the best of cabbage. A box about three feet in length, and six or seven inches wide, with a sharp blade fixed across the bottom, something on the principle of the jack-plane, is used for cutting the cabbage. The head being separated from the stalk, and stripped of its outer leaves, is placed in this box, and run back and forth. The cabbage thus cut up is placed in a barrel, a little salt sprinkled on from time to time, then pressed down very closely, and covered over at the open head. In the course of three or four weeks it acquires a sourish taste, and to persons accustomed to the use of it, is a very agreeable and wholesome food. It is said that the use of it, within the last few years, on board of ships, has proved it to be the best preventive known for the scurvy. The use of it is becoming pretty general among all classes of people in the valley.

Previous to the war of the revolution, and for several years after, considerable quantities of tobacco were raised in the lower counties of the valley. The cultivation of this crop was first introduced and pursued by immigrants from the eastern counties of Virginia. From the newly cleared lands, two crops of tobacco in succession were generally taken, and it was then appropriated to the culture of other crops. The crop of tobacco left the soil in the finest possible state for the production of other crops. Corn, wheat, rye, flax, oats, potatoes, and every thing else, were almost certain to produce abundant crops, after the crop of tobacco.

In the year 1789 the French revolution broke out, when bread-stuffs of every kind suddenly became enormously high; in consequence of which, the farmers in the valley abandoned the cultivation of tobacco and turned their attention to wheat, which they raised in vast quantities for several years. It was no uncommon thing for the farmer, for several years after the commencement of the French revolution, to sell his crops of wheat from one to two, and sometimes at two and a half dollars per bushel, and his flour from ten to fourteen dollars per barrel in our seaport towns.

RICHMOND.

RICHMOND was created in 1692, when the old county of Rappahannock was extinguished, and Essex, with this county, made from it. It is 30 miles long, with an average breadth of 7 miles. The Rappahannock forms its southwestern boundary. Pop. in 1840, whites 3,092, slaves 2,363, free colored 510; total 5,963.

Richmond C. H. is centrally situated in the county, 56 miles NE. of Richmond. It is a small village containing only about a dozen dwellings.

RUSSELL.

RUSSELL was formed in 1786, from Washington county, and named from Gen. Wm. Russell. Its mean length is 40, mean breadth 34 miles. It is drained by branches of the Sandy, and by the Clinch River; the latter runs through its eastern portion. The principal portion of the population is included between Clinch mountain and a distance of 15 miles from its base. The northern, and a greater portion of its territory, is so mountainous, sterile, and difficult of access, that its inhabitants are few and far between. There are some rich sections of land in Russell; and its mineral wealth—coal, iron ore, marble, &c.—is considerable. About 100,000 pounds of maple sugar are annually produced in the county. Pop. in 1840, whites 7,152, slaves 700, free colored 26; total, 7,878.

Lebanon, the county-seat, is 325 miles sw. of Richmond, and 130 miles from Knoxville, Tenn. It is beautifully situated on a branch of Clinch River, and commands a fine view of mountain scenery. It was founded in 1816, and although a small village, it is the only one in the county.

SCOTT.

SCOTT was formed in 1814, from Lee, Washington, and Russell, and named from Gen. Winfield Scott: its mean length is 24, mean breadth 23 miles. It is drained by the north fork of Holston and Clinch Rivers, each of which affords the facilities of boat navigation in times of freshets. Big and Little Moccasin and Sinking creeks, also water the county. The face of the country is mountainous and uneven, and much of the soil is good. Iron, coal, marble, limestone, and freestone, are found within its limits. About 60,000 pounds of maple sugar are annually produced. Pop. in 1840, whites 6,911, slaves 344, free colored 48 ; total, 7,303.

Estillville, the county-seat, is 344 miles sw. of Richmond, and 40 from Abingdon. It contains 3 stores, a Methodist church, and about 60 dwellings. The *Holston Springs* are on the north fork of Holston, 4 miles from the C. H. The medicinal qualities of the water are excellent, and its growing reputation, together with the improvements lately made, draw a large number of visitors. The water contains all the ingredients of the White Sulphur possessing any medical efficacy. The principal difference is the existence, in the latter, of sulphureted hydrogen. The uniform temperature of the water is 68½°, which renders it a natural medicated bath of the most agreeable degree of heat.

The NATURAL TUNNEL is situated upon Stock creek, about 12 miles westerly from Estillville. That part of the description in fine type, is extracted from the communication of Lieut.-Col. Long, of the U. S. Army, published in the Monthly American Journal of Geology for Feb., 1832 :

To form an adequate idea of this remarkable and truly sublime object, we have only to imagine the creek, to which it gives a passage, meandering through a deep narrow valley, here and there bounded on both sides by walls or *revêtements*, rising to the height of two or three hundred feet above the stream ; and that a portion of one of these chasms, instead of presenting an open *thorough cut* from the summit to the base of the high grounds, is intercepted by a continuous unbroken ridge more than three hundred feet high, extending entirely across the valley, and perforated transversely at its base, after the manner of an artificial tunnel, and thus affording a spacious subterranean channel for the passage of the stream.

The entrance to the natural tunnel, on the upper side of the ridge, is imposing and picturesque, in a high degree ; but on the lower side, the grandeur of the scene is greatly heightened by the superior magnitude of the cliffs, which exceed in loftiness, and which rise perpendicularly—and in some instances in an impending manner—more than three hundred feet ; and by which the entrance on this side is almost environed, as it were, by an amphitheatre of rude and frightful precipices.

The observer, standing on the brink of the stream, at the distance of about one hundred yards below the débouchure of the natural tunnel, has, in front, a view of its arched entrance, rising seventy or eighty feet above the water, and surmounted by horizontal stratifications of yellowish, white, and gray rocks, in depth nearly twice the height of the arch. On his left, a view of the same mural precipice, deflected from the springing of the arch in a manner to pass thence in a continuous curve quite to his rear, and towering, in a very impressive manner, above his head. On his right, a sapling growth of buckeye, poplar, lindens, &c., skirting the margin of the creek, and extending obliquely to the right, and upwards through a narrow, abrupt ravine, to the summit of the ridge,

THE NATURAL TUNNEL.

The Natural Tunnel is in the southwestern part of Virginia, three hundred and fifty-six miles from Richmond, near the line of Tennessee. This passage through a mountain is about four hundred and fifty feet in length. A stream of water passes through it and a stage road over it. The above is an internal view, taken near the lower entrance, looking out upon the wall of rock beyond, shown on page 466. At the point where the figures are seen, the roof is estimated at about ninety feet above the stream, and the strata is there arranged in concentric circles, bearing a striking resemblance to a dome.

THE NATURAL TUNNEL.

The Natural Tunnel is in the southwestern part of Virginia, three hundred and fifty-six miles from Richmond, near the line of Tennessee. This passage through a mountain is about four hundred and fifty feet in length. A stream of water passes through it and a stage road over it. The above is an internal view, taken near the lower entrance, looking out upon the wall of rock beyond, shown on page 466. At the point where the figures are seen, the roof is estimated at about ninety feet above the stream, and the strata is there arranged in concentric circles, bearing a striking resemblance to a dome.

which is here, and elsewhere, crowned with a timber-growth of pines, cedar, oaks, and shrubbery of various kinds.   On his extreme right, is a gigantic cliff lifting itself up perpendicularly from the water's edge, to the height of about three hundred feet, and accompanied by an insulated cliff, called the chimney, of about the same altitude, rising in the form of a turret, at least sixty feet above its basement, which is a portion of the imposing cliff just before mentioned.

The following passages are from Col. Long's private journal, which he gives in addition to the above:

The creek, which is about seven yards wide, and has a general course of about s. 15 w., here passes through a hill elevated from two to three hundred feet above the surface of the stream, winding its way through a huge subterraneous cavern, or grotto, whose roof is vaulted in a peculiar manner, and rises from seventy to eighty feet above its floor. The sides of this gigantic cavern rise perpendicularly in some places to the height of fifteen or twenty feet, and in others, are formed by the springing of its vaulted roof immediately from its floor.   The width of the tunnel varies from fifty to one hundred and fifty feet; its course is that of a continuous curve, resembling the letter S—first winding to the right as we enter on the upper side, then to the left, again to the right, and then again to the left, on arriving at the entrance on the lower side.   Such is its peculiar form, that an observer, standing at a point about midway of its subterranean course, is completely excluded from a view of either entrance, and is left to grope in the dark through a distance of about twenty yards, occupying an intermediate portion of the tunnel.   When the sun is near the meridian, and his rays fall upon both entrances, the light reflected from both extremities of the tunnel contributes to mollify the darkness of this interior portion into a dusky twilight.

The extent of the tunnel from its upper to its lower extremity, following its meanders, is about one hundred and fifty yards, in which distance the stream falls about ten feet, emitting, in its passage over a rocky bed, an agreeable murmur, which is rendered more grateful by its reverberations upon the roof and sides of the grotto.   The discharge of a musket produces a crash-like report, succeeded by a roar in the tunnel, which has a deafening effect upon the ear.   The hill through which this singular perforation leads, descends in a direction from east to west, across the line of the creek, and affords a very convenient passage for a road which traverses it at this place, having a descent in the direction just mentioned of about four degrees.

In the view of the lower entrance to the Natural Tunnel, there is represented an occurrence which took place many years since. At this point the deep gorge, through which the creek passes, is bounded on three sides by a perpendicular wall of rock over 300 feet in height, the fourth side being open to allow the passage of the creek after leaving the mouth of the tunnel.   The rocks at this place have several small caves, or fissures, in which the nitrous earth from which saltpetre is extracted has been found.   One or more of these are in the sides of the tunnel itself.   A gentleman informed us that the first time he visited the tunnel, some persons were inside extracting saltpetre, and that the smoke belching forth from its mouth and curling up the gorge, enhanced the natural gloom and hideousness of the scene.   In the late war, when saltpetre was very scarce, the small fissure in the wall of rock—at that place over 300 feet high—shown in the view, attracted attention, and it was determined to explore it.   An adventurous individual, by the name of George Dotson, was accordingly lowered from the top by a rope running over a log, and held by several men.   The rope not being sufficiently long, the last length, which was tied around his waist, was made of the bark of leatherwood. When down to the level of the fissure, he was still 12 or 14 feet from it horizontally, being thrown so by the overhanging of the wall of rock.   With a long pole, to which was attached a hook, he attempted to pull himself to the fissure. He had nearly succeeded, when the hook slipped, and he swung out into the middle of the ravine, pendulum-like, on a rope of perhaps 150 feet in length. Returning on his fearful vibration, he but managed to ward himself off with his pole from being dashed against the rock,

Lower Entrance to the Natural Tunnel.

when away he swung again. One of his companions, stationed on the opposite side of the ravine to give directions, instinctively drew back, for it appeared to him that he was slung at him across the abyss. At length the vibrations ceased. At that juncture Dotson heard something crack above his head: he looked, and saw that a strand of his bark rope had parted. Grasping, with both hands, the rope immediately above the spot, he cried out hastily, "Pull! for —— sake pull!" On reaching the top he fainted. On another occasion, the bark rope being replaced by a hempen one, he went down again and explored the cave. His only reward was the satisfaction of his curiosity. The hole extended only a few feet.

SHENANDOAH.

SHENANDOAH was established in 1772, from Frederick, under the name of Dunmore; but in October, 1777, after Lord Dunmore had taken a decided stand against the colonists, one of the delegates from the county stated, "that his constituents no longer wished to live in, or he to represent, a county bearing the name of such a tory; he therefore moved to call it Shenandoah, after the beautiful stream which passes through it;" and it was accordingly done. It is 32 miles long, with a mean width of 15 miles. The eastern and western portions are mountainous. The central part of the county is watered by the north fork of the Shenandoah, and the soil is extremely fertile. Population in 1840, whites 10,320, slaves 1,033, free colored 265; total, 11,618.

Woodstock, the county-seat, is 150 miles NW. of Richmond, and 32 ssw. of Winchester, on the Staunton and Winchester macadamized turnpike, and about a mile from the N. fork of the Shenandoah. The town was established in March, 1761. It contains several mercantile stores, 1 newspaper printing-office, an academy, a masonic hall, 1 German Reformed, 1 Lutheran, and 1 Methodist church, and a population of over 1,000. New Market was established in 1784. It is situated on the main turnpike through the valley of Virginia, about 20 miles south of Woodstock, and 18 N. of Harrisonburg: it contains six mercantile stores, 1 Lutheran, 1 Baptist, and 1 Methodist church, an academy, and a population of about 700. The Massanutten Fall, a beautiful cataract of nearly 50 feet perpendicular descent, is situated on a mountain of the same name, about three miles east of this village. The north fork of the Shenandoah runs within a mile on the west of the town, and is navigable, at high water, for large boats, to the Plain Mills. Strasburg is on the main turnpike, and on the N. branch of the Shenandoah, 12 miles N. of Woodstock: it contains 1 free, 1 Presbyterian, and 1 Lutheran church, and 85 dwellings. Edinburg, formerly called Stony Creek, is 5 miles ssw. of Woodstock: it is flourishing, and contains about 30 dwellings. Stony Creek, on which it is situated, is a bold stream, containing excellent sites for manufactories.

The Orkney or Yellow Springs, are about 18 miles southwest of Woodstock. "The waters are composed of several lively springs, and are strongly chalybeate. Every thing the water passes through, or over, is beautifully lined with a bright yellow fringe or moss. The use of this water is found beneficial for the cure of several complaints. A free use of this water acts as a most powerful cathartic, as does also a small quantity of the fringe, or moss, mixed with common water." There is, high up on Cedar creek, an *ebbing and flowing spring.* It is "a beautiful spring of clear mountain water, issuing from the western side of the Little North mountain, in a glen. It ebbs and flows twice in every twenty-four hours; and if care is not particularly taken at every flow, its current is so strong as to overset the vessels of milk placed in the water."

This county was settled by Germans from Pennsylvania, a plain, frugal, and industrious people. Within the memory of those living, the German language was universally spoken among them, and is now, to a considerable extent. A traveller in this section during the French and Indian war, draws a glowing description of their condition. He says:

The low grounds upon the banks of the Shenandoah are very rich and fertile. They are chiefly settled by Germans, who gain a sufficient livelihood by raising stock for the troops, and sending butter down into the lower parts of the country. I could not but reflect with pleasure on the situation of these people; and think, if there is such a thing as happiness in this life, they enjoy it. Far from the bustle of the world, they live in the most delightful climate and richest soil imaginable. They are everywhere surrounded with beautiful prospects and sylvan scenes—lofty mountains, transparent streams, falls of water, rich valleys, and majestic woods; the whole interspersed with an infinite variety of flowering shrubs, constitute the landscape surrounding them. They are subject to few diseases, are generally robust, and live in perfect liberty. They are ignorant of want, and are acquainted with but few vices. Their inexperience of the elegances of life, precludes any regret that they have not the means of enjoying them; but they possess what many princes would give half their dominions for—health, content, and tranquillity of mind

---

The Historian of the Valley has given the particulars of several incursions of the Indians into this region, from which we select the following:

In the year 1758, a party of about fifty Indians and four Frenchmen penetrated into the Mill Creek neighborhood, about nine miles south of Woodstock, and committed some murders, and carried off forty-eight prisoners. Among them was a young lad of the name of Fisher, about thirteen years of age.

After six days' travel they reached their villages west of the Alleghany mountains, where they held a council, and determined to sacrifice their helpless prisoner, Jacob Fisher. They first ordered him to collect a quantity of dry wood. The poor little fellow shuddered, burst into tears, and told his father they intended to burn him. His father replied, "I hope not;" and advised him to obey. When he had collected a sufficient quantity of wood to answer their purpose, they cleared and smoothed a ring around a sapling, to which they tied him by one hand, then formed a trail of wood around the tree, and set it on fire. The poor boy was then compelled to run round in this ring of fire until his rope wound him up to the sapling, and then back, until he came in contact with the flame, while his infernal tormentors were drinking, singing, and dancing around him, with "horrid joy." This was continued for several hours; during which time the savage men became beastly drunk, and as they fell prostrate to the ground, the squaws would keep up the fire. With long sharp poles, prepared for the purpose, they would pierce the body of their victim whenever he flagged, until the poor and helpless boy fell, and expired with the most excruciating torments, while his father and brothers, who were also prisoners, were compelled to be witnesses of the heart-rending tragedy.

In 1766, two men by the name of Sheetz and Taylor, had taken their wives and children in a wagon, and were on their way to the fort at Woodstock. At the Narrow Passage, three miles south of Woodstock, five Indians attacked them. The two men were killed at the first onset, and the Indians rushed to seize the women and children. The women, instead of swooning at the sight of their bleeding, expiring husbands, seized their axes, and with Amazonian firmness, and strength almost superhuman, defended themselves and children. One of the Indians had succeeded in getting hold of one of Mrs. Sheetz's children, and attempted to drag it out of the wagon; but with the quickness of lightning she caught her child in one hand, and with the other made a blow at the head of the fellow, which caused him to quit his hold to save his life. Several of the Indians received pretty sore wounds in this desperate conflict, and all at last ran off, leaving the two women with their children to pursue their way to the fort.

Gen. PETER MUHLENBURG was a native of Pennsylvania, and by profession a clergyman of the Lutheran order. At the breaking out of the revolution, he was a young man about 30 years of age, and pastor of a Lutheran church at Woodstock. In 1776, he received the commission of colonel, and was requested to raise his regiment among the Germans of the valley. Having in his pulpit inculcated the principles of liberty, he found no difficulty in enlisting a regiment. He entered the pulpit with his sword and cockade, preached his farewell sermon, and the next day marched at the head of his regiment to join the army. His regiment was the 8th Virginia, or, as it was commonly called, the German regiment. This corps behaved with honor throughout the war. They were at Brandywine, Monmouth, and Germantown, and in the southern campaigns. In 1777, Mr. Muhlenburg was promoted to the rank of brigadier-general. After the war he returned to Pennsylvania, and was appointed treasurer of that state, where he ended his days. In person, Gen. Muhlenburg was tall and well-proportioned, and in his address, remarkably courteous. He was a fine disciplinarian, an excellent officer, and esteemed and beloved by both officers and soldiers.

———

Human bones of extraordinary size—thigh bones three feet in length, and skeletons seven feet in length—have been discovered on Flint run, in this county, on Hawksbill creek, Tuscarora creek, and in Hardy county. (See p. 300.) Capt. Smith's "Generall Historie," vol. I., p. 120, gives an account of a prodigious giant tribe of Indians, the Sasquesahanocks, whom he met with at the head of Chesapeake Bay. This relation has been rejected as incredible, and considered as on a footing with the stories of Baron Munchausen, or Sinbad the Sailor; but these evidences would seem to confirm it.[*]

SMYTH.

Smyth was formed in 1831, from Washington and Wythe, and named from Gen. Alexander Smyth, an officer of the late war, and a M. C. from 1817 to 1825, and 1827 to 1830. It is 30 miles long, with a mean width of 22 miles. It has three valleys; the north, south, and middle forks of the Holston running parallel with each. The mountains are lofty, the bottom lands rich and productive. There are three quarries of gypsum, of the best quality, on the N. fork of the Holston, and several other quarries on Cove creek. It is now extensively and advantageously used in agriculture. About 60,000 pounds of maple sugar are annually produced. Pop., whites 5,539, slaves 838, free colored 145; total, 6,522.

Marion, the county-seat, is a recently established village, near the centre of the county; 275 miles sw. of Richmond, 29 NE. of Abingdon, and 26 sw. of Wytheville, on the great turnpike from Baltimore to Nashville, Tenn. It is a small, but neat town, containing 3 mercantile stores, and about 30 dwellings. The Chilhowee Sulphur Springs are on, or near the great turnpike, within 18 miles of Abingdon. The settlement called Saltville, derives its name from the justly celebrated salt-works of Preston and King, which are on the line of this and Washington counties, in a narrow plain between the Rich Valley and the north fork of the Holston. There are two wells here, and the salt manufactured from them is of an excellent quality. About 100 persons are employed at these works. The only fossil salt yet discovered in the Union, is found at this place.

SOUTHAMPTON.

Southampton was formed in 1748, from Isle of Wight. Its length is 40, mean width 15 miles. The rail-road from Portsmouth to Welden, N. C., runs across the county. It is watered by the Meherrin, Nottoway, and Blackwater Rivers. The Nottoway is navigable for vessels of 70 tons, as far as Monroe, from which place produce and lumber are shipped to Norfolk. The Blackwater is navigable for large vessels to South Quay, in Nansemond. There were in 1840, whites 5,171, slaves 6,555, free colored 1,799; total, 14,525. Jerusalem, the county-seat, is on Nottoway River, 70 miles SSE. of Richmond, and contains about 30 dwellings.

In this county are the relics of the once powerful tribe of Nottoway Indians. They have a reservation of good land, about 15 miles square, on the Nottoway River, near Jerusalem. These, with the relics of the Pamunkey* tribe at Indian Town, in King William county, are the last remains of the Indians of eastern Virginia. Col. Byrd, in 1728, thus speaks of the Nottoways in his journal:

In the morning we dispatched a runner to the Nottoway Town, to let the Indians know we intended them a visit that evening, and our honest landlord was so kind as to be our pilot thither, being about four miles from his house. Accordingly, in the afternoon we marched in good order to the town, where the female scouts, stationed on an eminence for that purpose, had no sooner spied us, but they gave notice of our approach to their fellow-citizens by continual whoops and cries, which could not possibly have been more dismal at the sight of their most implacable enemies. This signal assembled all their great men, who received us in a body, and conducted us into the fort. This fort was a square piece of ground, enclosed with substantial puncheons, or strong palisades, about ten feet high, and leaning a little outwards, to make a scalade more difficult. Each side of the square might be about a hundred yards long, with loop-holes at proper distances, through which they might fire upon the enemy. Within this enclosure we found bark cabins sufficient to lodge all their people, in case they should be obliged to retire thither. These cabins are no other but close arbors made of saplings, arched at the top, and covered so well with bark as to be proof against all weather. The fire is made in the middle, according to the Hibernian fashion, the smoke whereof finds no other vent but at the door, and so keeps the whole family warm, at the expense both of their eyes and complexion. The Indians have no standing furniture in their cabins but hurdles to repose their persons upon, which they cover with mats and deer-skins. We were conducted to the best apartments in the fort, which just before had been made ready for our reception, and adorned with new mats that were very sweet and clean. The young men had painted themselves in a hideous manner, not so much for ornament as terror. In that frightful equipage they entertained us with sundry war-dances, wherein they endeavored

---

* Since the account of the Pamunkey Indians was printed (see p. 349) we have accidentally met, in the Family Magazine for 1838, a description of an Indian ornament, accompanied by an engraved representation. The description, signed "J. M.," and dated at Fredericksburg, here follows:

"There is now before me a silver frontlet, obviously, I think, part of a crown. The engraving upon it is, first, the *crest*, a crown surmounted by a lion passant. The escutcheon, as delineated, field argent. Beneath this is a scroll containing the words, 'THE QUEENE OF PAMUNKEY.' Those nondescript things in the dexter, chief, and sinister base quarters are lions passant, and the whole is bordered with a wreath. Just within the wreath you will see inscribed, 'CHARLES THE SECOND, KING OF ENGLAND, SCOTLAND, FRANCE, IRELAND, AND VIRGINIA,' and within that the words, 'HONI SOIT QVI MAL Y PENSE,' [EVIL TO HIM WHO EVIL THINKS.] The ornament was purchased of some Indians many years ago by Alexander Morson, of Falmouth, the grandfather of the present proprietor.

"You know that the Pamunkey tribe still occupies its old ground in King William county, exercising to a certain extent its own laws, an '*imperium in imperio*.'"

to look as formidable as possible. The instrument they danced to was an Indian drum, that is, a large gourd with a skin braced tight over the mouth of it. The dancers all sang to the music, keeping exact time with their feet, while their heads and arms were screwed into a thousand menacing postures. Upon this occasion the ladies had arrayed themselves in all their finery. They were wrapped in their red and blue match coats, thrown so negligently about them that their mahogany skins appeared in several parts, like the Lacedæmonian damsels of old. Their hair was braided with white and blue peak, and hung gracefully in a large roll upon their shoulders.

This peak consists of small cylinders cut out of a conch-shell, drilled through, and strung like beads. It serves them both for money and jewels, the blue being of much greater value than the white, for the same reason that Ethiopian mistresses in France are dearer than French, because they are more scarce. The women wear necklaces and bracelets of these precious materials, when they have a mind to appear lovely. Though their complexions be a little sad-colored, yet their shapes are very straight and well-proportioned. Their faces are seldom handsome, yet they have an air of innocence and bashfulness, that, with a little less dirt, would not fail to make them desirable. Such charms might have had their full effect upon men who had been so long deprived of female conversation, but that the whole winter's soil was so crusted on the skins of those dark angels, that it required a very strong appetite to approach them. The bear's oil, with which they anoint their persons all over, makes their skins soft, and at the same time protects them from every species of vermin that use to be troublesome to other uncleanly people.

The little work that is done among the Indians is done by the poor women, while the men are quite idle, or at most employed only in the gentlemanly diversions of hunting and fishing. In this, as well as in their wars, they use nothing but fire-arms, which they purchase of the English for skins. Bows and arrows are grown into disuse, except only amongst their boys. Nor is it ill policy, but on the contrary very prudent, thus to furnish the Indians with fire-arms, because it makes them depend entirely upon the English, not only for their trade, but even for their subsistence. Besides, they were really able to do more mischief while they made use of arrows, of which they would let silently fly several in a minute with wonderful dexterity ; whereas now they hardly ever discharge their firelocks more than once, which they insidiously do from behind a tree, and then retire as nimbly as the Dutch horse used to do now and then formerly in Flanders. We put the Indians to no expense, but only of a little corn for our horses, for which in gratitude we cheered their hearts with what rum we had left, which they love better than they do their wives and children. Though these Indians dwell among the English, and see in what plenty a little industry enables them to live, yet they choose to continue in their stupid idleness, and to suffer all the inconveniences of dirt, cold, and want, rather than to disturb their heads with care, or defile their hands with labor.

The whole number of people belonging to the Nottoway Town, if you include women and children, amount to about two hundred. These are the only Indians of any consequence now remaining within the limits of Virginia. The rest are either removed, or dwindled to a very inconsiderable number, either by destroying one another, or else by the smallpox and other diseases. Though nothing has been so fatal to them as their ungovernable passion for rum, with which, I am sorry to say it, they have been but too liberally supplied by the English that live near them.

In August, 1831, a body of 60 or 70 slaves arose upon the white inhabitants of this county, and massacred 55 men, women, and children. The subjoined account of this event, known as the "Southampton Insurrection," was published at the time :

The leader of this insurrection and massacre was a slave by the name of *Nat Turner*, about thirty-one years of age, born the slave of Mr. Benjamin Turner, of Southampton county. From a child, Nat appears to have been the victim of superstition and fanaticism. He stimulated his comrades to join him in the massacre, by declaring to them that he had been commissioned by Jesus Christ, and that he was acting under inspired direction in what he was going to accomplish.

In the confession which he voluntarily made to Mr. Grey, while in prison, he says : "That in his childhood a circumstance occurred which made an indelible impression on his mind, and laid the groundwork of the enthusiasm which terminated so fatally to many. Being at play with other children, when three or four years old, I told them something, which my mother overhearing, said it happened before I was born. I stuck to my story, however, and related some things which went, in her opinion, to confirm it ; others being called on were greatly astonished, knowing these things had happened, and caused them to say in my hearing, I surely would be a prophet, as the Lord had showed me things which happened before my birth." His parents strengthened him in this belief, and said in his presence, that he was intended for some great purpose, which they had always thought from certain marks on his head and breast. Nat, as he grew up, was fully persuaded he was destined to accomplish some great purpose ; his powers of mind appeared much superior to his fellow slaves ; they looked up to him as a person guided by divine inspiration, which belief he ever inculcated by his austerity of life and manners.

After a variety of revelations from the spiritual world, Nat says, in his confession, that, "On the 12th of May, 1828, I heard a loud noise in the heavens, and the Spirit instantly appeared to me, and said the serpent was loosened, and Christ had laid down the yoke he had borne for the sins of men ; and that I should take it on, and fight against the serpent, for the time was fast approaching when the first should be last and the last should be first—and by signs in the heavens that it would make known to me when I should commence the great work—and until the first sign appeared, I should conceal it from the knowledge of men. And on the appearance of the sign, (the eclipse of the sun last February, 1831,) I should arise and prepare myself, and slay my enemies with their own weapons. And immediately on the sign appearing in the heavens, the seal was removed from my lips, and I communicated the great work laid out for me to do, to four, in whom I had the greatest confidence, (Henry, Hark, Nelson, and Sam.) It was intended by us to have begun the work of death on the 4th July last. Many were the plans formed and rejected by us ; and it affected my mind to such a degree, that I fell sick, and the time passed without our coming to any determination how to commence—still forming new schemes and rejecting them, when the sign appeared again, which determined me not to wait longer."

Nat commenced the massacre by the murder of his master and family. He says : "Since the commencement of 1830, I had been living with Mr. Joseph Travis, who was to me a kind master, and placed the greatest confidence in me. In fact, I had no cause to complain of his treatment to me. On Saturday evening, the 20th of August, it was agreed between Henry, Hark, and myself, to prepare a dinner the next day for the men we expected, and then to concert a plan, as we had not yet determined on any. Hark, on the following morning, brought a pig, and Henry, brandy ; and being joined by Sam, Nelson, Will, and Jack, they prepared in the woods a dinner, where, about three o'clock, I joined them. I saluted them on coming up, and asked Will how came he there ; he answered, his life was worth no more than others, and his liberty as dear to him. I asked him if he thought to obtain it ? He said he would, or lose his life. This was enough to put him in full confidence. Jack, I knew, was only a tool in the hands of Hark. It was quickly agreed we should commence at home, (Mr. J. Travis',) on that night ; and, until we had armed and equipped ourselves, and gathered sufficient force, neither age nor sex was to be spared, (which was invariably adhered to.) We remained at the feast until about two hours in the night, when we went to the house and found Austin ; they all went to the cider press and drank, except myself. On returning to the house, Hark went to the door with an axe for the purpose of breaking it open, as we knew we were strong enough to murder the family, if they were awakened by the noise ; but reflecting that it might create an alarm in the neighborhood, we determined to enter the house secretly, and murder them while sleeping. Hark got a ladder and set it against the chimney, on which I ascended, and hoisting a window, entered and came down stairs, unbarred the door, and removed the guns from their places. It was then observed that I must spill the first blood. On which, armed with a hatchet, and accompanied by Will, I entered my master's chamber ; it being dark, I could not give a death-blow ; the hatchet glanced from his head, he sprang from the bed and called his wife ; it was his last word. Will laid him dead with a blow of his axe, and Mrs. Travis shared the same fate as she lay in bed. The murder of this family, five in number, was the work of a moment, not one of them awoke ; there was a little infant sleeping in a cradle, that was forgotten until we had left the house and gone some distance, when Henry and Will returned and killed it ; we got here four guns that would shoot, and several old muskets, with a pound or two of powder. We remained some time at the barn, where we paraded ; I formed them in a line as soldiers, and after carrying them through all the manœuvres I was master of, marched them off to Mr. Salathiel Francis', about six hundred yards distant."

They proceeded in this manner from house to house, murdering all the whites they could find, their force augmenting as they proceeded, till they amounted to fifty or sixty in number, all mounted, armed with guns, axes, swords, and clubs. They then started for Jerusalem, and proceeded a few miles, when they were met by a party of white men who fired upon them, and forced them to retreat. " On my way back, (says Nat,) I called at Mrs. Thomas's, Mrs. Spencer's, and several other places ; the white families having fled, we found no more victims to gratify our thirst for blood. We stopped at Major Ridley's quarter for the night, and being joined by four of his men, with the recruits made since my defeat, we mustered now about forty strong.

" After placing out sentinels, I lay down to sleep, but was quickly roused by a great racket ; starting up, I found some mounted, and others in great confusion. One of the sentinels having given the alarm that we were about to be attacked, I ordered some to ride round and reconnoitre ; and on their return the others being more alarmed, not knowing who they were, fled in different ways, so that I was reduced to about twenty again ; with this I determined to attempt to recruit, and proceeded on to rally in the neighborhood I had left. Dr. Blunt's was the nearest house, which we reached just before day ; on riding up the yard, Hark fired a gun. We expected Dr. Blunt and his family were at Major Ridley's, as I knew there was a company of men there ; the gun was fired to ascertain if any of the family were at home ; we were immediately fired upon and retreated, leaving several of my men. I do not know what became of them, as I never saw them afterwards. Pursuing our course back, and coming in sight of Capt. Harris's, where we had been the day before, we discovered a party of white men at the house, on which all deserted me but two, (Jacob and Nat.) We concealed ourselves in the woods until near night, when I sent them in search of Henry, Sam, Nelson, and Hark ; and directed them to rally all they could, at the place we had had our dinner the Sunday before, where they would find me ; and I accordingly returned there as soon as it was dark, and remained until Wednesday evening, when, discovering white men riding around the place, as though they were looking for some one, and none of my men joining me, I concluded Jacob and Nat had been taken, and compelled to betray me. On this I gave up all hope for the present, and on Thursday night, after having supplied myself with provisions from Mr. Travis', I scratched a hole under a pile of fence-rails in a field, where I concealed myself for six weeks, never leaving my hiding-place but for a few minutes in the dead of the night to get water, which was very near ; thinking by this time I could venture out, I began to go about in the night, and evesdrop the houses in the neighborhood ; pursuing this course for about a fortnight, and gathering little or no intelligence, afraid of speaking to any human being, and returning every morning to my cave before the dawn of day. I know not how long I might have led this life, if accident had not betrayed me. A dog in the neighborhood, passing by my hiding-place one night while I was out, was attracted by some meat I had in my cave, and crawled in and stole it, and was coming out just as I returned. A few nights after, two negroes having started to go hunting with the same dog, and passed that way, the dog came again to the place, and having just gone out to walk about, discovered me and barked, on which, thinking myself discovered, I spoke to them to beg concealment. On making myself known they fled from me. Knowing then they would betray me, I immediately left my hiding-place, and was pursued almost incessantly, until I was taken a fortnight afterwards, by Mr. Benjamin Phipps, in a little hole I had dug out with my sword, for the purpose of concealment, under the top of a fallen tree. On Mr. Phipps' discovering the place of my concealment, he cocked his gun and aimed at me. I requested him not to shoot, and I would give up, upon which he demanded my sword. I delivered it to him and he brought me to prison."

Nat was executed according to his sentence, at Jerusalem, Nov. 11th, 1831. The following is a list of the persons murdered in the insurrection, on the 21st and 22d of August, 1831 :

Joseph Travis and wife and three children, Mrs. Elizabeth Turner, Hartwell Prebles, Sarah Newsome, Mrs. P. Reese and son William, Trajan Doyle, Henry Bryant and wife and child, and wife's mother ; Mrs. Catharine Whitehead, son Richard, four daughters and grand-child ; Salathiel Francis, Nathaniel Francis' overseer and two children, John T. Barrow, George Vaughan, Mrs. Levi Waller and ten children, William Williams, wife and two boys ; Mrs. Caswell Worrel and child, Mrs. Rebecca Vaughan, Ann Elizabeth Vaughan and son Arthur, Mrs. John K. Williams and child, Mrs. Jacob Williams and three children, and Edward Drury—amounting to fifty-five.

SPOTTSYLVANIA.

SPOTTSYLVANIA was formed in 1720, from Essex, King William, and King and Queen, and named from Alexander Spotswood, then governor of Virginia. It is 23 miles long, and 17 wide. It is drained by head branches of the North Anna and Mattapony, and the Rappahannock forms its northern boundary. The soil on the streams is fine; but on the ridges, the land, originally thin, has much deteriorated by the wretched system of agriculture introduced by the first settlers, and long persisted in by their descendants. Gold has been found in the county, and at present it is obtained in considerable quantities. Pop. in 1840, whites 6,787, slaves 7,590; total, 15,161. There are several small places in the county, though none of much note, except the city of Fredericksburg. The C. H. is situated about the centre of the county, on the river Po.

The subjoined historical sketch of Spottsylvania, was published in the year 1836:

The earliest authentic information we have of that portion of our state now called Spottsylvania, is found in an act passed " at a grand assemblie held at James cittie," between the 20th September, 1674, and the 17th March, 1675, in which war is declared against the Indians; and among other provisions for carrying it on, it is ordered that " one hundred and eleven men out of Gloucester county be garrisoned at one ' ffort,' or place of defence, at or neare the ffalls of Rapahanack River, of which ffort Major Lawrence Smith to be captain or chiefe commander;" and that this " ffort" be furnished with " ffour hundred and eighty pounds of powder, ffourteen hundred and fforty-three pounds of shott." This " ffort" was built in 1676, as appears by the preamble of a subsequent act.

In the year 1679, Major Lawrence Smith, upon his own suggestion, was empowered, provided he would settle or seate downe at or neare said fort, by the last day of March, 1681, and have in readiness upon all occasions on beat of drum, fifty able men, well armed, with sufficient ammunitions, &c., and two hundred men more within the space of a mile along the river, and a quarter of a mile back from the river, prepared always to march twenty miles in any direction from the fort; or should they be obliged to go more than such distance, to be paid for their time thus employed at the rate of other " souldiers;" " to execute martiall discipline" among the said fifty " souldiers and others so put in arms," both in times of war and peace; and said Smith, with two others of said privileged place, to hear and determine all causes, civil and criminal, that may arise within said limits, as a county court might do, and to make by-laws for the same. These military settlers were privileged from arrest for any debts save those due to the king, and those contracted among themselves—and were free from taxes and levies save those laid within their own limits.

The exact situation of this fort cannot now be determined with absolute certainty; but as it is known that there was once a military post at Germanna, some ruins of which are still occasionally turned up by the plough, it is probable that this is the spot selected by Col. Smith for his colony.

The earliest notice we have of Spottsylvania county, as such, is found in 7th Geo. I. 1720, passed at Williamsburg, of which the preamble declares, by way of inducement, " that the frontiers towards the high mountains are exposed to danger from the Indians, and the late settlements of the French to the westward of the said mountains. There-fore it is enacted, that Spottsylvania county bounds upon Snow creek up to the mill, thence by a sw. line to the North Anna, thence up the said river as far as convenient, and thence by a line to be run over the high mountains to the river on the nw. side thereof, so as to include the northern passage through the said mountains, thence down the said river until it comes against the head of Rappahannock, thence by a line to the head of Rappahannock River and down that river to the mouth of Snow creek, which tract of lands from the 1st of May, 1721, shall become a county by the name of Spottsylvania county."

The act goes on to direct that "fifteen hundred pounds, current money of Virginia, shall be paid by the treasurer to the governor, for these uses, to wit : £500 to be expended in a church, court-house, prison, pillory, and stocks, in said county ; £1,000 to be laid out in arms, ammunition, &c., of which each ' Christian tytheable' is to have ' one firelock, musket, one socket, bayonet fixed thereto, one cartouch-box, eight pounds bullet, and two pounds powder.' " The inhabitants were made free of public levies for ten years, and the whole county made one parish, by the name of St. George.

From the following clause of the same act, it is presumed that this new county had been cut off from Essex, King and Queen, and King William ; for the act declares that " until the governor shall settle a court in Spottsylvania," the justices of these counties " shall take power over them by their warrants, and the clerks of said courts by their process returnable to their said courts, *in the same manner as before the said county was constituted,*" &c.

In the year 1730 an act was passed directing that the Burgesses for this county should be allowed for four days journey in passing to Williamsburg, and the same returning. In the same year, St. George's parish was divided by a line running from the mouth of Rappahannock to the Pamunkey ; the upper portion to be called St. Mark's parish ; the lower part to retain the name of St. George's parish. Four years after this the county was thus divided : St. George's parish to be still called Spottsylvania ; and St. Mark's parish to be called Orange, and all settlers beyond the " Sherrando" river to be exempt for three years from the " paiment" of public and parish dues.

The governor fixed the seat of justice at Germanna, where the first court sat on the 1st day of August, 1722, when Augustine Smith, Richard Booker, John Taliaferro, Wm. Hunsford, Richard Johnson, and Wm. Bledsoe, were sworn as justices, John Waller as clerk, and Wm. Bledsoe as sheriff; this place being found "inconvenient to the people," it was directed by law that from and after the 1st of August, 1732, the court should be held at Fredericksburg, which law was repealed seventeen years afterwards, because it was " derogatory to his majesty's prerogative to take from the governor or commander-in-chief of this colony his power and authority of removing or adjourning the courts ;" and because " it might be inconvenient in a case of smallpox or other contagious distemper."

In 1769 the county, which had theretofore been one parish, was thus divided : all that part lying between the rivers Rappahannock and Po retained the name of St. George's parish—the rest of the county was erected into a new parish called Berkeley. In 1778 an act was passed authorizing the justices to build a court-house at some point near the centre of the county, to which the court should be removed, provided a majority of the justices should concur in deeming it advisable. It appears that the justices determined to avail themselves of this privilege, for an act of 1780, passed, as is therein stated, in consequence of a representation that the court-house in Fredericksburg was " unfit to hold courts in," authorizes the county court to be held at the house of John Holladay, " *until the new court-house now building in the said county shall be completed.*"

The first regular stage coaches that passed through this county were established by Nathaniel Twining, by virtue of an exclusive privilege granted him in 1784, for the term of three years, to be paid at the rate of five pence per mile by each passenger.

In the foregoing sketch mention is made of the ancient town of Germanna, founded by Governor Spotswood, and the original seat of justice for the county. There was a massacre of the inhabitants of this town shortly after its establishment, "perpetrated by the Indians, and sternly revenged by the whites—an event now learned only from the weakest and most feeble of all traditions."[*] Hugh Jones, in his "Present Condition of Virginia," published about 1724, thus describes Germanna:

Beyond Col. Spotswood's furnace, above the Falls of Rappahannock River, within view

---

[*] This quotation is from a communication by W. G. Minor, to the late Gov. Gilmer, and published in the Southern Literary Messenger for February, 1841, entitled, "Colonial History of Virginia—a plea for its preservation." It is an able article, evincing much research, and vividly depicting the imperfections of the annals of Virginia.

of the vast mountains, he has founded a town called Germanna, from some Germans sent over by Queen Anne, who are now removed up further. Here he has servants, and workmen of most handicraft trades ; and he is building a church, court-house, and dwelling-house for himself; and with his servants and negroes, he has cleared plantations about it, proposing great encouragement for people to come and settle in that uninhabited part of the world, lately divided into a county.

Beyond this is seated the colony of Germans of Palatines, with allowance of good quantity of rich land, who thrive very well and live happily, and entertain generously. These are encouraged to make wines ; which by the experience (particularly) of the late Robert Beverly, who wrote the History of Virginia, was done easily, and in large quantities in those parts ; not only from the cultivation of the wild grapes, which grow plentifully and naturally in all the lands thereabouts, and in the other parts of the country ; but also from the Spanish, French, Italian, and German wines.

Col. Byrd, in his " Progress to the Mines," in 1732, gives the following notice of Germanna, and " the accomplished Governor Spotswood," and family. The governor had, nine years previously, vacated the gubernatorial chair, and was at this time extensively engaged in the iron-mining business :

This famous town [Germanna] consists of Col. Spotswood's enchanted castle on one side of the street, and a baker's dozen of ruinous tenements on the other, where so many German families had dwelt some years ago ; but are now removed ten miles higher, in the fork of Rappahannock, to land of their own. There had also been a chapel about a bowshot from the colonel's house, at the end of an avenue of cherry-trees, but some pious people had lately burnt it down, with intent to get another built nearer to their own homes. Here I arrived about three o'clock, and found only Mrs. Spotswood at home, who received her old acquaintance with many a gracious smile. I was carried into a room elegantly set off with pier-glasses, the largest of which came soon after to an odd misfortune. Among other favorite animals that cheered this lady's solitude, a brace of tame deer ran familiarly about the house, and one of them came to stare at me as a stranger. But unluckily spying his own figure in the glass, he made a spring over the tea-table that stood under it, and shattered the glass to pieces, and falling back upon the tea-table, made a terrible fracas among the china. This exploit was so sudden, and accompanied with such a noise, that it surprised me, and perfectly frightened Mrs. Spotswood. But it was worth all the damage, to show the moderation and good humor with which she bore this disaster. In the evening, the noble colonel came home from his mines, who saluted me very civilly, and Mrs. Spotswood's sister, Miss Theky, who had been to meet him *en cavalier*, was so kind too as to bid me welcome. We talked over a legend of old stories, supped about nine, and then prattled with the ladies, till it was time for a traveller to retire. In the mean time I observed my old friend to be very uxorious, and exceedingly fond of his children. This was so opposite to the maxims he used to preach up before he was married, that I could not forbear rubbing up the memory of them. But he gave a very good-natured turn to his change of sentiments, by alleging that whoever brings a poor gentlewoman into so solitary a place, from all her friends and acquaintance, would be ungrateful not to use her and all that belongs to her with all possible tenderness.

We all kept snug in our several apartments till nine, except Miss Theky, who was the housewife of the family. At that hour we met over a pot of coffee, which was not quite strong enough to give us the palsy. After breakfast, the colonel and I left the ladies to their domestic affairs, and took a turn in the garden, which has nothing beautiful but three terrace-walks that fall in slopes one below another. I let him understand, that besides the pleasure of paying him a visit, I came to be instructed by so great a master in the mystery of making iron, wherein he had led the way, and was the Tubal Cain of Virginia. He corrected me a little there, by assuring me he was not only the first in this country, but the first in North America, who had erected a regular furnace

The city of Fredericksburg is in a handsome valley on the south side of the Rappahannock River, 56 miles from Washington City, and 62 miles from Richmond, on the line of the great southern rail-road. It is at the head of tide on the river, about 150 miles

VIEW OF FREDERICKSBURG FROM THE WASHINGTON FARM.

from its mouth. The Rappahannock is navigable for vessels of 140 tons, to the Falls of the Rappahannock, a short distance above the town.

Fredericksburg was founded by law in 1727, and named from Prince Frederick, father of George III. The neighboring village of Falmouth was founded at the same time. The preamb.e of the act establishing Fredericksburg says:

"Whereas great numbers of people have of late seated themselves and their families upon and near the river Rappahannock, and the branches thereof above the falls; and great quantities of tobacco and other commodities are every year brought down to the upper landings upon the said river, to be shipped off and transported to other parts of the country; and it is necessary that the poorer part of said inhabitants should be supplied from thence, with goods and merchandise in return for their commodities; but for want of some convenient place, where traders may cohabit and bring their goods to, such supplies are not to be had, without great disadvantages; and good houses are greatly wanted upon some navigable part of said river, near the falls, for the reception and safe keeping of such commodities as are brought thither; and for the entertainment and sustenance of those who repair thither from remote places with carriages drawn by horses or oxen. And forasmuch as the inhabitants of the county of Spottsylvania have made humble supplication to this General Assembly, that a town may be laid out in some convenient place near the falls of the said river, for the cohabitation of such as are minded to re side there for the purposes aforesaid, whereby the peopling that remote part of the country will be en couraged, and trade and navigation may be increased. Be it enacted," &c.

The town originally comprehended fifty acres, and was laid out on what was then called "the lease land." In 1742 and in 1759, its boundaries were enlarged. In 1738, a law was passed directing that "fairs should be held in Fredericksburg twice a year, for the sale of cattle, provisions, goods, wares, and all kinds of merchandise whatsoever." All persons at such fairs, going to or from them, were privileged from arrest and execution during the fairs, and for two days before and two days after them, except for capital offences, breaches of the peace, or for any controversies, suits, and quarrels, that might arise during the time. The fairs were continued, from time to time, by various acts, until 1769, when the right of holding them was made perpetual.

When Fredericksburg was incorporated, there was a warehouse on its site. The act appointed John Robinson, Henry Willis, Augustine Smith, John Taliaferro, Harry Beverly, John Waller, and Jeremiah Clowder, trustees. The first church was built on the site of the present Episcopal church. Col. Byrd, in 1732, five years after the town was established, notices it as follows:

I was obliged to rise early here, that I might not starve my landlord, whose constitution requires him to swallow a beefsteak before the sun blesses the world with its genial rays. However, he was so complaisant as to bear the gnawing of his stomach till eight o'clock, for my sake. Col. Waller, after a score of loud hems to clear his throat, broke his fast along with us. When this necessary affair was dispatched, Col. Willis walked me about his town of Fredericksburg. It is pleasantly situated on the south shore of Rappahannock River, about a mile below the falls. Sloops may come up and lie close to the wharf, within thirty yards of the public warehouses, which are built in the figure of a cross. Just by the wharf is a quarry of white stone that is very soft in the ground, and hardens in the air, appearing to be as fair and fine-grained as that of Portland. Besides that, there are several other quarries in the river bank, within the limits of the town, sufficient to build a large city. The only edifice of stone yet built, is the prison; the walls of which are strong enough to hold Jack Sheppard, if he had been transported thither. Though this be a commodious and beautiful situation for a town, with the advantages of a navigable river, and wholesome air, yet the inhabitants are very few. Besides Col. Willis, who is the top man of the place, there are only one merchant, a tailor, a smith, and an ordinary keeper; though I must not forget Mrs. Levistone, who acts here in the double capacity of a doctress and coffee woman. And were this a populous city, she is qualified to exercise two other callings. It is said the court-house and the church are going to be built here, and then both religion and justice will help to enlarge the place.

Fredericksburg is regularly laid out, and compactly built; many of its buildings are of brick. The principal public buildings are a court-house, clerk's office, and jail, a market-house, an orphan asylum, 1 Episcopal, 1 Presbyterian, 1 Methodist, 1 Baptist, and 1

Reformed Baptist church. The orphan asylum and a charity school are for females. The town also contains 2 banks, and 1 male and 1 female seminary of the higher class. It is supplied with water from the river, by subterraneous pipes; and is governed by a mayor and common council. A canal, extending from the town to Fox's Mill, a point on the Rappahannock 35 miles above, has been commenced and partly completed. Fredericksburg enjoys considerable trade, chiefly in grain, flour, tobacco, maize, &c., and considerable quantities of gold are exported. Its exports have been computed at over $4,000,000 annually. The Falls of the Rappahannock in the vicinity afford good water-power. There were in 1840, by the U. S. statistics, 73 stores, cap. $367,961; 2 tanneries, paints, drugs, &c., cap. $37,000; 1 grist-mill, 2 printing-offices, 4 semi-weekly newspapers; cap. in manufactures, $141,200; 5 academies, 256 students; 7 schools, 156 scholars. Population in 1830, whites 1,797, slaves 1,124, free blacks 387; total, 3,308. Population in 1840, 3,974.

Gen. Hugh Mercer and Gen. George Weedon, both of the army of the revolution, resided here before the war. Gen. Mercer was then a physician. His house, in which was his apothecary-shop, stood on the sw. corner of Princess Ann and Amelia sts.: it was a long frame building, of antique architecture, and a story and a half in height. Gen. Weedon was an inn-keeper. An English traveller, Dr. J. F. D. Smyth, in his tour published in London in 1784, says of these gentlemen:

I arrived at Fredericksburg, and put up at the inn kept by *one Weedon*, who is now a general officer in the American army, and was then *very active and zealous in blowing the flames of sedition.* . . . In Fredericksburg I called upon a worthy and intimate friend, *Dr. Hugh Mercer*, a physician of great merit and eminence, and, as a man, possessed of almost every virtue and accomplishment. . . . Dr. Mercer was afterwards a brigadier-general in the American army, to accept of which appointment I have reason to believe he was greatly influenced by Gen. Washington, with whom he had been long in intimacy and bonds of friendship. For Dr. Mercer was generally of a just and a moderate way of thinking, and possessed liberal sentiments, and a generosity of principle very uncommon among those with whom he embarked.

The interesting memoir subjoined, of Gen. Hugh Mercer, is principally abridged from the Southern Literary Messenger for April, 1838:

Gen. Hugh Mercer was a native of Scotland, and graduated at an early age in the science of medicine. At the memorable battle of Culloden, he acted as an assistant surgeon, and, with a multitude of the vanquished, sought a home of freedom in the wilderness of America. He landed in Pennsylvania, where he remained but a short time. From thence he removed to Fredericksburg, where he married, and became distinguished for his skill in medicine. In the Indian war of 1755, he served as a captain under Washington. In one of the engagements with this wily foe, he was wounded in the right wrist by a musket ball; and in the irregular warfare then practised, his company scattered and became separated from him. Faint from loss of blood, and exhausted by fatigue, he was closely pursued by the savage foe, their thrilling war-whoop ringing through the forest, and stimulating to redoubled energy the footsteps of their devoted victim. Fortunately the hollow trunk of a large tree presented itself. In a moment he concealed himself in it, and though his pursuers reached the spot and seated themselves around him, he yet miraculously escaped! Leaving his place of refuge, he sought the abodes of civilization, through a trackless wild of more than one hundred miles in extent; and after supporting life on roots and the *body of a rattlesnake*, which he encountered and killed, he finally reached Fort Cumberland in safety. For his gallantry and military skill in this war—proved, in a distinguished degree, by the destruction of the Indian settlement at Kittaning, Pennsylvania—the corporation of Philadelphia presented to him an honorable and appropriate medal.

The commencement of the American revolution found him in the midst of an extensive medical practice, surrounded by affectionate friends, and enjoying in the bosom of a happy family all the comforts of social life. Stimulated to action by a lofty spirit of patriotism, he broke from the endearments of domestic life, and gave to his country, in that trying hour, the energy and resources of a practised and accomplished soldier. In 1775, he was in command of three regiments of minute-men; and early in 1776 we find him zealously engaged, as a colonel of the army of Virginia, in drilling and organizing the raw and ill-formed masses of men who, under the varied names of sons of liberty, minute-men, volunteers, and levies, presented the bulk without the order—the mob without the discipline of an army. To produce obedience and subordination among men who considered military discipline as a restraint on personal liberty, and who had entered into the war unpaid and unrestricted by command, was a severe and invidious task. The courage, the fortitude, the self-possession of Col. Mercer quailed not at these adverse circumstances; and, by the judicious exercise of mingled severity and kindness, he soon succeeded in reducing a mutinous soldiery to complete submission. Tradition has preserved the following anecdote, illustrating, in a striking manner, his characteristic promptitude and bravery:

Among the troops which arrived at Williamsburg, then the metropolis of Virginia, was a company of riflemen from beyond the mountains, commanded by Capt. Gibson. A reckless insubordination, and a violent opposition to military restraint, had gained for this corps the sarcastic name of "Gibson's Lambs." They had not been long in camp before a mutiny arose among them, producing much excitement in the army, and alarming the inhabitants of the city. Freed from all command, they roamed through the camp, threatening with instant death any officer who should presume to exercise authority over them. In the height of the rebellion, an officer was dispatched with the alarming tidings to the quarters of Col. Mercer. The citizens of the town vainly implored him not to risk his life and person amid this infuriated mob. Reckless of personal safety, he instantly repaired to the barracks of the mutinous band, and directing a general parade of the troops, he ordered Gibson's company to be drawn up as offenders and violators of law, and to be disarmed in his presence. The ringleaders were placed under a strong guard, and, in the presence of the whole army, he addressed the offenders in an eloquent and feeling manner, impressing on them their duties as citizen-soldiers, and the *certainty of death* if they continued to disobey their officers, and remained in that mutinous spirit, equally disgraceful to them and hazardous to the sacred interests they had marched to defend. Disorder was instantly checked, and, after a short confinement, those under imprisonment were released; and the whole company were ever after as exemplary in their deportment and conduct as any troops in the army.

Col. Mercer now joined the continental army, Congress having conferred upon him the rank of brigadier-general; and throughout the whole of the stormy and disastrous campaign of 1776, he was a bold, fearless, and efficient officer. At the battle of Princeton, Gen. Mercer was mortally wounded. The circumstances were these:—In the march from Trenton to Princeton, Gen. Mercer led the vanguard of Washington's army. Reaching Princeton about sunrise, Gen. Mercer encountered three British regiments, who had encamped there on the previous night, and who were leaving the town to join the rear of their troops at Maidenhead. A fierce and desperate conflict immediately ensued. The American militia, constituting the front, hesitated, became confused, and soon gave way, while the few regulars in the rear could not check the dastardly retreat. Ere the fortune of the day was changed, and ere victory perched on the patriot standard, the heroic Mercer fell. Rushing forward to rally his broken troops, and stimulating them by his voice and example, his horse was shot from under him, and he fell, dangerously wounded, among the columns of the advancing enemy. Being thus dismounted, he was instantly surrounded by a party of British soldiers, with whom, when they refused him quarter, he fought desperately with his drawn sword until he was completely overpowered. Excited to brutality by the gallantry of his resistance, they stabbed him with their bayonets in *seven* different parts of his body, inflicted many blows on his head with the butt-ends of their muskets, and did not cease their butchery until they believed him to be a crushed and mangled corpse. Nine days after the battle, he died in the arms of Major Geo. Lewis of the army, the nephew of Gen. Washington, whom the uncle had commissioned to watch over the last moments of his expiring friend. His latter hours were soothed by the skilful and affectionate attendance of the distinguished Dr. Rush.

In a small house, a few yards distant from that blood-red plain of carnage and of death, far away from the soothing consolations of domestic affection, this distinguished martyr of liberty breathed his last. The victorious flag of his country proudly floated over a field of triumph, and without a murmur he sank into a soldier's grave, finding a hallowed sepulchre in the hearts of his countrymen, and a fadeless epitaph in their institutions.

The remains of this gifted and accomplished soldier now sleep in Christ church, Philadelphia, under a plain marble slab, bearing the simple yet expressive inscription—" In memory of Gen. Hugh Mercer, who fell at Princeton, Jan. 3d, 1777."

The valor of Gen. Mercer was only equalled by his modesty. When Virginia organized the third regiment, there were numerous applications for commissions, but scarcely one for less than the rank of a field-officer. " During the sitting of the House of Burgesses upon the question, a plain but soldierly-looking individual handed up to the speaker's chair a scrap of paper, on which was written, ' Hugh Mercer will serve his adopted country, and the cause of liberty, in any rank or station to which he may be appointed.' This from a veteran soldier bred in European camps—the associate of Washington in the war of 1755, and known to stand high in his confidence and esteem, was all-sufficient for a body of patriots and statesmen such as composed the Virginia House of Burgesses in the revolution. The appointment of Mercer to the command of the 3d Virginia regiment was carried instanter."

In Wilkinson's Memoirs, several interesting particulars of the life and services of Gen. Mercer are related, and, in alluding to his death, that writer remarks : " In Gen. Mercer we lost, at Princeton, a chief who, for education, talents, disposition, integrity, and patriotism, was second to no man but the commander-in-chief, and was qualified to fill the highest trusts of the country." The same author remarks, that an evening or two before the battle of Princeton, Gen. Mercer being in the tent of Gen. St. Clair with several officers, the conversation turned on some promotions then just made in the army. Gen. Mercer remarked, " they were not engaged in a war of ambition, or that he should not have been there ; and that every man should be content to serve in that station in which he could be most useful ; *that for his part he had but one object in view, and that was the success of the cause, and that God could witness how cheerfully he would lay down his life to secure it.*" Little, adds the writer, did he or any of the company then think that a few fleeting hours would seal the compact.

———

Col. Fielding Lewis, who married Elizabeth, a sister of Washington, resided in Fredericksburg on the farm where lies buried Mary, the mother of Washington. He was proprietor of half the town, and of an extensive territory adjoining. He was an ardent patriot of the revolutionary war, and superintended the great manufactory of arms in this neighborhood at that time. He was also a magistrate, and represented the county in the legislature. He died in Dec., 1781, aged 55, universally respected and esteemed. His valuable estate was divided equally among his sons. His children were Capt. Fielding Lewis ; Capt. George Lewis, a captain of Washington's life guard ; Elizabeth Lewis, who married Charles Carter, Esq. ; Maj. Lawrence Lewis, who was aid to Gen. Morgan in suppressing the Whiskey Insurrection ; and Capt. Robert Lewis, who was one of Washington's private secretaries.

———

Opposite Fredericksburg, on the east side of the Rappahannock, below the rail-road bridge, and within the limits of Stafford county, is " The Washington Farm," at present the property of the Rev. Thomas Teasdale. A few years after the birth of Washington, his father, Augustine Washington, removed with his family to this place, where he resided until his death, April 12th, 1743, at the age of 49. The house in which he resided has long since been gone : it stood near the present residence of Mr. King, from which spot the view of Fredericksburg in this volume was taken. Here it was that Washington spent his early youth ; and here, says tradition, is the place where, when a young man, he threw a stone across the Rappahannock,—a feat that no one, it is said, has since succeeded in accomplishing.

Sparks, in his life of Washington, says that his father was buried at Bridge's Creek, Westmoreland county, in the tomb of his ancestors. " Little is known," says the same author, " of his character or his acts. It appears by his will, however, that he possessed a large and valuable property in lands ; and as this had been acquired chiefly by his own industry and enterprise, it may be inferred that in the concerns of business he was methodical, skilful, honorable, and energetic. His occupation was that of a planter, which, from the first settlement of the country, had been the pursuit of nearly all the principal gentlemen of Virginia.

" Each of his sons inherited from him a separate plantation. To the eldest, Lawrence, he bequeathed an estate near Hunting creek, afterwards Mount Vernon, which then consisted of 2,500 acres ; and also other lands, and shares in iron works situated in Maryland and Virginia, which were productive. The second son had for his part an estate in Westmoreland. To George were left the lands where his father lived at the time of his decease ; and to each of the other sons, an estate of six or seven hundred acres. The youngest daughter died when an infant, and for the only remaining one a suitable provision was made in the will. It is thus seen that Augustine Washington, although suddenly cut off in the vigor of manhood, left all his children in a state of comparative independence. Confiding in the prudence of the mother, he directed that all the proceeds of the property of her children should be at her disposal, till they should respectively come of age.

" This weighty charge of five children, the eldest of whom was eleven years old, the superintendence of their education, and the management of complicated affairs, demanded no common share of resolution, resource of mind, and strength of character. In these important duties Mrs. Washington acquitted herself with great fidelity to her trust, and with entire success. Her good sense, assiduity, tenderness, and vigilance, overcame every obstacle ; and as the richest reward of a mother's solicitude and toil, she had the happiness to see all her children come forward with a fair promise into life, filling the sphere allotted to them in a manner equally honorable to themselves and to the parent who had been the only guide of their principles, conduct, and habits. She lived to witness the noble career of her illustrious son, till, by his own rare merits, he was raised to the head of a nation, and applauded and revered by the whole world. It has been said, that there never was a great man, the elements of whose greatness might not be traced to the original characteristics or early influence of his mother. If this be true, how much do mankind owe to the mother of Washington."

The maiden name of the mother of Washington was MARY BALL, and she was the second wife of her husband. Her father, Col. Ball, resided in Lancaster county. The dwelling alluded to in the succeeding extract from Alden's Collection is now standing in Fredericksburg, on the SE. corner of Charles and Lewis streets, and is at present the residence of Richard Sterling, Esq. It is a plain, substantial two-story dwelling, of the ordinary architecture, and painted white.

She died in this house, in the autumn of 1789, at the age of 85 years. She was buried on a beautiful swell of land which belonged to her son-in-law, Col. Fielding Lewis, on a spot which she had selected for her grave. " Within a few steps from the place where she lies interred is a romantic ledge of rocks, to which she used often to resort for private meditation and devotion. She was a lady of uncommon excellence, and was greatly endeared to all who had the happiness of her acquaintance. She was truly estimable in all the relations of life ; but among the distinguished traits of her character, none was more remarkable than her constant and generous attentions to the necessities of the poor. She for years was expecting the approach of death from a deep-rooted cancer in her breast ; and was long desirous to lay aside her clayey tabernacle to depart and be with Christ, in whom was all her hope ; yet she was enabled to exercise a becoming resignation to the will of God under all the sufferings she endured from her excruciating disorder." There is now over her grave a beautiful, though unfinished monument.

In the grave-yard at Fredericksburg lie the remains of LEWIS LITTLEPAGE, who was born in Hanover co., Dec. 19, 1762, and died in this place, July 19, 1802, in the 40th year of his age. He lost his father when young. At the request of his uncle, Benjamin Lewis, Mr. Jay, minister at Madrid, was induced to patronise him, and received him into his family. He volunteered in the expedition against Minorca, under the Duke de Crillon, in 1781 ; and afterwards accompanied the Count Nassau to the siege of Gibraltar, and thence to Constantinople and Warsaw. He was " honored for many years with the esteem and confidence of the unfortunate Stanislaus Augustus, king of Poland, he held under that monarch, until he lost his throne, the most distinguished offices, among which was that of ambassador to Russia. He was by him created Knight of the Order of St. Stanislaus, chamberlain and confidential secretary in his cabinet, and acted as his special envoy among the most important negotiations. Of talents, military as well as civil, he served with credit as an officer of high rank, in different armies. In private life he was charitable, generous, and just, and in various public offices which he filled, he acted with uniform magnanimity, fidelity, and honor."* When he was in New York in 1785, Mr. Jay arrested him for a debt of $1,000, without interest, for money lent him years before. In consequence, Littlepage challenged him. The correspond. ence between them was published, in which Mr. Jay " complained not only of the pecuniary imposition, but also of other abuse, as he expresses himself, from the young man, with my money in his pocket, and my meat still sticking in his teeth.' "

JOHN FORSYTH of Georgia, " a man of talents and eloquence, who had been long distinguished in public life, and held many important offices, was born at Fredericksburg, in 1781. He was graduated at New Jersey College in 1799 ; was member of Congress from Georgia in 1813–18, and in 1827–29 ; United States senator in 1818–19, and in 1829–35 ; governor of Georgia in 1827–29 ; minister to Spain 1819–22 ; and was appointed secretary of state by Gen. Jackson in 1835, which office he held till the end of Mr. Van Buren's administration. ' The high offices which, during a great portion of his life, he successfully filled, both in his own particular state and the general government, attest at once the superiority of his abilities and the public estimation of them. To the high advantage of superior talents, he added, also, that of elegance and dignity of manners, which shed a grace on the exalted stations which he filled.' " He died at Washington city, Oct. 22, 1841, at the age of 61 years.

STAFFORD.

STAFFORD was formed in 1675, from Westmoreland. Its length is 20, mean width 12 miles. The Rappahannock runs on its sw. border, the Potomac on its E. boundary ; the rail-road from Fredericksburg to the Potomac runs through it. On the streams there is considerable good land, elsewhere the soil is generally worn out by injudicious agriculture. Gold exists in the county. Pop. in 1840, whites 4,489, slaves 3,596, free colored 369 ; total 8,454.

Falmouth lies on the left bank of the Rappahannock, at the foot of the falls, about one mile above the town of Fredericksburg. A substantial bridge connects it with the Spottsylvania shore. It was incorporated and laid out in 1727, the same year with Fredericksburg, and was at one time the rival of that town. It contains 1 free church, 6 or 7 mercantile stores, 2 extensive flouring mills, and 1 large cotton factory, and a population of about 500.

Stafford C. H. lies near the centre of the county, and contains about a dozen dwellings. The following biographical sketch of Col. Washington, is from the pen of his brother officer, Col. Henry Lee, or, as he was commonly called, " Legion Harry :"

WILLIAM WASHINGTON, lieutenant-colonel commandant of a continental regiment of dragoons during the revolutionary war, was the eldest son of Baily Washington, Esq., of Stafford county, in the state of Virginia.

First among the youth of Virginia who hastened to the standard of his country, on the rupture between Great Britain and her colonies, he was appointed to the command of a company of infantry in the third regiment of the Virginia line, commanded by colonel, afterwards brigadier-general, Mercer. In no corps in our service was the substantial knowledge of the profession of arms more likely to be acquired.

Here young Washington learned the rudiments of war. He fought with this gallant regiment at York island, and on the retreat through New Jersey, sharing with distin-

---

* Alden's Collections.

guished applause in that disastrous period, its difficulties, its dangers, and its glory. When afterwards the commander-in-chief struck at Colonel Ralle, stationed with a body of Hessians in Trenton, Capt. Washington was attached to the van of one of the assailing columns, and in that daring and well-executed enterprise, received a musket-ball through his hand, bravely leading on his company against the arraying enemy.

The commander-in-chief having experienced the extreme difficulties to which he had been exposed during the preceding campaign, by his want of cavalry, was, shortly after this period, in consequence of his suggestion to Congress, authorized to raise three regiments of light dragoons. To the command of one of these he appointed Lieut.-Col. Baylor, one of his aid-de-camps. To this regiment Captain Washington was transferred, with the rank of major, and returned to Virginia for the purpose of assisting in recruiting the regiment.

As soon as the corps was completed, Baylor joined the main army; his regiment was, in 1778, surprised by a detachment of the British, led by Major-Gen. Gray, and suffered extremely. Washington fortunately escaped; and in the course of the succeeding year, or early in 1780, he was detached, with the remains of Bland's, Baylor's, and Moylan's regiments of horse, to the army of Major-Gen. Lincoln, in South Carolina, where he was constantly employed with the light troops, and experienced, with some flashes of fortune, two severe blows; first at Monk's Corner, where he commanded our horse, and last at Leneau's ferry, when he was second to Lieut.-Col. White, of Moylan's regiment. These repeated disasters so reduced our cavalry, that White and Washington retired from the field, and repaired to the northern confines of North Carolina for the purpose of repairing their heavy losses. It was here that they applied to Gen. Gates for the aid of his name and authority to expedite the restoration and equipment of their regiments, that they might be ready to take the field under his orders. This salutary and proper request was, as has been mentioned, injudiciously disregarded; from which omission very injurious consequences seem to have resulted in the sequel.

After the defeat of Gen. Gates on the 16th of the following August, it will be recollected that the American general retired to Hillsborough, from whence he returned to Salisbury.

Lieut.-Col. Washington, with his cavalry, now accompanied him, and formed a part of the light corps placed by Gates under the direction of Brigadier Morgan. He resumed his accustomed active and vigorous service, and was highly useful in the execution of the trust confided to Morgan.

One of his partisan exploits was the result of a well-conceived stratagem. Having learned, during a scouting excursion, that a large party of loyalists, commanded by Col. Rudgley, was posted at Rudgley's mill, 12 miles from Camden, he determined on attacking them. Approaching the enemy, he found them so secured in a large log-barn, surrounded by abattis, as to be perfectly safe from the operations of cavalry. Forbidden, thus, to attempt his object by direct attack, his usual and favorite mode of warfare, he determined, for once, to have recourse to policy. Shaping, therefore, a pine log in imitation of a field-piece, mounting it on wheels, and staining it with mud, to make it look like iron, he brought it up in military style, and affected to make arrangements to batter down the barn. To give to the stratagem solemnity and effect, he dispatched a flag, warning the garrison of the impending destruction, and to prevent bloodshed, summoned them to submission. Not prepared to resist artillery, Col. Rudgley obeyed the summons, and with a garrison of 103 rank and file, surrendered at discretion.

Greene now succeeded Gates, when Brigadier Morgan, with the light corps, was detached to hang upon the enemy's left flank, and to threaten Ninety-Six.

The battle of the Cowpens ensued, in which Washington, at the head of our horse, acquired fresh laurels. He continued with the light troops, performing with courage and precision the duties assigned him, until the junction of the two divisions of the American army at Guilford Court-House. Soon after this event a more powerful body of horse and foot was selected by Gen. Greene, and placed under Col. Williams, of which Washington and his cavalry were a constituent part.

In the eventful and trying retreat which ensued, Lieut.-Col. Washington contributed his full share to the maintenance of the measures of Williams, which terminated so propitiously to our arms, and so honorably to the light troops and their commander. After our repassage of the Dan, Washington and his horse were again placed in the van, and with Howard and Lee, led by Williams, played that arduous game of marches, countermarches, and manœuvres, which greatly contributed to baffle the skilful display of talents and enterprise exhibited by Lord Cornwallis, in his persevering attempt to force Greene, at the head of an inferior army, to battle, or to cut him off from his approaching reinforcements and supplies.

We have seen the distinguished part this officer successively bore in the battles of Guilford, Hobkick's Hill, and Eutaw ; and we have found him, throughout the arduous campaign of 1781, always at his post, decided, firm, and brave, courting danger, and contemning difficulty. His eminent services were lost to the army from the battle of Eutaw ; where, to its great regret, he was made prisoner; nor did he afterwards take any part in the war, as from the period of his exchange nothing material occurred, the respective armies being confined to minor operations, produced by the prospect of peace. While a prisoner in Charleston, Washington became acquainted with Miss Elliot, a young lady in whom concentred the united attractions of respectable descent, opulence, polish, and beauty. The gallant soldier soon became enamored with his amiable acquaintance, and afterwards married her.

This happened in the spring of 1782 ; and he established himself in South Carolina, at Sandy Hill, the ancestral seat of his wife.

Washington seems to have devoted his subsequent years to domestic duties, rarely breaking in upon them by attention to public affairs ; and then only as a member of the state legislature.

He possessed a stout frame, being six feet in height, broad, strong, and corpulent. His occupations and his amusements applied to the body, rather than to the mind ; to the cultivation of which he did not bestow much time or application, nor was his education of the sort to excite such habits, being only calculated to fit a man for the common business of life. In temper he was good-humored, in disposition amiable, in heart upright, generous, and friendly, in manners lively, innocent, and agreeable.

His military exploits announce his grade and character in arms. Bold, collected, and persevering, he preferred the heat of action to the collection and sifting of intelligence, to the calculations and combinations of means and measures, and was better fitted for the field of battle, than for the drudgery of camp and the watchfulness of preparation. Kind to his soldiers, his system of discipline was rather lax, and sometimes subjected him to injurious consequences, when close to a sagacious and vigilant adversary.

The Washington family emigrated from England, and settled in Virginia, always respectable and respected. The consanguinity of its numerous ramifications is involved in doubt ; but it is generally believed that they sprung from the same source.

Lieut.-Col. Washington was selected by his illustrious relation when he accepted the command of the army, during the presidency of Mr. Adams, as one of his staff, with the rank of brigadier-general, a decided proof of the high value attached by the best judge in America to his military talents.

Leading a life of honor, of benevolence, and hospitality, in the bosom of his family and friends, during which, until its last two years, he enjoyed high health, this gallant soldier died, after a tedious indisposition, leaving a widow, and a son and a daughter, the only issue of his marriage.

SURRY.

SURRY was formed in 1652 : it measures each way about 18 miles. The James runs on its northern, and the Blackwater River on a portion of its southern line. Pop. in 1840, whites 2,557, slaves 2,853, free colored 1,070 ; total, 6,480.

The C. H. is situated 5 miles s. of James River, and 55 southeasterly from Richmond. There is in this county, on or near the James, an antique mansion, called "BACON'S CASTLE," supposed by some to have been once fortified by Nathaniel Bacon, the leader of "the Rebellion" in 1676. On what ground this supposition rests, we have been unable to ascertain.

SUSSEX.

SUSSEX was formed in 1754, from Surry: it is about 32 miles long, and 18 wide. The rail-road from Petersburg to Weldon, N. C., runs through a portion of it on the west. The Nottoway runs centrally through it, and the Blackwater forms a part of its NE. boundary. About 500,000 pounds of cotton are annually produced in the county. Pop. in 1840, whites 3,584, slaves 6,384, free colored 811 ; total, 11,229.

The C. H. is situated near the centre of the county, 48 miles SSE. of Richmond.

TAYLOR.

TAYLOR was formed Jan. 19th, 1844, from Harrison, Barbour, and Marion, and named from John Taylor of Caroline. Williamsport, sometimes called Prunty Town, is the county-seat. It is situated near the ferry across Tygart's Valley River, 209 miles northwesterly from Richmond, and 18 NE. by E. from Clarksburg. It contains 3 stores, 1 Methodist and 1 Baptist church, and about 30 dwellings. Rector College, an institution founded in 1839, is located here ; it had, by the census of 1840, 110 students.

As this county has been so recently formed, we are unable to give its statistics or geographical boundaries, and the counties from which it has been formed have, in those particulars, been described in this volume as though it had no existence.

TAZEWELL.

TAZEWELL was formed in 1799, from Russell and Wythe, and named from Henry Tazewell, a member of the U. S. Senate, from 1794 to 1799. It is 60 miles long, with a mean width of 25 miles. The Tug Fork of Big Sandy runs on part of the northern border ; the Clinch River rises near Jeffersonville, and the Great Kanawha receives many branches from the eastern section of the county. It is traversed by mountains, some of which rise to an immense height; the chief are, Clinch, Rich, East River, and Paint Lick. Between some of them are beautiful valleys, of a black, deep soil, very fertile. Abb's Valley, a delightful tract, 10 miles long, and about 40 rods wide, with no stream running through it, and bounded by lofty mountains, possesses a soil of extraordinary fertility. It derives its name from Absalom Looney, a hunter, who is supposed to have been the first white person ever in it. Inexhaustible quarries of limestone exist in the county, and extensive

beds of excellent coal. The principal staples are cattle, horses,
hogs, feathers, tow and flax linen, beeswax, ginseng, seneca snake-
root, &c., &c. The mean height of the arable soil is about 2,200
feet above the level of the ocean. Pop. in 1840, whites 5,466,
slaves 786. colored 38; total, 6,290.

Mountain Scenery.

Jeffersonville, the county-seat, is 284 miles southwesterly from
Richmond, and 30 west of Wythe C. H. It is situated on the south
side of Clinch River, one mile from its bank, and contains 1 church,
3 stores, and about 25 dwellings. Burke's Garden, 10 miles E. of
Jeffersonville, is a remarkable spot. It is completely surrounded
by Clinch mountain, except a narrow pass, through which flows
Wolf creek. It is 11 miles long, and 5 wide, and is a beautiful
and perfect level; the soil is naturally fertile. A post-office is in
it, and the settlement contains a church and about 500 inhabitants.
It was late in a November evening that we ascended the lofty

Clinch mountain, after leaving Tazewell C. H. for Abingdon, and put up for the night at a miserable hut on its summit. The next morning the sun shone bright and clear as we buckled on our knapsack and resumed our journey through a light snow which covered the mountain-road that winds with great steepness down the declivity. In about half a mile was presented a scene of which none but a painting in the highest style of art can convey an adequate impression. The whole of a vast landscape was filled with a sea of mountains beyond mountains, in an apparently interminable continuity. Near, were huge mountains, dark and frowning, in the desolation of winter. Beyond, they assumed a deep blue color, and then grew fainter and fainter, until far away in the horizon—fifty or sixty miles—their jagged outlines were softened by distance, and sky and mountain met and mingled in the same light cerulean hue. Not a clearing was to be seen—not even a solitary smoke from some cabin curled up the intervening valleys to indicate the presence of man. It was—

> " A wild and lonely region, where, retired
> From little scenes of art, great Nature dwelt
> In awful solitude."

From a worthy pastor of a church in the Shenandoah valley, we have received the following account of the *captivity and destruction of the Moore family*, by the Indians, a few years after the close of the revolution :

JAMES MOORE, Jr., was a lineal descendant of the Rev. Samuel Rutherford, of Scotland ; the latter being a descendant of the Rev. Joseph Allein, the author of the "Alarm to the Unconverted." Mr. Moore's parents were among those who, during the persecutions under Charles I., emigrated from Scotland to the north of Ireland, the descendants of whom, in this country, come under the general name of "Scotch Irish." From Ireland he emigrated to Virginia, and settled in what is now Rockbridge county, on Walker's creek. There he married Jane Walker, and there James Moore, the subject of this sketch, was born. When the latter grew up he married Martha Podge, of the same county, and settled near the Natural Bridge, at a place long known as "Newel's Tavern." There his three oldest children, John, James, and Joseph, were born. About the year 1775, he removed to what is now Tazewell county, and settled in Abb's valley, on the waters of Blue Stone, a branch of New River. He was induced to emigrate to that country on account of the fertility of the soil, and its adaptedness to raising stock. There, with the aid of an old Englishman whose name was John Simpson, he erected his cabin ; and with his pious wife, both being members of the Presbyterian church, he erected his altar to God, cleared a piece of ground, and there resided with his family until they were destroyed ; frequently going into a fort, which was almost every summer. The first of his family who was captured was James, his second son, a lad in the 14th year of his age. This occurred September 7th, 1784. Mr. Moore, the captive, who is still living, gives this account of that event :

My father had sent me to a waste plantation, about 2½ miles distant, to catch a horse on which I might go to mill. As we lived about 12 miles from the mill, and the road for the whole distance thither leading through a dreary wilderness, I had frequently to come home a considerable part of the way after night, when it was very dark. Being accustomed to this, I set out for the horse without the least intimidation, or apprehension of danger. But notwithstanding this, I had not proceeded more than half the distance to the field, before a sudden dread, or panic, came on me. The appearance of the Indian who took me was presented to my mind, although at the time I did not think of an Indian, but rather that some wild animal in human shape would devour me. Such was my alarm that I went on trembling, frequently looking back, expecting to see it. Indeed

I would have returned home, but for the fear that with such an excuse my father would be displeased, and perhaps send me back. I therefore proceeded on until I came near the field, when suddenly three Indians sprang from behind a log, one of whom laid hold of me. Being much alarmed at the time with the apprehension of being devoured, and believing this to be the animal I had dreaded, I screamed with all my might. The Indian who had hold of me laid his hand on my head, and, in the Indian language, told me to hush. Looking him in the face, and perceiving that it was an Indian, I felt greatly relieved, and spoke out aloud, " It is an Indian, why need I fear ;" and thought to myself, "All that is in it is, I will have to go to the Shawnee towns." In this company there were only three Indians, a father and son, and one other ; the former bearing the name of the " Black Wolf," a middle-aged man, of the most stern countenance I ever beheld, about six feet high, having a black beard. The others I suppose were about 18 years of age, and all of the Shawnee tribe. I belonged to the Black Wolf, who had captured me. We immediately proceeded to an old cabin, near to which were the horses. Here we made a halt, and the old Wolf told me to catch the horses, and gave me some salt for that purpose. My object was to catch one and mount, and make my escape ; but suspecting my intention, as often as I would get hold of a horse they would come running up, and thus scare him away. Finding that I could not get a horse for myself, I had no wish, and did not try to catch one for them, and so, after a few efforts, abandoned the attempt. This I suppose was about one o'clock in the afternoon. The Indians then went into a thicket where were concealed their kettle and blankets, after which we immediately proceeded on our journey. In consequence of the high weeds, green briers, logs, and the steep and mountainous character of the country, the walking was very laborious, and we travelled that evening only about 8 miles. The two younger Indians went before, myself next, with the old Wolf in the rear. If marks were made, he would carefully remove them with his tomahawk. I frequently broke bushes, which he discovered, and shook his tomahawk over my head to let me know the consequences if I did not desist. I would then scratch the ground with my feet. This he also discovered, and made me desist, showing me how to set my feet flat, so as not to leave any mark. It then became necessary to cease my efforts to make a trail for others, as they were all immediately detected. In the evening, about sundown, the old Wolf gave a tremendous war-whoop, and another the next morning at sunrise. These were repeated evening and morning during our whole journey. It was long, loud, and shrill, and intended to signify that they had one prisoner. Their custom is to repeat it as frequent as the number of prisoners. It is different from their whoop when they have scalps, and in this way it can be known as far as the whoop is heard, whether they have prisoners or scalps, and also the number. But to return, the night was rainy. We lay down in a laurel thicket, without food or fire. Previous to this, the old Wolf had searched me carefully, to see whether I had a knife. After this he tied one end of a leading-halter very tightly around my neck, and wrapped the other end around his hand, so as to make it secure, as well as very difficult for me to get away without waking him. Notwithstanding my situation was thus dreary, gloomy, and distressing, I was not altogether prevented from sleep. Indeed, I suppose few prisoners were ever more resigned to their fate. The next morning we resumed our journey about daybreak, and continued down Tug creek about two miles, until we reached the main ridge of Tug mountain, along which we descended until we came to Maxwell's Gap.* At this place the old Wolf went off and brought in a middle-sized Dutch-oven, which had been secreted on their former expedition. The carriage of this was assigned to me. At first it was fastened to my back, but after suffering much I threw it down, saying I would carry it no more. Upon this the old Wolf placed down his bundle and told me to carry it, but on finding that I could not lift it I became more reconciled, took up the oven again, and after some days filled it with leaves, and carried it with more ease. We continued on the same ridge the whole of that day, and encamped on it at night. In the evening there came on a rain, and the son of the Black Wolf pulled off my hat. This I resented, struck him, and took it from him. He then showed me by signs that with it he wished to protect his gunlock from the rain. I then permitted him to have it, and after the rain he returned it. For three days we travelled without sustenance of any kind, save some water in which poplar bark had been steeped. On the 4th day we killed a buffalo, took out the paunch, cut it open, rinsed it a little in the water, cut it up, and put it into the kettle with some pieces of the flesh, and made broth. Of this we drank heartily, without eating any of the meat. After

---

* This gap took its name from a man by the name of Maxwell, who was there killed by the Indians while in pursuit of the wife of Thomas English, of Burke's Garden, who had been taken by a party of Indians, at the head of which was this same Wolf.

night we made another kettle of broth, but ate no meat. This is Indian policy after fasting.

I travelled the whole route barefooted ; the consequence was that I had three stone-bruises on each foot, and at this time my sufferings were very great. Frequently I would walk over rattlesnakes, but was not permitted to kill any, the Indians considering them their friends.

Some few days after this, we killed a buffalo that was very fat, and dried as much of the meat as lasted us for several days. After this we killed deer and buffaloes as our wants required, until we reached their towns, near what is now called Chillicothe, in Ohio, just 20 days from the time we set out. We crossed the Ohio between the mouth of Guyandot and Big Sandy, on a raft made of dry logs, and tied together with grape-vines. On the banks of the Scioto we remained one day. Here they made pictures to represent three Indians, and me their prisoner. Near this place the old Wolf went off and procured some bullets which he had secreted.

When we came near the towns the Indians painted themselves black, but did not paint me. This was an omen of my safety. I was not taken directly into the town, but to the residence of Wolf's half-sister, to whom I was sold for an old horse. The reason why I was not taken directly to the town, was, I suppose, 1st, because it was a time of peace ; 2dly, that I might be saved from running the gauntlet, which was the case with prisoners taken in war. Shortly after I was sold, my mistress left me entirely alone for several days in her wigwam, leaving a kettle of hommony for me to eat. In this solitary situation I first began to pray, and call upon God for mercy and deliverance, and found great relief. Having cast my burdens on the Lord, I would arise from my knees and go off cheerfully. I had been taught to pray. My father prayed in his family ; and I now found the benefit of the religious instruction and example I had enjoyed.

On one occasion while on our journey, I was sent some distance for water. Suppo-sing that I was entirely out of view, I gave vent to my feelings, and wept abundantly. The old Indian, however, had watched me, and noticing the marks of tears on my cheeks, he shook his tomahawk over my head to let me know I must not do so again. Their object in sending me off, was, I suppose; to see whether I would attempt to escape, as the situation appeared favorable for that purpose. After this I was no longer fastened with a halter.

In about two weeks after I was sold, my mistress sent me, with others, on a hunting excursion. In this we were very unsuccessful. The snow being knee-deep, my blanket too short to cover me, and having very little other clothing, my sufferings from hunger and cold were intense. Often after having lain down, and drawn up my feet to get them under the blanket, I became so benumbed that it was with difficulty I could straighten myself again. Early in the morning the old Indian would build up a large fire, and make me and the young Indians plunge all over in cold water. This, I think, was of great benefit, as it prevented us from taking cold.

When we returned from hunting in the spring, the old man gave me up to Capt. Elliot, a trader from Detroit. But my mistress, on learning this, became very angry, threatened Elliot, and got me back.

Some time in April, there was a dance at a town about two miles from where I resided. This I attended, in company with the Indian to whom I belonged. Meeting with a French trader from Detroit, by the name of Batest Ariome, who took a fancy to me on account of my resemblance to one of his sons, he bought me for 50 dollars in Indian money.* Before leaving the dance I met with a Mr. Sherlock, a trader from Ky., who had formerly been a prisoner to this same tribe of Indians, and who had rescued a lad by the name of Moffit, who had been captured by the Indians on the head of the Clinch, and whose father was an intimate and particular friend of my father's.† I re-quested Mr. Sherlock to write to my father, through Mr. Moffit, informing him of my captivity, and that I had been purchased by a French trader, and was gone to Detroit. This letter, I have reason to believe, father received, and that it gave him the first infor-mation of what had become of me.

But we must pause in this narrative, to notice the destruction and captivity of the remaining part of Mr. Moore's family.

There being only a few families in the part of Va. where Mr. Moore resided, the Indians from the Shawanee towns made frequent incursions upon them. Consequently

---

* This consisted of silver brooches, crosses, &c.
† Mr. Moffit had removed to Ky., and was then living there.

most of the families returned to the more thickly settled parts of what is now Montgomery co., &c., but Mr. Moore still remained. Such was the fertility of the soil, and the adaptedness of the country to grazing, that Mr. M. kept about 100 head of horses, and a good stock of cattle, which principally wintered themselves. On the 14th of July, 1786, early in the morning, a gang of horses had come in from the range to the lick-blocks, about 100 yards from the house, and Mr. Moore had gone out to salt them. Two men also, who were living with him, had gone out, and were reaping wheat. The Indians, about 30 in number, who were lying in ambush, watching the house, supposing that all the men were absent, availed themselves of the opportunity and rushed forward with all speed. As they advanced they commenced firing, and killed two of the children, viz. William and Rebecca, who were returning from the spring, and Alexander in the yard. Mr. Moore attempted to get to the house, but finding it surrounded, ran past it through a small pasture in which the house stood. When he reached the fence he made a halt, and was shot through with seven bullets. The Indians said he might have escaped if he had not stopped on the fence. After he was shot he ran about 40 yards, and fell. He was then scalped by the Indians, and afterwards buried by the whites at the place where the body lay, and where his grave may yet be seen. It was thought that when he saw his family about to be massacred, without the possibility of rendering them assistance, he chose to share a like fate. There were two fierce dogs, which fought like heroes until the fiercest one was killed. The two men who were reaping, hearing the alarm, and seeing the house surrounded, fled, and alarmed the settlement. At that time the nearest family was distant 6 miles. As soon as the alarm was given, Mrs. Moore and Martha Ivins* barred the door, but this was of no avail. There was no man in the house at the time except John Simpson, the old Englishman already alluded to, and he was on the loft sick, and in bed. There were five or six guns in the house, but having been shot off the evening before, they were then empty. It was intended to have loaded them after breakfast. Martha Ivins took two of them and went up stairs where Simpson was, and handing them to him, told him to shoot. He looked up, but had been shot in the head through a crack, and was then near his end. The Indians then proceeded to cut down the door, which they soon effected. During this time Martha Ivins went to the far end of the house, lifted up a loose plank, and went under the floor, and requested Polly Moore, (then eight years of age,) who had the youngest child, called Margaret, in her arms, (which was crying,) to set the child down and come under. Polly looked at the child, clasped it to her breast, and determined to share its fate. The Indians having broken into the house, took Mrs. Moore and her children, viz.: John, Jane, Polly, and Peggy, prisoners, and having taken every thing that suited them, they set it and the other buildings on fire, and then went away. Martha Ivins remained under the floor a short time, and then came out and hid herself under a log that lay across a branch not far from the house. The Indians having tarried a short time with the view of catching horses, one of them walked across this log, sat down on the end of it, and began to fix his gun-lock. Miss Ivins supposing that she was discovered, and that he was preparing to shoot her, came out and gave herself up. At this he seemed much pleased. They then set out for their towns. Perceiving that John Moore was a boy weak in body and mind, and unable to travel, they killed him the first day. The babe they took two or three days, but it being fretful, on account of a wound it had received, they dashed its brains out against a tree. They then moved on with haste to their towns. For some time it was usual to tie very securely each of the prisoners at night, and for a warrior to lie beside each of them with tomahawk in hand, so that in case of pursuit the prisoners might be speedily dispatched. Their manner of travelling was very much like that described by James Moore. Not unfrequently they were several days without food, and when they killed game, their habit was to make broth as described by him. When they came to the banks of the Scioto, they carefully pointed out to Mrs. Moore and the prisoners, the hieroglyphics mentioned in the narrative of James Moore. When they reached their town, (which was the one to which James Moore had been taken,) they were soon assembled in council, when an old man made a long speech to them dissuading them from war; but at the close of it the warriors shook their heads, and retired. This old man afterwards took Polly Moore into his family, where he and his wife seemed greatly to commiserate her situation, and showed all possible kindness.

Shortly after they reached the towns, Mrs. Moore and her daughter Jane were put to death, being burned and tortured at the stake. This lasted some time, during which

---

* Miss Ivins was living in the family at the time, helping them to spin; Joseph Moore, another son was in Rockbridge co., going to school.

she manifested the utmost Christian fortitude, and bore it without a murmur—at intervals conversing with her daughter Polly and Martha Ivins, and expressing great anxiety for the moment to arrive when her soul should wing its way to the bosom of her Saviour. At length an old squaw, more humane than the rest, dispatched her with a tomahawk.*

This tribe of Indians proving very troublesome to the whites, it was repeatedly contemplated to send an expedition against their town. This it is probable Martha Ivins in some measure postponed, by sending communications through the traders, urging the probable fate of the prisoners, if it were done immediately. In November, two years afterwards, however, such an expedition did go out. The Indians were aware of it from about the time it started, and when it drew near they concealed what they could not carry off, and with the prisoners, deserted their towns. About this time Polly Moore had serious thoughts of concealing herself until the arrival of the whites; but fearing the consequences of a greater delay in their arrival than she might anticipate, she did not attempt it.

Late in November, however, the expedition did arrive, and after having burned their towns, destroyed their corn, &c., returned home. After this the Indians returned to their towns; but winter having set in, and finding themselves without houses or food, they were greatly dispirited, and went to Detroit, where, giving themselves up to great excess in drinking, they sold Polly Moore to a man who lived in or near a little village by the name of French Town, near the western end of Lake Erie, for half a gallon of rum. Though at this time the winter was very severe, the released captive had nothing to protect her feet but a pair of deerskin moccasins, and the state of her other clothing will presently appear. But it is now time to resume the narrative of James Moore.

" Mr. and Mrs. Ariome were to me parents indeed. They treated me like one of their own sons. I ate at their table, and slept with their sons in a good feather-bed. They always gave me good counsel, and advised me, (particularly Mrs. Ariome,) not to abandon the idea of returning to my friends. I worked on the farm with his sons, and occasionally assisted him in his trading expeditions. We traded at different places, and sometimes went a considerable distance into the country. On one of these occasions, four young Indians began to boast of their bravery, and among other things said that one Indian could whip four white men. This provoked me, and I told them that I could whip all four of them. They immediately attacked me; but Mr. Ariome hearing the noise, came and took me away. This I consider a kind Providence; for the Indians are very unskilful in boxing, and in this manner of fighting, I could easily have whipped all of them; but when they began to find themselves worsted, I expected them to attack me with clubs, or some other weapon, and if so, had laid my plans to kill them all with a knife which I had concealed in my belt, mount a fleet horse which was close at hand, and escape to Detroit.

" It was on one of these trading expeditions that I first heard of the destruction of father's family. This I learned through a Shawnee Indian with whom I had been acquainted when I lived with them, and who was one of the party on that occasion. I received this information some time in the same summer after it occurred. In the following winter I learned that my sister Polly had been purchased by a Mr. Stogwell, an American by birth, but unfriendly to the American cause. He was a man of bad character—an unfeeling wretch—and treated my sister with great unkindness. At that time he resided a considerable distance from me. When I heard of my sister, I immediately prepared to go and see her; but as it was then in the dead of winter, and the journey would have been attended with great difficulties, on being told by Mr. S. that he intended to remove to the neighborhood where I resided in the following spring, I declined it, When I heard that Mr. Stogwell had removed, as was contemplated, I immediately went to see her. I found her in the most abject condition, almost naked, being clothed with only a few dirty and tattered rags, exhibiting to my mind an object of pity indeed. It is impossible to describe my feelings on that occasion; sorrow and joy were both combined; and I have no doubt the feelings of my sister were similar to my own. On being advised, I applied to the commanding officer at Detroit, informing him of her treatment, with the hope of effecting her release. I went with Mr. Simon Girty to Col, McKee, the superintendent for the Indians, who had Mr. Stogwell brought to trial to answer to the complaint against him. But I failed to procure her release. It was de-

---

* James Moore says that he learned from Martha Ivins that the murder of these prisoners was committed by a party of Cherokee Indians, who were returning from a war excursion, in which they had lost some of their party. That in consequence of this they became exasperated, fell upon the prisoners, and put them to death.

cided, however, that when an opportunity should occur for opr returning to our friends, she should be released without remuneration. This was punctually performed on application of Mr. Thomas Ivins, who had come in search of his sister Martha, already alluded to, who had been purchased from the Indians by some family in the neighborhood, and was at that time living with a Mr. Donaldson, a worthy and wealthy English farmer, and working for herself.

"All being now at liberty, we made preparations for our journey to our distant friends, and set out, I think, some time in the month of October, 1789, it being little more than five years from the time of my captivity, and a little more than three years from the time of the captivity of my sister and Martha Ivins.* A trading boat coming down the lakes, we obtained a passage for myself and sister to the Moravian towns, a distance of about 200 miles, and on our route to Pittsburg. There, according to appointment, we met with Mr. Ivins and his sister, the day after our arrival. He had in the mean time procured three horses, and we immediately set out for Pittsburg. Fortunately for us, a party of friendly Indians, from these towns, were about starting on a hunting excursion, and accompanied us for a considerable distance on our route, which was through a wilderness, and the hunting-ground of an unfriendly tribe. On one of the nights during our journey, we encamped near a large party of these hostile Indians. The next morning four or five of their warriors, painted red, came into our camp. This much alarmed us. They made many inquiries, but did not molest us, which might not have been the case if we had not been in company with other Indians. After this nothing occurred worthy of notice until we reached Pittsburg. Probably we would have reached Rockbridge that fall if Mr. Ivins had not unfortunately got his shoulder dislocated. In consequence of this, we remained until spring with an uncle of his in the vicinity of Pittsburg. Having expended nearly all his money in travelling, and with the physician, he left his sister, and proceeded on with sister Polly and myself to the house of our uncle, Wm. McPhoetus, about 10 miles southwest of Staunton, near the Middle River.† He received from uncle Joseph Moore, the administrator of father's estate, compensation for his services, and afterwards returned and brought in his sister."

Here the narrative of Mr. Moore closes. He remained several years with his friends in Rockbridge county, but subsequently returned to the plantation of his father, where he still resides, having raised a large family : himself a highly respectable member of the Methodist church ; in connection with which, also, are many of his children, and his brother Joseph, who is a resident of the same county. Martha Ivins married a man by the name of Hummer, emigrated to Indiana, and reared a family of children. Two of her sons are ministers in the Presbyterian church—one in the presbytery of Crawfordsville, and the other in the presbytery of Iowa.

An incident in the captivity of Polly Moore has been omitted, too interesting to be passed over without notice.

At the time she became a prisoner, notwithstanding her father, two brothers, and a sister had just been murdered, herself and the rest captured, and the house set on fire, she took up two New Testaments, one of which she kept the whole time of her captivity, and that too when she was but eight years of age.‡ She did not long continue with Mr. McPhoetus, but lived with her uncle Joseph Walker, on Buffalo creek, about six miles south of Lexington, in Rockbridge county.§ At the age of twelve she was baptized, and admitted into full communion with the Presbyterian church. When she grew up, she married the Rev. Samuel Brown, a distinguished Presbyterian clergyman of the same county, and pastor of New Providence congregation. She became the mother of eleven children. Of these, one died in infancy, another while quite young, and of the others, one is ruling elder in the church, another married a pious physician, another a clergyman, five are Presbyterian ministers in Virginia, and the remaining one is a communicant in the church. Her last legacy was a Bible to each of her children.

At the north end of the grave-yard near New Providence church, 14 miles north of Lexington, is the grave of Mary Moore.

The following tragical song, commemorative of the death and

---

* James Moore had, in the mean time, become so much attached to the family of Mr. Ariome, and especially to one of his daughters, that he would have been contented to remain had it not been for his sister.

† This property is now in the possession of Mr. George Shue. The Rev. Dr. Wm. McPhoetus informed the writer that he remembered the time.

‡ The other was stolen from her while with the Indians.

§ This plantation was afterwards owned by Mr. John Donahoe, who kept a tavern. It is now owned by a Mr. Maſht.

captivity of the Moore family, was written many years since, and is still much sung among the mountaineers of this region. We insert it as a curiosity:

MOORE'S LAMENTATION.

Assist me with words, Melpomene, assist me with skill to impart
The dolorous sorrow and pain that dwelt upon every heart,
When Moore and his infantile throng the savages cruel did slay.
His wife they led captive along; with murmuring voice she did say,
Farewell! ye soft bowers so green, I'll traverse these valleys no more,
Beside yon murmuring stream lies bleeding the man I adore,
And with him my sweet innocent babes, these barbarous Indians have slain,
Were I but in one of their graves, then I would be free from my pain.
Once more on them she cast her eyes and bade them forever farewell,
Deep sobs from her bosom did rise, while she thus in anguish did wail.
The heathen her sorrows to crown, led her without further delay,
A victim to their Shawnee towns, and now comes her tragical day.
A council upon her was held, and she was condemned for to die;
On a rock they a fire did build, while she did their torments espy;
With splints of light wood they prepared to pierce in her body all round,
Her flesh for to mangle and tear. With sorrow she fell to the ground,
But her senses returning again, the mercy of God did implore.
"Thou Saviour that for me wast slain and bathed in a bloody gore,
Have mercy now on me in death, and Heaven will sing forth thy praise
Soon as I have yielded my breath in a raging fiery blaze."
Then to her destruction proceeds each cruel blood-thirsty hell-hound:
With lightwood they cause her to bleed, streaming from every wound.
The smoke from her body doth rise; she begs for their pity in vain:
These savages hear her cries, and with dancing laugh at her pain.
Three days in this manner she lay, tormented and bleeding the while,
But God his mercy displayed, and on her with pity did smile,
Growing angry at their cruel rage her soul would no longer confine,
Her torments he soon assuaged, and in praise she her breath did resign.
Let each noble, valorous youth, pity her deplorable end,
Awhile from your true loves part; join me each brother and friend,
For I have been where cannons roared and bullets did rapidly fly,
And yet I would venture once more, the Shawnees to conquer or die.

Beside the above, we here insert another song, derived, like the other, from a mountain cabin in this region. It was made on the battle of Point Pleasant, "sometimes called the *Shawnee Battle*." (See Mason county.)

Let us mind the tenth day of October,
Seventy-four, which caused woe,
The Indian savages they did cover
The pleasant banks of the Ohio.

The battle beginning in the morning,
Throughout the day it lashed sore,
Till the evening shades were returning down
Upon the banks of the Ohio.

Judgment precedes to execution,
Let fame throughout all dangers go,
Our heroes fought with resolution
Upon the banks of the Ohio.

Seven score lay dead and wounded
Of champions that did face their foe,

By which the heathen were confounded,
Upon the banks of the Ohio.

Col. Lewis and some noble captains,
Did down to death like Uriah go,
Alas! their heads wound up in napkins,
Upon the banks of the Ohio.

Kings lamented their mighty fallen
Upon the mountains of Gilboa,
And now we mourn for brave Hugh Allen,
Far from the banks of the Ohio.

O bless the mighty King of Heaven
For all his wondrous works below,
Who hath to us the victory given,
Upon the banks of the Ohio.

TYLER.

TYLER was formed in 1814, from Ohio, and named from John Tyler, gov. of Va. from 1808 to 1811, and father of the late President of the U. S. It is 40 miles long, with a mean breadth of 18 miles. This county declines to the west towards the Ohio, and is drained by Middle Island and Fishing creeks, both running through the county and emptying into the Ohio. The surface is exceedingly hilly and broken, but the soil is of a fair quality, and on the creek and river bottoms, excellent. About 50,000 pounds of maple sugar are annually produced. Pop. in 1840, whites 6,854, slaves 85, free colored 5 ; total, 6,954.

Middlebourn, the county-seat, is 307 miles northwesterly from Richmond, 52 miles s. of Wheeling, near the centre of the county, on Middle Island creek. It contains 3 mercantile stores, a Methodist church, and about 50 dwellings. Sistersville, 48 miles below Wheeling, is one of the best landings on the Ohio. This town was laid out in 1814 as the county-seat ; but in 1816 it was removed to Middlebourn, 9 miles east of here. It is a flourishing village, containing 4 mercantile stores and about 80 dwellings. Martinsville, at the mouth of Fishing creek, 40 miles below Wheeling, contains 1 store and about 40 dwellings. Centreville, situated on the west bank of Middle Island creek, 7 miles E. of the C. H., contains from 30 to 40 dwellings.

This county, being upon the Ohio River, has, in common with those counties situated upon this great artery, a facility in transporting its produce to market not possessed by the country further inland. The introduction of steamboats has greatly increased these facilities. In the infancy of the country every species of water-craft was employed in navigating this beautiful river ; and that unique and hardy race that once spent their lives upon its waters have vanished. The graphic and lively picture given below from Flint's Recollections of the lives of the boatmen, is now a part of the history of our country :

The way of life which the boatmen lead, is in turn extremely indolent and extremely laborious ; for days together requiring little or no effort, and attended with no danger, and then, on a sudden, laborious and hazardous beyond Atlantic navigation. The boats float by the dwellings of the inhabitants on beautiful spring mornings, when the verdant forests, the mild and delicious temperature of the air, the delightful azure of the sky, the fine bottom on one hand and the romantic bluff on the other, the broad and smooth stream rolling calmly down the forest and floating the boat gently onward—all combine to inspire the youthful imagination. The boatmen are dancing to the violin on the deck of their boat. They scatter their wit among the girls on the shore, who come down to the water's edge to see the pageant pass. The boat glides on until it disappears behind a point of wood. At this moment, perhaps, the bugle, with which all the boats are provided, strikes up its notes in the distance over the water. These scenes and these notes, echoing from the bluffs of the beautiful Ohio, have a charm for the imagination, which, although I have heard a thousand times repeated, and at all hours, is, even to me, always new and always delightful.

WARREN.

WARREN was formed in 1836, from Frederick and Shenandoah : it is 20 miles long and 12 wide. The Shenandoah River runs through it at the base of the Blue Ridge, and receives in its passage the waters of its North Fork, which enters it from the west. There is considerable mountain land in the sw. part of the county, and the surface is generally hilly, yet there is much excellent soil

Pop. in 1840, whites 3,851, slaves 1,434, free colored 342 ; total, 5,627.

Front Royal, the county-seat, is 139 miles NW. of Richmond and 20 SE. of Winchester, between the Shenandoah and the Blue Ridge, about a mile from the former. It was established in 1788, on 50 acres of land, the property of Solomon Vanmeter, James Moore, Robert Haines, William Cunningham, Peter Halley, John Smith, Allen Wiley, Original Wroe, George Chick, William Morris, and Henry Trout ; was laid into lots and streets, and Thomas Allen, Robert Russell, William Headly, William Jennings, John Hickman, Thomas Hand, and Thomas Buck, appointed trustees. The town is neatly built, and is surrounded by beautiful scenery. It contains 1 Presbyterian, 1 Baptist, and 1 Episcopal church, 5 mercantile stores, and about 400 inhabitants. About 7 miles south of this village is a copper-mine, which has recently been opened. It is conducted with spirit, and promises to be valuable.

About three miles southwest of Front Royal is *Allen's Cave*. In beauty and magnificence it is said to equal Weyer's Cave. It extends about 1200 feet. The sparry incrustations and concretions of "Sarah's Saloon," one of its principal apartments, presents a gorgeous scene. Its innumerable cells and grottoes form a complete labyrinth.

WARWICK.

WARWICK was one of the eight original shires into which Virginia was divided in 1634 : its extreme length is 20, and greatest breadth 5 miles. It occupies a portion of the narrow peninsula between York and James Rivers, the latter of which forms its southwestern boundary. Pop. in 1840, whites 604, slaves 831, free colored 21 ; total, 1,456.

The C. H. lies about 3 miles N. of the James, and 77 miles southeasterly from Richmond.

WASHINGTON.

WASHINGTON was formed in 1776, from Fincastle county : it is 40 miles long, and 18 broad. This county occupies part of the valley between the Blue Ridge and Clinch mountains, and is watered by the North, Middle, and South Forks of Holston, which rise in Wythe and flow through this county, dividing it into three fertile valleys. Gypsum of a superior quality abounds, and over 60,000 pounds of maple sugar are annually produced. Pop. in 1840, whites 11,731, slaves 2,058, free colored 212 ; total, 13,001.

On the bank of the Middle Fork of Holston, about 15 miles SE.

of Abingdon, is an ebbing and flowing spring. | At irregular intervals of from 3 to 4 hours, this spring, with a rushing noise, sends forth a volume of water in two or three successive waves, when it suddenly subsides until again agitated by this irregular tide.

Westerly from Abingdon, between Three Springs and the North Fork of Holston, on Abram's creek, in a narrow, gloomy ravine, bounded by a high perpendicular ledge, is a waterfall, which in one single leap descends perpendicularly 60 feet, and then falls about 40 feet more ere it reaches the bottom; the stream is about 20 feet wide.

Emory and Henry College.

Emory and Henry College is 10 miles from Abingdon, in a beautiful and secluded situation. It was founded in 1838, under the patronage of the Holston Annual Conference of the Methodist Episcopal church. It is yet in its infancy, but is efficiently organized, and is already exerting a salutary influence upon the cause of education in sw. Virginia. The faculty consists of a president, Rev. Charles Collins, A. M., who is the professor of moral and mental science, two other professors, and a tutor; number of pupils about 125, including those in the preparatory department. The name, Emory and Henry, was given in honor of Patrick Henry, and the Rev. Bishop Emory of the M. E. church. The post-office of the college is Glade Spring.

Abingdon, the county-seat, is 304 miles sw. of Richmond, 8 N. of the Tennessee line, 56 from Wytheville, and 130 from Knoxville, Tenn. This, by far the most considerable and flourishing town in sw. Virginia, was established by law in Oct. 1778, on 120 acres of land given for the purpose by Thomas Walker, Joseph Black, and Samuel Briggs, Esqs., and the following gentlemen were appointed trustees: Evan Shelby, William Campbell, Daniel Smith, William

Edmondson, Robert Craig, and Andrew Willoughby. The town stands on an elevation; it is substantially built, with many brick buildings; the principal street is macadamized, and the town is surrounded by a fertile, flourishing, and thickly-settled agricultural

Abingdon.

country. It contains several large mercantile stores, 2 newspaper printing offices, 1 Presbyterian, 2 Methodist, and 1 Swedenborgian church, a variety of mechanical and manufacturing establishments, and a population of over 1000.

In regard to the early settlement of the tract of Virginia west of New River, it is said, that in 1754, six families only were residing on it—two on Back creek, in (now) Pulaski county; two on Cripple creek, in Wythe county; one at the Town house, now in Smyth county; and Burke's family, in Burke's Garden, Tazewell county. On the breaking out of the French war, the Indians in alliance with the French made an irruption into this valley, and massacred Burke and his family. The other families, finding their situation too perilous to be maintained, returned to the eastern side of New River. The renewal of the attempt to settle this part of the country was not made until after the close of that war. A small fort, called Black's Fort, was erected when the country around Abingdon was settled, at a point about 100 yards south of that village, on the western bank of a small creek. It was one of those rude structures which the pioneers were accustomed to make for defence against the Indians, consisting of a few log cabins surrounded by a stockade, to which they always fled whenever Indian signs appeared.

Southwestern Virginia, at that day, had ceased to be the permanent residence of the aborigines, but was the thoroughfare through which those tribes inhabiting the Rockcastle hills, in the wilderness of Kentucky, passed to the old settlements of Virginia. About two and a half miles northwest of the village, an old gentleman, by the name of Cummings—familiarly known as Parson Cummings—resided. It frequently happened, during times of excitement, when the whole population had repaired to the fort, that provisions grew scarce, and it became necessary for some of the most fearless and athletic to go out to the *clearings* and bring in supplies. On one occasion, several started with a wagon to the *clearing* of Parson Cummings, and among the rest, the parson accompanied them. About half a mile from the fort, upon what is called Piper's hill, the company was surprised by a party of Indians, and one of their number killed. The others, unprepared for such a reception, took to the bushes. The parson being somewhat portly, and wearing one of those large powdered wigs deemed an essential accompaniment of the gown in those days, rendered him conspicuous, and, of course, an object

500 WASHINGTON COUNTY.

of more particular pursuit. Accordingly, in his precipitate retreat, he was closely followed by an active savage, with upraised tomahawk. The parson, in dodging under
the undergrowth, left the aforesaid wig suspended upon a bramble, seeing which, the Indian, taking it for the parson's head, made a bound or two and grasped it, but, on finding the head was not there, with a violent gesture, and all the lineaments of disappointment drawn upon his face, he threw it upon the ground, exclaiming, " d——d lie !"
and doggedly gave up the chase. The parson, in the mean time, was concealed in the
bushes, within a few feet of the spot. The man who was killed was buried at a place
since comprising the village burial-place, and the spot where his ashes repose, is marked
with a rude, unhewn stone, with the inscription, " William Creswell, July 4, 1776."

_____

As an evidence of the superstition even now occasionally existing among the lower
class of the country, there resided, in 1838, in the hills, a few miles from Abingdon, a
man by the name of Marsh, who was deemed by his neighbors not only honest and industrious, but possessed of as much intelligence as most people in the lower walks of
life. This man was severely afflicted with scrofula, and imagined his disease to be the
effects of a *spell*, or *pow-wow*, practised upon him by a *conjurer*, or *wizard*, in the
neighborhood, by the name of Yates. This impression taking firm hold of Marsh's
mind, he was thoroughly convinced that Yates could, if he chose, remove the malady.
The latter, being termed an Indian doctor, was sent for, and administered his nostrums.
The patient, growing worse, determined to try another remedy, which was to take the
life of Yates. To accomplish this, he sketched a rude likeness of Yates upon a tree,
and shot at it repeatedly with bullets containing a portion of silver. Yates, contrary to
his expectations, still survived. Marsh then determined to *draw a head* upon the original, and, accordingly, charged an old musket with two balls, an admixture of silver
and lead, watched an opportunity, and shot his victim as he was quietly passing along
the road, both balls entering the back of the neck. Yates, however, survived, and
Marsh was sent to the penitentiary.

_____

The annexed historical sketch of Washington county is abridged
from the ms. memoirs of Southwestern Virginia by Col. John
Campbell, Esq. Treasurer of the United States in the administration of President Jackson :

About one hundred years ago—viz., in 1738—the counties of Frederick and Augusta
were formed out of Orange. These two western counties then embraced within their
jurisdiction the whole colony of Virginia west of the Blue Ridge. With the exception
of the few first settlers of Augusta and Frederick, it was all a howling and savage wilderness. . . . As late as the year 1756, eighteen years after Frederick and Augusta
were formed into counties, the Blue Ridge was regarded, as Judge Marshall says, as the
northwestern frontier of Virginia, and she found an immense difficulty in completing a
single regiment to protect the inhabitants from the horrors of the scalping-knife, and the
still greater horrors of being led into captivity by those who added terrors to death by the
manner of inflicting it. Carlisle in Pennsylvania, Frederick in Maryland, and Winchester in Virginia, were then *frontier posts*.
This division of the territory west of the Blue Ridge into counties, continued for 31
years, up to the year 1769, when the county of Botetourt was formed out of Augusta.
Botetourt then embraced all southwestern Virginia, south and west of Augusta. Three
years afterwards—viz., in 1772—the county of Fincastle was formed out of Botetourt.
The county of Fincastle then embraced all sw. Va. south and west of the Botetourt
line, which was near New River. In 1776, four years afterwards, the county of Fincastle was divided into three counties, and called Kentucky, Washington, and Montgomery counties, and the name of Fincastle became extinct.
Washington county, during the whole of the revolution and up to 1786, embraced
within its limits all southwestern Va., sw. of the Montgomery line. It included parts of
Grayson, Wythe, and Tazewell, all of Smyth, Scott, Russell, and Lee, with its present
limits.
The act establishing the county of Washington passed in October, 1776, but it was
not to go into operation until January, 1777. It received its military and civil organization on the 28th of January, 1777. It is the oldest county of *Washington* in the U.
S., being the first that was called after the father of his country. The act establishing

the county passed in the first year of the commonwealth, and the county was organized the first month of the new year.

The following are the first records made, in which the county received its civil and military organization:

"January 28th, in the first year of the commonwealth of Virginia, and in the year of our Lord Christ 1777, being the day appointed by act of the General Assembly of the commonwealth of Virginia, for holding the first court of the county of Washington at 'Black's Fort.' A commission of the Peace and Dedimus for this county, directed to Arthur Campbell, William Campbell, Evan Shelby, Daniel Smith, William Edminston, John Campbell, Joseph Martin, Alexander Buchanan, James Dysart, John Kincaid, John Anderson, James Montgomery, John Coalter, John Snody, George Blackburn, and Moses' Masten, gentlemen, bearing date the 21st day of December, 1776, were produced and read. Thereupon, pursuant to the Dedimus, William Campbell and Joseph Martin, two of the aforesaid justices, administered the oath of a justice of the peace, and of a justice of the county court of chancery, to Arthur Campbell, the first justice named in said commission, and he afterwards administered the aforesaid oaths to William Campbell, William Edminston, and others named as aforesaid in the said commission." . . The records also state that James Dysart produced a commission as county sheriff from Gov. Patrick Henry, and securities being given, he took the oath.

The sheriff having opened the court in the name of the commonwealth of Virginia, David Campbell, afterwards Judge Campbell of Tennessee, was inducted into the office of county clerk.

The same records exhibit the following as the military organization of the county in this the first year of the commonwealth, and morning of the American revolution:— Arthur Campbell, county lieutenant or colonel-commandant; Evan Shelby, colonel; William Campbell, lieutenant-colonel; William Edminston and Daniel Smith, majors; Captains, John Campbell, Joseph Martin, John Shelby, Sen., James Montgomery, Robert Buchanan, Aaron Lewis, John Duncan, Gilbert Christian, James Shelby, James Dysart, Thomas Masten, John Kinkead, John Anderson, William Bowen, George Adams, Robert Craig, Andrew Colvill, and James Robertson. Some time after this organization, Col. Evan Shelby resigned his commission, and William Campbell was appointed in his place.

Among the records illustrating the times, is this:

"John Findlay making it appear to the satisfaction of the court of Washington county, that he, upon the 20th day of July, 1776, received a wound in the thigh in the battle fought with the Cherokees, near the Great Island,* and it now appears to the said court that he, in consequence of the said wound, is unable to gain a living by his labor as formerly; therefore his case is recommended to the consideration of the General Assembly of the commonwealth of Virginia."

The Cherokee Indians were defeated in this action, and massacre prevented upon the frontier settlements. The savages were led on, it is said, by a bold chieftain called "Dragon Canoe." He led his men, in some places, within thirty or forty paces of the opposing party; and although he fought with the courage and skill of a Tecumseh or Oceola, he was completely beaten in his own mode of warfare. Both parties fought behind trees, with rifles, and both were girded with tomahawks, as weapons of self-defence with the white, when in close personal conflict with his savage foe, and of massacre on the part of the Indian, when his wounded enemy had fallen into his power. There was no American officer in this well-fought action, of a higher rank than captain. Three of that grade commanded volunteer companies from Washington county, Va., viz.: John Campbell, James Shelby, and James Thompson. William Cocke commanded a company from Tennessee, then the territory of North Carolina. There were other captains out of Va., whose names are unknown to the writer.

The condition of the country is further disclosed by these annexed extracts:

Jan. 29th, 1777. "Ordered, that William Campbell, Wm. Edminston, John Anderson, and George Blackburn, be appointed commissioners to hire wagons to bring up the county salt, allotted by the governor and council, and to receive and distribute the same agreeably to said order of council." "Ordered, that Capt. Robert Craig and Capt. John Shelby be added to the commissioners appointed to receive and distribute the flour contributed in Augusta, or elsewhere, for the distressed inhabitants of the county."

Without flour, and without salt, these brave pioneers of a new county, cheerful and gay, social and kind to each other, and linked together like a band of brothers, thought of nothing but the sublime objects of the American revolution—the great cause of American liberty. Avarice had not won its way to their patriotic souls. They fought for freedom, and with their own weapons and war-steeds they volunteered and marched in every direction, at their own expense, in which the cries of suffering humanity reached them. These gallant Highlanders volunteered on the expedition against the Shawnees at Pt. Pleasant, against the Cherokees at Long Island, and against the British at King's Mountain and Guilford; against the Cherokees, under Col. Christian, and afterwards under Col. Arthur Campbell in 1781. Col. Campbell, on this expedition, commanded 700 mounted riflemen. History gives him the credit of having first made the experiment

---

* This Island lies in Holston River, East Tennessee, near Kingsport, a few miles south of the Virginia line.

of attacking Indians with *mounted riflemen*, a mode of fighting on this occasion proving completely successful.* He destroyed in this expedition 14 Indian towns, and burnt 50,000 bushels of corn. The cruel necessity also devolved upon him of destroying several scattered settlements, and a large quantity of provisions, after supplying his own army for their return.

Mr. Jefferson, then governor of Virginia, in a letter dated the 17th of Feb., 1781, to the Continental Congress, enclosing the account of this expedition, remarks:

"Our proposition to the Cherokee chiefs to visit Congress, for the purpose of preventing or delaying a rupture with that nation, was too late. The storm had gathered to a head when Major Martin (the agent) had got back. It was determined, therefore, to carry the war into their country, rather than wait it in ours; and I have it in my power to inform you that, thus disagreeably circumstanced, the issue has been successful. I enclose the particulars as reported to me." Col. Arthur Campbell's report to Mr. Jefferson is dated Washington county, Jan. 15, 1781. "The militia (he says) of this and the two western North Carolina counties (now Tennessee) have been fortunate enough to frustrate the designs of the Cherokees. On my reaching the frontiers, I found the Indians meant to annoy us by small parties. To resist them effectually, the apparently best measure was to transfer the war *without delay* into their own borders.

"To raise a force sufficient, and provide them with provisions and other necessaries, was a work of time, that would be accompanied with uncommon difficulties, especially in the winter season. Our situation was critical, and nothing but an extraordinary effort could save us, and disappoint the views of the enemy. All the calamities of 1776 came fresh in remembrance, and to avoid a like scene, men flew to their arms and marched to the field."

The following message was sent to the Indian chiefs and warriors after this expedition was completed:

"*Chiefs and Warriors*—We came into your country to fight your young men. We have killed many of them, and destroyed your towns. You know you began the war, by listening to the bad counsels of the King of England, and the falsehoods told you by his agents. We are now satisfied with what is done, as it may convince your nation that we can distress you much at any time when you are so foolish as to engage in war against us. If you desire peace, as we understand you do, we, out of pity to your women and children, are disposed to treat with you on that subject.

"We therefore send this by one of your young men, who is our prisoner, to tell you if you are disposed to make peace, six of your head men must come to our agent, Major Martin, at the Great Island, within two moons, so as to give him time to meet them with a flag guard on Holston river, at the boundary line. To the wives and children of those men of your nation who protested against the war, if they are willing to take refuge at the Great Island until peace is restored, we will give a supply of provisions to keep them alive.

"Warriors, listen attentively:

"If we receive no answer to this message until the time already mentioned expires, we shall then conclude that you intend to continue to be our enemies. We will then be compelled to send another strong force into your country, that will come prepared to remain in it, to take possession of it as a conquered country, without making you any compensation for it. Signed at Kai-a-tee, the 4th of Jan., 1781, by

"ARTHUR CAMPBELL, Col.,

"JOHN SEVIER, Col.,

"JOSEPH MARTIN, Agent and Major of Militia."

A few days after the return of the army across the Dan, Gen. Greene received a communication from Col. Arthur Campbell, announcing the fortunate result of the expedition, and stating that the Indians were desirous of submitting, and negotiating a treaty with the proper authorities. It being at that early day doubtful in whom such a power rested, Gen. Greene deemed the necessity of the case sanctioned him in nominating commissioners for that purpose. On the 20th of February, 1781, he issued a commission to Wm. Christian, Wm. Preston, Arthur Campbell, and Joseph Martin, of Virginia, and to Robert Sevier, Evan Shelby, Joseph Williams, and John Sevier, of North Carolina, to enter into a treaty for restoring peace, and *establish the limits* between the two states and the Indian tribes; but with the wary precaution of limiting their powers by the laws of those states, and the duration of the commission by the will of Congress or the

---

* On this point see Morse's Hist. Sketch of Tenn., prepared for the Am. Atlas, pub. in 1827, by Carey & Lee.

commander-in-chief. Under this commission was concluded that treaty which took place the ensuing year.

During the summer of 1780, the militia of southwestern Virginia were kept constantly on the alert, in consequence of the movements of the British army in South Carolina. In August and September, 150 men from Washington county were in service on New River, about the lead mines, and over the mountains in North Carolina, under Col. Campbell, to prevent and suppress insurrections among the tories in those quarters. In the fall of this year the regiment of Col. William Campbell was in the battle of King's Mountain, and behaved with great bravery. The signal defeat which the enemy experienced on that occasion crushed the hopes of the tories, and did much towards giving a favorable turn to the tide of war in the southern states.*

The annexed biographical sketches of Col. Arthur Campbell, and of Gen. William Campbell, are from the MS. history of Washington county. The notice of the latter was written by the former, who was both a cousin and a brother-in-law:

ARTHUR CAMPBELL was born in 1742, in Augusta county. When about fifteen years old he volunteered as a militiaman, to perform a tour of duty in protecting the frontier settlements against the incursions of the Indians, and was stationed in a fort which had been erected about that period, near where the road leading from Staunton to the Warm Springs at this time crosses the stream called the Cow Pasture. While engaged in this service, a party of men from the fort, of which he was one, went some distance to a plum thicket, in quest of plums. The Indians, lying in ambush, fired upon them, and one of their balls grazed the knee of Arthur, then in one of the plum-trees. He sprang to the ground, and the shock, together with the injury from the wound, although slight, caused him to fall, and he was captured ere he could recover himself. The others made their escape without injury.

This youth, a mere stripling, was loaded with Indian packs, and made to carry them for seven days. The Indians, who were of one of the tribes in the vicinity of Lakes Erie and Michigan, immediately set out for their country. He was soon exhausted, unable to travel, and was treated with great severity. The aged chief in command interfered, took him from the others, and protected him from further injury ; and when the party reached the Indian towns, this chief adopted him, and he remained in his family during his captivity.

The young man now turned his attention to studying the Indian character, learning their language and customs ; and soon acquiring the confidence of his chief, became his companion in all his hunting excursions, in which they rambled over the whole country now forming Michigan, and the northern portions of Ohio, Indiana, and Illinois. In 1759, some portion of the British army was marched towards the upper lakes and the country bordering on Lake Erie, with a view of bringing the Indian tribes to submission. In what particular direction the force marched, the writer hereof has not now the means of ascertaining. It was moving towards the borders of Lake Erie when runners and traders made known to the Indians that such a force was marching towards their country. Campbell knew that although they were several hundred miles distant, the Indians would watch his every movement with the greatest suspicion ; he, however, formed the bold resolution of escaping to them. To accomplish it required skill and cool determination, and the result showed he possessed both in a high degree. A hunting excursion was soon projected, in which he joined ; and after several days march in an opposite direction somewhat from the army, the party left their camp one morning, each separating for the day's hunt. Campbell took what he judged to be the proper course, and in two weeks reached the British army. In this journey of several hundred miles, partly through an unknown country, great peril was encountered in avoiding Indian hunting parties ; but he escaped all, furnishing himself meat with his rifle. On reaching the outposts, he requested to be conducted to the commander. The officer was deeply interested in his narrative, and being struck with the intelligence of the young

* We learn from tradition, that after the battle, the American officers held a council, and hung some fifteen or twenty of their tory prisoners. Many more were condemned; but, disgusted with this work of blood, their lives were spared. Among those who suffered was an Irishman, a noble-looking young man, who had by his own exertions raised a company of royalists. As the rope was being adjusted around his neck, he was offered his life if he would join the Americans. He spurned the offer with indignation, and as they were about swinging him off, cried, "*Long live King George!*"—H. H.

man, engaged him to pilot the army. In this he rendered them important service, and soon after returned home.

During his three years of captivity, his friends had not heard of his destiny, and time in some measure had healed the wounds inflicted by his supposed horrible fate. In their imaginations his name had long been numbered with the dead, and to sooth the feelings of his pious parents, it had been ceased to be mentioned in the midst of a numerous family of brothers and sisters. A letter is unexpectedly received from him, dated at Pittsburg, announcing his safety, and that in a few days he would have the pleasure of meeting them at the parental hearth. The parents and children are overwhelmed with joy at the prospect of once beholding and embracing their long-lost son and brother. The eldest son starts immediately to meet him, and they meet in the road alone. The captive boy has grown a tall youth, with the erect, manly step, and lofty air of the red man. He reaches home, the neighbors flock to see him. He has acquired the taciturnity of the Indian, and the thousand inquisitive interrogatories annoy him. Soon as he becomes settled, instead of devoting his leisure to social amusements, he is acquiring a knowledge from books that places him above his cotemporaries, and to the astonishment of all, writes an elegant epistle to the governor of the state, detailing his captivity, escape, and services rendered to the army as a guide ; upon which the government then allows him a thousand acres, near Louisville, Kentucky.

About four years before the commencement of the revolution, David Campbell (his father) and family, (Arthur and one sister having emigrated two years previous,) moved, and settled at a place called " the Royal Oak," on Holston River, then a wilderness and an Indian hunting-ground. Arthur was soon appointed a major in the Fincastle county militia, and in the spring of 1776 was elected to the Virginia assembly, and was a member of the convention forming the constitution. In this convention he took a decided stand against an established church, and although not a public speaker, influenced some of the first members of the convention. While a member of the Assembly, he became intimately acquainted with Edmund Pendleton, Richard Henry Lee, and George Mason, and afterwards with Jefferson and Madison, with all of whom he corresponded. Previous to this, he married the third sister of Gen. William Campbell, a lady of beauty, sprightliness, and intelligence. When Washington county was formed, he was appointed county lieutenant, or colonel-commandant. At this period there was a general military spirit, and no officers resigned their commissions. Col. Campbell retained command of this regiment (the 70th) for nearly thirty years ; and there were in his corps several captains with heads perfectly white with age. Before Col. Campbell reached the command of a regiment, he was engaged in and commanded several military expeditions, as well as after. The public documents at Richmond giving authentic accounts of public affairs, were destroyed (it is supposed) by Arnold, and therefore previous to the date of his colonelship, little can be learned about his public services. The crowning act of his life, his brilliant services against the Cherokees, are elsewhere detailed.

Col. Campbell resided on the farm he first settled after coming to Holston, about thirty-five years. He then removed to Yellow Creek, Knox county, Kentucky, where he died of a cancer in the face, in the 74th year of his age. Col. Campbell was tall, of a dignified air, a man of extensive reading, and fine conversational talents. With the mass of society he was unpopular, although respected, owing mainly to his not relaxing in his manner to suit it. His temper being hasty and overbearing, occasioned violent quarrels and bitter enemies. He was a zealous whig, and in the gloomiest hour had not a doubt of an auspicious result to the contest.

Col. Arthur Campbell had two sons, who died in the army during the late war. Capt. James Campbell died at Mobile, and Col. John B. Campbell fell at Chippewa, where he commanded the right wing of the army under Gen. Winfield Scott. He was a gallant and a humane officer, and in the winter of 1813, commanded an expedition against the Indians on the Wabash, and had a bloody battle with them at Mississinewa, and finally destroyed their towns.

Gen. WILLIAM CAMPBELL, the subject of this memoir, was a native of Augusta, in the state of Virginia, of the true Caledonian race by the maternal line, as well as that by the father. Being an only son, he received a liberal education under the best teachers of those times. He had an ardent mind, very susceptible of literary improvement, and acquired early in life a correct knowledge of the English language, of ancient and modern history, and of several branches of the mathematics. Nature had formed him for a commander in military capacity. His personal appearance was grave and masculine, being something about six feet high, and well proportioned ; in conversation rather reserved and thoughtful ; in his written communications expressive and elegant. His patriotism was not of a timid cast. He never balanced between his military duty and prudential maxims. When his ire was excited, he showed in his countenance the fury of an Achilles. The trusty *Andreferrara*, the sword he wore on the day of battle, was once the property of his grandfather from Scotland, and he had an arm and a spirit that could wield it with effect. In the year 1775, he was of the first regular troops raised in Virginia, being honored with a captain's commission in the first regiment. Here he acquired a practical knowledge of tactics and the discipline of an army. In the latter part of the year 1776, he resigned his commission on account of the Indian war breaking out, by which his family and friends were exposed to immediate danger. Soon after he was promoted to be lieut.-colonel of the militia of Washington county, and the next year, on the resignation of Evan Shelby, sen., to that of colonel of the regiment. In this rank he remained until after the battle of King's Mountain, and of Guilford, when he was appointed by a vote of the legislature of Virginia, to rank as a brigadier-general, and was ordered to join the Marquis Lafayette, to oppose the invasion of the enemy in 1781. After the defeat of Ferguson, the British general, Cornwallis, imbibed a personal resentment, and had the temerity to threaten if Gen. Campbell fell into his hands, he would have instantly been put to death for his rigor against the tories. This, instead of intimidating, had the contrary effect, and in turn the American general resolved, if the fortune of war should place Cornwallis in his power, he should meet the fate of Ferguson. This soon after, at the battle of Guilford, had nearly been the case, for had the militia behaved with the same firmness and courage as on the wing where Gen. Campbell commanded, the British army must have met with a total defeat. On forming the army in Virginia, under the Marquis Lafayette, in 1781, Gen. Campbell became a favorite of that gallant nobleman, who gave him the command of the brigade of light infantry and riflemen. A few weeks before the siege of Yorktown, he took sick of a complaint in his breast, which obliged him to retire from the army to a friend's house in the country, and there, after a short sickness, to end his days in the thirty-sixth year of his age, much lamented by the friends of liberty who knew him. Of his military character we have given a short sketch. His moral sentiments and social demeanor in civil life were exemplary. Although an only son, and an heir to a considerable property, he never gave way to the fashionable follies of young men of fortune. He well knew that vice, at any time of life, or in any shape, darkens the understanding, perverts the will, and thus injures social order in every grade of society. He kept a strict guard on his own passions, and was by some deemed too severe in punishing the deviations of others. His military career was short but brilliant. Warren and Montgomery acted on a conspicuous stage, and deserved the eulogiums so often repeated. Campbell undertook a no less arduous task, with an inferior number of undisciplined militia. He marched in a few days near two hundred miles, over vast mountains, in search of the enemy, who were commanded by an experienced officer, of known bravery and military skill, and who had chosen his field for battle. It was [King's Mountain] rather a fortification than an open space for combatants to meet upon. The assault of the Americans was impetuous and irresistible, and the event was victory to a wish. This victory resulted in the retreat of the main British army a considerable distance, and their relinquishment of the scheme of invading Virginia that year. It also reanimated all the friends of liberty in the southern states, and was the prelude of adverse events to the enemy, which, in the course of the next campaign, terminated in their final overthrow.*

Judge PETER JOHNSON, who resided in this vicinity in the latter part of his life, was originally intended for the church. At the breaking out of the revolution he clandestinely left his father's house, and joined the legion of Lee. Proving a most vigilant and prudent soldier, he was promoted to a lieutenancy. At the siege of Augusta, a ditch of the besiegers was occupied by Lieut. Johnson and 24 men. Early in the night information was received that a party of 40 British soldiers and Indians were approaching. Johnson immediately ordered his men, who had their muskets loaded, to sit on their

---

* The Virginia legislature presented this officer with a sword, horse, and pistols, for his conduct at King's Mountain, and named a county after him. The Continental Congress passed in his favor a highly complimentary resolution. His conduct at Guilford drew from Gen. Greene, and from Col. Henry Lee, (to whose legion he was attached,) flattering letters. And when the scene closes, and death has befallen him, Lafayette issues a funeral order, regretting the decease of "an officer whose services must have endeared him to every citizen, and in particular to every American soldier;" as one who has acquired "a glory in the affairs of King's Mountain and Guilford Court-House, that will do his memory everlasting honor, and ensure him a high rank among the defenders of liberty in the American cause."

hams on the reverse of the ditch. In a few minutes the enemy were heard stealthily advancing. When they were within a few yards, he gave the order, and his men suddenly rising took deliberate aim and poured in upon them a deadly fire. They were completely routed, and instead of surprising Johnson were themselves surprised. His intrepidity and coolness on this occasion saved his detachment from being cut off.

While his brother officers were spending their time in dissipation, Johnson was pursuing his studies. After the war he acquired distinction at the bar, was elected speaker of the House of Representatives, and finally received the appointment of judge. He left a numerous family, some of whom are now residing in this county.

WAYNE.

WAYNE is a new county, formed in 1842 from the southwestern part of Cabell. It is about 35 miles long, with a mean breadth of 10 miles. The Ohio forms its NW. boundary, the Tug Fork of Big Sandy divides it from Kentucky, and Twelve Pole creek rises in Logan and runs through it centrally. The surface of the county is considerably broken, and it is sparsely inhabited. The court-house is at Trout's Hill.

The following description of this section of country is extracted from the history of a voyage from Marietta to New Orleans in 1805, and communicated to the American Pioneer, by Dr. S. P. Hildreth:

At the mouth of the Big Sandy, the dividing line between Virginia and Kentucky, the Ohio makes its extreme southern bend, and approaches nearer to the climate of the cane, (*arundinaria macrosperma*,) than at any other point between Pittsburg and Cincinnati. At this period it grew in considerable quantities near the falls, 30 miles from the mouth, and had been visited in 1804 by Thomas Alcock, of Marietta, for the purpose of collecting its stems to manufacture weavers' reeds. It was the highest point, near the Ohio, where this valuable plant was known to grow, and has long since been destroyed by the domestic cattle of the inhabitants. In Tennessee and Kentucky it furnished the winter food for their cattle and horses many years after their settlement. The head waters of the Sandy and Guyandotte interlock with those of the Clinch and the Holston, amid the spurs of the Cumberland mountains. In their passage to the Ohio, they traverse the most wild and picturesque region to be found in western Virginia; abounding in immense hills of sand rocks, cut into deep ravines by the water-courses, containing caverns of various sizes and extent. At this period it was the most famous hunting-ground for bears in all the country. In the years 1805-6 and 7, eight thousand skins were collected by the hunters from the district traversed by these rivers and a few adjacent streams. It was the paradise of bears; affording their most favorite food in exhaustless abundance. The bear is not strictly a carnivorous animal, but, like the hog, feeds chiefly on vegetable food. On the ridges were whole forests of chestnuts, and the hillsides were covered with oaks, on whose fruits they luxuriated and fattened, until their glossy hides afforded the finest peltry imaginable. The war in Europe created a great demand for their skins, to decorate the soldiers of the hostile armies; and good ones yielded to the hunters four and five dollars each.

Since that day the attention of the sojourners of this wild region has been turned to the collection of the roots of the ginseng. This beautiful plant grows with great luxuriance, and in the most wonderful abundance, in the rich virgin soil of the hill and mountain sides. For more than thirty years the forests have afforded a constant supply of many thousand pounds annually, to the traders stationed at remote points along the water-courses. No part of America furnishes a more stately growth of forest trees, embracing all the species of the climate. The lofty Liriodendron attains the height of eighty and a hundred feet without a limb, having a shaft of from four to six feet in diameter. The white and yellow oak are its rivals in size. The magnolia acuminata towers aloft to an altitude uncommon in any other region; while its more humble relatives, the tripetala and mycrophilla, flourish in great beauty by its side. It may be considered the storehouse for building future cities, when the prolific pines of the Alleghany River are exhausted. In addition to all these vegetable riches, the hills are full of fine beds of bituminous coal, and argillaceous iron ores.

WESTMORELAND.

WESTMORELAND lies on the Potomac, in the NE. section of the state. It is about 30 miles long, with a width of from 8 to 10 miles. The first mention which has been found of this county, is in an act of the " Grand Assembly" of July, 1653, by which " It is ordered that the bounds of the county of Westmoreland be as followeth, (viz.,) from Machoactoke River, where Mr. Cole lives, and so upwards to the falls of the great river Pawtomake, above the Nescostin's towne." From this, it would seem the county was previously in existence, but it is not ascertained at what time it was taken from the older colony of Northumberland, (at first called Chicawane or Chickown,) which was established in 1648, and declared by an act of that year to contain the " neck of land between Rappahannock River and Potomack River." Its surface is indented with numerous tributaries of the Potomac, the waters of which generally abound with the finest fish, oysters, and wild-fowl. The face of the country is diversified by hills and flatland. The soil on the streams is fertile, and the middle or forest-lands are covered with a thick growth of pine and cedar, and exhibit all the symptoms of early exhaustion from the successive culture of tobacco. They are not, however, irreclaimable, and in many instances, by a proper system of agriculture, give abundant crops. Large quantities of cord-wood are exported to the Baltimore market. Pop. in 1840, whites 3,466, slaves 3,590, free colored 963 ; total, 8,019. The Court-House is situated near the line of Richmond co., 70 m. NE. of Richmond, and contains a few dwellings only.

Westmoreland has been called " the Athens of Virginia." Some of the most renowned men in this country have been born within her borders. Among these may be mentioned WASHINGTON, Richard Henry Lee, and his three brothers, Thomas, Francis, and Arthur, Gen. Henry Lee, Monroe, and the late Judge Bushrod Washington.

President Monroe was born at the head of Monroe's creek. *Chantilly*, situated upon the Potomac, now in ruins, was once the residence of Richard Henry Lee. Upon the same stream, a few miles further up, is *Stratford*, the family seat of the Lees for many generations. The BIRTHPLACE of Washington was destroyed previous to the revolution. It stood about half a mile from the junction of Pope's creek with the Potomac. A stone has lately been placed there to mark its site, by G. W. Custis, Esq. It bears the simple inscription, " HERE, ON THE 11TH OF FEBRUARY, (O. S.) 1732, GEORGE WASHINGTON WAS BORN."

" The spot is of deep interest, not only from its association but its natural beauties. It commands a view of the Maryland shore ; of the Potomac, one of the most majestic of rivers, and of its course for many miles towards Chesapeake Bay. The house was a low-pitched, single-storied, frame building, with four rooms on the first floor, and an enormous chimney at each end on the outside. This was the style of the better sort of houses in those days, and they are still occasionally seen in the old settlements of Virginia."

The fac-simile in the engraving, of the record of the birth of Washington, is from the family record in the Bible which belonged to his mother. The original entry is supposed to have been made by her. This old family Bible is in the possession of George W. Bassett, Esq., of Farmington, Hanover co., who married a grand-niece of Washington. It is in the quarto form, much dilapidated by age, and with the title-page missing. It is covered by the striped Virginia cloth, anciently much used.

The portrait of Washington which we give, is engraved from the original painting by his aid, Col. John Trumbull. When Lafayette was on his visit to this country, he pronounced it the best likeness of Washington he had seen. It was taken at the time of life when they were both together in the army of the revolution.

It is unnecessary here to give a biographical sketch of Washington, as it is to be presumed that the reader is already familiar with the events of his life. But we insert the tribute paid to his character by Lord Brougham, where he contrasts him with Napoleon:

How grateful the relief which the friend of mankind, the lover of virtue experiences when, turning from the contemplation of such a character, his eye rests upon the greatest man of our own or any other age. . . . In Washington we truly behold a marvellous contrast to almost every one of the endowments and the vices which we have been contemplating; and which are so well fitted to excite a mingled admiration, and sorrow, and abhorrence. With none of that brilliant genius which dazzles ordinary minds; with not even any remarkable quickness of apprehension; with knowledge less than almost all persons in the middle ranks, and many well educated of the humbler class possess; this eminent person is presented to our observation clothed with attributes as modest, as unpretending, as little calculated to strike or astonish, as if he had passed through some secluded region of private life. But he had a judgment sure and sound; a steadiness of mind which never suffered any passion, or even any feeling to ruffle its calm; a strength of understanding worked, rather than forced its way through all obstacles—removing or avoiding, rather than overleaping them. His courage, whether in battle or in council, was as perfect as might be expected from this pure and steady temper of soul. A perfectly just man, with a thoroughly firm resolution never to be misled by others, any more than by others to be overawed; never to be seduced, or betrayed, or hurried away by his own weakness, or self-delusions, any more than by other men's arts; nor even to be disheartened by the most complicated difficulties, any more than be spoilt on the giddy heights of fortune—such was this great man—whether we regard him alone sustaining the whole weight of campaigns, all but desperate, or gloriously terminating a just warfare by his resources and his courage; presiding over the jarring elements of his political council, alike deaf to the storms of all extremes—or directing the formation of a new government for a great people, the first time so vast an experiment had been tried by man; or finally retiring from the supreme power to which his virtue had raised him over the nation he had created, and whose destinies he had guided as long as his aid was required—retired with the veneration of all parties, of all nations, of all mankind, in order that the rights of men might be preserved, and that his example might never be appealed to by vulgar tyrants.

This is the consummate glory of the great American; a triumphant warrior, where the most sanguine had a right to despair; a successful ruler in all the difficulties of a course wholly untried; but a warrior whose sword only left its sheath when the first law of our nature commanded it to be drawn; and a ruler who, having tasted of supreme power, gently and unostentatiously desired that the cup might pass from him, nor would suffer more to wet his lips than the most solemn and sacred duty to his country and his God required!

To his latest breath did this great patriot maintain the noble character of a captain, the patron of peace; and a statesmen, the friend of justice. Dying, he bequeathed to his heirs the sword he had worn in the war for liberty, charging them "never to take it from the scabbard but in self-defence, or in defence of their country and her freedom;"

George Washington to Augustine & Mary his Wife was Born
y.e 11.th Day of February 173½ about 10 in the Morning & was Baptized the 3:.d of April
following Mr Beverley Whiting & Capt. Christopher Brooks Godfathers and
Mrs. Mildred Gregory Godmother

Fac-simile of the entry of the birth of Washington in the Bible of his mother.

He wrote on a certain 25.th of July when you ought to
have been at Church; praying in as becomes every so I
Christian Man

D.r Sir I.m me Affect.e & Obe.t

Geo Washington

28.th August 1762

Fac-simile of the writing of Washington.

and commanding them that when it should thus be drawn, they should never sheath it, nor ever give it up, but prefer falling with it in their hands to the relinquishment thereof —words, the majesty and simple eloquence of which are not surpassed in the oratory of Athens and Rome. It will be the duty of the historian and the sage in all ages, to omit no occasion of commemorating this illustrious man ; and until time shall be no more, will be a test of the progress which our race has made in wisdom and in virtue, to be derived from the veneration paid to the immortal name of WASHINGTON !

We now insert notices drawn from various public sources, of some of the other distinguished men of Westmoreland :

RICHARD HENRY LEE, a signer of the Declaration of Independence, was born at Stratford, Jan. 20th, 1732. He spent several years in an academy in England, from which he returned to his native country in his 19th year. His fortune being ample, he devoted his time principally to the elegant pursuits of literature. In 1755 he offered his services as a captain of provincials to Braddock ; but he refused to accept any more assistance from the provincials than he was obliged to. In his 25th year, Lee was appointed a justice of the peace, and was shortly after first chosen a delegate to the House of Burgesses, where he soon acquired distinction in debate, and his voice was always raised in support of republican principles. In all the questions of controversy that came up between the mother country and her colonies, Mr. Lee took an active part. He was appointed on the most important committees of the House of Burgesses, and drew up some of the most important papers, which " contained the genuine principles of the revolution, and abounded in the firm and eloquent sentiments of freemen."

It is stated that the celebrated plan of corresponding committees between the different colonies, adopted in 1773 by the House of Burgesses, originated with Mr. Lee. The same idea had, about the same time, been conceived by Mr. Samuel Adams of Massachusetts, which circumstance has occasioned much dispute. Mr. Lee doubtless followed the suggestions of his own mind, as he had, five years previously, requested Mr. Dickinson of Pennsylvania, in a letter, to bestow his consideration upon the advantage of plans which he communicated to him of the same purport.*

Wirt, in describing him at this time, says : " Richard Henry Lee was the Cicero of the house. His face itself was on the Roman model ; his nose Cæsarean ; the port and carriage of his head, leaning persuasively and gracefully forward ; and the whole contour noble and fine. Mr. Lee was by far the most elegant scholar in the house. He had studied the classics in the true spirit of criticism. His taste had that delicate touch which seized with intuitive certainty every beauty of an author, and his genius that native affinity which combined them without an effort. Into every walk of literature and science he had carried this mind of exquisite selection, and brought it back to the business of life, crowned with every light of learning, and decked with every wreath that all the Muses and all the Graces could entwine. Nor did those light decorations constitute the whole value of its freight. He possessed a rich store of historical and political knowledge, with an activity of observation, and a certainty of judgment that turned that knowledge to the very best account. He was not a lawyer by profession, but he understood thoroughly the constitution both of the mother country and of her colonies, and the elements also, of the civil and municipal law. Thus, while his eloquence was free from those stiff and technical restraints which the habits of forensic speaking are so apt to generate, he had all the legal learning which is necessary to a statesman. He reasoned well, and declaimed freely and splendidly. The note of his voice was deeper and more melodious than that of Mr. Pendleton. It was the canorous voice of Cicero. He had lost the use of one of his hands, which he kept constantly covered with a black silk bandage neatly fitted to the palm of his hand, but leaving his thumb free ; yet, notwithstanding this disadvantage, his gesture was so graceful and so highly finished, that it was said he had acquired it by practising before a mirror. Such was his promptitude that he required no preparation for debate. He was ready for any subject as soon as it was announced ; and his speech was so copious, so rich, so mellifluous, set off with such bewitching cadence of voice, and such captivating grace of action, that while you listened to him you desired to hear nothing superior, and indeed thought him perfect. He had a quick sensibility and a fervid imagination, which Mr. Pendleton wanted. Hence his orations were warmer and more delightfully interesting ; yet still, to him those keys were not consigned, which could unlock the sources either of the

---

* Wirt, in his Life of Henry, says that in Virginia " the measure was brought forward by Mr. Dabney Carr, a new member from the county of Louisa." (See p. 258.) Both Mr. Carr and Mr. Lee were appointed upon the standing committee of correspondence consequent upon the adoption of the measure.

strong or tender passions. His defect was, that he was too smooth and too sweet. His style bore a striking resemblance to that of Herodotus, as described by the Roman orator: 'he flowed on, like a quiet and placid river, without a ripple.' He flowed, too, through banks covered with all the fresh verdure and variegated bloom of the spring; but his course was too subdued, and too beautifully regular. A cataract, like that of Niagara, crowned with overhanging rocks and mountains, in all the rude and awful grandeur of nature, would have brought him nearer to the standard of Homer and of Henry."

In 1774, he was a member of the first general Congress, where he at once took a prominent stand, and was on all the leading committees. From his pen proceeded the memorial of Congress to the people of British America. In the succeeding Congress, Washington was appointed commander-in-chief of the army, and his commission and instructions were furnished by Mr. Lee, as chairman of the committee appointed for that purpose. The second address of Congress to the people of Great Britain—a composition unsurpassed by any of the state papers of the time—was written by him this session. But the most important of his services in this term was his motion, June 7, 1776, to declare independence. His speech on introducing this bold and glorious measure, was one of the most brilliant displays of eloquence ever heard on the floor. After a protracted debate, it was determined, June 10, to postpone the consideration of this resolution until the first Monday of the July following ; but a committee was appointed to prepare a declaration of independence. Of this committee he would have been chairman, according to parliamentary rules, had not the illness of some of his family called him home. Mr. Jefferson was substituted for him, and drew up the declaration. He shortly resumed his seat, in which he continued until June, 1777, when he solicited leave of absence on account of ill health, and to clear up some stains which malice or overheated zeal had thrown upon his reputation in Virginia. He demanded an investigation from the Assembly, which resulted in a most triumphant and flattering acquittal, by a vote of thanks for his patriotic services.

In consequence of Mr. Lee's great and persevering exertions to procure the independence of his country, and to promote the cause of liberty, the enemy made great exertions to secure his person. Twice he narrowly escaped being taken. Once his preservation was owing to the fidelity of his slaves, and on the other occasion his safety was owing to his own dexterity and presence of mind.

In August, 1778, he was again elected to Congress, but declining health forced him to withdraw, in a great degree, from the arduous labors to which he had hitherto devoted himself. In 1780 he retired from his seat, and declined returning to it until 1784. In the interval he served in the Assembly of Virginia, and, at the head of the militia of his county, protected it from the incursions of the enemy. In 1784, he was unanimously chosen president of Congress, but retired at the end of the year, and in 1786 was again a member of the Virginia Assembly. He was a member of the convention which adopted the federal constitution, and although personally hostile to it, he joined in the vote to submit it to the people. He was subsequently, with Mr. Grayson, chosen the first senators from Virginia under it, and in that capacity moved and carried through several amendments. In 1792, he was forced by ill health to retire from public life, when he was again honored by a vote of public thanks from the legislature of Virginia. He died June 19, 1794.

FRANCIS LIGHTFOOT LEE, a signer of the Declaration of Independence, was born Oct. 10, 1734. His education was directed by a private tutor, and he inherited a fortune. In 1765 he became a member of the House of Burgesses, and continued in that body until 1775, when the convention of Virginia chose him a member of the Continental Congress, in which he remained until 1779, when he entered the legislature of Va. He died in Richmond in 1797.

HENRY LEE, a governor of Va. and a distinguished officer of the revolution, was born Jan. 29, 1756. His family was one of high respectability and distinction. At 18 years of age he graduated at Princeton College. In 1776, when but 20 years of age, he was appointed captain of one of the six companies of cavalry composing the regiment of Col. Theodorick Bland. In Sept., 1777, Capt. Lee, with his company, joined the main army. He introduced excellent discipline into his corps, and rendered most effectual service, in attacking light parties of the enemy, in procuring information, and in foraging.

As Capt. Lee, in general, lay near the British lines, a plan was formed in the latter part of January, 1778, to cut off both him and his troop. A body of 200 cavalry made an extensive circuit, and seizing four of his patrols, came unexpectedly upon him in his quarters, a stone house. He had then with him only ten men ; yet with these he made so desperate a defence, that the enemy were beaten off with a loss of 4 killed, and an officer and 3 privates wounded. His heroism in this affair drew forth from Washington a complimentary letter, and he was soon after raised to the rank of a major, with the command of an independent partisan corps of two companies of horse, which afterwards was enlarged to three, and a body of infantry. On the 19th of July, 1779, Major Lee, at the head of about 300 men, completely surprised the British garrison at Powles' Hook—now Jersey City—and after taking 160 prisoners, retreated with the loss of but 2 men killed, and 3 wounded. For his " prudence, address, and bravery," in this affair, Congress voted him a gold medal.

In the commencement of the year 1780, he joined, with his legion, the army of the south, having been previously promoted to the rank of lieutenant-colonel. In the celebrated retreat of Greene before Cornwallis, Lee's legion formed the rear-guard of the army. So hot was the pursuit, that Col. Lee at one time came in contact with Tarleton's corps, and, in a successful charge, killed 18 of them, and made a captain and several privates prisoners. Shortly after, Lee with his legion, and Col. Pickens with some militia, attacked a party of 400 loyalist militia under Col. Pyle, killed 90, and wounded many others. At the battle of Guilford, Lee's legion distinguished itself; previous to the action, it drove back Tarleton's dragoons with loss, and afterwards maintained a sharp and separate conflict until the retreat of the main army. After this, Greene, in pursuance of the advice of Lee, determined to advance at once into South Carolina, and endeavor to reannex to the Union that and its sister state of Georgia, instead of watching the motions of Cornwallis. The results were as fortunate as the design was bold and judicious. In pursuance of this plan, Greene advanced southward, having previously detached Lee, with the legion, to join the militia under Marion, and, in cooperation with him, to attempt the minor posts of the enemy. By a series of bold and vigorous operations, Forts Watson, Motte, and Granby, speedily surrendered; after which, the legion was ordered to join Gen. Pickens, and attempt to gain possession of Augusta. On the way, Lee surprised and took Fort Galphin. The defences of Augusta consisted in two forts—Fort Cornwallis and Fort Grierson; the latter was taken by assault, the former after a siege of 16 days. In the unfortunate assault upon Ninety-Six, Lee was completely successful in the part of the attack intrusted to his care. In the battle at Eutaw Springs, his exertions contributed much to the successful issue of the day. After the surrender of Yorktown, Lee retired from the army, carrying with him, however, the esteem and affection of Greene, and the acknowledgment that his services had been greater than those of any one man attached to the southern army.

Soon after his return to Virginia, he married a daughter of Philip Ludwell Lee, and settled at Stratford in this county. In 1786, he was a delegate to Congress; in 1788, a member of the Virginia convention to ratify the constitution, in defence of which he greatly distinguished himself. From 1792 to 1795, he was governor of Virginia. On the breaking out of the Whiskey Insurrection, in 1755, he was appointed by Washington to the command of the forces ordered against the insurgents, and received great credit for his conduct. In 1799 he was again a delegate in Congress, and upon the death of Washington, he was appointed to pronounce his eulogium. It was upon this occasion he originated the celebrated sentence : " First in war, first in peace, and first in the hearts of his countrymen." On the election of Jefferson he retired to private life.

His last years were clouded by pecuniary troubles. The hospitable and profuse style of living so common in Virginia, ruined his estate, and even abridged his personal liberty. It was in 1809, while confined for debt, that he composed his elegantly written Memoirs of the Southern Campaign.

General Lee was in Baltimore in 1812, at the time of the riot occasioned by the publication of some strictures on the war in the Federal Republican, an anti-war paper. After the destruction of the printing-office, an attack on the dwelling of the editor was apprehended. Lee, from motives of personal friendship to the editor, with a number of others, assembled for the purpose of protecting it. On being attacked, two of the assailants were killed, and a number wounded. The military arriving soon after, effected a compromise with the mob, and conveyed the inmates of the house to the city-jail for their greater safety. In the night the mob reassembled in greater force, broke open the jail, killed, and mangled its inmates in a shocking manner. From injuries then received, Lee never recovered. He went to the West Indies for his health. His hopes proved futile. He returned in 1818 to Georgia, where he died.

Gen. Lee was about five feet nine inches, well-proportioned, of an open, pleasant countenance, and a dark complexion. His manners were frank and engaging ; his disposition generous and hospitable. By his first wife, he had a son and a daughter ; by his second, (a daughter of Charles Carter, of Shirley,) he had three sons and two daughters.

Engraved by A Daggett from the original Painting by Colonel Trumbull.

WASHINGTON.

ARTHUR LEE, M. D., minister of the United States to the court of Versailles, was a native of Virginia, and the brother of Richard Henry Lee. He was educated at the University of Edinburg, where he also pursued for some time the study of medicine. On his return to this country, he practised physic four or five years in Williamsburg. He then went to London, and commenced the study of the law in the Temple. During his residence in England he kept his eye on the measures of government, and rendered the most important services to his country, by sending to America the earliest intelligence of the plans of the ministry. When the instructions to Gov. Bernard were sent over, he at the same time communicated information to the town of Boston respecting the nature of them. He returned, it is believed, before 1769, for in that year he published the Monitor's Letters, in vindication of the colonial rights. In 1775 he was in London, as the agent of Virginia ; and he presented, in August, the second petition of Congress to the king. All his exertions were now directed to the good of his country. When Mr. Jefferson declined the appointment of a minister to France, Dr. Lee was appointed to his place, and he joined his colleagues, Dr. Franklin and Mr. Deane, at Paris, in December, 1776. He assisted in negotiating the treaty with France. In the year 1779, he and Mr. Adams, who had taken the place of Deane, were recalled, and Dr. Franklin was appointed sole minister to France. His return had been rendered necessary by the malicious accusations with which Deane had assailed his public conduct.

In the preceding year Deane had left Paris, agreeably to an order of Congress, and came to this country in the same ship with the French minister Gerard. On his arrival, as many suspicions hovered around him, he thought it necessary to repel them by attacking the character of his colleague, Dr. Lee. In an inflammatory address to the public he vilified him in the grossest terms, charging him with obstructing the alliance with France, and disclosing the secrets of Congress to British noblemen. He at the same time impeached the conduct of his brother, William Lee, Esq., agent for Congress at the courts of Vienna and Berlin. Dr. Lee, also, was not on very good terms with Dr. Franklin, whom he believed to be too much under the influence of the French court. Firm in his attachment to the interest of his country, honest, zealous, he was inclined to question the correctness of all the commercial transactions in which the philosopher had been engaged. These dissensions among the ministers produced corresponding divisions in Congress ; and Monsieur Gerard had so little respect for the dignity of an ambassador, as to become a zealous partisan of Deane. Dr. Lee had many friends in Congress, but Dr. Franklin more. When the former returned to America in the year 1780, such was his integrity, that he did not find it difficult to reinstate himself fully in the good opinion of the public. In 1784 he was appointed one of the commissioners for holding a treaty with the Indians of the Six Nations. He accordingly went to Fort Schuyler, and executed this trust in a manner which did him much honor. In February, 1790, he was admitted a counsellor of the supreme court of the United States, by a special order. After a short illness, he died, December 14th, 1792, at Urbanna, in Middlesex county, Virginia. He was a man of uniform patriotism, of a sound understanding, of great probity, of plain manners, and strong passions.

During his residence for a number of years in England, he was indefatigable in his exertions to promote the interests of his country. To the abilities of a statesman he united the acquisitions of a scholar. He was a member of the American Philosophical Society. Besides the Monitor's Letters, written in the year 1769, which have been mentioned, he published " Extracts from a Letter to Congress, in answer to a Libel by Silas Deane," 1780 ; and " Observations on certain Commercial Transactions in France," laid before Congress 1780.

BUSHROD WASHINGTON was born in this county, and educated at William and Mary. He studied law in Philadelphia, and commenced its practice with great success in this county. He was a member of the House of Delegates in 1781. He afterwards removed to Alexandria, and thence to Richmond, where he published two volumes of the decisions of the supreme court of Virginia. He was appointed, in 1798, an associate-justice of the supreme court of the United States, and continued to hold this situation until his death, in November, 1829. He was the favorite nephew of Gen. Washington, and was the devisee of Mount Vernon. He was noted for sound judgment, rigid integrity, and unpretending manners.

WYTHE.

WYTHE was formed in 1790, from Montgomery, and named from George Wythe, an eminent jurist, and a signer of the Declaration of Independence ; it is 24 miles long and 20 wide. The greater part of the county is a mountain valley, included between Walker's mountain on the NW. and Iron mountain on the SE. Wythe valley is an elevated table-land, about 2,200 feet above the level of the ocean. The surface is drained, principally, by New River and its tributaries. The soil is good, and peculiarly adapted to the cultivation of grass. Gypsum is advantageously used in agriculture. Wythe is rich in minerals, in iron, lead, and coal. Pop. in 1840, whites 7,632, slaves 1,618, free colored 125 ; total, 9,375.

View in Wytheville.

Wytheville, the county-seat, is on the main turnpike from Harper's Ferry to Knoxville, Tenn., 248 miles southwesterly from Richmond, 55 miles from Abingdon, and 27 from Newbern. This town was established by law in 1792, on land given by Stophel Zimmerman and John Davis; and the following gentlemen were appointed trustees: Alexander Smyth, Walter Crockett, William Ward, Robert Adams, James Newell, David McGavock, William Caffee, and Jesse Evans; it bore the name of Evansham, until changed to its present one in 1838. It contains 8 mercantile stores, 2 newspaper printing-offices, 1 Presbyterian, 1 Protestant Methodist, 1 German Lutheran, and 1 Catholic church, and about 700 inhabitants. The village is neat, well built, and flourishing.

About nine miles easterly of Wytheville, on the great road, anciently stood *Fort Chiswell*, which was occupied by British troops in Braddock's war. This spot was once the county-seat of Montgomery, and there is now standing a log tenement that was used for a jail. Tradition points to a stump at this place, as being the remains of the identical tree to which Daniel Morgan was tied and whipped for beating a British officer. We doubt the authenticity of the tradition. This occurrence, we believe, took place several hundred miles further north. The circumstances have been variously stated. We here give them as we received them from the lips of an officer of the revolution, who served under Morgan.

Morgan at that time had charge of wagons transporting baggage. An officer on this occasion came out and asked him why the wagons were not ready for the march. He replied that he had been delayed, but would have them ready as soon as possible. The other insultingly replied, if he did not hurry he would run him through with his sword. Morgan gave him a tart reply. The officer thereupon fell into a passion, and made a lunge at him with his sword. The latter parried the blow with a heavy wagon whip, broke his sword, and gave him a severe drubbing. A court-martial sentenced him to receive 500 lashes. After receiving 450 of them, Morgan fainted. He was then allowed to go free, as it was feared the complement would kill him. The officer afterwards becoming convinced of his error, asked Morgan's pardon.

The LEAD MINES of Wythe are about 13 miles easterly from the C. H., on New River, opposite the mouth of Cripple creek. Formerly they were worked with great profit ; but the discovery of lead in the far west has operated disadvantageously to the interest of the proprietors of these works, situated, as they are, so far inland, and away from easy means of transportation. These mines were discovered very early, and were extensively worked in the revolution. The first proprietor was Col. Chiswell, an English gentleman, who built a frame house—the first frame house erected in this section of the country—which is now standing, in a dilapidated condition, near the mouth of Mill creek. The Col. attempted unsuccessfully to extract silver from the ore. He killed a man in a quarrel, and died in prison. Col. Lynch then came in possession, and after him, Moses and Stephen Austin,* who worked the mines for several years until 1796. Since, the mines have passed through the hands of several proprietors. They are now owned by the heirs of Col. James White, David Pierce, and Thomas Jackson. Formerly, shafts were sunk perpendicularly at the top of the hill, from 50 to 150 feet, until the ore was struck, when the excavations were nearly horizontal. From the bottom of the shafts the ore was raised by windlasses. In 1840 an excavation was commenced at the level of the plain on New River, and runs in horizontally, at the present time, 1000 feet in solid limestone rock. The material excavated is carried off by a railroad. Dr. Morse, in the 1st edition of his geography, published in 1789, has a description of these mines.

WOOD.

WOOD was formed in 1799, from Harrison, and named from James Wood, governor of Virginia from 1796 to 1799 ; it is 35 miles long, and 30 wide. Nearly the whole of its territory is embraced in the valley of the Little Kanawha and its tributaries,

---

* Stephen Austin, whose name is intimately connected with the early history of Texas, was a son of the above. He was born at the mines.

Hughes River, and N. fork of Hughes River.   The surface is much broken, but the soil for the most part is good.   Pop. in 1840, whites 7,243, slaves 624, free colored 56; total, 7,923.

Parkersburg, the county-seat, is a neat village, beautifully situated on the Ohio at the mouth of the Little Kanawha, 335 miles

Blannerhasset's Island.

northwesterly from Richmond, 94 below Wheeling, 12 below Marietta, and 264 miles above Cincinnati.   It is the most flourishing river village in the state, below Wheeling; it contains 9 mercantile stores, a bank, 1 newspaper printing office, 2 steam grist and 2 steam saw mills, 1 steam carding factory, 1 iron foundry, 2 extensive tanneries, 1 Presbyterian, 1 Baptist, 1 Episcopalian, and 1 Methodist church, and a population of about 1,100.   A turnpike, about 280 miles in length, has lately been finished from Winchester to Parkersburg; and it is contemplated to continue the Baltimore and Ohio rail-road to this place.

Elizabeth is on the Little Kanawha, and has one Methodist and 1 Baptist church, a store, some mills, and about 25 dwellings. Belville, about 18 miles below the C. H., is a small village, on a beautiful and fertile bottom of the Ohio.   The settlement at Belville was commenced in the year 1786, by a mercantile house at Philadelphia.   This spot was the site of a strong garrison during the Indian war, and many tragic events transpired around it, an interesting account of which is given in Dr. Hildreth's history of Belville.

About two miles below Parkersburg, in the Ohio River, is Blannerhasset's Island, a beautifully wooded tract.   Its original owner was Col. P. Devoll, of Virginia.   He sold it to Mr. Elijah Backus about the period of the settlement of the Ohio company.   In 1798 he disposed of the upper half of it to Mr. Blannerhasset, who shortly after commenced improving it.   An English traveller, by the name of Ashe, who was here in 1806, thus describes the island and its accomplished occupants:

The island hove in sight to great advantage from the middle of the river, from which point of view little more appeared than the simple decorations of nature; trees, shrubs, flowers, of every perfume and kind. The next point of view on running with the current, on the right hand side, varied to a scene of enchantment. A lawn, in the form of a fan inverted, presented itself, the nut forming the centre and summit of the island, and the broad segment the borders of the water. The lawn contained one hundred acres of the best pasture, interspersed with flowering shrubs and clumps of trees, in a manner that conveyed a strong conviction of the taste and judgment of the proprietor. The house came into view at the instant I was signifying a wish that such a lawn had a mansion. It stands on the immediate summit of the island, whose ascent is very gradual; is snow white; three stories high, and furnished with wings which interlock the adjoining trees, confine the prospect, and intercept the sight of barns, stables, and out-offices, which are so often suffered to destroy the effect of the noblest views in England.

The full front of the house being the signal for pulling in for the island, we did so immediately, and fell below a small wharf that covered an eddy and made the landing both easy and secure. There was no resisting the friendly importunity of my fellow passengers; no excuse would be taken; to stop the night at least, was insisted upon, and with a convincing expression that showed the desire flowed from hearts desirous not to be refused. There is something so irresistible in invitations of such a nature that they cannot be denied. I gave instructions respecting the boat, and giving the lady my arm, we walked up the beautiful lawn, through which a winding path led to the house. It was tea-time. That refreshment was served and conducted with a propriety and elegance I never witnessed out of Britain. The conversation was chaste and general, and the manners of the lady and gentleman were refined, without being frigid; distinguished, without being ostentatious; and familiar, without being vulgar, importunate, or absurd.

Before the decline of day we walked into the gardens, which were elegantly laid out in your country's style; produced remarkably fine vegetables, and had a very favorable show of standard peaches, and other fruit. The island abounds with vines, which grow to great height and strength, but never produce to any perfection. The path we had taken led to the water, the border of which brought us to the boat, where it seems all the servants of the family had assembled to hear what news my people might have brought into their little world. We found them seated on the green around Mindreth, who, proud to be their historian, related tales of such peril and affright, that they gazed on him with sensations of wonder and astonishment. The poor Mundanean, excluded by his color and aspect from participating in the social pleasures of the whites, had built himself a good fire, made himself the section of a tent, and was preparing his rod and line to catch some fish for supper. I saw the lady so pleased with this scene, and so delighted with Cuff's truly rural establishment, that I proposed supping on the shore, and by displaying a specimen of my evenings on the river, give some idea of former times, and the innocent enjoyments of primitive life. The night being perfectly fine, and the moon out, and some light clouds hindering the dew from falling, my proposition was joyfully acceded to, and instructions were given accordingly.

This determination gave life and interest to a scene that before was calm and pleasing. All was action and bustle. The historian no more attended. Every one assumed an occupation, and Cuff saw his tent surrounded by twenty willing assistants. The lady being busy instructing the servants, and sending them to the house for a few necessary articles, I proposed to the gentlemen to take the canoe across the current, and under the shade of the trees of the bank, with a lighted torch, attract the fish to the surface, and spear them while gazing at the blaze. We crossed over, and met with the success of striking seven large cat and sunfishes, in less than half an hour. We returned with the torch still burning, and the hands singing "The Beauteous Month of May," in cadence to the paddles, which rose and struck with a preconcerted regularity. This mode of nocturnal fishing was quite novel to the inhabitants of the little insulated world. The lady was charmed with it, and declared that the view of the canoe by torchlight, across the water; the conversation, obscurely heard; the sudden bursts of exultation announcing every success; and the cheerful return, with mirth and song, was an improvement of the finest sort to a scene she before deemed incapable of augmentation. After chatting some time on subjects immediately arising out of occurring incidents, and admiring the versatility of mind which one time finds felicity in towns and midnight masquerades, and at another acknowledges happiness on the contrasted theatre of the rivers and wilderness, we sat down to our repast, and in a short time paid the encomium of a satiated appetite. After which we returned to the house, where, over a bottle of wine, one hour longer we conversed on the pleasures of our rural sports, and retired to rest with that heartfelt ease which follows an innocent and well-spent day. Next morning, after breakfast, I with difficulty tore myself from this interesting family. You will excuse me for omitting the names of this amiable couple. They were from Ireland.

Such is the description which this traveller gives, ere the island became the scene of those events which attracted the attention of the whole country. It was at this time in the zenith of its beauty, and answered fully the glowing description of Wirt in the trial of Burr at Richmond, in the year succeeding. Much mystery has hung over the history of Blannerhasset and his connection with Burr. From a lecture given upon the subject, in New York, in February, 1845, by William Wallace, Esq., the following is principally derived. The lecturer had in his possession the papers of the Blannerhasset family, and other authentic sources of information:

Herman Blannerhasset was from a distinguished and wealthy Irish family, and was born in England while his mother was there on a visit. He received part of his education in England, and afterwards graduated at the University of Dublin, and acquired the profession of the law. He married Miss Adeline Agnew, a grand-daughter of the Gen. Agnew who was with Wolfe at Quebec. Being in principle a republican, he sold his estates, and coming to this country, landed at New York, where he was hospitably received by the first families. About the year 1798, he commenced his improvements on the island. His workmen were principally from Philadelphia. While his house was building, himself and family resided at Marietta. One who knew Mrs. Blannerhasset informed the writer that she was the most beautiful and accomplished lady she ever knew. She was gay and dressy, and an elegant dancer. She was fond of walking and riding, and on one occasion walked up to Marietta, a distance of ten or twelve miles. She was also a splendid equestrian, and was accustomed to ride attired in a scarlet riding-dress, and made her horse leap fences and ditches with ease. While at the island, Mr. Blannerhasset " possessed a voluminous library of choice and valuable books; a full set of chemical apparatus, and philosophical instruments, to the accommodation of which one wing of the dwelling-house was appropriated. He was a fine scholar, well versed in the languages, and refined in taste and manners. So tenacious was his memory, that he could repeat the whole of Homer's Iliad in the original Greek. With an ample fortune to supply every want, a beautiful and highly accomplished wife, and children just budding into life, he seemed surrounded with every thing which can make existence desirable and happy. The adjacent settlements of Belprie and Marietta, although secluded in the wilderness, contained many men of cultivated minds and refined manners, with whom he held constant and familiar intercourse; so that he lacked none of the benefits of society which his remote and insular situation would seem to indicate. Many were the cheerful and merry gatherings of the young people of these two towns beneath his hospitable roof, while the song and the dance echoed through the halls."[*]

In 1805, Aaron Burr, then sailing down the Ohio, landed uninvited on the island, where he was received with frank hospitality by the family. He remained but three days; but afterwards frequently visited the island, and finally enticed Blannerhasset into his plans. These were to settle an armed force on the Washita, for the purpose of colonizing that region, and, in case of war between Spain and the United States—at that time threatened—to subjugate Mexico. It was charged against Burr at his trial, that he meditated the severing of the eastern from the western states; but the folly of such a scheme was too absurd for the sagacity of this artful man. And he solemnly declared on his death-bed that he never meditated treason against the United States. If he did, Blannerhasset was not aware of the fact, as the letters of himself and wife evince. Burr did not, however, impart to him all his plans. He only wished to excite the cu-

---

* Dr. S. P. Hildreth, American Pioneer, vol. i. p. 93.

pidity of Blannerhasset with the prospect of great gains from his land speculations on the Washita, so as to gain access to his purse. Burr gave security for moneys advanced, on his son-in-law, Mr. Allston, of South Carolina; and while their plans were consummating, the accomplished daughter of Burr, Mrs. Allston, was a guest of Mrs. Blannerhasset. In the mean time Mr. Blannerhasset had constructed a flotilla of about twenty barges, in the vicinity of Marietta, for the expedition. The peculiar form of these boats excited curiosity and apprehension. In December, 1806, he went down the Ohio with them, having on board about thirty men, and loaded with parched corn meal. In the mean time an order was received by Col. Phelps, the commandant of the militia of Wood county, for his arrest, with his associates. Mrs. Blannerhasset met the military with unblanched cheeks, and forbade their touching any thing not mentioned in the warrant; but " the mob spirit of the militia ran riot, the well-stored cellars of the mansion were assailed, fences were destroyed to feed the sentinel's fires, the shrubbery was trampled under foot, and for amusement, balls fired into the rich gilded ceiling of the wall." " By the aid of some of her kind neighbors in Belprie, who were friendly to her husband, and greatly pitied her unpleasant condition, she was enabled to embark a few days after, with her two little sons, the most valuable of her effects, and black servants, in a boat; but did not rejoin Mr. Blannerhasset until he reached Louisville. Well might they look back in after years with fond regret, to the fair Eden from which they had been expelled by their own indiscretion, and the deceptive blandishments of Aaron Burr. In the year 1812, the dwelling-house and offices were destroyed by an accidental fire. The garden, with all its beautiful shrubbery, was converted into a corn-field, the ornamental gateway which graced the gravelled avenue from the river to the house, was thrown down; and for many years not a vestige has been left of the splendid and happy home of Herman Blannerhasset but the name. Nearly forty years have elapsed since some of these events were transacted, and the thousands of passengers who annually travel up and down the Ohio in steamboats, still eagerly inquire after, and gaze upon the 'island of Blannerhasset' with wonder and delight."*

At the time of the trial of Burr at Richmond, Blannerhasset had been arrested, and was placed in the penitentiary at Richmond. His description of the trial, as preserved in his correspondence, the graphic picture of Judge Marshall, of Wirt, and the celebrated Luther Martin, is drawn with the skill of a master.

As the jury failed to convict Burr, the principal, his accomplice Blannerhasset was not brought to trial, and was set at liberty. He was, however, about ruined. The security which Burr gave for moneys advanced failed, and Blannerhasset, from being a very wealthy man, was reduced to indigence. He had gone through this fiery ordeal with a character unimpeached, although subjected to the severest calumnies. This is evinced by his continuing to enjoy the friendship of that worthy patriot Thomas Addis Emmet, and of many other men of standing.

Mr. Blannerhasset after this settled on a cotton plantation in Mississippi. At the close of the war he came on to the north to educate his children, from whence he removed to Canada, where he practised his profession as a lawyer. In 1822 he went to England with his family; and finally died on the island of Guernsey, at the age of sixty-three years. He left his wife and three children. Mrs. Blannerhasset came to America, and preferred claims against the United States, but without success. She died in New York city, in 1842, where one of her sons is now residing.

YORK.

York was one of the eight original counties into which Virginia was divided in 1634. Chesapeake Bay bounds it on the east, and York River on the NE. It is 30 miles long, with a mean width of 5 miles. Population in 1840, 4,720.

Yorktown, the seat of justice, is on York River, 11 miles from its mouth, 33 from Norfolk, and 70 from Richmond. It was established by law in 1705, and was once a flourishing village, and had

---

* Dr. S. P. Hildreth.

considerable commerce. There are now only about 40 dwellings, many of which are dilapidated and fast going to decay. The Swan tavern, in this town, is said to be the oldest in Virginia.

The water scenery at York is fine. The river, full a mile wide, is seen stretching far away until it merges into Chesapeake Bay— an object of beauty when rolling in the morning light, its ripples sparkling in the sun, or when its broad bosom is tinged with the

Ruins at Yorktown.

cloud-reflected hues of an autumnal sunset. On its banks stand the ruins of the old church. Silence reigns within its walls, and the ashes of the illustrious dead repose at its base.

This church was built about 150 years ago: it was destroyed by the great fire in 1814. The old bell, now preserved, bears the inscription, "*County of York, Virginia, 1725.*" The Hon. Francis Nicholson contributed 20 pounds sterling to its cost, as appears by the following paper that appeared some time since in the Richmond Inquirer, being a literal copy from the records of York county court:

"York county October ye 26th, 1696. I promise to give five pounds sterling towards building the cott. house at Yorké Town, and twenty pounds sterl'g if within two years they build a brick church att the same towne. As witness my hand ye day and year above written.

                                  "FFRA: NICHOLSON.

"Stiphen ffoward.
"Robt. Bill; November ye 24th: 1696.

"The above writing p'ented in cott: and according to order is committed to Record. p.   "WILLIAM SEDGWICK, cl. cur."

The walls "are composed of stone marl, which, it is said, is soft when taken out of its native bed, and becomes hardened by time and exposure, until it acquires the hardness and durability of solid stone."*

---

* Article "Yorktown," by C. C., in Southern Lit. Mess., Jan., 1844.

In the above view the ruins of the church are partly shown on the left; in front the tomb of Gov. Nelson, and monuments of the Nelson family; and in the distance York River, stretching away towards the ocean. We annex two inscriptions from tombstones beautifully sculptured. The first is upon a quadrangular monument, about 4 feet high, 3 wide, and 6 long. It is the work of "Mr. Saunders, Cannon-street, London." Upon one end are sculptured two angel's faces; one of which is breaking out from a cloud, on which is written, "All glory be to God." The other face below, with trumpet in mouth, is heralding the above inscription. Upon the other end are also two angel's heads: one is about receiving a crown from the hand of an invisible body hidden behind the clouds. This monument is that of the progenitor of the Nelson family in Virginia, and the grandfather of Gov. Nelson. He emigrated from Penrith, Cumberland county, England, which county had been transferred by Henry III. to the crown of Scotland, and upon failure of male heirs, reverted as a base fee to England; he was from this circumstance called Scotch Tom. On top is the Nelson coat-of-arms, then follows the inscription:

" Hic jacet, spe certa resurgendi in Christi, THOMAS NELSON, generosus, Filius Hugonis et Sariæ Nelson de Penrith, in Comitatu Cumbriæ, natus 20mo die Februarii Anno Domini 1677, vitæ bene gestæ finem implevit 7mo die Octobris 1745, ætatis suæ 68."

[*Translation.*]

" Here lies, in certain hope of a resurrection in Christ, THOMAS NELSON, gentleman, son of Hugo and Sarah Nelson, of Penrith, in the county of Cumberland: born February 20, A. D. 1677, died October 7, 1745, aged 68."

The other monument, that of Gov. Nelson's father, is also beautifully ornamented by carved work. Below is the inscription:

Here lies the body of the Hon. William Nelson, late president of his Majesty's council in this Dominion, in whom the love of man and the love of God so restrained and enforced each other, and so invigorated the mental powers in general, as not only to defend him from the vices and follies of his age and country, but also to render it a matter of difficult decision in what part of laudable conduct he most excelled; whether in the tender and endearing accomplishments of domestic life, or in the more arduous duties of a wider circuit; whether as a neighbor, gentleman, or a magistrate; whether in the graces of hospitality, charity, or piety. Reader, if you feel the spirit of that exalted ardor which aspires to the felicity of conscious virtue, animated by those stimulating and divine admonitions, perform the task and expect the distinction of the righteous man. Obit. 19th of Nov., Anno Domini 1772, ætatis 61.

The Nelson mansion is a large two-story brick building, fronting the river, on the main street of the town. It is built on the old English model. It is now the residence of William Nelson, Esq., and in the war of the revolution was that of Gov. Thomas Nelson, by whose father, the Hon. William Nelson, it was erected. Portraits of this last-named gentleman and wife, which were mutilated by the British at Hanover, where they were sent for safety, adorn its walls. A view of this building is shown in the background to the frontispiece to this volume. During the siege of York, the house was bombarded by the American army, and now bears marks of cannon shot. Gov. Nelson, then in Washington's army, had command of the first battery which opened upon

the town. Rightly supposing it was occupied by some of the
British officers, he pointed the first gun against his own dwelling,
and offered a reward to the soldiers of five guineas for every
bomb-shell that should be fired into it. The following is a brief
sketch of this genuine patriot:

THOMAS NELSON, jun., a signer of the Declaration of Independence, was born at York,
Dec. 26, 1738. When in his fifteenth year, according to the prevailing fashion among
gentlemen of affluence at the south, he was sent to England to receive his education.
His first appearance in public life was in 1774, as a member of the House of Burgesses.
He was a member of the conventions of 1774 and 1775; and evinced such a boldness
and promptitude in opposing British aggression, as to alarm some of his personal friends,
particularly when he proposed the organization of a military force among the colonists.
In the military organization of Virginia he was appointed to the command of a regiment. In September, 1775, he first took his seat in the general Congress, to which he
was reappointed the following year. In the summer of 1777, ill health compelled him
to resign his seat and return to Virginia. The state was at that time threatened with invasion, and Mr. Nelson was appointed brigadier-general and commander-in-chief of all its
military forces. His popularity was unbounded, and his appointment gave universal satisfaction. About this time a motion was made to sequester the debts due in this state to
English merchants. His inflexible and zealous opposition to the proposition in the legislature redounded to his honor, and evinced the lofty integrity of his character. At
this period the American cause was threatened with annihilation, and Congress made an
appeal to the patriotism of the young men of property and standing. When the appeal
was published, Gen. Nelson embarked in the cause with his characteristic ardor. He
published an animating address, and succeeded in enlisting about seventy young Virginians in a volunteer corps, and furnished a number of them with the means of defraying their expenses, from his own purse. At the head of this Spartan band he marched
to the north; but a change of circumstances occurring, their services were not required.
In this enterprise Gen. Nelson expended large sums of money, which were never repaid.
   Early in 1779, he was again a short time in Congress, but ill health again compelled
him to return to Virginia. In 1780, when the state undertook to borrow two millions of
dollars for the aid of Congress, Gen. Nelson opened a subscription. Calling on several
friends, they declared that they would not lend him a shilling on the security of the
commonwealth, but they would lend *him* all they could possibly raise; upon which he
added his own personal security to that of the state, and succeeded in raising a large proportion of the sum required. By this and similar patriotic exertions, he suffered severe
pecuniary losses, but never relaxed his exertions. He had at the beginning anticipated
sufferings and sacrifices in effecting the independence of his country, and prepared
his mind to meet and sustain them. In 1781, when the storm of war burst upon Virginia, Gen. Nelson was actively employed in effecting plans to oppose the enemy; and,
succeeding Mr. Jefferson as governor, he was compelled to unite in himself the two
offices of governor and commander of the military forces. By great exertions Gov. Nelson kept his forces together until the capture of Cornwallis. To do this, he exerted his
personal influence, his official authority, and his private fortune, to the utmost extent.
After the surrender, Washington, in his account of it, made a very honorable acknowledgment of the valuable services of Gov. Nelson, and the militia under his command,
during the siege, in securing its important issue.
   In a month after, ill-health compelled Gov. Nelson to retire again to private life,
where malice and envy preferred base accusations against him for mal-administration
of his office. But he was most honorably exculpated by the legislature. He never
again entered public life. His time was passed in retirement at his plantation in Hanover, and at York. His health gradually declining, he died in Hanover, Jan. 4th, 1789,
aged fifty years.

────────

   About a mile and a half below Yorktown, on what is called the
Temple Farm, are many old chimneys, indicating the site of an
ancient settlement. About a quarter of a mile from the York, on
the margin of a forest, are to be seen the vestiges of an ancient
temple. It was surrounded, a few yards distant, by a wall,

probably intended for defence against sudden attacks from the Indians. Within the enclosure are several defaced and broken monuments. One only is legible, a flat slab adorned with the insignia of heraldry. It bears this inscription:

Major William Gooch, of THIS Parish, dyed Octob. 29, 1655.

Within this tomb there doth interred lie,
No shape but substance, true nobility ;
Its self though young, in years, but twenty-nine,
Yet graced with vertues morall and divine ;
The church from him did good participate
In counsell rare fit to adorn a state.

Yorktown is memorable in American history as being the spot where, on the 19th of October, 1781, the army of Cornwallis surrendered to the combined armies of America and France. Dr. Thatcher, a surgeon in Washington's army, has given in his journal a full account of the siege and surrender, which gives its incidents as they transpired from day to day. From this lucid narration we subjoin the following:

27th Sept.—We arrived at Yorktown yesterday from Jamestown, and have encamped within one mile of the enemy's line of redoubts.

28th.—The French troops have arrived, and encamped on our left. Yorktown is situated on the south bank of the river, about fifteen miles from its entrance into Chesapeake Bay. In this little village, Lord Cornwallis, with about seven thousand troops, has taken his station, and is endeavoring to fortify himself against the impending danger of our combined operations. His communication by water is entirely cut off by the French ships of war stationed at the mouth of the river, preventing both his escape and receiving succor from Sir Henry Clinton at New York. The allied army is about twelve thousand strong, exclusive of the militia under Gov. Nelson. The Americans form the right, and the French the left wing of the combined forces, each extending to the borders of the river, by which the besiegers form a half circle round the town. His Excellency General Washington commands in person, and is assisted by Major-General Lincoln, Baron Steuben, the Marquis de Lafayette, General Knox, &c. The French troops are commanded by General the Count Rochambeau, a brave and experienced officer, having under him a number of officers of distinguished character. Unbounded confidence is reposed in our illustrious commanders, the spirit of emulation and military ardor universally prevail, and we are sanguine in our expectations that a surrender of the royal army must be his lordship's fate.

A cannonade commenced yesterday from the town, by which one man received a wound, and I assisted in amputating his leg. *30th.*—We were agreeably surprised this morning, to find that the enemy had, during the preceding night, abandoned three or four of their redoubts, and retired within the town, leaving a considerable extent of commanding ground which might have cost us much labor and many lives to obtain by force. Our light infantry and a party of French were ordered to advance and take possession of the abandoned ground, and to serve as a covering party to our troops, who are employed in throwing up breastworks. Considerable cannonading from the besieged in the course of the day, and four militiamen were wounded by a single shot, one of whom died soon after. An occurrence has just been announced which fills our hearts with grief and sorrow. Col. Alexander Scammel being officer of the day, while reconnoitring the ground which the enemy had abandoned, was surprised by a party of their horse, and after having surrendered, they had the baseness to inflict a wound which we fear will prove mortal ; they have carried him into Yorktown.

October 1st and *2d.*—Our troops have been engaged in throwing up two redoubts in the night-time ; on discovery, the enemy commenced a furious cannonade, but it does not deter our men from going on vigorously with their work. Heavy cannon and mortars are continually arriving, and the greatest preparations are made to prosecute the siege in the most effectual manner.

3d and *4th.*—A considerable cannonading from the enemy, one shot killed three men, and mortally wounded another. While the Rev. Mr. Evans, our chaplain, was standing near the commander-in-chief, a shot struck the ground so near as to cover his hat with sand; being much agitated, he took off his hat and said, "See here, general." "Mr. Evans," replied his Excellency, with his usual composure, "you had better carry that home and show it to your wife and children." Two soldiers from the French, and one from us, deserted to the enemy, and two British soldiers deserted to our camp the same night. The enemy, from the want of forage, are killing off their horses in great numbers; six or seven hundred of these valuable animals have been killed, and their carcasses are almost continually floating down the river. The British are in possession of a place called Gloucester, on the north side of the river, nearly opposite Yorktown; their force consists of one British regiment, and Col. Tarleton's legion of horse and infantry. In opposition to this force the French legion, under the command of the Duke de Luzerne, and a detachment of French infantry and militia, are posted in that vicinity. Tarleton is a bold and impetuous leader, and has spread terror through the Carolinas and Virginia for some time past. In making a sally from Gloucester yesterday, they were attacked by the French, and defeated, with the loss of the commanding officer of their infantry, and about fifty men killed and wounded; among the latter is Tarleton himself. The duke lost three men killed, and two officers and eleven men wounded. It is with much concern we learn that Col. Scammel died at Williamsburg, of the wound which he received a few days since, when he was taken prisoner; the wound was inflicted after he had surrendered. At the request of Gen. Washington, Lord Cornwallis allowed him to be carried to Williamsburg, where he died this day, universally lamented, as he was while living universally respected and esteemed. The commander-in-chief was well apprized of his merit, and bestowed on him marks of his friendly regard and confidence. For some time he sustained the office of adjutant-general to our army, but preferring a more active command and the post of danger, he was put at the head of a regiment of light infantry for this enterprising campaign. The British have sent from Yorktown a large number of negroes sick with the smallpox, probably for the purpose of communicating the infection to our army; thus our inhuman enemies resort to every method in their power, however barbarous or cruel, to injure and distress, and thus to gain an advantage over their opposers.

7th.—A large detachment of the allied army, under command of Major-General Lincoln, were ordered out last evening, for the purpose of opening intrenchments near the enemy's lines. This business was conducted with great silence and secrecy, and we were favored by Providence with a night of extreme darkness, and were not discovered before daylight. The working party carried on their shoulders fascines and intrenching tools, while a large part of the detachment was armed with the implements of death. Horses, drawing cannon and ordnance, and wagons loaded with bags filled with sand for constructing breastworks, followed in the rear. Thus arranged, every officer and soldier knowing his particular station, orders were given to advance in perfect silence, the distance about one mile. My station on this occasion was, with Dr. Munson, my mate, in the rear of the troops, and as the music was not to be employed, about twenty drummers and fifers were put under my charge to assist me in case of having wounded men to attend. Our troops were indefatigable in their labors during the night, and before daylight they had nearly completed the first parallel line of nearly two miles in extent, besides laying a foundation for two redoubts, within about six hundred yards of the enemy's lines. At daylight, the enemy having discovered our works, commenced a severe cannonade; but our men being under cover received no injury. A French soldier deserted to the enemy, after which there was a constant firing against the French lines, and one officer was killed, and fifteen men were killed or wounded. In the latter part of the night it rained severely, and being in the open field, cold, and uncomfortable, I entered a small hut made of brush, which the enemy had abandoned; soon after, a man came to the door, and seeing me standing in the centre, instantly drew his sword, and put himself in an attitude to plunge it into me. I called out *friend, friend,* and he as speedily to my great joy responded, "Ah, Monsieur, *friend,*" and returning his sword to its place he departed. I think he was a French soldier, and it is doubtful whether he or myself was the most frightened.

8th and *9th.*—The duty of our troops has been for several days extremely severe; our regiment labors in the trenches every other day and night, where I find it difficult to avoid suffering by the cold, having no other covering than a single blanket in the open field. We erected a battery last night in front of our first parallel, without any annoyance from the enemy. Two or three of our batteries being now prepared to open on the town, his Excellency Gen. Washington put the match to the first gun, and a furious discharge of cannon and mortars immediately followed, and Earl Cornwallis has received his first salutation.

From the 10th to the 15th, a tremendous and incessant firing from the American and French batteries is kept up, and the enemy return the fire, but with little effect. A red hot shell from the French battery set fire to the Charon, a British 44 gun ship, and two or three smaller vessels at anchor in the river, which were consumed in the night. From the bank of the river, I had a fine view of this splendid conflagration. The ships were wrapped in a torrent of fire, which, spreading with vivid brightness among the combustible rigging, and running with amazing rapidity to the tops of the several masts, while all around was thunder and lightning from our numerous cannons and mortars, and in the darkness of night, presented one of the most sublime and magnificent spectacles which can be imagined. Some of our shells, overreaching the town, are seen to fall into the river, and bursting, throw up columns of water like the spouting of the monsters of the deep. We have now made further approaches to the town, by throwing up a second parallel line, and batteries within about three hundred yards ; this was effected in the night, and at daylight the enemy were roused to the greatest exertions—the engines of war have raged with redoubled fury and destruction on both sides, no cessation day or night. The French had two officers wounded, and fifteen men killed or wounded, and among the Americans two or three were wounded. I assisted in amputating a man's thigh. The siege is daily becoming more and more formidable and alarming, and his lordship must view his situation as extremely critical, if not desperate. Being in the trenches every other night and day, I have a fine opportunity of witnessing the sublime and stupendous scene which is continually exhibiting. The bomb-shells from the besiegers and the besieged are incessantly crossing each other's path in the air. They are clearly visible in the form of a black ball in the day, but in the night they appear like a fiery meteor with a blazing tail, most beautifully brilliant, ascending majestically from the mortar to a certain altitude, and gradually descending to the spot where they are destined to execute their work of destruction. It is astonishing with what accuracy an experienced gunner will make his calculations, that a shell shall fall within a few feet of a given point, and burst at the precise time, though at a great distance. When a shell falls, it whirls round, burrows, and excavates the earth to a considerable extent, and bursting, makes dreadful havoc around. I have more than once witnessed fragments of the mangled bodies and limbs of the British soldiers thrown into the air by the bursting of our shells, and by one from the enemy, Capt. White, of the seventh Massachusetts regiment, and one soldier were killed, and another wounded near where I was standing. About twelve or fourteen men have been killed or wounded within twenty-four hours ; I attended at the hospital, amputated a man's arm, and assisted in dressing a number of wounds. The enemy having two redoubts, about three hundred yards in front of their principal works, which enfiladed our intrenchment and impeded our approaches, it was resolved to take possession of them both by assault. The one on the left of the British garrison, bordering on the banks of the river, was assigned to our brigade of light infantry, under the command of the Marquis de Lafayette. The advanced corps was led on by the intrepid Col. Hamilton, who had commanded a regiment of light infantry during the campaign, and assisted by Col. Gimat. The assault commenced at eight o'clock in the evening, and the assailants bravely entered the fort with the point of the bayonet without firing a single gun. We suffered the loss of eight men killed, and about thirty wounded, among whom Col. Gimat received a slight wound in his foot, and Major Gibbs, of his Excellency's guard, and two other officers, were slightly wounded. Major Campbell, who commanded in the fort, was wounded and taken prisoner, with about thirty soldiers ; the remainder made their escape. I was desired to visit the wounded in the fort, even before the balls had ceased whistling about my ears, and saw a sergeant and eight men dead in the ditch. A captain of our infantry, belonging to New Hampshire, threatened to take the life of Major Campbell, to avenge the death of his favorite, Col. Scammel, but Col. Hamilton interposed, and not a man was killed after he ceased to resist. During the assault, the British kept up an incessant firing of cannon and musketry from their whole line. His Excellency Gen. Washington, Generals Lincoln and Knox, with their aids, having dismounted, were standing in an exposed situation waiting the result. Col. Cobb, one of Gen. Washington's aids, solicitous for his safety, said to his Excellency, " Sir, you are too much exposed here, had you not better step a little back ?" " Col. Cobb," replied his Excellency, " if you are afraid, you have liberty to step back." The other redoubt, on the right of the British lines, was assaulted at the same time, by a detachment of the French, commanded by the gallant Baron de Viominel. Such was the ardor displayed by the assailants, that all resistance was soon overcome, though at the expense of nearly one hundred men killed and wounded.* Of the defenders of the redoubt, eighteen were killed, and one captain and two subaltern officers and forty-two rank and file captured.† Our second parallel line was immediately connected with the two redoubts now taken from the enemy, and some new batteries were thrown up in front of our second parallel line, with a covert way, and angling work approaching to less than three hundred yards of their principal forts. These will soon be mantled with cannon and mortars, and when their horrid thundering commences, it must convince his lordship that his post is not invincible, and that submission must soon be his only alternative. Our artillerymen, by the exactness of their aim, make every discharge take effect, so that many of the enemy's guns are entirely silenced, and their works are almost in ruins.

16th.—A party of the enemy, consisting of about four hundred men, commanded by Col. Abercrombie, about four in the morning, made a vigorous sortie against two unfinished redoubts occupied by the French; they spiked up seven or eight pieces of cannon, and killed several soldiers, but the French advanced and drove them from the redoubts, leaving several killed and wounded. Our New England troops have now become very sickly; the prevalent diseases are intermittent and remittent fevers, which are very prevalent in this climate during the autumnal months.

17th.—The whole of our works are now mounted with cannon and mortars, not less than one hundred pieces of heavy ordnance have been in continual operation during the last twenty-four hours. The whole peninsula trembles under the incessant thunderings of our infernal machines; we have levelled some of their works in ruins and silenced their guns; they have almost ceased firing. We are so near as to have a distinct view of the dreadful havoc and destruction of their works, and even see the men in their lines torn to pieces by the bursting of our shells. But the scene is drawing to a close. Lord Cornwallis, at length realizing the extreme hazard of his deplorable situation, and finding it in vain any longer to resist, has this morning come to the humiliating expedient of sending out a flag, requesting a cessation of hostilities for twenty-four hours, that commissioners may be appointed to prepare and adjust the terms of capitulation. Two or three flags passed in the course of the day, and Gen. Washington consented to a cessation of hostilities for two hours only, that his lordship may suggest his proposals as a basis for a treaty, which being in part accepted, a suspension of hostilities will be continued till to-morrow.

18th.—It is now ascertained that Lord Cornwallis, to avoid the necessity of a surrender, had determined on the bold attempt to make his escape in the night of the 16th, with a part of his army, into the country. His plan was to leave sick and baggage behind, and to cross with his effective force over to Gloucester Point, there to destroy the French legion and other troops, and to mount his infantry on their horses and such others as might be procured, and thus push their way to New York by land. A more preposterous and desperate attempt can scarcely be imagined. Boats were secretly prepared, arrangements made, and a large proportion of his troops actually embarked and landed on Gloucester Point, when from a moderate and calm evening, a most violent storm of wind and rain ensued. The boats with the remaining troops were all driven down the river, and it was not till the next day that his troops could be returned to the garrison at York. At an early hour this forenoon, Gen. Washington communicated to Lord Cornwallis the general basis of the terms of capitulation, which he deemed admis-

---

* The cause of the great loss sustained by the French troops in comparison with that of the Americans, in storming their respective redoubts, was that the American troops when they came to the abattis, removed a part of it with their hands, and leaped over the remainder. The French troops, on coming up to theirs, waited till their pioneers had cut away the abattis secundum artem, which exposed them longer to the galling fire of the enemy. To this cause also is to be ascribed the circumstance, that the redoubt assailed by the Americans was carried before that attacked by the French troops. The Marquis de Lafayette sent his aid, Major Barbour, through the tremendous fire of the whole line of the British, to inform the Baron Viominel, that "he was in his redoubt, and to ask the Baron where he was." The major found the Baron waiting the clearing away of the abattis, but sent this answer: "Tell the Marquis I am not in mine, but will be in five minutes." He instantly advanced, and was within or nearly so, within his time.

† Gen. Dumas, in "The Memoirs of his own Time," republished in this country in 1839, says, in relation to the attack on these redoubts, " I must here make mention of a circumstance which characterizes the courage of the French grenadiers. The grenadiers of the regiment of Gatinais, which had been formed out of that of Auvergne, were to lead the attack. The moment it was decided, I said to them, ' My friends, if I should want you this night, I hope you have not forgotten we have served together in that brave regiment of Auvergne, " Sans Tâche," an honorable name, which it has deserved ever since its creation.' They answered, if I promised to have their name restored to them, they would suffer themselves to be killed even to the last man. They kept their word, charged like lions, and lost one-third of their number. The king, on the report I made of this affair, signed the ordinance restoring to this regiment the name of Royale Auvergne."

sible, and allowed two hours for his reply. Commissioners were soon after appointed to prepare the particular terms of agreement. The gentlemen appointed by Gen. Washington are Col. Laurens, one of his aid-de-camps, and Viscount Noaille of the French army. They have this day held an interview with the two British officers on the part of Lord Cornwallis, the terms of capitulation are settled, and being confirmed by the commanders of both armies, the royal troops are to march out to-morrow and surrender their arms. It is a circumstance deserving of remark, that Col. Laurens, who is stipulating for the surrender of a British nobleman, at the head of a royal army, is the son of Mr. Henry Laurens, our ambassador to Holland, who being captured on his voyage, is now in close confinement in the tower of London.

19*th*.—This is to us a most glorious day, but to the English one of bitter chagrin and disappointment. Preparations are now making to receive as captives, that vindictive, haughty commander, and that victorious army, who by their robberies and murders have so long been a scourge to our brethren of the southern states. Being on horseback, I anticipate a full share of satisfaction in viewing the various movements in the interesting scene. The stipulated terms of capitulation are similar to those granted to Gen. Lincoln at Charleston the last year. The captive troops are to march out with shouldered arms, colors cased, and drums beating a British or German march, and to ground their arms at a place assigned for the purpose. The officers are allowed their side-arms and private property, and the generals and such officers as desire it, are to go on parole to England or New York. The marines and seamen of the king's ships are prisoners of war to the navy of France, and the land forces to the United States. All military and artillery stores to be delivered up unimpaired. The royal prisoners are to be sent into the interior of Virginia, Maryland, and Pennsylvania, in regiments, to have rations allowed them equal to the American soldiers, and to have their officers near them. Lord Cornwallis to man and dispatch the Bonetta sloop of war with dispatches to Sir Henry Clinton at New York, without being searched; the vessel to be returned, and the hands accounted for. At about twelve o'clock, the combined army was arranged and drawn up in two lines extending more than a mile in length. The Americans were drawn up in a line on the right side of the road, and the French occupied the left. At the head of the former the great American commander, mounted on his noble courser, took his station, attended by his aids. At the head of the latter was posted the excellent Count Rochambeau and his suite. The French troops, in complete uniform, displayed a martial and noble appearance; their band of music, of which the timbrel formed a part, is a delightful novelty, and produced, while marching to the ground, a most enchanting effect. The Americans, though not all in uniform, nor their dress so neat, yet exhibited an erect soldierly air, and every countenance beamed with satisfaction and joy. The concourse of spectators from the country was prodigious, in point of numbers probably equal to the military; but universal silence and order prevailed. It was about two o'clock when the captive army advanced through the line formed for their reception. Every eye was prepared to gaze on Lord Cornwallis, the object of peculiar interest and solicitude; but he disappointed our anxious expectations; pretending indisposition, he made Gen. O'Hara his substitute as the leader of his army. This officer was followed by the conquered troops in a slow and solemn step, with shouldered arms, colors cased, and drums beating a British march. Having arrived at the head of the line, Gen. O'Hara, elegantly mounted, advanced to his Excellency the commander-in-chief, taking off his hat, and apologized for the non-appearance of Earl Cornwallis. With his usual dignity and politeness, his Excellency pointed to Major-General Lincoln for directions, by whom the British army was conducted into a spacious field where it was intended they should ground their arms. The royal troops, while marching through the line formed by the allied army, exhibited a decent and neat appearance, as respects arms and clothing, for their commander opened his store and directed every soldier to be furnished with a new suit complete, prior to the capitulation. But in their line of march we remarked a disorderly and unsoldierly conduct; their step was irregular, and their ranks frequently broken. But it was in the field, when they came to the last act of the drama, that the spirit and pride of the British soldier were put to the severest test—here their mortification could not be concealed. Some of the platoon officers appeared to be exceedingly chagrined when giving the word " *ground arms*," and I am witness that they performed this duty in a very unofficer-like manner, and that many of the soldiers manifested a *sullen temper*,* throwing their arms on the pile with violence, as if determined to render

* Gen. Dumas says, "The garrison defiled between the two lines, beyond which I caused them to form in order of battle, and pile their arms. The English officers manifested the most bitter mortification, and I remember that Col. Abercrombie of the English Guards—the same who afterwards perished in Egypt

them useless. This irregularity, however, was checked by the authority of Gen. Lincoln. After having grounded their arms, and divested themselves of their accoutrements, the captive troops were conducted back to Yorktown, and guarded by our troops till they could be removed to the place of their destination. The British troops that were stationed at Gloucester surrendered at the same time, and in the same manner, to the command of the Duke de Luzerne. This must be a very interesting and gratifying transaction to Gen. Lincoln, who having himself been obliged to surrender an army to a haughty foe the last year, has now assigned him the pleasing duty of giving laws to a conquered army in return, and of reflecting that the terms which were imposed on him are adopted as a basis of the surrender in the present instance. It is a very gratifying circumstance that every degree of harmony, confidence, and friendly intercourse subsisted between the American and French troops during the campaign ; no contest except an emulous spirit to excel in exploits and enterprise against the common enemy, and a desire to be celebrated in the annals of history for an ardent love of great and heroic actions. We are not to be surprised that the pride of the British officers is humbled on this occasion, as they have always entertained an exalted opinion of their own military prowess, and affected to view the Americans as a contemptible, undisciplined rabble. But there is no display of magnanimity when a great commander shrinks from the inevitable misfortunes of war ; and when it is considered that Lord Cornwallis has frequently appeared in splendid triumph at the head of his army, by which he is almost *adored*, we conceive it incumbent on him cheerfully to participate in their misfortunes and degradations, however humiliating ; but it is said he gives himself up entirely to vexation and despair.

20th.—In the general orders of this day our commander-in-chief expresses his entire approbation, and his warmest thanks to the French and American officers and soldiers of all descriptions, for the brave and honorable part which they have acted during the siege. He congratulates the combined army on the momentous event which closes the campaign, and which crowns their heads with unfading laurels, and entitles them to the applause and gratitude of their country. Among the general officers whom his Excellency particularly noticed, for the important services which they rendered during the siege, are Generals Lincoln, de Lafayette, Steuben, Knox, and Du Portail, his Excellency Count Rochambeau, and several other distinguished French officers. To Gov. Nelson, of Virginia, he returned his grateful and sincere acknowledgments for the essential succors afforded by him and the militia under his command. The commander-in-chief, wishing that every heart should participate in the joy of this memorable day, ordered that all those who are under arrest or confinement should be immediately pardoned and set at liberty, a circumstance which I believe has never before occurred in our army. He closed by ordering that divine service shall be performed in the several brigades tomorrow, and recommends that the troops attend with a serious deportment, and with that sensibility of heart which the recollection of the surprising and particular interposition of Providence in our favor claims.

22d.—Yesterday being Sunday, our brigade of infantry, and the York brigade were drawn up in the field to attend divine service performed by Mr. Evans. After offering to the Lord of hosts, the God of battles, our grateful homage for the preservation of our lives through the dangers of the siege, and for the important event with which Divine Providence has seen fit to crown our efforts, he preached an excellent and appropriate sermon. Generals Lincoln and Clinton were present. In the design and execution of this successful expedition, our commander-in-chief fairly *outgeneralled* Sir Henry Clinton, and the whole movement was marked by consummate military address, which reduced the royal general to a mortifying dilemma that no skill or enterprise could retrieve. A siege of thirteen days, prosecuted with unexampled rapidity, has terminated in the capture of one of the greatest generals of which the English can boast, and a veteran and victorious army which has for several mon'hs past spread terror and desolation throughout the southern states. The joy on this momentous occasion is universally diffused, and the hope entertained that it will arrest the career of a cruel warfare, and advance the establishment of American Independence. In the progress of the royal army through the state of Virginia the preceding summer, they practised the most abominable enormities, plundering negroes and horses from almost every plantation, and reducing the country to ruin. Among the prodigious assemblage of spectators at the time of surrender, were a number of planters searching for the property which had been thus purloined from their estates. The famous Col Tarleton, mounted on a horse remarkable

on the field of battle where he had just triumphed—at the moment when his troops laid down their arms, withdrew rapidly, *covering his face, and biting his sword.*"

for elegance and noble appearance, while riding in company with several French officers with whom he was to dine, was met by a gentleman, who instantly recognised the animal as his own property. Tarleton was stopped, and the horse peremptorily demanded; observing a little hesitation, the British General O'Hara, who was present, said, "You had better give him his horse, Tarleton," on which the colonel dismounted and delivered the horse to the original proprietor; after which, being remounted on a very miserable animal, he rejoined his company, and the French officers were greatly surprised that he should be so humbly mounted. The British prisoners were all sent off yesterday, conducted by a party of militia on their way to the interior of Virginia and Maryland. I have this day visited the town of York, to witness the destructive effects of the siege. It contains about sixty houses, some of them are elegant; many of them are greatly damaged, and some totally ruined, being shot through in a thousand places, and honey-combed ready to crumble to pieces. Rich furniture and books were scattered over the ground, and the carcasses of men and horses half covered with earth, exhibited a scene of ruin and horror beyond description. The earth in many places is thrown up into mounds by the force of our shells, and it is difficult to point to a spot where a man could have resorted for safety.

The loss on the part of the French during the siege, was fifty killed and one hundred and twenty-seven wounded. Americans twenty-seven killed and seventy-three wounded, officers included. Cornwallis' account of his loss during the siege is one hundred and fifty-six, three hundred and twenty-six wounded, and seventy missing, probably deserted, total five hundred and fifty-two. The whole number surrendered by capitulation, seven thousand two hundred and forty-seven.[*] The amount of artillery and military stores, provisions, &c., is very considerable; seventy-five brass and one hundred and sixty-nine iron cannon, seven thousand seven hundred and ninety-four muskets; regimental standards, German eighteen, British ten. From the military chest we received two thousand one hundred and thirteen pounds six shillings sterling.

Dr. Thatcher, in the preceding account, has made mention of Dr. Æneas Munson, who was with him at the siege, in the capacity of surgeon's mate. From the lips of this gentleman, now living, we have derived the following:

Col. Scammel was the highest officer in rank in the American army, killed at the siege. He was shot after he had surrendered, by two Hessian horsemen, and was buried at Williamsburg. The annexed lines, forming part of his epitaph, were written by Col. Humphreys:

> What tho' no friend could ward thine early fall,
> Nor guardian angels turn the treacherous ball,
> Bless'd shade, be sooth'd! thy virtues all are known,
> Thy fame shall last beyond this mould'ring stone,
> Which conquering armies, from their toils return'd,
> Rear to thy glory, while thy fate they mourn'd.

During the siege almost all the Americans had the fever and ague. The dews were very heavy, and wet through the tents. The soldiers were divided into two divisions, and on alternate nights slept in the trenches in the open air.

On the attack of the two advanced redoubts of the British, on the night of the 15th, in a great measure depended the result of the siege. Washington, surrounded by a group of officers, among whom was our informant, stood in the grand battery looking through the embrasures, while the two divisions of the attacking party advanced to the assault. Col. Alexander Hamilton led on the Americans, with empty muskets and fixed bayonets. When he arrived at the right redoubt, which he was to attack, he made a short but eloquent address, which was distinctly heard by the silent but deeply-interested witnesses in the grand battery. "Did you ever hear such a speech?" remarked Lieut. D. to Dr. M.; "with such a speech I could storm ——." Shortly after, the French officer arrived with his division before the other redoubt, when he was challenged by the sentinel:

Sentinel.—"Who comes there?"

French officer.—"French."

Sentinel—mistakes it for "friend," and again demands, "Who comes there?"

---

[*] Another list which has been published, makes their total loss by death and capture to be eleven thousand eight hundred, including two thousand sailors, one thousand eight hundred negroes, one thousand five hundred tories, eighty vessels large and small.

French officer.—" French Grenadiers and Chasseurs, s-h-a-r-g-e ! s-H-A-R-G-E ! S-H-A-R-G-E !"

The word " charge" was drawled out with so much deliberation, and with such imperfect pronunciation, as to excite hearty laughter from the witnesses in the grand battery. The clash of bayonets succeeded, and the next morning the trench was seen filled five or six feet deep with the bodies of the gallant Frenchmen.

While the attack was progressing, a musket-ball rolled along a cannon, and fell at the feet of Washington. Gen. Knox seized him by the arm, and exclaimed, " My dear general, we can't spare you yet !" Washington replied, " It is a spent ball, and no harm is done." When it was all over, and the redoubts in possession of the two parties, Washing turned to Knox and said, " The work is done, and *well done* " and then exclaimed to his servant, " William, hand me my horse."

The Moore House, Yorktown.

The first night the American army reposed after the investment of Yorktown, Washington slept in the open air under a mulberry tree, the root forming his pillow. Cornwallis's head-quarters were originally in a splendid brick house, belonging to Secretary Nelson, (see p. 295,) the ruins of which are now visible in the large and continuous redoubt constructed by the British at the E. end of the town. He remained there until a servant was killed, and the building much injured by the American artillery, when he removed into the town. Fifty or sixty yards from this dwelling, on the hill-side at the lower end of the redoubt, he had a cave excavated in the earth. It was hung with green baize, and used solely for holding councils of war. There is a cave in the solid mass of stone marl which forms the river bank, improperly called Cornwallis's cave. This was used for a sutlery ; it is now a piggery. The Moore House, on Temple Farm, is yet standing on the banks of the river, about a mile below Yorktown. It is memorable as being the dwelling where the articles of capitulation were signed by Lord Cornwallis : it was then the property of a widow Moore.

The place of surrender was about half a mile from the E. limits of the town, on the s. side of the road to Hampton.

The frontispiece to this volume, representing the *Surrender of Cornwallis at Yorktown*, is copied from the painting of Col. John Trumbull. It is a faithful copy of the original, and the portraits and minor details are imitated with accuracy. Col. Trumbull, who died in 1843, was the son of Gov. Trumbull of Connecticut, and one of Washington's aid-de-camps in 1775, and in 1776 the deputy adjutant-general of the northern department, under the command of Major-Gen. Gates. He retired from the service in 1777, and afterwards became the great historical painter of the revolution. This was one of his series of pictures in commemoration of the principal events of the revolution, in which series he preserved, as far as possible, faithful portraits of its conspicuous actors, with accurate details of dress, manners, arms, &c., of the times. In the prosecution of his plan he was encouraged by John Adams and Thomas Jefferson, whose friendship he enjoyed. The portraits of the French officers he painted in 1787, at the house of Mr. Jefferson, in Paris. In 1791 he visited Yorktown, and made the drawing of the place of surrender.

Explanation of the Engraving.—The scene represents the moment when the principal officers of the British army, conducted by Gen. Lincoln, are passing the two groups of American and French officers, and entering between the two lines of victors. By this means the principal officers of the three nations are brought near together, so as to admit of distinct portraits. In the centre of the view, in the distance, is seen the entrance of the town, with the captured troops marching out, following their officers ; and also a distant glimpse of York River, and the entrance of the Chesapeake Bay, as seen from the spot.

The prominent figure on horseback in the centre, is Gen. Lincoln, by whose side stands the British general, O'Hara. Washington, on horseback, is a little in the rear and on the left of Gen. Lincoln. Count Rochambeau, the French general, is on horseback at the end of the line of French officers, and on the right and back of Gen. O'Hara. On the reader's right, the four American officers on foot are, respectively—commencing with the one nearest the margin—Col. Nicholas Fish, New York ; Col. Walter Stuart, Phila. ; Col. John Laurens, S. Carolina ; and Col. Alexander Hamilton, commander of light-infantry. On the reader's right, those on horseback—commencing with the figure nearest the margin—are, respectively, Col. Timothy Pickering, Lieut.-Col. E. Huntington, aid to Lincoln ; Maj.-Gen. Knox, commander of artillery ; Gen. Peter Muhlenburg, Virginia ; Gen. Hand, adjutant-general, Pennsylvania ; Gen. Anthony Wayne, Maryland ; Gen. Gist, Maryland ; Major-Gen. James Clinton, New York ; Col. Trumbull, secretary to Washington ; Col. Cobb, aid to Washington ; Baron Steuben ; Lafayette ; and Gov. Nelson, of Virginia. In the distance, the small figure on horseback, beyond some of the cannon, is Col. Ebenezer Stevens, of the American artillery. Those drawn up on the left side of the reader, are the French officers. The three first on foot—commencing with the one nearest the margin—are Count Deuxponts, colonel of French infantry ; Duke de Laval Montmorency, colonel of do. ; and Count Custine, colonel of do. The first figure on horseback, (who has a plume in his cap,) is the Duke de Lauzun, col. of cavalry ; and those next in order, as follows—Gen. Choizy ; Viscount Viomenil ; Marquis de St. Simon ; Count Fersen, aid to Rochambeau ; Count Charles Dumas, aid to do. ; Marquis Chastellux ; Baron Viomenil ; Count de Barras, admiral ; and Count de Grasse, admiral.

ADDENDA.

Since the first edition of this work was put to press, the following counties have been created :—

Appomattox was formed Feb. 8th, 1845, from parts of Prince Edward, Charlotte, and Campbell.

Doddridge was formed Feb. 4th, 1845, from Harrison, Tyler, Ritchie, and Lewis.

Gilmer was formed Feb. 3d, 1845, from parts of Lewis and Kanawha.

HISTORICAL AND DESCRIPTIVE SKETCH

OF THE

DISTRICT OF COLUMBIA.

THE DISTRICT OF COLUMBIA* was ceded to the United States in 1790, by the states of Virginia and Maryland, and in 1800 the seat of government was removed here from Philadelphia. Its site was selected by GEORGE WASHINGTON, by authority from Congress, after great research and observation, to become the metropolis of this republic. It forms an exact square of 10 miles on a side, lying upon both banks of the Potomac. The location being determined upon, the first stone to mark its boundary was set in Jones's Point, the uppermost cape of Hunting creek, April 15, 1791, in the presence of a large concourse of spectators.

The District is divided into two counties. Washington county is on the N. side of the Potomac, and includes Washington city and Georgetown. Alexandria county is on the S. side of the Potomac, and has the city of Alexandria. In the former, the laws of Maryland continue in force ; in the latter, those of Virginia. The District has never been represented in the Congress of the United States. Congress, however, makes what laws it pleases for both, which meets annually on the first Monday of December, unless otherwise provided by law.

The surface of the District is gently undulating, furnishing fine sites for cities. The soil is naturally sterile, but it possesses a fine, healthy climate. This District has become the centre of a considerable and active commerce, though it cannot at all compete with Baltimore, in its vicinity. Vessels of the largest class come up to Alexandria, 6 miles below Washington, where the Potomac is a mile wide, and from 30 to 50 feet deep ; and vessels of a large size come up to the U. S. Navy Yard, at the junction of the East Branch with the Potomac, at Washington. A very considerable quantity of flour, and other produce, comes down the Potomac, and centres chiefly at Alexandria, and some at Georgetown. The chief business of Washington city has relation to the accommodation of the national legislature, and of the officers of the general government. In 1800, the population was 14,093; in 1810, 24,023; in 1820, 33,039 ; in 1830, 39,858 ; in 1840, 43,712, of which 30,657 were whites, 8,361 were free colored persons, and 4,694 were slaves.

The valley at the foot of Capitol Hill, washed by the Tiber creek, it is stated on the authority of some of the early settlers, was periodically visited by the Indians, who named it their fishing-ground,

---

* We are indebted to Sherman and Smith's valuable Gazetteer of the United States for much information respecting the District.

in contradistinction to their hunting-ground; and that they assembled there in great numbers in the spring months to procure fish. Greenlief's Point was the principal camp, and the residence of their chiefs, where councils were held among the various tribes thus gathered there. The coincidence of the location of the national legislatures so near the council-house of an Indian nation, cannot fail to excite interesting reflections in intelligent minds. It is highly probable that Washington was acquainted with this tradition.

Washington City, the capital of the United States, is situated on the E. side of the Potomac, 295 miles from the ocean, by the course of the river and bay. It is 38 miles sw. from Baltimore; 136 from Philadelphia; 225 from New York; 432 from Boston; 856 from St. Louis; 544 from Charleston, S. C.; 662 from Savannah, Ga.; 1,203 from New Orleans. The population in 1800, was 3,210; in 1810, 8,208; in 1820, 13,247; in 1830, 18,827; in 1840, 23,364; in 1844, 30,429. Employed in commerce, 103; in manufactures and trades, 886; navigating the ocean, 45; do. rivers and canals, 25; learned professions, 83.

The city stands on a point of land between the Potomac and the Anacostia or Eastern branch. It contains a little over 8 square miles, and upwards of 5,000 acres. The ground is, in general, about 40 feet above the level of the river, and there are some moderate elevations, on two of which stand the Capitol and the President's house. The city is regularly laid out in streets running north and south, and crossed by others at right angles, running east and west. But the different parts of the city are connected by broad avenues, which traverse the rectangular divisions diagonally. Where the intersection of these avenues with each other and with the streets would form many acute angles, considerable rectangular or circular open grounds are left, which, when the city shall be built up, will give it an open appearance. The avenues and streets leading to public places are from 120 to 160 feet wide, and the other streets are from 70 to 110 feet wide. The avenues are named after the states of the Union, and the other streets, beginning at the capitol, are denoted by the letters of the alphabet, as A. north and A. south, B. north and B. south, &c.; and east and west, they are designated by numbers, as 1st east, 1st west, &c. Pennsylvania avenue, between the capitol and the president's house, contains the most dense population, and is much the finest street in the city. Five of the avenues radiate from the capitol, and five others from the president's house, giving these prominent places the most ready communication with all parts of the city. The buildings of Washington consist of scattered clusters; nor is it probable that the magnificent plan of the city will soon be built up, although it has greatly increased within the last few years. Three things are requisite to sustain a large city, one of which, it is to be hoped, will never be found in the United States. There must be extensive commerce, or manufactures, or an expensive and luxurious court, with the multitudes which a luxurious court draws around it, to expend their money. This last constitutes a great item in the support of some European cities. Washington cannot be expected to become a very great commercial or manufacturing place; and though the chief men of the government, and the national legislature, and the multitudes whom they draw around them, do much towards the prosperity of Washington, the money thus expended is too small in amount to constitute a main reliance of a large city. Baltimore, in the vicinity, will be likely to surpass Washington in commerce and manufactures, for a long time to come. The growth of Washington, however, has been considerably extensive, and it is continually increasing; and probably the bustle of a large city would not much improve it as a seat for the national congress. It enjoys the two important requisites for health, pure air and good water; and there is much elegant and refined society, rendering it a pleasant place of residence.

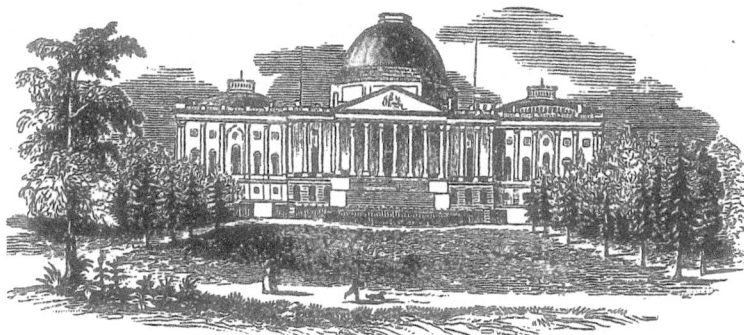

The Capitol at Washington.

The public buildings of Washington have a splendor becoming a great nation. The Capitol is probably the finest senate-house in the world, and it is fit that the most august legislative assembly on earth should be thus accommodated. The ground on which the capitol stands is elevated 73 feet above the level of the tide, and affords a commanding view of the different parts of the city, and of the surrounding country. The building, which is of freestone, covers an area of more than an acre and a half; the length of the front is 352 feet, including the wings; the depth of the wings is 121 feet. The centre building is surmounted by a lofty dome; and there are 2 less elevated domes, one towards each end. A projection on the east or main front, including the steps, is 65 feet wide; and another on the west front, with the steps, is 83 feet wide. In the projection on the east front, there is a noble portico of 22 lofty Corinthian columns; and in the west front there is a portico of 10 Corinthian columns. The height of the building to the top of the dome is 120 feet. Under the dome in the middle of the building is the rotunda, a circular room 95 feet in diameter, and of the same height, adorned with sculptures, representing in relief Smith delivered by Pocahontas, the Pilgrims landing at Plymouth, Penn treating with the natives, and a fight of Boone with the Indians ; and 4 magnificent paintings by Trumbull, with figures as large as life, representing the presentation to Congress of the Declaration of Independence, the capture of Burgoyne, the surrender of Cornwallis, and Washington resigning his commission to Congress. Another painting, the baptism of Pocahontas, by Chapman, has recently been added. The rotunda has recently received a splendid additional ornament in Greenough's statue of Washington, a colossal figure in a sitting posture, twice as large as life. On the west of the rotunda is the library-room of Congress, 92 feet by 34, and is 36 feet in height, containing, in arched alcoves, 20,000 volumes. In the second story of the south wing of the capitol, is the hall of the House of Representatives, of a semicircular form, 96 feet long and 60 high, with a dome supported by 24 beautiful columns of variegated marble from the Potomac, with capitals of Italian marble, of the Corinthian order. The circular wall is surrounded by a gallery for men, and the chord of the arc, back of the speaker's chair, has a gallery for the ladies. The room is ornamented with some fine statuary and paintings, and the whole furniture of it is elegant. The Senate chamber is in the second story of the north wing of the capitol, and is semicircular like that of the Representatives, but smaller, being 75 feet long and 45 feet high. The vice-president's chair is canopied by a rich crimson drapery, held by the talons of a hovering eagle. A gallery of light bronze running round the arc in front of the vice-president's chair, is mainly appropriated to ladies. There is another gallery above and behind the chair, supported by fine Ionic columns of variegated marble. A magnificent chandelier hangs in the centre of the room, and the whole appearance and furniture of the room are splendid. Below the Senate chamber, and of nearly the same form and dimensions, but much less elegant, is the room of the Supreme Court of the United States ; and there are in the building 70 rooms for the accommodation of committees and officers of Congress. The grounds around the capitol are spacious, containing 22 acres, highly ornamented with gravelled walks, shrubbery, and trees, a naval monument ornamented with statuary, and fountains, and the whole is enclosed by a handsome iron railing. The whole cost of the building has exceeded $2,000,000.

The President's house, a mile and a half NW. from the Capitol, is an elegant edifice of freestone, 2 stories high, with a lofty basement, and is 170 feet long, and 86 wide, the N. front of which is ornamented with a fine portico of 4 lofty Ionic columns, projecting with 3 columns. The outer intercolumniation is for carriages to drive under, to place company under shelter. It stands in the centre of a plat of ground of 20 acres, beautifully laid out and highly

WASHINGTON,

as it is seen from the President's House looking down Pennsylvania Avenue towards the Capitol in the distance.

ornamented. It is elevated 44 feet above tide-water, and the southern front presents a grand and beautiful prospect. The apartments within are admirably fitted to their purpose, and splendidly

U. S. Treasury, Washington.

furnished. On the E. side of the President's house are two large buildings, and on the w. side two large buildings for the departments of State, of the Treasury, of War, and of the Navy. The General Post-Office and the Patent-Office are also extensive build-

The General Post-Office, Washington.

ings. These, with the new Treasury building, have been recently erected, to supply the place of those which were burned a few years since. The new Treasury building contains 150 rooms, and when completed, will contain 250. It has a splendid colonnade, 457 feet in length. The General Post-Office contains about 80 rooms, and is of the Corinthian order, with columns and pilasters, on a rustic base. The Patent-Office, in addition to other spacious apartments, has one room in the upper story 275 feet by 65, and when completed by wings, according to the original design, will

The Patent-Office, Washington.

be upwards of 400 feet in length. It is considered one of the most splendid rooms in America, and is devoted to the grand and increasing collections of the national institution. The portico of this building is of the same extent as that of the Parthenon, at Athens, consisting of 16 columns, in double rows, 50 feet high. In the war-office was formerly kept the fine collection of Indian portraits, painted from the original heads by King. These valuable pictures are now in the custody, and adorn the collections of the national institution, in the patent-office.

The Navy Yard is on the Eastern branch, about three-fourths of a mile SE. of the Capitol, and contains 27 acres. It has houses for the officers, and shops and warehouses, and 2 large ship-houses, a neat armory, and every kind of naval stores. Several ships of war, some of which were of the largest class, have been built at this yard. There are also in the city an Arsenal, a City Hall, an Hospital, a Penitentiary, a Theatre, &c.

Washington is separated from Georgetown by Rock creek, over which are 2 bridges. A substantial pile bridge, over a mile in length, crosses the Potomac, and leads to Alexandria. There is a bridge, also, over the Anacostia, or Eastern branch. This river has water of sufficient depth for frigates to ascend to the navy yard, without being lightened. Vessels requiring 14 feet of water can come up to the Potomac bridge. By means of the Chesapeake and Ohio canal, a communication is opened with a rich back country; and it may be expected that the commerce of Washington will increase. The Washington canal is a continuation of this canal through the city. It extends from the Chesapeake and Ohio canal, at 17th street, west, to which it is connected by a lock at that street, to the Eastern branch. The canal and all the basins are walled with stone on both sides. From 17th to 14th street, is a spacious basin, 500 feet wide; from 14th to 6th street, where there is another ample basin, its width is 150 feet; and from 6th street to its termination in the Eastern branch, its width varies from 45 to 80 feet; and its depth is 4 feet below tide throughout. At its eastern termination is another spacious basin and wharf, which extends to the channel. This canal has been greatly neglected, and is much out of repair. The expense of this canal has been over $230,000.

There were in the city in 1840, 106 stores, cap. $926,040; 6 lumber yards, cap. $57,000; precious metals manufactured to the amount of $13,000; various other metals $17,300; 2 tanneries, cap. $2,000; 1 brewery, cap. $63,000; 2 potteries, cap. $3,250; 1 ropewalk, 1 grist m., 11 printing offices, 9 binderies, 3 daily, 5 weekly, 5 semi-weekly newspapers, and 3 periodicals, cap. $149,500; 30 brick and stone, and 23 wooden houses built, cost $86,910. Total cap. in manufac. $336,275.

The Columbian College was incorporated by an act of Congress in 1821. It is delightfully situated on elevated ground n. of the President's house, about two and a half miles from the Capitol. The buildings are a college edifice, 5 stories high, including the basement and the attic, having 48 rooms for students, with 2 dormitories attached to each, 2 dwelling-houses for professors, and a philosophical hall, all of brick. It has a medical department attached. The Medical College is situated at the corner of 10th and E streets, at equal distances from the Capitol and the President's house. In the several departments are a president, 10 professors, and in the college proper, about 25 students. There are about 4,200 books in its libraries. The commencement is on the first Wednesday of October. The whole number of alumni is 97. It is under the direction of the Baptists.

There were in the city in 1840, 12 academies, with 609 students, 9 primary and common schools, with 380 scholars.

The National Institution for the Promotion of Science, was organized in May, 1840. The President of the United States is patron; the heads of departments constitute 6 directors on the part of the government, and 6 literary and scientific gentlemen are directors on the part of the institution. Its stated monthly meetings are held in the patent-office building. Its collections are deposited in the grand hall of this building, 275 feet long, and 65 feet wide, and constitute a rapidly increasing scientific museum. The United States exploring expedition has added largely to its curiosities. The Historical Society and the Columbian Institute have united with it, with their libraries and collections. They have a valuable mineralogical cabinet. It is proposed to bring out regularly volumes of transactions. If properly fostered, it may become an honor to the nation. The Union Literary Society has been in existence for many years, and holds a weekly discussion in the lecture room of the medical college, and is well attended. Sectarian religion and party politics are excluded from its discussions. The City Library contains about 6,000 volumes.

The city contains 25 places of worship, of which the Presbyterians have 4, the Episcopalians 5, the Baptists 3, the Methodists 3, Protestant do. 1, Roman Catholics 3, the Africans 2, and the Unitarians and Friends 1 each and the Luthrans 2.

There are 2 orphan asylums. There are 3 banks, with an aggregate capital of $1,500,000; and 2 insurance companies, with an aggregate capital of $450,000.

This city was fixed on as the future seat of the government in accordance with the suggestion of the great man whose name it bears, and the ground on which it stands was ceded to the United States in December, 1788. The owners of the land gave one half of it, after deducting streets and public squares, to the United States to defray the expenses of the public buildings. Such grounds as should be wanted by the United States was to be paid for at the rate of $66 66 cents per acre. It was laid out by 3 commissioners, in 1791, and surveyed under the direction of Andrew Ellicot. The seat of the federal government was removed to this place in 1800. The north wing of the Capitol was commenced in 1793, and finished in 1800, at an expense of $480,202. The south wing was commenced in 1803, and finished in 1808, at an expense of $308,808. The centre building was commenced in 1818, and finished in 1827, at an expense of $957,647. In August, 1814, Washington was captured by the British, under Gen. Ross, who set fire to the Capitol, the President's house, and the public offices, with the exception of the patent-office, which was saved by the solicitation of its superintendent. The library of Congress was burned, and was afterwards replaced by the purchase of that of Mr. Jefferson, consisting of 7,000 volumes, for $23,000, in 1815.

The congressional burial-ground is in the eastern section of Washington, about a mile and a half from the Capitol, and contains about 10 acres of ground, near the Eastern branch. The grounds are tastefully laid out and neatly kept. It has already received a number of distinguished men, and has some fine monuments, and a vault in which bodies are placed that are awaiting a removal.

The following are inscriptions from monuments in this yard. Those in columns are members of Congress, and include those interred up to the year 1841:

Sacred to the memory of PHILIP PENDLETON BARBOUR, associate-justice of the Supreme Court of the United States, who was born in Orange county, Virginia, on the 25th of May, 1783, intermarried with Frances Todd Johnson, on the 4th of October, 1804, and died at Washington city on the 24th of February, 1841.

This monument is erected by order of his majesty Frederick William III., king of Prussia, to the memory of his resident minister in the United States, the Chevalier FREDERICK GREUHM, who departed this life on the 1st of December, 1823, in the 53d year of his age.

Sacred to the memory of Gen. JACOB BROWN. . . . He was born in Bucks co., Pennsylvania, on the 9th of May, 1775, and died at the city of Washington, commanding general of the army, on the 24th of February, 1828.

> Let him who e'er in after days
> Shall view this monument of praise,
> For honor heave the patriot sigh,
> And for his country learn to die.

JOSEPH LOVELL, late surgeon-general of the army of the United States, born in Boston, Massachusetts, Dec. 22, 1788; died in the city of Washington, October 17, 1836.

PUSH-MA-TA-HA, a Choctaw chief, lies here. This monument to his memory is erected by his brother chiefs, who were associated with him in a delegation from their nation, in the year 1824, to the general government of the United States. He died in Washington, on the 24th of December, 1824, of the croup, in the 60th year of his age. Push-ma-ta-ha was a warrior of great distinction. He was wise in council, eloquent in an extraordinary degree, and on all occasions, and under all circumstances, *the white man's friend.* Among his last words were the following: "*When I am gone let the big guns be fired over me.*"

Beneath this monument rest the mortal remains of HUGH GEORGE CAMPBELL, late a captain in the navy of the United States. He was a native of the state of South Carolina. In the year 1775, he entered as a volunteer on board the first vessel of war commissioned by the council of his native state. He served his country upwards of 22 years as a commander, and died in this city on the 11th day of November, 1820, aged about 60 years.

Here lie the remains of TOBIAS LEAR. He was early distinguished as the private secretary and familiar friend of the illustrious Washington; and after having served his country with dignity, zeal, and fidelity, in many honorable stations, died accountant of the war department, 11th October, 1816, aged 54. His desolate *widow* and mourning *son* have erected this monument, to mark the place of his abode in the city of silence.

Name.	Where from.	Date of dec.	Age.	Name.	Where from.	Date of dec.	Age.
Ezra Darby, rep.	N. J.,	Jan. 28, 1808,	38.	Rich'd J. Manning, rep.	S. C.,	May 1, 1830.	
Uriah Tracy, sen.	Conn.,	July 19, 1807,	52.	Zalmon Wildman, rep.	Ct.,	Dec. 10, 1835,	60.
Francis Malbone, sen.	R. I.,	June 4, 1809,	50.	Elias K. Kane, sen.	Ill.,	Dec.,	1835.
Thomas Blount, rep.	N. C.,	Feb. 7, 1812,	52.	R. W. Habersham, rep.	Ga.,	Dec. 2, 1842,	67.
Elijah Brigham, rep.	Mass.,	Feb. 22, 1816,	64.	Jas. W. Williams, rep.	Md.,	Dec. 2, 1842.	
Richard Stanford, rep.	N. C.,	April 9, 1816,	48.	Alb. G. Harrison, rep.	Mo.,	Sept. 7, 1839,	39.
George Mumford, rep.	"	Dec. 31, 1818.		Wm. Lowndes, rep.	S. C.,	Dec. 12, 1822,	41.
David Walker, rep.	Ky.,	March 1, 1820.		Wm. W. Porter, rep.	Pa.,	Oct. 29, 1839,	47.
Nathaniel Hazard, rep.	R. I.,	Dec. 17, 1820,	47.	Davis Dimock, Jr., rep.	"	Jan. 13, 1842,	38.
Jesse Slocumb, rep.	N. C.,	Dec. 20, 1820,	40.	Nathan F. Dixon, sen.	R. I.,	Jan. 29, 1842,	67.
James Burrill, Jr., sen.	R. I.,	Dec. 26, 1820,	48.	Sam'l L. Southard, sen.	N. J.,	June 26, 1842,	55.
Wm. A. Trimble, sen.	O.,	Dec. 12, 1821,	35.	Joseph Lawrence, rep.	Pa.,	April 17, 1842,	54.
Wm. Pinkney, sen.	Md.,	Feb. 25, 1822,	58.	Wm. S. Ramsey, rep.	"	Oct. 18, 1840,	30.
Wm. L. Ball, rep.	Va.,	Feb. 29, 1824,	43.	Lewis Williams, rep.	N. C.,	Feb. 23, 1842.	
John Gaillard, sen.	S. C.,	Feb. 26, 1826,	60.	Charles Ogle, rep.	Pa.,	May 10, 1841,	43.
Chris. Rankin, rep.	Miss.,	Mar. 14, 1826,	38.	Henry Black, rep.	"	Nov. 28, 1841,	59.
Alexander Smyth, rep.	Va.,	April 17, 1830.		John Coffee, rep.	Ga.,		1836.
James Noble, sen.	Ia.,	Feb. 26, 1831,	48.	Benj. F. Deming, rep.	Vt.,		1834.
Chas. C. Johnson, rep.	Va.,		37.	Henry Wilson, rep.	Pa.,		1826.
Johathan ... t, rep.	"	May 15, 1832.		Charles Slade, rep.	Ill.,		1834.
Geo. E. Mitchell, rep.	Md.,	June 28, 1832.		Gabriel Holmes, rep.	N. C.,		1829.
James Jones, rep.	Ga.,	Jan. 11, 1801,	32.	Thomas Hartley, rep.	Pa.,	Jan. 1,	1801.
Levi Casey, rep.	S. C.,	Feb. 3, 1807,	54.	Daniel Hiester, rep.	Md.,	March 8,	1804.
Philip Doddridge, rep.	Va.,	Nov. 19, 1832,	59.	W. A. Burwell, rep.	Va.,	Feb. 16,	1821.
James Lent, rep.	N. Y.,	Feb. 22, 1833,	50.	Patrick Farrell, rep.	Pa.,	Jan. 12,	1826.
Thos. T. Bouldin, rep.	Va.,	Feb. 11, 1834,	53.	John Linn, rep.	N. J.,	Jan. 19,	1828.
James Blair, rep.	S. C.,	April 1, 1834.		J. Crowninshield, rep.	Mass.,	April 15,	1808.
Litt'n P. Dennis, rep.	Md.,	April 14, 1834,	50.	P. Goodwin, rep.	"	Feb. 21,	1818.
Warren R. Davis, rep.	S. C.,		41.	Thaddeus Betts, sen.	Ct.,	April,	1840.
Nathan Smith, sen.	Conn.,	Dec. 6, 1835.		Nathan Bryan, rep.	N. C.,	June 4,	1798, 49.
Jonathan Cilley, rep.	Me.,	Feb. 24, 1838.		David Dickson, rep.	Miss.,		1836.
Isaac McKim, rep.	Md.,	April 1, 1838.		Robert P. Henry, rep.	Ky.,		1826.
Timothy J. Carter, rep.	Me.,	March 14, 1838.		Geo. L. Kinnard, rep.	Ia.,	Nov.,	1836.
Th. D. Singleton, rep.	S. C.,	Dec.,	1833.	James Johnson, rep.	Ky.,		1826.
Hedge Thompson, rep.	N. J.,	July 23, 1828,	49.	Henry Wilson, rep.	Pa.,		1826.
Theodorick Bland, rep.	Va.,	June 13, 1790.		Wm. S. Hastings, rep.	Mass.,	June 17,	1842.
George Holcomb, rep.	N. J.,	Dec. 4, 1828.		Sim. H. Anderson, rep.	Ky.,	Aug. 11,	1840, 38.
Joab Lawler, rep.	Ala.,	May 8, 1828,	42.	Anson Brown, rep.	N. Y.,	June 14,	1840, 40.
Nais'thy Hunter, del.	Miss.,	March 1, 1802.		Jas. O. Alvord, rep.	Mass.,	Sept. 30,	1839, 31.
James Gillespie, rep.	N. C.,	Jan. 10, 1805.		John Smilie, rep.	Pa.,	Dec. 30,	1812, 71.
Jeremiah McLene, rep.	O.,	March 19, 1837,	71.	John Dawson, rep.	Va.,	March 13,	1814, 52.

The tomb of ELBRIDGE GERRY, Vice-President of the United States, who died suddenly in this city, on his way to the capitol as president of the Senate, November 23d, 1814, aged 70; thus fulfilling his own memorable injunction, "it is the duty of every citizen, though he may have but one day to live, to devote that day to the good of his country."

To the memory of GEORGE CLINTON. He was born in the state of New York, on the 26th July, 1739, and died at the city of Washington on the 20th April, 1811, in the 73d year of his age. He was a soldier and statesman of the revolution. Eminent in council, distinguished in war, he filled with unexampled usefulness, purity, and ability, among many other high offices, those of governor of his native state, and Vice President of the United States. While he lived, his virtue, wisdom, and valor, were the pride, the ornament, and security of his country; and when he died, he left an illustrious example of a well-spent life, worthy of all imitation.

Georgetown is in Washington county, on the NE. bank of the Potomac, 2 miles from Washington city, from which it is separated by Rock creek, over which are two bridges. It was originally laid out under an act of the colonial assembly of Maryland, passed May 15th, 1751. In 1789, the town was incorporated.

The situation is pleasant, commanding a fine view of the Potomac River, the city of Washington, and of the adjacent country; and it contains many elegant buildings and country seats. It has 4 banks, a market-house, 7 churches—2 Episcopal, 2 Methodist, 1 Presbyterian, 1 Roman Catholic, and 1 colored Methodist—and a Roman Catholic college, with 2 spacious brick edifices, finely situated, founded in 1789, which has a president and 16 professors, or other instructors, 90 alumni, 135 students, and 22,000 volumes in its libraries. The commencement is near the last of July. It was authorized by Congress, in 1815, to confer degrees. There is also a nunnery, called the Convent of Visitation, founded in 1798, which contains from 50 to 70 nuns, attached to which is a large female academy, which generally contains 100 young ladies, instructed by the nuns. The Chesapeake and Ohio canal commences at this place, which is designed to be extended to the Ohio River, and which has been recently continued to Alexandria. The aqueduct which connects the canal with Alexandria is a most stupendous work. The piers, nine in number, are built of granite, and imbedded 17 feet in the bottom of the river, with a foundation upon solid rock, so as to withstand the shock of the spring ice, which, rushing furiously from the stormy regions of the falls and narrows above, passes with almost resistless force against the bridges of the Potomac, sweeping every thing before it. These piers, built in the most masterly manner, will bear up against any force that may be brought against them. There were in 1840, 7 commercial and 2 commission houses, capital $310,000; 23 retail stores, capital $247,400; 2 lumber yards, capital $20,000; 2 tanneries, 1 printing-office, 1 semi-weekly newspaper, 1 flouring-mill, producing 10,500 barrels annually; 1 saw-mill. Capital in manufac. $154,700. Six academies, 484 students; 9 schools, 435 scholars. Pop. in 1810, 4,948; 1820, 7,360; 1830, 8,441; 1840, 7,312. Tonnage of the port, 9,964.

Alexandria, originally called Belhaven, is on the western bank of the Potomac, near the head of tide-water, 6 miles south of Washington. The town lies principally in the District of Columbia, but a small part of it is in Virginia. It was incorporated in 1779, by the state of Virginia, and that part of it within the District ceded to the general government in 1801. The laws of Virginia, previously ceded, remain in force in the town and county.

Alexandria is very handsomely situated. The streets are laid out on the plan of Philadelphia, crossing each other at right angles, and are generally well paved. It is considered remarkably healthy, and the view from the city is very fine. The town is situated in the bottom of a valley, which to the eye of an observer is terminated in every direction by lofty and verdant hills. To the north he sees the city of Washington,—the capitol with its beautiful columns, white walls, and towering dome, forming a most conspicuous object; to the south, the broad translucent expanse of the Potomac opens upon him, with Fort Washington, lying like a white line on its distant margin, opposite to Mount Vernon.

The river opposite to the town is a mile in breadth, and varies from 34 to 52 feet in depth, in the ship channel, which here washes the shore,—of course the harbor is naturally very fine, and it has been much improved by the erection of large and commodious wharves.

The population in 1800, was 4,196; in 1810, 7,227; in 1820, 8,218; in 1840, 8,459. The public buildings are a court-house, and 10 churches—2 Presbyterian, 2 Episcopal, 2 Methodist, 1 Baptist, 1 Friends, 1 colored Methodist, and 1 Roman Catholic. The city has considerable shipping, and exports wheat, Indian corn, and tobacco, to a considerable amount. The tonnage of the port in 1840, was 14,470. The Chesapeake and Ohio canal extends to this place, and may be expected to add to its prosperity. It has 2 banks, with an aggregate capital of $1,000,000; and 1 fire, and 1 marine insurance company. It is governed by a mayor, and a common council of 16 members.

About three miles from Alexandria, in Fairfax county, is the Virginia Theological Seminary, an institution founded in 1822, by the Protestant Episcopal Church of the diocese of Virginia. The bishop of the diocese, the Right Rev. William Meade, D. D., is president of the faculty. It has 4 professors, 53 students, and a library of about 4,000 volumes.

An interesting incident occurred at Alexandria in the life of Washington. It is given below, as it has often been published:

When Col. Washington was stationed at Alexandria, in 1754, there was an election for members of the Assembly, when Mr. W. Payne opposed the candidate supported by Washington. In the course of the contest, Washington grew warm, and said something offensive to Mr. Payne, who, at one blow, extended him on the ground. The regiment heard that their colonel was murdered by the mob, and they were soon under arms, and in rapid motion to the town to inflict punishment on the supposed murderers. To their great joy he came out to meet them, thanking them for such a proof of attachment, but conjuring them by their love for him and their duty, to return peaceably to their barracks. Feeling himself to be the aggressor, he resolved to make honorable reparation. Early next morning he wrote a polite note to Mr. Payne, requesting to see him at the tavern. Payne repaired to the place appointed, in expectation of a duel; but what was his surprise to see wine and glasses in lieu of pistols. Washington rose to meet him, and smiling as he offered his hand, began, "Mr. Payne, to err is nature; to rectify error is glory. I believe I was wrong yesterday; you have already had some satisfaction, and if you deem that sufficient, here is my hand—let us be friends." An act of such sublime virtue produced its proper effect, and Mr. Payne was from that moment an enthusiastic admirer of Washington.

THE END.

NOTE.

On page 282, evidence is presented to prove that Shelly, in Gloucester county, was the spot where Pocahontas rescued 'Capt. Smith. Since that form was printed, we have received a letter from the author of the article alluded to, in which he says: "From a description of Werowocomoco, the scene of Smith's rescue, in 'Newes from Virginia,' (by Smith) republished in the last [January 1845] number of the Southern Literary Messenger, and from other circumstances, I am now satisfied that I was mistaken in supposing the scene of the rescue was at Shelly, and that it was some miles lower down York river, at or near what is still known as 'Powhatan's Chimney;' which I take it, was attached to the house built for the Emperor by the English."

THE POTOMAC RIVER.

We have been permitted to publish the following beautiful lines, written by P. Thompson, Esq., on a visit to Loudoun county, in May, 1839, one month before the marriage of a grand-daughter of Washington's intimate friend, Bryan Lord Fairfax, now a Lady Manager of the Mount Vernon Association :

Hail, Old Potomac ! to thy rocky shore
My vagrant-wandering feet have stray'd once more :
In various aspects I have view'd thy stream,
Now tempest toss'd, now calm as childhood's dream.
I've seen thee roll thy waters to the bay,
Deep and majestic as an inland sea.
I've seen thee circumscrib'd and closely pent,
By lofty rocks, through which thy floods have rent
Their way, and rushed along with wild turmoil ;
And now, from Loudoun's hospitable soil,
I view thee once again. thou noble river,
In aspect new, but beautiful as ever !

Through ancient Egypt, Nilus rolls his flood,
Ilissus flows through plains where Troy once stood.
On classic Tiber's banks "imperial Rome
Still proudly stands"—Sophia's lofty dome
"By Hellas' streams"—see London's crowded mart,
That world of commerce, literature and art ;
By the "deep rolling Thames" supplied,
With wealth from every land, by every tide.

Though to these honored streams a fame belongs
Conferr'd by Heroes' deeds and Poets' songs ;
Yet thou, Potomac, shalt through coming time
Enjoy a fame more glorious, more sublime.
For on thy banks, beneath *Mount Vernon's* shade,
All that could *die* of WASHINGTON is laid !
Of Washington, the truly great and good,
Who firm in Freedom's cause undaunted stood—
George Washington appeared, that man might see
In him, how pure humanity might be—
And on the broad Potomac's wood-crown'd side
The Patriot Soldier lived, the Christian Hero died.

Thither shall pilgrim feet, in every age,
Bear *Freedom's* sons on Freedom's pilgrimage—
There shall they come from every distant shore,
To gaze on Freedom's altar, and adore.
And palsied be the hand which would remove
His relics from the place he lived to love.
There let HIS honor'd dust in peace remain
Till earth to Chaos shall return again.

No "monumental brass," no "storied urn,"
No sculptur'd "thoughts that breathe," no " words that burn,"
Are needed here to mark HIS place of rest,
His monument is every freeman's breast !
Let none presume his *epitaph* to write,
'Tis told in deeds as pure as Heaven's own light !
But if for him a monument we claim,
God grant the city, honor'd by his name,
May be that monument, and worthy prove
The name it bears ! Oh ! far from it remove
Intolerance and Pride, and all the train
That wait upon the frivolent and vain !
May'st thou, Potomac, on thy margin see
A city worthy of the good and free !
May Justice in its courts of Law preside,
And Wisdom all its councils ever guide !
May *Washington's* successors worthy prove
The place they hold, and guard the land we love
From foreign outrage and domestic strife,
And all the ills that poison social life !
Oh ! may Columbia's sons for ever aim
Thus to erect a monument of fame,
Whilst Time shall last, to *Washington's* loved name !

But, ere I turn, *Potomac*, from thy banks,
My fair conductress must receive my thanks,
For opening to my view another feature
Of thy mild, placid face, where beauteous nature
O'er all its matchless robe of beauty flings ;
And every breeze bears health upon its wings.
I feel their genial renovating power
And thank thee, fair Louisa, for this pleasant hour.

May every blessing in thy being blend.

EVERYNAME INDEX